PARENTS' MAGAZINE
COOKBOOK

ALL RECIPES
KITCHEN TESTED
BY PARENTS' MAGAZINE

PARENTS' MAGAZINE
COOKBOOK

Editor-in-Chief
RITA MOLTER
Food Editor, Parents' Magazine
Formerly, Food Editor, Family Circle Magazine

THOMAS NELSON, PUBLISHERS

NASHVILLE - NEW YORK

Recipes and photographs from Parents' Magazine,
Published by Parents' Magazine Enterprises Inc.,
reprinted by permission.

All rights reserved under International and Pan-American Conventions. Published in Nashville, Tennessee, by Thomas Nelson Inc., Publishers and simultaneously in Don Mills, Ontario, by Thomas Nelson & Sons (Canada) Limited. Manufactured in the United States of America.

Library of Congress Cataloging in Publication Data
Main entry under title:

Parents' magazine cookbook.

1. Cookery. I. Molter, Rita. II. Parents'
magazine & better homemaking.
TX715.P22   641.5   78-704

(USA) ISBN 0-8407-4327-0
(CANADIAN) ISBN 0-17-600700-8

Printed in the United States of America

CONTENTS

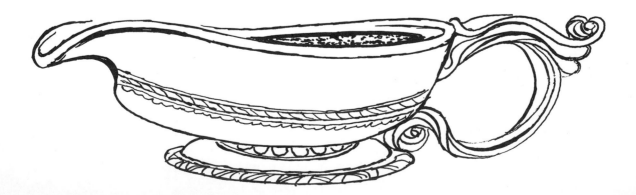

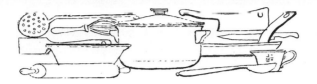

PUBLISHER'S ACKNOWLEDGMENTS

Editor-in-Chief
RITA MOLTER

Copy Editor	Elvin Abeles
Photographers	Will Rousseau
	William Pell
	Otto Fenn
	Alan Fontaine
	Sigrid Owen
	Irwin Horowitz
	Tom Yee
Illustrations	Oscar Liebman
Production	Norma S. Lloyd
	Diane Pearson
Composition	Edge Hill Typographic Service, Inc.
Created and produced by	STRAVON EDUCATIONAL PRESS

LIST OF
FULL-PAGE COLOR PHOTOGRAPHS

INTRODUCTION

THIS IS A BASIC ALL-PURPOSE COOKBOOK designed specifically to help you prepare wholesome and inviting meals and serve them with pride. Whether you're a beginner or a veteran cook, it tells you the how's and why's, and gives you a substantial collection of appealing kitchen-tested recipes as well. No matter what your budget, your time schedule, or the occasion, you'll find practical answers here to all of your day-by-day questions.

Over the years, there have been vast changes in ingredients, in styles of cooking, and in the appliances that make kitchen work easier. Individual interests and tastes have changed, too, and adults and children alike have become more adventurous in eating. Foods that used to be thought of solely as gourmet specialties or party dishes now hold routine places in everyday menus. With so many women working outside their homes today, time is more valuable than ever, and while most devote fewer hours to food fixing, they want to enjoy its creative side more. All of these trends are recognized and reflected throughout the pages of this book.

Between its covers, you'll find more than 1500 easy-to-follow recipes in every category from appetizers to desserts. All are top-rated choices that have been tested and tasted in the kitchens of *Parents' Magazine* to ensure perfect results for you.

Many of the recipes play up regional preferences of our own country or those of foreign lands; others reflect the popularity of ethnic cooking. Old favorites have been brought up to date, yet still retain the familiar taste and flavor you remember so well. Hundreds of new ones with built-in cooking secrets will give you inspiration for mealtime variety—for a minimum of effort. All can be depended upon to tempt your family and your friends, and at the same time, give everybody what counts towards a good diet.

Starting point for any meal-fixing job is a plan and an understanding of the principles of sound nutrition. So this book begins there, too, with a simple discussion of how to keep your family fit. Use this chapter as a handy reference or for brushing up on the major nutrients and the foods that contain them. Once you learn to think in terms of these two fundamentals, balanced meals will fall into place naturally and quickly.

Turn the pages for extensive sections on meats and poultry that include how-to's on buying, cooking timetables, serving variations, and carving guides, plus ideas for using leftovers in excitingly different second-day treats. There are dozens of suggestions for making fish, shellfish, eggs, and cheese into standouts as stand-ins for meats. Sprinkled through all of these chapters are recipes for hearty—and party—casseroles and one-dish meals that save time, money, effort, and waste.

For days when there's little time to dinnertime, there are lots of recipes that take advantage of instants, mixes, frozen products, and shortcuts to help you fix in minutes all kinds of dishes that taste as homemade as if hours had gone into their making. You'll find suggestions for salads, soups, and sandwiches that make a meal when everyone's in the mood for something light—or that complement one when more substantial fare is in order. To satisfy a sweet tooth, you can take your pick of the selections on desserts, pies, cakes, cookies, and candy.

Besides offering you new ways to prepare foods imaginatively and easily, another purpose of this book is to help you stick with your budget. Scattered all through its pages—and so worth reading and adopting—are literally hundreds of tips on shopping, storage, home canning, and freezing, in addition to a number of recipes developed, particularly, to pamper your pocketbook before payday or any day.

Second only to what's in a cookbook are the features that make it special and a joy to use in the kitchen. This one has many. All recipes start and end on the same page to eliminate mistakes and flipping pages with sticky hands. Since directions are paragraphed, it's simple to pick up where you left off or to find your place again if you're distracted.

Forty bright color photographs illustrate how some of the dishes should look when finished, and offer suggestions for trimming or arranging the food for the greatest serving style and appeal. Supplementing these pictures are decorative drawings plus simple sketches that give you step-by-step directions for tricky cooking jobs. And finally, a complete and detailed index will help you find what you want when you want it—in a jiffy.

Cooks of today, more than ever before, are concerned about feeding their families well at a reasonable cost in money and time. This is a book to cook with, and we hope it becomes your constant kitchen companion.

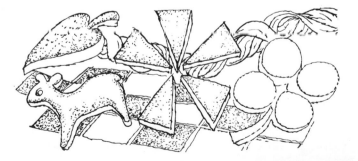

MEAL PLANNING AND NUTRITION

EVERY PENNY YOU SPEND ON FOOD should be an investment in good health. This doesn't mean that you have to devote hours every day to working with charts and slide rules. But to make the most of your food dollars, you do have to understand what kinds of food you need and what and how each contributes to basic nutritional requirements

Quite simply, good nutrition means meeting the body's needs for growth, maintenance, energy, and tissue repair. Good nutrition also means family meals that are satisfying and enjoyable.

Planning your menus

Well-balanced meals are easy to plan if you include a variety of foods that meet everyone's daily nutritional needs. While it's possible to provide a proper diet without following a daily plan, it's easier to stay within your budget while meeting your family's nutritional needs if you build your menus around the Basic Four Food Groups. All of us need something from each section every day, and since the foods within each group are similar in value, they can be used interchangeably for variety and interest. (The sample menu chart in this chapter shows you how to turn basic foods into excitingly different meals.) To review briefly, groups are:

1. *Dairy.* Included are milk, cheese, ice cream or ice milk—all of which supply calcium, riboflavin, protein, and Vitamin A, along with other essentials. *Daily need:* Three to four cups of milk for children and teenagers; two or more cups for adults; three or more cups for pregnant women; four cups for nursing mothers.

2. *Meats.* Other sources are poultry, fish, and eggs which we must have for animal protein, thiamine, riboflavin, niacin, and iron. *Daily need:* Two servings.

3. *Fruits and vegetables.* A daily must for nearly all of our Vitamin C and much of our Vitamin A, they also contribute minerals, calcium, iron, and some riboflavin. *Daily need:* Four or more servings, including one rich in Vitamin C and one of a dark green or yellow variety.

4. *Breads and cereals.* Alternates are spaghetti, macaroni, noodles, hominy, grits, rice, and crackers or other baked foods which provide essential B vitamins and iron. *Daily need:* Four or more servings.

Fortunately, all of the foods containing these nutrients are readily found in supermarkets. While each nutrient contributes to building, regulating, and repairing the

13

body, it's important to remember that they work together as a team. An extra supply of one can't take the place of another.

Only the amounts of food should vary to meet individual needs based on age and activity—for example, smaller servings for children and dieters, larger servings for very active adults and teenagers. In this chapter, you'll find a chart that lists the major nutrients, the reasons why they are needed, and their principal sources. Use it for quick reference; with a little practice, you'll notice that you soon think of each food in terms of what it provides.

Fiber. While it is not a nutrient, fiber is essential to health. It consists of the indigestible elements of foods which pass through our bodies primarily unchanged. To keep our digestive systems functioning properly, we all need a certain amount every day. Whole-grain cereals and breads—especially bran—fruits, vegetables, and nuts are top contributors.

Nutritional labeling—what's its use?

Labels that spell out what's inside are now found on any canned, frozen, processed, or packaged foods for which a manufacturer makes a nutritional claim, or on foods to which nutrients have been added (fortified cereals or enriched breads). Read these labels carefully, for they can help you:

(1) learn more about nutrition;
(2) plan better balanced meals;
(3) meet the nutritional needs of every member of your family;
(4) count calories;
(5) know how much of a specific nutrient a food contains.

At the same time, keep in mind that meats and fresh fruits and vegetables do not yet carry nutritional labels. Therefore, you can't use this information as your *only* guide to selecting foods.

Conveniently, all listings stated on the labels are given in single servings (2 slices, 1 cup, 1 ounce), along with the total servings in the container. This enables you to compare the nutritive values of different products, and as a result, find your best buys.

On the label, you'll also notice the term U.S. RDA. This means Recommended Daily Allowances, the nutritional standards based on the amounts of nutrients the National Research Council believes are adequate for most healthy people. Since RDA's are given in percentages of the day's total, they can help you keep tabs on how your menus stack up nutritionally.

A good breakfast

For good health and energy, everyone should start the day with at least a quarter of his daily needs for protein, vitamins, minerals, and calories. Children and adults who skip or skimp on the day's first meal slow down in mid- or late morning because of fatigue. With no breakfast, weight control is harder since noontime hunger is greater, and the dieter is more likely to overeat.

A sound, basic breakfast pattern can be as simple as fruit or juice, cereal and milk, toast with butter or margarine, and extra milk as a beverage for youngsters or coffee for adults. Even though a family eats in shifts, this menu is easy enough for most children of school age to fix for themselves.

How important are snacks?

For good health, at any age, it isn't necessary to eliminate them—just plan them so that they carry their weight in food value.

Children's energy needs are great, so most need something to keep them going between meals. Cereal and milk, pudding, ice cream, fruit, crackers, raw vegetables, cheese, and peanut butter are top nutritional choices. It's best not to allow snacking too close to mealtime, however, or appetites won't be up to par for the next meal.

For teenagers, snacks are a part of their social life, and for boys, particularly, a source of the extra calories they need. But whatever they eat should provide more than just calories. Wise choices are hamburgers or cheeseburgers, pizza, milk, milk shakes, and high-protein chocolate-flavored beverages that come in the soft drink section of the supermarket.

Girls benefit from meat and cheese sandwiches, ice cream, fruit and fruit juices, and dry cereals to eat out of hand. All of these supply particular nutrients that are often lacking—or low—in their diets.

Adults and waistline-watchers can also enjoy snacks if they select them wisely and count their calories as part of their day's permitted total. Fruit and vegetable juices, bouillon, skimmed milk or buttermilk, and raw vegetable relishes take the edge off hunger, yet contain few calories.

Cook to save nutrients

How you cook is equally as important as what you cook, since sloppy methods or overcooking can destroy food value. This is particularly true of vegetables that lose their bright color and fresh flavor when drowned in water or left on the heat too long. Check the chapter VEGETABLES for basic cooking tips; you'll find others throughout this book.

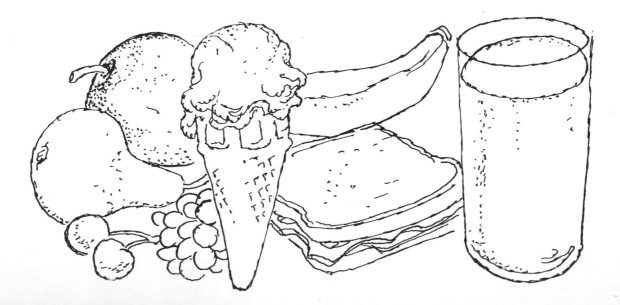

SAMPLE SEVEN-DAY MENU GUIDE
TO KEEP YOUR FAMILY FIT

BREAKFAST	LUNCH	DINNER
Chilled Grapefruit Juice 40% Bran Flakes Broiled Corned-beef Hash on Toasted Hamburger Buns Milk — Tea or Coffee	Chicken-vegetable Soup Tuna Scallop* Raw Carrot Sticks Fresh Fruit Compote Milk — Tea	Beef Patties Parslied Noodles Sesame Green Beans* Lemon Waldorf Salad* Strawberry Sundaes Pineapple Drop Cookies Milk — Tea or Coffee
Sliced Oranges Toasted Frozen Waffles with Hot Blueberry Sauce Milk — Tea or Coffee	Lentil Soup Toasted Italian Bread Shredded Cabbage Salad with Cranberry-mayonnaise Dressing Canned Apricot Halves Milk — Tea	Salmon Souffle* Baked Potatoes Pimiento Peas and Limas Marinated Yellow Squash Sticks on Lettuce Butterscotch Pudding Milk — Tea or Coffee
Sliced Bananas with Granola-type Cereal Raisin French Toast Maple-blended Syrup Milk — Tea or Coffee	Spanish Rice with Shrimp Tossed Green Salad with Oil-and-vinegar Dressing Raspberry Gelatin Cubes with Custard Sauce Milk — Tea	Lamb Stew with Mint Dumplings* Pear, Orange, and Avocado Salad with French Dressing Chocolate Layer Cake Milk — Tea or Coffee
Tangerine Sections Scrambled Eggs with Diced Ham Toasted English Muffins Milk — Tea or Coffee	Broiled Hamburger Patties Hamburger Buns with Mustard Butter Mixed Raw Relishes and Pickles Caramel Cup Custards Milk — Tea	Tijuana Chicken and Rice* Green Salad with Shredded Carrot and Sliced Cauliflowerets Corn Sticks Lemonade Cream Torte* Milk — Tea or Coffee
Chilled Mixed Vegetable Juice Hot Oatmeal Cinnamon Toast Milk — Tea or Coffee	Bologna Buns* Lettuce Wedges with Russian Dressing Chocolate Ice Cream Bars Milk — Tea	Consomme Baked Haddock Potatoes au Gratin Steamed Spinach Mixed Green Salad with Cherry Tomatoes Peach Betty with Cream Milk — Tea or Coffee
Grapefruit Halves Open-face Toasted Cheese Sandwich Milk — Tea or Coffee	Spaghetti with Meat Balls Hot Garlic French Bread Celery Spears Fresh Apples and Grapes Milk — Tea	Sauteed Liver and Onions Whipped Potatoes Steamed Broccoli Raw Relish Tray Baking Powder Biscuits Gingerbread with Lemon Sauce Milk — Tea or Coffee
Chilled Orange Juice Small Whole-wheat Pancakes Brown-and-serve Link Sausages Strawberry Preserves Milk — Tea or Coffee	Mushroom Omelets with Cheese Sauce Marinated Mixed Vegetables on Lettuce Italian Bread Sticks Lemon Pudding Milk — Tea	Beef Dinner Carbonnade* Romaine-radish Salad with Italian Dressing Hot Butterflake Rolls Dill Pickles Apricot-apple Pie* Milk — Tea or Coffee

*See index for starred recipes

MAJOR NUTRIENTS: THEIR ROLES AND SOURCES

NUTRIENT	WHY NEEDED	WHERE FOUND
Protein	Promotes growth and repair of body tissues; supplies energy; helps to fight infections; forms an important part of blood, enzymes, and hormones to regulate body functions.	Lean meats; poultry; fish; shellfish; eggs; milk; cheese. Next best are the vegetable proteins such as dry beans and peas; nuts; peanut butter; bread; cereals; wheat germ. If served with a complementary animal protein food such as cheese, the combined protein value is high.
Carbohydrates (Starches and sugars)	Supply energy; spare protein for body building and repair; also necessary for bulk and proper elimination.	Breads; cereals; grits; corn; rice; potatoes; the macaroni and noodle families; bananas; sugar; honey; syrup; jam; jelly; molasses.
Fats	Supply concentrated energy; improve taste of food; help body use other nutrients; help maintain temperature; lubricate intestinal tract.	Butter; margarine; whole milk; ice cream; cheese; egg yolk; shortening; lard; chocolate; chocolate candy; pies; puddings; salad oils.
Calcium	Builds sturdy bones and teeth; helps blood clot; helps to keep nerves, muscles, and heart healthy; aids in healing wounds; helps fight infections.	Milk; ice cream; cheese; cottage cheese; kale; collards; mustard and turnip greens; salmon; sardines.
Iodine	Helps thyroid gland work properly in regulating energy.	Iodized salt; salt-water fish and shellfish.
Iron	Necessary to form hemoglobin (red substance in blood) which carries oxygen from lungs to body cells.	Liver; heart; kidneys; oysters; lean meats; egg yolk; clams; whole-grain and enriched cereals; dry beans; molasses; raisins and other dried fruits; dark green leafy vegetables.
Sodium	Preserves water balance in body.	Salt; meat; fish; poultry; eggs; olives.
Potassium	Keeps nerves and muscles healthy; helps to maintain fluid balance.	Meat; fish; fruits; cereals.
Phosphorus	Essential (with calcium) for bones and teeth; helps fat do its job in the body; aids enzymes used in energy metabolism.	Milk; ice cream; cheese; meat; poultry; whole-grain, cereals; dry beans and peas; fish; nuts.
Magnesium	A must for strong bones and teeth; helps muscle contraction; aids in transmitting nerve impulses.	Cereals; dry beans; meats; milk; nuts.
Vitamin A	Helps maintain eyesight, especially in dim light; aids growth of healthy skin, bones, and teeth; promotes growth; helps resist infection.	Liver; broccoli; turnips; carrots; pumpkin; sweet potatoes; winter squash; apricots; butter; fortified margarine; egg yolk; fish-liver oils; cantaloupe.
Thiamine (Vitamin B₁)	Helps body cells obtain energy from food; aids in keeping nerves healthy; promotes good appetite and digestion.	Pork; lean meats; poultry; fish; liver; dry beans and peas; egg yolk; whole-grain and enriched cereals and breads; soybeans.
Riboflavin (Vitamin B₂)	Helps body use protein, fats, and carbohydrates for energy and for building tissues; aids in maintaining eyesight; promotes radiant skin.	Milk; cheese; liver; kidneys; heart; eggs; green leafy vegetables; enriched cereals and breads; yeast.
Niacin	Required for healthy nervous system, skin, and digestive tract; aids energy production in cells.	Lean meats; poultry; fish; variety meats; dark green leafy vegetables; whole-grain and enriched cereals and breads; peanuts; peanut butter.
Vitamin C (Ascorbic acid)	Aids in building the materials that hold cells together; helps in healing wounds and resisting infection; needed for healthy teeth, gums, and blood vessels.	Citrus fruits; strawberries; cantaloupe; tomatoes; potatoes; Brussels sprouts; raw cabbage; broccoli; green and sweet red peppers.
Vitamin D	Helps body use calcium and phosphorus to build bones and teeth.	Fortified milk; fish-liver oils; egg yolk; liver; salmon; tuna. Direct sunlight also produces Vitamin D.
Vitamin B₆	Aids body to use protein and maintain normal hemoglobin in blood.	Meats; wheat germ; liver; kidney; whole-grain cereals; soybeans; peanuts.
Vitamin B₁₂	A necessity for producing red blood cells and for building new proteins in the body.	Meats; liver; kidneys; fish; eggs; milk; cheese.
Vitamin E	Function is not clearly understood, although it is thought to help form red blood cells, muscle, and other tissue.	Wheat-germ oil; salad oils; green leafy vegetables; nuts; dry beans and peas; margarine.
Vitamin K	Promotes normal blood clotting.	Green leafy vegetables; cauliflower; egg yolk; liver; soybean oil.
Water	Forms a vital part of all cells; carries nutrients to cells and waste from body; necessary for digestion; regulates body temperature.	Water; beverages; soups; fruit juices; milk; fruits and vegetables.

APPETIZERS AND HORS D'OEUVRES

P ROBABLY NO OTHER FOOD-FIXING JOB promises as much fun or allows your imagination freer reign than appetizers do. Loosely defined, they include everything from bite-sized snacks for nibbling with beverages to light soups, salads, juices, and fruit cups that tempt appetites for a meal to come.

No one really needs to stick to any hard-and-fast rules for preparing appetizers, but there are a few guidelines to keep in mind that will make sure your food is always a hit.

For an open house where appetizers are the only food being served, offer an inviting assortment that complements each other in flavor, texture, and appearance. Depending on the size of the gathering and your time and mood, this can mean only two or three different kinds or a wide array, elaborately decorated. Either way, keep them small, sharply seasoned, and colorful. If the appetizer precedes a meal, plan something light and in keeping with the foods that are to follow.

Look through the next several pages for all kinds of suggestions for canapes and dinner starters to fit informal as well as formal occasions. There are dips to serve with raw vegetables and chips, dainty hot and cold hors d'oeuvres, spreads to go with wafers, crunchy nut and popcorn treats to munch on, and cracker and bread toppings that can be ready in minutes.

The most exciting appetizers are the ones you make yourself—imaginatively. But for spur-of-the-moment hospitality, you can also choose from—and depend on—a wide assortment of snacks in jars and packages at the supermarket. In fact, a few of these in your cupboard or freezer are good insurance for a planned party.

MOLDED PATE

1 can (3 ozs.) chopped mushrooms
1 can (10½ ozs.) condensed beef broth
1 envelope unflavored gelatin
10 pitted large ripe olives
2 cans (4¾ ozs. each) liverwurst spread
1 package (3 ozs.) cream cheese
   Few drops red-pepper seasoning
   Melba rounds

Drain liquid from mushrooms into a small saucepan; stir in beef broth; sprinkle gelatin over top to soften. Heat, stirring constantly, until gelatin dissolves.

Pour ½ cup of the gelatin mixture into a 1-quart mold; chill 20 minutes, or until syrupy-thick.

Cut 1 or 2 of the olives into rings or slices and arrange in a pretty pattern over gelatin in mold; chill again until sticky-firm.

While gelatin chills, combine remaining gelatin mixture, the rest of the olives, mushrooms, liverwurst spread, cream cheese, and red-pepper seasoning in an electric-blender container; cover; blend until smooth. Carefully spoon over layer in mold. Chill overnight until firm.

When ready to serve, loosen pâté around edge with a knife. Dip mold in and out of warm water; invert onto a serving plate; lift off mold. Frame with melba rounds or your favorite crackers.

Yield: 10 to 12 servings.

WIENER WRAPUPS

1 package (8 ozs.) cocktail wieners
3 small dill pickles
1 package refrigerated crescent rolls
16 small pimiento-stuffed green olives

Preheat oven to 375°.

Cut a slit in each wiener not quite to bottom. Cut each pickle lengthwise into 6 strips; stuff 1 strip into each wiener, trimming end of pickle, if needed, to fit.

Unroll crescent dough into 4 rectangles; pinch together at perforations. Cut each rectangle in half crosswise and lengthwise; place a stuffed wiener on each strip; roll up, jelly-roll fashion. Place, seam side down, on a cookie sheet.

Bake 15 minutes, or until golden.

Thread olives onto wooden picks; stick through centers of wieners. Serve hot with your favorite mustard sauce.

Yield: 16 appetizers.

CREAMY REMOULADE DIP

1 cup mayonnaise or salad dressing
½ cup dairy sour cream
3 tablespoons milk
1 small clove garlic, crushed
1 teaspoon prepared hot spicy mustard
1 tablespoon minced parsley
1 tablespoon freeze-dried chives
⅛ teaspoon salt

Combine all ingredients in a small bowl; mix well. Chill. (At serving time, if dip seems too thick, stir in 1 to 2 tablespoons more milk.)

Serve with shrimp or other seafoods.

Yield: About 1½ cups.

PIMIENTO PINWHEELS

1 package (3 ozs.) pimiento cream cheese
½ teaspoon Worcestershire sauce
2 teaspoons chopped parsley
1 package refrigerated crescent rolls

Preheat oven to 375°.

Blend cream cheese, Worcestershire sauce, and parsley in a small bowl.

Unroll crescent dough and separate into 4 rectangles; pinch together at perforations. Spread cheese mixture, dividing evenly, over rectangles. Starting at a long side of each, roll up tightly, jelly-roll fashion. Cut each roll into 6 small slices. Place, seam side down, on an ungreased cookie sheet.

Bake 12 minutes, or until golden. Serve hot.

Yield: 2 dozen.

NOEL APPETIZER TRAY

Creamy Remoulade Dip (recipe on page 19)
Romaine
1 lb. small shrimp, cooked, peeled, and deveined
1 large avocado, peeled, pitted, and cubed
2 tablespoons lemon juice
24 carrot curls
24 cherry tomatoes
24 celery fans
16 large pimiento-stuffed green olives

Make Remoulade Dip and chill.

When ready to serve, line a large serving tray or platter with romaine.

Spoon Creamy Remoulade Dip into a small serving bowl; place in center of tray; arrange shrimp in a circle around bowl.

Toss avocado cubes with lemon juice to prevent darkening; arrange avocado, carrot curls, tomatoes, celery, and olives in piles around shrimp. Set out a small container of cocktail picks to use for dunking.

Yield: 8 servings.

HAM CORNUCOPIAS

½ lb. ready-to-eat ham
½ lb. Edam cheese
½ cup finely diced water chestnuts
1 teaspoon prepared hot mustard
1 tablespoon chopped parsley
½ cup mayonnaise or salad dressing
30 large slices soft white bread
Parsley

Cut ham and cheese into chunks; put through a food grinder, using a medium-coarse blade. Combine with water chestnuts, mustard, parsley, and mayonnaise in a medium bowl; mix until well blended.

Roll each slice of bread with a rolling pin to flatten; cut three rounds from each with a 2¼-inch cookie cutter. Spread ham mixture on each; roll into a cornucopia shape. Place, seam side down, on a large tray or plate; cover with damp paper toweling, then transparent wrap to keep bread from drying; chill.

Just before serving, tuck a tiny sprig of parsley into the filling in wide end of each cornucopia.

Yield: 7½ dozen.

CRAB ROLLS

1 can (7½ ozs.) crab meat
¼ cup minced celery
1 tablespoon chopped parsley
3 tablespoons mayonnaise or salad dressing
1 tablespoon dry sherry
2 teaspoons lemon juice
¼ teaspoon salt
14 slices soft white bread
3 tablespoons butter or margarine

Drain liquid from crab. Flake meat fine in a medium bowl. Stir in celery and parsley.

Blend mayonnaise, sherry, lemon juice, and salt in a cup; stir into crab mixture; chill.

Roll each slice of bread with a rolling pin to flatten; trim off crusts to make even rectangles. Spread butter over each, then 1 tablespoon of the crab mixture, spreading to within ¼ inch of edges. Roll up tightly, jelly-roll fashion. Place rolls, seam side down and close together, in a shallow baking dish. Cover with damp paper toweling, then transparent wrap to keep bread from drying; chill several hours.

When ready to serve, cut each roll into thirds; stand on a serving plate. Tuck a tiny sprig of parsley into center of each roll if you like.

Yield: 3½ dozen.

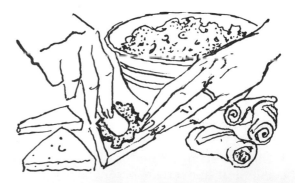

SALMON TOASTIES

1 loaf unsliced white bread
1 can (8 ozs.) salmon
¼ cup chopped celery
¼ cup chopped unpared raw cucumber,
    well drained
2 tablespoons finely chopped onion
1 hard-cooked egg, chopped
3 tablespoons mayonnaise or salad dressing
1 teaspoon lemon juice
½ teaspoon salt
    Cucumber slices, cut into tiny wedges

Trim crusts from top and sides of bread to make a rectangle; then cut loaf lengthwise into 4 thick slices. Cut each slice into 15 cubes; hollow out each to make a tiny basket. (A wooden pick makes a handy tool.) Place cubes in a single layer in a shallow baking pan.

Preheat oven to 325°. Bake cubes 15 minutes, or until golden; cool.

Drain salmon; remove skin and bones; flake meat in a medium bowl. Add celery, cucumber, onion, and egg.

Blend mayonnaise, lemon juice, and salt in a cup; stir into salmon mixture; chill.

About an hour before serving, drain any liquid from salmon mixture; spoon salmon into bread baskets. Garnish each with a tiny cucumber wedge; place on a large tray or plate. Chill until serving time.

Yield: 5 dozen.

SHRIMP SNACKS

1 can (4½ ozs.) deveined shrimp, drained and
    rinsed
¼ cup finely chopped celery
6 thin slices pared cucumber, chopped
2 tablespoons chopped green onion
2 tablespoons mayonnaise or salad dressing
¼ teaspoon salt
⅛ teaspoon pepper
6 large rye wafers
3 cherry tomatoes, quartered

Chop shrimp; combine with celery, cucumber, and green onion in a medium bowl; stir in mayonnaise, salt, and pepper. Chill several hours to blend flavors.

When ready to serve, spread a heaping 1½ tablespoons shrimp mixture onto each wafer; garnish with tomato quarters.

Yield: 6 servings.

TINY SHRIMP PUFFS

¼ cup butter or margarine
½ cup water
½ cup sifted all-purpose flour
    Salt
2 eggs
2 cans (4½ ozs. each) deveined shrimp, drained,
    rinsed, and chopped
1 cup chopped celery
2 tablespoons chopped green onions
3 hard-cooked eggs, chopped
⅔ cup mayonnaise or salad dressing
2 tablespoons lemon juice

Preheat oven to 400°.

Combine butter and water in a medium saucepan; heat to boiling. Stir in flour and a dash of salt all at once with a wooden spoon; continue stirring until batter forms a thick smooth ball that follows spoon around pan; remove from heat. Cool slightly; beat in eggs, one at a time, until mixture is thick and shiny-smooth.

Drop by level teaspoonfuls, 1 inch apart, on greased cookie sheets.

Bake 20 minutes, or until puffed and golden. Remove from cookie sheets to wire racks; cool completely.

Combine shrimp, celery, green onions, and eggs in a medium bowl. Blend mayonnaise, ¼ teaspoon salt, and lemon juice in a cup; fold into shrimp mixture; chill.

About an hour before serving, cut a thin slice from the top of each puff; scoop out any soft centers from bottoms. Spoon about 1 tablespoon shrimp mixture into each; replace tops. Arrange on a serving tray.

Yield: About 4 dozen.

BAKED CHICKEN STICKS

12 chicken wings
¼ cup all-purpose flour
1 teaspoon salt
¾ teaspoon paprika
1 egg
2 tablespoons water
½ cup fine bread crumbs
¼ cup butter or margarine

Cut through the biggest joint of each chicken wing to remove the large end. Set remaining pieces aside to simmer for broth for soup.

Mix flour, salt, and paprika in a transparent bag. Add wings, a few at a time, and shake until evenly coated with mixture.

Beat egg slightly with water in a pie plate; spread bread crumbs on waxed paper. Dip wings into egg mixture, then into bread crumbs to coat well.

Preheat oven to 425°.

Melt butter in a shallow baking pan; add wings, turning carefully to coat with butter.

Bake 15 minutes; turn. Bake 15 minutes longer, or until crusty brown and tender. Serve hot.

Yield: 6 servings.

BUTTON BURGERS

1 package hot roll mix
    Water
    Egg
10 tablespoons butter or margarine
2 lbs. ground beef
2 teaspoons seasoned salt
¼ teaspoon pepper
2 teaspoons prepared horseradish-mustard
8 small white onions, peeled and each
    cut into 6 slices
16 cherry tomatoes, stemmed and each
    cut into 3 slices

Prepare hot roll mix with water and egg and let rise as label directs. Turn out onto a lightly floured board and knead several times.

Divide dough into quarters; cut each quarter into 12 equal pieces. Shape each piece into a tiny ball; place in greased 1¾-inch muffin-pan cups; cover. Let rise again 45 minutes, or until doubled.

While dough rises, preheat oven to 400°. Melt 2 tablespoons of the butter in a small frying pan; brush over raised rolls.

Bake 15 minutes, or until rolls are golden and sound hollow when tapped with finger. Remove from pans to wire racks. Lower oven temperature to 350°.

Lightly mix ground beef with salt and pepper; shape into 48 tiny patties, using a tablespoonful for each. Place in a greased jelly-roll pan.

Bake 10 minutes, or until browned.

While meat cooks, blend remaining 8 tablespoons butter and horseradish-mustard in a cup.

Split rolls; spread butter mixture on each. Put each back together with an onion slice, a meat patty, and a tomato slice to make tiny sandwiches; hold in place with cocktail picks. Arrange on a serving tray. Serve hot.

Yield: 4 dozen.

CONTINENTAL CHEESE PLATE

½ lb. Swiss cheese, shredded (about 2 cups)
½ lb. sharp Cheddar cheese, shredded
    (about 2 cups)
 1 cup butter or margarine, softened
 2 teaspoons prepared mustard
    Finely chopped watercress
 2 large red apples
    Lemon juice
    Crisp crackers

Combine Swiss and Cheddar cheeses with butter in a medium bowl; beat until well blended; beat in mustard.

Chill until mixture is firm enough to handle, then spoon onto waxed paper and shape into a 4-inch ball. Wrap tightly; chill until very firm.

To decorate, cut three ½-inch-wide strips of waxed paper long enough to go around ball; press into cheese, spacing evenly. Roll ball in chopped watercress; wrap tightly in clean paper; chill.

About a ½ hour before serving, unwrap cheese; peel off paper strips; place ball on a serving plate. Let stand at room temperature to soften.

Halve apples, core, and slice thin; dip slices into lemon juice to prevent darkening. Arrange apples and crackers around cheese.

Yield: 12 generous servings.

HAM-AND-EGG CUTOUTS

 1 can (4½ ozs.) deviled ham
 3 hard-cooked eggs, chopped
½ cup finely chopped celery
 2 tablespoons finely chopped onion
 2 tablespoons mayonnaise or salad
    dressing
 1 tablespoon hot-dog relish
⅛ teaspoon salt
    Dash of pepper
 4 tablespoons butter or margarine
16 slices whole-wheat bread
    Carrot curls
    Parsley

Combine deviled ham, eggs, celery, and onion in a medium bowl.

Mix mayonnaise, relish, salt, and pepper in a cup; stir into ham mixture.

Spread butter on bread; spread ham mixture over 8 of the slices; top with remaining bread to make sandwiches. Cut two 2-inch rounds from each sandwich with a cookie cutter. (Wrap trimmings and save for nibbles.)

Arrange sandwiches in a circle on a large serving platter. Arrange carrot curls and parsley, bouquet fashion, in center.

Yield: 16 servings.

SHRIMP CRISPS

 2 dozen medium-sized fresh shrimp,
    shelled and deveined
 1 slice onion
 1 slice lemon
 1 teaspoon mixed pickling spices
 1 teaspoon salt
 1 can (8 ozs.) water chestnuts, drained
½ cup mayonnaise or salad dressing
 2 tablespoons sweet pickle relish
¼ teaspoon red-pepper seasoning
 2 dozen sesame crackers
    Parsley

Half-fill a large skillet with water; heat to simmering. Add shrimp, onion, lemon, pickling spices, and salt. Heat just to simmering again; cook 5 minutes, or until shrimp are tender. Lift from water with a slotted spoon; drain; chill.

Slice water chestnuts thin. Blend ¼ cup of the mayonnaise with pickle relish and red-pepper seasoning in a bowl.

Spread remaining ¼ cup mayonnaise on crackers; overlap water chestnut slices, dividing evenly, around edge on each. Spoon a heaping ½ teaspoon relish mixture onto center of each cracker; top with a shrimp and parsley.

Yield: 2 dozen.

Note: Assemble appetizers no sooner than an hour before serving so crackers stay crisp.

CHEESE KABOBS

4 long slices Muenster cheese
1 can (2¼ ozs.) deviled ham
24 tiny sweet pickles
24 small radishes, trimmed and cut in
    half crosswise

Let cheese stand at room temperature about an hour to warm.

Spread deviled ham over each slice to within ¼ inch of edges. Cut each slice in thirds lengthwise, then in half crosswise to make 6 short strips.

Place a pickle across one end of each strip, trimming to fit, if necessary; roll up tightly, jelly-roll fashion. Place, seam side down, on a tray or plate; chill.

When ready to serve, thread each roll between 2 radish halves onto a wooden pick.
Yield: 2 dozen.

RUBY CHEESE BALLS

2 jars (2½ ozs. each) dried beef
1 Gouda cheese, weighing 14 ozs.
1 package (3 ozs.) cream cheese
1 wedge (1¼ ozs.) Roquefort cheese,
    crumbled
  Thin pretzel sticks

Taste dried beef and if it's very salty, place in a sieve and rinse under running warm water; pat dry with paper toweling. Chop beef very fine. (To speed the job, place beef in a bowl and cut it with kitchen scissors.) Set aside.

Shred Gouda cheese. (There should be about 4½ cups.) Place in a medium bowl; stir in cream and Roquefort cheese until very well blended.

Shape mixture, a teaspoon at a time, into small balls; roll in chopped beef to coat generously. Place in a single layer on a large tray or plate; chill.

Just before serving, insert a pretzel stick into each ball for easy pickup.
Yield: About 5 dozen.

SHRIMP STICKS

1 jar (4¼ ozs.) cocktail shrimp
9 slices party-sized rye bread
1 tablespoon butter or margarine,
    softened
4½ teaspoons prepared tartar sauce
  Fresh dill

Empty shrimp into a sieve and rinse under running cold water; drain well, then pat dry.

Trim rounded ends from bread; spread butter lightly over each slice, then spread ½ teaspoon of the tartar sauce over each. Cut each slice into 2 small rectangles.

Arrange 2 shrimp on each rectangle; garnish with tiny sprigs of dill. Place on a tray or plate; chill until serving time.
Yield: 1½ dozen.

CHIP-AND-DIP TRAY

3 packages (3 ozs. each) cream cheese
    with chives
2 cans (4½ ozs. each) deviled ham
3 tablespoons prepared mustard with
    onions
2 tablespoons mayonnaise or salad
    dressing
  Few drops red-pepper seasoning
¼ cup finely chopped pitted ripe olives
  Corn chips, crackers, and cheese snacks

Blend cheese and deviled ham in a medium bowl; stir in mustard, mayonnaise, red-pepper seasoning, and olives. Chill several hours to blend flavors.

When ready to serve, spoon mixture into two or three small dip bowls; top each with a ring of sliced pitted ripe olives. Place bowls on a tray; surround with corn chips, crackers, and cheese snacks.
Yield: About 2½ cups.

MINIATURE CHICKEN ECLAIRS

4 tablespoons butter or margarine
½ cup water
½ cup sifted all-purpose flour
   Dash of salt
2 eggs
2 cans (4½ ozs. each) chicken spread
½ cup chopped unpared raw zucchini
⅓ cup chopped pitted ripe olives

Preheat oven to 400°.

Combine butter and water in a small saucepan; heat to boiling. Stir in flour and salt all at once with a wooden spoon; continue stirring until batter forms a thick smooth ball that follows spoon around pan. Remove from heat; cool slightly. Beat in eggs, one at a time, until mixture is thick and shiny smooth.

Fit plate #33 onto a cookie press; spoon half of the batter into press.

Press batter out onto greased large cookie sheets in double-high ribbons 1 inch long and about 1 inch apart. Repeat with remaining batter.

Bake 15 minutes, or until eclairs are puffed and golden. Remove from cookie sheets to wire racks; cool completely.

Combine chicken spread, zucchini, and olives in a small bowl; chill.

One to two hours before serving, cut a thin slice from the top of each eclair. (Handle carefully because they're fragile.) Pick out any soft centers from bottoms with a wooden pick, then fill each shell with chicken mixture; replace tops. Place in a single layer on a large tray or plate. Chill until serving time.

Yield: 6 dozen.

TOMATO-EGG THIMBLES

3 hard-cooked eggs
¼ cup minced celery
3 tablespoons mayonnaise or salad
   dressing
½ teaspoon curry powder
½ teaspoon salt
2 pints cherry tomatoes
8 small pitted ripe olives, sliced
   lengthwise

Press eggs through a sieve into a medium bowl; stir in celery, mayonnaise, curry powder, and salt.

Wash tomatoes and stem. Cut a thin slice from rounded end of each; scoop out insides with the ¼ teaspoon of a measuring spoon set; turn tomatoes upside down on paper toweling to drain.

Stuff egg mixture into tomatoes; garnish each with a slice of olive. Place on a plate or tray; cover; chill until serving time.

Yield: About 4 dozen.

PUNGENT PATE SPREAD

½ lb. liverwurst
1 package (8 ozs.) Neufchatel cheese,
   softened
1 tablespoon crumbled blue cheese
½ cup chopped celery
1 tablespoon finely chopped onion
2 tablespoons chopped parsley
¼ cup dairy sour cream
¼ teaspoon salt
2 teaspoons Worcestershire sauce
   Rye crackers

Peel casing from liverwurst; mash liverwurst well with a fork in a medium bowl. Beat in Neufchatel and blue cheeses until smooth.

Stir in celery, onion, parsley, sour cream, salt, and Worcestershire sauce. Chill.

When ready to serve, spoon into a small bowl; garnish with parsley. Place bowl on a large serving plate or tray; surround with crisp rye crackers.

Yield: 2½ cups spread.

BROWN-EYED SUSANS

1 lb. liverwurst
1 container (4 ozs.) whipped cream cheese
¼ cup chopped dill pickle
¼ cup minced green onion
2 tablespoons mayonnaise or salad dressing
¼ teaspoon salt
5 dozen plain round crackers
  Pitted ripe olives, sliced lengthwise
2 hard-cooked egg yolks
  Mayonnaise or salad dressing

Peel casing from liverwurst. Place liverwurst in a medium bowl and mash well with a fork. Stir in cream cheese, pickle, onion, the 2 tablespoons mayonnaise, and salt until well blended; cover; chill.

One to two hours before serving, spread liverwurst mixture generously on crackers; top each with several olive slices arranged in a flower design; place rounds on a large tray or plate.

Mash egg yolks in a small bowl; stir in just enough mayonnaise to moisten, spoon into centers of olive flowers. Cover tray; chill until serving time.

Yield: 5 dozen.

APPETIZER CHEESEBURGERS

1 lb. ground beef round
1 small onion, minced (¼ cup)
1 teaspoon prepared horseradish mustard
¾ teaspoon seasoned salt
  Dash of pepper
4 slices process American cheese
24 small sesame crackers
  Red pepper relish

Preheat oven to 400°.

Combine ground round, onion, mustard, salt, and pepper in a medium bowl; mix lightly until well blended. Shape into 24 small patties, using 1 tablespoon for each. Place on rack in broiler pan.

Bake 10 minutes, or until lightly browned.

While meat cooks, cut each slice of cheese into 6 strips, then each strip in half crosswise; crisscross 2 strips over each meat patty. Continue baking 1 minute, or until cheese starts to melt.

Place each patty on a cracker; top with a tiny spoonful of pepper relish. Serve hot.

Yield: 2 dozen.

PETITE BEEF BUNS

2 packages (20 to a package) party
  soft rolls
2 tablespoons butter or margarine,
  softened
1 can (12 ozs.) corned beef
1 jar (5 ozs.) relish cheese spread
1 small onion, minced (¼ cup)
¼ teaspoon salt
  Few drops red-pepper seasoning
  Small pimiento-stuffed green olives,
  sliced crosswise

Preheat oven to 325°.

Separate rolls. Cut a small round from the top of each, then hollow out inside to leave a shell; spread hollows with butter. Place rolls on a cookie sheet.

Bake 10 minutes, or until toasted; cool.

Shred corned beef with a fork in a medium bowl; stir in cheese spread, onion, salt, and red-pepper seasoning; chill.

About 1 hour before serving, spoon corned-beef mixture into rolls, packing in well. Garnish each with an olive slice.

Yield: 3⅓ dozen.

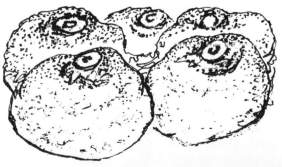

WAIKIKI FRANKS

1 can (20 ozs.) pineapple chunks in juice
1 cup orange marmalade
¼ teaspoon ground ginger
1 lb. frankfurters

Preheat oven to 350°.

Drain juice from pineapple into a bowl, then measure ½ cup and combine with marmalade and ginger in a baking pan, 13x9x2 inches. Heat in oven until bubbly; stir well.

Cut each frankfurter crosswise into 6 chunks. Place franks and pineapple chunks in a single layer in hot sauce.

Bake 15 minutes. Spoon sauce from bottom of pan over frankfurters and pineapple. Bake 15 minutes longer, or until bubbly and glazed.

Spoon into blazer pan of chafing dish. Set out wooden picks so everyone can spear his own serving.

Yield: 12 servings.

SAUSAGE FONDUE

2 tablespoons butter or margarine
2 tablespoons all-purpose flour
1 teaspoon salt
1 cup milk
2 tablespoons prepared horseradish-
    mustard
1 lb. frankfurters
1 package (8 ozs.) bacon-flavored
    brown-and-serve sausages
  Midget Sesame Rolls (recipe on page 377)
  Salad oil for frying

Melt butter in a small saucepan; stir in flour and salt. Cook, stirring constantly, until bubbly. Stir in milk; continue cooking and stirring until sauce thickens and boils 1 minute; stir in mustard; keep warm.

Cut frankfurters diagonally into 1-inch chunks; cut sausages in half crosswise; arrange on a tray. Spoon mustard sauce into 1 or 2 small dip bowls; split each Midget Sesame Roll about halfway through with a fork. Arrange sauce and rolls on a second tray.

Pour salad oil into fondue cooker to a depth of 2 inches; heat as manufacturer directs.

To serve, spear a piece of meat onto a fondue fork; heat in hot oil for 1 to 2 minutes. Dip into mustard sauce, then pop into a tiny roll to eat, sandwich fashion.

Yield: 12 servings.

TURKEY TWINKLES

15 slices white bread
 1 can (5 ozs.) boned turkey
 3 tablespoons mayonnaise or salad
    dressing
 2 tablespoons hot-dog relish
   Dash of salt
¼ cup coarsely chopped filberts
   Pimientos

Preheat oven to 325°.

Cut 2 rounds from each slice of bread with a 1½-inch cookie cutter; place rounds on a cookie sheet. Bake 10 minutes, or until golden; cool.

Drain turkey well; chop meat fine. Combine with mayonnaise, relish, salt, and filberts in a medium bowl; mix well. Spread on toast rounds. Trim each with a tiny star cut from pimiento; place on a large tray or plate. Chill until serving time.

Yield: 2½ dozen.

OLIVE HAM ROLLS

 1 package (4 ozs.) sliced boiled ham (4 slices)
 1 jar (5 ozs.) pimiento cheese spread
24 large pimiento-stuffed green olives

Cut ham slices in half crosswise and in thirds lengthwise to make 24 strips; spread cheese lightly over each. Roll each around an olive; fasten with a short wooden pick, if needed.

Place on a large serving plate; chill until serving time.

Yield: 2 dozen.

HERBED CHEESE SPREAD

1 package (8 ozs.) cream cheese, softened
2 tablespoons parsley flakes, crushed
¼ teaspoon dried basil, crushed
¼ teaspoon dried marjoram, crushed
¼ teaspoon dried thyme, crushed
⅛ teaspoon garlic powder
2 tablespoons milk
   Assorted crisp crackers

Combine cheese and seasonings in a small bowl; stir in milk until mixture is smooth and well blended. Chill at least 1 hour to season.

Spoon into a small serving bowl; garnish with a sprig of parsley. Place bowl on a large serving plate; surround with crackers.

Yield: About 1 cup.

MONTEREY OLIVE DIP

1 package (8 ozs.) cream cheese, softened
1 cup (8-oz. carton) dairy sour cream
¼ cup bottled chili sauce
½ cup chopped pitted ripe olives
½ teaspoon salt
   Few drops red-pepper seasoning

Combine cheese and sour cream in a medium bowl; beat until smooth. Stir in chili sauce, olives, salt, and red-pepper seasoning. Chill at least 1 hour to season.

Spoon into one or two small serving bowls; place on a large plate or tray. Surround with green-pepper squares, short celery sticks, and cauliflowerets.

Yield: 2½ cups.

NEW ENGLAND CLAM DIP

1 cup (8 oz. carton) large curd
   creamed cottage cheese
1 package (3 ozs.) cream cheese, softened
3 tablespoons chili sauce
2 teaspoons prepared horseradish
½ teaspoon salt
⅛ teaspoon liquid red-pepper seasoning
1 can (10½ ozs.) minced clams, drained

Beat cottage cheese vigorously in a medium

bowl to break up lumps; beat in cream cheese, chili sauce, horseradish, salt, and red-pepper seasoning until smooth. Stir in clams. Chill several hours to blend flavors.

When ready to serve, spoon into a small bowl; sprinkle paprika on top if you like. Place bowl on a large plate or tray; surround with your favorite crackers or raw vegetable sticks.

Yield: 2¼ cups.

SHRIMP REMOULADE

1 bag (16 ozs.) frozen shrimp
½ cup salad oil
¼ cup vinegar
2 teaspoons prepared mustard
1 teaspoon salt
½ teaspoon paprika
   Few drops red-pepper seasoning
½ cup minced green onions
½ cup minced celery
3 tablespoons chopped parsley
   Iceberg lettuce

Cook shrimp as label directs; drain. Place in a medium bowl.

Combine salad oil, vinegar, mustard, salt, paprika, and red-pepper seasoning in a small bowl; beat until blended. Stir in onions, celery, and parsley. Pour over shrimp; toss lightly to mix; cover. Chill at least 4 hours to season.

When ready to serve, line 6 salad plates with lettuce; spoon shrimp mixture and dressing onto each.

Yield: 6 servings.

GUACAMOLE

1 large firm ripe avocado
⅓ cup mayonnaise or salad dressing
2 tablespoons minced onion
2 tablespoons lemon juice
1 teaspoon salt
⅛ teaspoon liquid red-pepper seasoning
1 large firm ripe tomato, peeled,
    seeded, chopped, and drained
1 tablespoon bacon-flavored vegetable-protein
    bits
  Crisp corn chips

Cut avocado in half; peel, pit, and mash well in a medium bowl. Stir in mayonnaise, onion, lemon juice, salt, red-pepper seasoning, and tomato. Cover tightly; chill about an hour.

When ready to serve, spoon into a small bowl; sprinkle protein bits on top. Place bowl on a large serving plate; surround with corn chips.

Yield: About 2½ cups.

FROSTED GRAPEFRUIT CUPS

2 large grapefruits
1 tablespoon sugar
1 package (10 ozs.) frozen raspberries,
    partly thawed
½ pint lime sherbet

Pare grapefruits and section into a medium bowl; drain off juice and save to add to punch.

Sprinkle sugar over grapefruit; toss lightly to mix. Spoon into 4 sherbet glasses.

Spoon raspberries over grapefruit; top each serving with a small scoop of lime sherbet.

Yield: 4 servings.

CUCUMBER DIP

1 large cucumber
1 package (8 ozs.) cream cheese
3 tablespoons finely chopped green onions
2 tablespoons lemon juice
¼ teaspoon salt

Trim 3 thin slices from cucumber and set aside for garnish.

Pare remaining cucumber; grate into a bowl, then drain well. Beat cucumber into cream cheese until smooth; stir in onions, lemon juice, and salt; cover. Chill several hours.

Spoon into a small serving bowl; garnish with cucumber slices. Place bowl on a large plate or tray; surround with cherry tomatoes, carrot sticks, and celery chunks.

Yield: 1½ cups.

Note: If chilled dip seems too thick at serving time, thin with 1 to 2 tablespoons milk.

HOT TOMATO COCKTAIL

1 can (46 ozs.) tomato juice
2 cans (13¾ ozs. each) chicken broth
¼ cup lemon juice
1 tablespoon sugar
1 tablespoon Worcestershire sauce
  Celery sticks

Combine tomato juice, chicken broth, lemon juice, sugar, and Worcestershire sauce in a kettle; heat slowly to boiling.

Pour into mugs; garnish each with a celery stick for a stirrer.

Yield: 12 servings.

SUGAR 'N' SPICE WALNUTS

2 cups California walnuts
2 tablespoons butter or margarine
1 tablespoon cinnamon-sugar
⅛ teaspoon ground nutmeg

Combine walnuts and boiling water to cover in a medium skillet; reheat to boiling; drain well. Return to skillet.

Add butter and melt; toss walnuts until lightly coated; sprinkle cinnamon-sugar and nutmeg over top. Heat very slowly, stirring several times, 10 minutes, or until walnuts are toasted. Spread out on paper toweling to cool.

Store in a tightly covered container.

Yield: 2 cups.

APPETIZER SHRIMP MOLD

1 bag (16 ozs.) frozen shrimp
1 envelope unflavored gelatin
¾ cup water
¾ cup mayonnaise or salad dressing
⅓ cup catsup
1 small onion, minced (¼ cup)
1 tablespoon prepared horseradish
½ teaspoon salt
  Few drops red-pepper seasoning
  Escarole
  Lemon slices

Cook shrimp as label directs; drain; cool. Set aside 2 or 3 for garnish, then dice remainder.

Sprinkle gelatin over water in a small saucepan; heat, stirring constantly, until gelatin dissolves; cool.

Mix mayonnaise, catsup, onion, horseradish, salt, and red-pepper seasoning in a medium bowl; stir in cooled gelatin mixture; fold in shrimp. Spoon into a 3½-cup or 1-quart mold. Chill several hours or overnight until firm.

When ready to serve, loosen salad around edge with a knife; dip mold in and out of warm water; invert onto a serving plate; lift off mold.

Frame base of salad with small escarole leaves and garnish top with lemon slices and remaining shrimp.

Yield: 4 servings.

CRAB LOUIS

1 hard-cooked egg, chopped
1 green onion, trimmed and chopped
½ cup mayonnaise or salad dressing
¼ cup chili sauce
1 tablespoon prepared horseradish
1 can (7½ ozs.) crab meat
2 medium avocados
1 tablespoon lemon juice
  Boston lettuce

Blend egg, onion, mayonnaise, chili sauce, and horseradish in a small bowl. Chill.

Drain liquid from crab meat; cut meat into small pieces. Chill.

When ready to serve, cut avocados in half and pit; brush with lemon juice. Place each half on a lettuce-lined salad plate. Spoon crab evenly into avocados; spoon dressing over crab. Garnish each plate with a lemon wedge if you like.

Yield: 4 servings.

CHILI SCRAMBLE

2 cups pillow-shaped oat cereal
2 cups corn puff cereal
2 cups pretzel rings
1 can (6½ ozs.) peanuts
4 tablespoons butter or margarine
1½ teaspoons chili powder
1¼ teaspoons salt

Preheat oven to 300°.

Combine cereals, pretzels, and peanuts in a large shallow baking pan; heat in oven for 15 minutes.

Slice butter over mixture; return to oven for 5 minutes, or until butter melts; toss lightly with a spoon to mix with butter. Sprinkle chili powder and salt over top; toss again to mix.

Bake, stirring once or twice, 30 minutes; cool. Store in a tightly covered container.

Yield: About 7 cups.

STUFFED CELERY

1 package (8 ozs.) cream cheese
2 tablespoons parsley flakes
½ teaspoon seasoned salt
⅛ teaspoon dried thyme, crushed
⅛ teaspoon dried basil, crushed
2 tablespoons water
12 stalks of celery, 8 inches long

Combine cheese, parsley, seasoned salt, thyme, basil, and water in a medium bowl; mix well. Chill at least 1 hour to blend flavors.

Spread 4 teaspoons of the cheese mixture into each celery stalk; cut each into quarters.

Yield: 12 servings.

SCANDINAVIAN BERRY SOUP

1 package (10 ozs.) frozen raspberries
2 tablespoons cornstarch
2 tablespoons sugar
  Dash of salt
2 cups water
¼ cup lemon juice
1 pint fresh strawberries
  Unsweetened whipped cream

Thaw raspberries. Press berries with syrup through a sieve into a small bowl; discard seeds.

Mix cornstarch, sugar, and salt in a medium saucepan; stir in water and raspberry mixture. Cook, stirring constantly, until mixture thickens and boils 1 minute; remove from heat. Stir in lemon juice; cool.

While mixture cools, wash strawberries and hull. Set aside 4 whole ones for garnish, then slice remainder in half; stir into raspberry mixture. Chill several hours, or until frosty cold.

Ladle into small cups or bowls; garnish each serving with a puff of whipped cream and a strawberry.
Yield: 4 servings.

ANTIPASTO PLATES

1 package (6 ozs.) sliced large salami
1 package (4 ozs.) sliced cooked chicken
1 can (2 ozs.) flat anchovies, drained
1 jar (4 ozs.) pimientos, drained and cut in
    wide strips
6 pitted ripe olives
6 pimiento-stuffed green olives
  Romaine
1 jar (6 ozs.) marinated artichoke hearts,
    drained
12 celery fans
2 hard-cooked eggs, each cut in 6 wedges
6 radishes, trimmed
  Salad oil
  Vinegar

Lay salami slices flat on counter; top each with a slice of chicken, then anchovies and pimientos, dividing evenly. Roll up stacks, jelly-roll fashion; fasten with wooden picks; trim ends of picks with ripe and green olives.

Place each roll on a romaine-lined small serving plate. Arrange artichoke hearts, celery, egg wedges, and radishes attractively around meat. Serve with oil and vinegar to sprinkle over top.
Yield: 6 servings.

TANGY TOMATO CUP

1 can (18 ozs.) tomato juice
1 can (10¾ ozs.) condensed tomato soup
½ cup water
2 tablespoons lemon juice
½ teaspoon sugar
  Few drops red-pepper seasoning
1 tablespoon chopped parsley

Combine all ingredients in a large saucepan; heat just to boiling.

Pour into mugs or cups; serve hot.
Yield: 6 servings.

CONSOMME COCKTAIL

2 cans (10½ ozs. each) condensed consommé
2 cans (12 ozs. each) tomato juice
1 teaspoon Worcestershire sauce
1 large lemon, sliced thin

Combine consommé, tomato juice, and Worcestershire sauce in a medium saucepan; heat to boiling.

Pour into mugs or cups; float a slice of lemon on each serving.
Yield: 8 servings.

CALICO CORN

½ cup butter or margarine
4 quarts freshly popped popcorn
1 teaspoon parsley-garlic salt

Melt butter in a small saucepan; drizzle over popcorn in a large bowl. Sprinkle garlic salt over top; toss until popcorn is evenly coated.
Yield: 16 to 20 servings.

CHILI ALMONDS

1 tablespoon butter or margarine
¾ teaspoon chili powder
2 cups blanched shelled whole almonds
  Salt

Preheat oven to 350°.

Melt butter in a shallow baking pan in oven as it heats. Stir in chili powder and almonds; toss until almonds are well coated with butter mixture.

Bake, stirring several times, 20 minutes, or until toasted. Spread out on paper toweling to cool; sprinkle salt lightly over top.

Store in a tightly covered container.
Yield: 2 cups.

BARBECUED WALNUTS

2 tablespoons butter or margarine
⅓ cup bottled barbecue sauce
1 package (16 ozs.) California walnuts
  Salt

Preheat oven to 400°.

Melt butter in a baking dish, 13x9x2 inches, in oven as it heats. Stir in barbecue sauce and walnuts; toss until walnuts are evenly coated with mixture.

Bake, stirring several times, 20 minutes, or until toasted. Spread out on paper toweling to cool; sprinkle salt lightly over top.

Store in a tightly covered container.
Yield: 4 cups.

PARTY POPCORN

½ cup butter or margarine
4 quarts freshly popped popcorn
2 tablespoons baconion seasoning
½ teaspoon salt

Melt butter in a small saucepan; drizzle over popcorn in a large bowl; sprinkle baconion and salt over top. Toss until popcorn is evenly coated.
Yield: 16 to 20 servings.

ONION TWISTS

1¼ cups sifted all-purpose flour
1½ teaspoons baking powder
¼ teaspoon salt
1 envelope toasted onion dip mix
6 tablespoons butter or margarine
6 tablespoons cold water

Preheat oven to 425°.

Sift flour, baking powder, and salt into a medium bowl; stir in dip mix. Cut in butter with a pastry blender until mixture forms fine crumbs. Sprinkle cold water over top, a tablespoon at a time, mixing lightly until pastry holds together.

Roll out on a lightly floured cloth to a rectangle, 12x10 inches. Cut in half lengthwise, then cut each half crosswise into ½-inch-wide strips. Lift each strip carefully and twist several times; place on ungreased cookie sheets.

Bake 10 minutes, or until lightly golden. Remove from cookie sheets to wire racks; cool.
Yield: 4 dozen.

CHEESE CHIPS

1 package (8 ozs.) potato chips
½ cup shredded process Old English cheese

Preheat oven to 350°.

Spread potato chips in a jelly-roll pan, 15x10x1 inches; sprinkle cheese over chips.

Bake 5 to 8 minutes, or just until cheese melts.

Spoon into a napkin-lined basket; serve hot.
Yield: 6 servings.

(Clockwise from top)
HAM CORNUCOPIAS (p.20)
SHRIMP STICKS (p.24)
MINIATURE CHICKEN ECLAIRS (p.24)
TURKEY TWINKLES (p.27)
CRAB ROLLS (p.20)
BROWN-EYED SUSANS (p.26)
TOMATO-EGG THIMBLES (p.25)
SALMON TOASTIES (p.21)

BEVERAGES

For almost everyone, a mug of steaming coffee, a tumbler of frosty tea, a cup of sparkling punch, or a tall glassful of creamy chocolate milk are around-the-year, around-the-clock refreshers. And no wonder, for all are ideal ways to pick you up, to cool you off, to cheer you up, and to share with friends.

There are a few basic rules for making coffee and tea, but they aren't at all difficult, and once followed, soon become habit. Served plain, either beverage is equally at home on a breakfast table or a party table, and from there on, you can be as creative as you like in varying these two favorites or concocting endless other hot and cold treats.

To spark your imagination, look to the supermarkets for a vast assortment of instant mixers and flavor enhancers. There are fresh, frozen, and canned fruit juices, concentrates, ades, and drinks; carbonated beverages; powdered mixes in foil envelopes and family-sized canisters; milks; flavored syrups; whole and ground spices; mint; small fresh or frozen fruits such as lemons, limes, oranges, and strawberries; and ice creams, sherbets, and ices.

Whenever you're looking for a beverage recipe of any kind, browse through this chapter. You'll find suggestions that are appropriate for a backyard barbecue or a golden wedding celebration, for winter or summer, for children or adults—or for just anytime anyone needs a lift.

How to get the most from coffee

1. Keep your coffee maker scrupulously clean. After each use, wash it well in hot sudsy water and rinse it thoroughly with hot water. For electric coffee makers, follow manufacturer's directions for cleaning.

2. Start with fresh coffee and freshly drawn cold tap water, and always use the grind that's recommended for your coffee maker.

3. Measure accurately. Coffee-making directions are usually based on 2 level measuring tablespoons of coffee for each ¾ measuring cup of water. With a little experiment-

PAELLA (p. 178)
ARTICHOKE-ORANGE SALAD (p.330)
GARLIC-CHEDDAR LOAF (p.414)
SANGRIA FIZZ (p.47)

33

ing, you can adjust these amounts to suit your taste. Load drip or percolator baskets so that the coffee is evenly distributed rather than being mounded up on one side.

4. Be a clockwatcher and keep tabs on the brewing time. The best flavor is usually developed by perking the coffee between 5 and 8 minutes.

5. Serve coffee as soon as possible after it's made and serve it steaming hot. If it's necessary to let coffee stand after brewing, place the pot over very low heat so it holds at serving temperature. Never let coffee boil. (Economy tip: To avoid wasting leftover coffee, cool it first and freeze in ice cube trays. Use these cubes when making iced coffee.)

6. Store coffee properly. Keep the can covered tightly and place it in the coolest spot in the kitchen, away from the range. If you transfer the coffee from its original container to a canister, be sure the canister is air-tight. Under these conditions, coffee will hold its flavor up to two weeks.

For longer storage—from 6 to 8 weeks—call on your refrigerator, but remember that quickly-in-and-out is the key to freshness. Specifically, take out what you need from the container, reseal, and return it to the refrigerator at once. Otherwise, moisture condenses on the cold open can and hastens staling.

The instant variety

Coffees in powdered, freeze-dried, and decaffeinated forms save time and effort, and properly fixed, are just as acceptable and pleasing as brewed kinds.

To make a single serving, measure 1 to 2 teaspoons instant coffee into a cup and stir in enough boiling water to fill the cup.

If you need a larger quantity at a time, make it by the potful. For 6 servings, heat 4 cups cold water to boiling in a coffeepot or saucepan; turn off heat. Stir in 2 to 4 tablespoons instant coffee; cover container; let stand about 3 minutes. Pour and serve.

How to make iced coffee

Prepare coffee slightly stronger than usual since it will be diluted with ice. Three level tablespoons of coffee for each ¾ cup water is a good yardstick. Brew as usual and pour the hot coffee over cracked or crushed ice. Serve with sugar and cream—plain or whipped.

TIPS ON TEA

This popular beverage comes in a wide array of flavors and almost every brand or kind is a blend of many varieties carefully selected to produce a special flavor, aroma, and color. Despite all the differences, teas are usually divided into three categories, depending on how the leaves are processed. They are:

Black. Processing causes the leaves to oxidize and turn black, and they in turn, make a hearty, rich-flavored brew. Most of the tea sold in this country is the black type.

Oolong. Because leaves are only partly or semi-oxidized, they turn a greenish-brown. The brew is light-colored with a delicate flavor.

Green. Leaves stay green since they're not oxidized. The brew has a delicate green color and a mild but distinctive flavor.

Tea comes in loose form, as individual bags with about a teaspoonful of tea enclosed in special filter paper, or as instant tea in powdered and liquid varieties—some of which are flavored with lemon and sugar or low-calorie sweeteners.

Whether you use loose tea or tea bags, follow these fixing steps:

1. Start with a clean teapot. Preheat it by filling with boiling water; let it stand a few minutes, then pour it out.
2. Heat fresh cold tap water to a rapid boil. If water is not boiling, it produces a weak tea; water that has been standing or is reheated gives tea a flat taste.
3. Measure 1 teaspoonful loose tea (or use 1 regular tea bag) into the pot for each serving; pour in ¾ cup boiling water; cover. Brew 3 to 5 minutes to bring out the full flavor and aroma. Before pouring, stir the brew to make sure it's uniform. Pour into cups and serve plain, with milk, sugar, and lemon, lime, or orange wedges.

The instant varieties

Ready in minutes, this tea has been concentrated into powdered form. Whether you're making it hot by the cupful or potful or iced by the glassful or pitcherful, follow the directions on the label.

How to make iced tea

Follow the same directions as for hot tea, except double the amount of tea since it will be diluted with ice. After brewing, pour it hot over ice and serve with sugar and lemon, lime, or orange wedges. If possible, avoid refrigerating tea since it will turn cloudy. To make it clear again, pour a small amount of boiling water into the pitcher or jar.

To fix iced tea the cold-water way, combine 2 teaspoons loose tea or 2 regular tea bags and 1 cup cold water for each serving in a large glass jar or pitcher; cover. Chill overnight or for 24 hours. Serve over crushed or cracked ice.

COFFEE AND TEA

CAFE BRASILIA

2 envelopes premelted unsweetened
    chocolate
⅔ cup granulated sugar
⅓ cup water
⅓ cup whipping cream
6 cups freshly brewed, strong hot
    coffee

Combine chocolate, sugar, and water in a small saucepan. Heat slowly, stirring constantly, to boiling; cook 3 minutes, cool. (If syrup is made ahead, chill. Remove from refrigerator about an hour before serving and let stand at room temperature to warm.)

When ready to serve, beat cream in a small bowl until stiff; fold into chocolate mixture. Spoon 1 to 2 tablespoons into each of 8 cups or mugs; fill each with hot coffee. Pass extra sugar for those who prefer coffee sweeter.

Yield: 8 servings.

MEXICAN MOCHA

2 cups milk
2 tablespoons granulated sugar
2 teaspoons dry instant coffee
¼ cup chocolate syrup
    Cinnamon-sugar

Combine milk, sugar, instant coffee, and chocolate syrup in a medium saucepan. Heat slowly, stirring constantly, just until hot.

Pour into mugs; sprinkle cinnamon-sugar lightly over each serving.

Yield: 2 servings.

ESPRESSO CREAM

½ cup whipping cream
1 tablespoon confectioners'
    powdered sugar
4 tablespoons instant espresso coffee
4 cups boiling water
1 teaspoon shredded lemon rind

Beat cream with sugar in a small bowl until stiff.

Dissolve coffee in boiling water in a 4-cup measure; pour into 8 demitasse cups. Spoon cream on top of each; sprinkle lemon rind over cream. Serve very hot.

Yield: 8 servings.

JAVANESE COFFEE

¼ cup whipping cream
1 pint chocolate ice cream
4½ cups freshly brewed hot coffee
    Nutmeg

Beat cream in a small bowl until stiff.

Spoon ice cream into 6 tall mugs, pour ¾ cup hot coffee into each. Top with a spoonful of whipped cream; sprinkle nutmeg over cream.

Yield: 6 servings.

SPICED VIENNESE COFFEE

3 tablespoons freeze-dried instant coffee
6 whole cloves
1 three-inch stick of cinnamon
4 cups water
¼ cup granulated sugar
    Whipped cream
    Ground cinnamon

Combine coffee, cloves, cinnamon, and water in a medium saucepan. Heat to boiling; remove from heat; cover. Let stand 5 minutes. Remove cloves and cinnamon stick; stir in sugar; reheat to boiling.

Pour coffee into mugs or cups; spoon whipped cream over each serving; sprinkle cinnamon over cream.

Yield: 4 servings.

ICED TEA NECTAR

2 tablespoons instant tea
4 cups water
½ cup granulated sugar
1 can (12 ozs.) unsweetened pineapple juice
1 can (12 ozs.) apricot nectar
2 cups orange juice
1 cup lemon juice
 Ice cubes

Dissolve tea in water in a large pitcher or kettle; stir in sugar until dissolved, then add pineapple juice, apricot nectar, and orange and lemon juices.

Pour over ice in tall glasses. Trim edge of each glass with a wedge of orange if you like.

Yield: 10 servings.

SPICED TEA

6 whole cloves
1 two-inch stick of cinnamon
3 cups water
4 tea bags
¼ cup honey

Combine cloves, cinnamon stick, and water in a small saucepan; heat to boiling. Add tea bags; cover; remove from heat. Let stand 5 minutes; remove tea bags. Stir in honey.

Strain into cups and serve hot with milk. Or cool and pour over ice in tall glasses; serve with lemon wedges.

Yield: 4 servings.

MINTED TEA FIZZ

4 cups boiling water
6 tea bags
2 tablespoons mint jelly
 Ice cubes
 Ginger ale

Pour boiling water over tea bags in a teapot or saucepan; cover. Brew 5 minutes; remove tea bags. Stir in jelly until melted.

Pour over ice in tall glasses to fill half full; pour in enough ginger ale to fill glasses. Garnish each serving with a sprig of mint if you like.

Yield: 8 servings.

LEMON TEA SHRUB

2 cups boiling water
3 tea bags
½ cup granulated sugar
1 can (6 ozs.) frozen concentrate for
   orange juice
¼ cup lemon juice
1 cup cold water
1 pint lemon sherbet

Pour boiling water over tea bags in a teapot or medium saucepan; cover. Let stand 5 minutes; remove tea bags.

Stir in sugar until dissolved, then stir in orange concentrate, lemon juice, and cold water. Chill well.

Pour into tall glasses; float a spoonful of sherbet on each serving.

Yield: 6 servings.

CHOCOLATE AND COCOA

MOCHA FIZZ

½ cup instant cocoa mix
2 cups cold milk
1 pint chocolate ice cream
1 bottle (16 ozs.) carbonated
    coffee beverage, chilled
Frozen whipped topping, thawed

Dissolve cocoa mix in milk in a medium bowl. Beat in ice cream until smooth, then stir in coffee beverage.

Pour into mugs; spoon whipped topping over each serving.

Yield: 6 servings.

PEANUT COCOA

⅓ cup instant cocoa mix
4 cups milk
3 tablespoons creamy
    peanut butter

Dissolve cocoa mix in milk in a medium saucepan; beat in peanut butter with a rotary beater until well blended.

Heat slowly, stirring several times, until hot. (Do not boil.) Pour into mugs.

Yield: 4 servings.

CHOCO-BANANA FLIP

4 cups cold milk
2 large firm ripe bananas, peeled
    and cut into chunks
½ cup canned or bottled chocolate syrup
2 teaspoons vanilla
8 large ice cubes

Place half each of the milk, bananas, chocolate syrup, vanilla, and ice into an electric-blender container; cover. Blend until smooth. Repeat with other half of ingredients.

Serve at once in small glasses or cups.

Yield: 8 servings.

EARLY MORNING MOCHA

½ cup instant cocoa mix
¼ cup dry instant coffee
2 tablespoons granulated sugar
2 cups boiling water
2 cups milk
½ teaspoon orange extract

Combine cocoa mix, instant coffee, and sugar in a medium saucepan; stir in boiling water, then milk and orange extract. Heat very slowly until hot. (Do not boil.) Ladle into mugs. Serve hot.

Yield: 4 servings.

CINNAMON CHOCOLATE

5⅓ cups instant nonfat dry milk
1½ cups instant cocoa mix
2 tablespoons freeze-dried
    instant coffee
1 bottle (3 ozs.) cinnamon-sugar
    (about ½ cup)
4 quarts water
Tiny marshmallows

Mix milk powder, cocoa mix, dry coffee, and cinnamon-sugar in a kettle; stir in water. Heat very slowly, stirring often, just to boiling.

Ladle into cups or mugs; float a few marshmallows on each serving.

Yield: 16 servings.

DOUBLE CHOCOLATE WHIP

3 cups milk
½ cup chocolate syrup
1 pint chocolate ice cream
Chocolate sprinkles

Combine milk, chocolate syrup, and ice cream in an electric-blender container; cover. Blend until smooth.

Pour into tall glasses. Float chocolate sprinkles on each serving.

Yield: 6 servings.

MILK

PEANUT WHIP

1½ cups milk
  2 tablespoons peanut butter
  1 tablespoon honey

Combine all ingredients in an electric-blender container; cover. Beat until smooth. Or combine in a bowl and beat with rotary beater. Pour into glasses.
Yield: 2 servings.

PINEAPPLE SLUSH

  1 can (8 ozs.) crushed pineapple in syrup
  1 large seedless orange, pared and sectioned
1½ cups milk
  ¼ cup light corn syrup

Combine pineapple and syrup, orange sections, milk, and corn syrup in an electric-blender container; cover. Beat until smooth. Pour into tall glasses.
Yield: 3 servings.

PEACH NOG

¾ cup milk
¾ cup peach nectar
  2 teaspoons orange-flavored instant breakfast
      drink
  1 egg
½ teaspoon vanilla

Combine all ingredients in an electric-blender container; cover. Beat until smooth and frothy. Or combine mixture in a bowl and beat with a rotary beater. Pour into tall glasses.
Yield: 2 servings.

RASPBERRY SHAKE

  1 package (10 ozs.) frozen raspberries, thawed
  1 cup (8-oz. carton) vanilla yogurt
  ¼ cup regular wheat germ
  2 tablespoons granulated sugar
  ½ cup milk

Empty raspberries and syrup from package into an electric-blender container; cover. Beat until smooth. Strain into a small bowl to remove seeds; return to blender container.

Add yogurt, wheat germ, sugar, and milk; cover again. Beat several seconds until smooth. Pour into tall glasses.
Yield: 2 servings.

APRICOT FLIP

1½ cups milk
  1 cup apricot nectar
1½ teaspoons granulated sugar
  1 teaspoon vanilla
    Mace

Measure milk, apricot nectar, sugar, and vanilla into a shaker or jar with a tight lid; cover. Shake well to mix. Pour into tall glasses; sprinkle mace very lightly over each serving.
Yield: 2 servings.

BANANA TWIRL

1½ cups milk
  1 large firm ripe banana, peeled and cut up
  1 tablespoon honey
  ½ teaspoon vanilla

Combine milk, banana, honey, and vanilla in an electric-blender container; cover. Beat until smooth. Pour into tall glasses.
Yield: 2 servings.

APRICOT FROST

2 envelopes vanilla-flavored instant breakfast
2 cups milk
½ cup creamed cottage cheese
1 can (8 ozs.) apricot halves in syrup
1 teaspoon vanilla
1 cup crushed ice

Combine instant breakfast, milk, cottage cheese, apricots and syrup, and vanilla in an electric-blender container; cover. Blend until smooth.

Add ice; blend a few seconds more. Pour into tall glasses.

Yield: 4 servings.

STRAWBERRY-BANANA WHIP

⅔ cup instant nonfat dry milk
2 cups ice water
2 medium-sized ripe bananas
½ cup instant strawberry-flavored drink mix
1 teaspoon vanilla

Combine milk and water in an electric-blender container; cover. Blend until smooth.

Peel bananas and slice; add to blender container with drink mix and vanilla; cover again. Blend until smooth. Pour into tall glasses.

Yield: 4 servings.

MELBA MILK

1 package (10 ozs.) frozen sliced strawberries, thawed
1 can (8 ozs.) sliced cling peaches in syrup
2 cups milk
1 teaspoon vanilla

Combine strawberries and syrup and peaches and syrup in an electric-blender container; cover. Beat until smooth.

Add milk and vanilla; cover again; beat 1 to 2 seconds longer. Pour into tall glasses.

Yield: 4 servings.

FRUIT DRINKS

BLUSHING ORANGEADE

4 packages (3½ ozs. each) orange sugar-sweetened
    soft drink mix
4 quarts cold water
1 can (6 ozs.) frozen concentrate for cranberry juice
    cocktail, partly thawed

Dissolve drink mix in water in a kettle; stir in cranberry concentrate. Pour over ice in tall glasses.

Yield: 16 servings.

GRAPE COOLER

½ cup grape-flavored instant breakfast drink
 3 cups water
 1 can (6 ozs.) frozen lemonade, partly thawed
 1 bottle (28 ozs.) carbonated orange beverage
 Ice cubes

Combine grape drink powder and water in a large pitcher; stir until dissolved, then stir in lemonade and orange beverage.

Pour over ice in tall glasses. Garnish each serving with a sprig of mint if you like.

Yield: 8 servings.

APRICOT-ORANGE FROST

⅔ cup orange-flavored instant breakfast drink
 4 cups water
 2 cans (12 ozs. each) apricot nectar
½ cup lemon juice
 Ice cubes

Dissolve orange drink in water in a large pitcher. Stir in apricot nectar and lemon juice.

Pour over ice in tall glasses. Garnish each with a slice of orange if you like.

Yield: 8 servings.

PINK LEMON FIZZ

1 can (46 ozs.) fruit-juicy red Hawaiian punch
1 can (6 ozs.) frozen concentrate for lemonade
1 bottle (16 ozs.) lemon-lime carbonated beverage,
    chilled
 Ice

Combine punch and lemonade concentrate in a large pitcher; stir until lemonade melts; chill well.

Just before serving, stir in lemon-lime beverage; pour over ice in tall glasses. Float a slice of lemon or lime on each if you like.

Yield: 6 servings.

CRANBERRY-ORANGE FROST

1 can (6 ozs.) frozen concentrate for lemonade
1 pint cranberry juice cocktail
2 bottles (12 ozs. each) carbonated orange beverage
1 cup apple juice
 Ice

Combine lemonade concentrate and cranberry juice in a large pitcher; stir until lemonade thaws completely. Stir in orange beverage and apple juice.

Pour over ice in tall glasses. Float a lemon slice on each if you like.

Yield: 8 servings.

CRANBERRY CHEER

 1 bottle (32 ozs.) cranberry-juice cocktail, chilled
 1 can (18 ozs.) orange-grapefruit juice, chilled
¼ cup lime juice

Mix all ingredients in a large pitcher. Pour into tall glasses.

Yield: 8 servings.

CRANBERRY MIST

1 can (46 ozs.) lemon-pink Hawaiian punch
½ cup light corn syrup
1 bottle (32 ozs.) cranberry juice cocktail
1 bottle (28 ozs.) ginger ale
  Ice cubes

Empty punch into a large pitcher or kettle; stir in corn syrup until blended, then add cranberry juice and ginger ale.

Pour over ice in tall glasses. Garnish each with a thin lemon slice if you like.

Yield: 12 servings.

GRAPEFRUIT GROG

¼ cup light corn syrup
1 two-inch-long stick of cinnamon
6 whole cloves
4 cups water
¼ cup orange-flavored instant breakfast drink
¼ cup grapefruit-flavored instant breakfast drink

Combine corn syrup, cinnamon stick, cloves, and 2 cups of the water in a medium saucepan. Heat to boiling; simmer 5 minutes.

Dissolve orange and grapefruit drinks in remaining 2 cups water in a pitcher; strain hot syrup into pitcher; stir well.

Pour into mugs; serve warm.

Yield: 4 servings.

SPICED LEMONADE

3 whole cloves
1 four-inch stick of cinnamon, broken
2 cups cranberry-juice cocktail
3 cups water
½ cup lemonade-flavored drink mix
  Ice cubes

Combine cloves, cinnamon stick, cranberry juice, and water in a medium saucepan; heat to boiling; cover. Remove from heat; let stand 5 minutes. Strain into a pitcher; cool.

Stir in lemonade drink mix until dissolved. Pour over ice in tall glasses. Garnish each with a lemon slice if you like.

Yield: 6 servings.

RED GRAPE FIZZ

1 bottle (24 ozs.) red grape juice
¼ cup granulated sugar
2 cups orange juice
1 bottle (16 ozs.) carbonated lemon-lime beverage

Combine grape juice and sugar in a large pitcher; stir until sugar dissolves. Stir in orange juice and lemon-lime beverage.

Pour over ice in tall glasses. Garnish each with a slice of orange if you like.

Yield: 6 servings.

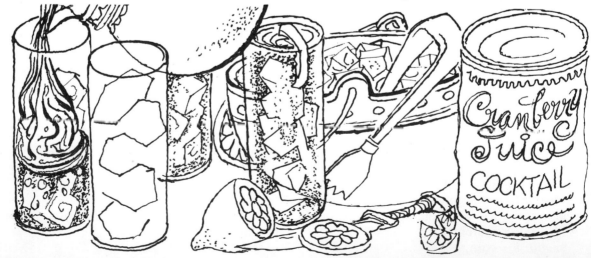

SHAKES, SODAS, AND FLOATS

MAPLE-NUT CREAM

3 cups milk
⅓ cup maple-blended syrup
1 pint maple-nut ice cream

Combine milk, syrup, and ice cream in an electric-blender container; cover. Blend until smooth.

Pour into tall glasses. Garnish each with crushed maple candy if you like.

Yield: 4 servings.

PURPLE MOO

2 cups milk
⅓ cup thawed frozen concentrate for grape juice
2 scoops vanilla ice milk

Measure milk into an electric-blender container; very slowly pour in grape concentrate. Add ice milk; cover. Beat until smooth. Pour into tall glasses.

Yield: 3 servings.

CHERRY SWIZZLE

1 pint cherry-vanilla ice cream
2 cans (12 ozs. each) noncarbonated cherry-flavored drink, chilled
1 bottle (16 ozs.) cola beverage, chilled

Beat ice cream into cherry drink in a medium bowl; divide evenly into 8 tall glasses. Pour ¼ cup cola beverage into each glass. (Do not stir.)

Yield: 8 servings.

APPLE BLOSSOM FREEZE

1 can (6 ozs.) frozen concentrate for tangerine juice
2 cups apple juice
2 cups milk
1 pint vanilla ice cream

Combine tangerine concentrate, apple juice, and milk in an electric-blender container; cover. Blend until smooth.

Add ice cream; blend just until smooth.

Pour into tall glasses. Garnish each with a sprig of fresh mint if you like.

Yield: 6 servings.

PEANUT FLUFF

⅓ cup creamy peanut butter
3 cups milk
1 pint butter-pecan ice cream
½ cup marshmallow topping for ice cream

Combine peanut butter and milk in an electric-blender container; cover. Beat until smooth.

Add ice cream and marshmallow topping; blend until smooth.

Pour into tall glasses. Garnish each with unsweetened chocolate curls if you like.

Yield: 4 servings.

AMBROSIA-IN-A-GLASS

1 large firm ripe banana
1 can (6 ozs.) unsweetened pineapple juice
⅓ cup honey
3 cups milk
1 pint orange sherbet

Peel banana and slice; combine with pineapple juice in an electric-blender container; cover. Beat until smooth.

Add honey, milk, and sherbet; blend until smooth.

Pour into tall glasses. Float flaked coconut on each if you like.

Yield: 8 servings.

SPICED PINEAPPLE SWIZZLE

½ cup granulated sugar
3 cups water
6 whole cloves
2 four-inch-long pieces stick cinnamon
1 can (6 ozs.) frozen concentrate for pineapple
   juice, thawed
2 tablespoons lemon juice
1 bottle (12 ozs.) ginger ale
   Ice cubes

Combine sugar, water, cloves, and cinnamon in a medium saucepan. Heat to boiling; cover. Simmer 10 minutes. Strain into a large pitcher. Stir in pineapple concentrate and lemon juice; chill.

Just before serving, stir in ginger ale. Pour over ice in tall glasses. Garnish each with a cinnamon stick if you like.

Yield: 4 servings.

STRAWBERRY SUNDAE SHAKE

3 cups milk
¼ cup instant strawberry-flavored drink mix
1 pint strawberry ice cream
   Frozen whipped topping, thawed
   Strawberries, hulled

Combine milk and drink mix in an electric-blender container; cover. Blend until drink mix dissolves.

Add ice cream; blend until smooth.

Pour into tall glasses. Garnish each with a spoonful of whipped topping and a strawberry.

Yield: 6 servings.

RASPBERRY COOLER

2 envelopes (.22 ozs. each) raspberry soft drink
   mix
¾ cup granulated sugar
⅔ cup instant nonfat dry milk
3 cups water
1 pint raspberry sherbet

Combine drink mix, sugar, milk powder, and water in an electric-blender container;

cover. Blend until drink mix and sugar are dissolved.

Add sherbet; blend until smooth. (If your blender container isn't large enough to hold all of the ingredients at one time, mix two batches.)

Pour into tall glasses. Float a few fresh or frozen raspberries on each if you like.

Yield: 6 servings.

CHOCO-ORANGE SODA

4 envelopes (1.1 ozs. each) dark chocolate instant
   cocoa mix
   Water
1 pint orange sherbet
2 bottles (12 ozs. each) carbonated orange
   beverage, chilled

Prepare cocoa mix with water in a pitcher as label directs; chill several hours until frosty cold.

When ready to serve, pour ½ cup of the cocoa into each of 6 tall glasses. Add a scoop of orange sherbet to each, then fill with orange beverage. Do not stir.

Yield: 6 servings.

PINK PINEAPPLE CREAM

1 can (6 ozs.) frozen concentrate for fruit-juicy red
   Hawaiian punch, thawed
3 cups milk
1 pint pineapple ice
1 bottle (12 ozs.) carbonated water

Combine half each of the Hawaiian punch, milk, and pineapple ice in an electric-blender container; cover. Blend until smooth. Pour into a large pitcher.

Repeat with other half of ingredients; pour into pitcher; stir in carbonated water.

Pour into tall glasses. Garnish each serving with pineapple chunks threaded onto a kabob stick if you like.

Yield: 6 servings.

LEMON-LIME FROST

3 cups milk
1 can (6 ozs.) frozen concentrate for limeade, partly
    thawed
1 pint lemon sherbet

Combine milk, limeade, and sherbet in an electric-blender container; cover. Blend until smooth.

Pour into tall glasses. Garnish each with a slice of lemon or lime if you like.

Yield: 6 servings.

STRAWBERRY FLOAT

1 package (10 ozs.) frozen sliced strawberries,
    thawed
1 can (46 ozs.) orange Hawaiian punch, chilled
1 bottle (10 ozs.) carbonated lemon-lime beverage,
    chilled
1 pint orange sherbet

Place strawberries and syrup in an electric-blender container; cover. Beat until smooth; pour into a large pitcher. Stir in orange punch and lemon-lime beverage.

Pour into tall glasses. Float a small scoop of sherbet on each serving.

Yield: 8 servings.

PEACH MEDLEY

2 cans (12 ozs. each) peach nectar
2 cups milk
3 tablespoons bottled grenadine syrup
1 teaspoon vanilla
1 pint peach ice cream
    Ground nutmeg

Combine half each of the peach nectar, milk, grenadine syrup, vanilla, and ice cream in an electric-blender container; cover. Blend until smooth. Repeat with rest of ingredients.

Pour into tall glasses; sprinkle nutmeg over each.

Yield: 8 servings.

TUTTI-FRUTTI SHAKE

1 can (8 ozs.) fruit cocktail
½ cup pineapple preserves
3 cups milk
1 pint vanilla ice milk

Pour fruit cocktail and syrup into an electric-blender container; cover. Beat until smooth.

Add preserves, milk, and ice milk; blend until smooth.

Pour into tall glasses. Garnish each with maraschino cherries and pineapple chunks threaded onto a drinking straw if you like.

Yield: 6 servings.

APRICOT MIST

2 tablespoons orange-flavored instant breakfast
    drink
¼ cup water
2 cans (12 ozs. each) apricot nectar
1 cup milk
1 pint vanilla ice cream

Combine breakfast drink and water in an electric-blender container; cover. Blend several seconds.

Add apricot nectar, milk, and ice cream; blend until smooth.

Pour into tall glasses. Garnish each with a slice or wedge of fresh orange if you like.

Yield: 6 servings.

HONEY-ORANGE CREAM

½ cup orange-flavored instant breakfast drink
2 cups water
½ cup honey
2 cups cold milk
½ pint vanilla ice cream

Dissolve orange drink in water in a medium bowl. Beat in honey, milk, and ice cream until smooth and frothy.

Pour into tall glasses. Garnish each with an orange slice if you like.

Yield: 6 servings.

PARTY PUNCHES

CRANBERRY-APPLE CRUSH

2 cups cranberry juice cocktail
2 tablespoons granulated sugar
1 can (46 ozs.) orange-flavored fruit drink
1 cup apple juice
1 can (6 ozs.) frozen concentrate for lemonade,
    thawed
  Ice cubes

Combine cranberry juice cocktail and sugar in a large pitcher or bowl, stir until sugar is dissolved.

Stir in orange drink, apple juice, and lemonade concentrate. Pour over ice in tall glasses. Float a slice of lemon on each if you like.

Yield: 10 servings.

TROPICAL FRUIT PUNCH

1 envelope (7¼ ozs.) red Hawaiian punch drink mix
1 can (6 ozs.) frozen concentrate for pineapple
    juice, thawed
6 cups water
1 bottle (32 ozs.) lemon-lime carbonated beverage
  Ice cubes

Combine drink mix, pineapple concentrate, and water in a large pitcher; stir until drink mix dissolves.

Just before serving, stir in carbonated beverage. Pour over ice in tall glasses. Garnish each with a long stick of fresh pineapple if you like.

Yield: 10 to 12 servings.

ST. NICK'S PUNCH

1 can (8 ozs.) pineapple chunks in juice
1 bottle (24 ozs.) white grape juice
1 can (46 ozs.) fruit-juicy red Hawaiian punch,
    chilled
1 can (6 ozs.) frozen concentrate for limeade,
    thawed
1 can (18 ozs.) pineapple juice
  Mint

Drain juice from pineapple and save for punch.

Place 1 pineapple chunk in each section of an ice-cube tray. (There should be about 18 chunks in can.) Pour grape juice over pineapple; pour remainder into a second tray; freeze both firm.

Just before serving, combine Hawaiian punch, limeade concentrate, and pineapple juice in a punch bowl; add pineapple-grape cubes. Float a few sprigs of mint on top. (Add plain grape cubes as needed.)

Ladle punch into cups, adding a pineapple cube to each cup.

Yield: 24 punch-cup servings.

DAIQUIRI PUNCH

1 can (46 ozs.) cool citrus Hawaiian punch
2 tablespoons granulated sugar
1 bottle (4/5 pint) light rum
1 bottle (28 ozs.) bitter lemon
  Cherry-lime ice ring (directions follow)

Combine punch and sugar in a punch bowl; stir until sugar dissolves. Stir in rum and bitter lemon.

Unmold ice ring onto a plate; carefully slide ring into punch bowl.

Yield: About 20 punch-cup servings.

Ice Ring: Slice 1 small lime; place slices in a circle in a 1- or 1½-quart ring mold. Place several maraschino cherries in a pretty pattern between lime slices. Slowly pour in ½ cup water; freeze firm. Add another 1 to 2 cups water; freeze firm. Add enough more water to fill mold; freeze overnight, or until serving time.

SANGRIA FIZZ

½ cup lemon juice
¼ cup orange juice
¼ cup granulated sugar
 1 bottle (4/5 quart) dry red wine, chilled
 1 bottle (12 ozs.) carbonated water, chilled
 Orange and lemon slices

Strain lemon and orange juices into a pitcher; stir in sugar until dissolved; chill.

Just before serving, stir in wine and carbonated water; add orange and lemon slices to pitcher. Serve in stemmed glasses.

Yield: 8 servings.

PARTY PINK PUNCH

 2 cans (46 ozs. each) red Hawaiian punch
½ cup light corn syrup
 1 three-inch-piece stick cinnamon
10 whole cloves
 1 bottle (4/5 quart) dry white wine, chilled
 Mint

Combine 1 cup of the punch, corn syrup, cinnamon, and cloves in a small saucepan. Heat to boiling, then simmer 10 minutes; chill.

Just before serving, strain spice mixture into a punch bowl; stir in remaining punch and wine.

Add ice to punch; float a few sprigs of mint on top.

Yield: 30 punch-cup servings.

CELEBRATION PUNCH

 1 can (12 ozs.) frozen fruit-juicy red Hawaiian
  punch, partly thawed
 1 can (6 ozs.) frozen pink lemonade, partly thawed
 1 can (6 ozs.) frozen limeade, partly thawed
10 cups water
 Ice cubes

Blend Hawaiian punch, lemonade, limeade, and water in a large bowl or pitcher; pour over ice cubes in tall glasses. If you like, garnish each serving with a lime slice and two maraschino cherries threaded onto a drinking straw.

Yield: 16 servings.

GOLDEN ANNIVERSARY PUNCH

 Ice Ring (directions on page 46)
1 cup granulated sugar
4 cups water
2 cans (12 ozs. each) apricot nectar, chilled
2 cans (6 ozs. each) frozen concentrate for orange
  juice, thawed
2 cups lemon juice
1 cup curacao
1 bottle (4/5 quart) champagne, chilled
1 bottle (28 ozs.) carbonated water, chilled
 Small mint leaves

Make Ice Ring, substituting small orange slices for lime and omitting cherries.

Combine sugar and water in a punch bowl; stir until sugar dissolves. Stir in apricot nectar, orange concentrate, lemon juice, and curacao.

Just before serving, stir in champagne and carbonated water.

Unmold ice ring onto a plate; carefully slide ring into punch bowl. Float mint leaves on top.

Yield: 40 punch-cup servings or about 5 quarts.

SOUPS

IF YOU'RE STUMPED BY THE HIGH PRICE OF MEAT, look to soups to rescue your meals and your budget. Almost anything goes, and a big bowlful of one that's thick and hearty makes a delightfully nourishing whole lunch or supper; a cupful of one that's light takes the edge off of appetites for other foods on a dinner menu.

Starting point can be as thrifty as a half pound or so of chicken wings, backs, or giblets; one or two beef shank crosscuts; or the bones left from a turkey or lamb roast or baked ham. All you need is just enough to simmer with seasonings for a savory broth base.

After the broth is made, look around your kitchen. You can stir in just about any other food and be assured that it will boost flavor. Small amounts of leftover fresh or cooked vegetables, liquids left from canned vegetables, dried peas and beans, macaroni, noodles, rice, or bits of leftover meat that aren't enough for a second meal are perfect ingredients. Just remember to add cooked foods at the end of the cooking time so they'll keep their shapes and textures.

When you're in a hurry, or for spur-of-the-moment meals, call on canned soups and packaged mixes as your starter. Although appealing as is, the combinations you can make by mixing kinds or adding your own extras can add almost endless variety to meal fixing—and pleasurable eating.

APPETIZER

HOT-WEATHER CARROT CREAM

1 medium onion, coarsely chopped (½ cup)
1 tablespoon butter or margarine
3 tablespoons all-purpose flour
1 envelope instant chicken broth
¼ teaspoon ground nutmeg
1 cup water
2 cups light cream
1 jar (8 ozs.) junior carrots
Few drops red-pepper seasoning

Sauté onion in butter in a small saucepan until soft. Stir in flour, chicken broth, and nutmeg; cook, stirring constantly, until bubbly. Stir in water; continue cooking and stirring until mixture thickens and boils 1 minute; pour into an electric-blender container.

Add 1 cup of the cream, carrots, and red-pepper seasoning; cover; blend until smooth. Stir in rest of cream. Chill several hours, or until frosty cold.

Pour into small cups or bowls; float a few paper-thin slices of carrot on each.

Yield: 4 servings.

ITALIAN CHICKEN CHOWDER

3 single-serving envelopes chicken-noodle soup mix
2 cups water
1 can (16 ozs.) stewed tomatoes
1 can (5 ozs.) boned chicken, cut up
¼ teaspoon dried oregano, crushed
¼ teaspoon sugar

Stir soup mix into water in a large saucepan; heat slowly, stirring several times, to boiling.

Stir in tomatoes, chicken, oregano, and sugar. Heat to boiling again; simmer 10 minutes to blend flavors.

Ladle into soup bowls or cups.

Yield: 4 servings.

SHRIMP BISQUE

1 small onion, chopped (¼ cup)
2 tablespoons butter or margarine
1 can (10¾ ozs.) condensed cream of shrimp soup
1 can (10¾ ozs.) condensed tomato soup
2 cups milk
⅛ teaspoon liquid red-pepper seasoning
1 cup light cream
1 tablespoon lemon juice
¼ cup whipping cream
1 teaspoon grated lemon rind

Sauté onion in butter in a large saucepan until soft; stir in soups, milk, and red-pepper seasoning.

Heat slowly, stirring several times, just to simmering. Stir in cream and lemon juice; heat again just until hot.

Beat cream until stiff in a small bowl; stir in lemon rind.

Ladle soup into small bowls or cups; float lemon cream on each serving.

Yield: 8 servings.

SUMMER BORSCH

1 envelope onion soup mix (2 to a package)
3 cups water
1 envelope unflavored gelatin
1 can (8 ozs.) diced beets
1 tablespoon lemon juice
1 cup (8-oz. carton) plain yogurt
2 tablespoons snipped chives

Stir onion soup mix into 2¾ cups of the water in a medium saucepan; heat, stirring several times, to boiling; simmer 10 minutes.

Soften gelatin in remaining ¼ cup water in a cup; stir into onion mixture until dissolved; remove from heat.

Drain liquid from beets; stir into gelatin mixture with lemon juice. Chill several hours, or until softly set; fold in beets.

When ready to serve, spoon beet mixture into 6 parfait glasses; spoon yogurt on top; sprinkle chives over yogurt.

Yield: 6 servings.

CHICKEN-VEGETABLE BROTH

1 can (10¾ ozs.) condensed vegetarian vegetable
   soup
1 can (13¾ ozs.) chicken broth
2 tablespoons freeze-dried chives
½ cup milk
   Plain croutons (from a package)

Combine soup, chicken broth, and chives in a medium saucepan. Heat slowly, stirring several times, to boiling. Stir in milk; heat again until bubbly.

Ladle into soup cups or small bowls; float a few croutons on each serving.

Yield: 6 servings.

JELLIED CHICKEN APPETIZER

1 envelope unflavored gelatin
2 cans (13¾ ozs. each) chicken broth
6 drops red-pepper seasoning
   Yellow food coloring
8 radishes

Soften gelatin in 1 cup of the chicken broth in a small saucepan. Heat, stirring constantly, until gelatin dissolves; stir into remaining chicken broth in a medium bowl, then stir in red-pepper seasoning and several drops food coloring to tint bright yellow. Chill several hours, or overnight, until softly set.

When ready to serve, spoon into 8 small soup cups or parfait glasses; garnish each serving with a radish which has been cut into a rose shape. Serve with crisp wheat wafers if you like.

Yield: 8 servings.

CLARET CONSOMME

3 cans condensed beef consommé
2 cups claret
2 cups water
2 tablespoons lemon juice
   Parsley
1 large lemon, sliced thin

Combine consommé, claret, and water in a large saucepan; heat to boiling. Stir in lemon juice.

Ladle into soup cups. Float parsley and lemon slices on top.

Yield: 8 servings.

TOMATO-CLAM CUP

2 cups boiling water
2 single-serving envelopes tomato soup mix
2 cans (8 ozs. each) minced clams
1 cup buttermilk
½ teaspoon salt
   Few drops red-pepper seasoning

Stir boiling water into soup mix in a medium bowl; pour into an electric-blender container. Add clams and liquid; cover; blend until smooth.

Pour back into bowl; stir in buttermilk, salt, and red-pepper seasoning. Chill several hours, or until frosty cold.

Ladle into small cups or bowls, garnish each serving with a thin slice of avocado if you like.

Yield: 6 servings.

PUMPKIN BISQUE

1 small onion, minced (¼ cup)
2 tablespoons butter or margarine
1 can (10¾ ozs.) condensed cream of potato soup
1½ cups water
1 cup canned pumpkin
1 cup light cream
¼ teaspoon pepper
¼ teaspoon ground nutmeg

Sauté onion in butter in a medium saucepan until soft; stir in potato soup and water. Heat, stirring once or twice, until blended.

Stir in pumpkin, cream, pepper, and nutmeg. Heat to boiling; simmer 20 minutes to blend flavors.

Ladle into soup cups. Float thin slices of raw zucchini on top of each serving if you like.

Yield: 6 servings.

PEA POTAGE

1 small onion, chopped (¼ cup)
1 tablespoon salad oil
3 single-serving envelopes green pea soup mix
2 cups water
1 can (8 ozs.) peas
4 tablespoons bacon-flavored vegetable-protein
    bits

Sauté onion in salad oil in a medium saucepan until soft.

Stir in soup mix, water, and peas and liquid. Heat to boiling; simmer 2 to 3 minutes to blend flavors.

Ladle into soup bowls or cups; sprinkle protein bits on top.

Yield: 4 servings.

ANDALUSIAN GAZPACHO

1 envelope unflavored gelatin
1 cup water
3 large tomatoes, stemmed and quartered
1 small green pepper, quartered, seeded, and cut
    up
1 small cucumber, pared, quartered, seeded, and
    cut into chunks
1 medium onion, peeled and cut into chunks
1 cup sliced celery
1 clove garlic, peeled
3 tablespoons lemon juice
2 tablespoons olive oil
1½ teaspoons salt
¼ teaspoon pepper
    Few drops red-pepper seasoning
    Plain croutons

Sprinkle gelatin over water in a small saucepan; let stand a minute to soften, then heat, stirring constantly, until gelatin dissolves; cool.

Pour half of the gelatin mixture into an electric-blender container; add half each of the tomatoes, green pepper, cucumber, onion, celery, garlic, lemon juice, and olive oil; cover. Chop or grate fine, but do not purée. Pour into a large bowl.

Repeat with second half of same ingredients; add to mixture in bowl; stir in salt, pepper, and red-pepper seasoning; cover. Chill mixture several hours, or overnight, until frosty cold.

Spoon into cups or small bowls; sprinkle a tablespoon of croutons over each serving.

Yield: 8 servings.

CHICKEN CREAM

3 tablespoons butter or margarine
3 tablespoons all-purpose flour
2 cans (13¾ ozs. each) chicken broth
1 can (5 ozs.) boned chicken, diced fine
1 jar (2 ozs.) pimientos, drained and chopped
1 cup light cream
2 tablespoons chopped parsley
2 tablespoons dry sherry

Melt butter in a large saucepan; stir in flour. Cook, stirring constantly, until bubbly. Stir in chicken broth and chicken; continue cooking and stirring until mixture thickens slightly; simmer 10 minutes.

Stir in pimientos, cream, parsley, and sherry. Reheat slowly just until bubbly. (Do not boil.)

Ladle into soup bowls or cups.

Yield: 6 servings.

CHICKEN-DUMPLING CUP

1 small onion, chopped (¼ cup)
2 tablespoons salad oil
6 medium carrots, pared and diced
1 cup thinly sliced celery
1 can (10½ ozs.) condensed chicken and
    dumplings soup
1½ cups water
2 cans (5 ozs. each) boned chicken, cut up

Sauté onion in salad oil in a large saucepan until soft; stir in carrots, celery, soup, and water; heat to boiling; cover. Simmer 10 minutes. Stir in chicken; heat to boiling again.

Ladle into soup bowls or cups.

Yield: 4 servings.

GREEN-ONION CREAM

4 bunches green onions, trimmed and sliced (2½ cups)
2 tablespoons butter or margarine
2 tablespoons all-purpose flour
½ teaspoon dried thyme, crushed
2 cans (13¾ ozs. each) chicken broth
1 cup reconstituted instant nonfat dry milk
Few drops red-pepper seasoning

Set aside 3 tablespoonfuls of the sliced green onion for garnish.

Sauté remaining onions in butter in a medium saucepan until soft; stir in flour and thyme. Cook, stirring constantly, until bubbly. Stir in 1 can of the chicken broth; continue cooking and stirring until mixture thickens and boils 1 minute; cool.

Pour mixture into an electric-blender container; cover; beat until smooth. Return to saucepan.

Stir in second can of chicken broth, milk, and red-pepper seasoning. Heat to boiling; simmer 5 minutes to blend flavors. Chill several hours, or overnight, until frosty cold.

Ladle into soup bowls or cups; sprinkle part of the remaining onions over each serving.

Yield: 6 servings.

EGG DROP SOUP

2 lbs. chicken wings or backs
1 small onion, peeled and sliced
Few celery tops
6 peppercorns
1 teaspoon salt
6 cups water
2 tablespoons cornstarch
1 egg
2 green onions, trimmed and sliced thin

Wash chicken; combine with onion, celery tops, peppercorns, salt, and water in a kettle; heat to boiling; cover. Simmer 1½ hours.

Remove chicken from broth and set aside to use in a casserole or sandwich filling. Strain broth into a bowl. Measure out ½ cup, then return remainder to kettle; cook rapidly until it measures 4 cups.

Mix the ½ cup broth and cornstarch in a small bowl until smooth; stir into kettle. Cook, stirring constantly, until mixture thickens slightly and boils 1 minute. Turn off heat.

Beat egg well (but not until foamy) in a small bowl; pour into hot soup in a thin stream, stirring constantly, so egg forms thin shreds.

Ladle soup into bowls; sprinkle green onions over each serving.

Yield: 4 to 6 servings.

CHICKEN CONGEE

1 roasting or stewing chicken, weighing about 3 lbs.
1 small onion, peeled and sliced
Few celery tops
1½ teaspoons salt
¼ teaspoon peppercorns
6 cups water
⅓ cup uncooked regular rice
1 cup finely shredded iceberg lettuce

Wash chicken inside and out. Combine with onion, celery tops, 1 teaspoon of the salt, peppercorns, and water in a kettle; heat to boiling; cover tightly. Simmer 2 hours, or until chicken is tender.

Remove chicken from broth and cool until easy to handle, then pull off skin and take meat from bones; dice enough to measure 1 cup. Chill remainder to use for a casserole or to chop or grind for a sandwich filling.

Strain broth, then return to kettle. (There should be 6 cups.) Reheat to boiling; stir in rice; cover. Simmer 15 minutes. Stir in diced chicken and remaining ½ teaspoon salt; heat again to boiling

Place lettuce in soup bowls or cups; ladle soup into each.

Yield: 4 to 6 servings.

HOT-WEATHER TUNA CREAM

1 can (10¾ ozs.) condensed cream of potato soup
1 small onion, chopped (¼ cup)
2 cups milk
1 can (3½ ozs.) tuna, drained and flaked
3 tablespoons chopped parsley
½ teaspoon salt
⅛ teaspoon pepper
  Few drops red-pepper seasoning

Combine soup and onion in a medium saucepan; heat slowly, stirring several times, to boiling; simmer 1 minute. Pour into an electric-blender container; add milk; cover. Beat until smooth. Pour into a medium bowl.

Stir in rest of ingredients. Chill until frosty-cold.

Ladle into small cups or bowls.

Yield: 4 servings.

CONFETTI CHICKEN CUP

1 can (10¾ ozs.) condensed cream of chicken soup
1 can (16 ozs.) mixed vegetables
¼ teaspoon dried rosemary, crushed
1 cup milk
  Dash of salt

Combine soup, vegetables and liquid, rosemary, milk, and salt in a large saucepan; heat slowly, stirring several times, to boiling. Simmer 5 minutes to blend flavors.

Ladle into soup cups or bowls.

Yield: 4 servings.

SEAFOOD BISQUE

1 small onion, chopped (¼ cup)
2 tablespoons butter or margarine
2 cans (10¾ ozs. each) condensed cream of shrimp soup
2 cups milk
⅛ teaspoon liquid red-pepper seasoning
1 cup light cream
1 can (7½ ozs.) crab meat, drained and cut into small chunks
1 lemon, cut into 8 slices

Sauté onion in butter in a kettle until soft; stir in soup, milk, and red-pepper seasoning. Heat slowly, stirring several times, to boiling.

Stir in cream and crab meat; heat again just until hot. (Do not boil.)

Ladle into soup cups or bowls; float a slice of lemon on each serving.

Yield: 8 servings.

SENEGALESE SOUP

2 cans (10¾ ozs. each) condensed cream of chicken soup
2½ cups milk
½ teaspoon curry powder
1 medium-sized red apple, quartered, cored, and finely diced
  Flaked coconut

Combine soup, milk, and curry powder in a medium saucepan; heat, stirring several times, just until smooth and hot. Chill several hours, or until frosty cold.

Pour into small cups or bowls; float diced apple and coconut on each serving.

Yield: 6 servings.

COUNTRY BEAN SOUP

3 slices bacon
1 small onion, chopped (¼ cup)
1 package (4 ozs.) pea soup mix
2½ cups water
1 can (11½ ozs.) condensed bean with bacon soup
1 can (8 ozs.) stewed tomatoes

Cut bacon into 1-inch pieces; sauté until crisp in a kettle; remove and drain on paper toweling; set aside for garnish.

Pour off all drippings, then measure 2 tablespoons and return to kettle. Add onion and sauté until soft. Stir in pea soup mix and water; heat to boiling; simmer 5 minutes. Stir in bean soup and tomatoes; heat slowly, stirring several times, to boiling again.

Ladle into soup bowls or cups; sprinkle bacon on top.

Yield: 4 servings.

MOCK BOUILLABAISSE

1 medium onion, chopped (½ cup)
1 tablespoon salad oil
1 medium carrot, pared and diced
¼ teaspoon dried thyme, crushed
⅛ teaspoon pepper
1 cup water
1 can (10¾ ozs.) condensed Manhattan-style clam chowder
1 can (8 ozs.) stewed tomatoes
1 can (about 7 ozs.) tuna, drained and flaked
1 can (4½ ozs.) shrimp, drained and rinsed

Sauté onion in salad oil in a large saucepan until soft. Stir in carrot, thyme, pepper, and water; cover. Cook 10 minutes, or until carrot is tender.

Stir in clam chowder and tomatoes and liquid; heat to boiling; add tuna and shrimp. Heat to boiling again; simmer 10 minutes to blend flavors.

Ladle into soup bowls or cups.
Yield: 6 servings.

CHICKEN VELVET SOUP

1 boneless chicken breast, weighing about 6 ozs.
2 cans (10¾ ozs. each) condensed chicken broth
2½ cups water
1 can (8 ozs.) cream-style corn
1 tablespoon cornstarch
1 tablespoon dry sherry
½ cup julienne strips cooked ham

Pull skin from chicken; cut chicken into pieces, then mince very fine with a sharp knife. (If you prefer, chop the meat in your blender.)

Combine chicken broth and water in a kettle; heat to boiling; stir in corn.

Mix cornstarch with 1 tablespoon water until smooth in a cup; stir in sherry; stir into broth mixture. Cook, stirring constantly, until mixture thickens slightly and boils 1 minute. Lower heat to simmer; stir in minced chicken. Heat slowly to boiling again.

Ladle into soup bowls or cups; top each serving with ham strips.
Yield: 6 servings.

MAIN DISH

EGGS BENEDICT SOUP

1 small onion, chopped (¼ cup)
2 tablespoons butter or margarine
1 can (10¾ ozs.) condensed cream of celery soup
1½ cups milk
1 can (8 ozs.) mixed vegetables
  Few drops red-pepper seasoning
1 package (4 or 5 ozs.) sliced boiled ham, diced
4 hard-cooked eggs, sliced
2 tablespoons chopped parsley

Sauté onion in butter in a large saucepan until soft. Stir in soup, milk, vegetables and liquid, red-pepper seasoning, and ham. Heat slowly to boiling. Stir in eggs and parsley.

Ladle into soup bowls.

Yield: 4 servings.

TURKEY CHOWDER PAPRIKASH

2 turkey drumsticks, about 2 lbs.
2 teaspoons salt
6 peppercorns
  Few celery tops
6 cups water
1 large onion, chopped (1 cup)
2 tablespoons salad oil
2 teaspoons paprika
1 envelope instant chicken broth
2 cups uncooked fine noodles
1 cup (8-oz. carton) dairy sour cream
2 tablespoons chopped parsley

Combine turkey, salt, peppercorns, celery tops, and water in a kettle; heat to boiling; cover. Simmer 1½ hours, or until turkey is tender; remove from broth and cool until easy to handle; take meat from bones and dice. Strain broth, then measure and add water, if needed, to make 6 cups.

Sauté onion in salad oil in kettle until soft; stir in paprika and chicken broth; cook 1 minute longer. Stir in the 6 cups broth; heat to boiling.

Stir in noodles. Cook 8 to 10 minutes, or until noodles are tender; stir in diced turkey.

Stir about 1 cup of the liquid from kettle into sour cream in a small bowl; stir back into kettle. Heat very slowly until bubbly. (Do not boil.) Add salt to taste, if needed.

Ladle into soup bowls; sprinkle parsley over each serving.

Yield: 6 servings.

DOUBLE BEEF BOWL

½ lb. ground beef
1 package (1¾ ozs.) vegetable-beef soup mix
3 cups water
½ cup uncooked elbow macaroni
½ teaspoon Italian seasoning
½ teaspoon salt
2 teaspoons chopped parsley

Brown ground beef in a medium saucepan; pour off fat. Stir in soup mix and water. Heat, stirring several times, to boiling, then simmer 5 minutes.

Stir in macaroni, Italian seasoning, and salt; cover. Cook 10 minutes, or until macaroni is tender.

Ladle into soup bowls; sprinkle parsley over each serving.

Yield: 4 servings.

HOT-DOG CHOWDER

1 can (8 ozs.) mixed vegetables
  Water
1 can (10¾ ozs.) condensed cream of potato soup
4 frankfurters, sliced thin crosswise
⅛ teaspoon dillweed or ½ teaspoon cut fresh dill

Drain liquid from vegetables into a 2-cup measure; add water to make 1½ cups. Combine with soup in a medium saucepan; heat slowly, stirring several times, to boiling.

Stir in vegetables, frankfurters, and dillweed. Heat to boiling again.

Ladle into soup bowls. Serve with chowder crackers.

Yield: 4 servings.

BAYOU CHOWDER

1 medium onion, chopped (½ cup)
1 small green pepper, quartered, seeded, and
    chopped (½ cup)
2 tablespoons salad oil
1 can (13¾ ozs.) chicken broth
1 can (16 ozs.) stewed tomatoes
1 bay leaf
½ teaspoon dried basil, crushed
3 cups water
1 can (4½ ozs.) deveined shrimp, drained and
    rinsed
1 can (5 or 6 ozs.) boned chicken, cut up
1 can (12 ozs.) pork luncheon meat, diced
¾ cup packaged precooked rice

Sauté onion and green pepper in salad oil in a kettle until soft. Stir in chicken broth, tomatoes, bay leaf, basil, and water; heat to boiling; cover. Simmer 10 minutes.

Stir in shrimp, chicken, and luncheon meat; heat to boiling. Stir in rice; cover; remove from heat. Let stand 5 minutes. Remove bay leaf.

Ladle into soup bowls; serve with thick slices of toasted French bread.

Yield: 6 servings.

OLD-FASHIONED VEGETABLE SOUP

2½ lbs. beef shank crosscuts
1 large onion, peeled, quartered, and sliced
1 cup sliced celery
3 teaspoons salt
¼ teaspoon pepper
10 cups water
6 medium carrots, pared and sliced
2 large potatoes, pared and diced
2 cups coarsely shredded green cabbage
1 package (10 ozs.) frozen whole-kernel corn
1 package (10 ozs.) frozen cut green beans
2 teaspoons mixed Italian herbs
1 can (16 ozs.) stewed tomatoes
¼ cup chopped parsley

Combine beef, onion, celery, salt, pepper, and water in a large kettle; heat to boiling. Skim top; cover. Simmer 2 hours.

Stir in carrots, potatoes, cabbage, corn, green beans, and herbs; heat to boiling again; cover. Simmer 1 hour longer, or until meat is tender.

Remove meat from kettle; cool until easy to handle, then take meat from bones, discarding bones and fat. Dice meat and return to kettle with tomatoes and parsley. Heat to boiling.

Ladle into soup bowls. Serve with toasted French bread or your favorite crackers.

Yield: 10 servings.

CHICKEN GUMBO

1 broiler-fryer, weighing about 3 lbs.
2 teaspoons salt
4 cups water
½ lb. ham, cubed
2 large onions, chopped (2 cups)
1 tablespoon salad oil
1 can (6 ozs.) tomato paste
¼ teaspoon cayenne
1 package (10 ozs.) frozen cut okra
2 cans (8 ozs. each) oysters
2 medium tomatoes, diced (2 cups)
  Hot cooked rice

Combine chicken, 1 teaspoon of the salt, and water in a kettle; heat to boiling; cover. Simmer 1 hour, or until chicken is tender. Remove from broth and cool until easy to handle, then pull skin from chicken and take meat from bones and cube. Strain broth into a medium bowl; skim off fat.

Sauté ham and onions lightly in salad oil in same kettle. Stir in tomato paste, chicken broth, cubed chicken, cayenne, remaining 1 teaspoon salt, and okra.

Drain liquor from oysters into a cup and stir into mixture in kettle. Heat to boiling; cover. Simmer 1 hour.

Stir in oysters and diced tomatoes; simmer 10 minutes.

Spoon rice into mounds in soup bowls; ladle soup mixture over top.

Yield: 8 generous servings.

SPANISH RICE BOWL

8 slices bacon, cut in 1-inch pieces
1 medium onion, chopped (½ cup)
¼ cup chopped green pepper
¼ teaspoon dried thyme, crushed
3 cups water
1 cup packaged precooked rice
1 can (10¾ ozs.) condensed tomato soup
1 can (8 ozs.) cut green beans

Sauté bacon in a large saucepan until crisp; remove and drain on paper toweling. Pour off all fat, then measure 2 tablespoons and return to pan.

Stir onion and green pepper into drippings; sauté until soft. Stir in thyme and water; heat to boiling. Stir in rice; cover; turn off heat. Let stand 10 minutes.

Stir in soup, green beans and liquid, and bacon. Heat to boiling.

Ladle into soup bowls.

Yield: 4 servings.

PASTA E FAGIOLI

1 large onion, chopped (1 cup)
2 tablespoons salad oil
1 can (13¾ ozs.) chicken broth
3½ cups water
1 package (8 ozs.) elbow macaroni
1 teaspoon garlic powder
1 teaspoon dried basil, crushed
1 teaspoon salt
2 cups diced cooked pork
1 can (15 ozs.) tomato sauce with onions, celery, and green peppers
1 can (16 ozs.) red kidney beans
Grated Romano cheese

Sauté onion in salad oil in a kettle until soft. Stir in chicken broth and water; heat to boiling. Stir in macaroni, garlic powder, basil, and salt. Reheat to boiling; cook 7 minutes, or until macaroni is almost tender.

Stir in pork, tomato sauce, and kidney beans and liquid; heat to boiling. Simmer 10 minutes longer.

Ladle into soup bowls; sprinkle Romano cheese over each serving. Serve with toasted Italian bread if you like.

Yield: 6 to 8 servings.

SOUTHWESTERN CHILI

1 package (16 ozs.) dried red kidney beans
8 cups water
1 lb. ground beef
2 large onions, chopped (2 cups)
2 tablespoons chili powder
1 can (15 ozs.) tomato sauce with onions, green pepper, and celery
2 teaspoons salt
1 teaspoon ground cumin

Rinse beans. Combine with water in a kettle. Heat to boiling; cook 2 minutes; remove from heat; cover. Let stand 1 hour. Reheat to boiling; simmer 2½ hours, or until beans are tender but still firm enough to hold their shape.

Shape ground beef into a large patty; place in a large skillet. Brown, turning once, in its own fat; break up into chunks; push to one side.

Stir onions and chili powder into drippings; sauté until onions are soft. Stir in tomato sauce, salt, and cumin; stir into bean mixture; heat to boiling. Simmer 30 minutes, or until slightly thickened.

Ladle into soup bowls.

Yield: 6 servings.

DUTCH OVEN LENTIL SOUP

1 package (16 ozs.) lentils
1 large onion, diced (1 cup)
2 large carrots, pared and diced (1 cup)
1 cup sliced celery
2 smoked pork hocks, weighing about 1 lb.
1 teaspoon dried basil, crushed
2 teaspoons salt
¼ teaspoon pepper
8 cups water
2 tablespoons chopped parsley

Rinse lentils. Place in a large Dutch oven; add onion, carrots, celery, pork hocks, basil, salt, pepper, and water. Heat to boiling; cover. Simmer 2 hours, or until pork is tender.

Remove pork hocks from soup; cool until easy to handle, then peel off skin and take meat from bones. Dice meat; return to soup; stir in parsley. Heat to boiling again. (If you prefer a thinner soup, stir in more water.)

Ladle into soup bowls.

Yield: 8 servings.

MANHATTAN COD CHOWDER

4 slices bacon, cut in 1-inch pieces
4 small onions, peeled, quartered, and sliced
1 cup thinly sliced celery
2 large potatoes, pared and cubed (2 cups)
1 clove garlic, minced
1 teaspoon dried thyme, crushed
1 teaspoon salt
1 bottle (8 ozs.) clam juice
1 cup water
1 package (16 ozs.) frozen cod, thawed and cut in ¾-inch cubes
1 can (28 ozs.) tomatoes

Sauté bacon in a kettle until crisp; remove and drain on paper toweling.

Stir onions and celery into drippings; sauté until onion is soft. Stir in potatoes, garlic, thyme, salt, clam juice, and water; heat to boiling; cover. Simmer 10 minutes.

Add cod cubes; cover. Simmer 5 minutes.

Stir in tomatoes and liquid; heat slowly, stirring several times, to boiling; simmer 5 minutes to blend flavors.

Ladle into soup bowls; sprinkle bacon over each serving.

Yield: 6 servings.

LUMBERJACK BURGOO

1 smoked pork hock, weighing about ¾ lb.
2 teaspoons salt
¼ teaspoon pepper
   Water
4 chicken thighs
2 large potatoes, pared and diced (about 2 cups)
1 large onion, chopped (1 cup)
1 package (10 ozs.) frozen whole-kernel corn
½ cup diced celery
½ cup chopped green pepper
1 can (16 ozs.) tomato purée
1 teaspoon leaf thyme, crushed
2 tablespoons Worcestershire sauce
6 slices French bread, cut ¼-inch thick
   Butter or margarine
1½ teaspoons sesame seeds

Combine pork hock, salt, pepper, and water to cover in a kettle; heat to boiling; cover. Simmer 1½ hours; add chicken to kettle. Simmer ½ hour longer, or until meats are tender. Remove from broth and cool until easy to handle.

Stir potatoes, onion, corn, celery, green pepper, tomato purée, and thyme into broth; heat to boiling; cover again. Simmer 30 minutes, or until vegetables are tender.

While vegetables cook, peel skin from pork hock and chicken; take meat from bones and dice. Stir into kettle with Worcestershire sauce; heat just to boiling.

Spread French bread with butter; sprinkle sesame seeds over slices; place on a cookie sheet. Toast in 350° oven.

Spoon soup mixture into bowls; place a slice of toast on top of each.

Yield: 6 servings.

COCK-A-LEEKIE SOUP

1 stewing chicken, weighing about 4 lbs., cut up
4 teaspoons seasoned salt
2 bay leaves
8 cups water
3 bunches of leeks
1 cup chopped celery
¾ cup packaged precooked rice
2 tablespoons chopped parsley

Combine chicken, seasoned salt, bay leaves, and water in a kettle. Heat to boiling; cover. Simmer 1½ hours, or until chicken is tender. Remove from broth and cool until easy to handle, then take meat from bones and dice. Remove bay leaves from broth; reheat broth to boiling.

While chicken cooks, trim leeks; slice white part thin. (There should be about 5 cups.) Stir leeks and celery into broth; cover again. Simmer 20 minutes.

Stir in rice; cover; turn off heat. Let stand 5 minutes. Stir in diced chicken; heat to boiling again.

Ladle into soup bowls; sprinkle parsley over each serving.

Yield: 8 servings.

NEW ORLEANS GUMBO

1 large onion, chopped (1 cup)
1 clove garlic, minced
2 tablespoons salad oil
2 envelopes instant vegetable broth
1 can (16 ozs.) stewed tomatoes
1 can (16 ozs.) cut okra
1 can (8 ozs.) minced clams
1½ cups tomato juice
½ teaspoon sugar
¼ teaspoon liquid red-pepper seasoning
2 tablespoons all-purpose flour
¼ cup water
2 cans (4½ ozs. each) deveined shrimp, drained and rinsed

Sauté onion and garlic in salad oil in a kettle until soft.

Stir in vegetable broth, tomatoes, okra and liquid, clams and juice, tomato juice, sugar,

and red-pepper seasoning. Simmer for 15 minutes.

Mix flour and water in a cup until smooth; stir into mixture in kettle. Cook, stirring constantly, until slightly thickened. Stir in shrimp; heat again until bubbly. Spoon into soup bowls.

Yield: 6 servings.

ANTIPASTO TURKEY SOUP

1 turkey carcass (from roasted bird)
1 medium onion, peeled and cut up
 Few celery tops
1 teaspoon salt
6 peppercorns
4 cups water
2 Italian hot sausages
1 can (20 ozs.) chick peas
1 can (16 ozs.) tomatoes
1 can (4 ozs.) pimientos, drained and chopped
1 teaspoon Italian seasoning
¼ cup sliced pitted ripe olives

Break up turkey carcass and place in a kettle with onion, celery tops, salt, peppercorns, and water. Heat to boiling; cover. Simmer 2 hours. Remove bones from broth and cool until easy to handle, then strip off meat and set aside. Strain broth into a large bowl.

Peel casings from sausages; break up meat. Sauté in its own fat in a kettle 10 minutes. Stir in turkey and a little salad oil, if needed; brown turkey.

Stir in 3 cups of the turkey broth, chick peas and liquid, tomatoes, pimientos, and Italian seasoning. Heat to boiling; simmer, stirring once or twice, 10 minutes to blend flavors.

Ladle into soup bowls; float olive slices on top. Serve with toasted sliced Italian bread.

Yield: 8 servings.

POT-AU-FEU

3 lbs. beef shortribs
1½ cups water
1 tablespoon salt
1 teaspoon fines herbes
¼ teaspoon pepper
8 small potatoes, pared
6 medium carrots, pared and cut in 1-inch pieces
4 medium onions, peeled and quartered
½ small head cabbage, cut in pieces
2 tablespoons chopped parsley

Trim as much fat as possible from short ribs; cut ribs into serving-sized pieces. Combine with water, salt, herbs, and pepper in a 4-quart pressure cooker; cover.

Heat to 15 pounds pressure as manufacturer directs; cook 15 minutes. Let pressure fall naturally; uncover. Skim fat from broth and remove bones from meat. Add potatoes, carrots, onions, and cabbage to cooker; cover. Heat again to 15 pounds pressure; cook 10 minutes, let pressure fall.

Ladle into soup bowls; sprinkle chopped parsley over each serving.

Yield: 8 servings.

CREOLE HOT-DOG CHOWDER

1 medium onion, chopped (½ cup)
¼ cup chopped green pepper
2 tablespoons butter or margarine
1 can (10¾ ozs.) condensed vegetarian vegetable soup
1 can (10¾ ozs.) condensed cream of potato soup
1½ cups milk
4 frankfurters, sliced thin
2 tablespoons chopped parsley

Sauté onion and green pepper in butter in a large saucepan until soft.

Stir in vegetable soup, potato soup, and milk; heat slowly, stirring constantly, to boiling; stir in frankfurters. Simmer 10 minutes to blend flavors. Stir in parsley.

Ladle into soup bowls. Serve with chowder crackers.

Yield: 4 servings.

TUNA CHEDDAR CHOWDER

1 small onion, chopped (¼ cup)
3 tablespoons butter or margarine
3 tablespoons all-purpose flour
½ teaspoon salt
3 cups milk
1 teaspoon Worcestershire sauce
4 slices process American cheese, cut up
1 can (about 7 ozs.) tuna, drained and broken into chunks
1 can (8 ozs.) peas

Sauté onion in butter in a large saucepan until soft. Stir in flour and salt; cook, stirring constantly, until bubbly.

Stir in milk and Worcestershire sauce; continue cooking and stirring until sauce thickens slightly and boils 1 minute.

Stir in cheese until melted, then tuna and peas and liquid; heat again just until hot.

Ladle into soup bowls. Serve with toasted buttered French bread.

Yield: 4 servings

CORN-AND-CLAM CHOWDER

½ cup diced salt pork
1 large onion, chopped (1 cup)
1 can (16 ozs.) small white potatoes, drained and diced
1 can (16 ozs.) cream-style corn
1 can (8 ozs.) minced clams
1 teaspoon salt
1 cup milk
1 cup light cream
2 tablespoons chopped parsley

Sauté salt pork in a large saucepan until crisp; remove from pan and set aside.

Stir onion and potatoes into drippings; sauté until onion is soft. Stir in corn, clams and juice, salt, and milk. Heat to boiling; simmer 20 minutes.

Stir in cream, salt pork, and parsley; heat again just until bubbly.

Ladle into soup bowls. Serve with chowder crackers.

Yield: 6 servings.

TUREEN SALMON

1 large onion, chopped (1 cup)
1 cup thinly sliced celery
4 tablespoons butter or margarine
2 medium potatoes, pared and diced (2 cups)
1 large carrot, pared and sliced (1 cup)
1 teaspoon salt
⅛ teaspoon pepper
3 cups water
1 cup instant nonfat dry milk powder or 1
    envelope (3.2 ozs.) nonfat dry milk
2 tablespoons all-purpose flour
1 can (8 ozs.) salmon, drained, boned, and broken
    into small chunks
1 tablespoon chopped parsley

Sauté onion and celery in butter in a kettle until soft; stir in potatoes, carrot, salt, pepper, and water. Heat to boiling; cover. Cook 20 minutes, or until vegetables are tender.

Mix milk powder and flour in a cup; slowly stir into vegetable mixture; cook, stirring constantly, until mixture thickens and boils for 1 minute.

Stir in salmon and parsley. Heat again just until hot.

Ladle into soup bowls. Serve with your favorite crackers.

Yield: 4 servings.

HAM-AND-CHEDDAR CHOWDER

1 cup coarsely chopped celery
2 tablespoons butter or margarine
2 cans (10¾ ozs. each) condensed cream of potato
    soup
2½ cups milk
1 package (4 ozs.) sliced boiled ham, cut in short
    julienne strips
⅛ teaspoon red-pepper seasoning
1 cup shredded sharp Cheddar cheese (4 ozs.)
3 tablespoons snipped chives

Sauté celery in butter in a large saucepan until soft.

Stir in soup, milk, ham, and red-pepper seasoning; heat slowly, stirring several times, to boiling; simmer 5 minutes. Stir in cheese until melted.

Ladle into soup bowls. Sprinkle chives over each serving.

Yield: 6 servings.

GREEN-PEA CHOWDER

1 small onion, chopped (¼ cup)
1 medium carrot, pared and diced (½ cup)
2 tablespoons salad oil
1 envelope (4 ozs.) pea soup mix
3 cups water
¾ cup tiny macaroni shells
½ teaspoon dried thyme, crushed
1 cup diced cooked ham
1 cup milk

Sauté onion and carrot in salad oil in a large saucepan until soft; stir in pea soup mix and water. Heat to boiling; simmer 3 minutes.

Stir in macaroni shells and thyme; simmer, stirring several times, 10 minutes, or until macaroni is tender. Stir in ham and milk; heat just to boiling. Taste and add salt, if needed.

Ladle into soup bowls. Serve with chowder crackers if you like.

Yield: 4 servings.

CHILI CHOWDER

1 medium onion, chopped (½ cup)
¼ cup chopped green pepper
2 tablespoons salad oil
1 can (about 16 ozs.) spaghetti in tomato sauce
    with cheese
1 can (16 ozs.) chili without beans
1 can (12 ozs.) mixed vegetable juice
½ cup shredded Cheddar cheese

Sauté onion and green pepper in salad oil in a large saucepan until soft.

Cut through spaghetti several times with a knife to break it up, then stir into onion mixture with chili and vegetable juice. Heat slowly to boiling; simmer, stirring several times, 10 minutes.

Spoon into soup bowls; sprinkle cheese over each serving.

Yield: 4 servings.

LAMB-AND-BEAN CHOWDER

1 package (16 ozs.) dried Great Northern beans
8 cups water
2 lbs. lamb neck slices
1 tablespoon salad oil
1 large onion, chopped (1 cup)
1 large green pepper, quartered, seeded, and
    chopped coarsely (1 cup)
1 cup coarsely chopped celery
2 teaspoons salt
1½ teaspoons dried Italian herbs
4 large carrots, pared and diced (2 cups)
2 tablespoons chopped parsley

Rinse beans; combine with water in a kettle. Heat to boiling; cook 2 minutes; turn off heat; cover. Let stand 1 hour.

Brown lamb in salad oil in a kettle; push to one side.

Stir onion, green pepper, and celery into drippings; sauté until onion is soft. Stir in beans and liquid, salt, and Italian herbs. Heat to boiling; cover. Simmer 1½ hours.

Stir in carrots; cover again. Simmer 30 minutes, or until lamb and beans are tender.

Remove lamb from kettle. Cool until easy to handle, then take meat from bones and dice, discarding bones and fat.

Spoon about 2 cups of the beans from kettle into a bowl and mash well; stir back into kettle with diced lamb and parsley. Heat slowly, stirring several times, to boiling.

Ladle into soup bowls.
Yield: 8 servings.

CHUNKY CORN CHOWDER

¼ cup diced salt pork
1 large onion, chopped (1 cup)
1 cup coarsely chopped celery
2 large potatoes, pared and diced (2 cups)
2 cups water
1½ teaspoons dillweed
1 teaspoon salt
2 knockwurst (½ lb.)
1 large can evaporated milk (1⅔ cups)
1 can (12 ozs.) whole-kernel corn
1 can (16 ozs.) cream-style corn

Sauté salt pork slowly until almost crisp in a kettle; push to one side.

Stir onion and celery into drippings; sauté until soft. Stir in potatoes, water, dillweed, and salt; heat to boiling; cover. Simmer 12 minutes, or until potatoes are tender.

While potatoes cook, peel skin from knockwurst; slice meat in thin rounds.

Stir milk, whole-kernel corn and liquid, cream-style corn, and knockwurst into mixture in kettle; heat slowly, stirring several times, just to boiling.

Ladle into soup bowls. Serve with Sesame Sticks (recipe on page 413).
Yield: 8 servings.

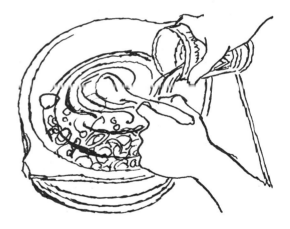

POTATO-CLAM CHOWDER

2 cans (10¾ ozs. each) condensed cream of potato
    soup
1 can (6½ ozs.) minced clams
1½ cups milk
    Few drops red-pepper seasoning
2 tablespoons butter or margarine
2 tablespoons chopped parsley

Combine soup, clams and juice, milk, and red-pepper seasoning in a large saucepan. Heat slowly, stirring several times, to boiling.

Stir in butter until melted; stir in parsley.

Ladle into soup bowls or cups. Serve with melba toast if you like.
Yield: 8 servings.

MINESTRONE

1 medium onion, chopped (½ cup)
1 clove garlic, minced
2 tablespoons salad oil or olive oil
1 can (10½ ozs.) condensed beef broth
1 cup water
1 cup diced celery
1 can (16 ozs.) tomatoes
1 teaspoon salt
1 teaspoon dried oregano, crushed
1 cup tiny noodle bows
2 medium zucchini, trimmed and sliced
1 can (20 ozs.) cannelli beans
¼ cup grated Parmesan cheese

Sauté onion and garlic in salad oil in a kettle until soft.

Stir in beef broth, water, celery, tomatoes, salt, and oregano; heat to boiling; cover. Simmer 15 minutes.

Stir in noodle bows and zucchini; simmer 7 minutes, or until noodles are tender. Stir in beans and liquid. Heat again just to boiling.

Ladle into soup bowls; sprinkle Parmesan cheese over each serving. Serve with Italian bread if you like.

Yield: 6 servings.

WHOLE-MEAL BARLEY BROTH

2 small lamb shanks, weighing about 1 lb.
½ cup medium barley
2½ teaspoons salt
½ teaspoon dried rosemary, crushed
6 cups water
2 medium carrots, pared and diced
1 medium onion, diced (½ cup)
1 cup diced celery
1 can (10¾ ozs.) condensed tomato soup

Trim any excess fat from lamb. Combine shanks with barley, salt, rosemary, and water in a kettle; heat to boiling; cover. Simmer 1½ hours, or until lamb is tender. Remove shanks from kettle to a plate.

Stir carrots, onion, and celery into barley mixture; cover. Simmer 15 minutes, or until vegetables are tender.

While vegetables cook, take lamb from bones, discarding bones and fat; dice meat.

Let barley mixture stand a minute or two, then skim off fat; stir tomato soup and lamb into kettle. Heat again just to boiling. (If you prefer a thinner soup, stir in a little more water.) Ladle into soup bowls.

Yield: 6 servings.

CHICKEN CHOWDER

1 broiler-fryer, weighing about 2 lbs.
1 bay leaf
5 sprigs parsley
Few celery tops
½ teaspoon dried rosemary, crushed
¼ teaspoon peppercorns
1½ teaspoons salt
4 cups water
¼ cup diced salt pork
1 large onion, chopped (1 cup)
½ cup uncooked regular rice
1 package (10 ozs.) frozen green peas
2 egg yolks
3 cups milk
2 hard-cooked eggs, chopped

Rinse chicken. Combine chicken, including giblets (except liver), with bay leaf, parsley, celery tops, rosemary, peppercorns, salt, and water in a kettle. Heat to boiling; cover. Simmer 1 hour, or until chicken is tender. Remove from broth and cool until easy to handle, then take meat from bones and dice. Strain broth into a large bowl. (There should be 4 cups.)

Sauté salt pork slowly until almost crisp in same kettle; push to one side. Stir onion into drippings and sauté until soft. Stir in rice, frozen peas, and the 4 cups chicken broth; heat to boiling; cover. Simmer 20 minutes, or until rice and peas are tender. Stir in diced chicken.

Beat egg yolks in a medium bowl; stir in milk; slowly stir into chicken mixture. Heat slowly, stirring constantly, until mixture thickens slightly. (Do not let mixture boil.)

Ladle into soup bowls; top each serving with a spoonful of chopped egg.

Yield: 8 servings.

MEATS

MOST MENUS CENTER AROUND A MEAT DISH, for here is where the biggest chunk of our food dollar goes. And while there's no particular magic to turning out a sizzling brown steak or a plump ham all a sparkle with a tangy glaze, it does pay to start with some know-how. This means being aware of what and when to buy as well as how to cook your purchase. So this chapter starts right at the meat counter with a simple discussion of signs to look for in selecting top-quality meats, plus hints for stretching your money just a little bit further.

As you read on, you'll find help with buying arithmetic and storing meat properly once you get it home. There are tips on tenderizers, basic how-tos on cooking methods, and a handy chart on when to use each that you'll refer to again and again. Though timetables, at best, can only be guides, those that are included here for roasting, broiling, braising, and baking will be a big help to you in getting everything to the table at the same time.

For your cooking inspiration and pleasure, more than 200 recipes for all types of meats and every kind of occasion follow. There are ideas for roasts that are elegant for holidays and entertaining—even better for family since most cuts are meaty enough to allow for some extra-savory second-day treats. Meat loaves and patties, the old stand-bys for many dinners, rate a special place for they can easily be turned into standouts if you vary the meat. Unquestionably, beef rates first choice, but ham, veal, lamb, corned beef, liver, and sausage are top contenders for variety and flavor.

Here, too, are fixing and serving suggestions aplenty for steaks, chops, pot roasts, stews, skewer specialties, meat pies, and timesaving one-dish meals to fix in skillets, kettles, and casseroles.

How to buy meat

Most of us can pick out firm, lean, well-marbled meat, but looks alone are not the only key to quality. Other factors that count are the age and breed of the animal, how it was fed, and how it was handled in the processing plant—and this information doesn't show up at the meat counter or on the label. You can also select meat by color, but this, too, has nothing to do with tenderness or quality. Variations from red to pink to gray may be due to exposure to light or air, so along with appearance, you need another

CHUNKY CORN CHOWDER (p.62) ▶
SESAME STICKS (p.413)

guide—and your most reliable one is a dependable brand name or a U.S. Government or packer grade. Make it a habit to look for such markings on every piece of meat you buy.

PRIME is the term used by the Government to designate the highest quality beef, veal, and lamb available. Some is carried by select butcher shops, but most of the supply goes to restaurants, and therefore, is hard to come by in supermarkets.

The next grade down the line is CHOICE and this is the most plentiful for everyday shoppers. It's leaner than PRIME meat, but still has enough marbling to be flavorful and juicy, and many of the cuts can be roasted or broiled.

Pork is a different story. While there are Government grades that apply, they are not widely used since pork is merchandised differently. When shopping, a reliable brand name is a good sign to go by.

How to trim costs

At the meat counter, there are many ways to save money or to spend it wisely. To help you get the most for your meat dollars, here are ten reminders, some general and some specific:

(1) Compare the price of one cut of meat with another by figuring the cost per serving—not the cost per pound. Also, think carefully about boneless cuts even though they appear to cost more. With no excess fat and no bone, the meat adds up to more servings per pound, and may even be thriftier than a bone-in piece that carries a lower price tag.

(2) Take advantage of meat sales or advertised specials on large cuts. Not only will you pay a more reasonable price per pound, but you'll have meat for several meals. Cook it all at once and turn what's left after dinner into a casserole, salad, soup, or sandwiches for another day. Or be your own meat cutter and divide large pieces into meal-sized portions to cook different ways.

(3) Learn all about the less tender cuts of meat and how to cook them with flair. Whatever the cost, all cuts have about the same good food value, and tenderizer and marinades will help make the economy buys just as juicy, flavorful, and inviting as their more expensive counterparts.

(4) Whatever meat you choose, buy in terms of meals. Leftovers that are not enough for a second time around are pointless extravagance.

(5) Consider chuck, bottom round, or shoulder steak when the prices of porterhouse, T-bone, and sirloin are beyond your budget. You can marinate or tenderize these choices, then broil them for a tempting steak meal.

(6) Always buy well-trimmed meat with an even layer of fat. Remember that any fat you trim away costs the same per pound as the meat.

(7) When buying fresh pork, compare the price of shoulder with fresh ham (leg). The shoulder may cost enough less that you can add on an extra pound or two of meat for the same total price.

(8) Keep in mind that there are three kinds of chops—loin, rib, and shoulder. All are equally flavorful and nourishing, but shoulder varieties give your budget a break.

◀ **OLD-FASHIONED VEGETABLE SOUP** (p.56)
BRAN PUFFS (p.378)

(9) You needn't always insist on ground beef for burgers. Ground lamb, pork, and veal make good patties and loaves and may cost the same or less than beef.

(10) Whatever kind of meat you buy, use every bit you pay for. Melt down fat trimmings for drippings and simmer bones and lean cuttings for soup stock or gravy.

How much to buy

It's a snap to count noses and buy enough chops or hot dogs for everyone, but beyond that, a little arithmetic is in order. Think first of the number of servings you will get from each pound, then consider individual appetites, what you're serving with the meat, and how you plan to cook it. All these factors should influence your decision on quantity. Handy buying rules are:

Boneless meats: Figure four servings per pound. These include rolled roasts, boneless roasts and steaks, stewing meats, sausages, liver, cutlets, cold cuts, ground meats, and pork tenderloin.

Small-bone meats: Figure two to three servings per pound. These include bone-in roast (rib, leg of lamb, pork loin, shoulder and chuck cuts) and beef, pork, veal, and ham steaks.

Bony meats: Figure one serving per pound. These include spareribs, shortribs, pork hocks, oxtails, lamb shanks, and lamb neck slices.

How to store meat properly

Fresh meat is perishable, and careful handling after you get it home not only helps you enjoy it at its best, but saves money, too. A couple of easy rules to remember are that the smaller the cut surfaces on a piece of meat, the better it will keep. And the bigger the piece, the longer it keeps.

For refrigerator storage, plan to hold roasts no longer than four or five days, steaks and chops for three days, and ground and cubed stewing meats no longer than two days. Variety meats are also short-term products, and should be used within a day after purchase. Place all meats in the meat compartment or coldest part of your refrigerator. For longer storage, look to your freezer. (See CANNING AND FREEZING.)

Large cuts that you buy and cook the same—or next—day can stay right in their store wrapper; otherwise, loosen the wrapper so air can circulate around the meat. To save yourself last-minute work, unwrap such cuts as steaks and chops, trim as needed, rewrap loosely in waxed paper or transparent wrap, and chill. Unwrap completely any special-order, market-wrapped cut and rewrap.

Store smoked meats—ham, bacon, cold cuts, and frankfurters—in their original wrappers alongside fresh meat in the refrigerator. Curing helps to preserve their flavor, but even so, it pays to use any of these foods within two weeks. Once the packages are opened, the leftovers should be used up quickly. Freezing is not usually recommended for cured meats because the salt used in preserving tends to change the flavor. Just remember to use the products within two months at the most.

Canned meats marked "perishable" are just that and should be stored in their unopened cans in the refrigerator. Use the meat within a week once it's opened. Some canned meats weighing two pounds or less do not need refrigeration, but for safety, always check the label. Never store canned meats in the freezer since the can may burst.

Store canned meats or meat products that are not marked "perishable" in a cool, dry place away from the kitchen range. Like all canned foods, they'll keep about a year, but faster turnover is a good habit to get into.

With cooked meat, take special care. Cool it quickly in the refrigerator after meal-time, then wrap properly for storage. A large roast will chill faster if you cut it in half first so that the cold air can circulate around it. When cold, wrap it loosely or pack it in a covered container and put it back into the refrigerator. Reheat just what you need at one time, but plan to use it all within a day or so.

Use a meat thermometer

While it is not absolutely essential, a meat thermometer is no longer considered a gadget but a helpful tool for roasting large cuts of meat. Timetables are primarily guides, and if you use a thermometer as a second check, you'll eliminate guesswork and be assured of having your roast the way you like it. In most housewares and department stores, you'll find thermometers in two styles, each costing just a few dollars. Either is a good investment.

Tenderizers—how they work

Cooking times for economy or less-tender cuts of meat can be speeded up if you start the tenderizing ahead. Here's how:

Meat tenderizers: These are pure food products that come from the papaya melon, and when sprinkled on meat, break down the connective tissue to make the cut tender. They look somewhat like salt and are available in small shaker-top jars at the meat counter or in the spice-and-herb section of the supermarket. Choose either seasoned or unseasoned varieties; use as labels direct.

Marinades: Letting meat stand in a liquid that contains acid—lemon juice, vinegar, or wine—will also shorten cooking time and add flavor to the meat as well. Almost any meat, except ground varieties, can be marinated. Times vary from several hours to several days; follow recipe directions.

Mechanical aids: Grinding and cubing also make meat tender by breaking down connective tissue. Pounding the meat with a cleaver or mallet as directed in some recipes not only achieves the same results but also makes the meat desirably thin.

How to cook meat

Cuts vary widely in tenderness, and it's important to match the cut and the cooking method if you're to enjoy the meat at its finest. As an overall guide, roast, broil, panbroil, or panfry tender cuts; less tender ones need to be steamed or simmered lazily in liquid. In general, use low to medium heat to keep in the juices and prevent shrinkage.

When in doubt about how to cook any number of cuts, refer to this handy chart.

CUT OF MEAT	HOW TO COOK
Beef	
Roasts: Rib, Boneless Rib, Ribeye, Tenderloin, Sirloin Tip, Boneless Rump	Roast
Roasts: Eye Round, Rolled Rump, Blade Chuck, Arm Chuck, Rolled Boneless Chuck	Braise
Steaks: Porterhouse, T-bone, Club, Rib, Delmonico, Sirloin, Filet Mignon, Top Round	Broil, panbroil, panfry
Steaks: Full-cut Round, Eye Round, Bottom Round, Blade Chuck, Arm Chuck, Cube	Braise, panbroil, panfry
Steak, Flank	Braise, broil
Shortribs	Braise, cook in liquid
Heel of round	Braise, cook in liquid
Plate	Braise
Brisket, fresh	Braise, cook in liquid
Brisket, corned	Cook in liquid
Shank Crosscuts	Braise, cook in liquid
Ground	Broil, panbroil, roast (bake)
Stewing cubes	Braise, cook in liquid
Pork	
Roasts: Center Loin, Crown, Sirloin, Rolled Boneless Loin, Loin Blade, Shoulder Arm, Boston, Tenderloin, Leg (fresh ham), Boston Butt, Shoulder Blade, Center Rib, Boneless Leg	Roast
Chops: Loin, Rib	Braise, panbroil, panfry
Chops, Shoulder	Braise

CUT OF MEAT	HOW TO COOK
Shoulder steak, arm or blade	Braise, panfry
Ham, whole or half	Roast (bake) cook in liquid
Ham, Steak or Center Slice	Broil, panbroil, panfry, roast
Shoulder (picnic), fresh	Roast, braise
Shoulder (picnic), smoked	Roast, cook in liquid
Shoulder Butt or Roll, smoked	Roast, cook in liquid, panfry
Sliced Bacon	Broil, panbroil, panfry
Canadian Bacon	Roast, broil, panbroil, panfry
Spareribs, Country-style Ribs, Back Ribs	Roast, braise, cook in liquid
Cube Steak	Braise, broil, panbroil
Sausage	Roast (bake), panbroil, braise, panfry
Hocks, fresh or smoked	Braise, cook in liquid
Pig's Feet	Braise, cook in liquid
Stewing Cubes	Braise, cook in liquid
Ground meat	Braise, panfry, panbroil, roast (bake)

Veal

Roast: Rib	Roast
Roasts: Leg, Rump, Rolled, Rump, Center Cut Leg, Loin, Sirloin, Blade, Arm, Round, Rolled Shoulder	Roast, braise
Steaks: Sirloin, Blade, Arm, Round, Cube	Braise, panfry
Cutlet	Braise, panfry
Chops: Loin, Kidney, Rib, Shoulder	Braise, panfry
Heel of Round	Braise, cook in liquid
Breast	Roast, braise, cook in liquid
Riblets	Braise, cook in liquid
Shanks	Braise, cook in liquid
Shank crosscuts	Braise, cook in liquid
City Chicken	Braise, panfry
Ground meat	Roast (bake), braise, panfry
Stewing cubes	Braise, cook in liquid

CUT OF MEAT	HOW TO COOK
Lamb	
Roasts: Whole Leg, Shank Half Leg, Boneless Rolled Leg, Rolled Shoulder, Rib (rack), Crown, Square Cut Shoulder	Roast
Chops: Loin, English, Sirloin, Rib, Leg, Frenched (rib)	Broil, panbroil, panfry
Chops: Arm Shoulder, Blade Shoulder, Saratoga	Broil, panbroil, panfry, braise
Riblets	Braise, cook in liquid
Breast	Braise, roast
Shanks	Braise, cook in liquid
Neck Slices	Braise, cook in liquid
Patties	Broil, panbroil, panfry
Stewing cubes	Braise, cook in liquid

Know your cooking terms

Basically, there are six different ways to cook meats—roasting, broiling, panbroiling, panfrying, braising, and cooking in liquid. Here's how to handle each:

Roasting: This is a dry heat method of cooking and one of the easiest for large tender cuts. Sprinkle the meat with salt and pepper or any special seasonings your recipe calls for. Place the meat, fat side up, on a rack in a shallow roasting pan. The rack allows air to circulate around the meat and keeps it out of the drippings.

If the roast is a rib cut, place it in the pan on the ribs—they form their own rack. Insert a meat thermometer into the thickest part of the roast so that the bulb doesn't touch bone or fat. Do not cover the pan, add water, or baste the meat as it cooks. Except for tenderloin and ribeye beef roasts, use an oven temperature of 325°.

Keep tabs on the time, using the Roasting Timetable on page 77, and remove the roast from the oven when the thermometer registers from five to ten degrees lower than the temperature you want (the heat in the meat causes it to continue cooking). For easier carving, let the roast stand 15 to 20 minutes at room temperature.

Broiling: This is today's popular way to cook beef and ham steaks, lamb chops, and meat patties. For broiling, steaks and chops should be at least an inch thick and a ham slice at least half an inch. Those that are thinner are best panbroiled.

Trim any excess fat from the edge of the meat so drippings won't flare up, then slash the remaining fat to keep the meat from curling. Grease the rack in the broiler pan with part of the trimmings, then place the meat on the rack. Turn the oven regulator to BROIL. Depending upon the thickness of the meat, place the broiler pan 3 to 5 inches from heat.

Broil until the top of the meat browns invitingly, season with salt or other flavorings, and turn with tongs. It's best to add the salt after the meat has cooked since salt tends to draw out the juices and delay browning—and as a result, the meat may unintentionally be overcooked.

Figure your cooking time carefully, using the timetable on page 78 as a guide. With a little experimentation, you'll soon learn the exact number of minutes you need. If you want to test for doneness, cut a small slit near the bone.

Panbroiling: Tender broiling cuts that are less than an inch thick are ideal cooked this way. It's also a convenient method of cooking a small steak, several hamburgers, or just a few chops at a time.

Preheat a heavy skillet or griddle but do not add any fat unless the meat is so lean that it's likely to stick. Add meat and cook over medium heat, turning it several times for even cooking. As the fat accumulates, pour it off—otherwise the meat will be sauteed. Keep a watchful eye on the clock, for panbroiling takes about half as long as broiling the same cut. Season the meat to taste after cooking.

When a recipe calls for browning ground beef before it's combined with other ingredients, panbroiling is the best way to do it. Shape the meat into a big patty and brown it well on the bottom. Pour off any fat that accumulates, turn the patty, and brown well on the second side. Then break it up into chunks and season.

Panfrying: Adding a little fat to the skillet before the meat goes in or cooking the meat in the fat as it accumulates are the simple characteristics that distinguish panfrying from panbroiling. Thin pieces of tender meat or those that have been pounded or breaded are often cooked this way.

To begin, measure a small amount of fat into a skillet and heat it slowly, then add the meat and brown it on both sides. Since meat that has been fried is supposed to be crisp, avoid covering the skillet—this steams the meat. Continue cooking, turning the pieces occasionally, until the meat is tender. Season it during cooking or afterwards as you prefer.

Braising: Less tender cuts of all varieties, plus veal and pork chops, steaks, and cutlets taste invitingly flavorful and juicy when braised. To start, roll or dip the meat in flour if you like, then brown it well on all sides in hot fat in a heavy skillet. Pour off the drippings but leave the crusty browned bits in the bottom of the skillet.

Season the meat with salt and pepper or any other spices and herbs of your choice, and pour in a small amount of broth, water, wine, vegetable juice, or bouillon; cover the skillet tightly. Finish the cooking on top of the range at a simmering temperature or in a 325° oven. The chart on page 76 will give you an idea on timing.

Cooking in liquid: Pot roasts and stews are two favorites that call for this type cooking.

Trim any excess fat from the meat, whether it's a large piece or cubes, and if you like, dust the meat with flour; brown on all sides in hot fat in a heavy kettle or Dutch oven. Exceptions to the browning rule are corned-beef brisket and cured or smoked pork that go into the kettle as they are.

After browning, pour any fat from the pan. Season the meat and add enough water or other liquid to cover it. Cover the pan tightly and simmer the meat until tender. Most important is the low temperature, for boiling toughens meat, causes shrinkage, and makes slicing difficult.

If you're adding vegetables to stew, work out your timing so they'll be done at the same time as the meat—but not overcooked.

Types of ham

A big baked ham is probably one of our most popular and easy to fix meats for family meals and party refreshments. Many kinds and sizes are available, and buying enough for more than one meal pays a bonus in both money and time. These are your choices:

Cook-before-eating: This is the familiar smoked variety that must be cooked thoroughly. Buy it whole with the bone in, partly boned, or boneless. Weights start at about eight pounds. When it is cut in half, the pieces are labeled BUTT HALF (chunky round shape) and SHANK HALF (tapered at one end because of leg bone). The pieces labeled SHANK AND BUTT PORTIONS tell you that thick center slices have been cut from each half to sell as steaks.

Fully-cooked: While this type looks like the cook-before-eating hams, it can be eaten with no further cooking. However, baking it for a short time brings out all its juiciness and mellow flavor. It, too, comes whole or cut, bone-in or boneless, halved, or sliced for steaks. Since processing has taken care of the cooking, there will be very little shrinkage, and even though the price tag may be slightly higher than for other types of ham, it may be a better buy.

Boneless rolls: A carver's delight, these are fully cooked hams with the bone taken out, the fat trimmed, and the meat rolled and wrapped in a transparent covering. They weigh from eight to twelve pounds, but can be bought cut up.

Canned: These appealing timesavers come boneless, skinless, trimmed, and fully cooked, and may be sliced and served hot or cold. All are cured but not all are smoked, so be sure to check the label if you have a preference. To fit every need, there are sizes from one to about thirteen pounds. All canned hams weighing two pounds or more are perishable and must be stored in the refrigerator until opened; one-pounders can be kept on a cupboard shelf. It's always good practice, however, to check every label for storage and baking instructions. Among canned hams, you'll also find flavored specialties with a seasoned sugar or honey glaze.

Country-style: Often referred to as old-fashioned hams, they carry names such as Tennessee, Virginia, Kentucky, and Smithfield. They are not available everywhere, but are favored by staunch ham fans because of their heavy curing and slow smoking. No refrigeration is needed with this type ham before it's cooked. Usually it's soaked overnight, simmered very slowly until tender, and then baked. Carve it into thin slices to eat with biscuits, or slice it and panbroil or panfry for breakfast or dinner.

Picnic: A budget choice clearly marked cook-before-eating or fully-cooked, it is cut from the shoulder of the animal. The meat is smoked and cured, and after simmering or baking, tastes just like ham.

Fresh: Not really ham but a leg of fresh pork, this choice is roasted the same as pork loin to an internal temperature of 170°.

Prosciutto or Italian-style: This ham is often cut in paper-thin slices and served with melon as an appetizer. It has a deep ruddy color and zesty flavor, and is ready to eat as purchased.

How to cook ham

These meats are most often baked, although picnics are sometimes simmered in water first, then baked and glazed. When shopping, it's most important that you look for a label that indicates whether the ham is ready-to-eat or needs cooking. If you have any doubt at all about which you bought, treat it as a cook-before-eating type.

For baking, place the ham, fat side up, on a rack in a shallow roasting pan. Do not add any water or cover the pan. Insert a meat thermometer into the thickest part of the ham, making sure that the bulb doesn't touch bone or fat. Bake, using the timetable below as a guide.

If you're glazing the ham, follow your recipe directions, or spread a ready-made glaze over the meat 30 minutes before baking is completed. For easier carving, let meat stand at room temperature 15 to 20 minutes before serving.

HAM BAKING TIMETABLE
Oven Temperature: 325°

Kind	Weight in Pounds	Approximate Total Hours§	Internal Temperature
Cook-before-eating	6 to 8	3¼	160°
	8 to 10	3¼ to 3½	160°
	10 to 15	3½ to 4½	160°
Picnic (cook-before-eating)	4 to 6	2½ to 3	170°
	6 to 8	3 to 4	170°
Fully-cooked	6 to 8	2¼	140°
	8 to 10	2¼ to 2½	140°
	10 to 15	2½ to 3½	140°
Picnic (fully-cooked)	3 to 5	1½ to 2	140°
	5 to 7	2 to 2½	140°
Boneless rolls	8 to 10	2½ to 3	140°
	10 to 12	3 to 3½	140°
Canned	3 to 7	1½ to 2	140°

§Times refer to meat taken directly from refrigerator and placed in a preheated oven.

How to cook bacon

Properly cooked bacon should be crisp, evenly cooked from end to end, and only slightly curled. Several cooking styles are given below, one ideal when you need only a few slices and the others, great timesavers when you're cooking for a crowd. Whichever you follow, it's important to keep the heat low. A temperature that's too high causes the drippings to smoke and may make the meat taste burned. In addition, there's more shrinkage; drippings may also spatter.

After the bacon is cooked, strain the drippings into a jar and chill to use for seasoning or cooking other foods.

Bacon slices, cold from the refrigerator, tear easily, so try to remember to take out what you need 10 to 15 minutes before cooking. If you forget, try this easy trick: Push the tip of a rubber spatula under one end of a slice and pull it slowly between the slices to the other end; you'll be amazed how easily they separate.

In cooking, follow these guides:

To pan-fry: Place slices in a cold frying pan. It isn't necessary to separate them—they fall apart as they heat. Place the pan over the heat and cook slowly, turning slices often with tongs, 6 to 8 minutes, or until meat is crisp and brown. Drain slices on paper toweling.

To bake: Place bacon slices on a rack in a shallow pan with the fat edge of one slice overlapping the lean of the next. Bake in a 400° oven for 12 to 15 minutes, or until crisp. Turning slices and draining off drippings are two jobs that can be eliminated here.

To broil: Arrange slices the same as for baking on rack in broiler pan. Broil about 4 inches from heat, turning once, 2 to 3 minutes on each side, or until meat is crisp and brown. Watch it carefully for cooking goes quickly.

Variety meats

Though often bypassed by those who claim they don't like them, these meats truly deserve a second look. Not only are they economical, but they offer a great deal nutritionally, and carefully prepared, can be as appealing as any other meat.

Liver: Packages may be marked beef, baby beef, calf's, lamb, veal, and pork liver; and as a group, these choices are probably the most popular and well known of all variety meats. Although calf's liver commands the highest price, all varieties work equally well in any recipe. Braise, panfry, or sauté liver, or grind for loaves or patties.

Heart: Most of our supply comes from beef and veal, and a beef heart is often sold split or cut. Heart falls into the category of less tender meat and should be cooked in liquid for several hours. It can also be stuffed, cubed and made into a stew, or ground and combined with other ground meats for loaves or patties.

Tongue: Popular for sandwiches, salads, or casseroles, it can be bought fresh, corned (pickled), or smoked. It, too, needs long slow cooking in a large amount of liquid. A thick skin covers the meat and should be peeled off after cooking. Some meat departments also sell tongue already cooked.

Kidneys: Considered a delicacy by many people, these meats—particularly beef kidneys—should be braised or cooked in liquid. Veal and lamb kidneys, although sold separately, are sometimes left attached to chops and labeled VEAL or LAMB KIDNEY CHOPS. Both can also be broiled, or cubed, wrapped in bacon, and cooked on a skewer.

Sweetbreads: Highest in price of all variety meats, they have a mild delicate flavor and are often featured on restaurant menus. Actually, they are the thymus glands from veal or young beef, and the thin membrane covering them is removed after cooking. Panfrying, broiling, or braising are popular ways to fix them.

How long to cook meat

The amount of time it takes to cook any cut depends upon the kind of meat, its size and shape, the temperature when it starts to cook, the accuracy of the oven, if used, the proportion of lean to fat and bone, how done you like it, and whether or not the meat has been tenderized. Thick cuts take longer than thinner ones of the same weight. If the meat has lots of fat, it will cook faster than a leaner piece. Roasts that are boned and rolled take longer than those with bone. With all these variables, it's easy to understand why any cooking chart can be only an approximate guide. Recipes in this chapter are based on meats that have been chilled until cooking time. If the meat is frozen or only partly thawed, it will, of course, need a longer cooking time.

BRAISING TIMETABLE

Cut	Approximate Weight or Thickness	Approximate Total Hours
Beef		
Pot roast	3 to 5 pounds	2½ to 3½
Shortribs	2x2x4-inch pieces	1½ to 2½
Flank Steak	1½ to 2 pounds	1½ to 2½
Round Steak	¾ to 1 inch	1 to 1½
Cubes for stewing	1½ inches	1½ to 2
Veal		
Breast, boneless	2 to 3 pounds	1½ to 2½
Riblets		2 to 3
Chops	½ to ¾ inch	¾ to 1
Cutlets	½ to ¾ inch	¾ to 1
Cubes for stewing	1 to 2 inches	¾ to 1
Pork		
Chops	¾ to 1½ inches	¾ to 1
Spareribs	2 to 3 pounds	1½
Shoulder Steaks	¾ inch	¾ to 1
Cubes for stewing	1½ inches	1¼
Lamb		
Chops, shoulder	¾ to 1 inch	¾ to 1
Breast, rolled	1½ to 2 pounds	1½ to 2
Riblets		1½ to 2½
Shanks	1 pound	1½
Cubes for stewing	1½ inches	1½ to 2
Neck Slices	¾ inch	1

ROASTING TIMETABLE
Oven Temperature: 325°

Cut	Weight in Pounds	Internal Temperature	Approximate Total Hours§
Beef			
Rib	6 to 8	140° (rare)	2½ to 3
		160° (medium)	3 to 3½
		170° (well-done)	3¾ to 4
Boneless Rib	5 to 7	140° (rare)	3¼ to 3½
		160° (medium)	3¾ to 4
		170° (well-done)	4½ to 4¾
Sirloin Tip (high quality)	4 to 5	140° (rare)	2 to 2½
		160° (medium)	2½ to 3
		170° (well-done)	3 to 3¼
Boneless Rump (high quality)	4	140° (rare)	1½
		160° (medium)	1¾
		170° (well-done)	2 to 2¼
Tenderloin (roast at 425°)	4 to 6	140° (rare)	¾ to 1
Ribeye (roast at 350°)	4 to 6	140° (rare)	1¼ to 1¾
		160° (medium)	1¾ to 2¼
		170° (well-done)	2¼ to 2½
Veal			
Leg	5 to 8	170°	2¾ to 3¾
Loin	4 to 6	170°	2½ to 3
Rolled Shoulder	4 to 6	170°	3½ to 3¾
Pork			
Loin Center	3 to 5	170°	2½ to 3
Loin Blade	3 to 4	170°	2¼ to 2¾
Boneless Loin	3 to 4	170°	2½ to 3
Boston	4 to 6	170°	3 to 4
Leg (fresh ham)	8 to 10	170°	4½ to 5½
Lamb			
Leg, whole	5 to 8	160° (medium)	2½ to 3½
		170° to 180° (well-done)	3 to 4
Leg, half	3 to 4	160° (medium)	2¼ to 2¾
		170° to 180° (well-done)	2½ to 3
Rib (rack) (roast at 375°)	1½ to 3	140° (rare)	1 to 1½
		160° (medium)	1¼ to 1¾
		170° to 180° (well-done)	2
Leg, boneless	3 to 5	160° (medium)	3¼ to 3¾
		170° to 180° (well-done)	3½ to 4

§Times refer to meat taken directly from refrigerator and placed in a preheated oven.

BROILING TIMETABLE

Cut	Weight	Thickness	Approximate Total Minutes
Beef Steaks			
Rib	1 to 1½ pounds	1 inch	15 (rare)
			20 (medium)
Ribeye	8 to 10 ounces	1 inch	15 (rare)
			20 (medium)
	1 to 1¼ pounds	2 inches	35 (rare)
			45 (medium)
T-bone	1 to 2 pounds	1½ inches	30 (rare)
			35 (medium)
Club	10 to 16 ounces	1 inch	15 (rare)
			20 (medium)
Sirloin	1½ to 3 pounds	1 inch	20 (rare)
			25 (medium)
	3 to 5 pounds	2 inches	40 (rare)
			45 (medium)
Porterhouse	2 to 3 pounds	1½ inches	30 (rare)
			35 (medium)
	2½ to 3½ pounds	2 inches	40 (rare)
			45 (medium)
Filet Mignon (tenderloin)	4 to 8 ounces		12 (rare)
			16 (medium)
Lamb Chops			
Rib	6 to 8 ounces	1½ inches	18
Loin	4 to 7 ounces	1 inch	12
Sirloin	6 to 12 ounces	¾ to 1 inch	12 to 14
Leg (steaks)	10 to 14 ounces	¾ to 1 inch	14 to 18
Ham Steak		1 inch	16 to 20
Bacon, sliced			4 to 5
Canadian Bacon, sliced		½ inch	8 to 10

THE ART OF CARVING

Equip yourself with good tools. The rest is easy; just follow these illustrated guides.

ROAST RIBS OF BEEF

Place roast, rib side to carver's left, on a board with a well to catch the juices. Insert a fork between the top two ribs to steady meat, then carve across roast from outside to bone side for end serving.

Remove knife, and holding it at an angle, cut all the way along rib to free entire slice.

Transfer slice to its individual serving plate with the fork and the flat side of the knife. Top with a spoonful of juices from the well. Carve remaining slices as needed, thick or thin as you like.

LEG OF LAMB

Place roast on a board or platter with shank or leg bone at carver's right. Steady roast with a fork and cut two or three thin slices from front to make a stand-up base, then turn roast upright on base.

Slice meat about ¼ inch thick, starting at shank end and cutting down each time until knife touches leg bone.

Run knife under slices along leg bone to loosen them; lift onto serving plates.

ROAST LOIN OF PORK

Cut away backbone, leaving as little meat on it as possible, before roast is taken to the table.

Place roast on platter with rib side facing carver. Insert fork in top of roast to steady it, then slice meat by cutting closely along each side of rib bone. One slice will contain a rib; the next one will be boneless.

WHOLE HAM

Place ham on platter with rounded meaty part on far side and shank end at carver's right. Steady meat with a fork and cut a few thin slices from front to make a flat base.

Turn ham upright so it rests on flat surface and cut a small wedge-shaped piece a few inches in from end of shank bone; lift it out and set aside on platter.

Slice meat ¼ inch thick, starting at wedge cut and cutting down each time to leg bone. Cut along leg bone to loosen slices.

PORTERHOUSE STEAK

Place steak on cutting board with large bone end at carver's right. Steady steak with fork and cut all around bone; lift out and set aside. Start at right side and carve across full width of steak, cutting each slice from ½ to ¾-inch thick.

BEEF

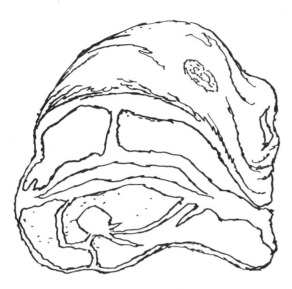

PARTY BEEF ROAST

  2 tablespoons all-purpose flour
  1 teaspoon dry mustard
  1 teaspoon seasoned salt
  ½ teaspoon seasoned pepper
  1 rolled beef rib roast, weighing about 4 lbs.
    Parsley-butter Potato Balls (recipe on page 305)

Preheat oven to 325°.

Mix flour, mustard, salt, and pepper in a cup. Using your hands, rub mixture all over roast; place roast on a rack in a shallow pan. Insert meat thermometer into center of roast. Do not cover pan or add any water.

Roast approximately 30 minutes per pound for rare, or until thermometer registers 140°. If you prefer medium beef, figure about 32 minutes per pound, or 160°. Remove meat from oven and let stand in pan 20 minutes.

Lift roast onto a large serving platter; spoon Parsley-butter Potato Balls around edge. Garnish platter with a few sprigs of watercress and 2 or 3 cherry tomatoes if you like. Carve into ¼-inch-thick slices with a sharp knife.

Yield: 6 servings.

COUNTRY BEEF ROAST

  1 beef bottom round roast, weighing about 5 lbs.
  2 teaspoons salt
  ¼ teaspoon pepper
  2 tablespoons salad oil
  1 large onion, chopped (1 cup)
  1 can (12 ozs.) mixed vegetable juice
  1 teaspoon dried thyme, crushed
  4 large carrots, pared and cut in 2-inch-long sticks
  1 cup sliced celery
  1 package (10 ozs.) frozen peas
  1 can (16 ozs.) whole white potatoes, drained
  2 tablespoons all-purpose flour

Rub beef with salt and pepper. Brown on all sides in salad oil in a Dutch oven; remove and set aside.

Stir onion into drippings; sauté until soft. Stir in vegetable juice and thyme; place beef in Dutch oven. Heat to boiling; cover.

Simmer, turning beef several times, 2½ hours, or until almost tender.

Place carrots, celery, and frozen peas in Dutch oven; heat to boiling; cover. Cook 10 minutes. Add potatoes; cook 5 minutes longer, or until beef and vegetables are tender.

Place beef on a large serving platter; remove vegetables from liquid with a slotted spoon and arrange around meat on platter.

Pour liquid from Dutch oven into a 4-cup measure; let stand a few minutes until fat rises to top, then skim off. Measure 2 tablespoons of the fat and return to Dutch oven; blend in flour. Cook, stirring constantly, until bubbly. Stir in 2 cups of the liquid; continue cooking and stirring until gravy thickens and boils 1 minute; pour into a serving bowl.

Cut strings from beef. Slice part of the meat; pass gravy to spoon over meat and vegetables.

Yield: 4 servings plus enough meat for a dividend dish.

BEEF DINNER CARBONNADE

1 beef bottom round roast, weighing about 4 lbs.
2 tablespoons salad oil
3 medium onions, peeled and sliced
1 clove of garlic, minced
2 teaspoons salt
2 teaspoons dried thyme, crushed
1 teaspoon sugar
1 teaspoon vinegar
1 can (12 ozs.) beer
½ cup water
12 small potatoes, pared
1 lb. carrots, pared and cut in chunks
3 tablespoons all-purpose flour

Brown roast slowly in salad oil in a Dutch oven; remove and set aside. Stir onions and garlic into drippings; sauté until soft.

Stir in salt, thyme, sugar, vinegar, beer, and water; heat, stirring constantly, to boiling. Place meat in liquid; cover. Simmer, turning meat several times, 2 hours and 15 minutes, or until almost tender.

Place potatoes and carrots around meat in Dutch oven; heat to boiling again; cover. Simmer 30 minutes, or until meat and vegetables are tender.

Place roast on a large serving platter; remove vegetables from broth with a slotted spoon and arrange around meat; keep warm.

Let broth stand in Dutch oven for a minute until fat rises to top, then skim off. Press broth with onions through a sieve into a bowl; return to Dutch oven. (There should be 2½ cups.) Reheat to boiling.

Mix flour with a little water in a cup until smooth; stir into boiling liquid. Cook, stirring constantly, until gravy thickens and boils 1 minute.

Cut strings from beef. Slice part of the meat; serve gravy separately to spoon over meat and vegetables.

Yield: 6 servings plus enough meat for a dividend dish.

BURGUNDY BEEF RAGOUT

1 beef round steak, weighing 2½ lbs. and cut 1 inch thick
3 tablespoons all-purpose flour
1 teaspoon salt
¼ teaspoon pepper
4 tablespoons salad oil
2 large onions, chopped (2 cups)
2 cloves garlic, minced
1 teaspoon dried basil, crushed
1½ cups Burgundy wine
1 can (10½ ozs.) condensed beef broth
½ lb. fresh mushrooms, trimmed and sliced
3 tablespoons butter or margarine
18 small white onions, peeled
12 medium carrots, pared and cut diagonally in 1-inch chunks
2 tablespoons chopped parsley

Cut steak into 1-inch cubes. Shake with mixture of flour, salt, and pepper in a transparent bag to coat well. Brown, a few pieces at a time, in salad oil in a Dutch oven; remove with a slotted spoon to a bowl.

Stir chopped onions and garlic into drippings in Dutch oven; sauté until soft. Stir in basil, wine, and beef broth; add beef. Heat to boiling; cover. Simmer 1½ hours, or until meat is almost tender.

While meat cooks, sauté mushrooms in butter in a large skillet 2 minutes; remove with a slotted spoon to a bowl.

Add whole onions and carrots to skillet; brown lightly, then spoon around meat in Dutch oven. Heat to boiling; cover. Simmer 20 minutes. Add mushrooms; cook 10 minutes longer, or until meat and vegetables are tender.

Just before serving, sprinkle chopped parsley over top. Serve from Dutch oven.

Yield: 6 servings.

BEEF RIB ROAST

1 tablespoon all-purpose flour
1 teaspoon dry mustard
1 teaspoon salt
½ teaspoon pepper
1 three-rib beef roast, weighing about 6 lbs.
  Watercress
  Radish roses

Preheat oven to 325°.

Combine flour, mustard, salt, and pepper in a cup; rub all over roast. Place roast, fat side up, in roasting pan. (Ribs form their own rack.) Insert meat thermometer into center of roast without touching bone or fat. Do not add water or cover pan.

Roast 2¼ to 3 hours, or until thermometer registers 140° for rare. If you prefer beef medium, roast 3 to 3½ hours, or to 160° on thermometer.

Place roast on a large serving platter; let stand 15 minutes for easier carving. Garnish platter with watercress and radish roses.

Yield: 8 servings.

PARMESAN STEAK

1 beef sirloin steak, weighing about 4 lbs. and cut
    2 inches thick
⅓ cup bottled Italian salad dressing
⅓ cup grated Parmesan cheese

Trim any excess fat from steak; slash remaining fat edge to prevent curling. Place steak in a large shallow dish; pour salad dressing over top. Let stand 2 to 3 hours at room temperature, turning several times, to season.

When ready to cook, preheat broiler. Remove steak from dish, place on rack in broiler pan. Brush dressing in dish over top.

Broil, 8 inches from heat, 15 minutes; turn. Broil 10 minutes; sprinkle Parmesan cheese on top; broil 5 minutes longer for rare, or until steak is as done as you like it.

Remove to a cutting board; carve into ¼-inch-thick slices.

Yield: 8 servings.

CHILI CON QUESO BEEF ROAST

1 beef chuck arm-bone roast, weighing about 4 lbs.
    and cut 2½ inches thick
2 canned whole pimientos
2 canned green chili peppers
1 envelope instant meat marinade
1 cup shredded sharp Cheddar cheese (4 ozs.)

With a sharp knife, cut 8 deep slits about 3 inches long in top of roast.

Cut pimientos and chili peppers in quarters; fold each piece of pimiento around a strip of chili pepper; stuff deep into slits in roast. Slash fat edge of roast every inch so it will lie flat.

Prepare meat marinade as label directs in a shallow dish. Place roast in dish; turn to coat all over with marinade; let stand 15 minutes.

When ready to cook, preheat broiler. Remove roast from dish; place on rack in broiler pan. Brush part of the marinade over top.

Broil, 8 inches from heat, 20 minutes; turn; brush again with marinade. Broil 20 minutes longer for rare, or until beef is as done as you like it. (To test, cut a small slit near bone.)

Sprinkle cheese over roast; heat 1 to 2 minutes until cheese melts.

Remove roast to a cutting board; carve diagonally into ¼-inch-thick slices.

Yield: 6 to 8 servings.

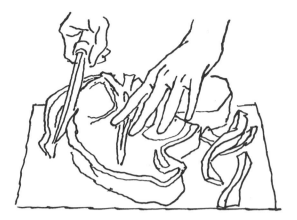

STEAK DIANE

1 beef sirloin steak, weighing about 4 lbs. and cut
    2 inches thick
½ lb. fresh mushrooms or 1 can (3 or 4 ozs.) sliced
    mushrooms
1 cup sliced green onions
½ cup butter or margarine
1½ teaspoons dry mustard
1 tablespoon Worcestershire sauce
¾ teaspoon salt
1 tablespoon lemon juice
3 tablespoons chopped parsley
¼ cup brandy

Preheat broiler.

Trim any excess fat from steak; slash remaining fat edge to prevent curling; place on rack in broiler pan.

Broil, 6 inches from heat, 16 minutes; turn. Broil 16 minutes longer for rare, or until steak is as done as you like it.

While steak cooks, trim fresh mushrooms and slice thin. If using canned ones, drain well. Sauté mushrooms and green onions lightly in butter in a medium skillet. Stir in mustard, Worcestershire sauce, and salt; heat to boiling. Stir in lemon juice and parsley.

Place steak on a large carving board; spoon onion mixture on top.

Heat brandy almost to boiling in same skillet; pour over steak; ignite with a match. When flame dies, carve steak into ¼-inch-thick slices.

Yield: 8 servings.

CAPE COD SKILLET STEAK

1 beef chuck arm-bone steak, weighing about 2
    lbs. and cut 1 inch thick
2 tablespoons salad oil
2 medium onions, peeled and sliced
1 can (10¾ ozs.) condensed bean with bacon soup
½ cup dry white wine

Trim any excess fat from steak.

Brown steak in salad oil in a large skillet; lay onions on top.

Mix soup and wine in a small bowl; pour over steak. Heat slowly to boiling; cover. Simmer 2 hours, or until meat is tender.

Lift steak onto a deep serving platter; spoon sauce over top.

Yield: 6 servings.

BOILED BEEF WITH HORSERADISH SAUCE

1 beef chuck arm-bone roast, weighing 3 lbs. and
    cut about 2½ inches thick
2 medium onions, peeled
1 tablespoon salt
6 peppercorns
1 bay leaf
    Water
    Horseradish Sauce (recipe on page 314)

Place roast in a Dutch oven; add onions, salt, peppercorns, bay leaf, and just enough water to cover. Heat to boiling; cover.

Simmer 2½ hours, or until meat is tender. Remove from broth and place on a large serving platter; keep warm.

Make Horseradish Sauce, using 1 cup of the broth to replace 1 cup of the milk called for in recipe; chill remainder to use for soup another day. Slice beef; serve with sauce.

Yield: 6 servings.

SAUERBRATEN

1 beef bottom round roast, weighing about 4 lbs.
1 cup wine vinegar
1 cup water
½ cup dry red wine
¼ cup firmly packed brown sugar
3 teaspoons salt
½ teaspoon pepper
½ teaspoon ground cloves
1 bay leaf
1 large onion, chopped (1 cup)
2 large carrots, pared and diced
2 cups diced celery
2 tablespoons salad oil
6 tablespoons all-purpose flour

Place roast in a large glass bowl.

Mix vinegar, water, wine, brown sugar, salt, pepper, cloves, bay leaf, onion, carrots, and celery in a medium bowl; pour over roast; cover. Place in refrigerator, turning several times, for 2 or 3 days to season.

When ready to cook roast, remove from marinade, pat dry with paper toweling. Brown slowly on all sides in salad oil in a kettle.

Remove vegetables from marinade with a slotted spoon; add to kettle; pour in marinade to a depth of 1 inch. Heat to boiling; cover.

Simmer, turning meat several times, 2 to 2½ hours, or until tender. Remove bay leaf. Place roast on a large platter.

Strain liquid into a bowl, pressing vegetables through sieve; measure and add water to make 3 cups; return to kettle.

Smooth flour with a little water in a cup to a paste; stir into mixture in kettle. Cook, stirring constantly, until gravy thickens and boils 1 minute. (If you prefer darker gravy, stir in ½ to 1 teaspoon gravy seasoning.)

Cut strings from beef. Slice meat; pass gravy separately to spoon over meat.

Yield: 8 servings.

BEEF BRISKET PROVENCALE

1 head of cabbage, weighing about 1¾ lbs.
1 oven cooking bag with sauce mix for beef stew
1 piece beef brisket, weighing about 3 lbs.
3 medium onions, chopped (1½ cups)
3 medium carrots, pared and sliced (1½ cups)
1 bay leaf
1½ cups dry red wine
½ cup chopped parsley
1 teaspoon dried thyme, crushed
½ teaspoon salt
1 package (10 ozs.) brown-and-serve sausages

Preheat oven to 350°.

Trim cabbage; quarter, core, and chop. (There should be about 8 cups.)

Fasten one end of cooking bag as label directs; place in a large shallow baking pan. Place cabbage in bag; lay beef on top of cabbage. Layer onions and carrots over meat; add bay leaf.

Empty sauce mix from cooking bag package into a 2-cup measure; stir in part of the wine until blended, then add remainder with parsley, thyme, and salt. Pour into bag with beef and vegetables; fasten bag and vent as label directs.

Bake 2¾ hours; remove from oven. Slit bag slightly and push sausages down into broth around meat. Bake 15 minutes longer, or until sausages are hot.

Push vegetables from beef into broth; remove beef to a cutting board and cut into thick slices. Pour vegetables and broth into baking pan, then spoon into soup bowls. Top each serving with a slice of beef and one or two sausages. Serve with French bread if you like.

Yield: 6 servings plus enough meat for a dividend dish.

DEVILED STEAK

1 beef round steak, weighing 2 lbs. and cut 1 inch
    thick
2 tablespoons salad oil
1 large onion, coarsely chopped (1 cup)
2 tablespoons prepared hot spicy mustard
1 tablespoon lemon juice
1 teaspoon salt
½ teaspoon garlic powder
½ teaspoon pepper
½ cup water
1 large green pepper, seeded and cut into rings

Preheat oven to 350°.

Cut steak into serving-sized pieces. Brown in salad oil in a large skillet; place pieces in a single layer in a baking dish, 12x8x2 inches.

Stir onion into drippings in skillet; sauté until soft; spoon over steak.

Mix mustard, lemon juice, salt, garlic powder, pepper, and water in a small bowl; pour over steak; cover tightly.

Bake 1 hour and 45 minutes.

Overlap green pepper rings around edge in dish; cover again. Bake 15 minutes longer, or until meat is tender.

Yield: 8 servings.

RIPPLED STEAK STICKS

1 beef round steak, weighing 2 lbs. and cut 1 inch
    thick
    Instant unseasoned meat tenderizer
4 small zucchini
1 can (16 ozs.) whole white potatoes, drained
1 cup bottled plain barbecue sauce
16 cherry tomatoes, stemmed

Moisten steak; sprinkle tenderizer all over and pierce meat with a fork as label directs. Cut steak across grain into long thin strips.

Trim zucchini; cut each crosswise into 4 chunks. Parboil, covered, in boiling water in a small saucepan 3 minutes, or until barely tender; drain.

Preheat broiler.

Thread steak strips, accordion style and alternating with zucchini chunks and potatoes,
onto 8 long skewers. Place on rack in broiler pan; brush part of the barbecue sauce over all.

Broil, 6 inches from heat, turning several times and brushing with remaining sauce, 3 to 5 minutes, or until steak is as done as you like it. Garnish end of each skewer with 2 cherry tomatoes.

Yield: 8 servings.

BACKWOODS BEEF STEW AND DUMPLINGS

1 piece lean boneless beef chuck, weighing 4 lbs.
    and cut 1 inch thick
¼ cup salad oil
3 medium onions, chopped (1½ cups)
3 teaspoons salt
2 teaspoons dried thyme, crushed
½ teaspoon pepper
4 cups water
4 envelopes (1½ ozs. each) brown gravy mix
4 cans (16 ozs. each) small whole carrots
4 cans (16 ozs. each) whole white potatoes
2 cans (16 ozs. each) whole boiled onions, drained
3 cups biscuit mix
1 cup milk

Trim any fat from beef; cut beef into 1-inch cubes. Brown in salad oil in a large kettle; push to one side.

Stir onions into drippings; sauté until soft. Stir in salt, thyme, pepper, and water; heat to boiling; cover. Simmer 1½ hours, or until meat is almost tender.

Sprinkle gravy mix over top, then stir in with carrots and liquid, potatoes and liquid, and onions; heat to boiling.

While stew heats, combine biscuit mix and milk in a medium bowl; stir until mixture is evenly moist. Drop by tablespoonfuls into 16 mounds on top of bubbling stew.

Cook, uncovered, 10 minutes; cover. Cook 10 minutes longer, or until dumplings are puffy-light. Serve from kettle.

Yield: 16 servings.

TERIYAKI STICKS

1 piece boneless beef chuck, weighing 1½ lbs.
   and cut 1 inch thick
1 can (8 ozs.) pineapple chunks in juice
   Water
1 package instant meat marinade
1 clove garlic, crushed
¾ teaspoon ground ginger
4 large carrots
2 tablespoons soy sauce
1 tablespoon honey

Trim any excess fat from beef; cut beef into sixteen 1-inch cubes.

Drain juice from pineapple into a 1-cup measure; add water to make ⅔ cup. Stir into meat marinade, garlic, and ginger in a shallow dish. Add meat cubes; turn to coat with marinade; pierce each deeply all over with a fork as marinade label directs. Let stand 15 minutes.

While meat seasons, pare carrots; cut each into four 1-inch chunks. Cook, covered, in boiling salted water in a medium saucepan 10 minutes, or until crisp-tender; drain.

Preheat broiler.

Remove meat from marinade. Thread cubes onto 4 long skewers, alternating with pineapple chunks and carrots. Place on rack in broiler pan.

Stir soy sauce and honey into remaining marinade in dish; brush part over meat, carrots, and pineapple.

Broil, 6 to 8 inches from heat, turning often and brushing with remaining marinade, 10 to 15 minutes, or until beef is as done as you like it. Serve as is or on a bed of buttered green beans if you like.

Yield: 4 servings.

HERBED BEEF ROULADES

¼ cup chopped celery
¼ cup chopped red pepper
4 tablespoons butter or margarine
3 cups water
1½ cups packaged herb stuffing mix
6 beef cube steaks, weighing about 1½ lbs.
2 tablespoons shortening
1 envelope onion soup mix
1 lb. wax beans, tipped and cut in 1-inch pieces
1 pint cherry tomatoes, stemmed
1 tablespoon all-purpose flour

Sauté celery and red pepper in butter in a medium saucepan until soft; stir in ½ cup of the water. Heat to boiling; stir in stuffing mix until evenly moist.

Place steaks flat on a cutting board; spoon about ¼ cup of the stuffing mixture onto each. Roll up, jelly-roll fashion; tie tightly with string.

Brown rolls in shortening in a large skillet.

Combine remaining 2½ cups water and soup mix in a 4-cup measure; pour over steak rolls. Heat to boiling; cover. Simmer, turning rolls once, 1 hour and 10 minutes.

Place beans in skillet; cover. Simmer 15 minutes, or until steak is tender and beans are still slightly crisp.

Add cherry tomatoes to skillet; cover. Heat 1 to 2 minutes, or just until hot.

Lift steak and vegetables from skillet with a slotted spoon and arrange in rows on a large deep platter; keep hot.

Mix flour with a little water in a cup until smooth; stir into liquid in pan. Cook, stirring constantly, until gravy thickens and boils 1 minute. Serve separately to spoon over steak rolls.

Yield: 6 servings.

BELGIAN BEEF STEW

1 beef round steak, weighing 2 lbs. and cut into
    1½-inch cubes
¼ cup salad oil
2 medium onions, peeled and sliced thin
1 clove garlic, minced
⅓ cup all-purpose flour
1 can (12 ozs.) beer
1 cup water
2 teaspoons salt
1 teaspoon sugar
1½ teaspoons cider vinegar
½ teaspoon leaf oregano, crushed
2 cups loose-pack frozen small whole carrots
2 cups loose-pack frozen peas

Brown beef cubes in 2 tablespoons of the
salad oil in a Dutch oven; remove beef and set
aside.

Add remaining oil to Dutch oven; stir in
onions and garlic; sauté, stirring several times,
until soft.

Stir in flour, then beer, water, salt, sugar,
vinegar, and oregano; cook, stirring constantly, until mixture thickens slightly and
boils 1 minute. Return beef to Dutch oven;
cover tightly. Simmer 1½ hours.

Stir in frozen carrots; cover; simmer 10
minutes.

Stir in peas; cover. Simmer 20 minutes
longer, or until beef and vegetables are tender.

Yield: 6 servings.

DEVILED SHORTRIBS

4 lbs. beef shortribs, cut into serving-sized pieces
    Water
¼ cup all-purpose flour
1 teaspoon seasoned salt
¼ teaspoon seasoned pepper
2 eggs
½ cup dry bread crumbs
3 tablespoons prepared hot mustard
3 tablespoons lemon juice
3 tablespoons butter or margarine, melted
2 tablespoons chopped parsley

Place shortribs in a Dutch oven; pour in
enough water to cover. Heat to boiling; cover.
Simmer 1½ hours, or until meat is almost tender; drain.

Mix flour, seasoned salt, and seasoned pepper in a pie plate. Beat eggs with 2 tablespoons
water in another pie plate; sprinkle bread
crumbs on waxed paper.

Preheat oven to 350°.

If any moisture clings to ribs, pat dry with
paper toweling. Dip ribs into seasoned flour,
then egg mixture, and bread crumbs. Place on
a rack in a shallow baking pan.

Mix mustard, lemon juice, melted butter,
and parsley in a cup; drizzle half over ribs.

Bake 20 minutes; turn ribs; drizzle remaining mustard mixture over top. Bake 20 minutes longer, or until ribs are tender and
crusty-brown.

Yield: 4 to 6 servings.

BEEF BURGUNDY

    1 beef round steak, weighing 2 lbs. and cut 1¼
        inches thick
    2 tablespoons salad oil
    2 tablespoons all-purpose flour
 1½ teaspoons salt
    ¼ teaspoon dried marjoram, crushed
    ¼ teaspoon dried thyme, crushed
    ¼ teaspoon seasoned pepper
    1 envelope instant beef broth
    1 cup Burgundy or other dry red wine
    1 cup water
   18 small white onions, peeled
    6 medium carrots, pared and cut in 1-inch lengths

Brown steak in salad oil in a large skillet. Sprinkle flour, salt, marjoram, thyme, pepper, and beef broth over meat; pour wine and water over top. Heat to boiling; cover. Simmer 1 hour.

Place onions and carrots around meat in skillet; cover again. Simmer 30 minutes, or until steak and vegetables are tender.

Place steak on a large serving platter; arrange vegetables in mounds around edge. Slice meat; serve gravy separately to spoon over top.

Yield: 6 servings.

ORIENTAL BEEF

    1 piece boneless beef chuck, weighing about 1½
        lbs. and cut ½ inch thick
    ¾ teaspoon seasoned instant meat tenderizer
    3 tablespoons salad oil
    1 large green pepper, quartered, seeded, and cut
        in strips
    1 large red pepper, quartered, seeded, and cut in
        strips
    2 cups diagonally sliced celery
    2 medium onions, peeled and sliced thin
    1 can (8 ozs.) water chestnuts, drained and sliced
    2 tablespoons cornstarch
    1 envelope instant beef broth
    2 teaspoons sugar
    ¾ teaspoon ground ginger
    ¼ teaspoon seasoned pepper
 1½ cups water
    3 tablespoons soy sauce

Trim any fat from beef. Moisten meat thoroughly with water, then sprinkle tenderizer over both sides; pierce meat deeply with a fork as tenderizer label directs. Cut meat into 3x½-inch strips with a sharp knife.

Heat 1 tablespoon of the salad oil in a large skillet; add meat and brown quickly; remove meat from skillet.

Add remaining 2 tablespoons salad oil to skillet; heat. Place green and red peppers, celery, onions, and water chestnuts in separate piles in skillet. Sauté, stirring once or twice, 3 minutes, or just until vegetables are crisp-tender; return meat to skillet.

While vegetables cook, mix cornstarch, beef broth, sugar, ginger, and seasoned pepper in a small saucepan; stir in water and soy sauce. Cook, stirring constantly, until sauce thickens and boils 1 minute. Pour over meat and vegetables; heat slowly just until hot. Serve as is or, if you like, with cooked rice seasoned with toasted slivered almonds or canned pineapple tidbits.

Yield: 6 servings.

MONTEREY BEEF DINNER

6 tablespoons all-purpose flour
2½ teaspoons salt
¼ teaspoon pepper
1 beef chuck roast, weighing about 3½ lbs.
2 tablespoons salad oil
1 large onion, chopped (1 cup)
2 cloves garlic, chopped
1 can (10½ ozs.) condensed consommé
2 cans (5½ ozs. each) apple juice
1 teaspoon dried thyme, crushed
1 package (16 ozs.) carrots, pared
1 lb. fresh green beans, tipped
12 small potatoes, pared

Mix 2 tablespoons of the flour with salt and pepper in a cup; rub over both sides of roast. Brown roast in salad oil in a Dutch oven; remove and set aside.

Add onion and garlic to drippings; sauté until soft. Stir in consommé, apple juice, and thyme; heat to boiling. Place meat in liquid; cover. Simmer, turning several times, 2 hours.

Add carrots to Dutch oven, cover again; cook 10 minutes. Add whole green beans and potatoes; cover. Cook 30 minutes longer, or until meat and vegetables are tender.

Remove meat to a large serving platter; place vegetables around edge; keep warm. Reheat liquid in Dutch oven to boiling.

Mix remaining 4 tablespoons flour with a little water until smooth in a cup; stir into boiling liquid. Cook, stirring constantly, until gravy thickens and boils 1 minute; add salt to taste, if needed. Pass gravy separately to spoon over meat.

Yield: 6 to 8 servings.

MANDARIN BEEF

1 piece boneless beef chuck, weighing 1 lb.
  Unseasoned instant meat tenderizer
4 tablespoons salad oil
2 cups diagonally sliced celery
2 small onions, peeled, sliced, and separated into rings
1 medium-sized green pepper, quartered, seeded, and cut in squares
¼ cup dry sherry
3 tablespoons soy sauce
1 envelope instant beef broth
1 tablespoon cornstarch
1 cup water
1 can (11 ozs.) mandarin orange segments, drained
1 can (3 ozs.) Chinese noodles

Trim any excess fat from beef. Moisten meat thoroughly with water, then sprinkle tenderizer over both sides; pierce meat deeply with a fork as tenderizer label directs. Cut into strips about ½ inch thick and 3 inches long.

Heat 2 tablespoons of the salad oil in a large skillet; add meat and brown quickly; remove from skillet.

Add remaining 2 tablespoons oil to skillet; stir in celery, onions, and green pepper; sauté 2 to 3 minutes. Stir in sherry, soy sauce, and instant beef broth.

Dissolve cornstarch in water in a cup; stir into onion mixture. Cook, stirring constantly, until mixture thickens and boils 3 minutes. Stir in beef and mandarin orange segments. Heat slowly 5 minutes, or until bubbly.

Spoon onto a large deep platter; sprinkle noodles in a ring around edge. Serve with extra soy sauce to drizzle over top.

Yield: 4 servings.

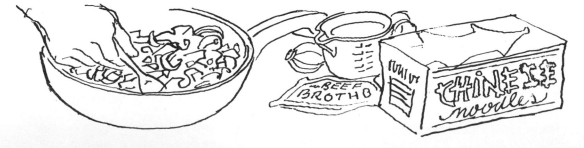

ITALIAN BEEF DINNER

1 beef chuck roast, weighing about 2½ lbs.
2 tablespoons all-purpose flour
1 tablespoon salad oil
1 large onion, chopped (1 cup)
1 clove of garlic, minced
1 can (16 ozs.) stewed tomatoes
1 can (8 ozs.) tomato sauce
1 can (3 or 4 ozs.) chopped mushrooms
2 teaspoons dried Italian herbs
1 teaspoon salt
1 teaspoon sugar
½ cup water
1 package (8 ozs.) spaghetti

Trim any excess fat from beef. Rub flour over both sides of roast; brown in salad oil in a Dutch oven; remove and set aside.

Stir onion and garlic into drippings; sauté until soft. Stir in tomatoes, tomato sauce, mushrooms and liquid, Italian herbs, salt, sugar, and water; heat to boiling. Place meat in sauce; cover.

Simmer, turning meat several times, 2½ hours, or until tender.

While meat simmers, cook spaghetti as label directs; drain; keep hot.

Place roast on a large serving platter; cut into ½-inch-thick slices. Spoon spaghetti around edge of meat.

Skim any fat from sauce; reheat to boiling. Spoon part over meat and spaghetti; serve remainder separately.

Yield: 4 servings.

BEEF SCALLOPINI WITH WINE SAUCE

1 envelope instant meat marinade
1 beef eye round roast, weighing 1½ lbs. and sliced ¼ inch thick
2 tablespoons salad oil
1 envelope Burgundy wine sauce mix
    Water
    Butter
2 tablespoons chopped parsley

Prepare meat marinade with water in a large shallow dish as label directs. Place beef slices in marinade, turning to coat both sides; pierce meat all over with a fork. Let stand just 15 minutes.

Brown slices quickly, several at a time, in salad oil in a large skillet; place, overlapping, on a large deep platter; keep hot.

While meat browns, prepare wine sauce mix with water and butter as label directs; spoon over meat. Sprinkle parsley on top.

Yield: 6 servings.

OVEN SUKIYAKI

1 piece lean boneless beef sirloin, weighing 1 lb.
1 tablespoon salad oil
1½ cups packaged precooked rice
1 cup thinly sliced celery
1 can (8 ozs.) water chestnuts, drained and sliced
1 package (10 ozs.) frozen spinach, thawed and drained well
6 medium carrots, pared and cut diagonally into thin slices
8 green onions, trimmed and sliced
1¼ cups water
2 envelopes instant beef broth
⅓ cup soy sauce
2 teaspoons sugar

Cut beef across grain into strips about ¼ inch thick and 2 inches long.

Heat salad oil in a large skillet; add beef strips and brown quickly.

Preheat oven to 350°.

Place rice in a 2-quart shallow baking dish to cover bottom; layer celery, water chestnuts, meat strips, spinach, carrots, and green onions on top.

Combine water, beef broth, soy sauce, and sugar in same skillet. Heat to boiling; pour over beef and vegetables; cover.

Bake 30 minutes, or until rice is tender and vegetables are still slightly crisp. Serve from baking dish with additional soy sauce to drizzle on top.

Yield: 4 servings.

PEPPER STEAK STEW

1 beef round steak, weighing 1½ lbs. and cut ¾
    inch thick
2 tablespoons all-purpose flour
½ teaspoon dried thyme, crushed
1 teaspoon salt
¼ teaspoon pepper
2 tablespoons salad oil
1 can (10¾ ozs.) condensed golden mushroom
    soup
¾ cup dry white wine
12 small white onions, peeled
3 small zucchini, trimmed and cut in ½-inch-thick
    rounds
1 small green pepper, seeded and cut into rings
1 small red pepper, seeded and cut into rings

Preheat oven to 350°.

Cut steak into serving-sized pieces.

Mix flour, thyme, salt, and pepper in a cup; rub into steak.

Brown pieces slowly, turning once, in salad oil in a Dutch oven with ovenproof handles.

Mix soup and wine in a small bowl; pour over steak. Heat to boiling; cover.

Bake 1 hour and 15 minutes. Add onions to Dutch oven; cover again. Bake 30 minutes.

Lay zucchini and pepper rings on top of steak; cover. Bake 15 minutes longer, or until meat and vegetables are tender.

Yield: 6 servings.

SOMBRERO BEEF

1 piece boneless beef chuck, weighing 2 lbs.
3 tablespoons all-purpose flour
2 tablespoons chili powder
2 teaspoons salt
¼ teaspoon pepper
¼ cup salad oil
1 large onion, chopped (1 cup)
2 cans (16 ozs. each) red kidney beans
2 cans (12 ozs. each) Mexican-style corn
1 can (16 ozs.) tomatoes
2 tablespoons chopped parsley
  Pitted ripe olives, sliced crosswise

Trim any excess fat from beef; cut beef into 1-inch cubes. Combine with flour, chili powder, salt, and pepper in a transparent bag; shake well to coat meat.

Preheat oven to 350°.

Brown meat, part at a time, in salad oil in a large skillet; remove with a slotted spoon and place in a 2½-quart baking dish.

Stir onion into drippings in skillet; sauté until soft. Drain liquids from beans and corn into a bowl; stir liquids and tomatoes into onion mixture; heat to boiling. Stir into beef; cover.

Bake 1¾ hours, or until beef is tender.

Stir beans into beef mixture; spoon corn in a ring on top; cover again. Bake 15 minutes longer, or until vegetables are heated through.

Garnish with chopped parsley and clusters of olive slices. Serve as is or with steamed rice, Mexican style, if you like.

Yield: 8 servings.

BARBECUED SHORTRIBS

4 lbs. beef shortribs
1 medium onion, chopped (½ cup)
1 clove garlic, minced
1 tablespoon brown sugar
2 teaspoons salt
1 cup catsup
3 tablespoons cider vinegar
3 tablespoons Worcestershire sauce
1 cup water
   Casserole Barley (recipe follows)

Preheat oven to 350°.

Cut shortribs, if needed, into serving-sized pieces; brown in their own fat in a large skillet. Place in a single layer in a shallow baking dish; cover.

Bake 1 hour.

Pour drippings from skillet, then measure 1 tablespoon and return to skillet. Stir in onion and garlic and sauté until soft. Stir in brown sugar, salt, catsup, vinegar, Worcestershire sauce, and water; heat to boiling.

Spoon all fat from ribs; pour sauce over top; cover again.

Bake, turning once or twice, 1½ hours, or until meat is tender.

Spoon Casserole Barley around edge on a large serving platter; spoon ribs and sauce in center.

Yield: 4 servings.

CASSEROLE BARLEY

¾ cup medium barley
1 envelope instant chicken broth
1 teaspoon salt
2¼ cups boiling water
2 tablespoons chopped parsley

Preheat oven to 350°.

Combine barley, chicken broth, and salt in a 1-quart baking dish. Stir in boiling water; cover tightly.

Bake 1 hour, or until barley is tender and liquid is absorbed. Add parsley to dish; toss lightly with a fork to mix.

Yield: 4 servings.

SPANISH STEAK

1 beef chuck steak, weighing about 2½ lbs. and
   cut 1¼ inches thick
¼ cup all-purpose flour
1½ teaspoons salt
½ teaspoon garlic salt
⅛ teaspoon pepper
2 tablespoons salad oil
3 large onions, peeled and cut in half crosswise
1 can (15 ozs.) tomato sauce with onions, celery,
   and green peppers
¼ cup wine vinegar

Trim any excess fat from steak.

Mix flour, salt, garlic salt, and pepper in a cup; pound into both sides of steak. Brown slowly, turning once, in salad oil in a large skillet; remove from pan.

Add onions to drippings and brown, turning carefully so as not to break halves; remove from skillet.

Stir in tomato sauce and vinegar; place steak in sauce. Heat to boiling; cover. Simmer 1¾ hours; place onions around edge in skillet; cover again. Simmer 15 minutes longer, or until meat is tender. Sprinkle chopped parsley over meat and serve with riced potatoes if you like.

Yield: 6 servings.

BOEUF EN BROCHETTE

1 piece beef round steak, weighing 2 lbs. and cut 1¼ inches thick
1 envelope instant meat marinade
⅓ cup wine vinegar
⅓ cup water
1 clove garlic, minced
½ teaspoon dried oregano, crushed
1 package (6 ozs.) long-grain and wild rice mix
2 medium-sized green peppers
½ lb. sliced bacon
1 can (16 ozs.) whole boiled onions, drained
6 cherry tomatoes

Cut steak into 18 even cubes.

Mix meat marinade, vinegar, water, garlic, and oregano in a shallow dish. Add steak cubes; pierce deeply all over with a fork; turn to coat well with marinade. Let stand 15 minutes. Remove from marinade; set marinade aside.

Prepare rice mix with water as label directs; keep warm.

Cut green peppers in half; seed and cut into 1-inch squares. Cook in boiling water 2 minutes; drain well.

Preheat broiler.

Thread bacon, accordion style, onto 6 long skewers with steak cubes, onions, and green pepper squares; place on rack in broiler pan. Brush marinade over bacon, steak, onions, and peppers.

Broil, 4 to 5 inches from heat, turning often and brushing with remaining marinade, 10 minutes, or until steak is as done as you like it.

Spoon rice onto a large flat serving platter. Place a cherry tomato on the end of each skewer; arrange skewers over rice.

Yield: 6 servings.

BEEF BALLS VERONIQUE

2 lbs. ground beef
2 medium-sized tart apples, pared, quartered, cored, and chopped fine
1 medium onion, chopped fine (½ cup)
1 medium-sized green pepper, quartered, seeded, and chopped fine (½ cup)
2 eggs
¾ cup fine dry bread crumbs
1 teaspoon salt
1 teaspoon ground nutmeg
⅛ teaspoon pepper
2 tablespoons butter or margarine
2 tablespoons cornstarch
2 envelopes instant chicken broth
1 teaspoon brown sugar
1½ cups water
1 jar (7¾ ozs.) junior applesauce
1 cup small seedless green grapes

Preheat oven to 400°.

Combine ground beef, apples, onion, green pepper, eggs, bread crumbs, salt, nutmeg, and pepper in a large bowl; mix lightly until well blended. Shape into 64 meatballs, using about 1 tablespoon for each. Arrange in a single layer in a greased large shallow baking pan.

Bake 20 minutes. Spoon meatballs into a 2½-quart baking dish. Lower oven temperature to 350°.

While meatballs bake, melt butter in a medium saucepan; stir in cornstarch, chicken broth, and brown sugar; cook, stirring constantly, until bubbly. Stir in water; continue cooking and stirring until sauce thickens and boils 1 minute; stir in applesauce. Pour over meatballs; cover.

Bake 30 minutes, or until bubbly. Stir in grapes. Serve as is or with hot steamed rice if you like.

Yield: 8 servings.

MEXICAN BEEF ROUND

1 can (10¾ ozs.) condensed cream of celery soup
2 lbs. meat-loaf mixture (ground beef, veal, and pork)
1½ cups fortified high-protein cereal flakes
1 medium onion, chopped (½ cup)
1 can (4 ozs.) green chili peppers, drained, seeded, and chopped
1 egg
1 teaspoon salt
¼ teaspoon pepper
⅓ cup milk
2 tablespoons chopped parsley

Preheat oven to 350°.

Combine ½ cup of the soup, meat-loaf mixture, cereal, onion, chili peppers, egg, salt, and pepper in a large bowl; mix lightly until well blended. Press into a 1½-quart mixing bowl; invert into a greased shallow baking pan.

Bake 1 hour, or until loaf is crusty brown.

While loaf bakes, combine remaining soup, milk, and parsley in a small saucepan; heat slowly, stirring several times, to boiling.

Lift loaf onto a large serving platter; cut into wedges. Pass sauce separately to spoon over meat.

Yield: 6 servings.

CASSEROLE BEEF BALLS

1 lb. green beans
   Salt
6 leeks
4 large ears of corn
1½ lbs. ground beef
¾ cup rolled oats
¼ teaspoon pepper
¾ cup milk
2 tablespoons all-purpose flour
2 tablespoons salad oil
1 jar (21 ozs.) Italian cooking sauce

Tip green beans and wash; cut in 1-inch pieces. (There should be 4 cups.) Cook, covered, in lightly salted boiling water 15 minutes, or just until crisp-tender; drain well.

Trim leeks and wash well; cut in ½-inch lengths.

Husk corn and remove silks; cut kernels from cobs.

Combine ground beef, rolled oats, 1 teaspoon salt, pepper, and milk in a large bowl; mix lightly until well blended. Shape into 30 medium balls.

Combine flour and ½ teaspoon salt in a pie plate; roll meatballs in mixture to coat well. Brown, a few at a time, in salad oil in a large skillet; place in a mound in the middle of a baking dish, 13x9x2 inches. Spoon beans around meatballs.

Preheat oven to 350°.

Stir leeks into drippings in skillet; sauté 2 to 3 minutes. Stir in cooking sauce; heat to boiling; spoon over meat and beans. Sprinkle corn on top; cover.

Bake 45 minutes, or until bubbly. Serve from baking dish.

Yield: 6 servings.

RIO BEEF PIE

½ lb. ground beef
1 can (16 ozs.) barbecue beans
½ teaspoon dried oregano, crushed
1 package (12 ozs.) corn muffin mix
½ cup milk
1 egg
¼ cup sliced pitted ripe olives
1 cup shredded sharp Cheddar cheese (4 ozs.)

Preheat oven to 400°.

Shape ground beef into a large patty; brown in its own fat, turning once, in a medium skillet; break up into chunks. Stir in beans and oregano; heat slowly to boiling.

Prepare muffin mix with the ½ cup milk and egg as label directs; spread evenly in a 14-inch pizza pan. Spread bean mixture on top; sprinkle olives and cheese over beans.

Bake 20 minutes, or until crust browns lightly around edge. Cut into wedges; serve hot.

Yield: 4 servings.

PETER PIPER BEEF PATTIES

1½ lbs. lean ground beef
　1 cup regular wheat germ
　1 can (3 or 4 ozs.) chopped mushrooms, drained
　1 medium onion, chopped (½ cup)
½ cup drained sweet pickle relish
½ cup milk
　1 egg, beaten
　1 tablespoon Worcestershire sauce
1½ teaspoons salt
⅛ teaspoon pepper

Preheat broiler.

Combine all ingredients in a large bowl; mix lightly until well blended. Shape into 6 patties about ¾ inch thick. Place on rack in broiler pan.

Broil, 4 inches from heat, 5 minutes; turn. Broil 5 to 8 minutes longer, or until beef is as done as you like it.

Place on a large serving platter; serve with fresh tomato wedges if you like.

Yield: 6 servings.

ITALIAN BEEF BAKE

　2 cups uncooked small macaroni shells
½ lb. ground beef
　1 tablespoon salad oil
　1 medium onion, chopped (½ cup)
　1 jar (15 ozs.) meatless spaghetti sauce
　1 can (8 ozs.) cut green beans
　1 cup shredded mozzarella cheese (4 ozs.)

Cook macaroni as label directs; drain. Place in a 1½-quart baking dish.

Preheat oven to 350°.

Shape ground beef into a patty; brown in salad oil, turning once, in a large skillet; break up into chunks and push to one side. Stir onion into drippings; sauté until soft.

Stir in spaghetti sauce, beans and liquid, and half of the cheese; heat to boiling; stir into macaroni. Sprinkle remaining cheese on top.

Bake 30 minutes, or until bubbly and cheese melts and browns lightly.

Yield: 4 servings.

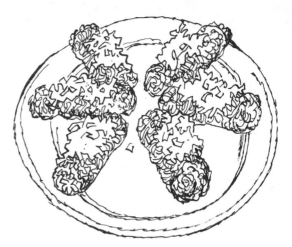

TERIYAKI BEEF ROLLS

　2 lbs. ground beef
　1 teaspoon salt
⅓ cup soy sauce
⅓ cup salad oil
⅓ cup orange juice
　1 teaspoon sugar
　1 teaspoon ground ginger
　1 clove garlic, crushed
　1 can (8 ozs.) crushed pineapple in juice
¼ cup thinly sliced green onions

Combine ground beef and salt in a medium bowl; mix lightly. Shape into 6 even logs about 5 inches long.

Mix soy sauce, salad oil, orange juice, sugar, ginger, and garlic in a large shallow dish. Place meat logs in mixture, turning to coat all over. Let stand, spooning soy mixture over meat several times, 1 hour to season.

Preheat broiler.

Remove meat from marinade and place on rack in broiler pan.

Broil, 6 inches from heat, turning and brushing several times with marinade, 8 minutes, or until beef is as done as you like it.

While meat cooks, heat pineapple in a small saucepan; drain off juice.

Place meat logs, spoke fashion, on a large serving platter; spoon fruit over meat; sprinkle green onions on top.

Yield: 6 servings.

MEATBALL TAMALE PIE

    1 lb. ground beef
    1 large onion, chopped (1 cup)
    1 large green pepper, quartered, seeded, and
        chopped (1 cup)
    2 tablespoons salad oil
    1 teaspoon chili powder
    1 can (16 ozs.) stewed tomatoes
    1 can (12 ozs.) Mexican-style corn, drained
    ½ cup sliced pitted ripe olives
    2 teaspoons sugar
    1 teaspoon garlic powder
    1 teaspoon salt
    1½ cups shredded sharp Cheddar cheese
    1 package (12 ozs.) corn muffin mix
        Egg
        Milk

Shape ground beef into 24 small balls.

Sauté onion and green pepper in salad oil in a large skillet until soft; push to one side. Add meatballs to skillet and brown. Stir in chili powder; cook 1 minute.

Stir in tomatoes, corn, olives, sugar, garlic powder, and salt; heat to boiling; cover. Simmer 30 minutes, or until slightly thickened. Stir in cheese until melted. Spoon into a baking dish, 12x8x2 inches.

Preheat oven to 375°.

Prepare muffin mix with egg and milk as label directs; spoon evenly over meat mixture.

Bake 20 minutes, or until topping is golden and a wooden pick inserted into center comes out clean. Just before serving, garnish with halved pitted ripe olives if you like.

Yield: 6 servings.

STUFFED BEEF PINWHEEL

    ¼ cup finely chopped celery
    2 tablespoons minced onion
    4 tablespoons butter or margarine
    3 cups fresh bread crumbs (6 slices)
    ½ cup regular wheat germ
    1¾ teaspoons salt
    ¼ teaspoon dried leaf sage, crumbled
        Pepper
    1½ lbs. lean ground beef
    1 egg
    ¾ cup milk
    1 teaspoon prepared hot spicy mustard

Sauté celery and onion in butter in a medium skillet; until soft; stir in 2 cups of the bread crumbs, ¼ cup of the wheat germ, ¼ teaspoon of the salt, sage, and ⅛ teaspoon pepper; toss lightly to mix.

Combine ground beef, remaining 1 cup bread crumbs, ¼ cup wheat germ, egg, milk, mustard, remaining 1½ teaspoons salt, and ¼ teaspoon pepper in a large bowl; mix lightly until well blended.

Pat meat mixture into a rectangle, 12x8, on a sheet of waxed paper.

Preheat oven to 350°.

Spread stuffing mixture over meat. Starting at an 8-inch side, roll up meat, jelly-roll fashion, using waxed paper as a guide. Place roll, seam side down, in a shallow baking pan.

Bake 50 minutes, or until loaf is crusty brown. Lift roll onto a large serving platter; cut crosswise into serving-sized slices.

Yield: 6 servings.

COUNTRY BEEF ROAST (p.80)
MOCK PEPPER STEAK (p.105)

ROAST BURGER ROLL

1 medium onion, chopped (½ cup)
½ cup chopped celery
¼ cup butter or margarine
¼ cup water
4 cups fresh bread crumbs (8 slices)
¼ cup chopped parsley
½ teaspoon dried basil, crushed
¼ teaspoon dried thyme, crushed
2 lbs. ground beef
1 teaspoon seasoned salt
¼ teaspoon seasoned pepper
3 slices bacon, cut in half

Sauté onion and celery in butter until soft in a small skillet. Stir in water; heat to boiling.

Combine bread crumbs, parsley, basil, and thyme in a medium bowl; drizzle onion mixture over top; toss until evenly moist.

Preheat oven to 375°.

Season ground beef with salt and pepper; pat into a rectangle, 16x10 inches, on a large sheet of foil. Spread stuffing mixture over rectangle to within ½ inch of edges. Starting at a short end, roll up, jelly-roll fashion, using foil as a guide; lay bacon slices diagonally on top. Wrap roll in same sheet of foil; seal edges and ends. Place package in a large shallow baking pan.

Bake 45 minutes. Carefully open foil and fold down around roll. Bake 10 to 15 minutes longer.

To serve, cut into thick slices; spoon juices from package on top.

Yield: 6 to 8 servings.

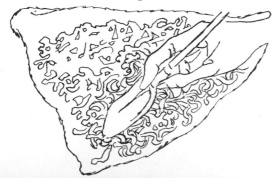

◄ **VEAL ROLL CORDON BLEU** (p.128)
ZUCCHINI AND TOMATOES POLONAISE (p.311)
MINIATURE BEEF LOAVES (p.105)

CHILI BEEF ROUND

12 square saltine crackers
1 can (8 ozs.) tomato sauce
1½ lbs. meat-loaf mixture (ground beef, veal, and pork)
1 medium onion, chopped (½ cup)
1 egg
3 tablespoons horseradish-mustard
1½ teaspoons salt
¼ teaspoon pepper
2 tablespoons light brown sugar
⅓ cup chili sauce

Preheat oven to 350°.

Combine crackers and tomato sauce in a large bowl; let stand until crackers are soft, then beat mixture with a spoon until blended.

Add meat-loaf mixture, onion, egg, 2 tablespoons of the mustard, salt, and pepper; mix lightly until well blended. Shape into a 6-inch round loaf in a greased large shallow baking pan.

Bake 45 minutes.

While loaf bakes, mix brown sugar, chili sauce, and remaining 1 tablespoon mustard until blended in a bowl; spread over loaf.

Bake 15 minutes longer, or until loaf is richly glazed. Lift onto a large serving platter with two pancake turners. Cut into wedges.

Yield: 6 servings.

LAREDO BEEF WHEEL

1 small onion, chopped (¼ cup)
¼ cup chopped red pepper
¼ cup chopped green pepper
2 tablespoons butter or margarine
¼ cup water
1½ cups packaged herb stuffing mix
1½ lbs. ground beef
¼ cup fine dry bread crumbs
5 tablespoons plain barbecue sauce
1 egg
½ teaspoon salt

Sauté onion, red pepper, and green pepper in butter until soft in a medium skillet. Stir in water; heat to boiling. Drizzle over stuffing mix in a medium bowl; toss lightly until evenly moist.

Combine ground beef, bread crumbs, 2 tablespoons of the barbecue sauce, egg, and salt in a large bowl; mix lightly until well blended.

Pat half of meat mixture into a greased 9-inch shallow round baking dish; spread stuffing mixture in an even layer on top; pat remaining meat mixture over stuffing.

Preheat oven to 350°.

Mark top of loaf into 6 wedges with a knife. Separate cuts slightly to make shallow ridges; spoon remaining 3 tablespoons barbecue sauce into ridges.

Bake 1 hour, or until loaf is firm and browned. Cut into 6 wedges, cutting between lines of barbecue sauce; place on a large round serving platter. Garnish center with parsley if you like.

Yield: 6 servings.

CHECKERBOARD CHEESEBURGERS

1 lb. ground beef
1 small onion, chopped (¼ cup)
1 teaspoon prepared hot spicy mustard
½ teaspoon salt
⅛ teaspoon pepper
4 slices process pimiento cheese
Pepper relish

Preheat oven to 400°.

Combine ground beef, onion, mustard, salt, and pepper in a medium bowl; mix lightly until well blended. Shape into 4 patties about ½ inch thick. Place in a shallow baking pan.

Bake 15 minutes.

Cut each slice of cheese into 6 strips; place 6 strips, crisscross fashion, over each patty.

Bake 2 to 3 minutes longer, or until cheese starts to melt. Serve with pepper relish.

Yield: 4 servings.

CARAWAY BEEF LOAF

½ cup milk
3 slices white bread
1½ lbs. ground beef
1 medium onion, chopped (½ cup)
1 egg
1 teaspoon salt
1 teaspoon caraway seeds
½ teaspoon ground nutmeg
½ teaspoon ground sage
¼ teaspoon pepper

Preheat oven to 350°.

Combine milk and bread in a large bowl; let stand a few minutes until liquid is absorbed, then beat with a spoon until blended.

Add ground beef, onion, egg, salt, caraway seeds, nutmeg, sage, and pepper; mix lightly until well blended. Shape into a loaf about 8x4 inches in a greased large shallow baking pan.

Bake 1 hour, or until loaf is firm. Lift onto a large serving platter with two pancake turners; garnish top with small white onion rings if you like.

Yield: 6 servings.

HUNGARIAN MEATBALL GOULASH

1½ lbs. meat-loaf mixture (ground beef, veal, and pork)
1 medium onion, chopped (½ cup)
1 clove garlic, crushed
1 egg
1 cup fresh bread crumbs (2 slices)
1 teaspoon salt
¼ teaspoon pepper
½ cup mixed vegetable juice
3 tablespoons salad oil
1 tablespoon all-purpose flour
1 envelope instant chicken broth
2 tablespoons paprika
1½ cups water
1 package (8 ozs.) fine noodles
1 cup (8-oz. carton) dairy sour cream
1 tablespoon chopped parsley

Combine meat-loaf mixture, onion, garlic, egg, bread crumbs, salt, pepper, and vegetable juice in a large bowl; mix lightly until well blended. Shape into 36 balls.

Brown meatballs, a few at a time, in salad oil in a large skillet; pour off any drippings.

Stir flour, chicken broth, paprika, and water into skillet; heat, stirring constantly, to boiling; place meatballs in sauce; cover. Simmer 30 minutes.

While meatballs cook, cook noodles as label directs; drain well. Spoon into a shallow serving dish or onto a deep platter; remove meatballs from sauce with a slotted spoon and arrange over noodles.

Slowly stir about 1 cup of the hot sauce into sour cream in a small bowl; stir back into remaining sauce in skillet; heat very slowly just until bubbly. Pour over meatballs; sprinkle parsley on top.

Yield: 6 servings.

HAMBURGER DRUMSTICKS

1 lb. ground beef
1 egg
1 teaspoon salt
Dash of pepper
¼ cup packaged cornflake crumbs
1 can (about 11 ozs.) pizza sauce

Preheat oven to 425°.

Combine ground beef, egg, salt, and pepper in a medium bowl; mix well; divide into 4 mounds. Shape each mound into a "drumstick" around the stick from an ice-cream pop. Roll in cornflake crumbs on waxed paper. Place in a greased shallow baking pan.

Bake 25 minutes, or until meat is crusty.

Heat pizza sauce to boiling in a small saucepan; serve as a dip with meat, or spoon over top.

Yield: 4 servings.

COWBOY BEEF

¾ lb. ground beef
½ teaspoon salt
Dash of pepper
1 tablespoon salad oil
1 small onion, chopped (¼ cup)
1 can (10¼ ozs.) beef gravy
¼ cup chili sauce
2 teaspoons prepared mustard
1 can (8 ozs.) cut green beans, drained
1 can (8 ozs.) small whole potatoes, drained and cubed

Season ground beef with salt and pepper; shape into 20 small meatballs. Brown in salad oil in a large skillet; push to one side.

Stir onion into drippings; sauté until soft.

Combine gravy, chili sauce, and mustard in a small bowl; stir into mixture in skillet; stir in green beans and potatoes. Heat slowly to boiling; cover. Simmer 10 minutes to blend flavors.

Ladle into soup bowls. Serve with baking powder biscuits or corn muffins if you like.

Yield: 4 servings.

GLAZED STEAKBURGER PLATTER

2 lbs. ground beef
2 teaspoons seasoned salt
¼ teaspoon seasoned pepper
½ cup chili sauce
2 tablespoons soy sauce
2 tablespoons light corn syrup
3 large tomatoes
2 tablespoons bottled thin French dressing
1 package (8 ozs.) frozen French fried onion rings

Preheat oven to 400°.

Combine ground beef, seasoned salt, and seasoned pepper in a large bowl; mix lightly. Shape into a large patty 1½ inches thick and place on rack in broiler pan.

Mix chili sauce, soy sauce, and corn syrup in a cup; spoon about three fourths over meat.

Bake 20 minutes.

While meat bakes, cut tomatoes in half; brush cut surfaces with salad dressing.

Place onions and tomatoes around meat in broiler pan; spoon remaining chili-sauce mixture over meat.

Bake 10 minutes longer, or until beef is as done as you like it and tomatoes and onions are hot.

Lift meat onto a large serving platter with two pancake turners; surround with tomatoes and onions.

Yield: 6 servings.

PEPPER PIZZA

1½ lbs. ground beef round
1 egg
1 medium onion, chopped (½ cup)
½ cup fresh bread crumbs (1 slice)
1 teaspoon salt
1 cup pizza sauce (from a 15½ oz. can)
1 teaspoon dried oregano, crushed
4 bacon-flavored brown-and-serve sausages, sliced in thin rounds
1 jar (2 ozs.) sliced pimientos, drained
1 small green pepper, quartered, seeded, and cut crosswise in thin strips
½ cup sliced small pimiento-stuffed green olives
4 long slices mozzarella cheese, cut in squares
3 tablespoons grated Romano cheese

Combine ground round, egg, onion, bread crumbs, and salt in a medium bowl; mix lightly until blended. Press evenly over bottom and up side of a 12-inch pizza pan.

Preheat oven to 400°.

Mix pizza sauce and oregano in a small bowl; spread over meat.

Arrange sausage rounds, pimientos, green-pepper strips, and olives in rings over sauce; arrange mozzarella squares on top; sprinkle Romano cheese over all.

Bake 30 minutes, or until cheese browns and beef is as done as you like it. (Meat crust will shrink slightly; before serving, spoon any drippings from pan.) Cut into wedges.

Yield: 8 servings.

CHEESEBURGER LOAF

2 lbs. ground beef
1 envelope onion soup mix (two to a package)
½ cup quick-cooking rolled oats
1 egg
½ cup milk
⅛ teaspoon pepper
3 long slices sharp Cheddar cheese
¼ cup chili sauce
½ teaspoon dry mustard

Preheat oven to 350°.

Combine ground beef, dry onion soup mix, rolled oats, egg, milk, and pepper in a large bowl; mix lightly until well blended. Pat half into a rectangle about ½ inch thick in a shallow baking pan.

Layer cheese slices over rectangle; pat remaining meat mixture over cheese, sealing in cheese and shaping into a neat loaf.

Mix chili sauce and mustard in a cup; spread over top of loaf.

Bake 1 hour, or until crusty and brown. Place loaf on a large serving platter; let stand 15 minutes. Cut crosswise into thick slices.

Yield: 8 servings.

TAMALE PIE

4 cups water
1 cup yellow cornmeal
2 teaspoons salt
1 lb. ground beef
1 large onion, chopped (1 cup)
¼ cup chopped green pepper
2 teaspoons chili powder
¼ teaspoon pepper
2 tablespoons all-purpose flour
1 can (16 ozs.) stewed tomatoes
1 can (12 ozs.) whole-kernel corn
½ cup shredded sharp Cheddar cheese
    Pitted ripe olives
    Parsley

Heat water to boiling in a medium saucepan; slowly stir in cornmeal and 1 teaspoon of the salt. Cook, stirring several times, 10 minutes, or until thick. Measure out 1 cup of the mixture and spread in an even layer in a loaf pan, 9x5x3 inches; chill until firm.

Spoon remaining cornmeal mixture into a 2-quart deep baking dish; let stand a few minutes until mixture starts to firm up, then spread over bottom and side of dish with back of spoon to line dish completely.

Brown ground beef in its own fat in a large skillet; push to one side. Add onion and green pepper to drippings in skillet; sauté until soft. Stir in remaining 1 teaspoon salt, chili powder, and pepper; cook 1 minute.

Sprinkle flour over meat mixture, then stir in with tomatoes and corn and liquid. Cook, stirring constantly, until mixture thickens slightly and boils 1 minute. Spoon into cornmeal-lined baking dish.

Preheat oven to 350°.

Loosen cornmeal layer from pan with a knife, then turn out onto a cutting board. Cut in half lengthwise; cut each half into 6 even triangles. Arrange around edge and in center of meat filling to make a pretty pattern. Sprinkle cheese over top.

Bake 45 minutes, or until bubbly in center. Just before serving, garnish with olives and parsley.

Yield: 6 servings.

MEATBALL GOULASH

½ pound ground beef
2 teaspoons instant minced onion
1 tablespoon salad oil
1 teaspoon chili powder
1 can (8 ozs.) tomato sauce
2½ cups water
1 package (7 ozs.) beef noodle dinner

Mix ground beef and onion in a small bowl; shape into tiny balls. Brown in salad oil in a large skillet; push to one side.

Add chili powder to skillet; cook 1 minute. Stir in tomato sauce, water, and sauce mix from noodle dinner; heat to boiling; stir in noodles. Simmer uncovered, stirring several times, 20 minutes. Spoon onto serving plates.

Yield: 4 generous servings.

CHEESEBURGER LOGS

1 can (8 ozs.) stewed tomatoes
¾ cup fresh bread crumbs (1½ slices)
1 lb. ground beef
1 egg
1 teaspoon horseradish-mustard
1 teaspoon salt
⅛ teaspoon pepper
¼ cup shredded process American cheese

Preheat oven to 350°.

Combine tomatoes and bread crumbs in a large bowl; let stand until liquid is absorbed. Lightly mix in ground beef, egg, mustard, salt, and pepper.

Divide mixture into quarters, then shape each into a 5-inch-long loaf; make a ridge down middle of each with finger. Place loaves on a rack in a shallow baking pan.

Bake 30 minutes. Spoon cheese into hollows. Bake 10 minutes longer, or until cheese melts and loaves are crusty brown.

Yield: 4 servings.

SPANISH PATTY-STEAKS

1 package (6 ozs.) Spanish rice mix
1 can (16 ozs.) tomatoes
   Butter or margarine
2 lbs. ground beef
1½ teaspoons salt
¼ teaspoon seasoned pepper
½ cup bottled plain barbecue sauce

Preheat oven to 350°.

Prepare Spanish rice mix with water, tomatoes, and butter as label directs. Combine with ground beef, salt, and pepper in a large bowl; mix lightly until well blended. Divide into 8 even mounds, then shape each into a patty about 1½ inches thick. Place in a single layer in a large shallow baking pan. Brush part of the barbecue sauce over each.

Bake 15 minutes; turn patties. Brush again with barbecue sauce. Bake 20 minutes longer, or until patties are richly glazed.

Yield: 8 servings.

CAMPER'S STEW

1½ lbs. ground beef
1 medium onion, chopped (½ cup)
¼ cup fine dry bread crumbs
1 teaspoon seasoned salt
¼ teaspoon seasoned pepper
2 tablespoons all-purpose flour
1 tablespoon salad oil
1 cup water
1 envelope instant beef broth
2 packages (10 ozs. each) frozen succotash
1 can (16 ozs.) stewed tomatoes
1 teaspoon dried Italian herbs

Combine ground beef, onion, bread crumbs, salt, and pepper in a large bowl; mix lightly. Shape into 24 small patties; dust each with flour.

Brown patties in salad oil in a Dutch oven; remove and set aside. Stir in water, beef broth, and frozen succotash; heat to boiling; cover. Simmer 5 minutes.

Stir in tomatoes, Italian herbs, and meat patties; cover. Simmer 20 minutes longer to blend flavors.

Ladle into soup bowls. Serve with thick slices of French bread if you like.

Yield: 6 servings.

BEEF GOULASH

1 medium onion, chopped (½ cup)
½ cup chopped celery
1 tablespoon salad oil
1½ cups cubed roast beef
1 can (15 ozs.) spaghetti with tomato sauce and cheese
1 can (8 ozs.) cut green beans, drained
½ teaspoon dried basil, crushed
¼ teaspoon salt

Sauté onion and celery in salad oil until soft in a medium skillet. Stir in beef; sauté 3 minutes.

Stir in remaining ingredients; cover. Simmer, stirring once or twice, 10 minutes to blend flavors.

Yield: 4 servings.

CREPES MARINARA

1 lb. ground beef
1 medium onion, chopped (½ cup)
½ cup chopped celery
1 can (8 ozs.) tomato sauce
1 teaspoon salt
½ teaspoon dried oregano, crushed
¼ teaspoon pepper
Basic Crêpes (recipe on page 412)
1 jar (15 ozs.) marinara sauce or meatless spaghetti sauce
1 cup shredded mozzarella cheese (4 ozs.)

Shape ground beef into a large patty. Brown in its own fat, turning once, in a large skillet; break up into small chunks and push to one side.

Stir onion and celery into drippings; sauté until soft. Stir in tomato sauce, salt, oregano, and pepper; heat to boiling. Simmer 5 minutes; keep hot.

Make Basic Crêpes.

Preheat oven to 350°.

As crêpes are baked, spread ¼ cup of the meat mixture over each; roll up tightly, jelly-roll fashion. Place, seam side down, in a greased baking dish, 13x9x2 inches.

Spoon marinara sauce over crêpes; sprinkle mozzarella cheese in a ribbon down center.

Bake 30 minutes, or until bubbly and cheese melts and browns lightly.

Yield: 6 servings.

BEEF PIE MORNAY

1 package piecrust mix
1 lb. meat-loaf mixture (ground beef, veal, and pork)
1 can (8 ozs.) mixed vegetables
Milk
1 envelope cheese sauce mix
1½ teaspoons prepared mustard

Preheat oven to 400°.

Prepare piecrust mix as label directs. Roll out half to an 11-inch round on a lightly floured cloth; fit into an 8-inch pie plate; trim overhang to ½ inch.

Shape meat-loaf mixture into a large patty in a medium skillet; brown, turning once, in its own fat, then break up into chunks; pour off all fat.

Drain liquid from vegetables into a 1-cup measure; add milk to make 1 cup.

Sprinkle cheese sauce mix over meat, then stir in with milk mixture and mustard. Cook slowly, stirring constantly, until mixture thickens and boils 1 minute; stir in vegetables. Spoon into prepared pastry shell.

Roll out remaining pastry to a 10-inch round; cut several slits in center to let steam escape; cover pie. Trim overhang to ½ inch; turn edge under with bottom crust, flush with rim of pie plate; flute to make a stand-up edge.

Bake 30 minutes, or until filling bubbles up and pastry is golden.

Yield: 4 servings.

SPANISH BEEF

¾ lb. ground beef
1 medium onion, chopped (½ cup)
½ small green pepper, seeded and chopped
1 teaspoon chili powder
1 teaspoon salt
¼ teaspoon pepper
1 can (16 ozs.) tomatoes
1 can (8 ozs.) whole-kernel corn
¾ cup packaged precooked rice

Shape ground beef into a large patty in a large skillet; brown, turning once, in its own fat, then break up into chunks and push to one side.

Stir onion, green pepper, and chili powder into drippings in skillet; sauté until onion is soft.

Stir in salt, pepper, tomatoes, and corn and liquid; heat to boiling; cover. Simmer 15 minutes.

Stir in rice; cover again. Turn off heat. Let stand 15 minutes. Fluff mixture with a fork; spoon onto serving plates.

Yield: 4 servings.

MINIATURE BEEF ROUNDS

1 cup fresh bread crumbs (2 slices)
½ cup milk
1 egg
1 small onion, chopped (¼ cup)
1 teaspoon salt
2 teaspoons Worcestershire sauce
1 lb. ground beef
2 tablespoons chili sauce

Preheat oven to 350°.

Combine bread crumbs and milk in a medium bowl; let stand until milk is absorbed.

Beat in egg, onion, salt, and Worcestershire sauce; lightly mix in beef. Divide mixture into quarters, then shape each into a round loaf; place in a greased shallow baking pan. Spread ½ tablespoon of the chili sauce over each.

Bake 45 minutes, or until loaves are crusty brown.

Yield: 4 servings.

GLAZED CORNED BEEF

4 lbs. mild-cure corned beef for oven roasting
¼ cup firmly packed brown sugar
⅓ cup catsup
2 tablespoons vinegar
2 tablespoons butter or margarine
1 teaspoon dry mustard
1 teaspoon prepared horseradish

Preheat oven to 325°.

Place corned beef on a rack in roasting pan; roast as label directs.

While roast cooks, combine brown sugar, catsup, vinegar, butter, mustard, and horseradish in a small saucepan. Heat slowly, stirring constantly, to boiling; brush half over corned beef.

Continue roasting, brushing once again with remaining sauce, 20 minutes, or until meat is tender and richly glazed.

Remove roast to a large serving platter. For easier slicing, let stand at least 20 minutes. Slice thin; serve plain or with mustard.

Yield: 6 servings.

DEVILED MEAT-LOAF PATTIES

1 lb. meat-loaf mixture (ground beef, veal, and pork)
1 can (2¼ ozs.) deviled ham
¼ cup regular wheat germ
2 tablespoons instant minced onion
1 egg
1 tablespoon parsley flakes
¾ teaspoon salt
⅛ teaspoon pepper
¼ cup milk

Preheat oven to 350°.

Combine meat-loaf mixture, deviled ham, wheat germ, onion, egg, parsley flakes, salt, pepper, and milk in a large bowl; mix lightly until well-blended.

Divide mixture into quarters, then shape each into a round about 1½ inches thick. Place in a greased shallow baking pan.

Bake 45 minutes, or until crusty.

Yield: 4 servings.

HEIDELBERG KRAUT BAKE

2 bags (16 ozs. each) sauerkraut (from dairy case)
¾ lb. cooked corned beef
1 bottle (8 ozs.) Thousand Island salad dressing
4 large oval slices dark rye bread
1 tablespoon butter or margarine
1 cup shredded Swiss cheese (4 ozs.)

Preheat oven to 375°.

Place sauerkraut in a strainer and rinse under running cold water to remove any excess salt; drain well again.

Cut corned beef into ½-inch cubes; place in a large bowl. Add sauerkraut and salad dressing; toss well to mix. Spoon into a 1½-quart shallow baking dish; cover.

Bake 45 minutes.

While sauerkraut mixture bakes, cut two 2-inch rounds from each slice of bread with a biscuit cutter; spread butter on each. Arrange around edge in baking dish; sprinkle cheese all over top.

Bake 15 minutes, or until cheese melts.

Yield: 4 servings.

MOCK PEPPER STEAK

3 cups thin strips cooked beef
2 tablespoons salad oil
8 green onions, trimmed and cut into 1-inch
    lengths
1 envelope instant beef broth
1½ cups water
3 tablespoons soy sauce
1 teaspoon garlic powder
2 medium-sized green peppers, quartered,
    seeded, and cut into ¾-inch squares
4 teaspoons cornstarch
2 medium tomatoes, each cut in 8 wedges
    Chinese noodles (from a 6-oz. package)

Brown beef in salad oil in a large skillet; remove from pan with a slotted spoon and set aside.

Stir onions into drippings; sauté 1 minute. Stir in beef broth, water, soy sauce, garlic powder, and green peppers; heat to boiling; cover. Simmer 3 minutes, or just until peppers are crisp-tender.

Mix cornstarch with a little water until smooth in a cup; stir into mixture in skillet. Cook, stirring constantly, until sauce thickens and boils 1 minute.

Stir in beef and tomatoes; cover. Heat just until hot. Serve with Chinese noodles.

Yield: 4 servings.

MINIATURE BEEF LOAVES

2 cups cornflakes
½ cup evaporated milk
1 egg
1 lb. ground beef
½ lb. sausage meat
½ cup chopped green onions
1½ teaspoons salt
¼ teaspoon pepper
1 jar (15 ozs.) meatless spaghetti sauce

Preheat oven to 350°.

Combine cornflakes, milk, and egg in a large bowl; let stand a few minutes until liquid is absorbed, then beat with a spoon until blended.

Add ground beef, sausage, green onions, salt, and pepper; mix lightly until well blended. Divide into 6 even portions; shape each into a loaf about 3½ inches long. Place in a greased large shallow baking pan.

Bake 50 minutes, or until firm and browned.

While loaves bake, heat spaghetti sauce to boiling in a medium saucepan.

Arrange loaves on a large serving platter; garnish with ruffled green onion tops if you like. Serve with spaghetti sauce.

Yield: 6 servings.

PORK

AUTUMN PORK ROAST

1 boned fresh pork shoulder, weighing about 5 lbs.
1 package (8 ozs.) herb-seasoned stuffing mix
1 can (12 ozs.) Mexican-style corn, drained
1 small onion, minced (¼ cup)
2 eggs, beaten
2 teaspoons salt
½ teaspoon pepper
 Water
4 tablespoons all-purpose flour

Trim any excess fat from pork.

Combine stuffing mix, corn, onion, eggs, salt, and pepper in a large bowl; mix until evenly moist. (Mixture will be crumbly.) Stuff into pocket in pork, packing in well; tie roast in several places to give meat a rounded shape. (If you have any stuffing left, place in a baking dish and bake, covered, in same oven with roast for 40 minutes.)

Preheat oven to 325°.

Brown roast, fat side down, in a kettle with ovenproof handles; pour in 1 cup water; heat to boiling; cover tightly.

Bake, turning roast once, 4 hours, or until tender; remove to a large serving platter; keep hot.

Strain liquid from kettle into a 2-cup measure; let stand a few minutes until fat rises to top, then skim off; return 4 tablespoons to kettle. Add water to liquid, if needed, to make 2 cups.

Blend flour into fat in kettle; cook, stirring constantly, until bubbly. Stir in the 2 cups liquid; continue cooking and stirring until gravy thickens and boils 1 minute. Season with salt and pepper, if needed.

Cut strings from roast; slice roast and serve with gravy.

Yield: 6 servings plus enough meat for a dividend dish.

HARVEST PORK

4 pork loin chops, cut 1 inch thick
1 teaspoon salt
⅛ teaspoon pepper
¼ cup firmly packed brown sugar
1 teaspoon grated orange rind
1 cup orange juice
1 tablespoon lemon juice
4 medium yams or sweet potatoes, pared and cut in ½-inch-thick slices
2 large seedless oranges, pared and sectioned
1 tablespoon cornstarch

Trim any excess fat from chops, rub salt and pepper into both sides of meat.

Sauté enough of the fat trimmings to make about 2 tablespoons drippings in a large skillet; discard trimmings.

Place pork in skillet and brown slowly, turning once; drain off any drippings.

Mix brown sugar, orange rind and juice, and lemon juice in a small bowl; pour over pork. Heat to boiling; cover. Simmer 45 minutes.

Place yam slices in sauce around pork; cover. Cook 15 minutes, or until chops and yams are tender.

Place orange sections in skillet; cover. Heat 2 to 3 minutes, or just until hot.

Lift pork, yams, and orange sections onto a large deep serving platter with a slotted spoon; keep hot.

Mix cornstarch with 1 tablespoon water until smooth in a cup; stir into liquid in skillet. Cook, stirring constantly, until sauce thickens and boils 1 minute. Spoon over pork and yams.

Yield: 4 servings.

DUXBURY PORK

5 lb. pork center-cut loin roast
1 teaspoon salt
¼ teaspoon pepper
½ teaspoon ground ginger
¾ cup currant jelly
½ cup frozen concentrate for cranberry-orange
    juice, thawed

Preheat oven to 325°.

Trim any excess fat from pork.

Mix salt, pepper, and ginger in a cup; rub into roast. Place on a rack in a shallow roasting pan. Insert meat thermometer into center of roast without touching bone.

Roast 2 hours, or until thermometer registers 160°.

Combine currant jelly and cranberry concentrate in a small saucepan; heat to boiling. Simmer 5 minutes; brush part over roast.

Continue roasting, brushing often with remaining sauce, ½ hour, or until thermometer registers 170°.

Remove roast to a large serving platter; carve into chops.

Yield: 6 to 8 servings.

CHINESE PORK ROAST

5 lb. pork center-cut loin roast
1 can (6 ozs.) frozen concentrate for
    orange-pineapple juice, thawed
½ cup catsup
¼ teaspoon ground nutmeg
¼ teaspoon ground cinnamon
⅛ teaspoon ground cloves
¼ teaspoon salt
¼ cup honey
1 tablespoon lemon juice
1 tablespoon prepared mustard

Trim any excess fat from pork. Thread roast on spit of rotisserie, following manufacturer's directions. Insert meat thermometer into center of roast without touching bone.

Roast 2 hours, or until thermometer registers 160°.

Combine all remaining ingredients in a small saucepan; heat to boiling; simmer 10 minutes. Brush part over pork.

Continue roasting, brushing often with more sauce, ½ hour, or until thermometer registers 170°.

Remove roast to a large serving platter; carve into chops.

Yield: 6 to 8 servings.

SCANDINAVIAN PORK

5 lb. pork center-cut loin roast
1 lime, quartered
6 large green onions
1½ teaspoons salt
1 teaspoon dried marjoram, crushed
¼ teaspoon seasoned pepper
3 tablespoons all-purpose flour

Preheat oven to 325°.

Trim any excess fat from pork. Rub lime wedges all over roast, then squeeze any remaining juice over top; place on a rack in a shallow roasting pan.

Trim onions; chop fine, including green tops. (There should be about 1 cup.) Mix onions with salt, marjoram, and pepper in a small bowl; pat about three fourths over roast. Insert meat thermometer into center of roast without touching bone.

Roast 2½ hours, or until thermometer registers 170°. Remove from pan to a large serving platter; sprinkle remaining onion mixture over top. Keep warm while making gravy.

Strain liquid from roasting pan into a 2-cup measure. Let stand a few minutes until fat rises to top, then skim off; return 3 tablespoons to pan. Add water to liquid to make 1½ cups.

Blend flour into fat in pan; cook, stirring constantly, until bubbly. Stir in the 1½ cups liquid; continue cooking and stirring until gravy thickens and boils 1 minute. Season with salt and pepper, if needed.

Carve roast into chops; serve with gravy.

Yield: 6 to 8 servings.

GLAZED STUFFED PORK

1 fresh pork shoulder, weighing 4 to 5 lbs., boned
1 teaspoon salt
½ teaspoon garlic powder
1 small onion, minced
1 large apple, pared, cored, and diced (1 cup)
2 tablespoons butter or margarine
1½ cups fresh bread crumbs (1½ slices)
⅓ cup dark raisins
1 tablespoon brown sugar
¼ cup peach preserves
1 teaspoon ground ginger
2 tablespoons water

Preheat oven to 325°.

Trim skin and excess fat from pork; sprinkle ½ teaspoon of the salt and garlic powder inside pocket.

Sauté onion and apple in butter until soft in a skillet; stir in bread crumbs, raisins, brown sugar, and remaining ½ teaspoon salt. Stuff into pocket in pork, packing in well; close opening with skewers, then tie meat with string.

Place pork, fat side up, on a rack in a shallow roasting pan. Insert meat thermometer into thickest part of pork, being careful not to touch stuffing or fat. Roast 2 hours.

Combine peach preserves, ginger, and water in a small saucepan; heat to boiling. Brush half over pork.

Roast, brushing again with remaining peach mixture, ½ hour, or until thermometer registers 170° and pork is richly glazed.

Remove to a large serving platter; take out skewers and cut away string. Carve pork into ¼-inch-thick slices. Garnish with watercress and apple slices if you like.

Yield: 6 servings.

BARBECUED PORK

1 fresh pork shoulder, weighing about 6 lbs.
1 cup bottled plain barbecue sauce
⅓ cup water
1 large onion, peeled, quartered, and sliced
1 teaspoon dried thyme, crushed

Preheat oven to 325°.

Trim skin and excess fat from pork.

Brown pork slowly in its own fat, turning once, in a kettle with ovenproof handles.

Mix barbecue sauce and water in a 2-cup measure; pour over pork. Stir in onion and thyme; cover tightly.

Bake 3 hours, or until pork is tender. Remove to a large serving platter.

Let sauce in kettle stand a few minutes until fat rises to top, then skim off; reheat sauce to boiling. Pour into a serving bowl.

Carve pork; spoon sauce over each serving.

Yield: 6 to 8 servings.

JAMAICAN HAM

1 rolled boned fresh ham, weighing about 5 lbs.
1 teaspoon salt
½ cup frozen concentrate for tangerine juice, thawed
¾ teaspoon ground ginger
¼ cup light corn syrup
2 tablespoons soy sauce

Preheat oven to 325°.

Rub ham with salt. Place on a rack in a shallow baking pan; insert meat thermometer into center of ham.

Roast 2 hours, or until thermometer registers 160°.

While ham cooks, combine tangerine concentrate, ginger, corn syrup, and soy sauce in a small saucepan; heat slowly to boiling; brush part over ham to coat generously.

Continue roasting, brushing several times with remaining tangerine mixture, 45 minutes, or until thermometer registers 170° and meat is richly browned and glazed.

Remove roast to a large serving platter; slice and serve with buttered peas and small whole carrots if you like.

Yield: 6 servings, plus enough meat for a dividend dish.

HAWAIIAN PORK ROAST

3 lb. pork center-cut loin roast
2 teaspoons ground cinnamon
2 teaspoons parsley-garlic salt
1 teaspoon curry powder
½ cup pineapple preserves
2 tablespoons lemon juice

Preheat oven to 325°.

Trim any excess fat from pork.

Mix cinnamon, garlic salt, and curry powder in a cup; rub into all sides of roast. Place roast on a rack in a shallow baking pan; insert meat thermometer into center of roast without touching bone.

Roast 1½ hours, or until thermometer registers 160°.

Combine preserves and lemon juice in a cup; brush half over roast.

Continue roasting, brushing again with remaining pineapple mixture, 30 minutes, or until thermometer registers 170° and meat is richly glazed.

Place roast on a large serving platter; surround with halved pineapple slices and watercress if you like. To serve, carve roast into chops.

Yield: 4 servings.

DANISH PORK DINNER

1 fresh pork shoulder, weighing about 5 lbs.
1 medium onion, chopped (½ cup)
1 cup apple juice
2 tablespoons brown sugar
1 teaspoon pumpkin-pie spice
1 teaspoon salt
4 medium-sized sweet potatoes or yams, pared and
    cut in half
1 cup dried pitted prunes
2 tablespoons cornstarch

Trim skin and excess fat from pork.

Brown pork on all sides in its own fat in a Dutch oven; remove and set aside.

Stir onion into drippings; sauté until soft. Stir in apple juice, brown sugar, pumpkin-pie spice, and salt; heat to boiling. Place pork in Dutch oven; cover. Simmer 1½ hours, or until pork is almost tender.

Place potatoes in Dutch oven; cover. Cook 20 minutes; add prunes to Dutch oven; cover again. Cook 1 to 2 minutes longer, or until potatoes and pork are tender.

Place pork on a large serving platter; spoon potatoes and prunes around pork; keep warm.

Strain liquid from Dutch oven into a 4-cup measure, pressing onion through sieve; let stand a few minutes until fat rises to top, then skim off. Measure 2 cups of the liquid and return to Dutch oven; heat to boiling.

Mix cornstarch with a little water until smooth in a cup; stir into boiling liquid. Cook, stirring constantly, until sauce thickens and boils 1 minute; pour into a serving bowl.

Carve part of the pork; pass sauce to spoon over meat and potatoes.

Yield: 4 servings plus enough meat for a dividend dish.

PORK CHOPS CACCIATORE

6 pork loin chops, cut 1 inch thick
1 large onion, chopped (1 cup)
1 can (35 ozs.) Italian tomatoes
1 envelope spaghetti sauce mix
¼ cup light molasses
1 teaspoon dried oregano, crushed
½ teaspoon salt

Preheat oven to 350°.

Trim any excess fat from chops. Brown chops in their own fat in a large skillet; place in a single layer in a baking dish, 13x9x2 incheses.

Stir onion into drippings; sauté until soft. Stir in tomatoes, spaghetti sauce mix, molasses, oregano, and salt; heat to boiling. Pour over chops; cover tightly.

Bake 1 hour and 15 minutes, or until chops are tender.

Serve over cooked spaghetti if you like.

Yield: 6 servings.

PORK CHOP PLATTER INDIENNE

6 pork rib or loin chops, cut 1 inch thick
1 medium onion, chopped (½ cup)
1 tablespoon all-purpose flour
2 teaspoons sugar
1½ teaspoons curry powder
⅛ teaspoon ground cardamom
¾ teaspoon salt
1 envelope instant beef broth
1 jar (4¾ ozs.) baby-pack strained peaches
2 tablespoons chili sauce
¾ cup water
3 cups hot cooked rice

Trim any excess fat from chops.

Brown chops in a large skillet; place in a single layer in a shallow baking pan. Pour off all drippings, then measure 1 tablespoon and return to skillet.

Preheat oven to 375°.

Stir onion into drippings and sauté until soft; stir in flour, sugar, curry powder, cardamom, salt, beef broth, peaches, chili sauce, and water. Heat, stirring constantly, to boiling; simmer 2 minutes, or until thick. Spoon half over chops.

Bake 20 minutes. Spoon remaining curry mixture over chops. Bake 20 minutes longer, or until chops are tender.

Spoon rice in the center of a large serving platter; stand chops around edge. Garnish rice with parsley. Serve with bottled cranberry-orange relish if you like.

Yield: 6 servings.

CHILI CHOP CASSEROLE

1 medium onion, chopped (½ cup)
½ cup chopped green pepper
1 clove garlic, minced
1 tablespoon butter or margarine
1½ teaspoons chili powder
1¼ teaspoons salt
   Dash of pepper
3 cups mixed vegetable juice
1 cup uncooked regular rice
4 pork loin chops, cut ¾ inch thick

Preheat oven to 350°.

Sauté onion, green pepper, and garlic in butter in a large skillet until soft; stir in 1¼ teaspoons of the chili powder, 1 teaspoon of the salt, and pepper; cook 1 minute.

Stir in vegetable juice; heat to boiling; stir in rice. Simmer 1 minute; pour into a greased 2-quart baking dish; cover. Bake 15 minutes.

While rice bakes, trim excess fat from pork chops; rub both sides with remaining ¼ teaspoon salt and ¼ teaspoon chili powder. Brown slowly in their own fat in a large skillet; place in a single layer over rice mixture in baking dish; cover again.

Bake 45 minutes longer, or until chops and rice are tender and liquid is absorbed. Garnish with sliced pitted ripe olives if you like.

Yield: 4 servings.

MIDWESTERN PORK BAKE

4 pork shoulder chops, cut ¾ inch thick
4 large carrots, pared and sliced
¾ teaspoon dried thyme, crushed
1 teaspoon salt
⅛ teaspoon pepper
1 can (16 ozs.) whole-kernel corn
4 green onions, trimmed and sliced

Trim any excess fat from chops.

Sauté a few of the trimmings in a large skillet until 2 tablespoons fat cook out; discard trimmings. Brown chops, turning once, in drippings; remove from heat.

Preheat oven to 350°.

Place carrots in a layer in a shallow baking dish; arrange chops, overlapping if needed, in a row on top.

Mix thyme, salt, and pepper in a cup; sprinkle half over chops and carrots.

Spoon corn and liquid along sides in dish; sprinkle remaining seasoning mix over top, then sprinkle green onions over all; cover.

Bake 1 hour, or until chops are tender. Serve from baking dish.

Yield: 4 servings.

PORK CHOPS WITH ORANGE STUFFING

8 pork rib chops, cut ½ inch thick
1¼ teaspoons salt
½ teaspoon dried thyme, crushed
⅛ teaspoon pepper
½ cup sliced celery
1 small onion, chopped (¼ cup)
2 tablespoons butter or margarine
½ cup water
2 teaspoons grated orange rind
6 cups cubed unfrosted raisin bread (12 to 14 slices)
2 medium-sized seedless oranges, pared and sectioned

Trim any excess fat from chops. Place trimmings in a large skillet; heat slowly until fat cooks out and drippings measure about 2 tablespoons; discard trimmings.

Mix ¼ teaspoon of the salt, thyme, and pepper in a cup; rub into both sides of chops. Brown in drippings in skillet; place in a single layer in a 2-quart shallow baking dish.

Preheat oven to 350°.

Sauté celery and onion in butter until soft in a large skillet. Stir in water, remaining 1 teaspoon salt, and orange rind. Pour over bread cubes and orange sections in a large bowl; toss lightly to mix. Spoon over chops in baking dish; cover.

Bake 50 minutes; uncover. Bake 10 minutes longer, or until chops are tender.

Yield: 4 servings.

ORANGE-GLAZED RIBS

4 lbs. country-style pork ribs
Salt
Pepper
½ cup frozen concentrate for orange juice, thawed
¼ cup honey
1 tablespoon light brown sugar

Preheat oven to 350°.

Trim any excess fat from ribs; cut ribs into serving-sized pieces. Lightly sprinkle salt and pepper over both sides. Place in a single layer in a shallow baking pan.

Bake 1¼ hours; remove from oven. Pour all drippings from pan.

While ribs cook, combine orange concentrate, honey, and brown sugar in a small saucepan; heat slowly, stirring constantly, to boiling; simmer 2 minutes. Brush part over ribs.

Continue baking, brushing twice more with remaining orange mixture, 30 minutes, or until ribs are richly glazed.

Yield: 4 to 6 servings.

APPLE-STUFFED PORK CHOPS

6 pork loin chops, cut 1 inch thick with pockets for stuffing
1½ teaspoons salt
1 large tart apple, pared, quartered, cored, and chopped (1 cup)
1 small onion, chopped (¼ cup)
1 tablespoon butter or margarine
½ cup plain wheat germ
½ cup fresh bread cubes (1 small slice)
Water
1 lemon, cut into 6 slices

Trim any excess fat from chops; sprinkle salt over both sides.

Sauté apple and onion in butter in a medium saucepan until soft; stir in wheat germ, bread cubes, and 1 tablespoon water. Stuff into pockets in chops; fasten each in several places with wooden picks.

Melt enough of the fat trimmings in a large skillet to make 2 tablespoons drippings; remove trimmings and discard. Place chops in drippings and brown slowly; top each with a slice of lemon. Pour ¼ cup water into skillet; cover.

Cook 45 minutes, or until chops are tender. Lift onto a large serving platter, leaving lemon slices in place.

Yield: 6 servings.

APRICOT-STUFFED PORK ROAST

1 fully-cooked pork picnic shoulder, weighing 5 to 6 lbs., boned
1 large onion, chopped (1 cup)
½ cup chopped celery
4 tablespoons butter or margarine
1 cup water
1 cup chopped dried apricots
8 cups small fresh bread cubes
1 teaspoon grated orange rind
1 cup apricot preserves
½ teaspoon dry mustard
½ cup thawed frozen concentrate for pineapple juice

Trim skin and excess fat from pork.
Preheat oven to 325°.

Sauté onion and celery in butter until soft in a small skillet; stir in water and apricots; heat to boiling. Pour over bread cubes and orange rind in a large bowl; toss lightly until evenly moist.

Stuff part into pocket in pork, packing in well to fill and give meat a rounded shape; close opening with skewers and tie roast in several places with string. Place on a rack in a roasting pan. (Spoon remaining stuffing into a small baking dish; cover; bake along with roast for 45 minutes.)

Roast meat 1½ hours.

Combine apricot preserves, mustard, and pineapple concentrate in a small saucepan; heat to boiling. Brush half over pork.

Continue roasting, brushing 2 or 3 more times with preserves mixture, 1 hour, or until pork is richly glazed.

Remove roast to a large serving platter; take out skewers and cut away string. Garnish platter with small inner celery leaves if you like. Carve roast and serve with extra stuffing.

Yield: 6 to 8 servings.

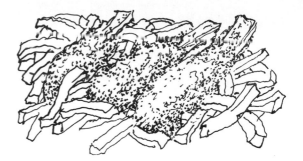

DEVILED PORK BONES

3½ lbs. country-style pork ribs
¼ cup all-purpose flour
1 teaspoon garlic powder
½ teaspoon salt
⅛ teaspoon crushed red pepper
1 egg
2 tablespoons water
½ cup fine dry bread crumbs
⅓ cup butter or margarine, melted
2 tablespoons prepared mustard
2 tablespoons lemon juice

Preheat oven to 350°.

Trim any excess fat from ribs; cut ribs into serving-sized pieces. Place in a single layer on rack in broiler pan.

Bake, turning several times, 1½ hours, or until meat is tender. Remove from oven; pour drippings from broiler pan.

Mix flour, garlic powder, salt, and red pepper in a pie plate. Beat egg with water in a second pie plate; sprinkle bread crumbs on waxed paper.

Dip meat into seasoned flour, then into egg mixture and crumbs to coat well. Return to rack in broiler pan.

Mix melted butter, mustard, and lemon juice in a cup; drizzle half over meat.

Bake 15 minutes; turn. Drizzle remaining mustard mixture over top. Bake 15 minutes longer, or until meat is crispy and brown. Serve with frozen prepared French fried potatoes if you like.

Yield: 4 servings.

PORK TERIYAKI

1 piece lean boneless pork shoulder, weighing 1½
    lbs. and cut into 1½-inch cubes
1 tablespoon salad oil
2 cups diagonally sliced celery
1 large onion, chopped (1 cup)
1 can (13¾ ozs.) chicken broth
1 can (20 ozs.) pineapple chunks in juice
2 tablespoons cornstarch
1 tablespoon brown sugar
2 teaspoons ground ginger
3 tablespoons soy sauce
1 can (16 ozs.) Chinese vegetables, drained
1 can (3 ozs.) chow mein noodles

Brown pork in salad oil in a large skillet 20 minutes; remove from skillet.

Stir celery and onion into drippings; sauté until soft. Stir in chicken broth; heat to boiling. Add pork; cover. Simmer 40 minutes, or until pork is tender.

Drain juice from pineapple into a 1-cup measure; add water, if needed, to make 1 cup; stir into skillet.

Mix cornstarch, brown sugar, and ginger in a cup; slowly stir into liquid in skillet. Cook, stirring constantly, until mixture thickens and boils 1 minute. Stir in soy sauce, pineapple chunks, and vegetables.

Spoon noodles around edge in a serving dish; spoon pork mixture into center. Garnish with green pepper strips and cherry tomatoes if you like.

Yield: 6 servings.

CANTONESE PORK

1 piece lean boneless pork shoulder, weighing
    1½ lbs.
2 tablespoons salad oil
2 envelopes instant chicken broth
1½ cups water
2 medium-sized green peppers
1½ cups diagonally sliced celery
1 can (20 ozs.) pineapple chunks in juice
3 tablespoons cornstarch
2 tablespoons brown sugar
½ teaspoon salt
⅓ cup white vinegar
3 tablespoons catsup
4 cups hot cooked rice

Trim any fat from pork; cut pork into thin strips. Brown in salad oil in a large skillet; pour off any excess fat.

Stir chicken broth and water into skillet; heat to boiling; cover. Simmer 20 minutes, or until pork is almost tender.

Cut green peppers in half; seed and cut into 1-inch squares. Stir into pork mixture with celery; cook, stirring once or twice, 5 minutes, or until pork is tender and vegetables are crisp-tender.

Drain juice from pineapple into a cup. Mix cornstarch, brown sugar, and salt in a small bowl; stir in pineapple juice and vinegar until mixture is smooth; stir into skillet. Cook, stirring constantly, until mixture thickens and boils 1 minute.

Stir in catsup and pineapple chunks; heat to boiling again.

Spoon onto a deep serving platter; spoon rice around edge.

Yield: 6 servings.

O'BRIEN PORK HASH

¾ lb. ground pork
2 tablespoons salad oil
1 medium onion, chopped (½ cup)
¼ cup diced green pepper
¼ cup diced red pepper
3 cups loose-pack frozen hashed brown potatoes
¾ teaspoon salt

Shape pork into a large flat patty. Brown, turning once, in salad oil in a large skillet; break up into chunks; push to one side.

Stir onion, green pepper, and red pepper into skillet; sauté until soft.

Stir in potatoes and salt; cook slowly, stirring once or twice, 3 minutes; cover. Continue cooking over low heat 5 minutes, or until potatoes are tender and crusty-brown on bottom. Spoon onto serving plates.

Yield: 4 servings.

POLYNESIAN SPARERIBS

6 lbs. pork spareribs
1 medium onion, peeled and sliced
  Salt
1½ cups sugar
⅓ cup cornstarch
½ teaspoon ground ginger
1½ cups water
⅔ cup cider vinegar
½ cup soy sauce

Place spareribs and onion in a kettle; add boiling water to cover. Salt lightly; cover kettle. Simmer 45 minutes, or until meat is almost tender but still clings to bones; drain.

While ribs simmer, mix sugar, cornstarch, and ginger in a small saucepan; stir in water, vinegar, and soy sauce. Cook, stirring constantly, until sauce thickens and boils 1 minute.

Preheat broiler.

Place ribs on rack in broiler pan; brush part of the sauce over top.

Broil, 0 inches from heat, turning often and brushing with more sauce, 15 minutes, or until richly glazed. Cut between ribs into serving-sized pieces.

Yield: 6 to 8 servings.

DEVILED PORK SKEWERS

1 piece lean boneless pork shoulder,
   weighing 2 lbs. and cut 1½ inches thick
1 teaspoon salt
1 cup water
12 small white onions
3 large carrots
3 tablespoons prepared hot mustard
⅓ cup salad oil
2 teaspoons dillweed
½ teaspoon sugar
  Dash of pepper

Trim any fat from pork; cut pork into 1½-inch cubes. Combine with ½ teaspoon of the salt and water in a medium saucepan; heat to boiling; cover. Simmer 1 hour, or until pork is almost tender; drain well and set aside.

Peel onions. Pare carrots; cut each into 4 chunks. Cook onions and carrots together, covered, in boiling salted water in a large saucepan 10 minutes, or until crisp-tender; drain.

Beat mustard with salad oil, dillweed, sugar, remaining ½ teaspoon salt, and pepper in a small saucepan; heat slowly just until hot.

Preheat broiler.

Thread pork cubes, alternately with onions and carrots, onto 6 long skewers. Place on rack in broiler pan; brush part of the mustard sauce over each.

Broil, 8 inches from heat, turning and brushing once with remaining sauce, 8 minutes, or until richly glazed.

Yield: 6 servings.

VENEZUELAN PORK

1 fresh pork butt, weighing about 5 lbs.
1 large onion, chopped (1 cup)
1 can (4 ozs.) pimientos, drained and chopped
1 clove garlic, crushed
¼ cup chopped parsley
½ teaspoon salt

Ask your meatman to bone and butterfly pork butt, trimming off any excess fat. Meat will resemble a rectangular steak about 1½ inches thick that can be broiled.

Preheat broiler to 425°.

Place meat, fat side down, on a cutting board; score top lengthwise and crosswise every inch, cutting about ½ inch deep. Place meat, scored side up, on rack in broiler pan.

Broil, 6 inches from heat, 1 hour; turn. Broil 25 minutes.

While meat cooks, combine onion, pimientos, garlic, parsley, and salt in a small bowl; spread over meat.

Broil 20 minutes longer, or until meat is thoroughly cooked and tender.

Place on a large serving platter. Slice into individual servings.

Yield: 4 servings plus enough meat for a dividend dish.

ORIENTAL PORK DINNER

1 lb. lean boneless fresh pork steak or cutlets, cut
  ½ inch thick
¼ teaspoon seasoned pepper
4 tablespoons salad oil
1 large green pepper, quartered, seeded, and cut
  in strips
1 large red pepper, quartered, seeded, and cut in
  strips
2 cups diagonally sliced celery
4 small onions, peeled, sliced, and separated into
  rings
1 package (6 ozs.) frozen pea pods with water
  chestnuts
2 tablespoons cornstarch
1 envelope instant chicken broth
2 teaspoons sugar
¾ teaspoon ground ginger
1½ cups water
3 tablespoons soy sauce
¼ cup diced roasted almonds
3 cups hot cooked rice

Trim any fat from pork. Sprinkle pepper over both sides; cut meat into very thin strips across grain.

Heat 2 tablespoons of the salad oil in a large skillet; add pork and brown slowly 20 minutes. Remove from skillet; keep hot.

Add remaining 2 tablespoons salad oil to drippings. Place green and red peppers, celery, onion rings, and frozen pea pods in separate piles in skillet; sauté 5 minutes until crisp-tender; return meat.

While vegetables cook, mix cornstarch, chicken broth, sugar, and ginger in a medium saucepan; stir in water. Cook, stirring constantly, until mixture thickens and boils 1 minute; stir in soy sauce. Pour over meat and vegetables in skillet; cover. Heat slowly just to boiling.

Stir almonds into rice; spoon onto a large serving platter; spoon pork mixture on top. Serve with additional soy sauce to drizzle over all.

Yield: 4 servings.

NORWEGIAN PORK BALLS

1¼ lbs. ground pork
 ¾ lb. ground beef
1 large apple, pared, quartered, cored, and
  chopped fine (1 cup)
1 large onion, chopped fine (1 cup)
2 cups fresh bread crumbs (4 slices)
2 eggs
¼ cup chopped parsley
3 teaspoons salt
½ teaspoon ground nutmeg
2 cups water
4 tablespoons butter or margarine
6 tablespoons all-purpose flour
1 teaspoon dillweed
2 cups milk

Preheat oven to 400°.

Combine ground pork, beef, apple, onion, bread crumbs, eggs, parsley, 2 teaspoons of the salt, and nutmeg in a large bowl; mix lightly until well blended. Shape into 48 balls, using a tablespoonful for each. Place in a single layer in a greased jelly-roll pan.

Bake 35 minutes, or until browned; remove from oven; lower temperature to 350°. Spoon meatballs into a 2-quart baking dish.

Pour water into baking pan; heat to boiling.

Melt butter in a medium saucepan; stir in flour, remaining 1 teaspoon salt, and dillweed; cook, stirring constantly, until bubbly. Stir in milk and liquid from baking pan; continue cooking and stirring until sauce thickens and boils 1 minute. Pour around meatballs in baking dish.

Bake 45 minutes, or until bubbly in center. Garnish with fresh dill and serve with hot steamed rice if you like.

Yield: 8 servings.

PORK RAGOUT

1 piece lean boneless pork shoulder, weighing 2
    lbs. and cut 1½ inches thick
1 can (5½ ozs.) apple juice
2 tablespoons light brown sugar
1 teaspoon ground ginger
1 teaspoon salt
¼ teaspoon pepper
12 small white onions, peeled
2 cans (24 ozs. each) yams in syrup
1 jar (12½ ozs.) spiced apple rings, drained

Preheat oven to 350°.

Trim any fat from pork; cut pork into 1½-
inch cubes.

Melt enough of the fat trimmings in a large
skillet to make about 2 tablespoonfuls drippings; remove trimmings. Add pork cubes and
brown slowly; spoon into a 2½-quart baking
dish.

Combine apple juice, brown sugar, ginger,
salt, and pepper in a cup; pour over pork;
cover.

Bake 1 hour. Place onions around pork in
dish; cover again. Bake 45 minutes, or until
pork is almost tender.

Drain syrup from yams into a small bowl;
arrange yams over pork in center of dish.
Overlap apple rings around edge; drizzle ¼
cup of the yam syrup over top; cover.

Bake 15 minutes, or until yams and apples
are hot. Serve from baking dish.

Yield: 6 servings.

PORK SCRAMBLE

1 lb. ground pork
1 small onion, chopped (¼ cup)
2 teaspoons chili powder
1 can (10¾ ozs.) condensed tomato soup
1½ cups water
1 cup uncooked elbow macaroni
1 package (10 ozs.) frozen peas
½ teaspoon salt
1 cup shredded process American cheese (4 ozs.)

Shape pork into a large patty; brown in its
own fat, turning once, in a medium skillet 20
minutes. Break meat into chunks; push to one
side.

Stir onion and chili powder into drippings;
sauté until onion is soft. Stir in soup and water;
heat to boiling. Stir in macaroni, frozen peas,
and salt; heat to boiling again; cover.

Simmer 15 minutes, or until macaroni is
tender. Sprinkle cheese over mixture; cover
again; heat just until cheese melts. Serve from
skillet.

Yield: 4 to 6 servings.

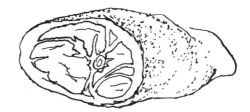

MANDARIN HAM ROAST

1 ready-to-eat ham steak, weighing about 3 lbs.
    and cut 3 inches thick
½ cup red currant jelly
2 tablespoons dry red wine
1 tablespoon prepared mustard
⅛ teaspoon ground cloves
1 can (11 ozs.) mandarin orange segments, drained

Preheat oven to 325°.

Score fat edge of ham; place on a rack in a
shallow baking pan.

Bake 45 minutes.

While ham bakes, melt jelly in a small
saucepan; stir in wine, mustard, and cloves;
heat to boiling. Brush part over ham.

Continue baking, brushing again with jelly
mixture, 20 minutes.

Arrange mandarin orange segments over
ham; brush with remaining jelly mixture.
Bake 10 minutes longer, or until fruit is hot
and glazed.

Lift ham, without moving fruit, onto a
heated serving platter. Circle platter with
watercress or parsley if you like. Carve ham
into ½-inch-thick slices.

Yield: 8 servings.

GLAZED HAM AND BANANAS

½ cup orange marmalade
2 tablespoons butter or margarine
1 tablespoon lemon juice
4 individual ham steaks, weighing about 4 ozs.
   each
2 large green-tipped bananas

Preheat oven to 350°.

Combine marmalade, butter, and lemon juice in a large skillet with ovenproof handle; heat slowly, stirring constantly, until marmalade melts and sauce is blended.

Place ham steaks in skillet; turn to coat well with sauce.

Bake 20 minutes. Peel bananas; cut in half lengthwise; place around steaks in skillet. Spoon sauce over bananas to cover.

Bake 15 minutes longer, or until bananas and steaks are bubbly and glazed. Serve from skillet.

Yield: 4 servings..

SUNBURST HAM

1 fully-cooked bone-in ham, weighing about 10
   lbs.
¾ cup peach preserves
⅓ cup lemon juice
1 teaspoon ground cloves
1 can (16 ozs.) cling peach slices, drained
4 to 6 maraschino cherries, drained

Preheat oven to 325°.

Trim skin, if any, and excess fat from ham; leave remaining fat layer plain or score in 1-inch squares or diamonds. Insert meat thermometer into thickest part of meat without touching bone. Place ham, fat side up, on a rack in a shallow roasting pan; do not add water or cover pan.

Bake 2 hours and 15 minutes.

Mix preserves, lemon juice, and cloves in a medium bowl; brush part over ham. Continue baking, brushing with more preserves mixture, 45 minutes, or until top is richly glazed and thermometer registers 140°.

Remove ham to a large serving platter. Arrange peach slices in sunburst designs over glaze, holding in place with short wooden picks, if needed; place a cherry in center of each. Garnish platter with buttered broccoli spears and lemon wedges if you like.

Yield: 8 servings plus enough meat for two or three dividend dishes.

GLAZED STUFFED HAM STEAKS

1 small onion, chopped (¼ cup)
1 medium apple, pared, quartered, cored, and
   diced (1 cup)
3 tablespoons butter or margarine
2 cups fresh bread crumbs (4 slices)
½ cup dark raisins
1 tablespoon light corn syrup
½ teaspoon salt
2 fully-cooked ham steaks, weighing about
   1½ lbs. and cut ½ inch thick
2 tablespoons orange marmalade
¼ teaspoon ground ginger

Preheat oven to 400°.

Sauté onion and apple in butter until soft in a medium skillet; stir in bread crumbs, raisins, corn syrup, and salt until mixture is evenly moist.

Place one ham steak in a shallow baking pan; spread stuffing over top. Cover with remaining ham steak; cover pan.

Bake 30 minutes; uncover.

While ham bakes, mix orange marmalade and ginger in a cup; spread over ham.

Bake, uncovered, 15 minutes longer, or until steaks are lightly glazed.

Lift steaks onto a large serving platter with two pancake turners. Garnish platter with parsley if you like. Slice steaks crosswise into serving-sized pieces.

Yield: 6 servings.

HAM ROUND AND APRICOTS

1½ lbs. ready-to-eat ham, and cut into chunks
1 medium onion, peeled and quartered
1½ cups fresh bread crumbs (3 slices)
1 egg
½ cup milk
½ teaspoon dried marjoram, crushed
⅛ teaspoon pepper
  Whole cloves
⅓ cup apple jelly
1 teaspoon prepared hot spicy mustard
1 can (16 ozs.) apricot halves in syrup
2 tablespoons brown sugar
¼ teaspoon ground ginger
1 tablespoon butter or margarine

Preheat oven to 350°.

Put ham and onion through a food grinder, using a medium blade. (Mixture should measure about 6 cups.) Place in a large bowl; add bread crumbs, egg, milk, marjoram, and pepper; mix lightly until well blended. Shape into a 7-inch round loaf about 2 inches thick; place in a greased shallow baking pan. Score top into squares or diamonds; stud with whole cloves.

Bake 30 minutes.

Combine jelly and mustard in a small saucepan; heat slowly, stirring constantly, until jelly melts; brush part over loaf.

Continue baking, brushing remaining jelly mixture over loaf once or twice, 30 minutes, or until richly glazed.

While loaf bakes, drain syrup from apricots into a cup; place fruit, rounded side up, in a pie plate; drizzle 2 tablespoons of the syrup over fruit.

Mix brown sugar and ginger in a cup; sprinkle over apricots; dot butter over top.

Bake in same oven with ham loaf, spooning syrup from bottom of pie plate over fruit once or twice, 20 minutes, or until glazed.

Place ham loaf on a serving platter; arrange apricots around edge. For serving, cut loaf into wedges.

Yield: 6 servings.

CREAMED HAM ON PANCAKES

1 ready-to-eat thin ham steak, weighing about ¾ lb.
1 can (10¾ ozs.) condensed cream of mushroom soup
½ cup milk
  Few drops red-pepper seasoning
2 hard-cooked eggs, sliced
1 package (10½ ozs.) frozen pancakes

Cut ham into small cubes. Combine with mushroom soup, milk, and red-pepper seasoning in a medium saucepan. Heat slowly, stirring several times, to boiling; stir in eggs. Keep hot.

Heat pancakes as label directs; stack each two on a serving plate; spoon ham mixture on top.

Yield: 4 servings.

GLAZED HAM LOGS

3 cups ground cooked ham
1 medium onion, finely chopped (½ cup)
1 egg
1½ cups fresh bread crumbs (3 slices)
2 tablespoons minced parsley
½ teaspoon salt
⅛ teaspoon pepper
½ cup apple cider
⅓ cup currant jelly
1 teaspoon lemon juice
¼ teaspoon ground nutmeg

Preheat oven to 350°.

Combine ham, onion, egg, bread crumbs, parsley, salt, pepper, and cider in a large bowl; mix lightly until well blended. Shape into 6 loaves about 4 inches long; score top of each; place in a greased shallow baking pan.

Bake 30 minutes.

While loaves bake, mix currant jelly, lemon juice, and nutmeg in a cup; spread over loaves.

Bake 10 minutes longer, or until loaves are glazed.

Yield: 6 servings.

PINWHEEL HAM PIE

¼ cup butter or margarine
¼ cup all-purpose flour
½ teaspoon salt
1 cup milk
1 package (10 ozs.) frozen peas
1½ cups cubed baked ham
1 package refrigerated crescent rolls
4 tablespoons pimiento cheese spread

Melt butter in a medium saucepan; stir in flour and salt; cook, stirring constantly, until bubbly. Stir in milk; continue cooking and stirring until sauce thickens and boils 1 minute. Stir in frozen peas and ham; heat to boiling. Spoon into a shallow 1½-quart baking dish.

Preheat oven to 400°. Place baking dish in oven to keep hot while oven heats.

Unroll crescent dough and separate into 4 rectangles, pinching triangles together at perforations; spread 1 tablespoon of the cheese over each. Roll up rectangles; slice each roll into 5 even rounds; arrange over hot ham mixture in baking dish.

Bake 35 minutes, or until topping is golden.
Yield: 4 servings.

BROCCOLI-HAM ROLLS

2 packages (10 ozs. each) frozen broccoli spears
4 tablespoons butter or margarine
⅓ cup all-purpose flour
2 cups milk
1 can (3 or 4 ozs.) chopped mushrooms
2 tablespoons dry sherry
8 thin slices cooked ham
¼ cup fresh bread crumbs
2 tablespoons grated Parmesan cheese

Cook broccoli as label directs; drain; keep hot.

Melt butter in a medium saucepan; stir in flour. Cook, stirring constantly, until bubbly. Stir in milk and mushrooms and liquid; continue cooking and stirring until mixture thickens and boils 1 minute; stir in sherry.

Preheat oven to 350°.

Roll each ham slice around 2 spears of broccoli; fasten with a wooden pick. Place rolls in a row in a baking dish, 12x8x2 inches. Pour sauce in a ribbon over center of rolls.

Mix bread crumbs and cheese in a cup; sprinkle over sauce.

Bake 30 minutes, or until bubbly and topping is toasted.
Yield: 4 servings.

POTATO-HAM SCALLOP

2 cans (16 ozs. each) whole white potatoes
3 tablespoons butter or margarine
¾ cup fresh bread crumbs (1½ slices)
3 tablespoons all-purpose flour
½ teaspoon salt
Few drops red-pepper seasoning
2 cups milk
1 cup shredded Swiss cheese (4 ozs.)
½ cup sliced green onions
¾ teaspoon dillweed
1 cup minced cooked ham

Drain liquid from potatoes; slice potatoes. (There should be about 4 cups.)

Melt butter in a medium saucepan; measure out 1 tablespoon and toss with bread crumbs in a small bowl.

Stir flour, salt, and red-pepper seasoning into remaining butter in saucepan; cook, stirring constantly, until bubbly. Stir in milk; continue cooking and stirring until sauce thickens and boils 1 minute; remove from heat.

Mix cheese, green onions, and dillweed in a small bowl.

Preheat oven to 350°.

Layer half of the potatoes into a 1½-quart baking dish; top with half each of the ham, cheese mixture, and sauce; repeat layers, lifting mixture at side of dish with a fork so sauce runs to bottom. Sprinkle buttered crumbs on top.

Bake 35 minutes, or until bubbly and topping is toasted.
Yield: 4 generous servings.

COBBLESTONE HAM PIE

½ cup diced celery
1 small onion, chopped (¼ cup)
1 tablespoon salad oil
1 can (10¾ ozs.) condensed cream of chicken
    soup
⅓ cup milk
1½ cups diced cooked ham
4 servings prepared instant mashed potatoes
¼ cup shredded sharp Cheddar cheese

Preheat oven to 350°.

Sauté celery and onion in salad oil in a medium saucepan until soft; stir in soup, milk, and ham. Heat slowly, stirring several times, to boiling; spoon into a 1½-quart shallow baking dish.

Drop mashed potatoes by small spoonfuls on top of ham mixture; sprinkle cheese over potatoes.

Bake 20 minutes, or until bubbly and cheese melts.

Yield: 4 servings.

GLAZED HAM RING

1½ lbs. lean boneless ham
1 large onion, peeled
½ lb. ground pork
2 eggs
1 cup fresh bread crumbs (2 slices)
1 tablespoon prepared hot spicy mustard
1 small can evaporated milk (⅔ cup)
½ cup apricot preserves
1 tablespoon lemon juice
⅛ teaspoon ground cloves

Preheat oven to 350°.

Cut ham and onion into chunks; put through a food grinder, using a coarse blade; place in a large bowl.

Add pork, eggs, bread crumbs, mustard, and evaporated milk to ham; mix lightly until well blended. Pack into a greased 1¾-quart ring mold.

Bake 1 hour; remove from oven but leave heat on.

While meat bakes, combine apricot pre-serves, lemon juice, and cloves in a small saucepan; heat very slowly, stirring several times, to boiling.

Loosen ham loaf around edge and center with a knife; invert into a shallow baking pan; brush part of the apricot mixture over top.

Continue baking, brushing remaining apricot mixture over loaf once or twice, 30 minutes, or until richly glazed.

Lift loaf very carefully onto a large serving platter with two pancake turners. Garnish with watercress if you like. Cut loaf into wedges; serve plain or with mustard sauce if you like.

Yield: 8 servings.

PORK-AND-APPLE PIE

4 medium yams or sweet potatoes
¼ cup butter or margarine
⅓ cup evaporated milk
1 teaspoon salt
3 cups cubed cooked pork
1 can (20 ozs.) pie-sliced apples
⅓ cup firmly packed light brown sugar
½ teaspoon mace
1 jar (4¾ ozs.) baby-pack applesauce
⅓ cup broken California walnuts

Pare potatoes; quarter. Cook, covered, in boiling salted water in a large saucepan 20 minutes, or until tender; drain well. Mash with a fork; beat in butter until melted, evaporated milk, and salt.

Preheat oven to 350°.

Place half of the pork in a 2-quart shallow baking dish; top with half of the apples; sprinkle half of the brown sugar and mace over top, then add remaining pork. Spread applesauce over pork.

Spoon potatoes in a ring around edge in dish; pile remaining apples in center; sprinkle the rest of the brown sugar and mace over apples. Sprinkle walnuts over potatoes.

Bake 40 minutes, or until bubbly in center.

Yield: 4 to 6 servings.

HAM PATTYCAKES

2 cups ground cooked ham
½ cup frozen hashed brown potatoes, thawed and chopped fine
1 small onion, minced (¼ cup)
1 egg, beaten
2 tablespoons cornmeal
4 tablespoons salad oil
1 can (8 ozs.) peas and carrots
1 can (10¾ ozs.) condensed cream of celery soup

Mix ham, potatoes, onion, and egg in a medium bowl; shape into 8 small patties. Dip each in cornmeal on waxed paper.

Brown patties slowly, turning once, in salad oil in a large skillet.

While patties brown, drain liquid from peas and carrots into a cup. Combine vegetables, 2 tablespoons of the vegetable liquid, and soup in a medium saucepan; heat, stirring several times, to boiling.

Place patties on serving plates; spoon vegetable mixture over top.

Yield: 4 servings.

HAM BALLS TROPICALE

2 lbs. ground ready-to-eat ham
1 lb. ground pork
1 cup regular wheat germ
1 medium onion, minced (½ cup)
¾ cup milk
3 eggs
3 tablespoons salad oil
1 can (20 ozs.) pineapple chunks in syrup
2 cans (11 ozs. each) mandarin orange segments
1 cup firmly packed brown sugar
6 tablespoons cornstarch
½ cup cider vinegar
¼ cup soy sauce
1½ cups halved, seeded green grapes

Combine ham, pork, wheat germ, onion, milk, and eggs in a large bowl; mix lightly until blended. Shape into balls, using 1 level tablespoon for each.

Brown meatballs, a few at a time, in salad oil in a kettle; remove to another pan; pour drippings from kettle.

Drain syrups from pineapple chunks and mandarin orange segments into a 4-cup measure; add water to make 3 cups.

Mix brown sugar and cornstarch in kettle; stir in the 3 cups fruit liquid, vinegar, and soy sauce. Cook, stirring constantly, until sauce thickens and boils 1 minute. Place meatballs in sauce; cover. Simmer 30 minutes.

Place pineapple, mandarin orange segments, and grapes on top of meatballs; heat 10 minutes longer, or until fruit is hot.

Spoon meatballs and sauce into a large serving bowl. Garnish with parsley and serve with hot cooked rice or pilaf if you like.

Yield: 12 servings.

SOUTHERN PORK HASH

1 small onion, chopped (¼ cup)
4 tablespoons butter or margarine
2 cups coarsely chopped cooked pork
1 can (16 ozs.) yams or sweet potatoes, drained and mashed
⅓ cup evaporated milk
½ teaspoon ground cinnamon
¼ teaspoon salt
1 can (8 ozs.) crushed pineapple in juice, drained
2 tablespoons brown sugar

Sauté onion in butter in a medium skillet until soft; stir in pork; brown lightly. Stir in yams, evaporated milk, cinnamon, and salt; cook slowly, uncovered, 10 minutes.

Spread pineapple over pork mixture; sprinkle brown sugar over pineapple; cover. Heat slowly 3 to 5 minutes, or until sugar melts.

Lift onto serving plates with a pancake turner to keep pineapple on top.

Yield: 4 servings.

PORK-AND-STUFFING LOAF

2 cups corn-bread stuffing mix
1 cup finely diced roast pork
1 small onion, chopped (¼ cup)
¼ cup chopped celery
7 tablespoons butter or margarine
⅓ cup water
¼ teaspoon dried thyme, crushed
1 egg, beaten
2 tablespoons all-purpose flour
¼ teaspoon salt
1 cup milk

Preheat oven to 350°.

Combine stuffing mix and pork in a medium bowl.

Sauté onion and celery in 5 tablespoons of the butter until soft in a large skillet. Stir in water and thyme; heat to boiling. Drizzle over stuffing mixture; toss lightly. Pour egg over top; toss to mix. Spoon into a greased baking pan, 8x4x2 inches.

Bake 30 minutes, or until loaf is crusty.

While loaf bakes, melt remaining 2 tablespoons butter in a small saucepan; stir in flour and salt; cook, stirring constantly, until bubbly. Stir in milk; continue cooking and stirring until sauce thickens and boils 1 minute.

Remove loaf from pan; slice crosswise. Serve with sauce.

Yield: 4 servings.

SPANISH PORK

3 cups thin strips cooked pork
2 tablespoons salad oil
1 medium onion, chopped (½ cup)
1 clove garlic, minced
1 teaspoon dried basil, crushed
1 teaspoon salt
⅛ teaspoon pepper
1 can (16 ozs.) stewed tomatoes
1 package (10 ozs.) frozen baby lima beans, cooked and drained
2 tablespoons all-purpose flour

Brown pork in salad oil in a large skillet; push to one side.

Stir onion and garlic into drippings; sauté until soft. Stir in basil, salt, pepper, and tomatoes; heat to boiling; cover. Simmer 20 minutes; stir in lima beans.

Mix flour with a little water in a cup until smooth; stir into pork mixture. Cook, stirring constantly, until mixture thickens and boils 1 minute. Serve from skillet as is or with cooked macaroni if you like.

Yield: 4 servings.

VEAL

PARISIAN VEAL ROAST

1 boneless veal shoulder roast, weighing about 5 lbs.
1 teaspoon salt
½ teaspoon pepper
2 tablespoons salad oil
1 medium onion, chopped (½ cup)
1 tube (2 ozs.) anchovy paste
2 tablespoons vinegar
2 teaspoons sugar
1 bay leaf
1 can (10½ ozs.) condensed beef broth
3 tablespoons all-purpose flour
¼ cup water
½ cup light cream

Rub veal with salt and pepper. Brown on all sides in salad oil in a Dutch oven; remove veal from Dutch oven.

Stir onion into drippings; sauté until soft. Stir in anchovy paste, vinegar, sugar, bay leaf, and beef broth; return veal to Dutch oven. Heat to boiling; cover.

Simmer, turning veal several times, 2¼ hours, or until tender. Remove to a large serving platter; keep warm.

Pour liquid from Dutch oven into a 4-cup measure; let stand a few minutes until fat rises to top, then skim off; remove bay leaf. Measure 2 cups of the liquid and return to Dutch oven; heat to boiling.

Mix flour and water in a cup until smooth; stir into boiling liquid. Cook, stirring constantly, until gravy thickens and boils 1 minute; stir in cream; continue heating just until hot. Pour into a serving bowl.

Cut strings from roast; slice part of the roast and serve with gravy and mashed potatoes if you like.

Yield: 4 servings plus enough meat for a dividend dish.

DAPPLED VEAL FRICASSEE

1½ lbs. boneless veal shoulder, and cut in 1½-inch cubes
2 tablespoons salad oil
1 medium onion, chopped (½ cup)
1 can (3 or 4 ozs.) chopped mushrooms
1 can (10¾ ozs.) condensed cream of mushroom soup
¼ cup dry white wine
1½ cups water
1 teaspoon dried thyme, crushed
2 cups biscuit mix
⅔ cup milk
3 tablespoons chopped parsley
1 cup (8-oz. carton) dairy sour cream
¼ cup whipping cream

Brown veal in salad oil in a Dutch oven; remove veal from Dutch oven and set aside.

Stir onion into drippings; sauté until soft.

Drain liquid from mushrooms into a cup; stir into onion mixture with soup, wine, water, and thyme. Heat to boiling; return veal to Dutch oven; cover.

Simmer 40 minutes, or until veal is almost tender; stir in mushrooms.

While veal cooks, combine biscuit mix, milk, and parsley in a medium bowl; mix with a fork until evenly moist.

Stir about 1 cup of the hot sauce from veal into sour cream in a small bowl; stir back into remaining mixture in Dutch oven; stir in cream; heat to boiling.

Drop dumpling dough in 12 even mounds on top. Cook slowly, uncovered, 10 minutes; cover. Cook 10 minutes longer, or until dumplings are puffed and dry. Serve from Dutch oven.

Yield: 6 servings.

GOLDEN VEAL RAGOUT

1 large onion, chopped (1 cup)
9 medium carrots, pared and quartered
12 small potatoes, pared
2 lbs. boneless veal shoulder, cut into
    1½-inch cubes
1 can (10¾ ozs.) condensed golden mushroom
    soup
¼ cup dry white wine
½ teaspoon dried oregano, crushed
2 tablespoons all-purpose flour

Place onion, carrots, potatoes, and veal in layers in a slow cooker.

Mix soup, wine, and oregano in a small bowl; pour over mixture in cooker, covering veal completely; cover. Cook on high 1 hour, then turn temperature setting to low and cook for 8 hours.

Remove veal and vegetables from liquid in cooker to a large deep serving platter; keep warm. Return temperature setting to high.

Blend flour with a little water in a cup until smooth; stir into liquid in cooker. Cook, stirring constantly, until gravy thickens. Serve separately to spoon over veal and vegetables.

Yield: 6 servings.

VEAL PARISIENNE

2 lbs. boneless veal shoulder, cut into
    1½-inch cubes
1 bay leaf
    Few sprigs of parsley
1½ teaspoons salt
½ cup chicken broth
½ cup dry white wine
    Water
12 small white onions, peeled
4 carrots, pared and sliced in 1-inch chunks
1 celery stalk, trimmed and chopped
1 clove garlic, minced
6 tablespoons butter or margarine
½ cup sifted all-purpose flour
¼ teaspoon ground thyme
1 can (3 or 4 ozs.) sliced mushrooms
2 tablespoons lemon juice
2 egg yolks
1 cup light cream

Place veal, bay leaf, parsley, salt, chicken broth, and wine in a kettle; pour in water to cover. Heat to boiling; cover. Simmer 1 hour.

Add onions and carrots to kettle; simmer ½ hour longer, or until veal and vegetables are tender. Pour liquid into a 4-cup measure; remove parsley and bay leaf from veal.

Sauté celery and garlic until soft in butter in a skillet. Sprinkle flour and thyme over top, then stir in with 3½ cups of the liquid from veal. Cook, stirring constantly, until mixture thickens and boils 1 minute. Stir in mushrooms and liquid and lemon juice; pour over veal and vegetables; heat slowly *just* to boiling.

Beat egg yolks and cream in a small bowl; slowly stir in 1 cup of the hot sauce, then stir back into mixture in kettle. Heat very slowly, stirring constantly, until hot. Serve with cooked white rice if you like.

Yield: 6 servings.

VEAL AND NOODLES

1 lb. ground veal
½ teaspoon seasoned salt
⅛ teaspoon pepper
¼ cup butter or margarine
1 package noodles with sour cream-cheese sauce
    mix
⅓ cup milk
2 teaspoons chopped parsley

Season veal with salt and pepper; shape into 16 small balls. Brown slowly in 2 tablespoons of the butter in a medium skillet until no pink remains.

While meat browns, cook noodles from package as label directs; drain; return to pan. Stir in remaining 2 tablespoons butter, then blend in milk and sour cream sauce mix; stir in parsley.

Spoon noodle mixture into nests on serving plates; spoon meatballs into centers.

Yield: 4 servings.

VEAL CORDON BLEU

6 even slices veal for scallopini, weighing about 2 lbs.
 Salt
 Pepper
3 long slices boiled ham
2 long slices Swiss cheese
1 tablespoon milk
1 package seasoned coating mix for chicken
2 tablespoons melted butter or margarine
2 tablespoons water
¼ cup dry red wine

Preheat oven to 350°.

Spread veal flat on counter; sprinkle each slice lightly on both sides with salt and pepper.

Cut ham slices in half crosswise; cut cheese in thirds crosswise. Place a piece of cheese, then a piece of ham on each slice of veal; roll up, jelly-roll fashion; fasten with wooden picks.

Brush rolls with milk; shake in coating mix. Place rolls, not touching, in a greased shallow baking pan. Drizzle butter over top.

Bake 40 minutes, or until rolls are golden brown and veal is tender. Arrange on a serving platter.

Stir water into drippings in pan; stir in wine; heat to boiling. Spoon over veal rolls.

Yield: 6 servings.

VEAL AND EGGPLANT COLOMBO

1½ lbs. veal for scallopini
 4 tablespoons all-purpose flour
1½ teaspoons salt
 ¼ teaspoon pepper
 6 tablespoons butter or margarine
 1 eggplant, weighing about 1 lb.
 1 tablespoon lemon juice
 1 large onion, chopped (1 cup)
 1 large green pepper, chopped (1 cup)
 1 clove garlic, minced
 ½ lb. mushrooms, trimmed and sliced
 1 can (8 ozs.) tomato sauce
 ½ teaspoon dried basil, crushed
 ¼ cup water

Cut veal into serving-sized pieces.

Mix flour, salt, and pepper in a pie plate; dip veal into flour mixture to coat both sides. Brown pieces, a few at a time, in 4 tablespoons of the butter in a large skillet.

While veal browns, pare eggplant; cut into ½-inch slices. Place in a single layer in a baking dish, 13x9x2 inches. Drizzle lemon juice over top. Arrange veal over eggplant.

Preheat oven to 350°.

Add remaining 2 tablespoons butter to drippings in skillet; stir in onion, green pepper, and garlic; sauté until vegetables are soft. Add mushrooms; sauté 2 minutes. Stir in tomato sauce, basil, and water; heat to boiling. Spoon over veal and eggplant; cover.

Bake 45 minutes, or until veal is tender; uncover. Bake 15 minutes longer to thicken sauce slightly.

Yield: 6 servings.

CAN-CAN STEW

½ lb. ground veal
 2 tablespoons salad oil
 2 tablespoons instant minced onion
½ teaspoon chili powder
 1 can (11¼ ozs.) condensed chili beef soup
 1 can (14¾ ozs.) macaroni and cheese
 1 can (8 ozs.) lima beans
¾ cup water
¼ teaspoon salt
½ cup coarsely broken corn chips

Shape veal into a large patty. Brown in salad oil in a large saucepan, turning once. Break up into chunks; push to one side.

Stir onion and chili powder into drippings; sauté 1 minute. Stir in soup, macaroni and cheese, lima beans and liquid, water, and salt. Heat slowly, stirring several times, to boiling; cover. Simmer 10 minutes to blend flavors.

Ladle into soup bowls. Sprinkle corn chips over each serving.

Yield: 4 servings.

BUDGET VEAL PARMIGIANA

1 egg
1 tablespoon water
½ cup packaged dry bread crumbs
6 veal cube steaks, weighing 1½ lbs.
2 tablespoons salad oil
1 can (16 ozs.) marinara sauce
1 small onion, chopped (¼ cup)
1 teaspoon garlic salt
½ teaspoon dried Italian herbs
⅛ teaspoon pepper
2 long slices Muenster cheese, cut crosswise into
    12 strips
¼ cup grated Romano cheese

Beat egg with water in a pie plate; sprinkle bread crumbs on waxed paper.

Dip veal into egg mixture, then into bread crumbs to coat well. Brown steaks in salad oil in a large skillet, turning once; place in a shallow baking dish. Pour drippings from skillet.

Preheat oven to 350°.

Combine marinara sauce, onion, garlic salt, Italian herbs, and pepper in same skillet; heat slowly to boiling; pour over veal. Arrange cheese strips, chevron fashion, on top; sprinkle Romano cheese over all.

Bake 30 minutes, or until bubbly.
Yield: 6 servings.

ITALIAN VEAL PLATTER

6 veal cube steaks, weighing 1½ lbs.
1½ teaspoons lemon-pepper
1½ teaspoons salt
6 tablespoons butter or margarine
2 large green peppers, quartered, seeded, and
    sliced
2 large red peppers, quartered, seeded, and
    sliced
2 large yellow squashes, trimmed and sliced
    crosswise
½ teaspoon dried Italian herbs
2 tablespoons water

Sprinkle steaks on both sides with lemon-pepper and 1 teaspoon of the salt; brown slowly in 2 tablespoons of the butter in a large skillet. Keep warm.

Melt remaining 4 tablespoons butter in a second skillet. Add green peppers, red peppers, and squashes, keeping each in a separate pile. Sprinkle remaining ½ teaspoon salt and Italian herbs over vegetables. Add water to skillet; cover. Steam 10 minutes, or until vegetables are crisp-tender.

Overlap steaks down center of a large serving platter; spoon squashes and peppers on each side of meat. Drizzle any remaining buttery liquid from skillet over top.
Yield: 6 servings.

VEAL PAPRIKA PIE

1 nine-inch frozen pastry shell
¾ lb. ground veal
¼ teaspoon salt
¼ teaspoon pepper
1 tablespoon salad oil
1 teaspoon paprika
1 can (10½ ozs.) mushroom gravy
1 can (16 ozs.) mixed vegetables, drained
½ cup dairy sour cream

Let pastry shell stand at room temperature at least 10 minutes to thaw.

Preheat oven to 400°.

Season veal with salt and pepper in a medium bowl; shape into 20 small balls. Brown in salad oil in a medium skillet; remove from pan; pour off drippings.

Sprinkle paprika into pan; heat 1 minute. Stir in gravy, vegetables, and sour cream; return meatballs. Heat, stirring constantly, to boiling; spoon into an 8-inch round shallow baking dish.

Carefully remove pastry shell from foil pie plate; cut several slits near center to let steam escape. Place over filling in baking dish; re-flute edge.

Bake 20 minutes, or until filling bubbles up and pastry is golden.
Yield: 4 servings.

VEAL IN SOUR CREAM

3 cups small noodle bows
1 tablespoon butter or margarine
1 teaspoon parsley flakes
4 veal cube steaks, weighing 1 lb.
1 teaspoon salad oil
1 teaspoon paprika
1 can (10½ ozs.) mushroom gravy
½ cup dairy sour cream
¼ teaspoon salt

Cook noodles in boiling salted water as label directs; drain; return to kettle. Add butter and parsley flakes; toss lightly to mix.

Cut veal steaks into bite-sized pieces. Sauté in salad oil in a large skillet until brown and no pink remains; remove from pan and set aside. Pour all drippings from pan.

Sprinkle paprika into pan; heat 1 minute; stir in gravy, sour cream, and salt. Heat very slowly, stirring constantly, until blended, then stir in veal. Heat again just until hot. (Do not boil.)

Spoon noodles onto serving plates; spoon veal mixture on top.

Yield: 4 servings.

VEAL ROLL ROMANO

1 cup coarse cheese-cracker crumbs
1 cup (8-oz. carton) cream-style cottage cheese
1 egg
1½ lbs. ground veal
1 medium onion, chopped (½ cup)
¼ cup finely chopped green pepper
1 teaspoon salt
¼ teaspoon pepper
½ teaspoon dried oregano, crushed
2 long slices mozzarella cheese

Preheat oven to 350°.

Combine cracker crumbs, cottage cheese, and egg in a large bowl; let stand a few minutes until crackers soften, then beat with a spoon until blended.

Add veal, onion, green pepper, salt, pepper, and oregano; mix lightly until well blended. Shape into a log about 10 inches long in a greased large shallow baking pan.

Bake 55 minutes, or until firm.

While loaf bakes, cut mozzarella cheese into 8 triangles; overlap on top of loaf.

Bake 5 minutes, or until cheese melts.

Lift loaf onto a large serving platter with two pancake turners. Garnish with several thin green-pepper rings if you like. Cut loaf crosswise into thick slices.

Yield: 6 servings.

MINIATURE VEAL ROLLS

1 lb. ground veal
2 medium carrots, pared and shredded
1 small onion, chopped (¼ cup)
½ cup fresh bread crumbs (1 slice)
1 egg
1 teaspoon salt
¼ teaspoon dried thyme, crushed
½ cup dairy sour cream
  Hamburger relish

Preheat oven to 350°.

Combine all ingredients except hamburger relish in a large bowl; mix lightly until well-blended.

Divide mixture into quarters, then shape each into a log about 5 inches long; place in a greased baking pan. Score tops of loaves with a knife.

Bake 45 minutes, or until loaves are crusty brown. Serve with hamburger relish.

Yield: 4 servings.

COUNTRY VEAL

3 cups cubed cooked veal
3 tablespoons butter or margarine
1 medium onion, chopped (½ cup)
1 can (10¾ ozs.) condensed cream of mushroom soup
½ cup dry white wine
¾ teaspoon dried oregano, crushed
1 cup (8-oz. carton) dairy sour cream
3 cups hot cooked rice
2 tablespoons chopped parsley

Brown veal in butter in a large skillet; push to one side.

Stir onion into drippings; sauté until soft. Stir in soup, wine, and oregano; heat to boiling; cover. Simmer 15 minutes.

Slowly stir about 1 cup of the hot sauce from skillet into sour cream in a small bowl; stir back into mixture in skillet. Heat slowly, stirring several times, until hot.

Spoon rice onto a large deep serving platter or onto individual plates; spoon veal mixture on top; sprinkle parsley over veal.

Yield: 4 servings.

VEAL ROLL CORDON BLEU

1 lb. ground veal
½ lb. ground beef
1 medium onion, chopped (½ cup)
¾ cup fine dry bread crumbs
⅓ cup dry sherry
3 tablespoons chopped parsley
1 egg
1 teaspoon salt
¼ teaspoon pepper
1 can (6¾ ozs.) chunked and ground ham, drained
1¼ cups shredded Swiss cheese
   Zucchini and Tomatoes Polonaise (recipe on page 311)

Combine ground veal and beef, onion, bread crumbs, sherry, 2 tablespoons of the parsley, egg, salt, and pepper in a large bowl; mix lightly until well blended.

Flake ham with a fork in a medium bowl; stir in 1 cup of the cheese and remaining 1 tablespoon parsley.

Preheat oven to 350°.

Pat veal mixture into a rectangle, 14x9 inches, on a large sheet of waxed paper; sprinkle ham mixture over rectangle to within ½ inch of edges. Using paper as a guide, roll up meat, jelly-roll fashion. Place, seam side down, in a greased large shallow baking pan.

Bake 50 minutes, or until loaf is firm. Sprinkle remaining ¼ cup cheese over top. Bake 5 minutes longer, or just until cheese melts.

Lift roll onto a large serving platter with two pancake turners. Serve with Zucchini and Tomatoes Polonaise.

Yield: 8 servings.

VEAL IN MUSHROOM SAUCE

1½ cups cubed cooked veal
2 tablespoons salad oil
1 medium onion, chopped (½ cup)
¼ teaspoon garlic powder
¼ teaspoon dried basil, crushed
¼ teaspoon salt
1 can (10½ ozs.) chicken gravy
1 can (3 or 4 ozs.) chopped mushrooms
2 cups uncooked regular noodles
2 tablespoons chopped parsley

Brown veal lightly in salad oil in a medium skillet; push to one side.

Stir onion into skillet; sauté until soft. Stir in garlic powder, basil, salt, gravy, and mushrooms and liquid. Heat slowly to boiling; cover. Simmer 10 minutes.

While veal simmers, cook noodles as label directs; drain; spoon onto serving plates. Spoon veal and sauce over noodles; sprinkle parsley on top.

Yield: 4 servings.

SHRIMP EN BROCHETTE (p.234)
BOLOGNA RUFFLES (p.153)
CURRIED LAMB KABOBS (p.131)
DUXBURY PORK (p.107)

DUCHESS VEAL LOAF

1½ lbs. ground veal
½ lb. ground pork
1 medium onion, chopped (½ cup)
1 egg
1 cup quick-cooking rolled oats
1 small can evaporated milk (⅔ cup)
   Salt
1 teasoon dried Italian herbs
¼ teaspoon pepper
   Instant mashed potatoes
   Water
   Milk
2 egg yolks
2 teaspoons finely cut chives

Preheat oven to 350°.

Combine ground veal, pork, onion, egg, rolled oats, evaporated milk, 2 teaspoons salt, Italian herbs, and pepper in a large bowl; mix lightly. Shape into a 9-inch-long loaf in a greased shallow baking pan.

Bake 1 hour, or until loaf is crusty brown.

While loaf bakes, prepare 3 cups instant mashed potatoes with water, milk, and salt as label directs (omit butter); beat in egg yolks and chives.

Remove loaf from oven; turn oven temperature control to broil. Spread mashed potatoes over loaf to cover completely.

Broil, 6 inches from heat, 3 to 5 minutes, or until potatoes are tipped with gold. Lift loaf onto a large serving platter. Garnish with cherry tomatoes lightly sautéed in butter if you like. Cut loaf crosswise into thick slices.

Yield: 8 servings.

SAVORY VEAL AND NOODLE MOLDS

1 package noodles with sour cream-cheese sauce
   mix
2 tablespoons butter or margarine
1 cup milk
1 egg
1½ cups diced cooked veal
1 can (10½ ozs.) chicken gravy
⅛ teaspoon dried rosemary, crushed

Preheat oven to 325°.

Prepare noodles with butter and ⅓ cup of the milk as label directs; spoon into 4 greased 6-ounce custard cups. Beat egg with remaining ⅔ cup milk in a small bowl. Pour evenly over noodle mixture; lift noodles with a fork so custard runs to bottom of cups. Set cups in a shallow pan of hot water.

Bake 35 minutes, or until set.

While noodles bake, combine remaining ingredients in a medium saucepan; heat to boiling.

Remove noodle molds from cups and place on serving plates; spoon veal mixture on top.

Yield: 4 servings.

◀ **HARVEST PORK** (p.106)

LAMB

BARBECUED LAMB

1 rolled boned lamb shoulder, weighing about 5
   lbs.
2 tablespoons salad oil
1 envelope onion soup mix
2 tablespoons brown sugar
2 teaspoons paprika
1 teaspoon dry mustard
¼ teaspoon chili powder
1½ cups tomato juice
½ cup catsup
¼ cup vinegar
2 tablespoons all-purpose flour
1 can (20 ozs.) cannelli beans, drained

Brown lamb on all sides in salad oil in a
Dutch oven.

Stir in soup mix, brown sugar, paprika, mustard, chili powder, tomato juice, catsup, and
vinegar. Heat to boiling; cover.

Simmer lamb, turning several times, 2
hours, or until tender; remove to a shallow
pan; keep warm.

Pour liquid from Dutch oven into a 4-cup
measure; let stand a few minutes until fat rises
to top, then skim off. Measure 2 cups of the
liquid and return to Dutch oven; heat to boiling.

Mix flour with a little water in a cup until
smooth; stir into boiling liquid. Cook, stirring
constantly, until sauce thickens and boils 1
minute. Stir in beans; beat again to boiling;
simmer 2 to 3 minutes.

Remove beans from Dutch oven with a slotted spoon and place on a deep serving platter;
slice part of the lamb and overlap slices on top.
Serve sauce in a separate bowl to spoon over
all.

Yield: 4 servings plus enough meat for a
dividend dish.

MOCK DUCK

3 slices bacon, cut into 1-inch pieces
1 rolled boned lamb shoulder, weighing about
   4 lbs.
1 small onion, chopped (¼ cup)
4 tablespoons all-purpose flour
1 tablespoon curry powder
1 tablespoon sugar
1 teaspoon salt
1 envelope instant beef broth
¾ cup water
1 jar (4¾ ozs.) baby-pack peaches

Sauté bacon until almost crisp in a 4-quart
pressure cooker; remove and drain on paper
toweling.

Brown lamb slowly on all sides in drippings; remove from cooker.

Stir in onion; sauté until soft. Stir in 2 tablespoons of the flour, curry powder, sugar,
salt, beef broth, water, and peaches; cook, stirring constantly, until bubbly. Add bacon and
lamb; cover cooker.

Heat to 15 pounds pressure as manufacturer
directs; cook 40 minutes. Let pressure fall
naturally. Uncover cooker; place roast on a
large serving platter; keep warm. Skim fat
from liquid; reheat liquid to boiling.

Blend remaining 2 tablespoons flour with 2
tablespoons water until smooth in a cup; stir
into boiling liquid. Cook, stirring constantly,
until sauce thickens slightly and boils 1
minute.

Cut strings from lamb; slice part of the meat;
serve sauce separately to spoon over meat.

Yield: 4 servings plus enough meat for a
dividend dish.

CUMBERLAND LAMB ROAST

1 leg of lamb, weighing about 8 lbs.
1½ teaspoons seasoned salt
½ teaspoon seasoned pepper
1 cup currant jelly
¼ cup horseradish
2 teaspoons dry mustard
   Peanut Pilaf (recipe on page 263)
   Peach Pickles (recipe on page 413)

Preheat oven to 325°.

Trim excess fat from lamb. Sprinkle salt and pepper over roast; place, fat side up, on a rack in a large roasting pan. Insert meat thermometer into thickest part of roast without touching bone. Do not cover pan or add any water.

Roast 3 hours.

Beat jelly with horseradish and mustard in a small bowl until blended; brush part over lamb.

Continue roasting, brushing every 15 minutes with more jelly mixture, 45 minutes, or until lamb is richly glazed and thermometer registers 170° for medium. (If you prefer lamb well-done, thermometer should register 180°.)

Place roast on a heated large serving platter; serve with Peanut Pilaf and Peach Pickles.

Yield: 6 servings plus enough meat for one or two dividend dishes.

CURRIED LAMB KABOBS

1 shank end leg of lamb, weighing about 3 lbs.
¾ cup pineapple-orange juice
¼ cup salad oil
2 tablespoons light brown sugar
1 clove garlic, minced
1 teaspoon salt
1 teaspoon curry powder
6 large ears of corn
18 large pimiento-stuffed green olives

Cut lamb into 1½-inch cubes, discarding bones and fat.

Combine pineapple-orange juice, salad oil, brown sugar, garlic, salt, and curry powder in a large shallow dish; place lamb in dish, turning cubes to coat well. Let stand at room temperature 3 hours to season.

Husk corn and remove silk; break each ear into 4 chunks.

Pour marinade from lamb into a small saucepan; cook rapidly until it measures ⅔ cup.

Preheat broiler.

Thread lamb cubes, corn, and olives, dividing evenly, onto 6 long skewers. Place on rack in broiler pan; brush part of the marinade over meat and vegetables.

Broil, 8 inches from heat, turning and brushing often with remaining marinade, 15 minutes, or until lamb is as done as you like it.

Yield: 6 servings.

KOREAN LAMB

4 lamb shanks, weighing about 1 lb. each
½ cup chopped green onions
½ cup soy sauce
½ teaspoon lemon-pepper
1 teaspoon garlic powder
¾ cup beer
⅓ cup honey

Trim any excess fat from lamb shanks.

Combine onions, soy sauce, lemon-pepper, garlic powder, and beer in a kettle; add lamb. Heat to boiling; cover. Simmer 1½ hours, or until meat is tender. Remove lamb from sauce; place on rack in broiler pan.

Preheat broiler.

Measure sauce, then return ½ cup to kettle; stir in honey; brush part over lamb.

Broil, 8 inches from heat, turning and brushing often with remaining sauce, 20 minutes, or until richly glazed.

Yield: 4 servings.

INDONESIAN LAMB

1½ lbs. lean boneless lamb shoulder
1 tablespoon salad oil
1 medium onion, chopped (½ cup)
2 teaspoons curry powder
1 teaspoon salt
¼ teaspoon ground ginger
⅛ teaspoon ground cardamom
¾ cup light raisins
1 jar (4¾ ozs.) baby-pack applesauce
1 cup water
1 tablespoon lemon juice
4 cups hot cooked rice

Trim all fat from lamb; cut lamb into 1-inch cubes. Brown in salad oil in a large skillet; remove meat from skillet. Pour off all fat, then measure 2 tablespoons and return to skillet.

Stir onion into drippings; sauté until soft. Stir in curry powder, salt, ginger, and cardamom; cook 1 minute longer. Stir in raisins, applesauce, water, and lamb; heat to boiling; cover.

Simmer 1½ hours, or until lamb is tender and sauce thickens slightly. Stir in lemon juice.

When ready to serve, spoon rice around edge in a large shallow serving bowl; spoon lamb mixture in center. Serve with finely diced, pared cucumbers, chopped slivered almonds, chopped preserved kumquats, and crisp diced bacon to sprinkle on top if you like.

Yield: 6 servings.

NEAR EAST LAMB SHANKS

4 lamb shanks, weighing about ¾ lb. each
2 teaspoons curry powder
1 tablespoon salad oil
1 large onion, chopped (1 cup)
1 cup chopped celery
1 clove garlic, chopped
1 jar (about 8 ozs.) junior peaches
⅓ cup catsup
2 teaspoons salt
½ cup water
3 cups hot cooked rice

Trim any excess fat from lamb shanks, rub shanks with curry powder. Brown in salad oil in a 4-quart pressure cooker; remove and set aside.

Add onion, celery, and garlic to drippings; sauté until soft. Stir in peaches, catsup, salt, and water; return lamb shanks; cover.

Heat cooker to 15 pounds pressure as manufacturer directs; cook 30 minutes; remove from heat. Let pressure fall naturally; uncover cooker.

Spoon rice around edge on a large serving platter; arrange lamb shanks in center. Let sauce in cooker stand a minute until fat rises to top, then skim off; spoon sauce over lamb.

Yield: 4 servings.

LAMB BALLS SCANDIA

2 lbs. ground lamb
1 envelope green onion dip mix
1 cup fresh bread crumbs (2 slices)
1 teaspoon salt
¼ teaspoon pepper
½ cup milk
2 cans (10½ ozs. each) chicken gravy
1 can (8 ozs.) tomato sauce
½ teaspoon dried rosemary, crushed

Preheat oven to 350°.

Combine lamb with dip mix, bread crumbs, salt, pepper, and milk in a large bowl; mix lightly until well blended. Shape into 24 balls; place in a baking dish, 13x9x2 inches.

Combine chicken gravy, tomato sauce, and rosemary in a medium saucepan; heat, stirring several times, to boiling; pour over lamb balls; cover.

Bake 40 minutes, or until bubbly and lamb is cooked through. Serve plain or with hot cooked noodles or mashed potatoes if you like.

Yield: 8 servings.

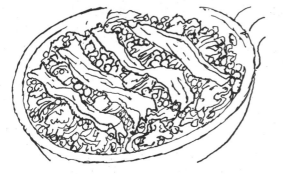

utes longer, or until bacon is crisp and lamb is tender. Remove bay leaf before serving.

Yield: 6 to 8 servings.

CASSOULET

1 package (16 ozs.) dried Great Northern beans
2 teaspoons salt
6 cups water
4 slices bacon
1 lb. lean boneless lamb shoulder, and cut into 1-inch cubes
1 large onion, chopped (1 cup)
¼ lb. salami, diced
1 can (16 ozs.) stewed tomatoes
1 teaspoon garlic powder
1 teaspoon dried thyme, crushed
¼ teaspoon pepper
1 large bay leaf

Rinse beans. Place in a kettle with 1 teaspoon of the salt and water. Heat to boiling; cook 2 minutes; remove from heat; cover. Let stand 1 hour. Reheat to boiling; simmer 2 hours, or until beans are tender but still firm enough to hold their shape.

Sauté bacon in a large skillet until fat starts to cook out; remove slices and drain on paper toweling.

Preheat oven to 375°.

Stir lamb into drippings and brown; remove with a slotted spoon and add to bean mixture.

Pour off all fat, then measure 2 tablespoons and return to skillet; stir in onion and salami; sauté until onion is soft. Stir in tomatoes, garlic powder, remaining 1 teaspoon salt, thyme, pepper, and bay leaf; heat to boiling; stir into bean mixture. Spoon into a 2½-quart baking dish; cover.

Bake 1 hour and 30 minutes; uncover. Place bacon slices on top. Bake, uncovered, 30 min-

LAMB STEW WITH MINT DUMPLINGS

2 lbs. lean boneless lamb shoulder, cut into 1-inch cubes
2 tablespoons salad oil
1 large onion, chopped (1 cup)
1 teaspoon dried marjoram, crushed
1 teaspoon salt
¼ teaspoon pepper
2½ cups water
1 yellow turnip, weighing about 1½ lbs., pared and cut into ¾-inch cubes
1 package (9 ozs.) frozen cut green beans
1 cup sliced celery
1 envelope mushroom gravy mix
1½ cups biscuit mix
1 teaspoon mint flakes, crushed
½ cup milk

Trim any fat from lamb. Brown cubes slowly in salad oil in a kettle; push to one side. Stir onion into drippings; sauté until soft.

Stir in marjoram, salt, pepper, and 2 cups of the water; heat to boiling; cover. Simmer 30 minutes.

Stir in turnip; heat to boiling; cover. Simmer 45 minutes, or until lamb and turnip are almost tender.

Stir in frozen green beans and celery; heat to boiling.

Blend remaining ½ cup water into gravy mix in a small bowl; stir into bubbling stew. Cook, stirring constantly, until mixture thickens.

While stew cooks, combine biscuit mix and mint in a medium bowl; stir in milk until mixture is evenly moist. Drop by tablespoonfuls in 8 mounds on top of bubbling stew.

Cook, uncovered, 10 minutes; cover. Cook 10 minutes longer, or until dumplings are puffy-light. Serve from kettle.

Yield: 8 servings.

LAMB LOAF WITH CURRY SAUCE

⅓ cup milk
2 slices slightly dry white bread, crumbled
1 egg
1½ lbs. ground lamb
3 medium carrots, pared and shredded (1 cup)
1 large onion, chopped (1 cup)
1 clove garlic, crushed
1½ teaspoons salt
¼ teaspoon pepper
1 teaspoon curry powder
1 tablespoon butter or margarine
1 tablespoon all-purpose flour
1 can (5½ ozs.) apple juice
1 jar (7¾ ozs.) junior apricots

Preheat oven to 350°.

Combine milk, bread, and egg in a large bowl; let stand a few minutes until liquid is absorbed, then beat with a spoon until blended.

Add lamb, carrots, ½ cup of the onion, garlic, salt, and pepper; mix lightly until well blended. Spoon into a greased baking pan, 8x4x2 inches; pack down lightly.

Bake 1 hour, or until loaf is firm and browned.

While loaf bakes, sauté remaining ½ cup onion with curry powder in butter until onion is soft in a medium saucepan. Stir in flour until blended; stir in apple juice and apricots. Cook, stirring constantly, until sauce thickens and boils 1 minute.

Loosen lamb loaf around edges with a knife; turn out onto a large serving platter. Garnish with carrot curls and parsley if you like. Cut crosswise into thick slices; serve with curry sauce.

Yield: 6 servings.

CABBAGE ROLLUPS

1 head of cabbage, weighing about 2 lbs.
1 medium onion, chopped (½ cup)
2 tablespoons salad oil
3 cups finely chopped cooked lamb
1 egg, beaten
½ cup fresh bread crumbs (1 slice)
1 jar (15 ozs.) meatless spaghetti sauce
1 teaspoon garlic salt
¼ teaspoon pepper
¼ teaspoon dried basil, crushed
½ cup water
1½ cups packaged precooked rice
2 tablespoons chopped parsley

Trim cabbage and cut out core; place head in a kettle. Pour in boiling water to cover cabbage; cover kettle. Cook 8 to 10 minutes, or until cabbage is almost tender; lift head from water with two slotted spoons and drain well. Carefully peel off 12 large outer leaves and set aside. (Chill remaining cabbage to dice and cream for another meal.)

Sauté onion in salad oil in a medium skillet until soft; remove from heat. Stir in lamb, egg, bread crumbs, ½ cup of the spaghetti sauce, garlic salt, pepper, and basil.

Preheat oven to 350°.

Lay cabbage leaves flat on counter top; spoon about 3 tablespoons of the lamb mixture on narrow end of each leaf. Fold ends of leaves, then sides over filling; roll up, jelly-roll fashion; fasten with wooden picks. Place in a baking dish, 13x9x2 inches.

Mix remaining spaghetti sauce and water in same skillet; heat to boiling. Pour over the cabbage rolls; cover.

Bake 45 minutes, or until cabbage is tender.

While rolls bake, prepare rice as label directs; add parsley and toss lightly to mix. Mound in center of a large serving platter; arrange cabbage rolls around edge. Spoon part of the sauce over rolls; pass remainder separately.

Yield: 6 servings.

CURRIED LAMB LOAF

    4 slices bacon, diced
    1 medium onion, chopped (½ cup)
    1 tablespoon curry powder
    3 cups ground cooked lamb
    1 egg
    1 jar (8 ozs.) unsweetened applesauce
    1 cup fresh bread crumbs (2 slices)
 ½ teaspoon salt
 ¼ teaspoon pepper
    6 preserved kumquats, sliced thin
    2 large green onions, trimmed and sliced
    1 large fresh tomato, chopped

Preheat oven to 350°.

Sauté bacon until almost crisp in a medium skillet; remove and drain on paper toweling. Stir onion into drippings; sauté until soft; push to one side. Stir in curry powder; cook 1 minute longer.

Combine lamb, egg, applesauce, bread crumbs, salt, and pepper in a large bowl. Add onion mixture and bacon; mix lightly until well blended. Shape into a round 1¼ inches thick in a greased baking pan.

Bake 45 minutes, or until loaf is crusty brown.

Carefully lift loaf onto a large serving platter. Spoon kumquats, green onions, and tomato in rows on top of loaf. Surround with oven-browned potato balls if you like.

Yield: 6 servings.

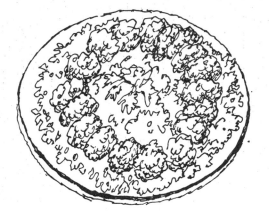

FINNISH LAMB

    2 slices bacon, cut into ½-inch pieces
 1½ lbs. ground lamb
 1½ cups fresh bread crumbs (3 slices)
    1 egg
    1 small onion, minced (¼ cup)
    2 tablespoons tomato juice
    2 tablespoons chopped parsley
    2 teaspoons salt
      Dash of pepper
 ¼ cup butter or margarine
 ¼ cup all-purpose flour
    2 cups milk
    1 tablespoon dillweed

Sauté bacon until crisp in a large skillet; remove and drain on paper toweling.

Combine lamb, bacon pieces, bread crumbs, egg, onion, tomato juice, parsley, 1 teaspoon of the salt, and pepper in a large bowl; mix lightly until well blended. Shape into 18 balls. Brown meatballs slowly in bacon drippings in skillet; place in a 2-quart baking dish.

Preheat oven to 350°.

Melt butter in a medium saucepan; blend in flour. Cook, stirring constantly, until bubbly. Stir in milk; continue cooking and stirring until sauce thickens and boils 1 minute. Stir in remaining 1 teaspoon salt and dillweed; pour over lamb balls; cover.

Bake 40 minutes, or until bubbly in center. Serve as is or with rice if you like.

Yield: 6 servings.

MOROCCAN LAMB BAKE

1 small eggplant, weighing about 1 lb.
⅔ cup salad oil
3 cups cubed cooked lamb
1 large onion, chopped (1 cup)
1 clove garlic, minced
1 can (16 ozs.) tomatoes
 Water
1 teaspoon dried Italian herbs
1 teaspoon salt
½ teaspoon sugar
¼ teaspoon pepper
¾ cup uncooked regular rice

Pare eggplant and cut into ½-inch-thick slices.

Preheat oven to 350°.

Heat part of the salad oil in a large skillet; place eggplant slices in skillet and brown, adding more oil as needed; remove slices from pan and drain well on paper toweling.

Stir lamb into drippings; brown lightly; remove with a slotted spoon; set aside.

Stir onion and garlic into drippings; sauté until soft.

Drain liquid from tomatoes into 2-cup measure; add water to measure 1¾ cups. Stir tomatoes, tomato liquid, herbs, salt, sugar, and pepper into onion mixture; heat to boiling.

Layer half each of the eggplant, lamb, rice, and sauce into a 2-quart baking dish; repeat layers; cover.

Bake 1 hour, or until rice is tender and liquid is absorbed.

Yield: 4 servings.

SHEEPHERDER'S STEW

1½ lbs. ground lamb
1 clove garlic, minced
1 teaspoon salt
¼ teaspoon pepper
1 cup fresh bread crumbs (2 slices)
⅓ cup milk
2 tablespoons salad oil
9 medium carrots, pared and quartered
 lengthwise
12 small potatoes, pared
1 cup thinly sliced celery
2 cups water
1 envelope onion soup mix
1 can (8 ozs.) stewed tomatoes
½ teaspoon dried thyme, crushed
1 package (10 ozs.) frozen lima beans

Combine lamb, garlic, salt, pepper, bread crumbs, and milk in a large bowl. Mix lightly until well blended; shape into 24 balls.

Brown in salad oil in a large skillet; remove with a slotted spoon and pile in the center of a 3-quart baking dish. Place carrots, potatoes, and celery around lamb in dish. Pour all drippings from skillet.

Preheat oven to 350°.

Stir water, onion soup mix, tomatoes, thyme, and limas into skillet; heat to boiling, breaking up limas with a fork. Spoon over lamb and vegetables; cover.

Bake 60 minutes, or until potatoes and carrots are tender. Serve in soup plates.

Yield: 6 servings.

LITTLE LAMB DINNER

4 lamb shanks, weighing about 1 lb. each
2 tablespoons salad oil
1 medium onion, chopped (½ cup)
1 can (10¾ ozs.) condensed golden mushroom
    soup
1 cup dry white wine
½ cup water
½ teaspoon dried rosemary, crushed
8 small carrots, pared
1 bunch broccoli, weighing about 1¼ lbs.

Trim any excess fat from lamb shanks.

Brown lamb slowly in salad oil in a Dutch oven; remove and set aside. Stir onion into drippings; sauté until soft.

Stir in soup, wine, water, and rosemary; place lamb in liquid. Heat to boiling; cover tightly. Simmer, turning lamb several times, 1½ hours.

Place carrots around lamb in Dutch oven; cover again. Cook 10 minutes.

While carrots cook, wash and trim broccoli. Cut off flowerets; cut stalks into 1-inch pieces. Place stalks, then flowerets in Dutch oven on top of lamb; cover.

Cook 10 minutes, or just until lamb is tender and vegetables are still slightly crisp. Serve from Dutch oven.

Yield: 4 servings.

MOUSSAKA

1 medium eggplant, weighing about 1¾ lbs.
  Salt
  Salad oil
2 cups very finely chopped cooked lamb
1 medium onion, chopped (½ cup)
⅓ cup water
1 tablespoon chopped parsley
2 tablespoons tomato paste
⅛ teaspoon pepper
2 eggs
2 tablespoons butter or margarine
2 tablespoons all-purpose flour
  Dash of nutmeg
1 cup milk
¼ cup dry bread crumbs
⅛ teaspoon paprika

Pare eggplant, and cut into ½-inch-thick slices. Sprinkle salt over slices; set aside.

Heat 3 tablespoons salad oil in a medium skillet; stir in lamb and onion; sauté until lamb is brown and onion is soft. Stir in water, parsley, tomato paste, 1 teaspoon salt, and pepper. Simmer 10 minutes; cool.

Beat 1 of the eggs in a small bowl; stir into lamb mixture.

Brown eggplant slices, a few at a time, in salad oil in a large skillet, adding more oil as needed; remove from skillet and drain on paper toweling.

Preheat oven to 350°.

Melt butter in a small saucepan; stir in flour, nutmeg, and ¼ teaspoon salt. Cook, stirring constantly, until bubbly. Stir in milk; continue cooking and stirring until sauce thickens and boils 1 minute. Beat remaining egg in a small bowl; stir in about half of the hot sauce, then stir back into pan; cook 1 minute longer.

Sprinkle bread crumbs into a baking dish, 9x9x2 inches. Top with half of the eggplant, all of the meat sauce, and remaining eggplant. Pour cream sauce over top; sprinkle paprika over sauce.

Bake 40 minutes, or until bubbly and lightly browned.

Yield: 4 servings.

CANNED MEATS

KANSAS PORK LOAF

1 one-pound canned ham
1 medium onion, peeled
12 unsalted soda crackers
1 lb. ground pork
2 eggs
¼ cup apple juice
2 tablespoons chopped parsley
½ teaspoon dried marjoram, crushed
⅛ teaspoon pepper
¼ cup maple-blended syrup
1½ teaspoons prepared mustard

Scrape gelatin coating from ham; cut ham into chunks; quarter onion. Put ham, onion, and crackers through a food grinder, using a coarse blade.

Preheat oven to 350°.

Place ham mixture in a large bowl; add pork, eggs, apple juice, parsley, marjoram, and pepper; mix lightly. Shape into a 7-inch round loaf in a large shallow baking pan; score top in squares.

Bake 45 minutes.

Mix syrup and mustard in a cup; brush part over loaf. Continue baking, brushing several times with remaining syrup mixture, 30 minutes, or until loaf is richly glazed.

Lift onto a serving platter with two pancake turners; slice in wedges. Serve with prepared mustard and creamed or scalloped potatoes if you like.

Yield: 6 to 8 servings.

BEEF-AND-BACON PIZZA

2 packages refrigerated plain or buttermilk biscuits
6 slices bacon, cut into 1-inch pieces
1 can (about 15 ozs.) barbecue sauce with beef
½ teaspoon dried Italian herbs, crushed
4 long slices mozzarella cheese

Preheat oven to 400°.

Separate biscuits; press together evenly into a lightly greased 14-inch pizza pan to form a crust.

Sauté bacon in a medium skillet until almost crisp; remove and drain on paper toweling; pour off all drippings into a cup.

Combine barbecue sauce and Italian herbs in same skillet. Heat slowly, stirring several times, to boiling; spread over crust; sprinkle bacon on top.

Cut cheese into strips or triangles; arrange over bacon.

Bake 20 minutes, or until crust browns lightly. Cut into wedges; serve hot.

Yield: 4 servings.

GYPSY CORNED BEEF

1 can (12 ozs.) corned beef
½ cup sliced green onions
1 can (16 ozs.) whole white potatoes, drained and sliced
1 can (16 ozs.) stewed tomatoes
1 can (8 ozs.) lima beans
Dash of pepper
1 tablespoon all-purpose flour

Break up corned beef with a fork; combine with onions, potatoes, tomatoes, lima beans and liquid, and pepper in a large skillet. Heat slowly to boiling; cover. Simmer 15 minutes.

Blend flour with a little water in a cup until smooth; stir into mixture in skillet. Cook, stirring gently but constantly, until mixture thickens and boils 1 minute.

Spoon into soup bowls. Serve with toasted corn muffins if you like.

Yield: 4 servings.

BAKED LIMAS AND HAM

1 package (16 ozs.) dried large lima beans
6 cups water
1 one-pound canned ham
1 medium onion, peeled and sliced
2 tablespoons salad oil
¼ cup firmly packed brown sugar
2 tablespoons sweet-pickle relish
1 teaspoon dry mustard
⅛ teaspoon ground cinnamon
⅛ teaspoon pepper
2 tablespoons chopped parsley

Rinse lima beans. Combine with water in a kettle. Heat to boiling; cook 2 minutes; remove from heat; cover. Let stand 1 hour. Reheat to boiling; simmer 1 hour, or until beans are tender but still firm enough to hold their shape.

Scrape gelatin coating from ham; dice meat. Preheat oven to 350°.

Sauté ham and onion in salad oil in a large skillet until onion is soft; stir in brown sugar, pickle relish, mustard, cinnamon, and pepper. Heat to boiling; stir into bean mixture. Spoon into a 2½-quart baking dish; cover.

Bake 30 minutes; uncover. Bake 30 minutes longer, or until bubbly. Before serving, sprinkle parsley over top.

Yield: 6 servings.

TOPSY-TURVY CORNED BEEF WEDGES

1 can (12 ozs.) corned beef, shredded
1 can (8 ozs.) whole white potatoes, drained and diced
1 small onion, minced (¼ cup)
2 tablespoons chopped parsley
1 container (4 ozs.) whipped cream cheese
1 package refrigerated buttermilk biscuits
½ cup dairy sour cream
¼ cup mayonnaise or salad dressing
1 tablespoon horseradish-mustard
  Few drops red-pepper seasoning

Preheat oven to 400°.

Combine corned beef, potatoes, onion, and parsley in a large bowl; stir in cream cheese until well blended. Spread evenly in a greased 9-inch pie plate.

Separate biscuits and place on a sheet of waxed paper; pat into a 9-inch round. Using paper as a lifter, invert round over corned beef mixture in pie plate.

Bake 20 minutes, or until topping is puffed and golden.

While pie bakes, combine sour cream, mayonnaise, mustard, and red-pepper seasoning in a small saucepan; heat very slowly just until hot. (Do not let mixture boil.)

Loosen pie around edge with a knife; invert onto a large serving plate. Cut into wedges; top with mustard sauce.

Yield: 4 servings.

CORNED-BEEF PILLOWS

1 can (12 ozs.) corned beef
1 small potato, cooked, peeled, and chopped
1 small onion, chopped (¼ cup)
1 egg
1 teaspoon prepared mustard
1 package refrigerated crescent rolls
1 can (10¾ ozs.) condensed cream of celery soup
⅓ cup milk

Preheat oven to 375°.

Shred corned beef in a large bowl; add potato, onion, egg, and mustard; mix lightly.

Separate crescent rolls into 4 rectangles; pinch together at perforations; roll each lightly into a rectangle, 6x5 inches.

Divide meat mixture into quarters; spoon into a loaf shape on each rectangle. Fold dough up around loaves to cover; pinch ends to seal. Place seam side down on an ungreased cookie sheet. Cut several slits in top of each to let steam escape.

Bake 20 minutes, or until golden.

While loaves bake, combine soup and milk in a small saucepan; heat to boiling. Serve over rolls.

Yield: 4 servings.

MEATBALL RAGOUT

1 medium onion, chopped (½ cup)
1 cup thinly sliced celery
2 tablespoons butter or margarine
1 can (15 ozs.) meatballs in gravy
1 can (8 ozs.) peas and carrots
½ teaspoon dried thyme, crushed
2 small fresh tomatoes
½ teaspoon sugar
2 cups cooked noodles
1 tablespoon butter or margarine

Sauté onion and celery in butter in a large skillet until soft.

Stir in meatballs and gravy, peas and liquid, and thyme; heat to boiling; cover. Simmer 10 minutes.

Cut tomatoes in thin wedges; place on top of meat mixture. Sprinkle sugar over tomatoes; cover. Cook 5 minutes.

Toss noodles with butter; spoon onto serving plates; spoon meat mixture on top.

Yield: 4 servings.

HAM-AND-SWISS PUFF

1 can (4½ ozs.) deviled ham
½ cup shredded process Swiss cheese
1 teaspoon prepared mustard
8 slices white bread
4 eggs
2¼ cups milk

Mix deviled ham with cheese and mustard; spread on 4 slices of bread; top with remaining bread to make sandwiches. Place in a single layer in a greased baking dish, 8x8x2 inches.

Beat eggs slightly with milk; pour over sandwiches. Cover; chill at least 4 hours or overnight.

When ready to bake, preheat oven to 325°; uncover baking dish; place in oven.

Bake 1 hour, or until sandwiches are puffed and a knife inserted near center comes out clean. To serve, cut between sandwiches; lift onto serving plates with a pancake turner.

Yield: 4 servings.

DUBLIN SKILLET BEANS

1 can (12 ozs.) corned beef
1 medium onion, chopped (½ cup)
¼ cup chopped green pepper
2 tablespoons salad oil
1 jar (18 ozs.) brick-oven baked beans
¼ cup chili sauce
2 tablespoons prepared mustard

Cut corned beef into small cubes. (If meat is well chilled before opening can, it will cut neatly.)

Sauté onion and green pepper in salad oil in a medium skillet until soft; push to one side. Add corned beef and brown.

Mix beans, chili sauce, and mustard in a medium bowl; stir into mixture in skillet. Heat slowly to boiling; simmer 5 minutes to blend flavors.

Serve with sliced Boston brown bread if you like.

Yield: 4 servings.

MEXICALI SHORTCAKES

1 large onion, chopped (1 cup)
1 cup chopped celery
2 tablespoons salad oil
1 tablespoon chili powder
1 can (12 ozs.) pork luncheon meat, diced
1 can (16 ozs.) kidney beans
1 can (15 ozs.) herb-tomato sauce
1 teaspoon salt
½ teaspoon sugar
¼ teaspoon pepper
6 toaster cornmeal cakes

Sauté onion and celery in salad oil in a large skillet until soft. Stir in chili powder; cook 1 minute.

Stir in luncheon meat, kidney beans and liquid, tomato sauce, salt, sugar, and pepper. Heat to boiling; simmer, uncovered, 20 minutes.

While mixture simmers, toast cornmeal cakes; place on serving plates; spoon meat mixture on top.

Yield: 6 servings.

SKILLET GUMBO

1 can (12 ozs.) pork luncheon meat, diced
1 cup chopped green pepper
1 large onion, chopped (1 cup)
1 package (10 ozs.) frozen cut okra
1 can (16 ozs.) stewed tomatoes
2 teaspoons garlic salt
¼ teaspoon pepper
1½ cups water
1 cup uncooked regular rice

Combine meat, green pepper, onion, okra, tomatoes and liquid, garlic salt, pepper, and water in a large skillet; heat to boiling; cover. Simmer 10 minutes, breaking okra apart with a fork.

Stir in rice; heat to boiling again; cover. Simmer 20 minutes, or until rice is tender and liquid is absorbed.

Yield: 6 servings.

HASH BALLS IN CREAM

1 can (15½ ozs.) corned beef hash
1 egg
1 tablespoon water
½ cup dry bread crumbs
1 package (8 ozs.) frozen mixed vegetables in onion sauce
Milk
Butter or margarine

Preheat oven to 400°.

Shape corned beef hash into 20 small balls, using 1 tablespoonful for each.

Beat egg with water in a pie plate; spread bread crumbs on waxed paper. Dip hash balls into egg mixture, then into bread crumbs to coat well. Place in a single layer in a greased shallow pan.

Bake 15 minutes, or until crusty.

While hash balls bake, prepare vegetables with milk and butter as label directs.

Place hash balls on serving plates; spoon creamed vegetables over top.

Yield: 4 servings.

QUICK BEEF POTPIE

1 can (24 ozs.) beef stew
1 can (8 ozs.) peas, drained
1 medium tomato, diced (1 cup)
½ teaspoon dried oregano, crushed
3 tablespoons butter or margarine
1 tablespoon grated Parmesan cheese
1 tablespoon chopped parsley
8 small slices French bread, cut ½ inch thick

Preheat oven to 350°.

Combine beef stew, peas, tomato, and oregano in a large bowl; toss lightly to mix; spoon into a 1½-quart shallow baking dish.

Bake 30 minutes.

Mix butter, Parmesan cheese, and parsley in a small bowl; spread on bread. Arrange slices, buttered side up, on top of hot meat mixture.

Bake 10 minutes longer, or until bread is crisp and lightly golden. Spoon onto serving plates.

Yield: 4 servings.

CORNED BEEF AND POTATO RINGS

1 can (12 ozs.) corned beef
1 small onion, chopped (¼ cup)
2 tablespoons butter or margarine
1 can (10¾ ozs.) condensed cream of celery soup
⅓ cup milk
2 tablespoons chopped parsley
Instant mashed potatoes

Cut corned beef into ½-inch cubes. (Meat will cut neatly if chilled first.)

Sauté onion in butter in a medium skillet until soft; stir in corned beef; brown lightly. Stir in soup, milk, and parsley. Heat, stirring gently several times, to boiling; keep hot.

Prepare enough instant mashed potatoes as label directs to make 4 servings. Spoon onto serving plates; press a hollow in center of each mound; spoon corned-beef mixture into hollows.

Yield: 4 servings.

RED FLANNEL HASH SQUARES

3 medium potatoes, pared and diced (3 cups)
1 can (12 ozs.) corned beef, shredded
1 can (8 ozs.) diced beets, drained and chopped
1 medium onion, chopped (½ cup)
½ teaspoon salt
  Dash of pepper

Cook potatoes, covered, in boiling water in a medium saucepan 15 minutes, or until tender; drain well; mash coarsely in a large bowl.

Preheat oven to 375°.

Add corned beef, beets, onion, salt, and pepper to potatoes; mix well. Spoon into a baking pan, 8x8x2 inches.

Bake 45 minutes, or until lightly browned on top. Cut into squares; lift onto serving plates with a pancake turner.

Yield: 4 to 6 servings.

GOLDEN CORNED-BEEF PIE

1 can (12 ozs.) corned beef
1 medium onion, chopped (½ cup)
2 tablespoons butter or margarine
1 tablespoon all-purpose flour
1 can (10¾ ozs.) condensed vegetarian vegetable
  soup
1 can (8 ozs.) peas and carrots
2 cups prepared instant mashed potatoes
½ cup shredded process American cheese

Cube corned beef. (Meat will cut neatly if chilled first.)

Preheat oven to 350°.

Sauté onion in butter in a medium skillet until soft; add corned beef and brown lightly.

Sprinkle flour over onion mixture, then gently stir in with soup and peas and carrots and liquid. Cook, stirring constantly, until mixture thickens and boils 1 minute. Spoon into a 1½-quart shallow baking dish.

Drop potatoes into 8 small mounds on top of corned-beef mixture; sprinkle cheese over potatoes.

Bake 20 minutes, or until bubbly and cheese melts.

Yield: 4 servings.

NEW ENGLAND HASH

1 package (5½ ozs.) hashed brown potatoes with
  onions
  Butter
  Salt
  Water
1 can (12 ozs.) corned beef, shredded
1 can (8 ozs.) peas, drained
½ cup dairy sour cream
2 teaspoons prepared mustard

Prepare potatoes with butter, salt, and water as label directs; stir in corned beef and peas.

Blend sour cream and mustard in a small bowl; spread over beef mixture; cover. Heat very slowly 5 minutes, or just until mixture is hot. Spoon onto serving plates.

Yield: 4 to 6 servings.

LOG CABIN PORK HASH

4 cups diced cooked potatoes
1 can (12 ozs.) pork luncheon meat, diced
1 large onion, chopped (1 cup)
1 small can evaporated milk (⅔ cup)
½ teaspoon salt
2 tablespoons butter or margarine
½ cup mayonnaise or salad dressing
2 tablespoons chopped parsley
1 tablespoon prepared mustard
¼ teaspoon Worcestershire sauce

Combine potatoes, luncheon meat, onion, evaporated milk, and salt in a large bowl. Mash coarsely with a fork or chop with a pastry blender.

Heat butter in a medium skillet with a broilerproof handle; spoon meat mixture into skillet; press down firmly with back of spoon. Cook slowly, without stirring, 25 minutes, or until crusty on bottom.

While hash cooks, preheat broiler.

Blend mayonnaise, parsley, mustard, and Worcestershire sauce in a small bowl.

Place skillet in broiler, 4 to 6 inches from heat; broil several minutes, or just until hash browns on top. Cut into wedges; pass mustard sauce separately to spoon on top.

Yield: 6 servings.

DUBLIN BEEF RING

2 cans (12 ozs. each) corned beef
1 can (16 ozs.) whole white potatoes, drained
2 eggs, beaten
1 medium onion, chopped (½ cup)
2 tablespoons prepared mustard
2 tablespoons chopped parsley
¼ teaspoon pepper
  Skillet Cabbage Salad (recipe follows)

Preheat oven to 350°.

Flake corned beef with a fork in a large bowl.

Chop potatoes fine. (There should be 2 cups.) Combine with corned beef, eggs, onion, mustard, parsley, and pepper; mix lightly until well blended. Spoon into a greased 1½- or 1¾-quart ring mold; pack down lightly.

Bake 1 hour, or until loaf is firm and browned on top.

Loosen carefully around edge and tube with a knife; invert onto a serving plate. Spoon part of the Skillet Cabbage Salad into center; serve remainder in a separate bowl.

Yield: 6 servings.

SKILLET CABBAGE SALAD

1 tablespoon butter or margarine
1 tablespoon all-purpose flour
½ teaspoon salt
  Dash of pepper
½ teaspoon dillweed
⅔ cup milk
⅓ cup mayonnaise or salad dressing
5 cups shredded cabbage
½ cup diced green pepper

Melt butter in a large skillet; stir in flour, salt, pepper, and dillweed. Cook, stirring constantly, until bubbly. Stir in milk; continue cooking and stirring until sauce thickens and boils 1 minute; remove from heat.

Stir in mayonnaise; fold in cabbage and green pepper. Serve warm.

Yield: 6 servings.

MEATBALLS SUPREME

3 cups uncooked regular noodles
1 can (15 ozs.) meatballs in brown gravy
¼ cup water
¼ teaspoon dried oregano, crushed
1 package (3 ozs.) cream cheese

Cook noodles as label directs; drain; keep hot.

Combine meatballs and gravy, water, and oregano in a medium saucepan; heat, stirring several times, until bubbly. Cut up cream cheese and stir in until melted.

Spoon noodles onto serving plates; spoon meatballs and sauce over top.

Yield: 4 servings.

PORK-AND-APPLE BAKE

1 can (12 ozs.) pork luncheon meat
1 can (16 ozs.) vacuum-packed yams or sweet
    potatoes
3 tablespoons butter or margarine, melted
½ teaspoon salt
2 large tart apples, pared, quartered, cored, and
    sliced thin
¼ cup firmly packed light brown sugar
½ cup crushed gingersnaps

Cut luncheon meat into 8 slices; stand around edge in a deep 1½-quart baking dish.

Preheat oven to 400°.

Mash yams in a medium bowl; stir in 2 tablespoons of the melted butter and salt; spoon into center of baking dish. Arrange apple slices over yams; sprinkle brown sugar over apples; cover.

Bake 30 minutes, or until apples are tender; uncover.

Toss gingersnap crumbs with remaining 1 tablespoon melted butter in a small bowl; sprinkle over apples.

Bake 10 minutes longer, or until topping is toasted.

Yield: 4 servings.

TERIYAKI HAM KABOBS

1 one-pound canned ham
1 can (29 ozs.) cling peach halves in syrup
1 can (8 ozs.) pineapple chunks in juice
¼ cup light corn syrup
2 tablespoons teriyaki sauce
2 teaspoons lemon juice
2 teaspoons salad oil

Scrape gelatin coating from ham; cut ham into 16 even chunks.

Drain syrup from peaches into a small bowl; measure ¼ cup into a small saucepan. Drain juice from pineapple and add to remaining peach syrup; chill to add to a breakfast beverage.

Stir corn syrup, teriyaki sauce, lemon juice, and salad oil into saucepan; heat to boiling; simmer 5 minutes, or until thickened slightly.

Preheat broiler.

Thread ham, peaches, and pineapple, alternately, onto 4 long skewers; place on rack in broiler pan. Brush part of the peach sauce over all.

Broil, 8 inches from heat, turning several times and brushing with more sauce, 10 minutes, or until richly glazed.

Yield: 4 servings.

YANKEE HAM DINNER

1 can (20 ozs.) pie-sliced apples, drained
1 one-pound canned ham
1 can (16 ozs.) vacuum-packed sweet potatoes
⅔ cup plum preserves
1 teaspoon dry mustard

Preheat oven to 400°.

Spread apple slices in a 1½-quart baking dish; top with ham; place sweet potatoes around ham.

Mix plum preserves with mustard; spread half over ham and sweet potatoes.

Bake 15 minutes; spread remaining plum mixture over ham. Bake 25 minutes longer, or until bubbly and ham is glazed.

Yield: 4 servings.

FRIZZLED HAM

1½ lbs. ham (from a 2-lb. canned ham)
3 tablespoons butter or margarine

Scrape gelatin coating from ham; cut meat into thin slices.

Melt butter in a large skillet; place ham slices in a single layer in butter. Sauté quickly, turning once, until lightly browned.

Yield: 6 servings.

HILO HAM

1 two-pound canned ham
Whole cloves
1 can (8 ozs.) pear halves in syrup
1 can (8 ozs.) cling peach slices in syrup
1 tablespoon cornstarch
Dash of salt
1 tablespoon lemon juice
2 tablespoons curaçao

Preheat oven to 350°.

Scrape gelatin coating from ham; stud ham with cloves; wrap in foil, sealing edges and ends. For easy handling, place in a shallow baking pan.

Bake 1 hour, or until heated through.

While meat heats, drain syrup from pears and peaches into a 1-cup measure; add water to make 1 cup. Dice pears and peaches.

Stir the 1 cup syrup into cornstarch and salt in a small saucepan; cook, stirring constantly, until mixture thickens and boils 1 minute. Stir in lemon juice, curaçao, and diced fruits; heat to boiling again.

Unwrap ham and place on a large cutting board; carve into slices; spoon sauce over each serving.

Yield: 8 servings.

EASTER SUNDAY BAKED HAM

1 five-pound canned ham
2 large seedless oranges
¾ cup orange marmalade
¼ cup orange juice
1 teaspoon Worcestershire sauce
Watercress

Preheat oven to 325°.

Place ham on a rack in a shallow baking pan. Bake 1½ hours.

While ham bakes, slice oranges thin; make even saw-tooth cuts into rind around edge of each if you like; cut slices in half.

Mix marmalade, orange juice, and Worcestershire sauce in a small saucepan; heat to boiling.

Remove ham from oven; make ¾-inch-deep slits every ½ inch across top; push orange slices down into slits. Brush half of the marmalade mixture over ham and oranges.

Continue baking, brushing again with marmalade mixture, 30 minutes, or until richly glazed. Place ham on a heated large serving platter; garnish with watercress and Apple-stuffed Yams (recipe on page 310) if like.

Yield: 6 servings plus enough meat for one or two dividend dishes.

LITTLE HAM TURNOVERS

1 one-pound canned ham
4 anchovy fillets, drained
1 egg
⅓ cup whipping cream
2 tablespoons dry bread crumbs
1 tablespoon chopped green onion
1 tablespoon chopped parsley
1 tablespoon lemon juice
½ teaspoon garlic powder
1 package piecrust mix
1 can (10½ ozs.) chicken gravy
2 tablespoons dairy sour cream

Scrape gelatin coating from ham; cut ham into chunks. Put through a food grinder, using a fine blade. (Loosely packed, meat should measure 3 cups.)

Mash anchovies in a medium bowl with a fork; add ground ham, egg, cream, bread crumbs, green onion, parsley, lemon juice, and garlic powder; mix lightly until well blended.

Prepare piecrust mix as label directs. Roll out half on a lightly floured cloth to a rectangle, 14x12 inches; cut into four 6-inch circles. Spoon ¼ cup of the ham filling onto each circle; moisten edges of pastry, then fold over to cover filling completely; press edges together with a fork to seal. Repeat with remaining pastry and filling.

Preheat oven to 425°.

Cut one or two small slits in top of each turnover; place on a cookie sheet.

Bake 20 minutes, or until golden.

While turnovers bake, blend gravy and sour cream in a small saucepan; heat slowly just to boiling. Pass separately to spoon over turnovers.

Yield: 4 servings.

CHILI BEAN BAKE

1 one-pound canned ham
2 tablespoons salad oil
1 cup sliced celery
1 large onion, chopped (1 cup)
1 can (16 ozs.) pork and beans in tomato sauce
1 can (16 ozs.) barbecue beans
¾ cup chili sauce

Preheat oven to 350°.

Scrape gelatin coating from ham; cut meat into cubes. Brown lightly in salad oil in a medium skillet; remove with a slotted spoon and place in a 2-quart baking dish.

Stir celery and onion into drippings; sauté until soft. Stir into ham with pork and beans and sauce, barbecue beans, and chili sauce; cover.

Bake 30 minutes; uncover. Bake 30 minutes longer, or until slightly thickened.

Yield: 6 servings.

MEXICAN CHILI PIE

1 package (10 ozs.) frozen succotash
1 can (15 ozs.) chili without beans
1 package (12 ozs.) corn-muffin mix
  Egg
  Milk
½ cup shredded sharp Cheddar cheese

Cook succotash as label directs; drain well. Stir into chili in a medium bowl; spoon into a baking dish, 8x8x2 inches.

Preheat oven to 400°.

Prepare muffin mix with egg and milk as label directs. Spoon evenly over meat mixture; sprinkle cheese on top.

Bake 30 minutes, or until topping is golden and a wooden pick inserted in center comes out clean.

Yield: 4 servings.

HAM JUBILEE

1 two-pound canned ham
2 cans (8¾ ozs. each) fruits for salad
1 tablespoon cornstarch
2 tablespoons brandy
1 teaspoon lemon juice

Preheat oven to 350°.

Cut ham into 8 even slices; place slices in a shallow baking dish; cover.

Bake 30 minutes, or until heated through.

While ham bakes, drain syrup from fruits into a cup; stir into cornstarch in a medium saucepan. Cook slowly, stirring constantly, until mixture thickens and boils 1 minute; stir in brandy and lemon juice. Add fruits; heat slowly just until hot.

Spoon over or around ham in baking dish.
Yield: 8 servings.

PARTY HAM LOAF

1 two-pound canned ham
3 medium onions, peeled
1½ cups packaged precooked rice
2 eggs, beaten
1 can (14 ozs.) sweetened condensed milk
½ cup chili sauce
2 tablespoons prepared horseradish

Preheat oven to 350°.

Cut ham and onions into chunks; put through a food grinder, using a coarse blade. Place in a large bowl.

Add dry rice, eggs, sweetened condensed milk, chili sauce, and horseradish; mix lightly until well blended. Spoon into a greased baking pan, 9x5x3 inches; pack down lightly.

Bake 1 hour and 10 minutes, or until firm and browned on top.

Loosen loaf around edges with a knife; turn out onto a large serving platter. Garnish with pineapple slices and parsley if you like.

Yield: 8 servings.

DIXIE HAM POTPIE

1 package (10 ozs.) frozen mixed vegetables
1 one-pound canned ham
1 cup thinly sliced celery
1 medium onion, chopped (½ cup)
¼ cup butter or margarine
¼ cup all-purpose flour
2 envelopes instant vegetable broth
2½ cups milk
1½ cups biscuit mix
½ cup yellow cornmeal
½ teaspoon sesame seeds

Cook vegetables as label directs; drain.

Scrape gelatin coating from ham; cut ham into ½-inch cubes.

Sauté celery and onion in butter in a medium saucepan until soft. Stir in flour and vegetable broth; cook, stirring constantly, until bubbly. Stir in 2 cups of the milk; continue cooking and stirring until sauce thickens and boils 1 minute. Stir in vegetables and ham; spoon into a 2-quart shallow baking dish.

Preheat oven to 400°; keep ham mixture hot in oven as it heats.

Combine biscuit mix and cornmeal in a medium bowl; stir in remaining ½ cup milk until mixture is evenly moist. (If mixture seems too dry, add 1 more tablespoon milk.) Turn dough out onto a lightly floured board; knead ½ minute; pat out to a rectangle ½ inch thick. Cut out 8 rounds with a 2½-inch floured biscuit cutter and 8 with a 1-inch cutter. Arrange large rounds on top of hot meat mixture; top each with a small round; sprinkle sesame seeds over both.

Bake 30 minutes, or until bubbly and biscuits are puffed and golden.

Yield: 4 to 6 servings.

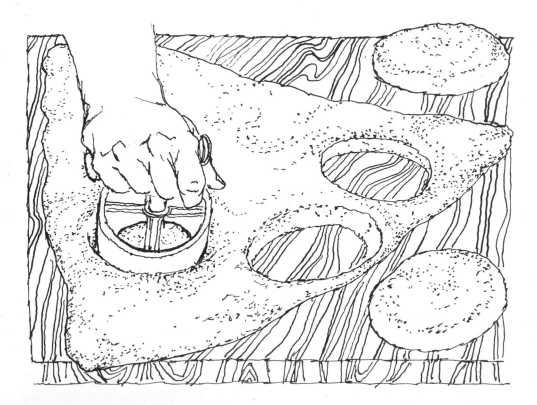

VARIETY MEATS

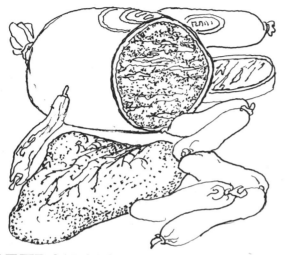

LIVER-SAUSAGE LOAF

1 lb. sliced beef liver
2 tablespoons salad oil
1 package (8 ozs.) brown-and-serve sausages
1 medium onion, peeled and quartered
2 eggs, beaten
1½ cups fresh bread crumbs (3 slices)
½ cup milk
Salt
Pepper
3 tablespoons chopped onion
3 tablespoons chopped green pepper
1 can (8 ozs.) tomato sauce

Trim any veiny parts from liver.

Heat 1 tablespoon of the salad oil in a medium skillet; add liver slices and sauté, turning once, 4 minutes; remove from skillet and drain on paper toweling.

Preheat oven to 350°.

Put liver, sausages, and onion through a food grinder, using coarse blade; place in a large bowl.

Add eggs, bread crumbs, milk, ½ teaspoon salt, and ¼ teaspoon pepper; mix lightly until well blended. Spoon into a greased baking pan, 8x4x2 inches; pack down lightly.

Bake 45 minutes, or until loaf is firm.

While loaf bakes, sauté chopped onion and green pepper in remaining 1 tablespoon salad oil until soft in a medium saucepan; stir in tomato sauce and a dash each of salt and pepper; heat slowly to boiling. Simmer 5 minutes.

Loosen loaf around edges of pan with a knife; turn out onto a large serving plate. Cut loaf crosswise into slices and top with tomato sauce.

Yield: 6 servings.

KIDNEY RAGOUT

1 lb. beef kidney
1 large onion, chopped (1 cup)
1 clove garlic, minced
1 can (10½ ozs.) condensed beef broth
1 cup water
¼ cup dry red wine
½ teaspoon dried thyme, crushed
¼ teaspoon salt
¼ teaspoon pepper
8 small potatoes, pared
1 package (10 ozs.) frozen peas
2 large carrots, pared and cut in ¼-inch rounds
1 tablespoon all-purpose flour

Rinse kidney well in cold water; cut in 1-inch cubes, trimming away any membranes, fat, and hard parts. Combine cubes with onion, garlic, beef broth, water, wine, thyme, salt, and pepper in a kettle; heat to boiling; cover.

Simmer 1¼ hours, or until meat is almost tender. Add potatoes to kettle; cover. Cook 20 minutes.

Add frozen peas and carrots; cover. Cook 15 minutes, or until meat and vegetables are tender.

Blend flour with a little water until smooth in a cup; stir into mixture in kettle. Cook, stirring constantly, until mixture thickens and boils 1 minute. Serve in soup plates.

Yield: 4 servings.

LIVER CREOLE

1 lb. sliced beef liver
1 medium onion, chopped, (½ cup)
1 medium-sized green pepper, quartered, seeded, and chopped (½ cup)
½ cup chopped celery
4 tablespoons salad oil
1 can (15 ozs.) tomato sauce with tomato pieces
2 teaspoons sugar
½ teaspoon dried thyme, crushed
½ teaspoon salt
¼ teaspoon pepper
Few drops red-pepper seasoning

Slice liver into ¼-inch-wide strips, trimming away any veiny parts.

Sauté onion, green pepper, and celery in 2 tablespoons of the salad oil in a medium saucepan until soft; stir in tomato sauce, sugar, thyme, salt, pepper, and red-pepper seasoning. Heat slowly to boiling; cover. Simmer 15 minutes.

While sauce cooks, heat remaining 2 tablespoons salad oil in a large skillet; add liver and sauté, turning once, 5 to 7 minutes, or until brown and meat is no longer pink.

Pour sauce over liver; heat slowly just until hot. Spoon onto a deep serving platter. Garnish with several thin green-pepper rings if you like.

Yield: 4 servings.

COUNTRY LIVER LOAF

1 lb. sliced beef liver
1 cup water
¾ lb. pork sausage meat
1 small onion, minced
2 eggs
1½ cups fresh bread crumbs (3 slices)
¼ cup chili sauce
¼ cup milk
1 tablespoon Worcestershire sauce
1½ teaspoons salt
¼ teaspoon pepper
Green Bean Sauce (recipe on page 316)

Trim any veiny parts from liver. Place liver and water in a skillet; heat to boiling; cover.

Simmer 5 minutes; drain. Put liver through a food grinder, using a coarse blade.

Preheat oven to 350°.

Combine liver, sausage, onion, eggs, bread crumbs, chili sauce, milk, Worcestershire sauce, salt, and pepper in a large bowl; mix lightly until well blended. Pack into a 1½-quart bowl, then turn out into a greased large shallow baking pan.

Bake 45 minutes, or until loaf is crusty-brown. Slice into wedges; serve with Green Bean Sauce.

Yield: 6 servings.

SWEETBREADS ROYALE

1 lb. sweetbreads
1 teaspoon salt
1 teaspoon lemon juice
4½ cups water
2 tablespoons butter or margarine
2 tablespoons all-purpose flour
1 envelope instant chicken broth
1 cup light cream
¼ teaspoon dried tarragon, crushed
4 slices toast, cut in triangles

Rinse sweetbreads in cold water; combine with salt, lemon juice, and 4 cups of the water in a large saucepan. Heat to boiling; cover. Simmer 20 minutes, or until sweetbreads are tender; drain. Cool until easy to handle, then trim away white membranes, fat, and any connective tissue. Cut sweetbreads into bite-sized pieces.

Sauté pieces in butter until golden in a medium skillet; push to one side. Stir in flour and chicken broth; cook, stirring constantly, until bubbly. Stir in remaining ½ cup water, cream, and tarragon. Continue cooking and stirring until mixture thickens and boils 1 minute; cover. Simmer 5 minutes.

Place toast triangles on serving plates; spoon sweetbreads and sauce on top.

Yield: 4 servings.

SMOKED TONGUE WITH ORANGE-RAISIN SAUCE

1 smoked beef tongue, weighing about 4 lbs.
1 medium onion, peeled and sliced
¼ teaspoon peppercorns
6 whole cloves
1 bay leaf
  Few celery tops
8 cups water
  Orange-raisin Sauce (recipe on page 313)

Rinse tongue in cold water. Place in a large kettle with onion, peppercorns, cloves, bay leaf, celery tops, and water; heat to boiling; cover.

Simmer 2¾ hours, or until tongue is tender. Let stand in liquid until cool enough to handle, then drain. Make a shallow cut with a small sharp knife down middle of tongue through skin on underside; peel off skin and discard. Cut out any fat, gristle, and bones from large end.

Slice meat thin and serve with hot Orange-raisin Sauce.

Yield: 6 servings plus enough meat for a dividend dish.

HEART FRICASSEE

2 veal hearts, weighing about 1½ lbs.
3 tablespoons all-purpose flour
¼ teaspoon salt
⅛ teaspoon pepper
¼ cup salad oil
1 medium onion, chopped (½ cup)
1 can (10¾ ozs.) condensed golden mushroom
    soup
½ cup dry white wine
½ cup water
½ teaspoon dried basil, crushed
2 tablespoons chopped parsley
3 cups hot cooked rice

Rinse hearts in cold water. Cut each in half lengthwise; trim away any fat and hard parts from center; cut meat crosswise into ¼-inch thick slices. Shake slices with a mixture of flour, salt, and pepper in a paper or plastic bag to coat well.

Brown meat in salad oil in a heavy kettle; push to one side. Stir in onion and sauté until soft.

Stir in soup, wine, water, and basil; heat to boiling; cover. Simmer, stirring several times, 2 hours, or until meat is tender; stir in parsley.

Spoon rice onto a large serving platter; spoon meat mixture in a ring on top.

Yield: 6 servings.

SPANISH LIVER

1 package (6 ozs.) Spanish rice mix
  Water
  Butter or margarine
1 lb. sliced beef liver
2 tablespoons all-purpose flour
2 tablespoons salad oil
1 medium onion, chopped (½ cup)
⅓ cup catsup
1 teaspoon salt
⅛ teaspoon dried thyme, crushed
⅛ teaspoon lemon-pepper
2 tablespoons chopped parsley

Prepare rice mix with water and butter as label directs; keep hot.

While rice cooks, trim any veiny parts from liver; cut liver into thin strips about 1½ inches long. Shake with flour in a transparent bag until strips are well coated. Brown in salad oil in a medium skillet.

Stir onion, catsup, salt, thyme, pepper, and ¾ cup water into skillet; heat to boiling; cover. Simmer 3 minutes, or until liver is no longer pink.

Spoon Spanish rice around edge on a deep serving platter; spoon liver mixture in center. Sprinkle parsley over liver.

Yield: 4 servings.

SAUSAGES AND COLD CUTS

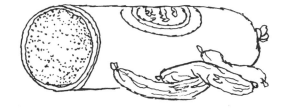

CREOLE BEANS AND SAUSAGES

1 package (16 ozs.) dried pea beans
1 teaspoon salt
6 cups water
1 medium onion, chopped (½ cup)
½ cup chopped celery
½ cup chopped green pepper
2 tablespoons salad oil
1 can (6 ozs.) tomato paste
½ cup chili sauce
1 teaspoon garlic salt
1 package (8 ozs.) brown-and-serve sausages, split lengthwise

Rinse beans. Combine with salt and water in a kettle. Heat to boiling; cook 2 minutes; remove from heat; cover. Let stand 1 hour. Reheat to boiling; simmer 1 hour, or until beans are tender but still firm enough to hold their shape.

Preheat oven to 350°.

Sauté onion, celery, and green pepper in salad oil in a medium skillet until soft. Stir in tomato paste, chili sauce, and garlic salt; heat to boiling; stir into bean mixture. Spoon half into a 2½-quart baking dish; place half of the sausage pieces on top. Repeat with remaining bean mixture and sausages, arranging sausages, spoke fashion, to make a pretty top; cover.

Bake 15 minutes; uncover. Bake 45 minutes longer, or until bubbly.

Yield: 6 servings.

SAUSAGE SWIRLS

1 lb. pork sausage meat
1 medium onion, chopped (½ cup)
½ cup chopped celery
½ cup regular wheat germ
1 can (10¾ ozs.) condensed cream of mushroom soup
2¼ cups all-purpose flour
3 teaspoons baking powder
1 teaspoon salt
⅓ cup shortening
1 cup shredded sharp Cheddar cheese (4 ozs.)
1½ cups milk

Sauté sausage slowly in a large skillet until fat cooks out and meat is no longer pink; push to one side. Drain off all but 1 tablespoon fat.

Stir onion and celery into drippings in skillet; sauté until soft. Stir in ¼ cup of the wheat germ and ½ cup of the mushroom soup; set aside.

Preheat oven to 400°.

Sift flour, baking powder, and salt into a medium bowl; stir in remaining ¼ cup wheat germ. Cut in shortening and ½ cup of the cheese with a pastry blender until mixture forms coarse crumbs. Stir in 1 cup of the milk with a fork until mixture is evenly moist.

Turn out onto a lightly floured board; knead 20 times; roll out to a 12-inch square. Spread sausage mixture evenly over square; roll up tightly, jelly-roll fashion; pinch edges to seal. Cut into 12 one-inch-thick slices; place, flat sides down and close together, on an ungreased cookie sheet.

Bake 20 minutes, or until golden.

While rolls bake, combine remaining soup, cheese, and milk in a small saucepan; heat slowly, stirring constantly, until cheese melts and mixture bubbles. Serve separately to spoon over sausage rolls.

Yield: 6 servings.

SAUSAGE SPOONBURGERS

2 lbs. pork sausage meat
1 lb. ground beef
1 large onion, chopped (1 cup)
1 cup chopped celery
1 cup chopped green pepper
1½ teaspoons chili powder
1 can (16 ozs.) barbecue beans
1 cup catsup
2 teaspoons salt
1 teaspoon dry mustard
½ teaspoon garlic powder
1 tablespoon Worcestershire sauce
1 can (10¾ ozs.) condensed tomato soup
1 cup water
12 hamburger buns, toasted
1½ cups shredded Monterey Jack cheese

Lightly mix sausage and ground beef; shape into a large patty. Brown slowly in a kettle 8 minutes on each side; break up into chunks; remove from kettle.

Pour off all drippings, then measure 2 tablespoons and return to kettle. Stir in onion, celery, and green pepper; sauté until soft; push to one side. Stir in chili powder; cook 1 minute.

Stir in beans and liquid, catsup, salt, mustard, garlic powder, Worcestershire sauce, soup, water, and browned meat. Heat to boiling; cover. Simmer 45 minutes, or until thick.

Spoon into hamburger buns; sprinkle cheese over filling.

Yield: 12 servings.

SAUSAGE ROLLS

2 tablespoons butter or margarine
2 tablespoons all-purpose flour
½ teaspoon salt
¼ teaspoon ground nutmeg
   Dash of pepper
1 cup milk
1 can (8 ozs.) mixed vegetables, drained
8 brown-and-serve sausages
1 cup complete pancake mix
1 cup water

Melt butter in a small saucepan. Blend in flour, salt, nutmeg, and pepper. Cook, stirring constantly, until bubbly. Stir in milk; continue cooking and stirring until sauce thickens and boils 1 minute; stir in vegetables; keep hot.

Heat sausages as label directs; keep hot.

Combine pancake mix and water in a small bowl; stir until almost smooth. Using a scant 2 tablespoons batter for each, bake eight 4-inch pancakes on greased heated griddle.

Roll a pancake around each sausage, jelly-roll fashion; place two rolls on a serving plate. Spoon vegetable sauce over top. Serve hot.

Yield: 4 servings.

KNOCKWURST BAKE

1 medium onion, chopped (½ cup)
1 small green pepper, quartered, seeded, and
   chopped (½ cup)
¾ cup chopped celery
2 tablespoons salad oil
1 lb. knockwurst
2 tablespoons prepared hot spicy mustard
1 can (10¾ ozs.) condensed bean with bacon soup
1⅓ cups water
1 package (12 ozs.) corn-muffin mix
   Egg
   Milk

Sauté onion, green pepper, and celery in salad oil until soft in a large skillet; push to one side.

Peel casings from knockwurst; slice knockwurst ¼ inch thick; stir into skillet and brown lightly.

Stir in mustard, soup, and water; heat, stirring several times, to boiling. Spoon into a shallow baking dish, 11¾x7½x1¾ inches.

Preheat oven to 375°.

Prepare corn-muffin mix with egg and milk as label directs; spoon over meat mixture in baking dish.

Bake 30 minutes, or until topping is puffed and golden.

Yield: 6 servings.

CONFETTI SAUSAGE BAKE

2 cans (12 ozs. each) Mexican-style corn
  Milk
3 eggs
½ teaspoon salt
⅛ teaspoon pepper
1 package (8 ozs.) brown-and-serve sausages

Preheat oven to 325°.

Drain liquid from corn into a 2-cup measure; add milk to make 1½ cups.

Beat eggs in a medium bowl until blended; stir in the 1½ cups liquid, corn, salt, and pepper. Pour into a 1½-quart shallow baking dish. Bake 30 minutes.

While corn bakes, brown sausages in a skillet; arrange in a row on top of partly baked corn mixture.

Bake 20 minutes longer, or until custard is set.

Yield: 4 servings.

KIELBASA AND CABBAGE

1 head green cabbage, weighing about 2 lbs.
3 tablespoons butter or margarine
¼ cup firmly packed brown sugar
⅓ cup cider vinegar
2 teaspoons caraway seeds
1 teaspoon salt
1 ring fully-cooked kielbasa (Polish sausage),
    weighing about 1 lb.

Trim cabbage and cut into quarters, then shred, discarding core. (There should be 8 cups.)

Melt butter in a large skillet; add cabbage and sauté, stirring several times, 3 minutes. Stir in brown sugar, vinegar, caraway seeds, and salt.

Cut kielbasa into 8 pieces; arrange over cabbage; cover tightly.

Simmer 15 minutes, or until cabbage is crisp-tender.

Serve from skillet, or arrange kielbasa around edge on a deep serving platter; spoon cabbage in a mound in center.

Yield: 4 servings.

GLAZED COLD-CUT STEAKS

1 lb. piece chopped ham
⅓ cup light molasses
2 tablespoons prepared mustard
2 tablespoons cider vinegar
1 teaspoon Worcestershire sauce
  Few drops red-pepper seasoning

Preheat broiler.

Peel casing, if there is one, from chopped ham; cut meat into 4 thick slices. Cut each slice in half diagonally; thread onto 2 long skewers; place on rack in broiler pan.

Combine molasses, mustard, vinegar, Worcestershire sauce, and red-pepper seasoning in a small saucepan; heat to boiling. Brush part over meat.

Broil, 8 inches from heat, turning often and brushing with remaining molasses mixture, 15 minutes, or until richly glazed.

Yield: 4 servings.

BOLOGNA RUFFLES

⅓ cup orange marmalade
1 teaspoon prepared mustard with onions
1 tablespoon water
2 packages (6 ozs. each) sliced large round
    bologna
12 preserved kumquats
8 large pitted prunes
2 large firm bananas, peeled and each cut into 4
    chunks

Combine orange marmalade, mustard, and water in a small saucepan; heat slowly until marmalade melts.

Preheat broiler.

Fold each slice of bologna around a kumquat to form a flower; thread onto 4 long skewers, alternately with prunes and banana chunks. Place on rack in broiler pan. Brush part of the orange sauce over each.

Broil, 6 inches from heat, turning several times and brushing with remaining sauce, 10 minutes, or until heated through and richly glazed.

Yield: 4 servings.

QUICK POLENTA PIE

1 package (8 ozs.) brown-and-serve sausages
1 package (12 ozs.) corn muffin mix
1 egg
¼ cup milk
1 can (8 ozs.) cream-style corn
1 tablespoon chopped parsley
1 cup boiling water
2 single-serving envelopes tomato soup mix
½ teaspoon Worcestershire sauce

Preheat oven to 400°. Grease a 1½-quart shallow baking dish; line with waxed paper; grease paper.

Brown sausages in a medium skillet; arrange, spoke fashion, in baking dish.

Prepare muffin mix with egg and milk as label directs; stir in corn and parsley; pour evenly over sausages.

Bake 35 minutes, or until puffed and golden.

While pie bakes, stir boiling water into soup mix in a small bowl; stir in Worcestershire sauce.

Loosen pie around edge with a knife; invert onto a large serving plate; peel off paper. Cut pie into wedges; spoon tomato sauce over each serving.

Yield: 4 servings.

SAUSAGE-STUFFED SQUASH BOATS

2 medium acorn squashes
1 can (8 ozs.) apricot halves, drained well
1 lb. sausage meat
½ cup quick-cooking rolled oats
1 small onion, chopped (¼ cup)
1 egg
1 tablespoon chopped parsley
¼ cup milk
   Salt
   Pepper

Preheat oven to 350°.

Cut squashes in half lengthwise; scoop out seeds. Place halves, cut sides down, in a shallow baking pan; pour ¼ cup water into pan.

Bake 15 minutes.

Chop apricots; combine with sausage, rolled oats, onion, egg, parsley, milk, and ¼ teaspoon salt in a large bowl; mix well. (Mixture will be soft.) Shape into 16 small balls; place, not touching, in a single layer in a second shallow baking pan.

Bake in same oven with squashes 30 minutes.

Remove squashes from oven; turn halves rightside up. Sprinkle salt and pepper lightly into hollows; place sausage balls in hollows.

Bake 30 minutes longer, or until squashes are tender and sausage is crusty brown.

Lift squashes onto a large serving platter. Garnish with parsley if you like.

Yield: 4 servings.

OVEN SAUSAGES AND BEANS

1 medium onion, chopped (½ cup)
1 tablespoon salad oil
1 can (16 ozs.) red kidney beans, drained
1 can (16 ozs.) pork-and-beans in tomato sauce
⅓ cup firmly packed light brown sugar
½ cup catsup
1 tablespoon prepared hot spicy mustard
½ teaspoon salt
1 package (12 ozs.) smoked sausage links

Sauté onion in salad oil until soft in a large skillet; stir in kidney beans, pork-and-beans and sauce, brown sugar, catsup, mustard, and salt. Heat slowly, stirring several times, to boiling.

Preheat oven to 350°.

Set aside 3 of the sausages for topping; slice remainder; stir into bean mixture. Spoon into a 1½-quart baking dish.

Bake 45 minutes.

Split remaining 3 sausages; arrange, spoke fashion, on top of beans.

Bake 15 minutes longer, or until sausages are hot.

Yield: 6 servings.

SAUSAGE ROLL UPS

1 can (21 ozs.) cherry pie filling
½ teaspoon ground cinnamon
¼ cup water
1 package (8 ozs.) brown-and-serve sausages
1½ cups complete pancake mix
1½ cups milk
Salad oil

Combine cherry pie filling, cinnamon, and water in a medium saucepan; heat slowly to boiling; keep hot while making pancakes.

Heat sausages as label directs; keep hot.

Heat griddle as manufacturer directs.

Combine pancake mix and milk in a medium bowl; stir until batter is almost smooth.

Grease griddle lightly with salad oil. For each 4-inch pancake, ladle a scant ¼ cup batter onto griddle. Bake 2 to 3 minutes, or until underside is golden; turn; bake 1 to 2 minutes longer until bottom browns. (If batter thickens as you work, stir in a few more tablespoons milk.)

As each pancake is baked, roll around a sausage; place on serving plates; top with hot cherry sauce.

Yield: 4 to 6 servings.

SAUSAGE PIZZA

2 cups biscuit mix
½ cup water
1 jar (15 ozs.) meatless spaghetti sauce
½ teaspoon dried oregano, crushed
1 can (3 or 4 ozs.) sliced mushrooms, drained
1 package (8 ozs.) brown-and-serve sausages, split lengthwise
1 cup shredded mozzarella cheese (4 ozs.)

Preheat oven to 425°.

Combine biscuit mix and water in a medium bowl; mix until evenly moist. Turn out onto a lightly floured board; knead 1 minute. Press evenly into a lightly greased 12-inch pizza pan; flute edge.

Combine spaghetti sauce and oregano in a medium saucepan; heat to boiling; spread over crust.

Sprinkle mushrooms over sauce; arrange sausage halves, spoke fashion, on top; sprinkle cheese over all.

Bake 20 minutes, or until crust is lightly browned. Cut into wedges.

Yield: 4 servings.

STUFFED HAM ROLLS

2 tablespoons finely chopped onion
2 tablespoons butter or margarine
½ cup water
1½ cups packaged corn-bread stuffing mix
½ teaspoon dried rosemary, crushed
3 packages (4 or 5 ozs. each) long slices boiled ham
1 can (29 ozs.) cling peach halves in syrup
⅓ cup orange marmalade
1 tablespoon cider vinegar
½ teaspoon dry mustard

Sauté onion in butter until soft in a small skillet; stir in water; heat to boiling. Pour over stuffing mix and rosemary in a medium bowl; toss until evenly moist.

Spoon stuffing mixture evenly over ham slices; starting at a short end of each, roll up, jelly-roll fashion; fasten with wooden picks. Place in a greased large shallow baking pan.

Preheat oven to 375°.

Drain syrup from peaches into a small bowl; arrange peaches around ham in pan. Combine ¼ cup of the peach syrup, marmalade, vinegar, and mustard in a small saucepan; heat, stirring constantly, to boiling. Brush part over ham and fruit.

Bake, turning several times and brushing with remaining marmalade mixture, 40 minutes, or until richly glazed.

Arrange ham rolls, spoke fashion, on a large serving platter; overlap peach halves in center.

Yield: 6 servings.

MEXICAN FRANKS AND BEANS

1 large onion, chopped (1 cup)
1 cup chopped celery
2 tablespoons salad oil
1 lb. frankfurters, sliced in ½-inch rounds
1½ teaspoons chili powder
¼ teaspoon dried thyme, crushed
1 can (8 ozs.) tomato sauce
2 cans (16 ozs. each) home-style pork and beans
1 cup shredded sharp Cheddar cheese (4 ozs.)

Preheat oven to 350°.

Sauté onion and celery in salad oil in a large skillet until soft; push to one side. Add frankfurters and brown lightly. Stir in chili powder and thyme; cook 1 minute longer.

Stir in tomato sauce and beans and liquid; heat slowly to boiling; spoon into a 2-quart shallow baking dish. Sprinkle cheese over top.

Bake 20 minutes, or until bubbly in center and cheese melts.

Yield: 6 servings.

HOT-DOG WINDERS

8 frankfurters
2 large dill pickles
1 package refrigerated crescent rolls
2 tablespoons sesame seeds
2 tablespoons butter or margarine
2 tablespoons all-purpose flour
1 teaspoon salt
1 cup milk
1 egg
2 tablespoons horseradish-mustard

Preheat oven to 400°.

Slit frankfurters lengthwise not quite to bottom. Quarter pickles lengthwise; stuff a strip into each frankfurter.

Unroll crescent dough and place the two halves, long sides together, to form a large rectangle; pinch dough together at perforations so it will be smooth. Cut crosswise into 8 even strips. Wrap each strip around a stuffed frankfurter to resemble a barber pole; roll in sesame seeds on waxed paper. Place on a cookie sheet.

Bake 15 minutes, or until golden.

While frankfurters bake, melt butter in a small saucepan; blend in flour and salt. Cook, stirring constantly, until bubbly. Stir in milk; continue cooking and stirring until mixture thickens and boils 1 minute.

Beat egg in a small bowl; beat in about half of the hot mixture, then stir back into saucepan. Cook 1 minute; remove from heat. Stir in horseradish-mustard. Spoon over frankfurters or serve hot as a dip.

Yield: 4 servings.

JAMAICAN BOLOGNA STEAKS

¾ lb. chunk of large bologna
1 can (13¼ ozs.) pineapple chunks in syrup
2 tablespoons water
¼ cup firmly packed brown sugar
1 teaspoon dry mustard
¼ teaspoon ground allspice
3 gingersnaps, crushed

Peel casing from bologna; cut meat into 4 even slices; place in a single layer in a shallow baking dish.

Preheat oven to 350°.

Drain syrup from pineapple into a small saucepan; stir in water, brown sugar, mustard, and allspice; heat, stirring constantly, to boiling. Pour over bologna; cover.

Bake 20 minutes; uncover.

Spoon pineapple over meat, then spoon sauce in dish over all.

Bake, spooning syrup over top several times, 20 minutes longer, or until pineapple and meat are lightly glazed.

Lift meat and fruit onto a large serving platter with a slotted pancake turner; keep warm.

Pour sauce into a small saucepan; stir in crushed gingersnaps. Heat, stirring several times, to boiling. Serve separately to spoon over meat.

Yield: 4 servings.

CURRIED FRANKFURTER KABOBS

8 frankfurters
2 medium-sized green peppers
4 medium-sized green-tipped bananas
16 pitted ripe olives
4 tablespoons butter or margarine
2 teaspoons curry powder
1 tablespoon all-purpose flour
1 envelope instant chicken broth
¾ cup water

Cut each frankfurter crosswise into thirds. Cut green peppers in half and seed; cut into 24 squares. Peel bananas and cut into quarters. Thread each 3 pieces of frankfurter onto a long skewer with 3 pieces green pepper, 2 pieces banana, and 2 olives.

Preheat broiler.

Melt butter in a small saucepan; stir in curry powder; cook 2 minutes. Stir in flour and chicken broth; cook, stirring constantly, until bubbly. Stir in water; continue cooking and stirring until mixture thickens and boils 1 minute.

Place skewers on rack in broiler pan; brush part of the curry sauce over each.

Broil, 8 inches from heat, turning and brushing several times with remaining curry sauce, 10 minutes, or until hot and glazed.

Yield: 4 servings.

FRANKFURTERS TERIYAKI

8 frankfurters
½ cup soy sauce
2 tablespoons dry sherry
1 tablespoon salad oil
1 small onion, grated
1 small garlic clove, crushed
1 teaspoon ground ginger
1 can (about 15 ozs.) sliced pineapple, drained
1 tablespoon butter or margarine
8 spiced whole crabapples, well drained

Score frankfurters every ¼ inch; arrange in a single layer in a shallow dish.

Mix soy sauce, sherry, salad oil, onion, gar-

lic, and ginger in a cup; pour evenly over frankfurters. Let stand, turning once or twice, 2 hours to season.

Preheat broiler.

Sauté pineapple slices in butter in a large skillet until lightly browned; keep warm.

Remove frankfurters from soy mixture; place at least 2 inches apart on rack in broiler pan. (Frankfurters will curl as they cook.)

Broil, 8 inches from heat, turning and brushing often with soy mixture, 10 minutes, or until puffed and richly glazed.

Place each two frankfurters on a serving plate; top each with a pineapple slice. Tuck crabapples into hollows in pineapple slices.

Yield: 4 servings.

MOCK QUICHE

1½ cups finely crushed unsalted crackers
2 tablespoons butter or margarine, melted
1 package (6 ozs.) sliced boiled ham, diced (about 1½ cups)
1 large onion, chopped (1 cup)
2 tablespoons salad oil
6 slices process Swiss cheese, cut into strips
3 eggs
1¼ cups milk
1 teaspoon salt
¼ teaspoon pepper

Preheat oven to 325°.

Toss cracker crumbs with melted butter in a 9-inch pie plate; pat over bottom and up side of plate to form a crust.

Sauté ham and onion in salad oil in a medium skillet until onion is soft; spread in bottom of crust. Place cheese strips over ham mixture.

Beat eggs slightly with milk, salt, and pepper in a small bowl; pour into crust.

Bake 30 minutes, or until a knife inserted near center comes out clean. Cool 5 minutes on a wire rack; cut into wedges.

Yield: 6 servings.

FRANK-POTATO BAKE

1 package white sauce mix
  Milk
½ teaspoon instant minced onion
3 medium potatoes, cooked, peeled, and sliced
6 frankfurters, sliced diagonally
1 can (8 ozs.) lima beans, drained
2 slices process American cheese, shredded

Prepare white sauce mix with milk as label directs to make 1 cup sauce; stir in onion.

Preheat oven to 350°.

Layer half of the potatoes into a 1-quart baking dish. Top with half of the frankfurters, all of the lima beans, remaining potatoes, and remaining frankfurters. Pour sauce over all; sprinkle cheese on top.

Bake 30 minutes, or until bubbly in center.

Yield: 4 servings.

WESTERN PANCAKE PLATES

4 medium apples
¼ cup butter or margarine
⅓ cup pancake syrup
1 small onion, minced (¼ cup)
2 tablespoons minced green pepper
  Salad oil
2 cups biscuit mix
1 egg
1½ cups milk
1 package (8 ozs.) brown-and-serve sausages

Quarter apples, but do not pare; core; cut each quarter into 3 wedges.

Melt butter in a large skillet; stir in syrup; heat to boiling. Place apples in a single layer in skillet, turning to coat with syrup.

Simmer, spooning syrup over slices several times, 7 minutes, or until apples are richly glazed and tender but still firm enough to hold their shape; keep hot.

Sauté onion and green pepper in 2 tablespoons salad oil until soft in a medium skillet; remove from heat.

Combine biscuit mix, egg, and milk in a medium bowl; beat until smooth; stir in onion mixture.

Heat griddle as manufacturer directs; grease lightly with salad oil. For each pancake, pour ¼ cup batter onto griddle; spread into a 5-inch round. Bake 2 minutes, or until bubbles appear on top and underside is golden; turn. Bake 1 to 2 minutes longer, or until golden on bottom.

As pancakes bake, heat sausages as label directs.

For each serving, stack 3 or 4 pancakes on a serving plate; arrange sausages and apple wedges around edge. Serve with butter or margarine and pancake syrup.

Yield: 4 servings.

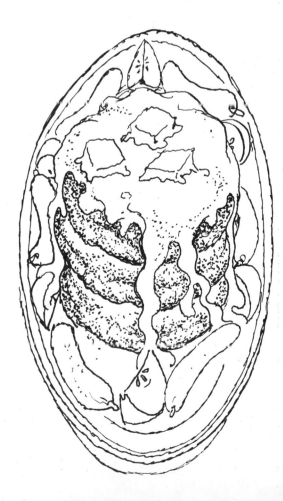

STUFFED FRANKFURTERS

8 slices bacon
1 small onion, minced (¼ cup)
¼ cup chopped celery
⅓ cup water
2 cups cereal wheat flakes, coarsely crushed
1 teaspoon dried shredded parsley
¼ teaspoon salt
8 frankfurters

Sauté bacon in a medium skillet just until fat starts to cook out; remove slices and drain on paper toweling. Pour off all fat, then measure 1 tablespoon and return to skillet.

Add onion and celery to drippings; sauté until soft. Stir in water; heat to boiling.

Combine cereal, parsley, and salt in a medium bowl; pour onion mixture over top; toss until evenly moist.

Preheat oven to 400°.

Cut a slit in each frankfurter almost to bottom; spoon stuffing mixture into slits, using a heaping tablespoon for each. Wrap a slice of bacon around each, holding in place at ends with wooden picks. Place frankfurters, stuffing side up, in a 1½-quart shallow baking dish.

Bake 20 minutes, or until stuffing is brown and crusty and bacon is crisp.

Yield: 4 servings.

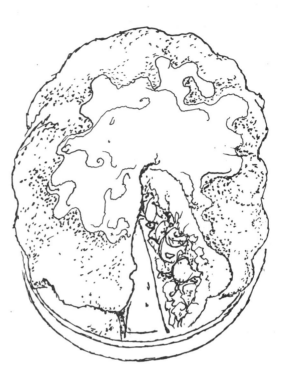

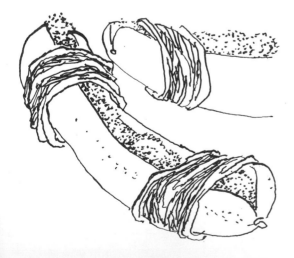

OVEN HOT-DOG HASH

3 cups frozen hashed brown potatoes, slightly thawed
1 small onion, finely chopped (¼ cup)
2 tablespoons all-purpose flour
½ teaspoon salt
⅛ teaspoon pepper
¼ cup evaporated milk
6 frankfurters, sliced thin
2 tablespoons butter or margarine
½ cup shredded process American cheese

Preheat oven to 400°.

Combine potatoes, onion, flour, salt, and pepper in a medium bowl; mix lightly.

Stir in milk and frankfurters. Spoon into a 9-inch pie plate; dot butter over top; cover.

Bake 45 minutes; uncover. Sprinkle cheese over top.

Bake 5 minutes longer, or until cheese melts and browns lightly.

Cut in wedges; lift onto serving plates with a pancake turner.

Yield: 4 servings.

POULTRY

CHICKEN AND TURKEY SET A STYLISH PACE THESE DAYS, and supermarkets go all out the year round to offer you a wide selection of packs and parts to suit your taste, your purse, or a special recipe. Cooking for two or two dozen poses no problem either, for you can easily count noses and buy enough drumsticks for everyone, or splurge on a showy 25-pound bird to carve with a flourish. Luckily, both are such versatile meats that no one ever seems to tire of seeing them on a menu.

Knowing how to buy any kind of poultry is as important as understanding how to cook it properly, so this chapter starts with a rundown on what's available. For beginner cooks, it's a learning guide, and because so many new products come on the market constantly, experienced hands will find it a simple brush-up course.

Read on for dozens of recipes and ideas on how to bake, broil, sauté, simmer, and roast these adaptable choices. Many suggest easy, economical dishes for family meals and informal parties as well as ways to turn leftovers into second-day treats; others are the elegant specialties that everyone looks for at holiday time. If your taste turns to duckling and goose, you'll find help here, too.

In planning your family's menus, remember that when you consider poultry you also think good health, for chicken and turkey, particularly, are high in protein and some of the B vitamins and low in fat, cholesterol, and calories.

TYPES OF CHICKEN

What kind you buy depends upon how you plan to cook it and how many servings you need. Except for Rock Cornish hens, allow ¾ pound for each serving. A whole 1-pound Cornish hen, or a half if the bird weighs 1½ pounds, makes an individual serving. These are your choices:

Broiler-fryer–A versatile all-purpose bird, it weighs from 1½ to 3 pounds, and is sold whole, split, quartered, or cut in pieces. Regardless of the name, it may be roasted, fried, simmered, baked, or broiled. Many markets now pack two or three whole broiler-fryers in a transparent bag for several cents a pound less than those that are cut up. If you have a freezer or entertain often, you can save a little—even more if you buy at sales—by being your own meat cutter. These birds are so tender they're a snap to cut with poultry shears or a knife.

EASTER SUNDAY BAKED HAM (p.145)
APPLE-STUFFED YAMS (p.310)
MACARONI CARBONARA (p.279)
BROCCOLI-HAM ROLLS (p.119)

Roaster–A little older and larger than the broiler-fryer, it usually weighs from 3½ to 6 pounds. The smaller ones are ideal for a small family dinner roast with no leftovers. If you're making a salad or a casserole that calls for cooked chicken meat, you'll be pennies ahead if you start with a roaster since it yields more meat than a younger bird.

Capon–Birds in this class weigh from 4 to 7 pounds and have a generous quantity of white meat. They usually carry a higher price tag than other types of chicken, but are popular when roasted for holiday meals.

Stewing hen or fowl–Both are plump, meaty, mature hens about 1½ years old and weigh from 4½ to 6 pounds. Most come whole or cut up and are attractively priced. Because of their age, they take long simmering to make them tender, but say some cooks, are the only choices for soup, stew, or old-fashioned fricassee with fluffy dumplings.

Rock Cornish Hen–These small, specially bred chickens weigh 1½ pounds or less and may be roasted, baked, broiled, or fried.

TYPES OF TURKEY

In figuring what size turkey to buy, remember that the giblets and neck are included in the weight of a whole bird. A good rule of thumb is to allow 1 pound per serving if the turkey weighs 12 pounds or less, or ½ to ¾ pound per serving for heavier birds. If the turkey is already stuffed, figure about 1½ pounds per serving. These are your choices:

Whole Turkey–Some are available fresh, but most come frozen. These are ready-to-cook birds with the giblets and neck packed in a little bag and tucked into the body cavity. Weights range from 4 to 25 pounds; the 10- to 12-pounders are the most popular sizes. Many of these birds are also self-basting.

Half Turkey—Large whole birds are split lengthwise to make 8- to 12-pound roasts. A good point to remember is that half of a 20-pound bird will probably cost less than a whole 10-pound one, and have more meat in proportion to bone. In some stores, you'll also find turkey quarters, and in this case, the bird has been split lengthwise and crosswise.

Frozen Stuffed Turkey–Available in a wide range of sizes, these birds should go directly from freezer to oven. Follow roasting directions exactly as printed on the label.

Fryer-roaster–These tender young birds average 4 to 9 pounds and are a perfect size to fry, roast, broil, or spin on a rotisserie.

Turkey Breast–One of the newest members of the turkey family, it is also fast becoming one of the most popular among those who prefer white meat. Look for this elegant roast either fresh or frozen in weights from 3 to 9 pounds.

Frozen Boneless Roasts–Some are available as boned, tied rolls weighing 3 to 5 pounds; others, as small 2-pound loaf-shaped roasts that come in their own foil roasting pans. You'll find a selection of dark or light meat or a combination of the two.

Turkey Parts–Following the popularity of cut-up chicken, turkey drumsticks, wings,

◀ **HAM JUBILEE** (p.146)
SUNSHINE SUCCOTASH (p.309)

thighs, necks, half breasts, and cutlets (thin slices of breast meat) are now being featured, both fresh and frozen.

Smoked Turkey–Choose either ready-to-eat or ready-to-cook varieties. Since the meat is rich, slice it paper-thin. These roasts are most popular for parties and holidays.

DUCKLING

These birds are now enjoyed for everyday family meals and barbecues as well as for holidays. In some areas they're sold fresh, but most come frozen. They usually weigh about 5 pounds—a perfect size for 4 servings. For the easiest, neatest way of carving, simply quarter the bird with poultry shears.

GOOSE

While some markets stock these birds year round, you'll find them most often in the freezer cabinets at Christmastime. Stores that accept special orders may even be able to get one for you fresh.

Like duckling, goose is a fatty bird, so pull out as much of the fat from the body cavity and from under the skin as possible before roasting. Weights range from 6 to 14 pounds, although most weigh from 8 to 10 pounds. Allow from ½ to ¾ pound for a serving.

How to store poultry

Chill any type fresh bird as soon as possible after you buy it. Place the bird on a plate or tray, cover loosely with waxed paper or transparent wrap, and store it in the coldest part of the refrigerator. Store giblets separately in a covered container. Plan to use any fresh bird within two days after purchase.

For longer storage, depend on your freezer. Remove all store wrappings and giblets from bird, then rewrap in regular freezer paper that keeps out air and moisture; seal, label, date, and freeze. Two important points to remember: Never freeze an uncooked stuffed bird and never refreeze poultry that's thawed unless it has been cooked first.

Remember safety first when storing cooked poultry. Place it in the refrigerator immediately after mealtime, and use it within two days. If it must be held longer, divide the meat into meal-sized amounts and freeze it. Chill leftover gravy and stuffing separately from the meat.

How to thaw poultry

It's always best to thaw unstuffed frozen poultry in its original wrapper in the refrigerator. A 3-pound chicken will take about 12 hours, a 12- to 16-pound turkey from two to three days, and a 6- to 10-pound goose from one to two days.

If you must speed up the thawing, place the wrapped bird in a large pan and cover with cold water. Change the water often so it stays cold. As soon as the bird is thawed, remove it from the wrapper, take out the giblets and neck, rinse the bird well, and place it in the refrigerator until cooking time. Any bird that's been thawed in water should be cooked within a day.

How to roast whole chickens

Remove giblets from cavity of chicken and save to simmer for gravy or soup. Rinse chicken inside and out and pat dry with paper toweling. Sprinkle salt and pepper lightly inside body and neck cavities and on the outside of the bird.

If bird is to be stuffed, make your choice of stuffings (see index for recipes) just before roasting time. Pack stuffing lightly into neck cavity; smooth neck skin over stuffing and skewer to back of bird. Twist wing tips flat against back. Stuff body cavity; close with poultry pins and string; tie legs together. Place bird, breast side up, on a rack in a shallow roasting pan; brush melted butter or margarine all over bird. Do not cover pan or add any water.

If you're roasting smaller chickens without stuffing, place a quartered onion or a handful of celery tops or parsley in the body cavity for extra flavor, and truss the same as stuffed birds.

Roast bird, using the timetable on page 165 as a guide. During roasting, brush bird several more times with melted butter. To test for doneness, pinch the thickest part of a drumstick; it should feel very soft. When the chicken is tender, the drumstick should also move up and down easily.

When figuring roasting time, plan to take the chicken out of the oven about 20 minutes before serving. It's easier to carve if it stands for awhile.

Place finished chicken on its serving platter; take out skewers and cut away string; keep bird warm while making gravy.

How to roast a whole turkey

If turkey is frozen, thaw it in its original wrapper in the refrigerator. Allow one or two days for an 8- to 11-lb. bird, two to three days for one weighing 11 to 14 lbs., and slightly longer for larger weights. Plan to cook a thawed bird within two days and keep it chilled until cooking time.

Remove giblets and neck from cavities of bird, and set aside for GIBLET GRAVY (recipe on page 191). Rinse bird inside and out and pat dry with paper toweling. Salt cavities lightly; stuff with your choice of dressings suggested on page 190, allowing ¾ cup stuffing for each pound of turkey. Skewer neck skin to back and twist wing tips flat against back. Depending on the brand of turkey, push drumsticks under band of skin at the tail, close with the stuffing clamp that comes with the bird, or close body opening with poultry pins and string and tie legs to tail.

Place bird, breast side up, on a rack in a shallow roasting pan. Brush melted butter, margarine, or salad oil generously over skin to keep it from drying. Insert meat thermometer into center of thigh next to body, making sure that the bulb does not touch bone or stuffing. Do not cover pan or add any water.

Roast at 325°, following timetable on page 165. (If turkey is not stuffed, figure about 1 hour less cooking time.) Remember, too, that timetables are guides only, since the temperature of the bird when it goes into the oven and the accuracy of the oven affect cooking. So it pays to start checking for doneness during the last hour of roasting.

If turkey is prebasted, there's no need to baste during the roasting period; otherwise, brush the bird several times as it cooks with the drippings in the pan or more melted butter or margarine. If, during cooking, the turkey seems to be browning too fast, cover it loosely with a sheet of foil.

When the bird is done, the thermometer should register 180° to 185°, a drumstick should move up and down and twist easily at the joint, and the thickest part of the drumstick should feel very soft when pressed with fingers.

Place roasted bird on a large serving platter; let stand at room temperature 20 minutes for easier carving. Garnish platter with any of the suggestions from GAR-NISHES chapter.

How to make pan gravy

Gravy tastes best when prepared right in the roasting pan since the baked-on brown bits in the bottom add a savory flavor.

No matter how much gravy you're making, always use 1 tablespoon fat and 1 tablespoon flour with 1 cup of liquid for thin gravy; if you prefer it thicker, use 2 tablespoons fat, 2 tablespoons flour, and 1 cup liquid.

After the bird comes from the oven, pour all the fat from the roasting pan into a small bowl, then measure the amount you need back into the roasting pan. Stir in the flour until mixture is smooth. Cook slowly, stirring constantly, until mixture bubbles. Slowly stir in the liquid; continue cooking and stirring until gravy thickens and boils 1 minute. Season with salt and pepper as needed.

For the liquid, use giblet broth, water, or consommé, or part of any of these with part wine. For cream gravy, substitute milk or light cream for all or part of the liquid you need.

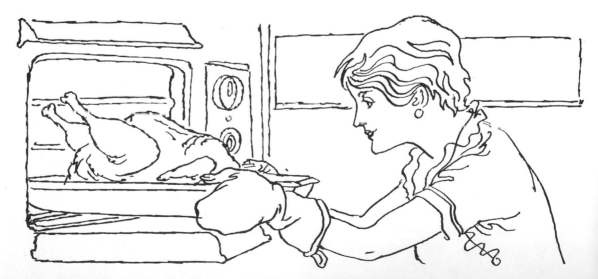

ROASTING TIMETABLE FOR WHOLE CHICKENS

Kind	Purchased Weight	Oven Temperature	Approximate Time*
Broiler-fryer	1½ to 2 lbs.	400°	1 to 1¼ hours
Broiler-fryer	2 to 2½ lbs.	400°	1¼ to 1½ hours
Broiler-fryer	2½ to 3 lbs.	375°	1½ to 2 hours
Roaster	3½ to 5 lbs.	350°	2½ to 3½ hours
Capon	5 to 8 lbs.	350°	2½ to 3½ hours
Cornish Hen	1 to 2 lbs.	375°	1 to 1½ hours

*Times given refer to stuffed birds. Subtract from 15 to 30 minutes from the total if bird is not stuffed.

ROASTING TIMETABLE FOR WHOLE TURKEY
Oven Temperature: 325°

Purchased Weight	Approximate Time
8 to 11 lbs.	4½ to 4¾ hours
11 to 14 lbs.	4¾ to 5½ hours
14 to 20 lbs.	5½ to 6 hours
20 to 24 lbs.	6 to 7 hours

THE ART OF CARVING ROAST TURKEY OR CHICKEN

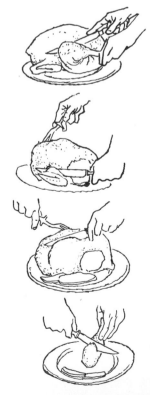

Place bird on platter with drumsticks to carver's right. Holding onto leg, gently bend it down toward platter, cutting through thigh joint to separate the whole piece from frame. Set piece on another plate; cut through joint to separate thigh and drumstick.

Steady bird by sticking a fork into meat near breastbone, then cut off wing the same as leg. Slanting the knife in slightly may make it easier to hit the joint. Place wing on plate with drumstick.

Slice white meat, starting at tip of breastbone and cutting down to wing joint. Slice enough for first servings, then carve dark meat.

Hold drumstick upright and slice meat downward, turning drumstick as needed to get uniform slices. Carve thigh meat in long thin slices parallel to bone. If you need seconds, turn platter and start over again. Drumsticks and thighs from small birds are usually served whole.

CHICKEN

ORANGE-GLAZED ROAST CHICKEN

1 roasting chicken, weighing about 5½ lbs.
  Salt
5 tablespoons butter or margarine
1 small onion, chopped (¼ cup)
½ cup water
1 can (6 ozs.) frozen concentrate for orange juice (¾ cup)
1 package (8 ozs.) herb-seasoned stuffing mix
¼ cup light corn syrup
½ teaspoon dry mustard

Rinse chicken inside and out; pat dry with paper toweling. Salt cavities lightly.

Melt butter in a small saucepan; measure out 1 tablespoon and set aside for brushing chicken.

Preheat oven to 350°.

Stir onion into rest of melted butter in saucepan; sauté until soft. Stir in water and ½ cup of the orange concentrate; heat to boiling. Pour over stuffing mix in a bowl; toss until evenly moist.

Stuff into neck and body cavities of chicken. Skewer neck skin to back; twist wing tips flat against back. Fasten body opening with skewers and string; tie legs to tail. Place chicken, breast side up, on a rack in a small roasting pan. Brush the melted butter over chicken.

Roast 2¼ hours.

While chicken cooks, combine remaining ¼ cup orange concentrate, corn syrup, and mustard in a small saucepan; heat to boiling; brush part over chicken.

Continue roasting, brushing two or three more times with remaining orange mixture, 45 minutes, or until chicken is tender and richly glazed. Lift onto a large serving platter; pull out skewers and cut away string. Carve chicken into serving-sized pieces.

Yield: 6 to 8 servings.

DUTCH OVEN CHICKEN

1 roasting chicken, weighing about 3½ lbs.
1½ teaspoons salt
¼ teaspoon pepper
1 can (10¾ ozs.) condensed golden mushroom soup
½ cup dry white wine
8 small potatoes, pared
6 medium carrots, pared and cut diagonally into 1-inch chunks
4 small zucchini, trimmed and cut in 1-inch rounds

Preheat oven to 350°.

Rinse chicken inside and out; pat dry with paper toweling.

Mix salt and pepper in a cup; sprinkle into cavities and over outside of chicken. Place in a Dutch oven or large baking dish.

Mix soup and wine in a small bowl; pour around chicken; cover.

Bake 1 hour and 15 minutes. Place potatoes and carrots in gravy around chicken; cover. Bake 45 minutes.

Place zucchini in Dutch oven; cover. Bake 15 minutes, or until chicken and vegetables are tender.

Lift chicken onto a large serving platter; remove vegetables with a slotted spoon and arrange around chicken. Pour gravy into a serving bowl and pass separately to spoon over chicken.

Yield: 4 to 6 servings.

CHICKEN MONTEREY

6 chicken breasts, weighing about 10 ozs. each
1 cup chopped dried apricots
½ cup water
⅔ cup chopped celery
1 medium onion, chopped (½ cup)
½ cup butter or margarine
5 cups fresh bread cubes (about 10 slices)
1 teaspoon salt
1 can (5½ ozs.) apricot nectar
2 tablespoons honey
1 tablespoon Worcestershire sauce
2 tablespoons cornstarch
  Sweet Potatoes Almondine (recipe on page 310)
  Chicory or curly endive

Rinse chicken breasts and dry on paper toweling. Bone each, leaving skin in place.

Combine apricots and water in a small saucepan. Heat to boiling, then cook 3 minutes; set aside.

Sauté celery and onion in ¼ cup of the butter in a small skillet until soft; drizzle over bread cubes in a medium bowl; add apricots and liquid and salt; toss until evenly moist.

Place chicken breasts flat, skin side down, on counter top. Divide stuffing mixture evenly onto each breast; fold sides over stuffing to cover completely; fasten with wooden picks. Place, skin side up, in a baking pan, 13x9x2 inches.

Preheat oven to 350°.

Melt remaining ¼ cup butter; brush over chicken breasts.

Bake 30 minutes.

Mix ¼ cup of the apricot nectar, honey, and Worcestershire sauce in a cup; brush part over chicken. Continue baking, brushing once with remaining honey mixture, 30 minutes, or until chicken is tender. Remove to another pan; keep warm while making sauce.

Pour drippings from pan into a 2-cup measure; let stand a few minutes until fat rises to top, then skim off; add remaining apricot nectar and water, if needed, to drippings to make 1½ cups. Return to pan; heat to boiling.

Blend cornstarch with a little water until smooth in a cup; stir into boiling liquid. Cook, stirring constantly, until sauce thickens and boils 3 minutes.

Take wooden picks from chicken breasts. Arrange breasts, spoke fashion, on a heated large serving platter; overlap Almondine Sweet Potatoes in between. Tuck sprigs of chicory around potatoes. Pass sauce separately to spoon over chicken.

Yield: 6 servings.

CHICKEN CHASSEUR

1 cooked whole broiler-fryer (from Pot-roasted
    Chicken on page 170)
1 small onion, chopped (¼ cup)
2 tablespoons butter or margarine
4 large fresh mushrooms, trimmed and sliced
1 tablespoon all-purpose flour
¾ cup dry white wine
1 tablespoon lemon juice
1 teaspoon sugar
⅛ teaspoon salt
2 medium tomatoes, peeled and diced

Preheat oven to 350°.

Cut chicken into quarters or pieces with poultry shears; place in a single layer in a large shallow baking dish.

Sauté onion in butter until soft in a medium skillet; push to one side. Add mushrooms and sauté 2 to 3 minutes. Sprinkle flour over top, then stir in with wine, lemon juice, sugar, salt, and tomatoes. Heat, stirring constantly, to boiling; pour over chicken; cover.

Bake 30 minutes; uncover. Bake 15 minutes longer, or until sauce thickens slightly.

Yield: 4 servings.

CHICKEN AND HAM SCANDIA

3 whole chicken breasts, weighing about 14 ozs.
  each
1 teaspoon salt
  Few celery tops
3 cups water
½ lb. cooked ham
½ small onion, peeled
1 egg
1 cup fresh bread crumbs (2 slices)
1 package (10 ozs.) frozen peas and carrots
6 tablespoons butter or margarine
6 tablespoons all-purpose flour
1 teaspoon dillweed
2 cups milk
2 cups packaged precooked rice
1 jar (2 ozs.) sliced pimientos, drained

Rinse chicken breasts and dry on paper toweling.

Combine chicken breasts, ½ teaspoon of the salt, celery tops, and water in a large saucepan; heat to boiling; cover. Simmer 45 minutes, or until chicken is tender. Remove from broth and cool until easy to handle; strain broth into a 4-cup measure.

Cut each chicken breast in half, then pull off skin and take meat from each section off bones in one large piece. Cut each piece crosswise into three or four large chunks; set aside.

Put ham and onion through a food grinder, using a medium-course blade; place in a large bowl. Stir in egg and bread crumbs until mixture is well blended. Shape into 32 tiny balls, using a heaping teaspoon for each; chill while making sauce.

Cook peas and carrots as label directs; drain. Preheat oven to 350°.

Melt butter in a large saucepan; stir in flour, dillweed, and remaining ½ teaspoon salt; cook, stirring constantly, until bubbly. Stir in 2 cups of the chicken broth and milk; continue cooking and stirring until sauce thickens and boils 1 minute.

Measure rice into a 3-quart baking dish; stir in about half of the sauce. Top with chicken and ham balls; sprinkle peas and carrots and pimientos over meat; pour remaining sauce over all; cover.

Bake 45 minutes, or until meat is bubbly and rice is tender. Garnish with fresh dill if you like.

Yield: 8 servings.

CANTONESE CHICKEN

4 boneless chicken breasts, weighing about 1½
  lbs.
5 tablespoons salad oil
1 large green pepper, quartered, seeded, and cut
  in thin strips
1 large red pepper, quartered, seeded, and cut in
  thin strips
2 cups diagonally sliced celery
2 medium onions, peeled, sliced, and separated
  into rings
1 can (8 ozs.) water chestnuts, drained and sliced
2 tablespoons cornstarch
1 envelope instant chicken broth
1 teaspoon sugar
1 teaspoon ground ginger
½ teaspoon seasoned pepper
1½ cups water
¼ cup soy sauce
  Hot cooked rice

Rinse chicken and dry on paper toweling; cut into thin strips.

Heat 3 tablespoons of the salad oil in a large skillet; add chicken and sauté, stirring often, 10 minutes; push to one side.

Add remaining 2 tablespoons salad oil to skillet; heat. Place green and red peppers, celery, onions, and water chestnuts in separate piles in skillet; sauté 3 minutes, or just until vegetables are crisp-tender.

While vegetables cook, mix cornstarch, chicken broth, sugar, ginger, and seasoned pepper in a small saucepan; stir in water and soy sauce. Cook, stirring constantly, until sauce thickens and boils 1 minute. Pour over chicken and vegetables; heat slowly just until hot. Serve as is from skillet with cooked rice, or toss all ingredients together first, if you prefer.

Yield: 6 servings.

CONTINENTAL CHICKEN CREPES

1 broiler-fryer, about 2½ lbs., cut up
4 peppercorns
1 teaspoon salt
    Few celery tops
2 cups water
    Basic Crepes (recipe on page 412)
4 tablespoons butter or margarine
4 tablespoons all-purpose flour
¼ teaspoon dried rosemary, crushed
½ cup light cream
2 egg yolks
2 tablespoons grated Parmesan cheese

Rinse chicken and dry on paper toweling. Combine chicken, peppercorns, salt, celery tops, and water in a large skillet; heat to boiling; cover. Cook 45 minutes, or until chicken is tender.

Remove from broth; cool until easy to handle, then take meat from bones and dice. (There should be about 3 cups.)

Strain broth; return to skillet; cook down rapidly until it measures 1½ cups.

Make Basic Crepes; keep warm.

Melt butter in a medium saucepan. Stir in flour and rosemary; cook, stirring constantly, until bubbly. Stir in the 1½ cups chicken broth; continue cooking and stirring until sauce thickens and boils 1 minute. Stir in cream.

Beat egg yolks in a small bowl; slowly stir in about half of the hot sauce, then stir back into saucepan; cook 1 minute longer; remove from heat. Measure ¾ cup of the sauce and stir into chicken in a medium bowl.

Preheat broiler

Spoon ¼ cup of the chicken mixture onto each crepe; roll up, jelly-roll fashion; place, seam side down, in a lightly buttered baking dish, 13x9x2 inches. Spoon remaining sauce in a ribbon down center of crepes; sprinkle Parmesan cheese evenly over sauce.

Broil, 6 to 8 inches from heat, 2 to 3 minutes, or until top browns lightly.

Yield: 6 servings.

HERBED CHICKEN

8 chicken thighs, weighing about 1½ lbs.
1 egg
1 tablespoon water
1½ cups herb-seasoned stuffing mix
½ teaspoon salt
¼ teaspoon pepper
¼ cup butter or margarine, melted

Rinse chicken and dry on paper toweling. Preheat oven to 400°.

Beat egg with water in a pie plate. Measure stuffing mix into a transparent or paper bag; crush fine with a rolling pin; stir in salt and pepper.

Dip chicken pieces, one at a time, into beaten egg, then shake in crumb mixture to coat well. Place in a single layer in a greased shallow baking pan; drizzle melted butter over top.

Bake 45 minutes, or until chicken is crisp and tender.

Yield: 4 servings.

CHEF'S CHICKEN

1 broiler-fryer, weighing about 3½ lbs.
1 can (8 ozs.) tomato sauce
⅓ cup salad oil
⅓ cup orange juice
¼ cup lemon juice
1 teaspoon dried thyme, crushed
1 teaspoon salt
½ teaspoon garlic powder
¼ teaspoon pepper
2 tablespoons honey
1 teaspoon prepared hot mustard

Rinse chicken inside and out; pat dry with paper toweling. Close body opening with skewers and string; skewer neck skin to back; twist wing tips flat against back. Place chicken in a transparent bag.

Combine tomato sauce, salad oil, orange juice, lemon juice, thyme, salt, garlic powder, and pepper in a small bowl; pour over chicken in bag; fasten bag. For easy handling, place bag in a large bowl. Chill chicken, turning bag several times, overnight to season.

When ready to cook chicken, preheat oven to 350°.

Remove chicken from bag and place on a rack in a small roasting pan; for a compact shape, tie legs to tail. Pour marinade from bag into a small bowl.

Bake chicken 1 hour; brush generously with marinade. Bake 30 minutes; brush again with marinade; bake 15 minutes.

Mix honey and mustard in a cup; brush over chicken. Bake 15 minutes longer, or until chicken is tender.

Place on a large serving platter; cut away strings and take out skewers. Garnish platter with parsley and tomato wedges if you like. Carve chicken into serving-sized pieces.

Yield: 4 to 6 servings.

POT-ROASTED CHICKEN

2 broiler fryers, weighing about 3 lbs. each
1 teaspoon dried rosemary, crushed
1 teaspoon salt
4 tablespoons butter or margarine
1 medium onion, chopped (½ cup)
1 can (13¾ ozs.) chicken broth
2 tablespoons all-purpose flour
1 small can evaporated milk (⅔ cup)
3 cups medium noodles, cooked and drained
2 tablespoons chopped parsley

Rinse chickens inside and out; pat dry with paper toweling.

Mix rosemary and salt in a cup; sprinkle half into body cavities of chickens. Skewer neck skin to backs; twist wing tips flat against backs; tie legs to tails. Rub remaining seasoning mixture over outside of chickens.

Preheat oven to 350°.

Brown chickens, one at a time, in 3 tablespoons of the butter in a small roasting pan; remove and set aside.

Stir onion into drippings in pan; sauté until soft. Stir in chicken broth; place chickens in pan; heat to boiling; cover.

Bake 1 hour and 15 minutes, or until tender.

Remove one chicken to a large serving platter; take out skewer and cut away string; keep warm. Set second chicken aside for another meal.

Strain liquid from pan into a 4-cup measure, pressing onion through sieve. Let stand a few minutes until fat rises to top, then skim off. Measure 2 tablespoons of the fat and return to roasting pan; stir in flour. Cook, stirring constantly, until bubbly. Stir in 1¼ cups of the liquid; continue cooking and stirring until gravy thickens and boils 1 minute. Stir in evaporated milk; heat again to boiling. Pour into a serving bowl.

Toss noodles with remaining 1 tablespoon butter and parsley; spoon around chicken on platter. Serve with gravy to spoon over all.

Yield: 4 servings plus one chicken for a dividend dish. (*see* CHICKEN CHASSEUR)

FRENCH CHICKEN DINNER

 4 chicken drumsticks with thighs
¼ cup all-purpose flour
 1 teaspoon salt
⅛ teaspoon pepper
¼ cup salad oil
12 small white onions, peeled
 1 clove garlic, minced
 1 can (16 ozs.) tomatoes
¼ cup dry white wine
¼ cup water
 2 cups loose-pack frozen small carrots
 2 medium zucchini, trimmed and sliced
 2 tablespoons sliced ripe olives

Cut drumsticks and thighs apart at the joints with a sharp knife; rinse chicken and dry on paper toweling.

Combine chicken with a mixture of flour, salt, and pepper in a transparent bag; shake well to coat pieces. Brown slowly in salad oil in a Dutch oven or large skillet; remove all chicken from pan.

Stir onions and garlic into drippings; brown onions lightly. Stir in remaining flour mixture from bag, tomatoes, wine, and water; heat to boiling. Return chicken to Dutch oven; cover.

Simmer 20 minutes. Add carrots; reheat to boiling; cover. Simmer 15 minutes. Add zucchini; simmer 5 minutes longer, or until chicken and vegetables are tender. Sprinkle olive slices over top.

Serve from Dutch oven.

Yield: 4 servings.

DEVILED CHICKEN RAMEKINS

 3 tablespoons butter or margarine
 1 cup coarsely crushed cornflakes
¼ cup chopped celery
 1 small onion, chopped (¼ cup)
 2 cups cubed cooked chicken
 3 tablespoons all-purpose flour
 4 teaspoons prepared hot spicy mustard
¾ teaspoon salt
   Few drops red-pepper seasoning
1½ cups milk
 2 tablespoons chopped pimientos
 1 package (10 ozs.) frozen baby lima beans,
   cooked and drained

Preheat oven to 375°.

Melt butter in a medium skillet; measure out 1 tablespoon and toss with cornflakes in a small bowl.

Stir celery and onion into remaining butter in skillet; sauté until soft. Stir in chicken; sauté 2 minutes. Sprinkle flour over mixture, then stir in with mustard, salt, red-pepper seasoning, and milk; cook, stirring constantly, until mixture thickens and boils 1 minute. Stir in pimientos and lima beans. Spoon into four 10-ounce custard cups. Sprinkle buttered cornflakes over each. For easy handling, set cups in a large shallow pan.

Bake 20 minutes, or until chicken is bubbly and topping is toasted.

Yield: 4 servings.

BOMBAY CHICKEN

12 chicken drumsticks, weighing about 2 lbs.
¼ cup salad oil
 1 large onion, chopped (1 cup)
 1 clove garlic, minced
⅔ cup all-purpose flour
 5 teaspoons curry powder
 1 teaspoon salt
½ teaspoon ground ginger
 1 can (13¾ ozs.) chicken broth
 1 cup water
½ cup light cream
 1 jar (about 8 ozs.) junior apricots
 4 cups cooked rice
 1 can (29 ozs.) apricot halves, drained
    Bottled chutney

Rinse chicken and dry on paper toweling. Brown drumsticks slowly, a few at a time, in oil in a Dutch oven; remove and set aside.

Stir onion and garlic into drippings in Dutch oven; sauté until soft. Stir in flour, curry powder, salt, and ginger. Cook, stirring constantly, until bubbly; stir in chicken broth and water. Continue cooking and stirring until mixture thickens and boils 1 minute.

Stir in cream and junior apricots; return chicken to Dutch oven; cover. Simmer 35 minutes, or until chicken is tender.

Spoon rice onto a large deep serving platter; spoon chicken and part of the sauce on top. Place apricot halves around chicken; fill hollows with chutney. Serve remaining sauce separately.

Yield: 6 servings.

BARBECUED CHICKEN

 2 broiler-fryers, weighing about 2½ lbs. each, quartered
    Salad oil
1½ teaspoons salt
 ⅛ teaspoon pepper
 1 small onion, finely chopped (¼ cup)
 1 clove garlic, minced
 1 can (10¾ ozs.) condensed tomato soup
 2 tablespoons brown sugar
 1 tablespoon vinegar
 1 tablespoon Worcestershire sauce
 1 teaspoon prepared hot spicy mustard
    Few drops red-pepper seasoning

Preheat oven to 400°.

Rinse chicken and dry on paper toweling. Brush salad oil over both sides; sprinkle salt and pepper over all. Place pieces, skin side down, in a single layer in a large shallow baking pan.

Bake 30 minutes.

While chicken bakes, sauté onion and garlic in 2 tablespoons salad oil in a small saucepan until soft; stir in soup, brown sugar, vinegar, Worcestershire sauce, mustard, and red-pepper seasoning. Heat, stirring several times, to boiling; simmer 15 minutes. Brush part over chicken.

Bake 10 minutes; turn pieces; brush sauce over top.

Continue baking, brushing once or twice more with remaining sauce, 30 minutes, or until chicken is tender.

Yield: 8 servings.

CHICKEN CHOP SUEY

2 boneless chicken breasts, weighing about 1 lb.
3 tablespoons salad oil
3 small onions, peeled and sliced
1 cup diagonally sliced celery
1 small red pepper, quartered, seeded, and diced
    (½ cup)
1 can (13¾ ozs.) chicken broth
3 tablespoons soy sauce
1 can (16 ozs.) bean sprouts, drained
1 can (8 ozs.) water chestnuts, drained and sliced
1 can (8 ozs.) bamboo shoots, drained
2 cups shredded Chinese cabbage
2 tablespoons cornstarch
2 tablespoons water
  Hot cooked rice

Rinse chicken and dry on paper toweling; cut into thin strips.

Measure salad oil into a large skillet; heat; add chicken and sauté, stirring often, 5 minutes; push to one side.

Stir in onions, celery, and red pepper; sauté 1 minute. Stir in chicken broth and soy sauce; heat to boiling; cover. Simmer 5 minutes.

Stir in bean sprouts, water chestnuts, bamboo shoots, and cabbage.

Mix cornstarch with water in a cup until smooth; stir into mixture in skillet. Cook, stirring constantly, until mixture thickens and boils 1 minute.

Spoon into a serving bowl. Serve with cooked rice.

Yield: 4 servings.

MANDARIN CHICKEN SKILLET

1 package main dish mix for creamy noodles and
    tuna
3 cups water
½ cup diagonally sliced celery
2 tablespoons soy sauce
2 cans (5 ozs. each) boned chicken, broken up
½ cup sliced green onions
½ cup sliced water chestnuts
1 package (4 ozs.) shredded Cheddar cheese

Combine noodles, sauce mix, and water in a

large skillet; heat, stirring constantly, to boiling.

Stir in celery and soy sauce; cover. Simmer, stirring several times, 20 minutes, or until noodles are tender.

Stir in chicken, green onions, and water chestnuts; sprinkle cheese over top; cover. Heat slowly 2 to 3 minutes, or until chicken and vegetables are hot and cheese melts. Garnish with more green onions if you like.

Yield: 4 servings.

SWEET-SOUR CHICKEN

3 chicken breasts, weighing about 10 ozs. each,
    cut in half
3 tablespoons salad oil
1 large onion, chopped (1 cup)
⅔ cup water
2 envelopes instant chicken broth
1 can (20 ozs.) pineapple chunks in syrup
2 tablespoons cornstarch
2 tablespoons cider vinegar
2 tablespoons soy sauce
1 small green pepper, seeded and cut in rings
¼ cup toasted slivered almonds

Rinse chicken breasts and dry on paper toweling.

Brown in salad oil in a large skillet; remove from skillet and place on a plate.

Stir onion into drippings; sauté until soft. Stir in water and chicken broth; return chicken to skillet. Heat to boiling; cover tightly. Simmer 40 minutes, or until chicken is tender. Remove from skillet and arrange on a large deep serving platter; keep hot.

Drain syrup from pineapple and stir into cornstarch until smooth in a small bowl; stir in vinegar and soy sauce. Stir into liquid in skillet. Cook, stirring constantly, until sauce thickens and boils 1 minute. Stir in pineapple and green-pepper rings; heat again just until hot. Spoon over chicken on platter; sprinkle almonds on top. Serve with hot cooked rice if you like.

Yield: 6 servings.

GOURMET CHICKEN FRICASSEE

1 broiler-fryer, weighing about 3 lbs., cut into
　　serving-sized pieces
3 tablespoons all-purpose flour
¼ teaspoon salt
¼ teaspoon pepper
3 tablespoons salad oil
1 medium onion, chopped (½ cup)
1 teaspoon dried oregano, crushed
1 can (10¾ ozs.) condensed cream of mushroom
　　soup
½ cup dry white wine
1 package (10 ozs.) frozen green peas
1 can (16 ozs.) small whole carrots, drained
1 package (8 ozs.) medium noodles
2 tablespoons chopped parsley
1 cup (8-oz. carton) dairy sour cream

Rinse chicken and dry on paper toweling. Shake chicken in mixture of flour, salt, and pepper in a transparent bag. Brown slowly in salad oil in a large skillet; remove from pan.

Stir onion, oregano, mushroom soup, and wine into drippings in skillet; heat, stirring several times, to boiling; return chicken; cover.

Simmer 45 minutes; stir in frozen peas and carrots; heat to boiling; cover. Simmer 15 minutes longer, or until chicken is tender.

While chicken simmers, cook noodles as label directs; drain. Add parsley; toss to mix.

Place chicken on a large deep serving platter; spoon noodles around edge; keep hot.

Stir about 1 cup of the hot sauce from skillet into sour cream in a small bowl, then stir back into remaining mixture in skillet; heat slowly just until hot. (Do not boil.) If you prefer sauce thinner, stir in ¼ cup water or milk. Spoon over chicken.

Yield: 4 servings.

CHICKEN CHOW MEIN

2 boneless chicken breasts, weighing about 1 lb.
2 tablespoons salad oil
1 cup diagonally sliced celery
1 large onion, chopped (1 cup)
1 small green pepper, quartered, seeded, and
　　diced (½ cup)
1 can (13¾ ozs.) chicken broth
3 tablespoons soy sauce
½ teaspoon monosodium glutamate
1 can (16 ozs.) chop suey vegetables, drained
1 can (3 ozs.) sliced mushrooms
1 jar (2 ozs.) sliced pimientos, drained
2 tablespoons brown gravy sauce (molasses-type)
3 tablespoons cornstarch
2 tablespoons water
　Chow mein noodles

Rinse chicken and dry on paper toweling; cut into thin strips.

Measure salad oil into a large skillet; heat; add chicken and sauté, stirring often, 5 minutes; push to one side.

Stir in celery, onion, and green pepper; sauté 1 minute.

Stir in chicken broth, soy sauce, and monosodium glutamate. Heat to boiling; cover. Simmer 5 minutes.

Stir in chop suey vegetables, mushrooms and liquid, pimientos, and brown gravy sauce.

Mix cornstarch with water until smooth in a cup; stir into mixture in skillet. Cook, stirring constantly, until mixture thickens and boils 1 minute.

Spoon into a serving bowl. Serve with chow mein noodles and hot cooked rice if you like.

Yield: 4 servings.

DIETER'S CHICKEN KIEV

4 ozs. Neufchatel cheese
4 teaspoons freeze-dried chives
4 boneless chicken breasts or cutlets, weighing 10 ozs. each
1 teaspoon seasoned salt
2 tablespoons diet margarine
1 envelope instant chicken broth
¼ cup water

Blend cheese and chives in a small bowl; spread into a 4x1-inch rectangle on waxed paper; wrap in paper. Place in freezer for 10 to 20 minutes, or until very firm.

Rinse chicken breasts and dry on paper toweling. Cut each in half; pound thin between sheets of waxed paper. Sprinkle seasoned salt evenly over chicken. Place flat, skin side down, on counter.

Cut cheese into 8 equal pieces; place each on a half chicken breast. Fold edges up over cheese, then roll up meat, jelly roll fashion; fasten in several places with wooden picks.

Brown chicken rolls slowly in margarine in a large skillet; stir in chicken broth and water. Heat to boiling; cover. Simmer 40 minutes, or until chicken is tender. Place on a large serving platter; take out picks. Pass sauce separately to spoon over chicken.

Yield: 8 servings.

GOURMET CHICKEN TOWERS

4 boneless chicken breasts or chicken cutlets, weighing about 6 ozs. each
Salt
Pepper
Dried oregano, crushed
2 tablespoons butter or margarine
1 tablespoon salad oil
2 tablespoons dry white wine
1 package (10 ozs.) frozen asparagus spears
1 package hollandaise sauce mix
8 slices white bread

Rinse chicken and dry on paper toweling.

Cut each in half; sprinkle lightly with salt, pepper, and oregano. Brown very slowly in butter and salad oil in a large skillet. Add wine to skillet; cover. Cook 30 minutes, or until chicken is tender.

While chicken cooks, cook asparagus as label directs; drain; keep hot.

Prepare hollandaise sauce mix with water as label directs. Trim crusts from bread; toast slices.

Place 2 slices of toast on each of four serving plates. Top each slice with asparagus and a half chicken breast; spoon sauce over all. Serve with buttered cooked frozen peas and celery if you like.

Yield: 4 servings.

ONION CHICKEN

2 broiler-fryers, weighing about 2½ lbs. each, cut
    in serving-sized pieces
1 cup fine saltine crumbs (about 26 crackers)
1 envelope green-onion dip mix
1½ teaspoons salt
¼ teaspoon pepper
2 eggs
2 tablespoons milk
4 tablespoons butter or margarine

Rinse chicken and dry on paper toweling;
pull off skin.

Mix saltine crumbs, dip mix, salt, and pepper in a shallow dish. Beat eggs with milk in a
pie plate.

Dip chicken into egg mixture, letting any
excess drip back into pie plate; roll in crumb
mixture to coat well. Place, meaty side up, in a
single layer in two greased baking pans, each
13x9x2 inches.

Preheat oven to 350°.

Melt butter in a small skillet; drizzle over
chicken.

Bake 1 hour, or until tender and brown.
Yield: 6 to 8 servings.

QUICK CHICKEN STROGANOFF

1 medium onion, chopped (½ cup)
1 tablespoon butter or margarine
2 cans (5 ozs. each) boned chicken, cut in bite-sized
    pieces
1 can (10½ ozs.) chicken gravy
1 tablespoon catsup
1 cup (8-oz. carton) dairy sour cream
3 cups hot cooked noodles.

Sauté onion in butter in a medium skillet
until soft. Stir in chicken, gravy, and catsup.
Heat to boiling; simmer 10 minutes.

Stir about ½ cup of the hot chicken mixture
into sour cream in a small bowl, then stir back
into skillet. Heat very slowly just until hot.
(Do not boil.) Serve over cooked noodles.
Yield: 4 servings.

CHICKEN CARBONNADE

1 broiler-fryer, weighing about 3 lbs., cut in
    serving-sized pieces
6 tablespoons all-purpose flour
2 teaspoons salt
¼ teaspoon pepper
3 tablespoons salad oil
16 small white onions, peeled
1 large clove garlic, minced
1 can (12 ozs.) beer
¼ cup water
1 teaspoon dried Italian herbs
2 medium carrots, pared and sliced
3 cups uncooked fine noodles
1 tablespoon chopped parsley

Rinse chicken and dry on paper toweling.

Combine 5 tablespoons of the flour, salt,
and pepper in a transparent bag; add chicken
pieces and shake until well coated.

Brown, a few pieces at a time, in salad oil in
a large skillet or Dutch oven; remove all
chicken from skillet.

Stir onions and garlic into drippings; brown
onions lightly. Stir in any remaining seasoning mixture from bag. Add beer, water, Italian
herbs, and carrots; heat to boiling. Return
chicken to skillet; cover. Simmer 45 minutes,
or until chicken is tender.

While chicken simmers, cook noodles as
label directs; spoon onto a large serving platter. Remove chicken and vegetables from skillet and arrange over noodles; keep hot.

Blend remaining 1 tablespoon flour with a
little water in a cup until smooth; stir into
liquid in skillet. Cook, stirring constantly,
until sauce thickens and boils 1 minute. Pour
over chicken and noodles; sprinkle parsley on
top.
Yield: 4 servings.

TWIN CHICKEN PLATTER

2 roasting chickens, weighing about 4 lbs. each
  Salt
4 chicken livers
  Water
3 cups herb-seasoned stuffing mix
1 tablespoon chopped parsley
¼ teaspoon poultry seasoning
1 can (4 ozs.) chopped mushrooms
1 cup chopped celery
1 medium onion, chopped (½ cup)
¾ cup butter or margarine
1 can (29 ozs.) cling peach halves, drained
¼ cup all-purpose flour
  Lemon Potatoes (recipe on page 308)
1 cup bottled cranberry-orange relish
  Watercress

Rinse chickens inside and out; pat dry with paper toweling. Salt cavities lightly.

Place livers in a small saucepan; add water to cover. Heat to boiling; drain. Let cool until easy to handle, then chop and combine with stuffing mix, parsley, poultry seasoning, and 1 teaspoon salt in a medium bowl.

Drain liquid from mushrooms into a 1-cup measure; add water to make ⅔ cup.

Preheat oven to 350°.

Sauté celery, onion, and mushrooms in ¼ cup of the butter in a skillet about 5 minutes; stir in the ⅔ cup mushroom liquid. Heat to boiling; pour over stuffing mixture; toss until evenly moist. Stuff into body cavities of chickens; fasten openings with skewers and string. Tie legs of each chicken to tail; skewer neck skin to back; twist wing tips flat against back. Place chickens, breast side up, on a rack in a shallow roasting pan.

Melt remaining ½ cup butter in a small saucepan; brush part over chickens.

Roast, brushing every half hour with more butter, 2 hours, or until a drumstick feels soft and moves easily at the joint.

While chickens roast, place peach halves in a shallow pan. Brush lightly with butter. Heat in oven with chickens 10 minutes, or until hot.

Remove chickens to a large serving platter; take out skewers and cut away strings. Let stand 15 minutes for easier carving.

Pour drippings from pan into a 4-cup measure; let stand a few minutes until fat rises to top, then skim off. Measure 4 tablespoons fat and return to pan; add water to drippings to make 2 cups.

Blend flour into fat in pan; cook, stirring constantly, until bubbly. Stir in the 2 cups drippings mixture. Continue cooking and stirring until gravy thickens and boils 1 minute. Season with salt and pepper as needed.

Spoon Lemon Potatoes at sides of chickens on platter. Arrange peaches at ends; spoon cranberry relish into peach hollows. Tuck watercress around peaches. Serve gravy separately to spoon over meat and stuffing.

Yield: 8 to 10 servings.

DEVILED CHICKEN LIVERS

1 lb. chicken livers
1 egg
1 tablespoon water
¾ cup dry bread crumbs
1 teaspoon garlic powder
¾ teaspoon salt
⅓ cup butter or margarine, melted
2 tablespoons prepared hot spicy mustard
1 tablespoon lemon juice

Cut chicken livers in half; snip out any veiny parts.

Preheat broiler.

Beat egg with water in a pie plate; mix bread crumbs, garlic powder, and salt in a second pie plate. Dip livers into egg mixture, then into crumbs to coat generously. Place on rack in broiler pan.

Mix melted butter, mustard, and lemon juice in a small bowl; drizzle half over livers.

Broil, 6 inches from heat, 7 minutes; turn. Drizzle remaining butter mixture over top. Broil 5 minutes longer. Serve as is or with sautéed cherry tomatoes if you like.

Yield: 4 servings.

CHICKEN FRIED RICE

  1 large onion, chopped (1 cup)
  2 tablespoons salad oil
  1 envelope instant chicken broth
1½ cups water
  ½ cup uncooked regular rice
  1 can (5 ozs.) boned chicken, cut in bite-sized
     pieces
  1 tablespoon soy sauce
  4 eggs

Sauté onion in salad oil in a medium skillet until soft. Stir in chicken broth and water; heat to boiling. Stir in rice; cover. Cook 15 minutes, or until rice is tender and liquid is absorbed. Stir in chicken and soy sauce.

Beat eggs until blended in a small bowl; pour over rice mixture. Cook slowly 2 to 3 minutes, or until eggs start to set on bottom, then stir lightly to mix. Cook 5 to 6 minutes longer, or until eggs are as firm as you like them.

Yield: 4 servings.

PAELLA

  4 boneless chicken breasts, weighing about 8 ozs.
     each
  2 tablespoons olive oil
  ½ lb. salami, cut in small cubes
  3 medium onions, chopped (1½ cups)
  1 large green pepper, quartered, seeded, and
     chopped (1 cup)
  2 cloves garlic, minced
1½ cups uncooked regular rice
  ¼ teaspoon saffron, crushed
  3 teaspoons paprika
  2 teaspoons salt
  1 can (28 ozs.) tomatoes
     Water
  1 package (10 ozs.) frozen peas
  1 package (16 ozs.) frozen shrimp, thawed
  1 jar (4 ozs.) pimientos, drained and cut in short
     strips
  1 can (24 ozs.) clams in shells

Rinse chicken breasts and dry on paper toweling. Cut each in half. Brown slowly in olive oil in a large skillet; remove and set aside.

Stir salami into drippings in skillet; sauté until brown; remove with a slotted spoon to a bowl.

Stir onions, green pepper, and garlic into drippings; sauté until soft. Stir in rice and saffron; sauté until rice is golden. Stir in paprika and salt.

Drain juice from tomatoes into a 1-quart measure; add water to make 3 cups. Stir into rice mixture in skillet; add tomatoes; heat to boiling.

Run hot water over peas to separate.

Preheat oven to 375°.

Layer half each of the chicken, salami, shrimp, peas, rice mixture, and pimientos into a 4-quart baking dish; repeat to make a second layer of each; cover.

Bake 1 hour, or until rice and chicken are tender.

Drain juice from clams. Rinse clams and shells under running cold water; arrange on top of rice mixture; cover again. Bake 10 minutes longer, or until clams are hot.

Yield: 8 servings.

NEAPOLITAN CHICKEN DINNER

2 broiler-fryers, each weighing about 2 lbs., split
¼ cup all-purpose flour
1 teaspoon seasoned salt
¼ teaspoon pepper
¼ cup salad oil
1 jar (15 ozs.) marinara sauce
½ cup dry red wine
1 teaspoon dried oregano, crushed
1 cup shredded mozzarella cheese
1 package (8 ozs.) small macaroni shells
2 tablespoons chopped parsley

Rinse chicken and dry on paper toweling. Preheat oven to 350°.

Shake chicken halves in a mixture of flour, salt, and pepper in a transparent bag to coat well.

Brown slowly, part at a time, in salad oil in a large skillet; place in a single layer in a baking dish, 13x9x2 inches. Pour all drippings from skillet.

Stir marinara sauce, wine, and oregano into skillet; heat, stirring several times, to boiling. Pour over chicken; cover.

Bake 1 hour; uncover. Sprinkle cheese on top.

Bake 15 minutes longer, or until chicken is tender and topping browns lightly.

While chicken bakes, cook macaroni as label directs; drain; spoon onto a large deep platter. Arrange chicken on top.

Let sauce in dish stand a minute until fat rises to top; skim off. Ladle sauce around chicken; sprinkle with parsley.

Yield: 4 servings.

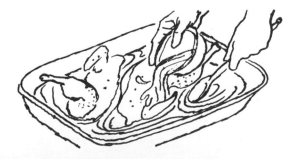

WALNUT CHICKEN

4 boneless chicken breasts, weighing about 1½ lbs.
3 tablespoons cornstarch
1 cup California walnut pieces
⅓ cup salad oil
1 teaspoon minced pared gingerroot
1 cup diagonally sliced celery
1 can (8 ozs.) water chestnuts, drained and sliced
1½ cups water
2 envelopes instant chicken broth
3 tablespoons soy sauce
2 tablespoons dry sherry
1 teaspoon sugar

Rinse chicken and dry on paper toweling; cut into 1-inch squares. Toss with 1 tablespoon of the cornstarch in a medium bowl.

Combine walnuts and enough water to cover in a small saucepan; heat to boiling. Simmer 3 minutes; drain and dry well on paper toweling.

Heat half of the salad oil in a large skillet; add walnuts and sauté, stirring often, until golden-brown; remove from skillet with a slotted spoon and set aside.

Add remaining salad oil to drippings in skillet; heat. Add chicken and sauté, stirring often, 6 minutes; push to one side. Stir in gingerroot, celery, and water chestnuts; sauté 2 minutes.

Stir in 1 cup of the water, chicken broth, soy sauce, sherry, and sugar; heat slowly to boiling. Mix remaining 2 tablespoons cornstarch with ½ cup water until smooth in a cup; stir into mixture in skillet. Cook, stirring constantly, until sauce thickens and boils 1 minute; stir in walnuts. Spoon into a serving bowl. Serve with hot cooked rice if you like.

Yield: 6 servings.

DEVILED CHICKEN

12 chicken thighs
⅓ cup chili sauce
2 tablespoons prepared mustard
¼ teaspoon garlic powder
¼ teaspoon liquid red-pepper seasoning
½ cup all-purpose flour
2 teaspoons salt
¾ teaspoon dried basil, crushed
¼ teaspoon pepper
3 tablespoons salad oil

Preheat oven to 350°.

Rinse chicken and dry on paper toweling; place, skin side up, on counter.

Mix chili sauce, mustard, garlic powder, and red-pepper seasoning in a cup; mix flour, salt, basil, and pepper on waxed paper.

Spread chili-sauce mixture over chicken, then dredge each piece in seasoned flour to coat well. Brown slowly in salad oil in a large skillet; place in a single layer in a large shallow baking pan.

Bake 45 minutes, or until chicken is tender and golden. Serve warm or cold.

Yield: 6 servings.

CHINESE CHICKEN AND VEGETABLES

8 chicken thighs, weighing about 2 lbs.
3 tablespoons salad oil
2 cloves garlic, minced
1 teaspoon minced pared gingerroot
2 cups diagonally sliced celery
1 can (8 ozs.) water chestnuts, drained and sliced
1 can (8 ozs.) bamboo shoots, drained
¼ lb. mushrooms, washed, trimmed, and sliced
1 package (6 ozs.) frozen pea pods or snow peas
1 can (13¾ ozs.) chicken broth
3 tablespoons cornstarch
½ teaspoon salt
½ teaspoon sugar
3 tablespoons dry sherry
3 green onions, trimmed and sliced thin

Rinse chicken and dry on paper toweling. Bone thighs this way: Make a slit all along thinner side to bone. Scrape and cut meat from bone all around; lift out bone. Pull off skin and trim away any small pieces of cartilage. Cut meat into 1½-inch squares.

Measure salad oil into a large skillet; heat; add chicken and sauté, stirring often, 10 minutes; push to one side.

Stir in garlic and gingerroot; sauté, 2 minutes.

Stir in celery, water chestnuts, bamboo shoots, mushrooms, and frozen pea pods. Cook quickly, stirring constantly, 2 minutes, or just until pea pods are thawed. Stir in 1 cup of the chicken broth; heat to boiling; simmer 1 minute.

Mix remaining chicken broth with cornstarch, salt, sugar, and sherry until smooth in a small bowl; stir into mixture in skillet. Cook, stirring constantly, until mixture thickens and boils 1 minute.

Spoon into a serving bowl; sprinkle green onions over top. Serve with hot cooked rice if you like.

Yield: 4 to 6 servings.

DIXIE CHICKEN PIE

1 broiler-fryer, weighing about 2½ lbs., cut up
Few celery tops
1 small onion, peeled and sliced
4 peppercorns
1¾ teaspoons salt
3 cups water
1 ham steak, weighing about 1 lb.
6 tablespoons butter or margarine
6 tablespoons all-purpose flour
¼ teaspoon pepper
1 can (16 ozs.) whole boiled onions, drained
1 package (10 ozs.) frozen mixed vegetables
¾ teaspoon dried rosemary, crushed
½ package piecrust mix

Rinse chicken and dry on paper toweling.

Combine chicken, celery tops, onion, peppercorns, 1 teaspoon of the salt, and water in a large skillet; heat to boiling; cover. Simmer 1 hour, or until chicken is tender. Remove from broth and cool until easy to handle. Strain broth into a 4-cup measure; add water, if needed, to make 2½ cups.

Pull skin from chicken and take meat from bones; dice chicken and ham.

Melt butter in same skillet; stir in flour, remaining ¾ teaspoon salt, and pepper; cook, stirring constantly, until bubbly. Stir in the 2½ cups broth; continue cooking and stirring until sauce thickens and boils 1 minute. Stir in chicken and ham, boiled onions, mixed vegetables, and rosemary; heat, breaking up vegetables with a fork, to boiling; pour into a 1¾-quart baking dish.

Preheat oven to 425°; keep chicken mixture hot in oven as it heats.

Prepare piecrust mix as label directs. Roll out to an oval, round, or square 1 inch larger than baking dish; trim even. Using a small cookie cutter, make two or three cutouts in pastry to let steam escape. (Or cut several slits in pastry with a knife.) Place pastry over filling in baking dish; turn overhang under, flush with rim; flute edge.

Bake 30 minutes, or until pastry is golden.
Yield: 6 servings.

CHILI CHICKEN

1 broiler-fryer, weighing about 3 lbs., cut into serving-sized pieces
2 tablespoons salad oil
1 large green pepper, quartered, seeded, and chopped (1 cup)
1 medium-sized red pepper, quartered, seeded, and chopped (½ cup)
1 medium onion, chopped (½ cup)
1 tablespoon chili powder
3 tablespoons all-purpose flour
1½ teaspoons salt
1 can (16 ozs.) tomatoes
½ cup water

Rinse chicken and dry on paper toweling.

Brown pieces, part at a time, in salad oil in a large skillet; remove from skillet. Pour off drippings, then measure 2 tablespoons and return to skillet.

Stir green and red peppers and onion into drippings; sauté until soft. Stir in chili powder; cook 1 minute.

Sprinkle flour and salt over pepper mixture, then stir in with tomatoes and water. Cook, stirring constantly, until sauce thickens and boils 1 minute. Place chicken in sauce; heat to boiling; cover.

Simmer 45 minutes; uncover. Simmer 15 minutes longer, or until chicken is tender.

Arrange chicken on a large serving platter; garnish with several red and green pepper rings if you like. Serve sauce in a separate bowl to spoon over chicken.
Yield: 4 servings.

DOUBLE CHICKEN CASSEROLE

1¼ cups packaged precooked rice
1 can (10¾ ozs.) condensed cream of chicken soup
1 package (8 ozs.) process American cheese, shredded
1 can (5 ozs.) boned chicken, cut up
¼ cup thinly sliced green onions
1 can (8 ozs.) peas, drained
1 jar (2 ozs.) sliced pimientos, drained and diced
2 tablespoons grated Romano cheese

Preheat oven to 350°.

Prepare rice as label directs.

Combine soup, cheese, chicken, green onions, peas, and pimientos in a medium bowl; mix well. Spoon one third into a 1¾-quart baking dish; top with half of the rice, half of the remaining sauce, remaining rice, and rest of sauce. Sprinkle Romano cheese on top.

Bake 45 minutes, or until bubbly.

Yield: 4 servings.

CHICKEN BENEDICT

2 boneless chicken breasts or cutlets, weighing about 8 ozs. each
2 tablespoons all-purpose flour
½ teaspoon salt
  Dash of pepper
2 tablespoons salad oil
1 envelope hollandaise sauce mix
  Water
1 package (3 ozs.) sliced Canadian bacon
2 English muffins, split
  Paprika

Rinse chicken and dry on paper toweling.

Cut each breast in half; shake with a mixture of flour, salt, and pepper in a transparent bag to coat well.

Brown chicken in salad oil in a large skillet; cover. Cook slowly 30 minutes, or until chicken is tender; keep hot.

While chicken cooks, prepare hollandaise sauce mix with water as the label directs.

Preheat broiler.

Sauté Canadian bacon, turning once, in a second skillet until brown; keep hot.

Place muffin halves on a cookie sheet; toast in broiler. Top each half with bacon, then chicken; spoon hollandaise sauce over chicken; sprinkle paprika over sauce.

Broil, 6 inches from heat, 2 to 3 minutes, or until sauce bubbles up. Serve with spiced peaches and crisp radishes if you like.

Yield: 4 servings.

PILGRIM'S DRUMSTICKS

12 chicken drumsticks
¾ cup corn-bread stuffing mix
½ cup grated Romano cheese
1 teaspoon dried thyme, crushed
½ teaspoon salt
⅓ cup undiluted evaporated milk

Rinse chicken and dry on paper toweling. Preheat oven to 400°.

Crush stuffing mix with rolling pin; mix with Romano cheese, thyme, and salt in a pie plate. Pour milk into a second pie plate.

Dip drumsticks, one at a time, into milk, then roll in crumb mixture to coat generously. Place, not touching, in a single layer in a well-buttered jelly-roll pan.

Bake 50 minutes, or until chicken is tender and coating is crusty golden. Serve hot or cold.

Yield: 6 servings.

CHICKEN CLUBS

8 slices bacon, cut in half crosswise
1 can (about 5 ozs.) chicken spread
2 tablespoons chopped celery
1 tablespoon sweet pickle relish
2 teaspoons prepared mustard
1 can (10½ ozs.) chicken gravy
⅛ teaspoon poultry seasoning
1 cup complete pancake mix
1 cup water
2 medium tomatoes, each cut in 4 slices

Sauté bacon in a small skillet until crisp; remove and drain on paper toweling; keep hot.

Blend chicken spread with celery, relish, and mustard in a small bowl.

Combine gravy and poultry seasoning in a small saucepan; heat to boiling; keep hot.

Combine pancake mix and water in a small bowl; stir until almost smooth. Using 1 tablespoon batter for each, bake 24 three-inch pancakes on greased heated griddle.

Spread 1 tablespoon of the chicken mixture over each of 8 pancakes; top each with another pancake, a tomato slice, 2 pieces of bacon, and a third pancake. Place each two stacks on a serving plate. Spoon gravy over all.

Yield: 4 servings.

CALICO CHICKEN BAKE

1 broiler-fryer, weighing about 2½ lbs.
1 small onion, peeled and quartered
   Few celery tops
1½ teaspoons salt
2 cups water
4 tablespoons butter or margarine
1 cup fresh bread crumbs (2 slices)
2 cups diced celery
1 medium onion, chopped (½ cup)
5 tablespoons all-purpose flour
1 cup milk
2 cups shredded Tybo or Havarti cheese
1 can (12 ozs.) Mexican-style corn
⅓ cup chopped parsley

Rinse chicken; combine with quartered onion, celery tops, 1 teaspoon of the salt, and water in a kettle; heat to boiling; cover.

Simmer 45 minutes, or until chicken is tender. Remove from broth and cool until easy to handle. Strain broth into a 2-cup measure and set aside.

Pull skin from chicken and take meat from bones; cube meat. (There should be 2 cups.)

Melt butter in a large saucepan; measure out 1 tablespoon and toss with bread crumbs in a small bowl.

Stir celery and chopped onion into remaining melted butter in saucepan; sauté until soft. Stir in flour and remaining ½ teaspoon salt; cook, stirring constantly, until bubbly. Stir in milk and 1 cup of the chicken broth; continue cooking and stirring until sauce thickens and boils 1 minute. Stir in cheese until melted, then corn and liquid and parsley.

Preheat oven to 350°.

Layer half of the chicken into a shallow baking dish, 11¾x7½x2 inches; spoon half of the sauce over chicken; repeat layers. Top with bread crumbs.

Bake 35 minutes, or until bubbly.

Yield: 6 servings.

CHICKEN IN CREAM

1 jar (2½ ozs.) sliced dried beef
3 large boneless chicken breasts or cutlets,
    weighing about 10 ozs. each
3 slices bacon, cut in half crosswise
1 can (10¾ ozs.) condensed cream of mushroom
    soup
1 cup (8-oz. carton) dairy sour cream
¾ teaspoon dried oregano, crushed

Preheat oven to 350°.

Place dried beef in a sieve and rinse under running cold water to remove excess salt; dry on paper toweling. Shred coarsely; spread over bottom of a baking dish, 12x8x2 inches.

Rinse chicken and dry on paper toweling. Pull off skin; cut each breast in half. Place in a single layer over beef in dish; top each with a half slice of bacon.

Bake, uncovered, 30 minutes.

While chicken bakes, combine mushroom soup, sour cream, and oregano in a medium bowl; spoon over chicken; stir to mix with juices in dish.

Bake 25 minutes longer, or until chicken is tender. Serve from baking dish with mashed potatoes or steamed rice if you like.

Yield: 6 servings.

KOREAN CHICKEN

2 broiler-fryers, weighing 1½ lbs. each, split
1 small onion, finely chopped (¼ cup)
1 tablespoon honey
1 teaspoon garlic salt
½ cup water
¼ cup soy sauce

Rinse chickens and dry on paper toweling. Place halves, skin side down, in a large shallow baking dish.

Combine onion, honey, garlic salt, water, and soy sauce in a small bowl; pour over chicken. Let stand at room temperature, turning once or twice, 2½ hours.

Preheat oven to 350°. Cover chicken; place in oven.

Bake 45 minutes; uncover; turn chicken. Bake uncovered, spooning drippings in dish over chicken once or twice, 45 minutes longer, or until chicken is tender.

Place chicken on a large serving platter; spoon any sauce from dish over top.

Yield: 4 servings.

HERB-STUFFED CHICKEN BREASTS

3 boneless chicken breasts or cutlets, weighing
    about 10 ozs. each
1½ cups fresh bread crumbs (3 slices)
½ cup finely diced salami
¼ cup chopped parsley
6 tablespoons butter or margarine
2 tablespoons salad oil
1 can (10¾ ozs.) condensed cream of mushroom
    soup
¼ cup milk
¼ cup chili sauce

Rinse chicken and dry on paper toweling. Cut each breast in half; place, skin side down, on a cutting board.

Combine bread crumbs, salami, and parsley in a medium bowl; cut in butter until well blended and mixture seems slightly pasty.

Carefully pull each half breast apart at large muscle to make a pocket for stuffing; stuff 2 to 3 tablespoons of the salami mixture into each; fasten in several places with short wooden picks.

Brown chicken slowly in salad oil in a large skillet; place in a single layer in a baking dish. Pour off drippings.

Preheat oven to 350°.

Combine soup, milk, and chili sauce in skillet; heat slowly, stirring several times, to boiling; pour over chicken; cover.

Bake 1 hour, or until chicken is tender. Garnish with parsley if you like. Serve from baking dish.

Yield: 6 servings.

MANDARIN CHICKEN

    4 boneless chicken breasts or cutlets, weighing
       about 6 ozs. each
    3 tablespoons butter or margarine
    2 tablespoons brown sugar
    1 teaspoon salt
    ½ teaspoon dried rosemary, crushed
    1¼ cups orange juice
    2 tablespoons cornstarch
    1 can (11 ozs.) mandarin orange segments,
       drained
    3 cups hot cooked rice

Rinse chicken and dry on paper toweling. Brown pieces, one or two at a time, in butter in a 4-quart pressure cooker; remove all meat from cooker.

Stir in brown sugar, salt, rosemary, and orange juice; place chicken in sauce; cover. Heat to 15 pounds pressure as manufacturer directs; cook 15 minutes. Let pressure fall naturally; uncover.

Remove chicken from liquid; pour liquid into a 2-cup measure. Let stand a minute until fat rises to top, then skim off. Add more orange juice or water to liquid, if needed, to make 2 cups. Stir slowly into cornstarch in cooker; cook, stirring constantly, until sauce thickens and boils 1 minute.

Stir in mandarin oranges; return chicken to sauce; heat until bubbly.

Arrange chicken in center of a large serving platter; spoon rice around edge. Serve sauce separately to spoon over all.

Yield: 4 servings.

TWIRLY BIRDS

    2 broiler-fryers, weighing about 3 lbs. each
    1½ teaspoons salt
    ¼ teaspoon pepper
    ½ cup bottled thin French dressing
    3 tablespoons chili sauce
    1 tablespoon light molasses
    2 tablespoons lemon juice
    1 tablespoon Worcestershire sauce
    1½ teaspoons onion salt

Rinse chickens inside and out; pat dry with paper toweling. Sprinkle salt and pepper lightly into cavities and over outsides; thread on spit of rotisserie, following manufacturer's directions.

Mix French dressing, chili sauce, molasses, lemon juice, Worcestershire sauce, and onion salt in a small saucepan; heat to boiling. Brush part lightly over chickens. Set spit in position in oven or in countertop rotisserie-broiler; start rotisserie.

Roast 45 minutes; brush more sauce over chickens.

Continue roasting, brushing several times with remaining sauce, 45 minutes, or until meat is tender. Remove chickens from spit to a cutting board; cut each into quarters with kitchen shears or a sharp knife.

Yield: 8 servings.

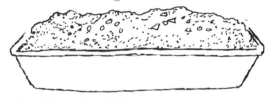

CHICKEN PUFF

    3 eggs
    1 cup milk
    1 can (5 ozs.) boned chicken, cut up
    1 small onion, chopped (¼ cup)
    1¼ cups coarsely crumbled cheese crackers
    1 teaspoon dried shredded parsley
    ½ teaspoon salt
       Dash of pepper
    1 tablespoon butter or margarine, melted

Preheat oven to 325°.

Beat eggs in a medium bowl until blended; stir in milk, chicken, onion, 1 cup of the cracker crumbs, parsley, salt, and pepper. Pour into a 1-quart deep baking dish.

Toss remaining ¼ cup cracker crumbs with melted butter in a small bowl; sprinkle over chicken mixture.

Bake 1 hour, or until puffed and set.

Yield: 4 servings.

EASY CHICKEN BAKE

3 boneless chicken breasts or cutlets, weighing
    about 10 ozs. each
1 teaspoon paprika
¼ teaspoon salt
¼ teaspoon pepper
1 package (8 ozs.) medium noodles
1 can (16 ozs.) cut green beans
1 jar (2 ozs.) sliced pimientos, drained and diced
2 cans (10¾ ozs. each) condensed cream of
    chicken soup
1 cup dry white wine
2 tablespoons grated Parmesan cheese

Rinse chicken and dry on paper toweling.
Pull off skin; cut each breast in half.

Combine paprika, salt, and pepper in a cup;
rub into both sides of chicken.

Place uncooked noodles in a layer in a baking dish, 13x9x2 inches.

Drain liquid from beans into a cup; layer
beans and pimientos over noodles; place
chicken in a single layer on top.

Preheat oven to 375°.

Combine soup, wine, and ½ cup of the
liquid from beans in a medium saucepan;
heat, stirring several times, to boiling. Pour
around chicken into dish; cover.

Bake 1 hour; uncover. Sprinkle Parmesan
cheese on top. Bake 10 minutes longer, or
until chicken and noodles are tender.

Yield: 6 servings.

PARISIAN CHICKEN RAGOUT

1 broiler-fryer, weighing about 3 lbs., cut into
    serving-sized pieces
4 slices bacon, cut in 1-inch pieces
⅓ cup all-purpose flour
1 teaspoon salt
¼ teaspoon pepper
1 medium onion, chopped (½ cup)
1 clove garlic, minced
1 envelope instant chicken broth
1 cup dry red wine
1 cup water
½ teaspoon dried mixed Italian herbs, crushed
¼ teaspoon dried marjoram, crushed
8 small potatoes, pared
4 medium carrots, pared and cut diagonally into
    1-inch lengths
¼ lb. mushrooms, washed, trimmed, and sliced
4 small zucchini, trimmed and cut in 1-inch
    rounds
2 tablespoons chopped parsley

Rinse chicken and dry on paper toweling.

Sauté bacon until crisp in a Dutch oven;
remove with a slotted spoon and drain on
paper toweling.

Shake chicken in mixture of flour, salt, and
pepper in a transparent bag to coat well;
brown in bacon drippings in Dutch oven; remove and set aside.

Stir onion and garlic into drippings; sauté
until soft. Stir in remaining flour mixture,
chicken broth, wine, water, Italian herbs, and
marjoram. Place chicken and bacon in liquid;
heat to boiling cover. Simmer 20 minutes.

Add potatoes and carrots to Dutch oven;
cover again. Simmer 20 minutes.

Place mushrooms and zucchini in Dutch
oven; cover. Cook 10 minutes, or until chicken
and vegetables are tender. Sprinkle parsley
over top.

Yield: 4 servings.

COUNTRY ROAST CHICKEN

2 broiler-fryers, weighing 3 lbs. each
2 teaspoons salt
5 medium onions, chopped (2½ cups)
7 large carrots, pared and diced (3½ cups)
2½ cups diced celery
1½ teaspoons dried Italian herbs
2 cups water
2 teaspoons butter or margarine, melted

Rinse chickens inside and out; pat dry with paper toweling. Sprinkle ½ teaspoon of the salt into cavities.

Combine onions, carrots, celery, Italian herbs, remaining 1½ teaspoons salt, and water in a large saucepan; heat to boiling; cover. Simmer 15 minutes, or until vegetables are tender and liquid is absorbed.

Preheat oven to 375°.

Stuff 1¾ cups of the vegetable mixture into neck and body cavity of each chicken; skewer neck skin to back; twist wingtips flat against back. Fasten body openings with skewers and string; tie legs to tail. Place chickens, breast side up, on a rack in a shallow roasting pan. Brush melted butter over each.

Spoon remaining vegetable mixture into a 1-quart baking dish; cover.

Roast chickens 2 hours, or until golden and a drumstick feels soft and moves easily at the joint. Bake extra vegetable stuffing in same oven for the last 30 minutes of roasting time.

Remove chickens to a large serving platter; take out skewers and cut away strings. Garnish platter with carrot curls and celery leaves if you like.

Yield: 8 servings.

APRICOT CHICKEN PLATTER

8 chicken thighs, weighing about 2 lbs.
1 tablespoon instant minced onion
16 dried apricot halves
16 small California walnut halves
2 tablespoons butter or margarine, melted
1⅓ cups packaged precooked rice
½ cup dairy sour cream
⅓ cup apricot preserves
1 tablespoon prepared hot spicy mustard

Rinse chicken and dry on paper toweling.

Bone this way: Make a cut all along thinner side of thigh to bone. Scrape and cut meat away from bone all around; lift out bone. Trim off any small pieces of cartilage.

Preheat oven to 400°.

Place thighs, skin side down, on a cutting board; sprinkle onion over each. Place 2 apricot and 2 walnut halves at one end of each thigh; roll up, jelly-roll fashion; fasten each in several places with wooden picks.

Place rolls seam side down, in a shallow baking dish. Brush melted butter over each.

Bake 50 minutes, or until chicken is tender and golden.

While chicken cooks, prepare rice as label directs; keep hot.

Combine sour cream, apricot preserves, and mustard in a small saucepan; heat slowly just until hot. (Do not boil.)

Spoon rice onto a large serving platter; arrange rolls in a row on top. Spoon sauce in a ribbon over chicken.

Yield: 4 servings.

CHICKEN ROYALE

4 boneless chicken breasts or cutlets weighing
    about 10 ozs. each
1 egg
¼ cup evaporated milk
¾ cup dry bread crumbs
1 teaspoon dried rosemary, finely crushed
1 teaspoon salt
¼ teaspoon pepper
4 tablespoons butter or margarine
2 tablespoons all-purpose flour
1 cup chicken broth
2 tablespoons brandy

Rinse chicken and dry on paper toweling; cut each breast in half.

Preheat oven to 350°.

Beat egg with evaporated milk in a pie plate; mix bread crumbs, rosemary, salt, and pepper in a second shallow dish. Dip chicken into egg mixture, then into crumb mixture to coat well. Place pieces in a single layer in a baking pan, 13x9x2 inches.

Melt butter in a small saucepan, drizzle over chicken.

Bake 1 hour, or until chicken is tender and golden. Arrange pieces on a large serving platter; keep warm.

Stir flour into drippings in baking pan; cook, stirring constantly, until bubbly. Stir in chicken broth; continue cooking and stirring until mixture thickens and boils 1 minute; stir in brandy. Taste and add salt if needed. Serve separately to spoon over chicken.

Yield: 8 servings.

BRUNSWICK STEW

1 broiler-fryer, weighing about 3 lbs., cut into
    serving-sized pieces
1 medium onion, peeled and sliced
2 teaspoons salt
1 teaspoon dried basil, crushed
¼ teaspoon pepper
4 cups water
3 medium potatoes, pared and cut in half
1 package (10 ozs.) frozen cut green beans
1 package (10 ozs.) frozen cut okra
1 can (16 ozs.) stewed tomatoes
1 can (8 ozs.) whole-kernel corn
3 tablespoons all-purpose flour

Rinse chicken and combine with onion, salt, basil, pepper, and water in a kettle; heat to boiling; cover. Simmer 20 minutes.

Add potatoes and green beans to kettle; heat to boiling; cover. Simmer 10 minutes.

Add okra, tomatoes, and corn and liquid; simmer 10 minutes longer, or until chicken and vegetables are tender.

Smooth flour and a little water to a paste in a cup; stir into bubbling stew mixture. Heat, stirring gently but constantly, until mixture thickens slightly and boils 1 minute.

Place chicken pieces in 6 soup bowls or individual serving dishes; spoon vegetable mixture over each. Serve with bread sticks or thick slices of crusty bread if you like.

Yield: 6 servings.

ORIENTAL CHICKEN

2 boneless chicken breasts or cutlets, weighing 1 lb.
2 tablespoons butter or margarine
1 can (10¾ ozs.) condensed golden mushroom soup
⅓ cup water
2 tablespoons soy sauce
3 tablespoons dry sherry
Few drops red-pepper seasoning
1 cup sliced celery
1 medium onion, peeled and sliced thin
1 can (3 or 4 ozs.) sliced mushrooms
1 can (8 ozs.) water chestnuts, drained and cut in half crosswise
1 jar (2 ozs.) sliced pimientos, drained
1 can (3 ozs.) chow mein noodles

Rinse chicken and dry on paper toweling. Pull off skin; cut meat into strips about 1½ inches long. Brown in butter in a large skillet.

Stir in soup, water, soy sauce, sherry, and red-pepper seasoning; heat to boiling; cover. Simmer 10 minutes.

Stir in celery, onion, mushrooms and liquid, water chestnuts, and pimientos; heat to boiling again; cover. Simmer 10 minutes, or until vegetables are crisp-tender.

Spoon onto a deep serving platter; sprinkle noodles around edge. Serve with additional soy sauce to drizzle on top.
Yield: 4 servings.

CHICKEN CHILI

2 lbs. chicken thighs
2 tablespoons salad oil
1 large onion, chopped (1 cup)
1 large green pepper, quartered, seeded, and chopped (1 cup)
1 clove garlic, minced
1 tablespoon chili powder
1 teaspoon salt
¼ teaspoon pepper
1 can (16 ozs.) tomatoes
1 can (16 ozs.) red kidney beans
1 can (12 ozs.) Mexican-style corn
½ cup shredded sharp Cheddar cheese

Rinse chicken thighs; pull off skin. Cut meat from each bone in one large piece, then cut into 1-inch cubes, trimming away cartilage.

Brown cubes in salad oil in a heavy kettle; push to one side.

Stir in onion, green pepper, and garlic; sauté until soft. Stir in chili powder, salt, and pepper; cook 1 minute.

Stir in tomatoes; heat to boiling; cover. Simmer 45 minutes, or until chicken is tender.

Stir in kidney beans and liquid and corn and liquid; cover. Simmer 15 minutes.

Ladle into soup plates; sprinkle cheese over each serving.
Yield: 4 servings.

TANGERINE CHICKEN

1 broiler-fryer, weighing about 3 lbs. quartered
2 tablespoons butter or margarine
2 tablespoons salad oil
4 tablespoons all-purpose flour
2 tablespoons sugar
1½ teaspoons salt
¾ teaspoon ground ginger
2 cups reconstituted frozen tangerine juice
3 cups hot cooked rice
2 tablespoons chopped slivered almonds

Rinse chicken and dry on paper toweling. Brown pieces slowly in butter and salad oil in a large skillet; place in a single layer in a shallow baking dish. Pour off all drippings, then measure 2 tablespoons and return to skillet.

Preheat oven to 350°.

Stir flour, sugar, salt, and ginger into drippings; cook, stirring constantly, until bubbly. Stir in tangerine juice; continue cooking and stirring until sauce thickens and boils 1 minute; pour over chicken; cover.

Bake 60 minutes, or until chicken is tender.

Toss hot rice with almonds; spoon onto a large serving platter. Arrange chicken on top. Pass sauce separately to spoon over all.
Yield: 4 servings.

TURKEY

SOUTHERN OYSTER STUFFING

    1 large onion, chopped (1 cup)
    1 cup thinly sliced celery
 ¾ cup butter or margarine
    2 cans (8 ozs. each) oysters
1¼ cups light cream
 ⅓ cup chopped parsley
 ½ teaspoon salt
 ⅛ teaspoon liquid red-pepper seasoning
    3 packages (3½ ozs. each) unsalted soda crackers,
        coarsely crushed

Preheat oven to 350°.

Sauté onion and celery in butter in a medium skillet until soft.

Drain liquid from oysters; stir into onion mixture with cream, parsley, salt, and red-pepper seasoning; heat to boiling.

Drizzle over crackers in a large bowl; add oysters; toss to mix.

Yield: About 10 cups or enough to stuff a 12- to 14-lb. turkey.

CORN-AND-ONION STUFFING

    1 can (12 ozs.) whole-kernel corn
        Turkey or chicken broth
    6 cups herb-seasoned stuffing mix (about 1½
        packages)
1¼ teaspoons salt
 ¼ teaspoon dried basil, crushed
    3 cups chopped green onions
    1 cup chopped celery
    6 tablespoons butter or margarine

Drain liquid from corn into a 2-cup measure; add enough turkey or chicken broth to measure 1½ cups.

Combine corn, stuffing mix, salt, and basil in a large bowl.

Sauté green onions and celery in butter until soft in a large skillet. Stir in the 1½ cups corn liquid; heat to boiling. Pour over stuffing mixture; toss until evenly moist.

Yield: About 9 cups or enough to stuff a 12-lb. turkey.

SAGE STUFFING

    4 large onions, chopped (4 cups)
    2 tablespoons butter or margarine
    8 cups small cubes white bread (about 1 loaf)
    1 tablespoon dried sage, crushed
    2 teaspoons salt
 ¼ teaspoon pepper

Sauté onions slowly in butter in a large skillet until wilted; spoon over bread cubes in a large bowl. Sprinkle sage, salt, and pepper over top; toss until evenly moist.

Yield: About 10 cups or enough to stuff a 12-lb. turkey.

SAUSAGE STUFFING

    1 lb. sweet Italian sausages
    8 cups small white bread cubes (about 1 loaf)
    4 tablespoons butter or margarine
    1 large onion, chopped (1 cup)
    1 cup chopped celery
 ½ cup chopped parsley
    1 teaspoon dried oregano, crushed
    1 teaspoon salt
 ¾ cup water

Peel casings from sausages and crumble meat. Sauté slowly in a medium skillet until all fat cooks out and meat is lightly browned. Remove with a slotted spoon and place in a large bowl with bread. Pour off all drippings, then return 2 tablespoons to skillet. Add butter and heat.

Stir in chopped onion and celery; sauté until soft. Stir in parsley, oregano, salt, and water; heat to boiling. Pour over bread mixture; toss until evenly moist.

Yield: About 10 cups or enough to stuff a 12-lb. turkey.

GIBLET GRAVY

    Turkey giblets and neck
1 medium onion, peeled and sliced
    Few celery tops
    Few peppercorns
1 teaspoon salt
4 cups water
    Turkey fat and drippings
½ cup all-purpose flour

Rinse giblets and neck. Combine all but liver with onion, celery tops, peppercorns, salt, and water in a medium saucepan; cover. Simmer 2 hours; add liver. Simmer 20 minutes longer, or until meat is tender. Strain broth into a medium bowl; chop giblets and neck meat.

After turkey has roasted, pour drippings from roasting pan into a 4-cup measure; let stand a few minutes until fat rises to top, then skim off into a bowl. Measure ½ cup and return to roasting pan; add giblet broth to drippings to make 4 cups.

Blend flour into fat in pan; cook, stirring constantly, until bubbly. Stir in the 4 cups liquid; continue cooking and stirring until gravy thickens and boils 1 minute; stir in chopped giblets. Season with salt and pepper if needed.

Yield: 4 cups.

TURKEY ROAST ROYALE

1 frozen self-basting turkey breast, weighing
    about 5 lbs.
1 medium onion, chopped (½ cup)
½ cup chopped celery
¼ cup chopped red pepper
4 tablespoons butter or margarine
2 tablespoons chopped parsley
½ teaspoon dried thyme, crushed
1 teaspoon salt
⅛ teaspoon pepper
⅓ cup water
6 slices white bread, toasted and cut in small
    cubes (3 cups)
    Chicory or curly endive

Thaw turkey breast; rinse inside and out; pat dry with paper toweling.

Sauté onion, celery, and red pepper in butter until soft in a medium skillet. Stir in parsley, thyme, salt, pepper, and water; heat to boiling. Pour over bread cubes in a medium bowl; toss to mix.

Preheat oven to 325°.

Lightly stuff part of the bread mixture into neck cavity; smooth neck skin over stuffing and skewer to back of neck. Stuff remaining bread mixture into breast cavity; pull edges of skin over stuffing and hold in place with skewers. Place breast, skin side up, on a rack in a shallow roasting pan. Insert meat thermometer into thickest part of breast without touching bone.

Roast 2 hours, or until turkey is tender and thermometer registers 180°. Lift onto a heated large serving platter. Surround with chicory leaves.

Yield: 8 servings.

TURKEY RAGOUT

1 medium onion, chopped (½ cup)
2 tablespoons butter or margarine
2 cups cubed cooked turkey
1 can (8 ozs.) small white potatoes, drained and
    diced
1 can (10¾ ozs.) condensed cream of mushroom
    soup
1 can (8 ozs.) diced carrots
½ teaspoon dried oregano, crushed
1 tablespoon chopped parsley

Sauté onion in butter in a medium skillet until soft; push to one side.

Stir in turkey and potatoes; brown lightly. Stir in soup, carrots and liquid, and oregano; heat slowly, stirring several times, to boiling; cover. Simmer 10 minutes to blend flavors; sprinkle parsley over top. Serve from skillet.

Yield: 4 servings.

SWEET-SOUR TURKEY

1 two-pound frozen boneless white and dark meat
  turkey roast
1 egg
5 tablespoons cornstarch
2 tablespoons salad oil
1 can (20 ozs.) pineapple chunks in juice
½ cup vinegar
⅔ cup firmly packed light brown sugar
1 tablespoon soy sauce
1 large green pepper, quartered, seeded, and cut
  in strips
1 can (8 ozs.) water chestnuts, drained and sliced
  Chinese noodles

Cook turkey roast as label directs; remove from foil pan; cool. Cut into ¾-inch cubes. (There should be 4 cups.)

Beat egg in a medium bowl; add turkey cubes and toss until evenly coated. Sprinkle 3 tablespoons of the cornstarch over top; toss again until coated.

Brown quickly in salad oil in a large skillet; remove from skillet.

Drain juice from pineapple into a 1-cup measure. (There should be 1 cup.) Stir pineapple juice, vinegar, brown sugar, and soy sauce into drippings in skillet; heat, stirring constantly, to boiling. Stir in green-pepper strips; simmer 2 minutes.

Blend remaining 2 tablespoons cornstarch with a little water in a cup until smooth; stir into mixture in skillet. Cook, stirring constantly, until mixture thickens and boils 1 minute. Stir in turkey, pineapple, and water chestnuts; heat slowly just until hot.

Spoon Chinese noodles around edge on a large deep serving platter. Spoon turkey mixture in center.

Yield: 6 servings.

DEVILED DRUMSTICKS

6 medium-sized turkey drumsticks, weighing
  about 4 lbs.
2 tablespoons salad oil
1 medium onion, chopped (½ cup)
2 envelopes instant chicken broth
  Water
1 teaspoon salt
1 egg
⅔ cup fine dry bread crumbs
1 teaspoon garlic powder
6 tablespoons butter or margarine
3 tablespoons prepared hot spicy mustard
2 tablespoons lemon juice

Preheat oven to 350°.

Rinse drumsticks and pat dry with paper toweling. Brown in salad oil in a large skillet; place in a single layer in a baking pan, 13x9x2 inches.

Stir onion into drippings; sauté until soft. Stir in chicken broth, 1 cup water, and ½ teaspoon of the salt; pour over drumsticks; cover.

Bake 1½ hours, or until drumsticks are tender. Remove from pan; cool just until easy to handle. (Chill cooking liquid to use for soup.)

Preheat broiler.

Beat egg with 2 tablespoons water in a pie plate; mix bread crumbs, garlic powder, and remaining ½ teaspoon salt in a second pie plate. Dip drumsticks into egg mixture, then into crumbs to coat generously. Place on rack in broiler pan.

Melt butter in a small saucepan; stir in mustard and lemon juice; drizzle half over drumsticks.

Broil, 6 inches from heat, 5 minutes; turn drumsticks; drizzle remaining butter mixture over top. Broil 3 to 4 minutes longer, or until golden-brown.

Arrange drumsticks on a heated large serving platter. Garnish with parsley and sliced tomatoes if you like.

Yield: 6 servings.

CHEF'S CHICKEN (p.170) ▶
SAN FERNANDO SPINACH SALAD (p.329)
BOURBON BAKED BEANS (p.291)

CARIBBEAN TURKEY

4 small turkey drumsticks, weighing about 2 lbs.
¼ cup all-purpose flour
1½ teaspoons salt
¼ teaspoon pepper
¼ cup salad oil
1 large onion, chopped (1 cup)
1 medium-sized green pepper, quartered, cored,
    and chopped
1 clove garlic, chopped
2 teaspoons curry powder
1 can (16 ozs.) tomatoes
¼ cup currants
1 tablespoon cornstarch
3 cups hot cooked rice
    Baked Bananas (recipe on page 369)

Rinse drumsticks and pat dry with paper toweling. Shake in mixture of flour, ½ teaspoon of the salt, and pepper in a transparent bag. Brown slowly in salad oil in a large skillet; place in a baking dish, 13x9x2 inches.

Preheat oven to 375°.

Stir onion, green pepper, garlic, and curry powder into drippings; sauté until onion and pepper are soft. Stir in remaining 1 teaspoon salt, tomatoes, and currants; heat to boiling. Pour over turkey; cover.

Bake 1¾ hours, or until turkey is tender; remove from dish; keep hot.

Pour sauce into a small saucepan; skim off any fat; reheat sauce to boiling.

Blend cornstarch with a little water in a cup until smooth; stir into boiling sauce. Cook, stirring constantly, until sauce thickens and boils 1 minutes.

Spoon rice onto a large serving platter; arrange drumsticks on top. Spoon part of the sauce over turkey, then serve remainder separately. Serve with Baked Bananas.

Yield: 4 servings.

◀ *(Clockwise from top)*
CANTONESE CHICKEN (p.168)
CHICKEN-SHRIMP FRIED RICE (p.270)
WALNUT CHICKEN (p.179)

MANDARIN TURKEY PLATTER

1 frozen boneless white and dark meat turkey
    roast, weighing about 4½ lbs.
½ cup pineapple preserves
¼ cup whole-berry cranberry sauce
3 tablespoons lemon juice
1 cup uncooked regular rice
2 tablespoons lime juice
4 tablespoons butter or margarine
½ cup sliced green onions
1 can (8 ozs.) water chestnuts, drained and
    chopped coarsely
1 can (11 ozs.) mandarin orange segments, drained

Prepare turkey and start roasting as label directs.

About 45 minutes before end of roasting time, combine pineapple preserves, cranberry sauce, and lemon juice in a small saucepan; heat slowly, stirring constantly, to boiling. Spoon half over turkey.

Continue roasting 15 minutes; spoon remaining cranberry mixture over turkey. Roast 15 minutes longer, or until thermometer registers 175° and turkey is tender.

While turkey cooks, cook rice in salted water as label directs; add lime juice and 2 tablespoons of the butter. Toss until butter melts; keep hot.

Sauté green onions in remaining 2 tablespoons butter in a large skillet until soft; stir in water chestnuts, mandarin orange segments, and rice mixture. Heat slowly, tossing lightly several times, just until hot.

Place turkey on a heated large serving platter; spoon rice mixture around edge. Garnish platter with ruffled green onion tops if you like. Slice turkey, removing strings as you slice.

Yield: 8 servings, plus enough turkey for a bonus meal.

STUFFED TURKEY CUTLETS

1 bag (16 ozs.) frozen chopped turnip greens
1 carton (12 ozs.) pot cheese or cottage cheese
¾ cup grated Parmesan cheese
7 tablespoons butter or margarine
⅛ teaspoon pepper
   Dash of ground nutmeg
1 cup packaged stuffing mix, crushed
1½ lbs. turkey cutlets

Cook turnip greens as label directs; drain well; press out liquid with back of spoon.

Combine greens, pot cheese, Parmesan cheese, 4 tablespoons of the butter, pepper, nutmeg, and stuffing mix in a large bowl; mix until completely blended.

Preheat oven to 350°.

Wipe turkey cutlets with paper toweling to remove any moisture. Brown slowly, part at a time, in remaining 3 tablespoons butter in a large skillet. Place half in a greased shallow baking dish, 12x8x2 inches to make a layer; spoon stuffing mixture evenly over turkey. Place remaining cutlets on top, arranging them in the same pattern as bottom layer; cover dish tightly with foil.

Bake 45 minutes, or until turkey is tender. Serve from baking dish, removing each serving with a pancake turner so stuffing is sandwiched between two layers of turkey.

Yield: 6 servings.

SICILIAN TURKEY

4 turkey tenderloin steaks, weighing about 1 lb.
2 tablespoons salad oil
4 large tomatoes, peeled and chopped (4 cups)
¼ cup water
¼ cup dry sherry
1 envelope spaghetti sauce mix
1 teaspoon salt
8 small white onions, peeled
2 lbs. lima beans, shelled (2 cups)
2 large carrots, pared and diced (2 cups)

Brown turkey steaks slowly in salad oil in a large skillet; remove and set aside.

Stir tomatoes, water, sherry, spaghetti sauce mix, and salt into drippings in skillet; heat, stirring constantly, to boiling; cover. Simmer 10 minutes.

Place turkey and onions in sauce; cover. Simmer 15 minutes.

Stir limas and carrots into skillet; heat to boiling; cover.

Cook 15 minutes, or until turkey and vegetables are tender. Serve as is or with cooked plain noodles if you like.

Yield: 4 servings.

SPANISH TURKEY

1 frozen self-basting turkey, weighing about 6 lbs., thawed
   Salad oil
1 envelope old-fashioned French salad dressing mix
2 tablespoons water
½ cup cider vinegar
1 can (15 ozs.) tomato sauce
1 tablespoon chili powder
1 teaspoon salt
½ teaspoon pepper

Remove giblets from turkey; rinse turkey inside and out; pat dry with paper toweling. Thread on spit of rotisserie, following manufacturer's directions; brush all over with salad oil. Insert meat thermometer into thickest part of a thigh so it doesn't touch bone or spit. Set spit in position; start rotisserie. Roast 2½ hours.

Combine salad dressing mix, water, vinegar, tomato sauce, chili powder, salt, and pepper in a small saucepan; brush part over turkey. Continue roasting, brushing several times with more tomato mixture, 1 hour, or until thermometer registers 180°.

Remove turkey from spit to a large cutting board; let stand 20 minutes for easier carving.

Simmer remaining tomato mixture, covered, 25 minutes, or until thickened slightly. Carve turkey; serve with extra sauce.

Yield: 8 to 10 servings.

SAUCY TURKEY AND TOAST

1 small onion, chopped (¼ cup)
1 tablespoon butter or margarine
2 cups cubed cooked turkey
1 can (10½ ozs.) chicken gravy
¼ cup milk
1 teaspoon Worcestershire sauce
¼ teaspoon salt
1 package (10 ozs.) frozen broccoli spears
4 slices white bread, toasted

Sauté onion in butter until soft in a medium skillet; stir in turkey; sauté several minutes.

Stir in gravy, milk, Worcestershire sauce, and salt; heat to boiling. Simmer 5 minutes to blend flavors.

While turkey mixture cooks, cook broccoli as label directs; drain well. Place spears, dividing evenly, on toast on four serving plates; spoon turkey mixture on top. Serve hot.

Yield: 4 servings.

BENGALI TURKEY DINNER

1 fresh or frozen turkey, weighing about 6 lbs.
1 carton (16 ozs.) plain yogurt
⅓ cup lemon juice
2 cloves garlic, minced
1 teaspoon salt
¼ teaspoon seasoned pepper
1 teaspoon ground ginger
½ teaspoon turmeric
¼ teaspoon cumin
Few drops red-pepper seasoning
1½ bags (16 ozs. each) frozen blackeye peas
1 can (10¾ ozs.) condensed chicken broth
1 medium onion, chopped (½ cup)
1 small carrot, pared and minced
¼ cup chopped celery

If using a frozen turkey, thaw completely. Rinse bird inside and out; pat dry with paper toweling. Fasten neck skin to back of bird with a plastic or wooden skewer; twist wing tips flat against back. Close body opening and tie legs to tail. Place turkey in a large glass or plastic dish.

Mix yogurt, lemon juice, garlic, salt, pepper, ginger, turmeric, cumin, and red-pepper seasoning in a medium bowl; spread over turkey; cover loosely. Chill several hours or overnight to season.

Preheat oven to 325°.

Lift turkey from marinade and place in a large shallow baking dish; coat turkey with marinade; place a tent of foil over dish. (Set remaining marinade aside.)

Bake 2 hours; remove foil. Drain liquid from baking dish into a bowl and set aside.

While turkey cooks, cook peas as label directs; drain well. Combine with chicken broth, onion, carrot, celery, and remaining turkey marinade; spoon around turkey in pan.

Bake, uncovered, 45 minutes, or until turkey is very tender and golden. (If pea mixture should start to look dry during baking, stir in some of the liquid drained from turkey.)

Place turkey on a cutting board and carve; arrange pieces on a large platter. Spoon peas into a serving bowl.

Yield: 8 servings.

ITALIAN TURKEY BAKE

1 two-pound frozen boneless turkey roast
1 package (8 ozs.) spaghetti, broken into 1-inch
    lengths
1 package (10 ozs.) frozen baby lima beans
4 tablespoons butter or margarine
1 cup crumbled plain crackers
1 large onion, chopped (1 cup)
1 large green pepper, quartered, cored, and
    chopped (½ cup)
2 cans (10½ ozs. each) chicken gravy
1 cup (8-oz. carton) dairy sour cream
¼ cup dry sherry
¼ teaspoon pepper
¼ cup grated Parmesan cheese

Roast turkey as label directs; cool. Pull off skin; cut meat into small cubes.

Cook spaghetti in a kettle as label directs; drain; return to kettle. Cook lima beans as label directs; drain. Add lima beans and turkey to spaghetti.

Preheat oven to 350°.

Melt butter in a medium saucepan; measure out 2 tablespoonfuls and toss with cracker crumbs in a small bowl.

Stir onion and green pepper into remaining melted butter in pan; sauté until soft. Stir in gravy; heat to boiling.

Slowly stir about 1 cup of the gravy mixture into sour cream in a small bowl, then stir back into pan; stir in sherry and pepper; heat just until bubbly. Stir into spaghetti mixture. Spoon into a baking dish, 13x9x2 inches. Spoon buttered crumbs diagonally in ribbons on top; sprinkle Parmesan cheese over all.

Bake 35 minutes, or until bubbly and topping is golden. Garnish with tiny cutouts of green pepper if you like.

Yield: 8 to 10 servings.

TARRAGON TURKEY ROLLS

2 cups finely diced cooked turkey
½ cup diced celery
¼ cup chopped green onions
⅓ cup mayonnaise or salad dressing
¼ teaspoon dried tarragon, crushed
¼ teaspoon salt
1 tablespoon lemon juice
2 cups biscuit mix
½ cup water
1 tablespoon instant minced onion
1 tablespoon butter or margarine
1 can (10¾ ozs.) condensed cream of chicken soup
½ cup milk

Preheat oven to 375°.

Combine turkey, celery, and green onions in a medium bowl. Blend mayonnaise, tarragon, salt, and lemon juice in a cup; fold into turkey mixture.

Combine biscuit mix and water in a medium bowl; stir lightly with a fork until dough holds together. Turn out onto a lightly floured cloth; knead ½ minute. Roll out to a square, 12x12 inches; cut in half lengthwise and in thirds crosswise to make 6 rectangles.

Spread about ⅓ cup of the turkey mixture over each rectangle; starting at a short end, roll up, jelly-roll fashion; pinch edges to seal. Place rolls seam side down on a greased large cookie sheet; cut two or three slits in top of each.

Bake 30 minutes, or until golden.

While rolls bake, sauté instant onion lightly in butter in a small saucepan; stir in soup and milk. Heat slowly to boiling. Serve over turkey rolls.

Yield: 6 servings.

TURKEY COLOMBO

1 lb. turkey cutlets
¼ cup milk
⅔ cup finely crushed four-grain cereal flakes
2 tablespoons all-purpose flour
½ teaspoon salt
½ teaspoon dried Italian herbs, crushed
¼ teaspoon garlic powder
⅛ teaspoon pepper
3 tablespoons salad oil
1 can (3 or 4 ozs.) sliced mushrooms
¼ cup tomato paste
¼ cup dry white wine
2 tablespoons chopped parsley

Wipe turkey cutlets with paper toweling to remove any moisture.

Measure milk into a pie plate. Combine crushed cereal, flour, salt, Italian herbs, garlic powder, and pepper in a second pie plate; mix well.

Dip turkey cutlets into milk, then into crumb mixture to coat both sides well. Sauté slowly, a few at a time, in salad oil until brown in a large skillet; remove all from pan.

Drain liquid from mushrooms into a 1-cup measure; add water, if needed, to make ⅓ cup. Stir into drippings in skillet with tomato paste, wine, and mushrooms. Heat slowly, stirring constantly, to boiling; place turkey in skillet; cover. Simmer 15 minutes, or until turkey is tender.

Arrange cutlets on a large serving platter; spoon sauce over top; sprinkle parsley over sauce.

Yield: 4 servings.

GOLDEN TURKEY PLATTER

1 two-pound frozen boneless white and dark meat
    turkey roast
2 medium-sized acorn squash
1 can (16 ozs.) whole unpeeled apricots
⅓ cup butter or margarine
3 tablespoons light molasses
2 tablespoons sweet sherry

Preheat oven to 375°.

Roast frozen turkey in its foil pan 1½ hours; remove from pan and place in a large shallow baking pan; leave oven on. (Save drippings in foil pan for making gravy if you like.)

While turkey cooks, cut each squash crosswise into ½-inch-thick slices; scoop out seeds, but do not pare.

Cook slices, covered, in boiling salted water in a large skillet 8 minutes, or just until barely tender; drain carefully. Place slices around roast in pan.

Drain syrup from apricots into a small bowl. Measure out ⅓ cup and combine with butter, molasses, and sherry in a small saucepan; heat to boiling; spoon half over turkey and squash.

Bake 15 minutes. Add apricots to pan; spoon remaining molasses mixture over turkey, squash, and apricots. Bake 15 minutes longer, or until lightly glazed.

Lift turkey onto a heated large serving platter; arrange squash rings at edges and apricots at ends. Garnish platter with a few sprigs of parsley if you like.

Yield: 6 servings.

TURKEY DIABLE

½ cup chopped celery
1 small onion, chopped (¼ cup)
5 tablespoons butter or margarine
¼ cup all-purpose flour
1 teaspoon salt
1 teaspoon dry mustard
2 cups milk
3 cups diced cooked turkey
⅛ teaspoon liquid red-pepper seasoning
1½ cups fresh bread crumbs (3 slices)

Preheat oven to 350°.

Sauté celery and onion in 4 tablespoons of the butter in a large skillet until soft. Stir in flour, salt, and mustard; cook, stirring constantly, until bubbly. Stir in milk; continue cooking and stirring until sauce thickens and boils 1 minute. Stir in turkey and red-pepper seasoning. Spoon into a 1½-quart baking dish.

Melt remaining 1 tablespoon butter in a small saucepan; stir in bread crumbs; sprinkle over turkey mixture.

Bake 30 minutes, or until bubbly.
Yield: 4 servings.

MEDITERRANEAN TURKEY BAKE

1 small eggplant, weighing about 1 lb.
½ cup salad oil
3 cups cubed cooked turkey
1 large onion, chopped (1 cup)
1 clove garlic, minced
1 can (29 ozs.) tomatoes
1 teaspoon dried Italian herbs
1¼ teaspoons salt
½ teaspoon sugar
¼ teaspoon pepper
1 cup uncooked regular rice

Pare eggplant and cut into ¾-inch cubes. Brown in part of the salad oil in a large skillet, adding more oil as needed; remove with a slotted spoon to a bowl.

Stir turkey into drippings in skillet; brown lightly; remove to a second bowl.

Stir onion and garlic into drippings; sauté until soft.

Drain liquid from tomatoes into a 4-cup measure; add water, if needed, to make 2¼ cups. Stir into onion mixture with tomatoes, herbs, salt, sugar, and pepper; heat to boiling.

Preheat oven to 350°.

Layer half each of the eggplant, turkey, rice, and sauce into a 2½-quart baking dish; repeat layers; cover.

Bake 1 hour and 15 minutes, or until rice is tender and liquid is absorbed.
Yield: 6 servings.

TURKEY MOLE

2 medium-sized green peppers, quartered, seeded, and cut up
2 small onions, peeled and quartered
2 cans (16 ozs. each) tomatoes
1 jar (4 ozs.) pimientos, drained
¼ cup salad oil
1 tablespoon chili powder
1¼ teaspoons salt
½ teaspoon liquid red-pepper seasoning
⅛ teaspoon ground cinnamon
⅛ teaspoon ground cloves
2 envelopes instant chicken broth
¼ cup fine dry bread crumbs
1 square unsweetened chocolate
4 cups cubed cooked turkey
Hot cooked rice

Combine half each of the green peppers, onions, tomatoes, and pimientos in an electric-blender container; cover. Blend until smooth. Pour into a bowl and repeat with rest of same ingredients.

Heat salad oil in a large skillet; stir in tomato mixture, chili powder, salt, red-pepper seasoning, cinnamon, cloves, and chicken broth. Heat slowly to boiling; cover. Simmer 30 minutes.

Stir in bread crumbs and chocolate until melted. Stir in turkey. Heat very slowly, stirring several times, 15 minutes, or until turkey is hot. Serve over rice.
Yield: 8 servings.

CURRIED TURKEY

2 tablespoons curry powder
¼ cup butter or margarine
1 large onion, chopped (1 cup)
3 tablespoons all-purpose flour
½ teaspoon ground ginger
1 can (13¾ ozs.) chicken broth
1 can (8 ozs.) crushed pineapple in syrup
1 can (8 ozs.) water chestnuts, drained and sliced
3 cups cubed cooked turkey
2 tablespoons lemon juice
3 cups hot cooked rice

Heat curry powder in butter in a large skillet 2 to 3 minutes. Stir in onion; sauté until soft.

Sprinkle flour and ginger over mixture, then stir in with chicken broth and pineapple and syrup. Heat to boiling; simmer 15 minutes.

Stir in water chestnuts and turkey; cover; simmer 15 minutes. Stir in lemon juice.

Spoon rice around edge in a shallow serving bowl; spoon turkey mixture in center. Serve as is or, if you like, with chopped peanuts, sieved hard-cooked egg, or chopped chutney to sprinkle on top.

Yield: 4 to 6 servings.

CONFETTI TURKEY LOAF

2 eggs
1 cup milk
2½ cups fresh bread crumbs (5 slices)
1 tablespoon minced onion
1½ teaspoons salt
1½ teaspoons poultry seasoning
½ teaspoon liquid red-pepper seasoning
¼ teaspoon dried thyme, crushed
3 cups finely chopped cooked turkey
½ cup cooked green peas
¼ cup diced drained pimientos
1 can (11 ozs.) condensed Cheddar cheese soup
1 teaspoon prepared hot spicy mustard

Grease a loaf pan, 8½x4½x2¾ inches; line bottom with a strip of foil, letting strip hang over ends of pan about ¼ inch; grease foil well.

Preheat oven to 375°.

Beat eggs in a large bowl; stir in ½ cup of the milk, bread crumbs, onion, salt, poultry seasoning, red-pepper seasoning, thyme, turkey, peas, and pimientos until well blended. Spoon into prepared pan, spreading top even.

Bake 45 minutes, or until loaf is firm and golden. Loosen around edges of pan with a knife; invert onto a serving platter; peel off foil.

While loaf bakes, combine cheese soup, remaining ½ cup milk, and mustard in a small saucepan; heat slowly, stirring several times, until mixture is smooth and hot.

Cut turkey loaf crosswise into 6 thick slices; top with cheese sauce.

Yield: 6 servings.

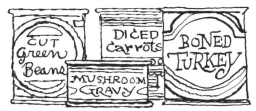

DAPPLED TURKEY FRICASSEE

1 can (10½ ozs.) mushroom gravy
1 can (8 ozs.) cut green beans, drained
1 can (8 ozs.) diced carrots, drained
1 can (5 ozs.) boned turkey, cut in bite-sized pieces
¼ teaspoon poultry seasoning
1 cup biscuit mix
1 teaspoon parsley flakes
⅓ cup milk

Preheat oven to 425°.

Combine gravy, green beans, carrots, turkey, and poultry seasoning in a medium saucepan. Heat to boiling; spoon into 4 individual baking dishes.

Combine biscuit mix and parsley flakes in a small bowl; stir in milk until mixture is evenly moist. Drop by teaspoonfuls on top of hot stew.

Bake 15 minutes, or until topping is puffed and golden.

Yield: 4 servings.

TURKEY STROGANOFF PIE

1 package (10 ozs.) frozen peas and carrots
1 cup sliced celery
¼ cup butter or margarine
¼ cup all-purpose flour
1½ teaspoons salt
1 teaspoon dried thyme, crushed
¼ teaspoon pepper
2 cups milk
1 cup (8-oz. carton) dairy sour cream
¼ cup whipping cream
3 cups cubed cooked turkey
1 can (16 ozs.) whole boiled onions, drained
½ package piecrust mix

Cook peas and carrots with celery in a small amount of boiling salted water in a medium saucepan 5 minutes; drain.

Melt butter in a large saucepan; stir in flour, salt, thyme, and pepper; cook, stirring constantly, until bubbly.

Stir in milk; continue cooking and stirring until mixture thickens and boils 1 minute. Stir about half into sour cream in a small bowl, then stir back into saucepan; stir in whipping cream, turkey, onions, and vegetable mixture. Spoon into a 2-quart shallow baking dish.

Preheat oven to 425°.

Prepare piecrust mix as label directs. Roll out on a lightly floured cloth to a rectangle, 8x6 inches; cut lengthwise into twelve ½-inch-wide strips. Weave 8 strips lengthwise and crosswise over filling to make a lattice top; trim ends even with edge of dish. Lay remaining 4 strips, overlapping slightly, around edge; press lightly to rim of dish.

Bake 40 minutes, or until bubbly and pastry is golden.

Yield: 6 servings.

TURKEY DIVAN

1 package (10 ozs.) frozen broccoli spears
2 large carrots, pared and cut in sticks
8 small slices cooked turkey
¼ cup butter or margarine
¼ cup all-purpose flour
1 envelope instant chicken broth
1¼ cups milk
2 tablespoons dry sherry
½ cup grated Parmesan cheese
½ cup whipping cream, whipped

Cook broccoli as label directs; drain. Cook carrot sticks in boiling water in a medium saucepan 10 minutes, or until tender; drain. Place vegetables in 4 individual broilerproof baking dishes; arrange turkey slices on top.

Preheat broiler.

Melt butter in a medium saucepan; stir in flour and chicken broth. Cook, stirring constantly, until bubbly. Stir in milk; continue cooking and stirring until mixture thickens and boils 1 minute; remove from heat. Stir in sherry and ¼ cup of the cheese; lightly fold in whipped cream. Pour over layers in baking dishes; sprinkle remaining ¼ cup cheese on top.

Broil, 4 to 6 inches from heat, 2 to 3 minutes, or until tops brown lightly.

Yield: 4 servings.

DUCKLING AND GOOSE

GOLDEN GLAZED DUCKLING

1 frozen duckling, weighing about 5 lbs., thawed
1 small onion, peeled and sliced
  Few celery tops
½ teaspoon salt
¼ teaspoon peppercorns
3 cups water
1 tablespoon sugar
1 teaspoon cornstarch
1 teaspoon ground cinnamon
½ cup frozen concentrate for tangerine juice,
    thawed
2 tablespoons lemon juice
2 tablespoons butter or margarine

Remove giblets from duckling. Rinse duckling inside and out; prick skin all over with a fork so fat will cook out. Skewer neck skin to back; twist wing tips flat against back. To prevent overcooking, wrap wings in foil. Close body cavity with poultry pins and string.

Place duckling in a kettle with onion, celery tops, salt, peppercorns, and water; heat to boiling; cover. Simmer 1 hour and 15 minutes, or until almost tender; drain; unwrap wings.

While duckling simmers, mix sugar, cornstarch, and cinnamon in a small saucepan; stir in tangerine concentrate and lemon juice. Cook, stirring constantly, until sauce thickens

and boils 1 minute; stir in butter.

Preheat broiler.

Place duckling on rack in broiler pan; brush part of the sauce over top and sides. Broil, 10 inches from heat, turning and brushing often with remaining sauce, ½ hour, or until a leg moves easily at the joint and duckling is a rich golden color.

Remove to a cutting board; take out skewers and cut away strings. Cut duckling into quarters with kitchen shears.

Yield: 4 servings.

ROAST STUFFED GOOSE

1 frozen goose, weighing about 10 lbs., thawed
  Salt
Sage Stuffing (recipe on page 190)

Remove giblets and neck from cavities of goose and simmer for broth for gravy if you like. Pull all fat from cavities; rinse goose inside and out; pat dry with paper toweling. Sprinkle salt lightly into cavities.

Spoon Sage Stuffing lightly into neck cavity; smooth neck skin over stuffing and skewer to back of bird. Spoon remaining stuffing into body cavity; close opening with poultry pins and string and tie legs to tail. Prick skin all over with a fork so fat will cook out.

Place goose, breast side up, on a rack in a shallow roasting pan. Insert meat thermometer into center of thigh next to body, making sure that the bulb does not touch bone or stuffing. Do not cover pan or add any water.

Roast 2 hours; spoon fat from pan. Roast 1½ hours longer, or until a drumstick feels soft and moves up and down and twists easily at the joint. Thermometer should register 190°.

Place goose on a large serving platter; take out skewers and cut away strings. Let stand 20 minutes for easier carving. Garnish platter with one of the suggestions from GARNISHES chapter.

Yield: 10 servings.

GOURMET DUCKLING PLATTER

1 frozen duckling, weighing about 5 lbs., thawed
  Salt
1 medium onion, peeled and halved
  Few celery tops
¼ cup dry white wine
½ cup chopped celery
2 tablespoons butter or margarine
1½ cups orange juice
1 teaspoon grated orange rind
½ cup light raisins
1⅓ cups packaged precooked rice
3 tablespoons all-purpose flour
1 can (11 ozs.) mandarin orange segments,
    drained
  Parsley

Preheat oven to 450°.

Remove giblets from duckling. Rinse duckling inside and out; pat dry with paper toweling. Sprinkle salt lightly into body and neck cavities; tuck onion and celery tops into body cavity. Tie legs to tail; skewer neck skin to back; twist wing tips flat against back. Place duckling, breast side up, on a rack in a shallow roasting pan. Prick skin all over with a fork so fat will cook out.

Roast 30 minutes; lower oven temperature to 350°. Pour all fat from pan; brush duckling with part of the wine.

Continue roasting, brushing every half hour with more of the wine, 1½ hours, or until richly browned and a drumstick moves up and down easily at the joint.

While duckling roasts, sauté celery in butter until soft in a medium skillet. Stir in orange juice and rind, raisins, and ½ teaspoon salt; heat to boiling. Stir in rice; cover; remove from heat. Let stand 10 minutes.

Remove duckling to another pan; keep warm while making gravy.

Pour drippings from roasting pan into a 2-cup measure; let stand a few minutes until fat rises to top, then skim off. Measure 3 tablespoons fat and return to pan. Add remaining wine and water to drippings to make 1½ cups.

Blend flour into fat in pan; cook, stirring constantly, until bubbly. Stir in the 1½ cups drippings mixture. Continue cooking and stirring until gravy thickens and boils 1 minute. Season with salt and pepper as needed.

Fluff rice mixture with a fork; spoon onto a large serving platter. Place duckling on top; take out skewer and cut away string.

Arrange orange segments to form small pumpkin shapes; top each with a sprig of parsley for a stem. Place in rice at one end of platter. Serve gravy separately to spoon over duckling.

Yield: 4 servings.

ROAST DUCKLING JUBILEE

1 frozen duckling, weighing about 5 lbs., thawed
  Salt
¼ cup orange juice
1 can (16 ozs.) pitted dark sweet cherries
1 tablespoon cornstarch
1 tablespoon butter or margarine
2 tablespoons curaçao

Preheat oven to 450°.

Remove giblets from duckling; rinse duckling inside and out; pat dry with paper toweling. Sprinkle salt lightly into body and neck cavities.

Tie legs to tail; skewer neck skin to back; twist wing tips flat against back. Place, breast side up, on a rack in a shallow roasting pan. Prick skin all over with a fork so fat will cook out.

Roast 30 minutes; lower oven temperature to 350°. Pour all fat from roasting pan.

Brush part of the orange juice over duckling. Continue roasting, brushing again with remaining orange juice, 1½ hours, or until golden and a drumstick moves up and down easily at the joint.

While duckling cooks, drain syrup from cherries into a 1-cup measure; add water to make 1 cup. Stir into cornstarch in a medium saucepan. Cook slowly, stirring constantly, until sauce thickens and boils 1 minute; stir in butter, curaçao, a dash of salt, and cherries. Heat again just until bubbly.

Place duckling on a large serving platter; take out skewer and cut away string. Garnish platter with watercress and halved orange slices if you like. Cut duckling into quarters with kitchen shears; serve with cherry sauce.

Yield: 4 servings.

CAPON AND CORNISH HENS

BUTTER-BAKED CAPON PLATTER

1 frozen capon, weighing about 7 lbs., thawed
  Salt
  Few celery tops
1 small onion, peeled and sliced
4 peppercorns
  Water
½ cup sesame seeds (about 3 ozs.)
½ cup butter or margarine
1 tablespoon instant minced onion
1 teaspoon ground sage
  Dash of pepper
1 package (8 ozs.) corn-bread stuffing mix
¼ cup all-purpose flour
  Onion-carrot Cups (recipe on page 300)
  Parsley

Remove giblets and neck from capon; rinse capon inside and out; pat dry with paper toweling. Salt cavity lightly.

Combine giblets (except liver) and neck, celery tops, sliced onion, ½ teaspoon salt, peppercorns, and 3 cups water in a medium saucepan. Heat to boiling; cover. Simmer 1 hour; add liver. Simmer 30 minutes longer, or until meat is tender. Strain broth into a small bowl. Chop giblets and neck meat and set aside for gravy.

Place sesame seeds in a medium skillet; heat very slowly, stirring often, until lightly toasted; remove from skillet.

Melt ¼ cup of the butter in same skillet; add 1 cup of the giblet broth, instant onion, sage, ½ teaspoon salt, and pepper; heat to boiling. Pour over stuffing mix in a large bowl; toss until evenly moist. Stir in sesame seeds.

Preheat oven to 350°.

Stuff breast cavity of capon lightly; smooth neck skin over stuffing and skewer to back of bird. Twist wing tips flat against back. Stuff body cavity lightly with rest of stuffing; close opening with poultry pins and string; tie legs to tail. Place capon, breast side up, on a rack in a shallow roasting pan. Insert meat thermometer into thickest part of a thigh, making sure that it doesn't touch bone or stuffing. Do not cover pan or add any water.

Melt remaining ¼ cup butter in a small saucepan; brush part over capon.

Roast, brushing once or twice with remaining melted butter and drippings in pan, 2½ hours, or until thermometer registers 190°.

Remove capon to a large serving platter; take out skewers and cut away strings. Let stand 15 minutes for easier carving.

Pour drippings from pan into a 4-cup measure; let stand a few minutes until fat rises to top, then skim off. Measure ¼ cup fat and return to pan; add remaining broth from giblets and water, if needed, to drippings to make 2 cups.

Blend flour into fat in pan; cook, stirring constantly, until bubbly. Stir in the 2 cups drippings mixture. Continue cooking and stirring until gravy thickens and boils 1 minute; stir in giblets. Season with salt and pepper if needed.

Place Onion-carrot Cups around capon on platter; tuck parsley sprigs around onions. Serve gravy separately to spoon over meat and stuffing.

Yield: 6 servings.

CORNISH HENS SEVILLE

6 Rock Cornish game hens, weighing about 1 lb.
   each
   Salt
   Pepper
2 packages (6 ozs. each) long-grain and wild-rice
   mix
1 cup thinly sliced celery
½ cup sliced green onions
4½ cups water
1 can (8 ozs.) water chestnuts, drained and diced
3 tablespoons butter or margarine, melted
½ cup orange juice
¼ cup light corn syrup

Thaw Cornish hens, if frozen, as label directs. Rinse inside and out; pat dry with paper toweling. Sprinkle salt and pepper lightly inside cavities.

Prepare rice mix with celery, green onions, and water in a large saucepan as label directs; remove from heat. Stir in water chestnuts.

Preheat oven to 400°.

Stuff rice mixture into neck and body cavities of hens, using ½ cup for each. Smooth neck skin over stuffing and skewer to backs; twist wing tips flat against backs. Close body openings with poultry pins and string; tie legs to tails. Place hens, breast side up, on a rack in a large shallow roasting pan. Brush part of the melted butter all over hens. Spoon extra rice mixture into a 1-quart baking dish; cover. Bake in same oven with hens for last 30 minutes.

Roast hens, brushing again with remaining melted butter, 45 minutes.

While hens bake, combine orange juice and

corn syrup in a small saucepan; heat to boiling. Simmer 5 minutes, or until mixture thickens slightly. Brush over hens.

Roast 15 minutes longer, or until hens are tender and richly glazed.

Fluff rice in baking dish with a fork and spoon into a layer on a large serving platter. Cut strings from hens and take out pins; arrange over rice. Garnish platter with Frosted Grapes and serve with Spiced Cranberries (see index) if you like.

Yield: 6 servings.

Note: If you prefer to stuff hens but skip the extra stuffing on the platter, one package of rice mix will be enough.

OVEN-FRIED CORNISH HENS

3 Rock Cornish game hens, weighing 1½ lbs.
   each
1 small can evaporated milk (⅔ cup)
½ envelope green-onion dip mix
¾ teaspoon salt
1½ cups dry bread crumbs
½ cup butter or margarine, melted

Thaw Cornish hens, if frozen, as label directs. Rinse inside and out; pat dry with paper toweling; split each hen in half.

Preheat oven to 400°.

Mix milk, dip mix, and salt in a pie plate; let stand 5 minutes. Sprinkle bread crumbs on waxed paper.

Dip hens in milk mixture, then in crumbs to coat well. Place in a single layer in a greased large shallow baking pan; drizzle melted butter over top.

Bake 1 hour, or until tender and golden.

Yield: 6 servings.

FISH AND SHELLFISH

THESE DAYS, FISH OR SHELLFISH, appear on most tables once or twice a week, and that's good menu planning—for this versatile food family is rich in protein, a big booster for vitamins and minerals, a boon to calorie watchers, and what's best, has a delicate flavor almost everyone likes. Thanks, also, to frozen foods and modern transportation, any homemaker, anywhere in the country, can have these treats anytime she wishes.

Among fresh-water or ocean seafoods, depend on your own regional specialties because here is the key to savings. And whether it's Boston scrod, Florida red snapper, Alaska king crab, Maine lobster, Colorado trout, Washington salmon, or Great Lakes whitefish, all are delicacies to be enjoyed for any dinner.

It pays, too, to get acquainted with all of the new varieties that are showing up constantly in the marketplace. Because we're eating so much more fish than ever before, the supplies of traditional favorites just can't keep up with the demand. As a result, you're likely to see names such as whiting, turbot, or pollock alongside cod, flounder, and haddock. Since they are less familiar, they usually carry lower price tags and will be among your best buys. All can be used as alternates in most recipes, although you may have to do a little experimenting with cooking times and seasonings to determine what your family likes best.

In the canned-food area, there are those old stand-bys that most of us rely on for sandwiches, salads, and casseroles. Depending on how they're prepared, tuna, salmon, shrimp, and crab—to name just a few—can go as obligingly into company menus as they do into family meals. The recipes and buying hints on the following pages will help you serve all kinds of fish and shellfish in all kinds of new ways.

FISH

How to buy

This popular food appears on the market in many different forms. To be sure of what you're getting, it pays to know the meanings of these basic terms:

Whole or round–This is fish just as it comes from the water. Before cooking, it must be scaled and eviscerated. Usually the head, fins, and tail are removed.

Drawn—Here the fish is left whole but eviscerated. Before cooking, remove the scales. Again, the head, fins, and tail may be removed.

Dressed or pan-dressed—Just as the term implies, these fish have been scaled and eviscerated with head, tail, and fins removed. In other words, they are ready for the cooking pan. Available fresh or frozen.

Steaks—These are cross-section slices cut from a large dressed fish. Most will be from ⅝ to 1 inch thick with a piece of the backbone intact. Available fresh or frozen.

Fillets—Virtually boneless and waste-free, these pieces come from the sides of fish, and are cut lengthwise away from the backbone. The skin may be left on or removed. No further fixing is necessary before cooking. Available fresh or frozen.

Butterfly fillet—For this treat, a piece is cut from both sides of the same fish and held together by flesh and skin. Available fresh, and in some areas, frozen.

Portions—Uniform in size, these pieces are cut from blocks of frozen boneless fish. They come frozen and breaded.

Sticks—Like portions, these are even stick-like sections cut from blocks of frozen boneless fish and have a seasoned crumb coating. Available frozen.

In buying whole or round fresh fish, look for sparkly-clear, slightly bulging eyes, reddish gills, brightly colored tight scales, shiny skin, and a firm springy flesh with the bones adhering securely to the meat. If you want to test the meat, press it lightly with your finger—it should spring back. Pay attention, too, to the odor—freshly caught fish has almost no fishy aroma.

In buying fresh steaks or fillets, look for firm flesh that appears freshly cut. Avoid any pieces that have started to discolor, or that tend to be dry and curled at the edges.

In buying frozen fish of any kind, check the package. It should be almost odor-free and solidly frozen with no ice crystals clinging to the outside.

How to store

Since all kinds of fresh fish are extremely perishable, be sure to keep them refrigerated from the time of purchase to use.

Wrap the fish in moisture- and vaporproof paper before chilling, or store in a tightly covered container. Plan to use it within one or two days. If the fish is cooked first, then placed in a covered container and chilled, you can hold it safely for three to four days.

How to cook

Here are a few of the easiest and most popular ways to cook small whole or split fish, fillets, or steaks—and have them richly golden on the outside, flaky-moist on the inside. The only secrets to remember are to handle the fish gently and to cook quickly.

To pan-fry—First dip the fish in slightly beaten egg, then in seasoned cracker, bread, or cereal crumbs, or cornmeal to make a generous coating.

Heat about a quarter inch of melted shortening, salad oil, or bacon drippings in a large skillet. Place the fish, a few pieces at a time (don't crowd), into the hot fat and cook over medium heat, turning once, 5 to 8 minutes. Exact time will depend on the thickness of the fish, so watch carefully.

To test for doneness, stick a fork into the fish—the meat will come away easily in little flakes if the fish has cooked long enough. Lift the pieces onto a platter with a pancake turner or wide slotted spatula. Serve plain or with one of your favorite sauces.

To broil—Grease the rack of your broiler pan. Arrange the fish, not touching, in a single layer on rack. Brush melted butter or salad oil over all. Place pan about 4 inches from the heat. Broil split fish or fillets from 6 to 10 minutes—without turning. Since steaks are thicker, they will need to be turned—but only once. Allow from 5 to 8 minutes cooking time on each side. Broil whole fish, again turning only once, 5 to 10 minutes on each side. Season with a sprinkle of salt, pepper, and lemon juice; lift onto platter and serve plain or with sauce.

To poach—Use a saucepan or skillet big enough to hold the fish without crowding and add enough liquid to cover the fish. Water, milk, or water and white wine combined, all seasoned to taste, are popular choices. Heat the liquid to boiling and add the fish in a single layer. Reheat just to simmering, cover, and continue simmering just until the fish is cooked. It will take about 5 minutes for flat fillets and from 7 to 10 minutes for steaks and small whole fish, depending upon the thickness. Since fish is tender long before it's cooked, it is always best to start testing for doneness about halfway through the time your recipe suggests.

Lift the fish from the liquid with a wide spatula and drain well before serving.

To bake—Brush the fish with melted butter or margarine and sprinkle with salt and pepper, or use one of the coatings suggested under pan-frying. Place it in a greased shallow baking dish. Bake plain fish at 350°, allowing about 30 minutes for a small whole fish, and from 10 to 20 minutes for fillets and steaks. To prevent drying, brush the fish several times during baking with more melted butter or a sauce of your choice.

Bake breaded fish at 400° for 10 to 20 minutes, or until cooked. Before baking, drizzle a little melted butter or margarine or salad oil over the top. In either case, you needn't turn the fish.

To deep-fry—Bread the fish the same as for pan-frying. Pour enough salad oil into a deep-fat fryer or deep saucepan to fill halfway; heat to 350°. Add fish, a few pieces at a time, and fry until golden. Turned once, fillets will cook in 3 to 5 minutes. Lift pieces from fat with a slotted spatula and drain well on paper toweling.

SHELLFISH

How to buy

In most areas, you can take your pick of fresh or frozen shellfish—and of course, those familiar stand-bys and specialties in cans and jars. If available fresh, it may be live, partly prepared, or cooked and ready to eat. Here are pointers to remember:

Shrimp—Fresh varieties come cooked or uncooked, in the shell or shelled and de-veined. Depending on the variety, the shell will be light gray, grayish-pink, or deep red. As the shrimp cook, the shells should turn bright red and the meat should become pink.

In the frozen food department, shrimp are available shelled and ready to cook, cooked and ready to eat, or breaded in cooked and uncooked forms.

Crabs and lobsters—If buying them live, it is important that they be *alive* and actively moving their legs. If cooked, look for bright red shells on both lobsters and hard-shell crabs. Soft-shell crabs should be a bright blue-gray color. Both kinds of meat are also available fresh or frozen, and with either, it should be odor-free and a clear white with patches of pink. Lobster tails also come frozen; follow the same guidelines as for buying frozen fish.

Oysters, clams, and mussels—Take your choice of fresh in the shell, fresh-shucked or removed from the shell and packed in a clear liquid, or frozen. If you buy them fresh in the shell, make sure that they are alive with the shells tightly closed. (Or if partly opened, the shells should close again when tapped.)

Scallops—Look for these delicacies fresh, frozen, or breaded and frozen. Fresh ones—either the large sea scallops or the smaller bay variety—should be plump, creamy-white, almost free of liquid, and have a slightly sweet aroma.

How to store
Wrap and chill shellfish the same as fresh fish. Cook live varieties immediately, then place the meat in a covered container, chill, and use within one or two days.

How to cook
To poach shrimp—Whether you shell and devein the shrimp before or after cooking depends on your own preference, but either way, here's how: Holding the shrimp, shell side down, break off the feelers. Then gently run your thumb between the shell and the meat, bending shell back as you go and easing shrimp out; break or cut off tail if still intact. To remove the sand vein, make a shallow cut down the back of each shrimp; then, holding it under running cold water, lift out the thin black line with the tip of a small knife.

Half-fill a large skillet with water (or enough to cover shrimp); season with lemon slices or juice, salt, onion, and a few pickling spices or packaged shrimp spice. Heat to boiling; add shrimp; reheat just to simmering; cover. Cook 4 to 5 minutes, depending on the size, or until the shrimp curl, turn pink, and are tender. Remove from water at once. Serve chilled as a cocktail with sauce, or use in recipes calling for cooked shrimp.

To poach scallops—Wash scallops under running cold water. Pour enough water into a skillet to cover scallops; season with a slice each of onion and lemon and a few peppercorns; heat to boiling. Add scallops; reheat to simmering, cover, and cook 3 to 4 minutes, depending on size. When cooked through, they will be opaque and tender. Remove from water at once. Serve chilled as a cocktail with sauce, or use in recipes calling for cooked scallops.

To boil live lobster—Plunge the lobster, head first, into a kettle of boiling salted water;

cover; reheat to boiling. Cook 12 to 15 minutes, or until the shell turns bright red; drain.

To remove the meat to use in other dishes, place the lobster on its back on a cutting board. Break off the claws; then, using kitchen shears, slit the soft shell on the underside from head to tail and gently pull out the meat. Make a shallow cut down the center of the meat (flat side) and remove the dark vein. Save the red roe or coral and the green liver or tomalley to use as garnishes or to add to a salad. Discard the stomach sac back of the head; pick meat from head with a small fork. Crack claws with a lobster cracker or nutcracker and pull out meat.

To serve in the shell, slit the undershell from head to tail as described above; spread open and remove the dark vein and stomach sac. Leave the roe and tomalley in place. For easier eating, crack the large claws. Serve hot with lemon and melted butter as a dipping sauce. To serve cold, chill the lobster after cooking, then split just before mealtime. Serve with tartar sauce or lemon-seasoned mayonnaise.

To broil lobster—Place live lobster on its back on a cutting board. Insert the point of a heavy sharp knife into lobster where tail and body meet, pushing it through to the back shell to sever the spinal cord. Split lobster from head to tail, being careful not to cut through back shell. Spread lobster open and remove the dark vein and stomach sac. Leave roe and tomalley in place; crack large claws. Place lobster, cut side up, on rack in broiler pan; brush generously with melted butter or margarine and sprinkle with salt. Broil, 4 inches from heat, and brushing several times with more melted butter, 10 to 15 minutes, or until lightly golden. Large sizes may take a few minutes longer. Serve with lemon and melted butter or margarine as a dipping sauce.

To steam clams—Scrub soft-shell or steamer clams well with a brush under running cold water. Pile into a large kettle or rack in steamer. Pour about an inch of water, or enough to cover bottom, into kettle; heat to boiling; cover. Steam 5 to 8 minutes, or just until shells open wide. (Discard any that do not open.) Serve in soup bowls with tiny cups of clam broth and melted butter or margarine. Allow about a dozen clams for each serving.

To fry clams—Dip shucked clams into beaten egg seasoned with salt and pepper, then into fine bread or cracker crumbs to coat generously. Fry in deep fat heated to 375° about 6 minutes, or until golden. Lift from fat with a slotted spatula and drain well on paper toweling. Serve with tartar or cocktail sauce.

To fry oysters—Follow directions above for frying clams.

To steam mussels—Follow directions for steaming clams, with this exception: After scrubbing mussels, cut away beards with kitchen scissors.

To boil hard-shell crab—Scrub crab thoroughly under running cold water. Holding it with tongs, plunge it, head first, into a large kettle of salted boiling water. Reheat to boiling; cover. Cook 10 to 15 minutes, or until shell turns red. Drain, rinse in cold water, and cool until easy to handle.

Twist off claws and legs and crack them with a mallet or hammer; pull out meat with a pick or the tip of a small sharp knife. Run knife under "apron" on back shell and break it off. Pull body shells apart, discarding top one. Scrape away spongy fingers on the inside of the shell and wash again. Grasping body with both hands, break it in half; cut away thin shells from around edges. Remove meat in large lumps with your fingers or a knife. Serve chilled as a cocktail with sauce, or use in recipes calling for cooked crab meat.

To sauté soft-shell crabs—With kitchen shears, remove head of crab. Pull away shell, starting from the middle of the back; remove spongy fingers underneath. Repeat on the other side. Break off "apron," the same as for hard-shell crabs. Rinse well under running cold water. Leave claws and legs intact.

Season crabs with salt and pepper. Sauté in butter or margarine in a skillet, turning once, 5 to 6 minutes, or until golden. Spoon onto toast wedges on serving plates. Stir Worcestershire sauce, lemon juice, and chopped parsley to taste into drippings in skillet; spoon over crabs.

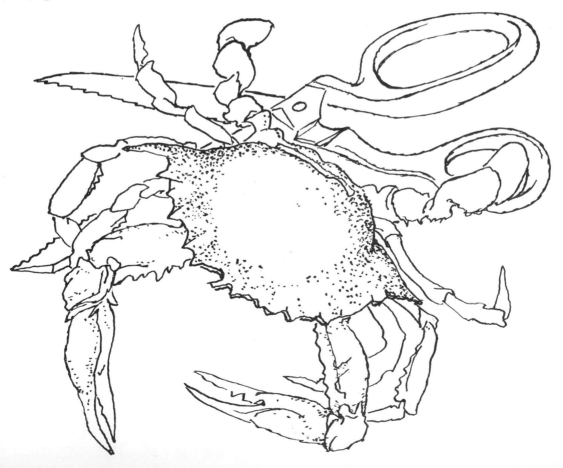

FRESH FISH

FLOUNDER DINNER AU GRATIN

2 packages (10 ozs. each) frozen cut
    asparagus
4 flounder fillets, weighing about 1 lb.
2 tablespoons butter or margarine
1 tablespoon lime juice
½ teaspoon salt
    Dash of pepper
1 cup shredded sharp Cheddar cheese
    (4 ozs.)
⅓ cup evaporated milk
½ teaspoon dry mustard

Preheat broiler.
Cook asparagus as label directs; drain well.
Spoon into a broilerproof baking dish to make
a layer. (Or spoon into 4 individual baking
dishes.)
Grease rack on broiler pan; place flounder
in a single layer on rack.
Melt butter in a small saucepan; stir in lime
juice. Brush generously over flounder;
sprinkle salt and pepper over top.
Broil, 6 inches from heat, 5 minutes; brush
remaining butter mixture over top.
Broil 2 minutes longer, or until flounder
flakes easily when tested with a fork. Arrange
over asparagus in dish.
While flounder cooks, combine cheese,
evaporated milk, and mustard in a small
saucepan; heat very slowly, stirring constantly, until cheese melts and sauce is
smooth; spoon in a ribbon over flounder.
Broil, 6 inches from heat, 4 minutes, or until
sauce bubbles up and browns lightly. Garnish
with lime slices if you like.
Yield: 4 servings.

ISLAND SALMON STEAKS

4 salmon steaks, weighing about 1½ lbs.
⅓ cup soy sauce
2 tablespoons salad oil
1 tablespoon light molasses
1 small clove garlic, crushed
1 teaspoon ground ginger
1 teaspoon dry mustard

Place salmon steaks in a single layer in a
shallow dish.
Combine soy sauce, salad oil, molasses, garlic, ginger, and mustard in a cup; pour over
salmon. Let stand at room temperature, turning once, 1 hour to season.
Preheat broiler.
Lift salmon from marinade and place on
rack in broiler pan.
Broil, 4 inches from heat, 7 minutes: turn.
Brush marinade from dish over top. Broil 5
minutes longer, or until salmon flakes easily
when tested with a fork.
Place salmon on a large serving platter.
Garnish with lime wedges and parsley if you
like.
Yield: 4 servings.

SAUCY FLOUNDER WITH RICE

4 flounder fillets, weighing about 1 lb.
1 can (10¾ ozs.) condensed cream of
    shrimp soup
¼ cup milk
1 tablespoon lemon juice
1 cup packaged precooked rice

Preheat oven to 350°.
Place flounder in a single layer in a shallow
baking dish.
Blend soup, milk, and lemon juice in a small
bowl; pour over flounder; cover.
Bake 30 minutes, or until flounder flakes
easily when tested with a fork.
While flounder cooks, prepare rice as label
directs; spoon onto serving plates. Top with
fillets; spoon sauce over all.
Yield: 4 servings.

RED SNAPPER WITH OYSTER STUFFING

1 whole red snapper, weighing about
    4½ lbs., dressed
1 medium onion, chopped (½ cup)
½ cup chopped celery
6 tablespoons butter or margarine
1 can (8 ozs.) oysters
½ cup light cream
2 tablespoons chopped parsley
    Salt
4 cups coarsely crushed unsalted
    soda crackers

Wash snapper inside and out; pat dry with paper toweling.

Sauté onion and celery in 4 tablespoons of the butter until soft in a medium skillet.

Drain liquid from oysters into a small bowl; stir in cream; stir into onion mixture with parsley and ½ teaspoon salt. Drizzle over crackers in a large bowl; add oysters; toss lightly until evenly moistened.

Preheat oven to 350°.

Sprinkle snapper lightly inside and out with salt; stuff oyster mixture into cavity; close opening with wooden picks. Place in a greased large shallow baking pan.

Melt remaining 2 tablespoons butter in a small skillet; brush part over snapper.

Bake, brushing once or twice more with remaining melted butter, 45 minutes, or until fish flakes easily when tested with a fork.

Lift snapper onto a large serving platter. Garnish top with thin slices of lemon and edge with parsley if you like.

Yield: 6 servings.

Note: If you have any stuffing leftover, spoon it into a casserole, cover, and bake in the same oven with fish for 35 minutes.

Some fish markets will also be happy to bone the fish for you if you like, or you can do it yourself, making a cut along each inside edge of the backbone and snipping through rib bones with poultry shears just deep enough to loosen the bone. (Be careful not to cut through the meat on the back.) Next cut through the backbone at each end, then carefully pull out the backbone, scraping meat away from the bone with a knife as you go.

FILLET OF SOLE ROULADE

3 large carrots, pared and cut in
    3-inch-long sticks
1 package (10 ozs.) frozen whole
    green beans
6 large fillets of sole, weighing 2 lbs.
1 teaspoon salt
¼ teaspoon lemon-pepper
½ cup dry white wine
½ cup water
1 tablespoon instant minced onion
½ teaspoon dried tarragon, crushed
2 tablespoons butter or margarine
2 tablespoons all-purpose flour

Cook carrots, covered, in boiling salted water in a large saucepan 8 minutes. Add green beans to pan; cook 8 minutes longer, or until vegetables are crisp-tender; drain carefully.

Lay fillets flat on counter; sprinkle salt and lemon-pepper over each. Place green beans and carrots, dividing evenly, crosswise over one end of each fillet; roll up; fasten with wooden picks.

Combine wine, water, onion, and tarragon in a large skillet; heat to boiling; place fish rolls in liquid. Heat to boiling again; cover. Poach 8 minutes, or until fish flakes easily when tested with a fork.

Lift rolls onto a serving platter with a slotted spoon; keep warm. Strain cooking liquid into a 1-cup measure; add water, if needed, to make 1 cup.

Melt butter in same skillet; stir in flour. Cook, stirring constantly, until blended. Stir in the 1 cup liquid; continue cooking and stirring until sauce thickens and boils 1 minute. Spoon over fish rolls. Garnish platter with thin cucumber or zucchini slices if you like.

Yield: 6 servings.

FLOUNDER WITH CIOPPINO SAUCE

1 small onion, chopped (¼ cup)
¼ cup chopped green pepper
1 medium carrot, pared and shredded
½ cup thinly sliced celery
1 can (8 ozs.) tomato sauce
1 envelope instant vegetable broth
1 teaspoon dried oregano, crushed
½ teaspoon garlic powder
¼ teaspoon lemon-pepper
½ cup water
2 tablespoons dry red wine
6 flounder fillets, weighing about
   ¼ lb. each
2 tablespoons butter or margarine,
   melted

Combine onion, green pepper, carrot, celery, tomato sauce, dry vegetable broth, oregano, garlic powder, lemon-pepper, and water in a small saucepan; heat to boiling; cover. Simmer 30 minutes.

Stir in wine; simmer, uncovered, 10 minutes or until thick.

Preheat broiler.

Sprinkle salt lightly over flounder; place flounder in a single layer on rack in broiler pan. Brush half of the butter over top.

Broil, 6 inches from heat, 5 minutes. Brush rest of butter over top. Broil 2 minutes longer, or until fish flakes easily when tested with a fork.

Place flounder on a large serving platter; spoon a ribbon of sauce over center. Serve rest of sauce separately.

Yield: 6 servings.

HALIBUT PARMESAN

6 halibut steaks, weighing about
   2 lbs.
1 cup (8-oz. carton) dairy sour cream
¼ cup grated Parmesan cheese
1 tablespoon minced onion
1 tablespoon lemon juice
½ teaspoon salt
   Paprika

Preheat oven to 375°.

Place steaks in a single layer in a greased shallow baking dish.

Mix sour cream, cheese, onion, lemon juice, and salt in a small bowl; spread over steaks; sprinkle paprika generously on top.

Bake 25 minutes, or until halibut flakes easily when tested with a fork. Place on a large serving platter. Garnish with clusters of watercress if you like.

Yield: 6 servings.

SNOWCAP SALMON STEAKS

1 cup thinly sliced celery
1 large carrot, pared and diced (1 cup)
½ cup diced green pepper
1 small onion, chopped (¼ cup)
4 salmon steaks, cut ¾ inch thick
   and weighing about 1½ lbs.
2 tablespoons butter or margarine, melted
1 tablespoon lemon juice
½ teaspoon seasoned salt
½ cup dairy sour cream
   Paprika

Preheat oven to 400°.

Toss celery with carrot, green pepper, and onion in a 12x8x2-inch baking dish; spread in an even layer. Arrange salmon steaks in a single layer on top.

Mix melted butter and lemon juice in a cup; brush over salmon; sprinkle salt over top; cover.

Bake 20 minutes; uncover.

Spread sour cream over steaks, dividing evenly; sprinkle paprika lightly over cream.

Bake, uncovered, 10 minutes longer, or until fish flakes easily when tested with a fork and topping is set. Serve from baking dish.

Yield: 4 servings.

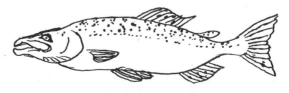

FLOUNDER FINLANDIA

1 package (10 ozs.) frozen peas
5 tablespoons butter or margarine
1 large cucumber, pared, seeded, and
    diced (1 cup)
½ teaspoon dillweed
  Salt
2 tablespoons lemon juice
½ teaspoon paprika
4 flounder fillets, weighing about 1½ lbs.

Cook peas as label directs in boiling salted water in a medium saucepan; drain well and set aside.

Melt 2 tablespoons of the butter in same saucepan; add cucumber and sauté just until wilted. Stir in dillweed, ¼ teaspoon salt, and peas; keep hot while cooking flounder.

Preheat broiler.

Melt remaining 3 tablespoons butter in a small saucepan; stir in lemon juice and paprika. Brush half over flounder; place fillets, seasoned side down, on rack in broiler pan. Brush rest of butter mixture over top; sprinkle salt lightly over all.

Broil, 6 inches from heat, 7 minutes, or until fish flakes easily when tested with a fork.

Overlap fillets in center of a large deep serving platter; spoon peas around edge. Garnish with cherry tomatoes and fresh dill if you like.

Yield: 4 servings.

PARTY PERCH BAKE

2 lbs. fresh perch or 2 packages
    (16 ozs. each) frozen perch
2 packages (10 ozs. each) frozen
    chopped broccoli
1 package (8 ozs.) medium noodles
5 tablespoons butter or margarine
1 cup fresh bread crumbs (2 slices)
¼ cup all-purpose flour
1 teaspoon dry mustard
1 teaspoon salt
1 teaspoon Worcestershire sauce
3 cups milk
1 package (8 ozs.) process Old English
    cheese, cut in small pieces
2 tablespoons chopped drained pimientos

If using frozen perch, thaw as label directs; separate into fillets.

Thaw broccoli; drain thoroughly.

Cook noodles in a kettle as label directs; drain; return to kettle.

Preheat oven to 350°.

Melt butter in a medium saucepan; measure out 1 tablespoon and toss with bread crumbs in a small bowl.

Stir flour, mustard, salt, and Worcestershire sauce into remaining butter in pan; cook, stirring constantly, until bubbly. Stir in milk; continue cooking and stirring until sauce thickens and boils 1 minute; stir in cheese until melted, then add pimientos.

Pour half of the sauce over noodles; toss to mix; spoon into a 13x9x2-inch baking dish to make a layer. Spread thawed broccoli in a layer over noodles; arrange perch over broccoli, overlapping fillets slightly if needed. Pour rest of sauce over perch; sprinkle buttered bread crumbs on top.

Bake 45 minutes, or until perch flakes easily when tested with a fork and topping is toasted. Garnish with tiny fish shapes cut from pimientos if you like.

Yield: 8 servings.

HADDOCK TROPICALE

1½ lbs. haddock
 3 tablespoons butter or margarine,
   melted
 ¼ cup orange juice
 ½ teaspoon salt
 ⅛ teaspoon ground nutmeg
 2 tablespoons shredded orange rind

Cut haddock into serving-sized pieces, if needed; place in a single layer in a greased shallow baking pan.

Preheat oven to 350°.

Combine melted butter, orange juice, salt, and nutmeg in a cup; pour over and around haddock; sprinkle orange rind on top.

Bake 25 minutes, or until haddock flakes easily when tested with a fork.

Lift pieces onto a large deep serving platter; spoon juices from dish over top. Garnish with orange slices and watercress if you like.

Yield: 6 servings.

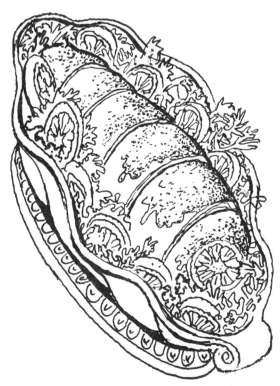

BAKED STUFFED FLOUNDER

 6 medium flounder fillets,
   weighing about 1½ lbs.
2½ cups fresh bread crumbs (5 slices)
 2 tablespoons minced onion
 1 cup (8-oz. carton) small curd
   creamed cottage cheese
 1 tablespoon chopped fresh dill
 ¼ teaspoon salt
   Dash of pepper
 2 tablespoons butter or margarine, melted
   Dash of paprika

Preheat oven to 350°.

Place 3 flounder fillets in a single layer in a 9x9x2-inch baking dish.

Mix bread crumbs, onion, cottage cheese, dill, salt, and pepper in a medium bowl. Spoon in a layer over fillets in dish; place remaining fillets on top. Brush with melted butter; sprinkle paprika over top.

Bake 20 minutes, or until fish flakes easily when tested with a fork. Cut into serving-sized blocks; lift out with a pancake turner.

Yield: 6 servings.

SCALLOPED HADDOCK EN COQUILLES

1 medium onion, peeled and sliced
2 lemon slices
3 sprigs of parsley
1 bay leaf
1½ teaspoons salt
3 cups water
1 lb. haddock
2 tablespoons butter or margarine
2 tablespoons all-purpose flour
1½ teaspoons dry mustard
Few drops red-pepper seasoning
2 cups milk
1 tablespoon lemon juice
1 cup fresh bread crumbs (2 slices)
3 hard-cooked eggs

Combine onion, lemon slices, parsley, bay leaf, ½ teaspoon of the salt, and water in a large skillet; heat to boiling. Add haddock; cover. Poach 5 minutes, or until fish flakes easily when tested with a fork; drain; cool. Break fish into large flakes, removing any bones.

Preheat oven to 350°.

Melt butter in a large saucepan; stir in flour, mustard, red-pepper seasoning, and remaining 1 teaspoon salt; cook, stirring constantly, until bubbly.

Stir in milk; continue cooking and stirring until sauce thickens and boils 1 minute; remove from heat. Stir in lemon juice, haddock, and ½ cup of the bread crumbs.

Chop 1½ eggs; fold into fish mixture; spoon into 4 large scallop shells. Sprinkle remaining ½ cup bread crumbs on top. For easy handling, set shells in a large shallow pan.

Bake 20 minutes, or until bubbly and topping is golden.

Slice remaining 1½ eggs; arrange over shells as a garnish.

Yield: 4 servings.

CRAB-STUFFED SOLE

1 package (6 ozs.) frozen Alaska king
   crab meat
1½ cups fresh bread crumbs (3 slices)
1 egg, beaten
½ teaspoon salt
6 fillets of sole, weighing about 1½ lbs.
3 tablespoons butter or margarine
2 tablespoons lemon juice
1 package (1 oz.) white wine sauce mix
   Milk
   Water
⅛ teaspoon dried tarragon, crushed

Thaw crab meat and drain well; flake in a medium bowl. Stir in bread crumbs, egg, and salt until well blended.

Preheat oven to 375°.

Lay fillets flat on waxed paper. Spread crab mixture over each; roll up, jelly-roll fashion; fasten with wooden picks. Place rolls, seam side down, in a shallow baking dish. Dot 2 tablespoons of the butter over top, then sprinkle lemon juice over all; cover.

Bake 20 minutes, or until fish flakes easily when tested with a fork.

While rolls cook, prepare sauce mix with milk, water, and remaining 1 tablespoon butter in a small saucepan; stir in tarragon.

Place rolls around edge on a large serving platter. Pour sauce into a small bowl; place in center. Or serve rolls on a bed of buttered carrots and lima beans; spoon some of the sauce over rolls, then serve remainder separately.

Yield: 6 servings.

FROZEN FISH

COD IN MUSHROOM SAUCE

1 package (16 ozs.) frozen cod
2 tablespoons chopped green onion
3 tablespoons butter or margarine
3 tablespoons all-purpose flour
½ teaspoon salt
⅛ teaspoon pepper
1 can (4 ozs.) sliced mushrooms
   Milk
1 teaspoon grated lemon rind
2 tablespoons lemon juice
1 tablespoon chopped parsley

Place block of frozen cod in a shallow 1½-quart baking dish.

Preheat oven to 350°.

Sauté onion in butter until soft in a medium saucepan; stir in flour, salt, and pepper. Cook, stirring constantly, until bubbly.

Drain liquid from mushrooms into a 1-cup measure; add milk to make 1 cup; stir into onion mixture. Continue cooking and stirring until sauce thickens and boils 1 minute: stir in mushrooms, and lemon rind and juice. Spoon over cod; cover.

Bake 45 minutes, or until cod flakes easily when tested with a fork.

Lift cod onto a deep serving platter; cut crosswise into quarters. Spoon sauce from dish over top; sprinkle parsley over sauce.

Yield: 4 servings.

BAKED HALIBUT WITH HERBS

2 packages (16 ozs. each) frozen halibut, partly
   thawed
4 tablespoons butter or margarine
¼ cup finely chopped green onions
1 teaspoon salt
½ teaspoon dried marjoram, crushed
⅛ teaspoon pepper
3 tablespoons minced parsley
2 tablespoons lemon juice

Preheat oven to 350°.

Cut halibut into 6 serving-sized blocks; place in a single layer in a shallow baking dish.

Cream butter with green onions, salt, marjoram, pepper, and parsley in a small bowl; stir in lemon juice. Spread over halibut; cover.

Bake 35 minutes, or until fish flakes easily when tested with a fork. Garnish with sprigs of parsley and lemon wedges if you like. Serve from baking dish.

Yield: 6 servings.

CONTINENTAL FLOUNDER

1 cup sliced green onions
4 tablespoons butter or margarine
3 medium-sized potatoes, pared and sliced thin
   Salt
   Pepper
2 large tomatoes, peeled, chopped, and drained (2
   cups)
2 medium-sized yellow squash, trimmed and sliced
3 tablespoons chopped parsley
1 package (16 ozs.) frozen flounder, thawed slightly
   Paprika

Preheat oven to 350°.

Sauté onions in 2 tablespoons of the butter in a small saucepan until soft; spoon into a baking dish, 12x8x2 inches, to make a layer.

Top with a layer of potatoes; sprinkle lightly with salt and pepper. Repeat with tomatoes and squash, sprinkling salt and pepper over each layer; sprinkle parsley over squash.

Cut block of flounder into 4 serving-sized pieces; arrange over vegetables. Spread remaining 2 tablespoons butter over flounder; sprinkle salt and paprika lightly over top; cover.

Bake 55 minutes, or until vegetables are tender and fish flakes easily when tested with a fork. Serve from baking dish.

Yield: 4 servings.

BARBECUED HALIBUT

2 packages (12 ozs. each) frozen halibut, thawed
¾ cup tomato juice
1 tablespoon minced onion
¾ teaspoon salt
½ teaspoon dried basil, crushed
¼ teaspoon sugar
1 tablespoon lemon juice
1½ teaspoons Worcestershire sauce

Preheat oven to 350°.

Place halibut in a single layer in a shallow baking dish.

Mix rest of ingredients in a small saucepan; heat to boiling. Cook 3 minutes, or until slightly thickened; brush half over halibut.

Bake 15 minutes; turn halibut; brush remaining sauce over top.

Bake 15 minutes longer, or until fish flakes easily when tested with a fork.

Yield: 4 servings.

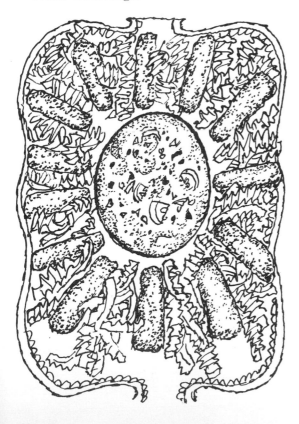

FISH-AND-TOMATO STACKS

1 package (9 ozs.) frozen fish sticks
1 large tomato, cut in 4 thick slices
1 tablespoon salad oil
1 teaspoon sugar
½ teaspoon salt
½ teaspoon dried basil, crushed
2 slices process American cheese
4 slices white toast

Preheat oven to 425°.

Place fish sticks in a shallow baking pan; heat in oven as label directs.

While fish heats, place tomato slices in a single layer in a shallow pan; brush salad oil over each. Mix sugar, salt, and basil in a cup; sprinkle over tomatoes. Heat in oven with fish 5 minutes, or until hot.

Cut cheese into 8 strips. Place fish on top of tomatoes; crisscross 2 cheese strips over each stack.

Bake 5 minutes longer, or until cheese melts. Place toast on 4 serving plates; top each slice with a fish stack.

Yield: 4 servings.

FISH AND CHIPS

1 package (9 ozs.) frozen fish sticks
1 package (9 ozs.) frozen French fried potatoes
½ cup mayonnaise or salad dressing
1 teaspoon prepared mustard
1 tablespoon catsup
1 tablespoon cider vinegar
2 small sweet pickles, minced

Preheat oven to 425°.

Place fish sticks and frozen potatoes in separate shallow baking pans; heat in oven as labels direct.

While fish heats, mix mayonnaise, mustard, catsup, vinegar, and pickles in a small bowl; place in center of a large serving plate. Arrange fish sticks and potatoes around edge. To serve, let everyone pick up fish and potatoes in his fingers and dip into sauce.

Yield: 4 servings.

SKILLET FISH BAKE

1 small onion, minced (¼ cup)
¼ cup chopped green pepper
1 tablespoon salad oil
1 can (10¾ ozs.) condensed tomato soup
1½ cups water
¼ teaspoon dried thyme, crushed
¼ teaspoon salt
¾ cup uncooked regular rice
1 package (9 ozs.) frozen fish sticks
2 long slices Cheddar cheese
4 pitted ripe olives, sliced

Sauté onion and green pepper in salad oil in a medium skillet until soft. Stir in soup, water, thyme, and salt; heat to boiling. Stir in rice; cover. Cook slowly, stirring several times, 25 minutes, or until rice is almost tender.

Lay frozen fish sticks, spoke fashion, on top of rice mixture; cover again. Heat 10 minutes.

Cut cheese into triangles; place in a circle around edge in pan. Pile olives in center; cover. Heat 5 to 7 minutes longer, or until cheese melts and fish is hot.

Yield: 4 servings.

CREOLE COD

2 packages (16 ozs. each) frozen cod, partly thawed
1 large green pepper, quartered, seeded, and diced (1 cup)
1 medium onion, chopped (½ cup)
½ cup thinly sliced celery
4 tablespoons butter or margarine
1 can (8 ozs.) tomato sauce
1 teaspoon dried thyme, crushed
1 teaspoon salt
⅛ teaspoon pepper

Preheat oven to 350°.

Cut cod into 6 serving-sized blocks; place in a single layer in a 12x8x2-inch baking dish.

Sauté green pepper, onion, and celery in butter until soft in a large skillet; stir in tomato sauce, thyme, salt, and pepper; heat, stirring several times, to boiling. Spoon over fish; cover.

Bake 45 minutes, or until fish flakes easily when tested with a fork. Serve from baking dish with small whole white potatoes and thin cucumber slices if you like.

Yield: 6 servings.

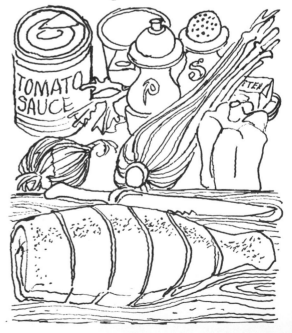

CANNED FISH

TUNA-VEGETABLE LOAF

1 package (10 ozs.) frozen peas and carrots
1 can (about 7 ozs.) tuna, drained and
    flaked
1 small onion, chopped (¼ cup)
½ teaspoon dried thyme, crushed
 4 tablespoons butter or margarine
 4 tablespoons all-purpose flour
½ teaspoon salt
 2 cups milk
 4 eggs
 1 cup shredded Gouda cheese (4 ozs.)

Grease a loaf pan, 8x4x2 inches; line bottom with waxed paper; grease paper.

Cook peas and carrots as label directs; drain well. Combine with tuna, onion, and thyme in a medium bowl.

Preheat oven to 350°.

Melt butter in a medium saucepan; stir in flour and salt; cook, stirring constantly, until bubbly. Stir in milk; continue cooking and stirring until sauce thickens and boils 1 minute. Measure out ½ cupful and stir into tuna mixture.

Beat eggs in a small bowl; stir into tuna mixture until well blended; spoon into prepared pan.

Bake 45 minutes, or until loaf is firm and a knife inserted into center comes out clean.

While loaf bakes, stir cheese into remaining sauce in pan; heat slowly, stirring constantly, until cheese melts and sauce is smooth. (If sauce seems too thick, stir in another ¼ cup milk.)

Loosen loaf around edges with a knife; invert onto a serving plate; peel off waxed paper. Slice loaf crosswise and serve with cheese sauce.

Yield: 4 servings.

TUNA EMPANADAS

1 can (about 7 ozs.) tuna
1 hard-cooked egg, chopped
1 small onion, chopped (¼ cup)
2 tablespoons chopped parsley
½ teaspoon salt
   Few drops red-pepper seasoning
¼ cup mayonnaise or salad dressing
 1 package refrigerated flaky biscuits
 1 small can evaporated milk (⅔ cup)
⅓ cup water
 4 slices process American cheese, cut up
½ teaspoon Worcestershire sauce

Preheat oven to 400°.

Drain liquid from tuna; flake tuna in a medium bowl. Stir in egg, onion, parsley, salt, red-pepper seasoning, and mayonnaise until blended.

Separate biscuits; roll each to a 5-inch round on a lightly floured cloth; spoon a scant 2 tablespoons of the tuna mixture onto half of each. Moisten one edge of each round and fold dough over to cover filling completely; press edges with a fork to seal. Cut several slits in top of each to let steam escape; place on a cookie sheet.

Bake 15 minutes, or until golden.

While turnovers bake, combine evaporated milk, water, cheese, and Worcestershire sauce in a small saucepan; heat slowly, stirring constantly, until cheese melts and sauce is smooth and hot.

Place turnovers on serving plates; spoon cheese sauce over top.

Yield: 4 to 6 servings.

SALMON TIMBALES

1 can (16 ozs.) salmon, drained, boned,
    and flaked
1 medium onion, minced (½ cup)
2 eggs
1 cup coarse saltine crumbs
1¼ cups milk
3 teaspoons lemon juice
1 can (10¾ ozs.) condensed cream
    of shrimp soup
1 teaspoon chopped parsley

Preheat oven to 375°. Grease four 6-ounce custard cups.

Combine salmon, onion, eggs, saltine crumbs, 1 cup of the milk, and lemon juice in a large bowl; mix lightly until well blended. Spoon into custard cups. For easy handling, set cups in a shallow pan.

Bake 35 minutes, or until firm and lightly golden.

While salmon bakes, combine soup and remaining ¼ cup milk in a small saucepan. Heat slowly, stirring several times, to boiling; stir in parsley.

Loosen salmon molds from cups with a knife; invert onto serving plates. Spoon shrimp sauce generously over each.

Yield: 4 servings.

LASAGNA PINWHEELS

12 lasagna noodles
1 can (12½ ozs.) tuna
1 package (8 ozs.) cream cheese
1 small onion, minced (¼ cup)
¼ cup minced celery
2 tablespoons chopped parsley
¼ teaspoon salt
2 jars (15½ ozs. each) marinara sauce
1 teaspoon dried oregano, crushed
1 package (8 ozs.) mozzarella cheese,
    shredded

Cook noodles as label directs; drain; return to kettle and cover with cold water to keep noodles from sticking together.

Drain liquid from tuna; flake meat fine in a medium bowl; stir in cream cheese, onion, celery, parsley, and salt until well blended.

Preheat oven to 350°.

Lift noodles, one at a time, from water and drain well; spread a scant ¼ cup of the tuna mixture over each; roll up tightly, jelly-roll fashion.

Combine marinara sauce and oregano in a medium saucepan; heat to boiling; spoon half into a baking dish, 11¾x7½x1¾ inches. Place tuna rolls, seam side down, in two rows in dish; spread remaining sauce evenly over top. Sprinkle cheese over sauce to make a crisscross pattern, or sprinkle evenly over top.

Bake 30 minutes, or until bubbly and cheese browns lightly. Let stand on a wire rack 10 minutes before serving.

Yield: 6 servings.

SALMON PATTYCAKES

1½ cups fresh bread crumbs (3 slices)
½ cup milk
1 can (8 ozs.) salmon
1 egg
2 tablespoons chopped onion
2 tablespoons chopped parsley
4 slices process pimiento cheese

Preheat oven to 350°.

Combine bread crumbs and milk in a medium bowl; let stand 5 minutes until milk is absorbed.

Drain liquid from salmon; remove bones and skin; flake meat and add to milk mixture with egg, onion, and parsley; mix well. Shape into 4 even patties. Place in a greased shallow baking dish.

Bake 30 minutes, or until firm.

Cut each slice of cheese into two triangles; arrange two over each salmon patty.

Bake 5 minutes longer, or until cheese starts to melt.

Yield: 4 servings.

TUNA HAWAIIAN

1 medium-sized green pepper, quartered,
   seeded, and cut in strips
1 medium onion, chopped (½ cup)
2 tablespoons butter or margarine
½ teaspoon ground ginger
1 tablespoon soy sauce
¼ cup cider vinegar
1 can (20 ozs.) pineapple chunks in juice
1 tablespoon cornstarch
2 cans (about 7 ozs. each) tuna,
   drained and broken into chunks
½ teaspoon salt
2 teaspoons sugar
3 cups hot cooked rice

Sauté green pepper and onion in butter in a medium skillet until soft. Stir in ginger, soy sauce, and vinegar.

Drain juice from pineapple into a 1-cup measure; add water to make 1 cup. Stir into cornstarch in a small bowl, then stir into green pepper-onion mixture. Cook, stirring constantly, until mixture thickens slightly and boils 1 minute.

Stir in pineapple, tuna, salt, and sugar; simmer 10 minutes. Serve over rice.

Yield: 4 servings.

GOLDEN TUNA FLORENTINE

2 packages (10 ozs. each) spinach
7 tablespoons butter or margarine
1 cup fresh bread crumbs (2 slices)
4 tablespoons all-purpose flour
   Salt
¼ teaspoon pepper
¼ teaspoon dry mustard
2 cups milk
1 cup shredded sharp Cheddar cheese
   (4 ozs.)
2 cans (about 7 ozs. each) tuna, drained
   and broken into chunks
2 medium tomatoes, sliced thin

Wash spinach thoroughly; dry well with paper toweling; chop coarsely.

Melt butter in a medium saucepan; measure out 2 tablespoons and toss with bread crumbs in a small bowl. Measure 1 tablespoon into a cup and set aside.

Stir flour, ½ teaspoon salt, pepper, and mustard into rest of butter in saucepan; cook, stirring constantly, until bubbly. Stir in milk; continue cooking and stirring until sauce thickens and boils 1 minute; stir in cheese until melted.

Preheat oven to 350°.

Place tuna in a 2-quart shallow baking dish to make a layer; spoon half of the cheese sauce over top.

Stir rest of sauce into spinach in a medium bowl; spread in an even layer over tuna; sprinkle buttered bread crumbs on top.

Bake 25 minutes, or until bubbly. Arrange tomato slices, overlapping, around edge in dish; brush remaining 1 tablespoon melted butter over slices; sprinkle lightly with salt.

Bake 10 minutes longer, or just until tomatoes are hot.

Yield: 6 servings.

CALICO SALMON

1 package tuna-macaroni dinner with
   Newburg sauce
2 cans (about 8 ozs. each) salmon, drained,
   boned, and broken into chunks
1 package (10 ozs.) frozen peas and celery
½ teaspoon dillweed
4 cups boiling water
1 cup coarsely crumbled cheese crackers
1 tablespoon butter or margarine, melted

Preheat oven to 400°.

Combine macaroni and sauce mix from dinner package, salmon, peas and celery, and dillweed in a 2½-quart baking dish. Stir in boiling water; cover.

Bake 45 minutes; uncover; stir gently.

Toss crackers with butter in a small bowl; sprinkle over macaroni mixture.

Bake 10 minutes longer.

Yield: 6 servings.

TUNA IIIGII-HATS

1 can (about 7 ozs.) tuna, drained
    and flaked
½ cup chopped celery
2 hard-cooked eggs, chopped
¼ cup chopped dill pickle
½ teaspoon instant minced onion or
    1 teaspoon grated onion
½ teaspoon salt
    Dash of pepper
¼ cup dairy sour cream
4 frankfurter rolls
2 egg whites
¼ cup mayonnaise or salad dressing
2 teaspoons lemon juice

Preheat oven to 350°.

Combine tuna, celery, eggs, dill pickle, onion, salt, and pepper in a medium bowl; fold in sour cream.

Separate rolls to make 8 pieces; place on a cookie sheet. Spoon tuna mixture on each half roll.

Beat egg whites in a small bowl until they form firm peaks; fold in mayonnaise and lemon juice. Spread over tuna mixture on each roll.

Bake 20 minutes, or until topping is puffed and golden. Place on serving plates. Serve hot.

Yield: 4 servings, 2 rolls each.

TUNA FONDUE

2 cups half-inch cubes French bread
1 can (about 7 ozs.) tuna, drained
    and flaked
1 small onion, minced (¼ cup)
1 cup shredded Swiss cheese (4 ozs.)
2 eggs
1½ cups milk
1½ teaspoons prepared mustard
¼ teaspoon salt
6 drops red-pepper seasoning
2 tablespoons grated Romano cheese

Layer ⅓ of the bread cubes into a 1½-quart shallow baking dish. Top with ⅓ each of the tuna, onion, and Swiss cheese; repeat to make two more layers of each.

Beat eggs in a medium bowl until blended; stir in milk, mustard, salt, and red-pepper seasoning. Pour over layers in baking dish; sprinkle Romano cheese on top. Cover dish with transparent wrap; chill overnight.

About 1 hour before serving, preheat oven to 350°. Uncover baking dish.

Bake 45 minutes, or until puffed and golden. Serve at once.

Yield: 4 servings.

CASSEROLE SALMON

Cucumber Sauce (recipe on page 313)
1 can (16 ozs.) salmon
1 small onion, finely chopped (¼ cup)
¼ cup butter or margarine
¾ cup milk
2 cups whole-wheat cereal flakes
3 eggs, separated
3 tablespoons chopped parsley
1 tablespoon lemon juice
¼ teaspoon Worcestershire sauce
1 teaspoon salt
⅛ teaspoon pepper

Make Cucumber Sauce; chill.

Preheat oven to 350°.

Drain liquid from salmon; remove bones and skin; flake salmon.

Sauté onion lightly in butter in a large saucepan; remove from heat. Stir in milk and cereal flakes; let stand 5 minutes until liquid is absorbed; add salmon.

Beat egg whites in a medium bowl until they form soft peaks. Beat egg yolks in a small bowl; stir into salmon mixture with parsley, lemon juice, Worcestershire sauce, salt, and pepper; fold in beaten egg whites. Spoon into a greased 1-quart shallow baking dish. Set dish in a large shallow pan; pour boiling water into pan to a 1-inch depth.

Bake 40 minutes, or until puffed and firm. Serve hot with cold Cucumber Sauce.

Yield: 6 servings.

(Clockwise from top)▶
FLOUNDER FINLANDIA (p.215)
CREOLE COD (p.220)
SEAFOOD SPAGHETTI BOWL (p.231)

DEVILED SALMON

2 cans (8 ozs. each) salmon
1 cup thinly sliced celery
4 tablespoons butter or margarine
¼ cup all-purpose flour
2 tablespoons prepared hot mustard
1 teaspoon salt
3 cups milk
　Few drops red-pepper seasoning
1 tablespoon lemon juice
3 hard-cooked eggs, diced
1½ cups coarsely crushed saltines

Drain liquid from salmon; remove bones and skin; break salmon into chunks.

Preheat oven to 350°.

Sauté celery in butter until soft in a medium saucepan; stir in flour; cook, stirring constantly, until bubbly. Stir in mustard, salt, milk, and red-pepper seasoning; continue cooking and stirring until mixture thickens and boils 1 minute; remove from heat. Stir in lemon juice; fold in salmon and eggs.

Spoon about one third into a 1½-quart baking dish; top with one third of the cracker crumbs. Repeat layers.

Bake 45 minutes, or until bubbly. Garnish with hard-cooked egg quarters and parsley if you like.

Yield: 6 servings.

TIMESAVER'S TUNA PIE

　Single Crust Pastry (recipe on page 497)
2 cans (about 7 ozs. each) tuna, drained and broken into chunks
½ cup catsup
¼ teaspoon pepper
1 can (10¾ ozs.) condensed cream of celery soup
1 cup shredded sharp Cheddar cheese (4 ozs.)
1 teaspoon Worcestershire sauce

Prepare Single Crust Pastry.

Roll out to a 12-inch round on a lightly floured cloth; fit into a 9-inch pie plate. Trim

◀ *(Clockwise from top)*
STUFFED LOBSTER THERMIDOR (p.230)
SCALLOPS CREOLE (p.228)
CRAB-STUFFED SOLE (p.217)

overhang to ½ inch; turn edge under flush with rim of pie plate; pinch to make a stand-up edge; flute.

Preheat oven to 400°.

Combine tuna, catsup, and pepper in a medium bowl; toss lightly to mix. Spoon into prepared pastry shell.

Combine soup, cheese, and Worcestershire sauce in a small saucepan; heat slowly, stirring constantly, until hot. Pour evenly over tuna mixture in shell.

Bake 25 minutes, or until sauce bubbles up and pastry is golden. Cool 10 minutes on a wire rack; cut into wedges.

Yield: 4 servings.

TUNA SCALLOP

1 can (about 7 ozs.) tuna, drained and broken into chunks
1 can (16 ozs.) cream-style corn
1 package (8 ozs.) sharp Cheddar cheese, shredded
2 cups coarsely crumbled unsalted crackers
2 tablespoons chopped parsley
¼ teaspoon salt
⅛ teaspoon pepper
¾ cup milk
2 tablespoons butter or margarine
2 tablespoons instant minced onion

Preheat oven to 350°.

Combine tuna, corn, three fourths of the cheese, cracker crumbs, parsley, salt, and pepper in a large bowl.

Combine milk, butter, and onion in a small saucepan; heat until butter melts. Pour over corn mixture; stir lightly to mix. Spoon into a 1½-quart baking dish. Sprinkle remaining cheese over top.

Bake 40 minutes, or until golden and a knife inserted into center comes out clean. Let stand in dish on a wire rack 10 minutes before serving.

Yield: 4 servings.

PALOS VERDES STEW

1 medium onion, chopped (½ cup)
2 tablespoons salad oil
1 can (10¾ ozs.) condensed tomato soup
1 can (8 ozs.) green peas
1 can (12 ozs.) Mexican-style corn
1 can (about 7 ozs.) tuna, drained and broken into chunks
¼ teaspoon dried basil, crushed
¼ teaspoon salt
1 cup packaged precooked rice

Sauté onion in salad oil until soft in a medium saucepan. Stir in tomato soup, peas and liquid, corn and liquid, tuna, basil, and salt. Heat to boiling; simmer 10 minutes.

Prepare rice as label directs; spoon onto serving plates; spoon tuna mixture on top.

Yield: 4 servings.

PARTY TUNA PIE

1¼ cups sifted all-purpose flour
¾ teaspoon salt
½ cup shortening
⅔ cup grated sharp Cheddar cheese
3 tablespoons cold water
2 cans (about 7 ozs. each) tuna, drained and flaked
1 cup thinly sliced celery
2 tablespoons minced onion
1 can (11 ozs.) mandarin orange segments, well drained
½ cup chopped slivered almonds
1 cup (8-oz. carton) dairy sour cream
¾ cup mayonnaise or salad dressing
Pitted ripe olives, sliced lengthwise

Preheat oven to 400°.

Sift flour and ½ teaspoon of the salt into a medium bowl; cut in shortening and ⅓ cup of the cheese with a pastry blender until mixture forms fine crumbs. Sprinkle water over top, 1 tablespoon at a time, mixing lightly until pastry holds together and cleans the side of bowl.

Roll out to a 12-inch round on a lightly floured pastry cloth; fit into a 9-inch pie plate.

Trim overhang to ½ inch; turn edge under flush with rim of pie plate, pinch to make a stand-up edge; flute. Prick shell well all over with a fork.

Bake 12 minutes, or until pastry is golden. Cool completely in pie plate on a wire rack.

Combine tuna, celery, onion, orange segments, and almonds in a medium bowl.

Blend sour cream, mayonnaise, and remaining ¼ teaspoon salt in a small bowl; fold 1 cup into tuna mixture; spoon into prepared pastry shell. Spread rest of cream mixture over top; sprinkle remaining ⅓ cup cheese over cream layer. Chill at least an hour.

Just before serving, garnish pie with sliced olives arranged in flower designs. Cut pie into wedges.

Yield: 6 servings.

YANKEE DOODLE TUNA BAKE

2 cans (10¾ ozs. each) condensed cream of celery soup
2 cups milk
1 package (8 ozs.) spaghetti, broken into 2-inch lengths
2 cans (about 7 ozs. each) tuna, drained and broken into chunks
1 package (8 ozs.) process American cheese, shredded
3 hard-cooked eggs, sliced
1 can (4 ozs.) sliced pimientos, drained and diced
1 medium onion, chopped (½ cup)
⅓ cup grated Romano cheese

Preheat oven to 375°.

Blend soup and milk in a large bowl; stir in spaghetti, tuna, shredded cheese, eggs, pimientos, and onion; mix well. Spoon into a 3-quart baking dish; cover tightly.

Bake 1 hour and 15 minutes; uncover. Sprinkle Romano cheese on top.

Bake 10 minutes longer, or until cheese browns lightly.

Yield: 8 servings.

FRESH SHELLFISH

SCAMPI

2 lbs. large shrimp in shells
½ cup butter or margarine
2 cloves garlic, crushed
2 tablespoons dry white wine
  Salt

Shell shrimp, leaving tails on; devein. Place in a single layer in bottom of broiler pan.

Preheat broiler.

Melt butter in a small saucepan; stir in garlic and wine; simmer 2 minutes. Brush half over shrimp; sprinkle salt lightly on top.

Broil, 4 inches from heat, 3 minutes; turn. Brush rest of butter mixture over top. Broil 3 minutes longer, or until shrimp are curled and pink.

Pile onto a large serving platter. Pour buttery juices from pan into a small bowl; place in center of platter for a dipping sauce.

Yield: 4 to 6 servings.

CLAMS ROCKEFELLER

24 cherrystone clams on the half shell
 1 package (10 ozs.) frozen chopped spinach
¼ cup minced green onions
 3 tablespoons minced parsley
½ teaspoon garlic salt
 1 teaspoon lemon juice
   Few drops red-pepper seasoning
 4 tablespoons butter or margarine
½ cup fine dry bread crumbs

Remove clams from shells; scrub shells, rinse, and dry; return clams. Place in a single layer in a large shallow baking pan. (If you like, spread a layer of salt in pan first to keep shells from tipping.)

Preheat oven to 450°.

Combine spinach, onions, 2 tablespoons of the parsley, garlic salt, lemon juice, red-pepper seasoning, and butter in a medium skillet; heat, stirring several times, until spinach thaws completely and starts to bubble. Stir in 6 tablespoons of the bread crumbs. Spread mixture evenly over clams to cover completely.

Mix remaining 1 tablespoon parsley and bread crumbs in a cup; sprinkle on top.

Bake 10 minutes, or until topping is toasted. Serve hot.

Yield: 6 servings.

SCALLOPS EN BROCHETTE WITH ONION RISOTTO

 1 lb. fresh sea scallops
16 cherry tomatoes, stemmed
 6 tablespoons butter or margarine
½ teaspoon dried basil, crushed
¼ teaspoon salt
 3 green onions, trimmed and sliced thin
 1 envelope instant chicken broth
 1 cup water
 1 cup packaged precooked rice

Preheat oven to 350°.

Rinse scallops under running cold water; drain.

Thread scallops and cherry tomatoes onto 4 long skewers, dividing evenly; place in a large shallow baking pan.

Melt 4 tablespoons of the butter in a small saucepan; stir in basil and salt; brush part over scallops.

Bake 10 minutes; turn and brush all over again with butter mixture. Bake 20 minutes longer, or until scallops are tender when tested with a fork.

While scallops cook, sauté green onions lightly in remaining 2 tablespoons butter in a small saucepan; stir in chicken broth and water. Heat to boiling; stir in rice; cover; turn off heat. Let stand 5 minutes, or until liquid is absorbed and rice is tender.

Spoon rice mixture onto a large serving platter; arrange skewers on top.

Yield: 4 servings.

SHRIMP ORIENTALE

1 large onion, chopped (1 cup)
2 cups diagonally sliced celery
2 tablespoons butter or margarine
1 lb. shrimp, shelled and deveined
1 package (7 ozs.) frozen snow peas
2 cups sliced Chinese cabbage
1 can (8 ozs.) water chestnuts, drained and sliced
1 envelope instant chicken broth
⅓ cup water
¼ cup soy sauce
1 tablespoon sugar
3 cups hot cooked rice

Sauté onion and celery in butter in a large skillet until soft; push to one side. Add shrimp; sauté 5 minutes; push to side. Place frozen snow peas, cabbage, and water chestnuts in piles in skillet.

Mix chicken broth, water, soy sauce, and sugar in a cup; pour in and around vegetables. Heat to boiling; cover.

Steam 10 minutes, or until shrimp are tender. Serve with rice and extra soy sauce to sprinkle on top.

Yield: 4 servings.

SCALLOPS MORNAY

1½ lbs. bay scallops
1 can (10 ¾ ozs.) condensed cream of mushroom soup
1 cup shredded Swiss cheese (4 ozs.)
¼ cup dry sherry
¾ cup fresh bread crumbs (1½ slices)
2 tablespoons butter or margarine, melted
2 tablespoons chopped parsley
6 slices white bread, toasted and cut into triangles

Preheat oven to 350°.

Rinse scallops under running cold water; pat dry with paper toweling. Place in a 1½-quart shallow baking dish.

Mix soup, cheese, and sherry in a small bowl; spoon over scallops.

Toss bread crumbs with melted butter and

parsley in a small bowl; sprinkle over top.

Bake 35 minutes, or until scallops are tender and topping is golden.

Place toast triangles on serving plates; spoon scallops and sauce over top.

Yield: 6 servings.

SCALLOPS CREOLE

1 lb. bay or sea scallops
1 medium onion, chopped (½ cup)
½ cup chopped green pepper
½ cup chopped celery
4 tablespoons butter or margarine
1 can (14½ ozs.) sliced baby tomatoes
½ teaspoon dried basil, crushed
½ teaspoon salt
2 cups hot cooked rice
1 tablespoon chopped parsley

Rinse scallops under running cold water; drain.

Sauté onion, green pepper, and celery in butter in a medium skillet until soft. Stir in tomatoes and liquid, basil, and salt; heat to boiling; simmer 2 minutes.

Stir in scallops; heat to boiling; cover. Simmer 5 minutes.

Spoon rice into 4 large scallop shells; spoon scallop mixture on top; sprinkle parsley over scallops.

Yield: 4 servings.

FROZEN SHELLFISH

COQUILLES SAINT-JACQUES

⅓ cup dry white wine
1 cup water
½ teaspoon garlic salt
1 lb. frozen sea scallops
1 can (4 ozs.) chopped mushrooms
1 small onion, chopped (¼ cup)
4 tablespoons butter or margarine
2 tablespoons all-purpose flour
½ teaspoon salt
¼ teaspoon pepper
¼ cup light cream
2 egg yolks
1 cup fresh white bread crumbs (2 slices)
2 tablespoons grated Parmesan cheese
2 tablespoons chopped parsley

Combine wine, water, and garlic salt in a large skillet; heat to boiling.

Quarter scallops. (No need to thaw first.) Place in boiling liquid; cover. Simmer 5 to 7 minutes, or until tender. Lift from liquid with a slotted spoon and place in a small bowl. Cook down liquid rapidly until it measures ¾ cup. Drain liquid from mushrooms and add to cup.

Sauté onion in 2 tablespoons of the butter until soft in same skillet; stir in flour, salt, and pepper; cook, stirring constantly, until bubbly. Stir in the mushroom-scallop liquid and cream. Continue cooking and stirring until mixture thickens and boils 1 minute.

Beat egg yolks slightly in a small bowl. Slowly stir in about ½ cup of the hot mixture, then stir back into rest of mixture in skillet; cook 1 minute longer. Stir in mushrooms and scallops. Spoon evenly into 4 large scallop shells. For easy handling, place shells in a large shallow pan.

Preheat broiler.

Melt remaining 2 tablespoons butter in a small saucepan; add bread crumbs; toss lightly. Sprinkle over scallop mixture; sprinkle cheese on top.

Broil, 4 inches from heat, 3 to 4 minutes, or until topping is toasted. Sprinkle parsley over each serving.

Yield: 4 servings.

SHRIMP MARENGO

1 medium onion, chopped (½ cup)
1 cup thinly sliced celery
1 small clove garlic, minced
2 tablespoons water
1 can (16 ozs.) stewed tomatoes
½ teaspoon salt
¼ teaspoon dried basil, crushed
⅛ teaspoon pepper
3 tablespoons dry white wine
1 can (4 ozs.) sliced mushrooms
1 bag (16 ozs.) frozen shrimp
1 tablespoon mixed pickling spices
3 cups hot cooked rice

Combine onion, celery, garlic, and water in a medium saucepan; heat to boiling; cover. Steam 5 minutes, or until onion and celery are tender.

Stir in tomatoes, salt, basil, pepper, wine, and mushrooms and liquid. Heat to boiling; simmer 10 minutes, or until thickened slightly.

While sauce simmers, cook shrimp as label directs, seasoning water with pickling spices; drain. Stir into sauce; heat again until bubbly.

Spoon rice onto serving plates; spoon shrimp sauce over top.

Yield: 4 servings.

STUFFED LOBSTER THERMIDOR

3 packages (7 ozs. each) frozen South African rock
    lobster tails
5 tablespoons butter or margarine
¾ cup fresh bread crumbs (1½ slices)
2 tablespoons grated Romano cheese
1 can (4 ozs.) sliced mushrooms
  Milk
4 tablespoons all-purpose flour
½ teaspoon salt
1 cup light cream
2 tablespoons dry sherry
2 tablespoons chopped parsley

Cook lobster tails as label directs; drain; cool until easy to handle. With scissors, snip away membranes from undersides and pull out meat; cut into small cubes. Place shells in a shallow baking pan.

Melt butter in a large skillet; measure out 1 tablespoon and toss with bread crumbs in a small bowl; stir in cheese.

Drain liquid from mushrooms into a 1-cup measure; add milk to make 1 cup.

Preheat oven to 400°.

Add lobster and mushrooms to remaining butter in skillet; sauté 3 minutes. Sprinkle flour and salt over top, then stir in with cream and mushroom-milk mixture. Cook, stirring constantly, until mixture thickens and boils 1 minute; stir in sherry and parsley. Spoon into shells; sprinkle seasoned crumbs on top.

Bake 10 minutes, or until topping is toasted. Arrange lobster on a large serving platter. Garnish with parsley and lemon wedges or slices if you like.

Yield: 4 servings.

LOUISIANA SHRIMP

1 bag (16 ozs.) frozen shrimp
1½ cups packaged precooked rice
1 can (4 ozs.) whole mushrooms, drained
2 tablespoons butter or margarine
1 can (10¾ ozs.) condensed cream of shrimp soup
1 cup (8-oz. carton) dairy sour cream
2 tablespoons dry sherry
¾ cup shredded sharp Cheddar cheese

Cook shrimp as label directs; drain well.

Prepare rice as label directs; spread in a layer in a 2-quart shallow broiler-proof baking dish.

Preheat broiler.

Sauté mushrooms in butter in a large skillet 2 minutes; stir in soup, sour cream, and sherry. Heat very slowly, stirring several times, until bubbly. (Do not boil.) Stir in shrimp; heat again until hot; spoon over rice. Sprinkle cheese on top.

Broil, 4 to 6 inches from heat, 3 to 5 minutes, or until bubbly and cheese browns.

Yield: 4 servings.

SHRIMP EN BROCHETTE

1 bag (12 ozs.) frozen shrimp
2 medium green peppers
8 fresh mushrooms
⅓ cup butter or margarine
¼ cup bottled thick meat sauce
1 tablespoon lemon juice
1 small lime, cut in 4 wedges

Place shrimp in a colander; run hot water over top to thaw just enough to separate.

Cut green peppers in half, seed, and cut in 1-inch squares. Wash mushrooms; trim. Thread shrimp, pepper squares, and mushrooms onto 4 long skewers, dividing evenly.

Preheat broiler.

Melt butter in a small saucepan; stir in meat sauce and lemon juice; heat slowly until mixture bubbles.

Place skewers on rack in broiler pan; brush part of the sauce over top.

Broil, 6 inches from heat, turning and brushing several times with rest of sauce, 8 minutes, or until shrimp are tender. Garnish each skewer with a wedge of lime.

Yield: 4 servings.

onto individual serving plates; spoon seafood sauce on top. Pass cheese to sprinkle over each serving.

Yield: 6 servings.

SHRIMP LOUIS BAKE

1½ cups uncooked regular rice
 1 bag (16 ozs.) frozen shrimp
 8 tablespoons butter or margarine
 1 cup fresh bread crumbs (2 slices)
 6 tablespoons all-purpose flour
1¼ teaspoons salt
1¼ teaspoons dry mustard
 3 cups milk
 ½ cup mayonnaise or salad dressing
 ½ cup chili sauce
 ¼ cup chopped green onions
 1 package (10 ozs.) frozen green peas
    Parsley

Cook rice as label directs; spoon into a 2½-quart baking dish.

Cook shrimp as label directs; drain.

Preheat oven to 350°.

Melt 7 tablespoons of the butter in a medium saucepan; measure out 1 tablespoonful and toss with bread crumbs in a small bowl.

Stir flour, salt, and mustard into remaining melted butter in pan; cook, stirring constantly, until bubbly. Stir in milk; continue cooking and stirring until sauce thickens and boils 1 minute; remove from heat. Stir in mayonnaise and chili sauce until mixture is smooth and blended. Stir in green onions; pour over rice.

Set aside 2 or 3 shrimp for garnish, then add rest to rice mixture; stir lightly until blended. Sprinkle buttered bread crumbs evenly over top.

Bake 45 minutes, or until bubbly and topping is toasted.

While casserole bakes, cook peas as label directs; drain. Season with remaining 1 tablespoon butter. Spoon around edge in baking dish. Garnish with saved shrimp and parsley.

Yield: 8 servings.

SEAFOOD SPAGHETTI BOWL

 1 package (7 ozs.) frozen South African rock
    lobster tails
 1 package (16 ozs.) spaghetti
 8 tablespoons butter or margarine
 1 clove garlic, minced
 2 cans (8 ozs. each) minced clams
 1 cup sliced green onions
 2 tablespoons chopped parsley
 ½ teaspoon salt
 ¼ teaspoon pepper
    Grated Parmesan cheese

Cook lobster tails in boiling salted water as label directs; drain; cool until easy to handle. With scissors, snip away membranes from undersides of shells and pull out meat; cut into small cubes.

Cook spaghetti as label directs; drain; return to kettle. Add 2 tablespoons of the butter and toss until butter melts and spaghetti is coated; keep hot.

Melt remaining 6 tablespoons butter in a skillet; stir in garlic; sauté until soft.

Stir in lobster, clams and liquid, green onions, parsley, salt, and pepper; heat to boiling; cover. Simmer 5 minutes.

Spoon spaghetti into a large serving bowl or

SHRIMP ROYALE

1 bag (16 ozs.) frozen shrimp
1¼ cups uncooked regular rice
1 envelope instant chicken broth
1¼ cups boiling water
2 tablespoons chopped parsley
1 can (10¾ ozs.) condensed cream of shrimp soup
1 cup milk
2 teaspoons lemon juice
4 tablespoons butter or margarine
1½ cups fresh bread crumbs (3 slices)
1 package (10 ozs.) frozen peas

Cook shrimp as label directs; drain well; set aside.

Cook rice as label directs; remove from heat. Stir in chicken broth, boiling water, and parsley; let stand until liquid is absorbed.

Preheat oven to 350°.

Combine shrimp soup and milk in a large saucepan; heat very slowly, stirring several times, until sauce is smooth and hot; remove from heat. Stir in lemon juice until blended, then fold in shrimp.

Layer half each of the rice, then shrimp sauce, into a 2½-quart deep baking dish; repeat layers.

Melt 3 tablespoons of the butter in a small saucepan; add bread crumbs and toss to mix; sprinkle over layers in dish.

Bake 45 minutes, or until bubbly and topping is toasted.

While rice bakes, cook peas as label directs; drain. Add remaining 1 tablespoon butter; toss to mix. Spoon around edge in baking dish. Garnish with a lemon wedge, shrimp, and watercress if you like.

Yield: 6 servings.

INDIENNE SHRIMP

1 bag (16 ozs.) frozen shrimp
5 tablespoons butter or margarine
2 teaspoons curry powder
5 tablespoons all-purpose flour
Dash of pepper
2½ cups chicken broth (from two 13¾-oz. cans)
1 jar (4 ozs.) baby-food apricots
4 small green-tipped bananas
3 cups hot cooked rice

Cook shrimp as label directs; drain. Set aside.

Melt butter in a large skillet; stir in curry powder; cook 1 minute. Stir in flour and pepper; cook, stirring constantly, until bubbly. Stir in chicken broth; continue cooking and stirring until sauce thickens and boils 1 minute; stir in baby apricots. Taste and add salt, if needed.

Preheat oven to 375°.

Peel bananas; cut diagonally into ¾-inch slices; place in a pie plate. Spoon about 1 cup of the curry sauce over top.

Bake 5 minutes; remove from oven; keep hot.

Stir shrimp into rest of sauce; heat slowly to boiling.

Spoon rice around edge on a large deep serving platter; spoon shrimp mixture into center; spoon banana mixture around shrimp.

Yield: 6 servings.

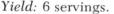

CANNED SHELLFISH

NEW ENGLAND CLAM PIE

 1 large potato, pared and diced (2 cups)
 1 medium onion, chopped (½ cup)
   Water
 2 cans (8 ozs. each) minced clams
   Milk
 3 tablespoons butter or margarine
2⅓ cups sifted all-purpose flour
 2 teaspoons salt
 ⅛ teaspoon pepper
 1 tablespoon lemon juice
 2 tablespoons chopped parsley
 ¾ cup shortening
 1 egg

Combine potato, onion, and 1 cup water in a small saucepan; heat to boiling; cover. Cook 10 minutes, or until potato is tender; drain well.

Drain liquid from clams into a 2-cup measure; add milk to make 1½ cups. Combine potato mixture and clams in a large bowl.

Melt butter in a medium saucepan; stir in ⅓ cup of the flour, 1 teaspoon of the salt, and pepper; cook, stirring constantly, until bubbly. Stir in the 1½ cups clam liquid; continue cooking and stirring until mixture thickens and boils 1 minute; stir in lemon juice and parsley. Stir into potato mixture.

Preheat oven to 400°.

Sift remaining 2 cups flour and 1 teaspoon salt into a medium bowl; cut in shortening with a pastry blender until mixture forms fine crumbs. Sprinkle 6 tablespoons cold water over top, 1 tablespoon at a time, mixing lightly until pastry holds together and cleans the side of bowl.

Roll out half to a 12-inch round on a lightly floured cloth; fit into a 9-inch pie plate; trim overhang to ½ inch. Spoon clam mixture into crust.

Roll out rest of pastry to an 11-inch round; cut several slits near center to let steam escape; place over filling. Trim overhang to ½ inch; turn top and bottom edges under flush with rim of pie plate; flute.

Beat egg with 1 tablespoon water in a small bowl; brush lightly over top crust.

Cut several fish shapes from pastry trimmings with a truffle cutter; arrange over pie; brush egg mixture over cutouts.

Bake pie 40 minutes, or until golden. Cool in pie plate on a wire rack 5 minutes; cut into wedges.

Yield: 9-inch pie.

CRAB SOUFFLE

 1 can (6½ ozs.) crab meat
 1 tablespoon grated onion
 4 tablespoons butter or margarine
 4 tablespoons all-purpose flour
 ½ teaspoon salt
1½ cups milk
 6 eggs, separated
   Swiss Cheese Sauce (recipe on page 313)

Drain liquid from crab meat; flake meat fine.

Sauté onion in butter in a medium saucepan until soft; stir in flour and salt. Cook, stirring constantly, until bubbly. Stir in milk; continue cooking and stirring until sauce thickens and boils 1 minute; cool while beating eggs.

Preheat oven to 350°.

Beat egg whites in a medium bowl until they stand in soft peaks. Beat egg yolks in a large bowl until thick and creamy; slowly beat in cooled sauce and crab; fold in beaten egg whites. Pour into a 2½-quart soufflé dish; gently run a spatula through mixture 1 inch in from edge of dish.

Bake 50 minutes, or until puffed and firm in center. Serve at once with Swiss Cheese Sauce.

Yield: 6 servings.

CRAB CANNELLONI

6 tablespoons butter or margarine
3 tablespoons all-purpose flour (for sauce)
¾ teaspoon salt
¼ teaspoon dried tarragon, crushed
1½ cups light cream
2 cans (6½ ozs. each) crab meat, drained and
   flaked
1 tablespoon freeze-dried chives
1 tablespoon lemon juice
¾ cup sifted all-purpose flour (for batter)
2 eggs
1 cup milk
2 tablespoons grated Parmesan cheese

Melt 3 tablespoons of the butter in a medium saucepan; stir in the 3 tablespoons flour, ½ teaspoon of the salt, and tarragon; cook, stirring constantly, until bubbly. Stir in cream; continue cooking and stirring until sauce thickens and boils 1 minute.

Stir ½ cup of the sauce into crab meat and chives in a medium bowl; stir lemon juice into the remaining sauce in pan and set aside for topping.

Mix the ¾ cup flour and remaining ¼ teaspoon salt in a medium bowl.

Beat eggs in a small bowl; stir in milk; beat into flour mixture until smooth.

Melt 1 tablespoon of the remaining butter in a small skillet; stir into batter.

Heat a 7-inch skillet slowly; lightly grease with part of the remaining butter.

Measure 2 tablespoons of the batter into skillet; quickly tilt skillet until batter covers bottom. Bake 1 to 2 minutes until brown on bottom; turn; bake 1 minute longer. Repeat with rest of batter, lightly buttering skillet between bakings, to make 12 crêpes.

Preheat oven to 450°.

As crêpes are baked, measure about 2 tablespoons of the crab mixture onto each; roll up tightly, jelly-roll fashion. Place, seam side down, in a single layer in a greased baking dish, 13x9x2 inches. Spread remaining sauce in a ribbon over top of rolls. (If sauce has become too thick upon standing, stir in 2 to 3 tablespoons more cream or milk.) Sprinkle cheese over sauce.

Bake 12 minutes, or until rolls are hot and top browns lightly.

Yield: 6 servings.

SHRIMP SPAGHETTI

1 large onion, chopped (1 cup)
3 tablespoons salad oil
2 jars (15½ ozs. each) marinara sauce
1 can (4 ozs.) sliced mushrooms
1½ teaspoons dried oregano, crushed
1 teaspoon salt
2 cans (4½ ozs. each) deveined shrimp, drained
   and rinsed
1 package (16 ozs.) spaghetti
Grated Parmesan cheese

Sauté onion in 2 tablespoons of the salad oil in a large skillet until soft. Stir in marinara sauce, mushrooms and liquid, oregano, and salt. Heat to boiling; simmer 10 minutes. Stir in shrimp; simmer 10 minutes longer.

While sauce simmers, cook spaghetti as label directs; drain. Toss with remaining 1 tablespoon salad oil; spoon onto serving plates. Spoon sauce on top. Pass Parmesan cheese to sprinkle over all.

Yield: 6 servings.

WHITE CLAM SAUCE

2 large cloves garlic, minced
6 tablespoons butter or margarine
1 can (6 ozs.) sliced mushrooms
2 cans (8 ozs. each) minced clams
⅛ teaspoon pepper
⅔ cup chopped parsley

Sauté garlic in butter in a medium saucepan until soft; stir in mushrooms and liquid, clams and juice, and pepper. Heat to boiling; simmer 10 minutes. Stir in parsley. Serve over hot cooked spaghetti.

Yield: 6 servings.

DEVILED CLAMS

2 cans (8 ozs. each) minced clams
1 small onion, minced (¼ cup)
3 tablespoons minced green pepper
6 tablespoons butter or margarine
1 tablespoon Worcestershire sauce
1 tablespoon dried parsley flakes
4 drops red-pepper seasoning
½ teaspoon salt
¾ cup coarse unsalted cracker crumbs

Preheat oven to 375°.

Drain juice from clams into a cup.

Sauté onion and green pepper in 4 tablespoons of the butter in a medium skillet until soft; stir in ½ cup of the clam juice, Worcestershire sauce, parsley flakes, red-pepper seasoning, salt, ¼ cup of the cracker crumbs, and clams.

Spoon into 6 scrubbed clam shells or individual baking dishes. Sprinkle remaining ½ cup cracker crumbs over tops; dot with remaining 2 tablespoons butter.

Bake 15 minutes, or until topping is toasted. Serve hot.

Yield: 6 servings.

CRAB STRATA

1 can (6½ ozs.) crab meat, drained
3 cups half-inch cubes French bread
2 cups shredded sharp Cheddar cheese (8 ozs.)
3 tablespoons all-purpose flour
3 tablespoons melted butter or margarine
4 eggs
3 cups milk
1 teaspoon salt
2 teaspoons prepared horseradish mustard

Flake crab meat.

Place one third of the bread cubes in a 2-quart deep baking dish; top with one third each of the crab meat and cheese. Sprinkle 1 tablespoon of the flour over cheese, then drizzle 1 tablespoon of the butter on top. Repeat layers.

Beat eggs in a medium bowl; stir in milk, salt, and mustard; pour over layers in baking dish; cover. Chill overnight.

Preheat oven to 350°.

Bake casserole, uncovered, 1 hour and 10 minutes, or until puffed and golden. Let stand 10 minutes before serving.

Yield: 6 servings.

RED CLAM SAUCE

1 large onion, chopped (1 cup)
½ clove garlic, minced
1 tablespoon butter or margarine
1 can (16 ozs.) tomatoes
1 can (8 ozs.) tomato sauce
1 teaspoon dried parsley flakes
1 tablespoon mixed Italian seasoning
1 teaspoon salt
2 teaspoons sugar
2 cans (8 ozs. each) minced clams

Sauté onion and garlic in butter until soft in a kettle. Stir in tomatoes, tomato sauce, and seasonings.

Drain liquid from clams and stir into kettle. Heat to boiling; cover. Simmer 45 minutes, or until thick. Stir in clams. Serve over hot cooked spaghetti.

Yield: 6 servings.

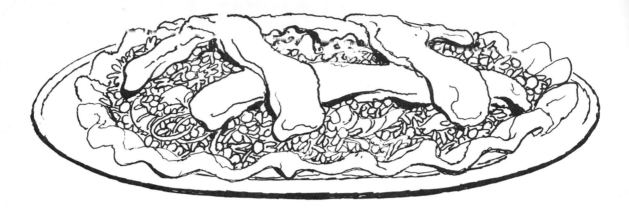

CRAB DIVAN

1 package (10 ozs.) frozen broccoli spears
1 can (6½ ozs.) crab meat
2 hard-cooked eggs, diced
1 tablespoon butter or margarine
1 tablespoon all-purpose flour
1 tablespoon minced onion
½ teaspoon salt
1 cup milk
2 egg whites
¼ cup mayonnaise or salad dressing
2 tablespoons lemon juice

Cook broccoli as label directs; drain well; place in 4 large scallop shells. For easy handling, set shells in a large shallow pan.

Drain liquid from crab. Break meat into small chunks in a medium bowl; add diced eggs.

Preheat oven to 350°.

Melt butter in a small saucepan; stir in flour, onion, and salt; cook, stirring constantly, until blended. Stir in milk; continue cooking and stirring until mixture thickens and boils 1 minute. Fold into crab-meat mixture; spoon evenly over broccoli.

Beat egg whites in a small bowl until they form firm peaks; fold in mayonnaise and lemon juice. Spoon over crab mixture.

Bake 30 minutes, or until topping is puffed and golden.

Yield: 4 servings.

CAJUN SHRIMP PIE

1 cup uncooked regular rice
4 tablespoons butter or margarine
2 eggs, beaten
1 small onion, chopped (¼ cup)
2 tablespoons all-purpose flour
½ teaspoon salt
¼ teaspoon dried thyme, crushed
1 cup milk
1 can (4½ ozs.) shrimp, drained and rinsed
1 can (8 ozs.) peas
4 slices process Old English cheese

Cook rice in salted water as label directs; remove from heat. Stir in 2 tablespoons of the butter until melted, then beaten eggs. Press mixture into a greased 9-inch pie plate, hollowing center to form a shell.

Preheat oven to 375°.

Sauté onion in remaining 2 tablespoons butter until soft in a medium saucepan; stir in flour, salt, and thyme; cook, stirring constantly, until bubbly.

Stir in milk; continue cooking and stirring until mixture thickens and boils 1 minute; stir in shrimp and peas and liquid. Spoon into rice shell.

Cut each cheese slice into 4 strips; arrange over filling to form a crisscross top.

Bake 25 minutes, or until bubbly in center and cheese melts and browns.

Yield: 4 servings.

EGGS AND CHEESE

LUCKILY FOR MEAL PLANNERS, these versatile foods are always in—in season, in favor, and in almost every dish you can imagine. Because they're both rich in protein, they make perfect alternates for meat, and fortunately for us, too, there are so many ways to serve them that we need never be stumped for a main dish idea for any meal.

For many people, the day must start with soft- or hard-cooked, scrambled, poached, or fried eggs. But don't stop there. Carry them to the dinner table as well in a handsome soufflé, an inviting casserole, or a different vegetable dish, and you'll not only please your family, but provide mealtime variety and help to stretch your food budget.

Of all types of cheese, American and Cheddar rank at the top in popularity. Flavors range from mild to sharp to tempt every taste, they mix well with other foods, and most important, they give us what counts to help us keep fit. Depend on these favorites, of course, but also branch out and take advantage of the dozens of other specialties to add excitement to your meal planning.

EGGS

How to store

Eggs lose quality quickly and it's important to get them from the store's refrigerated case into your home refrigerator as fast as possible, especially during hot weather. Leave them in their original carton, or transfer them to the egg holder of your refrigerator, always placing them large end up to help keep yolks centered. Stored properly, they will keep for several weeks, although for peak freshness, it's better to buy only what you need for a week to ten days at a time.

If your recipe calls for whites or yolks only, save the leftovers to use another time. Place whites in a tightly covered jar, chill, and plan to use them within a week. Place yolks in a small jar, cover with 1 to 2 tablespoons of cold water, cover tightly, and chill no longer than two to three days.

How to cook

Whatever method you use, the two most important rules are: Go easy on the heat and watch your timing. Heat that's too high or cooking time that's too long simply toughens eggs. Follow these basic cooking directions:

To soft-cook—Place eggs in a saucepan and add enough water to cover generously. Heat to boiling; remove from heat; cover; let stand from 1 to 3 minutes, depending on your preference. Cool promptly in cold water to stop the cooking. Crack the shell around the middle with a spoon, then scoop out each half into a serving dish.

To hard-cook—Follow the same method as for soft-cooking, but allow the eggs to stand in the water for 15 to 20 minutes; cool immediately in cold water. Tap the shell lightly against something hard to crack it in several places, then roll it between your palms to loosen all over. Holding egg under running cold water, peel from the large end.

To fry—Measure 1 tablespoon salad oil or butter or margarine into a small skillet; heat slowly just until it sizzles. Break egg into a custard cup first, then slide it into the skillet. Cook slowly, spooning the drippings in skillet over egg several times, just until the yolk is as firm as you like it. Or turn the egg once to cook both sides. Another way: Instead of basting the egg, add about a half teaspoonful water to the skillet after the egg has cooked a minute, cover the skillet to hold in the steam, and continue cooking to desired firmness.

To poach—Pour a 2-inch depth of water or milk into a shallow saucepan or skillet; heat to simmering. Break egg into a custard cup first, then slip it into the water, holding cup near the surface. Simmer 3 to 5 minutes, depending on taste. Remove the egg with a slotted spatula and drain before serving.

To scramble—Combine each 2 eggs with 2 tablespoons milk or cream and a dash each of salt and pepper in a small bowl. Beat until blended. Measure 1 tablespoon butter or margarine into a small skillet and heat just until it sizzles. Pour in egg mixture. Cook slowly, lifting mixture with a spatula around edge of pan as it sets to let soft part run to bottom; continue cooking just until eggs are softly firm but still creamy and moist on top. Cooking time for two eggs should be from 3 to 5 minutes.

To bake—Break egg into a lightly buttered custard cup; sprinkle salt and pepper over top. Bake at 325° for 15 to 20 minutes, or until as firm as you like it. Serve from cup.

CHEESE

Know what you're buying

Cheese products vary widely, and the label is your guide to the type that's best for your purpose. Get acquainted with these basic kinds:

Natural cheese—Just as its name implies, it's made from milk, then stored under carefully controlled conditions to age or ripen by itself and develop its special characteristics. Flavors range from mild to very sharp.

Pasteurized process cheese—Here, freshly made and aged natural cheeses are shredded, combined, and heated to stop further ripening. Texture and flavor are always the same, and because process cheese is attractively priced, it's one of the most popular

choices for cooking and sandwich-making. Buy it sliced, in blocks, or in ½-, 1-, and 2-pound loaves.

Pasteurized process cheese food—Made the same way as process cheese, it has nonfat dry milk, water, or whey solids added. That's why it is milder, softer, spreads easier, and melts faster than process cheese. It's packaged as slices, rolls, links, and loaves.

Pasteurized process cheese spread—Similar to process cheese food, it spreads easier because it contains more moisture. It may also have pimientos or other vegetables, meat, or fruit added for variety in flavor. Convenient packages include jars, pressurized cans, tubes, and loaves.

Coldpack cheese—This term confuses some consumers, but it needn't. It simply means that the product is a blend of one or more fresh and aged natural cheeses that are mixed without heating. Whatever natural cheese is used determines the flavor, although it may be smoked. Because it's soft and spreads easily, it's a popular item for appetizer trays and sandwiches. Look for it packed in jars, or as rolls and links.

How to store

Many kinds of natural cheese are good keepers, but it pays to remember that these products are perishable. The best rule of thumb is to buy often and only what you can use within a reasonable time.

At home, keep cheeses chilled, the same as milk. Use soft varieties such as cream, cottage, cheese foods, and cheese spreads within a week. Leave natural types in their original wrappers, or rewrap tightly in moistureproof paper, and store in the refrigerator. Properly handled, they will keep for weeks.

To freeze or not to freeze

Freeze cheese only if you must—for it may lose flavor and become crumbly or mealy. Keep the pieces small—one pound or less and not more than one-inch thick—and wrap tightly in moisture- and vaporproof paper, pressing the paper against the surface to prevent drying. Then freeze it quickly at zero degrees or less.

Among the varieties that can be frozen most successfully for up to four months are Brick, Cheddar, Edam, Gouda, Muenster, Port du Salut, Swiss, Provolone, Mozzarella, and Camembert. Cheeses packaged in small sizes, such as Camembert, may be frozen in their original packages.

Thaw frozen cheese, still wrapped, in the refrigerator, then use it as soon as possible.

EGGS

SCRAMBLED EGGS BENEDICT

1 package hollandaise sauce mix
1 thin ready-to-eat ham steak, weighing
　　about ¾ lb.
4 eggs
　Dash of pepper
¼ cup milk
2 tablespoons butter or margarine
2 English muffins, split and toasted

　Prepare hollandaise sauce mix with water as label directs; keep warm.

　Brown ham steak slowly, turning once, in a large skillet; cut into 4 pieces.

　While ham heats, beat eggs with pepper and milk until blended in a bowl. Melt butter in a medium skillet; pour in egg mixture. Cook slowly, lifting mixture around edge of pan as it sets to let soft part run to bottom; continue cooking just until eggs are softly set but still creamy-moist on top.

　Place each muffin half on a serving plate; top with a slice of ham, scrambled eggs, and hollandaise sauce.

　Yield: 4 servings.

SAUSAGE-EGG SCRAMBLE

1 package (8 ozs.) brown and
　　serve sausages
6 eggs
⅓ cup milk
1 single-serving envelope
　　onion soup mix

　Preheat oven to 350°.

　Brown sausages slowly in a medium skillet with ovenproof handle; arrange, spoke fashion, in skillet.

　Beat eggs with milk until blended in a medium bowl; stir in soup mix; pour over sausages.

　Bake 10 minutes, or until eggs are softly set but still creamy-moist on top. Cut into wedges.

　Yield: 6 servings.

DENVER SCRAMBLE

¼ cup chopped green pepper
1 small onion, chopped (¼ cup)
¼ cup chopped celery
4 tablespoons butter or margarine
1 cup diced cooked ham
6 eggs
1 can (11 ozs.) condensed Cheddar
　　cheese soup

　Sauté green pepper, onion, and celery in butter until soft in a large skillet; stir in ham; sauté 1 minute.

　Beat eggs well in a medium bowl; stir in cheese soup; pour over ham mixture.

　Cook slowly, lifting egg mixture around edge of pan as it sets to let soft part run to bottom; continue cooking just until eggs are softly set but still creamy-moist on top.

　Spoon onto serving plates. Serve with toasted buttered hamburger buns if you like.

　Yield: 4 servings.

MEXICAN OMELET

        5 tablespoons butter or margarine
        3 tablespoons all-purpose flour
        ½ teaspoon salt
        ⅛ teaspoon pepper
        1½ cups milk
        1 cup shredded Monterey Jack
            cheese (4 ozs.)
        8 eggs
        2 tablespoons minced seeded
            green chili peppers

Melt 3 tablespoons of the butter in a medium saucepan; stir in flour, ¼ teaspoon of the salt, and pepper; cook, stirring constantly, until bubbly.

Measure 2 tablespoons of the milk into a medium bowl for omelet mixture; stir remaining milk into saucepan. Cook, stirring constantly, until sauce thickens and boils 1 minute; stir in cheese until melted; keep hot.

Add eggs and remaining ¼ teaspoon salt to milk in bowl; beat until well blended; stir in chili peppers.

Heat remaining 2 tablespoons butter in a 10-inch skillet; pour in egg mixture. Cook slowly, lifting mixture around edge of pan as it sets to let soft part run to bottom; continue cooking just until eggs are softly set but still creamy-moist on top.

Gently fold omelet into thirds and lift onto a serving plate. Spoon part of the cheese sauce over top, then serve remainder separately.

Yield: 4 servings.

WESTERN OMELET FOLDOVER

        4 eggs, separated
        ¼ cup milk
        1 teaspoon prepared mustard
            Dash of pepper
        3 tablespoons butter or margarine
        1 small onion, minced
        1 package (6 ozs.) sliced boiled ham,
            diced (about 1¼ cups)
        ¼ cup minced green pepper

Preheat oven to 350°.

Beat egg whites in a medium bowl until stiff. Beat egg yolks with milk, mustard, and pepper in a medium bowl until blended; fold in egg whites.

Melt 2 tablespoons of the butter in a 10-inch skillet with ovenproof handle; pour in egg mixture. Cook slowly on top of the range 5 minutes, or until golden on bottom; place in oven. Bake 10 minutes, or until puffed and golden on top.

While omelet bakes, sauté onion, ham, and green pepper in remaining 1 tablespoon butter in a small skillet.

Halve omelet with a knife, cutting not quite to bottom; spoon ham mixture on top of one half; fold other half over filling. Lift onto a serving plate.

Yield: 4 servings.

FARMER'S OMELET

        1 small potato, peeled and sliced thin
        1 small onion, coarsely chopped
        3 tablespoons butter or margarine
        1 can (4 ozs.) Vienna sausages, drained
            and sliced thin
        4 eggs
        2 tablespoons milk
        ¼ teaspoon salt

Sauté potato and onion in 2 tablespoons of the butter until tender in a large skillet. Break up potatoes slightly with a spoon, then stir in sausages and remaining 1 tablespoon butter.

Beat eggs with milk and salt until blended in a medium bowl; pour over potato mixture. Cook slowly, lifting egg mixture around edge of pan as it sets to let soft part run to bottom; continue cooking just until mixture is softly firm. Cut in 4 wedges.

Yield: 4 servings.

A LA CARTE OMELETS

    1 can (15 ozs.) corned beef hash
 ½ teaspoon dried basil, crushed
    8 eggs
 ½ cup milk
    Salt
    Pepper
    4 tablespoons butter or margarine

Combine corned beef hash and basil in a medium skillet; heat slowly while preparing omelets.

For one omelet, beat 2 eggs with 2 tablespoons of the milk and a dash each of salt and pepper in a small bowl.

Melt 1 tablespoon of the butter in an 8-inch skillet; tilt skillet until butter coats bottom and side; pour in egg mixture.

Cook slowly, lifting mixture around edge of pan as it sets to let soft part run to bottom; continue cooking just until eggs are softly set but still creamy-moist on top.

Spoon one fourth of the corned beef hash mixture onto half of omelet; fold other half over top; lift onto a serving plate. Prepare and fill 3 more omelets the same way.

Yield: 4 servings.

HOT-DOG OMELET

    1 can (11¼ ozs.) condensed hot-dog bean soup
 ½ cup water
    4 eggs
    2 tablespoons milk
    Dash of salt
    Dash of pepper
    1 tablespoon butter or margarine

Blend soup and water in a medium saucepan; heat, stirring several times, to boiling; keep warm.

Beat eggs with milk, salt, and pepper until blended in a medium bowl.

Melt butter in a 10-inch skillet; when it starts to foam, pour in egg mixture.

Cook slowly, lifting mixture around edge of pan as it sets to let soft part run to bottom;

continue cooking just until eggs are softly set but still creamy-moist on top.

Spoon part of the bean mixture over one half of the omelet; fold other half over top. Lift onto a serving plate; spoon remaining bean mixture on top. Cut crosswise in 4 sections.

Yield: 4 servings.

SAUCY OMELET WEDGES

    4 tablespoons butter or margarine
    2 tablespoons all-purpose flour
 ¾ teaspoon salt
    Dash of pepper
 1¼ cups milk
    1 can (8 ozs.) peas and carrots, drained
    6 eggs, separated
 1½ teaspoons prepared mustard
 ¼ teaspoon dried thyme, crushed

Melt 2 tablespoons of the butter in a small saucepan; stir in flour, ½ teaspoon of the salt, and pepper. Cook, stirring constantly, until bubbly. Stir in 1 cup of the milk; continue cooking and stirring until sauce thickens and boils 1 minute; stir in peas and carrots. Keep warm.

Preheat oven to 350°.

Beat egg whites in a medium bowl until they form firm peaks. Beat egg yolks with remaining ¼ cup milk, ¼ teaspoon salt, mustard, and thyme in a large bowl until blended; fold in beaten egg whites.

Melt remaining 2 tablespoons butter in a 10-inch skillet with ovenproof handle; pour in egg mixture. Cook slowly on top of the range 5 minutes, or until brown on bottom, then bake 10 minutes, or until puffed and golden.

Cut in 4 wedges; spoon creamed vegetables over each serving.

Yield: 4 servings.

BACON-TOMATO OMELET

6 slices of bacon, cut in ½-inch pieces
1 medium tomato
6 eggs, separated
¼ cup milk
1 teaspoon prepared mustard
¼ teaspoon salt
2 tablespoons butter or margarine
¼ cup process cheese spread

Sauté bacon until crisp in a small skillet; remove and drain on paper toweling. Chop tomato fine.

Preheat oven to 350°.

Beat egg whites in a medium bowl until they form firm peaks. Beat egg yolks with milk, mustard, and salt in a large bowl until blended; fold in beaten egg whites.

Melt butter in a 10-inch skillet with oven-proof handle; pour in egg mixture. Cook slowly on top of the range 5 minutes, or until brown on bottom, then bake 10 minutes, or until puffed and golden.

Spoon cheese over omelet; let stand a minute to melt, then spread over top; sprinkle bacon and tomatoes over cheese. Cut in 4 wedges.

Yield: 4 servings.

DEVILED EGGS

8 hard-cooked eggs
2 tablespoons milk
1 tablespoon lemon juice
1½ teaspoons prepared mustard
½ teaspoon salt
Dash of pepper
1 tablespoon chopped pimiento-stuffed
green olives
Parsley

Cut eggs in half lengthwise; scoop out yolks into a small bowl; mash well.

Stir in milk, lemon juice, mustard, salt, pepper, and olives; pile back into whites. Trim each half with a small tuft of parsley.

Yield: 8 servings.

STUFFED EGG SALADS

8 hard-cooked eggs
2 slices salami, minced (¹/₃ cup)
2 tablespoons minced green pepper
¼ cup mayonnaise or salad dressing
⅛ teaspoon salt
Dash of pepper
1 package (10 ozs.) frozen green peas
3 tablespoons bottled French dressing
1 teaspoon instant minced onion
¼ cup chopped celery
Boston lettuce

Cut eggs in half lengthwise; scoop out yolks into a small bowl; mash well.

Stir in salami, green pepper, mayonnaise, salt, and pepper until blended; pile back into whites; chill.

Cook peas as label directs; drain. Toss with French dressing, onion, and celery in a medium bowl; chill.

When ready to serve, spoon pea mixture onto 4 lettuce-lined salad plates. Arrange egg halves around edge.

Yield: 4 servings.

EGG SALAD CARBONARA

1½ cups broken spaghetti
4 hard-cooked eggs, diced
4 slices ham-bologna, diced (1 cup)
½ cup mayonnaise or salad dressing
2 teaspoons instant minced onion
2 tablespoons milk
2 tablespoons chopped parsley
2 tablespoons grated Parmesan cheese
¼ teaspoon salt

Cook spaghetti as label directs; drain. Place in a medium bowl; add eggs and ham-bologna.

Blend mayonnaise, onion, milk, parsley, Parmesan cheese, and salt in a cup; fold into spaghetti mixture. Serve warm.

Yield: 4 servings.

COUNTRY EGG SALAD

2 medium potatoes, pared and diced (2 cups)
2 tablespoons butter or margarine
2 tablespoons all-purpose flour
½ teaspoon salt
⅛ teaspoon pepper
1 cup milk
½ cup mayonnaise or salad dressing
½ cup sliced celery
2 tablespoons chopped onion
2 tablespoons chopped parsley
6 hard-cooked eggs, diced
½ cup small cubes sharp Cheddar cheese
2 small tomatoes, each cut into 8 thin wedges

Cook potatoes, covered, in boiling salted water in a small saucepan 8 minutes, or until tender; drain well.

Melt butter in a large saucepan; stir in flour, salt, and pepper; cook, stirring constantly, until bubbly. Stir in milk; continue cooking and stirring until sauce thickens and boils 1 minute; remove from heat.

Stir in mayonnaise; fold in potatoes, celery, onion, parsley, three fourths of the eggs and cheese cubes.

Spoon onto serving plates; sprinkle remaining diced eggs on top. Garnish each plate with 4 tomato wedges. Serve warm.

Yield: 4 servings.

PICKLED STUFFED EGGS

½ cup cider vinegar
¼ cup sugar
1 tablespoon mixed pickling spices
½ cup water
  Red food coloring
6 hard-cooked eggs, shelled
2 tablespoons mayonnaise or salad dressing
1 teaspoon prepared horseradish-mustard
¼ teaspoon salt
  Dash of pepper

Combine vinegar, sugar, pickling spices, and water in a small saucepan. Heat, stirring several times, to boiling; simmer 10 minutes; tint deep pink with food coloring.

Strain over eggs in a medium bowl. Let stand, turning eggs several times to tint evenly, until bright pink; remove from liquid.

Cut each egg in half lengthwise; scoop out yolks into a small bowl. Mash well, then stir in mayonnaise, mustard, salt, and pepper. Pile back into whites; chill.

Yield: 6 servings.

PICKLED BEETS AND EGGS

1 can (16 ozs.) small whole beets
¾ cup vinegar
⅓ cup sugar
1 tablespoon mixed pickling spices
½ cup water
6 hard-cooked eggs, shelled
  Iceberg lettuce

Drain liquid from beets into a small saucepan. (There should be about ¾ cup.) Place beets in a small bowl.

Stir vinegar, sugar, and pickling spices into beet liquid; heat, stirring several times, to boiling. Simmer 5 minutes; strain into a 2-cup measure. Pour 1 cup of liquid over beets; cover; chill several hours.

Stir water into remaining liquid; pour over eggs in a medium bowl. Let stand, turning often, 25 minutes, or until evenly tinted a deep pink. Drain off liquid; cover eggs; chill several hours.

When ready to serve, drain liquid from beets; pile beets in the center of a lettuce-lined serving platter. Cut each egg in half lengthwise; arrange around edge. Serve plain or with mayonnaise, if you like, to spoon over eggs.

Yield: 6 servings.

FRYING PAN SOUFFLE

⅓ cup butter or margarine
⅓ cup all-purpose flour
1 teaspoon salt
  Dash of pepper
1½ cups milk
6 eggs, separated
¼ teaspoon cream of tartar
1 cup shredded process American cheese
  (4 ozs.)
6 green onions, trimmed and sliced thin
1 medium-sized red pepper, quartered, seeded,
  and chopped

Preheat oven to 325°.

Melt butter in a medium saucepan; stir in flour, salt, and pepper. Cook, stirring constantly, until bubbly. Stir in milk; continue cooking and stirring until mixture thickens and boils 1 minute; cool while beating eggs.

Beat egg whites in a large bowl until foamy; add cream of tartar and continue beating until mixture forms soft peaks.

Beat egg yolks in a second large bowl until creamy; slowly beat in cooled sauce; fold in beaten egg whites. Pour into a buttered 10-inch skillet with ovenproof handle.

Bake 35 minutes, or until puffed and golden. Sprinkle cheese over top; return to oven just until cheese starts to melt; remove from oven. Sprinkle green onions and red pepper on top. Cut into wedges; serve at once.

Yield: 6 servings.

HAM-AND-SWISS SOUFFLE

4 tablespoons butter or margarine
4 tablespoons all-purpose flour
1½ cups milk
1 cup shredded Swiss cheese (4 ozs.)
1 cup ground cooked ham
1 teaspoon prepared hot spicy mustard
¼ teaspoon salt
⅛ teaspoon pepper
6 eggs, separated

Melt butter in a medium saucepan; stir in flour; cook, stirring constantly, until bubbly.

Stir in milk; continue cooking and stirring until mixture thickens and boils 1 minute. Stir in cheese until melted, then ham, mustard, salt, and pepper. Cool while beating eggs.

Preheat oven to 350°.

Beat egg whites in a medium bowl until they form soft peaks. Beat egg yolks in a large bowl until thick and creamy; slowly stir in ham-cheese mixture; fold in beaten egg whites. Pour into a 2½-quart soufflé dish; gently run a spatula through mixture 1 inch in from edge of dish.

Bake 50 minutes, or until puffed and golden and firm in center. Serve at once.

Yield: 4 servings.

CLAM PUFFS

1 can (8 ozs.) minced clams
  Milk
3 tablespoons butter or margarine
3 tablespoons all-purpose flour
¾ teaspoon salt
1 teaspoon Worcestershire sauce
4 eggs, separated

Drain juice from clams into a 1-cup measure; add milk to make 1 cup.

Melt butter in a medium saucepan; stir in flour and salt; cook, stirring constantly, until bubbly. Stir in the 1 cup liquid; continue cooking and stirring until sauce thickens and boils 1 minute. Stir in clams and Worcestershire sauce; cool while beating eggs.

Preheat oven to 350°.

Beat egg whites in a medium bowl until they form soft peaks. Beat egg yolks in a large bowl until thick and creamy; slowly beat in cooled clam sauce; fold in beaten egg whites. Spoon into four 10-ounce baking dishes. Set dishes, not touching, in a large shallow baking pan.

Bake 25 minutes, or until puffed and golden and firm in center. Serve at once.

Yield: 4 servings.

SALMON SOUFFLE

    4 tablespoons butter or margarine
    4 tablespoons all-purpose flour
    ¼ teaspoon salt
      Few drops red-pepper seasoning
 1½ cups milk
    1 cup shredded Swiss cheese (4 ozs.)
    1 can (8 ozs.) salmon, drained, boned, and
      flaked
    6 eggs, separated
    ¼ teaspoon cream of tartar

Melt butter in a medium saucepan; stir in flour, salt, and red-pepper seasoning; cook, stirring constantly, until bubbly. Stir in milk; continue cooking and stirring until mixture thickens and boils 1 minute. Stir in cheese until melted, then salmon. Cool while beating eggs.

Preheat oven to 350°.

Beat egg whites with cream of tartar in a medium bowl until they form soft peaks.

Beat egg yolks in a large bowl until thick and creamy; slowly beat in cooled salmon sauce; fold in beaten egg whites.

Pour into a 2½-quart soufflé dish; gently run a spatula through mixture 1 inch in from edge of dish.

Bake 50 minutes, or until puffed and golden and firm in center. Serve at once.

Yield: 4 servings.

SCOTCH EGGS

 1½ lbs. ground beef
    1 tablespoon instant minced onion
    1 teaspoon seasoned salt
    ⅛ teaspoon pepper
    6 hard-cooked eggs, shelled
    2 tablespoons milk
    ¼ cup dry bread crumbs
    1 envelope spaghetti sauce mix with mushrooms
    1 tablespoon salad oil
    1 can (6 ozs.) tomato paste
 1½ cups water
    3 cups hot cooked noodles
    1 tablespoon butter or margarine
    1 tablespoon chopped parsley

Preheat oven to 400°.

Combine ground beef, onion, salt, and pepper in a large bowl; mix lightly. Divide into 6 mounds; shape each mound around a hard-cooked egg to cover completely.

Measure milk into a pie plate; sprinkle bread crumbs on waxed paper. Roll meat in milk, then in bread crumbs to coat well. Place in a greased shallow pan.

Bake 30 minutes, or until beef is as done as you like it.

While meat cooks, prepare spaghetti sauce mix with salad oil, tomato paste, and water as label directs.

Toss noodles with butter and parsley in a medium bowl; spoon in center of a large serving platter. Cut each meatball in half; arrange around edge. Pass sauce separately.

Yield: 6 servings.

FRENCH HAM PUFF

 8 slices white bread
 2 teaspoons prepared mustard
 1 package (4 ozs.) sliced boiled ham
 4 wedges (1 oz. each) process Gruyere cheese
 4 eggs
 2 cups milk
   Few drops red-pepper seasoning

Toast bread; spread mustard on 4 of the slices; place in a single layer in an 8x8x2-inch baking dish. Top with ham, cutting slices to fit toast.

Shred cheese; sprinkle over ham; top with remaining toast to make sandwiches.

Beat eggs in a medium bowl; stir in milk and red-pepper seasoning; pour over sandwiches; cover. Chill overnight.

Preheat oven to 325°. Uncover dish.

Bake sandwiches 40 minutes until puffed and custard is set in center. Cut apart with a knife; lift onto serving plates with a pancake turner. Serve hot.

Yield: 4 servings.

EASTER EGG PIE

1 large onion, chopped (1 cup)
2 tablespoons butter or margarine
6 eggs
1 tablespoon all-purpose flour
3 cups light cream
  Salt
1 package (6 ozs.) process Gruyere cheese,
    shredded
12 stalks fresh asparagus
  Water
1 hard-cooked egg, sliced

Preheat oven to 325°.

Sauté onion in butter until soft in a small skillet; spread in an even layer in a 2-quart shallow baking dish.

Beat eggs in a medium bowl until blended; beat in flour; stir in cream, ½ teaspoon salt, and cheese. Pour over onion mixture in dish.

Bake 50 minutes, or until a knife inserted into center comes out clean.

While pie bakes, wash asparagus; cut stalks to 5-inch lengths. Remove scales with a small sharp knife; wash stalks again. Tie in a bundle; stand in a deep saucepan.

Pour boiling water into pan to a 1-inch depth; salt lightly; cover. Cook 15 minutes, or just until asparagus is crisp-tender; drain carefully.

Arrange asparagus, spoke fashion, on top of pie; overlap egg slices in center.

Yield: 6 servings.

EGG ROLY-POLY

2 cups biscuit mix
1 cup milk
6 hard-cooked eggs, diced
¾ cup diced celery
¼ cup diced pimiento-stuffed green olives
⅓ cup mayonnaise or salad dressing
2 tablespoons dairy sour cream
½ teaspoon salt
1 can (10¾ ozs.) condensed cream of
    celery soup

Preheat oven to 400°.

Prepare biscuit mix with ⅔ cup of the milk as label directs. Turn out onto a lightly floured pastry cloth; pat into a rectangle, 10x8 inches.

Combine eggs, celery, and olives in a medium bowl. Blend mayonnaise, sour cream, and salt in a cup; fold into egg mixture. Spread over biscuit rectangle; starting at an 8-inch end, roll up, jelly-roll fashion. Cut into 1-inch-thick slices; place about ½ inch apart on a greased large cookie sheet.

Bake 20 minutes, or until firm and lightly golden.

While rolls bake, combine soup and remaining ⅓ cup milk in a small saucepan; heat slowly, stirring several times, to boiling. Serve over egg rolls.

Yield: 4 servings.

EGG CUPS FLORENTINE

1 package (10 ozs.) frozen chopped spinach
1 package white sauce mix
1 cup milk
2 tablespoons grated Parmesan cheese
1 package (6 ozs.) sliced boiled ham, chopped
    (about 1¼ cups)
4 eggs
  Paprika

Preheat oven to 350°. Grease four 10-ounce custard cups.

Cook spinach in unsalted water as label directs; drain well.

Prepare white sauce mix with milk as label directs; stir in cheese. Stir ¼ cup of the sauce into spinach; spoon evenly into custard cups; place ham on top.

Break an egg into each cup; spoon remaining sauce over eggs; sprinkle paprika on top.

Bake 20 minutes, or until eggs are as firm as you like them.

Yield: 4 servings.

SPANISH EGGS

1 small onion, chopped (¼ cup)
½ small green pepper, chopped (¼ cup)
2 tablespoons salad oil
2 tablespoons all-purpose flour
½ teaspoon salt
¼ teaspoon pepper
1 can (8 ozs.) stewed tomatoes
½ cup shredded process American cheese
1 can (15 ozs.) spaghetti with ground beef
4 hard-cooked eggs, sliced
2 tablespoons butter or margarine
1 cup fresh white bread crumbs (2 slices)

Preheat oven to 350°.

Sauté onion and green pepper in salad oil in a medium skillet until soft. Blend in flour, salt, and pepper; cook, stirring constantly, until bubbly. Stir in tomatoes; continue cooking and stirring until sauce thickens and boils 1 minute; stir in cheese until melted.

Layer one fourth of the spaghetti into each of four individual baking dishes; cover with sliced eggs, then sauce.

Melt butter in a small saucepan; add bread crumbs; toss to mix. Sprinkle over layers in baking dishes.

Bake 30 minutes, or until bubbly and topping is toasted.

Yield: 4 servings.

CHILI-EGG RAMEKINS

1 lb. ground beef
1 medium-sized green pepper, quartered, seeded, and diced (¾ cup)
1 medium onion, chopped (½ cup)
½ cup diced celery
1 tablespoon chili powder
1½ teaspoons salt
⅛ teaspoon pepper
1 can (16 ozs.) tomatoes
1 can (16 ozs.) red kidney beans
8 eggs
⅓ cup milk
3 tablespoons butter or margarine
2 tablespoons chopped parsley

Shape ground beef into a large patty; place in a kettle. Brown in its own fat, turning once; break up into chunks; push to one side.

Stir green pepper, onion, celery, and chili powder into drippings; sauté until onion is soft. Stir in 1 teaspoon of the salt, pepper, tomatoes, and kidney beans and liquid. Heat to boiling; cover. Simmer 30 minutes; uncover. Simmer 30 minutes longer, or until thick.

While chili simmers, beat eggs with milk and remaining ½ teaspoon salt in a medium bowl until well blended.

Melt butter in a medium skillet; pour in egg mixture. Cook slowly, lifting mixture around edge of pan as it cooks to let soft part run to bottom; continue cooking just until eggs are softly set but still creamy-moist on top.

Spoon chili mixture into 6 individual serving bowls; spoon eggs in a ring around edge on each. Sprinkle parsley over all.

Yield: 6 servings.

QUICK CREAMED EGGS

1 can (10¾ ozs.) condensed cream of chicken soup
¼ cup milk
6 hard-cooked eggs
2 English muffins, split
1 can (2¼ ozs.) deviled ham
Paprika

Preheat broiler.

Combine soup and milk in a medium saucepan; heat to boiling.

Slice eggs and stir into sauce; heat again until hot.

Place muffins on a cookie sheet; toast in broiler. Spread deviled ham over each half; place each on a serving plate. Spoon creamed eggs over top; sprinkle paprika over eggs.

Yield: 4 servings.

CHEDDAR EGG CUPS

1 can (11 ozs.) condensed Cheddar cheese soup
1 teaspoon Worcestershire sauce
8 eggs
2 tablespoons butter or margarine
½ cup dry bread crumbs

Preheat oven to 325°.

Mix soup and Worcestershire sauce in a small bowl; spoon into eight 6-ounce custard cups; break an egg into each cup. For easy handling, set cups in a large shallow pan.

Melt butter in a small saucepan; stir in bread crumbs; sprinkle over eggs.

Bake 20 minutes, or until eggs are set and topping is toasted.

Yield: 8 servings.

MOCK EGGS BENEDICT

½ cup dairy sour cream
½ cup mayonnaise or salad dressing
2 tablespoons lemon juice
1 package (4 ozs.) sliced Canadian-style bacon
2 hamburger buns, split
2 tablespoons salad oil
4 eggs
Paprika

Preheat broiler.

Combine sour cream, mayonnaise, and lemon juice in the top of a small double boiler; heat over hot water while fixing bacon and eggs.

Arrange bacon slices on rack in broiler pan; broil, 5 to 6 inches from heat, 2 to 4 minutes, or until hot and lightly browned; keep warm.

While bacon cooks, place bun halves on a cookie sheet; toast in oven; keep warm.

Heat salad oil in a large skillet; break eggs, one at a time, into a cup and place in skillet. Cook gently, spooning oil in skillet over eggs several times, 3 to 4 minutes, or until as firm as you like them.

Place each bun half on a serving plate; top with bacon, then eggs; spoon sauce over all. Sprinkle paprika over tops.

Yield: 4 servings.

EGG-AND-TUNA BAKE

4 hard-cooked eggs
2 tablespoons mayonnaise or salad dressing
1 teaspoon prepared mustard
⅛ teaspoon salt
⅛ teaspoon pepper
2 cups uncooked medium noodles
1 package (3 ozs.) cream cheese with chives
1 can (10¾ ozs.) condensed cream of mushroom soup
¼ cup milk
1 can (3 ozs.) tuna, drained and broken up
2 tablespoons chopped onion
½ cup crushed potato chips

Preheat oven to 375°.

Cut eggs in half lengthwise; scoop out yolks into a small bowl; mash well. Stir in mayonnaise, mustard, salt, and pepper; pile back into whites.

Cook noodles as label directs; drain; return to kettle.

Blend cream cheese with mushroom soup and milk in a medium bowl; stir in tuna and onion. Spoon over noodles; toss lightly to mix.

Spoon one third of the noodle mixture into a 1-quart baking dish; top with half of the deviled eggs. Repeat layers; spoon remaining tuna mixture on top. Sprinkle potato chips around edge in dish.

Bake 30 minutes, or until bubbly in the center.

Yield: 4 servings.

EGG-AND-SHRIMP BOATS

4 small hero rolls
4 hard-cooked eggs, cubed
1 can (about 5 ozs.) deveined shrimp, drained
   and diced
½ cup chopped celery
2 tablespoons chopped onion
2 tablespoons chopped dill pickle
½ cup mayonnaise or salad dressing
2 tablespoons chili sauce
1 teaspoon prepared horseradish

Cut around top of each roll about ¼ inch in from edge; scoop out insides to make boat-shaped shells. (Use insides for croutons or a crumb topping for a casserole.)

Combine eggs, shrimp, celery, onion, and pickle in a medium bowl.

Mix mayonnaise, chili sauce, and horseradish in a cup; fold into shrimp mixture until well blended. Spoon evenly into rolls.

Yield: 4 servings.

BAKED BACON AND EGGS

½ cup whipping cream
1 package (4 ozs.) sliced Canadian-style
   bacon
1 can (3 or 4 ozs.) chopped mushrooms,
   drained
4 eggs
   Seasoned salt
   Pepper

Preheat oven to 350°.

Measure 1 tablespoon of the cream into each of four 6-ounce custard cups. Place bacon in cups, dividing evenly; spoon mushrooms over bacon.

Break an egg into each cup; sprinkle lightly with salt and pepper; spoon another 1 tablespoon cream over each egg. For easy handling, place cups in a large shallow pan.

Bake 20 minutes until eggs are softly set, or until as firm as you like them. Serve hot.

Yield: 4 servings.

LEMON CUSTARD FRENCH TOAST

8 slices French bread, cut 1 inch thick
4 eggs
2 teaspoons sugar
1 teaspoon grated lemon rind
   Dash of salt
1 cup milk
¾ cup coarsely crushed bite-sized
   corn cereal squares
   Golden Apricot Syrup (recipe follows)

Place bread in a single layer in a shallow glass baking dish.

Beat eggs in a medium bowl until blended; stir in sugar, lemon rind, salt, and milk; pour over bread. Let stand 2 minutes, then turn slices. Let stand 15 minutes longer at room temperature, or overnight in refrigerator, until milk is absorbed completely.

Preheat oven to 400°.

Sprinkle cereal on a sheet of waxed paper. Lift bread slices from dish and dip in cereal to coat both sides generously; place in a single layer on a lightly greased large cookie sheet.

Bake 20 minutes, or until puffed and crisp. Serve hot with Golden Apricot Syrup.

Yield: 4 servings.

GOLDEN APRICOT SYRUP

1 can (12 ozs.) apricot nectar
¼ cup honey
1 tablespoon lemon juice
1 teaspoon grated orange rind
2 tablespoons butter or margarine

Combine apricot nectar, honey, lemon juice, and orange rind in a small saucepan. Heat slowly, stirring constantly, to boiling; simmer, stirring once or twice, 15 minutes, or until syrupy-thick. Stir in butter until melted.

Pour into a pitcher; serve hot.

Yield: About 1 cup.

BAKED HAM-AND-EGG BALLS

4 hard-cooked eggs
¼ cup chopped celery
2 tablespoons chopped green onion
2 tablespoons mayonnaise or salad dressing
½ teaspoon prepared mustard
⅛ teaspoon salt
1 package (4 ozs.) sliced boiled ham
1 package (10 ozs.) frozen green peas and
   cauliflower with cream sauce
  Milk
  Butter or margarine
½ cup shredded process American cheese

Cut eggs in half lengthwise; scoop out yolks into a small bowl; mash well. Stir in celery, onion, mayonnaise, mustard, and salt. Pile mixture into whites; press each two halves back together.

Fold each slice of ham in half lengthwise; wrap around an egg; place, seam side down, in a 10-ounce custard cup.

Preheat oven to 350°.

Prepare peas and cauliflower with milk and butter as label directs; spoon over eggs in cups; sprinkle cheese on top.

Bake 20 minutes, or until cheese melts and mixture is bubbly.

Yield: 4 servings.

THOUSAND ISLAND EGGS

½ cup dairy sour cream
¼ cup chili sauce
¼ teaspoon salt
  Dash of pepper
2 teaspoons butter or margarine
4 eggs
4 frankfurter rolls
1 jar (5 ozs.) process bacon cheese spread

Mix sour cream, chili sauce, salt, and pepper in a small bowl.

Preheat oven to 350°.

Measure ½ teaspoon of the butter into each of four 6-ounce custard cups. For easy handling, set cups in a large shallow pan. Heat in oven until butter melts.

Break an egg into each cup; spoon sour cream mixture over eggs.

Bake 15 minutes, or until eggs are as firm as you like them.

While eggs bake, open frankfurter rolls; place on a cookie sheet. Toast in same oven. Spread cheese over each.

Bake 3 to 4 minutes longer, or until cheese melts. Serve hot with eggs.

Yield: 4 servings.

DEVILED EGG BAKE

1 cup uncooked regular rice
6 hard-cooked eggs
2 tablespoons mayonnaise or salad dressing
1 teaspoon prepared mustard
¼ teaspoon salt
⅛ teaspoon pepper
2 cans (10¾ ozs. each) condensed cream of
   shrimp soup
½ cup milk
½ cup fresh bread crumbs (1 slice)
½ cup shredded Swiss cheese

Cook rice as label directs; spread in a shallow 2-quart baking dish.

Preheat oven to 350°.

Cut eggs in half lengthwise; scoop out yolks into a small bowl; mash well. Stir in mayonnaise, mustard, salt, and pepper. Pile back into whites; arrange in rows over rice in dish.

Mix soup and milk in a small bowl; spoon over rice mixture.

Mix bread crumbs and cheese on waxed paper; sprinkle evenly over sauce.

Bake 40 minutes, or until bubbly in center.

Yield: 6 servings.

CARAWAY EGG TOASTIES

4 slices whole-wheat bread
2 teaspoons prepared hot spicy mustard
4 hard-cooked eggs, sliced
1 large tomato, cut in 4 slices
4 square slices caraway cheese

Preheat broiler.

Place bread on a cookie sheet and toast in broiler; spread mustard over untoasted sides. Top each with egg slices, then a tomato and cheese slice.

Broil, 6 inches from heat, 3 to 4 minutes, or until cheese melts and sandwiches are heated through. Serve hot.

Yield: 4 servings.

CASSEROLE EGGS

2 cups cooked rice
4 hard-cooked eggs, sliced
1 can (11 ozs.) condensed Cheddar
    cheese soup
½ cup milk
1 small tomato, sliced thin

Preheat oven to 350°.

Layer half of the rice, then sliced eggs and remaining rice into a 1-quart baking dish.

Blend cheese soup and milk in a small bowl; pour over rice mixture; lift mixture around edge with a knife so sauce will seep to bottom.

Bake 30 minutes; overlap tomato slices around edge in dish. Bake 10 minutes longer, or until bubbly in center.

Yield: 4 servings.

CHEESE

HAVARTI CHEESE SOUFFLE

3 tablespoons butter or margarine
3 tablespoons all-purpose flour
¼ teaspoon salt
¼ teaspoon cayenne
¾ cup milk
1½ cups shredded Danish Havarti cheese (6 ozs.)
5 eggs, separated
¼ teaspoon cream of tartar
    Green-pea Sauce (recipe follows)

Preheat oven to 350°.

Melt butter in a medium saucepan; stir in flour, salt, and cayenne; cook, stirring constantly, until bubbly. Stir in milk; continue cooking and stirring until mixture thickens and boils 1 minute. Stir in cheese until melted. Cool while beating eggs.

Beat egg whites with cream of tartar in a medium bowl until they form soft peaks.

Beat egg yolks in a large bowl until thick and creamy; slowly beat in cooled cheese sauce; fold in beaten egg whites. Pour into a 2-quart soufflé dish. Gently run a spatula through mixture 1 inch in from edge of dish.

Bake 50 minutes, or until puffed and golden and firm in center. Serve at once with Green-pea Sauce.

Yield: 4 servings.

GREEN-PEA SAUCE

1 cup loose-pack frozen green peas
2 tablespoons butter or margarine
2 tablespoons all-purpose flour
¼ teaspoon salt
1 cup milk

Cook peas in boiling salted water as label directs; drain.

Melt butter in a small saucepan; stir in flour and salt; cook, stirring constantly, until bubbly. Stir in milk; continue cooking and stirring until sauce thickens and boils 1 minute. Stir in peas.

Yield: 2 cups.

TRIPLE CHEESE MANICOTTI

1 carton (16 ozs.) ricotta cheese (2 cups)
½ cup grated Parmesan cheese
1 cup chopped fresh spinach
2 eggs
1½ teaspoons salt
⅛ teaspoon pepper
8 manicotti shells
5 tablespoons butter or margarine
5 tablespoons all-purpose flour
2 cups milk
½ teaspoon Worcestershire sauce
1 package (8 ozs.) sharp Cheddar cheese,
    cut in small pieces

Combine ricotta cheese, ¼ cup of the Parmesan cheese, spinach, eggs, 1 teaspoon of the salt, and pepper in a large bowl; stir until well blended.

Cook manicotti shells as label directs; drain. Return to kettle; cover with cold water.

While shells cook, melt butter in a medium saucepan; stir in flour and remaining ½ teaspoon salt; cook, stirring constantly, until bubbly. Stir in milk and Worcestershire sauce; continue cooking and stirring until sauce thickens and boils 1 minute; stir in Cheddar cheese until melted. Spoon half into a baking dish, 11¾x7½x1¾ inches.

Preheat oven to 350°.

Lift manicotti shells from water and drain well; stuff a generous ⅓ cup of the ricotta mixture into each, using a small spatula or two spoons. Place in a row in sauce in dish. Spoon remaining cheese sauce over shells in a ribbon down center; sprinkle remaining ¼ cup Parmesan cheese on top.

Bake 35 minutes, or until bubbly and cheese browns lightly.

Yield: 4 servings.

PIZZA BEANS

1 can (16 ozs.) pork and beans in
    tomato sauce
4 brown-and-serve link sausages,
    sliced thin
1 small onion, minced (¼ cup)
½ teaspoon dried oregano, crushed
1 cup shredded mozzarella cheese (4 ozs.)
2 tablespoons grated Romano cheese

Preheat oven to 375°.

Combine pork and beans, sliced sausages, onion, and oregano in a medium bowl; mix well. Spoon into a 1-quart shallow baking dish. Sprinkle mozzarella, then Romano cheese over top.

Bake 20 minutes, or until bubbly and topping melts and browns lightly.

Yield: 4 servings.

LITTLE GRUYERE PUFFS

3 tablespoons butter or margarine
3 tablespoons all-purpose flour
1 tablespoon freeze-dried chives
½ teaspoon prepared mustard
½ teaspoon salt
1 cup milk
1 package (6 ozs.) Gruyere cheese, shredded
3 eggs, separated

Preheat oven to 350°.

Melt butter in a medium saucepan; blend in flour, chives, mustard, and salt. Cook, stirring constantly, until bubbly. Stir in milk; continue cooking and stirring until mixture thickens and boils 1 minute; stir in cheese until melted. Cool while beating eggs.

Beat egg whites in a medium bowl until they form firm peaks.

Beat egg yolks in a medium bowl until thick and creamy; slowly beat in cooled sauce; fold in egg whites. Spoon into 4 ungreased 10-ounce custard cups. Set cups in a shallow pan for easy handling.

Bake 40 minutes, or until puffed and golden and firm in center. Serve at once.

Yield: 4 servings.

MACARONI CHEESE SCALLOP

1 package (8 ozs.) small macaroni shells
1 package (10 ozs.) frozen peas
1 jar (2 ozs.) sliced pimientos, drained and
    diced
½ cup bottled thin French dressing
6 tablespoons butter or margarine
1 cup fresh bread crumbs (2 slices)
¼ cup chopped green onions
½ cup diced celery
4 tablespoons all-purpose flour
1 teaspoon salt
⅛ teaspoon pepper
2 cups milk
1 package (8 ozs.) sliced process Old English
    cheese

Cook macaroni and peas separately as labels direct; drain. Combine in a large bowl with pimientos; fold in French dressing until well mixed. Let stand while making sauce.

Preheat oven to 375°.

Melt butter in a medium saucepan; measure out 2 tablespoons and toss with bread crumbs in a small bowl.

Stir onions and celery into remaining melted butter; sauté until soft.

Stir in flour, salt, and pepper; cook, stirring constantly, until bubbly. Stir in milk; continue cooking and stirring until sauce thickens and boils 1 minute. Cut up cheese and stir in until melted. Fold sauce into macaroni mixture.

Spoon into an 11¾x7½x1¾-inch baking dish. Spoon buttered crumbs in diagonal rows on top.

Bake 40 minutes, or until bubbly and topping is toasted.

Yield: 8 servings.

CHEESE BEIGNETS

½ cup butter or margarine
1 cup water
1¼ cups sifted all-purpose flour
1 teaspoon dry hot mustard
½ teaspoon salt
4 eggs
1 package (6 ozs.) process Gruyere cheese,
    shredded
    Salad oil for frying

Combine butter and water in a medium saucepan; heat slowly to boiling. Stir in flour, mustard, and salt all at once with a wooden spoon; continue stirring until batter forms a thick smooth ball that follows spoon around pan; remove from heat and cool slightly.

Beat in eggs, 1 at a time, until mixture is thick and shiny-smooth; beat in cheese.

Pour enough salad oil into a deep fat fryer to fill about half way; heat to 375°.

Drop batter, a heaping teaspoon at a time, into hot oil; fry 2 to 3 minutes; turn. (Some may turn by themselves.) Fry 1 to 2 minutes longer, or until golden all over. Remove from oil and drain on paper toweling. Place on cookie sheets lined with paper toweling and keep hot in a low oven until all are cooked. Serve hot.

Yield: 5 dozen.

MONTEREY TAMALE DINNER

2 cans (16 ozs. each) barbecued beans
1 can condensed chili-beef soup
1 can (15 ozs.) tamales in chili gravy
1 cup shredded Monterey Jack cheese
    (4 ozs.)
1½ cups shredded iceberg lettuce

Preheat oven to 375°.

Combine beans and soup in a 2-quart shallow baking dish. Remove wrappings from tamales; arrange tamales, chevron style, on top of bean mixture; sprinkle cheese over all.

Bake 45 minutes, or until bubbly and cheese melts. Sprinkle shredded lettuce around edge in dish.

Yield: 6 servings.

CHEDDAR NOODLE RING

1 package (8 ozs.) medium noodles
1 can (4 ozs.) green chili peppers, drained, seeded, and minced
1 package (8 ozs.) sharp Cheddar cheese, shredded
2 cups (16-oz. container) dairy sour cream
1 teaspoon salt

Cook noodles as label directs; drain; return to kettle.

Preheat oven to 350°.

Add peppers, cheese, sour cream, and salt to noodles; stir lightly until well blended. Spoon into a well-greased 1¾-quart ring mold, packing mixture down firmly with back of spoon. Set mold in a shallow baking pan; pour hot water into pan to a depth of 1 inch.

Bake 45 minutes, or until set. Remove mold from water and let stand 10 minutes on a wire rack. Loosen ring around edge and center with a knife; invert onto a large serving plate; lift off mold. Serve plain with a roast for dinner, or fill center with creamed peas and serve as a main dish for luncheon.

Yield: 6 servings.

PORK-AND-PINEAPPLE RABBIT

1 can (12 ozs.) pork luncheon meat
1 can (8 ozs.) sliced pineapple, drained
¼ cup butter or margarine
¼ cup all-purpose flour
  Dash of salt
  Dash of pepper
1 cup milk
4 slices process American cheese, cut up
4 slices frozen French toast

Cut luncheon meat into 8 slices; brown lightly on both sides in a medium skillet; remove from skillet.

Brown pineapple lightly in drippings in skillet; keep hot.

While meat and pineapple brown, melt butter in a medium saucepan; stir in flour, salt, and pepper; cook, stirring constantly, until bubbly. Stir in milk; continue cooking and stirring until sauce thickens and boils 1 minute. Stir in cheese until melted.

Heat French toast as label directs; place each slice on a serving plate. Top with two slices of meat and a slice of pineapple; spoon cheese sauce over all.

Yield: 4 servings.

ALL-AMERICAN POTATO SCALLOP

4 large potatoes
5 tablespoons butter or margarine
¼ cup all-purpose flour
1½ teaspoons salt
1 teaspoon dry mustard
1½ cups milk
1 package (8 ozs.) process American cheese, cut up
  Few drops red-pepper seasoning
1 jar (2 ozs.) pimientos, drained and chopped
½ cup fine bread crumbs

Scrub potatoes. Cook, covered, in boiling salted water in a large saucepan 30 minutes, or until tender; drain. Cool, then peel and slice ⅛ inch thick.

Preheat oven to 350°.

Melt 4 tablespoons of the butter in a medium saucepan; stir in flour, salt, and mustard. Cook, stirring constantly, until bubbly. Stir in milk; continue cooking and stirring until sauce thickens and boils 1 minute. Stir in cheese until melted, then red-pepper seasoning and pimientos.

Layer one third of the potatoes into a deep 1½-quart baking dish; top with one third of the sauce. Repeat layers.

Melt remaining 1 tablespoon butter in a small saucepan; stir in bread crumbs; sprinkle over potato mixture.

Bake 45 minutes, or until sauce bubbles up.

Yield: 8 servings.

BUSY DAY MACARONI AND CHEESE

1½ cups uncooked elbow macaroni
1 can (3 ozs.) tuna, drained and flaked
2 tablespoons finely chopped onion
1 can (10¾ ozs.) condensed cream of
    mushroom soup
½ cup milk
1 cup shredded sharp Cheddar cheese
    (4 ozs.)

Preheat oven to 350°.

Cook macaroni as label directs; drain; return to pan. Stir in tuna, onion, mushroom soup, and milk; spoon half into a 1-quart baking dish. Sprinkle half of the cheese on top. Repeat layers.

Bake 45 minutes, or until bubbly.

Yield: 4 servings.

TUNA RABBIT

2 tablespoons butter or margarine
4 tablespoons all-purpose flour
¼ teaspoon dry mustard
½ teaspoon salt
⅛ teaspoon pepper
2 cups milk
1 cup shredded process Old English cheese
    (4 ozs.)
2 tablespoons chopped pimientos
1 can (about 7 ozs.) tuna, drained and
    broken into chunks
8 small frozen waffles

Melt butter in a medium skillet; stir in flour, mustard, salt, and pepper; cook, stirring constantly, until bubbly.

Stir in milk; continue cooking and stirring until mixture thickens and boils 1 minute; stir in cheese until melted, then add pimientos and tuna. Heat slowly just until bubbly.

While tuna mixture heats, toast waffles as label directs; place on serving plates; spoon tuna mixture over each.

Yield: 4 servings.

OLD ENGLISH HASH BAKE

1 can (16 ozs.) corned beef hash
1 teaspoon Worcestershire sauce
2 hard-cooked eggs, sliced
1 cup shredded process Old English Cheese
    (4 ozs.)

Preheat oven to 350°.

Mix hash and Worcestershire sauce in a medium bowl; spread half into a buttered 8-inch pie plate.

Arrange egg slices over layer, then sprinkle ½ cup of the cheese over eggs. Top with remaining hash mixture and cheese.

Bake 20 minutes, or until bubbly in center. Cut into wedges; lift out with a pancake turner.

Yield: 4 servings.

CAN-CAN GOULASH

1 cup thinly sliced celery
1 medium onion, chopped (½ cup)
2 tablespoons salad oil
1 can (15 ozs.) macaroni and beef in
    tomato sauce
1 can (8 ozs.) red kidney beans, drained
⅛ teaspoon pepper
1 cup shredded process American cheese
    (4 ozs.)

Sauté celery and onion in salad oil until soft in a medium skillet. Stir in macaroni and beef, kidney beans, and pepper. Heat slowly to boiling; simmer, stirring once or twice, 10 minutes

Sprinkle cheese over macaroni mixture; cover. Let stand 2 to 3 minutes, or just until cheese melts. Spoon onto serving plates.

Yield: 4 servings.

FRYING PAN SOUFFLE (p.245) ▶

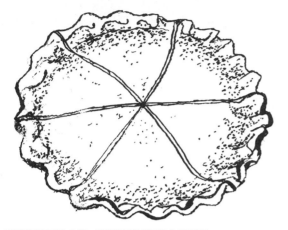

CHEDDAR CHICKEN PIE

Single Crust Pastry (recipe on page 497)
3 eggs
3 tablespoons cornstarch
½ teaspoon salt
⅛ teaspoon pepper
1 can (13¾ ozs.) chicken broth
1 cup shredded sharp Cheddar cheese
   (4 ozs.)
1 jar (2 ozs.) pimientos, drained and
   chopped
1 can (5 ozs.) boned chicken, minced
½ cup minced green pepper

Preheat oven to 425°.

Prepare Single Crust Pastry. Roll out to a 12-inch round on a lightly floured pastry cloth; fit into a 9-inch pie plate. Trim overhang to ½ inch; turn edge under flush with rim of pie plate; flute to make a stand-up edge.

Beat eggs in a large bowl until thick and creamy.

Mix cornstarch, salt, and pepper in a small bowl; slowly stir in chicken broth until smooth; slowly beat into eggs. Stir in cheese, pimientos, chicken, and green pepper. Pour into prepared pastry shell.

Bake 15 minutes; lower oven temperature to 325°. Bake 30 minutes longer, or until filling is set. Cool 10 minutes on a wire rack before serving. Cut into wedges.

Yield: 6 servings.

GREEN ENCHILADAS

1 carton (8 ozs.) cream-style cottage cheese
1 package (8 ozs.) sharp Cheddar cheese,
   shredded (2 cups)
1 medium onion, chopped (½ cup)
¼ cup chopped ripe olives
1¼ teaspoons salt
½ cup salad oil
12 tortillas
4 tablespoons butter or margarine
4 tablespoons all-purpose flour
   Water
1 can (13¾ ozs.) chicken broth
1 can (4 ozs.) green chili peppers, drained,
   seeded, and chopped
1 cup (8-oz. carton) dairy sour cream

Combine cottage cheese, 1½ cups of the Cheddar cheese, onion, olives, and ½ teaspoon of the salt in a medium bowl; mix well.

Heat salad oil in a medium skillet; place tortillas, only 1 at a time, in oil and heat for about 15 seconds on each side; remove from skillet and drain on paper toweling. As each is heated, measure about 2 tablespoons of the cheese mixture onto one edge; roll up, jelly roll fashion. Place, seam side down, in a 11¾x7½x1¾-inch baking dish.

Preheat oven to 375°.

Melt butter in a medium saucepan; stir in flour and remaining ¾ teaspoon salt; heat, stirring constantly, until bubbly.

Add enough water to chicken broth to measure 2 cups; stir into flour mixture. Continue cooking and stirring until sauce thickens and boils 1 minute; stir in chili peppers.

Slowly stir about 1 cup of the hot sauce into sour cream in a small bowl, then stir back into saucepan; heat just until hot. (Do not boil.) Pour over filled tortillas; sprinkle remaining ½ cup Cheddar cheese in a ribbon down center.

Bake 20 minutes, or until bubbly.

Yield: 4 to 6 servings.

CHEESE CRUNCHIES

1⅓ cups sifted all-purpose flour
½ cup yellow cornmeal
1 tablespoon sugar
2 teaspoons baking powder
1 teaspoon salt
⅓ teaspoon baking soda
2 eggs
1 cup buttermilk
½ cup butter or margarine, melted
⅓ cup chopped pitted ripe olives
½ lb. bacon
2 large tomatoes, each cut in 4 slices
1 cup shredded sharp Cheddar cheese
   (4 ozs.)

Heat waffle iron as the manufacturer directs.

Sift flour, cornmeal, sugar, baking powder, salt, and soda into a large bowl.

Beat eggs in a medium bowl; stir in buttermilk and melted butter. Add all at once to flour mixture; stir just until blended; stir in olives.

Ladle batter into hot waffle iron. Bake as manufacturer directs until golden. As waffles are baked, place in a single layer on a large cookie sheet.

While waffles bake, sauté bacon until crisp in a large frying pan; remove and drain on paper toweling; cut each slice in half. Arrange 4 pieces on each waffle; top with tomato slices; sprinkle cheese over all, dividing evenly.

Broil, 6 inches from heat, 2 to 3 minutes, or until cheese melts and bubbles up. Serve hot.
Yield: 4 to 6 servings.

CHEDDAR CHILI BEANS

1 package (16 ozs.) dried pinto beans
   Water
1 medium onion, chopped (½ cup)
1 tablespoon salad oil
1 can (4 ozs.) green chili peppers, drained,
   seeded, and chopped
1 can (10½ ozs.) condensed tomato soup
1 package (8 ozs.) sharp Cheddar cheese,
   shredded (2 cups)
2 tablespoons chopped parsley

Rinse beans. Combine with 8 cups water in a kettle. Heat to boiling; cook 2 minutes; remove from heat; cover. Let stand 1 hour. Reheat to boiling; simmer 1 hour, or until beans are tender but still firm enough to hold their shape; drain. Spoon beans into a 2-quart baking dish.

Sauté onion in salad oil until soft in a large skillet; stir in chili peppers, soup, and ½ cup water; heat to boiling. Stir into beans in baking dish.

Preheat oven to 350°.

Mix shredded cheese and parsley in a small bowl; sprinkle evenly, or in ribbons, over bean mixture.

Bake 30 minutes, or until bubbly and cheese melts.
Yield: 6 servings.

GOLDEN MACARONI CUPS

1½ cups uncooked elbow macaroni
1 can (8 ozs.) diced carrots
   Milk
2 eggs
1 tablespoon freeze-dried chives
¾ teaspoon salt
   Few drops red-pepper seasoning
1 package (8 ozs.) sliced process Old
   English cheese, diced
2 tablespoons butter or margarine
1 cup fresh bread crumbs (2 slices)

Preheat oven to 350°.

Cook macaroni as label directs; return to pan.

Drain liquid from carrots into a 1-cup measure; add milk to make ⅔ cup. Beat eggs slightly with milk mixture, chives, salt, and red-pepper seasoning in a small bowl; stir into macaroni with cheese and carrots. Spoon into four 10-ounce custard cups. For easy handling, set cups in a large shallow pan.

Melt butter in a small skillet; stir in bread crumbs; sprinkle over macaroni mixture.

Bake 35 minutes, or until mixture is softly set and topping is toasted.
Yield: 4 servings.

JUAREZ BEAN BAKE

1 large onion, chopped (1 cup)
½ cup thinly sliced celery
2 tablespoons salad oil
1 teaspoon chili powder
1 can (4 or 5 ozs.) Vienna sausages, sliced
½ teaspoon Italian herbs
1 can (8 ozs.) tomato sauce
2 jars (18 ozs. each) brick-oven baked beans
1 package (8 ozs.) process Monterey Jack
   cheese, shredded

Preheat oven to 350°.

Sauté onion and celery in salad oil in a large skillet until soft; stir in chili powder; cook 1 minute.

Stir in sausages, Italian herbs, tomato sauce, and beans and sauce. Heat to boiling; spoon into a 1½-quart baking dish. Sprinkle shredded cheese on top.

Bake 35 minutes, or until bubbly.
Yield: 6 servings.

DOUBLE CHEESE PIZZA

2 packages refrigerated plain or buttermilk
   biscuits
1 can (15 ozs.) spaghetti and beef in
   pizza sauce
1 can (3 or 4 ozs.) chopped mushrooms,
   drained
4 slices process white American cheese
½ cup grated Parmesan cheese

Preheat oven to 400°.

Separate biscuits; press together evenly into a lightly greased 12-inch pizza pan; flute edge.

Heat spaghetti to boiling in a small saucepan; spread over crust. Sprinkle mushrooms over spaghetti.

Cut American cheese into strips; arrange over mushrooms; sprinkle Parmesan cheese over all.

Bake 20 minutes, or until crust browns lightly. Cut into wedges.
Yield: 4 servings.

SALMON-CHEESE IMPERIAL

3 or 4 salmon steaks, weighing about 1¼ lbs.
3 cups milk
¾ teaspoon salt
1 package (8 ozs.) medium noodles
1 package (8 ozs.) sliced Swiss cheese
5 tablespoons butter or margarine
5 tablespoons all-purpose flour
¼ teaspoon pepper
1 package (8 ozs.) cream cheese
⅓ cup sliced pimiento-stuffed green olives

Preheat oven to 350°.

Place salmon steaks in a single layer in a shallow baking dish; pour in ½ cup of the milk; sprinkle ¼ teaspoon of the salt over top.

Bake 25 minutes, or until salmon flakes easily when tested with a fork; drain. Cool until easy to handle; cut into ½-inch cubes, discarding bones and skin.

Cook noodles as label directs; drain. Cut each slice of cheese into 8 squares. Set aside 20 squares for topping.

Melt butter in a medium saucepan; stir in flour, remaining ½ teaspoon salt, and pepper; cook, stirring constantly, until bubbly. Stir in remaining 2½ cups milk; continue cooking and stirring until sauce thickens and boils 1 minute. Cut up cream cheese and stir in until melted; remove from heat; stir in olives.

Spoon about ½ cup of the sauce into a 2½-quart baking dish. Top with half each of the noodles and salmon, all of remaining Swiss cheese, and half of the remaining sauce. Repeat with rest of noodles, salmon, and sauce; arrange saved cheese squares to cover top.

Bake 45 minutes, or until bubbly and cheese browns. Garnish with parsley and small pimiento-stuffed green olives if you like.

Yield: 8 servings.

EGGPLANT PARMIGIANA

1 medium eggplant, weighing about 1¾ lbs.
2 eggs
2 tablespoons water
  Salad oil
1 large onion, chopped (1 cup)
1 clove of garlic, crushed
1 lb. ground beef
2 cans (15 ozs. each)
    tomato-herb sauce
1½ teaspoons dried oregano, crushed
½ teaspoon salt
1 package (8 ozs.) sliced mozzarella cheese
½ cup grated Parmesan cheese

Pare eggplant; slice ¼ inch thick.

Beat eggs with water in a pie plate. Dip eggplant slices into egg mixture to coat; brown, a few at a time, in salad oil in a large skillet, adding oil as needed; remove from skillet and drain on paper toweling.

Stir onion and garlic into drippings; sauté until soft; push to one side. Stir in ground beef and brown. Stir in tomato sauce, oregano, and salt; heat to boiling.

Preheat oven to 375°.

Layer one third of the eggplant slices into a shallow 2-quart baking dish; top with one third of the meat sauce.

Set aside 2½ slices of the mozzarella cheese for topping; cut remainder into strips and place half over sauce in dish; sprinkle one third of the Parmesan cheese on top. Repeat layers, ending with sauce.

Cut remaining mozzarella cheese into strips; arrange over layers in dish to form a crisscross top; sprinkle remaining Parmesan cheese over all.

Bake 45 minutes, or until bubbly in center.
Yield: 6 servings.

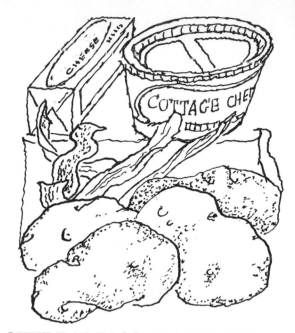

CHEDDAR-BACON POTATOES

4 large baking potatoes
4 slices bacon, cut in 1-inch pieces
½ cup creamed large-curd cottage cheese
¼ cup milk
½ teaspoon salt
⅛ teaspoon pepper
2 teaspoons finely cut chives
½ cup tiny cubes of Cheddar cheese

Preheat oven to 425°.

Scrub potatoes; place in a shallow pan.

Bake 1 hour, or until tender; remove from oven, but leave oven on.

While potatoes bake, sauté bacon until crisp in a small skillet; remove and drain on paper toweling.

Cut a thin slice from the top of each potato; scoop out centers into a medium bowl, being careful not to break shells; return shells to a cookie sheet.

Add cottage cheese, milk, salt, pepper, and chives to potatoes; beat until light and fluffy; fold in cheese cubes. Pile back into shells; sprinkle bacon on top.

Bake 10 minutes, or until cheese melts.
Yield: 4 servings.

RICE AND PASTA

BOTH OF THESE CUPBOARD MAINSTAYS offer matchless variety and versatility in meal fixing. Rare is the cook who doesn't have at least one kind on hand at all times to turn into a main or side dish, a salad, or in the case of rice, a dessert as well. Because of their mild flavor, both are good mixers with other foods and economical extenders for meat dishes and casseroles.

Rice takes a number of different forms, and which you buy depends upon your preference and purse. In most markets, you may choose from among these kinds:

Regular, in long-, medium-, or short-grain, with the outer hull and bran removed by polishing. Most come enriched which means that any vitamins and minerals lost in processing have been replaced. Long-grain cooks up lighter and fluffier than the short-grain type; all triple in volume during cooking.

Converted, a long-grain rice, especially processed to retain its food value. It cooks up very dry and fluffy and swells to almost four times its volume when cooked.

Precooked or instant, just as its name implies, processed to cook quickly. This type doubles in volume during cooking.

Brown, the whole unpolished form of rice with its outer bran layer intact. Of all types, brown contains the most vitamins and minerals and has a chewy, nutlike flavor. Count on a longer cooking time than for white varieties; figure on its tripling in volume when cooked.

Wild, not really a rice but the seed of an aquatic grass that grows wild. Because its price is high, it's considered a luxury to be used sparingly for holidays or other special occasions. Often it's mixed with white rice to stretch a little a long way. After cooking, it measures about three times its original volume.

Rice mixes, made up of quick-cooking or long-grain rice plus a variety of seasonings or flavorings. Available mostly in 6- or 7-ounce packages, they come in a wide variety of flavors.

Like rice, the pasta family is a large one that includes more than 150 different sizes and shapes of macaroni, spaghetti, and noodles. Just by changing shapes, you can create interesting new twists on some of your favorite dishes. Names of the various pasta vary by area and not all will be available where you shop, but you can always find one that's suitable for your recipe. Substitute by weight rather than cup measure since a cupful of one uncooked form may weigh more than a cupful of another. If you cook the product first, cup measure substitutions work fine.

All of the recipes in the pages that follow were especially chosen to show how adaptable and thrifty rice and pasta can be. There are many old dependables such as rice-and-ground beef casseroles or spaghetti and meatballs. But you'll also find dozens of new serving ideas to help you put an excitingly different flavor and look on your everyday and party tables.

How to cook rice

For any of the methods here, follow directions exactly and the grains will turn out plump, tender, and fluffy. The two points to remember: Measure accurately and use a saucepan or baking dish with a snug cover to keep in the steam.

White rice

Top-range way: Combine 1 cup regular long-grain rice, 2½ cups water, 1 tablespoon butter or margarine, and 1 teaspoon salt in a medium saucepan. Heat, stirring once or twice, to boiling; cover tightly. Simmer 25 minutes, or until rice is tender and liquid is absorbed. Fluff with a fork. Yield: 3 cups.

Oven way: Measure 1 cup regular long-grain rice into a 1-quart baking dish. Heat 2½ cups water, 1 tablespoon butter or margarine, and 1 teaspoon salt to boiling in a small saucepan; stir into rice; cover tightly. Bake at 350° for 1 hour, or until rice is tender and liquid is absorbed. Fluff with a fork. Yield: 3 cups.

Instant way: Fixing directions vary slightly by brand, so follow the specific instructions on the label. Yield: One cup from the package measures 2 cups prepared rice.

Brown rice

Top-range way: Combine 1 cup brown rice, 2½ cups water, and 1 teaspoon salt in a medium saucepan; heat, stirring once or twice, to boiling; cover tightly. Simmer 45 minutes, or until rice is tender and liquid is absorbed. Fluff with a fork. Yield: 3 cups.

Wild rice

Top-range way: Place rice in a sieve and rinse under cold running water, stirring several times with a spoon to make sure it's cleaned thoroughly. Combine 1 cup rice, 2½ cups water, and 1 teaspoon salt in a medium saucepan; heat, stirring once or twice, to boiling; cover tightly. Cook 45 minutes, or until rice is tender and liquid is absorbed. Yield: 3 cups.

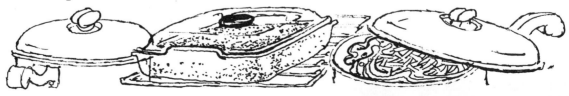

RICE

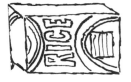

PEANUT PILAF

1⅓ cups uncooked regular rice
4 tablespoons salad oil
1 medium onion, chopped (½ cup)
½ cup chopped green pepper
½ cup chopped salted peanuts
1 can (13¾ ozs.) chicken broth
⅛ teaspoon pepper

Preheat oven to 325°.

Sauté rice in salad oil in a large skillet until golden. Stir in onion, green pepper, and peanuts; sauté 1 to 2 minutes longer.

Add water to chicken broth to make 2½ cups; stir into rice mixture in skillet with pepper; heat to boiling. Spoon into a 1½-quart baking dish; cover.

Bake 1 hour, or until liquid is absorbed and rice is tender. Fluff lightly with a fork.

Yield: 6 servings.

SWISS HAM SCALLOP

1 cup uncooked regular rice
5 tablespoons butter or margarine
5 tablespoons all-purpose flour
3 cups milk
¼ teaspoon pepper
Few drops red-pepper seasoning
1 package (8 ozs.) sliced Swiss cheese,
   shredded (2 cups)
½ cup chopped green pepper
2 cups cubed cooked ham (1 lb.)
1 package (10 ozs.) frozen peas, thawed
1 cup fresh bread crumbs (2 slices)

Cook rice in salted water as label directs; set aside.

Melt butter in a large saucepan; stir in flour. Cook, stirring constantly, until bubbly. Stir in milk, pepper, and red-pepper seasoning; continue cooking and stirring until sauce thickens and boils 1 minute. Stir in three fourths of the Swiss cheese until melted.

Preheat oven to 350°.

Layer half each of the rice, green pepper, ham, peas, and sauce into a 3-quart baking dish; repeat layers.

Mix bread crumbs and rest of cheese in a small bowl; sprinkle over rice mixture.

Bake 45 minutes, or until bubbly and topping is toasted.

Yield: 6 servings.

PIZZA RICE BAKE

1 cup uncooked regular rice
1 medium onion, chopped (½ cup)
½ cup chopped celery
2 tablespoons salad oil
2 cans (8 ozs. each) tomato sauce
¼ cup grated Parmesan cheese
1 teaspoon dried oregano, crushed
¾ teaspoon salt
1 package (6 ozs.) sliced mozzarella cheese

Cook rice as label directs.

While rice cooks, sauté onion and celery in salad oil in a medium skillet until soft. Stir in tomato sauce, Parmesan cheese, oregano, and salt; heat to boiling; stir in rice.

Preheat oven to 350°.

Cut mozzarella cheese crosswise into inch-wide strips; set aside about 6 strips for topping.

Spoon one third of the rice mixture into a 1½-quart baking dish; top with half of the cheese. Repeat layers; cover with rest of rice mixture. Arrange the saved cheese strips in a pattern on top.

Bake 30 minutes, or until bubbly. Serve with steamed frankfurters or broiled hamburgers.

Yield: 6 servings.

TIJUANA CHICKEN AND RICE

6 chicken drumsticks with thighs
2 tablespoons salad oil
1 large onion, chopped (1 cup)
1 tablespoon chili powder
1 can (16 ozs.) stewed tomatoes
1 teaspoon salt
1 can (12 ozs.) Mexican-style corn
1 can (8 ozs.) red kidney beans
   Water
1 package (8 ozs.) chicken-flavored rice
   and vermicelli mix

Cut drumsticks and thighs apart at joints; wash chicken; dry on paper toweling.

Brown pieces in salad oil in a large skillet; remove from skillet.

Stir onion and chili powder into drippings; sauté until onion is soft; stir in tomatoes and salt. Heat to boiling; place chicken in sauce; cover tightly. Simmer 20 minutes.

Drain liquids from corn and kidney beans into a 2-cup measure; add water to make 2 cups.

Stir rice and seasoning mix into chicken mixture; stir in the 2 cups liquid, beans, and corn. Heat to boiling again; cover. Simmer, stirring once or twice, 30 minutes, or until rice and chicken are tender and almost all liquid is absorbed. Serve from skillet.

Yield: 6 servings.

FRANKFURTER-RICE CROWN

1⅓ cups uncooked regular rice
  1 cup shredded sharp Cheddar cheese
    (4 ozs.)
1½ teaspoons salt
 ⅛ teaspoon pepper
  1 cup (8-oz. carton) dairy sour cream
  1 large onion, chopped (1 cup)
  2 tablespoons salad oil
  2 cans (8 ozs. each) tomato sauce
  1 tablespoon brown sugar
  1 tablespoon cider vinegar
  1 tablespoon prepared mustard
 ½ teaspoon dried thyme, crushed
  1 lb. frankfurters, sliced into 1-inch pieces

Cook rice as label directs; cool.
Preheat oven to 350°.

Mix rice with cheese, 1 teaspoon of the salt, and pepper in a large bowl; fold in sour cream. Spoon into a greased 1½-quart ring mold.

Bake 20 minutes, or until set. Cool in mold on a wire rack 10 minutes; loosen around edge and center ring with a knife; invert onto a large serving platter.

While rice bakes, sauté onion in salad oil in a large skillet until soft; stir in tomato sauce, brown sugar, vinegar, mustard, remaining ½ teaspoon salt, and thyme. Heat slowly to boiling; stir in frankfurters; cover. Simmer 15 minutes, or until frankfurters are puffed and hot.

Spoon frankfurters and part of the sauce into center of rice ring; serve remaining sauce separately.

Yield: 6 servings.

SKILLET RICE STUFFING

2 cups thinly sliced celery
1 large onion, chopped (1 cup)
½ cup butter or margarine
2 cups uncooked regular rice
  Water
1 can (13¾ ozs.) chicken broth
1 can (6 ozs.) chopped mushrooms
2 teaspoons salt
1 teaspoon poultry seasoning
¼ teaspoon pepper
1 cup broken California walnuts

Sauté celery and onion in butter in a large skillet until soft. Stir in rice; sauté, stirring several times, until golden.

Add enough water to chicken broth to measure 4 cups; stir into rice mixture with mushrooms and liquid, salt, poultry seasoning, and pepper; heat to boiling; cover.

Simmer 20 minutes, or until rice is tender and liquid is absorbed; stir in walnuts.

Yield: 11 cups or enough to stuff a 14- to 16-lb. turkey.

PECAN PILAF

5 cups packaged precooked rice
1 large green pepper, halved, seeded,
and chopped (1 cup)
¼ cup butter or margarine
1½ cups coarsely chopped pecans

Prepare rice as label directs; keep hot.

Sauté green pepper in butter in a small skillet until soft; stir in pecans. Pour over rice mixture; toss lightly.

Spoon into a large serving bowl. Garnish with several thin green pepper rings if you like.

Yield: 12 servings.

JAMBALAYA

2 chicken breasts, each weighing
about 10 ozs.
Water
Few celery tops
2 teaspoons salt
4 peppercorns
1 can (16 ozs.) stewed tomatoes
1 canned ham, weighing 1 lb.
1 large onion, chopped (1 cup)
1 small green pepper, halved, seeded,
and chopped
1 clove garlic, minced
2 tablespoons salad oil
1½ teaspoons dried thyme, crushed
1 bay leaf
Dash of pepper
1½ cups uncooked regular rice
1 can (4½ ozs.) deveined shrimp,
drained and rinsed

Combine chicken, 1½ cups water, celery tops, 1 teaspoon of the salt, and peppercorns in a large skillet; heat to boiling; cover. Simmer 30 minutes, or until chicken is tender. Remove from broth and cool until easy to handle. Strain broth into a 4-cup measure.

Drain juice from tomatoes; add to chicken broth, then add water, if needed, to make 3½ cups.

Take chicken from bones; cube chicken and ham; place in a 2-quart baking dish.

Preheat oven to 350°.

Sauté onion, green pepper, and garlic in salad oil until soft in same skillet. Stir in the 3½ cups broth mixture, tomatoes, remaining 1 teaspoon salt, thyme, bay leaf, and pepper. Heat to boiling; stir in rice. Pour into baking dish; stir lightly to mix; cover.

Bake 45 minutes, arrange shrimp on top; cover again. Bake 15 minutes longer, or until rice is tender and liquid is absorbed. Fluff mixture with a fork; remove bay leaf. Garnish with parsley if you like.

Yield: 8 servings.

TURKEY RISOTTO

1 large onion, chopped (1 cup)
1 cup chopped celery
2 tablespoons salad oil
3 cups cubed cooked turkey
1 can (16 ozs.) stewed tomatoes
1½ teaspoons salt
1 teaspoon sugar
½ teaspoon dried rosemary, crushed
¼ teaspoon pepper
1 cup water
1 can (6 ozs.) mixed vegetable juice
¾ cup uncooked regular rice
2 cups (8 ozs.) shredded sharp Cheddar cheese

Preheat oven to 350°.

Sauté onion and celery in salad oil in a large saucepan until soft; push to one side.

Add turkey to pan and brown lightly. Stir in tomatoes, salt, sugar, rosemary, pepper, water, and vegetable juice; heat to boiling. Spoon half into a 2-quart baking dish.

Sprinkle rice, then half of the cheese over layer in dish; top with rest of sauce and cheese; cover.

Bake 1 hour, or until rice is tender and liquid is absorbed.

Yield: 6 servings.

APRICOT STUFFING

1 cup sliced green onions
1 cup thinly sliced celery
4 tablespoons butter or margarine
1 cup snipped dried apricots
2 envelopes instant chicken broth
1 teaspoon salt
2½ cups uncooked regular rice
5 cups water

Sauté green onions and celery in butter in a kettle until soft; stir in apricots, instant chicken broth, salt, rice, and water. Heat to boiling; cover. Cook 20 minutes, or until liquid is absorbed and rice is tender; remove from heat; cool.

Yield: About 10 cups or enough to stuff a 12- to 14-lb. turkey.

BAKED CHICKEN AND RICE

⅓ cup sliced green onions
3 tablespoons butter or margarine
1 can (13¾ ozs.) chicken broth
   Water
1 teaspoon dried rosemary, crushed
1¼ teaspoons salt
1 cup brown rice
1 broiler-fryer, weighing about 3 lbs.,
   cut into serving-sized pieces
2 tablespoons all-purpose flour
⅛ teaspoon pepper
3 tablespoons salad oil
2 tablespoons chopped parsley

Preheat oven to 350°.
Sauté green onions lightly in butter in a large skillet.
Combine chicken broth and enough water to measure 3 cups; stir into onion mixture with rosemary and ¼ teaspoon of the salt. Heat to boiling; pour over rice in a shallow 2-quart baking dish; stir well to mix; cover.
Bake 30 minutes.
While rice bakes, shake chicken pieces in a mixture of flour, the remaining 1 teaspoon salt, and pepper in a paper or transparent bag. Brown slowly in salad oil in same skillet. Ar-range pieces in a single layer over partly cooked rice; cover again.
Bake 45 minutes longer, or until chicken and rice are tender and liquid is absorbed. Sprinkle parsley over top. Serve from baking dish.

Yield: 4 to 6 servings.

FRANK-AND-RICE BAKE

1 medium onion, chopped (½ cup)
¾ cup uncooked regular rice
2 tablespoons butter or margarine
6 frankfurters, cut in short sticks
1 can (18 ozs.) tomato juice
3 tablespoons chili sauce
2 tablespoons bottled steak sauce
1 teaspoon garlic salt
¼ teaspoon sugar
⅛ teaspoon pepper

Preheat oven to 350°.
Sauté onion and rice in butter in a medium skillet until rice is golden.
Stir in frankfurters, tomato juice, chili sauce, steak sauce, garlic salt, sugar, and pepper. Heat, stirring several times, to boiling; pour into a 1½-quart baking dish; cover.
Bake 45 minutes, or until rice is tender and liquid is absorbed.

Yield: 4 servings.

CHILI-RICE RINGS

1 cup packaged precooked rice
1 can (12 ozs.) Mexican-style corn,
   drained
1 can (15 ozs.) chili without beans
½ cup shredded process American cheese

Prepare rice with salt and water as label directs; add corn and toss lightly to mix. Keep hot.
Heat chili in a medium saucepan as label directs.
Spoon rice mixture into rings on serving plates; spoon chili in center of each; sprinkle cheese over chili.

Yield: 4 servings.

HAM-RICE CUPS

1 can (3 or 4 ozs.) chopped mushrooms
  Milk
4 tablespoons butter or margarine
5 tablespoons all-purpose flour
½ teaspoon dried basil, crushed
¼ teaspoon salt
⅛ teaspoon pepper
2 cups small thin strips cooked ham
1 cup packaged precooked rice
2 tablespoons grated Parmesan cheese

Drain liquid from mushrooms into a 4-cup measure; add milk to make 3 cups.

Preheat oven to 350°.

Sauté mushrooms in butter in a medium skillet 3 minutes. Sprinkle flour, basil, salt, and pepper over top; cook, stirring constantly, until bubbly. Stir in milk mixture; continue cooking and stirring until mixture thickens and boils 1 minute.

Stir in ham and rice; spoon into four 10-ounce custard cups. For easy handling, set cups in a large shallow pan; cover.

Bake 30 minutes, or until rice is tender; uncover. Sprinkle cheese on top. Bake 10 minutes longer.

Yield: 4 servings.

TURKEY PARISIENNE

1 package (6 ozs.) long grain and wild rice
9 tablespoons butter or margarine
1 bunch broccoli, weighing about
    1¼ lbs.
1½ lbs. turkey cutlets
2 cups fresh bread crumbs (4 slices)
¼ lb. mushrooms, trimmed and sliced
5 tablespoons all-purpose flour
½ teaspoon salt
¼ teaspoon pepper
2 cups milk
½ cup dry white wine

Prepare rice with water and 1 tablespoon of the butter as label directs; spread in a baking dish, 13x9x2 inches.

While rice cooks, trim broccoli; cut into 3-inch lengths. Cook, covered, in boiling salted water in a large skillet 5 minutes, or just until crisp-tender; drain well.

Wipe turkey cutlets with paper toweling to remove any excess moisture. Brown slowly on both sides in 2 tablespoons of the butter in same skillet; arrange in a single layer over rice; layer broccoli over turkey.

Preheat oven to 350°.

Melt remaining 6 tablespoons butter in same skillet; measure out 2 tablespoonfuls and toss with bread crumbs in a small bowl.

Stir mushrooms into rest of melted butter; sauté 2 minutes; push to one side.

Stir in flour, salt, and pepper; cook, stirring constantly, until bubbly. Stir in milk and wine; continue cooking and stirring until sauce thickens and boils 1 minute. Spoon over broccoli to cover completely; sprinkle buttered bread crumbs on top.

Bake 45 minutes, or until bubbly and topping is golden.

Yield: 6 servings.

CASSEROLE RISOTTO

1 package (7½ ozs.) saffron-flavored
    rice and vermicelli mix
2 tablespoons butter or margarine, melted
2¾ cups boiling water

Preheat oven to 350°.

Combine rice mixture and melted butter in a 1½-quart baking dish; stir in boiling water and seasoning mix from rice package; cover.

Bake 45 minutes, or until rice is tender and liquid is absorbed. Fluff rice with a fork. Serve from baking dish.

Yield: 6 servings.

ITALIAN SAUSAGE SUPPER

¾ cup uncooked regular rice
1 package (10 ozs.) frozen peas
1 lb. sweet Italian sausages
1 jar (21 ozs.) Italian cooking sauce
½ cup grated Romano cheese

Cook rice as label directs. Cook peas as label directs; drain; combine with rice.

Peel casings from sausages; place sausages in a large skillet. Sauté slowly until brown, breaking up meat with a spoon as it cooks; drain off all fat.

Stir sauce into skillet; heat, stirring several times, to boiling.

Preheat oven to 350°.

Spoon half of the rice mixture into a 2-quart shallow baking dish; top with half of the sauce; repeat layers; cover.

Bake 30 minutes; uncover. Sprinkle cheese diagonally in ribbons over top.

Bake 10 minutes longer, or until cheese browns lightly.

Yield: 6 servings.

HAM FRIED RICE

¼ cup chopped green onions
2 tablespoons salad oil
4 eggs
⅛ teaspoon salt
2½ cups cooked rice
1 cup diced cooked ham
½ cup cooked peas

Sauté onions in salad oil in a medium skillet just until wilted.

Beat eggs well with salt in a medium bowl; pour over onion mixture in pan; cook slowly 1 minute.

Stir in rice, ham, and peas; continue cooking, tossing mixture lightly several times, until heated through.

Spoon onto serving plates; serve as is or drizzle soy sauce lightly over top if you like.

Yield: 4 servings.

HAWAIIAN HAM AND CHICKEN

1 cup uncooked regular rice
1 large green pepper, quartered, seeded, and chopped (1 cup)
1 medium onion, chopped (½ cup)
2 tablespoons butter or margarine
2 cans (10¾ ozs. each) condensed cream of chicken soup
1 cup diced cooked ham
1 cup diced cooked chicken
1 can (8 ozs.) pineapple chunks in juice

Cook rice as label directs; keep warm.

While rice cooks, sauté green pepper and onion in butter in a large skillet until soft.

Stir in soup until well blended; stir in ham, chicken, and pineapple and juice. Heat slowly, stirring several times, to boiling.

Spoon rice onto a deep platter or onto individual serving plates; spoon ham mixture over rice. Sprinkle toasted slivered almonds over top if you like.

Yield: 4 servings.

PORK-AND-RICE SKILLET

4 slices bacon, cut in 1-inch pieces
1 medium onion, chopped (½ cup)
¼ cup chopped green pepper
2 cans (10¾ ozs. each) condensed tomato soup
1 cup water
¾ cup uncooked regular rice
1 cup diced cooked pork
½ teaspoon dried thyme, crushed

Sauté bacon until crisp in a large skillet; remove and drain on paper toweling. Pour off all drippings into a cup or bowl, then measure 2 tablespoonfuls and return to skillet.

Stir onion and green pepper into skillet; sauté until soft. Stir in soup, water, rice, pork, and thyme; heat slowly to boiling; cover tightly.

Simmer, stirring several times, 45 minutes, or until rice is tender and liquid is absorbed. Sprinkle bacon on top.

Yield: 4 servings.

RICE-TURKEY BAKE

1 frozen boneless turkey roast,
    weighing 2 lbs.
2 can (10¾ ozs. each) condensed cream of
    chicken soup
1 medium onion, finely chopped (½ cup)
2 tablespoons chopped parsley
½ teaspoon dried mixed Italian herbs,
    crushed
2 cups water
1 package (8 ozs.) chicken-flavored rice and
    vermicelli mix

Roast turkey as label directs; remove from foil pan; cool. Dice meat. (There should be 2 cups.)

Preheat oven to 350°.

Combine soup, onion, parsley, Italian herbs, water, and seasoning mix from vermicelli package in a medium saucepan; heat to boiling. Pour half into a greased 2½-quart baking dish.

Layer half each of the vermicelli mix and turkey on top; repeat layers. Pour rest of soup mixture over all; cover.

Bake 30 minutes; stir well. Continue baking 30 minutes longer, or until rice is tender and liquid is absorbed.

Just before serving, garnish with a wreath of parsley if you like.

Yield: 6 servings.

TRAILWAY HASH

½ lb. bacon, cut in 1-inch pieces
4 lbs. ground beef
3 large green peppers, quartered, seeded,
    and chopped (3 cups)
3 large onions, chopped (3 cups)
1 tablespoon sugar
3 teaspoons salt
2 teaspoons Italian seasoning
½ teaspoon pepper
1 can (46 ozs.) mixed vegetable juice
1½ cups water
6 cups packaged precooked rice

Sauté bacon until crisp in a large kettle; remove with a slotted spoon and drain well on paper toweling.

Shape ground beef into a large patty; place in drippings in kettle. Sauté until brown on bottom; turn; brown other side, then break up into chunks; push to one side. Stir in green peppers and onions; sauté until soft.

Stir in sugar, salt, Italian seasoning, pepper, vegetable juice, and water; heat to boiling.

Stir in rice and bacon; cover; remove from heat. Let stand 10 minutes. Fluff with a fork; serve from kettle.

Yield: 16 servings.

SIMPLE SALMON BAKE

1 cup packaged precooked rice
6 tablespoons butter or margarine
4 tablespoons all-purpose flour
1 teaspoon salt
¼ teaspoon pepper
2 cups milk
1 container (4 ozs.) whipped chive cream
    cheese
1 can (8 ozs.) salmon, drained, boned, and
    flaked
2 hard-cooked eggs, diced
1 cup coarsely crumbled cheese crackers

Prepare rice as label directs; spoon into a deep 1½-quart baking dish.

Preheat oven to 350°.

Melt 4 tablespoons of the butter in a medium saucepan; stir in flour, salt, and pepper; cook, stirring, constantly, until bubbly. Stir in milk; continue cooking and stirring until sauce thickens and boils 1 minute; stir in cheese until melted. Stir into rice in baking dish, then lightly stir in salmon and eggs.

Melt remaining 2 tablespoons butter in a small saucepan; toss with crackers; sprinkle over salmon mixture.

Bake 45 minutes, or until bubbly.

Yield: 4 servings.

CHICKEN-SHRIMP FRIED RICE

1 cup uncooked regular rice
4 tablespoons salad oil
1 cup cubed cooked chicken
1 cup cooked small whole shrimp
1 cup cooked peas
¼ cup sliced green onions
¼ cup soy sauce
½ teaspoon salt
¼ teaspoon pepper
2 eggs, beaten
1 cup shredded iceberg lettuce

Cook rice as label directs; keep hot.

Heat salad oil in a large skillet; add chicken, shrimp, peas, and onions; sauté quickly 2 minutes. Lightly stir in rice, soy sauce, salt, and pepper; heat 1 minute.

Slowly pour in eggs, stirring constantly; continue cooking just until eggs are set; remove from heat. Stir in lettuce lightly with a fork.

Spoon into a serving bowl, pulling several of the shrimp to top for a garnish. Serve with additional soy sauce to drizzle on top if you like.

Yield: 6 servings.

PASTA

ALMOND-BUTTER NOODLES

1 package (8 ozs.) medium noodles
2 tablespoons slivered blanched almonds
3 tablespoons butter or margarine

Cook noodles in a kettle as label directs; drain; return to kettle.

Sauté almonds in butter until lightly toasted and butter turns golden in a small skillet; pour over noodles; toss lightly to mix. Spoon into a serving bowl.

Yield: 6 servings.

CREAMY HERBED NOODLES

1 package (8 ozs.) medium noodles
1 package (8 ozs.) cream cheese
¼ cup milk
2 tablespoons parsley flakes
¼ teaspoon dried marjoram, crushed
¼ teaspoon ground thyme
¼ teaspoon dried basil, crushed
¼ teaspoon garlic powder
¼ teaspoon salt

Cook noodles in a kettle as label directs; drain; return to kettle.

While noodles cook, blend cream cheese with milk and seasonings until smooth in a small bowl. Spoon over hot noodles; toss lightly until evenly coated.

Spoon into a serving bowl.

Yield: 4 to 6 servings.

SPINACH NOODLES WITH MEAT SAUCE

½ lb. ground beef
½ lb. sausage meat
1 medium onion, chopped (½ cup)
½ cup chopped celery
1 can (29 ozs.) tomatoes
1 can (15 ozs.) herb tomato sauce
2 teaspoons garlic salt
1 teaspoon dried basil, crushed
2 packages (8 ozs. each) spinach noodles
Grated Parmesan cheese

Brown ground beef and sausage in their own fat in a kettle; push to one side.

Stir in onion and celery; sauté until soft. Stir in tomatoes, tomato sauce, garlic salt, and basil; heat, stirring constantly, to boiling; cover. Simmer 1 hour.

Uncover; stir again; simmer ½ hour longer, or until sauce is as thick as you like it.

While sauce simmers, cook noodles as label directs; drain. Spoon onto a large serving platter or onto individual plates; spoon sauce on top. Pass cheese separately to sprinkle over all.

Yield: 8 servings.

SICILIAN TURKEY BAKE

  1 package (8 ozs.) medium noodles
  3 cups cubed cooked turkey
½ cup sliced pimiento-stuffed green olives
  1 cup diced celery
  1 medium onion, diced (½ cup)
  6 tablespoons butter or margarine
⅓ cup all-purpose flour
½ teaspoon salt
  1 envelope instant chicken broth
2½ cups milk
  1 package (6 ozs.) sliced Muenster cheese,
     cut up
⅓ cup regular wheat germ
¼ cup grated Romano cheese

Cook noodles in a kettle as label directs; drain; return to kettle. Add turkey and olives.

Sauté celery and onion in 4 tablespoons of the butter in a medium saucepan until soft. Stir in flour, salt, and chicken broth; cook, stirring constantly, until bubbly. Stir in milk; continue cooking and stirring until sauce thickens and boils 1 minute; stir into turkey mixture.

Preheat oven to 350°.

Layer one third of the turkey mixture into a 2½-quart baking dish; top with half of the Muenster cheese. Repeat layers; top with rest of turkey mixture.

Melt rest of butter in a small saucepan; stir in wheat germ; sprinkle wheat-germ mixture, then Romano cheese, over layers in dish.

Bake 45 minutes, or until bubbly.

Yield: 8 servings.

SHRIMP LASAGNA

  1 package (8 ozs.) lasagna noodles
  1 tablespoon salad oil
  1 package (16 ozs.) frozen uncooked shrimp
  2 cans (10¾ ozs. each) condensed cream
     of shrimp soup
  1 package (8 ozs.) cream cheese, softened
  1 egg
  1 carton (16 ozs.) cream-style cottage cheese
  1 large onion, chopped (1 cup)
  1 teaspoon dillweed
  1 teaspoon salt
¼ teaspoon pepper
  3 medium fresh tomatoes, sliced
  1 cup shredded Edam cheese (4 ozs.)

Cook noodles with salad oil in a kettle of boiling water as label directs; drain; return to kettle. Cover with cold water to keep noodles from sticking together.

Cook shrimp as label directs; drain. Combine with soup in a medium bowl.

Beat cream cheese and egg until fluffy in a medium bowl; stir in cottage cheese, onion, dillweed, salt, and pepper.

Preheat oven to 350°.

Lift noodles, one at a time, from water and drain well; place 4 in the bottom of a greased baking dish, 13x9x2 inches to cover.

Spread half of the cheese mixture over noodles, cover with another layer of noodles, all of the shrimp sauce, rest of noodles, and rest of cheese mixture. Arrange tomato slices in rows on top; sprinkle each very lightly with salt if you like. Sprinkle shredded cheese evenly over tomatoes.

Bake 1 hour, or until bubbly and cheese melts and browns lightly. Let stand 15 minutes; cut into blocks.

Yield: 8 servings.

SOUTHWESTERN CHILI PIE

3½ cups uncooked medium noodles
  2 tablespoons butter or margarine
  1 egg, beaten
  1 can (15 ozs.) chili without beans
  1 can (8 ozs.) cut green beans, drained
¾ cup shredded sharp Cheddar cheese

Preheat oven to 350°.

Cook noodles in a kettle as label directs; drain well; return to kettle. Stir in butter until melted, then stir in beaten egg. Spoon into a lightly greased 9-inch pie plate, hollowing center and building up edge to form a shell.

Spoon chili into center; spoon green beans over chili; sprinkle cheese over beans.

Bake 25 minutes, or until crust is set and cheese browns lightly. Cut into wedges; lift onto serving plates with a wide spatula.

Yield: 4 servings.

CORNED BEEF BAKE

1 package (8 ozs.) curly noodles
1 can (12 ozs.) corned beef
1 package (8 ozs.) process American cheese
1 can (10¾ ozs.) condensed cream of
    celery soup
¾ cup milk
1 medium onion, chopped (½ cup)
2 tablespoons butter or margarine
1 cup fresh bread crumbs (2 slices)

Cook noodles in a kettle as label directs; drain; return to kettle.

Dice corned beef and cheese; add to noodles. (Corned beef will cut neatly if chilled first.)

Preheat oven to 350°.

Blend soup and milk in a medium bowl; stir in onion; stir into noodle mixture. Spoon into a 2-quart baking dish.

Melt butter in a small skillet; add bread crumbs and toss to mix well. Sprinkle over noodle mixture.

Bake 45 minutes, or until bubbly and topping is toasted.

Yield: 6 servings.

OLD WORLD LASAGNA

2 Italian hot sausages
1 lb. meat-loaf mixture (ground beef,
    pork, and veal)
1 large onion, chopped (1 cup)
1 clove garlic, minced
1 envelope (1⅝ ozs.) lasagna sauce mix
1 can (35 ozs.) Italian tomatoes
16 lasagna noodles
2 eggs
2 cups (16-oz. container) cream-style
    cottage cheese
2 packages (8 ozs. each) sliced mozzarella
    cheese
⅔ cup grated Romano cheese

Peel casing from sausages; crumble meat.

Shape meat-loaf mixture into a large patty; place in a large skillet. Brown on bottom in its own fat; turn; add sausage meat to skillet. Continue cooking until all meat is brown; break up into small chunks and push to one side.

Stir onion and garlic into drippings in skillet; sauté until soft. Stir in lasagna sauce mix and tomatoes; heat, stirring several times, to boiling, then simmer 30 minutes, or until thickened slightly.

While sauce simmers, cook noodles in kettle as label directs; drain; return to kettle and cover with cold water to keep noodles from sticking together.

Beat eggs in a medium bowl; stir in cottage cheese. Cut mozzarella cheese crosswise into strips.

Preheat oven to 350°.

Lift noodles, one at a time, from water and drain well; place enough in a single layer over bottom and around sides of a greased 13x9x2-inch baking dish to line completely.

Top with one-third each of the cottage cheese mixture, meat sauce, and mozzarella and Romano cheeses. Repeat to make two more layers of each, arranging mozzarella strips on top to form a criss-cross pattern.

Bake 30 minutes, or until bubbly and top is lightly browned. Let stand on a wire rack 10 minutes. Cut into squares.

Yield: 10 to 12 servings.

FETTUCINE ALFREDO

1 package (12 ozs.) medium noodles
½ cup butter or margarine
1 cup whipping cream
¾ cup freshly grated Parmesan cheese
½ teaspoon salt

Cook noodles in a kettle as label directs; drain; return to kettle.

Melt butter in a small saucepan; stir in cream, ½ cup of the cheese, and salt. Drizzle over noodles; toss until evenly coated.

Spoon into a serving bowl; sprinkle remaining cheese over top.

Yield: 6 servings.

CHECKERBOARD SALMON

1 package (8 ozs.) medium noodles
3 tablespoons butter or margarine
3 tablespoons all-purpose flour
1 teaspoon salt
⅛ teaspoon pepper
3 cups milk
1 package (8 ozs.) process Old English
   cheese
2 cans (8 ozs. each) salmon, drained, boned,
   and broken into chunks
½ cup sliced pimiento-stuffed green olives

Cook noodles in a kettle as label directs; drain; return to kettle.

Melt butter in a medium saucepan; stir in flour, salt, and pepper. Cook, stirring constantly, until bubbly. Stir in milk; continue cooking and stirring until sauce thickens and boils 1 minute.

Cut 4 slices of the cheese into small pieces and stir into sauce until melted; stir into noodles; fold in salmon and olives. Spoon into a 2-quart shallow baking dish.

Preheat oven to 350°.

Cut rest of cheese into 16 strips; arrange, checkerboard style, on top of noodle mixture.

Bake 35 minutes, or until bubbly and cheese melts. Garnish with more olive slices if you like.

Yield: 8 servings.

CHIPPED BEEF AND NOODLES

4 tablespoons butter or margarine
4 tablespoons all-purpose flour
1 envelope instant chicken broth
⅛ teaspoon pepper
2 cups milk
¼ cup mayonnaise or salad dressing
1 jar (5 ozs.) dried beef, shredded
3 cups medium noodles

Melt butter in a medium saucepan; stir in flour, chicken broth, and pepper; heat, stirring constantly, until bubbly. Stir in milk; continue cooking and stirring until sauce thickens and boils 1 minute; remove from heat. Stir in mayonnaise and dried beef; keep hot.

Cook noodles as label directs; drain; spoon onto serving plates. Spoon creamed beef over noodles.

Yield: 4 servings.

VIENNESE NOODLE SCRAMBLE

2 cups medium noodles
2 cans (5 ozs. each) Vienna sausages
1 can (8 ozs.) peas
1 tablespoon salad oil
1 can (10¾ ozs.) condensed tomato soup
¼ teaspoon dried oregano, crushed
⅛ teaspoon pepper

Cook noodles in boiling salted water as label directs; drain.

Drain liquids from sausages and peas into a small bowl; slice sausages.

Brown sausages lightly in salad oil in a large skillet; stir in noodles, peas, soup, liquids from meat and vegetables, oregano, and pepper.

Heat slowly to boiling; cover. Simmer 10 minutes to blend flavors. Spoon onto serving plates.

Yield: 4 servings.

PIE-PLATE PIZZA

2 cups fine noodles
1 can (15 ozs.) barbecue sauce with
   ground beef
½ teaspoon Italian seasoning
4 long slices mozzarella cheese
2 tablespoons grated Romano cheese

Preheat oven to 350°.

Cook noodles in a kettle as label directs; drain; return to kettle.

Stir in barbecue sauce and Italian seasoning. Spoon into a 9-inch pie plate.

Cut mozzarella cheese into strips; arrange over noodle mixture; sprinkle Romano cheese on top.

Bake 30 minutes, or until cheese melts.

Yield: 4 servings.

NEAPOLITAN CHICKEN BAKE

2 broiler-fryers, each weighing about
    2½ lbs., cut up
1 medium onion, peeled and sliced
    Few celery tops
3 teaspoons salt
4 peppercorns
    Water
1 package (8 ozs.) fine noodles
1 can (7 ozs.) whole pimientos, drained
1 can (6 ozs.) sliced mushrooms
10 tablespoons butter or margarine
 2 cups soft bread crumbs (4 slices)
 3 medium onions, chopped (1½ cups)
½ cup all-purpose flour
½ teaspoon pepper
 2 cups light cream
½ cup grated Romano cheese
    Watercress

Combine chickens, sliced onion, celery tops, 1 teaspoon of the salt, and peppercorns in a large skillet; pour in water to cover. Heat to boiling; cover. Simmer 1 hour, or until chicken is tender. Remove from broth and cool until easy to handle, then take meat from bones and cut into cubes. Strain broth into a 4-cup measure.

Cook noodles in a kettle as label directs; drain; return to kettle.

Cut 6 small flower shapes from one or two of the pimientos with a cookie cutter or knife; set aside for garnish. Chop remaining pimientos. Drain liquid from mushrooms into a 2-cup measure; add chicken broth to make 2 cups.

Preheat oven to 350°.

Melt butter in a large saucepan; measure out 2 tablespoons and toss with bread crumbs in a small bowl. Sauté chopped onions in rest of melted butter until soft. Blend in flour, 2 teaspoons salt, and pepper; cook, stirring constantly, until bubbly. Stir in the 2 cups broth mixture and cream; continue cooking and stirring until sauce thickens and boils 1 minute. Stir in cheese until melted, then chicken, chopped pimientos, and mushrooms; stir into noodles. Spoon into a 13x9x2-inch baking dish. Sprinkle bread crumbs evenly over top.

Bake 30 minutes, or until bubbly in center and topping is toasted. Garnish with pimiento cutouts and watercress.

Yield: 8 servings.

SALMON CUPS

 2 cups wide noodles
¼ cup thinly sliced celery
 2 tablespoons chopped onion
 1 tablespoon salad oil
 1 can (10¾ ozs.) condensed cream of
    mushroom soup
 1 can (7 ozs.) salmon, drained and
    broken into chunks
½ teaspoon dillweed
¼ cup regular wheat germ
 2 tablespoons butter or margarine, melted

Preheat oven to 350°.

Cook noodles in a kettle as label directs; drain; return to kettle.

Sauté celery and onion in salad oil in a medium saucepan until soft; stir in soup; heat to boiling. Stir in salmon and dillweed; fold into noodles. Spoon into 4 greased 10-ounce baking dishes.

Toss wheat germ with melted butter in a small bowl; sprinkle on top.

Bake 20 minutes, or until bubbly and topping is toasted.

Yield: 4 servings.

CHICKEN-NOODLE SCALLOP

2½ cups medium noodles
1 can (5 ozs.) boned chicken, cut in
 bite-sized pieces
1 can (8 ozs.) peas and carrots, drained
1 can (10¾ ozs.) condensed cream of
 celery soup
 Dash of Italian seasoning
1 tablespoon packaged seasoned bread
 crumbs

Preheat oven to 350°.

Cook noodles as label directs; drain; place in a 1-quart baking dish. Add chicken, peas and carrots, soup, and Italian seasoning; toss lightly to mix; sprinkle bread crumbs over top.

Bake 30 minutes, or until bubbly in center.

Yield: 4 servings.

SPAGHETTI AND MEATBALLS

1½ lbs. meat-loaf mixture (ground beef,
 veal, and pork)
3 large onions, chopped (3 cups)
3 cloves garlic, chopped
½ cup chopped parsley
½ cup fine dry bread crumbs
 Grated Parmesan cheese
1 egg
3½ teaspoons salt
¼ teaspoon pepper
 Dash of ground nutmeg
 Salad oil
1 can (35 ozs.) Italian tomatoes
1 can (8 ozs.) tomato sauce
1½ teaspoons Italian seasoning
1 teaspoon sugar
¼ teaspoon crushed red pepper
1 cup water
1 can (6 ozs.) chopped mushrooms
2 packages (16 ozs. each) spaghetti

Combine meat-loaf mixture, 1 cup of the chopped onion, 1 clove of the garlic, ¼ cup of the parsley, bread crumbs, ½ cup Parmesan cheese, egg, 1½ teaspoons of the salt, pepper, and nutmeg in a large bowl; mix lightly until well blended. Shape into ¾-inch balls.

Brown slowly, part at a time, in 2 table-spoons of salad oil in a Dutch oven; remove all meat from pan. Pour off drippings, then measure and add enough salad oil to make ¼ cup; return to Dutch oven.

Stir remaining 2 cups chopped onion and 2 cloves garlic into drippings; sauté until soft. Stir in tomatoes, tomato sauce, remaining ¼ cup parsley, Italian seasoning, sugar, red pepper, remaining 2 teaspoons salt, and water. Heat slowly, stirring constantly, to boiling; cover. Simmer 2 hours.

Add meatballs and mushrooms and liquid to sauce; simmer, uncovered, 1½ hours longer, or until slightly thickened.

Cook spaghetti as label directs; drain well. Spoon onto serving plates; ladle sauce and meatballs on top. Serve with additional grated Parmesan cheese to sprinkle over each serving.

Yield: 8 servings.

WAGON WHEEL BAKE

1 medium onion, chopped (½ cup)
2 tablespoons salad oil
2 cups diced cooked beef
2 teaspoons garlic salt
¾ teaspoon dried basil, crushed
¼ teaspoon pepper
1 can (15 ozs.) tomato sauce
1½ cups water
3 cups uncooked wheel-shaped macaroni
2 tablespoons grated Parmesan cheese

Preheat oven to 350°.

Sauté onion in salad oil in a large skillet until soft; push to one side.

Stir in beef; brown lightly. Stir in garlic salt, basil, pepper, tomato sauce, and water. Heat to boiling; pour into a 1¾-quart baking dish. Stir in macaroni; cover tightly.

Bake 1 hour, or until macaroni is tender; sprinkle cheese over top. Bake, uncovered, 10 minutes longer, or until cheese melts.

Yield: 4 servings.

OVEN SPAGHETTI

1½ packages (16 ozs. each) spaghetti,
    broken in 2-inch lengths
  1 large onion, chopped (1 cup)
  1 cup chopped celery
  1 clove garlic, chopped
  3 tablespoons salad oil
  4 jars (16 ozs. each) spaghetti sauce
  2 cans (12 ozs. each) Mexican-style corn
  2 cups grated Parmesan cheese

Cook spaghetti in a kettle as label directs; drain well; return to kettle.

Preheat oven to 375°.

Sauté onion, celery, and garlic in salad oil in a large skillet until soft; stir in spaghetti sauce and corn and liquid; heat to boiling. Stir in 1 cup of the Parmesan cheese; pour over spaghetti in kettle; toss lightly to mix. Spoon into two 2-quart baking dishes. Sprinkle half of the remaining cheese over each.

Bake 45 minutes, or until bubbly and cheese starts to brown. If you like, garnish each dish with small slices of salami rolled into cornucopia shapes and stuffed with parsley.

Yield: 16 servings.

SLOPPY JOE BAKE

  1 lb. ground beef
  1 small green pepper, quartered, seeded,
    and chopped (½ cup)
  1 medium onion, chopped (½ cup)
  1 can (16 ozs.) tomatoes
  1 can (8 ozs.) tomato sauce
  1 teaspoon dried thyme, crushed
½ teaspoon salt
¼ teaspoon pepper
  1 package (8 ozs.) mostaccioli (macaroni),
    cooked and drained
  1 package (8 ozs.) sliced process
    American cheese, shredded
¼ cup grated Romano cheese

Preheat oven to 350°.

Shape ground beef into a large patty; place in a large skillet. Brown, turning once, in its own fat; break up into chunks; push to one side.

Stir green pepper and onion into drippings in skillet; sauté until soft. Stir in tomatoes, tomato sauce, thyme, salt, and pepper; heat to boiling.

Layer half each of the mostaccioli, meat sauce, and American cheese into a 2-quart baking dish; repeat layers. Sprinkle Romano cheese on top.

Bake 30 minutes, or until bubbly and cheese melts and browns lightly.

Yield: 6 servings.

SOUP-PLATE SPAGHETTI SCRAMBLE

  1 small onion, chopped (¼ cup)
  1 tablespoon salad oil
  1 teaspoon chili powder
  1 can (15 ozs.) spaghetti with beef in
    tomato sauce
  1 can (12 ozs.) Mexican-style corn
  1 can (8 ozs.) red kidney beans
¼ teaspoon salt
  2 tablespoons chopped parsley

Sauté onion in salad oil in a medium skillet until soft; stir in chili powder.

Stir in spaghetti, corn and liquid, beans and liquid, and salt. Heat, stirring several times, to boiling; cover.

Simmer 10 minutes; uncover. Simmer 5 minutes longer, or until slightly thickened.

Spoon into soup plates; sprinkle parsley over each serving.

Yield: 4 servings.

OVEN SPAGHETTI STROGANOFF

4 tablespoons butter or margarine
1 cup fresh bread crumbs (2 slices)
1 small onion, chopped (¼ cup)
2 cans (15 ozs. each) spaghetti rings and
    little meatballs in tomato sauce
½ cup dairy sour cream
½ teaspoon dried thyme, crushed
¼ teaspoon salt
1 can (8 ozs.) cut green beans, drained

Preheat oven to 350°.

Melt butter in a large saucepan; measure out 2 tablespoons and toss with bread crumbs in a small bowl.

Stir onion into rest of melted butter; sauté until soft. Stir in spaghetti, sour cream, thyme, and salt. Spoon half into a 1½-quart baking dish; top with green beans, then rest of spaghetti mixture; sprinkle bread crumbs over all.

Bake 30 minutes, or until bubbly.
Yield: 4 generous servings.

MEXICAN SPAGHETTI

1 lb. ground beef
1 teaspoon salt
¼ teaspoon pepper
2 tablespoons salad oil
1 large onion, chopped (1 cup)
1 tablespoon chili powder
1 can (16 ozs.) stewed tomatoes
1 can (6 ozs.) tomato paste
1 can (16 ozs.) red kidney beans
1 package (8 ozs.) spaghetti

Season ground beef with salt and pepper in a medium bowl; shape into 40 tiny meatballs, using 1 teaspoon for each. Brown in salad oil in a large saucepan or Dutch oven; remove from pan.

Stir onion into drippings and sauté until soft. Stir in chili powder; cook 1 minute. Stir in tomatoes, tomato paste, kidney beans and liquid, and meatballs. Heat to boiling; cover. Simmer 10 minutes, or until the sauce is thick.

While sauce simmers, cook spaghetti as label directs; drain well. Spoon onto a large deep serving platter; spoon meatballs and sauce over top.
Yield: 4 servings.

SPAGHETTI MILANO

1 package (8 ozs.) spaghetti
½ cup light cream
1 package (8 ozs.) Neufchatel cheese
¼ cup grated Parmesan cheese
3 tablespoons salad oil
½ cup chopped parsley
¼ teaspoon garlic powder
¼ teaspoon salt

Cook spaghetti in a kettle as label directs; drain; return to kettle.

Stir cream, a little at a time, into Neufchatel cheese in a medium bowl; stir in Parmesan cheese, salad oil, parsley, garlic powder, and salt until sauce is smooth.

Spoon over hot spaghetti; toss lightly to mix.
Yield: 6 servings.

CHEESEBURGER SCRAMBLE

½ cup chopped green pepper
2 tablespoons butter or margarine
1 package (8 ozs.) cheeseburger-
    macaroni dinner
1 can (4½ ozs.) corned-beef spread
1 teaspoon Worcestershire sauce
1 small fresh tomato, cut in thin wedges

Sauté green pepper in butter in a medium skillet until soft. Stir in hot water and cheeseburger-macaroni dinner as label directs. Heat, stirring constantly, to boiling; cover. Simmer 15 minutes.

Stir in corned-beef spread and Worcestershire sauce. Place tomato wedges in a circle on top; cover again.

Heat slowly 5 minutes, or until tomatoes are heated through. Serve from skillet.
Yield: 4 to 6 servings.

OVEN SPAGHETTI AND CHEESE

1 package (8 ozs.) spaghetti
4 tablespoons butter or margarine
4 tablespoons all-purpose flour
¼ teaspoon pepper
2½ cups milk
1 package (8 ozs.) process Old English
    cheese, shredded
1 one-pound canned ham, cubed (2 cups)
2 medium fresh tomatoes, sliced
    Salt
½ cup fine dry bread crumbs

Break spaghetti into 2-inch lengths. Cook in boiling salted water in a kettle as label directs; drain well; return to kettle.

Preheat oven to 350°.

Melt butter in a medium saucepan; stir in flour and pepper. Cook, stirring constantly, until bubbly. Stir in milk; continue cooking and stirring until sauce thickens and boils 1 minute. Stir in three fourths of the cheese until melted. Pour over spaghetti; add ham; toss lightly to mix. Spoon into a 2½-quart shallow baking dish.

Arrange tomato slices in a pretty pattern on top; sprinkle salt lightly over tomatoes.

Mix rest of cheese and bread crumbs in a small bowl; sprinkle over tomatoes.

Bake 30 minutes, or until topping is golden and sauce bubbles up.

Yield: 6 servings.

CAMPFIRE SPAGHETTI

3 medium onions, chopped (1½ cups)
3 tablespoons salad oil
4 teaspoons chili powder
3 cans (15 ozs. each) herb tomato sauce
6 cans (15 ozs. each) meatballs in
    brown gravy
3 packages (16 ozs. each) spaghetti
    Grated Parmesan cheese

Sauté onions in salad oil in a large kettle until soft. Stir in chili powder; cook 1 minute.

Stir in tomato sauce and meatballs; heat very slowly, stirring several times, to boiling; cover. Simmer 30 minutes.

While sauce simmers, cook spaghetti in a separate kettle as label directs; drain. Spoon onto serving plates; spoon sauce and meatballs on top; sprinkle cheese over all.

Yield: 16 servings.

ITALIAN STEAK 'N' TWISTS

1 piece beef round steak, weighing
    about 2 lbs. and cut 1 inch thick
2 tablespoons salad oil
1 medium onion, chopped (½ cup)
1 teaspoon garlic powder
½ teaspoon salt
1 envelope (1½ ozs.) spaghetti sauce
    mix
1 can (16 ozs.) tomatoes
¾ cup water
2 long slices Muenster cheese,
    cut in strips
6 cups uncooked spaghetti twists

Brown steak on both sides in salad oil in a large skillet; place in a baking dish, 11¾x7½x1¾ inches.

Preheat oven to 350°.

Stir onion into drippings in skillet; sauté until soft. Stir in garlic powder, salt, spaghetti sauce mix, tomatoes, and water. Heat, stirring several times, to boiling; pour over steak; cover.

Bake 1¾ hours, or until steak is tender; uncover.

Place cheese strips over meat. Bake 10 minutes longer, or until cheese melts and browns lightly.

While meat bakes, cook spaghetti in a kettle as label directs; drain; return to kettle.

Lift steak onto a large serving platter. Pour sauce from baking dish over spaghetti; toss to mix; spoon around edge on platter. Slice meat crosswise into serving-sized pieces.

Yield: 8 servings.

COUNTRY SPAGHETTI

¾ lb. pork sausage meat
1 small onion, chopped (¼ cup)
½ cup chopped celery
1 package (8 ozs.) American-style
    spaghetti dinner
1 can (6 ozs.) tomato paste
1½ cups water
½ cup shredded process American cheese

Brown sausage slowly in a medium saucepan; push to one side. Stir onion and celery into pan; sauté until soft. Spoon off any fat.

Stir in sauce mix from spaghetti dinner package, then tomato paste and water. Heat, stirring several times, to boiling; simmer 10 minutes.

While sauce simmers, cook spaghetti from package as label directs; drain well. Spoon onto serving plates; spoon sauce over spaghetti, then sprinkle cheese on top.

Yield: 4 servings.

PIGGY-BANK SPAGHETTI

1 small onion, chopped (¼ cup)
1 tablespoon salad oil
2 cans (5 ozs. each) Vienna sausages
2 cans (15 ozs. each) spaghetti with
    tomato sauce
2 tablespoons chopped parsley
1 teaspoon dried oregano, crushed
¼ teaspoon salt
½ cup shredded sharp Chedder cheese

Sauté onion in salad oil in a large skillet until soft.

Drain liquid from sausages into a cup; cut each sausage in half crosswise. Stir sausages and liquid, spaghetti, parsley, oregano, and salt into onion mixture. Heat, stirring several times, to boiling, then simmer, uncovered, 10 minutes.

Sprinkle cheese over top; cover. Heat 1 minute longer to melt cheese.

Yield: 4 servings.

SKILLET BEEF AND MACARONI

1 package (7¼ ozs.) macaroni-and-
    cheese dinner
¾ lb. ground beef
1 tablespoon salad oil
1 small onion, chopped (¼ cup)
¼ teaspoon dried thyme, crushed
⅛ teaspoon pepper
1 small can (⅔ cup) evaporated milk
¼ cup butter or margarine

Cook macaroni from dinner package as label directs; drain.

Shape ground beef into a patty; brown in salad oil, turning once, in a large skillet; break up into chunks and push to one side.

Stir onion into drippings and sauté until soft. Stir in thyme, pepper, evaporated milk, butter, macaroni, and cheese from package. Heat very slowly, stirring several times, until hot and blended. Spoon onto serving plates.

Yield: 4 servings.

MACARONI CARBONARA

1 package (8 ozs.) elbow macaroni
2 cups cubed cooked ham
2 tablespoons salad oil
2 tablespoons bacon-flavored
    vegetable-protein bits
2 eggs
⅓ cup light cream
⅓ cup grated Romano cheese
2 tablespoons chopped parsley

Cook macaroni as label directs; drain.

Sauté ham in salad oil in a large skillet until lightly browned; stir in macaroni and protein bits.

Beat eggs with cream in a small bowl; slowly pour over macaroni mixture, tossing constantly to coat well. Sprinkle cheese over top; toss to mix.

Spoon into a serving bowl; sprinkle parsley over top.

Yield: 6 servings.

CLAMBAKE

1 package (8 ozs.) small shell macaroni
1 package (16 ozs.) frozen sole or
    flounder, thawed
2 cans (6½ ozs. each) minced clams
1 cup chopped celery
½ cup sliced green onions
5 tablespoons butter or margarine
6 tablespoons all-purpose flour
2 envelopes instant chicken broth
¼ teaspoon pepper
    Milk
1 cup coarsely crushed cornflakes
2 tablespoons chopped parsley

Cook macaroni in a kettle as label directs; drain; return to kettle.

Cut fish into ½-inch cubes; drain well. Drain liquid from clams into a 4-cup measure.

Preheat oven to 350°.

Sauté celery and green onions in butter in a large saucepan until soft; stir in flour, chicken broth, and pepper. Cook, stirring constantly, until bubbly.

Add milk to clam liquid to make 3 cups; stir into onion mixture. Cook, stirring constantly, until sauce thickens and boils 1 minute. Stir into macaroni with fish and clams. Spoon into a 2½-quart baking dish; cover.

Bake 30 minutes; uncover.

Mix cornflakes and parsley in a small bowl; sprinkle over top of macaroni mixture.

Bake 30 minutes, or until bubbly and topping is golden.

Yield: 6 servings.

FRANKFURTER RAGOUT

1 cup uncooked elbow macaroni
½ cup chopped celery
1 medium onion, chopped (½ cup)
2 tablespoons salad oil
6 frankfurters, cut diagonally in
    1-inch pieces
1 can (10¾ ozs.) condensed tomato soup
½ cup water
2 teaspoons Worcestershire sauce
2 tablespoons chopped parsley

Cook macaroni as label directs; drain. Keep warm.

Sauté celery and onion in salad oil in a medium skillet until soft; push to one side. Add frankfurters and brown lightly.

Stir in soup, water, Worcestershire sauce, and macaroni; heat slowly, stirring several times, to boiling; cover. Simmer 10 minutes to blend flavors. Sprinkle parsley over top.

Yield: 4 servings.

CHICKEN-FILLED SHELLS

2 cups finely chopped cooked chicken
1 small onion, minced (¼ cup)
¼ cup minced celery
1 egg
½ cup fresh bread crumbs (1 slice)
½ teaspoon dried rosemary, crushed
¼ teaspoon salt
⅛ teaspoon pepper
1 can (10¾ ozs.) condensed cream of
    chicken soup
16 jumbo macaroni shells
⅓ cup milk
    Few drops red-pepper seasoning

Combine chicken, onion, celery, egg, bread crumbs, rosemary, salt, and pepper in a large bowl; add 2 tablespoons of the soup; stir with a fork until well blended.

Cook macaroni shells as label directs; drain. Stuff a heaping tablespoon of the chicken mixture into each.

Preheat oven to 350°.

Blend rest of soup, milk, and red-pepper seasoning in a small bowl; pour about half over bottom of a 2-quart shallow baking dish. Arrange shells, stuffing side up, in rows in dish; pour rest of soup mixture over top.

Bake 30 minutes, or until bubbly. Sprinkle chopped parsley over top if you like.

Yield: 4 servings.

MINESTRONE TOSS

1 package (8 ozs.) elbow macaroni
1 can (20 ozs.) chick peas, drained
2 medium carrots, pared and
    shredded
1 small onion, chopped (¼ cup)
1 cup chopped celery
¼ cup chopped parsley
¾ cup bottled Italian salad dressing
1 jar (5 ozs.) Old English cheese spread
2 packages (8 ozs. each) sliced
    bologna
½ small head romaine

Cook macaroni as label directs; drain. Combine with chick peas, carrots, onion, celery, and parsley in a large bowl. Drizzle Italian dressing over top; toss lightly to mix; cover. Chill at least 2 hours to season.

Spread cheese over each of 12 slices of the bologna. Stack each 3 slices; top with a plain slice; wrap and chill.

When ready to serve, line a large shallow salad bowl with romaine; spoon macaroni mixture into center.

Cut each bologna stack into 6 even wedges; stand around edge in bowl.

Yield: 6 servings.

SPAGHETTI CHOWDER

1 medium onion, chopped (½ cup)
2 tablespoons butter or margarine
1 can (15 ozs.) spaghetti with tomato sauce
1 can (about 7 ozs.) tuna, drained and flaked
1 can (8 ozs.) peas
½ teaspoon dillweed
¼ teaspoon salt
2 cups milk

Sauté onion in butter in a large saucepan until soft.

Cut through spaghetti in can with a knife to break up long strands; stir into onion mixture with tuna, peas and liquid, dillweed, salt, and milk. Heat slowly, stirring several times, to boiling; cover. Simmer 5 minutes. Serve in soup bowls with chowder crackers if you like.
Yield: 4 servings.

MACARONI-AND-TUNA SUPREME

1 cup elbow macaroni, cooked and drained
1 can (7 ozs.) tuna, drained and flaked
1 small onion, minced
1 package (8 ozs.) process American
    cheese, shredded
3 eggs
½ teaspoon leaf oregano, crushed
1¾ cups milk

Preheat oven to 325°. Grease an 8x8x2-inch baking dish.

Combine macaroni, tuna, onion, and shredded cheese in a bowl; toss lightly to mix; spoon into baking dish.

Beat eggs slightly with oregano and milk; pour over macaroni mixture.

Bake 1 hour, or until set and lightly golden on top.
Yield: 6 servings.

DEVILED MACARONI BAKE

2 eggs
1 can (14¾ ozs.) elbow macaroni
    and cheese
1 cup (8-oz. carton) creamed cottage
    cheese
1 jar (2 ozs.) sliced pimientos,
    drained and diced
1 tablespoon instant minced onion
2 teaspoons prepared hot spicy mustard
¾ teaspoon salt
2 tablespoons plain wheat germ

Preheat oven to 350°.

Beat eggs in a medium bowl until blended. Stir in macaroni and cheese, cottage cheese, pimientos, onion, mustard, and salt until well blended. Spoon into a baking dish, 8x8x2 inches. Sprinkle wheat germ evenly over top.

Bake 30 minutes, or until set. Spoon onto serving plates.
Yield: 4 servings.

CHICKEN RAMEKINS

1½ cups 1-inch pieces uncooked
     spaghetti
1½ cups cubed cooked chicken
  2 pimientos, drained and chopped
  1 can (10¾ ozs.) condensed cream of
     mushroom soup
¾ cup milk
  1 cup shredded process American
     cheese (4 ozs.)
½ cup crumbled potato chips

Cook spaghetti in a kettle as label directs; drain; return to kettle. Stir in chicken and pimientos.

Preheat oven to 350°.

Combine soup, milk, and cheese in a small saucepan; heat slowly, stirring constantly, until cheese melts and sauce is smooth; stir into spaghetti mixture.

Spoon into four 10-ounce custard cups. Sprinkle potato chips in a ring around top of each. For easy handling, set cups in a large shallow pan.

Bake 25 minutes, or until bubbly in center.
Yield: 4 servings.

SUMMER SHRIMP TETRAZZINI

  1 bag (16 ozs.) frozen uncooked shrimp
⅓ cup bottled thin French dressing
  1 package (8 ozs.) spaghetti, broken in
    2-inch lengths
  1 package (3 ozs.) cream cheese
½ cup mayonnaise or salad dressing
  3 tablespoons grated Parmesan cheese
  2 tablespoons dry sherry
½ cup sliced green onions
½ cup sliced celery
  1 jar (2 ozs.) sliced pimientos, drained
    and diced
    Chicory or curly endive

Cook shrimp as label directs; drain; place in a medium bowl. Drizzle half of the French dressing over top; toss lightly to mix; cover.

Cook spaghetti as label directs; drain; place in a large bowl. Add rest of French dressing; toss lightly; cover. Chill shrimp and spaghetti mixtures at least 2 hours to season.

Combine cream cheese, mayonnaise, Parmesan cheese, and sherry in a small bowl; beat until smooth.

Add onions, celery, and pimientos to spaghetti mixture; fold in cheese mixture; fold in shrimp. Spoon into a chicory-lined bowl, pulling several shrimp to top for a garnish.
Yield: 6 servings.

VEGETABLES

WHATEVER YOU SPEND FOR VEGETABLES—fresh, frozen, or canned—is a sound investment in good health and good eating. These mealtime favorites abound in the vitamins and minerals everyone needs everyday, and it takes so little ingenuity to serve them a different way each time they go to the table. Remember that varieties, choices, and prices vary with the season, and comparing the three styles before you buy is the key to savings.

At the produce counter, look around you and pick what's freshest and what your family likes best. At home, keep tabs on your refrigerator and use the most perishable first—corn, peas, and greens. Wash, pare, and cut up fresh vegetables as near mealtime as possible—long soaking only destroys their food value. Other reminders: Go easy on the water you use for cooking, fix just enough for one meal at a time, cook in a tightly covered saucepan, and watch your timing so that the vegetables will be crisp-tender when served.

To help you keep interest and flavor high, here are a few other suggestions for fixing vegetables: Slice, dice, cube, or shred the vegetables to vary their shapes; sauté them lightly as the Orientals do; serve two or more kinds in one dish; team vegetables with fruit; try bouillon, tomato juice, consommé, or milk as the cooking liquid; turn vegetables into a casserole; combine with a flavorful sauce; and finally, use herbs, spices, and seasoning mixes to enhance their flavor.

On the next few pages you'll find basic directions for cooking fresh vegetables, along with a variety of recipes for individual kinds.

How to store
Pointers below tell you how to handle fresh vegetables to keep them looking and tasting their best from the time of purchase until they appear on your table.
Salad fixings—For leafy greens, follow the directions on page 327. Trim celery and radishes, then scrub them with a brush so they'll be ready to use. Simply wash peppers and cucumbers, and chill all. Tomatoes that are firm and ripe can go into the refrigerator at once, but any that are underripe are best kept at room temperature—away from sunlight—until they reach the rosy eating stage.

Year-round favorites–Fresh peas and beans, cabbage, cauliflower, yellow squash, zucchini, and eggplant no longer know any season, and most of these choices show up in our markets all year long. All are excellent values for once-a-week shoppers because they'll stay fresh through the middle of the week. Wait to trim them until you're ready to use them. Rinse any that are sandy and dry well—excess water clinging to pods or leaves only encourages spoilage. Store them in the vegetable crisper in your refrigerator or, if it's full, in transparent bags or wrapped loosely in foil to hold in their natural moisture.

Root varieties–Most of us think of vegetables that grow below ground as old standbys—for they rank high in popularity and menu versatility, keep for weeks, and usually save pennies. Most supermarkets pack potatoes, sweet potatoes, onions, and carrots in net or transparent bags to keep them clean and save you shopping time, and you'll find package sizes to fit every need. Leave these products in their bags and store in a cool, dry, dark place where there is plenty of air. Because of their strong odor, it's best to give onions a little corner to themselves.

Almost all vegetables taste great if they are boiled or steamed and simply dressed with butter or margarine. Based on the cooking times given here, the vegetables will be crisp-tender. However, to make sure they are cooked to your family's taste, test them with a fork before removing the saucepan from the heat.

ARTICHOKES

Cut off stems even with base. Slice about an inch from the tops with a sharp knife; snip off any spiny tips. Stand artichokes in a large saucepan; drizzle salad oil over tops, using 1 tablespoon for each artichoke. Pour boiling water into saucepan to a depth of 2 inches; salt lightly. Heat to boiling; cover. Cook 40 minutes, or until a leaf pulls easily from the base. Lift artichokes, one at a time, from water with a slotted spoon and drain well.

ASPARAGUS

Break tough woody ends from spears. (Stalks will snap easily at the point where tender part ends.) Wash spears; remove scales with a sharp knife; wash spears again. Tie in serving-sized bundles; stand upright in a deep saucepan. Pour in boiling water to a depth of 1 inch; salt lightly; cover. Cook 15 minutes. Lift bundles from water; drain well; cut away strings.

BEANS (Green and Wax)

Trim stems and tails from beans; wash beans well; leave whole. Cook, covered, in a 1-inch depth of boiling salted water, 15 minutes; drain. Or cut beans crosswise in half or into 1-inch lengths, or pull through a bean slicer to fix French-style. Cook the same as whole beans for 10 minutes.

BEANS (Lima)

Shell beans and wash. Cook, covered, in a small amount of boiling salted water 25 minutes; drain.

BEETS

Trim roots and tops to within 1 inch of beets; scrub beets well; do not pare. Cook, covered, in a small amount of boiling salted water, 30 to 60 minutes, depending upon size; drain. Cool until easy to handle, then peel off skins. Or pare beets first, slice or cut into cubes, and cook the same as whole ones for 15 minutes; drain.

BROCCOLI

Wash broccoli; trim leaves and any tough ends. Cut stalks into 3-inch lengths; for even cooking, pare thick stalks and split lengthwise. Place stalks in bottom and flowerets on top in a large saucepan. Pour in boiling water to a depth of 1 inch; salt lightly; cover. Cook 15 minutes; drain.

BRUSSELS SPROUTS

Trim off any wilted leaves; wash sprouts; leave whole. Cook, covered, in a small amount of boiling salted water, 12 minutes; drain.

CABBAGE (Green)

Trim off wilted outer leaves and base of core. Cut head into 6 or 8 wedges, depending upon size. Do not remove core or wedges will fall apart. Cook, covered, in a small amount of boiling salted water, 12 minutes; drain. Or shred cabbage, discarding core. Cook the same as wedges for 5 minutes; drain.

CARROTS

Wash carrots; pare or scrape; leave whole. Cook, covered, in a small amount of boiling salted water, 20 minutes; drain. Or cut carrots into chunks or sticks, or dice or slice. Cook the same as whole carrots for 12 minutes.

CAULIFLOWER

Trim leaves from head; break head into flowerets, discarding core. Wash flowerets. Cook, covered, in a small amount of boiling salted water, 10 minutes; drain. Or leave head whole but cut out core. Cook the same as flowerets for 20 minutes.

CELERY

Trim leaves and root end; wash celery well. Slice outside stalks; split heart. Cook, covered, in a small amount of boiling salted water, 10 minutes; drain.

CHARD

Wash leaves well; trim stems and any coarse ribs; drain leaves but do not dry. Pile leaves into a large saucepan. (No need to add any water—moisture that clings to leaves will be enough.) Salt lightly; cover pan. Steam 10 minutes, or until leaves wilt; drain.

CHINESE CABBAGE

Trim root end and any wilted leaves; cut stalk crosswise into ¼-inch-thick slices; wash well. Cook, covered, in a small amount of boiling salted water, 12 minutes; drain.

COLLARDS

Cook the same as CHARD

CORN

Husk corn; remove silks with a stiff brush; rinse ears. Cook, covered in a small amount of boiling salted water, 7 minutes; drain. Or cut kernels from cobs with a sharp knife. (Hold ear at tapered end and stand it on a cutting board; cut kernels from tip to bottom, letting them fall onto board.) Cook the same as whole ears for 5 minutes. Or cook kernels, covered, in a small amount of seasoned milk for 5 minutes; serve with the milky liquid as a sauce.

EGGPLANT

Wash eggplant; pare or not as you prefer. Cut crosswise into ½-inch-thick slices. Dip in beaten egg, then in seasoned dry bread crumbs. Sauté slowly in hot salad oil or drippings in a skillet, turning slices once, 4 minutes, or until golden.

KALE

Cook the same as CHARD

KOHLRABI

Trim off tops; wash, pare, and dice or slice. Cook, covered, in a small amount of boiling salted water, 15 minutes; drain.

LEEKS

Trim root ends and cut off green tops to within 1 inch of white part; wash leeks well. Cook, covered, in a small amount of boiling salted water, 15 minutes; drain.

MUSHROOMS

Trim stems; leave mushrooms whole; rinse lightly. Sauté in butter or margarine in a skillet, stirring several times, 5 minutes. Or slice mushrooms and cook the same as whole ones.

OKRA

Remove stems from pods; wash pods. Cook, covered, in a small amount of boiling salted water, 10 minutes; drain. Or slice pods crosswise in ½-inch lengths; cook the same as whole pods for 8 minutes.

ONIONS

Peel; leave whole. Cook, covered, in a small amount of boiling salted water, 25 minutes; drain. Or cut large onions into quarters or slices and cook the same as whole ones for 15 minutes. To peel small white onions, place onions in a bowl; pour in boiling water to cover; let stand a minute, then drain. Skins will peel off easily and quickly. Cook the same as quartered large onions.

PARSNIPS

Trim tops and root ends; pare or scrape parsnips; wash well. Cut in half lengthwise. Cook, covered, in a small amount of boiling salted water 18 minutes; drain. Or slice crosswise about ¼-inch thick; cook slices the same as halved parsnips for 15 minutes.

PEAS (Green)

Shell and wash peas. Cook, covered, in a small amount of boiling salted water, 10 minutes; drain.

PEPPERS (Sweet)
Cook, following specific recipes. To fix for stuffing, wash peppers; cut a thin slice from top of each; scoop out seeds. Parboil peppers, covered, in boiling salted water, 3 minutes; remove from water with a slotted spoon and turn upside down to drain.

POTATOES (White)
Pare and rinse, or scrub well and leave peeling on. Place in a saucepan; pour in boiling water to cover; salt lightly; cover. Cook 25 minutes; drain. Or cut potatoes into quarters or slices, or dice or cube; cook the same as whole potatoes for 10 to 20 minutes, depending upon the size of the pieces.

POTATOES (Sweet)
Pare and rinse, or scrub well and leave peeling on. Place in a saucepan; pour in boiling water to cover; salt lightly; cover. Cook 30 minutes; drain. Or cut potatoes into quarters or thick slices, or dice or cube; cook the same as whole potatoes for 10 to 20 minutes, depending upon the size of the pieces.

RUTABAGA (Yellow Turnip)
Wash and pare; cut in slices or cubes, or dice. Cook, covered, in a small amount of boiling salted water, 25 to 35 minutes, depending upon the size of the pieces; drain.

SPINACH
Trim stems and any coarse ribs; wash leaves well; drain but do not dry. Pile into a large saucepan; salt lightly; cover. (No need to add any water.) Steam 3 to 4 minutes, or until leaves wilt; drain.

SQUASH (Acorn or Butternut)
Wash squashes; cut in half; scoop out seeds. Place halves, cut side down, in a shallow baking pan. Bake at 350° for 45 to 60 minutes, depending upon size. Or pare squash, seed, and cut into cubes. Cook, covered, in a small amount of boiling salted water, 15 minutes; drain.

SQUASH (Hubbard)
Wash squash; cut in serving-sized pieces but do not pare; scoop out seeds. Place pieces, cut side up, in a large shallow baking pan; dot with butter or margarine; cover tightly. Bake at 350° for 1 hour, or until tender. Or pare squash; cut into cubes. Cook, covered, in a small amount of boiling salted water 15 minutes; drain.

SQUASH (Yellow)
Wash, but do not pare; cut crosswise into ¼-inch-thick slices. Cook, covered, in a small amount of boiling salted water 3 minutes; drain.

TOMATOES
Wash and peel. (Job goes quickly if you dip each tomato into boiling water for a few seconds.) Cut out cores. Leave tomatoes whole or cut up as you prefer. Cook, covered, with seasonings of your choice, but no extra water, for 10 minutes. Serve liquid in pan with tomatoes. Cherry tomatoes may be sautéed, without peeling, in a little seasoned butter or margarine. Cook 2 to 3 minutes, or just until the skins start to pop.

TURNIPS (White)
Wash and pare. Leave small ones whole. Cook, covered, in a small amount of boiling salted water, 20 minutes; drain. Or cut turnips into quarters, slices, or cubes. Cook the same as whole one for 15 minutes.

YAMS
Cook the same as SWEET POTATOES

ZUCCHINI
Wash, but do not pare. Slice crosswise, cube, or cut into thin sticks. Cook, covered, in a small amount of boiling salted water, 5 minutes; drain.

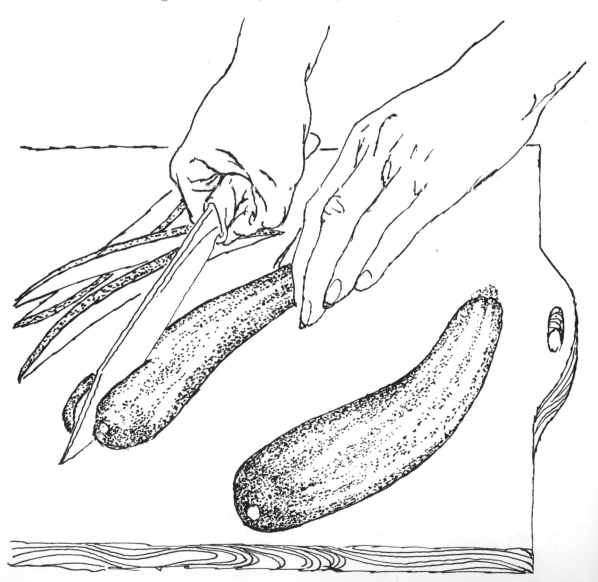

SHRIMP LASAGNA (p.271) ▶

ARTICHOKES MILANESE

3 cups fresh bread crumbs (6 slices)
1 small onion, minced (¼ cup)
½ cup minced pepperoni sausage
½ cup chopped parsley
½ teaspoon garlic salt
⅛ teaspoon pepper
⅓ cup grated Romano cheese
6 large artichokes
6 tablespoons salad oil
 Melted butter or margarine

Mix bread crumbs, onion, pepperoni, parsley, garlic salt, pepper, and cheese in a medium bowl.

Cut stems from artichokes to even the base. Slice about an inch from tops with a sharp knife; snip off any spiny tips. Carefully spread tops open; pull out any yellowed leaves from center, then scoop out fuzzy chokes. Wash artichokes; dry.

Spoon stuffing mixture into hollows in artichokes; stand them in a large saucepan; drizzle salad oil over each.

Pour boiling water into saucepan to a 2-inch depth; heat to boiling again; cover. Cook 40 minutes, or until a leaf pulls easily from the base. Lift artichokes from liquid with a slotted spoon; drain.

Place on serving plates; add individual bowls of melted butter to use as a dip.

Yield: 6 servings.

ASPARAGUS POLONAISE

3 packages (10 ozs. each) frozen asparagus spears
6 tablespoons butter or margarine
1½ cups fresh bread crumbs (3 slices)
2 tablespoons chopped parsley

Cook asparagus as label directs; drain. Place in a large shallow serving dish; keep warm.

While asparagus cooks, melt butter in a small skillet; stir in bread crumbs. Heat slowly until butter is absorbed and crumbs are toasted. Sprinkle over asparagus; sprinkle parsley on top.

Yield: 8 servings.

◀ TIJUANA CHICKEN AND RICE (p.264)
LEMONADE CREAM TORTE (p.419)

ASPARAGUS SEVILLE

1½ lbs. fresh asparagus
 Salt
1 package (8 ozs.) cream cheese
1 teaspoon grated orange rind
½ cup orange juice
1 tablespoon lemon juice
1 teaspoon sugar

Break tough woody ends from asparagus; wash spears. Remove scales with a small sharp knife; wash stalks again.

Tie stalks in serving-sized bundles; stand upright in a deep saucepan. Pour in boiling water to a 1-inch depth; salt lightly; cover.

Cook 15 minutes, or just until crisp-tender; drain. Keep warm.

Blend cream cheese, orange rind, orange and lemon juices, sugar, and ¼ teaspoon salt in a small saucepan; heat slowly, stirring constantly, until sauce is smooth and hot.

Place asparagus on a large serving platter; cut away strings. Spoon sauce in a ribbon on top.

Yield: 6 servings.

GARDEN BROCCOLI

2 bunches broccoli, weighing about 1½ lbs. each
1 small red pepper, halved, seeded, and cut in strips
⅓ cup butter or margarine.

Wash broccoli; trim flowerets about 3 inches from top. (Wrap stalks and chill to cook for another meal.) Separate any large flowerets.

Cook flowerets, covered, in a small amount of boiling salted water in a kettle 12 minutes, or until crisp-tender; drain carefully; keep warm.

Sauté red pepper in butter in same kettle about 5 minutes, or until crisp-tender; spoon over broccoli.

Yield: 8 servings.

BOK CHOY VEGETABLE BOWL

¼ cup salad oil
1 large onion, peeled and sliced
2 cups diagonally sliced celery
2 cups thinly sliced broccoli flowerets
2 tablespoons water
2 cups sliced Chinese cabbage
1 can (8 ozs.) water chestnuts, drained and sliced
1 can (16 ozs.) bean sprouts, drained
  Soy sauce

Heat salad oil in a large skillet; stir in onion. Sauté 2 to 3 minutes. Add celery, broccoli, and water; cover. Steam 5 minutes.

Place cabbage, water chestnuts, and bean sprouts in layers on top; cover. Steam 5 minutes, or just until cabbage is crisp-tender.

Toss vegetables, salad style; spoon into a large serving bowl. Serve with soy sauce to drizzle over top.

Yield: 6 servings.

BROCCOLI WITH MUSTARD CREAM

1 bunch broccoli, weighing about 1½ lbs.
  Salt
¼ cup butter or margarine
½ cup mayonnaise or salad dressing
1 tablespoon prepared mustard

Wash broccoli; trim leaves and tough ends. Cut stalks and flowerets into 3-inch lengths; for even cooking, pare thick stalks and split lengthwise.

Put stalks in the bottom and flowerets on top in a large saucepan. Pour in boiling water to a 1-inch depth; salt lightly; cover. Cook 12 minutes, or just until crisp-tender; drain. Place on a large serving platter; keep warm.

Melt butter in a small saucepan; remove from heat. Beat in mayonnaise, mustard, and a dash of salt until smooth; heat very slowly until hot. (Do not let mixture boil.)

Spoon sauce over broccoli. Garnish platter with lemon wedges if you like.

Yield: 6 servings.

COLONIAL BAKED BEANS

1 package (16 ozs.) dried navy or pea beans
8 cups water
¼ lb. salt pork
1 small onion, chopped (¼ cup)
¾ cup light or dark molasses
¼ cup catsup
1 teaspoon salt
½ teaspoon dry mustard
1 teaspoon Worcestershire sauce

Rinse beans. Combine with water in a kettle. Heat to boiling; cook 2 minutes; remove from heat; cover. Let stand 1 hour. Reheat to boiling; simmer 1 hour, or until beans are tender but still firm enough to hold their shape. Drain liquid into a medium bowl.

Preheat oven to 325°.

Cut 4 thin slices from salt pork, then dice remainder.

Combine beans, diced pork, onion, molasses, catsup, salt, mustard, and Worcestershire sauce in a medium bowl; stir in 1 cup of the bean liquid. Spoon into a 2-quart baking dish; lay pork slices over top; cover.

Bake 2 hours; pour in 1 more cup of the bean liquid; cover. Bake 1 hour; uncover. Continue baking 1 hour longer.

Yield: 6 servings.

DANISH BAKED BEANS

1 can (16 ozs.) brown-sugar beans or old-fashioned beans in molasses and brown-sugar sauce
1 cup diced cooked ham
1 medium-sized tart apple, pared, quartered, cored, and diced (1 cup)
2 teaspoons prepared hot spicy mustard
2 tablespoons pineapple juice

Preheat oven to 350°.

Combine beans, ham, apple, mustard, and pineapple juice in a medium bowl; stir lightly until well mixed. Spoon into a 1-quart baking dish; cover.

Bake 45 minutes; uncover; stir well. Bake 15 minutes longer, or until slightly thickened.

Yield: 4 servings.

BOURBON BAKED BEANS

1 can (28 ozs.) brick-oven baked beans
2 teaspoons freeze-dried instant coffee
3 tablespoons bourbon
1 can (8 ozs.) sliced pineapple in juice, drained
3 tablespoons brown sugar

Preheat oven to 350°.

Empty beans into a 1-quart baking dish.

Dissolve coffee in bourbon in a cup; stir into beans; cover.

Bake 1 hour.

While beans bake, cut each pineapple slice into thirds; stand around edge in baking dish; sprinkle brown sugar over top.

Bake 15 minutes longer, or until pineapple is hot and lightly glazed.

Yield: 4 servings.

CONFETTI BEANS

 1 small onion, chopped (¼ cup)
 2 tablespoons salad oil
½ lb. ground beef
 2 tablespoons brown sugar
¼ cup maple-blended pancake syrup
¼ cup catsup
½ teaspoon dry mustard
¼ teaspoon salt
 1 can (8¾ ozs.) red kidney beans, drained
 1 can (8½ ozs.) lima beans, drained
 1 can (8 ozs.) pork and beans in tomato sauce
 2 tablespoons bacon-flavored vegetable protein bits

Preheat oven to 350°.

Sauté onion in salad oil in a medium skillet until soft; push to one side.

Add ground beef to skillet and brown; spoon off fat. Stir in brown sugar, syrup, catsup, mustard, salt, kidney beans, limas, and pork and beans; heat slowly to boiling.

Spoon into a 1-quart baking dish. Sprinkle protein bits over top; cover.

Bake 30 minutes; uncover. Bake 30 minutes longer, or until thickened.

Yield: 4 servings.

SPRING VEGETABLE PLATTER

1 bag (16 ozs.) small carrots, pared
1 lb. fresh green beans, tipped and cut in 1-inch lengths
1 tablespoon instant minced onion
6 tablespoons butter or margarine
½ teaspoon seasoned salt
¼ cup peanuts, chopped

Cook carrots, covered, in boiling salted water in a medium skillet 30 minutes, or until crisp-tender; drain.

Cook green beans with onion, covered, in boiling salted water in a medium saucepan 20 minutes, or until crisp-tender; drain. Keep both vegetables warm.

Melt butter in a small saucepan; stir in seasoned salt and peanuts. Heat slowly, stirring several times, until peanuts are lightly toasted.

Arrange carrots, spoke fashion, on a serving platter; pile green beans in center. Drizzle butter mixture over all.

Yield: 6 servings.

ORIENTAL GREEN BEANS

3 cups loose-pack frozen cut green beans
3 tablespoons butter or margarine
2 tablespoons blanched slivered almonds
1 can (11 ozs.) mandarin orange segments, drained

Cook green beans in boiling salted water in a large saucepan as label directs; drain well.

Melt butter in same saucepan; stir in almonds. Heat slowly, stirring several times, just until almonds are golden; remove with a slotted spoon to a cup.

Stir beans into butter in pan; lay orange segments on top; cover. Heat 1 to 2 minutes, or just until hot. (To keep orange segments whole, be careful to heat mixture only—not cook.)

Spoon beans and orange segments into a serving bowl; sprinkle almonds on top.

Yield: 4 servings.

SESAME GREEN BEANS

3 cups loose-pack frozen cut green beans
2 tablespoons salad oil
2 tablespoons soy sauce
¼ teaspoon salt
¼ cup water
1 tablespoon sesame seeds

Combine beans, salad oil, soy sauce, salt, and water in a medium skillet; heat to boiling; cover. Cook 8 to 10 minutes, or until beans are crisp-tender.

While beans cook, measure sesame seeds into a small skillet. Heat very slowly, shaking skillet often, 2 to 3 minutes, or until seeds are toasty-golden; stir into bean mixture.

Spoon into a serving bowl. Serve with additional soy sauce if you like.

Yield: 4 servings.

SPANISH GREEN BEANS

2 lbs. fresh green beans
¼ cup butter or margarine
1 envelope instant onion broth
½ cup sliced small pimiento-stuffed green olives
½ teaspoon dried basil, crushed

Tip green beans; cut into 1-inch lengths. Cook, covered, in boiling salted water in a large saucepan 20 minutes, or until crisp-tender; drain.

Melt butter in same saucepan; stir in dry onion broth; cook 1 minute.

Stir in olives, basil, and beans; simmer 5 minutes to blend flavors. Taste and add salt, if needed; spoon into a large serving bowl.

Yield: 8 servings.

SAVORY LIMAS

2 packages (10 ozs. each) frozen baby lima beans
1 small onion, chopped (¼ cup)
8 whole cloves
2 tablespoons butter or margarine
1 small can evaporated milk (⅔ cup)

Cook lima beans as label directs; drain; return to pan.

While lima beans cook, sauté onion and cloves in butter in a small saucepan until onion is soft; stir in milk. Heat to simmering; simmer 5 minutes; remove cloves.

Pour sauce over beans; reheat to boiling. Serve in saucedishes.

Yield: 6 servings.

TARRAGON CELERY

1 medium-sized bunch of celery
2 tablespoons butter or margarine
1 envelope instant chicken broth
½ teaspoon dried tarragon, crushed
½ teaspoon salt
Dash of pepper
¼ cup water

Trim celery and separate stalks. Cut into 1-inch lengths; for even cooking, split any large pieces lengthwise. (Celery should measure about 6 cups.)

Melt butter in a large skillet; stir in chicken broth, tarragon, salt, pepper, and water; heat to boiling. Stir in celery; cover. Steam 10 minutes, or until celery is crisp-tender. Spoon into a serving bowl.

Yield: 6 servings.

INDIAN CORN

½ cup chopped green pepper
½ cup chopped red pepper
1 small onion, chopped (¼ cup)
½ cup butter or margarine
5 cups frozen whole-kernel corn (from a 2 lb. bag)
1 teaspoon salt
⅛ teaspoon pepper

Sauté green and red peppers and onion in butter in a large skillet until soft; stir in frozen corn, salt, and pepper. Heat to boiling; cover.

Cook stirring once or twice, 5 minutes, or until corn is tender. Spoon into a heated serving bowl.

Yield: 8 servings.

TOMATO-BEAN BOWL

2 slices bacon, cut in 1-inch pieces
1 can (8 ozs.) whole boiled onions, drained
1 can (16 ozs.) tomato wedges
1 can (16 ozs.) wax beans, drained
1 teaspoon dried basil, crushed
½ teaspoon salt
¼ teaspoon sugar
⅛ teaspoon pepper

Sauté bacon until crisp in a medium saucepan; remove from pan and drain on paper toweling.

Add onions to drippings and sauté until lightly browned. Stir in tomatoes and juice, beans, and seasonings. Heat to boiling; simmer 20 minutes.

Spoon into a serving bowl; pile bacon in center.

Yield: 6 servings.

BARBECUED WAX BEANS

2 packages (10 ozs. each) frozen wax beans
1 small onion, chopped (¼ cup)
¼ cup chopped green pepper
2 tablespoons salad oil
½ cup chili sauce
2 tablespoons water
1 tablespoon lemon juice
1 tablespoon brown sugar
1 teaspoon dry mustard
½ teaspoon salt
¼ teaspoon liquid red-pepper seasoning
2 tablespoons chopped parsley

Cook beans in 1 cup boiling water in a medium saucepan 5 to 7 minutes, or just until crisp-tender; drain.

Sauté onion and green pepper in salad oil in same saucepan until soft; stir in chili sauce, water, lemon juice, brown sugar, mustard, salt, and red-pepper seasoning. Heat to boiling; simmer 5 minutes.

Stir beans into sauce; simmer 5 minutes longer. Spoon into a serving bowl; sprinkle parsley on top.

Yield: 6 servings.

GREEN BEANS GRUYERE

1½ lbs. green beans, tipped and cut in 1-inch
    lengths
1 package (6 ozs.) process Gruyere cheese
½ cup milk
    Few drops red-pepper seasoning
    Paprika

Cook beans covered, in boiling salted water in a large saucepan 20 minutes, or until crisp-tender; drain; return to pan.

Cut cheese in small pieces; combine with milk in a small saucepan. Heat very slowly, stirring constantly, until cheese melts completely and sauce is smooth. Stir in red-pepper seasoning. Pour over beans; heat just until hot.

Spoon into a large serving bowl; sprinkle paprika over top.

Yield: 6 servings.

VEGETABLE SCRAMBLE

2 large ears of corn
3 medium carrots, pared and cut into 1-inch sticks
1 cup thin celery crescents
¼ cup salad oil
2 medium zucchini, trimmed and sliced into
    ¼-inch-thick rounds
1¼ teaspoons salt
1 teaspoon dried basil, crushed
⅛ teaspoon pepper
2 tablespoons water
1 small tomato, cut in 6 wedges

Husk corn and remove silk; cut kernels from cobs.

Sauté carrots and celery in salad oil in a large skillet 10 minutes. Stir in zucchini and corn; sauté 5 minutes.

Sprinkle salt, basil, and pepper over top. Add water; cover; steam 5 minutes.

Arrange tomato wedges on top of vegetables; cover. Heat 5 minutes, or just until tomatoes are hot. Serve from skillet.

Yield: 6 servings.

MEXICALI SUCCOTASH

6 large ears of corn
1 cup loose-pack frozen baby lima beans
½ cup boiling water
½ cup chopped celery
¼ cup butter or margarine
1 teaspoon chili powder
½ teaspoon salt
2 tablespoons finely chopped pimientos

Husk corn and remove silk; cut kernels from cobs.

Cook lima beans, covered, in ½ cup lightly salted boiling water in a medium saucepan 10 minutes; stir in corn. Cook 10 minutes longer, or until vegetables are tender; drain off liquid.

Sauté celery in butter in a medium skillet until soft; stir in chili powder and salt; cook 1 minute longer. Stir in vegetables; cover; heat slowly 5 minutes.

Spoon into a serving bowl; sprinkle pimientos over top.
Yield: 6 servings.

DOUBLE CORN CUSTARD

¼ cup finely chopped green pepper
1 small onion, finely chopped (¼ cup)
2 tablespoons butter or margarine
3 eggs
2 cups milk
1 teaspoon salt
½ teaspoon sugar
⅛ teaspoon pepper
1 can (16 ozs.) whole-kernel corn, drained
1 cup shredded process American cheese (4 ozs.)
2 cups bite-sized corn cereal squares, coarsely broken

Sauté green pepper and onion in butter in a small saucepan until soft.

Preheat oven to 325°.

Beat eggs with milk, salt, sugar, and pepper in a medium bowl until blended. Stir in corn, cheese, onion mixture, and 1¾ cups of the cereal. Spoon into a buttered 1½-quart shallow baking dish; sprinkle rest of the cereal over top.

Bake 50 minutes, or until a knife inserted into center comes out clean. Let stand 10 minutes on a wire rack before serving.
Yield: 6 servings.

GINGER CARROTS

1 bag (24 ozs.) frozen small whole carrots
6 tablespoons butter or margarine
½ cup honey
2 teaspoons grated orange rind
1 teaspoon ground ginger
¼ teaspoon salt

Cook carrots as label directs; drain well.

Melt butter in a large skillet; stir in honey, orange rind, ginger, and salt. Heat to boiling; add carrots; turn to coat with honey mixture.

Simmer, turning several times, 12 minutes, or until carrots are glazed. Spoon into a heated large serving bowl. Garnish with several thin slices of fresh orange if you like.
Yield: 8 servings.

MINTED CARROTS AND PEAS

1 bag (16 ozs.) small slender carrots, pared
3 lbs. peas in pods, shelled
¼ cup butter or margarine
¼ cup thawed frozen concentrated pineapple juice
½ teaspoon salt
2 tablespoons chopped fresh mint

Cook carrots whole, covered, in boiling salted water in a medium saucepan 15 minutes, or until crisp-tender; drain. Keep warm.

Cook peas, covered, in boiling salted water in a medium saucepan 15 minutes, or until tender; drain. Keep warm.

Melt butter in a small saucepan; stir in pineapple concentrate and salt; heat slowly to boiling.

Arrange carrots at ends of a deep serving platter; mound peas in center. Stir chopped mint into sauce; drizzle over vegetables.
Yield: 6 servings.

SAUCEDISH CORN

8 large ears of corn
¾ cup light cream
¼ cup butter or margarine
1 teaspoon sugar
1 teaspoon celery salt
 Dash of pepper

Husk corn and remove silk; cut kernels from cobs.

Combine corn with cream, butter, sugar, celery salt, and pepper in a medium saucepan; heat slowly to boiling; cover. Simmer 20 minutes, or until corn is tender.

Serve in saucedishes.

Yield: 6 servings.

GLAZED CARROTS

1 bag (16 ozs.) carrots, pared
⅓ cup orange marmalade
2 tablespoons butter or margarine

Cook carrots, covered, in boiling salted water in a skillet 20 minutes, or until crisp-tender; drain; return to skillet.

Spoon orange marmalade over carrots; dot with butter. Cook slowly, turning carrots once or twice, 10 minutes, or until richly glazed.

Yield: 4 to 6 servings.

DILLED CARROTS AND PEAS

6 medium carrots, pared and sliced diagonally
  into ¼-inch-thick slices
3 cups loose-pack frozen peas
½ teaspoon salt
¼ teaspoon dillweed
4 tablespoons butter or margarine
⅓ cup boiling water

Preheat oven to 400°.

Combine carrots with peas in a 1½-quart baking dish. Sprinkle salt and dillweed over top; add butter and water; cover.

Bake, stirring once, 1 hour, or until vegetables are tender. Serve from baking dish.

Yield: 6 servings.

ORANGE-BUTTER CARROTS

1 bag (16 ozs.) carrots, pared and shredded
1 teaspoon sugar
½ teaspoon salt
2 teaspoons grated orange rind
2 tablespoons orange juice
¼ cup butter or margarine

Preheat oven to 350°.

Place carrots in a 1-quart baking dish. Sprinkle sugar, salt, and orange rind over top; drizzle orange juice over all; dot evenly with butter; cover tightly.

Bake 30 minutes; stir lightly. Bake 30 minutes longer, or until carrots are tender.

Yield: 4 servings.

GOLDEN SUCCOTASH

2 medium carrots, pared and diced (1 cup)
1 cup water
½ teaspoon salt
1 package (10 ozs.) frozen whole-kernel corn
1 cup loose-pack frozen large lima beans
3 tablespoons butter or margarine
½ teaspoon dillweed

Combine carrots, water, and salt in a medium saucepan; heat to boiling; cover. Cook 5 minutes.

Add frozen corn and lima beans to pan; heat to boiling again; cover. Cook 5 minutes longer, or until all vegetables are tender; drain. Return to saucepan.

Add butter and dillweed; heat, tossing several times, until butter melts and vegetables are coated. Spoon into a serving bowl. Garnish with a sprig of fresh dill if you like.

Yield: 6 servings.

CASSEROLE CARROTS

12 medium-sized carrots, pared and shredded
1 tablespoon sugar
1 teaspoon salt
¼ teaspoon pepper
1 teaspoon grated lemon rind
4 tablespoons butter or margarine

Preheat oven to 325°.

Place carrots in a 1½-quart baking dish. Sprinkle sugar, salt, pepper, and lemon rind over carrots; toss lightly; dot butter over top; cover.

Bake, stirring once, 1 hour, or until carrots are tender.

Yield: 6 servings.

CUCUMBER-CELERY SCALLOP

4 medium cucumbers
1 cup sliced celery
6 tablespoons butter or margarine
6 tablespoons all-purpose flour
1 teaspoon salt
   Dash of pepper
1½ cups milk
¼ cup mayonnaise or salad dressing
¾ cup soft bread crumbs (1½ slices)

Pare cucumbers; cut in eighths lengthwise; cut out seeds. Cut cucumbers into 1-inch pieces.

Cook cucumbers and celery together, covered, in boiling salted water in a medium saucepan 7 minutes, or until tender; drain well. Place in a 1½-quart shallow baking dish.

Preheat oven to 350°.

Melt 4 tablespoons of the butter in a small saucepan; stir in flour, salt, and pepper; cook, stirring constantly, until bubbly. Stir in milk; continue cooking and stirring until mixture thickens and boils 1 minute; remove from heat. Stir in mayonnaise; pour over vegetables in dish; toss lightly.

Melt rest of the butter in a small skillet; toss with bread crumbs until butter is absorbed; sprinkle over vegetables.

Bake 20 minutes, or until bubbly and topping is toasted.

Yield: 6 servings.

INDIAN CABBAGE

4 tablespoons butter or margarine
1 small onion, chopped (¼ cup)
6 cups finely shredded green cabbage (about 1½ lbs.)
1 teaspoon sugar
½ teaspoon curry powder
½ teaspoon salt
1 large tart red cooking apple, quartered, cored, and sliced

Melt butter in a medium skillet; stir in onion and cabbage. Sprinkle sugar, curry powder, and salt over top; cover. Steam 5 minutes; stir well.

Arrange apple slices in a pretty pattern on top of cabbage mixture; cover again. Steam 5 minutes longer, or until apples and cabbage are crisp-tender. Serve from skillet.

Yield: 6 servings.

CAULIFLOWER-CARROT BOWL

1 medium head cauliflower, weighing about 1½ lbs.
1 bag (16 ozs.) frozen small whole carrots
6 tablespoons butter or margarine
2 tablespoons lemon juice
¼ teaspoon salt
2 tablespoons chopped parsley

Trim cauliflower and break into small flowerets.

Cook cauliflowerets and carrots together, covered, in boiling salted water in a large saucepan 10 minutes, or until crisp-tender; drain well.

Melt butter in same saucepan; stir in lemon juice and salt. Add vegetables; toss lightly to mix with butter; heat just until hot.

Spoon into a serving bowl; sprinkle parsley over top.

Yield: 8 servings.

BAVARIAN CABBAGE

    1 large onion, chopped (1 cup)
    2 tablespoons butter or margarine
    2 large tart apples, pared, quartered, cored, and
        diced
    2 tablespoons brown sugar
    8 cups finely shredded red cabbage (about 2 lbs.)
    ⅓ cup cider vinegar
    ½ cup water
    1½ teaspoons salt
    ¼ cup currant jelly

Sauté onion in butter in a large skillet until soft; stir in apples and brown sugar; sauté 2 minutes.

Add cabbage; toss lightly to mix with drippings, then stir in vinegar; heat to boiling. Stir in water; cover.

Simmer 45 minutes, or until cabbage is tender. Stir in salt and jelly; cover again; reheat to boiling. Spoon into a serving bowl. Garnish with thin apple slices if you like.

Yield: 6 servings.

CAULIFLOWER WITH BROWN BUTTER SAUCE

    1 small head cauliflower, weighing about 1 lb.
    ¼ cup butter or margarine
    2 tablespoons sliced almonds
    1 tablespoon lemon juice
        Dash of salt
        Dash of pepper

Trim cauliflower and break into flowerets; slice flowerets thin.

Cook, covered, in boiling salted water in a medium saucepan 5 minutes, or until crisp-tender; drain. Keep warm while making sauce.

Melt butter in a small skillet; add almonds. Continue heating, shaking skillet constantly, until butter foams up and turns golden brown. (Watch carefully, for butter browns quickly.) Remove from heat; slowly stir in lemon juice, salt, and pepper.

Spoon cauliflower into a serving bowl; drizzle almond-butter sauce evenly over the top.

Yield: 4 servings.

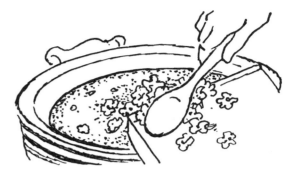

ONION SCALLOP

    6 medium onions, peeled and halved crosswise
    ¼ cup butter or margarine
    ¼ cup all-purpose flour
    1 envelope instant chicken broth
    1 teaspoon dried thyme, crushed
    ½ teaspoon salt
        Dash of pepper
    1 large can evaporated milk (1⅔ cups)
    ⅔ cup water
    1½ cups corn-bread stuffing mix

Cook onions, covered, in boiling salted water in a large skillet 15 minutes, or until crisp-tender; drain, being careful not to break halves.

Preheat oven to 350°.

Melt butter in a medium saucepan; stir in flour, chicken broth, thyme, salt, and pepper; cook, stirring constantly, until bubbly. Stir in evaporated milk and water; continue cooking and stirring until sauce thickens and boils 1 minute.

Layer half of the onions into a 2½-quart baking dish; top with half each of the sauce and stuffing mix. Repeat layers.

Bake 30 minutes, or until sauce bubbles up and topping is toasted.

Yield: 8 servings.

CAJUN EGGPLANT

3 small eggplants
1 large green pepper, quartered, seeded, and chopped (1 cup)
1 cup chopped celery
1 large onion, chopped (1 cup)
2 tablespoons salad oil
½ cup uncooked regular rice
2 large tomatoes, peeled and chopped (2 cups)
¾ cup water
1½ teaspoons salt
¼ teaspoon pepper
1 teaspoon dried basil, crushed
2 teaspoons Worcestershire sauce
1 package (8 ozs.) process Old English cheese, shredded (2 cups)

Cut each eggplant in half lengthwise; scoop out insides to leave shells ¼-inch thick. Dice eggplant.

Preheat oven to 350°.

Sauté green pepper, celery, and onion in salad oil in a large skillet until soft; push to one side.

Stir rice into drippings; sauté, stirring constantly, until golden.

Stir in diced eggplant, tomatoes, water, salt, pepper, basil, and Worcestershire sauce; heat to boiling; cover. Simmer 20 minutes, or until rice is tender. Stir in half of the cheese until melted. Spoon into eggplant shells; sprinkle rest of the cheese on top. Place shells in a greased shallow baking pan.

Bake 25 minutes, or until cheese melts and filling is hot.

Lift eggplants onto a large serving platter with a pancake turner; garnish with celery leaves if you like.

Yield: 6 servings.

PUMPKIN PUFF

3 eggs, separated
1 can (16 ozs.) pumpkin
¼ cup butter or margarine, melted
¼ cup firmly packed light brown sugar
1 teaspoon pumpkin-pie spice
1 tablespoon grated orange rind
½ cup light cream

Preheat oven to 325°.

Beat egg whites in a medium bowl until they form stiff peaks.

Beat egg yolks in another medium bowl; stir in pumpkin, melted butter, brown sugar, spice, orange rind, and cream; fold in beaten egg whites. Spoon into a 1-quart soufflé dish.

Bake 1 hour and 15 minutes, or until puffed and firm in center. Serve as a vegetable with melted butter or margarine to drizzle over each serving.

Yield: 6 servings.

HERBED ONION HALVES

4 medium onions, peeled and halved crosswise
4 tablespoons butter or margarine, softened
1 teaspoon dried marjoram, crushed
½ teaspoon salt

Preheat oven to 325°.

Place onions in a baking pan.

Blend butter, marjoram, and salt in a cup; spread a heaping teaspoonful on each onion half.

Bake 30 minutes; turn onions. Bake 30 minutes longer, or until crisp-tender.

Yield: 4 servings.

CARAWAY ONIONS

4 large onions, peeled and sliced
3 tablespoons butter or margarine
3 tablespoons all-purpose flour
¼ teaspoon salt
¾ cup milk
4 long slices caraway cheese, cut up
½ teaspoon Worcestershire sauce
½ cup coarsely crushed saltines

Preheat oven to 350°.

Cook onions in boiling salted water in a medium saucepan 10 minutes, or until tender but still firm enough to hold their shape; drain very well. Place in a deep 1-quart baking dish.

Melt butter in a medium saucepan; stir in flour and salt; cook, stirring constantly, until bubbly. Stir in milk; continue cooking and stirring until sauce thickens and boils 1 minute. Stir in cheese until melted, then Worcestershire sauce. Pour over onions, lifting onions with a fork so sauce seeps to bottom. Sprinkle saltine crumbs in a ring around edge in dish.

Bake 30 minutes, or until bubbly in center and topping is toasted.

Yield: 6 servings.

CANDIED ONIONS

18 small white onions (about 1½ lbs.)
¼ cup butter or margarine
⅓ cup maple-blended syrup
2 teaspoons lemon juice
¼ teaspoon ground nutmeg
1 teaspoon grated lemon rind

Place onions in a large bowl; pour in boiling water to cover. Let stand 5 minutes; peel.

Cook onions, covered, in boiling salted water in a medium skillet 15 minutes, or until tender; drain.

Melt butter in same skillet; stir in syrup, lemon juice, nutmeg, and onions. Simmer, turning several times, 15 minutes, or until glazed.

Spoon into a serving bowl; sprinkle lemon rind over top.

Yield: 6 servings.

GOLDEN SPINACH NESTS

1 package (10 ozs.) frozen chopped spinach
1 can (10¾ ozs.) condensed cream of potato soup
2 tablespoons minced onion
4 eggs
Dash of salt
Dash of pepper
½ cup shredded process American cheese

Preheat oven to 325°.

Cook spinach in unsalted water as label directs; drain well. Place in a medium bowl; stir in soup and onion. Spoon mixture into four 10-ounce custard cups; hollow each with back of spoon to form a nest.

Break an egg into each hollow; sprinkle salt and pepper lightly over eggs, then sprinkle cheese on top.

Bake 25 minutes, or until eggs are as firm as you like them. Serve from cups.

Yield: 4 servings.

PARISIAN PEAS

3 large iceberg lettuce leaves
1 bag (24 ozs.) frozen peas
1 small onion, chopped (¼ cup)
1 teaspoon sugar
½ teaspoon salt
¼ teaspoon dried basil, crushed
⅛ teaspoon pepper
3 tablespoons butter or margarine
3 tablespoons water

Place lettuce in a large saucepan; add peas, onion, sugar, salt, basil, pepper, butter, and water; cover. Heat slowly to boiling, then cook 5 minutes, or until peas are tender.

Spoon peas into a heated serving bowl, removing lettuce. Garnish bowl with several small white onion rings if you like.

Yield: 8 servings.

ONION-CARROT CUPS

6 large onions, peeled
6 medium carrots, pared and cut into strips about
　　1½ inches long
¼ cup butter or margarine
2 tablespoons finely cut chives
¼ teaspoon salt
　Dash of pepper

Cut a half-inch thick slice from top of each onion, then scoop out centers to leave shells about ½-inch thick. (Wrap centers and top slices to use another day.)

Place onion shells in a single layer in a large skillet; add about 2 cups water; cover. Steam 12 minutes, or until tender but still firm enough to hold their shape. Lift each from pan with a slotted spoon and drain well; keep warm.

Cook carrots, covered, in boiling salted water in a medium saucepan 5 minutes, or until crisp-tender; drain; return to pan. Add butter, chives, salt, and pepper. Heat slowly, tossing lightly, until butter melts and bubbles up. Spoon into onion cups.

Yield: 6 servings.

SPINACH PUFF

1 package (10 ozs.) frozen chopped spinach
4 eggs
2 cups milk
1 small onion, chopped (¼ cup)
1½ cups small fresh bread cubes
1½ teaspoons salt

Cook spinach as label directs; drain well, pressing out as much liquid as possible with back of spoon. (There should be 1 cup spinach.)

Preheat oven to 350°.

Beat eggs in a medium bowl until blended; stir in milk, onion, bread cubes, salt, and spinach. Pour into a 1-quart baking dish. Set dish in a shallow baking pan on oven rack; fill pan with hot water.

Bake 1 hour and 20 minutes, or until puffed and golden and a knife inserted into center comes out clean. Remove from hot water. Serve at once.

Yield: 4 servings.

CONFETTI PEAS IN SQUASH RINGS

2 medium-sized acorn squash
½ teaspoon salt
2 packages (10 ozs. each) frozen peas
6 tablespoons butter or margarine
1 teaspoon dillweed
2 small tomatoes, peeled, seeded, and diced

Trim ends from squash; cut each squash crosswise into 4 even rings; scoop out seeds.

Place rings in a single layer in a large shallow pan; pour in boiling water to a depth of ½ inch. Sprinkle ¼ teaspoon of the salt over top; cover. Heat to boiling on top of the range; simmer 10 to 12 minutes, or until squash is tender. Carefully lift rings from water with a slotted pancake turner; drain well; keep hot.

While squash cooks, cook peas as label directs; drain well; return to saucepan. Add butter, dillweed, remaining ¼ teaspoon salt, and tomatoes; heat just until butter melts and vegetables are hot.

Arrange squash rings on a large flat serving plate; spoon peas into centers, drizzling any remaining butter mixture in pan over squash. To serve, lift rings onto individual plates with a wide spatula or pie server.

Yield: 8 servings.

PIMIENTO PEAS AND LIMAS

  1 package (10 ozs.) frozen large lima beans
  1 package (10 ozs.) frozen peas
⅔ cup water
½ teaspoon salt
¼ cup chopped drained pimientos
  2 tablespoons butter or margarine
¼ teaspoon dried thyme, crushed

Combine limas, peas, water, and salt in a medium saucepan; heat to boiling; cover. Cook 5 minutes, or until vegetables are tender; drain; return to pan.

While vegetables cook, sauté pimientos in butter in a small saucepan 2 minutes; stir into vegetables; stir in thyme. Heat slowly 2 to 3 minutes, or until bubbly hot. Spoon into a serving bowl.

Yield: 6 servings.

STUFFED YELLOW SQUASH

  3 small yellow squashes, trimmed and halved
     lengthwise
1½ cups fresh bread crumbs (3 slices)
  1 cup (8-oz. carton) small-curd creamed cottage
     cheese
  1 small onion, minced (¼ cup)
¾ teaspoon fines herbes
¼ teaspoon salt
⅛ teaspoon pepper
¾ cup shredded sharp Cheddar cheese

Parboil squash halves in boiling salted water in a large skillet 10 minutes; drain well. Carefully scoop pulp from each half with a teaspoon to make a boat-shaped shell; place shells in a single layer in a large shallow baking pan. Chop pulp fine; drain again.

Preheat oven to 350°.

Mix bread crumbs with cottage cheese, onion, herbs, salt, pepper, and chopped squash in a medium bowl; pile back into shells. Sprinkle cheese over filling.

Bake 30 minutes, or until cheese melts and filling is set.

Yield: 6 servings.

DOUBLE SQUASH SCALLOP

  3 medium-sized zucchini
  3 medium-sized yellow squashes
  2 medium-sized tomatoes
  1 small onion, chopped (¼ cup)
¼ cup butter or margarine
  1 teaspoon sugar
  1 teaspoon salt
½ teaspoon dried basil, crushed
⅛ teaspoon seasoned pepper
  2 tablespoons grated Romano cheese

Trim zucchini and yellow squashes, but do not pare; cut in sticks. Cut tomatoes in thin wedges.

Sauté onion in 2 tablespoons of the butter until soft in a large skillet. Place squashes in separate piles over onion mixture; place tomato wedges between squashes. Sprinkle sugar, salt, basil, and pepper over all; dot with remaining 2 tablespoons butter; cover.

Steam 10 minutes, or until squashes are crisp-tender. Sprinkle cheese on top.

Yield: 6 servings.

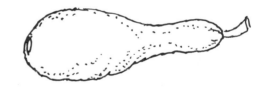

DILLED YELLOW SQUASH

  4 medium-sized yellow squashes
¼ teaspoon salt
½ cup water
  2 tablespoons butter or margarine
¼ teaspoon dillweed

Wash squashes; trim ends and quarter each lengthwise; cut into sticks about 2 inches long. Combine with salt and water in a medium skillet; heat to boiling; cover. Cook 8 minutes, or until squashes are crisp-tender; drain well; return to skillet.

Add butter; sprinkle dillweed over top. Heat, stirring gently several times, 1 to 2 minutes, or until butter melts and sticks are coated.

Yield: 6 servings.

DIXIE SQUASH

2 medium-sized acorn squashes, halved
    lengthwise
1 tablespoon butter or margarine, melted
1 teaspoon salt
⅔ cup uncooked regular rice
¼ cup thinly sliced green onions
8 slices bacon, cooked and crumbled
½ cup dairy sour cream
1 teaspoon prepared hot spicy mustard

Preheat oven to 400°.

Scoop out seeds from squash halves. Brush melted butter over hollows; season with ½ teaspoon of the salt. Place, cut sides down, in a greased shallow baking pan.

Bake 45 minutes, or until tender; turn halves right side up in pan.

While squashes bake, cook rice as label directs; remove from heat; stir in onions and bacon. Blend sour cream, mustard, and remaining ½ teaspoon salt in a cup; fold into rice mixture. Spoon into hollows in squashes.

Bake 15 minutes, or until hot.

Yield: 4 servings.

GEORGIAN SQUASH BOATS

3 medium-sized acorn squashes
4 tablespoons butter or margarine
¾ teaspoon salt
1 jar (about 5 ozs.) baby-pack applesauce
1 package (8 ozs.) bacon-flavored brown and serve
    sausages, sliced thin crosswise
2 tablespoons chopped salted peanuts

Preheat oven to 400°.

Halve squashes lengthwise; scoop out seeds. Melt 2 tablespoons of the butter and brush over hollows, then sprinkle ¼ teaspoon of the salt over top. Place halves, cut sides down, in a shallow baking pan.

Bake 45 minutes, or until tender.

Cool squashes slightly, then scoop pulp from shells into a medium bowl, being careful not to break shells; return shells to pan.

Add remaining 2 tablespoons butter, ½ teaspoon salt, and applesauce to squash; beat until light and fluffy; fold in sausages. Pile back into shells; sprinkle peanuts over top.

Bake 25 minutes longer, or until sausages are hot.

Yield: 6 servings.

SESAME TOMATO CUPS

8 medium-sized firm ripe tomatoes
2 lbs. fresh asparagus
    Salt
1 teaspoon sesame seeds
¼ cup butter or margarine
1 tablespoon lemon juice

Cut a thin slice from the top of each tomato; scoop out insides with a teaspoon to make shells about ⅛ inch thick. (Save pulp to add to soup.) Turn shells upside down on paper toweling to drain.

Break tough woody ends from asparagus; wash spears. Remove scales with a small sharp knife; wash stalks again; cut into 1-inch lengths.

Place asparagus in a medium saucepan with tips on top; pour in boiling water to a depth of 1 inch; salt lightly; cover. Cook 10 minutes, or until asparagus is crisp-tender; drain carefully.

Heat sesame seeds in a small skillet, shaking pan constantly, until toasted. Add butter to skillet; heat until melted; remove from heat. Stir in lemon juice.

Preheat oven to 350°.

Place tomato cups in a large shallow pan; spoon asparagus into tomatoes; drizzle butter mixture over top.

Bake 10 minutes, or just until tomatoes are hot.

Yield: 8 servings.

BROILED TOMATOES SCANDIA

1 cup (8-oz. carton) dairy sour cream
¾ teaspoon dried basil, crushed
¾ teaspoon salt
3 large firm ripe tomatoes, halved crosswise
2 tablespoons bottled Italian rosé salad dressing
1 teaspoon sugar
Dash of pepper

Blend sour cream, basil, and ¼ teaspoon of the salt in a small bowl; chill several hours to blend flavors.

Preheat broiler.

Place tomato halves in a large shallow baking pan; brush salad dressing over cut surfaces. Mix sugar, remaining ½ teaspoon salt, and pepper in a cup; sprinkle over tomatoes.

Broil, 4 to 6 inches from heat, 5 minutes, or until bubbly. Place on serving plates or on a large platter; spoon cold sour-cream sauce over each.

Yield: 6 servings.

BAKED HASH-STUFFED TOMATOES

4 large firm ripe tomatoes
1 can (15½ ozs.) corned-beef hash
1 egg
1 cup corn-bread stuffing mix
2 teaspoons prepared hot spicy mustard
½ teaspoon dried oregano, crushed
¼ cup shredded mozzarella cheese

Preheat oven to 350°.

Cut a thin slice from the top of each tomato; scoop out insides into a bowl, then drain pulp and chop. Turn tomato shells upside down on paper toweling to drain.

Combine corned-beef hash, egg, stuffing mix, mustard, oregano, and chopped tomato pulp in a medium bowl; mix well. Pile into tomato shells. Place tomatoes in a shallow baking pan; sprinkle cheese over stuffing. (If you have any stuffing leftover, bake in a small casserole, uncovered, alongside tomatoes.)

Bake tomatoes 20 minutes, or until stuffing is hot and cheese melts and browns lightly.

Yield: 4 servings.

TOMATO-MACARONI CUPS

4 large firm ripe tomatoes
1 package (7¼ ozs.) macaroni and cheese dinner
2 tablespoons milk
1 can (2¼ ozs.) deviled ham
1½ teaspoons prepared hot spicy mustard
¼ cup fresh bread crumbs
1 tablespoon butter or margarine, melted

Cut a thin slice from the top of each tomato; scoop out insides with a teaspoon to make shells about ⅛ inch thick. (Set pulp aside to add to soup.) Turn shells upside down on paper toweling to drain.

Preheat oven to 400°.

Cook macaroni in salted water as label directs; drain; return to pan. Stir in milk, grated cheese from dinner package, deviled ham, and mustard until well blended; spoon into tomato cups. Place in a baking dish.

Toss bread crumbs with melted butter; sprinkle over stuffing in tomatoes.

Bake 15 minutes, or until tomatoes are hot and topping is toasted.

Yield: 4 servings.

CHERRY TOMATOES ITALIENNE

2 tablespoons butter or margarine
1 pint cherry tomatoes, stemmed
½ teaspoon sugar
¼ teaspoon Italian seasoning
¼ teaspoon salt

Melt butter in a medium skillet; add tomatoes. Sprinkle sugar, Italian seasoning, and salt over top. Toss lightly to mix.

Sauté slowly, turning several times, 2 to 3 minutes, or just until skins start to pop. Spoon into a serving bowl.

Yield: 4 servings.

STUFFED PEPPERS

6 large green peppers
1 cup uncooked tiny macaroni tubes or rings
½ cup chopped celery
2 tablespoons salad oil
1 can (15¼ ozs.) barbecue sauce with beef
¾ teaspoon salt
½ teaspoon dried thyme, crushed
1 package (8 ozs.) sliced provolone cheese, shredded

Cut a thin slice from the top of each pepper; scoop out insides. Chop tops to make ⅓ cup.

Stand peppers in a large kettle; pour in boiling water to cover; heat to boiling; cover. Cook 5 minutes, or until peppers are tender but still firm enough to hold their shapes; drain well.

Cook macaroni as label directs; drain well.

Preheat oven to 350°.

Sauté chopped pepper and celery in salad oil in a large saucepan until soft; stir in barbecue sauce, salt, thyme, macaroni, and three fourths of the cheese. Pile into pepper shells; sprinkle remaining cheese over filling. Stand peppers in a shallow baking dish.

Bake 30 minutes, or until filling is hot and cheese melts and browns lightly.

Yield: 6 servings.

CALICO PEPPER CUPS

⅔ cup uncooked regular rice
3 large red peppers
3 large green peppers
½ lb. chicken livers
4 slices bacon, cut in ½-inch pieces
1 large onion, chopped (1 cup)
1 cup diced celery
6 small mushrooms, trimmed and sliced
1 clove garlic, minced
1 teaspoon salt
⅛ teaspoon pepper
½ cup fresh bread crumbs (1 slice)
1 tablespoon melted butter or margarine
1 tablespoon chopped parsley

Cook rice as label directs; keep hot.

Cut a thin slice from the top of each pepper; scoop out insides. Cook peppers, covered, in boiling water in a kettle 5 minutes, or until tender but still firm enough to hold their shapes. Lift from water with a slotted spoon and turn upside down on paper toweling to drain; stand in a shallow baking dish.

Dice chicken livers, trimming off fat or veiny parts.

Preheat oven to 350°.

Sauté bacon until almost crisp in a large skillet. Stir in chicken livers, onion, celery, mushrooms, and garlic; sauté slowly, stirring several times, until vegetables are soft. Stir in rice, salt, and pepper. Spoon into pepper cups.

Mix bread crumbs, melted butter, and parsley until blended in a small bowl; sprinkle over filling in peppers.

Bake 20 minutes, or until filling is hot and topping is toasted.

Yield: 6 servings.

PIMIENTO POTATO PUFF

5 large potatoes
1 package (8 ozs.) cream cheese, softened
2 eggs
1 small onion, chopped (¼ cup)
¼ cup chopped pimientos
1 teaspoon salt
⅛ teaspoon pepper
2 tablespoons grated Romano cheese

Pare potatoes; cut in small chunks. Cook, covered, in boiling salted water in a large saucepan 15 minutes, or until tender; drain well.

Preheat oven to 325°.

Place potatoes in a large bowl; mash well. (There should be about 4 cups.) Beat in cream cheese, eggs, onion, pimientos, salt, and pepper; spoon into a 1¾-quart baking dish. Sprinkle cheese over top.

Bake 1 hour, or until puffed and golden. Serve at once.

Yield: 8 servings.

BUTTER-BROILED POTATOES

8 large oblong potatoes
¼ cup butter or margarine
2 tablespoons finely cut chives

Pare potatoes. Cook whole, covered, in boiling salted water 30 minutes, or until tender; drain well. Cool just until easy to handle.

Cut each potato diagonally in 4 or 5 slices almost to bottom. Place in a single layer in a large shallow baking pan.

Preheat broiler.

Melt butter in a small saucepan; brush over potatoes.

Broil, 6 inches from heat, 10 minutes, or until golden. Place on a heated serving platter; sprinkle chives over potatoes.

Yield: 8 servings.

PARSLEY-BUTTER POTATO BALLS

4 tablespoons butter or margarine
1 bag (24 ozs.) frozen small white potatoes
½ teaspoon salt
¼ teaspoon pepper
2 teaspoons dried parsley flakes

Preheat oven to 325°.

Melt butter in a large shallow baking pan. Place potatoes in pan and toss around with a fork until evenly coated with butter; sprinkle salt and pepper over top.

Bake 30 minutes; turn potatoes with a fork; sprinkle parsley over top.

Bake 30 minutes longer, or until potatoes are tender and golden.

Yield: 6 servings.

SAUSAGE-STUFFED POTATOES

4 baking potatoes
1 small onion, chopped (¼ cup)
3 tablespoons salad oil
1 can (5 ozs.) Vienna sausages, drained and sliced
1 teaspoon sugar
1 teaspoon salt
2 tablespoons vinegar
2 tablespoons chopped parsley

Preheat oven to 425°.

Scrub potatoes; place in a shallow pan.

Bake 1 hour, or until tender. Remove from oven and cool until easy to handle. Cut a thin slice from the top of each potato; scoop out insides in large chunks; dice, if needed. Set shells aside.

Sauté onion in salad oil in a skillet until soft; stir in sausages; brown lightly.

Stir in sugar, salt, vinegar, and diced potatoes; heat, stirring gently several times, 5 minutes, or until potatoes are hot and dressing is absorbed. Pile back into shells; sprinkle parsley over tops.

Yield: 4 servings.

GOURMET BAKED POTATOES

4 baking potatoes
2 packages (3 ozs. each) cream cheese
4 teaspoons parsley flakes
¼ teaspoon dried marjoram, crushed
¼ teaspoon dried thyme, crushed
¼ teaspoon dried basil, crushed
¼ teaspoon garlic salt
¼ cup milk

Preheat oven to 425°.

Scrub potatoes; place in a shallow pan.

Bake 1 hour, or until tender.

While potatoes bake, mix cream cheese with parsley, marjoram, thyme, basil, garlic salt, and milk until smooth in a small bowl.

Cut a crisscross in the top of each potato; squeeze ends lightly until centers pop up; spoon cheese mixture onto each.

Yield: 4 servings.

SCALLOPED POTATOES AND LEEKS

6 medium potatoes
4 leeks
3 tablespoons butter or margarine
3 tablespoons all-purpose flour
1 teaspoon salt
⅛ teaspoon pepper
  Few drops red-pepper seasoning
2 cups milk
1 cup shredded Swiss cheese (4 ozs.)
½ cup wheat flakes cereal, coarsely crushed

Pare potatoes and slice. (There should be about 6 cups.) Trim leeks; wash well; cut in ½-inch lengths.

Cook potatoes and leeks, covered, in boiling salted water in a large saucepan 8 minutes, or until barely tender; drain. Place in a 2-quart shallow baking dish.

Preheat oven to 350°.

Melt butter in a medium saucepan; stir in flour, salt, pepper, and red-pepper seasoning. Cook, stirring constantly, until bubbly. Stir in milk; continue cooking and stirring until sauce thickens and boils 1 minute; stir in ½ cup of the cheese until melted. Pour over vegetables in dish.

Mix cereal and remaining ½ cup cheese in a small bowl; sprinkle diagonally in ribbons over vegetables.

Bake 30 minutes, or until bubbly and golden.

Yield: 6 servings.

BLUSHING POTATO BALLS

3 tablespoons butter or margarine
2 cans (16 ozs. each) small whole white potatoes, drained
1¼ teaspoons paprika
¾ teaspoon salt

Preheat oven to 350°.

Melt butter in a shallow baking pan; add potatoes and stir to coat all over with butter. Sprinkle paprika and salt over top.

Bake, stirring several times, 30 minutes, or until potatoes are heated through. Spoon into a serving bowl.

Yield: 6 servings.

POTATO STICKS MILANESE

3 tablespoons salad oil
¼ teaspoon liquid red-pepper seasoning
3 cups loose-pack frozen French fried potatoes
½ teaspoon Italian seasoning
½ teaspoon salt

Preheat oven to 450°.

Mix salad oil and red-pepper seasoning in a large shallow baking pan. Add potatoes to pan, then turn to coat all over with oil mixture; spread out in a single layer. Sprinkle Italian seasoning and salt over top.

Bake 20 minutes, or until tender, crisp, and golden.

Yield: 4 servings.

POTATO-BEEF BOATS

6 tablespoons butter or margarine
4 tablespoons all-purpose flour
1 envelope instant chicken broth
2½ cups milk
¼ cup mayonnaise or salad dressing
1 jar (5 ozs.) dried beef, shredded
4 hot baked potatoes

Melt 4 tablespoons of the butter in a medium saucepan; stir in flour and chicken broth. Cook, stirring constantly, until bubbly. Stir in 2 cups of the milk; continue cooking and stirring until sauce thickens and boils 1 minute; remove from heat. Stir in mayonnaise and dried beef.

Cut each potato in half lengthwise; scoop out centers into a large bowl, being careful not to break shells; place each two shells on a serving plate.

Add remaining 2 tablespoons butter and ½ cup milk to potatoes; beat until light and fluffy.

Spoon potatoes into one shell on each plate and dried-beef mixture into the other. Serve hot.

Yield: 4 servings.

POTATOES AND ONIONS MIMOSA

18 small new potatoes
3 bunches green onions
1 cup (8-oz. carton) large-curd creamed cottage
    cheese
¼ cup butter or margarine
¼ cup all-purpose flour
1½ teaspoons salt
    Dash of pepper
2 cups milk
1 hard-cooked egg yolk

Pare potatoes. Trim green onions and cut into 1-inch lengths.

Cook potatoes, covered, in boiling salted water in a large saucepan 15 minutes, or until tender; drain. Keep warm. Cook green onions, covered, in boiling salted water in a medium saucepan 5 minutes, or until crisp-tender; drain.

Press cottage cheese through a sieve.

Melt butter in a medium saucepan; stir in flour, salt, and pepper; cook, stirring constantly, until bubbly. Stir in milk; continue cooking and stirring until mixture thickens and boils 1 minute. Stir in cottage cheese.

Mound potatoes in the center of a large deep serving platter; spoon green onions around edge. Pour sauce over potatoes. Press egg yolk through a sieve over sauce.

Yield: 6 to 8 servings.

TANGY POTATO SCALLOP

4 medium potatoes
4 tablespoons butter or margarine
⅓ cup plain wheat germ
2 tablespoons all-purpose flour
2 tablespoons bacon-flavored seasoning
½ teaspoon salt
¼ teaspoon pepper
1½ cups milk
1 package (8 ozs.) Neufchatel cheese

Scrub potatoes. Cook, covered, in boiling salted water in a large saucepan 20 minutes, or until tender; drain. Cool until easy to handle, then peel and cut into 1-inch cubes. (There should be 4 cups.)

Preheat oven to 350°.

Melt butter in a medium saucepan; measure out 2 tablespoonfuls and toss with wheat germ in a small bowl; set aside. Stir flour, bacon seasoning, salt, and pepper into rest of butter in saucepan; cook, stirring constantly, until bubbly. Stir in milk; continue cooking and stirring until mixture thickens and boils 1 minute. Cut up cheese and stir in until melted.

Layer half of the potatoes into a 1½-quart baking dish; top with half of the sauce; repeat layers. Sprinkle wheat-germ mixture over top.

Bake 45 minutes, or until sauce bubbles up and topping is toasted.

Yield: 4 to 6 servings.

EASY SCALLOPED POTATOES

1 bag (24 ozs.) frozen plain or onion-seasoned
    hashed brown potatoes
3 tablespoons all-purpose flour
1 teaspoon salt
⅛ teaspoon pepper
2 tablespoons butter or margarine
1 package (8 ozs.) process American cheese,
    shredded
1 tall can evaporated milk

Preheat oven to 350°.

Layer one third of the potatoes into a 1¾-quart baking dish.

Mix flour, salt, and pepper in a cup; sprinkle one third over potato layer; dot with one third of the butter and top with one third of the cheese. Repeat layering two more times, making sure cheese on top covers potatoes. Pour evaporated milk down one side into dish. (Mixture will appear to overflow dish, but will sink down as it cooks.)

Bake 1½ hours, or until potatoes are tender.
Yield: 6 servings.

DOUBLE POTATO BOWL

6 medium-sized white potatoes
4 large yams
½ cup butter or margarine
½ cup milk
1 teaspoon salt
⅓ cup firmly packed light brown sugar
1 tablespoon grated orange rind
¼ cup orange juice
2 tablespoons toasted slivered almonds

Pare white potatoes and yams; quarter. Cook, covered, in boiling salted water in separate large saucepans 20 minutes, or until tender; drain.

Heat 3 tablespoons of the butter and milk in a small saucepan until butter melts.

Mash white potatoes; beat in hot milk mixture and ½ teaspoon of the salt until fluffy-light; keep hot.

Mash yams; beat in 3 tablespoons of butter, brown sugar, orange rind and juice, and ½ teaspoon salt; keep hot.

Sauté almonds in remaining 2 tablespoons butter until golden in a small skillet.

Spoon white potatoes into half of a large serving bowl and yams in the other half. Spoon almond mixture in a row between sections.

Yield: 8 servings.

LEMON POTATOES

1½ packages (24 ozs. each) frozen small whole
      potatoes
⅓ cup butter or margarine
4 teaspoons lemon juice
1½ teaspoons shredded lemon rind

Cook potatoes in boiling salted water in a large saucepan as label directs; drain; return to pan.

Add butter and lemon juice to pan; heat slowly, tossing potatoes lightly, until butter melts and potatoes are coated. Just before serving, sprinkle lemon rind over top.

Yield: 8 to 10 servings.

OVEN POTATO SALAD

4 medium potatoes
½ cup sliced pimiento-stuffed olives
3 tablespoons butter or margarine
2 tablespoons all-purpose flour
1 teaspoon onion powder
½ teaspoon salt
1 cup milk
⅔ cup mayonnaise or salad dressing
⅓ cup regular wheat germ

Scrub potatoes. Cook, covered, in boiling salted water in a medium saucepan 25 minutes, or until tender; drain. Cool until easy to handle, then peel and dice. Combine with olives in a medium bowl.

Preheat oven to 350°.

Melt 2 tablespoons of the butter in a small saucepan; blend in flour, onion powder, and salt. Cook, stirring constantly, until bubbly. Stir in milk; continue cooking and stirring until sauce thickens and boils 1 minute; remove from heat. Stir in mayonnaise. Pour over potato mixture; toss lightly to mix. Spoon into a 1½-quart shallow baking dish.

Melt remaining 1 tablespoon butter in a small skillet; toss with wheat germ; sprinkle over potato mixture.

Bake 20 minutes, or just until hot and topping is toasted.

Yield: 6 servings.

HOT POTATO-CELERY SALAD

4 hot baked potatoes
2 hard-cooked eggs, chopped
¼ cup chopped celery
2 tablespoons chopped green onion
3 tablespoons pepperoni-flavored
  vegetable-protein bits
1 teaspoon salt
⅛ teaspoon pepper
⅓ cup mayonnaise or salad dressing

Cut a thin slice from the top of each potato; cut out centers in bite-sized pieces, being careful not to break shells; place each shell on a serving plate.

Combine potato chunks with eggs, celery, green onion, and protein bits in a large bowl. Sprinkle salt and pepper over top, then fold in mayonnaise. Pile back into potato shells. Serve warm.

Yield: 4 servings.

CINNAMON YAMS

4 large yams
2 large tart apples
½ cup firmly packed light brown sugar
1 teaspoon ground cinnamon
½ teaspoon salt
4 tablespoons butter or margarine, melted

Pare yams; cut into ½-inch-thick slices.

Cook, covered, in boiling lightly salted water 10 minutes or until slices are tender but still firm enough to hold their shape; drain carefully. Place half in a shallow 2-quart baking dish.

Preheat oven to 325°.

Pare apples, cut in half, core, and slice thin. Layer half over yams in dish.

Mix brown sugar, cinnamon, and salt in a small bowl; sprinkle half over apple layer. Repeat with remaining potatoes, apples, and seasonings. Drizzle melted butter over top; cover.

Bake 40 minutes; uncover. Bake 10 minutes longer, or until apples are tender. Garnish with thin apple slices and watercress if you like.

Yield: 8 servings.

HOT SALAD SPINACH

1 package (10 ozs.) fresh spinach
6 slices bacon, cut in 1-inch pieces
¼ cup cider vinegar
2 teaspoons soy sauce
1 teaspoon prepared mustard
1 teaspoon sugar
½ teaspoon seasoned salt
¼ teaspoon seasoned pepper
1 cup onion-flavored snack rings

Wash spinach; remove stems and any coarse ribs. Dry spinach well; break into bite-sized pieces; place in a salad bowl.

Sauté bacon until crisp in a medium skillet; remove and drain on paper toweling. Pour off all drippings, then measure ⅓ cup and return to skillet. Stir in vinegar, soy sauce, mustard, sugar, salt, and pepper; heat to boiling. Drizzle over spinach; add bacon; toss to mix. Garnish with onion snack rings. Serve hot.

Yield: 6 to 8 servings.

SUNSHINE SUCCOTASH

4 tablespoons butter or margarine
½ cup water
1 package (10 ozs.) frozen small lima beans
1 package (10 ozs.) frozen whole-kernel corn
3 small zucchini, trimmed and cut in 1½-inch long
  sticks
3 tablespoons lemon juice

Combine butter and water in a large skillet; heat to boiling. Stir in limas; heat to boiling again; cover. Cook 5 minutes.

Stir in corn and zucchini; heat to boiling again; cover. Cook 4 to 5 minutes, or just until vegetables are crisp-tender. Stir in lemon juice.

Spoon into a serving bowl. Garnish with several thin slices of lemon if you like.

Yield: 8 servings.

SWEET POTATOES ALMONDINE

**3 large sweet potatoes, pared and cut into
    ½-inch-thick rounds**
¼ cup butter or margarine
½ cup sliced almonds

Cook sweet potatoes, covered, in boiling salted water in a skillet 8 minutes, or until almost tender; drain.

Melt butter in same skillet; place sweet potatoes in a single layer in butter; add almonds. Cook slowly, turning potatoes once, 10 minutes.

Yield: 6 servings.

BAKED YAMS

6 small yams
1 tablespoon salad oil
6 tablespoons butter or margarine

Preheat oven to 400°.

Scrub yams well; dry on paper toweling. Rub salad oil all over each; for easy handling, place in a shallow baking pan. (If you prefer skin crisp, omit salad oil.)

Bake 1 hour, or until yams are tender.

Cut a crisscross in top of each; squeeze ends until some of the potato pops through opening; top each with butter.

Yield: 6 servings.

APPLE-STUFFED YAMS

6 medium yams
4 tablespoons butter or margarine
¾ cup applesauce
3 tablespoons honey
1 teaspoon ground cinnamon

Preheat oven to 400°.

Scrub yams; place in a shallow baking pan.

Bake 1 hour, or until tender. Remove from oven and cool until easy to handle, then cut a thin slice from top of each; scoop out insides into a medium bowl, being careful not to break shells; return shells to baking pan.

Mash yams; beat in butter until melted, applesauce, honey, and cinnamon. Pile back into shells. Return to oven; heat just until hot. Garnish each with small wedges of unpared apple if you like.

Yield: 6 servings.

ISLAND YAMS

3 large yams or sweet potatoes
¼ cup butter or margarine
1 can (about 9 ozs.) crushed pineapple
1 teaspoon grated orange rind
2 tablespoons orange juice
¾ teaspoon salt
2 tablespoons brown sugar
3 tablespoons flaked coconut

Scrub potatoes. Cook, covered, in boiling water in a large saucepan 30 minutes, or until tender; drain. Cool just until easy to handle.

Preheat oven to 350°.

Peel potatoes. Mash with a fork in a large bowl; beat in butter until melted, then add pineapple and syrup, orange rind and juice, and salt. Spoon into a 1½-quart baking dish; sprinkle brown sugar over top; cover.

Bake 30 minutes; sprinkle coconut over top. Bake 15 minutes longer, or until coconut is lightly toasted.

Yield: 6 servings.

ZUCCHINI AND TOMATOES POLONAISE

6 medium zucchini, trimmed and sliced ¼-inch thick
6 tablespoons butter or margarine
½ teaspoon salt
¼ teaspoon pepper
1 tablespoon lemon juice
3 small tomatoes, cut in wedges
1 cup fresh bread crumbs (2 slices)
2 teaspoons grated lemon rind

Sauté zucchini in 4 tablespoons of the butter in a large skillet 3 minutes; cover. Cook, stirring several times, 10 minutes, or just until zucchini is crisp-tender; stir in salt, pepper, lemon juice, and tomato wedges. Heat just until tomatoes are hot.

While zucchini cooks, melt remaining 2 tablespoons butter in a small skillet; stir in bread crumbs. Heat slowly, stirring several times, until crumbs are toasted; stir in lemon rind.

Spoon zucchini mixture into a serving bowl; sprinkle lemon crumbs on top.

Yield: 6 servings.

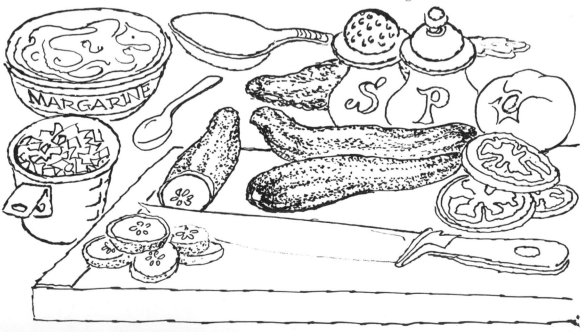

SAUCES

BORROW A SECRET FROM THE FRENCH—as well as great chefs everywhere—and use sauces as a tantalizing change of pace with meats, vegetables, and desserts.
No mystery goes into their making. All you need are a little imagination and a few on-hand ingredients to create literally dozens of different flavor combinations to vary favorite foods.

Butter sauces are probably the simplest and most popular—and adaptable, too. By itself, melted butter dresses any vegetable perfectly. With the addition of herbs, spices, seeds, onions, garlic, wine, or cheese, it turns into a distinctive topper to complement many meats and seafoods as well.

Another familiar and economical seasoner that lends itself to almost endless variations is white—or cream—sauce. Follow either of two basic recipes included here. If you're using the sauce for cooked vegetables, a handy rule to remember: 1 cup of sauce for each 2 cups vegetables.

Zesty sour cream—so often spooned right from the carton over steaming baked potatoes— ranks high as another starting point for sauces. So do mayonnaise or salad dressing, bottled dressings and mixes in foil envelopes, and convenient, versatile canned soups.

In cooking with sour cream and mayonnaise, handle them carefully so they'll stay creamy and smooth. Specifically, this means to keep the heat low and avoid boiling.

In using canned soups, pick a variety that enhances—not overpowers—the flavor of the food it goes with. Depending on what you add to the soup as it comes from the can, you can figure on 1½ to 2 cups sauce—a guide worth remembering when you're cooking for a crowd.

Following all kinds of recipes that call for each of these basic ingredients are a number of suggestions for dessert go-withs to top everything from puddings, ice cream, fruit, and custards to baked and molded treats. All will help you develop a few of your own specialties of the house.

MAIN DISH SAUCES

ORANGE-RAISIN SAUCE

1 tablespoon cornstarch
3 tablespoons light brown sugar
  Dash of salt
½ teaspoon grated orange rind
1 cup orange juice
¼ cup water
½ cup raisins

Mix cornstarch, sugar, salt, and orange rind in a small saucepan; stir in orange juice and water.

Cook slowly, stirring constantly, until sauce thickens and boils 1 minute. Stir in raisins; heat to boiling again. Serve hot with baked ham or cooked tongue.

Yield: About 1⅓ cups.

GREEN-ONION BUTTER

4 tablespoons butter or margarine
2 teaspoons chopped green-onion tops
1 teaspoon lemon juice

Mix butter with onions and lemon juice in a small bowl until blended. Spread over hot broiled steaks, hamburgers, or chicken.

Yield: ¼ cup.

MUSTARD BUTTER

4 tablespoons butter or margarine
¼ teaspoon dry mustard
¼ teaspoon salt

Melt butter in a small skillet; stir in mustard and salt. Heat 1 minute longer. Serve over broiled steak or hamburger patties.

Yield: ¼ cup.

SWISS CHEESE SAUCE

4 tablespoons butter or margarine
4 tablespoons all-purpose flour
½ teaspoon salt
  Dash of pepper
2 cups milk
1 package (8 ozs.) Swiss cheese, cut into small pieces
  Few drops red-pepper seasoning

Melt butter in a medium saucepan; stir in flour, salt, and pepper; cook, stirring constantly, until bubbly.

Stir in milk; continue cooking and stirring until sauce thickens and boils 1 minute.

Stir in cheese until melted, then add red-pepper seasoning. Spoon over a fish or vegetable soufflé.

Yield: About 3 cups.

CUCUMBER SAUCE

½ cup chopped pared cucumber
¼ cup mayonnaise or salad dressing
2 teaspoons sugar
½ teaspoon salt
1 cup (8-oz. carton) dairy sour cream
2 tablespoons lemon juice

Blend all ingredients in a small bowl. Chill until serving time. Serve over salmon or tuna loaf.

Yield: About 2 cups.

BEARNAISE SAUCE

½ cup dry white wine
 1 tablespoon tarragon vinegar
 1 teaspoon chopped shallots
   Dash of pepper
 2 sprigs parsley
½ teaspoon dried tarragon, crushed
 2 egg yolks
½ cup butter or margarine, melted

Combine wine, vinegar, shallots, pepper, parsley, and tarragon in a small saucepan; heat to boiling. Simmer 5 minutes, or until liquid measures ⅓ cup; strain into a cup.

Beat egg yolks in the top of a double boiler; stir in one third of the melted butter. Place top over simmering water.

Beat in wine mixture, alternately with remaining melted butter, until mixture is fluffy-thick; remove from heat. Serve hot with broiled steak, roast beef, or broiled or poached fish.

Yield: 1 cup.

HORSERADISH SAUCE

 2 tablespoons butter or margarine
¼ cup all-purpose flour
1½ cups milk
⅓ cup prepared horseradish
½ teaspoon salt
 1 egg yolk
 2 tablespoons chopped parsley

Melt butter in a small saucepan; stir in flour. Cook, stirring constantly, until bubbly. Stir in milk; continue cooking and stirring until mixture thickens and boils 1 minute.

Stir in horseradish and salt. Heat slowly just to boiling; remove from heat.

Beat egg yolk in a small bowl; slowly stir in about half of the hot sauce, then stir back into remaining sauce in pan. Heat slowly, stirring constantly, 1 minute; stir in parsley. Serve over plain boiled beef or broiled hamburger patties.

Yield: 2 cups.

BARBECUE SAUCE SEVILLE

 2 tablespoons sugar
 2 tablespoons cornstarch
½ teaspoon ground allspice
¼ teaspoon ground ginger
 1 cup orange juice
 2 tablespoons lemon juice
¼ cup butter or margarine

Mix sugar, cornstarch, and spices in a small saucepan; stir in orange and lemon juices. Cook slowly, stirring constantly, until mixture thickens and boils 1 minute; stir in butter until melted. Use as a brush-on sauce for broiled chicken or spareribs.

Yield: 1¼ cups.

NIPPY APRICOT SAUCE

 1 cup apricot preserves
⅓ cup prepared mustard
 4 tablespoons prepared horseradish

Combine all ingredients in a small saucepan; heat slowly, stirring constantly, just until hot. Serve hot with roast chicken or baked ham.

Yield: About 1½ cups.

DILL SAUCE

 1 tablespoon butter or margarine
 1 tablespoon all-purpose flour
¼ teaspoon salt
½ cup water
½ cup dairy sour cream
½ teaspoon dillweed

Melt butter in a small saucepan; stir in flour and salt. Cook, stirring constantly, until bubbly. Stir in water; continue cooking and stirring until sauce thickens and boils 1 minute.

Slowly stir hot mixture into sour cream in a small bowl; stir back into pan; stir in dillweed. Heat very slowly just until hot. Serve over plain cooked beef or as a dip for beef, veal, or pork balls.

Yield: About 1 cup.

CURRY SAUCE

½ cup mayonnaise or salad dressing
2 tablespoons catsup
1 teaspoon grated orange rind
1 tablespoon orange juice
¼ teaspoon curry powder

Blend all ingredients in a small bowl. Serve over broiled or poached fish.
Yield: ⅔ cup.

QUICK MUSTARD CREAM

1 cup (8-oz. carton) dairy sour cream
¼ cup prepared horseradish mustard

Combine ingredients in a small saucepan; heat very slowly, stirring constantly, just until warm. Serve with baked ham, plain boiled beef, or pot roast.
Yield: 1¼ cups.

MUSHROOM SAUCE MORNAY

1 can (10¾ ozs.) condensed cream of mushroom
    soup
⅓ cup milk
¾ cup shredded process Old English cheese

Combine soup and milk in a small saucepan; stir in cheese. Heat slowly, stirring constantly, until cheese melts and sauce is hot and smooth. Serve over open-face chicken or ham sandwiches, broiled hamburgers, or broiled fish.
Yield: About 2 cups.

CREOLE SAUCE

¼ cup chopped green pepper
1 small onion, chopped (¼ cup)
1 clove garlic, minced
2 tablespoons salad oil
1 can (10¾ ozs.) condensed tomato soup
⅓ cup water

Sauté green pepper, onion, and garlic in salad oil in a medium saucepan until soft; stir

in soup and water. Heat slowly, stirring several times, to boiling. Spoon over broiled hamburger patties or broiled or poached fish fillets.
Yield: 1⅔ cups.

SPICED PLUM SAUCE

1 cup plum preserves
2 teaspoons minced onion
1 tablespoon vinegar
¼ teaspoon ground ginger
¼ teaspoon ground cinnamon
⅛ teaspoon ground cloves

Combine all ingredients in a small saucepan; heat slowly, stirring constantly, to boiling; pour into a small bowl. Chill. Serve cold with roast pork or duckling.
Yield: 1 cup.

CAPER CREAM

½ cup mayonnaise or salad dressing
½ cup light cream
2 tablespoons drained capers
½ teaspoon Worcestershire sauce

Combine all ingredients in a small saucepan; heat slowly, stirring constantly, just until warm. Spoon over broiled or poached fish or fish loaves.
Yield: 1 cup.

SHRIMP SAUCE

1 can (10¾ ozs.) condensed cream of shrimp soup
¼ cup milk
1 tablespoon dry sherry
2 tablespoons chopped parsley

Combine soup, milk, and sherry in a small saucepan; heat slowly, stirring several times, until sauce is hot and smooth. Stir in parsley. Serve over broiled or poached fish, crab soufflé, or tuna loaf.
Yield: About 1½ cups.

GREEN-BEAN SAUCE

1 package (10 ozs.) frozen cut green beans
2 tablespoons butter or margarine
2 tablespoons all-purpose flour
¼ teaspoon salt
 Dash of pepper
1 cup milk

Cook green beans as label directs; drain.

Melt butter in a small saucepan; stir in flour, salt, and pepper; cook, stirring constantly, until bubbly.

Stir in milk; continue cooking and stirring until sauce thickens and boils 1 minute. Stir in beans; heat slowly until bubbly. Serve over a salmon, tuna, or meat loaf.

Yield: 2 cups.

TARTARE SAUCE

⅔ cup mayonnaise or salad dressing
¼ cup chopped sweet pickles
1 teaspoon finely minced onion
2 teaspoons chopped parsley

Combine all ingredients in a small bowl; chill. Serve with any kind of fish or shellfish.

Yield: About 1 cup.

LOUIS COCKTAIL SAUCE

½ cup mayonnaise or salad dressing
½ cup dairy sour cream
¼ cup bottled chili sauce
1 tablespoon lemon juice
¼ teaspoon sugar
1 teaspoon finely minced onion
½ teaspoon salt

Combine all ingredients in a small bowl; stir well to mix. Chill several hours to blend flavors. Serve over seafood cocktails.

Yield: 1⅓ cups.

GARLIC BUTTER

4 tablespoons butter or margarine
1 clove garlic, mashed
 Dash of salt

Melt butter in a small skillet. Stir in garlic and salt; heat 1 minute longer. Spoon over broiled steak or hamburgers.

Yield: ¼ cup.

CHEDDAR CHEESE SAUCE

Basic White Sauce (recipe on page 317)
1 cup shredded sharp Cheddar cheese (4 ozs.)
 Few drops red-pepper seasoning

Make Basic White Sauce; stir in cheese and red-pepper seasoning; heat slowly, stirring constantly, until cheese melts and sauce is smooth. Spoon over broiled hamburger patties, broiled, baked, or pan-fried fish, or just about any fish or vegetable soufflé.

Yield: 1½ cups.

RUBY COCKTAIL SAUCE

1 cup catsup
2 tablespoons prepared horseradish
1 tablespoon lemon juice
 Dash of salt
 Dash of pepper

Combine all ingredients in a small bowl; stir to mix; chill. Serve over shrimp or mixed seafood cocktails.

Yield: About 1 cup.

LEMON BUTTER

4 tablespoons butter or margarine
1 tablespoon lemon juice
¼ teaspoon salt
2 teaspoons chopped parsley

Melt butter in a small skillet; stir in lemon juice and salt; heat 1 minute longer. Stir in parsley. Spoon over broiled or pan-fried fish.

Yield: ⅓ cup.

VEGETABLE SAUCES

BASIC WHITE SAUCE

2 tablespoons butter or margarine
2 tablespoons all-purpose flour
½ teaspoon salt
1 cup milk

Melt butter in a small saucepan; stir in flour and salt; cook, stirring constantly, until mixture is bubbly.

Stir in milk; continue cooking and stirring until sauce thickens and boils 1 minute.

Yield: 1 cup.

To make thin white sauce: Follow recipe above, using 1 tablespoon each butter and flour.

To make thick white sauce: Follow recipe above, using 3 tablespoons each butter and flour.

WHITE SAUCE MIX

2¾ cups instant nonfat dry milk
½ cup cornstarch
1 teaspoon salt

Combine dry milk, cornstarch, and salt in a medium bowl; stir well to mix. Store in a tightly covered jar at room temperature. Stir again just before each use.

To make thin white sauce: Melt 2 tablespoons butter or margarine in a small saucepan; remove from heat. Stir in ⅓ cup White Sauce Mix and 1 cup cold water. Heat slowly, stirring constantly, to boiling; cook 1 minute. *Yield:* About 1 cup.

To make thick white sauce: Follow method for thin sauce, using 2 tablespoons butter or margarine, ⅔ cup White Sauce Mix, and 1 cup cold water. *Yield:* About 1 cup.

CHIVE CREAM

Basic White Sauce (recipe on page 317)
¼ cup mayonnaise or salad dressing
1 tablespoon freeze-dried chives

Make Basic White Sauce; stir in mayonnaise and chives; heat very slowly 1 minute longer. Spoon over cooked whole-kernel corn, carrots, or potatoes.
Yield: 1¼ cups.

FRENCH ALMOND SAUCE

Basic White Sauce (recipe on page 317)
1 envelope instant chicken broth
¼ cup chopped toasted slivered almonds

Make Basic White Sauce, omitting salt. Stir in chicken broth and almonds; heat 1 minute longer. Spoon over cooked green beans, broccoli, potatoes, cauliflower, peas, limas, asparagus, or carrots.
Yield: 1¼ cups.

PINK GLOW SAUCE

Basic White Sauce (recipe on page 317)
3 tablespoons catsup
2 teaspoons prepared horseradish

Make Basic White Sauce; stir in catsup and horseradish; heat 1 minute longer. Spoon over cooked cauliflower or green beans.
Yield: 1¼ cups.

HOLLANDAISE SAUCE

¼ cup butter or margarine
2 tablespoons water
2 egg yolks
1 tablespoon lemon juice
Dash of salt
Dash of pepper

Melt butter in a small heavy saucepan; stir in water; remove from heat.

Beat in egg yolks all at once with a rotary or electric beater; continue beating 2 to 3 minutes, or until mixture doubles in volume. Stir in lemon juice, salt, and pepper. Return saucepan to *very* low heat.

Cook, stirring constantly, 3 minutes, or until thick and fluffy. Spoon over cooked asparagus or broccoli.
Yield: ½ cup.

BROWN BUTTER SAUCE

4 tablespoons butter or margarine
Dash of salt

Melt butter in a small skillet. Continue heating slowly, shaking skillet constantly, until butter foams up and turns brown. Stir in salt. Spoon over any cooked vegetable.
Yield: ¼ cup.

TOASTED PECAN BUTTER

4 tablespoons butter or margarine
¼ cup broken pecans
1 tablespoon lemon juice
¼ teaspoon salt

Melt butter in a small skillet; stir in pecans. Sauté slowly, stirring several times, until pecans are lightly toasted. Stir in lemon juice and salt; heat 1 minute longer. Spoon over cooked green beans, asparagus, cauliflower, broccoli, or carrots.
Yield: ⅓ cup.

COLD CHIVE CREAM

½ cup dairy sour cream
½ cup mayonnaise or salad dressing
2 tablespoons chopped chives
2 teaspoons lemon juice
¼ teaspoon seasoned salt

Combine all ingredients in a small bowl; chill well. Serve cold over hot boiled or baked potatoes.
Yield: About 1 cup.

PARMESAN-PARSLEY BUTTER

4 tablespoons butter or margarine
1 tablespoon grated Parmesan cheese
2 teaspoons chopped parsley

Melt butter in a small skillet. Stir in Parmesan cheese and parsley; heat 1 minute longer. Serve over cooked Italian or snap green beans.
Yield: ¼ cup.

SESAME BUTTER

1 tablespoon sesame seeds
4 tablespoons butter or margarine
1 teaspoon lemon juice

Measure sesame seeds into a small skillet; heat slowly, shaking skillet constantly, until seeds are toasted.

Add butter to skillet; heat slowly until butter melts. Stir in lemon juice; heat 1 minute longer. Spoon over cooked carrots, green beans, Chinese cabbage, or celery.
Yield: ¼ cup.

MINT BUTTER

4 tablespoons butter or margarine
½ teaspoon dried mint flakes, crushed
¼ teaspoon salt

Melt butter in a small skillet. Stir in mint flakes and salt; heat 1 minute longer. Spoon over cooked carrots and peas or either vegetable separately.
Yield: ¼ cup.

HERB BUTTER

4 tablespoons butter or margarine
¼ teaspoon paprika
¼ teaspoon dried marjoram, crushed
¼ teaspoon dried basil, crushed
½ teaspoon salt
Dash of pepper

Melt butter in a small skillet; stir in remain-ing ingredients; heat 1 minute longer. Spoon over cooked whole-kernel corn or mushrooms.
Yield: ¼ cup.

CINNAMON BUTTER

4 tablespoons butter or margarine
½ teaspoon ground cinnamon
½ teaspoon sugar

Melt butter in a small skillet. Stir in cinnamon and sugar; heat 1 minute longer. Spoon over sweet potatoes or yams or acorn or Hubbard squash.
Yield: ¼ cup.

BLUE-CHEESE CREAM

1 cup (8-oz. carton) creamed cottage cheese
½ cup mayonnaise or salad dressing
⅓ cup crumbled blue cheese

Blend all ingredients in a small bowl; chill. Serve cold over hot baked potatoes or broiled tomato halves.
Yield: 1⅔ cups.

AU GRATIN SAUCE

1 can (10¾ ozs.) condensed cream of celery soup
1 cup shredded Swiss cheese (4 ozs.)
⅓ cup milk
Few drops red-pepper seasoning
Buttered bread crumbs

Preheat oven to 350°.
Combine soup, cheese, milk, and red-pepper seasoning in a medium saucepan. Heat slowly, stirring constantly, until cheese melts and sauce is smooth. Pour over cooked broccoli, asparagus, or green beans in a shallow baking dish. Sprinkle buttered bread crumbs on top.

Bake 15 to 20 minutes, or until topping bubbles and browns.
Yield: 1¾ cups or enough for 6 servings.

HONEY BUTTER

4 tablespoons butter or margarine
2 tablespoons honey
¼ teaspoon grated orange rind

Melt butter in a small skillet; stir in honey and orange rind. Heat 1 minute longer. Serve over cooked carrots, acorn or butternut squash, or yams or sweet potatoes.
Yield: ⅓ cup.

BROWN ONION SAUCE

1 can (10¾ ozs.) condensed cream of onion soup
⅓ cup milk
2 tablespoons soy sauce

Combine all ingredients in a medium saucepan; heat slowly, stirring constantly, until bubbly. Spoon over cooked green beans.
Yield: 1½ cups.

CARAWAY CREAM SAUCE

1 cup (8-oz. carton) dairy sour cream
1 teaspoon caraway seeds
Dash of salt
Few drops red-pepper seasoning

Combine all ingredients in a small saucepan; heat very slowly, stirring constantly, just until warm. Spoon over boiled potatoes, cooked yellow turnips, or cooked green cabbage.
Yield: 1 cup.

CREAMY DILL SAUCE

1 package (3 ozs.) cream cheese
½ cup dairy sour cream
½ teaspoon dillweed
⅛ teaspoon salt
Dash of pepper

Cream cheese until soft in a small saucepan; stir in remaining ingredients. Heat very slowly, stirring constantly, just until warm.

Spoon over broiled or baked tomato halves.
Yield: ¾ cup.

GREEN-ONION CREAM SAUCE

1 cup (8-oz. carton) dairy sour cream
¼ cup chopped green onions
1 teaspoon seasoned salt

Combine sour cream, onions, and seasoned salt in a small saucepan. Heat very slowly, stirring constantly, just until warm. Spoon over baked potatoes, or cooked lima or green beans.
Yield: About 1 cup.

PINK CLOUD CREAM SAUCE

1 cup (8-oz. carton) dairy sour cream
2 tablespoons bottled chili sauce
1 teaspoon prepared hot spicy mustard
Dash of salt
Dash of pepper

Combine all ingredients in a small saucepan. Heat very slowly, stirring constantly, just until warm. Spoon over cooked whole-kernel corn, lima beans, or boiled onions.
Yield: About 1 cup.

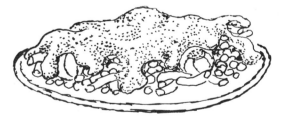

MILANO BUTTER

4 tablespoons butter or margarine
2 teaspoons dry Italian salad dressing mix

Melt butter in a small saucepan; stir in salad dressing mix; continue heating just until hot. Spoon over cooked green, wax, or lima beans.
Yield: ¼ cup.

DANISH POTATO SALAD PLATTER (p.339) ▶

BLUE-CHEESE SAUCE

½ cup mayonnaise or salad dressing
¼ cup dairy sour cream
2 tablespoons crumbled blue cheese
1 teaspoon prepared hot spicy mustard

Blend all ingredients in a small saucepan; heat very slowly; stirring constantly, until warm. Spoon over boiled potatoes, or cooked green or lima beans.
Yield: About ¾ cup.

CUCUMBER CREAM SAUCE

1 cup (8-oz. carton) dairy sour cream
2 tablespoons lemon juice
1 tablespoon sugar
½ teaspoon Worcestershire sauce
¼ teaspoon salt
½ cup chopped seeded pared cucumber

Mix all ingredients in a small saucepan. Heat very slowly, stirring constantly, just until warm. Spoon warm over cold sliced tomatoes, or hot cooked zucchini or yellow squash.
Yield: 1½ cups.

GOLDENROD SAUCE

½ cup mayonnaise or salad dressing
¼ cup milk
½ teaspoon dry mustard
1 hard-cooked egg, chopped

Blend mayonnaise, milk, and mustard in a small saucepan; heat slowly, stirring constantly, until warm. Stir in egg. Spoon over cooked broccoli or asparagus.
Yield: About 1 cup.

FRENCH BACON SAUCE

2 slices bacon, cut in ½-inch pieces
1 small onion, chopped (¼ cup)
½ cup bottled chunky blue cheese salad dressing

(Clockwise from top)
SPAGHETTI SALAD CARBONARA (p.354)
CUCUMBER-RICE SALAD (p.344)
PERUVIAN POTATO SALAD (p.340)

Sauté bacon in a small skillet until crisp; remove from skillet and drain on paper toweling. Pour off all drippings, then measure 1 tablespoon and return to skillet.

Stir onion into drippings; sauté until soft. Stir in salad dressing. Heat very slowly, stirring constantly, until hot. Spoon over cooked green or wax beans; sprinkle bacon on top.
Yield: ⅔ cup.

DAPPLED HORSERADISH SAUCE

½ cup mayonnaise or salad dressing
¼ cup milk
2 tablespoons sweet-pickle relish
½ teaspoon prepared horseradish

Blend all ingredients in a small saucepan; heat very slowly, stirring constantly, until warm. Spoon over cooked green beans or beet greens.
Yield: About 1 cup.

SOUFFLE SAUCE

2 egg whites
½ cup mayonnaise or salad dressing
2 tablespoons lemon juice

Preheat oven to 400°.

Beat egg whites in a medium bowl until they form soft peaks; fold in mayonnaise and lemon juice. Spread over cooked broccoli or cauliflower in a shallow baking dish.

Bake 12 minutes, or until sauce is puffed and golden.
Yield: 2 cups or enough for 6 servings.

NUTMEG SAUCE

½ cup mayonnaise or salad dressing
¼ cup milk
1 teaspoon lemon juice
¼ teaspoon ground nutmeg

Blend all ingredients in a small saucepan; heat very slowly, stirring constantly, until warm. Spoon over cooked asparagus or peas.
Yield: ¾ cup.

PIQUANT PIMIENTO SAUCE

1 canned pimiento, drained and chopped
½ cup bottled thin French dressing

Combine pimiento and French dressing in a small saucepan; heat very slowly just until hot. Spoon over cooked lima beans or broccoli.
Yield: About ½ cup.

DOUBLE LEMON SAUCE

½ cup bottled coleslaw dressing
1 teaspoon grated lemon rind
1 tablespoon lemon juice

Combine all ingredients in a small saucepan; heat very slowly, stirring constantly, just until hot. Spoon over cooked shredded green cabbage or cabbage wedges.
Yield: ½ cup.

ZIPPY CHEESE SAUCE

1 container (4 ozs.) whipped cream cheese
1 can (11 ozs.) condensed Cheddar cheese soup
1 tablespoon bottled steak sauce

Combine all ingredients in a medium saucepan. Heat slowly, stirring constantly, until sauce is smooth and hot. Spoon over just about any cooked vegetable.
Yield: 1⅔ cups.

MOCK HOLLANDAISE SAUCE

1 envelope (1 oz.) hollandaise sauce mix
¾ cup water
1 can (10¾ ozs.) condensed cream of chicken soup

Combine hollandaise sauce mix and water in a medium saucepan; beat until smooth. Stir in soup; heat, stirring constantly, to boiling; simmer 3 minutes. Spoon over cooked broccoli, asparagus, or cauliflower.
Yield: About 2 cups.

DESSERT SAUCES

RIO FUDGE SAUCE

3 tablespoons butter or margarine
3 tablespoons light corn syrup
2 teaspoons dry instant coffee
1 package (6 ozs.) semisweet chocolate pieces
2 tablespoons water
½ cup chopped California walnuts

Melt butter in a small saucepan; stir in corn syrup, coffee, chocolate, and water. Heat very slowly, stirring several times, just until chocolate melts. Stir in walnuts.

Serve warm over ice cream, custard, or pudding.

Yield: 1¼ cups.

ROYAL BUTTERSCOTCH SAUCE

1 cup firmly packed light brown sugar
⅓ cup light corn syrup
½ cup water
1 tablespoon butter or margarine
1 teaspoon vanilla

Combine sugar, corn syrup, and water in a small saucepan; heat slowly, stirring constantly, to boiling. Simmer, uncovered, 5 minutes; remove from heat.

Stir in butter until melted and vanilla. Serve warm or cold over ice cream, pudding, or baked desserts.

Yield: 1¼ cups.

PRALINE SUNDAE SAUCE

⅔ cup firmly packed light brown sugar
4 tablespoons butter or margarine
2 tablespoons light corn syrup
½ cup broken pecans
¼ cup water
1 teaspoon vanilla

Combine brown sugar, butter, corn syrup, and pecans in a small saucepan. Heat slowly, stirring constantly, to boiling; stir in water. Cook 5 minutes, or until mixture thickens slightly; remove from heat. Stir in vanilla; cool. Serve warm or cold over ice cream, vanilla pudding, or plain custard.

Yield: 1¼ cups.

BURNT SUGAR SAUCE

1⅓ cups granulated sugar
½ cup boiling water
1 teaspoon vanilla

Measure sugar into a medium-sized heavy skillet. Heat slowly, stirring constantly, just until sugar melts and turns golden. Very slowly stir in boiling water; heat to boiling; cook 2 to 3 minutes, or just until a little of the syrup forms a soft ball when dropped into a cup of cold water; remove from heat. Pour into a small bowl; stir in vanilla. Serve warm over ice cream or plain puddings.

Yield: About 1 cup.

DEVONSHIRE CREAM

1 package (3¾ ozs.) vanilla instant pudding mix
1½ cups milk
1 cup (8-oz. carton) dairy sour cream
¼ teaspoon lemon extract

Combine pudding mix, milk, sour cream, and lemon extract in a small deep bowl; beat as pudding mix label directs. Chill until set.

Just before serving, beat mixture until creamy and smooth. Serve over fruits, raisin-bread pudding, or warm gingerbread.

Yield: About 2¼ cups.

VANILLA CUSTARD SAUCE

2 egg yolks
2 tablespoons granulated sugar
1½ cups milk
  Dash of salt
1 teaspoon vanilla

Beat egg yolks with sugar, milk, and salt in a small saucepan. Cook slowly, stirring constantly, until mixture thickens slightly and coats a spoon. (Do not let mixture boil.) Strain into a small bowl; cool.

Stir in vanilla. Chill until serving time. Serve over pudding, fruit compotes, or plain cake squares.

Yield: About 1½ cups.

NUTMEG CUSTARD SAUCE

2 eggs
2 tablespoons granulated sugar
  Dash of salt
¼ teaspoon ground nutmeg
1 cup milk
½ teaspoon vanilla

Beat eggs slightly in a small saucepan. Stir in sugar, salt, nutmeg, and milk until blended.

Cook very slowly, stirring constantly, until mixture thickens slightly and coats a spoon. Strain into a small bowl; stir in vanilla. Serve warm over baked fruit puddings.

Yield: About 1 cup.

BUTTER-RUM SAUCE

½ cup butter or margarine
¾ cup granulated sugar
½ cup whipping cream
3 tablespoons rum

Melt butter in a small saucepan. Stir in sugar and cream. Heat very slowly, stirring several times, just to boiling; remove from heat. Stir in rum. Serve warm over baked or steamed fruit puddings.

Yield: About 1½ cups.

CINNAMON CREAM

1 egg
¼ cup granulated sugar
  Dash of salt
¼ teaspoon ground cinnamon
¼ cup butter or margarine, melted
1 cup whipping cream

Beat egg in a small bowl until fluffy-thick. Slowly beat in sugar, salt, and cinnamon, then stir in melted butter.

Beat cream in a medium bowl until stiff; fold into cinnamon mixture. Serve over baked or steamed puddings.

Yield: About 2¼ cups.

VANILLA HARD SAUCE

½ cup butter or margarine
2 cups sifted confectioners' powdered sugar
2 teaspoons light cream
1 teaspoon vanilla

Cream butter until fluffy-light in a medium bowl; beat in sugar, alternately with cream, until smooth and creamy; beat in vanilla. Serve over steamed puddings, warm gingerbread, or baked apples.

Yield: About 2 cups.

FLUFFY LEMON SAUCE

4 tablespoons butter or margarine
¾ cup sugar
2 eggs
⅓ cup water
1 teaspoon grated lemon rind
3 tablespoons lemon juice

Cream butter and sugar in a small saucepan; beat in eggs and water.

Cook very slowly, stirring constantly, until mixture thickens; remove from heat. Stir in lemon rind and juice until blended. Serve warm over steamed puddings.

Yield: About 1 cup.

LEMON SAUCE

1 egg
2¾ cups water
½ cup granulated sugar
1 package (3¼ ozs.) lemon pudding and
    pie filling mix
1 tablespoon lemon juice

Beat egg in a medium saucepan; stir in water, sugar, and pudding mix. Cook as pudding mix label directs. Remove from heat; stir in lemon juice. Cool. Serve over baked puddings or warm gingerbread.
Yield: 3½ cups.

QUICK EGGNOG SAUCE

1 tablespoon cornstarch
1 tablespoon sugar
2 cups bottled eggnog

Mix cornstarch and sugar in a small saucepan; stir in eggnog. Cook slowly, stirring constantly, until mixture thickens. Serve warm or cold over plain pudding or fruit.
Yield: 2 cups.

STRAWBERRY SAUCE

2 pints strawberries
⅓ cup sugar
¼ cup water

Wash strawberries and hull. Mash half with a fork in a medium saucepan; slice remaining half and set aside.
Stir sugar and water into mashed berries. Heat slowly, stirring until sugar dissolves, to boiling; simmer 10 minutes. Pour into a bowl; cool about an hour.
Stir in sliced berries and a few drops food coloring to tint deeper red if you like. Chill until serving time. Serve over ice cream, pudding, or a fruit soufflé.
Yield: 3 cups.

MELBA SAUCE

1 package (10 ozs.) frozen raspberries
1 tablespoon sugar
2 teaspoons cornstarch

Thaw raspberries; press berries and syrup through a sieve into a small bowl.
Mix sugar and cornstarch in a small saucepan; stir in raspberry purée. Cook, stirring constantly, until sauce thickens and boils 1 minute; remove from heat. Cool, then chill until serving time. Serve over ice cream, puddings, or a creamy fruit mold.
Yield: About 1 cup.

ORANGE FLUFF

1 package (8 ozs.) cream cheese
½ cup sifted confectioners' powdered sugar
3 tablespoons light cream
1 teaspoon grated orange rind

Beat cheese until fluffy in a small bowl; beat in sugar, alternately with cream, until mixture is smooth. Beat in orange rind. Spoon over warm baked puddings.
Yield: 1¼ cups.

BRAZILIAN VELVET

1 package (3 ozs.) cream cheese
⅓ cup dairy sour cream
1 cup sifted confectioners' powdered sugar
1 envelope premelted unsweetened chocolate
¼ teaspoon ground cinnamon

Beat cheese until fluffy in a small bowl; slowly beat in sour cream, sugar, chocolate, and cinnamon until mixture is smooth. Serve over warm baked chocolate pudding or squares of chocolate or yellow cake.
Yield: About 1 cup.

SALADS, DRESSINGS, AND RELISHES

ALL YEAR LONG, NATURE'S COLORFUL FRUIT AND PRODUCE BASKETS give you the opportunity for easy mealtime showmanship, and give your family what counts toward good health. With such a vast array of foods to choose from, it's fun to put together a combination that makes a meal or complements one—and depending on your time and mood, you can be forthright or fancy.

To put new zest in your meal-making, leaf through the next few pages for inspiration. You'll find suggestions for lush salad bowls built around bright crisp vegetables; homespun coleslaw, potato, and bean salads that go round and round the table at picnics and barbecues; sparkly make-ahead molds studded with rainbow-gay fruits; sunny citrus plates to add a ray of sunshine to winter tables; big platter arrangements of meat, cheeses, or fish to serve for buffets or summer suppers; and simple bowlfuls of mixed greens to toss with just the right dressing.

No, mealtime monotony need never be a problem when you serve salads—all pretty enough to feast an eye on, then eat with special enjoyment.

Follow these steps to a great salad

Whether your menu calls for a green salad, a fruit combination, a cool main dish, or a sparkling mold, make your choice as tempting to look at as it is to taste. The rules are few and this simple:

• Consider contrast in color, texture, and flavor as you do your planning. Combine the delicate hues of greens with the bright tones of fruits and vegetables; mix soft foods with crisp, or raw ones with cooked; blend sweet fruits with a tart dressing, and pungent vegetables with one that's mild.

• Take advantage of all of the salad greens to keep interest and flavor high. Of course, buy your favorites—escarole; romaine; curly endive or chicory; Bibb, Boston, leaf, and iceberg lettuce; spinach; parsley; and watercress. But for variety, once in a while try something new—fennel or finochio, Swiss chard, dandelion or beet greens, Chinese or plain cabbage, Belgian endive, or any other regional specialties that you may find in your area. Just a few of these, chopped up and mixed in with regular greens, add excitement to any salad.

• Clean and store greens properly—and promptly after shopping—to keep them crackly-crisp and save all of the vitamins you paid for. Trim off stems and any droopy leaves, then wash solid heads and dry well with paper toweling or drain in a colander, and store in the vegetable crisper in your refrigerator. Swish leafy varieties up and down in a sinkful of warm water, changing the water as needed. Contrary to what you might think, warm water won't wilt the leaves and makes it easier and faster to wash away soil or sand. For a final rinse, dunk the leaves in very cold water and dry well on paper toweling, wrap in a clean towel and pat dry, or place in a salad basket and hang to drain. (If you live in an open area and want to do as the French do, twirl the basket until the moisture is gone.) Bundle the greens into transparent bags and chill until salad-making time.

• Tear salad greens—rather than cut—into bite-sized pieces. Torn greens not only look more appealing, but they absorb the dressing better. Place in a bowl that's big enough for tossing without spilling over onto the table.

• Choose the right dressing but keep it simple, adding seasoning touches such as herbs, spices, or grated cheese for variety. As a general rule, thin French or Italian dressings go well with greens; mayonnaise or creamy dressings enhance fish, seafood, vegetable, and meat salads. And be a miser with the dressing—too much makes a soggy, heavy salad. You need only enough to make each leaf glisten.

• Toss salads lightly, using a long-handled spoon and fork. Reach into the bottom of the bowl each time, and gently roll the salad over as you bring the utensil up to the top. Keep tossing until all of the leaves are evenly coated with dressing. Serve at once—for salads do not wait well.

How to make a perfect molded salad

If you understand how to work with gelatin, it's easy to master the art of jellied salads. Foremost to remember is that one envelope of unflavored gelatin or a 3-ounce package of the fruit-flavored kind will set two cups of liquid. Go on from there like this:

Mixing: When dissolving gelatin, follow your recipe directions carefully. The mixture should be smooth and sparkly with no tiny granules clinging to the side of pan or bowl.

Fruit-flavored gelatins dissolve easily in boiling water. Unflavored gelatin recipes in this book call for dissolving the gelatin in one of these ways: (1) Soften the gelatin first in cold water, then dissolve it in a hot liquid or heat the softened gelatin slowly until dissolved; or (2) mix the dry gelatin with sugar, then add liquid and heat until dissolved.

Chilling: Place dissolved gelatin in the refrigerator to chill until *syrupy-thick*—the consistency of unbeaten egg white. Gelatin sets first at the bottom and side of the bowl so stir it occasionally for even thickening.

If you're in a hurry, pour the gelatin mixture into a shallow pan and place it in the refrigerator. Or set the bowl of gelatin in a larger pan of ice and water. Keep it on the kitchen counter where you can watch it, for it sets quickly.

If, during chilling, the gelatin sets too quickly, place the bowl over hot or simmering water and heat, stirring constantly, until it's melted. Then start chilling again the same as you would for freshly mixed gelatin.

Layering: If you like a fancy design on top, place your mold in a large pan of ice and water that's deep enough to allow the water to come to within 1 inch of the top of mold. Spoon in a ¼-inch-thick layer of syrupy-thick gelatin; chill just until it starts to become *sticky-firm.* (This means that the mixture appears set but is still sticky when you touch it.) Arrange foods in the pattern you want on top; carefully spoon in another thin layer of syrupy-thick gelatin—just barely enough to cover foods; chill until sticky-firm. This is the key phrase when you're adding one layer to another so they'll hold together when the salad is turned out. If the gelatin has set firmly, the layers will slip apart.

As you work, keep any remaining syrupy-thick gelatin at room temperature or watch it carefully if it's necessary to store it in the refrigerator.

Folding: If you're adding other ingredients to the gelatin, fold them in when it reaches the syrupy-thick stage, and spoon this mixture on top of already-set layer while it's still sticky-firm. Fruits, vegetables, meats, or fish should be mixed evenly throughout the gelatin. If you add them before the mixture is syrupy-thick, they may either sink to the bottom or float to the top.

Setting: Place mold in the back of the refrigerator where it can chill without being disturbed. Most molds will turn out neatly if chilled overnight. Allow at least 12 hours for large ones that are heavy with fruits or vegetables. Small or individual ones are usually firm enough to turn out after three to four hours chilling time.

Unmolding: Follow these illustrated directions.

Loosen edge of mold with knife.

Plunge in hot water.

Put a plate on top of mold and turn upside down.

SALADS

CONTINENTAL SALAD BOWL

⅓ cup salad oil
3 tablespoons lime juice
2 tablespoons honey
⅛ teaspoon salt
½ medium honeydew melon
1 package (6 ozs.) process Gruyere cheese
1 large head Boston lettuce
1 lb. seedless green grapes, stemmed
    (2 cups)

Combine salad oil, lime juice, honey, and salt in a small jar with a tight lid; shake well; chill.

Remove seeds from honeydew; cut in half lengthwise; pare and slice into thin crescents. Cut cheese into cubes.

When ready to serve, break lettuce into bite-sized pieces and place in a large salad bowl. Add honeydew, grapes, and cheese. Shake dressing well; pour over salad; toss lightly.

Yield: 6 servings.

CAESAR SALAD

3 slices white bread
1 large head romaine
⅓ cup olive oil
¼ cup wine vinegar
2 tablespoons lemon juice
1 clove garlic, crushed
1 teaspoon salt
1 egg
1 can (2 ozs.) anchovy fillets, drained
3 tablespoons freshly grated
    Parmesan cheese
⅛ teaspoon freshly ground pepper

Preheat oven to 300°.

Cut bread into small cubes; place in a single layer in a shallow baking pan. Toast in oven 20 minutes, or until golden. Set aside.

Separate romaine leaves; wash and dry well; cut out any coarse ribs.

Combine olive oil, vinegar, lemon juice, garlic, and salt in a large salad bowl; break romaine into bite-sized pieces and add to bowl. (There should be about 10 cups.)

Half fill a small saucepan with water; heat to boiling; add egg; cover. Remove from heat; let stand 1 minute to coddle egg; drain.

Add anchovies to romaine; sprinkle cheese and pepper over top; break coddled egg over all. Toss lightly to mix; add croutons; toss again.

Yield: 8 servings.

SAN FERNANDO SPINACH SALAD

1 package (10 ozs.) fresh spinach
2 seedless oranges, pared, sectioned,
    and drained
½ medium sweet onion, peeled, sliced thin,
    and separated into rings
6 slices bacon, cut into 1-inch pieces
⅓ cup bottled thin French dressing

Trim stems and any coarse ribs from spinach; wash leaves; dry well. Break into bite-sized pieces and place in a large salad bowl. Add orange sections and onion rings.

Sauté bacon until crisp in a small skillet; remove and drain on paper toweling. Pour all drippings into a cup, then measure 1 tablespoonful back into skillet. Stir in French dressing; heat very slowly just until warm. Drizzle over spinach mixture; add bacon; toss until leaves are evenly coated.

Yield: 8 servings.

ALL GREEN SALAD

1 head Boston lettuce, broken
    into bite-sized pieces
2 cups bite-sized pieces fresh spinach
2 cups bite-sized pieces escarole
1 cup parsley leaves (no stems)
¼ cup finely cut chives
½ cup salad oil
2 tablespoons lemon juice
1 tablespoon minced onion
1 teaspoon paprika
½ teaspoon sugar
½ teaspoon salt
¼ cup crumbled blue cheese
    (about 1 oz.)

Combine lettuce with spinach, escarole, parsley, and chives in a large salad bowl.

Combine salad oil, lemon juice, onion, paprika, sugar, salt, and blue cheese in a jar with a tight lid; cover. Shake vigorously to mix. Pour over greens; toss lightly until evenly coated.

Yield: 8 servings.

ARTICHOKE-ORANGE SALAD

1 package (9 ozs.) frozen artichoke hearts
1 large head romaine
3 large seedless oranges, peeled and
    sectioned
½ small sweet onion, peeled, pared thin,
    and separated into rings
⅓ cup bottled oil-and-vinegar salad
    dressing
¼ cup chopped ripe olives

Cook artichoke hearts as label directs; drain well; chill.

When ready to serve, line a large salad bowl with small inner romaine leaves; break remainder into bite-sized pieces and place in bowl.

Arrange artichoke hearts, orange sections, and onion rings over romaine. Drizzle dressing over salad; toss lightly to mix. Sprinkle olives evenly on top.

Yield: 8 servings.

LETTUCE SLAW

1 cup (8-oz. carton) dairy sour cream
¼ cup crumbled Roquefort cheese
½ teaspoon Worcestershire sauce
½ teaspoon salt
1 tablespoon milk
1 medium head iceberg lettuce
12 cherry tomatoes, stemmed and cut
    in half
2 small white onions, peeled, sliced, and
    separated into rings
1 can (8 ozs.) red kidney beans, drained

Combine sour cream, Roquefort cheese, Worcestershire sauce, salt, and milk in a small bowl; beat until well blended; chill.

Just before serving, cut head of lettuce in half, then shred fine, discarding core. (There should be about 8 cups.) Place in a large salad bowl. Add tomatoes, onion rings, and beans; spoon dressing over top. Toss lightly until evenly mixed.

Yield: 6 servings.

SESAME SPINACH SALAD

6 cups bite-sized pieces fresh spinach
½ small red onion, peeled, sliced thin,
    and separated into rings
4 large radishes, trimmed and sliced thin
1 medium tomato, cut into thin wedges
2 teaspoons sesame seeds
3 tablespoons salad oil
1 tablespoon vinegar
½ teaspoon garlic powder
¼ teaspoon salt
⅛ teaspoon pepper

Combine spinach, onion rings, radishes, and tomato wedges in a large salad bowl.

Measure sesame seeds into a small skillet; heat slowly, shaking skillet constantly, until seeds are toasty-golden. Stir in salad oil, vinegar, garlic powder, salt, and pepper; heat slowly until hot.

Drizzle hot dressing over spinach mixture; toss lightly to mix. Serve warm.

Yield: 4 servings.

EASTER EGG SALAD

  Red, yellow, and green food colorings
8 hard-cooked eggs, shelled
1 large head Boston lettuce
¼ small head chicory
1 small firm ripe avocado, cut in half, peeled, and
    pitted
1 small tomato
¼ cup mayonnaise or salad dressing
¼ cup dairy sour cream
2 teaspoons grated onion
½ teaspoon salt
2 tablespoons lemon juice

Fill several small deep cups with water. Stir a few drops food coloring into each to tint pink, green, yellow, orange, or other colors of your choice. Place 1 egg in each cup; let stand, turning several times, until delicately tinted. Remove from water; drain on paper toweling. Repeat with remaining eggs; chill.

Wash lettuce and chicory; dry well. Separate leaves; chill.

Mash avocado well in a small bowl. Dice tomato; stir into avocado with mayonnaise, sour cream, onion, salt, and lemon juice; chill.

Just before serving, line a large salad bowl with small lettuce leaves; break remaining leaves into bite-sized pieces and place in bowl; top with chicory. Nestle eggs in greens. Pass dressing separately to spoon over each serving.

Yield: 8 servings.

CUCUMBER SALAD BOWL

1 envelope onion salad dressing mix
  Vinegar
  Water
  Salad oil
1 medium cucumber
1 large head romaine, broken into
    bite-sized pieces
1 can (11 ozs.) mandarin orange segments, drained

Combine salad dressing mix, vinegar, water, and salad oil in a jar as label directs; chill.

Draw a fork lengthwise through rind of cucumber to make a ridged design; slice cucumber in thin rounds.

Place romaine in a large salad bowl. (There should be 8 cups.) Tuck cucumber slices and orange segments into bowl around romaine. Drizzle ½ cup of the salad dressing over top; toss until evenly mixed. (Chill remaining salad dressing to use another day.)

Yield: 6 servings.

AUTUMN SALAD

⅓ cup salad oil
2 tablespoons lemon juice
1 teaspoon minced onion
1 teaspoon sugar
½ teaspoon salt
1 large head romaine
1 large firm ripe avocado
1 pint cherry tomatoes, stemmed

Combine salad oil, lemon juice, onion, sugar, and salt in a small jar with a tight lid; shake well to mix; chill.

Just before serving, line a large salad bowl with small inner romaine leaves; break remainder into bite-sized pieces and place in bottom of bowl.

Peel avocado, cut in half, and pit; slice halves crosswise. Arrange around edge in bowl.

Cut each tomato in half; pile in center of bowl. Drizzle dressing over top; toss lightly to mix.

Yield: 8 servings.

RAINBOW SALAD BOWL

1 medium head iceberg lettuce, broken
    into bite-sized pieces
1 medium head romaine, broken into
    bite-sized pieces
2 cups bite-sized pieces fresh spinach
1 pint cherry tomatoes, stemmed and
    cut in half
2 small white onions, peeled, sliced thin,
    and separated into rings
2 large carrots, pared and sliced thin
¼ small head cauliflower, separated
    into flowerets and sliced thin
½ cup salad oil
¼ cup lemon juice
1 tablespoon sugar
1 teaspoon salt
    Dash of pepper
2 tablespoons chopped parsley

Mix lettuce, romaine, and spinach; place in a large salad bowl. Arrange cherry tomatoes, onion rings, carrots, and cauliflower in rows over greens.

Combine salad oil, lemon juice, sugar, salt, pepper, and parsley in a jar with a tight lid; shake well.

Just before serving, drizzle dressing over salad; toss lightly to mix.

Yield: 12 servings.

coarse ribs, then break leaves into bite-sized pieces in a large salad bowl. Dice eggs and add to spinach.

Slice onion thin and separate into rings; peel avocado, pit, and slice; add to spinach mixture.

Drizzle dressing over all; toss lightly to mix. *Yield:* 6 servings.

SPINACH CHIFFONADE SALAD

⅓ cup salad oil
2 tablespoons vinegar
1 small clove garlic, crushed
¾ teaspoon sugar
½ teaspoon paprika
¼ teaspoon salt
    Dash of pepper
1 package (10 ozs.) fresh spinach
3 hard-cooked eggs
½ medium Spanish sweet onion
1 small firm ripe avocado

Combine salad oil, vinegar, garlic, sugar, paprika, salt, and pepper in a jar with a tight lid; shake well to mix; chill.

Wash spinach leaves; dry well. Remove any

DOUBLE PEAR SALAD BOWL

    Lemon juice
1 medium firm ripe avocado, cut in half,
    peeled, pitted, and sliced lengthwise
1 head Boston lettuce, broken into
    bite-sized pieces
1 can (16 ozs.) pear halves, drained and
    sliced lengthwise
½ cup bottled blue-cheese salad dressing

Brush lemon juice over cut surfaces of avocado. Place lettuce in a large salad bowl; alternate pear and avocado slices in a ring on top. Spoon salad dressing over all; toss lightly to mix.

Yield: 6 servings.

ANTIPASTO TOSS

2 lbs. fresh lima beans, shelled (2 cups)
⅔ cup bottled Italian salad dressing
1 large head iceberg lettuce
1 large red pepper, quartered, seeded,
  and cut into strips
1 small red onion, peeled, sliced,
  and separated into rings
1 package (8 ozs.) sliced provolone
  cheese, cut in strips
1 package (6 ozs.) sliced salami, cut
  in strips
½ cup small pimiento-stuffed olives

Cook lima beans, covered, in boiling salted water in a medium saucepan 15 minutes, or until crisp-tender; drain. Place in a medium bowl; stir in 3 tablespoons of the Italian dressing; chill.

When ready to serve, break lettuce into bite-sized pieces; place on a large deep platter. Arrange limas, pepper strips, onion rings, cheese, salami, and olives in rows on top. Drizzle remaining salad dressing over all.

Yield: 6 to 8 servings.

WESTERN BROCCOLI RING

1 tablespoon sesame seeds
⅔ cup salad oil
⅓ cup tarragon vinegar
1 teaspoon salt
½ teaspoon dry mustard
¼ teaspoon pepper
1 tablespoon sugar
2 tablespoons grated Romano cheese
1½ lbs. fresh broccoli
3 medium fresh mushrooms
3 medium tomatoes
  Escarole

Measure sesame seeds into a small skillet, Heat slowly, shaking pan constantly, until seeds are toasted; remove from heat.

Combine salad oil, vinegar, salt, mustard, pepper, and sugar in a jar with a tight lid; shake well. Add sesame seeds and cheese; shake again; set aside.

Trim broccoli; cut stalks into 3-inch lengths. For even cooking, split any thick stalks. Cook, covered, in boiling salted water in a medium saucepan 12 minutes, or until crisp-tender; drain carefully. Place in a large shallow dish; drizzle ¼ cup of the dressing over top. Chill several hours to season.

Just before serving, trim mushrooms; wash and dry well; slice thin lengthwise. Slice tomatoes thin.

Line a large serving platter with escarole leaves; overlap tomato slices around edge on platter. Arrange broccoli in a circle next to tomatoes; pile mushrooms in center. Drizzle part of the remaining dressing over tomatoes and mushrooms; pass the rest separately.

Yield: 6 servings.

WALDORF RELISH

1 large apple, quartered,
  cored, and diced
1 tablespoon lemon juice
1 large carrot, pared and shredded
  (1 cup)
1 cup finely shredded cabbage
¼ cup broken California walnuts
½ cup thinly sliced celery
¼ cup mayonnaise or salad dressing
2 tablespoons dairy sour cream
½ teaspoon sugar
¼ teaspoon salt
  Romaine

Toss apple with lemon juice in a large bowl, then stir in carrot, cabbage, walnuts, and celery.

Mix mayonnaise, sour cream, sugar, and salt in a cup; stir into apple mixture. Spoon into a romaine-lined bowl. Garnish with several red apple wedges if you like.

Yield: 4 servings.

SALAD PEAS

1 can (16 ozs.) green peas with tiny
 onions, drained
1 can (5 ozs.) water chestnuts,
 drained and sliced
3 tablespoons salad oil
1 tablespoon cider vinegar
½ teaspoon salt
½ teaspoon sugar
¼ teaspoon dry mustard
½ cup tiny cubes Cheddar cheese
¼ cup sliced pitted ripe olives
¼ cup mayonnaise or salad dressing
⅛ teaspoon pepper
 Iceberg lettuce
1 small fresh tomato, cut in wedges
 Parsley

Combine peas and water chestnuts in a shallow dish.

Combine salad oil, vinegar, ¼ teaspoon of the salt, sugar, and mustard in a small jar with a tight lid; cover. Shake well to mix. Pour over vegetables. Chill at least an hour to season.

Just before serving, add cheese and olives to vegetable mixture.

Blend mayonnaise, pepper, and remaining ¼ teaspoon salt in a cup; fold into vegetable mixture; spoon into a lettuce-lined bowl. Arrange tomato wedges on top to form a flower; tuck parsley in center.

Yield: 6 servings.

BROCCOLI TOSS

1½ lbs. fresh broccoli
1 small head cauliflower, weighing
 about 1 lb.
½ cup diced salami
⅓ cup salad oil
¼ cup cider vinegar
2 tablespoons soy sauce
1 teaspoon prepared mustard
¾ teaspoon sugar
½ teaspoon salt

Trim broccoli; cut flowerets from stems. (Save stems to dice and cook for another meal.)
Trim cauliflower; break into flowerets.
Wash broccoli and cauliflower; slice flowerets very thin lengthwise.

Sauté salami in salad oil in a large skillet 3 minutes; stir in vinegar, soy sauce, mustard, sugar, and salt; heat very slowly until warm. Add broccoli and cauliflower; toss lightly to mix with dressing; continue heating 1 minute. Spoon into a large serving bowl. Serve warm.

Yield: 6 servings.

TRIPLE BEAN TOSS

1 package (10 ozs.) frozen baby lima beans
1 package (9 ozs.) frozen wax beans
1 can (16 ozs.) red kidney beans, drained
1 small onion, chopped fine (¼ cup)
⅓ cup bottled oil-and-vinegar salad dressing
⅔ cup mayonnaise or salad dressing
⅔ cup dairy sour cream
2 tablespoons prepared hot spicy mustard
½ teaspoon salt
1 medium head romaine

Cook limas and wax beans in separate saucepans as labels direct; drain. Place limas, wax beans, and kidney beans in separate shallow dishes.

Mix onion and oil-and-vinegar dressing in a cup; drizzle one third over each dish of beans; toss lightly to mix; cover. Chill at least an hour to season.

Mix mayonnaise, sour cream, mustard, and salt in a small bowl; chill.

Just before serving, break romaine into bite-sized pieces and place in a large salad bowl. Spoon kidney beans and wax beans in rings on top; pile limas in center. Spoon mustard dressing over top; toss lightly to mix.

Yield: 6 servings.

GAZPACHO SALAD BOWL

1 envelope old-fashioned French salad
    dressing mix
2 tablespoons water
⅔ cup salad oil
⅔ cup tomato juice
¼ cup vinegar
1 small head iceberg lettuce
1 small avocado
    Lemon juice
1 small cucumber, scored and sliced
1 small red onion, peeled, sliced, and
    separated into rings
1 large carrot, pared and shredded
2 hard-cooked eggs, sliced
1 cup packaged cheese croutons

Combine dressing mix and water in a jar with a tight lid; shake well. Add salad oil, tomato juice, and vinegar; shake well again; chill.

Just before serving, break lettuce into bite-sized pieces and place in a large salad bowl.

Peel avocado; cut in half and pit; slice halves crosswise. Dip slices in lemon juice in a pie plate to prevent darkening.

Arrange avocado, cucumber slices, onion rings, carrot, and eggs in sections, spoke fashion, on top of lettuce; pile croutons in center.

Drizzle ¾ cup of the tomato dressing over top; toss lightly to mix. (Chill remaining dressing to use another day.)

Yield: 8 servings.

MACARONI-BEAN BOWL

1 package (8 ozs.) elbow macaroni
1 bottle (8 ozs.) creamy onion salad
    dressing
1 can (16 ozs.) red kidney beans, drained
1 cup thinly sliced celery
1 cup small cubes sharp Cheddar cheese
1½ teaspoons salt
⅛ teaspoon pepper

Cook macaroni as label directs; drain. Toss with 2 tablespoons of the onion dressing; cool at room temperature, then chill.

Just before serving, lightly stir in beans, celery, and cheese.

Mix remaining salad dressing with salt and pepper in a cup; fold into macaroni mixture. Spoon into a serving bowl. Garnish with sliced radishes and parsley if you like.

Yield: 8 servings.

MINESTRONE SALAD

1 package (16 ozs.) elbow macaroni
2 cans (12 ozs. each) Mexican-style corn,
    drained
1 can (16 ozs.) cut green beans, drained
3 medium carrots, pared and shredded
    (1 cup)
1 cup sliced green onions
¾ cup bottled Italian salad dressing
1 cup thinly sliced celery
1½ cups mayonnaise or salad dressing
1 tablespoon prepared hot mustard
2 teaspoons salt
4 medium tomatoes

Cook macaroni as label directs; drain. While warm, combine with corn, green beans, carrots, onions, and Italian dressing in a large bowl; toss lightly to mix. Chill at least 2 hours to season and blend flavors.

Just before serving, add celery to macaroni mixture.

Mix mayonnaise, mustard, and salt in a small bowl; stir into macaroni mixture until evenly coated.

Slice tomatoes; cut each slice in half; arrange evenly around edge in bowl.

Yield: 16 servings.

TOMATO SALAD VINAIGRETTE

3 medium-sized firm ripe tomatoes
1 small white onion
⅓ cup salad oil
2 tablespoons vinegar
1½ teaspoons sugar
¼ teaspoon salt
  Dash of pepper
4 cups bite-sized pieces romaine

Slice tomatoes; place in a shallow dish. Peel onion and slice thin; separate into rings; place over tomatoes.

Mix salad oil, vinegar, sugar, salt, and pepper in a 1-cup measure; pour over tomatoes. Chill at least an hour to season.

When ready to serve, place romaine in a large salad bowl or divide among 6 individual salad bowls; arrange tomatoes and onion rings on top; spoon dressing from dish over all.

Yield: 6 servings.

BUFFET VEGETABLE TRAY

1 medium zucchini
1 medium-sized yellow squash
3 tablespoons bottled oil-and-vinegar
  salad dressing
2 cups cut fresh wax beans
1 package (10 ozs.) frozen Fordhook
  lima beans
  Salt
⅔ cup mayonnaise or salad dressing
2 tablespoons sweet pickle relish
2 teaspoons prepared hot spicy mustard
2 teaspoons prepared horseradish
  Iceberg lettuce
2 medium tomatoes, cut in thin wedges

Trim zucchini and yellow squash; slice ¼-inch thick. Cook together, covered, in a small amount of boiling salted water 3 minutes, or until crisp-tender; drain well. Place in a shallow dish; drizzle 1 tablespoon of the oil-and-vinegar dressing over top; cover. Chill.

Combine wax beans and frozen limas in a large saucepan; pour in ¾ cup boiling water; salt lightly; cover. Cook 12 minutes, or until crisp-tender; drain well, place in a second shallow dish. Drizzle remaining 2 tablespoons oil-and-vinegar dressing over top; toss lightly to mix; cover. Chill.

Mix mayonnaise, pickle relish, mustard, and horseradish in a small bowl; chill.

Just before serving, line a large serving tray with lettuce. Spoon squashes and bean mixture at ends of platter; arrange tomato wedges in between. Serve dressing separately to spoon over all.

Yield: 6 servings.

Note: If you prefer, combine 6 cups broken mixed greens with squashes, beans, tomatoes, and dressing and serve as a tossed salad.

CHINESE COLESLAW

1 small head cabbage, weighing about
  1½ lbs.
1 cup parsley leaves
1 can (11 ozs.) mandarin orange
  segments, drained
1 can (8 ozs.) water chestnuts, drained
  and sliced
1 small onion, peeled, sliced, and
  separated into rings
¼ cup salad oil
2 tablespoons lime juice
1 tablespoon honey
¼ teaspoon ground ginger
¼ teaspoon salt

Trim cabbage; cut head into quarters. Shred fine, discarding core. (There should be about 8 cups.)

Combine cabbage with parsley, orange segments, water chestnuts, and onion rings in a large bowl; cover; chill.

Combine salad oil, lime juice, honey, ginger, and salt in a small jar with a tight lid; shake well to mix; chill.

Just before serving, pour dressing over cabbage mixture; toss lightly to mix. Spoon into a serving bowl.

Yield: 6 servings.

SPINACH SALAD PROVENCE

⅓ cup salad oil
2 tablespoons wine vinegar
½ teaspoon garlic powder
1 egg, beaten
¼ cup grated Parmesan cheese
4 cups bite-sized pieces fresh spinach
2 cups bite-sized pieces curly endive
     or chicory
2 cups bite-sized pieces Boston lettuce
1 small cucumber, pared and sliced thin
1 pint cherry tomatoes, stemmed and
     cut in half

Combine salad oil, vinegar, and garlic powder in a small jar with a tight lid; shake well to mix. Add egg and cheese; shake again; chill.

Just before serving, combine spinach, endive, Boston lettuce, cucumber, and tomatoes in a large salad bowl. Drizzle dressing over top; toss lightly until greens and vegetables are coated.

Yield: 6 servings.

FRENCH TOMATO SALAD

6 medium firm ripe tomatoes
⅓ cup salad oil
3 tablespoons lemon juice
2 tablespoons chopped parsley
1 tablespoon prepared hot spicy mustard
1½ teaspoons sugar
1 teaspoon seasoned salt
¾ teaspoon garlic powder
   Boston lettuce

Peel tomatoes and core; cut each into 4 even slices, then re-stack into tomato shape; stand in a shallow dish.

Combine salad oil, lemon juice, parsley, mustard, sugar, salt, and garlic powder in a small jar with a tight lid; shake well to mix. Drizzle over tomatoes; cover. Chill several hours to season.

When ready to serve, place each tomato on a lettuce-lined salad plate; spoon dressing from dish over top.

Yield: 6 servings.

TOSSED WINTER SALAD

5 cups bite-sized pieces romaine
6 radishes, trimmed and sliced
½ small cucumber, sliced thin
1 small onion, peeled, sliced thin, and
     separated into rings
¼ cup pitted ripe olives, sliced
3 tablespoons salad oil
1 tablespoon lemon juice
½ teaspoon sugar
¼ teaspoon garlic salt
¼ teaspoon dried basil, crushed

Place romaine in a medium salad bowl; top with sliced radishes, cucumber, onion rings, and olives.

Mix salad oil, lemon juice, sugar, garlic salt, and basil in a cup; drizzle over vegetables; toss lightly to mix.

Yield: 6 servings.

IRISH COLESLAW

1 small head cabbage, weighing
     about 1½ lbs.
1 large onion, chopped (1 cup)
3 tablespoons sugar
½ teaspoon salt
1 can (12 ozs.) corned beef
1 cup (8-oz. carton) dairy sour cream
3 tablespoons lemon juice
2 teaspoons caraway seeds
   Romaine

Quarter cabbage; shred fine, discarding core. (There should be about 8 cups.) Place cabbage in a large bowl; pour in enough boiling water to cover; let stand 2 minutes; drain. Stir in onion; sprinkle sugar and salt over top; toss lightly. Chill several hours.

When ready to serve, cut corned beef into small cubes. (If meat is chilled in can for several hours, it will cut neatly.) Add to cabbage mixture.

Blend sour cream, lemon juice, and caraway seeds in a cup; stir lightly into cabbage mixture. Spoon into a romaine-lined salad bowl.

Yield: 6 servings.

STUFFED SQUASH BOATS

3 medium yellow squashes
1 envelope Italian salad dressing mix
  Salad oil
  Vinegar
  Water
1 medium zucchini
2 green onions, trimmed and sliced
  Boston lettuce
½ cup chopped celery
1 cup cherry tomatoes, quartered
  lengthwise

Trim yellow squashes, but do not pare; cut each in half lengthwise. Parboil in boiling salted water in a large skillet 7 minutes, or until crisp-tender; lift from water with a slotted spoon; drain. With a teaspoon, carefully scoop centers from each to make boat-shaped shells. Turn halves upside down on paper toweling to drain again.

Prepare Italian dressing mix with salad oil, vinegar, and water as label directs. Place squash halves in a single layer in a large shallow dish; drizzle ¼ cup of the dressing over top; chill several hours to season.

Trim zucchini, but do not pare; slice in thin rounds. Cook in boiling salted water in a medium saucepan 4 minutes, or until crisp-tender; drain well. Combine with green onions in a medium bowl; toss with 2 tablespoons of the Italian dressing; chill.

Just before serving, arrange yellow squashes on a lettuce-lined platter. Stir celery and cherry tomatoes into zucchini mixture; spoon into hollows in squashes. Serve with extra dressing to spoon over top.

Yield: 6 servings.

LEMON-GINGER CARROTS

1 bag (20 ozs.) frozen small whole carrots
¼ cup salad oil
2 tablespoons lemon juice
1 tablespoon minced onion
2 tablespoons chopped parsley
1 teaspoon sugar
½ teaspoon salt
½ teaspoon ground ginger
  Romaine

Cook carrots as label directs; drain. Place in a medium bowl.

While carrots cook, combine salad oil, lemon juice, onion, parsley, sugar, salt, and ginger in a jar with a tight lid; shake well to mix. Pour over warm carrots; stir lightly to coat; cover. Chill several hours to season.

When ready to serve, line a medium salad bowl with romaine; spoon carrot mixture into center. Garnish with several small white onion rings if you like.

Yield: 6 servings.

CARAWAY CABBAGE TOSS

6 cups shredded Chinese cabbage
12 cherry tomatoes, stemmed and cut
  in half
½ cup mayonnaise or salad dressing
¼ cup dairy sour cream
1 tablespoon sugar
½ teaspoon salt
½ teaspoon caraway seeds
1 tablespoon lemon juice
  Iceberg lettuce

Combine cabbage and tomatoes in a medium bowl; chill.

Blend mayonnaise, sour cream, sugar, salt, caraway seeds, and lemon juice in a small bowl; chill.

Just before serving, stir dressing into cabbage mixture. Spoon into a lettuce-lined salad bowl, arranging some of the tomato halves on top as a garnish.

Yield: 6 servings.

SUMMER GARDEN SALAD BOWL

1 envelope cheese-garlic salad
    dressing mix
Water
Vinegar
Salad oil
1 medium head Boston lettuce
¼ small head curly endive or chicory
2 cups thinly sliced cauliflowerets
1 small green pepper, quartered,
    seeded, and sliced thin
1 cup sliced radishes (about 12)
¼ cup sliced ripe olives

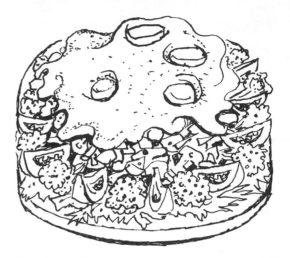

Prepare salad dressing mix with water, vinegar, and salad oil as label directs; chill.

Line a large salad bowl with lettuce leaves. Break remaining lettuce and endive into bite-sized pieces and place in bottom of bowl. (There should be about 6 cups.) Tuck cauliflowerets, green pepper slices, radishes, and olives among greens.

Just before serving, pour ¾ cup of the dressing over mixture; toss until evenly mixed. (Chill remaining dressing to use another day.)
Yield: 6 servings.

DANISH POTATO SALAD PLATTER

1 bag (16 ozs.) frozen hashed brown
    potatoes
½ cup water
1½ teaspoons seasoned salt
1 medium onion, chopped (½ cup)
1 small green pepper, quartered,
    seeded, and cut in thin strips
½ medium red pepper, seeded and
    diced (½ cup)
4 hard-cooked eggs
1 package (8 ozs.) cream cheese,
    softened
½ cup bottled chunky blue cheese
    salad dressing
1 tablespoon milk
    Few drops red-pepper seasoning
1 bunch fresh broccoli, weighing about
    1½ lbs.
2 tablespoons bottled thin French dressing
    Boston lettuce
2 medium tomatoes, sliced thin

Combine frozen potatoes, water, and ½ teaspoon of the salt in a large skillet; heat to boiling; cover. Simmer 5 minutes, or until potatoes are tender and liquid is absorbed. Combine potatoes with onion and green and red peppers in a large bowl.

Dice three of the eggs and remaining white; add to potato mixture. Set remaining yolk aside for garnish.

Combine cream cheese, blue cheese dressing, milk, red-pepper seasoning, and remaining 1 teaspoon salt in a small bowl; beat until smooth. Fold into potato mixture; cover. Chill several hours to season.

Wash broccoli; trim leaves and tough ends. Cut stalks and flowerets into 3-inch lengths; for even cooking, pare thick stalks and split lengthwise.

Place stalks on botton and flowerets on top in a large skillet. Pour in boiling water to a 1-inch depth; cover. Cook 12 minutes, or just until crisp-tender; drain well; place in a shallow dish. Drizzle French dressing over top; cover. Chill at least an hour to season.

When ready to serve, spoon potato salad into the center of a large, lettuce-lined platter or tray; press remaining egg yolk through a sieve on top. Arrange broccoli at ends of platter; overlap tomato slices along sides.
Yield: 6 servings.

PICNIC POTATO SALAD

6 large potatoes, pared and cubed
1½ cups thinly sliced celery
½ cup sliced green onions
½ cup bottled oil-and-vinegar salad dressing
4 hard-cooked eggs
1 package (6 ozs.) sliced boiled ham, diced
1 cup (8-oz. carton) dairy sour cream
½ cup mayonnaise or salad dressing
2 teaspoons prepared mustard
2 teaspoons salt
　Iceberg lettuce
　Parsley

Cook potatoes, covered, in boiling salted water in a large saucepan until tender; drain well.

Combine with celery and green onions in a large bowl; drizzle oil-and-vinegar dressing over top; toss lightly to mix. Chill several hours to season.

When ready to serve, dice three of the eggs; add to potato mixture with ham.

Blend sour cream, mayonnaise, mustard, and salt in a small bowl; fold into potato mixture. Spoon into a lettuce-lined bowl.

Cut remaining egg into 6 wedges; arrange, flower fashion, on top of salad. Tuck parsley into center.

Yield: 8 servings.

PERUVIAN POTATO SALAD

4 medium potatoes, pared and cubed
　(4 cups)
　Salt
1 medium onion, chopped (½ cup)
1 green chili pepper, seeded and chopped
4 hard-cooked eggs
2 tablespoons salad oil
¼ teaspoon pepper
½ cup whipping cream
1 cup shredded sharp Cheddar cheese (4 ozs.)
　Chicory or curly endive
3 radishes, trimmed and sliced

Cook potatoes, covered, in boiling salted water in a medium saucepan 15 minutes, or until tender; drain. Place in a large bowl; cool. Add onion and chili pepper to bowl.

Cut up 2 of the eggs and combine with salad oil, 1¼ teaspoons salt, pepper, and cream in an electric-blender container; cover. Blend just until smooth; drizzle over potato mixture. Sprinkle cheese over top; toss lightly to mix; cover. Chill several hours to blend flavors.

When ready to serve, spoon into a chicory-lined salad bowl. Slice remaining 2 eggs and arrange around edge in bowl; overlap radish slices in center.

Yield: 6 servings.

POTATO SALAD CUPS

4 large potatoes, pared and diced
¼ cup bottled oil-and-vinegar salad
     dressing
1 small onion, chopped (¼ cup)
1 cup thinly sliced celery
½ lb. fresh peas, shelled (½ cup)
2 tablespoons snipped fresh dill
½ cup dairy sour cream
2 tablespoons mayonnaise or salad
     dressing
½ teaspoon salt
6 medium-sized firm ripe tomatoes
  Boston lettuce

Cook potatoes, covered, in boiling salted water in a medium saucepan until tender; drain well. Place in a medium bowl; drizzle oil-and-vinegar dressing over top; toss lightly to mix. Let stand at room temperature until dressing is absorbed. Stir in onion, celery, peas, and dill.

Mix sour cream, mayonnaise, and salt in a cup; fold into potato mixture. Chill several hours to season.

When ready to serve, cut a thin slice from the blossom end of each tomato; scoop out centers with a spoon and set aside to use for soup. Turn tomato cups upside down on paper toweling to drain.

Spoon potato salad into tomatoes; garnish each with a small sprig of dill if you like. Place each on a lettuce-lined salad plate.

Yield: 6 servings.

CHEF'S POTATO SALAD

5 medium potatoes, pared and cubed (5 cups)
1 medium onion, chopped (½ cup)
½ cup thinly sliced celery
2 tablespoons chopped parsley
⅔ cup bottled Italian salad dressing
3 long slices Swiss cheese, cut in strips
1 package (4 ozs.) sliced boiled ham,
     cut in strips
3 long slices sharp Cheddar cheese,
     cut in strips
1 pint cherry tomatoes, stemmed and
     cut in half
  Escarole

Cook potatoes, covered, in boiling salted water in a large saucepan 15 minutes, or until tender; drain. Combine with onion, celery, and parsley in a large bowl. Drizzle ⅓ cup of the Italian dressing over top; toss lightly to mix; cover. Chill several hours to season.

Place Swiss cheese, ham, Cheddar cheese, and tomatoes in separate piles in a large shallow dish; drizzle remaining ⅓ cup dressing over top; cover. Chill several hours.

When ready to serve, spoon potato mixture into an escarole-lined large salad bowl. Spoon ham, Swiss cheese, and Cheddar cheese in piles on top to divide into six sections; spoon tomatoes between and in center. Drizzle any remaining dressing from dishes on top.

Yield: 6 servings.

HOT POTATO SALAD

5 medium potatoes, pared and diced
1 package (10 ozs.) frozen green peas
4 slices bacon, cut in 1-inch pieces
3 tablespoons sugar
2 tablespoons all-purpose flour
½ teaspoon salt
⅛ teaspoon pepper
3 tablespoons cider vinegar
½ cup sliced green onions
½ cup sliced celery

Cook potatoes, covered, in boiling salted water in a large saucepan until tender; drain, saving ¾ cup of the cooking liquid; return potatoes to pan.

Cook peas as label directs; drain. Add to potatoes; keep hot.

Sauté bacon until crisp in a medium skillet; remove and drain on paper toweling. Pour off drippings, then measure 3 tablespoonfuls and return to skillet.

Mix sugar, flour, salt, and pepper in a cup; stir into drippings in skillet, then stir in the ¾ cup potato liquid and vinegar. Cook, stirring constantly, until mixture thickens and boils 1 minute.

Lightly stir into potato mixture with green onions and celery. Spoon into a serving bowl; garnish with bacon and sieved hard-cooked egg yolk if you like. Serve warm.

Yield: 6 servings.

SCANDINAVIAN POTATO SALAD

4 large carrots, pared and diced (2 cups)
  Salt
2 large potatoes, pared and cubed (3 cups)
1 small onion, sliced thin and separated
  into rings
1 jar (12 ozs.) herring in wine sauce
1 tablespoon vinegar
⅛ teaspoon pepper
  Iceberg lettuce
1 jar (16 ozs.) sliced pickled beets, drained

Cook carrots, covered, in boiling salted water in a small saucepan 10 minutes, or until crisp-tender; drain well. Place in a medium bowl.

Cook potatoes, covered, in boiling salted water in a medium saucepan 15 minutes, or until tender; drain. Add potatoes and onion rings to carrots.

Drain liquid from herring into a cup. Remove skin and bones, if any, from herring; cut herring into bite-sized pieces; add to potato mixture.

Stir vinegar, ¼ teaspoon salt, and pepper into wine sauce from herring; fold into potato mixture; cover. Chill several hours to season.

When ready to serve, spoon herring mixture onto a lettuce-lined serving plate; overlap beets around edge.

Yield: 6 servings.

DEVILED POTATO SALAD

4 medium potatoes, pared and diced (4 cups)
  Salt
2 tablespoons bottled thin French dressing
1 cup diced celery
¼ cup chopped green onions
1 small green pepper, quartered, seeded, and chopped (¼ cup)
1 small red pepper, quartered, seeded, and chopped (¼ cup)
3 hard-cooked eggs, chopped
½ cup mayonnaise or salad dressing
½ cup dairy sour cream
2 tablespoons prepared hot spicy mustard
  Boston lettuce
1 package (8 ozs.) sliced small bologna
1 small zucchini, trimmed and sliced paper thin

Cook potatoes, covered, in boiling salted water in a medium saucepan 8 minutes, or until tender; drain. Place in a large bowl. Drizzle French dressing over top; toss lightly to mix. Chill until cold.

Add celery, green onions, green and red peppers, and eggs to potato mixture.

Blend mayonnaise, sour cream, mustard, and ½ teaspoon salt in a small bowl; fold into potato mixture; cover. Chill several hours to season.

When ready to serve, spoon potato mixture in a mound in center of a lettuce-lined large serving platter; garnish with red and green pepper rings if you like.

Roll bologna slices into cornucopia shapes; fasten with wooden picks; place at ends of platter. Overlap zucchini slices at sides. Serve with extra salt to sprinkle over zucchini.

Yield: 6 servings.

GOLDEN GATE POTATO SALAD

1 envelope Parmesan salad dressing mix
  Water
  Vinegar
  Salad oil
6 medium-sized potatoes, scrubbed
  Salt
2 cans (6 ozs. each) tuna, drained and broken into chunks
1 medium-sized red onion, peeled, sliced thin, and separated into rings
  Romaine
1 tablespoon chopped parsley
3 medium-sized tomatoes, sliced thin

Prepare salad dressing mix with water, vinegar, and salad oil as label directs.

Cook potatoes, covered, in boiling salted water in a large saucepan 30 minutes, or until tender; drain. Cool just until easy to handle, then peel; slice ⅛ inch thick; place slices in a shallow dish. Drizzle ½ cup of the Parmesan dressing over top; cover. Chill several hours to season.

Place tuna and onion rings in separate pie plates; drizzle ¼ cup of the dressing over tuna and 2 tablespoons over onion; cover plates. Chill several hours.

When ready to serve, spoon potatoes in a layer on a lettuce-lined large flat serving platter. Spoon onion rings, then tuna in layers on top; sprinkle chopped parsley over tuna. Arrange tomato slices around edge of platter. Spoon any remaining dressing in dishes over tomatoes.

Yield: 6 servings.

HOT GERMAN RICE SALAD

1½ cups packaged precooked rice
1 package (10 ozs.) frozen peas
9 slices bacon
½ cup chopped celery
1 small onion, chopped (¼ cup)
⅓ cup sugar
3 tablespoons cider vinegar
½ teaspoon salt
2 tablespoons chopped parsley

Prepare rice and cook peas in separate saucepans as labels direct; drain peas; keep both warm.

Sauté 4 slices of the bacon until almost crisp in a large skillet; before removing, wind each slice around the tines of a fork to make a curl; drain on paper toweling. Cut remaining bacon into 1-inch pieces; sauté until crisp in same skillet; remove and drain.

Pour off all drippings, then measure ¼ cupful and return to skillet. Stir in celery and onion and sauté until soft. Stir in sugar, vinegar, and salt; heat to boiling; remove from heat.

Add rice, peas, bacon pieces, and parsley to dressing; toss lightly until dressing is absorbed. Spoon into a serving bowl; garnish with bacon curls and parsley. Serve warm.

Yield: 8 servings.

CUCUMBER-RICE SALAD

1½ cups packaged precooked rice
1 teaspoon salt
Water
1 medium cucumber
1 small onion, chopped (¼ cup)
¾ cup mayonnaise or salad dressing
2 tablespoons milk
1 tablespoon vinegar
3 tablespoons snipped fresh dill
Boston lettuce

Prepare rice with ½ teaspoon of the salt and boiling water as label directs; spoon into a medium bowl.

Cut three or four thin slices from cucumber and set aside for garnish. Pare remaining cucumber; cut in quarters, seed, and dice. (There should be about 1 cup.) Add cucumber and onion to rice.

Blend mayonnaise with milk, vinegar, remaining ½ teaspoon salt, and dill in a small bowl; fold into rice mixture; cover. Chill several hours to blend flavors.

Just before serving, spoon into a lettuce-lined salad bowl. Garnish with cucumber slices and dill sprigs if you like.

Yield: 6 servings.

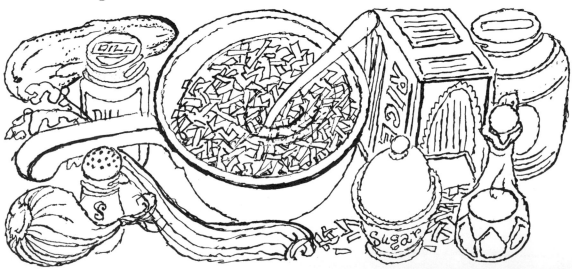

AMBROSIA SALAD BOWL

¼ cup sugar
½ teaspoon celery seeds
½ teaspoon dry mustard
¼ teaspoon paprika
¼ teaspoon salt
3 tablespoons lemon juice
⅓ cup salad oil
1 medium head romaine, broken into
    bite-sized pieces (6 cups)
2 large seedless oranges, pared and
    sectioned
1 large grapefruit, pared and sectioned
2 large firm ripe bananas, peeled and
    sliced

Combine sugar, celery seeds, mustard, paprika, salt, and lemon juice in a small bowl; slowly beat in salad oil until mixture is blended and thick; chill.

Place romaine in a large salad bowl; arrange orange and grapefruit sections in rings on top; pile bananas in center. Drizzle dressing over all; toss lightly until romaine and fruits are evenly coated.

Yield: 6 servings.

APPLE-CRANBERRY COLESLAW

1 small head green cabbage, weighing
    about 1½ lbs., cut in quarters
½ small head red cabbage, cut in half
2 tablespoons sugar
1 tablespoon lemon juice
½ teaspoon salt
1 large red apple, quartered, cored,
    and diced
1 cup mayonnaise or salad dressing
⅓ cup bottled cranberry-orange relish

Shred green and red cabbages, discarding cores. Combine cabbages in a large bowl. Sprinkle sugar, lemon juice, and salt over top; toss to mix. Chill mixture several hours to season and crisp cabbage.

Just before serving, drain any liquid from bowl; add apple to cabbage. Mix mayonnaise and cranberry relish in a small bowl; spoon over cabbage mixture; toss lightly.

Yield: 8 to 10 servings.

PARTY FRUIT PLATTER

1 cup bottled chunky blue cheese
    salad dressing
Lemon juice
1 large head romaine
1 bunch watercress
1 can (29 ozs.) cling peach halves,
    drained
2 cups seedless green grapes
½ lb. Swiss cheese, cut in small cubes
½ lb. sharp Cheddar cheese, cut in
    small cubes
1 pint strawberries, hulled and cut
    in half
1 can (8 ozs.) water chestnuts, drained
    and sliced

Blend blue cheese dressing and 1 tablespoon lemon juice in a small bowl; cover; chill.

Just before serving, line a large platter with romaine leaves; break remainder into bite-sized pieces and place on bottom. Pull watercress leaves from stems and toss over romaine.

Arrange peach halves at ends of platter. Then, working from both ends, arrange grapes, cheeses, and strawberries in rows next to peaches. Place water chestnuts in center.

Serve with blue cheese dressing and blueberry or apple muffins.

Yield: 8 servings.

MANDARIN RICE BOWL

1 cup uncooked regular rice
¼ cup bottled oil-and-vinegar salad dressing
3 tablespoons lemon juice
1 can (11 ozs.) mandarin orange segments, drained
1 cup thinly sliced celery
2 large leeks, trimmed and sliced thin (1 cup)
¾ cup mayonnaise or salad dressing
  Iceberg lettuce
  Parsley

Cook rice as label directs; fold in oil-and-vinegar dressing and lemon juice while rice is warm; cover. Let stand at room temperature until cold.

Set aside a few mandarin orange segments for garnish, then add remainder to rice mixture with celery and leeks; fold in mayonnaise until blended.

Spoon into a lettuce-lined serving bowl; garnish with remaining mandarin orange segments and parsley. Serve with a cold-cut platter or cold baked ham.

Yield: 6 to 8 servings.

CHRISTMAS SALAD

3 seedless pink grapefruits
1 medium cucumber
¼ cup salad oil
2 tablespoons wine vinegar
1 teaspoon sugar
½ teaspoon salt
1 large head romaine
  Seeds from one small pomegranate

Pare grapefruits and section over a bowl to catch the juice; drain sections well, saving juice for dressing.

Score rind of cucumber with a fork; slice cucumber thin. Chill cucumber and grapefruit.

Combine salad oil, vinegar, 2 tablespoons grapefruit juice, sugar, and salt in a jar with a tight lid; shake well to mix.

When ready to serve, line a large salad bowl with romaine; break remainder into bite-sized pieces and place in bowl. Arrange cucumber slices and grapefruit sections in a wheel design on top. Spoon pomegranate seeds in center.

Drizzle dressing over salad; toss lightly to mix.

Yield: 8 servings.

MONTEREY MEDLEY

½ cup salad oil
¼ cup lemon juice
2 teaspoons sugar
1 teaspoon dry mustard
¼ teaspoon salt
2 medium seedless oranges
½ medium Bermuda onion
1 small firm ripe avocado
2 large firm ripe bananas
1 head iceberg lettuce, broken into bite-sized pieces

Combine salad oil, lemon juice, sugar, mustard, and salt in a jar with a tight lid; shake well to mix; chill.

Just before serving, pare oranges, slice thin, and cut each slice in half. Slice onion and separate into rings. Cut avocado in half; peel, pit, and slice lengthwise. Peel bananas and slice diagonally.

Place lettuce in a large salad bowl; arrange oranges, onion rings, avocado, and bananas in sections on top. Drizzle dressing over all; toss lightly to mix.

Yield: 8 servings.

RASPBERRY RIBBON FRUIT PLATTER

    1 can (16 ozs.) cling peach slices
    1 package (3 ozs.) orange-flavored
        gelatin
3½ cups boiling water
    1 package (8 ozs.) cream cheese,
        softened
    1 tablespoon lemon juice
    2 packages (3 ozs. each) raspberry-
        flavored gelatin
    1 package (10 ozs.) frozen raspberries
        Curly endive or chicory
        Frosted Green Grapes (directions follow)
        Banana Cuts (directions follow)
        Raspberry Cream Dressing (recipe
            on page 365)

Drain syrup from peaches into a small bowl; dice peaches; set syrup and fruit aside.

Dissolve orange gelatin in 1 cup of the boiling water in a medium bowl; stir in peach syrup. Very slowly beat into cream cheese in a medium bowl; stir in lemon juice. Chill about 50 minutes, or until syrupy-thick. Stir in diced peaches.

Dissolve raspberry gelatin in remaining 2½ cups boiling water in a medium bowl; stir in raspberries and syrup. Chill about 50 minutes, or until syrupy-thick.

Place a 2-quart mold in a deep pan of ice and water to speed setting; pour orange mixture into mold. Chill until sticky-firm. Carefully spoon raspberry mixture on top. Remove mold from ice and place in refrigerator; chill overnight until firm.

Just before serving, loosen salad around edge with a knife; dip mold quickly in and out of warm water. Invert onto a serving platter; lift off mold.

Frame salad with endive. Arrange Frosted Green Grapes at corners of platter; place Banana Cuts in between. Serve with Raspberry Cream Dressing.

Yield: 8 servings.

To make Frosted Green Grapes: Beat 1 egg white slightly with 1 tablespoon water in a small bowl; sprinkle granulated sugar on waxed paper. Dip small clusters of green grapes into egg mixture, then into sugar to coat well. Let stand on a wire rack until sugar dries.

To make Banana Cuts: Peel 3 or 4 large firm ripe bananas and draw a fork over fruit to make a ridged design; cut fruit into 1½-inch chunks. Dip in lemon juice in a pie plate to prevent darkening.

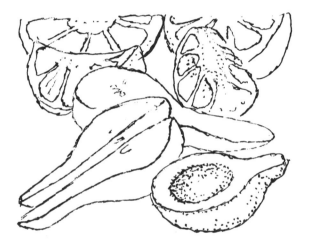

PEAR, ORANGE, AND AVOCADO SALAD

    1 small head romaine, broken into
        bite-sized pieces
    1 can (16 ozs.) pear halves, drained and
        sliced lengthwise
    1 medium-sized firm ripe avocado, cut in half,
        peeled, pitted, and sliced lengthwise
    3 medium seedless oranges, pared
        and sectioned
⅓ cup bottled thin French dressing

Place romaine in a large salad bowl; arrange pear and avocado slices in a ring around edge; pile orange sections in center.

Drizzle dressing over all; toss lightly to mix.
Yield: 6 servings.

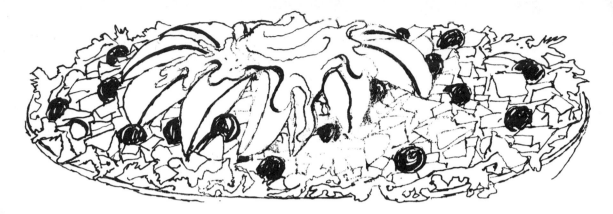

SPICED PEACH CROWN

  1 can (16 ozs.) cling peach slices
  1 3-inch piece stick cinnamon
  1 teaspoon whole cloves
⅓ cup white vinegar
    Water
  2 packages (3 ozs. each) orange-
    flavored gelatin
  1 cup (8-oz. carton) dairy sour cream
¼ cup mayonnaise or salad dressing
  1 teaspoon sugar
  1 teaspoon grated orange rind
    Chicory or curly endive
  1 can (8 ozs.) jellied cranberry sauce

Drain syrup from peaches into a small saucepan; add cinnamon, cloves, and vinegar to syrup.

Heat to boiling; simmer 10 minutes. Strain into a 2-cup measure; add water to make 2 cups. Return to saucepan; reheat to boiling. Stir into gelatin in a small bowl until gelatin dissolves, then stir in 1 cup cold water.

Arrange enough of the peach slices in the bottom of a 1-quart mold to make a pretty pattern; pour in ½ cup of the gelatin mixture. Place mold in a pan of ice and water to speed setting. Let stand just until gelatin is sticky-firm.

Dice any remaining peach slices; stir into remaining orange gelatin; spoon over layer in mold. Chill in refrigerator several hours, or until firm.

Combine sour cream, mayonnaise, sugar, and orange rind in a small bowl; chill.

Just before serving, loosen salad around edge with a knife; dip mold in and out of warm water. Invert onto a serving plate; lift off mold. Frame with chicory.

Slice cranberry sauce; cut each slice in half; overlap around base of mold. Serve with sour-cream dressing.

Yield: 6 servings.

LEMON WALDORF SALAD

  1 large red eating apple
½ cup sliced celery
  1 can (8 ozs.) fruit cocktail, drained
¼ cup thawed frozen concentrate for
    lemonade
  3 tablespoons mayonnaise or salad
    dressing
  1 large firm ripe banana
    Lettuce

Quarter apple, core, and cut into bite-sized wedges. Combine with celery and fruit cocktail in a medium bowl.

Beat lemonade concentrate with mayonnaise until smooth in a cup; stir into apple mixture; chill.

When ready to serve, peel banana and slice; stir into apple mixture. Spoon onto lettuce-lined plates.

Yield: 4 servings.

ALL-AMERICAN HAM-AND-POTATO PLATTER

5 medium potatoes, pared and cubed
1 cup thinly sliced celery
½ cup chopped dill pickle
1 small onion, chopped (¼ cup)
1 jar (2 ozs.) sliced pimientos,
    drained and chopped
½ cup mayonnaise or salad dressing
1½ teaspoons salt
1 tablespoon lemon juice
    Egg Salad (recipe follows)
2 packages (6 ozs. each) sliced
    boiled ham
    Escarole
    Parsley
    Radish roses

Cook potatoes, covered, in lightly salted boiling water in a medium saucepan 12 minutes, or until tender; drain. Combine with celery, dill pickle, onion, and pimientos in a large bowl.

Blend mayonnaise with salt and lemon juice in a cup; stir into potato mixture; cover. Chill several hours, or even overnight, to season.

Prepare Egg Salad; cover; chill.

Just before serving, curl each slice of ham into a cornucopia shape; fasten with a wooden pick. Spoon Egg Salad into cornucopias.

Spoon potato salad onto a large escarole-lined platter. Arrange ham cornucopias in a ring on top. Fill center with sprigs of parsley and radish roses.

Yield: 6 servings.

EGG SALAD

6 hard-cooked eggs, chopped
½ cup finely chopped celery
2 tablespoons finely chopped green pepper
¼ cup mayonnaise or salad dressing
½ teaspoon onion salt
2 tablespoons prepared horseradish mustard

Combine eggs, celery, and green pepper in a medium bowl.

Blend mayonnaise, onion salt, and mustard in a cup; stir into egg mixture.

Yield: 2⅓ cups.

TURKEY TETRAZZINI PLATTER

1 frozen boneless turkey roast, weighing
    2 lbs.
1 package (8 ozs.) spaghetti, broken in
    2-inch lengths
1 large red pepper, quartered, seeded,
    and cut into 1-inch slivers (1 cup)
½ cup diced celery
¼ cup thinly sliced green onions
⅓ cup salad oil
3 tablespoons lemon juice
¾ teaspoon salt
1 package (8 ozs.) Neufchatel cheese
3 tablespoons grated Parmesan cheese
½ cup mayonnaise or salad dressing
2 tablespoons milk
    Small spinach leaves
1 small cantaloupe, cut in half, seeded,
    and cut into balls (2 cups)
1 small honeydew melon, cut in quarters,
    seeded, pared, and sliced thin crosswise

The day before serving salad, roast turkey as label directs. Remove from foil pan; wrap and chill overnight.

Cook spaghetti as label directs; drain; place in a large bowl.

While spaghetti cooks, cube turkey. (There should be 4 cups.) Add to spaghetti with red pepper, celery, and green onions.

Combine salad oil, lemon juice, and ¼ teaspoon of the salt in a small jar with a tight cover; shake well to mix. Pour over spaghetti mixture; toss lightly; cover. Chill several hours to season.

Just before serving, combine Neufchatel and Parmesan cheeses, mayonnaise, milk, and remaining ½ teaspoon salt in a small bowl; beat until smooth. Fold into turkey mixture. Spoon onto center of a spinach-lined platter. Spoon cantaloupe balls at each end; arrange honeydew slices at each side.

Yield: 6 servings.

BUFFET BOUILLABAISSE

1 lb. fresh or frozen sea scallops
1 package (16 ozs.) frozen shrimp
1 package (12 ozs.) frozen halibut
4 medium carrots, pared, and cut into
    1-inch sticks
1 small red onion, peeled, sliced thin,
    and separated into rings
1 small green pepper, cut in half,
    seeded, and sliced
1 small cucumber, scored and sliced thin
1¼ cups salad oil
⅓ cup white vinegar
3 tablespoons finely cut dill or
    2 teaspoons dillweed
2 teaspoons sugar
1½ teaspoons salt
⅛ teaspoon pepper
1 small head romaine

Half fill a medium skillet with water. Heat to boiling; add scallops; cover. (If frozen, no need to thaw first.) Simmer 5 to 7 minutes, or until scallops are tender. Lift from liquid with a slotted spoon and place in a small bowl.

Cook shrimp and halibut as labels direct; drain. Cut halibut into 1-inch pieces; place shrimp and halibut in separate bowls. Chill all seafoods. Wrap each vegetable separately and chill.

Combine salad oil, vinegar, dill, sugar, salt, and pepper in a jar with a tight lid; cover; shake until sugar dissolves. Chill.

When ready to serve, line a large platter with small inner romaine leaves; break remainder into bite-sized pieces and place in center. Arrange seafoods and vegetables in rows on top. Serve dill dressing separately.

Yield: 8 servings.

NICOISE BUFFET PLATTER

1 lb. green beans, tipped
2 medium potatoes, pared and cubed
1 envelope old-fashioned French salad
    dressing mix
Water
Vinegar
Salad oil
1 medium head iceberg lettuce,
    broken into bite-sized pieces
2 cans (about 7 ozs. each) tuna, drained
    and broken into chunks
2 medium tomatoes, each cut into 6 wedges
2 hard-cooked eggs, sliced
1 cup pitted ripe olives
1 can (2 ozs.) rolled anchovy fillets,
    drained

Cook green beans, covered, in boiling salted water in a medium saucepan 25 minutes, or until crisp-tender; drain. Place in a pie plate.

Cook potatoes, covered, in boiling salted water in a small saucepan 12 minutes, or until tender, drain. Place in a second pie plate.

Prepare salad dressing mix with water, vinegar, and salad oil as label directs; drizzle 2 tablespoonfuls over each vegetable; toss lightly to mix; cover. Chill several hours to season.

Just before serving, place lettuce on a large platter. Pile tuna in center. Arrange green beans on platter to divide into 4 sections; place potatoes, tomatoes, eggs, and olives in between. Garnish tuna with anchovies. Pass remaining salad dressing to spoon over all.

Yield: 6 servings.

HOT-WEATHER CURRIED CHICKEN

1 cup uncooked regular rice
2 tablespoons lime juice
½ cup thinly sliced celery
¼ cup thinly sliced green onions
1 cup halved seedless green grapes
¼ cup coarsely chopped peanuts
1 cup mayonnaise or salad dressing
2 tablespoons milk
1 teaspoon curry powder
¼ teaspoon salt
 Escarole
 Green onions
2 packages (3 ozs. each) thinly sliced
 pressed cooked chicken

Cook rice in boiling salted water as label directs; place in a medium bowl. Drizzle lime juice over top; toss lightly to mix; cool.

Add celery, sliced onions, grapes, and peanuts to rice mixture.

Blend mayonnaise, milk, curry powder, and salt in a small bowl; fold into rice mixture; cover. Chill several hours to blend flavors.

When ready to serve, line a large shallow salad bowl with escarole; spoon rice mixture into center.

Cut green onions slightly longer than chicken slices; roll each slice around an onion, letting part of the green top show at one end. Pile rolls along side of bowl. Garnish center of salad with a small cluster of grapes if you like.

Yield: 6 servings.

PINWHEEL BEAN SALAD

2 packages (10 ozs. each) frozen baby
 lima beans
1 can (16 ozs.) red kidney beans, drained
1 cup thinly sliced celery
½ cup bottled thin French dressing
3 green onions, trimmed and sliced
½ cup chopped dill pickles
1 pimiento, drained and diced
½ teaspoon salt
¼ cup mayonnaise or salad dressing
2 packages (8 ozs. each) sliced boiled ham

Cook lima beans, covered, in boiling salted water as label directs; drain well. Place in a medium bowl with kidney beans and celery. Drizzle French dressing over top; toss lightly to mix. Let stand at room temperature until lima beans are cold.

Stir in green onions, pickles, pimiento, salt, and mayonnaise. Spoon into a shallow serving bowl; cover; chill.

When ready to serve, roll each slice of ham tightly. Arrange, spoke fashion, on top of bean mixture; tuck parsley in center if you like.

Yield: 8 servings.

SOUTHWESTERN CHILI SALAD BOWL

1 lb. cooked roast beef
⅔ cup bottled oil-and-vinegar salad
 dressing
1 teaspoon chili powder
2 tablespoons catsup
¼ teaspoon salt
 Few drops red-pepper seasoning
2 cans (16 ozs. each) red kidney beans,
 drained
1 medium head iceberg lettuce
½ small Bermuda onion, sliced thin and
 separated into rings
3 medium-sized firm ripe tomatoes, cut
 in wedges

Cut beef into julienne strips. (There should be 3 cups.) Place in a shallow dish.

Combine salad dressing, chili powder, catsup, salt, and red-pepper seasoning in a small jar with a tight cover; shake well to mix. Pour half over beef; toss lightly; cover.

Pour remaining dressing over beans in a shallow dish; toss; cover. Chill beef and beans at least 2 hours to season.

When ready to serve, line a large shallow salad bowl with lettuce; break remainder into bite-sized pieces and place in bowl. Arrange beef strips, beans, onion rings, and tomato wedges in sections on top. Drizzle any dressing left in dishes over all; toss lightly to mix.

Yield: 6 servings.

DUBLIN POTATO SALAD

4 medium potatoes
1 medium onion, chopped (½ cup)
½ cup sliced celery
1 small green pepper, quartered, seeded,
    and diced (½ cup)
⅔ cup dairy sour cream
⅓ cup mayonnaise or salad dressing
1 tablespoon lemon juice
1 teaspoon prepared hot spicy mustard
1 teaspoon caraway seeds
¼ teaspoon salt
1 lb. cooked corned beef
    Iceberg lettuce
3 hard-cooked eggs, sliced

Cook potatoes, covered, in boiling salted water in a large saucepan 15 minutes, or until tender; drain; cool.

Peel potatoes and cut into cubes. (There should be 4 cups.) Place in a large bowl with onion, celery, and green pepper.

Mix sour cream, mayonnaise, lemon juice, mustard, caraway seeds, and ¼ teaspoon salt in a small bowl; fold into potato mixture; cover. Chill several hours to season.

When ready to serve, cut corned beef into cubes. (There should be 3 cups.) Fold into potato mixture; spoon into a lettuce-lined bowl. Overlap egg slices around edge in bowl.

Yield: 6 servings.

HAM SALAD ROYALE

1 canned ham, weighing 1 lb.
1 can (8 ozs.) pineapple chunks in juice
1 cup thinly sliced celery
1 cup halved seedless green grapes
1 can (8 ozs.) water chestnuts, drained and diced
½ cup mayonnaise or salad dressing
½ cup dairy sour cream
½ teaspoon ground nutmeg
2 medium-sized firm ripe cantaloupes
    Boston lettuce

Scrape gelatin coating from ham; cut ham into ½-inch cubes. (There should be 2 cups.)

Place in a large bowl.

Drain juice from pineapple into a cup. Add pineapple, celery, green grapes, and water chestnuts to ham.

Blend mayonnaise, sour cream, 1 tablespoon of the pineapple juice, and nutmeg in a small bowl; fold into ham mixture. Chill about an hour to season.

When ready to serve, cut each cantaloupe crosswise into three even rings; pare and scoop out seeds. Trim ends slightly so rings will sit flat on plates.

Place each ring on a lettuce-lined serving plate; spoon ham salad into centers. Garnish each with a sprig of watercress if you like.

Yield: 6 servings.

HOT CHEF'S SALAD BOWL

4 slices bacon, cut in 1-inch pieces
1 small head iceberg lettuce, broken into
    bite-sized pieces
2 cups bite-sized pieces fresh spinach
4 green onions, trimmed and sliced
8 small slices salami, cut into strips
    (4 ozs.)
4 slices chopped ham, cut into strips
    (4 ozs.)
2 hard-cooked eggs, sliced
2 tablespoons crumbled blue cheese
¼ cup vinegar
2 tablespoons sugar
½ teaspoon Worcestershire sauce

Sauté bacon until crisp in a small skillet; remove and drain on paper toweling. Set drippings aside. (There should be ¼ cup.)

Combine lettuce, spinach, and onions in a large salad bowl. Place salami and ham strips in piles on top to divide into 4 sections; arrange bacon and eggs in remaining sections; pile blue cheese in center.

Stir vinegar, sugar, and Worcestershire sauce into bacon drippings; heat, stirring constantly, to boiling. Pour over salad; toss lightly until evenly mixed. Serve warm.

Yield: 4 to 6 servings.

CAPE COD TURKEY SALAD (p.354)▶

FRANKFURTER SALAD CROWN

4 medium potatoes
½ cup sliced pimiento-stuffed green olives
1 small onion, chopped (¼ cup)
2 tablespoons butter or margarine
2 tablespoons all-purpose flour
½ teaspoon salt
1 cup milk
⅔ cup mayonnaise or salad dressing
1 lb. frankfurters
1 hard-cooked egg, sliced

Scrub potatoes. Cook, covered, in boiling salted water in a medium saucepan 25 minutes, or until tender; drain. Cool until easy to handle, then peel and cube. (There should be 4 cups.) Combine potatoes and olives in a large bowl.

Sauté onion in butter until soft in a medium saucepan; stir in flour and salt. Cook, stirring constantly, until bubbly. Stir in milk; continue cooking and stirring until sauce thickens and boils 1 minute; remove from heat. Stir in mayonnaise. Pour over potato mixture; toss lightly to mix.

Preheat oven to 350°.

Cut each frankfurter in half crosswise; stand around edge in a 1¾-quart shallow baking dish; spoon potato mixture into center.

Bake 20 minutes, or just until hot. Garnish with egg slices. Serve hot.

Yield: 6 servings.

HAM SALAD ALOHA

1 canned ham, weighing 1 lb.
½ cup thinly sliced celery
¾ cup mayonnaise or salad dressing
2 tablespoons salad oil
2 tablespoons lemon juice
1 tablespoon honey
½ medium-sized firm ripe pineapple
1 firm ripe papaya
Boston lettuce

Scrape gelatin coating from ham; cube meat. (There should be 2 cups.) Combine with celery in a medium bowl.

Combine mayonnaise, salad oil, lemon juice, and honey in a small bowl; beat until smooth. Fold half into ham mixture; cover. Chill along with remaining dressing at least 1 hour.

Pare pineapple; remove core and eyes; slice fruit crosswise.

Pare papaya; cut in half; scoop out seeds. Slice fruit crosswise into thin crescents.

Line a medium salad bowl with lettuce; spoon ham mixture into center. Overlap pineapple and papaya slices, alternately, around edge. Garnish ham mixture with several thin lemon slices if you like. Serve with extra dressing to spoon over fruit.

Yield: 4 servings.

POLYNESIAN TUNA TOSS

1 small head romaine
2 cans (about 7 ozs. each) tuna, drained and broken into chunks.
1 can (11 ozs.) mandarin orange segments, drained
1 can (8 ozs.) water chestnuts, drained and sliced
1 cup diagonally sliced celery
½ cup sliced green onions
1 small green pepper, quartered, seeded, and cut into strips
⅔ cup mayonnaise or salad dressing
1 teaspoon grated orange rind
⅓ cup orange juice

Line a large salad bowl with romaine; break remainder into bite-sized pieces and place in bottom of bowl.

Arrange tuna, orange segments, water chestnuts, celery, onions, and pepper strips on top.

Blend mayonnaise, orange rind, and orange juice in a small bowl; drizzle over salad; toss lightly to mix. Or pass dressing separately to spoon over each serving.

Yield: 6 servings.

◀ **STEAK DIANE** (p.83)
CAESAR SALAD (p.329)
POPOVERS (p.409)

CAPE COD TURKEY SALAD

1 frozen boneless turkey roast, weighing 2 lbs.
1½ cups diagonally sliced celery
1 can (8 ozs.) jellied cranberry sauce
½ medium-sized firm ripe honeydew melon
½ cup whipping cream
¼ cup dairy sour cream
1 tablespoon lime juice
2 teaspoons finely chopped crystallized ginger
1 head Boston lettuce
2 tablespoons coarsely broken pecans

Roast turkey as label directs; remove from foil pan; chill. Cut meat into cubes. (There should be 3 cups.) Combine with celery in a large bowl.

Open cranberry can at both ends and push out sauce; cut into 6 slices, then cut into small cubes; place in a small bowl and chill.

Pare honeydew; scoop out seeds. Cut melon in half lengthwise, then cut crosswise into thin slices; cover and chill.

Just before serving, combine whipping cream and sour cream in a small bowl; beat until mixture forms soft peaks. Fold in lime juice and ginger; fold about three fourths into turkey mixture.

Line a large salad bowl with lettuce; break remainder into bite-sized pieces and place in bowl. Spoon turkey mixture on top. Overlap honeydew slices around edge in bowl; spoon cranberry cubes in a ring next to melon.

Spoon remaining dressing on top of turkey mixture; sprinkle pecans over dressing.

Yield: 6 servings.

SPAGHETTI SALAD CARBONARA

1 package (8 ozs.) spaghetti, broken into 2-inch lengths
1 tablespoon salad oil
4 slices bacon, cut into 1-inch pieces
1 package (4 ozs.) sliced boiled ham
1 cup thinly sliced celery
3 hard-cooked eggs, chopped
4 tablespoons chopped parsley
1 cup mayonnaise or salad dressing
2 tablespoons milk
⅓ cup grated Parmesan cheese
Romaine

Cook spaghetti as label directs; drain; place in a large bowl. Drizzle salad oil over top; toss lightly to mix; cool.

Sauté bacon in a small skillet until crisp; remove from skillet and drain on paper toweling. Cut ham slices in half lengthwise, then cut into thin strips; add to spaghetti mixture with bacon, celery, eggs, and 3 tablespoons of the parsley.

Blend mayonnaise, milk, and Parmesan cheese in a small bowl; stir into spaghetti mixture; cover. Chill several hours to season.

When ready to serve, spoon spaghetti mixture into a romaine-lined salad bowl; sprinkle remaining 1 tablespoon chopped parsley over top.

Yield: 6 servings.

DANISH SALMON STACKS

1 can (8 ozs.) salmon, drained,
  boned, and flaked
½ cup fresh unpared zucchini, finely
  chopped
1 small onion, chopped (¼ cup)
1 tablespoon snipped fresh dill
½ cup prepared sandwich spread
2 teaspoons lemon juice
¼ teaspoon salt
2 large carrots
2 large stalks celery
4 medium tomatoes
  Romaine
8 green onions, trimmed
1 small cucumber, scored and sliced
  thin

Combine salmon, zucchini, onion, and dill
in a medium bowl. Blend sandwich spread
with lemon juice and salt in a cup; stir into
salmon mixture; chill.

Pare carrots; cut into long thin strips with a
vegetable parer. Roll up each strip, jelly-roll
fashion; fasten with a wooden pick. Drop into
a large bowl of ice and water for several hours
to crisp and curl.

Trim celery stalks; cut into 3-inch lengths.
Working from each end, cut into narrow strips
to within ½ inch of center. Drop into bowl
with carrots until ends curl.

Just before serving, peel tomatoes; cut each
crosswise into 4 thick slices, keeping slices in
order. Spread salmon mixture over 3 slices of
each tomato; restack in tomato shape. Place on
a romaine-lined platter, stem end down. Garnish each with a cherry tomato held in place
with a wooden pick if you like.

Drain carrots and celery; remove picks from
carrots. Arrange carrots, celery, green onions,
and cucumber slices in piles around tomatoes.

Yield: 4 servings.

HAM MOUSSE VERONIQUE

2 envelopes unflavored gelatin
¼ cup sugar
⅛ teaspoon salt
1½ cups water
¼ cup lime juice
   Green and yellow food colorings
1 canned ham, weighing 1 lb.
1 can (8 ozs.) water chestnuts, drained
   and chopped
¼ cup chopped dill pickle
1 can (13¾ ozs.) chicken broth
½ cup seedless green grapes
¾ cup mayonnaise or salad dressing
2 teaspoons prepared mustard
   Chicory or curly endive
¼ small cucumber, scored and sliced thin

Mix 1 envelope of the gelatin with sugar and salt in a small saucepan; stir in ½ cup of the water. Heat, stirring constantly, until gelatin dissolves; remove from heat. Stir in remaining water and lime juice, then 1 drop green food coloring and 2 drops yellow to tint lime color. Set aside.

Scrape gelatin coating from ham; put meat through a food grinder, using a fine blade. Combine with water chestnuts and chopped pickle in a medium bowl.

Sprinkle remaining 1 envelope gelatin over 1 cup of the chicken broth in a small saucepan; heat, stirring constantly, until gelatin dissolves; remove from heat. Stir in remaining chicken broth. Chill in refrigerator 20 minutes, or until mixture starts to thicken.

Pour lime gelatin mixture into a 1¾-quart mold; set mold in a shallow pan of ice and water to speed setting. Let stand, stirring several times, until mixture starts to thicken; stir in grapes. Continue chilling just until sticky-firm to the touch.

Beat mayonnaise and mustard into thickened chicken-broth mixture; fold in ham mixture. Carefully spoon over sticky-firm layer in mold; remove from ice and water. Chill in refrigerator overnight until firm.

When ready to serve, loosen salad around edge with a knife. Dip mold in and out of warm water; invert on a large serving plate. Frame with sprigs of chicory and cucumber slices cut in half.

Yield: 6 servings.

SALMON SALAD SOUFFLE

2 envelopes unflavored gelatin
1½ cups water
1 envelope instant chicken broth
1 can (16 ozs.) salmon
1 small green pepper, quartered,
   seeded, and diced (½ cup)
1 jar (2 ozs.) sliced pimientos,
   drained and diced
½ cup diced celery
1 cup mayonnaise or salad dressing
¼ cup lemon juice
1 cup whipping cream
   Chicory or curly endive
1 small cucumber, cut into 2-inch
   sticks
2 small tomatoes, cut into wedges

Soften gelatin in water in a small saucepan. Heat, stirring constantly, until gelatin dissolves; stir in chicken broth; pour into a large bowl. Chill about 30 minutes, or just until mixture starts to thicken.

While gelatin mixture chills, drain liquid from salmon; remove skin and bones; flake salmon. Combine with green pepper, pimientos, and celery in a bowl.

Blend mayonnaise and lemon juice in a 2-cup measure; beat cream until stiff in a medium bowl. Beat mayonnaise mixture into thickened gelatin; fold in salmon mixture, then whipped cream. Spoon into a 1½-quart mold. Chill in refrigerator overnight until firm.

When ready to serve, loosen salad around edge with a knife; dip mold in and out of warm water; invert onto a large serving plate; lift off mold. Frame salad with chicory, cucumber sticks, and tomato wedges.

Yield: 6 servings.

STRAWBERRY-PINEAPPLE CROWN

1 package (3 ozs.) strawberry-flavored
   gelatin
1 cup boiling water
¾ cup cold water
1 can (20 ozs.) pineapple chunks in juice
1 package (3 ozs.) lemon-flavored gelatin
1 tablespoon lemon juice
1 package (8 ozs.) cream cheese, softened
1 container (4½ ozs.) frozen whipped
   topping, thawed
1 pint (2 cups) strawberries, washed,
   hulled, and sliced
   Boston lettuce

Dissolve strawberry gelatin in boiling water in a medium bowl; stir in cold water. Chill 20 minutes, or until mixture is syrupy-thick.

While gelatin chills, drain juice from pineapple into a 1-cup measure; add water to make 1 cup. Heat to boiling in a small saucepan; remove from heat. Stir in lemon gelatin until dissolved, then lemon juice; cool slightly.

Beat lemon gelatin mixture into cream cheese in a medium bowl until smooth; fold in whipped topping and pineapple. Chill until mixture starts to thicken.

Stir strawberries into thickened strawberry gelatin; spoon into a 2-quart mold. Place mold in a shallow pan of ice and water to speed setting. Chill strawberry layer until sticky-firm. Carefully spoon pineapple mixture on top; remove from water. Chill in refrigerator overnight until firm.

When ready to serve, loosen salad around edge with a knife; dip mold in and out of warm water; invert onto a serving plate; lift off mold. Garnish plate with small lettuce leaves and whole strawberries if you like.

Yield: 10 servings.

MOLDED TURKEY AND CRANBERRIES

1 envelope unflavored gelatin
1 cup cold water
3 tablespoons lime juice
1 cup (8-oz. carton) dairy sour cream
½ cup mayonnaise or salad dressing
1 tablespoon grated onion
1 package (3 ozs.) lemon-flavored gelatin
1 cup boiling water
1 can (8 ozs.) whole-berry cranberry sauce
2 cans (5 or 6 ozs. each) boned turkey,
   drained and cut up
⅓ cup chopped blanched slivered almonds
½ cup chopped celery

Soften unflavored gelatin in cold water in a small saucepan. Heat, stirring constantly, until gelatin dissolves; pour into a medium bowl; cool. Stir in lime juice, then beat in sour cream, mayonnaise, and onion. Chill, stirring several times, just until mixture starts to thicken.

While mayonnaise mixture chills, dissolve lemon gelatin in boiling water in a medium bowl; stir in cranberry sauce. Chill until mixture starts to thicken.

Fold turkey and almonds into thickened mayonnaise-gelatin mixture; spoon into a 7-cup tube mold. Place mold in a shallow pan of ice and water to speed setting; let stand just until sticky-firm to the touch.

Stir celery into cranberry mixture; carefully spoon over sticky-firm turkey layer. Remove mold from ice and water; chill in refrigerator overnight until firm.

When ready to serve, loosen salad around edge with a knife; dip mold in and out of warm water; invert onto a large serving plate; lift off mold. Garnish with romaine and celery fans if you like.

Yield: 6 servings.

PERFECTION MOLD

  2 packages (3 ozs. each) lemon-flavored
    gelatin
  2 cups boiling water
1½ cups cold water
  3 tablespoons cider vinegar
  2 teaspoons prepared horseradish
1½ teaspoons salt
  6 radishes, trimmed and sliced
1½ cups finely chopped Chinese cabbage
  ¾ cup chopped pared cucumber, well
    drained
  ½ cup chopped green pepper
    Escarole

Dissolve gelatin in boiling water in a medium bowl; stir in cold water, vinegar, horseradish, and salt. Chill 30 minutes, or until syrupy-thick.

Stir in radishes, cabbage, cucumber, and green pepper. Spoon into a shallow 1½-quart mold. Chill in refrigerator overnight until firm.

When ready to serve, loosen salad around edge with a knife; dip mold in and out of warm water; invert onto a serving plate; lift off mold. Garnish plate with escarole. Serve salad plain or with mayonnaise if you like.

Yield: 6 to 8 servings.

PEACH MELBA MOLD

  1 can (29 ozs.) cling peach slices
  1 package (3 ozs.) raspberry-flavored gelatin
  1 package (3 ozs.) lemon-flavored gelatin
  1 cup boiling water
  1 can (6 ozs.) pineapple juice
  ½ cup mayonnaise or salad dressing
    Leaf lettuce

Drain syrup from peaches into a 2-cup measure; add water to make 2 cups. Dice peaches and set aside.

Heat syrup to boiling in a small saucepan; remove from heat; stir in raspberry gelatin until dissolved. Pour into a 1¾-quart mold. Chill just until mixture is sticky-firm to the touch.

While raspberry mixture chills, dissolve lemon gelatin in boiling water in a medium bowl; stir in pineapple juice, then beat in mayonnaise. Chill until mixture starts to thicken; fold in peaches. Spoon over sticky-firm raspberry layer in mold. Chill in refrigerator overnight until firm.

When ready to serve, loosen salad around edge with a knife; dip mold in and out of warm water; invert on a large serving plate; lift off mold. Circle plate with lettuce. Garnish with additional peach slices and raspberries if you like.

Yield: 6 to 8 servings.

LIME VEGETABLE CREAM

  1 package (3 ozs.) lime-flavored gelatin
  ¾ cup boiling water
  1 large carrot
  1 large cucumber
  1 cup (8-oz. carton) dairy sour cream
  2 tablespoons minced onion
  ⅛ teaspoon salt
    Escarole
    Mayonnaise or salad dressing

Dissolve gelatin in boiling water in a medium bowl. Chill 20 minutes, or until syrupy-thick.

While gelatin chills, pare carrot and shred. (There should be 1 cup.) Pare cucumber; cut in half and scoop out seeds; shred cucumber and drain well. (There should be 1 cup.)

Beat sour cream into gelatin mixture until blended; stir in carrot, cucumber, onion, and salt. Spoon into a 3½-cup or 1-quart mold. Chill in refrigerator overnight until firm.

When ready to serve, loosen salad around edge with a knife; dip mold in and out of warm water; invert onto a serving plate; lift off mold.

Frame with small escarole leaves and garnish top with sliced ripe olives if you like. Serve with extra mayonnaise.

Yield: 6 servings.

CRANBERRY RING

1 can (20 ozs.) pineapple chunks in juice
2 envelopes unflavored gelatin
2 cups fresh cranberries, stemmed
1 cup sugar
　Salt
2 cups water
1½ cups thinly sliced celery
1 cup (8-oz. carton) dairy sour cream
1 tablespoon prepared horseradish
　Boston lettuce

Drain juice from pineapple into a small bowl; sprinkle gelatin over top of juice to soften.

Combine cranberries, sugar, a dash of salt, and water in a large saucepan; heat to boiling. Simmer 5 minutes, or until cranberries start to pop; stir in gelatin mixture until dissolved.

Place pan in a bowl of ice and water to speed setting. Chill, stirring several times, until syrupy-thick; fold in pineapple and celery. Spoon into a 1¾-quart ring mold. Chill in refrigerator overnight until firm.

Blend sour cream, horseradish, and ½ teaspoon salt in a small bowl; chill to blend flavors.

When ready to serve, loosen salad around edge and center with a knife; dip mold in and out of warm water; invert onto a serving plate; lift off mold. Garnish with small lettuce leaves. Serve with horseradish dressing.

Yield: 8 servings.

MOLDED GUACAMOLE SALAD

1 envelope unflavored gelatin
1 cup water
1 large firm ripe avocado
1 small onion, peeled and quartered
¼ cup mayonnaise or salad dressing
¼ cup dairy sour cream
2 tablespoons lemon juice
½ teaspoon salt
　Romaine
3 medium-sized ripe tomatoes, sliced thin

Sprinkle gelatin over water in a small saucepan; heat slowly, stirring constantly, until gelatin dissolves; cool.

Peel avocado, cut in half, and pit; cut avocado into chunks and place in an electric-blender container. Add onion, mayonnaise, sour cream, lemon juice, salt, and cooled gelatin mixture; cover. Blend until smooth. Pour into a 3-cup mold. Chill in refrigerator until firm.

When ready to serve, loosen avocado mixture around edge with a knife; dip mold quickly in and out of warm water; invert onto a large serving platter; lift off mold. Frame salad with small romaine leaves and tomato slices.

Yield: 6 servings.

MOLDED BEET RELISH

2 cans (8 ozs. each) diced beets
1 envelope unflavored gelatin
3 tablespoons lemon juice
1 teaspoon salt
4 teaspoons prepared horseradish
1 cup thinly sliced celery
⅓ cup thinly sliced pimiento-stuffed
　green olives
1 tablespoon grated onion
　Romaine
　Mayonnaise or salad dressing

Drain liquid from beets into a 2-cup measure; add water to make 1½ cups. Pour into a small saucepan; sprinkle gelatin over top to soften. Heat slowly, stirring constantly, until gelatin dissolves; pour into a medium bowl.

Stir in lemon juice, salt, and horseradish. Chill 40 minutes, or until mixture starts to thicken.

Stir in celery, olives, onion, and beets; spoon into a 1-quart mold. Chill in refrigerator until firm.

When ready to serve, loosen salad around edge with a knife; dip mold quickly in and out of warm water; invert onto a serving plate; lift off mold. Garnish salad with small romaine leaves and serve with mayonnaise.

Yield: 6 servings.

AVOCADO-SALMON MOUSSE

2 envelopes unflavored gelatin
2½ cups water
1 large firm ripe avocado
½ small onion, peeled and cut up
¾ cup mayonnaise or salad dressing
¼ cup dairy sour cream
2 tablespoons lemon juice
¾ teaspoon salt
1 can (16 ozs.) salmon
2 tablespoons chili sauce
2 tablespoons minced onion
1 tablespoon chopped parsley

Sprinkle 1 envelope gelatin over 1 cup of the water in a small saucepan; heat, stirring constantly, until gelatin dissolves; remove from heat; cool slightly.

Cut avocado in half; peel and pit; cut fruit into chunks. Place in an electric-blender container with gelatin mixture, cut onion, ¼ cup of the mayonnaise, sour cream, 1 tablespoon of the lemon juice, and ½ teaspoon of the salt; cover. Blend until smooth. Set aside while preparing salmon mixture.

Sprinkle remaining 1 envelope gelatin over 1½ cups water in a small saucepan; heat, stirring constantly, until gelatin dissolves; remove from heat.

Drain liquid from salmon; flake meat, removing bones and skin; place in a medium bowl. Stir in chili sauce, minced onion, parsley, remaining ½ cup mayonnaise, 1 tablespoon lemon juice, ¼ teaspoon salt, and gelatin mixture. Chill in refrigerator 30 minutes, or until mixture starts to thicken.

Pour avocado mixture into a 1½-quart mold; place mold in a shallow pan of ice and water to speed setting. Chill about 20 minutes, or until sticky-firm. Carefully spoon thickened salmon mixture on top; remove from water. Chill in refrigerator overnight until firm.

When ready to serve, loosen salad around edge with a knife; dip mold in and out of warm water; invert onto a serving plate; lift off mold.

Garnish salad with several tiny bouquets of parsley and ripe olives if you like.
Yield: 8 servings.

SUMMER RICE SUPPER

1 cup uncooked regular rice
1 envelope unflavored gelatin
2 tablespoons sugar
1½ teaspoons salt
1½ cups water
¼ cup lemon juice
1 cup chopped celery
½ cup chopped green pepper
½ cup sliced pimiento-stuffed green olives
½ small cucumber, sliced thin (about 16 slices)
1 cup mayonnaise or salad dressing
½ cup whipping cream, whipped
Pickled Stuffed Eggs (recipe on page 244)
Romaine

Cook rice as label directs; cool.

Mix gelatin, sugar, and ½ teaspoon of the salt in a small saucepan; stir in water. Heat, stirring constantly, until gelatin dissolves; remove from heat. Stir in lemon juice; cool.

Combine rice with celery, green pepper, and olives in a large bowl.

Place a 1½-quart mold in a shallow pan of ice and water to speed setting. Pour in ¼ cup of the gelatin mixture; let stand until syrupy-thick. Overlap cucumber slices on top of gelatin in mold; carefully pour in another ¼ cup gelatin; let stand until sticky-firm.

Stir remaining 1 teaspoon salt into the rest of the gelatin mixture; fold into rice mixture, then fold in mayonnaise and whipped cream. Spoon over cucumber layer in mold; remove from ice and water. Chill in refrigerator overnight until firm.

When ready to serve, loosen salad around edge with a knife; dip mold in and out of warm water; invert onto a large serving plate; lift off mold. Frame with Pickled Stuffed Eggs and romaine.
Yield: 6 to 8 servings.

MOLDED APPLE RELISH

1 package (3 ozs.) lemon-flavored
    gelatin
¼ teaspoon salt
1¼ cups boiling water
¼ cup mayonnaise or salad dressing
¼ cup dairy sour cream
1 large red eating apple
1 tablespoon lemon juice
1 large carrot, pared and shredded (1 cup)
½ cup thinly sliced celery
¼ cup broken California walnuts
    Chicory or curly endive

Dissolve gelatin and salt in boiling water in a medium bowl; chill 20 minutes, or until syrupy-thick. Beat in mayonnaise and sour cream.

Quarter apple, core, and dice; toss with lemon juice in a medium bowl; fold into gelatin mixture with carrot, celery, and walnuts. Spoon into a 1-quart mold. Chill in refrigerator overnight until firm.

When ready to serve, loosen salad around edge with a knife; dip mold in and out of warm water; invert onto a serving plate; lift off mold.

Frame base of salad with chicory and garnish top with carrot curls if you like.

Yield: 4 to 6 servings.

CRANBERRY-TURKEY RING

2 cups orange juice
1 cup water
1 package (6 ozs.) cherry-flavored gelatin
1 can (16 ozs.) whole-berry cranberry sauce
2 teaspoons grated orange rind
3 cups cubed cooked turkey
1 cup thinly sliced celery
1 cup seedless green grapes
1 small firm ripe papaya, quartered,
    pared, seeded, and diced
½ cup mayonnaise or salad dressing
1 tablespoon lemon juice
    Watercress

Heat 1 cup of the orange juice and water to boiling in a medium saucepan; remove from heat. Stir in gelatin until dissolved; stir in remaining 1 cup orange juice, cranberry sauce, and orange rind.

Chill mixture 50 minutes, or until syrupy-thick; stir well; pour into a 1½-quart ring mold. Chill in refrigerator overnight until firm.

Combine turkey, celery, grapes, and papaya in a medium bowl. Blend mayonnaise and lemon juice in a cup; stir into turkey mixture; chill at least an hour.

When ready to serve, loosen cranberry ring around edge and center with a knife; dip mold in and out of warm water; invert onto a serving plate; lift off mold.

Spoon turkey mixture into center of ring. Garnish plate with watercress.

Yield: 6 servings.

BLACK CHERRY WHIP

1 can (16 ozs.) pitted dark sweet cherries
1 package (3 ozs.) black cherry-flavored
    gelatin
1 cup boiling water
1 package (2 ozs.) whipped topping mix
    Milk
¼ cup mayonnaise or salad dressing
2 medium-sized firm ripe bananas, peeled
    and diced
    Mint

Drain syrup from cherries into a 1-cup measure; add water to make 1 cup.

Dissolve gelatin in boiling water in a medium bowl; stir in the 1 cup cherry liquid. Chill 20 minutes, or until syrupy-thick.

While gelatin chills, prepare topping mix with milk as label directs; beat in mayonnaise. Beat into thickened gelatin mixture; fold in cherries and bananas. Spoon into a 1½-quart mold. Chill in refrigerator until firm.

When ready to serve, loosen salad around edge with a knife; dip mold in and out of warm water; invert onto a serving plate; lift off mold. Garnish with a few sprigs of mint.

Yield: 8 servings.

TUNA-OLIVE SALAD

1 envelope unflavored gelatin
1 cup chicken broth
¾ cup water
¾ cup mayonnaise or salad dressing
2 tablespoons lemon juice
⅛ teaspoon pepper
2 tablespoons minced onion
1 can (about 7 ozs.) tuna, drained and
    flaked
½ cup sliced pitted ripe olives
1 cup shredded sharp Cheddar cheese
    Chicory or curly endive

Sprinkle gelatin over chicken broth in a medium saucepan. Heat, stirring constantly, until gelatin dissolves; remove from heat; stir in water. Chill 30 minutes, or until mixture is syrupy-thick.

Beat in mayonnaise, lemon juice, and pepper until smooth; stir in onion, tuna, olives, and cheese. Spoon into a 1-quart mold. Chill in refrigerator until firm.

When ready to serve, loosen salad around edge with a knife; dip mold in and out of warm water; invert onto a serving plate; lift off mold. Garnish salad with small chicory leaves and cherry tomatoes if you like.

Yield: 4 servings.

CURRIED CHICKEN SALAD

1 broiler-fryer, weighing about 3 lbs.
1 small onion, peeled and quartered
    Few celery tops
1½ teaspoons salt
2 cups water
1 envelope unflavored gelatin
¾ teaspoon curry powder
¼ teaspoon lemon-pepper
2 egg whites
1 cup whipping cream
1 cup mayonnaise or salad dressing
1 can (8 ozs.) water chestnuts, drained
    and diced
    Romaine
2 hard-cooked eggs, sliced

Combine chicken, onion, celery tops, 1 teaspoon of the salt, and water in a kettle. Heat to boiling; cover. Simmer 45 minutes, or until chicken is tender. Remove from broth and cool until easy to handle, then take meat from bones and dice. (There should be 2½ cups.) Strain broth into a small bowl; cool.

Measure 1 cup of the broth into a small saucepan; sprinkle gelatin over top to soften. Heat, stirring constantly, until gelatin dissolves; remove from heat. Stir in curry powder, lemon-pepper, and remaining ½ teaspoon salt. Chill 20 minutes, or until mixture is syrupy-thick.

While gelatin mixture chills, beat egg whites until they stand in soft peaks in a small bowl; beat cream until stiff in a medium bowl.

Beat mayonnaise into thickened gelatin mixture; stir in diced chicken and water chestnuts; fold in beaten egg whites and whipped cream. Spoon into a 1¾-quart mold. Chill in refrigerator overnight until firm.

When ready to serve, loosen salad around edge with a knife; dip mold in and out of warm water; invert onto a large serving plate; lift off mold. Circle salad with small romaine leaves and egg and cucumber slices if you like.

Yield: 8 servings.

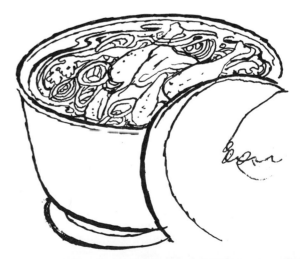

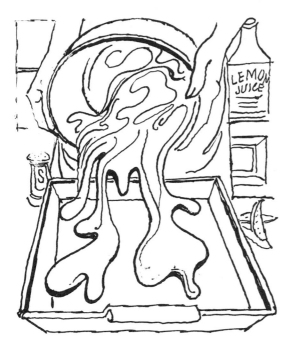

CRANBERRY RELISH SOUFFLE

1 package (3 ozs.) orange-flavored
    gelatin
¼ teaspoon salt
1 cup boiling water
½ cup mayonnaise or salad dressing
1 tablespoon grated orange rind
1 tablespoon lemon juice
1 can (16 ozs.) whole-berry cranberry
    sauce
1 large seedless orange, pared and
    diced
    Chicory

Dissolve gelatin and salt in boiling water in a medium bowl; beat in mayonnaise, orange rind, and lemon juice. Pour into a shallow pan. Chill in freezer until mixture starts to freeze around edge but is still soft in center.

Scoop mixture into a medium bowl; beat until smooth and fluffy; beat in cranberry sauce; stir in diced orange. Pour into a 1-quart mold. Chill in refrigerator until firm.

When ready to serve, loosen salad around edge with a knife; dip mold in and out of warm water; invert onto a serving plate; lift off mold.

Garnish plate with small chicory leaves and a few orange wedges if you like.
Yield: 8 servings

DEVONSHIRE FRUIT RING

2 envelopes unflavored gelatin
½ cup water
2 cartons (16 ozs. each) creamed
    cottage cheese (4 cups)
1 cup light cream
1 teaspoon grated lime rind
¼ cup lime juice
3 tablespoons sugar
2 teaspoons salt
¾ cup pre-sweetened wheat germ
⅔ cup salad oil
1 teaspoon grated lemon rind
⅓ cup lemon juice
1 pint strawberries
1 can (20 ozs.) pineapple chunks in juice
    Watercress

Soften gelatin in water in a small saucepan. Heat, stirring constantly, until gelatin dissolves; pour into a large bowl. Stir in cottage cheese, cream, lime rind and juice, 1 tablespoon of the sugar, and 1½ teaspoons of the salt. Chill 20 minutes, or just until mixture starts to thicken.

Fold in wheat germ; spoon into a 1½-quart ring mold. Chill in refrigerator until firm.

Combine salad oil, lemon rind and juice, remaining 2 tablespoons sugar, and remaining ½ teaspoon salt in a jar with a tight lid; cover; shake until sugar dissolves. Chill.

Just before serving, wash strawberries; hull and cut in half. Drain juice from pineapple and save to make punch; combine pineapple and strawberries.

Loosen salad around edge and center ring with a knife; dip mold in and out of warm water; invert onto a large serving plate; lift off mold. Garnish plate with a cluster of watercress; spoon fruit mixture into center. Serve with lemon dressing.
Yield: 8 servings.

DRESSINGS

BASIC FRENCH DRESSING

¾ cup salad oil
¼ cup vinegar
¾ teaspoon salt
¾ teaspoon sugar
½ teaspoon dry mustard
¼ teaspoon paprika
   Dash of pepper

Combine ingredients in a jar with a tight lid; shake well to mix. Chill. Serve with vegetable, meat, or tossed green salads.
Yield: About 1 cup.

THOUSAND ISLAND DRESSING

1 cup mayonnaise or salad dressing
3 tablespoons catsup
2 tablespoons sweet-pickle relish
1 hard-cooked egg, chopped
¼ teaspoon salt

Combine all ingredients in a small bowl; stir until well blended. Chill. Serve over lettuce wedges or with mixed greens.
Yield: 1½ cups.

BLUE-CHEESE DRESSING

1 cup (8-oz. carton) creamed cottage cheese
1 package (4 ozs.) blue cheese
2 green onions, trimmed and cut up
¾ cup milk
¼ teaspoon salt
   Few drops of red-pepper seasoning

Combine all ingredients in an electric-blender container; cover. Beat until smooth. Chill. Serve over lettuce or tomato slices.
Yield: 2 cups.

QUICK RUSSIAN DRESSING

½ cup mayonnaise or salad dressing
2 tablespoons finely chopped celery
2 tablespoons chopped pimiento
1 tablespoon finely chopped green pepper
2 tablespoons chili sauce

Combine all ingredients in a small bowl; stir well to mix. Chill. Serve with seafood or tossed green salads.
Yield: 1 cup.

CREOLE SALAD DRESSING

1 cup mayonnaise or salad dressing
½ cup catsup
2 teaspoons prepared horseradish
1 teaspoon Worcestershire sauce
   Dash of salt

Combine all ingredients in a small bowl; stir well to mix. Chill. Serve with seafood salads.
Yield: 1½ cups.

GREEN GODDESS DRESSING

1 cup mayonnaise or salad dressing
½ cup dairy sour cream
2 tablespoons minced onion
3 tablespoons minced parsley
2 tablespoons lemon juice
1 tablespoon vinegar
¾ teaspoon garlic salt

Combine all ingredients in a small bowl; beat until well blended. Chill. Serve with mixed green or egg salads.
Yield: 1¾ cups.

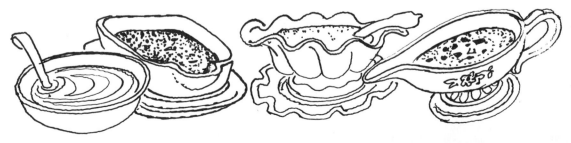

STRAWBERRY-LIME DRESSING

⅓ cup strawberry jelly
½ cup salad oil
¼ cup lime juice
1 teaspoon dry mustard
¾ teaspoon celery seeds
¼ teaspoon salt

Combine all ingredients in an electric-blender container; cover. Beat until smooth. Chill. Serve with fruit salads.
Yield: 1 cup.

PINK LEMONADE DRESSING

½ cup honey
½ cup lemon juice
½ cup salad oil
¼ cup currant jelly
1 teaspoon salt

Combine all ingredients in an electric-blender container; cover. Beat until smooth. Chill. Serve with fruit salads.
Yield: 1½ cups.

ORANGE CREAM DRESSING

1 package (8 ozs.) cream cheese, softened
1 teaspoon grated orange peel
½ cup orange juice
2 tablespoons lemon juice
¾ teaspoon sugar
¼ teaspoon salt

Combine all ingredients in a small bowl; beat until smooth. Chill. Serve with fruit salads.
Yield: 1½ cups.

PINEAPPLE CREAM DRESSING

1 cup dairy sour cream
½ cup pineapple preserves
2 tablespoons unsweetened pineapple juice
⅛ teaspoon ground nutmeg

Blend sour cream with pineapple preserves and juice, and nutmeg. Chill if made ahead, then stir lightly just before serving.
Serve with fruit or fruited gelatin salads.
Yield: about 1½ cups.

RASPBERRY CREAM DRESSING

⅓ cup seedless red raspberry preserves
¼ cup mayonnaise or salad dressing
1 tablespoon lime juice
Dash of salt
½ cup whipping cream, whipped

Combine raspberry preserves, mayonnaise, lime juice, and salt in a small bowl; beat until blended. Fold in whipped cream. Chill until serving time. Serve with fruit salads.
Yield: 1⅓ cups.

RELISHES

PICKLED MUSHROOMS

1 lb. small whole fresh mushrooms
2 tablespoons salad oil
1 tablespoon lemon juice
2 tablespoons sugar
½ teaspoon salt
⅓ cup white vinegar
2 tablespoons water

Rinse mushrooms; trim stem ends.

Sauté mushrooms in salad oil in a medium skillet 2 minutes; stir in lemon juice, then stir in sugar, salt, vinegar, and water; heat just to boiling.

Spoon into a medium bowl; cover. Chill several hours to season.

Yield: About 2 cups.

CARROT-RAISIN RELISH

4 large carrots
¾ cup dark raisins
½ cup mayonnaise or salad dressing
2 tablespoons cream
1 tablespoon lemon juice
2 teaspoons sugar
⅛ teaspoon salt

Pare carrots and shred. (There should be about 4 cups.) Combine with raisins in a medium bowl.

Blend mayonnaise with cream, lemon juice, sugar, and salt in a cup; stir into carrot mixture. Chill at least a half hour to season.

Yield: About 4 cups.

HOT APPLE-CRANBERRY RELISH

4 medium apples, pared, quartered, cored, and sliced
1½ cups cranberries, stemmed
1¼ cups sugar
1 tablespoon grated orange rind
1½ teaspoons ground cinnamon
½ teaspoon ground nutmeg
¼ teaspoon ground allspice
Dash of salt
2 tablespoons butter or margarine

Preheat oven to 350°.

Combine apples and cranberries in a 1¾-quart baking dish. Stir in sugar, orange rind, spices, and salt; dot butter over top; cover.

Bake 50 minutes; stir mixture lightly. Bake, uncovered, 10 minutes longer, or until apples and cranberries are tender. Serve hot.

Yield: 4 cups.

CABBAGE CHOP-CHOP

1 head cabbage, weighing about 1½ lbs.
1 medium-sized green pepper
Ice water
2 tablespoons vinegar
2 tablespoons sugar
1½ teaspoons salt

Trim cabbage; cut into quarters and core. Chop cabbage coarsely and place in a medium bowl. (There should be about 6 cups.) Cut green pepper in half; seed and dice; combine with cabbage.

Pour enough ice water into bowl to cover vegetables; chill in refrigerator 1 hour. Drain vegetables, pressing out as much liquid as possible with back of spoon; return vegetables to bowl.

Mix vinegar, 2 tablespoons water, sugar, and salt in a cup; stir into cabbage mixture; cover. Chill several hours to season. Drain well before serving.

Yield: About 6 cups.

PIMIENTO CORN RELISH

2 cans (12 ozs. each) whole-kernel corn
1 large onion, chopped (1 cup)
1 jar (2 ozs.) sliced pimientos, drained and diced
2 teaspoons mustard seeds
1 teaspoon dry mustard
½ teaspoon salt
¼ teaspoon pepper
¾ cup white vinegar
2 tablespoons salad oil

Drain liquid from corn into a medium saucepan; combine corn with onion and pimientos in a medium bowl.

Stir mustard seeds, dry mustard, salt, pepper, and vinegar into corn liquid. Heat to boiling; simmer 5 minutes. Stir in salad oil, then stir into vegetable mixture. Cool; cover; chill at least 12 hours to blend flavors.

Yield: 4⅓ cups.

HILO CRANBERRY RELISH

1 package (15 ozs.) cranberries
1 small firm ripe pineapple
2 large seedless oranges
1 cup sugar

Wash cranberries and stem. Cut leafy top from pineapple, then pare fruit. Cut into large chunks; remove eyes and core. Cut oranges into quarters, leaving rind in place.

Put fruits, part at a time, through a food grinder, using a coarse blade; place in a medium bowl. Stir in sugar. Cover and chill 12 hours or more to blend flavors.

Yield: About 4½ cups.

RIPE OLIVE RELISH

2 cans (7¾ ozs. each) unpitted large ripe olives
1 can or jar (3 ozs.) mushroom caps
⅔ cup salad oil
¼ cup cider vinegar
1 clove garlic, crushed
½ teaspoon salt
¼ teaspoon pepper
2 pints cherry tomatoes, stemmed

Drain liquids from olives and mushrooms.

Mix salad oil, vinegar, garlic, salt, and pepper in a medium bowl; stir in olives and mushrooms; cover. Chill at least overnight to season. Stir in whole cherry tomatoes. Chill 6 or more hours before serving.

Yield: 10 to 12 servings.

PEACH PICKLES

1 can (29 ozs.) cling peach halves in syrup
6 whole cloves
6 whole allspice
1 four-inch piece stick cinnamon

Drain syrup from peaches into a small saucepan; add spices. Heat to boiling; simmer 10 minutes.

Pour over peaches in a medium bowl. Let stand at room temperature until cool, then chill at least overnight to season. Drain before serving.

Yield: 6 to 8 servings.

BOMBAY FRUITS

1 can (29 ozs.) pear halves in syrup
1 can (20 ozs.) sliced apples in syrup
1 can (16 ozs.) apricot halves in syrup
1 can (11 ozs.) mandarin orange segments in syrup
¼ cup butter or margarine
1 tablespoon curry powder
⅓ cup firmly packed light brown sugar
¼ cup toasted slivered almonds.

Preheat oven to 325°.

Drain syrup from pears, apples, apricots, and mandarin orange segments and save to make fruit punch. Arrange fruits in a 1½-quart shallow baking dish.

Melt butter in a small saucepan; stir in curry powder; cook 1 minute. Drizzle over fruits; sprinkle brown sugar and almonds over top.

Bake 45 minutes. Serve warm as an accompaniment to meat.

Yield: 6 servings.

QUICK CRANBERRY CHUTNEY

1 can (8 ozs.) whole-berry cranberry sauce
1 large tart apple, pared, quartered, cored, and diced (1 cup)
½ cup light raisins
1 tablespoon chopped onion
1 tablespoon sweet-pickle relish

Combine all ingredients in a medium bowl; cover. Chill overnight to blend flavors.
Yield: 2½ cups.

QUICK SPICED APRICOTS

1 can (17 ozs.) whole peeled apricots in syrup
1 tablespoon mixed pickling spices

Drain syrup from apricots into a small saucepan; place apricots in a medium bowl.

Stir pickling spices into syrup; heat to boiling; cover. Simmer 5 minutes. Strain over apricots; cover. Chill overnight to season.
Yield: 4 servings.

TANGY CUCUMBER STRAWS

1 large cucumber
¼ teaspoon salt
Vinegar

Pare cucumber; slice lengthwise into sixths; cut crosswise into ¼-inch-wide strips. Place in a pie plate. Sprinkle salt over top, then pour in enough vinegar to cover cucumbers; cover. Chill several hours to season.

Before serving, drain off liquid.
Yield: About 2 cups.

TANGY OLIVES

1 can (7¾ ozs.) ripe olives, drained
1 small green pepper, quartered, seeded, and cut into strips
1 small red pepper, quartered, seeded, and cut into strips
½ cup vinegar
3 tablespoons salad oil

Combine olives, green pepper, and red pepper in a medium bowl.

Combine vinegar and salad oil in a jar with a tight lid; shake well to mix. Pour over olive mixture; toss lightly to mix; cover. Chill overnight to season.
Yield: About 3 cups.

SUCCOTASH RELISH

1 can (16 ozs.) green lima beans
1 can (12 ozs.) whole-kernel corn
1 jar (2 ozs.) sliced pimientos, drained
1 medium onion, chopped fine (½ cup)
½ cup chopped celery
⅓ cup white vinegar
½ teaspoon salt
¼ teaspoon liquid red-pepper seasoning
⅓ cup salad oil

Drain liquids from lima beans and corn into a small bowl; measure ½ cup into a small saucepan. Combine limas, corn, pimientos, onion, and celery in a medium bowl.

Stir vinegar, salt, and red-pepper seasoning into liquid in saucepan. Heat to boiling; simmer 10 minutes. Remove from heat; stir in salad oil, then stir into lima mixture; cover. Chill 1 or 2 days to season.
Yield: 4 cups.

GINGER PEARS

1 can (29 ozs.) pear halves in syrup
1½ teaspoons ground ginger
1 two-inch piece stick cinnamon
Salt
1 tablespoon lemon juice

Drain syrup from pears into a medium saucepan; place pears in a shallow dish.

Add ginger, cinnamon, and a dash of salt to syrup; heat to boiling, then simmer 5 minutes; remove from heat.

Stir in lemon juice; pour over pears; cover. Chill at least overnight to season.
Yield: 6 servings.

PETER RABBIT RELISH

3 cups chopped green cabbage
1 medium-sized cucumber, pared, quartered,
    seeded, and chopped
1 medium-sized red pepper, quartered, seeded,
    and chopped
2 medium-sized carrots, pared and shredded
2 tablespoons lemon juice
1 tablespoon water
1 tablespoon sugar
½ teaspoon salt

Combine cabbage, cucumber, red pepper, and carrots in a medium bowl.

Combine lemon juice, water, sugar, and salt in a cup. Stir until sugar dissolves; stir into cabbage mixture; cover. Chill at least an hour to blend flavors. Drain before serving.

Yield: About 5 cups.

DILLED CUCUMBER SLICES

1 medium cucumber
½ teaspoon salt
⅛ teaspoon pepper
¼ teaspoon dillweed
2 tablespoons vinegar
2 tablespoons water

Pare cucumber; slice thin; place slices in a pie plate. Sprinkle salt, pepper, and dillweed over top.

Mix vinegar and water in a cup; pour over cucumber mixture; toss lightly to mix; cover. Chill several hours to season.

Yield: About 1½ cups

GREEN CHILI SALSA

2 large tomatoes
1 large onion, peeled
1 can (4 ozs.) chopped green chili peppers,
    drained
1 clove garlic, minced
½ teaspoon salt

Chop tomatoes and onion coarsely; combine with chili peppers and garlic in a

medium bowl. Stir in salt; cover. Chill at least an hour to season.

Yield: About 3½ cups.

CRANBERRY-PEAR RELISH

1 can (16 ozs.) pear halves in syrup
½ cup sugar
2 tablespoons chopped crystallized ginger
2 tablespoons cider vinegar
1 cup cranberries, stemmed and chopped

Drain syrup from pears into a medium saucepan; dice pears and place in a medium bowl.

Stir sugar, ginger, and vinegar into syrup; heat to boiling. Stir in cranberries; heat to boiling again; simmer 10 minutes.

Pour over pears; stir lightly to mix. Chill at least overnight to blend flavors.

Yield: 2 cups.

BAKED BANANAS

2 tablespoons butter or margarine
4 medium-sized green-tipped bananas
Dash of salt

Preheat oven to 375°.

Melt butter in a baking dish, 8x8x2 inches. Peel bananas and place in dish, turning to coat well with butter; sprinkle salt lightly over top.

Bake 12 minutes, or until bananas are tender. Serve immediately.

Yield: 4 servings.

CRANBERRY-ORANGE RELISH

1 package (15 ozs.) cranberries, washed and
    stemmed
2 medium-sized seedless oranges, quartered
2 cups sugar

Put cranberries and oranges through a food grinder, using a coarse blade; place in a medium bowl. Stir in sugar; cover. Chill at least 12 hours to blend flavors.

Yield: About 4 cups.

SPICED CRANBERRIES

1 cup sugar
⅓ cup orange juice
½ teaspoon grated orange rind
1 two-inch piece stick cinnamon
2 cups cranberries, washed and stemmed

Combine sugar, orange juice and rind, and cinnamon stick in a medium saucepan; heat slowly, stirring constantly, to boiling. Stir in cranberries.

Cook rapidly 3 minutes, or just until berries start to pop; remove from heat.

Pour into a bowl; chill. Just before serving, remove cinnamon stick.

Yield: 2 cups.

RUTABAGA RELISH

2 cups shredded pared rutabaga or yellow turnip
2 cups shredded Chinese cabbage
1 large red eating apple, quartered, cored, and
    diced
½ cup bottled coleslaw dressing
½ teaspoon grated lemon rind
1 tablespoon lemon juice

Combine rutabaga with cabbage and apple in a medium bowl.

Mix coleslaw dressing, lemon rind, and lemon juice in a cup; stir into rutabaga mixture. Chill at least 30 minutes to blend flavors.

Yield: 6 servings.

MANDARIN PINEAPPLE

1 can (20 ozs.) pineapple chunks in juice
1 can (11 ozs.) mandarin orange segments in syrup
½ cup firmly packed brown sugar
⅓ cup chopped crystallized ginger
1 tablespoon lemon juice

Drain juice from pineapple and syrup from

orange segments into a small saucepan; combine fruits in a medium bowl.

Stir brown sugar and ginger into liquid; heat to boiling. Simmer 10 minutes; remove from heat; stir in lemon juice. Cool slightly; pour over fruits; cover. Chill overnight to blend flavors.

Yield: 2½ cups.

RAW APPLE CHUTNEY

4 medium-sized tart apples
1 medium-sized onion
3 medium-sized dill pickles, drained
¼ cup sugar
¼ cup vinegar

Cut apples in quarters; core. Peel onion and quarter. Put apples, onion, and dill pickles through a food grinder, using coarse blade; place in a medium bowl.

Stir in sugar and vinegar; cover. Chill overnight to blend flavors.

Yield: 3 cups.

BLUSHING APPLE WEDGES

½ cup red cinnamon candies
1½ cups water
3 large tart apples, pared, quartered, and cored
¼ cup sugar

Combine cinnamon candies and water in a medium skillet; heat, stirring constantly, until candies dissolve.

Place apple wedges in a single layer in skillet; heat to boiling; cover. Simmer 5 minutes, or just until apples are tender but still firm enough to hold their shape. Remove from skillet with a slotted spoon and place in a shallow dish.

Stir sugar into liquid in skillet; cook rapidly 3 minutes, or until syrup thickens slightly; pour over apples; cover. Chill several hours to season.

Yield: 6 servings.

BREADS

ALMOST EVERYONE AGREES that nothing quite matches the tantalizing aroma that wafts from the kitchen as plump loaves of yeast bread puff and bake to a rich golden brown. And for good eating, a big thick slice still warm from the oven and topped with butter or jelly is hard to beat for a snack or a meal.

Baking your own bread, rolls, and coffee-cake specialties won't save you time, but who watches the clock when it comes to cooking for the love of cooking and giving your family so much pleasure? The how-to's are simple, although it pays to know a few basic rules for handling yeast. You'll find them given here, along with pictured steps on kneading and shaping to guide you to success.

Besides yeast breads, there are all of the quick varieties—fruit and nut loaves, biscuits, muffins, corn bread, pancakes, waffles, and French toast—to tempt your family from morning to night and give everyday meals an extra lift. When you can't start from scratch, depend on packaged mixes and refrigerated doughs to streamline fixing. With a few of your own special flavoring tricks and shaping twists, they can be turned into homemade tempters in a hurry.

When you work with yeast

There are two types of yeast—*active dry* and *compressed*—and whichever you choose depends primarily on availability and your own preference. Active dry yeast comes in small airtight envelopes, and if stored in a cool, dry cupboard, it will stay fresh until the expiration date stamped on the package. Compressed, or fresh, yeast is sold as 0.6-ounce, 1-ounce, and 2-ounce cakes. Since it's perishable, it must be stored in the refrigerator. Both kinds work equally well in recipes, with one package of active dry interchangeable with one 0.6-ounce cake.

In our recipes, you'll find that there are two different methods of dissolving the yeast; both give excellent results if followed carefully. One calls for sprinkling the yeast into very warm water and stirring it until dissolved; the other specifies mixing the undissolved yeast with part of the dry ingredients from your recipe, then beating in warmed liquid. In either case, it is important that the temperature of the liquid be right. If it's too hot, it will kill the yeast and prevent rising; if it's too cool, the rising time will be slowed down considerably.

The "very warm water" referred to in the first method means a temperature of from 105° to 115°. Test it with a thermometer if you have one, or drop a little of the water onto the inside of your wrist—it should feel comfortably warm but not hot.

In the second method, the temperature of the liquid should range from 120° to 130°, or about the same as very hot tap water.

How to knead and shape a perfect loaf

1. Mix dough as your recipe directs, then sprinkle a bit of flour onto a board. Turn dough out onto board and shape it into a ball. If dough becomes sticky as you work, sprinkle a tablespoon or so more flour underneath to prevent sticking.

2. Fold the far edge of dough toward you, then, using the heels of your hands, push it away with a quick rocking motion. Give dough a quarter turn and continue folding and pushing until it is smooth and elastic—about 8 to 10 minutes. Shape into a ball again; place in a greased bowl, turning ball to coat with shortening; cover.

3. Let dough rise in a warm, draft-free place until doubled—45 minutes to 1 hour. To test, press the tips of your first two fingers about a half inch into dough. If dents remain, dough is right for shaping. During rising, grease your baking pan so it will be ready when the dough is rolled.

4. Punch dough down by pushing your fist into the center. Then pull the edges of the dough to the center. Lift it out of the bowl, turn it over, and shape into a ball again. Set on lightly floured board.

5. Roll the dough to an even, thick rectangle, about 14x9 inches. If air bubbles appear on top, press them out with sides of hands, working from the center toward edges and ends. Use a light touch.

6. Start with upper end of rectangle and roll it toward you. Roll tightly but be careful not to stretch dough. After each turn, press roll at bottom edge with your thumbs to seal. Turn seam side down.

7. Seal ends by pressing sides of hands down on each end; fold sealed ends under. Press firmly but do not tear dough.

8. Place loaf, seam side down, in greased pan. Although recipes don't always say so, it's a good idea at this point to brush top of loaf with melted shortening to keep crust from drying during second rising. For baking directions, follow your recipe.

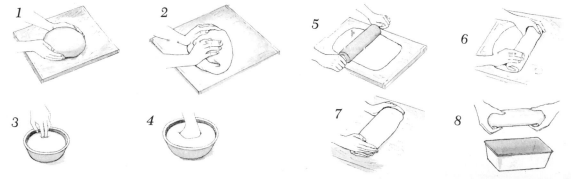

YEAST BREADS

BASIC WHITE BREAD

6½ cups sifted all-purpose flour
3 tablespoons sugar
2 teaspoons salt
1 envelope active dry yeast
1 cup milk
1 cup water
3 tablespoons shortening

Mix 2 cups of the flour, sugar, salt, and yeast in a large bowl.

Combine milk, water, and shortening in a small saucepan; heat until warm. Very slowly beat into yeast mixture; continue beating 2 minutes, scraping side of bowl once or twice. Beat in 1 cup flour; beat 2 minutes. By hand, stir in 3 cups more flour to make a stiff dough.

Turn out onto a lightly floured board; knead 8 minutes until smooth and elastic, adding only enough of the remaining ½ cup flour to keep dough from sticking. Shape into a ball; place in a greased large bowl; turn to coat all over with shortening; cover. Let rise in a warm place, away from drafts, 1 hour, or until dough is doubled.

Punch dough down; knead a few times; divide in half; cover. Let stand 15 minutes.

Roll out each half on a lightly floured board to a rectangle, 14x9 inches. Starting at a short end, roll up tightly, jelly-roll fashion. Fold ends of loaves under; place each, seam side down, in a greased baking pan, 8½x4½x2¾ inches, cover. Let rise again 45 minutes, or until doubled.

Preheat oven to 400°.

Bake 30 minutes, or until golden and loaves sound hollow when tapped with finger. Loosen around edges with a knife; turn out onto wire racks. Brush tops with melted butter or margarine if you prefer a soft crust; cool completely.

Yield: 2 loaves.

SWISS CHEESE BREAD

5¾ cups sifted all-purpose flour
2 tablespoons sugar
3 teaspoons salt
¼ teaspoon baking soda
1 envelope active dry yeast
1 cup buttermilk
1 cup water
1 tablespoon shortening
2 cups grated Swiss cheese (8 ozs.)

Mix 2½ cups of the flour, sugar, salt, baking soda, and yeast in a large bowl.

Combine buttermilk, water, and shortening in a small saucepan; heat until warm. Very slowly beat into yeast mixture; continue beating 2 minutes, scraping side of bowl once or twice.

Beat in cheese and 1 cup flour; beat 2 minutes. By hand, stir in 2 cups more flour to make a stiff dough.

Turn out onto a lightly floured board; knead 8 minutes until smooth and elastic, adding only enough of the remaining ¼ cup flour to keep dough from sticking. Shape into a ball; place in a greased large bowl; turn to coat all over with shortening; cover. Let rise in a warm place, away from drafts, 1 hour, or until dough is doubled.

Punch dough down; knead a few times; divide in half.

Roll out each half on a lightly floured board to a rectangle, 14x9 inches. Starting at a short end, roll up tightly, jelly-roll fashion. Fold ends of loaves under; place each, seam side down, in a greased baking pan, 9x5x3 inches; cover. Let rise again 1 hour, or until doubled.

Preheat oven to 375°.

Bake 45 minutes, or until golden and loaves sound hollow when tapped with finger. Loosen around edges with a knife; turn out onto wire racks. Brush tops with melted butter or margarine if you prefer a soft crust; cool completely.

Yield: 2 loaves.

RAISIN-OATMEAL BREAD

    4 tablespoons butter or margarine
    2 cups milk
    2 tablespoons sugar
 1½ teaspoons salt
    2 envelopes active dry yeast
    ½ cup very warm water
 5½ cups sifted all-purpose flour
    2 cups quick-cooking rolled oats
    1 cup dark raisins

Combine butter, milk, sugar, and salt in a small saucepan; heat to scalding; cool to lukewarm.

Dissolve yeast in very warm water in a large bowl. (Very warm water should feel comfortably warm when dropped on wrist.) Beat in cooled milk mixture and 2 cups of the flour until smooth. Stir in rolled oats, raisins, and 3¼ cups flour to make a soft dough.

Turn out onto a lightly floured board; knead 8 minutes until smooth and elastic, adding only enough of the remaining ¼ cup flour to keep dough from sticking. Shape into a ball; place in a greased large bowl; turn to coat all over with shortening; cover. Let rise in a warm place, away from drafts, 1 hour, or until dough is doubled.

Punch dough down; knead a few times; divide in half.

Roll out each half on a lightly floured board to a rectangle, 14x9 inches. Starting at a short end, roll up tightly, jelly-roll fashion. Fold ends of loaves under; place each, seam side down, in a greased baking pan, 8½x4½x2¾; cover. Let rise again 40 minutes, or until dough is doubled.

Preheat oven to 375°.

Bake 45 minutes, or until golden and loaves sound hollow when tapped with finger. Loosen around edges with a knife; turn out onto wire racks. Brush tops with melted butter or margarine if you prefer a soft crust; cool completely.

Yield: 2 loaves

CINNAMON PINWHEEL LOAF

⅓ cup shortening
  Milk
⅓ cup granulated sugar (for dough)
 1 teaspoon salt
 1 envelope active dry yeast
 ¼ cup very warm water
 1 egg
3¾ cups sifted all-purpose flour
 3 tablespoons granulated sugar (for filling)
 1 teaspoon ground cinnamon
 ½ cup sifted confectioners' powdered sugar
 ½ teaspoon vanilla

Combine shortening, ¾ cup milk, the ⅓ cup sugar, and salt in a small saucepan; heat to scalding; cool to lukewarm.

Dissolve yeast in very warm water in a large bowl. Beat in egg, cooled milk mixture, and 2 cups flour until smooth. Beat in 1½ cups more flour to make a stiff dough.

Turn out onto a lightly floured board; knead 5 minutes until smooth and elastic, adding only enough of the remaining ¼ cup flour to keep dough from sticking. Shape into a ball; place in a greased large bowl; turn to coat all over with shortening; cover. Let rise in a warm place, away from drafts, 1 hour, or until dough is doubled.

Punch dough down; knead a few times. Roll out on a lightly floured board to a rectangle, 16x9 inches.

Mix the 3 tablespoons sugar and cinnamon in a cup; sprinkle evenly over rectangle. Starting at a short end, roll up tightly, jelly-roll fashion. Fold ends of loaf under; place, seam side down, in a greased baking pan, 9x5x3 inches; cover. Let rise again 45 minutes, or until doubled.

Preheat oven to 375°.

Bake 45 minutes, or until golden and loaf sounds hollow when tapped with finger. Loosen around edges with a knife; turn out onto a wire rack; cool.

Blend confectioners' sugar, vanilla, and 1 to 2 teaspoons milk in a cup to make a smooth thin glaze; drizzle over loaf. Let stand until glaze is firm.

Yield: 1 loaf.

FRUIT BREAD

1 cup whole bran cereal
2 tablespoons butter or margarine
1 tablespoon sugar
½ teaspoon salt
½ cup boiling water
1 package hot roll mix
1 package active dry yeast
½ cup very warm water
2 eggs
½ cup chopped mixed candied fruits
½ cup chopped light raisins

Combine bran, butter, sugar, salt, and boiling water in a medium bowl; let stand about 10 minutes.

Dissolve yeast from hot roll mix plus extra package in warm water in a small bowl.

Beat eggs into cereal mixture. Stir in dissolved yeast and flour mixture from hot roll mix until well blended and smooth; stir in candied fruits and raisins; cover. Let rise in a warm place, away from drafts, 1 hour, or until dough is doubled.

Stir dough down; beat several times; spoon into a greased baking pan, 9x5x3 inches; cover. Let rise again 1 hour, or until doubled.

Preheat oven to 375°.

Bake loaf 45 minutes, or until deep brown and it sounds hollow when tapped with finger. (If loaf seems to be browning too fast, cover with a sheet of foil or heavy brown paper after 30 minutes.)

Remove loaf from pan to a wire rack; cool completely.

Yield: 1 loaf.

ITALIAN RAISIN LOAVES

  3 cups sifted all-purpose flour
¼ cup granulated sugar
½ teaspoon salt
  1 envelope active dry yeast
  1 small can evaporated milk (⅔ cup)
  5 tablespoons butter or margarine
  2 eggs
¼ cup finely chopped citron
¼ cup dark raisins
  2 teaspoons grated orange rind
  1 cup sifted confectioners' powdered sugar
  1 tablespoon milk
  1 teaspoon vanilla

Mix 1 cup of the flour, granulated sugar, salt, and yeast in large bowl of electric mixer.

Combine evaporated milk and 4 table-spoons of the butter in a small saucepan; heat until warm. (Butter need not melt.) Very slowly beat into yeast mixture; continue beating for 2 minutes at medium speed, scraping side of bowl once or twice.

Beat in eggs and ½ cup flour; beat 2 minutes. Stir in citron, raisins, orange rind, and 1¼ cups flour until blended. (Dough will be soft and sticky.)

Sprinkle remaining ¼ cup flour onto a board; turn dough out onto board. Knead 8 to 10 minutes until smooth and elastic; shape into a ball. Place in a greased large bowl; turn to coat all over with shortening; cover. Let rise in a warm place, away from drafts, 1 hour, or until doubled.

Punch dough down; knead a few times; divide in half. Shape each half into a smooth ball; place in a greased 1-pound coffee can; cover both. Let rise again 1 hour, or until doubled.

Preheat oven to 350°.

Melt remaining 1 tablespoon butter in a small saucepan; brush over raised dough.

Bake 35 minutes, or until golden and loaves sound hollow when tapped with finger. Cool in cans on a wire rack 5 minutes; turn out onto rack.

Combine confectioners' sugar, milk, and vanilla in a small bowl; beat until smooth. Drizzle over loaves, letting mixture run down sides. Sprinkle shredded orange rind on top if you like. Slice loaves crosswise into rounds or lengthwise into wedges; serve warm or cold.

Yield: 2 four-inch round loaves.

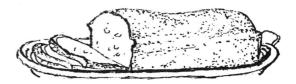

CASSEROLE DILL BREAD

4½ cups sifted all-purpose flour
  3 tablespoons sugar
  1 teaspoon salt
  2 envelopes active dry yeast
  1 can (10¾ ozs.) condensed cream of potato soup
⅔ cup water
  1 tablespoon grated onion
  2 tablespoons butter or margarine
  1 egg
  2 teaspoons dillweed

Mix 2 cups of the flour, sugar, salt, and yeast in a large bowl.

Combine soup, water, onion, and butter in a small saucepan; heat until warm. Beat mixture vigorously to break up potato lumps, then very slowly beat into yeast mixture.

Beat in egg, dillweed, and remaining 2½ cups flour; beat 2 minutes, or 100 strokes by hand. (Dough will be very sticky and heavy.) Cover; let rise in a warm place, away from drafts, 1 hour, or until doubled.

Stir dough down; beat about 50 strokes; spoon into a greased 2½-quart baking dish; cover. Let rise again 45 minutes, or until almost doubled.

Preheat oven to 375°.

Bake loaf 45 minutes, or until it sounds hollow when tapped with finger. Remove from dish. Brush top with butter or margarine if you prefer a soft crust. To serve, cut into wedges.

Yield: 1 loaf.

CINNAMON WHIRLIGIG

1 package hot roll mix
  Egg
  Warm water
3 tablespoons granulated sugar
2 teaspoons ground cinnamon
4 tablespoons butter or margarine
⅔ cup confectioners' powdered sugar
½ teaspoon vanilla
¼ cup chopped mixed candied fruits

Prepare hot roll mix with egg and warm water and let rise as label directs.

While dough rises, mix granulated sugar and cinnamon in a cup.

Punch dough down; roll out on a lightly floured board to a rectangle, 20x6 inches. Spread 3 tablespoons of the butter over rectangle; sprinkle cinnamon mixture over top. Starting at a short end, roll up dough, jelly-roll fashion; seal ends. Place in a greased baking pan, 9x5x3 inches; cover. Let rise 45 minutes, or until doubled.

Preheat oven to 375°. Melt remaining butter in a small skillet; brush over raised dough.

Bake 45 minutes, or until golden and loaf sounds hollow when tapped with finger. Loosen around edges with a knife; turn out onto a wire rack; cool.

Blend confectioners' sugar and vanilla with just enough water to make a thin frosting; drizzle over loaf. Sprinkle candied fruits on top. Serve warm or cold.

Yield: 1 loaf.

MIDGET SESAME ROLLS

1 package hot roll mix
  Warm water
  Egg
2 tablespoons butter or margarine
3 teaspoons sesame seeds

Prepare hot roll mix with water and egg and let rise as label directs. Turn out onto a floured board and knead several times.

Divide dough in half, then cut each half into 20 equal pieces. Shape each piece into a ¾-inch ball; place in 4 rows of 5 balls each in 2 greased, baking pans, 8x8x2 inches. Let rise again 30 minutes, or until doubled.

Preheat oven to 400°.

Melt butter in a small saucepan; brush over raised rolls; sprinkle sesame seeds over top.

Bake 15 minutes, or until rolls are golden and sound hollow when tapped with finger. Remove from pans to wire racks. Serve hot.

Yield: 40 rolls.

SAVORY TURBAN LOAF

1 package hot roll mix
  Warm water
2 eggs
3 tablespoons butter or margarine, melted
½ teaspoon ground nutmeg
½ teaspoon dried sage, crushed

Dissolve yeast from roll mix package in warm water in a large bowl as label directs; beat in one of the eggs and melted butter. Stir in flour mixture, nutmeg, and sage until well blended; cover. Let rise in a warm place, away from drafts, 45 minutes, or until doubled.

Punch dough down; turn out onto a lightly floured board; knead about a minute until dough is no longer sticky.

Roll out to a rectangle, 20x12 inches. Starting at one long side, roll up tightly, jelly-roll fashion; pinch ends to seal. Place roll, seam side down, on a greased large cookie sheet; working from inside out, shape into a coil; cover. Let rise again 45 minutes, or until almost doubled.

Preheat oven to 350°.

Beat remaining egg in a small bowl; brush over raised coil.

Bake 30 minutes, or until loaf is golden and sounds hollow when tapped with finger. Remove from cookie sheet to a wire rack; cool. To serve, cut in wedges.

Yield: 1 ten-inch round loaf.

HERB BALLS

1 package hot roll mix
Warm water
1 egg, beaten
1½ teaspoons caraway seeds
½ teaspoon ground sage
¼ teaspoon ground nutmeg
1 egg white, slightly beaten

Dissolve yeast from hot roll mix in warm water in a large bowl as label directs; stir in beaten egg, 1 teaspoon of the caraway seeds, sage, nutmeg, and flour mixture until well-blended; cover. Let rise in a warm place 45 minutes, or until doubled.

Turn dough out onto a well-floured board; knead several times until no longer sticky. Divide into quarters, then cut each quarter into 9 even pieces. Shape each into a small ball; place in a greased ¾-inch muffin-pan cup; cover. Let rise again, 45 minutes, or until doubled.

Preheat oven to 400°.

Brush beaten egg white over raised dough; sprinkle remaining ½ teaspoon caraway seeds over top.

Bake 15 minutes, or until rolls are golden and sound hollow when tapped with finger. Remove from pans to wire racks. Serve hot.

Yield: 3 dozen miniature rolls.

BRAN PUFFS

½ cup milk
½ cup shortening
⅓ cup sugar
1 teaspoon salt
1 cup whole bran cereal
2 envelopes active dry yeast
½ cup warm water
1 egg
3 cups sifted all-purpose flour
½ cup dark raisins

Scald milk with shortening, sugar, and salt in a small saucepan; pour over bran in a large bowl. Let stand until liquid is almost absorbed and mixture is lukewarm.

Dissolve yeast in warm water in a medium bowl. Beat egg into bran mixture, then beat in yeast mixture and 2 cups of the flour until smooth. Stir in just enough of the remaining 1 cup flour to make a soft dough; stir in raisins.

Turn dough out onto a lightly floured board; knead about 5 minutes until smooth and elastic, adding only enough of any remaining flour to keep dough from sticking. Shape into a ball; place in a greased large bowl, turning to coat all over with shortening; cover. Let rise in a warm place, away from drafts, 1 hour, or until doubled.

Punch dough down; cut into 18 equal pieces. Shape each into a ball; place in a greased medium-sized muffin-pan cup; cover. Let rise again 1 hour, or until doubled.

Preheat oven to 375°.

Bake 25 minutes, or until rolls are golden and sound hollow when tapped with finger. Remove from pans to wire racks. Serve warm or cold.

Yield: 18 rolls.

CARAWAY CRESCENTS

 1 envelope active dry yeast
 ⅔ cup very warm water
2½ cups biscuit mix
 1 tablespoon caraway seeds
 ½ teaspoon ground nutmeg
 ¼ teaspoon ground sage
 1 tablespoon butter or margarine, softened

Sprinkle yeast over warm water in a large bowl; stir until yeast dissolves. Stir in biscuit mix, caraway seeds, nutmeg, and sage; beat vigorously for 2 minutes.

Turn dough out onto a lightly floured board; knead 20 times, or until smooth. Roll out to a rectangle, 12x9 inches; spread butter lightly over top.

Cut rectangle crosswise into quarters and lengthwise into thirds to make 12 three-inch squares. Roll up each, jelly-roll fashion; place, several inches apart and seam side down, on a greased cookie sheet. Make cuts in top of each roll every half inch, cutting halfway to bottom, with a sharp knife. Curve rolls slightly so cuts will open during baking; cover.

Let rise in a warm place, away from drafts, 45 minutes, or until doubled.

Preheat oven to 400°.

Bake 15 minutes, or until rolls are golden. Remove from cookie sheet to wire racks. Serve hot.

Yield: 1 dozen.

CARAWAY RYE ROUNDS

2 cups sifted rye flour
⅓ cup light molasses
¼ cup shortening
2 teaspoons salt
2 cups boiling water
1 envelope active dry yeast
½ cup very warm water
6 cups sifted all-purpose flour
1 egg
  Caraway seeds

Combine rye flour, molasses, shortening, and salt in a large bowl; stir in boiling water until shortening melts; cool to lukewarm.

Dissolve yeast in warm water in a cup; beat into cooled rye mixture. Beat in 2 cups of the all-purpose flour until mixture is smooth. By hand, beat in 3½ cups of the remaining flour to make a soft dough.

Turn out onto a lightly floured board; knead 10 minutes until smooth and elastic, adding only enough of the remaining ½ cup flour to keep dough from sticking. Shape into a ball; place in a greased large bowl, turning to coat all over with shortening; cover. Let rise in a warm place, away from drafts, 1½ hours, or until doubled.

Punch dough down; cover. Let rise again 30 minutes, or until almost doubled.

Turn dough out onto board; knead several times; divide in half. Shape each half into a ball; place on a greased cookie sheet; cover. Let rise 1 hour, or until almost doubled.

Preheat oven to 350°.

Beat egg in a small bowl; brush over raised loaves; sprinkle caraway seeds over each.

Bake loaves 40 minutes, or until dark brown and they sound hollow when tapped with finger. Remove from cookie sheets to wire racks; cool completely.

Yield: 2 eight-inch round loaves.

DILLED BUBBLE STICKS

1 package hot roll mix
Egg
Warm water
2 teaspoons dillweed
¼ cup butter or margarine

Prepare hot roll mix with egg and warm water as label directs, adding dillweed with flour mixture; cover. Let rise in a warm place, away from drafts, 45 minutes, or until doubled.

Punch dough down. Pat into a 6-inch square on a lightly floured board. Cut lengthwise, then crosswise into thirds to make 9 squares; cut each square into quarters; shape each piece into a small ball. For each roll, place 3 balls close together in a straight line on a greased large cookie sheet; cover. Let rise again 45 minutes, or until doubled.

Preheat oven to 400°.

Melt butter in a saucepan; brush half over raised dough.

Bake 15 minutes, or until rolls are golden and sound hollow when tapped with finger. Remove from cookie sheet to wire racks; brush with remaining melted butter. Serve warm.

Yield: 12 rolls.

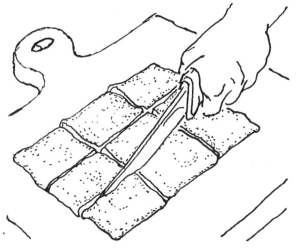

ONION CREAM BUNS

1 envelope active dry yeast
¼ cup very warm water
1 carton (8 ozs.) dairy sour cream
2 tablespoons sugar
1 teaspoon salt
1 egg
2 tablespoons salad oil
2 tablespoons minced green onions
2½ cups sifted all-purpose flour

Dissolve yeast in warm water in a large bowl.

Heat sour cream very slowly just until warm in a saucepan; beat into yeast mixture with sugar, salt, egg, salad oil, onions, and 1 cup of the flour until smooth. By hand, beat in remaining flour to make a soft dough; cover bowl.

Let rise in a warm place, away from drafts, 45 minutes, or until doubled.

Stir batter down. Spoon into 16 greased muffin-pan cups, filling each about half full. Level tops with fingertips; cover. Let rise again 30 minutes, or until dough is even with tops of cups.

Preheat oven to 400°.

Bake 15 minutes, or until buns are puffed and golden. Loosen around edges with a knife; remove from cups to wire racks. Brush softened butter or margarine lightly over tops if you prefer a soft crust; cool. Serve warm or cold.

Yield: 16 buns.

SESAME BRAID

1⅓ cups milk
  1 tablespoon sugar
  2 tablespoons salt
  3 tablespoons shortening
  1 envelope active dry yeast
  ¼ cup very warm water
4¼ cups sifted all-purpose flour
  1 egg
  1 tablespoon sesame seeds

Combine milk, sugar, salt, and shortening in a small saucepan; heat to scalding; cool to lukewarm.

Dissolve yeast in very warm water in a large bowl. Stir in cooled milk mixture and 2 cups of the flour until smooth. Beat in 2 more cups flour to make a stiff dough.

Sprinkle part of the remaining ¼ cup flour onto a board; turn dough out onto board. Knead until smooth and elastic, adding only enough of the remaining flour to keep dough from sticking. Shape into a ball; place in a greased large bowl; turn to coat all over with shortening; cover. Let rise in a warm place, away from drafts, 1 hour, or until doubled.

Punch dough down; knead a few times; divide in half. Cut one half into 3 equal pieces. Roll each to a 15-inch-long log with hands. Place logs, side by side, on a greased large cookie sheet; pinch together at one end, then braid; pinch other end to seal.

Divide remaining dough into 3 equal pieces; roll each to a 12-inch-long log; braid; seal. Place on top of larger braid; cover. Let rise again, 45 minutes, or until doubled.

Preheat oven to 350°.

Beat egg well in a cup; brush over braid; sprinkle sesame seeds generously over top.

Bake 45 minutes, or until braid is golden and sounds hollow when tapped with finger. Remove from cookie sheet to a large wire rack; cool.

Yield: 1 loaf about 15 inches long.

HERB BATTER BREAD

1½ cups milk
  2 tablespoons butter or margarine
  3 tablespoons sugar
  3 teaspoons salt
  1 small onion, finely chopped (¼ cup)
  2 envelopes active dry yeast
  ½ cup very warm water
4½ cups sifted all-purpose flour
  2 teaspoons caraway seeds
  ¾ teaspoon ground nutmeg
  ¾ teaspoon dried sage, crushed

Combine milk, butter, sugar, salt, and onion in a small saucepan; heat to scalding; cool to lukewarm.

Dissolve yeast in warm water in a large bowl; stir in cooled milk mixture. Stir in 2 cups of the flour, caraway seeds, nutmeg, and sage until smooth, then stir in remaining 2½ cups flour; beat vigorously 100 strokes. (Dough will be sticky.) Cover; let rise in a warm place, away from drafts, 1 hour, or until doubled.

Stir dough down; beat vigorously 25 strokes. Spoon into a greased 2½-quart ovenproof mixing bowl; cover. Let rise again 30 minutes, or until almost doubled.

Preheat oven to 375°.

Bake 1 hour, or until loaf is golden and sounds hollow when tapped with finger. Loosen around edges with a knife; turn out onto a wire rack, then turn right side up. Brush top with butter or margarine if you prefer a soft crust. Cool completely. Slice into wedges.

Yield: 1 large loaf.

YEAST COFFEE CAKES AND SWEET ROLLS

PETALED YEAST CROWN

  1 cup milk
¾ cup granulated sugar
¼ cup shortening
  1 teaspoon salt
  2 envelopes active dry yeast
¼ cup very warm water
  2 eggs
  5 cups sifted all-purpose flour
¼ cup honey
½ cup finely chopped California walnuts
  2 teaspoons grated orange rind
1½ teaspoons ground cinnamon
  1 tablespoon butter or margarine, melted
  1 cup sifted confectioners' powdered sugar
½ teaspoon vanilla
  3 teaspoons warm water

Combine milk, ½ cup of the sugar, shortening, and salt in a small saucepan; heat to scalding; cool to lukewarm.

Dissolve yeast in very warm water in a large bowl. Beat in cooled milk mixture, eggs, and 2 cups of the flour until smooth. Stir in 2¾ cups of the remaining flour to make a soft dough.

Sprinkle remaining ¼ cup flour onto a board; turn out dough; knead several minutes until smooth and elastic. Shape into a ball; place in a greased large bowl; turn to coat all over with shortening; cover. Let rise in a warm place, away from drafts, 1 hour, or until dough is doubled.

While dough rises, mix honey, walnuts, remaining ¼ cup sugar, orange rind, and cinnamon in a small bowl.

Punch dough down; turn out onto lightly floured board; divide in half.

Roll out half to a 12-inch square; brush half of the melted butter over square, then spread half of the honey mixture on top. Roll up,

jelly-roll fashion; pinch ends and edge to seal. Cut into 12 even slices. Place a layer of 6 slices, flat side down, in a greased 10-inch angel-cake pan; place remaining 6 slices on top so they overlap edges of those underneath.

Repeat with second half of dough; place slices in pan as before; cover. Let rise again 45 minutes, or until doubled.

Preheat oven to 350°.

Bake 55 minutes, or until loaf is golden and sounds hollow when tapped with finger. (If loaf seems to be browning too fast, lay a sheet of heavy brown paper over top for the last 20 minutes of baking.)

Cool loaf in pan on a wire rack 10 minutes. Loosen around edge and tube with a knife; turn out onto rack; turn right side up; cool.

Blend confectioners' sugar, vanilla, and warm water until smooth in a small bowl; drizzle over loaf; decorate with more walnuts if you like. Cut into wedges.

Yield: 1 ten-inch loaf.

HOUSKA

5 cups sifted all-purpose flour
1 envelope active dry yeast
1 cup milk
⅓ cup butter or margarine
½ cup sugar
2 teaspoons salt
2 eggs
1 teaspoon grated lemon rind
½ teaspoon ground nutmeg
½ cup light raisins
¾ cup chopped slivered blanched almonds
1 egg white

Mix 3 cups of the flour and yeast in large bowl of electric mixer.

Combine milk, butter, sugar, and salt in a small saucepan; heat until warm. (Butter need not melt.) Very slowly beat into yeast mixture; continue beating for 2 minutes at medium speed, scraping side of bowl once or twice.

Beat in eggs, lemon rind, and nutmeg; beat for 2 minutes at high speed. By hand, beat in 1¾ cups flour, raisins, and ½ cup of the almonds to make a soft dough. Turn out onto a lightly floured board; knead until smooth and elastic, adding only enough of the remaining ¼ cup flour to keep dough from sticking. Shape into a ball; place in a greased large bowl; turn to coat all over with shortening; cover. Let rise in a warm place, away from drafts, 1 hour, or until doubled.

Punch dough down; knead a few times; divide into 5 even pieces. With palms of hands, roll each piece to an 18-inch log on a lightly floured board. Place 3 logs, side by side, on a greased large cookie sheet; braid. Twist remaining 2 strips together to form a rope; place on top of braid; tuck ends under; cover. Let rise again 45 minutes, or until doubled.

Preheat oven to 350°.

Beat egg white slightly in a cup; brush over raised braid; sprinkle remaining ¼ cup chopped almonds on top.

Bake 40 minutes, or until loaf is golden and sounds hollow when tapped with finger. Remove from cookie sheet to a wire rack; cool. Slice crosswise.

Yield: 1 sixteen-inch-long loaf.

CHERRY-COCONUT BABKA

2¼ cups sifted all-purpose flour
¾ cup sugar
1 envelope active dry yeast
½ cup milk
⅓ cup butter or margarine
3 eggs
1 container (3½ ozs.) candied red cherries, chopped (½ cup)
½ cup flaked coconut
¼ cup water
2 tablespoons lemon juice

Combine ¾ cup of the flour, ¼ cup of the sugar, and yeast in large bowl of electric mixer.

Combine milk and butter in a small saucepan; heat until warm. (Butter need not melt.) Very slowly beat into yeast mixture; continue beating for 2 minutes at medium speed, scraping side of bowl once or twice.

Add eggs and ½ cup flour; beat 2 minutes to form a thick batter. By hand, beat in remaining 1 cup flour; cover. Let rise in a warm place, away from drafts, 1 hour, or until doubled.

Stir cherries and coconut into batter. Spoon into a greased 2-quart tube mold; cover. Let rise again 1 hour, or until doubled.

Preheat oven to 350°.

Bake 40 minutes, or until loaf is golden and a long metal skewer inserted near center comes out clean. Cool in mold on a wire rack 5 minutes; loosen around edges and tube with a knife; turn out onto rack.

While loaf cools, combine remaining ½ cup sugar and water in a small saucepan; heat to boiling; simmer 2 minutes. Remove from heat; stir in lemon juice. While hot, brush over warm loaf until all is absorbed. Slice loaf into wedges. Serve warm or cold.

Yield: 1 eight-inch round loaf.

CRISSCROSS PINEAPPLE ROUNDS

4¼ cups sifted all-purpose flour
⅓ cup sugar
1 teaspoon salt
1 envelope active dry yeast
¾ cup milk
¼ cup water
½ cup butter or margarine (for dough)
2 eggs
1 can (8 ozs.) crushed pineapple in syrup
1 tablespoon cornstarch
½ cup orange marmalade
1 tablespoon butter or margarine (for filling)

Mix 1 cup of the flour, sugar, salt, and yeast in large bowl of electric mixer.

Combine milk, water, and the ½ cup butter in a small saucepan; heat until warm. (Butter need not melt.) Very slowly beat into yeast mixture; continue beating for 2 minutes at medium speed, scraping side of bowl once or twice.

Beat eggs in a small bowl; measure 1 tablespoonful into a cup and set aside for brushing loaves. Beat remainder into yeast mixture with 1 cup flour; beat 2 minutes at medium speed. By hand, stir in 1¾ cups flour until smooth. (Dough will be soft and sticky.)

Sprinkle remaining ½ cup flour onto a board; turn dough out onto board. Knead 8 to 10 minutes, or until smooth and elastic; shape into a ball. Place in a greased large bowl; turn to coat all over with shortening; cover. Let rise

in a warm place, away from drafts, 1½ hours, or until doubled.

While dough rises, stir pineapple and syrup into cornstarch in a small saucepan until smooth; stir in marmalade. Cook slowly, stirring constantly, until mixture thickens and boils 1 minute. Remove from heat; stir in the 1 tablespoon butter; cool.

Punch dough down; knead a few times. Cut off one third and set aside for crisscross tops; divide remainder in half.

Roll out each half to a 10-inch round on a lightly floured board; place on a greased large cookie sheet. Spread pineapple mixture over rounds to within ½ inch of edges.

Divide remaining dough into 20 pieces. With hands, roll each to a pencil-thin log; weave 10 pieces across filling on each round to make a crisscross top, cutting and fitting pieces as needed; pinch to edge of rounds to hold in place; cover loaves. Let rise again 1 hour, or until doubled.

Preheat oven to 350°.

Stir 1 tablespoon water into beaten egg in cup; brush over loaves.

Bake 25 minutes, or until loaves are golden and sound hollow when tapped with finger. Remove from cookie sheets to wire racks; cool. Slice into wedges.

Yield: 2 ten-inch round loaves.

(Clockwise from top) ▶
CINNAMON PINWHEEL LOAF (p.375)
BASIC WHITE BREAD (p.373)
RAISIN-OATMEAL BREAD (p.374)

CANDIED FRUIT COBBLECAKE

5¼ cups sifted all-purpose flour
½ cup granulated sugar
1 teaspoon salt
1 teaspoon ground cinnamon
2 envelopes active dry yeast
¾ cup milk
½ cup water
½ cup butter or margarine
2 eggs
1 cup chopped mixed candied fruits
1 tablespoon butter or margarine, melted
1 cup sifted confectioners' powdered sugar
2 tablespoons orange juice

Mix 2 cups of the flour, granulated sugar, salt, cinnamon, and yeast in large bowl of electric mixer.

Combine milk, water, and the ½ cup butter in a small saucepan; heat until warm. Very slowly beat into yeast mixture; continue beating for 2 minutes at medium speed, scraping side of bowl once or twice.

Beat in eggs and 1 cup flour; beat 2 minutes. By hand, beat in candied fruits and 2 cups flour until completely blended.

Sprinkle remaining ¼ cup flour onto a pastry board; turn dough out onto board. Knead 8 to 10 minutes, or until smooth and elastic. Shape into a ball; place in a greased large bowl; turn to coat all over with shortening; cover. Let rise in a warm place, away from drafts, 1½ hours, or until doubled.

Punch dough down; knead a few times; divide in half. With palms of hands, roll each half on a lightly floured board to an even log 9 inches long. Cut into 1-inch slices; shape each into a ball. Place balls in 3 rows of 3 each in 2 greased baking pans, 8x8x2 inches; cover. Let rise again 1¼ hours, or until doubled.

Preheat oven to 375°. Brush melted butter over raised dough.

Bake 30 minutes or until cakes are golden and sound hollow when tapped with finger. Cool in pans on wire racks 10 minutes; turn out onto racks.

Combine confectioners' sugar and orange juice in a small bowl; beat until smooth. Drizzle over coffee cakes. Break apart into rolls. Serve warm or cold.

Yield: 2 coffee cakes of 9 rolls each.

PRUNE BRAID

1 package hot roll mix
Egg
Warm water
½ cup chopped pitted prunes
Sugar
½ teaspoon ground cardamom
½ cup water
½ cup chopped pecans
1 tablespoon butter or margarine, melted

Prepare hot roll mix with egg and warm water and let rise as label directs.

While dough rises, combine prunes, ½ cup sugar, cardamom, and the ½ cup water in a small saucepan. Heat to boiling; simmer 5 minutes, or until thick. Cool; stir in pecans.

Punch dough down; divide into thirds. Roll out each third on a lightly floured board to a rectangle, 14x4 inches; spread one third of the prune mixture over each rectangle. Starting at a long side, roll up dough, jelly-roll fashion. Place rolls side by side on a greased large cookie sheet; pinch at one end to seal, then braid and seal other end; cover. Let rise 45 minutes, or until doubled.

Preheat oven to 375°.

Brush melted butter over raised dough; sprinkle sugar generously over top.

Bake 30 minutes, or until braid is golden and sounds hollow when tapped with finger. Remove from cookie sheet to a wire rack; cool. Serve warm or cold.

Yield: 1 sixteen-inch braid.

CHRISTMAS FRUIT CRESCENTS

½ cup milk
½ cup granulated sugar
1 teaspoon salt
⅓ cup butter or margarine
2 envelopes active dry yeast
½ cup very warm water
3 eggs
5 cups sifted all-purpose flour
2 teaspoons vanilla
1 container (8 ozs.) mixed candied fruits,
     chopped
1½ cups confectioners' powdered sugar

Combine milk, granulated sugar, salt, and butter in a small saucepan; heat until butter melts; cool to lukewarm.

Dissolve yeast in very warm water in a large bowl.

Beat eggs in a small bowl; measure 2 tablespoons into a cup and set aside for brushing loaves. Stir remaining beaten eggs and milk mixture into dissolved yeast.

Beat in 2 cups of flour until smooth, then 1 teaspoon of the vanilla and candied fruits. Beat in 2½ cups more flour to make a smooth soft dough.

Turn dough out onto a lightly floured board; knead until smooth and elastic, adding only enough of the remaining ½ cup flour to keep dough from sticking. Place in a greased large bowl; turn to coat all over with shortening; cover. Let rise 1½ hours, or until doubled.

Punch dough down; divide in half. Roll each half into an oval 12x8 inches; fold in half lengthwise. Place on a greased cookie sheet; cover. Let rise again 1 hour, or until doubled.

Preheat oven to 350°.

Stir 1 tablespoon water into beaten egg in cup; brush over raised loaves.

Bake 30 minutes, or until loaves are golden and sound hollow when tapped with finger. Remove from cookie sheets to wire racks; cool.

Mix confectioners' sugar, remaining 1 teaspoon vanilla, and 5 teaspoons water until smooth in a small bowl; drizzle over loaves. If you like, decorate with whole blanched almonds arranged around candied cherry halves to form flowers. Let stand until frosting is firm. Cut crosswise into thick slices.

Yield: 2 loaves.

CHERRY-GO-ROUND

1 package hot roll mix
¾ cup warm water
1 egg, slightly beaten
2 tablespoons granulated sugar
10 tablespoons cherry preserves
¾ cup sifted confectioners' powdered sugar
2½ teaspoons milk
½ teaspoon vanilla

Prepare hot roll mix with water, egg, and granulated sugar, and let rise as label directs.

Turn out onto a lightly floured board; knead several times until dough is no longer sticky. Roll out to a 15-inch circle; cut into quarters, then cut each quarter into 5 pie-shaped wedges.

Twist each two wedges together to form a rope; pinch ends to seal; curl each into a coil. Place one coil in the center of a greased large cookie sheet; arrange remaining coils around edge, touching center one; cover. Let rise again 45 minutes, or until doubled.

Preheat oven to 375°.

Press a hollow in center of each coil with thumb; spoon 1 tablespoon of the cherry preserves into each hollow.

Bake 30 minutes, or until cake is golden and sounds hollow when tapped with finger. Remove from cookie sheet to a wire rack; cool.

Mix confectioners' sugar, milk, and vanilla until smooth in a small bowl; drizzle over coffee cake.

Yield: 1 coffee cake of 10 buns.

BABA

4½ cups sifted all-purpose flour
½ cup sugar
1 teaspoon salt
1 envelope active dry yeast
1 cup milk
½ cup water
½ cup butter or margarine
3 eggs
2 teaspoons grated lemon rind
2 teaspoons vanilla
¾ cup apricot preserves
1 tablespoon lemon juice
1 tablespoon rum flavoring

Mix 2 cups of the flour, sugar, salt, and yeast in large bowl of electric mixer.

Combine milk, water, and butter in a small saucepan; heat until warm. (Butter need not melt.) Very slowly beat into yeast mixture; continue beating for 2 minutes at medium speed, scraping side of bowl once or twice.

Beat in eggs and 1 cup flour; beat at high speed 2 minutes. By hand, beat in lemon rind, vanilla, and remaining 1½ cups flour until blended. (Batter will be very soft.) Beat vigorously 150 strokes; cover. Let rise in a warm place, away from drafts, 1½ hours, or until doubled.

Stir batter down; beat vigorously 50 strokes. Spoon into a greased 3-quart tube pan or 10-inch angel-cake pan; cover. Let rise again 1½ hours, or until doubled.

Preheat oven to 375°.

Bake 50 minutes, or until loaf is golden and a long metal skewer inserted near center comes out clean. Cool in pan on a wire rack 15 minutes. Loosen around side and tube with a knife; invert onto a deep serving plate.

While loaf cools, heat apricot preserves to boiling in a small saucepan; press through a sieve into a small bowl; stir in lemon juice and rum flavoring. Spoon part over warm loaf. (Glaze will soak in.) Spoon remainder over top, spooning any that drips onto plate back over loaf.

Slice loaf into wedges; serve warm or cold.
Yield: 1 ten-inch round loaf.

CHERRY CROWN

4½ cups sifted all-purpose flour
½ cup sugar
1 teaspoon salt
1 envelope active dry yeast
1 cup milk
½ cup water
½ cup butter or margarine
3 eggs
½ cup chopped candied red cherries
2 teaspoons grated lemon rind
2 teaspoons vanilla
Confectioners' powdered sugar

Mix 2 cups of the flour, sugar, salt, and yeast in large bowl of electric mixer.

Combine milk, water, and butter in a small saucepan; heat until warm. (Butter need not melt.) Very slowly beat into yeast mixture; continue beating for 2 minutes at medium speed, scraping side of bowl once or twice.

Beat in eggs and 1 cup flour; beat at high speed, scraping side of bowl, 2 minutes. Stir in cherries, lemon rind, vanilla, and rest of flour until blended. (Batter will be very soft.) Beat vigorously 150 strokes; cover. Let rise in a warm place, away from drafts, 1½ hours, or until doubled.

Stir batter down; beat vigorously 50 strokes. Spoon into a greased 3-quart Bundt pan or 10-inch angel-cake pan; cover. Let rise again 1½ hours, or until doubled.

Preheat oven to 375°.

Bake 50 minutes, or until ring is golden and a long metal skewer inserted near center comes out clean. Cool 15 minutes in pan on a wire rack. Loosen around side and tube with a knife; invert onto a large serving plate. Sprinkle confectioners' sugar lightly over top of coffee cake. Slice into wedges; serve warm or cold.

Yield: 1 ten-inch round loaf.

APRICOT LOAVES

½ cup milk
½ cup granulated sugar
1 teaspoon salt
⅓ cup butter or margarine
2 envelopes active dry yeast
½ cup very warm water
3 eggs
5 cups sifted all-purpose flour
½ teaspoon mace
1 cup chopped dried apricots
1 cup chopped California walnuts
1½ cups sifted confectioners' powdered sugar
1 teaspoon vanilla

Combine milk, granulated sugar, salt, and butter in a small saucepan; heat until butter melts; cool to lukewarm.

Dissolve yeast in very warm water in a large bowl.

Beat eggs in a small bowl; measure 2 tablespoons into a cup and set aside for brushing loaves. Stir remaining beaten eggs and milk mixture into dissolved yeast.

Beat in 2 cups of flour until smooth; stir in mace, apricots, and walnuts. Beat in 2½ cups flour to make a smooth stiff dough.

Turn dough out onto a lightly floured board; knead until smooth and elastic, adding only enough of the remaining ½ cup flour to keep dough from sticking; shape into a ball. Place in a greased large bowl; turn to coat all over with shortening; cover. Let rise in a warm place, away from drafts, 2 hours, or until doubled.

Punch dough down; divide in half. Roll each half into an oval, 12x8 inches; roll each side of oval, jelly-roll fashion, to center; curve into a horseshoe shape. Place on a greased large cookie sheet; cover. Let rise again 1½ hours, or until doubled.

Preheat oven to 375°.

Stir 1 tablespoon water into beaten egg in cup; brush over raised loaves.

Bake 35 minutes, or until loaves are golden and sound hollow when tapped with finger. Remove from cookie sheets to wire racks; cool.

Mix confectioners' sugar, vanilla, and about 5 teaspoons water until smooth in a small bowl; drizzle over loaves. Garnish with finely chopped dried apricots if you like. Let stand until frosting is firm. Cut into thick slices.

Yield: 2 loaves.

FROSTED DATE RING

1 package hot roll mix
Egg
Warm water
2 tablespoons granulated sugar
1 package (8 ozs.) pitted dates
¼ cup firmly packed brown sugar
½ cup water
¾ teaspoon ground cinnamon
½ cup sifted confectioners' powdered sugar
1½ teaspoons lemon juice

Prepare hot roll mix with egg and warm water as label directs, adding granulated sugar to flour mixture; cover. Let rise in a warm place, away from drafts, 1 hour, or until doubled.

While dough rises, chop dates; combine with brown sugar, the ½ cup water, and cinnamon in a small saucepan; heat to boiling. Simmer 20 minutes, or until thick; cool.

Punch dough down; roll out on a lightly floured board to a rectangle, 16x12 inches. Spread date mixture over rectangle; starting at a long side, roll up, jelly-roll fashion. Place, seam side down, on a greased cookie sheet; curve into a ring; pinch ends to seal.

Cut slits every ¾ inch from outer edge of ring to within ½ inch of center; twist each slice on its side; cover. Let rise again 45 minutes, or until doubled.

Preheat oven to 375°.

Bake 30 minutes, or until ring is golden and it sounds hollow when tapped with finger. Remove from cookie sheet to a wire rack; cool.

Combine confectioners' sugar and lemon juice in a small bowl; beat until smooth. Drizzle over ring. Slice into wedges; serve warm or cold.

Yield: 1 large loaf.

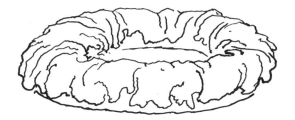

CINNAMON RING

1 package hot roll mix
Egg
Warm water
6 tablespoons granulated sugar
2½ teaspoons ground cinnamon
1 cup chopped California walnuts
4 tablespoons butter or margarine
½ cup confectioners' powdered sugar
¼ teaspoon vanilla

Prepare hot roll mix with egg and warm water and let rise as label directs.

While dough rises, mix granulated sugar, cinnamon, and walnuts in a bowl.

Punch dough down; roll out on a lightly floured board to a rectangle, 14x10 inches. Spread 3 tablespoons of the butter evenly over dough; sprinkle cinnamon mixture over top. Starting at a long side, roll up dough, jelly-roll fashion. Curve into a ring; pinch ends to seal. Place, seam side down, in a greased 10-inch angel-cake pan. Snip deep cuts, 1 inch apart, in top of loaf with scissors. Cover again; let rise 45 minutes, or until doubled.

Preheat oven to 375°.

Melt remaining butter; brush over raised dough.

Bake 35 minutes, or until ring is golden and sounds hollow when tapped with finger. Cool in pan on a wire rack 10 minutes; loosen around edge and tube with a knife; turn out onto rack; cool.

Blend confectioners' sugar and vanilla with just enough water to make a thin frosting; drizzle over ring. Slice in thick wedges. Serve warm or cold.

Yield: 1 ten-inch ring.

WALNUT MINIATURES

    3 cups sifted all-purpose flour
    ¼ cup granulated sugar
    ½ teaspoon salt
    1 envelope active dry yeast
    ⅓ cup milk
    ¼ cup water
    ¾ cup butter or margarine
    1 egg
    ⅓ cup firmly packed light brown sugar
    1 tablespoon honey
    ⅓ cup chopped California walnuts
    4 tablespoons cinnamon-sugar

Mix 1 cup of the flour, granulated sugar, salt, and yeast in large bowl of electric mixer.

Combine milk, water, and ¼ cup of the butter in a small saucepan; heat until warm. Very slowly beat into yeast mixture; continue beating 2 minutes at medium speed.

Beat in egg and 1 cup flour; beat 2 minutes at medium speed. By hand, stir in ¾ cup of the remaining flour to make a smooth stiff dough.

Turn out onto a lightly floured board, knead until smooth and elastic, adding only enough of the remaining ¼ cup flour to keep dough from sticking. Shape into a ball; place in a greased large bowl; turn to coat all over with shortening; cover. Let rise in a warm place, away from drafts, 1½ hours, or until doubled.

While dough rises, melt 6 tablespoons of the remaining butter in a small saucepan; stir in brown sugar and honey until mixture is smooth; spoon about ½ teaspoon into each of 36 greased 1¾-inch muffin-pan cups. Sprinkle a scant ½ teaspoon of the walnuts into each cup.

Punch dough down; divide in half. Roll out each half to a 9-inch square on a lightly floured board. Spread 1 tablespoon of the remaining butter over each square; sprinkle 2 tablespoons of the cinnamon-sugar over butter; roll up tightly, jelly-roll fashion. Cut each roll into 18 half-inch slices; place over butter mixture in pans; cover. Let rise again 1 hour, or until doubled.

Preheat oven to 350°.

Bake 20 minutes, or until rolls are golden and sound hollow when tapped with finger. Let stand 5 minutes in pans on wire racks. Loosen around edges with a knife; invert onto large serving plates; lift off pans. Serve warm or cold.

Yield: 3 dozen small rolls.

PARISIAN RAISIN RING

    1¼ cups milk
    ¾ cup butter or margarine
    ½ cup sugar
    1 teaspoon salt
    1 envelope active dry yeast
    ¼ cup very warm water
    2 eggs
    4 cups sifted all-purpose flour
      Whole blanched almonds
    1 cup dark raisins

Combine milk, butter, sugar, and salt in a small saucepan; heat to scalding; cool to lukewarm.

Dissolve yeast in very warm water in a large bowl. Stir in cooled milk mixture; beat in eggs and 1 cup of the flour until smooth. Beat in remaining 3 cups flour; beat vigorously 5 minutes to make a thick batter; cover. Let rise in a warm place, away from drafts, 1½ hours, or until doubled.

Grease a 2½-quart ring mold; arrange two circles of almonds in mold.

Stir batter down; stir in raisins. Spoon over almonds in mold; cover. Let rise again 1¼ hours, or until doubled.

Preheat oven to 350°.

Bake 55 minutes, or until ring is golden and a long metal skewer inserted near center comes out clean. Cool ring in mold on a wire rack 5 minutes; turn out onto rack. Serve warm or cold.

Yield: 1 ten-inch ring.

CHERRY FOLDOVERS

4 cups sifted all-purpose flour
⅓ cup sugar
1 teaspoon salt
1 envelope active dry yeast
¾ cup milk
¼ cup water
½ cup butter or margarine
2 eggs
1 can (21 ozs.) cherry pie filling
½ cup chopped California walnuts
¼ teaspoon almond extract
Sugar

Mix 1 cup of the flour, the ⅓ cup sugar, salt, and yeast in large bowl of electric mixer.

Combine milk, water, and butter in a small saucepan; heat until warm. (Butter need not melt.) Very slowly beat into yeast mixture; continue beating for 2 minutes at medium speed, scraping side of bowl once or twice.

Beat in 1 of the eggs and 1 cup flour; beat 2 minutes. Stir in 1¾ cups flour until smooth. (Dough will be soft and sticky.)

Sprinkle remaining ¼ cup flour onto a board; turn dough out onto board. Knead 8 to 10 minutes, or until smooth and elastic; shape into a ball. Place in a greased large bowl; turn to coat all over with shortening; cover. Let rise in a warm place, away from drafts, 1½ hours, or until doubled.

While dough rises, mix cherry pie filling, walnuts, and almond extract in a small bowl.

Punch dough down; knead a few times; divide in half. Roll out half on lightly floured board to a rectangle, 13x9 inches. Spoon half of the cherry mixture in a 3-inch-wide strip down center, leaving a ½-inch border on each end. With a sharp knife or scissors, cut slits every inch in dough on each side, cutting from outside edge not quite to filling. Fold strips, alternating from side to side, at an angle across filling. Place coffee cake on a greased large cookie sheet. Repeat rolling, filling, and shaping with remaining dough; place on a second cookie sheet; cover both. Let rise again 1 hour, or until doubled.

Preheat oven to 350°.

Beat remaining egg with 1 tablespoon water in a cup; brush over raised dough; sprinkle sugar generously over tops.

Bake 25 minutes, or until cakes are golden and sound hollow when tapped with finger. Remove from cookie sheets to wire racks; cool. Cut into slices; serve warm or cold.

Yield: 2 twelve-inch-long loaves.

SUGAR CRUNCH SQUARES

1 cup firmly packed light brown sugar
2¼ cups sifted all-purpose flour
½ teaspoon mace
⅓ cup butter or margarine (for topping)
1 cup chopped California walnuts
1 envelope active dry yeast
¼ cup very warm water
2½ teaspoons baking powder
½ teaspoon salt
½ cup butter or margarine (for batter)
½ cup granulated sugar
1 egg
¼ cup milk

Preheat oven to 350°.

Mix brown sugar, ¼ cup of the flour, and mace in a small bowl; cut in the ⅓ cup butter with a pastry blender until mixture forms coarse crumbs; stir in walnuts.

Sprinkle yeast over very warm water in a cup; let stand.

Sift remaining 2 cups flour, baking powder, and salt onto waxed paper.

Cream the ½ cup butter and granulated sugar in a medium bowl until fluffy; beat in egg and half of the flour mixture. Beat in milk and yeast mixture, then remaining flour just until blended. Spread half into a greased baking pan, 8x8x2 inches. Sprinkle half of the walnut mixture on top; repeat layers.

Bake 1 hour, or until a wooden pick inserted in center comes out clean. Cool in pan on a wire rack. Serve warm or cold.

Yield: 1 eight-inch coffee cake.

JULEKAKE

½ cup milk
½ cup granulated sugar
1 teaspoon salt
½ cup butter or margarine
2 envelopes active dry yeast
½ cup very warm water
3 eggs
5½ cups sifted all-purpose flour
1½ teaspoons ground cardamom
½ cup mixed candied fruits, finely chopped
½ cup dark raisins
½ cup chopped California walnuts
1¾ cups sifted confectioners' powdered sugar
½ teaspoon vanilla
   Red and green candied cherries, slivered

Combine milk with granulated sugar, salt, and butter in a small saucepan; heat just until butter melts. Cool to lukewarm.

Dissolve yeast in very warm water in a large bowl.

Beat eggs in a small bowl; measure 2 tablespoons into a cup and set aside for brushing loaves. Beat remaining eggs and milk mixture into yeast mixture, then beat in 2 cups of the flour and cardamom until smooth. Beat in fruits, raisins, and walnuts.

Beat in 3 cups flour to make a soft, sticky dough.

Turn out onto a lightly floured board; knead until smooth and elastic, adding only enough of the remaining ½ cup flour to prevent sticking. Place in a greased large bowl; turn to coat all over with shortening; cover. Let rise in a warm place, away from drafts, 1½ hours, or until doubled.

Punch dough down; knead a few times; divide in half. Shape each half into a ball; place several inches apart on a greased large cookie sheet; flatten tops slightly; cover. Let rise again 1½ hours, or until doubled.

Preheat oven to 350°.

Stir 1 teaspoon water into remaining beaten egg; brush over raised dough.

Bake 35 minutes, or until loaves are golden and sound hollow when tapped with finger. Loosen from cookie sheet; remove to wire racks; cool.

Blend confectioners' sugar, vanilla, and just enough water to make a medium thin frosting; spread over loaves. Decorate with cut cherries to resemble Christmas trees or holly wreaths.

Yield: 2 loaves.

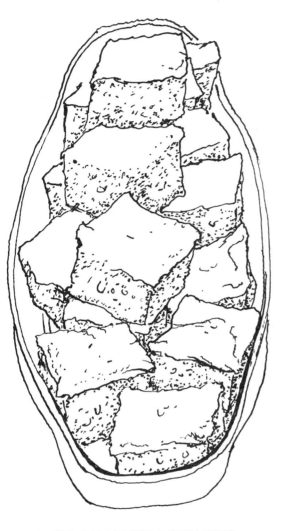

LATTICE ORANGE SQUARES

  5 cups sifted all-purpose flour
½ cup sugar (for dough)
  1 teaspoon salt
  2 envelopes active dry yeast
½ cup milk
½ cup water
¾ cup butter or margarine
  2 eggs
  1 jar (12 ozs.) orange marmalade
  6 tablespoons sugar (for filling)
⅔ cup chopped slivered almonds

    Mix 2 cups of the flour, the ½ cup sugar, salt, and yeast in large bowl of electric mixer.

    Combine milk, water, and ¼ cup of the butter in a small saucepan; heat until warm. (Butter need not melt.) Very slowly beat into yeast mixture; continue beating for 2 minutes at medium speed, scraping side of bowl once or twice.

    Beat eggs in a small bowl. Measure 1 tablespoon into a cup; stir in 2 teaspoons water; set aside for brushing coffee cakes. Beat remaining eggs and 1 cup of flour into yeast mixture; beat 2 minutes. Stir in 1¾ cups flour until smooth. (Dough will be soft and sticky.)

    Sprinkle remaining ¼ cup flour onto a board; turn dough out onto board. Knead 8 to 10 minutes, or until smooth and elastic; shape into a ball. Place in a greased large bowl; turn to coat all over with shortening; cover. Let rise in a warm place, away from drafts, 1 hour, or until doubled.

    While dough rises, combine remaining ½ cup butter, orange marmalade, and the 6 tablespoons sugar in a small saucepan. Heat to boiling; simmer 25 minutes. Cool; stir in almonds.

    Punch dough down; knead a few times. Cut off one quarter and set aside for crisscross tops. Divide rest of dough in half; pat each half into a greased baking pan, 9x9x2 inches. Spread half of the orange-almond mixture over each.

    Divide the quarter of dough that was set aside into 20 even pieces. With your palms, roll each on a lightly floured board to a pencil-size log. Weave 10 pieces diagonally across filling in each pan, cutting and piecing together as needed to fit; cover. Let rise again 1 hour, or until doubled.

    Preheat oven to 375°.

    Brush saved egg mixture over raised dough.

    Bake 25 minutes, or until cakes are golden and sound hollow when tapped with finger. Cool in pans on wire racks. Cut into squares; serve warm or cold.

    Yield: 2 nine-inch square coffee cakes.

APPLE DATE TWIST

⅓ cup shortening
⅓ cup granulated sugar (for dough)
1 teaspoon salt
½ cup milk
1 envelope active dry yeast
¼ cup very warm water
1 egg
1 tablespoon grated orange rind
3½ cups sifted all-purpose flour
1 package (8 ozs.) pitted dates, chopped (1 cup)
1 medium apple, pared, quartered, cored, and
   diced (1 cup)
⅓ cup firmly packed light brown sugar
⅔ cup water
1 teaspoon ground cinnamon
1 tablespoon lemon juice
1 tablespoon butter or margarine, melted
2 tablespoons granulated sugar (for topping)

Combine shortening, the ⅓ cup sugar, salt, and milk in a small saucepan; heat to scalding; cool to lukewarm.

Dissolve yeast in very warm water in a large bowl. Beat in egg, orange rind, cooled milk mixture, and flour to make a stiff dough.

Turn out onto a lightly floured board; knead until smooth and elastic. Shape into a ball; place in a greased large bowl; turn to coat all over with shortening; cover. Let rise in a warm place, away from drafts, 1 hour and 15 minutes, or until doubled.

While dough rises, combine dates, apple, brown sugar, water, cinnamon, and lemon juice in a small saucepan; heat slowly, stirring several times, to boiling. Cook 10 minutes, or until thick; cool.

Punch dough down; roll out on a lightly floured board to a rectangle, 16x15 inches; cut lengthwise into 3 strips. Spread ½ cup of the date mixture over each strip to within ½ inch of edges. Starting at a long side of each, roll up tightly, jelly-roll fashion. Place rolls, side by side, on a greased large cookie sheet; braid. Pinch ends to seal, then tuck under slightly; cover. Let rise again 1 hour, or until doubled. Preheat oven to 350°.

Brush melted butter over raised braid; sprinkle the 2 tablespoons sugar on top.

Bake 40 minutes, or until loaf is golden and sounds hollow when tapped with finger. Remove from cookie sheet to a wire rack; cool. Serve warm or cold.

Yield: 1 seventeen-inch-long loaf.

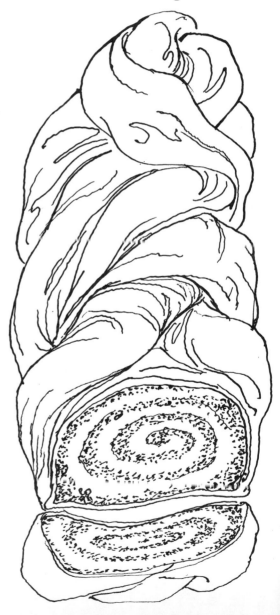

LUCIA BUNS

5½ cups sifted all-purpose flour
½ cup sugar
½ teaspoon salt
⅛ teaspoon powdered saffron
3 packages active dry yeast
½ cup butter or margarine, softened
1 cup very warm water
2 eggs
  Dark raisins

Mix 1 cup of the flour, sugar, salt, saffron, and yeast in large bowl of electric mixer; add butter.

Beat in water slowly; continue beating, scraping side of bowl, 2 minutes.

Beat eggs in a small bowl; measure 1 tablespoonful into a cup and set aside for brushing buns. Beat remainder into yeast mixture with another ¼ cup flour; beat 2 minutes. Stir in 4 cups of the flour to make a stiff dough. Turn out onto a lightly floured board; knead 8 to 10 minutes; or until smooth and elastic, adding only enough of the remaining ¼ cup flour to keep dough from sticking.

Divide dough in half, then cut each half into 16 even pieces. Roll each into a 12-inch-long log with palms of hands; coil ends of strips toward center to form an "S." Place on greased cookie sheets.

Stir 1 tablespoon water into egg in cup; brush over buns; place a raisin in center of each coil. Cover with foil; freeze until firm, then place in transparent bags; seal, date, and return to freezer. (Plan to use within a month.)

When ready to finish buns, place on ungreased cookie sheets; cover with a clean towel. Let stand about 2 hours, or until completely thawed, then let rise in a warm place, away from drafts, 45 minutes, or until doubled.

Preheat oven to 350°.

Bake 15 minutes, or until buns are golden and sound hollow when tapped with finger. Remove from cookie sheets to wire racks. Serve warm.

Yield: 32 buns.

MINIATURE BABKAS

2¼ cups sifted all-purpose flour
¼ cup sugar
¼ teaspoon salt
1 envelope active dry yeast
½ cup milk
⅓ cup butter or margarine
3 eggs
1 teaspoon grated lemon rind
½ cup light raisins
3 tablespoons chopped slivered almonds

Combine ¾ cup of the flour, sugar, salt, and yeast in large bowl of electric mixer.

Combine milk and butter in a small saucepan; heat until warm. Very slowly beat into yeast mixture; continue beating for 2 minutes at medium speed, scraping side of bowl once or twice.

Separate 1 of the eggs, placing yolk in a cup to set aside for brushing rolls. Beat white and remaining 2 whole eggs, lemon rind, and ½ cup of the flour into yeast mixture until smooth. By hand, beat in remaining 1 cup flour to form a thick batter; cover. Let rise in a warm place, away from drafts, 1 hour, or until doubled.

Stir raisins into batter; spoon into 12 greased medium-sized muffin-pan cups; cover. Let rise again 45 minutes, or until dough is doubled.

Preheat oven to 350°.

Beat 1 tablespoon water into saved egg yolk; brush over raised rolls; sprinkle almonds on top.

Bake 30 minutes, or until rolls are golden and sound hollow when tapped with finger. Cool in pan on a wire rack 5 minutes; loosen around edges with a knife; turn out onto rack. Serve warm or cold.

Yield: 12 rolls.

PRUNE CRESCENTS

½ cup milk
1 cup granulated sugar
1 teaspoon salt
½ cup butter or margarine
2 envelopes active dry yeast
½ cup very warm water
3 eggs
5 cups sifted all-purpose flour
2 teaspoons grated lemon rind
1 package (12 ozs.) pitted dried prunes, snipped
1 cup water (for filling)
2 teaspoons ground cinnamon
2 tablespoons confectioners' powdered sugar

Combine milk, ½ cup of the granulated sugar, salt, and butter in a small saucepan; heat to scalding; cool to lukewarm.

Dissolve yeast in very warm water in a large bowl.

Beat eggs in a small bowl; measure 2 tablespoons into a cup and set aside for brushing loaves. Stir remaining beaten eggs and milk mixture into dissolved yeast.

Beat in 2 cups of the flour until smooth, then lemon rind. Beat in 2¾ cups more flour to make a smooth stiff dough. Turn out onto a lightly floured board; knead until smooth and elastic, adding only enough of the remaining ¼ cup flour to keep dough from sticking. Shape into a ball; place in a greased large bowl; turn to coat all over with shortening; cover. Let rise in a warm place, away from drafts, 1 hour, or until doubled.

While dough rises, combine prunes, remaining ½ cup sugar, water, and cinnamon in a medium saucepan; heat, stirring constantly, to boiling. Simmer 12 minutes, or until thick; cool.

Punch dough down; knead a few times; divide into 12 even pieces. Roll each to an oval, 8x4 inches, on a lightly floured board. Spread 2 tablespoons of the prune mixture down center of each. Brush part of the remaining beaten egg on edges; fold over to cover filling completely; press edges with a fork to seal. Curve each into a crescent shape; place, 2 inches apart, on greased large cookie sheets; cover. Let rise again 45 minutes, or until dough is doubled.

Preheat oven to 350°.

Stir 1 tablespoon water into remaining beaten egg; brush over raised dough.

Bake 25 minutes, or until crescents are golden and sound hollow when tapped with finger. Remove from cookie sheets to wire racks; cool.

Just before serving, sprinkle confectioners' sugar over each.

Yield: 12 crescents.

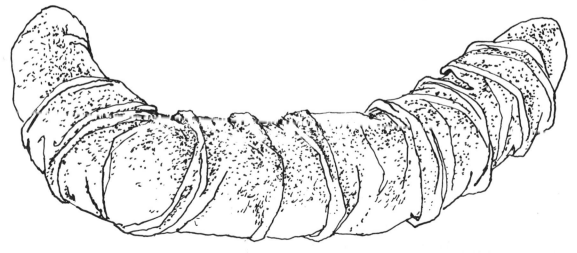

QUICK FRUIT AND NUT LOAVES

CRANBERRY-BANANA LOAVES

1 cup fresh cranberries, stemmed and chopped
1¼ cups sugar
3 cups sifted all-purpose flour
3 teaspoons baking powder
½ teaspoon baking soda
1 teaspoon salt
1 cup chopped California walnuts
1 egg
¼ cup milk
3 tablespoons butter or margarine, melted
3 medium-sized ripe bananas, peeled and mashed (1 cup)

Preheat oven to 350°.

Combine cranberries and ¼ cup of the sugar in a small bowl; set aside.

Sift flour, remaining 1 cup sugar, baking powder, baking soda, and salt into a large bowl; stir in walnuts.

Beat egg in a medium bowl; stir in milk, melted butter, mashed bananas, and cranberry mixture. Add all at once to flour mixture; stir just until mixture is evenly moist. Spoon evenly into 4 greased small loaf pans, each 5¾x3¼x2¼ inches.

Bake 45 minutes, or until loaves are golden and a wooden pick inserted into centers comes out clean. Cool in pans on wire racks 10 minutes. Loosen loaves around edges with a knife; turn out onto racks; cool completely.

For easy, neat slicing, wrap loaves in foil and store overnight.

Yield: 4 small loaves.

Note: Bread may also be baked in one large loaf pan, 9x5x3 inches. Bake at 350° for 1 hour, or until a wooden pick inserted into center comes out clean.

STREUSEL PRUNE BREAD

2½ cups sifted all-purpose flour
¾ cup sugar
⅔ cup wheat germ
¾ cup chopped California walnuts
2 tablespoons butter or margarine
3 teaspoons baking powder
1 teaspoon salt
1 teaspoon ground cinnamon
½ teaspoon ground nutmeg
¼ teaspoon ground cloves
1 egg
¾ cup milk
¼ cup salad oil
1 cup chopped drained cooked prunes or drained canned prunes

Combine 2 tablespoons of the flour, 3 tablespoons of the sugar, 2 tablespoons of the wheat germ, and 3 tablespoons of the walnuts in a small bowl; cut in butter with a pastry blender until coarse crumbs form; set aside for topping.

Preheat oven to 350°.

Sift remaining flour, sugar, baking powder, salt, cinnamon, nutmeg, and cloves into a large bowl; stir in remaining wheat germ and walnuts with a fork to mix well.

Beat egg in a small bowl; stir in milk and salad oil. Add all at once to flour mixture; stir just until mixture is evenly moist; stir in prunes. Spoon into a greased baking pan, 9x5x3 inches; sprinkle crumb mixture over top.

Bake 1 hour, or until a wooden pick inserted into center comes out clean. Cool in pan on a wire rack 10 minutes. Loosen loaf around edges with a knife; turn out onto rack; cool completely.

For easy, neat slicing, wrap loaf in foil and store overnight.

Yield: 1 loaf.

BANANA-CHERRY BREAD

2 cups sifted all-purpose flour
1½ teaspoons baking powder
½ teaspoon baking soda
½ teaspoon salt
½ cup butter or margarine
1 cup granulated sugar
2 eggs
3 large ripe bananas, peeled and mashed (1½ cups)
1 teaspoon grated lemon rind
1 container (3½ ozs.) candied red cherries, chopped
Confectioners' powdered sugar

Preheat oven to 350°.

Sift flour, baking powder, baking soda, and salt onto waxed paper.

Cream butter with granulated sugar until fluffy-light in a large bowl; beat in eggs, mashed bananas, and lemon rind. Add flour mixture all at once; stir just until mixture is evenly moist; stir in cherries. Spoon into a greased 1¾-quart tube mold.

Bake 55 minutes, or until loaf is golden and a wooden pick inserted near center comes out clean. Cool in mold on a wire rack 10 minutes. Loosen around edge and tube with a knife; invert onto rack; cool completely.

For easy, neat slicing, wrap loaf in foil and store overnight. Just before serving, sprinkle confectioners' sugar lightly over top; cut into thin wedges.

Yield: 1 nine-inch ring.

CARROT-WALNUT LOAF

1½ cups sifted all-purpose flour
1 teaspoon baking soda
1 teaspoon ground cinnamon
½ teaspoon salt
¼ cup shortening
⅔ cup sugar
2 eggs
1 cup grated pared raw carrots
1 cup chopped California walnuts

Preheat oven to 325°.

Sift flour, baking soda, cinnamon, and salt onto waxed paper.

Cream shortening with sugar in a medium bowl; beat in eggs; stir in carrots.

Add flour mixture all at once; stir just until mixture is evenly moist; stir in walnuts. Spoon into a greased baking pan, 8½x4½x2¾ inches.

Bake 1 hour, or until loaf is golden and a wooden pick inserted into center comes out clean. Cool in pan on a wire rack 10 minutes. Loosen around edges with a knife; turn out onto rack; cool completely.

For easy neat slicing, wrap loaf in foil and store overnight.

Yield: 1 loaf.

PEANUT BREAD

3 cups sifted all-purpose flour
2 teaspoons baking powder
2 teaspoons baking soda
1 teaspoon salt
2 teaspoons ground cinnamon
1 cup firmly packed light brown sugar
3 cups high-protein cereal flakes
4 eggs
½ cup peanut oil
½ cup peanut butter
1 jar (15 ozs.) applesauce
1 cup light raisins

Preheat oven to 350°.

Sift flour, baking powder, baking soda, salt, and cinnamon into a large bowl; stir in brown sugar and cereal.

Combine eggs, peanut oil, peanut butter, and applesauce in a medium bowl; beat until well blended. Stir into flour mixture until evenly blended; stir in raisins. Pour into two greased loaf pans, 8½x4½x2¾ inches.

Bake 50 minutes, or until loaves are firm and brown. Cool in pans on wire racks 10 minutes. Loosen loaves around edges with a knife; turn out onto racks; cool completely.

For easy, neat slicing, wrap loaves in foil and store overnight.

Yield: 2 loaves.

BLUEBERRY KUCHEN

2⅓ cups sifted all-purpose flour
½ cup firmly packed light brown sugar
¼ teaspoon ground cinnamon
¼ teaspoon ground nutmeg
¼ cup butter or margarine
½ cup chopped California walnuts
⅔ cup granulated sugar
2½ teaspoons baking powder
½ teaspoon salt
1 egg
¾ cup milk
¼ cup salad oil
1 can (15 ozs.) blueberries, drained well

Mix ⅓ cup of the flour, brown sugar, cinnamon, and nutmeg in a small bowl. Cut in butter with a pastry blender until mixture forms coarse crumbs; stir in walnuts; set aside.

Preheat oven to 350°.

Sift remaining 2 cups flour, granulated sugar, baking powder, and salt into a medium bowl.

Beat egg in a small bowl; stir in milk and salad oil. Add all at once to flour mixture; stir just until mixture is evenly moist; fold in blueberries. Spoon into a greased baking pan, 8x8x2 inches. Sprinkle brown sugar mixture over top.

Bake 50 minutes, or until a wooden pick inserted into center comes out clean. Cool in pan on a wire rack 30 minutes; cut into squares; serve warm.

Yield: 1 eight-inch square loaf.

PUMPKIN-WALNUT TEA BREAD

1 egg
½ cup canned pumpkin
2 tablespoons milk
1 package spice muffin mix
½ cup chopped California walnuts
1 tablespoon butter or margarine
2 tablespoons honey

Preheat oven to 350°.

Beat egg with pumpkin and milk until blended in a small bowl. Add all at once to muffin mix in a large bowl; stir just until mixture is evenly moist. Stir in walnuts. Spoon into a greased baking pan, 8½x4½x2¾ inches.

Bake 35 minutes, or until a wooden pick inserted in center comes out clean. Cool loaf in pan on a wire rack 10 minutes; loosen around edges with a knife; turn out onto rack.

Melt butter in a small saucepan; stir in honey. Heat until warm; drizzle over loaf. (Glaze will soak in.) Cool loaf completely.

Yield: 1 loaf.

APRICOT-ALMOND BREAD

1½ cups whole bran cereal
1¼ cups milk
¾ cup slivered blanched almonds
1¾ cups sifted all-purpose flour
½ cup sugar
3 teaspoons baking powder
½ teaspoon salt
2 eggs
⅓ cup melted shortening
½ cup finely cut dried apricots

Combine bran and milk in a medium bowl; let stand until milk is absorbed.

Chop enough of the almonds to make ½ cup; set the rest aside for topping.

Preheat oven to 350°.

Sift flour, sugar, baking powder, and salt into a large bowl; stir in chopped almonds.

Beat eggs in a small bowl; stir in shortening and apricots; stir into bran mixture. Add all at once to flour mixture; stir just until mixture is evenly moist. Spoon into a greased baking pan, 9x5x3 inches; sprinkle remaining slivered almonds on top.

Bake 55 minutes, or until a wooden pick inserted into center comes out clean. Cool in pan on a wire rack 10 minutes. Loosen loaf around edges with a knife; turn out onto rack; cool completely.

For easy, neat slicing, wrap loaf in foil and store overnight.

Yield: 1 loaf.

RAISIN-WHEAT BREAD

    3 cups sifted all-purpose flour
 1½ teaspoons baking soda
    ½ teaspoon salt
    1 cup firmly packed dark brown sugar
    1 cup dark raisins
    ¾ cup uncooked granulated whole-wheat cereal
    2 eggs
 1½ cups buttermilk
    3 tablespoons butter or margarine, melted

Preheat oven to 350°.

Sift flour, baking soda, and salt into a large bowl; stir in brown sugar, raisins, and dry cereal.

Beat eggs in a small bowl; stir in buttermilk and melted butter. Add all at once to flour mixture; stir just until mixture is evenly moist. Spoon into greased baking pan, 9x5x3 inches.

Bake 1 hour and 15 minutes, or until a wooden pick inserted in center comes out clean. Cool loaf in pan on a wire rack 10 minutes. Loosen around edges with a knife; turn out onto rack; cool completely.

For easy, neat slicing, wrap loaf in foil and store overnight.

Yield: 1 loaf.

OLIVE-CHEESE LOAF

 2½ cups sifted all-purpose flour
 3½ teaspoons baking powder
 1¼ teaspoons salt
    ¼ cup shortening
    ½ cup sugar
    1 egg
    1 cup milk
    ½ cup grated sharp Cheddar cheese
    ½ cup chopped pitted ripe olives
    ½ cup chopped California walnuts

Preheat oven to 350°.

Sift flour, baking powder, and salt onto waxed paper.

Cream shortening and sugar until fluffy in a large bowl; beat in egg. Stir in flour mixture, alternately with milk, just until blended. Stir in cheese, olives, and walnuts. Spoon into a greased baking pan, 9x5x3 inches.

Bake 1 hour, or until loaf is golden and a wooden pick inserted into center comes out clean. Cool in pan on a wire rack 10 minutes. Loosen loaf around edges with a knife; turn out onto rack; cool completely.

For easy, neat slicing, wrap loaf in foil and store overnight.

Yield: 1 loaf.

PINEAPPLE-CHERRY RING

    1 cup chopped pecans
    3 cups sifted all-purpose flour
    ½ cup sugar
    4 teaspoons baking powder
    ½ teaspoon salt
    2 tablespoons grated orange rind
    1 can (8 ozs.) crushed pineapple in juice
      Orange juice
    1 egg
    ¼ cup butter or margarine, melted
    ½ cup chopped candied red cherries

Preheat oven to 350°.

Grease a 1¾-quart ring mold; sprinkle 3 tablespoons of the pecans over bottom.

Sift flour, sugar, baking powder, and salt into a large bowl; stir in orange rind and remaining pecans.

Drain juice from pineapple into a 1-cup measure; add orange juice to make ¾ cup.

Beat egg in a small bowl; stir in melted butter, pineapple, and orange-juice mixture. Add all at once to flour mixture; stir just until mixture is evenly moist; stir in cherries. Spoon evenly into prepared mold.

Bake 45 minutes, or until golden and a wooden pick inserted near center comes out clean. Cool in mold on a wire rack 10 minutes. Loosen ring around edge and center with a knife; turn out onto rack; cool completely.

For easy, neat slicing, wrap ring in foil and store overnight.

Yield: 1 seven-inch ring.

BANANA-COCONUT ROUND

2 cups biscuit mix
2 tablespoons granulated sugar
2 tablespoons salad oil
1 egg
¾ cup mashed ripe bananas
¼ cup orange juice
3 tablespoons butter or margarine
⅓ cup firmly packed brown sugar
2 tablespoons cream
½ cup flaked coconut

Preheat oven to 400°.

Combine biscuit mix, granulated sugar, salad oil, egg, bananas, and orange juice in a medium bowl. Stir until blended, then beat vigorously ½ minute; spoon into a well-greased 9-inch round layer-cake pan.

Bake 30 minutes, or until loaf is golden; remove from oven. Turn temperature control to broil.

Melt butter in a small saucepan; stir in brown sugar, cream, and coconut; spread over hot loaf.

Broil, 5 to 6 inches from heat, 2 to 3 minutes, or until topping bubbles up. Cool slightly in pan on a wire rack. Cut into wedges; serve warm.

Yield: 1 nine-inch round loaf.

DATE-PECAN LOAF

1 package (8 ozs.) pitted dates, finely cut
¾ cup boiling water
6 tablespoons butter or margarine
1¼ cups firmly packed light brown sugar
1 egg
1 cup applesauce
2¼ cups sifted all-purpose flour
1½ teaspoons baking soda
1 teaspoon ground cinnamon
1 teaspoon salt
½ cup chopped pecans

Preheat oven to 350°.

Combine dates and boiling water in a medium bowl; stir in butter until melted, then add brown sugar.

Beat egg in a small bowl; stir in applesauce; stir into date mixture.

Sift flour, soda, cinnamon, and salt into a large bowl; stir in pecans. Add date mixture all at once; stir just until mixture is evenly moist. Spoon into a greased baking pan, 9x5x3 inches.

Bake 1 hour, or until a wooden pick inserted into center comes out clean. Cool in pan on a wire rack 10 minutes. Loosen loaf around edges with a knife; turn out onto rack; cool completely.

For easy, neat slicing, wrap loaf in foil and store overnight.

Yield: 1 loaf.

RAISIN-NUT LOAF

3 cups sifted all-purpose flour
¾ cup sugar
1 teaspoon salt
1½ teaspoons baking soda
1½ teaspoons baking powder
1½ teaspoons ground cinnamon
1 cup dark raisins
1 cup finely chopped filberts
1 egg
1½ cups sour milk
¼ cup salad oil

Preheat oven to 350°.

Sift flour, sugar, salt, baking soda, baking powder, and cinnamon into a large bowl; stir in raisins and filberts.

Beat egg in a small bowl; stir in sour milk and salad oil. Add all at once to flour mixture; stir just until mixture is evenly moist. Spoon into a greased baking pan, 9x5x3 inches.

Bake 1 hour, or until a wooden pick inserted into center comes out clean. Cool in pan on a wire rack 10 minutes. Loosen loaf around edges with a knife; turn out onto rack; cool completely.

For easy, neat slicing, wrap loaf in foil and store overnight.

Yield: 1 loaf.

BISCUITS, POPOVERS, FRITTERS, MUFFINS, AND CORN BREAD

BAKING POWDER BISCUITS

2 cups sifted all-purpose flour
3 teaspoons baking powder
1 teaspoon salt
¼ cup shortening
⅔ cup milk

Preheat oven to 425°.

Sift flour, baking powder, and salt into a medium bowl. Cut in shortening with a pastry blender until fine crumbs form.

Stir in milk all at once with a fork just until mixture is evenly moist. Turn out onto a lightly floured board; knead ½ minute.

Roll out dough to a circle ½-inch thick; cut into rounds with a floured 2-inch biscuit cutter; place on a lightly greased cookie sheet.

Bake 12 minutes, or until biscuits are golden. Remove from cookie sheet. Serve hot.

Yield: 1 dozen 2-inch biscuits.

BUTTERMILK BISCUITS

2 cups sifted all-purpose flour
1 teaspoon baking powder
½ teaspoon baking soda
⅛ teaspoon salt
¼ cup shortening
¾ cup buttermilk

Preheat oven to 425°.

Sift flour, baking powder, baking soda, and salt into a medium bowl. Cut in shortening with a pastry blender until fine crumbs form.

Stir in buttermilk all at once with a fork to make a soft dough; turn out onto a lightly floured board; knead ½ minute.

Roll out dough to a circle ½ inch thick; cut into rounds with a 2-inch biscuit cutter. Place on an ungreased cookie sheet.

Bake 15 minutes, or until biscuits are golden. Remove from cookie sheet. Serve hot with butter or margarine.

Yield: 1 dozen 2-inch biscuits.

Note: If biscuits are placed about an inch apart on cookie sheet, they will have crusty sides when baked. If you prefer soft sides, arrange rounds close together in an ungreased baking pan.

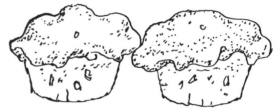

BLUEBERRY SUGAR PUFFS

2 cups sifted all-purpose flour
6 tablespoons sugar
2½ teaspoons baking powder
½ teaspoon salt
1 egg
⅓ cup salad oil
½ cup milk
1 cup thawed frozen blueberries, well drained
  (from a 10-oz. package)
2 teaspoons grated lemon rind

Preheat oven to 400°.

Sift flour, 4 tablespoons of the sugar, baking powder, and salt into a medium bowl.

Beat egg slightly in a small bowl; stir in salad oil and milk. Add all at once to flour mixture; stir just until mixture is evenly moist; fold in blueberries. Spoon into greased medium-sized muffin-pan cups.

Mix remaining 2 tablespoons sugar and lemon rind in a cup; sprinkle over batter.

Bake 30 minutes, or until muffins are puffed and golden. Cool 10 minutes in pan on a wire rack; remove from pan. Serve warm.

Yield: 1 dozen.

CHEDDAR BISCUITS

2 cups sifted all-purpose flour
3 teaspoons baking powder
½ teaspoon salt
¼ cup shortening
⅔ cup shredded sharp Cheddar cheese
1 tablespoon chopped parsley
⅔ cup milk

Preheat oven to 425°.

Sift flour, baking powder, and salt into a medium bowl. Cut in shortening with a pastry blender until fine crumbs form; stir in cheese and parsley.

Stir in milk all at once with a fork to make a soft dough; turn out onto a lightly floured board; knead ½ minute.

Roll out dough to a circle ½ inch thick; cut into rounds with a 2-inch biscuit cutter. Place on a greased cookie sheet.

Bake 15 minutes, or until biscuits are golden. Remove from cookie sheet. Serve hot with butter or margarine.

Yield: 1 dozen.

QUICK WALNUT PUFFS

¼ cup butter or margarine
¼ cup firmly packed light brown sugar
¼ cup chopped California walnuts
2 cups biscuit mix
2 tablespoons granulated sugar
⅔ cup milk

Preheat oven to 425°.

Measure one teaspoon each of the butter and brown sugar into 12 medium-sized muffin-pan cups. Set in oven to melt as oven preheats; measure 1 teaspoon of the walnuts into each cup.

Combine biscuit mix, granulated sugar, and milk in a medium bowl; stir until well blended; spoon over sugar-nut mixture in cups.

Bake 15 minutes, or until biscuits are puffed and golden. Loosen biscuits around edges of cups with a knife; invert pan onto a cookie sheet. Let stand several minutes; lift off pan. Serve biscuits hot.

Yield: 1 dozen.

REFRIGERATOR BRAN MUFFINS

1 cup bran flakes cereal
1 cup boiling water
2 cups whole-bran cereal
2 cups buttermilk
3 cups sifted all-purpose flour
2½ teaspoons baking soda
½ teaspoon baking powder
½ teaspoon salt
½ cup shortening
1 cup sugar
2 eggs
¼ cup unsulphured molasses

Combine bran flakes and boiling water in a medium bowl; set aside.

Combine whole-bran cereal and buttermilk in a medium bowl; set aside.

Sift flour, baking soda, baking powder, and salt onto waxed paper.

Cream shortening and sugar in a large bowl until fluffy-light; beat in eggs and molasses. Stir in bran-flake mixture, alternately with flour mixture, just until evenly moist; stir in buttermilk mixture.

Spoon batter into one or more refrigerator containers; cover tightly. Store in refrigerator up to two weeks.

Preheat oven to 400°.

Spoon batter into greased medium-sized muffin-pan cups.

Bake 20 minutes, or until muffins are puffed and golden. Cool in pans on wire racks 10 minutes; remove from pans. Serve warm.

Yield: 2½ dozen.

Note: If you prefer to bake batter immediately after mixing, use same temperature and time as given above.

MINIATURE BANANA-OAT MUFFINS

1½ cups sifted all-purpose flour
1 teaspoon salt
1 teaspoon ground cinnamon
½ teaspoon baking soda
⅓ cup butter or margarine
⅔ cup firmly packed dark brown sugar
2 eggs
2 large ripe bananas, peeled and mashed (1 cup)
1½ cups oat cereal flakes

Preheat oven to 400°.

Sift flour, salt, cinnamon, and baking soda onto waxed paper.

Cream butter with brown sugar until fluffy in a large bowl; beat in eggs, one at a time, until fluffy again. Stir in flour mixture, alternately with bananas, just until evenly moist; fold in oat flakes. Spoon into greased 1¾-inch muffin-pan cups to fill each two thirds full.

Bake 15 minutes, or until muffins are puffed and golden. Cool in pans on wire racks 1 to 2 minutes, remove from pans. Serve warm

Yield: 3 dozen.

APRICOT MUFFINS

1 cup sifted all-purpose flour
⅓ cup sugar
2½ teaspoons baking powder
½ teaspoon salt
1 cup whole-bran cereal
¾ cup milk
1 egg
¼ cup soft shortening
½ cup finely chopped dried apricots

Preheat oven to 400°.

Sift flour, sugar, baking powder, and salt onto waxed paper.

Stir bran into milk in a medium bowl; let stand until milk is absorbed. Beat in egg and shortening; stir in apricots.

Add flour mixture all at once; stir just until mixture is evenly moist. Spoon into greased medium-sized muffin-pan cups.

Bake 30 minutes, or until muffins are puffed and golden. Cool in pan on a wire rack 10 minutes; remove from pan. Serve warm.

Yield: 1 dozen.

BACON-BRAN MUFFINS

1 cup whole-bran cereal
1 cup milk
¼ cup sugar
1 egg
4 tablespoons butter or margarine, melted
2 cups biscuit mix
¼ cup crumbled crisp bacon or bacon-flavored vegetable-protein bits

Preheat oven to 400°.

Combine bran and milk in a large bowl; let stand 5 minutes until liquid is absorbed.

Stir in sugar, egg, melted butter, and biscuit mix; beat vigorously ½ minute; stir in protein bits. Spoon into greased medium-sized muffin-pan cups.

Bake 25 minutes, or until muffins are puffed and golden. Cool in pan on a wire rack 10 minutes; remove from pan. Serve warm.

Yield: 1 dozen.

BACON-CORN MUFFINS

1 package (12 ozs.) corn muffin mix
Egg
Milk
3 tablespoons bacon-flavored vegetable-protein bits, coarsely broken
3 tablespoons chopped drained pimientos

Preheat oven to 400°.

Prepare muffin mix with egg and milk as label directs; fold in protein bits and pimientos. Spoon into greased medium-sized muffin-pan cups.

Bake 15 minutes, or until muffins are puffed and golden. Cool in pan on a wire rack 10 minutes; remove from pan. Serve warm.

Yield: 1 dozen.

STRAWBERRY STREUSEL PUFFS

2⅓ cups biscuit mix
2 tablespoons granulated sugar
1 egg
⅔ cup cold water
½ cup chopped California walnuts
2 tablespoons strawberry preserves
⅓ cup firmly packed brown sugar
¼ cup butter or margarine

Preheat oven to 400°.

Combine 2 cups of the biscuit mix, granulated sugar, egg, and water in a medium bowl; beat until blended; stir in walnuts. Spoon 1 rounded tablespoonful into each of 12 greased medium-sized muffin-pan cups.

Drop ½ teaspoon strawberry preserves onto center of batter in each cup; spoon in remaining batter.

Combine brown sugar and remaining ⅓ cup biscuit mix in a bowl; cut in butter with a pastry blender until mixture forms coarse crumbs; sprinkle over batter.

Bake 15 minutes, or until muffins are golden. Remove from pan to a wire rack. Serve warm.

Yield: 1 dozen.

APPLE FANS

3 small tart apples
7 tablespoons sugar
1 teaspoon ground cinnamon
½ teaspoon ground nutmeg
2¼ cups sifted all-purpose flour
3 teaspoons baking powder
½ teaspoon salt
1 egg
¾ cup milk
¼ cup melted shortening

Pare apples; cut each in half and core. Finely chop 1 apple to measure ½ cup; set aside. Cut remaining 2 apples into 24 thin slices.

Mix 3 tablespoons of the sugar, cinnamon, and nutmeg in a medium bowl; add apple slices and toss to coat well.

Preheat oven to 400°.

Sift flour, remaining 4 tablespoons sugar, baking powder, and salt into a medium bowl.

Beat egg slightly with milk and melted shortening in a small bowl. Add all at once to flour mixture; stir just until mixture is evenly moist; stir in chopped apple. Spoon evenly into 12 greased medium-sized muffin-pan cups. Push two apple slices deep into batter in each cup; sprinkle any remaining spice mixture in bowl over tops.

Bake 30 minutes, or until muffins are golden. Cool in pan on a wire rack 10 minutes; remove from pan. Serve warm.

Yield: 1 dozen.

SESAME CORN MUFFINS

1 package (12 ozs.) corn muffin mix
Egg
Milk
1½ teaspoons sesame seeds

Preheat oven to 400°.

Prepare muffin mix with egg and milk as label directs; spoon into greased 1¾-inch muffin-pan cups to fill each two thirds full. Sprinkle sesame seeds over top.

Bake 15 minutes, or until muffins are puffed and golden. Cool in pans on wire racks 1 to 2 minutes; remove from pans. Serve warm.

Yield: 2½ dozen.

PINEAPPLE-CHERRY MINIATURES

2 cups biscuit mix
2 tablespoons sugar
1 egg
1 can (8 ozs.) crushed pineapple in syrup
⅓ cup milk
½ teaspoon vanilla
⅓ cup chopped maraschino cherries
⅓ cup flaked coconut

Preheat oven to 400°.

Combine biscuit mix and sugar in a medium bowl.

Beat egg slightly in a small bowl; stir in pineapple and syrup, milk, and vanilla. Stir into sugar mixture until evenly moist, then beat vigorously ½ minute; stir in cherries and coconut. Spoon into greased 1¾-inch muffin-pan cups to fill each two thirds full.

Bake 15 minutes, or until muffins are puffed and golden. Cool in pans on a wire rack 10 minutes; remove from pans. Serve warm.

Yield: 3 dozen.

DILL PUFFS

1 package (12 ozs.) corn muffin mix
1 cup biscuit mix
¾ teaspoon dillweed
1 egg
¾ cup milk

Preheat oven to 400°.

Combine muffin and biscuit mixes with dillweed in a medium bowl.

Beat egg slightly in a small bowl; stir in milk; add all at once to biscuit mixture. Stir until evenly moist, then beat ½ minute; spoon into greased medium-sized muffin-pan cups.

Bake 15 minutes, or until muffins are golden. Cool in pan on a wire rack 10 minutes; remove from pan. Serve warm.

Yield: 1 dozen.

PEANUT BUTTER MUFFINS

2 cups sifted all-purpose flour
3 tablespoons sugar
3 teaspoons baking powder
1 teaspoon salt
1 egg
1 cup milk
⅓ cup crunchy peanut butter

Preheat oven to 400°.

Sift flour, sugar, baking powder, and salt into a medium bowl.

Beat egg with milk in a small bowl; beat in peanut butter. Add all at once to flour mixture; stir just until mixture is evenly moist. Spoon into greased medium-sized muffin-pan cups.

Bake 20 minutes, or until muffins are puffed and golden. Cool in pan on a wire rack 10 minutes; remove from pan. Serve warm.

Yield: 1 dozen.

PINEAPPLE-BRAN MUFFINS

1 cup sifted all-purpose flour
2 tablespoons sugar
2½ teaspoons baking powder
¼ teaspoon salt
1 egg
⅔ cup milk
1 can (8 ozs.) crushed pineapple in syrup, well drained
3 tablespoons salad oil
1½ cups bran flakes cereal

Preheat oven to 400°.

Sift flour, sugar, baking powder, and salt into a medium bowl.

Beat egg with milk until blended in a small bowl; stir in pineapple and salad oil. Add all at once to flour mixture; stir just until mixture is evenly moist; fold in bran flakes. Spoon into greased 1¾-inch muffin-pan cups to fill each two thirds full.

Bake 20 minutes, or until muffins are firm and golden. Cool in pans on wire racks 1 to 2 minutes; remove from pans. Serve warm.

Yield: 2½ dozen.

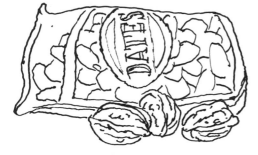

DATE-WALNUT MUFFINS

　2 cups sifted all-purpose flour
　3 tablespoons sugar
2½ teaspoons baking powder
　½ teaspoon salt
　1 egg
　⅓ cup melted shortening
　¾ cup milk
　½ teaspoon vanilla
　½ cup chopped dates
　½ cup chopped California walnuts

Preheat oven to 400°.

Sift flour, sugar, baking powder, and salt into a medium bowl.

Beat egg in a small bowl; stir in shortening, milk, and vanilla. Add all at once to flour mixture; stir just until mixture is evenly moist; fold in dates and walnuts. Spoon into greased medium-sized muffin-pan cups.

Bake 25 minutes, or until muffins are puffed and golden. Cool in pan on a wire rack 10 minutes; remove from pan. Serve warm.

Yield: 1 dozen.

HONEY-RAISIN BRAN MUFFINS

1⅓ cups sifted all-purpose flour
　¼ cup sugar
　3 teaspoons baking powder
　½ teaspoon salt
　3 cups raisin-bran cereal flakes
1¼ cups milk
　¼ cup honey
　1 egg
　⅓ cup salad oil
　1 teaspoon grated orange rind

Preheat oven to 400°.

Sift flour, sugar, baking powder, and salt into a large bowl.

Combine cereal, milk, and honey in a medium bowl; beat in egg, salad oil, and orange rind. Add all at once to flour mixture; stir just until mixture is evenly moist. Spoon into greased medium-sized muffin-pan cups.

Bake 25 minutes, or until muffins are puffed and golden. Cool in pan on a wire rack 10 minutes; remove from pan. Serve warm.

Yield: 1 dozen.

ORANGE-PRUNE MUFFINS

1¾ cups sifted all-purpose flour
　½ cup regular wheat germ
　⅓ cup sugar (for batter)
　3 teaspoons baking powder
　½ teaspoon mace
　½ teaspoon salt
　1 cup snipped dried prunes
　2 eggs
　¼ cup salad oil
　⅔ cup milk
　¼ cup sugar (for topping)
　1 teaspoon grated orange rind
　2 tablespoons orange juice

Preheat oven to 400°.

Mix flour, wheat germ, the ⅓ cup sugar, baking powder, mace, and salt in a large bowl; stir in prunes.

Beat eggs slightly in a small bowl; stir in salad oil and milk. Add all at once to flour mixture; stir just until mixture is evenly moist. Spoon into greased medium-sized muffin-pan cups.

Bake 20 minutes, or until muffins are puffed and golden. Cool in pan on a wire rack 10 minutes; remove from pan.

While muffins cool, combine the ¼ cup sugar, orange rind, and juice in a small saucepan. Heat, stirring constantly, to boiling; cook 1 minute. Brush hot glaze over muffins. (Mixture will soak in.) Serve muffins warm.

Yield: 1 dozen.

APPLE RAISIN MUFFINS

1½ cups sifted all-purpose flour
2½ teaspoons baking powder
¼ cup sugar
½ teaspoon pumpkin-pie spice
½ teaspoon salt
2 cups raisin-bran cereal flakes
1 egg
3 tablespoons salad oil
¾ cup milk
1 large apple, pared, quartered, cored, and
    chopped fine (1 cup)

Preheat oven to 400°.

Sift flour, baking powder, sugar, pumpkin-pie spice, and salt into a large bowl; stir in raisin bran.

Beat egg in a small bowl; stir in salad oil and milk. Add all at once to flour mixture; stir just until mixture is evenly moist; fold in apple. Spoon into greased medium-sized muffin-pan cups.

Bake 30 minutes, or until muffins are puffed and golden. Cool in pan on a wire rack 10 minutes; remove from pan. Serve warm.

Yield: 1 dozen.

CHOCOLATE MARBLE MUFFIN SQUARES

1 tablespoon butter or margarine
⅔ cup flaked coconut
5 tablespoons sugar
½ teaspoon ground cinnamon
2 squares semisweet chocolate
2 tablespoons milk (for chocolate)
2 cups biscuit mix
¾ cup milk (for batter)
1 egg
2 tablespoons salad oil

Preheat oven to 400°.

Melt butter in a small saucepan; remove from heat. Stir in coconut, 1 tablespoon of the sugar, and cinnamon.

Combine chocolate and the 2 tablespoons milk in a medium saucepan; heat slowly, stirring constantly, until chocolate melts and mixture is smooth; cool.

Combine biscuit mix, remaining 4 tablespoons sugar, the ¾ cup milk, egg, and salad oil in a medium bowl; stir until blended, then beat vigorously ½ minute. Stir half into chocolate mixture until well blended.

Drop spoonfuls of chocolate batter, alternately with spoonfuls of remaining plain batter, into a greased baking pan, 8x8x2 inches. Cut through batter with a knife to marble. Sprinkle coconut mixture evenly over batter.

Bake 30 minutes, or until a wooden pick inserted in center comes out clean. Cool in pan on a wire rack. Cut into serving-sized pieces.

Yield: 8 servings.

MOCK BOSTON BROWN BREAD

1¼ cups sifted all-purpose flour
¾ teaspoon baking soda
1½ teaspoons dry mustard
⅛ teaspoon ground cloves
¼ teaspoon salt
¾ cup regular wheat germ
½ cup dark molasses
⅓ cup hot water
¼ cup butter or margarine
¼ cup sugar
1 egg

Preheat oven to 350°.

Sift flour, baking soda, mustard, cloves, and salt into a medium bowl; stir in wheat germ.

Mix molasses and hot water in a small bowl.

Cream butter with sugar in a medium bowl; beat in egg. Stir in flour mixture, alternately with molasses mixture, until blended. Spoon into a well-greased baking pan, 8x8x2 inches.

Bake 30 minutes, or until a wooden pick inserted into center comes out clean. Cool in pan on a wire rack.

Cut into squares. Serve warm.

Yield: 9 servings.

POPOVERS

2 eggs
1 cup milk
1 cup sifted all-purpose flour
¼ teaspoon salt
1 teaspoon melted butter or margarine

Preheat oven to 400°.

Beat eggs slightly in a medium bowl. Slowly beat in milk, flour, and salt until blended, then beat briskly, scraping side of bowl once, 2 minutes; stir in melted butter. Pour evenly into 8 generously greased small deep custard cups, filling each half full. For easy handling, place cups, not touching, in a shallow pan.

Bake 45 minutes, or until popovers are puffed and golden. Remove from cups. Serve hot.

Yield: 8 popovers.

BLUEBERRY FRITTERS

1½ cups sifted all-purpose flour
¼ cup granulated sugar
2 teaspoons baking powder
¼ teaspoon salt
½ teaspoon mace
1 cup fresh blueberries
2 eggs
½ cup milk
1 tablespoon melted shortening
Salad oil for frying
½ cup sifted confectioners' powdered sugar

Sift flour, 3 tablespoons of the granulated sugar, baking powder, salt, and mace into a large bowl. Combine remaining 1 tablespoon sugar with blueberries in a small bowl; toss to coat well.

Beat eggs in a small bowl; stir in milk and melted shortening. Stir into flour mixture until smooth; fold in blueberry mixture.

Pour enough salad oil into an electric cooker and deep fryer to fill about half way; heat to 375°.

Drop batter, a tablespoon at a time, into hot oil; fry 2 minutes, or until golden on bottoms; turn. Fry 2 to 3 minutes longer, or until fritters are golden on second sides. Remove from oil with a slotted spoon and drain on paper toweling. While hot, roll in confectioners' sugar on waxed paper. Serve warm.

Yield: About 2½ dozen.

CORN BREAD

1 cup yellow cornmeal
1 cup sifted all-purpose flour
3½ teaspoons baking powder
3 tablespoons sugar
1 teaspoon salt
1 egg
1 cup milk
¼ cup melted shortening or salad oil

Preheat oven to 425°.

Sift cornmeal, flour, baking powder, sugar, and salt into a medium bowl.

Beat egg in a small bowl; stir in milk and melted shortening. Add all at once to cornmeal mixture; stir just until evenly moist and smooth. Pour into a greased baking pan, 8x8x2 inches.

Bake 25 minutes, or until loaf is firm and golden. Cut into squares. Serve hot.

Yield: 8 to 10 servings.

BACON-CORN LOAF

6 slices bacon, cut in ½-inch pieces
1 package (12 ozs.) corn muffin mix
1 cup sifted all-purpose flour
1 egg
1 cup milk

Sauté bacon until crisp in a small skillet; remove and drain on paper toweling.

Preheat oven to 400°.

Combine muffin mix and flour in a medium bowl.

Beat egg with milk in a small bowl; stir into flour mixture until almost smooth; fold in bacon. Spoon into a greased baking pan, 9x5x3 inches.

Bake 35 minutes, or until loaf is golden. Loosen loaf around edges with a knife; turn out onto a wire rack; cool. Cut crosswise in thick slices; serve warm.

Yield: 1 loaf.

PANCAKES, WAFFLES, AND FRENCH TOAST

GOLDEN GRIDDLE CAKES

1½ cups sifted all-purpose flour
 3 teaspoons baking powder
 2 tablespoons sugar
 ¾ teaspoon salt
 1 egg
1¼ cups milk
 3 tablespoons shortening, melted
    Salad oil

Sift flour, baking powder, sugar, and salt into a medium bowl.

Beat egg with milk in a small bowl; add to flour mixture all at once; stir just until batter is almost smooth; stir in melted shortening.

Preheat griddle as manufacturer directs; grease lightly with salad oil.

For each pancake, pour a scant ¼ cup of the batter onto hot griddle. Bake 2 to 3 minutes, or until bubbles appear on top and underside is golden; turn. Bake 1 to 2 minutes longer, or until pancake is golden on bottom. Serve hot with butter or margarine and pancake syrup.

Yield: 12 four-inch pancakes.

BLUEBERRY WHEAT CAKES

 1 egg
 1 cup buttermilk
    Salad oil
 ½ cup sifted all-purpose flour
 ½ cup uncooked granulated whole-wheat cereal
 1 tablespoon sugar
 1 teaspoon baking powder
 ½ teaspoon baking soda
 ½ teaspoon salt
 1 can (21 ozs.) blueberry pie filling
 4 tablespoons butter or margarine
 2 tablespoons water

Beat egg in a medium bowl; stir in buttermilk and 2 tablespoons salad oil. Add flour, dry cereal, sugar, baking powder, baking soda, and salt; beat until smooth.

Preheat griddle as manufacturer directs; grease lightly with salad oil.

For each pancake, pour a generous ¼ cup of the batter onto hot griddle; spread into a 5-inch round. Bake 2 to 3 minutes, or until bubbles appear on top and underside is golden; turn. Bake 1 to 2 minutes longer, or until pancake is golden on bottom.

While pancakes bake, combine blueberry pie filling, butter, and water in a medium saucepan; heat slowly, stirring several times, to boiling.

When ready to serve, stack two or three pancakes on each serving plate; top with blueberry sauce.

Yield: 4 servings.

BANANA GRIDDLE CAKES

 2 cups complete pancake mix
1¾ cups milk
 2 large ripe bananas, peeled and mashed (1 cup)
 1 teaspoon vanilla
    Salad oil

Combine pancake mix, milk, mashed bananas, and vanilla in a medium bowl; stir until batter is almost smooth.

Preheat griddle as manufacturer directs; grease lightly with salad oil.

For each pancake, pour ¼ cup batter onto hot griddle; spread into a 4-inch round. Bake 2 to 3 minutes, or until bubbles appear on top and underside is golden; turn. Bake 1 to 2 minutes longer, or until pancake is golden on bottom. Serve hot with butter or margarine and pancake syrup.

Yield: 14 four-inch pancakes.

CHEDDAR WAFFLES

2 cups sifted all-purpose flour
3 teaspoons baking powder
½ teaspoon salt
2 eggs, separated
1⅓ cups milk
3 tablespoons salad oil
½ cup grated sharp Cheddar cheese

Preheat waffle iron as manufacturer directs.

Sift flour, baking powder, and salt into a medium bowl.

Beat egg whites in a small bowl until they form firm peaks.

Beat egg yolks with milk and salad oil in a small bowl; add all at once to flour mixture; stir just until blended. Stir in cheese; fold in beaten egg whites.

Ladle batter into hot waffle iron. Bake as manufacturer directs until waffle is golden. Serve hot with butter or margarine and pancake syrup.

Yield: 8 five-inch square waffles.

BLUEBERRY PANCAKES

1½ cups sifted all-purpose flour
2½ teaspoons baking powder
3 tablespoons sugar
½ teaspoon salt
1 egg
1¼ cups milk
3 tablespoons butter or margarine, melted
¾ cup fresh blueberries
    Salad oil

Sift flour, baking powder, sugar, and salt into a medium bowl.

Beat egg in a small bowl; stir in milk and melted butter. Add to flour mixture all at once; stir until batter is almost smooth; fold in blueberries.

Preheat griddle as manufacturer directs; grease lightly with salad oil.

For each pancake, measure 1 tablespoon batter onto hot griddle. Bake 1 to 2 minutes, or until bubbles appear on top and underside is golden; turn. Bake 1 to 2 minutes longer, or until pancake is golden on bottom. Serve hot with butter or margarine and pancake syrup.

Yield: 32 three-inch pancakes.

SPICED RICE WAFFLES

1¾ cups sifted all-purpose flour
3 teaspoons baking powder
1 teaspoon pumpkin-pie spice
½ teaspoon salt
2 eggs, separated
1 cup cooled cooked rice
1½ cups milk
⅓ cup butter or margarine, melted (for batter)
1 can or jar (15 ozs.) applesauce
½ cup pancake syrup
⅓ cup butter or margarine (for topping)

Preheat waffle iron as manufacturer directs.

Sift flour, baking powder, pumpkin-pie spice, and salt into a large bowl.

Beat egg whites in a small bowl until they form firm peaks.

Beat egg yolks well in a medium bowl; stir in rice, milk, and melted butter. Add all at once to flour mixture; stir just until blended; fold in beaten egg whites.

Ladle batter into hot waffle iron. Bake as manufacturer directs until golden.

While waffles bake, combine applesauce, syrup, and ⅓ cup butter in a medium saucepan; heat slowly to boiling.

Place waffles on serving plates: spoon hot apple mixture over top.

Yield: 6 servings.

BASIC CREPES

¾ cup sifted all-purpose flour
¼ teaspoon salt
2 eggs
1 cup milk
3 tablespoons butter or margarine

Combine flour and salt in a medium bowl.

Beat eggs in a small bowl; stir in milk; beat into flour mixture until smooth. Melt 1 tablespoon of the butter in a small saucepan; stir into batter.

Heat a 7-inch skillet slowly. (Test temperature by sprinkling in a few drops of water; when drops bounce about, skillet is ready for baking.) Lightly butter skillet.

Measure 2 tablespoons of the batter into skillet; quickly tilt skillet until batter covers bottom. Bake 1 to 2 minutes until brown on bottom; turn; bake 1 minute longer. Repeat with remaining batter, lightly buttering skillet between bakings. As crêpes are baked, stack between sheets of paper toweling on a plate and keep warm.

Yield: 12 crêpes.

CUSTARD FRENCH TOAST

12 slices French bread, cut 1 inch thick
5 eggs
2 teaspoons sugar
1 teaspoon grated orange rind
Dash of salt
1½ cups milk
1 cup coarsely crushed cornflakes
½ cup butter or margarine
½ cup honey

Place bread in a single layer in a baking dish, 13x9x2 inches.

Beat eggs in a medium bowl until blended; stir in sugar, orange rind, salt, and milk; pour over bread. Let stand 2 minutes, then turn slices. Let stand 15 minutes, or until milk mixture is absorbed completely.

Preheat oven to 400°.

Sprinkle cornflakes on waxed paper. Lift bread slices from dish and dip in cornflakes to coat both sides generously; place in a single layer on a lightly greased large cookie sheet.

Bake 20 minutes, or until toast is puffed and crisp.

Melt butter in a small saucepan; stir in honey; heat until bubbly. Serve hot over French toast.

Yield: 6 servings.

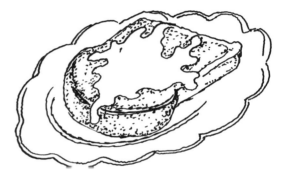

BUTTERMILK WAFFLES

1½ cups sifted all-purpose flour
2 teaspoons sugar
1½ teaspoons baking powder
¼ teaspoon baking soda
¼ teaspoon salt
2 eggs, separated
1½ cups buttermilk
6 tablespoons butter or margarine, melted

Preheat waffle iron as manufacturer directs.

Sift flour, sugar, baking powder, baking soda, and salt into a large bowl.

Beat egg whites in a small bowl until they form firm peaks.

Beat egg yolks well in a small bowl; stir in buttermilk and melted butter. Add all at once to flour mixture; stir just until blended; fold in beaten egg whites.

Ladle batter into hot waffle iron. Bake as manufacturer directs until golden. Serve hot with butter or margarine and pancake syrup.

Yield: 10 five-inch square waffles.

DRESS-UPS FOR REFRIGERATED ROLLS AND READY-BAKED BREAD

ORANGE-PINEAPPLE LOAF

  2 packages refrigerated orange Danish rolls with icing
  1 can (8 ozs.) crushed pineapple, drained
  ¼ cup butter or margarine, melted
  6 maraschino cherries, halved

Preheat oven to 350°.

Combine icing (from roll packages), drained pineapple, and butter in a small bowl; blend well. Spread in a greased baking pan, 9x5x3 inches. Arrange cherries in a pattern over pineapple mixture.

Separate rolls; stand, slightly overlapping, in two rows in pan.

Bake 45 minutes, or until loaf is golden. Loosen loaf around edges with a knife; invert onto a large serving plate. Let stand 10 minutes; lift off pan.

With two forks, break loaf apart into rolls; serve warm.

Yield: 8 servings.

ONION SAUCERS

1 package refrigerated flaky buttermilk biscuits
2 tablespoons butter or margarine, melted
5 teaspoons instant toasted onions

Preheat oven to 400°.

Separate biscuits; roll each to a 5-inch round on a lightly floured cloth; place on ungreased cookie sheets.

Brush butter or margarine over rounds; sprinkle toasted onion over each.

Bake 6 minutes, or until rounds are golden. Serve hot.

Yield: 10 biscuits.

SESAME STICKS

1 package refrigerated crescent rolls
1 egg
  Sesame seeds

Preheat oven to 375°.

Separate rolls into 4 rectangles; pinch together at diagonal perforations.

Roll each to a 10-inch-long rectangle on a lightly floured board. Starting at a long side, roll up tightly, jelly-roll fashion. Cut in half; place, seam side down, on a large cookie sheet.

Beat egg in a small bowl; brush over shaped dough; sprinkle sesame seeds on each.

Bake 12 minutes, or until sticks are golden. Remove from cookie sheet to a wire rack. Serve warm.

Yield: 8 sticks.

CARAWAY LOAVES

  2 packages refrigerated butterflake rolls
  1 tablespoon butter or margarine
  ¾ teaspoon caraway seeds

Preheat oven to 375°.

Grease three small loaf pans, each 5¾x3¼x2 inches.

Separate each package of rolls into 12 pieces. Stand 8 of the pieces in each pan to form a small loaf.

Melt butter in a small saucepan; brush over loaves; sprinkle caraway seeds over tops.

Bake loaves 25 minutes, or until loaves are puffed and golden. Let stand 10 minutes in pans on wire racks; loosen around edges with a knife; turn out onto racks. Serve warm, letting each person break off serving-sized sections.

Yield: 6 servings or 3 small loaves.

ROQUEFORT ROLLS

6 crusty French rolls
4 tablespoons butter or margarine
2 tablespoons crumbled Roquefort cheese
1 tablespoon chopped parsley

Preheat oven to 400°.

Cut each roll into thirds diagonally, cutting not quite to bottom crust.

Cream butter and cheese in a small bowl; stir in parsley. Spread lightly over cut surfaces of rolls. Wrap tightly in foil.

Bake 10 minutes, or until rolls are hot and cheese mixture melts. Serve hot.

Yield: 6 servings.

GARLIC-CHEDDAR LOAF

1 large round loaf unsliced white bread
¼ cup butter or margarine
½ cup grated sharp Cheddar cheese
1 clove garlic, crushed

Cut loaf into 8 wedges, but leave in loaf shape.

Preheat oven to 400°.

Mix butter, cheese, and garlic until well blended in a small bowl; spread over cut surfaces of bread. Wrap loaf in foil.

Bake 10 minutes, or until loaf is hot. Serve hot.

Yield: 8 servings.

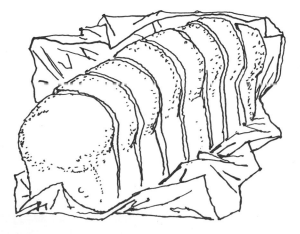

ITALIAN CHEESE CRESCENTS

1 cup pot cheese or uncreamed cottage cheese
3 tablespoons all-purpose flour
½ teaspoon salt
1 egg
¼ teaspoon Italian herbs
2 packages refrigerated crescent rolls
2 tablespoons butter or margarine, melted
1 teaspoon sesame seeds

Preheat oven to 375°.

Combine cheese, flour, salt, egg, and Italian herbs in a small bowl; beat until well blended.

Separate crescent rolls into triangles as label directs; spoon 1 tablespoon of the cheese mixture on wide end of each. Roll up; place, point up, on a cookie sheet. Brush melted butter over rolls; sprinkle sesame seeds on top.

Bake 18 minutes, or until rolls are golden. Remove from cookie sheet. Serve hot.

Yield: 16 crescents.

STRAWBERRY CRESCENTS

¼ cup strawberry preserves
¼ cup chopped pecans
1 package refrigerated crescent rolls
1 tablespoon butter or margarine

Preheat oven to 375°.

Mix preserves and pecans in a bowl.

Separate crescent rolls into triangles; spread butter lightly over each, then spread a teaspoonful of the preserves mixture on top; roll up as label directs. Place, point side down, on an ungreased cookie sheet; curve into crescent shapes.

Bake 15 minutes, or until rolls are golden. Remove from cookie sheet. Serve hot.

Yield: 8 crescents.

PEANUT FINGERS

⅓ cup chunky peanut butter
⅓ cup currant jelly
6 slices white bread
1 egg
1 tablespoon water
½ cup crushed cornflakes

Preheat oven to 400°.

Spread peanut butter, then jelly on 3 slices of the bread; top with remaining bread to make sandwiches; trim crusts. Cut each sandwich into 3 strips.

Beat egg well with water in a pie plate; sprinkle cornflakes on waxed paper. Dip each strip into egg mixture, then into cornflakes to coat well. Place on a greased cookie sheet.

Bake 10 minutes, or until strips are crusty-golden. Serve hot.

Yield: 4 servings.

PIMIENTO SQUARES

1 loaf unsliced white bread
½ cup butter or margarine
1 whole pimiento, drained and mashed (about 2 tablespoons)
Few drops red-pepper seasoning

Preheat oven to 400°.

Slice bread lengthwise into quarters; place rectangles on a cookie sheet.

Blend butter, pimiento, and red-pepper seasoning in a cup; spread over bread.

Heat 10 minutes, or until bread is crusty around edges. Cut into squares.

Yield: 8 servings.

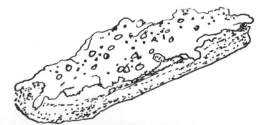

JOLLY JELLIES

1 package (3 ozs.) cream cheese, softened
8 slices fresh soft white bread
4 tablespoons butter or margarine, melted
4 tablespoons strawberry jelly

Preheat oven to 400°.

Cut cream cheese into 8 equal pieces.

Trim crusts from bread; spread cream cheese over each slice; fold slices in half crosswise to make rectangles. Press edges of each all around with finger to seal. then press a ridge in top with fingertip. Place on a cookie sheet.

Brush melted butter over rectangles; spoon ½ tablespoon jelly into ridge in each.

Bake 10 minutes, or until bread is toasted. Serve hot.

Yield: 4 servings.

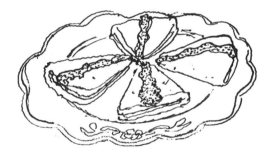

HERBED FRENCH BREAD

1 small loaf French bread
4 tablespoons butter or margarine
2 teaspoons chopped parsley
1 tablespoon grated Parmesan cheese
Dash of garlic salt

Cut loaf in half lengthwise, cutting not quite to bottom crust, then cut crosswise in 1-inch-thick slices.

Preheat oven to 350°.

Mix butter, parsley, cheese, and garlic salt in a cup; spread over cut sides of bread. Wrap loaf in foil.

Bake 15 minutes, or until loaf is hot. Serve hot.

Yield: 6 servings.

ONION ROLLS

4 hero rolls
½ cup butter or margarine
1 single-serving envelope onion soup mix

Cut each roll diagonally in quarters almost to bottom.

Preheat oven to 400°.

Blend butter and onion soup mix in a cup; spread between cuts and over tops of rolls; wrap each in foil.

Bake 15 minutes, or until rolls are hot. Serve hot.

Yield: 4 to 6 servings.

PUMPERNICKEL-CHEESE ROUND

1 large round loaf pumpernickel
¼ cup butter or margarine
1 jar (5 ozs.) olive-pimiento cheese spread
1 tablespoon chopped parsley
2 teaspoons Worcestershire sauce

Cut loaf in quarters; cut each quarter into 3 wedges, keeping wedges in order.

Preheat oven to 400°.

Blend butter, cheese spread, parsley, and Worcestershire sauce in a small bowl; spread over wedges; put back together in loaf shape. Wrap tightly in foil.

Bake 20 minutes, or until cheese melts and loaf is hot. Serve hot.

Yield: 6 servings.

JUMBO BREAD STICKS

2 loaves Italian bread
½ cup butter or margarine
1 teaspoon dried basil, crushed

Preheat oven to 375°.

Cut each loaf of bread in half lengthwise, then crosswise; split each quarter.

Melt butter in a small saucepan; stir in basil; brush over cut surfaces of bread. Place on cookie sheets.

Bake 15 minutes, or until bread is golden. Serve hot.

Yield: 16 servings.

STRAWBERRY-LIME CREAM CAKE (p.451) ▶

DESSERTS

ITT'S FUN TO CONCOCT A SPECIAL SWEET for family and friends that are special to you. An everyday meal, a party dinner, a kaffeeklatsch, or a late-evening get-together are excuses enough to get out the mixing spoons and bowls and show off your creativity.

The recipes in this chapter will give you plenty of inspiration. The choices are many and varied and planned to see you through any occasion, simple or elaborate, that calls for something sweet.

Check over the pages. Perhaps you'll prefer one of the home-style specialties—cobblers, shortcakes, custards, baked puddings, turnovers, or dumplings that all taste so tantalizing served warm from the oven. Maybe you're in the mood for a fancy gelatin or bavarian mold, or a parfait flecked or layered with colorful fruits and crowned with cream. Or would you rather go all out on a lavishly rich cheesecake, a stately soufflé, a many-layered torte, deluxe crêpes, wait-in-the freezer cream puffs, or a variety of suggestions that start with cake or ice cream? If you're short on time, there are ideas to help you turn store-bought helpers into your own homemades.

Whatever you choose, make it suit your menu and the occasion. Simple fruit treats are best after filling meals, and a rich dessert makes a fitting conclusion to a light bridge luncheon or a come-for-coffee party. Remember, too, that desserts can be more than just sweet-tooth pleasers. Fixed with milk, eggs, and fruit, they're top contributors to good health.

◄ *(Clockwise from left)*
PEACH CREAM (p.426)
JAMAICAN MELON COMPOTE (p.426)
LEMON SPONGE MOLDS (p.426)
RAINBOW MELON BOATS (p.425)

FRUIT DESSERTS

RAINBOW FRUIT SAMPLER

1 egg
2 tablespoons sugar
¼ cup salad oil
1 teaspoon grated orange rind
2 tablespoons orange juice
¼ teaspoon salt
2 large seedless oranges, pared and sectioned
½ small honeydew melon, pared and cubed
2 packages (10 ozs. each) frozen sliced peaches, thawed and drained
2 cups seedless green grapes, stemmed
2 large ripe bananas, peeled and sliced diagonally
1 pint strawberries, hulled and sliced
½ cup whipping cream

Beat egg with sugar in the top of a small double boiler. Heat over hot water, stirring constantly, 3 minutes, or until sugar dissolves; remove top from water.

Beat mixture until fluffy; beat in salad oil, orange rind and juice, and salt; chill.

When ready to serve, layer orange sections, honeydew, peaches, grapes, and bananas into a large deep glass serving bowl; arrange strawberries on top.

Beat cream until stiff in a small bowl; fold into chilled orange mixture. Pass separately to spoon over fruits.

Yield: 8 to 10 servings.

STRAWBERRY TORTE

1 package (3⅛ ozs.) vanilla pudding and pie filling mix
1¾ cups milk
1 teaspoon grated orange rind
1 packaged angel cake, weighing about 10 ozs.
1 container (4½ ozs.) frozen whipped topping, thawed
1 pint strawberries, washed, hulled, and cut in half

Prepare pudding mix with milk as label directs; stir in orange rind; cool.

Tear angel cake into 1-inch cubes. (There should be about 5 cups.) Place in a shallow 1½-quart dish to make an even layer.

Fold whipped topping into pudding mixture until no streaks of white remain; fold in half of the strawberries. Spoon over cake cubes to cover completely; place rest of strawberries on top; cover. Chill overnight.

To serve, cut into squares; place on dessert plates. Serve as is or with more whipped topping if you like.

Yield: 8 servings.

OVEN POACHED PEARS

6 medium-sized firm ripe pears
¾ cup sugar
¾ cup water
2 small tangerines, peeled and separated into sections
1 cinnamon stick, about 3 inches long

Preheat oven to 350°.

Peel pears, leaving core and stem in place. Stand pears in a deep baking dish.

Combine sugar and water in a small saucepan; heat, stirring constantly, to boiling; pour over pears. Add tangerine sections and cinnamon stick, pushing fruit down into syrup.

Bake, spooning syrup in dish over pears once or twice, 45 minutes, or until pears are tender. Serve warm.

Yield: 6 servings.

LEMONADE CREAM TORTE

1 cup cornflake crumbs
6 tablespoons butter or margarine, melted
1 can (6 ozs.) frozen concentrate for pink
    lemonade, thawed
⅔ cup water
1 bag (10 ozs.) large marshmallows
1 package (2 ozs.) whipped dessert topping mix
  Milk
  Red food coloring

Preheat oven to 325°.

Mix cornflake crumbs and melted butter in a medium bowl until blended; measure out ⅓ cup and set aside for topping. Press remainder over bottom of a baking dish, 8x8x2 inches.

Bake 10 minutes; cool on a wire rack.

Combine lemonade concentrate and water in a large saucepan; add marshmallows. Heat very slowly, stirring constantly, until marshmallows melt completely and mixture is smooth and syrupy. Pour into a medium bowl; chill 45 minutes, or until mixture thickens slightly.

While marshmallow mixture chills, prepare topping mix with milk as label directs; fold into thickened marshmallow mixture; tint pink with food coloring.

Spoon over crumb layer in dish; sprinkle remaining ⅓ cup crumb mixture on top. Chill several hours, or overnight until firm. Cut into squares.

Yield: 9 servings.

SCANDINAVIAN FRUIT COMPOTE

2 tablespoons quick-cooking tapioca
2 tablespoons sugar
  Dash of salt
1½ cups water
1 can (6 ozs.) frozen concentrate for orange juice,
    partly thawed
1 can (20 ozs.) pineapple chunks in juice
½ pint strawberries, hulled and cut in half
1 large firm ripe banana, peeled and sliced

Combine tapioca, sugar, salt, and water in a small saucepan; heat, stirring constantly, to a full rolling boil. Stir into orange concentrate in a medium bowl; stir in pineapple chunks and juice. Chill at least 4 hours or overnight until frosty cold.

Just before serving, stir strawberries and banana into orange mixture. Spoon into sherbet glasses. Garnish each serving with a sprig of mint if you like.

Yield: 6 generous servings.

BAKED APPLES ALOHA

6 large baking apples
1 can (8 ozs.) crushed pineapple in syrup
  Water
6 maraschino cherries, sliced
½ cup sugar
1 tablespoon lemon juice
  Red food coloring
  Light cream

Core apples almost to bottom; pare top third of each; stand in a shallow baking dish.

Preheat oven to 350°.

Drain syrup from pineapple into a 2-cup measure; add water to make 1 cup. Mix pineapple and cherries in a small bowl; spoon into hollows in apples.

Stir sugar and lemon juice into syrup mixture; add a few drops food coloring to tint bright red; pour around apples in dish; cover.

Bake 30 minutes; uncover. Continue baking 20 minutes longer, or until apples are tender but still firm enough to hold their shapes. Cool in dish on a wire rack, spooning syrup over apples several times to glaze lightly.

Spoon apples into serving dishes; serve warm or cold with cream.

Yield: 6 servings.

CHANTILLY CHERRY CUPS

1 carton (8 ozs.) whipped cream cheese
⅓ cup sifted confectioners' powdered sugar
1 teaspoon vanilla
10 packaged dessert shells
1 cup flaked coconut
⅛ teaspoon almond extract
1 can (21 ozs.) cherry pie filling

Combine cream cheese, confectioners' sugar, and vanilla in a medium bowl; beat until smooth.

Spread around sides of dessert shells, using a generous 1½ tablespoons for each; roll shells in coconut on waxed paper; place on a tray or large flat plate.

Stir almond extract into cherry pie filling; spoon into shells. Chill.

Yield: 10 servings.

RASPBERRY RIBBON CAKE

1 frozen poundcake (11 ozs.), thawed
½ cup seedless red raspberry preserves
1 can (8 ozs.) cling peach slices, drained
1 package (2 ozs.) whipped topping mix
Milk
Vanilla

Split poundcake lengthwise into three even layers. Spread preserves over each; stack back together, preserves side up, on a serving plate. Arrange peach slices in a pretty pattern on top.

Prepare topping mix with milk and vanilla as label directs; spread over sides of cake, making deep swirls with spatula. (Let peaches show through on top.) Chill cake at least an hour.

Cut crosswise into slices; serve with any remaining whipped topping.

Yield: 8 servings.

QUICK BUTTERSCOTCH APPLES

½ cup butterscotch-flavor pieces
¼ cup water
4 large apples, pared, quartered, cored, and sliced
½ cup whipping cream

Combine butterscotch pieces, water, and apple slices in a medium saucepan; heat to boiling; cover.

Cook slowly, stirring gently several times, 10 minutes, or until apples are tender. Cool in pan on a wire rack at least 30 minutes.

Just before serving, beat cream in a small bowl until stiff.

Spoon warm apple mixture into serving dishes; top each with whipped cream.

Yield: 4 servings.

BLUSHING PEARS

1 can (16 ozs.) whole-berry cranberry sauce
3 tablespoons sugar
2 tablespoons lemon juice
2 cinnamon sticks, about 2 inches long
4 medium-sized firm ripe pears, cut in half and cored

Mix cranberry sauce, sugar, lemon juice, and cinnamon in a large skillet; heat slowly, stirring several times, to boiling.

Place pear halves in a single layer in sauce; heat to boiling again; cover. Simmer, turning once, 15 minutes, or until pears are tender.

Spoon pears into serving dishes; spoon sauce from skillet over each. Serve warm.

Yield: 4 servings.

PIE-PLATE APPLE PUDDING

3 large tart apples, pared, quartered, cored, and
    sliced
2 tablespoons lemon juice
½ teaspoon mace
⅓ cup honey
¾ cup firmly packed light brown sugar
2 tablespoons all-purpose flour
3 tablespoons butter or margarine
½ cup coarsely chopped California walnuts
    Light cream

Preheat oven to 375°.

Place apple slices in a 9-inch pie plate.
Sprinkle lemon juice, then mace over top;
drizzle 2 tablespoons of the honey over all.
Cover pie plate with foil.

Bake 25 minutes, or until apples are tender;
remove from oven. Turn oven temperature to
broil.

While apples bake, mix brown sugar and
flour in a small bowl; cut in butter until mixture forms a paste; stir in remaining honey and
walnuts. Drop by teaspoonfuls over hot apple
mixture.

Broil, 6 inches from heat, 3 to 4 minutes, or
until topping melts and bubbles up. Cool in
pie plate on a wire rack at least 30 minutes.

Spoon into serving dishes; serve warm or
cold with cream.

Yield: 6 servings.

RHUBARB COMPOTE

1 can (20 ozs.) pineapple chunks in juice
1 package (10 ozs.) frozen rhubarb
1 teaspoon grated orange rind

Drain juice from pineapple into a medium
saucepan. Add block of frozen rhubarb to
juice; heat slowly, breaking up rhubarb with a
fork as it thaws, to boiling. Simmer 2 minutes,
or until rhubarb is tender but still firm enough
to hold its shape.

Stir in pineapple chunks and orange rind;
cool. Serve warm or cold.

Yield: 6 servings.

TRIPLE ORANGE CUP

1 package (3 ozs.) orange-flavored gelatin
1 cup boiling water
2 cups orange juice
1 can (11 ozs.) mandarin orange segments, drained

Dissolve gelatin in boiling water in a
medium bowl; stir in orange juice. Chill until
softly set.

Fold in mandarin orange segments. Chill
until serving time.

Yield: 6 servings.

PLUM COMPOTE

1 can (16 ozs.) orange and grapefruit sections in
    syrup
1 can (30 ozs.) purple plums in syrup
⅓ cup sugar
½ teaspoon mace

Drain syrup from orange and grapefruit sections into a 2-cup measure. Drain syrup from
plums, adding enough to orange syrup to
make 1¼ cups. Arrange fruits in a shallow
serving bowl.

Combine the 1¼ cups syrup with sugar and
mace in a small saucepan. Heat, stirring several times, to boiling; simmer 5 minutes; pour
over fruits. Let stand ½ hour to season. Serve
warm.

Yield: 6 servings.

CALICO FRUIT PARFAITS

2 tablespoons brown sugar
½ teaspoon ground cinnamon
1 cup (8-oz. carton) dairy sour cream
1 can (29 ozs.) fruit cocktail, drained
4 maraschino cherries with stems

Stir brown sugar and cinnamon into sour
cream in a small bowl.

Spoon ¼ cup of the fruit into each of four
parfait glasses; top with 2 tablespoons of the
cream mixture. Repeat layers; garnish each
with a maraschino cherry.

Yield: 4 servings.

WENATCHEE VALLEY APPLE CRISP

5 large apples, pared, quartered, cored, and sliced
    thin (6 cups)
⅓ cup granulated sugar
½ cup instant nonfat dry milk
⅔ cup quick-cooking rolled oats
¼ cup firmly packed light brown sugar
¼ cup flaked coconut
2 tablespoons presweetened wheat germ
2 teaspoons sesame seeds
¼ cup sliced almonds
½ teaspoon ground cinnamon
¼ teaspoon ground nutmeg
4 tablespoons butter or margarine, melted
    Vanilla ice cream

Preheat oven to 400°.

Combine apple slices, granulated sugar, and nonfat dry milk in a large bowl; toss lightly to mix. Spoon into a shallow 1½-quart baking dish.

Combine rolled oats, brown sugar, coconut, wheat germ, sesame seeds, almonds, and spices in a medium bowl. Stir in melted butter until mixture is evenly moist; sprinkle evenly over apple mixture in dish.

Bake 30 minutes, or until apples are tender and topping is browned. Cool in dish on a wire rack at least 30 minutes.

Spoon into serving dishes; serve warm with ice cream.

Yield: 6 servings.

CRANBERRY DREAM SQUARES

2 cups cranberries, stemmed and finely chopped
⅔ cup granulated sugar
1 large firm ripe banana, peeled and diced
1 tablespoon grated orange rind
½ cup butter or margarine
1 cup confectioners' powdered sugar
2 eggs
2 cups crushed sugar cookies
1 cup chopped California walnuts
1 package (2 ozs.) whipped topping mix
    Milk
    Vanilla

Mix cranberries, granulated sugar, banana, and orange rind in a bowl.

Cream butter and confectioners' sugar in a medium bowl until fluffy-light; beat in eggs, 1 at a time, until fluffy again.

Sprinkle half of the cookie crumbs in an even layer in a baking dish, 8x8x2 inches. Spread butter mixture over crumb layer; top with cranberry mixture and walnuts.

Prepare topping mix with milk and vanilla as label directs; spread over walnut layer. Sprinkle remaining cookie crumbs over top; pat down lightly; cover. Chill overnight to mellow flavors.

When ready to serve, cut dessert into squares; place on serving plates. Serve as is or with more whipped topping.

Yield: 9 servings.

PEACH TRIFLE

1 package (3⅛ ozs.) vanilla pudding and pie
    filling mix
2¼ cups milk
½ of a frozen 11-oz. plain poundcake, thawed
2 tablespoons dry white wine
¼ cup seedless raspberry preserves
1 can (16 ozs.) cling peach slices, drained
½ cup whipping cream
2 tablespoons toasted slivered almonds

Prepare pudding mix with milk as label directs; pour into a bowl. Press a sheet of transparent wrap directly onto pudding; chill until cold.

Cut poundcake into 4 slices; place on a cookie sheet. Drizzle wine over each, then spread preserves on top. Cut each crosswise into thirds

Stand strips around edge in a deep glass serving bowl; spoon in pudding mixture. Arrange peach slices in a pretty pattern over pudding. Chill.

Beat cream until stiff in a small bowl; spoon over peaches; garnish cream with almonds.

Yield: 6 servings.

CRANBERRY CREAM SQUARES

1 cup graham-cracker crumbs
4 tablespoons butter or margarine, melted
3 tablespoons sugar (for crust)
½ cup flaked coconut
2 packages (3⅛ ozs. each) vanilla pudding and pie filling mix
3½ cups milk
1 container (4½ ozs.) frozen whipped topping, thawed
1½ cups cranberries, washed and stemmed
½ cup sugar (for cranberries)
1¾ cups water
1 envelope unflavored gelatin

Blend graham-cracker crumbs, melted butter, and the 3 tablespoons sugar in a small bowl; press firmly over bottom of a baking dish, 8x8x2 inches. Set aside.

Preheat oven to 325°.

Spread coconut in a pie plate. Toast in oven, stirring several times, 15 minutes, or until golden; cool. Set aside.

Combine pudding mix and milk in a medium saucepan; cook as label directs; cool. Fold in 1 cup of the whipped topping. Pour over crumb layer in dish. Chill several hours, or until firm.

While pudding mixture chills, combine cranberries, the ½ cup sugar, and 1½ cups of the water in a medium saucepan; heat to boiling; cover. Simmer 10 minutes.

Sprinkle gelatin over remaining ¼ cup water in a small bowl; let stand a few minutes to soften, then stir into cranberry mixture until gelatin dissolves. Chill 30 minutes, or until syrupy-thick; spoon over cream layer in dish. Chill several hours, or until firm.

When ready to serve, spread rest of whipped topping over cranberry layer; sprinkle coconut on top. Cut into squares.

Yield: 9 servings.

STRAWBERRY SHORTCAKE SUPREME

3 pints strawberries
4⅔ cups biscuit mix
⅔ cup sugar
¾ cup butter or margarine, melted
1 cup milk
½ cup chopped California walnuts
1 egg
2 teaspoons vanilla
1½ cups whipping cream

Wash strawberries, hull, and slice into a large bowl; sweeten to taste. Let stand while preparing shortcake and sauce.

Preheat oven to 425°.

Combine biscuit mix, ⅓ cup of the sugar, 6 tablespoons of the melted butter, and milk in a large bowl; stir just until blended to make a soft dough; stir in walnuts.

Turn dough out onto a lightly floured board; knead 8 to 10 times; divide in half. Pat each half into an ungreased 9-inch round layer-cake pan.

Bake 15 minutes, or until golden; remove from pans to wire racks.

While shortcake bakes, beat egg in a medium bowl until fluffy and thick. Slowly beat in remaining ⅓ cup sugar and vanilla. Stir in remaining 6 tablespoons melted butter.

Beat cream until stiff in a medium bowl; fold into egg mixture.

Place one shortcake layer on a large serving plate; top with half each of the strawberries and whipped-cream sauce, then second shortcake layer and rest of berries and sauce. Cut into wedges; serve warm.

Yield: 8 to 10 servings.

CHERRY TORTE

1 package (2 to a package) dessert layers
1 jar (12 ozs.) cherry preserves (about 1¼ cups)
1 container (9 ozs.) frozen whipped topping, thawed

Split each dessert layer in half crosswise. Spread about ¼ cup of the cherry preserves over each of three layers; spread part of the whipped topping over preserves. Stack layers on a serving plate; place remaining plain layer on top.

Frost side of torte with remaining whipped topping, spreading it 1½ inches up over top edge; spread remaining preserves in center. Chill at least an hour. Cut into wedges.

Yield: 8 servings.

WATERMELON FRUIT BOWL

1 end cut of watermelon, about 8 inches long
1 small firm ripe cantaloupe
2 firm ripe peaches or nectarines
1 cup seedless green grapes
½ pint strawberries, washed, hulled, and cut in half
1 cup dry white wine

Cut a thin slice from the round end of watermelon so it will sit flat. Cut meat from rind to within 1 inch of bottom to form a bowl. Wrap shell and chill.

Remove seeds from watermelon and cut meat into bite-sized pieces; place in a large bowl.

Quarter cantaloupe; scoop out seeds and pare; cut meat into bite-sized pieces and add to watermelon.

Peel peaches, cut in half, pit, and slice. (If using nectarines, there's no need to peel them.) Add peaches, grapes, and strawberries to other fruits in bowl. Drizzle wine over top; toss lightly to mix; cover. Chill several hours.

When ready to serve, place watermelon shell on a large flat plate or tray. Spoon fruits into shell. Garnish with fresh mint if you like.

Yield: 12 servings.

BANANA CREAM CAKE

1 package (2 to a package) 8-inch dessert layers
⅓ cup butter or margarine
¾ cup firmly packed light brown sugar
¼ cup undiluted evaporated milk
1 cup chopped pecans
2 medium-sized firm ripe bananas
1 container (9 ozs.) frozen whipped topping, thawed

Preheat broiler. Place dessert layers on a cookie sheet.

Cream butter with brown sugar in a small bowl; stir in evaporated milk and pecans.

Peel bananas; slice crosswise and arrange slices in a single layer over cake; spread pecan mixture over bananas to cover.

Broil, 8 inches from heat, 2 to 3 minutes, or until topping bubbles up; cool.

Stack cake layers on a serving plate with 1 cup of the whipped topping between layers; spread the rest over side and top of cake, making swirls with spatula. Chill until serving time.

Yield: 8 servings.

CHERRY-ALMOND CREPES

2 cups (16-oz. carton) ricotta cheese
1 teaspoon grated lemon rind
5 tablespoons sugar
1 teaspoon salt
½ teaspoon vanilla
1 cup sifted all-purpose flour
3 eggs
1 cup milk
3 tablespoons butter or margarine
1 can (21 ozs.) cherry pie filling
¼ cup water
¼ teaspoon almond extract
¼ cup toasted slivered almonds

Mix cheese, lemon rind, 2 tablespoons of the sugar, ½ teaspoon of the salt, and vanilla in a medium bowl.

Sift flour, remaining 3 tablespoons sugar and ½ teaspoon salt into a medium bowl.

Beat eggs in a small bowl; stir in milk; beat into flour mixture until smooth. Melt 1 tablespoon of the butter in a small skillet; stir into batter until blended.

Heat a 6-inch skillet slowly; grease lightly with butter. Measure a scant ¼ cup of the batter into skillet; quickly tilt skillet until batter covers bottom. Bake 1 to 2 minutes until brown on bottom; turn; bake 1 minute longer until brown. Repeat with rest of batter, lightly buttering skillet between bakings.

As crêpes are baked, spread 2 tablespoons of the cheese mixture over each; roll up tightly, jelly-roll fashion; place, seam side down, in a large shallow baking dish. Keep warm until all are baked and filled.

Combine cherry pie filling, water, and almond extract in a small saucepan; heat until bubbly. Spoon over crêpes. Sprinkle almonds on top. Serve warm.

Yield: 6 servings.

RHUBARB CRUNCH

1¼ lbs. rhubarb, trimmed and cut in ½-inch pieces
    (4 cups)
¾ cup sifted all-purpose flour
½ cup honey
¾ cup firmly packed light brown sugar
¾ cup cornflake crumbs
½ cup butter or margarine
  Vanilla ice milk

Preheat oven to 350°.

Combine rhubarb and ¼ cup of the flour in a medium bowl; toss to mix well; spoon into a 1½-quart shallow baking dish. Drizzle honey over top; cover.

Bake 25 minutes; uncover; stir well.

While rhubarb bakes, combine remaining ½ cup flour, brown sugar, and cornflake crumbs in a medium bowl; cut in butter with a pastry blender until fine crumbs form. Spoon evenly over hot rhubarb mixture.

Bake, uncovered, 30 minutes, or until topping is golden. Cool at least ½ hour on a wire rack. Spoon into serving dishes; top each serving with a spoonful of ice milk.

Yield: 6 servings.

RAINBOW MELON BOATS

½ large cantaloupe
½ small honeydew melon
1 pint lime sherbet

Remove seeds from melons; cut each half into 3 wedges. Cut balls from wedges with a melon-ball cutter, then place cantaloupe balls in honeydew wedges and honeydew balls in cantaloupe. Wrap and chill well.

At serving time, place melon wedges on dessert plates; top each with a scoop of lime sherbet.

Yield: 6 servings.

PEACH CREAM

1 package (3 ozs.) peach-flavored gelatin
1 package (3⅛ ozs.) vanilla pudding and pie filling
   mix
2 cups water
¼ cup brandy
1 container (4½ ozs.) frozen whipped topping,
   thawed
3 medium-sized firm ripe peaches, peeled,
   quartered, seeded, and sliced (1½ cups)

Combine gelatin, pudding mix, and water in a medium saucepan. Heat slowly, stirring constantly, to boiling; remove from heat. Stir in brandy. Pour mixture into a bowl.

Place bowl in a pan of ice and water to speed setting. Chill, stirring several times, 20 minutes, or until mixture is syrupy-thick. Keeping bowl over ice, fold in whipped topping and peaches. Spoon into sherbet glasses. Chill several hours, or until firm.

Just before serving, garnish with more whipped topping and peach slices if you like.

Yield: 8 servings.

LEMON SPONGE MOLDS

1 package (3¼ ozs.) lemon pudding and pie filling
   mix
¾ cup granulated sugar
2 eggs, separated
   Water
1 tablespoon lemon juice
1 pint strawberries

Prepare pudding mix with ½ cup of the sugar, egg yolks, and water as label directs; remove from heat. Stir in lemon juice.

Beat egg whites in a small bowl until foamy; slowly beat in 2 tablespoons of the remaining sugar until meringue forms firm peaks; fold into pudding mixture. Spoon into eight ½-cup pudding molds or custard cups. Chill several hours, or until firm.

Wash strawberries and hull; mash about 1 cup in a small bowl; slice remainder and stir in with remaining 2 tablespoons sugar. Let stand at least 10 minutes until sugar dissolves.

When ready to serve, unmold puddings into dessert dishes. Spoon strawberries and syrup on top.

Yield: 8 servings.

JAMAICAN MELON COMPOTE

1 two-pound wedge of watermelon
1 small cantaloupe
½ medium honeydew melon
¼ cup white rum

Cut watermelon meat from rind; cut into cubes, removing seeds. (There should be about 2 cups.) Place in a medium bowl.

Cut cantaloupe in half; remove seeds and pare; cut meat into cubes. (There should be about 2 cups.) Add to watermelon.

Cut enough balls from honeydew with a melon-ball cutter to measure 2 cups; combine with other melons. Pour rum over top; toss lightly to mix; cover and chill.

When ready to serve, spoon melons into sherbet or parfait glasses. Garnish with mint if you like.

Yield: 6 servings.

MANDARIN RHUBARB COMPOTE

1 can (11 ozs.) mandarin orange segments in syrup
1 lb. rhubarb, trimmed and cut in ½-inch pieces (3
   cups)
½ cup sugar

Drain syrup from mandarin orange segments into a small bowl.

Combine rhubarb, ⅓ cup of the mandarin orange syrup, and sugar in a medium saucepan. Heat, stirring several times, to a full rolling boil; cover; remove from heat. Cool to room temperature.

Stir in orange segments; chill.

Spoon into serving dishes; garnish each with a sprig of mint if you like.

Yield: 4 servings.

PUDDINGS AND PARFAITS

PEANUT ROCKY ROAD CUPS

1 can (18 ozs.) prepared chocolate pudding
3 tablespoons creamy peanut butter
1 container (4½ ozs.) frozen whipped topping, thawed
½ cup tiny marshmallows
  Peanuts

Combine pudding and peanut butter in a medium bowl; beat until blended and smooth.

Set aside about ½ cup of the whipped topping for garnish; fold the rest into pudding mixture with marshmallows. Spoon into 6 dessert dishes. Garnish each with a spoonful of remaining topping and several peanuts. Chill ½ hour, or until serving time.

Yield: 6 servings.

FRUIT CUP CUSTARD

1 package (3 ozs.) egg custard mix
½ teaspoon ground nutmeg
3 cups milk
2 medium-sized firm ripe bananas
1 can (29 ozs.) fruit cocktail, drained

Combine egg custard mix with nutmeg in a medium saucepan; prepare with the milk as label directs. Chill at least 2 hours until completely cold; beat until smooth.

Peel bananas and slice; combine with fruit cocktail; spoon evenly into 6 deep dessert dishes. Pour ½ cup of the custard mixture over each. Chill again until softly set, or until serving time.

Yield: 6 servings.

STRAWBERRY RICE PUDDING

1 package (3⅛ ozs.) vanilla pudding and pie filling mix
  Milk
1 cup cooked rice
1 package (2 ozs.) whipped topping mix
½ teaspoon vanilla
8 tablespoons strawberry preserves

Prepare pudding mix with 2 cups milk as label directs; pour into a medium bowl; stir in rice. Cool until mixture is completely cold.

Prepare whipped topping mix with milk and vanilla as label directs; fold into cold pudding mixture.

Measure 2 teaspoons of the strawberry preserves into each of 8 dessert dishes. Spoon pudding mixture evenly over preserves. Garnish each with 1 teaspoon of the remaining preserves. Chill until serving time.

Yield: 8 servings.

CHERRY-RICE PUDDING

1 cup uncooked regular rice
½ cup sugar
1½ teaspoons vanilla
1 package (2 ozs.) whipped topping mix
½ cup cold milk
½ teaspoon almond extract
1 can (21 ozs.) cherry pie filling

Cook rice as label directs; stir in sugar and 1 teaspoon of the vanilla; let stand until cold.

Prepare topping mix with milk and remaining ½ teaspoon vanilla as label directs; fold into rice mixture. Spoon into sherbet glasses; chill.

Just before serving, stir almond extract into cherry pie filling in a medium bowl; spoon over pudding.

Yield: 8 servings.

MANDARIN CREAM

1 package (2 ozs.) whipped topping mix
1½ cups milk
Vanilla
1 package (about 4 ozs.) vanilla instant pudding mix
2 tablespoons orange-flavored instant breakfast drink
½ cup gingersnap crumbs
1 can (11 ozs.) mandarin orange segments, drained

Prepare topping mix with ½ cup of the milk and vanilla as label directs.

Mix dry pudding mix and orange drink powder in a medium bowl; add remaining 1 cup milk; beat as label directs. Fold in three fourths of the prepared topping.

Spoon one third of the pudding into a medium serving bowl; top with half of the gingersnap crumbs and one third of the mandarin oranges. Repeat with another third of the pudding, the rest of gingersnap crumbs, another third of mandarin oranges, and the rest of pudding. Chill at least 1 hour, or until set.

Just before serving, spoon the rest of whipped topping in a pouf in center of dessert; garnish with the rest of mandarin oranges.

Yield: 6 servings.

GLAZED PINEAPPLE CREAM

1 package (3¾ ozs.) instant pineapple cream pudding mix
2 cups milk
1 can (8 ozs.) crushed pineapple in syrup
⅓ cup orange juice
2 teaspoons cornstarch
Dash of salt

Prepare pudding mix with milk as label directs; spoon into 4 dessert dishes; let stand about 5 minutes until softly set.

Drain syrup from pineapple into a cup; spoon pineapple evenly over pudding in dishes.

Add orange juice to pineapple syrup; slowly stir into cornstarch and salt in a small saucepan. Cook, stirring constantly, until mixture thickens and boils 3 minutes; cool slightly. Spoon over pineapple. Chill until glaze sets, or until serving time.

Yield: 4 servings.

STEAMED PUMPKIN PUDDING

1½ cups sifted all-purpose flour
1 teaspoon baking powder
½ teaspoon baking soda
1 teaspoon pumpkin-pie spice
½ teaspoon salt
½ cup regular wheat germ
½ cup shortening
1 cup firmly packed light brown sugar
2 eggs
1 cup canned pumpkin
¼ cup buttermilk
Cinnamon Cream (recipe on page 324)

Sift flour, baking powder, baking soda, pumpkin-pie spice, and salt into a medium bowl; stir in wheat germ.

Cream shortening and brown sugar in a large bowl until fluffy; beat in eggs, one at a time, until fluffy again. Stir pumpkin into buttermilk in a bowl.

Stir flour mixture, part at a time, into creamed mixture, adding alternately with pumpkin mixture; stir just until well blended. Spoon into a well-greased 1½-quart mold. Cover mold with a double thickness of foil; tie with string to hold tightly. Place mold on a rack or trivet in a kettle; pour boiling water into kettle to half the depth of mold; cover kettle tightly.

Steam pudding 1 hour and 45 minutes, or until a long skewer inserted in center comes out clean. Cool in mold on a wire rack 10 minutes; loosen around edge with knife; invert onto rack. Cut into wedges; serve warm with Cinnamon Cream.

Yield: 8 servings.

MOCHA PARFAITS

1 package (4 ozs.) chocolate-flavored whipped
    dessert mix
1 tablespoon dry instant coffee
  Cold milk
  Cold water
8 thin chocolate wafers, coarsely crushed
4 tablespoons flaked coconut

Combine dessert mix and instant coffee in a small deep bowl; prepare with milk and water as label directs.

Spoon half of mixture into 4 parfait glasses to make a layer in each; top with wafer crumbs; spoon in remaining chocolate mixture. Sprinkle 1 tablespoon coconut in a ring around edge on each. Chill at least an hour.

Yield: 4 servings.

HEAVENLY HASH PARFAITS

 1 package (3 ozs.) cherry-flavored gelatin
 1 cup boiling water
¾ cup cold water
 1 package (3⅛ ozs.) vanilla pudding and pie
    filling mix
1½ cups milk
 1 can (8 ozs.) crushed pineapple in syrup, drained
½ cup tiny marshmallows
¼ cup chopped drained maraschino cherries
½ cup cooked rice
 1 cup thawed frozen whipped topping

Dissolve gelatin in boiling water in a medium bowl; stir in cold water. Pour into a shallow pan, 8x8x2 inches. Chill until firm.

Prepare pudding mix with milk as label directs; pour into a medium bowl; press a sheet of waxed paper directly onto surface of pudding. Chill until completely cold. Fold in remaining ingredients.

Rice gelatin mixture with a fork.

Spoon half of the pudding mixture into 8 parfait glasses to make a layer in each; spoon all of the gelatin on top; spoon rest of pudding mixture over gelatin. Chill until serving time.

Serve as is or garnish each parfait with more whipped topping and a maraschino cherry.

Yield: 8 servings.

PEACH CREAM PARFAITS

1 can (21 ozs.) peach pie filling
¼ teaspoon almond extract
1 package (3¾ ozs.) vanilla instant pudding mix
  Milk

Combine pie filling and almond extract in a medium bowl; stir lightly to blend. Spoon half into 6 parfait glasses to make a layer in each.

Prepare pudding mix with milk as label directs; let stand 5 minutes. Spoon over peach layers in glasses; spoon remaining peach mixture on top. Chill.

Serve plain or garnish each serving with whipped cream and a maraschino cherry if you like.

Yield: 6 servings.

MAPLE FLAN

4 tablespoons maple-blended pancake syrup
5 eggs
⅔ cup sugar
1 teaspoon vanilla
3 cups milk, scalded

Preheat oven to 325°.

Measure ½ tablespoon of the syrup into each of eight 6-oz. custard cups; tilt and turn cups until syrup coats sides.

Beat eggs in a medium bowl just until blended; stir in sugar and vanilla; slowly stir in scalded milk. Strain mixture and pour over syrup in cups. For easy handling, set cups in a baking pan, 13x9x2 inches; place pan on oven shelf. Pour very hot water into pan to within ½ inch of tops of cups.

Bake 40 minutes, or until a knife inserted into custard halfway between edge and center comes out clean. Remove cups from water; cool on a wire rack, then chill.

When ready to serve, run a knife around inside edges of cups to loosen custards; invert into serving dishes. Serve plain or with whipped cream if you like.

Yield: 8 servings.

BAKED DESSERTS

OATMEAL CHERRY SQUARES

1 can (21 ozs.) cherry pie filling
¼ teaspoon almond extract
4 tablespoons butter or margarine
1 package (18 ozs.) oatmeal cookie mix
¼ cup chopped California walnuts
  Light cream

Preheat oven to 350°.

Combine cherry pie filling and almond extract in a small bowl.

Cut butter into cookie mix until mixture forms coarse crumbs; pat 2 cupfuls into a baking pan, 8x8x2 inches. Spread cherry mixture over layer in pan.

Stir walnuts into rest of oatmeal mixture in bowl; sprinkle over cherry filling; pat down lightly.

Bake 40 minutes, or until bubbly and golden. Cool at least 30 minutes in pan on a wire rack.

Cut into squares; place in serving dishes. Serve warm or cold with cream.
Yield: 9 servings.

STRAWBERRY TRIFLE CAKE

1 package (2-layer size) yellow cake mix
2 medium-sized ripe bananas
2 eggs
⅔ cup water
⅓ cup strawberry preserves
¾ teaspoon sherry flavoring
2 pints strawberries
2 tablespoons sugar
1½ cups whipping cream

Preheat oven to 350°. Grease two 9-inch round layer-cake pans; dust lightly with flour.

Empty cake mix into large bowl of electric mixer.

Peel bananas and mash with a fork. (There should be 1 cup.) Add to cake mix with eggs and water; beat 4 minutes with electric mixer as cake mix label directs. Pour evenly into prepared pans.

Bake 30 minutes, or until a wooden pick inserted into center comes out clean. Cool layers 10 minutes in pans on wire racks. Loosen around edges with a knife; turn out onto racks; cool.

Mix strawberry preserves and sherry flavoring in a small bowl; spread half over each cake layer while it's still slightly warm; place one layer on a serving plate.

Wash strawberries and hull; cut strawberries in half and place in a medium bowl. Sprinkle sugar over top; toss to mix.

Beat cream in a medium bowl until stiff; spread about half over cake layer on plate; spoon half of the strawberries over cream. Top with second cake layer, rest of cream, and rest of strawberries. To serve, cut into wedges.
Yield: 6 generous servings.

AUTUMN APPLE TORTE

1 egg
1 cup sugar
½ cup sifted all-purpose flour
1½ teaspoons baking powder
Dash of salt
1 tablespoon melted butter or margarine
1½ teaspoons vanilla
4 medium-sized tart apples, pared, quartered, cored, and diced (4 cups)
½ cup chopped dates
¾ cup chopped California walnuts
Nutmeg Custard Sauce (recipe on page 324)

Preheat oven to 375°.

Beat egg slightly in a large bowl; stir in sugar, flour, baking powder, salt, melted butter, and vanilla just until mixture is moist. (Do not beat.) Fold in apples, dates, and walnuts. Spoon evenly into a greased baking pan, 8x8x2 inches.

Bake 55 minutes, or until firm and golden. Cool at least 20 minutes in pan on a wire rack.

Cut in serving-sized pieces; place on dessert plates. Serve warm with Nutmeg Custard Sauce.

Yield: 8 servings.

CHANTILLY PEACH SHORTCAKE

1¼ cups sifted cake flour
1 teaspoon baking powder
¼ teaspoon salt
½ cup butter or margarine
1¼ cups granulated sugar
4 eggs, separated
½ teaspoon almond extract
¼ cup milk
1 teaspoon vanilla
½ cup coarsely chopped California walnuts
1½ cups whipping cream
2 tablespoons confectioners' powdered sugar
3 firm ripe peaches, peeled, pitted, and sliced

Preheat oven to 350°. Grease two 8-inch round layer-cake pans; dust lightly with flour.

Sift flour, baking powder, and salt onto waxed paper.

Cream butter with ¾ cup of the granulated sugar in a medium bowl until fluffy-light; beat in egg yolks until fluffy again; stir in almond extract and milk. Stir in flour mixture, part at a time, until well blended. Spread batter evenly into prepared pans.

Beat egg whites in a medium bowl until foamy; beat in remaining ½ cup sugar, 1 tablespoon at a time, until meringue stands in firm peaks; beat in vanilla. Spread evenly over batter in pans; sprinkle walnuts on top.

Bake 35 minutes, or until golden. (Meringue will crack slightly during baking and seem to overflow pans, but will settle and smooth out as it cools.)

Cool layers 15 minutes in pans on wire racks. Loosen around edges with a knife; carefully turn out each layer onto the palm of one hand, then place, meringue side up, on racks; cool layers completely.

Just before serving, combine cream and confectioners' sugar in a medium bowl; beat until stiff. Place one cake layer on a serving plate; top with half of the cream and peaches, then second layer, rest of cream, and rest of peaches. To serve, cut into wedges.

Yield: 8 to 10 servings.

PLUM KUCHEN

2 cups sifted all-purpose flour
3 teaspoons baking powder
½ teaspoon salt
1 cup sugar
½ cup butter or margarine
1 egg
¾ cup milk
2 lbs. plums, quartered and seeded (4 cups)
1 teaspoon ground cinnamon
½ teaspoon ground nutmeg

Preheat oven to 400°.

Sift flour, baking powder, salt, and ¼ cup of the sugar into a large bowl; cut in 6 tablespoons of the butter with a pastry blender until mixture forms fine crumbs.

Beat egg with milk in a small bowl; stir into flour mixture until well blended. Pour into a greased baking pan, 13x9x2 inches. Arrange plum quarters, overlapping, in rows on top. Melt remaining 2 tablespoons butter in a small skillet; drizzle over plums.

Mix remaining ¾ cup sugar, cinnamon, and nutmeg in a small bowl; sprinkle over plums.

Bake 40 minutes, or until plums are tender and a wooden pick inserted into center comes out clean. Cool at least 30 minutes in pan on a wire rack. Cut into squares; serve warm or cold, either plain or with soft vanilla ice cream if you like.

Yield: 12 servings.

CRANBERRY CRUMBLE

1½ cups sifted all-purpose flour
1 cup firmly packed light brown sugar
½ teaspoon salt
¾ cup butter or margarine
1½ cups quick-cooking rolled oats
1 can (16 ozs.) whole-berry cranberry sauce
1 teaspoon grated orange rind
1 carton (4½ ozs.) frozen whipped topping, thawed

Preheat oven to 350°.

Mix flour, brown sugar, and salt in a medium bowl; cut in butter with a pastry blender until mixture forms coarse crumbs; stir in rolled oats.

Measure out 1½ cups of the mixture and set aside. Press the rest into a greased baking pan, 9x9x2 inches, to make an even layer.

Break up cranberry sauce with a fork; stir in orange rind; spread evenly over layer in pan. Sprinkle the 1½ cups crumb mixture on top; pat down lightly.

Bake 55 minutes, or until golden. Cool in pan on a wire rack.

Cut in serving-sized pieces; serve warm or cold with whipped topping.

Yield: 8 servings.

GEORGIA PEACH SHORTCAKE

2 packages butter-pecan muffin mix
Eggs
Milk
¼ cup butter or margarine
⅓ cup firmly packed brown sugar
2 packages (2 ozs. each) whipped topping mix
¼ teaspoon almond extract
1 can (29 ozs.) cling peach slices, drained

Preheat oven to 375°.

Prepare both packages of muffin mix with eggs and milk as label directs; spoon evenly into 2 greased 9-inch round layer-cake pans.

Bake 25 minutes, or until golden and tops spring back when touched with finger. Cool in pans on wire racks 5 minutes; turn out onto racks.

Cream butter and brown sugar in a small bowl; spread half over each hot muffin layer.

Prepare topping mix with milk and almond extract as label directs.

Put muffin layers together, shortcake fashion, on a serving plate with half of the peach slices and whipped topping between and the remainder on top. Cut into wedges; serve warm.

Yield: 12 servings.

CHERRY CRUNCH CUPS

  1 can (21 ozs.) cherry pie filling
1½ cups biscuit mix
  ⅓ cup firmly packed light brown sugar
  1 teaspoon grated orange rind
  1 egg
  4 tablespoons butter or margarine, melted
    Vanilla ice cream

Preheat oven to 400°.

Spoon cherry pie filling into six 6-ounce custard cups, dividing evenly.

Combine biscuit mix, brown sugar, and orange rind in a medium bowl.

Beat egg well in a small bowl; stir into sugar mixture until coarse crumbs form; sprinkle over cherry filling. Drizzle melted butter over top. For easy handling, place cups in a large shallow pan.

Bake 25 minutes, or until topping is golden. Cool slightly on a wire rack. Serve warm with ice cream.

Yield: 6 servings.

BLUEBERRY COBBLER

  2 cans (15 ozs. each) blueberries in syrup
  5 teaspoons cornstarch
  2 tablespoons sugar
¼ teaspoon ground nutmeg
  2 tablespoons butter or margarine
  1 tablespoon lemon juice
  1 package refrigerated orange Danish rolls

Preheat oven to 400°.

Drain syrup from blueberries into a medium saucepan.

Mix cornstarch, sugar, and nutmeg in a cup; stir into syrup. Cook, stirring constantly, until mixture thickens and boils 1 minute; stir in butter, lemon juice, and blueberries. Spoon into a 1½-quart shallow oblong baking dish.

Set icing from orange rolls aside. Separate rolls as label directs, then unwind five to make long strips. Twist each several times; place lengthwise over blueberry mixture.

Unwind remaining 3 rolls; cut each in half crosswise; twist. Place crosswise over other strips in dish.

Bake 25 minutes, or until topping is golden. Cool slightly on a wire rack; drizzle icing over topping. Serve warm.

Yield: 6 servings.

APPLE-ORANGE COBBLER CUPS

  1 can (21 ozs.) apple pie filling
½ cup dark raisins
  1 teaspoon grated orange rind
1½ cups biscuit mix
  ⅓ cup firmly packed light brown sugar
½ teaspoon ground cinnamon
  1 egg
  4 tablespoons butter or margarine melted
    Light cream

Preheat oven to 400°.

Combine apple pie filling, raisins, and orange rind in a medium bowl; stir until well blended; spoon into six 6-ounce custard cups.

Combine biscuit mix, brown sugar, and cinnamon in a medium bowl; stir with a fork to mix.

Beat egg well in a small bowl; stir into biscuit mixture until fine crumbs form; sprinkle over apple mixture. Drizzle melted butter evenly over top. For easy handling, place cups in a large shallow pan.

Bake 25 minutes, or until topping is golden. Cool slightly on a wire rack. Serve warm with cream.

Yield: 6 servings.

APPLE DUMPLINGS

    2 cups sifted all-purpose flour
    1 tablespoon granulated sugar
    ¼ teaspoon salt
    ¼ teaspoon ground cardamom
    ⅔ cup shortening
    1 egg, separated
    ¼ cup cold water
    2 tablespoons butter or margarine
    ⅓ cup firmly packed brown sugar
    ¼ cup dark raisins
    ⅓ cup chopped California walnuts
    4 large baking apples, pared and cored
      Light cream

Preheat oven to 425°.

Sift flour, granulated sugar, salt, and cardamom into a medium bowl; cut in shortening with a pastry blender until mixture forms fine crumbs. Beat egg yolk and water in a cup; stir into flour mixture until pastry holds together and cleans the side of bowl.

Cream butter and brown sugar in a small bowl; stir in raisins and walnuts. Stuff evenly into centers of apples.

Divide pastry into quarters. Roll out, one quarter at a time, to an 8-inch square on a lightly floured cloth. Stand a stuffed apple in center; fold pastry up around apple to cover completely; pinch edges to seal. Place about 1 inch apart in a shallow baking pan.

Bake 30 minutes.

Beat egg white slightly in a cup; brush over pastry. Bake 10 minutes longer, or until apples are tender and pastry is golden. Serve warm with cream.

Yield: 4 servings.

TOASTED STRAWBERRY-RHUBARB CRUNCH

1¼ lbs. rhubarb, trimmed and cut in ½-inch pieces
      (4 cups)
    1 cup sugar
    1 tablespoon grated orange rind
    2 tablespoons cornstarch
      Red food coloring
    4 tablespoons butter or margarine
    2 cups sugar-cookie crumbs
    1 teaspoon ground cinnamon
    1 pint strawberries
    ½ cup whipping cream

Preheat oven to 350°.

Place rhubarb in a 1-quart baking dish; sprinkle sugar and orange rind over top; cover.

Bake, stirring gently several times, 45 minutes, or until rhubarb is tender but still firm enough to hold its shape. Drain syrup into a small saucepan. (There should be from 1½ to 2 cups.)

Blend cornstarch with a little water until smooth in a cup; stir into syrup. Cook, stirring constantly, until mixture thickens and boils 1 minute; remove from heat. Stir in a few drops food coloring to tint bright pink; gently fold into rhubarb; cool.

Melt butter in a shallow baking pan; stir in cookie crumbs and cinnamon. Bake, stirring several times, 15 minutes, or until toasted; cool.

About an hour before serving, wash strawberries, hull, and cut in half; fold into rhubarb. Spoon one third into a deep serving dish; top with one third of the crumb mixture; repeat layers two more times.

Beat cream until stiff in a small bowl; spoon on top. Chill until serving time.

Yield: 6 servings.

CHERRY-BERRY COBBLER

1 can (15 ozs.) blueberries in syrup
1 can (16 ozs.) tart red cherries in juice
⅔ cup sugar (for fruit)
3 tablespoons cornstarch
1 package orange muffin mix
  Egg
  Milk
2 tablespoons sugar (for topping)
2 teaspoons grated orange rind

Preheat oven to 350°.

Drain syrup from blueberries into a 2-cup measure. Drain juice from cherries, adding enough to blueberry syrup to make 1½ cups.

Mix the ⅔ cup sugar and cornstarch in a medium saucepan; stir in the 1½ cups syrup mixture. Cook, stirring constantly, until mixture thickens and boils 1 minute. Fold in blueberries and cherries; spoon into a 2-quart shallow baking dish.

Prepare muffin mix with egg and milk as label directs; spoon over fruit mixture. Mix the 2 tablespoons sugar and orange rind in a cup; sprinkle over batter.

Bake 35 minutes, or until topping is puffed and golden and a wooden pick inserted in center comes out clean. Cool on a wire rack at least 30 minutes. Serve warm, plain or with cream or ice cream if you like.

Yield: 6 servings.

BAKED PEAR PUDDING

½ cup sifted all-purpose flour
2 teaspoons baking powder
½ teaspoon salt
½ cup granulated sugar
½ cup firmly packed light brown sugar
1 egg
2 tablespoons butter or margarine, melted
1 teaspoon grated orange rind
1 teaspoon vanilla
4 large firm ripe pears, pared, quartered, cored, and diced (4 cups)
½ cup snipped dates
  Light cream

Preheat oven to 375°.

Sift flour, baking powder, and salt into a medium bowl; stir in granulated and brown sugars.

Beat egg with butter in a small bowl; stir in orange rind and vanilla. Stir into flour mixture until smooth; fold in pears and dates. Spoon evenly into a greased baking pan, 9x9x2 inches.

Bake 45 minutes, or until firm and golden. Cool at least 30 minutes in pan on a wire rack. Cut into serving-sized pieces; serve warm with cream.

Yield: 6 to 8 servings.

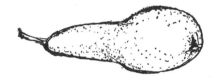

PEACH PUDDING CAKE

1⅓ cups sifted all-purpose flour
¾ cup sugar
½ teaspoon salt
½ teaspoon mace
¼ teaspoon baking powder
½ cup butter or margarine
1 can (29 ozs.) peach halves, drained
1 egg
1 cup whipping cream

Preheat oven to 350°.

Sift flour, sugar, salt, mace, and baking powder into a medium bowl; cut in butter with a pastry blender until mixture is very well blended. Measure out ½ cup; press the rest over bottom and 1 inch up sides of a shallow 1½-quart baking dish to form a shell.

Arrange peach halves, rounded side up, in shell; sprinkle the ½ cup flour mixture on top.

Bake 15 minutes; remove from oven but leave heat on.

While fruit bakes, beat egg slightly with cream in a bowl; pour over peaches.

Bake 35 minutes longer, or until topping is set. Cool in dish. Cut into squares; serve warm or cold.

Yield: 8 servings.

APPLE FLUDEN

3¾ cups sifted all-purpose flour
1 teaspoon baking powder
½ teaspoon salt
¾ cup butter or margarine (for dough)
1¾ cups sugar
2 eggs
1 teaspoon vanilla
2 tablespoons orange juice
1 teaspoon ground cinnamon
½ teaspoon ground nutmeg
4 large apples, pared, quartered, cored, and
  sliced paper-thin (4 cups)
1 cup dark raisins
1 cup coarsely chopped California walnuts
  Butter or margarine (for filling)
  Vanilla ice cream

Measure ¼ cup of the flour and set aside. Sift remaining 3½ cups with baking powder and salt onto waxed paper.

Cream butter with ¾ cup of the sugar until fluffy-light in a large bowl; beat in eggs and vanilla until fluffy again. Stir in flour mixture, alternating with orange juice, until well blended. Chill dough at least 4 hours or overnight until firm enough to roll.

Mix the ¼ cup flour, remaining 1 cup sugar, cinnamon, and nutmeg in a small bowl.

Preheat oven to 350°.

Divide chilled dough into quarters; roll out one fourth to a 9-inch square on a well-floured pastry cloth; place in a greased 9x9x2-inch baking pan. (Trim square even, if needed.) Top with one third each of the apple slices, raisins, and walnuts; sprinkle one third of the sugar mixture over top; dot butter lightly over all. Repeat layering two more times. Roll out rest of dough; place over filling; prick well all over with a fork.

Bake 1 hour, or until pastry is golden and a wooden pick inserted in center comes out clean. Cool in pan on a wire rack at least an hour.

Cut into serving-sized pieces; serve warm with ice cream.

Yield: 8 servings.

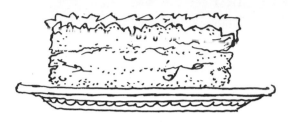

PLANTATION PUDDING

2¼ cups sifted all-purpose flour
¾ cup firmly packed light brown sugar
1 teaspoon ground cinnamon
½ teaspoon ground nutmeg
¼ teaspoon salt
½ cup butter or margarine
1 cup light molasses
1 cup water
1 teaspoon baking soda
  Lemon Sauce (recipe on page 325)
2 containers (4 ozs. each) whipped cream cheese
1 tablespoon granulated sugar

Preheat oven to 350°.

Combine flour, brown sugar, cinnamon, nutmeg, and salt in a medium bowl; cut in butter with a pastry blender until mixture forms fine crumbs.

Mix molasses, water, and baking soda in a 1-quart measure.

Spread 1½ cups of the crumb mixture into a greased baking pan, 8x8x2 inches; pat down lightly to make an even layer. Drizzle half of the molasses mixture over top. Repeat layers, using two thirds of the remaining crumb mixture and all of the molasses mixture; sprinkle remaining crumb mixture on top.

Bake 45 minutes, or until a wooden pick inserted into center comes out clean. Cool pudding completely in pan.

Make Lemon Sauce and cool.

When ready to serve, mix cream cheese and granulated sugar in a bowl.

Cut pudding into squares; place in dessert dishes. Top each with a spoonful of cheese mixture; pour Lemon Sauce over top.

Yield: 9 servings.

BLUEBERRY CRISP

2 pints blueberries, washed and stemmed
1 cup sugar
¼ cup all-purpose flour
1 teaspoon ground cinnamon
¼ teaspoon salt
2 tablespoons lemon juice
2 cups plain granola-type cereal
¼ cup butter or margarine, melted
   Light cream

Preheat oven to 350°.

Combine blueberries, sugar, flour, cinnamon, salt, and lemon juice in a large bowl; toss lightly to mix. Spoon into a 1½-quart shallow baking dish.

Mix cereal and melted butter in a medium bowl; sprinkle over blueberry mixture.

Bake 40 minutes, or until juices bubble up and topping is toasted.

Serve warm or cold with cream.

Yield: 6 servings.

APPLE KUCHEN

3 large tart apples, pared, halved, and cored
2¼ cups sifted all-purpose flour
½ cup granulated sugar
2½ teaspoons baking powder
1 teaspoon salt
½ cup butter or margarine
2 eggs
½ cup milk
1 teaspoon vanilla
⅔ cup firmly packed light brown sugar
1 teaspoon pumpkin-pie spice
1 teaspoon grated lemon rind
3 tablespoons butter or margarine, melted

Cut each half apple into 10 thin slices.

Sift flour, granulated sugar, baking powder, and salt into a large bowl; cut in the ½ cup butter until mixture forms fine crumbs.

Beat eggs slightly with milk and vanilla in a small bowl; stir into flour mixture until evenly moist. Spread in a greased baking pan, 13x9x2 inches. Arrange apple slices, overlapping, in three rows on top to cover dough completely.

Preheat oven to 375°.

Mix brown sugar, pumpkin-pie spice, lemon rind, and melted butter in a small bowl; drop by tiny spoonfuls over apples.

Bake cake 35 minutes, or until a wooden pick inserted into center comes out clean. Cool in pan on a wire rack at least 30 minutes.

Cut into squares; serve warm, plain or with whipped cream if you like.

Yield: 12 servings.

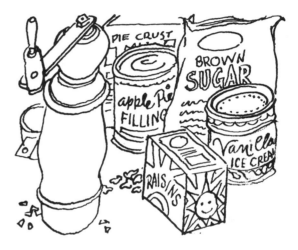

APPLE STREUSEL SQUARES

1 package piecrust mix
¾ cup firmly packed brown sugar
¼ teaspoon ground nutmeg
½ cup dark raisins
1 can (25 ozs.) apple pie filling
1 pint vanilla ice cream

Preheat oven to 425°.

Combine piecrust mix, brown sugar, and nutmeg in a medium bowl; mix well. Press half into a baking pan, 9x9x2 inches.

Stir raisins into apple pie filling in a medium bowl; spoon over layer in pan. Sprinkle remaining crumb mixture over top.

Bake 30 minutes, or until golden. Cool in pan on a wire rack. Cut into serving-sized pieces; place on dessert plates. Top each serving with a big spoonful of ice cream.

Yield: 8 servings.

CHERRY-PEACH TURNOVERS

    4 cups sifted all-purpose flour
    2 teaspoons salt
1½ cups shortening
  12 tablespoons cold water
    1 can (21 ozs.) cherry pie filling
    1 can (21 ozs.) peach pie filling
    2 tablespoons grated orange rind
    3 tablespoons butter or margarine
    2 tablespoons milk
      Sugar

Sift flour and salt into a large bowl; cut in shortening with a pastry blender until mixture forms fine crumbs. Sprinkle water over top, 1 tablespoon at a time, mixing lightly until pastry holds together and cleans side of bowl.

Mix cherry and peach pie fillings with orange rind in a large bowl.

Preheat oven to 425°.

Roll out pastry, one quarter at a time, ⅛ inch thick on a lightly floured cloth; cut into 4½-inch rounds. Spoon a generous tablespoonful fruit mixture onto half of each round; dot about ¼ teaspoon butter over each. Moisten edges of rounds with water, then fold dough over filling to cover completely; press edges with a fork to seal.

Cut several small slits in top of each turnover to let steam escape. Brush milk over tops; sprinkle sugar generously over each. Place on ungreased cookie sheets.

Bake 20 minutes, or until pastry is golden and filling bubbles up. Remove from cookie sheets to wire racks; cool.

Yield: About 2½ dozen.

CHERRY CHEESECAKE

1½ cups graham-cracker crumbs
  ⅓ cup melted butter or margarine
    2 cups sugar
    5 packages (8 ozs. each) cream cheese
    3 tablespoons all-purpose flour
    2 teaspoons grated lemon rind
    1 teaspoon vanilla
    5 eggs
    2 egg yolks
  ¼ cup whipping cream
    1 can (21 ozs.) cherry pie filling
    1 teaspoon grated orange rind

Blend graham-cracker crumbs with melted butter and ¼ cup of the sugar in a medium bowl; press over bottom of a 9-inch springform pan.

Preheat oven to 500°.

Beat cream cheese until fluffy-light in a large bowl; beat in remaining 1¾ cups sugar, flour, lemon rind, and vanilla.

Beat in eggs and egg yolks, one at a time, until mixture is fluffy again; stir in cream. Pour into prepared pan.

Bake 10 minutes; lower oven temperature to 200°. Bake 1 hour; turn off heat. Let cake stand in oven 2 to 3 hours, or until cool. Chill 4 hours, or overnight.

Loosen cake around edge in pan with a knife; release spring and carefully lift off side of pan. Place cake, on its metal base, on a serving plate.

Mix cherry pie filling and orange rind in a small bowl; spoon over top of cake. Chill until serving time.

Yield: 12 servings.

RHUBARB COBBLECAKE

1¾ lbs. rhubarb, trimmed and cut in ½-inch pieces
    (6 cups)
1¾ cups sugar
 3 tablespoons quick-cooking tapioca
 2 tablespoons water
 1 tablespoon grated orange rind
1½ cups sifted all-purpose flour
 3 teaspoons baking powder
 ¼ teaspoon salt
 ⅓ cup shortening
 1 egg
 ½ cup milk
   Light cream

Place rhubarb, 1½ cups of the sugar, tapioca, and water in a medium saucepan; heat slowly, stirring constantly, to a full rolling boil; remove from heat. Stir in orange rind. Pour into a 2½-quart shallow baking dish.

Preheat oven to 400°. Place baking dish in oven as it heats to keep rhubarb mixture hot.

Sift flour, 2 tablespoons of the remaining sugar, baking powder, and salt into a medium bowl; cut in shortening with a pastry blender until mixture forms fine crumbs.

Beat egg with milk until well blended in a small bowl; add all at once to flour mixture; stir just until mixture is evenly moist. Drop by small spoonfuls over hot rhubarb mixture to cover fruit completely. Sprinkle remaining 2 tablespoons sugar over topping.

Bake 25 minutes, or until puffed and golden. Cool at least ½ hour on a wire rack. Spoon into serving dishes; serve warm with cream.
Yield: 8 servings.

PURPLE PLUM COBBLER

 2 cans (16 ozs. each) purple plums
 2 tablespoons cornstarch
 ¼ teaspoon ground nutmeg
 2 tablespoons butter or margarine
1½ cups sifted all-purpose flour
 ¼ cup sugar
 3 teaspoons baking powder
 ¼ teaspoon salt
 ⅓ cup shortening
 1 egg
 ½ cup milk
   Light cream

Drain syrup from plums into a small bowl. Pit plums and place in a 2-quart shallow baking dish.

Mix cornstarch and nutmeg in a small saucepan; stir in plum syrup. Cook, stirring constantly, until mixture thickens and boils 1 minute; stir in butter until melted; pour over plums.

Preheat oven to 400°. Place baking dish in oven to keep hot as oven preheats.

Sift flour, 2 tablespoons of the sugar, baking powder, and salt into a medium bowl; cut in shortening with a pastry blender until mixture forms fine crumbs.

Beat egg with milk until blended in a small bowl; add all at once to flour mixture; stir just until mixture is evenly moist. Drop by small spoonfuls over hot plum mixture to cover completely. Sprinkle remaining 2 tablespoons sugar over topping.

Bake 25 minutes, or until puffed and golden. Cool at least a half hour on a wire rack. Spoon into serving dishes; serve warm with cream.
Yield: 6 servings.

TOASTED PEACH CRISP

1 can (29 ozs.) cling peach slices in syrup
¼ cup butter or margarine
¼ cup firmly packed light brown sugar
½ teaspoon ground nutmeg
2 cups oven-toasted rice cereal
Light cream

Preheat oven to 375°.

Drain syrup from peaches into a cup; place peaches in a 9-inch pie plate. Drizzle ¼ cup of the syrup over top.

Melt butter in a medium saucepan; stir in brown sugar, nutmeg, and cereal; sprinkle over peaches.

Bake 20 minutes, or until hot and topping is toasted. Cool 10 minutes on a wire rack. Spoon into serving dishes; serve warm with cream.

Yield: 4 servings.

MINCEMEAT-APPLE SQUARES

1 egg
1 cup sugar
¾ cup sifted all-purpose flour
1½ teaspoons baking powder
Dash of salt
1 tablespoon butter or margarine, melted
2 cups prepared mincemeat
2 medium-sized tart apples, pared, quartered, cored, and diced (1½ cups)
½ cup chopped California walnuts
Vanilla Custard Sauce (recipe on page 324)

Preheat oven to 375°.

Beat egg slightly in a large bowl; stir in sugar, flour, baking powder, salt, melted butter, and mincemeat until blended. (Do not beat.) Fold in apples and walnuts. Spoon evenly into a greased baking pan, 8x8x2 inches.

Bake 55 minutes, or until firm and brown. Cool in pan.

Cut into serving-sized pieces; place on dessert plates. Spoon Custard Sauce over each serving.

Yield: 9 servings.

MINCEMEAT TORTE

1½ cups prepared mincemeat
1 large tart apple, pared, quartered, cored, and chopped (1 cup)
1 teaspoon grated lemon rind
½ cup chopped California walnuts
1½ cups sifted all-purpose flour
1 cup firmly packed light brown sugar
1 teaspoon ground cinnamon
½ teaspoon salt
¾ cup butter or margarine
1½ cups quick-cooking rolled oats
Vanilla ice cream

Mix mincemeat, apple, lemon rind, and walnuts in a medium bowl.

Preheat oven to 350°.

Combine flour, brown sugar, cinnamon, and salt in a large bowl. Cut in butter with a pastry blender until mixture forms fine crumbs; stir in rolled oats.

Press half of mixture evenly over bottom of a greased baking pan, 9x9x2 inches; spread mincemeat mixture over layer. Sprinkle remaining flour mixture on top; pat down lightly.

Bake 1 hour, or until firm and golden. Cool completely in pan on a wire rack.

When ready to serve, cut into small squares; place on serving plates; top with small scoops of ice cream.

Yield: 12 servings.

LEMON TORTE

    2 cups sifted all-purpose flour
    1 teaspoon salt
    ¾ cup shortening
    ¾ cup flaked coconut
    6 tablespoons cold water (for pastry)
    1¼ cups sugar
    5 tablespoons cornstarch
    1 egg
    1¾ cups water (for filling)
    2 tablespoons butter or margarine
    1 teaspoon grated lemon rind
    ⅓ cup lemon juice
    ½ cup whipping cream

Preheat oven to 400°.

Sift flour and salt into a medium bowl; cut in shortening with a pastry blender until mixture forms fine crumbs; stir in coconut. Sprinkle the 6 tablespoons water over top, 1 tablespoon at a time, mixing lightly with a fork until pastry holds together and cleans the side of bowl. Divide into 6 equal pieces.

Roll out, 1 piece at a time, to a 7-inch circle on a lightly floured cloth; place on ungreased cookie sheets; prick each well with a fork.

Bake 6 minutes, or until lightly golden; remove carefully from cookie sheets to wire racks. Cool completely.

Mix sugar and cornstarch in a medium saucepan. Beat egg in a small bowl; stir in the 1¾ cups water; stir into cornstarch mixture. Cook slowly, stirring constantly, until mixture thickens and boils 3 minutes; remove from heat. Stir in butter until melted, then lemon rind and juice. Chill until completely cold.

Place one pastry layer on a serving plate; spread a heaping ⅓ cup of the lemon filling over layer. Stack second layer on top; spread with filling. Continue with remaining layers and filling. Chill at least 2 hours.

Just before serving, beat cream in a small bowl until stiff; spread over filling on top of torte. Cut into wedges with a sharp knife. (For neat serving, cut all pieces first, then remove them to individual plates.)

Yield: 8 servings.

PRUNE COBBLECAKE

    2 cups sifted all-purpose flour
    2 teaspoons baking powder
    ½ teaspoon salt
    ¾ cup milk
    3 tablespoons butter or margarine
    3 eggs
    2 cups firmly packed light brown sugar
    1 teaspoon vanilla
    2 cups plain granola-type cereal
    1 cup cut-up dried pitted prunes
    1 teaspoon ground cinnamon
    ½ cup melted butter or margarine

Sift flour, baking powder, and salt onto waxed paper.

Scald milk with the 3 tablespoons butter in a small saucepan; set aside.

Beat eggs until fluffy and thick in a large bowl; slowly beat in 1½ cups of the brown sugar until mixture is fluffy again; beat in vanilla until blended.

Stir in flour mixture until blended, then scalded milk mixture. Pour into a greased baking pan, 13x9x2 inches.

Preheat oven to 350°.

Mix cereal, remaining ½ cup brown sugar, prunes, and cinnamon in a medium bowl; drizzle melted butter over top; toss until well blended. Sprinkle over batter in pan.

Bake 35 minutes, or until golden and a wooden pick inserted into center comes out clean. Cool in pan on a wire rack. Serve warm or cold.

Yield: 12 servings.

MOLDED DESSERTS

LEMON CREAM

1 envelope unflavored gelatin
¼ cup water
4 eggs, separated
1¼ cups sugar
½ cup lemon juice
¼ teaspoon salt
2 teaspoons grated lemon rind
1 cup whipping cream
   Strawberry Sauce (recipe on page 325)

Fold a 22-inch-long strip of regular foil in half lengthwise. Wrap around a straight-sided 1-quart dish to make a 2-inch stand-up collar; hold in place with cellophane tape.

Soften gelatin in water in a medium saucepan.

Beat egg yolks in a small bowl; stir into gelatin mixture with ¾ cup of the sugar, lemon juice, and salt. Cook slowly, stirring constantly, until gelatin dissolves; remove from heat. Stir in lemon rind; pour into a large bowl.

Place bowl in a pan of ice and water to speed setting. Let stand, stirring several times, until mixture starts to thicken.

While gelatin mixture chills, beat egg whites in a medium bowl until foamy; slowly beat in remaining ½ cup sugar until meringue forms firm peaks. Beat cream until stiff in another medium bowl.

Fold meringue, then whipped cream into thickened gelatin mixture. Spoon into prepared dish. Chill several hours, or until firm.

Remove foil collar. Garnish dessert with a ring of strawberries cut in half if you like.

To serve, spoon into sherbet glasses; top with Strawberry Sauce.

Yield: 8 servings.

AMBROSIA CROWN

1 package (6 ozs.) orange-flavored gelatin
1 can (8 ozs.) crushed pineapple in syrup
   Water
1 pint orange sherbet
1 can (11 ozs.) mandarin orange segments, drained
1 can (3½ ozs.) flaked coconut
1 package (10 ozs.) frozen raspberries
2 teaspoons cornstarch
1 teaspoon lemon juice

Place gelatin in a medium bowl.

Drain syrup from pineapple into a 2-cup measure; add water to make 1¼ cups. Heat to boiling in a small saucepan; pour over gelatin; stir until gelatin dissolves. Stir in sherbet, a few spoonfuls at a time, until melted. (If mixture is not thickened at this point, chill until it starts to set.)

Stir in pineapple, orange segments, and coconut; spoon into a 1¼- or 1½-quart mold. Chill several hours or overnight until firm.

Thaw raspberries as label directs; press berries with syrup through a sieve into a small bowl.

Measure cornstarch into a small saucepan; stir in raspberry purée. Cook, stirring constantly, until mixture thickens and boils 1 minute; remove from heat. Stir in lemon juice; chill.

When ready to serve, loosen dessert around edge with a knife; dip mold quickly in and out of warm water; invert onto a serving plate; lift off mold.

Drizzle several spoonfuls of the sauce over dessert; serve remainder separately.

Yield: 8 servings.

PUMPKIN MOUSSE

1 cup butter-cookie crumbs
2 tablespoons butter or margarine, melted
2 envelopes unflavored gelatin
1¼ cups sugar
1 teaspoon ground cinnamon
½ teaspoon ground nutmeg
½ teaspoon ground ginger
½ teaspoon salt
4 eggs, separated
1 cup milk
1 can (16 ozs.) pumpkin
¼ cup curacao
1½ cups whipping cream
¼ cup sliced almonds

Blend cookie crumbs with melted butter in a small bowl; press evenly over bottom of a 9-inch springform pan.

Mix gelatin, ¾ cup of the sugar, cinnamon, nutmeg, ginger, and salt in a medium saucepan.

Beat egg yolks with milk in a small bowl; stir into gelatin mixture; stir in pumpkin. Heat slowly, stirring constantly, until gelatin dissolves; pour into a large bowl; stir in curaçao.

Set bowl in a large pan of ice and water to speed setting. Chill, stirring several times, 30 minutes, or until mixture starts to thicken.

While pumpkin mixture chills, beat egg whites in a medium bowl until foamy; beat in remaining ½ cup sugar, 1 tablespoon at a time, until meringue forms soft peaks. Beat 1 cup of the cream until stiff in a second bowl.

Fold meringue, then whipped cream into thickened gelatin mixture until no streaks of white remain. Spoon into prepared pan. Chill overnight.

Just before serving, loosen dessert around edge with a knife; release spring on pan and carefully lift off side; slide dessert, still on its metal base, onto a large serving plate.

Beat remaining ½ cup cream in a small bowl until stiff; spoon on top of dessert. Sprinkle almonds over cream. Cut dessert into wedges.
Yield: 8 to 10 servings.

APRICOT BAVARIAN

2 cans (16 ozs. each) whole peeled apricots in syrup
2 envelopes unflavored gelatin
4 eggs, separated
2 tablespoons lemon juice
1 teaspoon vanilla
⅛ teaspoon cream of tartar
¼ cup sugar
1 cup whipping cream

Drain syrup from apricots into a small bowl. Set aside 1 apricot for garnish if you like, then seed remainder and purée in a blender or press through a sieve into a small bowl. (There should be about 1½ cups purée.)

Soften gelatin in ¾ cup of the apricot syrup in a small saucepan. Beat egg yolks in a small bowl; stir into syrup mixture. Cook, stirring constantly, until gelatin dissolves and mixture coats spoon; pour into a large bowl. Stir in puréed apricots, lemon juice, and vanilla.

Place bowl in a pan of ice and water to speed setting; let stand, stirring several times, just until mixture starts to thicken.

While gelatin mixture chills, beat egg whites with cream of tartar in a medium bowl until foamy; slowly beat in sugar until meringue stands in firm peaks. Beat ¾ cup of the cream in a small bowl until stiff. Fold meringue, then whipped cream into thickened apricot mixture; continue folding until mixture mounds softly. Spoon into a 1¾-quart mold. Chill several hours, or overnight, until firm.

Just before serving, beat remaining ¼ cup cream until stiff in a small bowl.

Loosen dessert around edge with a knife; dip mold quickly in and out of warm water; invert onto a serving plate; lift off mold. Garnish with whipped cream and remaining apricot cut into quarters.
Yield: 8 to 10 servings.

APRICOT RICE MOLD

⅓ cup uncooked regular rice
1 can (29 ozs.) apricot halves, drained
1½ cups milk
1 envelope unflavored gelatin
⅔ cup sugar
3 egg yolks
1½ cups whipping cream
1 teaspoon vanilla

Cook rice as label directs.

Set aside 6 to 8 apricot halves for garnish; purée remaining apricots in an electric blender or mash well in a bowl.

Combine cooked rice and 1¼ cups of the milk in a medium saucepan. Heat slowly, stirring constantly, until milk is absorbed; remove from heat.

Mix gelatin and sugar in a medium saucepan; beat in remaining ¼ cup milk, egg yolks, and apricot purée. Heat slowly, stirring constantly, until gelatin dissolves; fold into rice mixture. Chill until very cold.

Combine 1 cup of the cream and vanilla in a medium bowl; beat until stiff; fold into rice mixture. Spoon into a 1½-quart mold. Chill several hours, or overnight, until firm.

Just before serving, loosen dessert around edge with a knife; dip mold quickly in and out of warm water; invert onto a serving plate; lift off mold.

Beat remaining ½ cup cream in a small bowl until stiff. Spoon part into saved apricot halves; place around base of mold. Spoon remaining whipped cream on top.

Yield: 6 servings.

STRAWBERRY-RHUBARB SOUFFLE

1 lb. rhubarb, trimmed and cut in ½-inch pieces (3 cups)
¾ cup water
1½ cups sugar
1½ pints strawberries
2 envelopes unflavored gelatin
3 egg whites
1 cup whipping cream

Fold a 22-inch-long strip of waxed paper in half lengthwise. Wrap around a straight-sided 1-quart dish to make a 2-inch stand-up collar; hold in place with cellophane tape.

Combine rhubarb, water, and ½ cup of the sugar in a medium saucepan; heat to boiling; cook 1 minute. Remove from heat; cover; let stand 5 minutes. Drain syrup into a 2-cup measure.

Set aside several of the prettiest strawberries for garnish, then wash remainder, hull, and mash in a large bowl; stir in ½ cup of the remaining sugar.

Soften gelatin in 1 cup of the rhubarb syrup in a small saucepan. (Save any remaining syrup to add to punch.)

Heat gelatin mixture slowly, stirring constantly, until gelatin dissolves; cool slightly. Stir into mashed strawberries; stir in rhubarb. Place bowl in a pan of ice and water to speed setting. Chill, stirring several times, until syrupy-thick.

While gelatin mixture chills, beat egg whites in a medium bowl until foamy; slowly beat in remaining ½ cup sugar until meringue forms soft peaks. Beat cream in a medium bowl until stiff.

Fold meringue, then whipped cream into thickened gelatin mixture; pour into prepared dish. Chill several hours, or until firm.

When ready to serve, remove paper collar from dish. Garnish soufflé with saved strawberries. Serve plain or with more whipped cream if you like.

Yield: 8 to 10 servings.

STRAWBERRY CREAM TORTE

¼ cup butter or margarine
1 cup graham-cracker crumbs
6 tablespoons sugar (for crust and filling)
1 envelope unflavored gelatin
1 egg, separated
½ cup milk
1 package (8 ozs.) cream cheese, cut up
2 tablespoons lemon juice
1 cup whipping cream
1 pint strawberries
  Water
⅓ cup sugar (for sauce)
2 tablespoons cornstarch
  Red food coloring

Preheat oven to 350°.

Melt butter in a small saucepan; blend in graham-cracker crumbs and 2 tablespoons of the sugar. Press evenly over bottom and 1 inch up sides of a baking dish, 8x8x2 inches.

Bake 10 minutes, or until set; cool completely in dish on a wire rack.

Mix 2 tablespoons of the sugar and gelatin in the top of a small double boiler. Beat egg yolk with milk in a small bowl; strain into gelatin mixture. Cook over hot water, stirring constantly, about 10 minutes, or until gelatin dissolves and custard coats spoon.

Stir in cheese until melted and smooth; remove from heat. Stir in 1 tablespoon of the lemon juice. Chill 15 minutes, or until mixture mounds softly.

While gelatin mixture chills, beat egg white in a small bowl until foamy. Beat in remaining 2 tablespoons sugar until meringue forms soft peaks. Beat cream in a medium bowl until stiff.

Beat gelatin mixture until fluffy-light; fold in meringue, then whipped cream; spoon into crust. Chill at least 4 hours, or until firm.

Wash strawberries and hull; mash in a medium bowl or purée in an electric blender. Measure, then add water, if needed, to make 1¾ cups. Combine with the ⅓ cup sugar in a small saucepan. Cook, stirring constantly, 2 minutes.

Blend ¼ cup water and cornstarch until smooth in a cup; stir into strawberry mixture. Cook, stirring constantly, until mixture thickens and boils 1 minute; remove from heat. Stir in remaining 1 tablespoon lemon juice and a few drops food coloring to tint deep red; cool.

Cut torte into serving-sized pieces; place on dessert plates; spoon strawberry sauce over each serving.

Yield: 12 servings.

COFFEE RUM BAVARIAN

2 envelopes unflavored gelatin
½ cup sugar
2 tablespoons dry instant coffee
3 cups milk
3 tablespoons rum
1 container (9 ozs.) frozen whipped topping, thawed

Mix gelatin, sugar, and coffee in a medium saucepan; stir in milk. Heat very slowly, stirring constantly, until gelatin dissolves; remove from heat. Stir in rum; pour into a large bowl.

Place bowl in a pan of ice and water to speed setting; chill, stirring several times, until syrupy-thick; fold in whipped topping. Continue folding, still over ice, until mixture mounds very softly; pour into a 1½-quart mold. Chill several hours or overnight until firm.

When ready to serve, loosen dessert around edge with a knife; dip mold quickly in and out of warm water; invert onto a serving plate; lift off mold. Garnish dessert with more whipped topping and grated chocolate if you like.

Yield: 8 servings.

HONEYDEW CREAM

1 small honeydew melon
2 tablespoons lime juice
2 envelopes unflavored gelatin
½ cup sugar
½ cup water
1 teaspoon grated lime rind
1 container (4½ ozs.) frozen whipped topping,
    thawed
  Green food coloring

Cut honeydew in half; scoop out seeds. Wrap half and chill for garnish. Pare remaining half; cut in small chunks.

Combine a few honeydew chunks with lime juice in an electric-blender container, cover. Beat until smooth. Add remaining chunks and beat to make 2½ cups purée.

Mix gelatin and sugar in a small saucepan; stir in water. Heat, stirring constantly, until gelatin dissolves; pour into a large bowl. Stir in the 2½ cups honeydew purée and lime rind. Chill at least 50 minutes, or until mixture is as thick as unbeaten egg white; beat until fluffy. Fold in whipped topping and a few drops food coloring to tint a delicate green. Spoon into a 1¼- or 1½-quart mold. Chill at least 4 hours, or until firm.

Just before serving, cut remaining honeydew into balls with a melon-ball cutter or ¼ teaspoon of a measuring spoon set.

Loosen dessert around edge with a knife; dip mold quickly in and out of warm water; invert onto a serving plate; lift off mold. Arrange honeydew balls in a ring around dessert. Garnish with a few sprigs of mint if you like.

Yield: 6 servings.

APPLE-LIME WHIP

2 large apples, pared, quartered, cored, and cut
    into small pieces
¾ cup water
¾ cup sugar (for mold)
1 envelope unflavored gelatin
  Salt
1 teaspoon grated lime rind
2 tablespoons lime juice
  Green food coloring
2 eggs, separated
3 tablespoons sugar (for sauce)
1¼ cups milk
1 teaspoon vanilla

Combine apples with water in a small saucepan; heat to boiling; cover. Cook 5 minutes, or until apples are tender. Cool slightly, then pour mixture into an electric-blender container; cover. Blend until smooth.

Mix the ¾ cup sugar, gelatin, and a dash of salt in a small saucepan; stir in 1½ cups of the apple purée. Heat slowly, stirring constantly, until gelatin dissolves; pour into a medium bowl. Stir in lime rind and juice and a few drops food coloring to tint a delicate green.

Place bowl in a pan of ice and water to speed setting. Let stand, stirring several times, until mixture is syrupy-thick.

Stir in unbeaten egg whites. Keeping bowl over ice, beat rapidly until mixture triples in volume and starts to hold its shape; spoon into a 1½-quart mold. Chill several hours, or until firm.

Beat egg yolks slightly in the top of a double boiler; stir in the 3 tablespoons sugar, a dash of salt, and milk. Cook over simmering water, stirring constantly, until custard thickens slightly and coats spoon. Strain into a small bowl; stir in vanilla; chill.

When ready to serve, loosen dessert around edge with a knife; dip mold quickly in and out of warm water; invert onto a serving plate; lift off mold. Garnish with thin lime and apple slices if you like. Serve with custard sauce.

Yield: 6 servings.

ORANGE CREAM CAKE

¾ cup crushed vanilla wafers
2 tablespoons butter or margarine, melted
2 envelopes unflavored gelatin
1 cup sugar (for cake)
¼ teaspoon salt
2 eggs, separated
1 cup milk
2 packages (8 ozs. each) cream cheese, softened
1 tablespoon grated orange rind
1½ cups orange juice
1 cup whipping cream
1 tablespoon sugar (for glaze)
1½ teaspoons cornstarch
2 medium-sized seedless oranges, pared, sectioned, and drained

Blend vanilla wafer crumbs and melted butter in a small bowl; press over bottom of a 9-inch springform pan.

Mix gelatin, ¾ cup of the sugar, and salt in a medium saucepan. Beat egg yolks with milk in a small bowl; stir into gelatin mixture. Cook slowly, stirring constantly, until gelatin dissolves; remove from heat.

Cut up cream cheese and stir in until melted, then beat mixture until smooth; stir in orange rind and 1 cup of the orange juice. Chill 50 minutes, or until mixture mounds softly.

While gelatin mixture chills, beat egg whites in a small bowl until foamy; slowly beat in remaining ¼ cup sugar until meringue forms soft peaks. Beat cream in a medium bowl until stiff. Fold meringue, then whipped cream into gelatin mixture until no streaks of white remain. Spoon into prepared pan. Chill at least 6 hours until firm.

Mix the 1 tablespoon sugar and cornstarch in a small saucepan; stir in remaining ½ cup orange juice. Cook, stirring constantly, until mixture thickens and boils 1 minute; cool.

Arrange orange sections around edge on cake and in center to form a flower design; spoon glaze evenly on top. Chill until glaze sets.

When ready to serve, loosen cake around edge of pan with a knife; release spring and carefully lift off side of pan. Place cake, on its metal base, on a serving plate. Cut into wedges.

Yield: 12 servings.

PUMPKIN CHEESECAKE

1 cup gingersnap crumbs
3 tablespoons butter or margarine, melted
1 package (3⅛ ozs.) vanilla pudding and pie filling mix
2 envelopes unflavored gelatin
2 eggs, separated
2 cups milk
1 carton (8 ozs.) whipped cream cheese
1 can (16 ozs.) pumpkin
2 tablespoons lemon juice
⅓ cup sugar
1 cup whipping cream

Blend gingersnap crumbs and melted butter in a small bowl; pat ⅔ cup over bottom of a 9-inch springform pan. Set remainder aside.

Mix pudding mix and gelatin in a medium saucepan. Beat egg yolks and milk in a small bowl; stir into pudding mixture. Cook slowly, stirring constantly, until mixture starts to boil; slowly beat into cream cheese in a large bowl. Stir in pumpkin and lemon juice. Chill until mixture mounds softly.

Beat egg whites in a small bowl until foamy; slowly beat in sugar until meringue forms stiff peaks. Beat cream in a small bowl until stiff. Fold meringue, then whipped cream into pumpkin mixture; pour into prepared pan; sprinkle remaining crumb mixture on top. Chill cheesecake overnight until firm.

When ready to serve, loosen cake around edge of pan with a knife; release spring and carefully lift off side of pan. Place cake, on its metal base, on a serving plate. Slice into thin wedges.

Yield: 12 servings.

CHOCOLATE CHANTILLY CAKE

1 cup graham-cracker crumbs
3 tablespoons sugar (for crust)
4 tablespoons butter or margarine, melted
1 package (3¾ ozs.) dark chocolate or chocolate fudge pudding and pie filling mix
2 envelopes unflavored gelatin
3 eggs, separated
2½ cups milk
4 containers (4 ozs. each) whipped cream cheese
2 teaspoons rum extract
⅓ cup sugar (for filling)
1½ cups whipping cream

Combine cracker crumbs, the 3 tablespoons sugar, and melted butter in a medium bowl; blend well. Press two thirds of the mixture over bottom of a 9-inch springform pan. Set remaining crumb mixture aside for topping.

Combine pudding mix and gelatin in a medium saucepan. Beat egg yolks with milk in a medium bowl; stir into pudding mixture. Heat slowly, stirring constantly, to boiling; very slowly beat into cream cheese until smooth in a large bowl; beat in rum extract. Chill mixture 30 minutes, or until it mounds softly on a spoon.

While pudding mixture chills, beat egg whites in a medium bowl until foamy; slowly beat in the ⅓ cup sugar until meringue forms soft peaks. Beat 1 cup of the cream in a medium bowl until stiff. Fold meringue, then whipped cream into chocolate mixture; spoon into prepared crust. Sprinkle remaining crumb mixture over top. Chill at least 6 hours or overnight until firm.

When ready to serve, beat remaining ½ cup cream until stiff in a small bowl.

Loosen dessert around edge of pan with a knife; release spring and carefully lift off side of pan; slide dessert, on its metal base, onto a serving plate. Garnish with whipped cream and chocolate curls if you like. Cut into wedges.

Yield: 12 servings.

EGGNOG CREAM

2 packages (3 ozs. each) egg custard mix
1 envelope unflavored gelatin
½ teaspoon ground nutmeg
2 eggs, separated
2½ cups milk
1 teaspoon rum extract
¼ cup sugar
1½ cups whipping cream
¼ cup chopped red and green candied cherries

Fold a 22-inch-long strip of waxed paper in half lengthwise. Wrap around a straight-sided 1-quart dish to make a 2-inch stand-up collar; hold in place with cellophane tape.

Combine custard mix, gelatin, and nutmeg in a medium saucepan.

Beat egg yolks with milk in a medium bowl; stir into gelatin mixture. Heat slowly, stirring constantly, to boiling; stir in rum extract; pour into a large bowl.

Place bowl in a pan of ice and water to speed setting. Chill mixture, stirring several times, until slightly thickened.

While gelatin mixture chills, beat egg whites in a small bowl until foamy; beat in sugar until meringue forms soft peaks. Beat 1 cup of the cream in a medium bowl until stiff.

Beat thickened gelatin mixture until smooth and fluffy; fold in meringue, then whipped cream. Continue folding, keeping mixture over ice, until it mounds softly. Pour into prepared dish. Chill several hours, or overnight, until firm.

When ready to serve, beat remaining ½ cup cream until stiff in a small bowl.

Remove waxed paper from dish; spoon whipped cream in a ring on top of dessert; sprinkle cherries over cream.

Yield: 8 servings.

(Clockwise from top) ▶
HONEYDEW CREAM (p.446)
CANTALOUPE COUPE (p.454)
CHANTILLY PEACH SHORTCAKE (p.431)

STRAWBERRY CROWN

   1 cup cooked regular rice
1½ cups milk
   1 pint strawberries
 ¾ cup sugar
   1 envelope unflavored gelatin
   3 egg yolks
      Red food coloring
   1 cup whipping cream

Combine rice and 1 cup of the milk in a small saucepan; heat slowly, stirring often, until milk is absorbed; spoon into a large bowl; cool.

Set aside 3 or 4 pretty strawberries for garnish, then wash remainder, hull, and mash in a small bowl.

Mix sugar and gelatin in a small saucepan.

Beat remaining ½ cup milk and egg yolks in a small bowl; stir into gelatin mixture. Heat slowly, stirring constantly, until gelatin dissolves and custard coats spoon. Stir into rice mixture; stir in mashed strawberries and a few drops food coloring to tint bright pink. Chill mixture 30 minutes, stirring several times, just until it starts to set.

Beat cream in a medium bowl until stiff; fold into rice mixture; spoon into a 1½-quart mold. Chill overnight until firm.

When ready to serve, loosen dessert around edge with a knife; dip mold quickly in and out of warm water; invert onto a serving plate; lift off mold. Garnish with saved strawberries. Serve plain or with more whipped cream if you like.

Yield: 8 servings.

◀ **WATERMELON FRUIT BOWL** (p.424)
ONION CHICKEN (p.176)
POTATO SALAD CUPS (p.341)
PINWHEEL BEAN SALAD (p.351)
PEANUT CRINKLES (p.545)

MILK CHOCOLATE SOUFFLE

 ¾ cup sugar
   1 envelope unflavored gelatin
 ¾ cup water
   1 package (6 ozs.) semisweet chocolate pieces
   4 eggs, separated
   2 tablespoons curaçao
   1 teaspoon vanilla
1½ cups whipping cream

Fold a 22-inch-long strip of regular foil in half lengthwise. Wrap around a straight-sided 1-quart dish to make a 2-inch stand-up collar; hold in place with cellophane tape.

Mix ¼ cup of the sugar and gelatin in the top of a double boiler; stir in water and chocolate pieces; place over simmering water. Heat, stirring constantly, until gelatin dissolves, chocolate melts, and mixture is smooth.

Beat egg yolks in a small bowl; slowly stir in a few spoonfuls of the hot chocolate mixture, then stir back into top of double boiler. Cook, stirring constantly, 3 minutes; remove from heat. Pour into a large bowl; stir in curaçao and vanilla. Place bowl in a pan of ice and water to speed setting. Chill, stirring several times, until mixture starts to thicken.

While chocolate mixture chills, beat egg whites in a medium bowl until foamy; slowly beat in remaining ½ cup sugar until meringue stands in firm peaks. Beat 1 cup of the cream in a medium bowl until stiff. Fold meringue, then whipped cream into thickened chocolate mixture until no streaks of white remain. Spoon into prepared dish. Chill at least 4 hours or overnight until firm.

Just before serving, beat remaining ½ cup cream in a small bowl until stiff. Carefully remove foil collar from soufflé; spoon cream in a ring on top. Garnish with maraschino cherry halves if you like.

Yield: 6 servings.

PEACH MELBA
IMPERATRICE

1 can (16 ozs.) sliced cling peaches in syrup
2 packages (3¾ ozs. each) rice pudding mix
1 envelope unflavored gelatin
2 eggs, separated
3 cups milk
5 tablespoons sugar
1 cup whipping cream
1 teaspoon vanilla
1 package (10 ozs.) frozen red raspberries, thawed
1 tablespoon cornstarch
2 teaspoons lemon juice

Drain syrup from peaches and chill to add to a fruit compote. Chop peaches coarsely. (There should be about 1 cup.)

Combine pudding mix and gelatin in a medium saucepan.

Beat egg yolks with milk in a medium bowl; stir into pudding mixture. Heat slowly, stirring constantly, to boiling; remove from heat; cover. Let stand 5 minutes, then chill 20 minutes, or until mixture is completely cold.

While pudding mixture chills, beat egg whites in a small bowl until foamy; slowly beat in 4 tablespoons of the sugar until meringue forms soft peaks. Beat cream in a medium bowl until stiff.

Fold peaches and vanilla into pudding mixture, then fold in meringue and whipped cream until no streaks of white remain; spoon into a 2-quart mold. Chill several hours, or overnight, until firm.

Press raspberries with syrup through a sieve into a medium bowl. (Or purée in an electric blender and strain mixture to remove seeds.)

Mix cornstarch and remaining 1 tablespoon sugar in a medium saucepan; stir in raspberry purée. Cook slowly, stirring constantly, until mixture thickens and boils 1 minute; remove from heat. Stir in lemon juice. Cool, then chill.

Just before serving, loosen dessert around edge of mold with a knife; dip mold quickly in and out of warm water; invert onto a serving plate; lift off mold. Garnish with additional peach slices and raspberries if you like. Serve with raspberry sauce.

Yield: 10 to 12 servings.

LIME SHERBET SOUFFLES

1 envelope unflavored gelatin
1 cup sugar
4 eggs, separated
½ cup water
½ teaspoon grated lime rind
¼ cup lime juice
  Green food coloring
1 cup whipping cream

Tear off 4 sheets of regular foil 4 inches wide; fold in half lengthwise. Wrap each around an individual soufflé dish or deep straight-sided cup to make a 1½-inch stand-up collar; fasten with cellophane tape.

Mix gelatin and ½ cup of the sugar in a small saucepan.

Beat egg yolks in a small bowl; stir in water, then stir into gelatin mixture. Cook, stirring constantly, until gelatin dissolves and mixture coats spoon; remove from heat. Pour into a large bowl; stir in lime rind and juice and a few drops food coloring to tint green.

Place bowl in a pan of ice and water to speed setting; let stand, stirring several times, just until mixture starts to thicken.

While gelatin mixture chills, beat egg whites in a medium bowl until foamy; slowly beat in remaining ½ cup sugar until meringue stands in firm peaks. Beat ¾ cup of the cream in a small bowl until stiff.

Fold meringue, then whipped cream into thickened lime mixture; continue folding until mixture mounds softly. Spoon into prepared dishes. Freeze several hours, or overnight, until firm.

When ready to serve, beat remaining ¼ cup cream in a small bowl until stiff.

Remove collars from dishes; spoon cream onto center of each.

Yield: 4 servings.

STRAWBERRY-LIME CREAM CAKE

1 cup graham-cracker crumbs
3 tablespoons butter or margarine, melted
2 envelopes unflavored gelatin
1¾ cups sugar
6 eggs, separated
1 cup water
1 teaspoon grated lime rind
½ cup lime juice
  Green food coloring
1 cup whipping cream
1 pint strawberries
1 tablespoon cornstarch
  Red food coloring

Blend cracker crumbs and melted butter in a small bowl; press evenly over bottom of an 8-inch springform pan.

Mix gelatin and 1 cup of the sugar in a small saucepan. Beat egg yolks in a small bowl; stir in ¾ cup of the water; stir into gelatin mixture. Cook slowly, stirring constantly, until gelatin dissolves and mixture coats spoon; remove from heat. Pour into a large bowl; stir in lime rind and juice and a few drops food coloring to tint bright green. Place bowl in a pan of ice and water to speed setting. Chill, stirring several times, until mixture starts to thicken.

While gelatin mixture chills, beat egg whites in a medium bowl until foamy; slowly beat in ½ cup of the remaining sugar until meringue stands in soft peaks. Beat cream in a medium bowl until stiff. Fold meringue, then whipped cream into thickened lime mixture until no streaks of white remain. Spoon into prepared pan. Chill several hours, or overnight, until firm.

Wash strawberries and hull; mash enough to measure ½ cup; pour into a small saucepan.

Dissolve cornstarch in remaining ¼ cup water; stir into saucepan with remaining ¼ cup sugar. Cook, stirring constantly, until mixture thickens and boils 1 minute; remove from heat. Stir in a few drops food coloring to tint deep pink; cool.

Loosen cake around edge of pan with a knife; release spring and carefully lift off side of pan. Place cake, on its metal base, on a large serving plate.

Cut remaining strawberries in half and arrange in a pretty pattern on top of cake. Spoon glaze over berries to coat, letting some drip down side of cake. Chill 20 minutes until glaze sets, or until serving time.

Slice cake into wedges.
Yield: 10 to 12 servings.

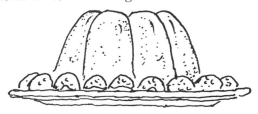

LEMON SNOW WITH STRAWBERRIES

1 package (6 ozs.) lemon-flavored gelatin
  Dash of salt
2 cups boiling water
1 can (6 ozs.) frozen concentrate for lemonade
1 cup cold water
2 egg whites
2 pints strawberries, washed, hulled, sliced, and sweetened

Dissolve gelatin and salt in boiling water in a large bowl; stir in lemonade concentrate and cold water. Place bowl in a pan of ice and water to speed setting. Chill, stirring several times, until mixture is syrupy-thick.

Stir in unbeaten egg whites. Keeping bowl over ice, beat rapidly until mixture triples in volume and starts to hold its shape; spoon into a 2½-quart mold. Chill several hours, or overnight, until firm.

When ready to serve, loosen dessert around edge with a knife; dip mold quickly in and out of warm water. Invert onto a rimmed serving plate; lift off mold. Spoon strawberries around edge on plate.
Yield: 10 servings.

PEACH-GLAZED CHEESECAKE

1½ cups zwieback crumbs
　1 tablespoon sugar (for crumb mixture)
　5 tablespoons butter or margarine, melted
　2 packages (8 ozs. each) cream cheese
　1 cup sugar (for filling)
　3 eggs
1⅓ cups dairy sour cream
⅔ cup whipping cream
　1 tablespoon grated orange rind
½ teaspoon vanilla
　1 package (10 ozs.) frozen sliced peaches
　1 tablespoon cornstarch
　2 teaspoons lemon juice

Preheat oven to 350°.

Lightly butter side of an 8-inch springform pan. Combine zwieback crumbs, the 1 tablespoon sugar, and melted butter in a medium bowl; mix until well blended. Press over bottom and 2 inches up side of pan. Set pan on a sheet of foil; fold foil up around side of pan to catch any butter that may drip out during baking. Chill crust while making filling.

Beat cream cheese with the 1 cup sugar until fluffy-light in a large bowl; very slowly beat in eggs, 1 at a time, until blended. Stir in sour cream, whipping cream, orange rind, and vanilla. Pour into prepared pan.

Bake 1 hour; turn off heat. Let cake stand in oven with door closed 1 hour. Cool in pan on a wire rack.

Thaw peaches as label directs. Drain syrup into a 1-cup measure, being careful not to break slices. Add water to syrup to make ¾ cup. Stir into cornstarch until smooth in a small saucepan; cook, stirring constantly, until mixture thickens and boils 1 minute; remove from heat. Stir in lemon juice; cool.

Arrange peach slices in a pretty pattern on top of cheesecake; spoon glaze over slices. Chill cake at least 6 hours, or overnight.

When ready to serve, loosen cake around edge of pan with a knife; release spring and carefully lift off side of pan. Place cake, on its metal base, on a serving plate. Cut into wedges.

Yield: 12 servings.

ICE CREAM DESSERTS

TOASTED ALMOND ALASKAS

1 frozen plain poundcake (11¼ ozs.), thawed
6 toasted almond ice-cream bars on sticks
3 egg whites
6 tablespoons sugar
1 teaspoon vanilla
¾ cup bottled butterscotch dessert topping

Cut cake crosswise into thirds, then split each piece; place in a single layer on a cookie sheet.

Let ice-cream bars stand at room temperature 3 to 4 minutes to soften, then remove sticks. (Job is easy if you place the bar on top of a piece of cake and slip the stick between the tines of a fork. Holding onto the end of the stick, gently pull while pushing bar in opposite direction.) Return to freezer while preparing meringue.

Preheat oven to 450°.

Beat egg whites in a medium bowl until foamy; slowly beat in sugar until meringue forms firm peaks; beat in vanilla. Spread over cake and ice cream, making swirls with spatula and spreading to bottom to seal in ice cream.

Bake 5 minutes, or until meringue is tipped with gold.

Remove at once to serving plates with a pancake turner; drizzle butterscotch topping over each.

Yield: 6 servings.

FROSTED LEMON CREAM

1 pint vanilla ice cream
3 tablespoons thawed frozen concentrate for lemonade
¼ cup coarsely crushed crisp macaroon cookies

Spread ice cream in a layer in an ice-cube tray. Drizzle lemonade concentrate on top, then swirl through ice cream with a knife. Sprinkle macaroon crumbs on top. Return to freezer until serving time.

Cut into blocks; lift onto dessert plates.
Yield: 4 servings.

APPLE-ORANGE CREAM

1 can (6 ozs.) frozen concentrate for orange juice
⅔ cup sugar
1 cup water
4 large apples, pared, halved, and cored
2 tablespoons cornstarch
2 tablespoons curaçao
1 quart vanilla ice cream

Combine orange concentrate, sugar, and water in a large skillet; heat to boiling. Place apple halves in a single layer in skillet. Heat to boiling again; simmer, turning apples once or twice, 10 minutes, or until tender but still firm enough to hold their shapes. Lift from syrup with a slotted spoon and place in a single layer in a large shallow dish.

Pour syrup into a 2-cup measure; add water, if needed, to make 2 cups. Stir slowly into cornstarch in a small saucepan. Cook, stirring constantly, until sauce thickens and boils 1 minute; stir in curaçao; pour over apples. Chill several hours.

When ready to serve, spoon ice cream into a mound in a shallow serving dish; stand apple halves around ice cream in dish. Garnish with a big spoonful of thawed frozen whipped topping and a slice of orange if you like. Serve sauce separately to spoon over each serving.

Yield: 8 servings.

CANTALOUPE COUPE

3 small cantaloupes
1 pint strawberries, hulled and cut in half
1 cup seedless green grapes
3 tablespoons sugar
3 tablespoons curaçao
1 pint orange-pineapple ice cream
⅔ cup flaked coconut
2 medium-sized firm ripe bananas

Cut cantaloupes in half crosswise; scoop out seeds. Cut fruit from rind in large pieces, leaving ¼-inch-thick shells. Turn shells upside down to drain, then wrap and chill.

Cut cantaloupe fruit into bite-sized pieces; combine with strawberries and grapes in a medium bowl. Sprinkle sugar and curaçao over top; toss lightly to mix; cover and chill.

Scoop ice cream into 6 small balls; roll each in coconut on waxed paper. Place on a plate and return to freezer.

When ready to serve, place each cantaloupe shell on a dessert plate. (If needed, trim a thin slice from rounded base so shell will sit flat on plate.)

Peel bananas and slice; stir into fruit mixture; spoon into cantaloupe shells. Top each with an ice-cream ball.

Yield: 6 servings.

Note: To cut cantaloupe basket, draw a line around the middle of the whole melon with a knife point, or mark with wooden picks. Then make even sawtooth cuts into cantaloupe above and below line, cutting to center. Gently pull halves apart.

CHOCOLATE CRUNCH PARFAITS

1 package (6 ozs.) semisweet chocolate pieces
3 cups plain granola-type cereal
1 quart butter-pecan ice cream

Melt chocolate until smooth in the top of a double boiler over hot water; remove from heat.

Stir in cereal until evenly coated. Spread out in a thin layer on a waxed-paper lined cookie sheet. Chill until cool and firm. Break into small pieces with a kitchen mallet or rolling pin.

Spoon half of the ice cream into 8 parfait glasses to make a layer in each; top with 3 to 4 tablespoons of the crumbled cereal mixture; repeat with remaining ice cream. Top with more cereal mixture. Place in freezer until serving time.

Yield: 8 servings.

Note: Store any leftover chocolate cereal mixture in a covered container in the refrigerator to use for another dessert or to serve as a candy-like treat.

CHERRY ALASKAS

1½ pints cherry-vanilla ice cream
6 tablespoons cherry preserves
6 packaged dessert shells
3 egg whites
6 tablespoons sugar
1 teaspoon vanilla

Scoop ice cream into 6 balls; place on a cookie sheet. Freeze several hours, or until very firm.

Spread 1 tablespoon of the cherry preserves on each dessert shell; place on a cookie sheet.

Preheat oven to 450°.

Beat egg whites in a medium bowl until foamy; very slowly beat in sugar until meringue forms firm peaks; beat in vanilla.

Place an ice-cream ball on each dessert shell; quickly frost with meringue, spreading to bottom to seal in ice cream. (If kitchen is warm and ice cream starts to melt, return to freezer until firm again. Meringue-covered shells may also be placed in freezer until all are finished.)

Bake 4 minutes, or until meringue is tipped with gold. Place on dessert plates. Serve at once.

Yield: 6 servings.

NESSELRODE CREAM CUPS

1 quart vanilla ice cream
½ cup Nesselrode dessert sauce
½ cup flaked coconut
4 large or 6 medium-sized seedless oranges
3 tablespoons chopped pistachio nuts

Soften ice cream slightly in a large bowl; stir in Nesselrode sauce and coconut. Spoon mixture into refrigerator trays; freeze until firm.

Slice off the top quarter of each orange; scoop out fruit, using a grapefruit knife or spoon. (Save fruit for breakfast another day.) Turn orange shells upside down on paper toweling to drain. For a festive look, make even sawtooth cuts around edges of shells.

Spoon ice cream into shells; sprinkle pistachio nuts on top. Stand cups in a large shallow pan; cover. Freeze until serving time.

Yield: 4 or 6 servings.

STRAWBERRY CREAM CAKE

2 pints strawberry ice cream
2 packaged 8-inch sponge layers
1 cup whipping cream
3 tablespoons sugar
1 pint strawberries

Line an 8-inch round layer-cake pan with waxed paper, allowing a 3-inch overhang. Pack ice cream into pan to make an even layer; fold waxed paper over top; freeze firm.

Place one sponge layer on a large freezer-proof serving plate. Uncover ice cream; unmold onto cake; peel off waxed paper. Top with second sponge layer; return to freezer.

Beat cream with 1 tablespoon of the sugar until stiff in a medium bowl; spread over side and top of cake; freeze.

Wash strawberries. Set aside 2 or 3 pretty ones for garnish, then hull remainder. Mash about half in a small bowl; slice the rest and stir in with remaining sugar.

About 20 minutes before serving, remove cake from freezer and let stand in refrigerator to soften. Cut into wedges; spoon strawberry sauce over each.

Yield: 8 servings.

COFFEE PUFFS

4 tablespoons butter or margarine
½ cup water (for batter)
½ cup sifted all-purpose flour
  Dash of salt
2 eggs
1 pint coffee ice cream
1 package (6 ozs.) semisweet chocolate pieces
5 tablespoons coffee-flavored liqueur
1 tablespoon water (for sauce)

Preheat oven to 400°.

Combine butter and the ½ cup water in a small saucepan; heat to boiling. Stir in flour and salt all at once with a wooden spoon; continue stirring until batter forms a thick smooth ball that follows spoon around pan. Remove from heat; cool slightly.

Beat in eggs, one at a time, until mixture is thick and shiny smooth. Drop into 6 even mounds, about 3 inches apart, on an ungreased cookie sheet.

Bake 35 minutes, or until golden. Remove puffs from cookie sheet to a wire rack; cool completely.

Cut a thin slice from the top of each puff; pull out any soft centers from bottoms with a fork. Spoon ice cream into shells; replace tops. Place on a flat plate or tray; place in freezer until serving time.

Combine chocolate, coffee liqueur, and the 1 tablespoon water in a small saucepan; heat very slowly, stirring constantly, until chocolate melts and sauce is smooth.

Remove puffs from freezer about 5 minutes before serving; place on dessert plates; spoon warm chocolate sauce over each. (If sauce is made ahead, reheat over hot water until warm.)

Yield: 6 servings.

CAKES AND FROSTINGS

MENTION A BIRTHDAY OR ANNIVERSARY and most of us think of a lavishly frosted and handsomely decorated cake as a lovely way to honor someone special. However, there's really no need to wait for a specific occasion like either of these; anytime is the right time for cake.

Most bakers consider cake-making a creative art and it truly is. But it's also an exacting one and not the time for improvising. Recipes are carefully worked out to blend ingredients perfectly and they must be put together in a certain way to be successful. Always follow your recipe accurately, and after the cake has baked and cooled, you can let your imagination get carried away, if you will, on the frosting and trimming.

Depending on your time and mood, you can make both cake and frosting from scratch or streamline the fixing with mixes and your own personal variations. This chapter is filled with how-to's for both.

You'll come across recipes for time-honored treats—gingerbread and upside-down cakes—that taste so good warm with a fluff of sauce or a dollop of ice cream or whipped cream. Some are the traveling kinds that conveniently go to picnics, barbecues, and church suppers right in their baking pans. Others, the types that especially please men, are moist and rich with fruits, nuts, sugar, and spice. Still another group includes pound cakes that are baked in attractive molds and topped with a simple glaze or a sprinkle of confectioners' sugar instead of frosting. There are angel, sponge, and chiffon cakes; jelly rolls; cupcakes; fruitcakes; party cakes for children; and dainty ones for teatime.

How to bake a perfect cake

Cake-making is neither difficult nor tricky if you keep in mind these basic pointers:
Follow directions exactly. Cakes fall into one of three categories—butter and shortening cakes, sponge and angel cakes that use no shortening, and chiffon cakes that are really a combination of the other two. All call for different ingredients and different methods of mixing. Trying to substitute ingredients or change the mixing method will only cause a failure.

Use the right pans; prepare them properly. For good size, shape, and texture, cakes should be baked in the pan called for in your recipe. If the pan is too large, the cake will be flat and underbrowned. If the pan is too small, the batter may overflow, bulge in the center, and lose its shape.

Use layer pans that are 1½ inches deep and squares or oblongs at least 2 inches in depth. Bright shiny metal pans are best for even, golden-brown crusts. Fill the pans only half full. If you want to use a fancy mold or odd-shaped pan such as a star, heart, or bell, measure the capacity first. Fill the pan with water, pour it into a large measure, divide in half, and use this amount of batter. If there's any left, bake it as cupcakes.

For butter and shortening cakes, grease bottoms and sides of pan generously with shortening, dust lightly with flour, and shake the pan until the flour coats the surface evenly. Tap out any excess. An alternate way: Grease the pan; line with waxed paper; grease the paper.

Tube pans that are used for angel, sponge, and chiffon cakes should not be greased. To rise properly and high, the batter must cling to the side and center tube. An exception to this rule is a jelly-roll pan. It should always be greased, lined with a rectangle of waxed paper cut ½-inch smaller than the pan, and the paper greased.

In baking fruitcakes, particularly large heavy ones, grease the pan, line the bottom with heavy brown paper or foil, and grease the paper.

Follow manufacturer's directions for all non-stick pans.

Mix the batter the right way. Before you start to make a cake, read the recipe carefully to make sure you understand the directions. For a conventional cake, start by creaming butter, margarine, or shortening thoroughly, then gradually add the sugar and continue creaming until the mixture is light and fluffy. If you're using an electric mixer, start creaming on low speed, then increase to medium as you add the sugar. Beat in the eggs, one at a time, beating about a minute after each is added; beat in flavorings next.

Return speed to low and beat in dry ingredients, alternately with liquid, beating only until flour disappears. During mixing, scrape the bowl several times to keep the batter blended.

One-bowl cakes, so called because everything is beaten together in a single bowl, are great time- and laborsavers, and were developed after the introduction of electric mixers and improved vegetable shortenings. Sifted dry ingredients go into the mixing bowl first, then add shortening and part of the liquid. Beat this mixture for 2 minutes at medium speed on a mixer; add remaining liquid, eggs, and flavorings; beat 2 minutes longer. For either the conventional or one-bowl methods, it's important not to overbeat the batter. Beating just enough to blend ingredients is the rule for conventional cakes; time and mixer speed are your guides for one-bowl cakes.

Angel, sponge, and chiffon cakes, often called the foam family, take their names from the light, airy texture of the batter that comes from meringue. In other ways, here's how they differ: Angel cakes contain no shortening and no egg yolks; sponge cakes call for both whites and yolks and may or may not contain cream of tartar or baking powder, but never shortening; chiffon cakes specify egg yolks and whites plus salad or vegetable oil.

Since all of these cakes rise high and light because of the air that's beaten into the eggs, remember these tips: Room temperature eggs will beat up best, although it's easier to separate yolks from whites if the eggs are cold from the refrigerator. Always beat the egg whites until they form stiff, straight peaks. Be sure your mixing bowl and beater are completely clean—the slightest trace of fat, oil, or egg yolks will keep whites from beating up.

Place pans correctly in oven. Start with the rack in the center of the oven. If you're baking only one cake, place the pan in the middle of the rack. Two pans should be placed on the rack at least 1 inch in from the edges of the oven and far enough from each other so the sides don't touch. For angel, sponge, and chiffon cakes, place the rack in the lower third of the oven, then set the pan in the middle of the rack.

Rely on these tests for doneness. Touch the center of a butter cake lightly with your fingertip; it will spring back, leaving no imprint, if the cake has baked completely. If done, the cake will also have started to shrink away from the side of the pan. Another tried-and-true test: Insert a wooden pick into the center of the cake. If the pick comes out clean, the cake is baked.

To test foam cakes, lightly touch cracks in the top; they should feel dry. Then touch an uncracked spot lightly, no imprint will remain if the cake is done. Regardless of the baking time given in any recipe, always be sure with one of these tests.

Cool cakes adequately and remove from pan. Cool a butter cake in its pan on a wire rack for 10 minutes, then loosen the cake from the side of the pan with a spatula or small-tip knife. Shake layer very gently to loosen the bottom; invert onto a wire rack; lift off pan; peel off waxed paper if pan was lined; turn layer right side up and cool completely.

Leave angel, sponge, and chiffon cakes in their pans until completely cold. As soon as the cake comes from the oven, turn it upside down on the feet around the side of the pan or stand it on the center tube if the tube is high enough. Otherwise, hang the tube over the neck of a bottle that's tall enough to keep the cake from touching the countertop or table.

To remove the cake from the pan, loosen it around side and tube with a knife, using an up-and-down motion. Invert the pan over a plate or wire rack, tap the side against the counter, and the cake will slip out easily.

Fill and frost a cake—prettily. Before frosting a layer cake, brush any loose crumbs from the edge. Place one layer, flat side up, on a plate or tray that's 1 to 2 inches larger than the cake. To keep plate clean, cut four strips of waxed paper and arrange under edge of cake to form a square.

Using a spatula, spread filling or about ½ cup frosting on layer to within ½ inch of edge; place second layer, flat side down, on top. (With flat sides of layers together, cake will be even.)

Spread a thin layer of frosting around side, then swirl on more, bringing the spatula up high enough to form a ¼-inch ridge of frosting above top of cake. Spread remaining frosting on top, working from center outward to meet the built up ridge. Make pretty swirls on top with spatula or leave smooth if you plan to add decorations. Gently pull out waxed-paper strips.

To frost an angel, sponge, or chiffon cake, leave cake, top side down, on plate. Brush off any loose crumbs. Coat side of cake with a thin layer of frosting to seal in any remaining crumbs, then swirl on more frosting, building up top edge the same as for butter cakes. Frost top last.

If you're glazing the cake, brush loose crumbs from top only. Pour or spoon a small amount of glaze mixture at a time onto top and spread to edge, letting it drip unevenly down side. Let cake stand until glaze is firm.

Cut cakes neatly. Use a sharp thin knife for butter cakes and a long serrated knife for angel, sponge, and chiffon cakes. With either, always cut with a sawing motion. If the frosting sticks to the knife, dip the knife in hot water and wipe it off with paper toweling after cutting each slice.

Store cakes properly. Wrap unfrosted layers or loaf cakes in foil or transparent wrap and keep at room temperature. If frosted with a creamy-type icing, place the cake in a covered cake keeper, or cover it with a large inverted bowl or pan. A cake with fluffy-type frosting tastes best served the same day it's made, but if you must store it overnight, cover it with a cake keeper or inverted bowl. Slip a knife or spoon handle under the edge of the container so it isn't airtight. Always store cakes with whipped cream frostings or cream fillings in the refrigerator.

HOW TO CUT ROUND CAKES

1. Cut an 8- or 9-inch double-layer cake into quarters; cut each quarter into 4 wedges.
2. Cut a small circle halfway to center in an 8- or 9-inch double-layer cake. Cut 24 pieces in outer circle and 4 wedges from inner one.
3. Cut an 8- or 9-inch double-layer cake into quarters; cut each quarter in 5 slices, then cut the two slices nearest the center in half.

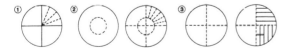

HOW TO CUT SQUARE CAKES

4. Cut an 8- or 9-inch single-layer cake in thirds or quarters lengthwise and crosswise.
5. Cut an 8- or 9-inch double-layer cake in quarters, then cut each quarter into 5 slices.

HOW TO CUT OBLONG CAKES

6. Cut a 13x9x2-inch cake into thirds lengthwise, then cut diagonally into 8 sections to make some triangles and some diamonds.
7. Cut a 15x10x1-inch cake into thirds crosswise and in sixths lengthwise. Cut middle section into squares and end sections into triangles to make dainty party servings.

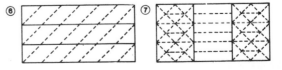

LAYERS AND LOAVES

ONE-BOWL CHOCOLATE CAKE

2¼ cups sifted cake flour (not self-rising)
2 cups granulated sugar
1½ teaspoons baking soda
1 teaspoon salt
2 teaspoons vinegar
1½ cups milk
½ cup shortening
2 eggs
4 squares unsweetened chocolate, melted and
    cooled
1 teaspoon vanilla

Grease two 9-inch round layer-cake pans;
dust lightly with flour.

Preheat oven to 350°.

Sift flour, sugar, baking soda, and salt into a
large bowl.

Stir vinegar into milk in a 2-cup measure; let
stand 10 minutes. Add to flour mixture with
shortening, eggs, cooled chocolate, and vanilla. Beat slowly until blended, then beat 3
minutes with electric mixer at medium speed,
scraping bowl once or twice. Pour into prepared pans.

Bake 30 minutes, or until centers spring
back when lightly pressed with fingertip.
Cool layers in pans on wire racks 10 minutes.
Loosen around edges with a knife; turn out
onto racks; cool completely.

Frost with Chocolate Rum Frosting (*see*
index for page of recipe) or any other frosting
of your choice.

Yield: One 9-inch double-layer cake.

OAHU PINEAPPLE CAKE

3 cups sifted cake flour (not self-rising)
1¾ cups granulated sugar (for cake)
4 teaspoons baking powder
1 teaspoon salt
⅔ cup shortening
1¼ cups milk
5 egg whites
2 teaspoons vanilla
2 tablespoons granulated sugar (for filling)
2 tablespoons cornstarch
1 can (20 ozs.) crushed pineapple in syrup
    White Mountain Frosting (recipe on page 491)
1 can (3½ ozs.) flaked coconut

Grease two 9-inch round layer-cake pans;
dust lightly with flour.

Preheat oven to 350°.

Sift flour, the 1¾ cups sugar, baking powder, and salt into a large bowl. Add shortening
and 1 cup of the milk; beat 2 minutes with
electric mixer at medium speed.

Add unbeaten egg whites, remaining ¼ cup
milk, and vanilla; beat 2 minutes longer at
medium speed until blended. Pour evenly
into prepared pans.

Bake 35 minutes, or until centers spring
back when lightly pressed with fingertip.
Cool in pans on wire racks 10 minutes. Loosen
around edges with a knife; turn out onto racks;
cool completely.

Mix the 2 tablespoons sugar and cornstarch
in a small saucepan; stir in pineapple and
syrup. Cook, stirring constantly, until mixture
thickens and boils 1 minute; remove from
heat; cool.

Prepare White Mountain Frosting.

Place one cake layer on a large serving
plate; spread half of the pineapple mixture on
top; cover with second layer.

Spread frosting around side of cake and 1
inch up over top. (A saucer or small paper
plate placed on center of cake makes a neat
guide.) Spread remaining pineapple mixture
in center. Pat coconut into frosting.

Yield: One 9-inch double-layer cake.

HAWAIIAN RIBBON CAKE

3¼ cups sifted cake flour (not self-rising)
2½ teaspoons baking powder
1 teaspoon salt
⅔ cup butter or margarine
1¾ cups granulated sugar
2 eggs
2 teaspoons vanilla
1¼ cups milk
1 teaspoon ground cinnamon
¼ teaspoon ground nutmeg
¼ teaspoon ground allspice
½ cup dark raisins
Pineapple-coconut Filling
(recipe on page 489)

Grease two 9-inch round layer-cake pans; line with waxed paper; grease paper.

Preheat oven to 350°.

Sift flour, baking powder, and salt onto waxed paper.

Cream butter and sugar in a large bowl until fluffy-light; beat in eggs, 1 at a time, until fluffy again; beat in vanilla.

Slowly beat in flour mixture, alternately with milk, just until blended. Pour half into one layer pan.

Stir cinnamon, nutmeg, allspice, and raisins into remaining batter in bowl; pour into second pan.

Bake 30 minutes, or until centers spring back when lightly pressed with fingertip. Cool layers in pans on wire racks 10 minutes. Loosen around edges with a knife; turn out onto racks; peel off waxed paper. Cool layers completely.

Make Pineapple-coconut Filling.

Split each cake layer evenly. Place one raisin layer, cut side up, on a large serving plate; top with about 1 cup of the pineapple mixture. Cover with a yellow layer; top with another cup filling. Repeat with remaining layers, using 1 cup filling between and the rest on top of cake. Garnish with a ring of candied red cherries and mint if you like.

Yield: One 9-inch four-layer cake.

SEAFOAM DEVIL'S FOOD

2 cups sifted cake flour (not self-rising)
2 cups granulated sugar
1 teaspoon baking soda
½ teaspoon salt
½ cup butter or margarine
¾ cup buttermilk
4 squares unsweetened chocolate, melted and cooled
2 teaspoons vanilla
3 eggs
⅓ cup water
Seafoam Frosting (recipe on page 490)
½ cup chopped California walnuts

Grease two 9-inch round layer-cake pans; dust lightly with flour.

Preheat oven to 350°.

Sift flour, sugar, baking soda, and salt into a large bowl. Add butter, buttermilk, chocolate, and vanilla; beat 2 minutes with electric mixer at high speed.

Add eggs and water; beat 2 minutes at medium speed. Pour evenly into prepared pans.

Bake 30 minutes, or until centers spring back when lightly pressed with fingertip. Cool layers in pans on wire racks 10 minutes. Loosen around edges with a knife; turn out onto racks; cool completely.

Prepare Seafoam Frosting. Spread about 1 cup over one cake layer; place on a serving plate; top with remaining layer. Spread remaining frosting on side and top of cake, making deep swirls with spatula. Trim with a ring of walnuts.

Yield: One 9-inch double-layer cake.

SWEETHEART BIRTHDAY CAKE

3¾ cups sifted cake flour (not self-rising)
3¾ teaspoons baking powder
¼ teaspoon salt
¾ cup butter or margarine
2¼ cups granulated sugar
4 teaspoons grated lemon rind
2 teaspoons vanilla
9 egg yolks
1¾ cups milk
    Raspberry Filling (recipe on page 490)
    Butter Cream Frosting (recipe on page 490)
    Red food coloring

Grease three 9-inch round layer-cake pans; dust lightly with flour.

Preheat oven to 350°.

Sift flour, baking powder, and salt into a large bowl.

Cream butter with sugar in a large bowl until fluffy-light; stir in lemon rind and vanilla. Beat in egg yolks, one at a time, until fluffy again. Slowly beat in flour mixture, alternately with milk, just until blended. Pour evenly into prepared pans.

Bake 25 minutes, or until centers spring back when lightly pressed with fingertip. Cool layers in pans on wire racks 10 minutes. Loosen around edges with a knife; turn out onto racks; cool completely.

Make Raspberry Filling. Spread over two of the cake layers; stack on a large serving plate; place plain layer on top.

Make Butter Cream Frosting. Measure ⅔ cup into a small bowl and tint pink with a few drops food coloring.

Spread remaining white frosting over side and top of cake, then spread into a smooth layer with spatula.

For decorating, you will need two star tubes (#27 and #30) and one round or writing tube (#2) for pastry bag.

Spoon pink frosting into bag; attach tube #27. Press out a border of small rosettes around top of cake. Change to tube #30; press out a larger border around base of cake. Change to tube #2 and pipe a swag around side of cake, attaching frosting to top edge every inch; pipe a smaller swag inside each large scallop. Change to tube #27; press out a small rosette inside each small scallop and a row around each large scallop, following curved line. Pressing constantly and using same tube, outline a heart on top of cake. Change to tube #2; write a birthday greeting inside heart. Let cake stand until frosting is firm.

Yield: One 9-inch triple-layer cake.

BASIC ONE-EGG CAKE

1⅓ cups sifted cake flour (not self-rising)
2 teaspoons baking powder
½ teaspoon salt
⅔ cup granulated sugar
½ cup shortening
½ cup milk
1 egg
1 teaspoon vanilla

Grease a baking pan, 8x8x2 inches; dust lightly with flour.

Preheat oven to 350°.

Sift flour, baking powder, salt, and sugar into a medium bowl. Add shortening and milk; beat slowly until blended, then beat 2 minutes with electric mixer at medium speed, scraping bowl once or twice.

Add egg and vanilla; beat 2 minutes longer. Spoon into prepared pan.

Bake 30 minutes, or until center springs back when lightly pressed with fingertip. Cool in pan on a wire rack 10 minutes. Loosen around edges with a knife; turn out onto rack; cool completely. Frost with Easy Fudge Frosting (recipe on page 491) or any other frosting of your choice.

Yield: One 8x8-inch square.

DOUBLE PRUNE CAKE

    2 cups sifted cake flour (not self-rising)
1½ cups granulated sugar
    2 teaspoons baking powder
    ¼ teaspoon baking soda
    ½ teaspoon ground cinnamon
    ½ teaspoon ground nutmeg
    ½ teaspoon ground allspice
        Salt
    ½ cup butter or margarine
    1 cup milk
    2 eggs
    1 cup dried pitted prunes (about 16)
    ½ cup water
    1 unbeaten egg white
    ½ cup firmly packed light brown sugar
    1 teaspoon vanilla
    1 teaspoon lemon juice

Grease two 8-inch round layer-cake pans; dust lightly with flour.

Preheat oven to 350°.

Sift flour, 1¼ cups of the granulated sugar, baking powder, soda, cinnamon, nutmeg, allspice, and ½ teaspoon salt into a large bowl; add butter and ¾ cup of the milk. Beat 2 minutes with electric mixer at medium speed, scraping bowl once or twice.

Add remaining ¼ cup milk and eggs; beat 2 minutes longer at medium speed, or until batter is smooth. Pour evenly into prepared pans.

Bake 25 minutes, or until centers spring back when lightly pressed with fingertip. Cool layers in pans on wire racks 10 minutes. Loosen around edges with a knife; turn out onto racks; cool completely.

While cake bakes and cools, combine prunes and water in a small saucepan; heat to boiling; cover. Cook 1 minute; remove from heat; let stand until cool. Drain liquid into a cup; chop prunes. (There should be about ¾ cup.)

Combine egg white, brown sugar, remaining ¼ cup granulated sugar, a dash of salt, and 3 tablespoons of the prune liquid in the top of a double boiler. Beat slowly until blended; place over boiling water. Beat constantly at high speed on electric mixer 7 minutes, or until frosting forms firm peaks; remove from heat; stir in vanilla.

Measure ½ cup of the frosting and combine with chopped prunes and lemon juice in a small bowl. Spread over one layer on a serving plate; top with second layer.

Spread remaining plain frosting on side and top of cake, making deep swirls with spatula. Garnish top with chopped or halved California walnuts if you like. Let cake stand until frosting sets.

Yield: One 8-inch double-layer cake.

CHOCOLATE CUPCAKES

1½ cups sifted cake flour (not self-rising)
    1 teaspoon baking soda
    ½ teaspoon salt
    ⅓ cup shortening
1¼ cups firmly packed light brown sugar
    2 eggs
    2 squares unsweetened chocolate, melted and
        cooled
    1 teaspoon vanilla
    ¾ cup milk

Line medium-sized muffin-pan cups with paper baking cups.

Preheat oven to 350°.

Sift flour, baking soda, and salt onto waxed paper.

Cream shortening with brown sugar in a large bowl until fluffy-light; beat in eggs, melted chocolate, and vanilla.

Beat in flour mixture, alternately with milk, just until blended. Spoon into cups, filling each half full.

Bake 20 minutes, or until centers spring back when lightly pressed with fingertip. Remove from cups to wire racks; cool completely. Frost with Easy Fudge Frosting (recipe on page 491) or any other frosting of your choice.

Yield: 18 medium cupcakes.

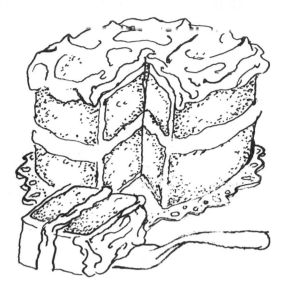

GOLDEN LAYER CAKE

  3 cups sifted cake flour (not self-rising)
2½ teaspoons baking powder
  ½ teaspoon salt
  ⅓ cup shortening
1¾ cups granulated sugar
  2 eggs
  2 teaspoons vanilla
1¼ cups milk

Grease two 9-inch round layer-cake pans; dust lightly with flour.

Preheat oven to 350°.

Sift flour, baking powder, and salt onto waxed paper.

Cream shortening and sugar in a large bowl until fluffy-light; beat in eggs and vanilla.

Beat in flour mixture, a third at a time, alternately with milk, just until blended. Pour into prepared pans.

Bake 30 minutes, or until golden and centers spring back when lightly pressed with fingertip. Cool layers in pans on wire racks 10 minutes. Loosen around edges with a knife; turn out onto racks; cool completely.

Frost with Coffee Cream Frosting (recipe on page 490) or any other frosting of your choice.

Yield: One 9-inch double-layer cake.

DOUBLE APPLE CAKE

2½ cups sifted cake flour (not self-rising)
1¼ cups granulated sugar
1½ teaspoons baking soda
  2 teaspoons pumpkin-pie spice
  ½ teaspoon salt
  ½ cup shortening
  1 can or jar (15 ozs.) applesauce
  2 eggs
  2 tablespoons butter or margarine
  3 cups confectioners' powdered sugar
  ½ cup apple butter

Grease two 8-inch round layer-cake pans; dust lightly with flour.

Preheat oven to 350°.

Sift flour, granulated sugar, baking soda, pumpkin-pie spice, and salt into a large bowl. Add shortening and applesauce; beat 2 minutes with electric mixer at medium speed.

Add eggs; beat 2 minutes longer at medium speed. Spread evenly into prepared pans.

Bake 35 minutes, or until centers spring back when lightly pressed with fingertip. Cool in pans on wire racks 10 minutes. Loosen around edges with a knife; turn out onto racks; cool completely.

Cream butter with ½ cup of the confectioners' sugar until fluffy in a medium bowl; slowly beat in remaining confectioners' sugar, adding alternately with apple butter, until frosting is smooth and easy to spread.

Place one cake layer on a large serving plate; spread about ¾ cup of the frosting over top; cover with second layer. Spread remaining frosting around side and top of cake, making swirls with spatula. If you like, garnish with red-skinned apple slices dipped in lemon juice.

Yield: One 8-inch double-layer cake.

GOLDEN CUPCAKES

2 cups sifted cake flour (not self-rising)
2 teaspoons baking powder
½ teaspoon salt
⅔ cup butter or margarine
¾ cup granulated sugar
1 egg
1 teaspoon vanilla
⅔ cup milk

Line medium-sized muffin-pan cups with paper baking cups.

Preheat oven to 350°.

Sift flour, baking powder, and salt onto waxed paper.

Cream butter with sugar in a large bowl until fluffy-light; beat in egg and vanilla.

Beat in flour mixture, alternately with milk, just until blended. Spoon into cups, filling each half full.

Bake 25 minutes, or until centers spring back when lightly pressed with fingertip. Remove from cups to wire racks; cool completely. Frost with Easy Fudge Frosting (recipe on page 491) or any other frosting of your choice.

Yield: 18 medium cupcakes.

YULETIDE PEPPERMINT CAKE

1¾ cups sifted cake flour (not self-rising)
2 teaspoons baking powder
¼ teaspoon salt
½ cup shortening
1 cup granulated sugar
3 eggs
2 teaspoons vanilla
⅔ cup milk
3 tablespoons hot water
2 squares unsweetened chocolate, melted and cooled
¼ teaspoon baking soda
1 tablespoon butter or margarine, melted
1 cup confectioners' powdered sugar
⅛ teaspoon peppermint extract
Red food coloring
1 small peppermint candy stick, crushed

Preheat oven to 350°.

Sift flour, baking powder, and salt onto waxed paper.

Cream shortening with granulated sugar in a large bowl until fluffy-light; beat in eggs, 1 at a time, until fluffy again; beat in vanilla.

Stir in flour mixture, alternating with milk, until blended.

Stir 2 tablespoons of the hot water into melted chocolate in a small bowl; stir in baking soda. Spoon one fourth of the cake batter into a medium bowl; stir in chocolate mixture until no streaks of yellow remain.

Spoon half of the yellow batter into a greased 1½-quart fluted tube pan; spread all of the chocolate batter on top; spoon remaining yellow batter over chocolate.

Bake 40 minutes, or until golden and a wooden pick inserted near center comes out clean. Cool in pan on a wire rack 10 minutes; loosen around edge and tube with a knife; turn out onto rack; cool completely.

Combine melted butter, confectioners' sugar, peppermint extract, and remaining 1 tablespoon water in a small bowl; beat until smooth. (If needed, stir in ½ to 1 teaspoonful more hot water to make glaze thin enough to pour from a spoon.) Tint pink with a few drops food coloring. Spoon over cake to cover completely. Sprinkle crushed candy on top. Let stand until glaze is firm.

Yield: One 9-inch tube cake.

STRAWBERRY TEA CAKES

    3 cups sifted cake flour (not self-rising)
1¼ teaspoons baking powder
  ¾ teaspoon salt
1½ cups butter or margarine, softened
    2 cups granulated sugar
    4 eggs
    1 tablespoon grated lemon rind
    2 tablespoons lemon juice
1¼ cups milk
    1 package (16 ozs.) confectioners' powdered
       sugar
    1 teaspoon vanilla
       Red food coloring
    3 tablespoons strawberry preserves
       Candy strawberries

Grease a baking pan, 13x9x2 inches; dust lightly with flour.

Preheat oven to 350°.

Sift flour, baking powder, and salt onto waxed paper.

Cream 1 cup of the butter in a large bowl until fluffy-light; add granulated sugar and eggs all at once; beat with electric mixer at high speed 3 minutes. (Do not underbeat.) Beat in lemon rind and juice.

Beat in flour mixture, a third at a time, adding alternately with 1 cup of the milk; beat at low speed just until blended. Spread evenly into prepared pan.

Bake 45 minutes, or until center springs back when lightly pressed with fingertip. Cool 10 minutes in pan on a wire rack. Loosen around edges with a knife; turn out onto rack; cool completely.

Beat remaining ½ cup butter and half of the confectioners' sugar in a large bowl until blended. Slowly beat in the rest of the confectioners' sugar, adding alternately with 3 tablespoons of the remaining milk until mixture is smooth and stiff; beat in vanilla and a few drops food coloring to tint bright pink.

Measure out 1 cup of the mixture and beat in strawberry preserves to make filling. Beat remaining 1 tablespoon milk into frosting mixture in large bowl.

Trim crusts from edges of cake, then cut cake crosswise into 8 even strips. Split each strip; put back together with strawberry filling between layers. Spread plain pink frosting over tops, making deep swirls with spatula. Cut each strip crosswise into 5 tiny cakes; trim each with a candy strawberry.

Yield: 40 miniature cakes.

BANANA JELLY SQUARES

2¼ cups sifted all-purpose flour
1½ cups granulated sugar
1¼ teaspoons baking soda
    1 teaspoon salt
  ¾ teaspoon baking powder
    1 tablespoon lemon juice
  ⅔ cup milk
  ⅔ cup shortening
    3 eggs
1½ cups mashed ripe bananas (3 medium)
    1 jar (10 ozs.) strawberry jelly
    1 can (3½ ozs.) flaked coconut

Grease a baking pan, 13x9x2 inches; dust lightly with flour.

Preheat oven to 350°.

Sift flour, sugar, baking soda, salt, and baking powder into a large bowl.

Stir lemon juice into milk in measuring cup; let stand several minutes. Add to flour mixture with shortening, eggs, and mashed bananas. Beat slowly with electric mixer until blended, then beat 3 minutes at high speed, scraping bowl several times. Pour into prepared pan, spreading top even.

Bake 35 minutes, or until golden and a wooden pick inserted into center comes out clean. Cool completely in pan on a wire rack.

Beat jelly with a fork or spoon in a small bowl until broken up; spread evenly over cake. Sprinkle coconut over jelly.

To serve, cut into squares.

Yield: 12 servings.

PICNIC PRUNE CAKE

  1 cup snipped pitted dried prunes
  ½ cup water (for prunes)
2½ cups sifted all-purpose flour
  1 teaspoon baking soda
  1 teaspoon salt
1½ teaspoons ground cinnamon
  1 teaspoon ground nutmeg
  3 eggs
1½ cups granulated sugar
  1 cup salad oil
  ½ cup buttermilk
  1 cup chopped California walnuts
  2 cups sifted confectioners' powdered sugar
  4 teaspoons lemon juice
  1 tablespoon water (for frosting)

Combine prunes and the ½ cup water in a small saucepan. Heat to boiling, then cook 5 minutes; pour into a 1-cup measure. (There should be 1 cup.)

Grease a baking pan, 13x9x2 inches; dust lightly with flour.

Preheat oven to 350°.

Sift flour, soda, salt, cinnamon, and nutmeg onto waxed paper.

Beat eggs well in a large bowl; slowly beat in granulated sugar until fluffy-light. Beat in salad oil, then buttermilk; stir in prune mixture. Slowly beat in flour mixture until well blended; fold in walnuts. Spread evenly into prepared pan.

Bake 45 minutes, or until center springs back when lightly pressed with fingertip. Cool in pan on a wire rack.

Mix confectioners' sugar and lemon juice in a small bowl. Stir in the 1 tablespoon water; blend until smooth; spread over cake. Decorate with walnut halves if you like. Cut lengthwise, then crosswise into quarters.

Yield: 16 servings.

POT O' GOLD CAKE

  2 cups granulated sugar
1¾ cups sifted all-purpose flour
  2 teaspoons baking soda
  1 teaspoon salt
  ⅓ cup presweetened wheat germ
  1 cup salad oil
  4 eggs
  3 cups grated pared raw carrots
  2 tablespoons butter or margarine
1½ cups sifted confectioners' powdered sugar
  4 teaspoons lemon juice
  1 tablespoon milk

Grease three 8-inch round layer-cake pans; dust lightly with flour.

Preheat oven to 350°.

Sift granulated sugar, flour, baking soda, and salt into a large bowl. Stir in wheat germ, then stir in salad oil until evenly moist.

Beat in eggs, 1 at a time, beating well after each addition; stir in carrots. Spoon batter evenly into prepared pans.

Bake 40 minutes, or until centers spring back when lightly pressed with fingertip. (Do not open oven door during first half hour of baking.) Cool layers in pans on wire racks 10 minutes. Loosen around edges with a knife; turn out onto racks; cool completely.

Cream butter in a medium bowl; slowly beat in confectioners' sugar, alternately with lemon juice and milk, until frosting is smooth and easy to spread.

Spread about ¼ cup over each layer; stack on a serving plate. (Do not frost side of cake.) Let stand until frosting is firm.

Yield: One 8-inch triple-layer cake.

MOCHA MARBLE LOAF

1¾ cups sifted cake flour (not self-rising)
2 teaspoons baking powder
¼ teaspoon salt
½ cup shortening
1 cup granulated sugar
3 eggs
2 teaspoons vanilla
⅔ cup milk
5 teaspoons freeze-dried instant coffee
6 tablespoons hot water
1 square unsweetened chocolate, melted and cooled
¼ teaspoon baking soda
0 tablespoons butter or margarine
1 package (about 15 ozs.) creamy white frosting mix
Chocolate curls

Grease a loaf pan, 9x5x3 inches; dust lightly with flour.

Preheat oven to 350°.

Sift flour, baking powder, and salt onto waxed paper.

Cream shortening with sugar in a large bowl until fluffy-light; beat in eggs, one at a time, until fluffy again; beat in vanilla.

Beat in flour mixture, part at a time, alternately with milk, just until blended.

Dissolve 3 teaspoons of the coffee in 2 tablespoons of the hot water in a medium bowl; stir in melted chocolate and soda. Stir in half of the cake batter until no streaks of yellow remain.

Spoon plain batter, alternating with spoonfuls of chocolate batter, into prepared pan; draw through batter with a knife to marble.

Bake 50 minutes, or until center springs back when lightly pressed with fingertip.

Cool in pan on a wire rack 10 minutes. Loosen around edges with a knife; turn out onto rack; cool completely. Place on a serving plate.

Dissolve remaining 2 teaspoons coffee in remaining 4 tablespoons hot water in a medium bowl; add butter and frosting mix; beat as frosting mix label directs. Spread over side and top of cake, making deep swirls with spatula. Garnish with chocolate curls. Let stand until frosting is set.

Yield: 1 loaf, 9x5x3 inches.

ORANGE POUNDCAKE

3 cups sifted cake flour (not self-rising)
1¼ teaspoons baking powder
¾ teaspoon salt
1 cup butter or margarine
2 cups granulated sugar
4 eggs
1 tablespoon grated orange rind
2 teaspoons orange extract
1 cup milk
Confectioners' powdered sugar

Grease a 3-quart tube pan or 10-inch angel-cake pan.

Preheat oven to 350°.

Sift flour, baking powder, and salt onto waxed paper.

Cream butter in a large bowl until fluffy-light; add granulated sugar and eggs all at once; beat 3 minutes with electric mixer at high speed. (Do not underbeat.) Beat in orange rind and extract.

Beat in flour mixture, a third at a time, adding alternately with milk; beat at low speed just until blended. Pour into prepared pan.

Bake 1 hour, or until a wooden pick inserted near center comes out clean. Cool in pan on a wire rack 10 minutes. Loosen around edge and tube with a knife; turn out onto rack; cool completely. Just before serving, sprinkle confectioners' sugar over top.

Yield: One 10-inch tube cake.

GINGERBREAD

1¾ cups sifted all-purpose flour
1 teaspoon baking soda
1 teaspoon ground ginger
½ teaspoon ground cinnamon
⅛ teaspoon ground cloves
¼ teaspoon salt
⅓ cup shortening
⅓ cup granulated sugar
¾ cup dark molasses
1 egg
½ cup hot water

Preheat oven to 350°.

Sift flour, baking soda, ginger, cinnamon, cloves, and salt onto waxed paper.

Cream shortening with sugar in a large bowl until fluffy-light; beat in molasses and egg.

Stir in flour mixture, half at a time, until blended; beat in hot water until mixture is smooth. Pour into a greased baking pan, 8x8x2 inches.

Bake 45 minutes, or until center springs back when lightly pressed with fingertip.

Cool in pan on a wire rack. Cut into squares. Serve plain or topped with a sprinkle of confectioners' sugar or lemon sauce if you like.

Yield: 9 servings.

DIXIE PRUNE CAKE

¾ cup snipped pitted dried prunes
   Water
2½ cups sifted all-purpose flour
1 teaspoon baking soda
1 teaspoon salt
1½ teaspoons ground cinnamon
1 teaspoon ground nutmeg
¼ teaspoon ground cloves
1 cup chopped California walnuts
½ cup milk
½ teaspoon vinegar
3 eggs
2 cups granulated sugar
1 cup salad oil
¼ cup butter or margarine
2 tablespoons lemon juice

Generously grease a 3-quart tube pan or 10-inch angel-cake pan; dust lightly with flour.

Preheat oven to 350°.

Combine prunes and ⅓ cup water in a small saucepan; heat to boiling; simmer 5 minutes. Pour prunes and liquid into a 1-cup measure. (There should be 1 cup.)

Sift flour, baking soda, salt, cinnamon, nutmeg, and cloves into a medium bowl; stir in walnuts.

Combine milk and vinegar in a cup; let stand several minutes.

Beat eggs well in a large bowl; slowly beat in 1½ cups of the sugar, then salad oil and milk mixture; stir in prune mixture. Beat in flour mixture, half at a time, until blended. Pour into prepared pan.

Bake 1 hour, or until top springs back when lightly pressed with fingertip. Cool in pan on a wire rack 15 minutes; remove from pan; place on a large serving plate.

While cake bakes, combine remaining ½ cup sugar, butter, and ¼ cup water in a small saucepan. Heat to boiling; simmer 5 minutes; remove from heat. Stir in lemon juice. While hot, spoon over warm cake, letting mixture soak in. Spoon any that drips onto plate back over cake. Let cake stand until cold. Cut into wedges.

Yield: One 10-inch tube cake.

CAROUSEL CAKE

1 package yellow cake mix
 Eggs
 Water
½ cup peanut butter
1 package (16 ozs.) confectioners' powdered sugar
7 tablespoons milk
10 peppermint candy sticks
10 animal crackers
¼ cup strawberry jelly
1 small green candy ball

Preheat oven to 350°.

Prepare cake mix with eggs and water, bake in two 8-inch round layer-cake pans, cool, and remove from pans as label directs.

Cream peanut butter and 1 cup of the confectioners' sugar until smooth in a medium bowl; beat in remaining confectioners' sugar, alternately with milk, until frosting is smooth and easy to spread. Measure out ⅓ cup and set aside for decorating top

Place one cake layer on a large serving plate; spread about ½ cup of the frosting over layer; cover with second layer. Spread remaining frosting on side and top, making top smooth. Press peppermint sticks, cutting to fit if needed, into frosting around side of cake.

Spoon the ⅓ cup frosting into a pastry bag or cake-decorating set; attach writing tube (#2). Press out just enough of the frosting around each animal cracker to outline; place a dot of frosting on back of each; press onto peppermint sticks to resemble animals on a merry-go-round.

Remove tube #2 from pastry bag and attach a rosette tube (#27). Press out some of the remaining frosting in ribbons on top of cake to divide into 8 or 10 wedge-shaped sections; press out the rest around top edge to make a border.

Spread jelly in alternate sections on top of cake; place candy ball in center. Let stand until frosting is firm.

Yield: 10 servings.

MOCHA RIBBON CAKE

4 tablespoons dry instant coffee (not freeze-dried)
1⅓ cups water
1 package marble cake mix
2 eggs
1 package (about 15 ozs.) creamy white frosting mix
1½ cups whipping cream
 Chocolate curls

Grease two 9-inch round layer-cake pans; dust lightly with flour.

Dissolve 2 tablespoons of the instant coffee in water in a 2-cup measure.

Prepare cake mix with eggs and the 1⅓ cups coffee as label directs; pour half of the batter into one pan.

Stir marbling mixture from cake mix package into remaining batter in bowl; spoon into second pan.

Bake layers, remove from pans, and cool as label directs.

While layers cool, stir frosting mix and remaining 2 tablespoons instant coffee into whipping cream in a medium bowl; chill 1 hour or longer. Beat mixture until stiff.

Split cake layers to make four thin layers; place one layer on a serving plate. Spread a scant one fourth of the frosting mixture over top. Cover with a coffee-flavored layer; spread another one fourth of the frosting over top. Repeat with remaining two layers; spread the rest of the frosting over side and top of cake. Garnish with chocolate curls. Chill cake until serving time.

Yield: One 9-inch four-layer cake.

CHEERY CHERRY CAKE

1 package chocolate cake mix
Eggs
Water
1 package fluffy white frosting mix
1½ cups whipping cream
1 teaspoon vanilla
1 can (about 21 ozs.) cherry pie filling
Red food coloring

Prepare cake mix with eggs and water, bake in two 8-inch round layer-cake pans, cool, and remove from pans as label directs.

Combine dry frosting mix and cream in a small deep bowl; chill at least an hour.

When ready to assemble cake, stir vanilla into cherry pie filling in a small bowl. Add a few drops food coloring to frosting mixture to tint pink; beat until stiff.

Place one cake layer on a serving plate. Spread ¾ cup of the frosting mixture over layer; top with about 1 cupful of the cherry pie filling, then second cake layer. Save about 3 tablespoons of the frosting mixture for center, then spread remainder around side of cake and 1 inch up over edge, making deep swirls with spatula. Spoon the 3 tablespoons in a small *pouf* in center. Pick out 3 or 4 cherries and trim center *pouf;* spoon remaining cherry mixture between rings of frosting. Chill cake until serving time.

Yield: 12 servings.

CHOCO-PEACH CAKE

1 package chocolate cake mix
Eggs
Water
1 package (1½ ozs.) whipped topping mix
¾ cup milk
1½ teaspoons vanilla
1 jar (10 ozs.) peach preserves
2 squares semisweet chocolate
½ cup butter or margarine
1 package (16 ozs.) confectioners' powdered
sugar, sifted
Chocolate sprinkles

Prepare cake mix with eggs and water, bake in two 8-inch round layer-cake pans, cool, and remove from pans as label directs. Split each layer.

Prepare whipped topping mix with ½ cup of the milk and ½ teaspoon of the vanilla as label directs.

Spread ¼ cup of the peach preserves, then ⅔ cup of the whipped topping on each of three cake layers; stack back together on a serving plate; top with remaining plain layer.

Melt chocolate in a cup over hot water; cool.

Cream butter with about 1 cup of the confectioners' sugar in a large bowl until fluffy; beat in cooled chocolate, then slowly beat in remaining confectioners' sugar, adding alternately with remaining ¼ cup milk, until frosting is smooth and easy to spread; beat in remaining 1 teaspoon vanilla.

Measure out ½ cup of the frosting and set aside; spread remainder over side and top of cake, building up top edge slightly.

Spoon the ½ cup frosting into a cake-decorating set; attach rosette tube (#27). Press frosting out around top edge of cake to form a scallop design. Spoon remaining peach preserves inside scallops. Press chocolate sprinkles into frosting around side of cake. Let stand until frosting is firm.

Yield: One 8-inch four-layer cake.

ORANGE PINEAPPLE TORTE

1 package orange cake mix
 Eggs
 Water
1 jar (12 ozs.) pineapple preserves
¼ cup thawed frozen concentrate for pineapple
    juice
2 packages fluffy white frosting mix

Preheat oven to 350°.

Prepare cake mix with eggs and water, bake in two 8-inch round layer-cake pans, cool, and remove from pans as label directs.

Split each layer in half to make 4 layers; spread pineapple preserves over 3 layers.

Heat ¼ cup water and pineapple concentrate to boiling in a small saucepan; stir into 1 package of the frosting mix in a small deep bowl; beat as label directs. Spread over preserves on layers; stack on a serving plate; top with plain layer.

Prepare second package of frosting mix with boiling water as label directs; frost side and top of cake. Decorate with fresh orange sections and chopped pistachio nuts if you like.

Yield: One 8-inch four-layer torte.

EMERALD ISLE COCONUT CAKE

1 package white cake mix
 Egg whites
 Water
 Lime Filling (recipe on page 489)
 Emerald Coconut (directions follow)
1 package fluffy white frosting mix
 Boiling water

Prepare cake mix with egg whites and water, bake in two 8-inch round layer-cake pans, remove from pans, and cool as label directs.

Prepare Lime Filling. Prepare Emerald Coconut.

Prepare frosting mix with boiling water as label directs.

Place one cake layer on a large serving plate; spread lime mixture over top; cover with second layer. Spread frosting over side and top of cake, making deep swirls with spatula. Pat Emerald Coconut over side and top.

Yield: One 8-inch double-layer cake.

Make Emerald Coconut: Empty 1 can (3½ ozs.) flaked coconut into a jar with a tight lid. Mix 1 teaspoon lime juice with 2 or 3 drops green food coloring in a cup; pour into jar; cover. Shake until coconut is evenly tinted.

APPLE-DATE CAKE

1 package spicecake mix
½ cup finely chopped dates
½ cup finely chopped California walnuts
2 eggs
1 can or jar (15 ozs.) applesauce
 Lemon Cream Frosting (recipe on page 492)

Grease two 8-inch round layer-cake pans; dust lightly with flour.

Preheat oven to 350°.

Measure ¼ cup of the cake mix and combine with dates and walnuts in a small bowl; toss to coat dates evenly.

Combine remaining cake mix, eggs, and applesauce in a large bowl; beat as label directs; fold in date mixture. Pour into prepared pans.

Bake 40 minutes, or until golden and centers spring back when-lightly pressed with fingertip. Cool layers in pans on wire racks 10 minutes. Loosen around edges with a knife; turn out onto racks; cool completely.

Prepare Lemon Cream Frosting. Fill and frost cake. Decorate with finely chopped walnuts sprinkled on top of cake in a petal design if you like.

Yield: One 8-inch double-layer cake.

LADY BALTIMORE CAKE

1 package white cake mix
2 egg whites
  Water
  Classic Seven-minute Frosting (recipe on
    page 491)
½ cup chopped dark raisins
⅓ cup finely snipped dried figs
⅓ cup chopped California walnuts

Prepare cake mix with egg whites and 1⅓ cups water, bake in two 8-inch round layer-cake pans, remove from pans, and cool as label directs.

Prepare Classic Seven-minute Frosting.

Spoon one third into a small bowl; stir in raisins, figs, and walnuts. Spread over one cake layer on a serving plate; cover with second layer. Spread remaining plain frosting over side and top of cake, making deep swirls with spatula. Garnish top with chopped candied red cherries if you like.

Yield: One 8-inch double-layer cake.

CRAZY CLOWN CAKE

1 package yellow cake mix
⅔ cup red Hawaiian punch drink mix
¼ cup cornstarch
4 eggs
⅔ cup salad oil
1 cup water
½ cup shortening
1 package (16 ozs.) confectioners' powdered
    sugar
6 tablespoons milk
1 can (3½ ozs.) flaked coconut
  Colored gum candies
  Foil

Grease and flour a 3-quart tube pan.

Preheat oven to 350°.

Combine cake mix, ⅓ cup of the Hawaiian punch drink mix, and cornstarch in a large bowl; stir to mix well.

Add eggs, salad oil, and water; beat until smooth with electric mixer at medium speed. Pour into prepared pan.

Bake 45 minutes, or until a wooden pick inserted near center comes out clean. Cool in pan on a wire rack 10 minutes. Loosen cake around edge and tube of pan with a knife; invert onto rack; cool completely.

Cream shortening with part of the confectioners' sugar until fluffy in a medium bowl; beat in milk and remaining sugar until frosting is smooth and easy to spread. Measure out ⅓ cup and set aside for clown's face.

Stir remaining ⅓ cup Hawaiian punch drink mix into remaining frosting in bowl.

Split cake into 3 layers with a serrated knife; place bottom layer on a large serving plate. Spread a scant ½ cup of the pink frosting over layer; cover with second layer and frosting; top with remaining layer.

Spread the ⅓ cup white frosting on cake to cover a 5-inch section of top and side. Spread pink frosting over rest of cake; pat coconut into pink frosting.

Press whole and cut candies into white frosting to resemble a clown's face. Make a long ruffle of foil and place under cake for collar. Make a pointed hat and a small ruffle of foil; place on cake to cover center hole.

Yield: 12 servings.

QUICK MARBLE NUT TORTE

1 package (13½ ozs.) yellow cake mix with
    chocolate frosting
  Water
1 square unsweetened chocolate, melted and
    cooled
½ cup thawed frozen whipped topping
3 tablespoons chopped California walnuts

Prepare cake mix with water as label directs. Drizzle melted chocolate in lines over top; carefully draw through batter with a knife to marble.

Bake cake as label directs; cool in pan. Loosen around edges with a knife; turn out onto a rectangular or square serving plate. Split cake to make two thin layers.

Empty chocolate frosting into a bowl; fold in whipped topping.

Spread about half of the chocolate mixture over bottom cake layer; top with second layer and remaining chocolate mixture. Garnish with walnuts. Chill until serving time.

Yield: 6 servings.

MINIATURE LIME LAYER CAKES

1 package yellow cake mix
1 package (1½ ozs.) whipped topping mix
4 eggs
1 cup cold water
1 tablespoon grated lemon rind
  Lime Filling (recipe on page 489)
  Vanilla Cream (recipe on page 493)
  Candied lime slices, cut in small wedges

Grease a jelly-roll pan, 15x10x1 inches, and a square pan, 9x9x2 inches; dust each lightly with flour.

Preheat oven to 350°.

Combine cake mix, dry topping mix, eggs, water, and lemon rind in a large bowl. Mix until moist, then beat 4 minutes with electric mixer at medium speed. Divide evenly into prepared pans.

Bake large cake 15 minutes and small cake 30 minutes, or until a wooden pick inserted in center comes out clean. Cool in pans on wire racks 15 minutes. Loosen each cake around edges with a knife; turn out onto racks; cool completely. Wrap small cake and set aside for another day.

Make Lime Filling; chill. Cut 24 rounds from large cake with a 2-inch cutter. Spread Lime Filling on 12 rounds; top each with a plain round; chill.

Make Vanilla Cream. Holding each cake on a fork, spread frosting generously over sides and tops; chill.

Just before serving, trim each cake with small wedges of candied lime slices.

Yield: 12 small cakes; one plain layer.

ALMOND ROSETTE CAKES

1 package white cake mix
1 package (3¾ ozs.) instant vanilla pudding mix
4 eggs
¾ cup salad oil
1 cup water
1 package (16 ozs.) confectioners' powdered
    sugar, sifted
¼ cup light corn syrup
¼ teaspoon almond extract
    Red food coloring
    Gumdrop roses (directions follow)

Grease 12 muffin-pan cups and a baking pan, 9x9x2 inches.

Preheat oven to 350°.

Combine cake and pudding mixes in a large bowl. Add eggs, salad oil, and ¾ cup of the water all at once. Beat 5 minutes with electric mixer at medium speed. Spoon part of the batter into prepared muffin pans to fill each ⅔ full; spoon remaining batter into square pan.

Bake cupcakes 20 minutes and layer 30 minutes, or until centers spring back when lightly pressed with fingertip. Cool cakes in pans on wire racks 10 minutes. Loosen around edges with a knife; turn out onto racks; cool completely. (Wrap layer and set aside to frost for another dessert.)

Combine confectioners' sugar, corn syrup, remaining ¼ cup water, and almond extract in the top of a double boiler; tint pink with a few drops food coloring. Place over hot water; heat just until lukewarm; remove from heat, but leave over hot water to keep glaze thin as you work.

Place cupcakes, several at a time, upside down on a wire rack set over a bowl. Using a small measuring cup, pour frosting over cakes, turning each cake as you glaze it to make sure side is completely covered and smooth.

After all cakes have one coat, scrape frosting that drips into bowl back into pan; stir in 1 tablespoon water and reheat to lukewarm. Pour over cakes again to cover with a second coat. Let stand until glaze is firm.

When ready to serve, decorate each with a Gumdrop rose.

Yield: 12 small cakes.

Make Gumdrop Roses: Sprinkle a cutting board generously with sugar. For each rose, roll out 2 large pink or red gumdrops to thin ovals about 2 inches long; cut each in half crosswise. Roll up one half tightly to form center of flower. Press remaining 3 halves, overlapping slightly, around center for petals. Press rose together tightly at base to hold in place.

ANGEL, CHIFFON, AND SPONGE CAKES

ANGEL CAKE

   1 cup sifted cake flour (not self-rising)
1½ cups granulated sugar
1½ cups unbeaten egg whites (about 11 large eggs)
   ½ teaspoon salt
   1 teaspoon cream of tartar
   2 teaspoons vanilla

Preheat oven to 375°.

Sift flour and ¾ cup of the sugar into a medium bowl.

Beat egg whites with salt and cream of tartar in a large bowl until foamy; beat in remaining ¾ cup sugar, 2 tablespoons at a time, until mixture forms firm peaks; beat in vanilla.

Sift flour mixture over top, a few tablespoons at a time, and gently fold in just until blended. Spoon into an ungreased 10-inch angel-cake pan, leveling top; gently cut through batter with a spatula.

Bake 30 minutes, or until golden and a long metal skewer inserted near center comes out clean.

Hang tube of pan upside down over a small-neck bottle; cool cake completely.

Loosen cake around edge and tube of pan with a knife; invert onto a large serving plate. Sprinkle top with confectioners' sugar or frost with flavored whipped cream or your favorite glaze.

Yield: One 10-inch cake.

DAFFODIL TORTE

2 tablespoons lemon juice
   Water
   Yellow food coloring
1 package angel-cake mix
1 teaspoon grated lemon rind
1 egg
1 package (3¼ ozs.) lemon pudding and pie filling mix
   Granulated sugar
1 cup whipping cream

Preheat oven to 375°.

Measure lemon juice into a 2-cup measure; add water to make 1⅓ cups; stir in a few drops food coloring to tint deep yellow. Combine with egg-white mixture from cake mix package in a large bowl; beat as label directs.

Beat in flour mixture and lemon rind. Spoon into a 10-inch angel-cake pan.

Bake, cool, and remove from pan as label directs.

Beat egg in a medium saucepan; stir in water, pudding mix, and sugar and prepare as label directs; chill until completely cold.

Split cake crosswise into three even layers; place bottom layer on a large serving plate. Top with one quarter of the pudding mixture, second layer, and another quarter of pudding; place plain layer on top.

Beat cream in a medium bowl until stiff; fold into remaining pudding until no streaks of white remain. Spread over side and top of cake. Chill at least an hour, or until serving time.

Slice cake into wedges with a sharp knife.
Yield: 10 to 12 servings.

MOCHA CHIFFON CAKE

½ cup cocoa powder (not cocoa mix)
¾ cup boiling water
2 cups sifted cake flour (not self-rising)
1¾ cups granulated sugar
3 teaspoons baking powder
1 teaspoon salt
½ cup salad oil
6 eggs, separated
2 teaspoons vanilla
½ teaspoon cream of tartar
1 package chocolate whipped frosting mix
2 teaspoons dry instant coffee
    Butter or margarine, softened
    Water

Preheat oven to 325°.

Stir cocoa into boiling water until smooth in a cup; cool.

Sift flour, sugar, baking powder, and salt into a large bowl. Make a well in center of flour mixture and add salad oil, egg yolks, cocoa mixture, and vanilla. Beat until smooth with electric mixer at medium speed.

Combine egg whites and cream of tartar in another large bowl; beat until mixture forms very stiff peaks.

Pour chocolate mixture in a thin stream over beaten egg whites; fold in until no streaks of white remain. Pour into an ungreased 10-inch angel-cake pan.

Bake 1 hour, or until top springs back when lightly pressed with fingertip. Hang tube of pan upside down over a small-neck bottle; cool cake completely.

Loosen cake around edge and tube of pan with a knife; invert onto a large serving plate.

Split cake in half crosswise to make two layers, using a sharp serrated knife and a sawing motion.

Mix frosting mix and instant coffee in a medium bowl; prepare with butter and water as label directs; fill and frost cake, making swirls on side and top with spatula.

Yield: One 10-inch tube cake.

BANANA CHIFFON CAKE

5 eggs
2 egg whites
2¼ cups sifted cake flour (not self-rising)
1½ cups granulated sugar
3 teaspoons baking powder
1 teaspoon salt
½ teaspoon cream of tartar
½ cup salad oil
1 cup mashed firm ripe bananas (2 large)
2 teaspoons grated lemon rind
    Confectioners' powdered sugar

Preheat oven to 325°.

Separate eggs, placing yolks in a cup and combining the 7 whites in a large bowl.

Sift flour, granulated sugar, baking powder, and salt into a medium bowl.

Add cream of tartar to egg whites; beat until mixture forms very stiff peaks.

Make a well in center of flour mixture and add salad oil, egg yolks, mashed bananas, and lemon rind; beat until smooth with electric mixer at medium speed. Gently spoon over beaten whites; fold in until no streaks of yellow remain. Pour into an ungreased 10-inch angel-cake pan.

Bake 55 minutes, or until top springs back when lightly pressed with fingertip. Hang tube of pan upside down over a small-neck bottle; cool cake completely.

Loosen cake around edge and tube of pan with a knife; invert onto a large serving plate. Sprinkle confectioners' sugar generously over top.

Yield: One 10-inch tube cake.

LIME ANGEL CROWN

¾ cup sugar
2 tablespoons cornstarch
　Dash of salt
¾ cup water (for filling)
1 tablespoon butter or margarine
2 tablespoons lime juice
　Green food coloring
1 packaged 8-inch angel cake
1 package fluffy white frosting mix
　Boiling water

Mix sugar, cornstarch, and salt in a small saucepan; stir in the ¾ cup water. Cook, stirring constantly, until mixture thickens and boils 1 minute; remove from heat. Stir in butter until melted, then lime juice and a few drops food coloring to tint pale green. Cool until completely cold.

Preheat oven to 400°.

Split angel cake to make 3 layers. Spread lime mixture over bottom two layers; stack on a cookie sheet or ovenproof serving plate; top with plain layer.

Prepare frosting mix with boiling water as label directs; spread over side and top of cake.

Bake 8 minutes, or until meringue is tipped with gold. Cool completely. Slice into wedges.

Yield: One 8-inch triple-layer cake.

SPICE CREAM ROLL

¾ cup sifted cake flour (not self-rising)
¾ teaspoon baking powder
2 teaspoons ground cinnamon
1 teaspoon ground nutmeg
½ teaspoon ground allspice
¼ teaspoon salt
4 eggs
1¼ cups granulated sugar
1 tablespoon light molasses
1 package (8 ozs.) cream cheese
4 tablespoons thawed frozen concentrate for
　orange juice
½ cup chopped California walnuts
⅓ cup sifted confectioners' powdered sugar

Grease a jelly-roll pan, 15x10x1 inches; line with waxed paper cut ½ inch smaller than pan, grease paper.

Preheat oven to 400°.

Sift flour, baking powder, cinnamon, nutmeg, allspice, and salt onto waxed paper.

Beat eggs in a medium bowl until foamy. Beat in ¾ cup of the granulated sugar, 1 tablespoon at a time; continue beating until mixture is very thick and light in color. Stir in molasses; fold in flour mixture. Spread evenly into prepared pan.

Bake 15 minutes, or until golden and center springs back when lightly pressed with fingertip.

Cut around cake ¼ inch in from edge of pan with a sharp knife; turn out onto a towel dusted lightly with confectioners' sugar; peel waxed paper from cake. Starting at a short end, roll up cake; wrap tightly in same towel; cool completely.

Soften cream cheese in a small bowl; beat in 2 tablespoons of the orange concentrate and remaining ½ cup granulated sugar until smooth; stir in walnuts.

Unroll cake carefully; spread cheese mixture over cake; reroll.

Mix remaining 2 tablespoons orange concentrate and confectioners' sugar in a cup until smooth; spread over top of roll, letting mixture drip down side. Chill cake 2 to 3 hours. To serve, slice crosswise.

Yield: 10 servings.

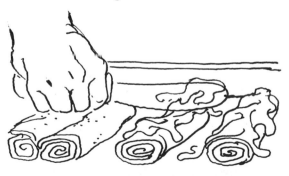

LEMON CROWN

1¾ cups sifted cake flour (not self-rising)
¼ teaspoon salt
6 eggs, separated
½ cup water
1½ cups granulated sugar
1 teaspoon lemon extract
¾ teaspoon cream of tartar
2 tablespoons butter or margarine
2 cups sifted confectioners' powdered sugar
½ teaspoon grated lemon rind
2 tablespoons lemon juice

Preheat oven to 325°.

Sift flour and salt onto waxed paper.

Beat egg yolks until thick in a large bowl; beat in water until well blended. Slowly beat in granulated sugar, beating constantly, until mixture is thick and fluffy; stir in lemon extract. Fold in flour mixture.

Combine egg whites and cream of tartar in a second large bowl; beat until mixture forms soft peaks. Fold into egg-yolk mixture until no streaks of white remain. Pour into an ungreased 10-inch angel-cake pan.

Bake 1 hour, or until top springs back when lightly pressed with fingertip. Hang tube of pan upside down over a small-neck bottle; cool cake completely.

Loosen cake around edge and tube of pan with a knife; invert onto a large serving plate.

Melt butter in a small saucepan; stir in confectioners' sugar, and lemon rind and juice, then stir in about 1 teaspoon water until mixture is smooth and thin enough to pour from spoon. Spoon over top of cake, letting glaze drip down side. Let stand until glaze is firm.

Yield: One 10-inch tube cake.

TOPSY-TURVY PINEAPPLE ROLL

4 tablespoons butter or margarine
¾ cup firmly packed light brown sugar
1 can (20 ozs.) crushed pineapple in juice, well drained
¼ cup chopped maraschino cherries, well drained
¾ cup sifted cake flour (not self-rising)
½ teaspoon baking powder
¼ teaspoon salt
4 eggs
¾ cup granulated sugar
1 teaspoon vanilla
Confectioners' powdered sugar

Preheat oven to 400°.

Melt butter in a jelly-roll pan, 15x10x1 inches, in oven as it preheats; remove from oven. Sprinkle brown sugar evenly over butter; spread pineapple and cherries over sugar mixture.

Sift flour, baking powder, and salt onto waxed paper.

Beat eggs in a medium bowl until foamy. Beat in granulated sugar, 1 tablespoon at a time; continue beating until mixture is very thick and light in color. Stir in vanilla; fold in flour mixture. Pour evenly over fruit in pan.

Bake 12 minutes, or until golden and center springs back when lightly pressed with fingertip. Loosen cake around edges of pan with a knife; invert onto a clean towel sprinkled with confectioners' sugar. Starting at a short end, roll up cake; wrap tightly in towel. Cool completely.

Just before serving, sprinkle more confectioners' sugar over roll. To serve, slice crosswise.

Yield: 10 servings.

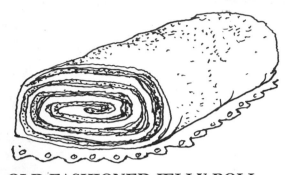

OLD-FASHIONED JELLY ROLL

¾ cup sifted cake flour (not self-rising)
½ teaspoon baking powder
¼ teaspoon salt
 4 eggs
¾ cup granulated sugar
 1 teaspoon vanilla
  Confectioners' powdered sugar
 1 jar (10 ozs.) strawberry jelly

Grease a jelly-roll pan, 15x10x1 inches; line with waxed paper cut ½ inch smaller than pan; grease paper.

Preheat oven to 400°.

Sift flour, baking powder, and salt onto waxed paper.

Beat eggs in a medium bowl until foamy. Beat in granulated sugar, 1 tablespoon at a time; continue beating until mixture is very thick and light in color. Stir in vanilla; fold in flour mixture. Spread evenly into prepared pan.

Bake 12 minutes, or until golden and center springs back when lightly pressed with fingertip.

Cut around cake ¼ inch in from edge of pan with a sharp knife; turn out onto a towel dusted with 1 tablespoon confectioners' sugar; peel waxed paper from cake. Starting at a short end, roll up cake; wrap tightly in same towel; cool completely.

Unroll cake carefully; spread jelly over cake; reroll. Dust confectioners' sugar over top. To serve, slice crosswise.

Yield: 10 servings.

STRAWBERRY ROLL

¾ cup sifted cake flour (not self-rising)
½ teaspoon baking powder
¼ teaspoon salt
 4 eggs
¾ cup granulated sugar
 1 teaspoon vanilla
  Confectioners' powdered sugar
 1 package (3 ozs.) strawberry-flavored gelatin
 1 cup boiling water
 1 cup strawberry ice cream
½ cup thinly sliced small strawberries
½ cup whipping cream

Grease a jelly-roll pan, 15x10x1 inches; line with waxed paper cut ½ inch smaller than pan; grease paper.

Preheat oven to 400°.

Sift flour, baking powder, and salt onto waxed paper.

Beat eggs in a medium bowl until foamy. Beat in sugar, 1 tablespoon at a time; continue beating until mixture is very thick and light in color. Stir in vanilla; fold in flour mixture. Spread evenly in prepared pan.

Bake 12 minutes, or until golden and center springs back when lightly pressed with fingertip.

Cut around cake ¼ inch in from edge of pan with a sharp knife; turn out onto a towel lightly dusted with confectioners' sugar; peel waxed paper from cake. Starting at a short end, roll up cake; wrap tightly in towel; cool completely.

Dissolve gelatin in boiling water in a medium bowl; stir in ice cream until melted; stir in strawberries. Chill until softly set.

Unroll cake carefully; spread gelatin mixture over top; reroll. Wrap in waxed paper or transparent wrap and chill.

Just before serving, beat cream until stiff in a small bowl. Unwrap cake; frost top with whipped cream. To serve, slice crosswise.

Yield: 10 servings.

HAWAIIAN RIBBON CAKE (p.461)▶

FROSTED PISTACHIO PINWHEEL

1¼ cups sifted cake flour (not self-rising)
 1 teaspoon baking powder
 ¼ teaspoon salt
 ¼ cup dry cocoa (not instant cocoa mix)
 3 eggs
 1 cup granulated sugar
 ⅓ cup water
1½ teaspoons vanilla
 3 tablespoons confectioners' powdered sugar
 1 pint pistachio ice cream, softened
 ½ cup whipping cream
 ⅛ teaspoon almond extract
   Green food coloring

Grease a jelly-roll pan, 15x10x1 inches; line with waxed paper; grease paper.

Preheat oven to 375°.

Sift flour, baking powder, salt, and cocoa onto waxed paper.

Beat eggs in a medium bowl until foamy. Beat in granulated sugar, one fourth at a time, until mixture is very thick and light in color; stir in water and 1 teaspoon of the vanilla.

Slowly beat in flour mixture just until blended. Pour evenly into prepared pan.

Bake 12 minutes, or until center springs back when lightly pressed with fingertip. Loosen cake around edges of pan with a knife; invert onto a towel sprinkled with 2 tablespoons of the confectioners' sugar; peel waxed paper from cake. Starting at a short end of cake, roll up tightly; wrap in towel. Cool completely on a wire rack.

Unroll cake carefully; spread ice cream quickly over cake to within ½ inch of edges; reroll. Place in freezer.

Combine cream with remaining 1 tablespoon confectioners' sugar, ½ teaspoon vanilla, almond extract, and a few drops food coloring in a small bowl. Beat until stiff; spread over top of roll. Sprinkle chopped pistachio nuts over topping if you like. Return cake to freezer until serving time. To serve, slice crosswise.

Yield: 10 servings.

◄ ARABIAN FRUITCAKE (p.488)
PUMPKIN-PINEAPPLE CHIFFON PIE (p.512)
NESSELRODE CREAM CUP (p.455)

UPSIDE-DOWN CAKES

PEACH CAKELETS

    4 tablespoons butter or margarine
    4 tablespoons light brown sugar
    1 can (16 ozs.) cling peach slices, well drained
1¼ cups sifted cake flour (not self-rising)
    ¾ cup granulated sugar
1¼ teaspoons baking powder
    ¼ teaspoon salt
    ¼ cup shortening, softened
3½ cups milk
    1 egg
    1 teaspoon vanilla
    1 package (3 ozs.) egg-custard mix
    ¼ teaspoon ground nutmeg

Preheat oven to 350°.

Measure ½ tablespoon of the butter into each of eight 6-ounce custard cups; set cups in a large shallow pan for easy handling. Place in oven while it preheats until butter melts; remove from oven. Sprinkle ½ tablespoon of the brown sugar into each cup; arrange two or three peach slices on sugar mixture in each.

Sift flour, granulated sugar, baking powder, and salt into a medium bowl; add shortening and ¼ cup of the milk; beat 2 minutes with electric mixer at medium speed. Add egg, another ¼ cup of the milk, and vanilla; beat 2 minutes longer. Spoon evenly over peaches in cups.

Bake 40 minutes, or until centers of cakes spring back when lightly pressed with fingertip. Cool cakes in cups on a wire rack 10 minutes. Loosen around edges with a knife; invert each cake onto a small serving plate. Let stand 5 minutes; lift off cups. Cool cakes.

While cakes bake, combine custard mix, remaining 3 cups milk, and nutmeg in a medium saucepan; cook as label directs; cool.

To serve, spoon custard sauce over each cake.

Yield: 8 servings.

UPSIDE-DOWN PEACH CAKE

    ¼ cup butter or margarine
    ½ cup firmly packed light brown sugar
    1 can (16 ozs.) cling peach slices, drained
    1 package cupcake mix
    1 egg
    1 cup milk
    ¼ cup chopped drained maraschino cherries
    1 package (1½ ozs.) whipped topping mix
        Vanilla

Preheat oven to 350°.

Melt butter in a baking pan, 8x8x2 inches, in oven as it heats; stir in brown sugar. Arrange peach slices in rows in sugar mixture.

Prepare cupcake mix with egg and ½ cup of the milk as label directs; fold in cherries. Spoon over peaches in pan.

Bake 45 minutes, or until center springs back when lightly pressed with fingertip. Cool cake in pan on a wire rack 5 minutes; loosen around edges with a knife; invert cake onto a large serving plate. Let stand 5 minutes; lift off pan.

Prepare whipped topping mix with remaining ½ cup milk and vanilla as label directs. Cut cake into serving-size pieces; place on serving plates; serve warm with whipped topping.

Yield: 8 servings.

APRICOT GINGER TORTE

6 tablespoons butter or margarine
⅔ cup firmly packed light brown sugar
2 cans (16 ozs. each) apricot halves, well drained
2 cups sifted all-purpose flour
1 teaspoon baking soda
½ teaspoon salt
¾ teaspoon ground ginger
¾ teaspoon ground cinnamon
⅓ cup shortening, softened
⅓ cup granulated sugar
1 egg
¾ cup light molasses
¾ cup hot water
1 cup whipping cream

Preheat oven to 350°.

Melt 3 tablespoons of the butter in each of two 8-inch round layer-cake pans in oven as it preheats; remove from oven. Sprinkle brown sugar evenly over butter. Arrange half of the apricots, hollow side up, in butter mixture in each pan.

Sift flour, baking soda, salt, ginger, and cinnamon onto waxed paper.

Cream shortening and granulated sugar in a medium bowl until fluffy; beat in egg and molasses. Stir in flour mixture, part at a time, until blended; beat in hot water. Pour half over apricots in each pan.

Bake 35 minutes, or until centers spring back when lightly pressed with fingertip. Cool layers in pans on wire racks 10 minutes. Loosen around edges with a knife; invert each layer onto a large serving plate. Let stand 5 minutes; lift off pans. Cool layers.

About 30 minutes before serving, beat cream until stiff in a medium bowl. Spread about one third over one cake layer; top with second layer. Spread remaining cream around side and on top of torte. Chill until serving time. Cut into wedges.

Yield: 8 servings.

CHERRY SUNDAE RING

1 can (21 ozs.) cherry pie filling
½ teaspoon almond extract
1 package yellow cake mix
  Eggs
  Water
2 pints cherry vanilla ice cream

Generously grease a 2½-quart ring mold with shortening.

Blend cherry pie filling and almond extract in a medium bowl; spoon into prepared mold.

Preheat oven to 350°.

Prepare cake mix with eggs and water as label directs; spoon over cherry mixture in mold.

Bake 1 hour and 10 minutes, or until top springs back when lightly pressed with fingertip. Cool cake in mold on a wire rack 10 minutes. Loosen around edge and ring with a knife; invert cake onto a serving plate. Let stand 5 minutes; lift off mold; cool cake.

While cake bakes, scoop ice cream into 12 small balls; place on a cookie sheet; return to freezer.

When ready to serve, pile ice cream balls in center of cake. Cut cake into wedges; serve each with ice cream.

Yield: 12 servings.

OLD-FASHIONED PINEAPPLE UPSIDE-DOWN CAKE

⅓ cup butter or margarine
⅔ cup firmly packed light brown sugar
2 cans (8 ozs. each) sliced pineapple in syrup, well drained
⅓ cup coarsely chopped California walnuts
1 cup sifted all-purpose flour
⅔ cup granulated sugar
1½ teaspoons baking powder
¼ teaspoon salt
¼ cup shortening
⅔ cup milk
1 egg
1 teaspoon vanilla
  Whipped cream

Preheat oven to 350°.

Melt butter in a heavy 10-inch skillet with ovenproof handle. Stir in brown sugar until melted; remove from heat. Arrange pineapple slices in a pretty pattern in sugar mixture; sprinkle walnuts over top.

Sift flour, granulated sugar, baking powder, and salt into a medium bowl. Add shortening and milk; beat slowly until blended, then beat 2 minutes with electric mixer at medium speed. Add egg and vanilla; beat 2 minutes longer. Pour over pineapple in skillet, leveling top.

Bake 40 minutes, or until golden and a wooden pick inserted into center comes out clean. Cool cake in skillet on a wire rack 5 minutes. Loosen around edge with a knife; invert cake onto a large serving plate; lift off skillet.

Serve warm or cold with whipped cream.
Yield: 8 servings.

CHERRY-ORANGE SQUARES

3 tablespoons butter or margarine
½ cup firmly packed light brown sugar
1 can (21 ozs.) cherry pie filling
2 teaspoons grated orange rind
1 package yellow cake mix
1 package (3¾ ozs.) vanilla instant pudding mix
4 eggs
¼ cup salad oil
1 cup water
2 packages (1½ ozs. each) whipped topping mix
  Milk
  Vanilla

Preheat oven to 350°.

Melt butter in a baking pan, 13x9x2 inches, in oven as it preheats; remove from oven. Sprinkle brown sugar evenly over butter.

Mix cherry pie filling and orange rind in a small bowl; spoon evenly over sugar mixture in pan.

Combine cake and pudding mixes, eggs, salad oil, and water in large bowl. Beat slowly with electric mixer until blended, then beat at medium speed 2 minutes; pour over fruit mixture in pan.

Bake 55 minutes, or until center springs back when lightly pressed with fingertip. Cool cake in pan on a wire rack 10 minutes. Loosen around edges with a knife; invert cake onto a large cutting board or serving plate; let stand 5 minutes; lift off pan. Cool cake.

When ready to serve, prepare topping mix with milk and vanilla as label directs. Cut cake into squares; spoon whipped topping over each serving.
Yield: 12 to 16 servings.

PEAR MERINGUE CAKE

4 tablespoons butter or margarine
¾ cup firmly packed light brown sugar
1 can (29 ozs.) pear halves, well drained
3 eggs
1 package spicecake mix
1⅓ cups water
¼ teaspoon mace
¼ cup chopped pecans

Preheat oven to 350°.

Melt butter in a 9-inch round layer-cake pan in oven as it preheats; remove from oven. Sprinkle ½ cup of the brown sugar over butter; arrange pear halves, hollow side up and spoke fashion, in sugar mixture in pan.

Separate 2 of the eggs, placing whites in a small bowl and yolks in a large bowl; add remaining whole egg, cake mix, and water to yolks; beat as label directs. Spoon about half of the batter over pears in pan and remainder into a greased baking pan, 8x8x2 inches.

Bake pear cake 45 minutes, or until center springs back when lightly pressed with fingertip. Bake plain layer, cool, and remove from pan as label directs; set aside to frost or turn into a different dessert for another day.

Cool pear cake in pan on a wire rack 10 minutes. Loosen around edge with a knife; invert cake onto a small cookie sheet. Let stand 5 minutes; lift off pan; cool cake.

About ½ hour before serving, preheat oven to 400°.

Beat egg whites in a small bowl until foamy; slowly beat in remaining ¼ cup brown sugar and mace until sugar dissolves completely and meringue forms firm peaks; spread over pears; sprinkle pecans over meringue.

Bake 10 minutes, or until meringue is lightly golden; cool on a wire rack. Cut into wedges; serve warm.

Yield: 8 servings.

CARAMEL-COCONUT RING

¾ cup butter or margarine
½ cup firmly packed light brown sugar
1 tablespoon warm water
⅔ cup flaked coconut
2 cups sifted cake flour (not self-rising)
2½ teaspoons baking powder
¼ teaspoon salt
2 eggs, separated
1 cup granulated sugar
1 teaspoon vanilla
1 can (8 ozs.) crushed pineapple in syrup
2 tablespoons milk
1 pint vanilla ice cream

Grease a 1¾-quart ring mold; dust lightly with flour.

Preheat oven to 350°.

Cream ¼ cup of the butter and brown sugar in a small bowl; stir in water. Spread evenly over bottom of mold; sprinkle coconut over sugar mixture.

Sift flour, baking powder, and salt onto waxed paper.

Beat egg whites until they form firm peaks in a small bowl.

Cream remaining ½ cup butter with granulated sugar in a medium bowl until fluffy; beat in egg yolks and vanilla.

Beat in flour mixture, alternately with pineapple and syrup and milk, just until blended; fold in beaten egg whites. Spoon over coconut in pan.

Bake 55 minutes, or until top springs back when lightly pressed with fingertip. Cool cake in mold on a wire rack 10 minutes. Loosen around edge and center with a knife; invert cake onto a large serving plate. Let stand 5 minutes; lift off mold. Cool cake.

Cut into wedges; serve warm or cold with ice cream.

Yield: 8 servings.

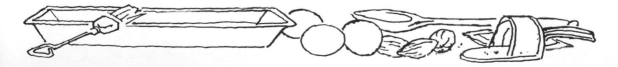

FRUITCAKES

RUM FRUIT RING

2¾ cups sifted all-purpose flour
1 teaspoon baking soda
¼ teaspoon salt
½ cup butter or margarine
2 cups granulated sugar
2 eggs
1 tablespoon grated orange rind
1 cup (8-oz. carton) plain yogurt
1 cup chopped mixed candied fruits
½ cup finely chopped California walnuts
   Butter Rum Glaze (recipe on page 493)

Preheat oven to 350°.

Sift flour, soda, and salt onto waxed paper.

Cream butter and granulated sugar until fluffy-light in a large bowl; beat in eggs and orange rind until fluffy again.

Stir in flour mixture, alternately with yogurt, until blended; fold in fruits and walnuts. Spoon into a greased 3-quart tube pan, spreading top even.

Bake 50 minutes, or until a wooden pick inserted near center comes out clean. Cool cake in pan on a wire rack 10 minutes. Loosen around edge and tube of pan with a knife; invert cake onto rack; cool completely.

Make Butter Rum Glaze. Spoon over top of cake, letting mixture drip down side. Let stand until glaze is firm.

Yield: One 10-inch tube cake.

REFRIGERATOR FRUITCAKE

1½ cups light raisins
   1 package (8 ozs.) pitted dates, each snipped into eighths
   1 cup quartered pitted dried prunes
   1 container (3½ ozs.) candied red cherries, sliced
   1 container (3½ ozs.) candied green cherries, sliced
   1 container (4 ozs.) candied orange peel, diced
   ½ cup chopped California walnuts
   ½ cup butter or margarine
   ½ cup confectioners' powdered sugar
   ½ cup orange marmalade
   ¼ cup light corn syrup
   1 teaspoon ground cinnamon
   ¼ teaspoon ground cloves
   ½ teaspoon salt
   3 cups fine graham-cracker crumbs
   2 cups regular wheat germ

Line 3 small loaf pans, each 6x3x2 inches, with waxed paper. Or use 1 large loaf pan, 9x5x3 inches.

Combine raisins, dates, prunes, cherries, orange peel, and walnuts in a large bowl.

Cream butter with confectioners' sugar until fluffy-light in a medium bowl; beat in marmalade, corn syrup, cinnamon, cloves, and salt. Stir into fruit mixture until well blended; cover. Let stand at room temperature 2 hours.

Stir in graham-cracker crumbs and wheat germ; mix well, using your hands.

Pack into paper-lined pans, pressing mixture down firmly with back of spoon and leveling tops. Wrap pans tightly in foil. Chill at least 48 hours.

When ready to serve, run a knife around inside edges of pans to loosen cakes; invert onto a cutting board; peel off waxed paper. Cut cakes into thin slices. Store any leftovers, tightly wrapped, in refrigerator.

Yield: 3 small loaf cakes.

WHITE FRUITCAKE

3¼ cups sifted all-purpose flour
1½ teaspoons baking powder
½ teaspoon salt
3 containers (3½ ozs. each) candied red cherries, cut in half
1 package (11 ozs.) dried apricots, snipped fine
3 containers (4 ozs. each) candied pineapple, diced
2 containers (4 ozs. each) candied orange peel, chopped
2 cups broken California walnuts
2 cups whole filberts
1 cup butter or margarine
2 cups granulated sugar
5 eggs
2 teaspoons brandy flavoring
½ cup apple juice
1 cup confectioners' powdered sugar
4 teaspoons orange juice
½ teaspoon vanilla

Generously grease a 10-inch angel-cake pan. Cut a circle of heavy brown paper to fit into bottom; fit into pan; grease paper.

Preheat oven to 275°.

Sift flour, baking powder, and salt onto waxed paper.

Combine cherries, apricots, pineapple, orange peel, walnuts, and filberts in a large bowl; sprinkle 3 tablespoons of the flour mixture over top; toss until fruits and nuts are evenly coated.

Cream butter and granulated sugar in a large bowl until fluffy-light; beat in eggs, one at a time, until fluffy again; beat in brandy flavoring.

Slowly beat in flour mixture, alternately with apple juice, just until blended. Pour over fruit mixture; fold in until well blended. Spoon into prepared pan. Push fruits down into batter with back of spoon to level top.

Bake 3 hours, or until a skewer inserted near center comes out clean. Cool 15 minutes in pan on a wire rack. Loosen around edge and tube with a knife; turn out onto rack. Peel waxed paper from cake; turn cake rightside up; cool completely. Wrap tightly in foil and store in refrigerator to mellow at least a week.

Just before serving, combine confectioners' sugar, orange juice, and vanilla in a small bowl; beat until smooth. Spread over top of cake, letting frosting drip down side. Decorate with sliced candied green cherries and leaves cut from red candied fruit slices if you like.

Yield: One 10-inch tube cake.

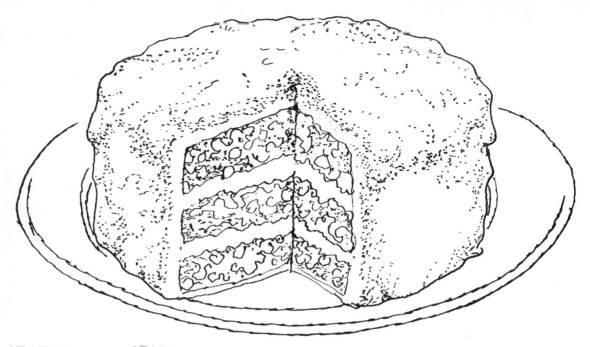

ARABIAN FRUITCAKE

4 cups sifted cake flour (not self-rising)
4 teaspoons baking powder
½ teaspoon salt
1 cup butter or margarine
2 cups granulated sugar
4 eggs
2 teaspoons vanilla
1 cup milk
1 container (3½ ozs.) candied red cherries,
**   chopped**
1 container (4 ozs.) candied pineapple, chopped
1 container (4 ozs.) candied orange peel, chopped
1 cup chopped California walnuts
**   Orange Filling (recipe on page 490)**
1 package fluffy white frosting mix
**   Boiling water**

Grease three 9-inch round layer-cake pans; line two with waxed paper; grease paper. Dust remaining pan with flour.

Preheat oven to 350°.

Sift flour, baking powder, and salt onto waxed paper.

Cream butter and sugar in a large bowl until fluffy light; beat in eggs, 1 at a time, until fluffy again; beat in vanilla.

Slowly beat in flour mixture, alternately with milk, just until blended. Measure out 2¼ cups of the batter and spread in floured pan.

Fold cherries, pineapple, orange peel, and walnuts into remaining batter; spread evenly in lined pans.

Bake layers in same oven 35 minutes, or until a wooden pick inserted into center of each comes out clean. Cool layers in pans on wire racks 10 minutes. Loosen around edges with a knife; turn out onto racks; peel waxed paper from layers; cool completely.

Make Orange Filling. Spread half on one fruit layer and remaining half on plain layer. Stack layers, placing plain one in middle, on a large serving plate.

Prepare frosting mix with boiling water as label directs; spread over side and top of cake, making deep swirls with spatula. Trim with chopped walnuts if you like.

Yield: One 9-inch triple-layer cake.

FILLINGS, FROSTINGS, AND GLAZES

LEMON FILLING

⅔ cup granulated sugar
3 tablespoons cornstarch
¼ teaspoon salt
¾ cup water
1 tablespoon grated lemon rind
⅓ cup lemon juice

Mix sugar, cornstarch, and salt in a medium saucepan; stir in water. Cook, stirring constantly, until mixture thickens and boils 1 minute; remove from heat.

Stir in lemon rind and juice. Chill until completely cold.

Yield: About 1 cup.

LIME FILLING

¾ cup granulated sugar
3 tablespoons cornstarch
¾ cup water
2 teaspoons grated lime rind
¼ cup lime juice
Dash of salt
Green food coloring

Mix sugar and cornstarch in a small saucepan; stir in water. Cook, stirring constantly, until mixture thickens and boils 1 minute; remove from heat.

Stir in lime rind and juice, salt, and a few drops food coloring to tint bright green. Cool, then chill.

Yield: 1 cup.

CUSTARD CREAM FILLING

¼ cup granulated sugar
2 tablespoons all-purpose flour
Dash of salt
1 egg
¾ cup milk
1 tablespoon butter or margarine
½ teaspoon vanilla

Combine sugar, flour, and salt in a small saucepan.

Beat egg with milk in a small bowl; slowly stir into flour mixture. Cook slowly, stirring constantly, until mixture thickens and boils 1 minute. Stir in butter until melted and vanilla. Pour into a small bowl; chill well.

Yield: 1 cup.

PINEAPPLE-COCONUT FILLING

1 can (20 ozs.) crushed pineapple in juice
Water
5 tablespoons cornstarch
2 cups granulated sugar
1 tablespoon grated orange rind
1 can (3½ ozs.) flaked coconut

Drain juice from pineapple into a 2-cup measure. (There should be about 1⅓ cups.) Add water to make 2 cups.

Mix cornstarch and sugar in a medium saucepan; stir in the 2 cups pineapple liquid and pineapple. Cook slowly, stirring constantly, until mixture thickens and boils 1 minute; remove from heat.

Stir in orange rind and coconut. Chill several hours, or until completely cold.

Yield: 4 cups, or enough to fill and top a 9-inch four-layer cake.

RASPBERRY FILLING

2 teaspoons unflavored gelatin
3 tablespoons cold water
1 jar (12 ozs.) raspberry preserves (1 cup)
1 cup thawed frozen whipped topping

Sprinkle gelatin over cold water in a small saucepan; let stand several minutes to soften.

Heat very slowly, stirring constantly, until gelatin dissolves and mixture is clear; stir into preserves in a small bowl; cool. Fold in whipped topping.

Yield: 2 cups or enough to fill a 9-inch triple-layer cake.

ORANGE FILLING

 1 cup granulated sugar
 4 tablespoons cornstarch
½ teaspoon salt
 1 cup orange juice
 2 tablespoons butter or margarine
 2 tablespoons grated orange rind
 1 tablespoon lemon juice

Mix sugar, cornstarch, and salt in a small saucepan; stir in orange juice.

Cook slowly, stirring constantly, until mixture thickens and boils 1 minute. Stir in butter until melted, then orange rind and lemon juice; cool.

Yield: About 1¼ cups.

BUTTER CREAM FROSTING

 ½ cup butter or margarine
 5 cups confectioners' powdered sugar, sifted
   (about 1½ packages)
1½ teaspoons vanilla
 6 tablespoons milk

Cream butter with a small amount of the confectioners' sugar in a medium bowl until fluffy; stir in vanilla.

Slowly beat in remaining sugar, alternately with milk, until frosting is smooth and easy to spread.

Yield: Enough to frost and decorate a 9-inch triple-layer cake.

COFFEE CREAM FROSTING

1 tablespoon dry instant coffee
3 tablespoons milk
1 package (3 ozs.) cream cheese
1 package (16 ozs.) confectioners' powdered sugar,
   sifted
1 teaspoon vanilla

Dissolve coffee in milk in a cup.

Beat cheese in a medium bowl until fluffy; slowly beat in confectioners' sugar, alternately with coffee mixture, until frosting is smooth and easy to spread. Beat in vanilla.

Yield: Enough to fill and frost an 8- or 9-inch double-layer cake.

SEAFOAM FROSTING

1½ cups firmly packed dark brown sugar
 2 egg whites
 1 tablespoon light corn syrup
   Dash of salt
 ¼ cup water
 2 teaspoons vanilla

Combine brown sugar, unbeaten egg whites, corn syrup, salt, and water in the top of a double boiler; place over boiling water.

Cook, beating constantly with a rotary or electric beater, 7 minutes, or until frosting triples in volume and forms soft peaks; remove from heat. Beat in vanilla.

Yield: Enough to fill and frost an 8- or 9-inch double-layer cake.

DECORATING FROSTING

 2 egg whites
 ⅛ teaspoon cream of tartar
3½ cups sifted confectioners' powdered sugar

Beat egg whites slightly in a medium bowl; beat in cream of tartar, then slowly beat in confectioners' sugar until mixture is smooth and stiff enough to hold its shape. (If any frosting is left over, cover bowl with wet paper toweling, then cover tightly with transparent wrap and store in the refrigerator to use another day.)

Yield: 2⅓ cups.

CLASSIC SEVEN-MINUTE FROSTING

1½ cups sugar
⅛ teaspoon cream of tartar
    Dash of salt
 2 egg whites
 1 tablespoon light corn syrup
¼ cup water
 2 teaspoons vanilla

Combine sugar, cream of tartar, salt, un-beaten egg whites, corn syrup, and water in the top of a double boiler; place over boiling water.

Cook, beating constantly with a rotary or electric beater, 7 minutes, or until frosting triples in volume and forms soft peaks; remove from heat. Beat in vanilla.

Yield: Enough to fill and frost an 8- or 9-inch double-layer cake.

WHITE MOUNTAIN FROSTING

¾ cup granulated sugar
    Dash of cream of tartar
    Dash of salt
 1 egg white
 2 tablespoons water
 1 teaspoon vanilla

Combine sugar, cream of tartar, salt, un-beaten egg white, and water in the top of a double boiler; place over boiling water. Cook, beating constantly, 5 minutes, or until mixture triples in volume and forms soft peaks. Remove from heat; beat in vanilla.

Yield: Enough to frost side and top of an 8- or 9-inch double-layer cake.

PENUCHE FROSTING

½ cup butter or margarine
 1 cup firmly packed light brown sugar
⅓ cup evaporated milk
 3 cups sifted confectioners' powdered sugar
 1 teaspoon vanilla

Melt butter in a medium saucepan; stir in brown sugar. Heat slowly, stirring constantly, to boiling; cook, stirring constantly, 2 minutes. Carefully stir in milk (mixture will bubble up); heat just until bubbly. Cool to lukewarm.

Slowly beat in confectioners' sugar until frosting is smooth and easy to spread; beat in vanilla.

Yield: Enough to fill and frost an 8- or 9-inch double-layer cake.

EASY FUDGE FROSTING

¼ cup butter or margarine
 2 squares unsweetened chocolate
 2 tablespoons light corn syrup
¼ cup milk
 3 cups sifted confectioners' powdered sugar
 1 teaspoon vanilla

Combine butter, chocolate, and corn syrup in a medium bowl; heat slowly until butter and chocolate melt. Stir in milk; heat slowly, stirring constantly, until bubbly; cool.

Beat in confectioners' sugar until frosting is smooth and easy to spread; beat in vanilla.

Yield: Enough to fill and frost an 8-inch double-layer cake or 18 cupcakes plus 1 layer, 8x8x2 inches.

BRAZILIAN CREAM FROSTING

1 cup whipping cream
3 tablespoons confectioners' powdered sugar
1 tablespoon dry instant coffee
½ teaspoon vanilla

Combine cream, confectioners' sugar, instant coffee, and vanilla in a medium bowl; beat until stiff.

Yield: Enough to frost a 10-inch angel or chiffon cake.

PEANUT BUTTER FROSTING

1 package (8 ozs.) cream cheese, softened
1 cup peanut butter
1 can (14 ozs.) sweetened condensed milk

Beat cream cheese in a medium bowl until fluffy; slowly beat in peanut butter and sweetened condensed milk until well blended.

Yield: Enough to fill and frost an 8- or 9-inch double-layer cake.
Note: Store frosted cake in refrigerator.

BROILER COCONUT FROSTING

⅓ cup butter or margarine
¾ cup firmly packed light brown sugar
½ cup flaked coconut
½ cup chopped California walnuts
2 tablespoons evaporated milk or light cream

Cream butter with brown sugar in a small bowl; stir in coconut, walnuts, and evaporated milk. Spread over cake while still hot from the oven.

Broil, 6 inches from heat, 3 minutes, or just until frosting bubbles up and turns golden. (Watch carefully, for mixture burns easily.)

Yield: Enough for two 8- or 9-inch layers or a sheet cake, 13x9x2 inches.

CHOCOLATE RUM FROSTING

½ cup butter or margarine
1 jar (7 ozs.) marshmallow cream
½ cup dry cocoa, sifted
3 cups sifted confectioners' powdered sugar
3 tablespoons rum

Cream butter in a medium bowl until fluffy; beat in marshmallow cream and cocoa.

Slowly beat in confectioners' sugar, alternately with rum, until frosting is smooth and easy to spread.

Yield: Enough to fill and frost an 8- or 9-inch double-layer cake.

LEMON CREAM FROSTING

½ cup butter or margarine
1 package (16 ozs.) confectioners' powdered sugar, sifted
2 tablespoons lemon juice
4 teaspoons water

Cream butter and 2 cups of the confectioners' sugar in a large bowl until fluffy. Beat in lemon juice, then slowly beat in remaining confectioners' sugar, alternately with water, until frosting is smooth and easy to spread.

Yield: Enough to fill and frost an 8- or 9-inch double-layer cake.

VANILLA CREAM

1 package (15 ozs.) creamy white frosting mix
2 cups cream for whipping

Combine dry frosting mix and cream in a large bowl; chill at least 1 hour.
Beat until stiff.
Yield: About 4 cups.

BROWN BUTTER ICING

¼ cup butter or margarine
3 cups confectioners' powdered sugar, sifted
3 tablespoons light cream
1 teaspoon vanilla

Melt butter in a small saucepan; continue heating, shaking pan gently, just until butter bubbles up and turns golden brown; remove from heat.
Slowly beat into confectioners' sugar, alternately with cream, until frosting is smooth and easy to spread; beat in vanilla.
Yield: Enough to fill and frost an 8- or 9-inch double-layer cake or 2½ dozen cupcakes.

BUTTER RUM GLAZE

1½ cups confectioners' powdered sugar, sifted
1 tablespoon butter or margarine, melted
3 tablespoons white rum

Combine confectioners' sugar, melted butter, and rum in a small bowl; beat until smooth.
Yield: About ⅔ cup.

DARK CHOCOLATE GLAZE

3 squares unsweetened chocolate
3 tablespoons butter or margarine
1 cup confectioners' powdered sugar, sifted
1 tablespoon hot water
½ teaspoon vanilla

Melt chocolate with butter in a small saucepan over low heat; remove from heat.
Stir in confectioners' sugar and hot water, 1 teaspoon at a time, until mixture is smooth and thin enough to pour from a spoon; stir in vanilla.
Yield: Enough to glaze a 10-inch angel or sponge cake.

ORANGE GLAZE

1 cup confectioners' powdered sugar, sifted
2 tablespoons orange juice
½ teaspoon vanilla

Combine all ingredients in a small bowl; beat until smooth and thin enough to pour from a spoon.
Yield: ⅓ cup.

CREAMY WHITE GLAZE

1 cup confectioners' powdered sugar, sifted
½ teaspoon vanilla
4 teaspoons water

Combine all ingredients in a medium bowl; beat until mixture is smooth and thin enough to pour from a spoon.
Yield: About ½ cup.

PIES AND TARTS

M ENTION THE WORD PIE and almost everyone will agree that it tops the list of dessert favorites. Not many will agree, however, on what the most popular kind might be. To some, it's juicy apple, peach, or cherry—sweet but still faintly tart, lightly spiced, and bubbling up through flaky golden pastry. To others, it's a billowy chiffon creation, rich with chocolate or tangy with lemon, and laced and crowned with cream.

Steps to praise-winning pies

A superb pie starts with tender, flaky pastry, and whether you're a beginner or an experienced hand at the making, it pays to keep these fundamentals in mind:

Equipment: The recipes in this book call for 8- or 9-inch pie plates or pans. Check the size stamped on the bottom or measure the plate across the top from rim to rim. For best results, always use the size called for in your recipe.

Equip yourself with a pastry cloth and stockinet for your rolling pin. Both make rolling easier and keep the pastry from sticking without absorbing excess flour. (These items come packaged together in department and housewares stores.) To keep the cloth from slipping when you're rolling pastry, smooth it over a large cutting board, and tuck the sides under the board.

Good pie bakers are fussy about their rolling pins, and you should have one that feels comfortable to you. One of the best has ball bearings to make rolling easier.

A pastry blender for cutting shortening into flour mixture is another essential, and a pastry wheel that cuts pretty fluted edges is nice to have.

Measuring: Always measure pastry ingredients exactly as your recipe directs. Too much or too little flour, water, or shortening will only give disappointing results.

Handling: Handle the pastry as little as possible. Overhandling toughens pastry.

Rolling: First shape prepared pastry into a ball and flatten it on the pastry cloth with your hand. This makes it easier to keep a circular shape during rolling.

Roll pastry round from center to outside in all directions, lifting the rolling pin at edge of dough to prevent edge from becoming too thin. If the edge begins to tear or crack, pinch it together, then continue rolling. From time to time, lift the edge of the pastry to make sure it isn't sticking. If it does stick, rub a little extra flour into the cloth at this spot. If you should tear a hole in the pastry, cut a little piece from the edge to fit the hole, lightly moisten with water and press the patch in place.

Rolled pastry should be about ⅛ inch thick and, for a bottom crust, 3 inches larger than the pie plate. To check the size, place your pie plate upside down over rolled round. Top crust needs to be only 2 inches larger than the pie plate.

Fitting: To lift rolled pastry from cloth to plate, fold the round carefully in half and lift into plate with the fold toward the center. Unfold the dough and ease it into the plate from outside edge to center, pressing lightly with your fingertips. Work gently, do not stretch the pastry. Trim overhanging edge and proceed as your recipe directs.

Finishing: For a sparkly top, especially on fruit pies, brush milk or cream over top crust and sprinkle lightly with sugar.

Overbrowning: To prevent the edge of a double crust pie from browning too quickly, cover it with a 2- to 3-inch-wide collar of foil. Place the collar on the pie before it goes into the oven, then remove it 15 minutes before the end of baking time.

Trimmings: If you have any pastry left, roll each piece separately and cut into squares, rectangles, or fancy shapes with small cookie or truffle cutters. Bake them on a cookie sheet and use to decorate an open-face pie.

How to turn a pretty pastry edge

Flute: Press right forefinger along inside edge of stand-up pastry rim between left thumb and forefinger on the outside to make V-shapes. Repeat every inch.

Rope: Press a skewer or clean pencil diagonally into stand-up pastry rim, twisting skewer slightly as you go. Continue all the way around, making even, widely spaced ridges.

Ruffle: Place left thumb and forefinger about ¾ inch apart on inside of stand-up pastry rim. With right forefinger between the other two, gently pull pastry toward the inside. Repeat every inch.

Braid: Trim overhang of pastry even with rim of pie plate. Roll pastry trimmings to a rectangle ⅛ inch thick; cut lengthwise into even strips ¼ inch wide. Braid each three strips, then piece together to make one braid to go around pie plate. Brush rim with water; press braid on top.

Leaf: Trim overhang of pastry even with rim of pie plate. Roll pastry trimmings ⅛ inch thick; cut into leaf shapes with a truffle cutter. Brush rim of pastry with water; place cutouts, overlapping slightly, on rim; press to hold in place.

FRUIT PIES

CRANBERRY-MINCE PIE

2½ cups fresh cranberries, stemmed
1¼ cups sugar
¼ cup water
1 can (22 ozs.) mincemeat pie filling
1 tablespoon lemon juice
  Double Crust Pastry (recipe follows)

Combine cranberries, sugar, and water in a medium saucepan; heat, stirring several times, to boiling. Simmer 5 minutes, or until cranberries start to pop, stir in pie filling and lemon juice; cool.

Preheat oven to 400°.

Prepare Double Crust Pastry or make piecrust from your favorite mix. Roll out two-thirds to a 12-inch round on a lightly floured cloth; fit into a 9-inch pie plate; trim overhang to ½ inch. Spoon cranberry mixture into crust.

Roll out rest of pastry to a rectangle 12x5 inches; cut lengthwise into ten ½-inch-wide strips with a pastry wheel or knife. Lay 5 strips evenly over filling in pie plate. Weave remaining 5 strips, over and under, at right angles to those on pie to make a crisscross top. Trim strips even with overhang of bottom crust; fold bottom edge up over strips and pinch to make a stand-up edge; flute. Brush strips lightly with milk and sprinkle with sugar if you like.

Bake 40 minutes, or until filling bubbles up and pastry is golden. Cool pie on a wire rack. Serve plain or with vanilla ice cream if you like.

Yield: 9-inch pie.

DOUBLE CRUST PASTRY

2 cups sifted all-purpose flour
1 teaspoon salt
¾ cup shortening
6 tablespoons cold water

Sift flour and salt into a medium bowl; cut in shortening with a pastry blender until mixture forms fine crumbs. Sprinkle water over top, 1 tablespoon at a time, mixing lightly until pastry holds together and cleans the side of bowl.

Yield: Enough for a 9-inch pie.

PLAIN-GOOD APPLE PIE

5 large tart apples, pared, quartered, cored, and
    sliced (6 cups)
¾ cup sugar
3 tablespoons quick-cooking tapioca
1 teaspoon ground cinnamon
½ teaspoon ground nutmeg
  Double Crust Pastry
2 tablespoons butter or margarine

Combine sliced apples, sugar, tapioca, cinnamon, and nutmeg in a large bowl; toss lightly to mix. Let stand while preparing pastry.

Preheat oven to 400°.

Prepare Double Crust Pastry or make piecrust from your favorite mix.

Roll out half to a 12-inch round on a lightly floured cloth; fit into a 9-inch pie plate; trim overhang to ½ inch. Spoon apple mixture into crust; dot butter over top.

Roll out rest of pastry to an 11-inch round; cut several slits near center to let steam escape; place over filling. Trim overhang to ½ inch; turn top and bottom edges under flush with rim of pie plate; pinch to make a stand-up edge; flute. Sprinkle sugar lightly over top crust if you like.

Bake 55 minutes, or until filling bubbles up and pastry is golden. Cool on a wire rack. Serve warm or cold.

Yield: 9-inch pie.

CARAMEL APPLE PIE

Double Crust Pastry (recipe on page 496)
¾ cup firmly packed light brown sugar
2 tablespoons all-purpose flour
1 teaspoon ground cinnamon
6 medium-sized tart apples, pared, quartered, cored, and sliced (6 cups)
¼ cup butter or margarine
Milk

Prepare Double Crust Pastry or make piecrust from your favorite mix. Roll out half to a 12-inch round on a lightly floured cloth; fit into a 9-inch pie plate; trim overhang to ½ inch.

Preheat oven to 425°.

Mix brown sugar, flour, and cinnamon in a small bowl; sprinkle over apples in a large bowl; toss lightly to mix. Spoon into crust; dot butter over top.

Roll out rest of pastry to an 11-inch round; cut several slits near center to let steam escape; place over filling. Trim overhang to ½ inch; turn top and bottom edges under flush with rim of pie plate; pinch to make a stand-up edge; flute. Brush top lightly with milk; sprinkle with sugar if you like.

Bake 45 minutes, or until filling bubbles up and pastry is golden. Cool pie on a wire rack. Serve warm or cold, plain or with ice cream.

Yield: 9-inch pie.

APPLE-STRAWBERRY PIE

Double Crust Pastry (recipe on page 496)
6 medium-sized tart apples, pared, quartered, cored, and sliced (6 cups)
1 tablespoon lemon juice
1 package (10 ozs.) frozen sliced strawberries, thawed
⅔ cup sugar
6 tablespoons all-purpose flour
1 tablespoon butter or margarine
Milk
Cinnamon Cream (recipe on page 324)

Prepare Double Crust Pastry or make piecrust from your favorite mix. Roll out half to a 12-inch round on a lightly floured cloth; fit into a 9-inch pie plate; trim overhang to ½ inch.

Preheat oven to 425°.

Place apples in a large bowl; drizzle lemon juice over top; stir in strawberries and syrup. Mix sugar and flour in a small bowl; sprinkle over apple mixture; toss lightly to mix. Spoon into crust; dot butter over top.

Roll out rest of pastry to a rectangle 12x5 inches; cut lengthwise into ten ½-inch-wide strips with a pastry wheel or knife. Lay 5 strips evenly across filling in pie plate. Weave remaining 5 strips, over and under, at right angles to those on pie to make a crisscross top. Trim strips even with overhang of bottom crust; fold bottom edge up over strips and pinch to make a stand-up edge; flute. Brush strips lightly with milk; sprinkle with sugar if you like.

Bake 45 minutes, or until filling bubbles up and pastry is golden. Cool pie on a wire rack. Serve with Cinnamon Cream.

Yield: 9-inch pie.

SINGLE CRUST PASTRY

1¼ cups sifted all-purpose flour
½ teaspoon salt
½ cup shortening
3 tablespoons cold water

Follow mixing directions given under Double Crust Pastry (recipe on page 496).

Yield: Enough for a 9-inch pie.

APPLE CREAM PIE

Single Crust Pastry (recipe on page 497)
5 large apples, pared, quartered, cored, and sliced
    paper thin (6 cups)
¾ cup granulated sugar
3 tablespoons all-purpose flour (for filling)
1 teaspoon ground nutmeg
1 tablespoon lemon juice
1 cup (8-oz. carton) dairy sour cream
½ cup firmly packed light brown sugar
½ cup sifted all-purpose flour (for topping)
4 tablespoons butter or margarine

Prepare Single Crust Pastry or make pie-crust from your favorite mix. Roll out to a 12-inch round on a lightly floured cloth; fit into a 9-inch pie plate. Trim overhang to ½ inch; turn edge under flush with rim of pie plate; pinch to make a high edge.

Preheat oven to 350°.

Combine apples, granulated sugar, the 3 tablespoons flour, nutmeg, lemon juice, and sour cream in a large bowl; toss lightly until well mixed. Spoon into crust.

Mix brown sugar and the ½ cup flour in a medium bowl; cut in butter with a pastry blender until mixture forms fine crumbs; sprinkle over apple mixture.

Bake 1 hour, or until apples are tender and pastry is golden. Cool on a wire rack.

Yield: 9-inch pie.

APRICOT-APPLE PIE

1 cup dried apricots, cut in small pieces
⅔ cup water
4 large apples, pared, quartered, cored, and sliced (5 cups)
1⅓ cups sugar
¼ cup sifted all-purpose flour
1 teaspoon ground nutmeg
    Salt
Double Crust Pastry (recipe on page 496)
2 tablespoons butter or margarine

Combine apricots and water in a small saucepan; heat to boiling. Simmer 5 minutes, or until water is absorbed. Combine apricots with apples in a large bowl. Sprinkle sugar, flour, nutmeg, and a dash of salt over fruit mixture; toss lightly to mix.

Preheat oven to 400°.

Prepare Double Crust Pastry or make pie-crust from your favorite mix. Roll out half to a 12-inch round on a lightly floured cloth; fit into a 9-inch pie plate; trim overhang to ½ inch. Spoon apple mixture into crust; dot butter over top.

Roll out rest of pastry to an 11-inch round; cut several slits near center to let steam escape; place over filling. Trim overhang to ½ inch; turn top and bottom edges under flush with rim of pie plate; pinch to make a stand-up edge; flute. Sprinkle sugar lightly over top crust if you like.

Bake 50 minutes, or until filling bubbles up and pastry is golden. Cool on a wire rack. Serve warm or cold.

Yield: 9-inch pie.

ROSY RHUBARB PIE

1¼ lbs. rhubarb, trimmed and cut in ½-inch pieces
    (4 cups)
1 cup sugar
¼ cup sifted all-purpose flour
1 teaspoon grated orange rind
½ teaspoon ground cinnamon
    Double Crust Pastry (recipe on page 496)
2 tablespoons butter or margarine

Combine rhubarb, sugar, flour, orange rind, and cinnamon in a large bowl; toss lightly to mix.

Preheat oven to 400°.

Prepare Double Crust Pastry or make pie-crust from your favorite mix. Roll out half to an 11-inch round on a lightly floured cloth; fit into an 8-inch pie plate; trim overhang to ½ inch. Spoon fruit mixture into crust; dot butter over top.

Roll out rest of pastry to a 10-inch round; cut several slits near center to let steam escape; place over filling. Trim overhang to ½ inch; turn top and bottom edges under flush with rim of pie plate; pinch to make a stand-up edge; flute. Brush milk lightly over top and sprinkle with sugar if you like.

Bake 40 minutes, or until filling bubbles up and pastry is golden. Cool pie on a wire rack. Serve plain or with ice cream.

Yield: 8-inch pie.

GOLDEN PEACH PIE

7 large firm ripe peaches, peeled, halved, seeded,
    and sliced (5 cups)
¾ cup sugar
3 tablespoons quick-cooking tapioca
½ teaspoon grated lemon rind
¼ teaspoon ground cinnamon
    Double Crust Pastry (recipe on page 496)
2 tablespoons butter or margarine

Combine peaches, sugar, tapioca, lemon rind, and cinnamon in a medium bowl; toss to mix well. Let stand while preparing pastry.

Prepare Double Crust Pastry or make pie-crust from your favorite mix. Roll out half to a 12-inch round on a lightly floured cloth; fit into a 9-inch pie plate; trim overhang to ½ inch. Spoon peach mixture into crust; dot butter over top.

Preheat oven to 400°.

Roll out rest of pastry to an 11-inch round; cut several slits near center to let steam escape; place over filling. Trim overhang to ½ inch; turn top and bottom edges under flush with rim of pie plate; flute. Brush milk lightly over top and sprinkle with sugar if you like.

Bake 45 minutes, or until filling bubbles up and pastry is golden. Cool on a wire rack.

Yield: 9-inch pie.

BLUEBERRY PIE

4 cups fresh blueberries, washed and stemmed
¾ cup sugar (for filling)
3 tablespoons quick-cooking tapioca
2 teaspoons grated orange rind
½ teaspoon ground cinnamon
    Double Crust Pastry (recipe on page 496)
2 tablespoons butter or margarine
    Milk
    Sugar (for topping)

Combine blueberries, the ¾ cup sugar, tapioca, orange rind, and cinnamon in a large bowl; toss lightly to mix. Let stand while preparing pastry.

Preheat oven to 400°.

Prepare Double Crust Pastry or make pie-crust from your favorite mix. Roll out half to a 12-inch round on a lightly floured cloth; fit into a 9-inch pie plate; trim overhang to ½ inch. Spoon blueberry mixture into crust; dot butter over fruit.

Roll out rest of pastry to an 11-inch round; cut several slits near center to let steam escape; place over filling. Trim overhang to ½ inch; turn top and bottom edges under flush with rim of pie plate; pinch to make a stand-up edge; flute. Brush milk lightly over top, then sprinkle with sugar.

Bake 45 minutes, or until filling bubbles up and pastry is golden. Cool pie on a wire rack.

Yield: 9-inch pie.

PLUM CRUMB PIE

2 lbs. plums, quartered, seeded, and sliced
   (4 cups)
¾ cup granulated sugar
1¼ cups sifted all-purpose flour
½ teaspoon bottled orange rind
½ cup firmly packed light brown sugar
½ cup butter or margarine
   Single Crust Pastry (recipe on page 497)

Combine plums with granulated sugar, ¼ cup of the flour, and orange rind in a medium bowl; toss lightly to mix.

Combine remaining 1 cup flour and brown sugar in a small bowl; cut in butter with a pastry blender until mixture forms coarse crumbs.

Preheat oven to 425°.

Prepare Single Crust Pastry or make pie-crust from your favorite mix. Roll out to a 12-inch round on a lightly floured cloth; fit into a 9-inch pie plate. Trim overhang to ½ inch; turn edge under flush with rim of pie plate; pinch to make a stand-up edge; flute. Spoon plum mixture into crust; sprinkle brown sugar mixture over top.

Bake 45 minutes, or until filling bubbles up and pastry is golden. Cool pie on a wire rack.
Yield: 9-inch pie.

BLUEBERRY-NECTARINE PIE

1 pint blueberries, washed and stemmed (2 cups)
3 large nectarines, peeled, cut in half, seeded,
   and sliced (3 cups)
1¼ cups sugar
3 tablespoons quick-cooking tapioca
½ teaspoon ground cinnamon
   Double Crust Pastry (recipe on page 496)
2 tablespoons butter or margarine.

Combine blueberries, nectarines, sugar, tapioca, and cinnamon in a large bowl; toss lightly to mix.

Prepare Double Crust Pastry or make pie-crust from your favorite mix. Roll out half to a 12-inch round on a lightly floured cloth; fit into a 9-inch pie plate; trim overhang to ½ inch. Spoon fruit mixture into crust; dot butter over top.

Preheat oven to 400°.

Roll out rest of pastry to an 11-inch round; cut several slits near center to let steam escape; place over filling. Trim overhang to ½ inch; turn top and bottom edges under flush with rim of pie plate; pinch to make a stand-up edge; flute. Brush milk lightly over top and sprinkle with sugar if you like.

Bake 45 minutes, or until filling bubbles up and pastry is golden. Cool pie on a wire rack. Serve warm or cold.
Yield: 9-inch pie.

CHERRY PIE

Double Crust Pastry (recipe on page 496)
6 tablespoons all-purpose flour
1 cup sugar
2 cans (16 ozs. each) pitted tart red cherries,
   drained
¼ teaspoon almond extract
   Red food coloring
2 tablespoons butter or margarine

Prepare Double Crust Pastry or make pie-crust from your favorite mix. Roll out half to a 12-inch round on a lightly floured cloth; fit into a 9-inch pie plate; trim overhang to ½ inch.

Preheat oven to 400°.

Mix flour and sugar in a medium bowl; stir in cherries, almond extract, and a few drops food coloring to tint bright red. Spoon into prepared crust; dot butter over top.

Roll out rest of pastry to an 11-inch round; cut several slits near center to let steam escape; place over filling. Trim overhang to ½ inch; turn top and bottom edges under flush with rim of pie plate; flute. Brush milk lightly over top and sprinkle with sugar if you like.

Bake 40 minutes, or until filling bubbles up and pastry is golden. Cool on a wire rack.
Yield: 9-inch pie.

STRAWBERRY-RHUBARB PIE

1 lb. rhubarb, trimmed and cut in ½-inch pieces
   (3 cups)
1 pint strawberries
1 cup sugar
3 tablespoons quick-cooking tapioca
¼ teaspoon ground nutmeg
¼ teaspoon ground cinnamon
   Dash of salt
   Double Crust Pastry (recipe on page 496)
1 tablespoon grated orange rind
1 tablespoon butter or margarine

Place rhubarb in a large bowl. Hull strawberries and cut each in half; add to rhubarb with sugar, tapioca, nutmeg, cinnamon, and salt; mix lightly.

Prepare Double Crust Pastry, stirring orange rind into flour mixture. Roll out half of pastry to a 12-inch round on a lightly floured cloth; fit into a 9-inch pie plate; trim overhang to ½ inch. Spoon fruit mixture into crust; dot butter over top.

Preheat oven to 400°.

Roll out rest of pastry to an 11-inch round; cut several slits near center to let steam escape; place over filling. Trim overhang to ½ inch; turn top and bottom edges under flush with rim of pie plate; pinch to make a stand-up edge; flute. Brush milk lightly over top crust and sprinkle with sugar if you like.

Bake 45 minutes, or until filling bubbles up and pastry is golden. Cool pie on a wire rack. Serve warm or cold.

Yield: 9-inch pie.

PRALINE PINEAPPLE-PEACH PIE

1 can (20 ozs.) pineapple chunks in juice
1 can (29 ozs.) cling peach slices in syrup
¼ cup granulated sugar
3 tablespoons quick-cooking tapioca
   Double Crust Pastry (recipe on page 496)
3 tablespoons butter or margarine
⅓ cup firmly packed light brown sugar
¼ cup chopped pecans
1 tablespoon light cream

Drain juice from pineapple; measure ¾ cup and combine with pineapple in a large bowl. Drain syrup from peaches and save for fruit punch. Add peaches, granulated sugar, and tapioca to pineapple; mix lightly. Let stand while making pastry.

Preheat oven to 400°.

Prepare Double Crust Pastry or make piecrust from your favorite mix. Roll out half to a 12-inch round on a lightly floured cloth; fit into a 9-inch pie plate; trim overhang to ½ inch. Spoon fruit mixture into crust; dot 1 tablespoon of the butter over top.

Roll out rest of pastry to an 11-inch round; cut several slits near center to let steam escape; place over filling. Trim overhang to ½ inch; turn top and bottom edges under flush with rim of pie plate; pinch to make a stand-up edge; flute.

Bake 40 minutes, or until pastry is lightly golden.

While pie bakes, melt remaining 2 tablespoons butter in a small saucepan. Stir in brown sugar, pecans, and cream; spread over top of hot pie. Bake 10 minutes longer, or until topping bubbles. Cool pie on a wire rack.

Yield: 9-inch pie.

NECTARINE CRUMB PIE

1¼ cups sifted all-purpose flour
½ cup firmly packed light brown sugar
½ cup butter or margarine
7 large nectarines, peeled, cut in half, seeded, and sliced (4 cups)
½ cup granulated sugar
½ teaspoon mace
   Single Crust Pastry (recipe on page 497)

Mix 1 cup of the flour and brown sugar in a medium bowl; cut in butter with a pastry blender until mixture forms fine crumbs. Set aside.

Combine nectarines, granulated sugar, mace, and remaining ¼ cup flour in a large bowl; toss lightly to mix.

Preheat oven to 400°.

Prepare Single Crust Pastry or make piecrust from your favorite mix. Roll out to a 12-inch round on a lightly floured cloth; fit into a 9-inch pie plate; trim overhang to ½ inch. Turn edge under flush with rim of pie plate; pinch to make a stand-up edge; flute. Spoon fruit mixture into crust; sprinkle brown sugar mixture evenly over top.

Bake 40 minutes, or until filling bubbles up and pastry and topping are golden. Cool pie on a wire rack. Serve warm or cold.

Yield: 9-inch pie.

PURPLE PLUM PIE

2 lbs. purple plums, cut in half, seeded, and sliced (4 cups)
⅓ cup sifted all-purpose flour
⅔ cup sugar
½ teaspoon grated orange rind
   Double Crust Pastry (recipe on page 496)
2 tablespoons butter or margarine

Combine plums, flour, sugar, and orange rind in a medium bowl; toss lightly to mix.

Prepare Double Crust Pastry or make piecrust from your favorite mix. Roll out half to a 12-inch round on a lightly floured cloth; fit into a 9-inch pie plate; trim overhang to ½ inch. Spoon plum mixture into crust; dot butter over top.

Preheat oven to 400°.

Roll out rest of pastry to an 11-inch round; cut several slits near center to let steam escape; place over filling. Trim overhang to ½ inch; turn top and bottom edges under flush with rim of pie plate; pinch to make a stand-up edge; flute. Brush milk lightly over top and sprinkle with sugar if you like.

Bake 40 minutes, or until filling bubbles up and pastry is golden. Cool pie on a wire rack. Serve warm or cold.

Yield: 9-inch pie.

BLUSHING PEAR PIE

1 can (29 ozs.) pear halves in syrup
2 tablespoons cornstarch
   Dash of salt
⅓ cup red cinnamon candies
   Sugar
2 tablespoons butter or margarine
1 tablespoon lemon juice
   Double Crust Pastry (recipe on page 496)
   Milk

Preheat oven to 425°.

Drain syrup from pears into a small bowl. Slice pears into a large bowl.

Mix cornstarch and salt in a small saucepan; stir in ½ cup of the pear syrup and cinnamon candies. Heat slowly, stirring constantly, until candies melt completely and mixture thickens; remove from heat. Stir in ¼ cup sugar, butter, and lemon juice. Pour over pears; toss lightly to mix.

Prepare Double Crust Pastry or make piecrust from your favorite mix. Roll out half to an 11-inch round on a lightly floured cloth; fit into an 8-inch pie plate; trim overhang to ½ inch. Spoon pear mixture into crust.

Roll out rest of pastry to a 10-inch round; cut several slits near center to let steam escape; place over filling. Trim overhang to ½ inch; turn top and bottom edges under flush with rim of pie plate; pinch to make a stand-up edge; flute. Brush milk lightly over top; sprinkle with sugar.

Bake 40 minutes, or until filling bubbles up and pastry is golden. Cool pie on a wire rack.

Yield: 8-inch pie.

CHERRY-PINEAPPLE PIE

1 can (16 ozs.) tart red cherries in juice
1 can (20 ozs.) crushed pineapple in syrup
¾ cup sugar
3 tablespoons cornstarch
½ teaspoon ground cinnamon
   Dash of salt
2 tablespoons butter or margarine
   Double Crust Pastry (recipe on page 496)

Drain liquids from cherries and pineapple into a 2-cup measure. (There should be 1½ cups.)

Mix sugar, cornstarch, cinnamon, and salt in a medium saucepan; stir in the 1½ cups liquid. Cook slowly, stirring constantly, until mixture thickens and boils 1 minute; stir in butter until melted, then cherries and pineapple. Set aside while making pastry.

Prepare Double Crust Pastry or make piecrust from your favorite mix. Roll out half to a 12-inch round on a lightly floured cloth; fit into a 9-inch pie plate; trim overhang to ½ inch. Spoon fruit mixture into crust.

Preheat oven to 400°.

Roll out rest of pastry to an 11-inch round; cut several slits near center to let steam escape; place over filling. Trim overhang to ½ inch; turn top and bottom edges under flush with rim of pie plate; pinch to make a stand-up edge; flute. Brush milk lightly over top and sprinkle with sugar if you like.

Bake 45 minutes, or until filling bubbles up and pastry is golden. Cool pie on a wire rack. Serve warm or cold.

Yield: 9-inch pie.

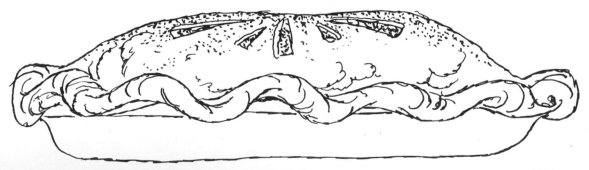

APRICOT-PINEAPPLE PIE

Double Crust Pastry (recipe on page 496)
1 can (20 ozs.) pineapple chunks in juice
1 can (29 ozs.) apricots in syrup
⅓ cup granulated sugar
2 tablespoons cornstarch
½ teaspoon mace
2 tablespoons butter or margarine

Prepare Double Crust Pastry or make pie-crust from your favorite mix. Roll out half to a 12-inch round on a lightly floured cloth; fit into a 9-inch pie plate; trim overhang to ½ inch.

Drain juice from pineapple into a 1-cup measure; drain syrup from apricots, adding enough to pineapple juice to measure 1 cup liquid. Cut apricots in half and pit; combine with pineapple in a large bowl.

Mix sugar and cornstarch in a small sauce-pan; stir in the 1 cup pineapple liquid. Cook, stirring constantly, until mixture thickens and boils 1 minute; stir in mace and butter. Pour over fruit mixture; toss to mix; spoon into crust.

Preheat oven to 425°.

Roll out rest of pastry to a rectangle 12x5 inches; cut lengthwise into ten ½-inch-wide strips with a pastry wheel or knife. Lay 5 strips evenly across filling in pie plate. Weave remaining 5 strips, over and under, at right angles to those on pie to make a crisscross top. Trim strips even with overhang of bottom crust. Fold bottom edge up over strips and pinch to make a stand-up edge; flute. Brush strips with milk and sprinkle with sugar if you like.

Bake 45 minutes, or until filling bubbles up and pastry is golden. Cool pie on a wire rack. Serve warm or cold.

Yield: 9-inch pie.

CREAM PIES

RAINBOW FRUIT PIE

Single Crust Pastry (recipe on page 497)
1 envelope unflavored gelatin
½ cup sugar (for filling)
Dash of salt
2 eggs, separated
½ cup milk
1 package (8 ozs.) cream cheese
1 teaspoon grated orange rind
1 cup orange juice
½ cup whipping cream
1 tablespoon sugar (for glaze)
1½ teaspoons cornstarch
1 pint strawberries, washed, hulled and halved
1 large banana
½ cup blueberries

Preheat oven to 400°.

Prepare Single Crust Pastry or make pie-crust from your favorite mix. Roll out to a 12-inch round on a lightly floured cloth; fit into a 9-inch pie plate. Trim overhang to ½ inch; turn edge under flush with rim of pie plate; flute to make a high edge. Prick shell well all over with a fork.

Bake 12 minutes, or until golden; cool shell completely on a wire rack.

Mix gelatin, ¼ cup of the sugar, and salt in a small saucepan.

Beat egg yolks with milk in a small bowl; stir into gelatin mixture. Cook slowly, stirring constantly, until gelatin dissolves; cut up cream cheese and stir in until melted, keeping saucepan over very low heat, if needed. Pour mixture into a medium bowl; beat until smooth; stir in orange rind and ½ cup of the orange juice. Chill 30 minutes, or until mixture mounds softly.

While gelatin mixture chills, beat egg whites in a small bowl until foamy; slowly beat in remaining ¼ cup sugar until meringue forms soft peaks. Beat cream in a small bowl until stiff. Fold meringue, then whipped cream into gelatin mixture until no streaks of white remain. Spoon into prepared pastry shell, spreading top even. Chill 2 hours, or until firm.

Mix the 1 tablespoon sugar and cornstarch in a small saucepan; stir in remaining ½ cup orange juice. Cook slowly, stirring constantly, until mixture thickens and boils 1 minute; cool just until lukewarm.

Arrange enough strawberry halves, over-lapping, on cream layer to form a circle around edge of shell. Peel banana and slice; overlap slices in a circle next to strawberries. Place blueberries in several rings next to bananas; arrange remaining strawberries in center. Brush cooled orange mixture over fruits to glaze generously. Chill pie until glaze sets.

Yield: 9-inch pie.

CHERRY CREAM PIE

2 cups crushed sugar cookies
4 tablespoons melted butter or margarine
1 cup whipping cream
2 cups tiny marshmallows
1 can (21 ozs.) cherry pie filling
¼ teaspoon orange extract

Preheat oven to 350°.

Blend cookie crumbs and melted butter in a medium bowl; measure out 3 tablespoons and set aside for topping. Press remainder over bottom and up side of a 9-inch pie plate to form a shell.

Bake 10 minutes; cool completely on a wire rack.

Beat cream in a medium bowl until stiff; fold in marshmallows; spread half into shell.

Mix cherry pie filling and orange extract in a medium bowl; spoon over cream layer in shell. Spoon rest of cream mixture on top, leaving a 2-inch opening in center. Sprinkle the 3 tablespoons crumb mixture over cream. Chill at least 8 hours, or overnight.

Yield: 9-inch pie.

PISTACHIO RIBBON PIE

2 egg whites
¼ teaspoon salt
¼ teaspoon cream of tartar
½ cup sugar
½ teaspoon vanilla
1 can (4 ozs.) flaked coconut
1 can (16 ozs.) pitted dark sweet cherries in syrup
4 teaspoons cornstarch
1 teaspoon lemon juice
1 package (3¾ ozs.) pistachio instant pudding mix
1¾ cups milk
1 cup thawed frozen whipped topping

Preheat oven to 275°.

Beat egg whites with salt and cream of tartar in a medium bowl until foamy. Beat in sugar, 1 tablespoon at a time, beating constantly until meringue stands in firm peaks; beat in vanilla. Fold in coconut.

Spread mixture over bottom and up side of a generously buttered 9-inch pie plate, hollowing center with a spoon, to form a shell.

Bake 1 hour, or until firm and lightly golden. Cool shell completely on a wire rack.

Drain syrup from cherries into a 1-cup measure. (There should be 1 cup.) Stir into cornstarch in a small saucepan; cook, stirring constantly, until mixture thickens and boils 1 minute. Stir in lemon juice and cherries; cool. Spread in prepared shell; chill 20 minutes.

Prepare pudding mix as label directs, using 1¾ cups milk; spoon over cherry layer in shell. Chill several hours, or until firm.

Just before serving, spoon whipped topping in a ruffle around edge on pie.

Yield: 9-inch pie.

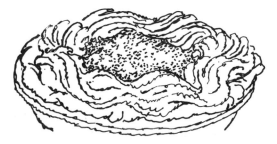

STRAWBERRY TART GLACE

1 package piecrust mix
4 tablespoons sugar
1 egg
1 cup milk
4 packages (3 ozs. each) cream cheese, softened
3 tablespoons curaçao
1 package (3¾ ozs.) vanilla-flavored instant pudding mix
2 pints strawberries, washed and hulled
¼ cup currant jelly

Preheat oven to 400°.

Combine piecrust mix and 2 tablespoons of the sugar in a medium bowl. Beat egg well in a small bowl; stir into piecrust mixture until evenly moist. (If mixture seems too dry to roll, stir in about 1 tablespoon ice water.)

Roll out pastry to a 13-inch round on a lightly floured cloth; fit into a 9-inch round layer-cake pan; trim edge even with rim of pan. Prick shell well all over with a fork. (Use any pastry trimmings to make a smaller shell for another dessert or to turn into nibbles for the children.)

Bake shell 12 minutes, or until golden. Cool completely on a wire rack, then remove carefully from pan and place on a large flat serving plate.

Blend milk and cream cheese until smooth in a medium bowl; beat in remaining 2 tablespoons sugar and 2 tablespoons of the curaçao. Add pudding mix; beat 1 minute; spread evenly in pastry shell. Chill while fixing strawberry topping.

Arrange strawberries, pointed ends up, over filling in shell to cover completely.

Heat jelly until melted in a small saucepan; stir in remaining 1 tablespoon curaçao; cool slightly. Brush over berries to glaze. Chill tart until glaze is firm or until serving time.

Yield: 8 servings.

RING-AROUND STRAWBERRY TART

2 packages piecrust mix
¼ cup sugar
2 eggs
2 tablespoons water
2 packages (3¼ ozs. each) vanilla pudding and pie filling mix
3 cups milk
1 teaspoon grated orange rind
4 pints fresh strawberries, washed and hulled
2 large firm ripe bananas
  Lemon juice
1 jar (10 ozs.) currant jelly
2 tablespoons orange juice

Preheat oven to 400°.

Combine piecrust mix and sugar in a large bowl. Beat eggs with water in a small bowl; stir into piecrust mixture with a fork until dough cleans side of bowl. Divide in half; press each half evenly into a 14-inch pizza pan; flute edges. Prick shells all over with a fork.

Bake 12 minutes, or until pastry is golden. Cool shells completely on wire racks.

Prepare pudding mix with milk as label directs; stir in orange rind. Chill 20 minutes, or until cool; spread half in each pastry shell.

Set aside 10 or 12 whole strawberries, then cut the rest in half lengthwise. Peel bananas and slice thin diagonally; dip slices in lemon juice in a pie plate to prevent darkening. Arrange halved strawberries and bananas in rings on top of filling in pastry shells; place whole strawberries in center.

Heat currant jelly until melted in a small saucepan; stir in orange juice; cool. Brush half over strawberries in each tart to glaze. Chill until glaze is firm. To serve, cut each tart into 8 wedges.

Yield: 16 servings.

PARISIAN CREAM PIE

Single Crust Pastry (recipe on page 497)
1 package (3¼ ozs.) vanilla pudding and pie filling mix
1¾ cups milk
1 egg, separated
1 teaspoon orange extract
1 tablespoon sugar
1 package (3 ozs.) orange-flavored gelatin
1½ cups boiling water
1 teaspoon lemon juice
1 can (11 ozs.) mandarin orange segments, drained

Preheat oven to 400°.

Prepare Single Crust Pastry or make piecrust from your favorite mix. Roll out to a 12-inch round on a lightly floured cloth; fit into a 9-inch pie plate. Trim overhang to ½ inch; turn edge under flush with rim of pie plate; pinch to make a stand-up edge; flute. Prick shell all over with a fork.

Bake 12 minutes, or until pastry is golden; cool shell completely on a wire rack.

Combine pudding mix and milk in a saucepan; beat in egg yolk. Cook as label directs; stir in orange extract; cool 15 minutes.

Beat egg white in a small bowl until foamy; beat in sugar until meringue forms soft peaks; fold into pudding mixture. Spoon into pastry shell. Chill several hours, or until layer is set.

While layer chills, dissolve gelatin in boiling water in a small bowl; stir in lemon juice. Chill 20 minutes, or until slightly thickened.

Arrange mandarin orange segments in a pretty pattern on top of layer in shell; spoon gelatin mixture over fruit. Chill several hours, or until firm. Serve plain or with whipped cream if you like.

Yield: 9-inch pie.

COCONUT CREME BRULEE PIE

Single Crust Pastry (recipe on page 497)
2 packages (3 ozs. each) egg custard mix
3 cups milk
1 cup light cream
1 egg, slightly beaten
½ cup toasted coconut
¼ cup firmly packed light brown sugar

Preheat oven to 400°.

Prepare Single Crust Pastry or make pie-crust from your favorite mix. Roll out to a 12-inch round on a lightly floured cloth; fit into a 9-inch pie plate. Trim overhang to ½ inch; turn edge under flush with rim of pie plate; pinch to make a stand-up edge; flute. Prick shell all over with a fork.

Bake 12 minutes, or until pastry is golden; cool shell completely on a wire rack.

Blend custard mix, milk, cream, and egg in a medium saucepan. Heat slowly just to boiling; remove from heat. Cool 15 minutes; stir in coconut. Pour into pastry shell. Chill at least 3 hours, or until filling is set.

Just before serving, preheat broiler.

Sprinkle brown sugar evenly over pie. Broil, 6 inches from heat, 2 minutes, or *just* until sugar melts. (Watch carefully so pastry doesn't burn and custard stays cold.)

Yield: 9-inch pie.

RUFFLED PEACH PIE

1 cup sifted all-purpose flour
¼ cup firmly packed light brown sugar
6 tablespoons butter or margarine
¼ cup finely chopped sliced almonds
1 can (29 ozs.) cling peach slices in syrup
2 packages (3¾ ozs. each) vanilla instant pudding mix
1 package (1½ ozs.) whipped topping mix
2¼ cups milk
½ teaspoon almond extract

Preheat oven to 400°.

Mix flour and brown sugar in a medium bowl. Cut in butter with a pastry blender until mixture is almost pastelike; stir in almonds. Press over bottom and up side of a 9-inch pie plate to form a shell.

Bake 12 minutes, or until set. Cool shell completely on a wire rack.

Drain syrup from peaches and save to sweeten fruit punch. Set aside 10 of the peach slices for topping, dice the rest.

Combine pudding mix, dry topping mix, milk, and almond extract in a medium bowl; beat slowly until blended, then beat at high speed on electric mixer 3 minutes, or until mixture forms soft peaks. Fold in diced peaches. Spoon into cooled crust.

Arrange rest of peach slices, rounded sides out, around edge on pie to form a scalloped design. Chill pie several hours, or until firm.

Yield: 9-inch pie.

CUSTARD PIES

CREAMY CUSTARD PIE

   Single Crust Pastry (recipe on page 497)
   4 eggs
   ⅔ cup sugar
   ¼ teaspoon salt
   ¼ teaspoon ground nutmeg
   2¾ cups milk
   1 teaspoon vanilla

Prepare Single Crust Pastry or make pie-crust from your favorite mix. Roll out to a 12-inch round on a lightly floured cloth; fit into a 9-inch pie plate. Trim overhang to ½ inch; turn edge under flush with rim of pie plate; flute.

Preheat oven to 425°.

Beat eggs just until blended in a medium bowl; stir in sugar, salt, nutmeg, milk, and vanilla; strain into pastry shell.

Bake 20 minutes; lower oven temperature to 350°.

Bake 25 minutes longer, or until a knife inserted into filling halfway between center and edge comes out clean. Cool pie on a wire rack.

   Yield: 9-inch pie.

APRICOT CUSTARD PIE

   ½ cup butter or margarine
   ¾ cup sugar
   1¼ cups sifted all-purpose flour
   ½ teaspoon salt
   ¼ teaspoon ground mace
   ¼ teaspoon baking powder
   1 can (29 ozs.) apricot halves, well drained
   1 egg
   ¾ cup whipping cream

   Preheat oven to 375°.

Cream butter and sugar in a large bowl; blend in flour, salt, mace, and baking powder. Measure out ½ cup of the mixture; press the rest over bottom and three quarters of the way up side of a deep 9-inch pie plate to form a shell.

Arrange apricot halves, hollow side down, in shell; sprinkle the ½ cup crumb mixture over apricots.

Bake 15 minutes.

Beat egg slightly in a small bowl; stir in cream. Pour over apricots. Bake 25 minutes longer, or until custard is set. Cool pie on a wire rack.

   Yield: 9-inch pie.

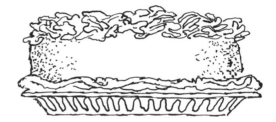

SOUTHERN PECAN PIE

   Single Crust Pastry (recipe on page 497)
   4 eggs
   ⅔ cup sugar
   3 tablespoons all-purpose flour
   ½ teaspoon salt
   1½ cups dark corn syrup
   3 tablespoons melted butter or margarine
   1 teaspoon vanilla
   1 cup pecans

Prepare Single Crust Pastry or make pie-crust from your favorite mix. Roll out to a 12-inch round on a lightly floured cloth; fit into a 9-inch pie plate. Trim overhang to ½ inch; turn edge under flush with rim of pie plate; pinch to make a stand-up edge; flute.

   Preheat oven to 375°.

Beat eggs until blended in a medium bowl; stir in sugar, flour, salt, corn syrup, butter, and vanilla until well blended. Pour into pastry shell. Arrange pecans over top.

Bake 45 minutes, or until filling is set. Cool pie on a wire rack at least 2 hours before cutting.

   Yield: 9-inch pie.

CANDIED PECAN PUMPKIN PIE

Single Crust Pastry (recipe on page 497)
3 eggs
1 can (16 ozs.) pumpkin
1 cup granulated sugar
⅓ cup firmly packed brown sugar
2 teaspoons pumpkin-pie spice
1 teaspoon salt
1 tall can evaporated milk (1⅔ cups)
½ cup coarsely broken pecans
½ teaspoon vanilla
1½ cups whipping cream

Prepare Single Crust Pastry or make pie-crust from your favorite mix. Roll out to a 12-inch round on a lightly floured cloth; fit into a 9-inch pie plate. Trim overhang to ½ inch; turn edge under flush with rim of pie plate; pinch to make a stand-up edge; flute.

Preheat oven to 425°.

Beat eggs in a medium bowl until blended; stir in pumpkin, ½ cup of the granulated sugar, brown sugar, pumpkin-pie spice, salt, and evaporated milk until blended; pour into crust.

Bake 15 minutes; lower temperature to 350°. Bake 25 minutes longer, or until filling is almost set but still soft in center. Cool pie completely on a wire rack.

While pie cools, measure remaining ½ cup granulated sugar into a small heavy skillet. Heat slowly, stirring constantly with a wooden spoon, until sugar melts and syrup turns golden. Quickly stir in pecans and vanilla. Spread on a foil-lined cookie sheet. (Work fast; mixture hardens quickly.) Let stand until cool and firm. Break into small pieces with a mallet.

When ready to serve pie, beat cream until stiff in a medium bowl; pile onto center. Sprinkle pecan brittle over cream.

Yield: 9-inch pie.

RHUBARB CREAM PIE

1¼ lbs. rhubarb, trimmed and cut in ½-inch pieces
    (4 cups)
1½ cups sugar
1 tablespoon grated orange rind
1 tablespoon water
1¼ cups sifted all-purpose flour
¼ teaspoon salt
½ teaspoon ground cinnamon
¼ teaspoon baking powder
½ cup butter or margarine
1 egg
1 cup whipping cream

Combine rhubarb, 1 cup of the sugar, orange rind, and water in a medium saucepan. Heat slowly, stirring several times, until sugar dissolves and juice starts to flow from rhubarb. Heat to boiling; cook 2 minutes; remove from heat; cover. Let stand until cold. Drain syrup from fruit and set aside to sweeten a breakfast beverage.

Preheat oven to 350°.

Sift flour, remaining ½ cup sugar, salt, cinnamon, and baking powder into a medium bowl; cut in butter with a pastry blender until mixture forms fine crumbs. Measure out ½ cup; press remainder over bottom and up side of a 9-inch pie plate to form a shell.

Spoon rhubarb into shell; sprinkle the ½ cup crumb mixture over rhubarb.

Bake 15 minutes; remove from oven, but leave heat on.

While pie bakes, beat egg slightly in a small bowl; stir in cream; pour over rhubarb.

Bake 25 minutes longer, or until topping sets. Cool pie on a wire rack.

Cut into wedges; serve warm or cold.

Yield: 9-inch pie.

MERINGUE PIES

LEMON MERINGUE PIE

Single Crust Pastry (recipe on page 497)
1¾ cups sugar
½ cup cornstarch
⅛ teaspoon salt
1¾ cups water
4 eggs, separated
2 tablespoons butter or margarine
2 teaspoons grated lemon rind
½ cup lemon juice
¼ teaspoon cream of tartar

Preheat oven to 400°.

Prepare Single Crust Pastry or make pie-crust from your favorite mix. Roll out to a 12-inch round on a lightly floured cloth; fit into a 9-inch pie plate. Trim overhang to ½ inch; turn edge under flush with rim of pie plate; pinch to make a stand-up edge; flute. Prick shell all over with a fork.

Bake 12 minutes, or until pastry is golden; cool completely in pie plate on a wire rack.

Mix 1¼ cups of the sugar with cornstarch and salt in a medium saucepan; stir in water. Cook slowly, stirring constantly, until mixture thickens and boils 1 minute.

Beat egg yolks well in a small bowl; slowly stir in about half of the hot cornstarch mixture; stir back into saucepan. Continue cooking and stirring 2 minutes; remove from heat.

Stir in butter until melted; stir in lemon rind and juice; pour into pastry shell.

Beat egg whites with cream of tartar in a medium bowl until frothy; beat in remaining ½ cup sugar, 1 tablespoon at a time, until meringue forms firm peaks. Pile onto lemon filling, spreading to edge of crust.

Bake 8 minutes, or until meringue is golden. Cool pie on a wire rack at least 4 hours before cutting.

Yield: 9-inch pie.

BUTTERSCOTCH-BANANA PIE

Single Crust Pastry (recipe on page 497)
2 cups milk
¾ cup firmly packed dark brown sugar
⅓ cup flour
⅛ teaspoon salt
3 eggs, separated
3 tablespoons butter or margarine
1 teaspoon vanilla
3 medium-sized firm ripe bananas
¼ teaspoon cream of tartar
6 tablespoons granulated sugar

Preheat oven to 400°.

Prepare Single Crust Pastry or make pie-crust from your favorite mix. Roll out to a 12-inch round on a lightly floured cloth; fit into a 9-inch pie plate. Trim overhang to ½ inch; turn edge under flush with rim of pie plate; pinch to make a stand-up edge; flute. Prick shell all over with a fork.

Bake 12 minutes, or until pastry is golden; cool shell completely on a wire rack. Lower oven temperature to 350°.

Scald milk in the top of a double boiler.

Mix brown sugar, flour, and salt in a small bowl; slowly stir into scalded milk. Cook, stirring constantly, until mixture thickens; cover. Continue cooking, stirring once or twice, 10 minutes longer.

Beat egg yolks well in a small bowl; slowly stir in about half of the hot mixture, then stir back into top of double boiler. Cook, stirring constantly, 2 minutes; remove from hot water. Stir in butter and vanilla.

Peel bananas and slice; layer half into pastry shell; top with half of the butterscotch mixture; repeat layers.

Beat egg whites with cream of tartar in a medium bowl until foamy; slowly beat in granulated sugar until meringue forms firm peaks. Pile onto butterscotch filling, spreading to edge of crust.

Bake 20 minutes, or until meringue is golden. Cool pie on a wire rack at least 4 hours before cutting.

Yield: 9-inch pie.

CHIFFON AND FREEZER PIES

REFRIGERATOR RASPBERRY PIE

¼ cup light corn syrup
2 tablespoons sugar
1 tablespoon butter or margarine
3 cups cornflakes
1 package (10 ozs.) frozen raspberries, thawed
    Water
1 package (3 ozs.) raspberry-flavored gelatin
1 pint vanilla ice cream
½ cup whipping cream
2 tablespoons confectioners' powdered sugar

Combine corn syrup, sugar, and butter in a medium saucepan. Heat slowly, stirring several times, until mixture starts to bubble; remove from heat. Stir in cornflakes until evenly coated. Press mixture firmly over bottom and up side of an 8-inch pie plate to form a shell with a high edge. Chill shell while preparing filling.

Drain raspberry syrup into a 1-cup measure; add water to make 1 cup. Heat to boiling in a small saucepan; pour over gelatin in a medium bowl; stir until gelatin dissolves. Stir in ice cream until melted and mixture is smooth.

Chill 10 minutes, or until partly thickened; fold in raspberries. Pour into prepared shell; chill several hours, or until firm.

Just before serving, beat cream with confectioners' sugar until stiff in a small bowl; spoon onto center of pie.

Yield: 8-inch pie.

PUMPKIN-PINEAPPLE CHIFFON PIE

Single Crust Pastry (recipe on page 497)
1 cup sugar
1 envelope unflavored gelatin
3 eggs, separated
¾ cup milk
1½ cups pumpkin
¾ teaspoon ground cinnamon
½ teaspoon ground ginger
½ teaspoon ground nutmeg
½ teaspoon salt
1 can (8 ozs.) crushed pineapple in syrup, well drained
1 cup whipping cream

Preheat oven to 400°.

Prepare Single Crust Pastry or make piecrust from your favorite mix. Roll out to a 12-inch round on a lightly floured cloth; fit into a 9-inch pie plate. Trim overhang to ½ inch; turn edge under flush with rim of pie plate; pinch to make a stand-up edge; flute. Prick shell all over with a fork.

Bake 12 minutes, or until pastry is golden. Cool shell completely on a wire rack.

Mix ½ cup of the sugar and gelatin in a large saucepan.

Beat egg yolks well with milk in a small bowl; stir into sugar mixture with pumpkin, spices, and salt. Cook slowly, stirring constantly, until gelatin dissolves and mixture thickens slightly; remove from heat. Cool slightly.

Beat egg whites in a medium bowl until foamy; slowly beat in remaining ½ cup sugar until meringue forms soft peaks; fold into pumpkin mixture. Spoon half into pastry shell; spread pineapple in a layer on top; spoon rest of pumpkin mixture over pineapple. Chill pie several hours or overnight until firm.

Just before serving, beat cream in a medium bowl until stiff; spoon in a ring on top of pie. Or press through a pastry bag onto pie to form a crisscross design.

Yield: 9-inch pie.

RAINBOW FRUIT PIE (p.505) ▶

PUMPKIN NESSELRODE PIE

   Single Crust Pastry (recipe on page 497)
   1 envelope unflavored gelatin
   6 tablespoons sugar
   ½ teaspoon salt
   3 eggs, separated
   ½ cup milk
   1 cup canned pumpkin
   ½ cup Nesselrode dessert sauce
   1½ cups whipping cream

Preheat oven to 400°.

Prepare Single Crust Pastry or make pie-crust from your favorite mix. Roll out to a 12-inch round on a lightly floured cloth; fit into a 9-inch pie plate. Trim overhang to ½ inch; turn edge under flush with rim of pie plate; pinch to make a stand-up edge; flute. Prick shell all over with a fork.

Bake 12 minutes, or until golden; cool shell completely on a wire rack.

Mix gelatin, 2 tablespoons of the sugar, and salt in a medium saucepan.

Beat egg yolks with milk in a small bowl; stir into gelatin mixture with pumpkin. Cook slowly, stirring constantly, until gelatin dissolves and mixture bubbles.

Pour into a large bowl; stir in Nesselrode sauce. Place bowl in a pan of ice and water to speed setting. Let stand, stirring several times, until mixture is cold.

Beat egg whites in a medium bowl until foamy; slowly beat in remaining 4 tablespoons sugar until meringue stands in firm peaks. Beat ½ cup of the cream in a small bowl until stiff. Fold meringue, then whipped cream into Nesselrode mixture. Continue folding until mixture mounds softly; spoon into pastry shell. Chill several hours, or until firm.

Just before serving, beat remaining 1 cup cream in a medium bowl until stiff; spoon around edge on pie. Sprinkle chopped candied cherries over cream if you like.

Yield: 9-inch pie.

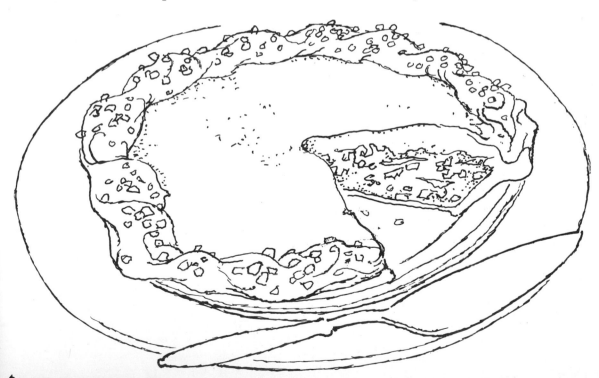

◀ CHOCOLATE CHIFFON PIE (p.515)

TANGERINE DREAM PIE

1 cup pre-sweetened wheat germ
½ cup finely crushed zwieback crumbs
⅓ cup melted butter or margarine
1 package (3 ozs.) lemon-flavored gelatin
¾ cup boiling water
1 cup sugar
1 can (6 ozs.) frozen concentrated tangerine juice, thawed
  Red food coloring
1 package (2 ozs.) whipped topping mix
  Cold milk
  Vanilla

Preheat oven to 350°.

Blend wheat germ, zwieback crumbs, and butter in a small bowl; press evenly over bottom and up side of a 9-inch pie plate.

Bake 8 minutes, or until crust is set; cool shell completely on a wire rack.

Dissolve gelatin in boiling water in a medium bowl; stir in sugar until dissolved, then tangerine concentrate and red food coloring to tint deep orange.

Place bowl in a pan of ice and water to speed setting. Chill, stirring several times, until mixture starts to thicken.

While gelatin mixture chills, prepare topping mix with milk and vanilla as label directs. Keeping mixture over ice, fold in whipped topping; continue folding until mixture mounds softly. Spoon into shell. Chill several hours, or until firm. Just before serving, garnish with more whipped topping and tangerine sections if you like.

Yield: 9-inch pie.

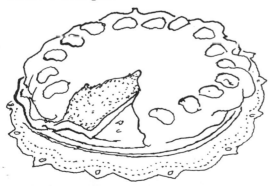

CARAMEL SUNDAE PIE

3 egg whites
¼ teaspoon cream of tartar
¾ cup granulated sugar
½ teaspoon salt
¾ teaspoon vanilla
3 pints vanilla ice cream
1 cup firmly packed light brown sugar
2 tablespoons light corn syrup
3 tablespoons water
1 teaspoon lemon juice
1 tablespoon butter or margarine

Preheat oven to 275°. Grease a 9-inch pie plate.

Beat egg whites with cream of tartar until foamy in a large bowl; very slowly beat in granulated sugar, 1 tablespoon at a time, beating constantly until sugar dissolves completely and meringue forms firm peaks; beat in ¼ teaspoon each of the salt and vanilla. (Beating will take about 20 minutes in all with an electric mixer.)

Spoon meringue into pie plate; with back of spoon, spread from center to outside edge, building up rim to form a shell.

Bake 1 hour, or until meringue is firm and lightly golden. Cool shell completely on a wire rack.

Scoop ice cream into balls; arrange in meringue shell. Freeze several hours, or overnight, until very firm.

Combine brown sugar, corn syrup, water, lemon juice, and remaining ¼ teaspoon salt in a small saucepan. Heat slowly, stirring constantly, to boiling, then cook, without stirring, 2 minutes, or until a little of the syrup forms a soft ball when dropped from a spoon into cold water. Remove from heat. Stir in butter and remaining ½ teaspoon vanilla; cool without stirring.

Remove pie from freezer about 10 minutes before serving and let stand in refrigerator to soften. When ready to serve, drizzle ¼ cup of the sauce over ice cream; serve remainder separately to spoon over each serving.

Yield: 9-inch pie.

CHOCOLATE CHIFFON PIE

Single Crust Pastry (recipe on page 497)
¼ cup finely chopped California walnuts
 1 envelope unflavored gelatin
 1 cup sugar
¼ teaspoon salt
 3 eggs, separated
 1 cup milk
 3 squares unsweetened chocolate
 1 teaspoon vanilla
⅛ teaspoon cream of tartar
 2 cups whipping cream
¼ cup semisweet chocolate pieces
½ teaspoon shortening

Preheat oven to 400°.

Prepare Single Crust Pastry or make pastry from your favorite mix, stirring walnuts into flour mixture before adding water. Roll out to a 12-inch round on a lightly floured cloth; fit into a 9-inch pie plate. Trim overhang to ½ inch; turn edge under flush with rim of pie plate; pinch to make a stand-up edge; flute. Prick shell all over with a fork.

Bake 12 minutes, or until pastry is golden; cool shell completely on a wire rack.

Mix gelatin, ½ cup of the sugar, and salt in a medium saucepan. Beat egg yolks in a small bowl; stir into gelatin mixture with milk; add chocolate squares. Heat slowly, stirring constantly, until gelatin dissolves and chocolate melts; pour into a large bowl; stir in vanilla.

Place bowl in a pan of ice and water to speed setting. Chill, stirring several times, until mixture starts to thicken.

While gelatin mixture chills, beat egg whites with cream of tartar in a medium bowl until foamy; slowly beat in remaining ½ cup sugar until meringue forms firm peaks. Beat 1 cup of the cream until stiff in a medium bowl.

Keeping gelatin mixture over ice, beat until smooth; fold in meringue, then whipped cream; continue folding until mixture mounds softly. Spoon into pastry shell. Chill several hours, or until firm.

Melt chocolate pieces with shortening in a cup over hot water; pour onto a foil-lined cookie sheet; spread into a rectangle 6x3 inches. Chill 15 minutes, or just until firm enough to cut. Using a truffle cutter or knife, cut chocolate into fan shapes; chill again until firm; peel off foil.

Just before serving, beat remaining 1 cup cream in a medium bowl until stiff. Spoon onto center of pie; trim with chocolate fans.

Yield: 9-inch pie.

STRAWBERRIES-AND-CREAM PIE

½ cup butter or margarine
½ cup firmly packed light brown sugar
 3 cups oven-toasted crisp rice cereal
½ cup flaked coconut
 2 pints strawberries, washed and hulled
⅔ cup granulated sugar
 1 tablespoon lemon juice
 1 envelope unflavored gelatin
¼ cup cold water
 1 cup whipping cream

Cream butter and brown sugar until fluffy in a medium bowl; stir in cereal and coconut until mixture is well blended. Press over bottom and up side of a 9-inch pie plate to form a shell. Chill while making filling.

Crush enough strawberries to measure 1½ cups. (It will take about 1½ pints.) Combine with granulated sugar and lemon juice in a medium bowl; let stand a half hour.

Sprinkle gelatin over water in a small saucepan; let stand a minute to soften, then heat slowly, stirring constantly, until gelatin dissolves. Cool slightly; stir into strawberry mixture. Chill 30 minutes, or until syrupy-thick.

While gelatin mixture chills, beat cream in a medium bowl until stiff; fold into thickened gelatin mixture until no streaks of white remain. Spoon into prepared shell. Chill several hours, or until firm.

When ready to serve, cut rest of strawberries in half; arrange, pointed ends toward center, around edge on pie.

Yield: 9-inch pie.

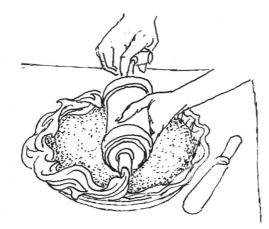

RASPBERRY RIPPLE PIE

Single Crust Pastry (recipe on page 497)
1 package (10 ozs.) frozen raspberries
1 tablespoon cornstarch
½ teaspoon lemon juice
1 envelope unflavored gelatin
1 cup sugar
¼ teaspoon salt
1¼ cups milk
1 teaspoon vanilla
3 egg whites
1 cup whipping cream

Preheat oven to 400°.

Prepare Single Crust Pastry or make pie-crust from your favorite mix. Roll out to a 12-inch round on a lightly floured cloth; fit into a 9-inch pie plate. Trim overhang to ½ inch; turn edge under flush with rim of pie plate; pinch to make a stand-up edge; flute. Prick shell all over with a fork.

Bake 12 minutes, or until pastry is golden. Cool shell completely on a wire rack.

Thaw raspberries just enough to pick out 6 pretty ones for garnish; stand on a plate; return to freezer. Press remaining raspberries with syrup through a sieve into a small saucepan; sprinkle cornstarch over top, then stir in. Cook, stirring constantly, until sauce thickens and boils 1 minute; cool. Stir in lemon juice.

Mix gelatin, ½ cup of the sugar, and salt in a small saucepan; stir in milk. Heat slowly, stir-ring constantly, until gelatin dissolves; pour into a large bowl; stir in vanilla.

Place bowl in a pan of ice and water to speed setting. Let stand, stirring several times, until mixture starts to thicken.

While gelatin mixture chills, beat egg whites in a medium bowl until foamy; slowly beat in remaining ½ cup sugar until meringue forms firm peaks. Beat ½ cup of the cream in a small bowl until stiff.

Keeping gelatin mixture over ice, fold in meringue, then whipped cream; continue folding until mixture mounds softly. Spoon half into pastry shell; drizzle half of the raspberry sauce over top. Repeat layers, then draw a knife through filling to marble. Chill pie several hours, or until firm.

Just before serving, beat remaining ½ cup cream in a small bowl until stiff. Spoon onto center of pie; garnish with remaining whole raspberries.

Yield: 9-inch pie.

CHOCO-LIME PIE

1 package (6 ozs.) semisweet chocolate pieces
2 tablespoons butter or margarine
2 cups cornflakes
2 pints lime sherbet
¼ cup bottled chocolate fudge topping

Combine chocolate pieces and butter in the top of a medium double boiler; place over hot, not boiling, water. Heat, stirring several times, until mixture is melted and smooth; remove from heat.

Stir in cornflakes until evenly coated. (Mixture will be very stiff.) Press over bottom and up side of a buttered 8-inch pie plate to form a shell. Chill until firm.

Spoon sherbet into shell; freeze.

When ready to serve, cut pie into wedges; place on serving plates; drizzle fudge topping over each.

Yield: 6 servings.

TARTS

PEACH CREAM TART

Double Crust Pastry (recipe on page 496)
1 package (3⅛ ozs.) vanilla pudding and pie
    filling mix
1¼ cups milk
½ cup whipping cream
¼ cup red currant jelly
1 can (29 ozs.) cling peach slices, well drained

Preheat oven to 425°.

Prepare Double Crust Pastry. Roll out on a lightly floured cloth to a 13-inch round; fit into a 9-inch round layer-cake pan; trim edge even with rim of pan. Prick shell well all over with a fork. (Reroll pastry trimmings; sprinkle with cinnamon sugar, and bake as nibbles for the children.)

Bake shell 10 minutes, or until golden; cool completely on a wire rack.

Prepare pudding mix with milk and cream as label directs; cool 5 minutes. Pour into pastry shell. Chill at least an hour, or until firm.

Melt currant jelly in a small saucepan; cool slightly. Arrange peach slices, overlapping, over filling in pastry shell; drizzle jelly in an even layer over peaches. Chill until glaze sets, or until serving time.

Yield: 8 servings.

Note: To remove shell from pan, cover with a wire rack and, grasping pan and rack firmly, turn upside down. Cover with a serving plate and carefully turn right side up again.

APRICOT CREAM TARTLETS

1 package piecrust mix
¼ cup sugar
3 tablespoons all-purpose flour
    Dash of salt
1 egg
1 cup milk
1 tablespoon butter or margarine
2 tablespoons curaçao
⅔ cup apricot preserves
1 tablespoon lemon juice
2 cans (16 ozs. each) apricot halves, well drained
½ cup whipping cream

Preheat oven to 425°.

Prepare piecrust mix as label directs; divide in half.

Roll out, half at a time, ⅛ inch thick on a lightly floured cloth; cut into 3½-inch rounds with a cookie cutter. Fit into 2½-inch tart-shell pans; prick each well all over with a fork. Reroll and cut out all trimmings. For eash handling, set tart pans in a large shallow baking pan.

Bake 10 minutes, or until golden; cool shells completely on a wire rack.

Mix sugar, flour, and salt in a small saucepan. Beat egg well with milk in a small bowl; stir into flour mixture. Cook slowly, stirring constantly, until mixture thickens and boils 1 minute; remove from heat. Stir in butter until melted, then curaçao; cool completely.

Heat apricot preserves in a small saucepan to boiling; press through a sieve into a small bowl. Stir in lemon juice; cool.

Carefully remove tart shells from pans; place on a large serving tray. Spoon a scant tablespoonful cream filling into each; top with an apricot half, rounded side up; brush apricots generously with preserves mixture. Chill about an hour.

When ready to serve, beat cream in a small bowl until stiff; spoon about a teaspoonful on each tart.

Yield: 2 dozen.

BLACK BOTTOM TARTLETS

1 package piecrust mix
1 envelope unflavored gelatin
¼ cup water
½ cup sugar
1 tablespoon cornstarch
4 eggs, separated
2 cups milk
½ cup semisweet chocolate pieces
1 teaspoon vanilla
¼ cup dark rum
½ cup whipping cream

Preheat oven to 425°.

Prepare piecrust mix as label directs; divide into 8 equal parts. Roll out each to a 6-inch round on a lightly floured cloth; fit into a 3-inch fluted tart-shell pan; trim edge even with rim. Prick shells well all over with a fork. For easy handling, set shells in a large shallow pan.

Bake 12 minutes, or until golden; cool completely on wire racks, then remove carefully from pans and place on a large flat plate or tray.

Soften gelatin in water in a cup; set aside.

Mix ¼ cup of the sugar and cornstarch in a medium saucepan; beat in egg yolks and milk. Cook slowly, stirring constantly, until mixture thickens slightly and coats spoon; remove from heat.

Measure out 1¼ cups; combine with chocolate pieces in a small bowl; stir until chocolate melts, then add vanilla. Spoon evenly into tart shells to make thin layers; chill until cold.

Stir softened gelatin into remaining custard in saucepan; heat slowly, stirring constantly, until gelatin dissolves. Pour into a large bowl; stir in rum. Place bowl in a pan of ice and water to speed setting; let stand, stirring several times, just until mixture starts to thicken.

While gelatin mixture chills, beat egg whites in a medium bowl until foamy; slowly beat in remaining ¼ cup sugar until meringue forms soft peaks. Fold into thickened gelatin mixture; continue folding until mixture mounds softly. Spoon evenly over chocolate layers in shells. Chill several hours, or until firm.

Just before serving, beat cream in a small bowl until stiff; spoon onto center of tarts. Garnish with chocolate curls if you like.

Yield: 8 tartlets.

PUMPKIN ICE-CREAM TARTLETS

2 cups sifted all-purpose flour
¾ cup sugar
⅔ cup shortening
1 egg, beaten
1 cup canned pumpkin
¾ teaspoon ground cinnamon
½ teaspoon ground ginger
¼ teaspoon mace
¼ teaspoon salt
1 quart vanilla ice cream
  Chopped pecans

Sift flour and ¼ cup of the sugar into a medium bowl; cut in shortening with a pastry blender until mixture forms fine crumbs. Stir in egg with a fork, then knead pastry in bowl until smooth. Chill at least ½ hour.

Preheat oven to 400°.

Divide pastry into 10 equal pieces. Roll out each to a 6-inch round on a lightly floured cloth; fit into a 3-inch tart-shell pan, pressing pastry firmly against bottom and side; trim overhang even with rim of pan. Prick well all over with a fork. For easy handling, place pans in a large shallow baking pan.

Bake 12 minutes, or until pastry is golden. Cool shells completely on wire racks; remove carefully from pans; return shells to large shallow pan.

Mix pumpkin, remaining ½ cup sugar, spices, and salt in a large bowl; beat in ice cream; spoon into shells. Top each with pecans. Freeze until serving time.

Yield: 10 servings.

NESSELRODE TARTLETS

1 package (12 ozs.) semisweet chocolate pieces
2 tablespoons shortening
½ cup sugar
1 envelope unflavored gelatin
¼ teaspoon salt
3 eggs, separated
1¼ cups milk
1 jar (10 ozs.) Nesselrode dessert sauce
½ teaspoon rum extract
¼ teaspoon cream of tartar
1 cup whipping cream
1 square unsweetened chocolate, grated

Place sixteen 2½-inch foil baking cups in medium muffin-pan cups.

Combine chocolate pieces and shortening in a medium saucepan. Heat very slowly, stirring constantly, until melted; measure 2 scant tablespoons into each cup. Chill 10 minutes, or until mixture starts to harden.

Using the back of a spoon, spread chocolate mixture up sides of cups to coat evenly. Chill until firm. Very carefully peel foil from each shell; stand shells on a cookie sheet; keep chilled while making filling.

Mix ¼ cup of the sugar, gelatin, and salt in a medium saucepan. Beat egg yolks with milk in a small bowl; stir into gelatin mixture. Cook over low heat, stirring constantly, until gelatin dissolves and mixture coats a spoon. Stir in Nesselrode sauce and rum extract; pour into a large bowl.

Set bowl in a large pan of ice and water to speed setting. Chill mixture, stirring several times, just until it starts to thicken.

While gelatin mixture chills, beat egg whites with cream of tartar in a medium bowl until foamy. Slowly beat in remaining ¼ cup sugar until meringue forms stiff peaks. Beat ½ cup of the cream until stiff in a small bowl. Fold meringue, then whipped cream into gelatin mixture. Spoon about ⅓ cup into each chocolate shell; chill until firm.

Just before serving, beat remaining ½ cup cream until stiff in a small bowl; spoon a dol-lop in center of each tartlet. Sprinkle grated chocolate over cream.

Yield: 16 tartlets.

PUMPKIN-PECAN TARTS

Double Crust Pastry (recipe on page 496)
2 tablespoons butter or margarine
¼ cup firmly packed brown sugar
¼ cup chopped pecans
1 egg
⅓ cup granulated sugar
1 cup canned pumpkin
Dash of salt
½ teaspoon ground cinnamon
¼ teaspoon ground ginger
¼ teaspoon mace
1 cup light cream
1 package (2 ozs.) whipped topping mix
Milk
Vanilla

Prepare Double Crust Pastry or make pie-crust from your favorite mix. Roll out half on a lightly floured cloth to a rectangle ⅛ inch thick. Cut into 3-inch rounds with a biscuit cutter; fit into 1¾-inch muffin-pan cups, pressing firmly against bottoms and sides. Repeat with second half of pastry, then reroll trimmings and cut out to make 36 shells in all.

Preheat oven to 425°.

Cream butter and brown sugar in a small bowl; stir in pecans; spread about ½ teaspoon over bottom of each shell.

Bake 10 minutes; remove from oven; lower oven temperature to 325°.

While shells bake, beat egg in a medium bowl until blended; stir in sugar, pumpkin, salt, spices, and cream. Spoon into partly baked shells.

Bake 15 minutes, or until pastry is golden and filling is set. Cool on wire racks 15 minutes; remove carefully from pans; cool completely.

Just before serving, prepare topping mix with milk and vanilla as label directs; spoon onto tarts.

Yield: 3 dozen.

LEMON ANGEL TART

1 package piecrust mix
1¼ cups sugar
6 eggs
1 envelope unflavored gelatin
½ teaspoon salt
½ cup lemon juice
¼ cup water
1 teaspoon grated lemon rind
1 package (2 ozs.) whipped topping mix
  Milk
  Vanilla

Preheat oven to 400°.

Combine piecrust mix and 2 tablespoons of the sugar in a medium bowl. Beat 1 of the eggs in a small bowl; stir into piecrust mixture until well blended.

Roll out to a 13-inch round on a lightly floured cloth; fit into a 9-inch round layer-cake pan; trim even with rim of pan. Prick shell well all over with a fork.

Bake 15 minutes, or until pastry is golden. Cool completely in pan, then carefully remove shell and place on a large flat serving plate.

Mix gelatin, ½ cup sugar, and salt in a medium saucepan.

Separate remaining eggs into two bowls; beat yolks well; stir in lemon juice and water; stir into gelatin mixture. Cook slowly, stirring constantly, until gelatin dissolves and mixture coats spoon; remove from heat. Stir in lemon rind. Chill 30 minutes, or until mixture mounds softly.

While gelatin mixture chills, beat egg whites in a medium bowl until foamy; slowly beat in rest of sugar until meringue stands in firm peaks; fold into thickened gelatin mixture until no streaks of white remain. Spoon into shell. Chill several hours, or until firm.

Just before serving, prepare whipped topping mix with milk and vanilla as label directs; spread over tart. Garnish with a slice of lemon dipped in sugar if you like.

Yield: 10 to 12 servings.

CHERRY JUBILEE TARTS

3 egg whites
½ teaspoon cream of tartar
  Salt
1 cup sugar
1 teaspoon vanilla
4 cups fresh dark sweet cherries
¾ cup water
2 tablespoons cornstarch
2 tablespoons brandy
½ cup whipping cream

Preheat oven to 250°. Grease 2 large cookie sheets; mark 6 four-inch circles on sheets with tip of knife or a wooden skewer.

Beat egg whites with cream of tartar and a dash of salt in a large bowl until foamy. Beat in ¾ cup of the sugar, 1 tablespoon at a time, beating constantly until sugar dissolves completely and meringue stands in firm peaks; beat in vanilla. (Beating will take about 15 minutes in all.)

Spoon meringue into circles on cookie sheets; spread to edges of circles with back of spoon, hollowing centers and building up edges to form shells.

Bake 50 minutes, or until firm but not brown. Loosen carefully from cookie sheets with a spatula; cool completely on wire racks.

Pit cherries. Combine with remaining ¼ cup sugar and water in a medium saucepan; heat to boiling; cover. Lower heat; simmer 5 minutes, or until cherries are tender.

Drain syrup from cherries into a 1-cup measure; add water, if needed, to make 1 cup; slowly stir into cornstarch in a small saucepan. Cook, stirring constantly, until mixture thickens and boils 1 minute; remove from heat. Stir in brandy, cherries, and a few drops red food coloring to darken sauce if you like; cool. Spoon into shells. Chill 1 to 2 hours to soften and mellow meringue.

When ready to serve, beat cream in a small bowl until stiff. Spoon onto centers of tarts.

Yield: 6 servings.

LEMONADE TARTLETS

Single Crust Pastry (recipe on page 497)
2 eggs, separated
1 package (3 ozs.) lemon-flavored gelatin
1 can (6 ozs.) frozen concentrate for lemonade,
    thawed
¼ cup sugar
1 cup thawed frozen whipped topping

Prepare Single Crust Pastry; divide into 8 even pieces. Roll out each to a 4½-inch round on a lightly floured cloth; fit into a 3-inch fluted tart-shell pan, pressing pastry firmly against bottom and side. Trim edge even with rim of pan. Prick shells well all over with a fork. For easy handling, set pans in a large shallow pan.

Preheat oven to 425°.

Bake shells 12 minutes, or until golden. Cool on wire racks; remove carefully from pans. Place shells on a large flat tray.

Beat egg yolks in a small bowl.

Combine gelatin and lemonade concentrate in a medium saucepan; stir in beaten egg yolks. Cook slowly, stirring constantly, until gelatin dissolves and mixture coats spoon; pour into a large bowl.

Place bowl in a pan of ice and water to speed setting. Chill, stirring several times, until syrupy-thick.

While gelatin mixture chills, beat egg whites in a small bowl until foamy; slowly beat in sugar until meringue stands in firm peaks.

Fold meringue, then whipped topping into thickened gelatin mixture until no streaks of white remain. Continue folding, still over ice, until mixture mounds softly. Spoon into tart shells, piling filling high. Chill several hours, or until firm.

Just before serving, garnish each tart with a small wedge of lemon if you like.

Yield: 8 servings.

LIMEADE TARTS

1¼ cups reconstituted frozen limeade
1 package (3 ozs.) lime-flavored gelatin
½ pint vanilla ice cream (1 cup)
6 packaged graham-cracker or pastry tart shells
1 cup thawed frozen whipped topping
    Chocolate curls

Combine limeade and gelatin in a small saucepan; heat slowly, stirring constantly, just until gelatin dissolves; remove from heat. Beat into ice cream in a small bowl. Chill in freezer 5 minutes, or until mixture starts to thicken.

Spoon into tart shells. Chill until firm.

When ready to serve, spoon whipped topping over each tart; garnish with chocolate curls.

Yield: 6 servings.

COOKIES

WHO CAN RESIST A PLUMP, GOLDEN-BROWN COOKIE, fresh and fragrant from the oven? Bite into one and you'll often find a delightful surprise—nuts, fruits, pieces of chocolate, or coconut. For versatility, cookies are hard to beat, and depending on the kind, they serve obligingly for every occasion from snacktime to tea parties.

Probably the most popular of all everyday varieties is drop cookies. They're simple and fun to make, and usually one of the first foods a beginner learns to bake. Some might take another viewpoint and claim that nothing ranks higher than bar cookies, and to them, this means only brownies—rich, moist, and fudgey.

During the holidays, more than at any other season of the year, making rolled cookies takes top priority in many kitchens. What home isn't familiar with the jaunty gingerbread men or twinkly stars dangling from the branches of Christmas trees? And with all the mixing, cutting, baking, and decorating that needs to be done, everyone in the family can get into the act.

For other fancy choices that are particularly fitting for party trays, open houses, gift boxes, or even edible centerpieces, there are molded, pressed, and bake-as-you please refrigerator cookies that will always provide suitable temptations.

The generous selection of recipes in this chapter includes all of these types. So whenever you're looking for cookie-baking ideas that are plain or elaborate, sweet or buttery-rich, homey or artistically shaped, crisp or chewy, big or little, frosted or unfrosted, you're sure to find a suggestion here to please your family and your guests.

Know-how for cookie bakers
Most cookies are easy to make, but if you're aware of a few simple rules, you can turn them out at their best every time.

Measuring: Be accurate. Cookie recipes are carefully balanced formulas, and while many call for the same basic ingredients, the proportions will vary, depending upon the kind of cookie. To measure correctly, use graduated or nested cups for dry ingredients and fill them loosely to overflowing, then level off the top with the edge of a spatula. Exceptions are brown sugar, solid shortenings, and butter or margarine which should be packed into the cup before leveling.

For liquids, a glass cup or any other designed specifically for liquids is a must. Not only does it have a pouring spout to eliminate spills, but it also has a small space above the top measuring mark to allow for accuracy. Always read liquid measurements at eye level.

In measuring with spoons, dip the spoon into dry ingredients or thick liquids such as honey or molasses and level off the same as for cups. Pour thin liquids (milk, for example) into the spoon until it's completely full. Avoid measuring liquids over your mixing bowl since your hand or the ingredient container may slip.

Mixing: Start with all ingredients at room temperature. For creaming fats and sugar and blending in eggs and flavorings, use your electric mixer or hand beater at medium speed, beating only as long as your recipe directs. Turn the speed to low for beating in dry ingredients.

Shaping: When making drop cookies, take the time to measure each spoonful of dough so the finished cookies will be neat, evenly shaped, and evenly baked. Some cooks find that they can shortcut the job by spooning the dough into a pastry bag and pressing it out into small mounds onto cookie sheets.

For bars and squares, use a spatula to spread the dough evenly into the corners of the pan, and always use the exact size pan your recipe specifies. Otherwise the cookies may be too thick and need longer baking, or be too thin, overbaked, dry, and crumbly.

In shaping refrigerator cookies, your hands are your best tools to form long smooth rolls of the size called for in your recipe. Wrap the roll in waxed paper, foil, or transparent wrap slightly larger than the roll and twist the ends to seal. Chill the dough until it's firm enough to slice neatly—usually from four hours to overnight, although longer will probably be even better. Use a long, thin, sharp knife for slicing the dough, and if dough tends to crumble, let it warm up just a bit. Most recipes call for a thickness of about ⅛ inch so the finished cookies will be thin and crisp.

Molded cookie doughs need to be chilled before shaping since the doughs are richer and softer than for other type cookies. Follow your recipe for chilling time. Work with only a small amount of the dough at one time, keeping the rest in the refrigerator until you're ready for it. Roll the dough between the palms of your hands to smooth even shapes. If the recipe calls for flattening the cookies, use the bottom of a glass dipped in flour, a fork, or your thumb.

Cutout cookie doughs, like pastry, should be rolled on a lightly floured cloth with a stockinet-covered rolling pin. Since most doughs have to be chilled before rolling, it's important here, too, to work with only a small quantity at a time. Roll lightly and evenly and cut with regular cookie cutters dipped in flour. To avoid breaking the dough or stretching the cookies, lift them onto the cookie sheet with a broad spatula or pancake turner.

If you can't find cutters in the designs you want, make your own from cardboard. Children's storybooks often provide excellent patterns. Grease one side of the pattern lightly, lay it greased-side down over rolled dough, and cut around it with a paring knife. To avoid rerolling any more dough than necessary, cut cookies close together. Rerolled cookies will be less tender than those rolled only once.

Pressed cookies, probably the most professional-looking of all since they can be made in so many dainty sizes and shapes, call for several very special rules. First, chill the dough only if specified in your recipe; otherwise, keep it at room temperature. Always press it out onto a cool or cold cookie sheet, and use ungreased sheets so the dough will stick when the cookie press is lifted. Today's cookie presses come in both manual and electric styles.

Baking: For best results with all kinds of cookies, use shiny bright baking sheets that are at least two inches narrower and shorter than your oven. This allows for even heat circulation.

Always place dough on a cool sheet so it will keep its shape. One that's too hot will cause the dough to spread. To speed baking, work with two or three sheets at a time. One can be cooling while you're filling and baking the others.

If you have only one sheet, use the back of a large shallow pan as a substitute. A jelly-roll pan or 13x9x2 work fine. Or cut a sheet of heavy foil the same size as your cookie sheet and fill it while one batch bakes. When done, remove cookies from the sheet, slip the foil onto the hot sheet, and put it into the oven at once.

Since cookies contain leavening, be sure your oven is heated to the proper temperature before you put the cookies in to bake. Place only one sheet at a time in the center of the oven. Use a timer and check for doneness about two minutes before the end of the baking time stated in your recipe. Ovens vary and one minute too long can make a great difference in the finished cookie.

Cooling: As soon as cookies are baked, take them off the sheet with a wide spatula and place them in a single layer on wire racks to cool. If you're cooling bars or squares in the pan, place the pan on a wire rack so the air can circulate underneath. Some recipes tell you to let the cookies stand on the sheet for a few minutes before they're removed. Usually, these types are rich and fragile, and break easily while hot.

Storing: Place thin, crisp cookies in a container with a loose cover. If you don't have enough regular containers, layer cookies in a roasting or jelly-roll pan, separating each layer with waxed paper or transparent wrap to avoid breakage. Then cover the pan loosely with more paper.

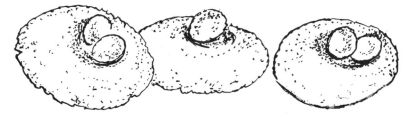

Store soft or rich buttery cookies in a container with a tight cover to keep out air.

Bar cookies stay moist and fresh longer if you leave them in their baking pan and wrap the pan tightly with foil. Or place the pan in a large transparent bag and seal. Cut them just before serving time.

Pack cookies for the freezer in sturdy, tightly covered plastic containers, separating each layer with crumpled transparent wrap. Most cookies freeze well, but it's best to frost or decorate them after they're thawed.

Mailing: Depending on the distance the cookies are traveling, use heavy cardboard boxes, empty metal coffee or shortening cans with plastic lids, or metal containers that are available in variety and housewares stores.

Wrap cookies in pairs, flat sides together, in foil long enough to allow a generous overlap; seal each packet with cellophane tape. Place a layer of crumpled foil in the bottom of the container for a cushion and arrange cookies on top; packing them in as tightly as possible to prevent their bouncing about. Stuff any holes between with more foil. Put the lid on the container and seal it tightly with tape.

Wrap the container in a layer of corrugated cardboard and then in double-thick brown paper. Tie securely with heavy string or twine and affix the label—to one side of the package only.

DROP COOKIES

SOUR CREAM JEWELS

1½ cups sifted all-purpose flour
½ teaspoon salt
¼ teaspoon baking powder
¼ teaspoon baking soda
6 tablespoons butter or margarine
¾ cup granulated sugar
1 egg
1½ teaspoons vanilla
½ cup dairy sour cream
1 square unsweetened chocolate
1½ cups sifted confectioners' powdered sugar
2 tablespoons milk
4 tablespoons apricot preserves
Crushed peppermint candy

Preheat oven to 375°.

Sift flour, salt, baking powder, and soda onto waxed paper.

Cream 4 tablespoons of the butter with granulated sugar in a large bowl until fluffy-light; beat in egg and 1 teaspoon of the vanilla. Stir in flour mixture, alternately with sour cream, until blended. Drop by teaspoonfuls, 1 inch apart, onto greased cookie sheets.

Bake 10 minutes, or until cookies are firm and lightly golden around edges. Remove from cookie sheets to wire racks; cool completely.

Melt chocolate and remaining 2 tablespoons butter in a small saucepan; remove from heat. Stir in confectioners' sugar, alternately with milk, until smooth; stir in remaining ½ teaspoon vanilla.

Attach a plain tip to a pastry bag; spoon frosting into bag. Press out in 1-inch rings on cookies. Let stand until frosting is firm; spoon apricot preserves inside chocolate rings. Or frost cookies, then sprinkle lightly with crushed peppermint candy.

Yield: About 4 dozen.

PENUCHE PUFFS

2¼ cups sifted all-purpose flour
½ teaspoon baking soda
¼ teaspoon salt
¾ cup butter or margarine
1½ cups firmly packed light brown sugar
1 egg
1½ teaspoons vanilla
3 squares unsweetened chocolate, melted
1 cup (8-oz. carton) dairy sour cream
1 cup chopped California walnuts
2 tablespoons milk
1¾ cups sifted confectioners' powdered sugar

Preheat oven to 350°.

Sift flour, baking soda, and salt onto waxed paper.

Cream ½ cup of the butter and 1 cup of the brown sugar in a large bowl until fluffy-light; beat in egg, 1 teaspoon of the vanilla, and melted chocolate.

Stir in flour mixture, alternately with sour cream, until well blended; stir in walnuts. Drop by slightly rounded tablespoonfuls, 2 inches apart, on lightly greased cookie sheets.

Bake 10 minutes, or until cookies are firm on top. Remove from cookie sheets to wire racks; cool completely.

Combine remaining ½ cup brown sugar, ¼ cup butter, and milk in a small saucepan; heat slowly, stirring constantly, just until sugar dissolves; remove from heat. Stir in confectioners' sugar until frosting is smooth and easy to spread; stir in remaining ½ teaspoon vanilla. Spread about 1 teaspoonful over each cookie. Let stand on wire racks until frosting is firm.

Yield: About 3½ dozen.

BUTTERSCOTCH CRISPIES

2 cups sifted all-purpose flour
1 teaspoon baking soda
1 teaspoon salt
1 cup shortening
2 cups firmly packed light brown sugar
3 eggs
1 teaspoon vanilla
2 cups quick-cooking rolled oats
2 cups oven-toasted rice cereal
1 cup chopped California walnuts

Preheat oven to 350°.

Sift flour, baking soda, and salt onto waxed paper.

Cream shortening with brown sugar in a large bowl until fluffy-light; beat in eggs, one at a time, until fluffy again; stir in vanilla.

Stir in flour mixture, a third at a time, until well blended; stir in rolled oats, rice cereal, and walnuts. Drop by teaspoonfuls, about an inch apart, onto greased large cookie sheets.

Bake 12 minutes, or until cookies are firm and lightly golden. Remove from cookie sheets to wire racks; cool completely.

Yield: 8½ dozen.

ORANGE-PUMPKIN CREAMS

2½ cups sifted all-purpose flour
 3 teaspoons baking powder
1½ teaspoons pumpkin-pie spice
 ½ teaspoon salt
 ½ cup shortening
1½ cups granulated sugar
 1 egg
 1 cup canned pumpkin
 ¾ cup chopped California walnuts
 1 can ready-to-spread orange frosting

Preheat oven to 375°.

Sift flour, baking powder, pumpkin-pie spice, and salt onto waxed paper.

Cream shortening with sugar in a large bowl until fluffy-light; beat in egg and pumpkin. Stir in flour mixture, a third at a time, until well blended; stir in walnuts. Drop by rounded teaspoonfuls, 1 inch apart, on greased cookie sheets.

Bake 15 minutes, or until cookies are firm and golden. Remove from cookie sheets to wire racks; cool completely.

Spread about ½ tablespoon of the orange frosting over each cookie. Top each with a walnut half if you like. Let stand until frosting is firm.

Yield: 5 dozen.

DATE HERMITS

 2 cups sifted all-purpose flour
 2 teaspoons ground cinnamon
 ½ teaspoon ground nutmeg
 ¼ teaspoon ground ginger
 ¼ teaspoon baking soda
 ¼ teaspoon salt
 ¾ cup butter or margarine
 1 cup firmly packed light brown sugar
 2 eggs
 2 tablespoons milk
 1 teaspoon lemon juice
 1 cup snipped dates
 1 cup chopped California walnuts
 1 cup confectioners' powdered sugar
 2 tablespoons orange juice

Preheat oven to 375°.

Sift flour, cinnamon, nutmeg, ginger, baking soda, and salt onto waxed paper.

Cream butter with brown sugar in a large bowl until fluffy-light; beat in eggs, one at a time, until fluffy again.

Combine milk and lemon juice in a cup; beat into egg mixture, alternately with flour mixture, until well blended; stir in dates and walnuts.

Drop by heaping teaspoonfuls, 2 inches apart, onto greased cookie sheets.

Bake 12 minutes, or until cookies are golden. Remove from cookie sheets to wire racks.

While cookies bake, combine confectioners' sugar and orange juice in a cup; beat until smooth. Brush over cookies while still hot to make a thin frosting. Let stand until frosting is firm.

Yield: About 5 dozen.

TOASTED COCONUT DROPS

  1 can (3½ ozs.) flaked coconut
  2 cups sifted all-purpose flour
  ¾ teaspoon baking powder
  1 teaspoon ground cinnamon
  ¼ teaspoon salt
  ¾ cup butter or margarine
  ½ cup firmly packed light brown sugar
  ½ cup granulated sugar
  2 eggs
  1 teaspoon vanilla
  1 package (6 ozs.) semisweet chocolate pieces

Preheat oven to 350°.

Spread coconut in a shallow baking pan; toast in oven, stirring once or twice, 10 to 12 minutes, or until golden. (Watch carefully so it doesn't burn.) Cool while mixing batter. Raise oven temperature to 375°.

Sift flour, baking powder, cinnamon, and salt onto waxed paper.

Cream butter with brown and granulated sugars until fluffy-light in a large bowl; beat in eggs and vanilla.

Stir in flour mixture, part at a time, until well blended; fold in coconut and chocolate pieces. Drop by teaspoonfuls, 2 inches apart, onto greased cookie sheets.

Bake 10 minutes, or until cookies are firm and golden. Remove from cookie sheets to wire racks; cool completely.

Yield: About 4 dozen.

BANANA PUFFS

3¼ cups sifted all-purpose flour
  ¾ teaspoon baking soda
  1 teaspoon ground cinnamon
  ½ teaspoon salt
  ¾ cup butter or margarine
  1 cup firmly packed light brown sugar
  1 egg
  2 large ripe bananas, peeled and mashed (1 cup)
  1 teaspoon vanilla
    Pecan halves

Preheat oven to 350°.

Sift flour, baking soda, cinnamon, and salt onto waxed paper.

Cream butter with brown sugar until fluffy-light in a large bowl; beat in egg, mashed bananas, and vanilla. Stir in flour mixture, part at a time, until well blended. Drop by heaping teaspoonfuls, 2 inches apart, onto greased cookie sheets; press a pecan half into top of each.

Bake 12 minutes, or until cookies are firm and lightly browned. Remove from cookie sheets to wire racks; cool completely.

Yield: About 6 dozen.

GINGER CAKES

2½ cups sifted all-purpose flour
  2 teaspoons baking soda
1¼ teaspoons ground cinnamon
  ½ teaspoon ground ginger
  ¼ teaspoon salt
  ⅓ cup butter or margarine
  ⅓ cup granulated sugar
  1 egg
  ⅔ cup light molasses
1½ teaspoons lemon juice
  ½ cup applesauce
    California walnut halves

Preheat oven to 400°.

Sift flour, baking soda, cinnamon, ginger, and salt onto waxed paper.

Cream butter and sugar in a large bowl until fluffy-light; beat in egg and molasses. Stir lemon juice into applesauce in a cup.

Stir flour mixture into egg mixture, alternately with applesauce mixture; blend well to make a thick batter.

Drop by level tablespoonfuls, 1½ inches apart, onto greased cookie sheets. Top each with a walnut half.

Bake 7 minutes, or until cakes are puffed and top springs back when pressed with finger. Remove from cookie sheets to wire racks; cool completely.

Yield: About 4½ dozen.

CARDAMOM SNAPS

2 cups sifted all-purpose flour
½ cup granulated sugar
½ teaspoon baking soda
½ cup dark corn syrup
½ cup butter or margarine
2 teaspoons grated orange rind
1 teaspoon ground cardamom
¼ teaspoon ground ginger
¼ teaspoon ground cloves
1 egg

Preheat oven to 375°.

Sift flour, sugar, and baking soda onto waxed paper.

Combine corn syrup, butter, orange rind, cardamom, ginger, and cloves in a medium saucepan. Heat slowly, stirring constantly, to boiling; remove from heat.

Beat egg well in a large bowl; very slowly stir in syrup mixture; stir in flour mixture until well blended. (Dough will be very soft.) Drop by rounded teaspoonfuls, 2 inches apart, onto greased cookie sheets.

Bake 10 minutes, or until cookies are firm. Remove from cookie sheets to wire racks; cool completely.

Yield: About 3½ dozen.

PINEAPPLE DROPS

2 cups sifted all-purpose flour
1 teaspoon baking powder
½ teaspoon baking soda
½ teaspoon salt
¼ cup shortening
¼ cup butter or margarine
1 cup firmly packed light brown sugar
1 egg
1 teaspoon vanilla
1 teaspoon grated orange rind
1 can (8 ozs.) crushed pineapple in juice, drained
1 cup chopped California walnuts

Preheat oven to 375°.

Sift flour, baking powder, baking soda, and salt onto waxed paper.

Cream shortening and butter with brown sugar in a large bowl until fluffy-light; beat in egg, vanilla, orange rind, and pineapple. Stir in flour mixture until well blended; stir in walnuts.

Drop dough by teaspoonfuls, 1 inch apart, onto lightly greased cookie sheets.

Bake 12 minutes, or until cookies are firm and lightly golden. Remove from cookie sheets to wire racks; cool completely.

Yield: 6 dozen.

FRUITCAKE DROPS

1 package (15 ozs.) dark raisins
½ cup rum
1¾ cups sifted all-purpose flour
1½ teaspoon baking soda
1 teaspoon ground cinnamon
½ teaspoon ground nutmeg
½ teaspoon ground ginger
¼ teaspoon salt
¼ cup butter or margarine
½ cup firmly packed light brown sugar
2 eggs
2 containers (4 ozs. each) candied pineapple, diced
2 containers (3½ ozs. each) candied green cherries, cut in half
2 containers (3½ ozs. each) candied red cherries, cut in half
4 cups coarsely broken California walnuts

Combine raisins and rum in a medium bowl; let stand while mixing batter.

Sift flour, baking soda, cinnamon, nutmeg, ginger, and salt onto waxed paper.

Preheat oven to 325°.

Cream butter with brown sugar in a large bowl until fluffy-light; beat in eggs. Stir in flour mixture until blended; stir in raisin mixture, pineapple, cherries, and walnuts until lightly coated with batter. Drop by half teaspoonfuls, 1 inch apart, onto greased cookie sheets.

Bake 15 minutes, or until cookies are firm and brown. Remove from cookie sheets to wire racks; cool completely.

Yield: 14 dozen small cookies.

APRICOT TWINKLES

1 package (10 ozs.) sugar cookie mix
Egg
Water
½ cup oven-toasted rice cereal
⅓ cup apricot preserves

Preheat oven to 375°.

Prepare cookie mix with egg and water as label directs; fold in cereal. Drop by teaspoonfuls, 1 inch apart, onto greased cookie sheets.

Press a hollow into center of each cookie with a spoon; fill each with a rounded ¼ teaspoon apricot preserves.

Bake 10 minutes, or until cookies are firm and lightly golden around edges. Remove from cookie sheets to wire racks; cool completely.

Yield: About 3½ dozen.

CHOCOLATE MERINGUES

2 egg whites
⅛ teaspoon cream of tartar
¼ teaspoon salt
⅔ cup granulated sugar
1 teaspoon vanilla
1 square unsweetened chocolate, grated
½ cup chopped California walnuts
½ cup semisweet chocolate pieces
⅓ cup chopped pistachio nuts

Preheat oven to 275°.

Beat egg whites with cream of tartar and salt in a medium bowl until foamy.

Slowly beat in sugar, 1 tablespoon at a time, beating constantly until sugar dissolves completely and meringue forms firm peaks. Beat in vanilla; fold in grated chocolate and walnuts. Drop by slightly rounded teaspoonfuls onto well-greased cookie sheets.

Bake 20 minutes, or until cookies are firm but not brown. Remove immediately from cookie sheets to wire racks; cool completely.

Melt chocolate pieces in a cup over hot water; cool. Spread over centers of cookies; sprinkle nuts over chocolate.

Yield: About 4½ dozen.

PRUNE JUMBLES

2 cups sifted all-purpose flour
1 teaspoon pumpkin-pie spice
½ teaspoon baking soda
⅛ teaspoon salt
¾ cup butter or margarine
1 cup firmly packed light brown sugar
2 eggs
2 cups snipped pitted prunes
1 cup chopped California walnuts

Preheat oven to 375°.

Sift flour, pumpkin-pie spice, baking soda, and salt onto waxed paper.

Cream butter with brown sugar in a large bowl until fluffy-light; beat in eggs.

Stir in flour mixture, part at a time, until well blended; stir in prunes and walnuts.

For each cookie, drop 2 tablespoonfuls of dough, 3 inches apart, onto greased cookie sheets; spread each into a 2½-inch round.

Bake 10 minutes, or until cookies are firm and golden. Remove from cookie sheets to wire racks; cool completely.

Yield: About 2½ dozen.

COCONUT KISSES

3 egg whites
¼ teaspoon salt
1 cup granulated sugar
1 teaspoon vanilla
1 can (3½ ozs.) flaked coconut
3 cups oven-toasted rice cereal
Red and green candied cherries, quartered

Preheat oven to 300°.

Beat egg whites with salt in a medium bowl until foamy. Beating constantly, add sugar, 1 tablespoon at a time; continue beating until sugar dissolves and meringue forms firm peaks.

Stir in vanilla; fold in coconut and cereal. Drop by teaspoonfuls onto greased cookie sheets. Decorate each with a piece of cherry.

Bake 20 minutes, or until cookies are firm but not brown. Remove from cookie sheets to wire racks; cool completely.

Yield: About 4½ dozen.

CHERRY CHEWS

2 packages (8 ozs. each) pitted dates
1 cup coarsely chopped toasted slivered almonds
1 container (3½ ozs.) candied green cherries,
    coarsely chopped
1 cup granulated sugar
3 egg whites
1 cup sifted all-purpose flour
    Dash of salt
1 teaspoon orange extract
    Candied green cherries, cut into quarters

Preheat oven to 350°.

Snip dates into small pieces with kitchen shears. Combine with almonds and chopped cherries in a large bowl; stir in sugar.

Beat egg whites in a bowl until stiff.

Stir flour, alternately with beaten egg whites, into fruit mixture until evenly blended; stir in salt and orange extract.

Drop by teaspoonfuls, 1 inch apart, onto greased cookie sheets; top each with a strip of cherry.

Bake 15 minutes, or until cookies are firm and pale golden. Remove from cookie sheets to wire racks; cool completely.

Yield: 6 dozen.

ORANGE FIG WAFERS

1 cup sifted all-purpose flour
½ cup granulated sugar
2 teaspoons baking powder
2 teaspoons baking soda
½ teaspoon salt
1 teaspoon ground ginger
2½ cups quick-cooking rolled oats
1 cup snipped dried figs
1 egg
⅔ cup salad oil
¾ cup light molasses
1 tablespoon butter or margarine
2 cups sifted confectioners' powdered sugar
1 teaspoon grated orange rind
2 tablespoons orange juice
    Candied orange slices, cut into small wedges

Preheat oven to 325°.

Sift flour, granulated sugar, baking powder, baking soda, salt, and ginger into a large bowl; stir in rolled oats and figs.

Beat egg with salad oil and molasses in a medium bowl; stir into flour mixture until evenly blended.

Drop by level measuring teaspoonfuls, 1 inch apart, onto greased cookie sheets.

Bake 15 minutes, or until cookies are firm. Remove from cookie sheets to wire racks; cool completely.

Cream butter and confectioners' sugar in a medium bowl; beat in orange rind and juice until frosting is smooth and easy to spread. Spread about ½ teaspoon on each cookie; trim with a wedge of candied orange slice. Let stand until frosting is firm.

Yield: About 8 dozen.

ORANGE LACE WAFERS

⅔ cup sifted all-purpose flour
½ cup finely chopped California walnuts
¼ teaspoon grated orange rind
¼ cup butter or margarine
⅓ cup firmly packed light brown sugar
¼ cup light corn syrup
2 tablespoons milk

Sift flour into a medium bowl; stir in walnuts and orange rind.

Preheat oven to 350°.

Combine butter, brown sugar, corn syrup, and milk in a medium saucepan; heat slowly, stirring constantly, to boiling; remove from heat. Stir in flour mixture until blended.

Drop batter by level half teaspoonfuls, 2 inches apart, onto foil-lined cookie sheets.

Bake 7 minutes, or until cookies are golden. Cool on cookie sheets 5 minutes; remove from foil and place on wire racks; cool completely.

Yield: 5 dozen 2-inch cookies.

Note: These cookies are very fragile, so handle carefully. In storing, it's a good idea to pack them between layers of crushed waxed paper or transparent wrap.

JELLY JEWELS

1¼ cups sifted all-purpose flour
½ teaspoon baking powder
¼ teaspoon salt
¼ cup butter or margarine
½ cup granulated sugar
1 egg
½ teaspoon lemon extract
1 tablespoon light cream
　 Large gumdrops, sliced crosswise

Preheat oven to 350°.

Sift flour, baking powder, and salt onto waxed paper.

Cream butter with sugar in a medium bowl until fluffy-light; beat in egg, lemon extract, and cream. Stir in flour mixture until well blended. (Dough will be soft.) Drop by half teaspoonfuls, 2 inches apart, onto greased cookie sheets; top each with a gumdrop slice, cut side up; press lightly into dough.

Bake 10 minutes, or until cookies are firm and lightly golden around edges. Remove from cookie sheets to wire racks, cool completely.

Yield: About 3 dozen.

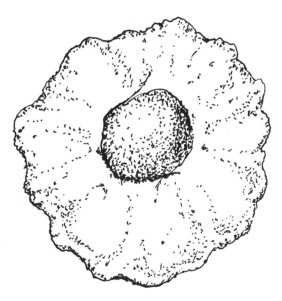

FRUIT DROPS

1 package date bar mix
　 Boiling water
1 egg
3 tablespoons brandy
½ cup chopped mixed candied fruits
½ cup chopped candied orange rind
¼ cup chopped candied red cherries
¼ cup chopped candied green cherries
1 cup chopped California walnuts

Preheat oven to 375°.

Place filling from date bar mix in a large bowl; stir in ⅔ cup boiling water; cool slightly.

Beat in egg and brandy; stir in crumbly mix from package; fold in fruits and walnuts. Drop by half teaspoonfuls onto greased cookie sheets.

Bake 15 minutes, or until cookies are firm. Remove from cookie sheets to wire racks; cool completely.

Yield: About 5 dozen.

BARS AND SQUARES

FIG BLOSSOMS

1¼ cups sifted all-purpose flour
1 teaspoon baking powder
½ teaspoon ground ginger
½ teaspoon salt
3 tablespoons butter or margarine
2 eggs
1 cup granulated sugar
1 tablespoon hot water
2 cups snipped dried figs
1 cup chopped California walnuts
2¼ cups sifted confectioners' powdered sugar
1 teaspoon grated orange rind
2 tablespoons orange juice

Preheat oven to 350°.

Sift flour, baking powder, ginger, and salt onto waxed paper.

Melt butter in a small saucepan; set aside.

Beat eggs in a large bowl until foamy; slowly beat in granulated sugar, 1 tablespoon of the melted butter, and hot water; fold in flour mixture until well blended, then figs and walnuts. Spread evenly into two greased baking pans, 8x8x2 inches.

Bake 25 minutes, or until layers are golden and top springs back when lightly pressed with finger. Cool completely in pans on wire racks.

Stir part of the confectioners' sugar into remaining melted butter; stir in orange rind and remaining confectioners' sugar, alternately with orange juice, until frosting is smooth. Spread over baked layers. Let stand until frosting is firm.

Cut each panful lengthwise and crosswise into six strips. Decorate each square with tiny flowers made from chopped and slivered candied orange rind or candied orange slices if you like.

Yield: 6 dozen.

CHOCO-PEPPERMINT TRIANGLES

1 cup sifted all-purpose flour
½ cup dry cocoa (not instant cocoa mix)
¼ teaspoon baking powder
¼ teaspoon salt
⅔ cup butter or margarine (for batter)
1 cup light corn syrup
2 eggs
1 teaspoon vanilla
½ cup chopped pecans
1 tablespoon butter or margarine (for frosting)
1½ cups sifted confectioners' powdered sugar
4 teaspoons milk
¼ teaspoon peppermint extract
Green food coloring
Crushed peppermint stick candy

Preheat oven to 350°.

Sift flour, cocoa, baking powder, and salt onto waxed paper.

Cream the ⅔ cup butter with corn syrup in a medium bowl until fluffy-light; beat in eggs and vanilla. Stir in flour mixture until smooth; stir in pecans. Spoon into a greased baking pan, 9x9x2 inches, spreading top even.

Bake 20 minutes, or until layer is almost firm but a slight imprint remains in top when touched with finger. (Do not overbake.) Cool completely in pan on a wire rack.

Cream the 1 tablespoon butter with confectioners' sugar in a medium bowl. Beat in milk and peppermint extract until frosting is smooth; tint green with a few drops food coloring. Spread over cooled baked layer; sprinkle crushed peppermint candy on top. Let stand until frosting is firm.

Cut lengthwise and crosswise into quarters to form 16 squares; cut each square diagonally in half.

Yield: 2⅔ dozen.

CHERRY SQUARES

1½ cups sifted all-purpose flour
½ teaspoon baking powder
¾ cup butter or margarine
 1 cup granulated sugar
 4 eggs
 1 teaspoon grated lemon rind
 1 tablespoon lemon juice
¼ cup sliced candied red cherries
¼ cup sliced candied green cherries
¼ cup chopped filberts

Preheat oven to 350°.
Sift flour and baking powder onto waxed paper.
Cream butter with ¾ cup of the sugar in a large bowl until fluffy-light; beat in eggs, 1 at a time, until fluffy again; beat in lemon rind and juice.
Stir in flour mixture until blended. Spread evenly in a greased baking pan, 13x9x2 inches.
Mix cherries, filberts, and remaining ¼ cup sugar in a small bowl; sprinkle over batter in pan. (Topping will sink to bottom of cake during baking.)
Bake 30 minutes, or until layer is golden and top springs back when lightly pressed with finger. Cool completely in pan on a wire rack. Cut lengthwise into sixths and crosswise into eighths.
Yield: 4 dozen.

NOEL FIG STRIPS

 2 cups sifted all-purpose flour
 1 teaspoon baking powder
 1 teaspoon ground ginger
¼ teaspoon salt
½ cup butter or margarine
 1 cup firmly packed light brown sugar
½ cup granulated sugar
 2 eggs
 1 cup snipped dried figs
 1 cup chopped pecans
 1 tablespoon butter or margarine, melted
 1 cup confectioners' powdered sugar
 1 tablespoon orange juice
 Candied orange slices

Sift flour, baking powder, ginger, and salt onto waxed paper.
Preheat oven to 350°.
Cream the ½ cup butter with brown and granulated sugars until fluffy-light in a large bowl; beat in eggs. Stir in flour mixture until blended; stir in figs and pecans. Spread evenly in a greased baking pan, 13x9x2 inches.
Bake 25 minutes, or until layer is golden and a wooden pick inserted into center comes out clean. Cool in pan on a wire rack 30 minutes.
Blend melted butter, confectioners' sugar, and orange juice until smooth in a small bowl; spread over warm layer to make a thin glaze. Let stand until glaze is firm.
Cut baked layer crosswise into twelve strips and lengthwise into four to make 48 small bars. Decorate each with a tiny wedge cut from a candied orange slice.
Yield: 4 dozen.

NOEL BARS

½ cup butter or margarine
1½ cups graham cracker crumbs
 1 can (14 ozs.) sweetened condensed milk
 1 package (8 ozs.) plain multi-colored chocolate candies
 1 can (3½ ozs.) flaked coconut
½ cup chopped pecans

Preheat oven to 350°.
Place butter in a baking pan, 13x9x2 inches; place in oven to melt as oven preheats.
Sprinkle graham cracker crumbs over melted butter in pan; pour sweetened condensed milk evenly over crumbs. Sprinkle candies, then coconut and pecans over top; press down gently.
Bake 30 minutes, or until layer is lightly browned. Cool completely in pan on a wire rack.
Cut lengthwise into sixths and crosswise into eighths with a sharp knife.
Yield: 4 dozen.

JEWELED FRUITCAKE BARS

    1 cup light raisins
 ½ cup dark raisins
    1 container (3½ ozs.) candied green cherries, cut
      in half
    1 container (4 ozs.) candied pineapple, diced
    1 teaspoon pumpkin-pie spice
 ½ teaspoon ground cinnamon
 ¼ cup dark rum
    1 cup sifted all-purpose flour
 ½ teaspoon baking soda
 ½ teaspoon salt
    5 tablespoons butter or margarine
 ¾ cup firmly packed light brown sugar
    1 egg
 ½ cup California walnut halves or quarters
 1½ cups sifted confectioners' powdered sugar
    4 teaspoons milk
 ¼ teaspoon vanilla
    2 squares semisweet chocolate
    1 teaspoon shortening

Combine raisins, cherries, pineapple, pumpkin-pie spice, cinnamon, and rum in a medium bowl; stir to mix well; cover. Let stand several hours or overnight.

Preheat oven to 350°.

Sift flour, baking soda, and salt onto waxed paper.

Cream 4 tablespoons of the butter with brown sugar in a large bowl until fluffy-light. Beat in egg; stir in flour mixture until well blended. Stir in fruit mixture and walnuts. Spoon into a greased baking pan, 9x9x2 inches, spreading top even.

Bake 35 minutes, or until a wooden pick inserted into center comes out clean. Cool completely in pan on a wire rack.

Cream remaining 1 tablespoon butter with confectioners' sugar in a medium bowl; stir in milk and vanilla until mixture is smooth. Spread over cooled baked layer in pan.

Melt chocolate with shortening in a cup over warm water; drizzle from tip of teaspoon over white frosting to form parallel lines lengthwise and crosswise. Let stand until frosting is firm.

Cut lengthwise into sixths and crosswise into eighths.

Yield: 4 dozen.

FIG MINIATURES

    1 lb. dried figs, snipped fine
 ½ cup granulated sugar
    2 teaspoons grated lemon rind
    2 tablespoons lemon juice
 ¾ cup water
    2 cups sifted all-purpose flour
 1¼ cups firmly packed light brown sugar
    2 cups quick-cooking rolled oats
    1 teaspoon ground ginger
    1 teaspoon salt
    1 cup butter or margarine

Combine figs, granulated sugar, lemon rind and juice, and water in a medium saucepan. Heat, stirring several times, to boiling; simmer 5 minutes, or until thick; remove from heat.

Preheat oven to 350°.

Mix flour, brown sugar, rolled oats, ginger, and salt in a medium bowl; cut in butter with a pastry blender until mixture is completely blended. Press half evenly over bottom of a greased baking pan, 13x9x2 inches.

Spread fig mixture evenly over layer in pan. Sprinkle rest of flour mixture on top; pat down lightly.

Bake 1 hour, or until layer is firm and golden. Cool completely in pan on a wire rack. Cut lengthwise into sixths and crosswise into eighths.

Yield: 4 dozen.

MINCE BARS

2 packages (9 ozs. each) condensed mincemeat
2½ cups water
1 tablespoon grated orange rind
1 cup chopped California walnuts
2 cups sifted all-purpose flour
1⅓ cups firmly packed light brown sugar
1½ teaspoons ground cinnamon
1 teaspoon salt
1 cup butter or margarine
2 cups quick-cooking rolled oats

Prepare mincemeat with water as label directs; cool. Stir in orange rind and walnuts.

Preheat oven to 350°.

Combine flour, brown sugar, cinnamon, and salt in a large bowl. Cut in butter with a pastry blender until mixture forms fine crumbs; stir in rolled oats.

Press half of mixture evenly over bottom of a greased baking pan, 13x9x2 inches; spread mincemeat mixture on top; pat rest of flour mixture over mincemeat.

Bake 1 hour, or until layer is firm and golden. Cool completely in pan on a wire rack.

Cut crosswise, then lengthwise into sixths.
Yield: 3 dozen.

HOLLY BARS

1 cup honey
2¼ cups sifted all-purpose flour
½ teaspoon baking soda
½ teaspoon salt
1½ teaspoons ground cinnamon
½ teaspoon ground nutmeg
¼ teaspoon ground cloves
½ cup currants
½ cup chopped almonds
½ cup chopped mixed candied fruits
¾ cup firmly packed dark brown sugar
1 egg
1½ teaspoons grated lemon rind
¼ cup granulated sugar
¼ cup water
⅓ cup sifted confectioners' powdered sugar
   Red and green candied cherries, cut in half and slivered

Preheat oven to 350°.

Heat honey until bubbly in a small saucepan; cool.

Sift flour, baking soda, salt, cinnamon, nutmeg, and cloves into a large bowl. Stir in currants, almonds, and candied fruits.

Stir brown sugar into honey; beat in egg and lemon rind. Stir into fruit mixture until evenly blended. Spread in a greased jelly-roll pan, 15x10x1 inches.

Bake 30 minutes, or until layer is firm. Cool in pan on a wire rack.

Combine granulated sugar and water in a small saucepan. Heat to boiling; simmer 3 minutes; remove from heat. Stir in confectioners' sugar. Brush over baked layer in pan.

Cut crosswise into 15 strips and lengthwise into 5 to make small bars. Decorate each with pieces of red and green cherries to resemble holly. Store in a tightly covered container for several days to soften and mellow flavors.

Yield: 6¼ dozen.

Note: Baked layer is very hard when it comes out of the oven. If you can spare the baking pan, leave the layer in the pan and wrap tightly in foil. Store layer in a cool dry place for several days to mellow and soften, then glaze, cut into bars, and decorate them.

WALNUT BARS

1 frozen poundcake (11¼ ozs.), thawed
3 tablespoons butter or margarine, softened
¼ cup honey
¾ cup finely chopped California walnuts

Preheat oven to 350°.

Cut cake into 8 even slices, then cut each slice in half lengthwise to form bars.

Blend butter and honey in a cup; sprinkle walnuts on waxed paper.

Spread butter mixture over three sides of each strip of cake; roll in walnuts. Place strips, plain side down, on a lightly buttered cookie sheet.

Bake 15 minutes, or until strips are toasted lightly. Remove from cookie sheet to a wire rack; cool.

Yield: 1⅓ dozen.

BANANA-CHERRY BARS

1¾ cups sifted all-purpose flour
2 teaspoons baking powder
½ teaspoon salt
6 tablespoons butter or margarine
1 cup granulated sugar
2 eggs
1 teaspoon vanilla
2 large ripe bananas, peeled and mashed (1 cup)
¼ cup chopped maraschino cherries
½ teaspoon grated lemon rind
1 teaspoon lemon juice
1 cup sifted confectioners' powdered sugar
1 tablespoon milk

Preheat oven to 350°.

Sift flour, baking powder, and salt onto waxed paper.

Cream 4 tablespoons of the butter with granulated sugar in a large bowl until fluffy-light; beat in eggs and vanilla. Stir in flour mixture, alternately with mashed bananas, just until blended; fold in cherries. Spread evenly in a greased baking pan, 13x9x2 inches.

Bake 30 minutes, or until layer is golden and top springs back when lightly pressed with finger. Cool completely in pan on a wire rack.

Cream remaining 2 tablespoons butter in a small bowl until soft; stir in lemon rind and juice. Stir in confectioners' sugar, alternately with milk, until mixture is smooth. Spread over baked layer; let stand until frosting is firm.

Cut crosswise, then lengthwise into sixths.
Yield: 3 dozen.

MOLASSES RAISIN BARS

2 cups sifted all-purpose flour
1 teaspoon ground cinnamon
½ teaspoon ground ginger
¼ teaspoon ground nutmeg
¼ teaspoon ground cloves
½ teaspoon baking soda
¼ teaspoon salt
⅔ cup shortening
⅔ cup granulated sugar
2 eggs
1 cup dark molasses
1 cup dark raisins
1 cup sifted confectioners' powdered sugar
1 tablespoon lemon juice

Preheat oven to 350°.

Sift flour, cinnamon, ginger, nutmeg, cloves, baking soda, and salt onto waxed paper.

Cream shortening with granulated sugar in a large bowl until fluffy-light; beat in eggs and molasses. Stir in flour mixture until well blended; stir in raisins. Spread evenly in a greased baking pan, 13x9x2 inches.

Bake 30 minutes, or until top springs back when lightly pressed with finger. Cool in pan on a wire rack.

Mix confectioners' sugar and lemon juice in a cup; stir in about 1 teaspoon water until mixture is smooth and thin enough to pour from a spoon. Drizzle over baked layer; let stand until frosting is firm.

Cut lengthwise into thirds and crosswise into eighths.
Yield: 2 dozen.

CHEWS

4 cups tiny marshmallows
¼ cup butter or margarine
1 tablespoon orange-flavored instant breakfast
   drink
¼ teaspoon salt
1 teaspoon vanilla
¼ teaspoon almond extract
4 cups presweetened wheat puffs
1 cup flaked coconut
¼ cup coarsely chopped California walnuts

Combine marshmallows and butter in a medium saucepan; heat very slowly, stirring constantly, until marshmallows melt and mixture is smooth. Remove from heat; stir in breakfast drink powder, salt, vanilla, and almond extract.

Combine wheat puffs, coconut, and walnuts in a large bowl; pour marshmallow mixture over top, then stir in until very well blended. (Mixture will be very stiff.) Spoon into a buttered baking pan, 9x9x2 inches; press down firmly into an even layer with back of spoon. Let stand until cold.

Cut lengthwise into 6 strips and crosswise into 8.
Yield: 4 dozen.

RASPBERRY ANGEL BARS

¾ cup butter or margarine
¾ cup granulated sugar
   Dash of salt
2 cups sifted all-purpose flour
1½ teaspoons vanilla
4 egg whites
1 can (3½ ozs.) flaked coconut
1 jar (12 ozs.) red raspberry preserves (about 1¼
   cups)

Preheat oven to 350°.
Cream butter with ¼ cup of the sugar and salt in a medium bowl; blend in flour; stir in vanilla. Press evenly into a baking pan, 13x9x2 inches.

Bake 25 minutes, or until lightly browned; remove from oven but leave oven on.

While layer bakes, beat egg whites in a medium bowl until foamy; beat in remaining ½ cup sugar, 1 tablespoon at a time, until meringue forms firm peaks; fold in coconut.

Spread preserves over layer in pan; spread meringue over preserves.

Bake 20 minutes longer, or until meringue is golden. Cool completely in pan on a wire rack. Cut lengthwise into sixths and crosswise into quarters.
Yield: 2 dozen.

TOFFEE COFFEE BARS

1 cup sifted all-purpose flour (for crust)
2 tablespoons granulated sugar
2 tablespoons instant coffee powder
½ cup butter or margarine
2 eggs
1 cup firmly packed light brown sugar
2 tablespoons all-purpose flour (for topping)
1 teaspoon vanilla
½ cup toasted coconut
½ cup chopped pecans

Preheat oven to 350°.
Mix the 1 cup flour, granulated sugar, and coffee powder in a large bowl; cut in butter with a pastry blender until mixture forms fine crumbs. Press evenly over bottom of an ungreased baking pan, 8x8x2 inches.

Bake 15 minutes; remove from oven.
While layer bakes, beat eggs until well blended in a medium bowl; stir in brown sugar, the 2 tablespoons flour, vanilla, coconut, and pecans. Pour over layer in pan.

Bake 30 minutes, or until layer is firm on top. Cool completely in pan on a wire rack.

Cut crosswise into quarters, then lengthwise into eighths.
Yield: 2⅔ dozen.

SNOWDRIFT BROWNIE SQUARES

1 package (8 ozs.) cornflakes
1 cup chopped California walnuts
  Confectioners' powdered sugar
1 teaspoon grated orange rind
1 package (8 ozs.) semisweet chocolate
1 cup evaporated milk

Crush cornflakes fine with a rolling pin. (There should be 2¾ cups crumbs.) Combine with walnuts, ½ cup confectioners' sugar, and orange rind in a large bowl.

Combine chocolate and evaporated milk in a medium saucepan; heat slowly, stirring constantly, until chocolate melts and mixture is smooth; stir into cornflake mixture until evenly blended. Press into a buttered pan, 9x9x2 inches. Chill 45 minutes, or until almost firm. Cut lengthwise and crosswise into sixths. Continue chilling until firm.

Jush before serving, sprinkle tops with confectioners' sugar.

Yield: 3 dozen.

ALMOND-CURRANT BARS

2 cups butter or margarine
2 cups granulated sugar
4 eggs
2¼ cups sifted all-purpose flour
1½ teaspoons vanilla
1 teaspoon grated lemon rind
½ cup currants
½ cup sliced almonds

Preheat oven to 375°.

Cream butter with sugar in a large bowl until fluffy-light; beat in eggs, one at a time, until blended. Stir in flour, vanilla, and lemon rind.

Spread evenly in a greased jelly-roll pan, 15x10x1 inches; sprinkle currants and almonds over top.

Bake 35 minutes, or until layer is golden and a wooden pick inserted in center comes out clean. Cool completely in pan on a wire rack.

Cut crosswise into sixths and lengthwise into fifths.

Yield: 2½ dozen.

PARTY BROWNIES

¾ cup butter or margarine (for cookies)
1 package (6 ozs.) semisweet chocolate pieces
1 cup sifted all-purpose flour
½ teaspoon baking powder
¼ teaspoon salt
2 eggs
1¼ cups granulated sugar
1½ teaspoons vanilla
1 cup chopped California walnuts
3 tablespoons butter or margarine (for frosting)
1 square unsweetened chocolate
2 cups sifted confectioners' powdered sugar
7 teaspoons milk
Red food coloring
Silver decorating candies

Preheat oven to 350°.

Melt the ¾ cup butter and chocolate pieces in a saucepan over very low heat; remove from heat.

Sift flour, baking powder, and salt onto waxed paper.

Beat eggs in a medium bowl until well blended; beat in granulated sugar and 1 teaspoon of the vanilla. Stir in chocolate mixture; fold in flour mixture and walnuts. Spread evenly in a greased baking pan, 13x9x2 inches.

Bake 40 minutes, or until layer is glossy on top. Cool completely in pan on a wire rack.

Melt 2 tablespoons of the butter for frosting with unsweetened chocolate in a small bowl over hot water; remove from heat. Stir in 1½ cups of the confectioners' sugar, alternately with 6 teaspoons of the milk, until frosting is smooth and easy to spread; stir in remaining ½ teaspoon vanilla. Spread over baked layer in pan. Let stand until frosting is firm. Cut lengthwise into six strips and crosswise into ten to make small squares.

Cream remaining 1 tablespoon butter with remaining ½ cup confectioners' sugar in a small bowl; slowly stir in enough of the remaining 1 teaspoon milk to make a stiff frosting; tint pink with red food coloring. Attach a rosette tip to a cake-decorating set; spoon frosting into tube. Press out onto each cookie to form a small rosette, trim each with a silver decorating candy.

Yield: 5 dozen.

REFRIGERATOR COOKIES

PISTACHIO PINWHEELS

2⅓ cups sifted all-purpose flour
¼ teaspoon salt
1 cup butter or margarine
⅔ cup sifted confectioners' powdered sugar
1¼ teaspoons vanilla
½ square unsweetened chocolate, melted and cooled
½ teaspoon almond extract
¼ cup finely chopped pistachio nuts
Green food coloring

Sift flour and salt onto waxed paper.

Cream butter with confectioners' sugar in a medium bowl until fluffy-light; stir in flour mixture until well blended; stir in vanilla. Measure half of the dough into a second bowl; stir in chocolate.

Stir almond extract and pistachio nuts into remaining plain dough in bowl; stir in a few drops food coloring to tint pale green. Chill both doughs several hours, or overnight, until firm enough to handle.

Preheat oven to 350°.

Pinch off a scant teaspoon of each flavor dough and roll into a 5-inch-long log with palms of hands on a lightly floured cloth. Place logs, side by side, on an ungreased cookie sheet; shape into a coil. Repeat with remaining dough.

Bake 10 minutes, or until cookies are firm but not brown. Remove from cookie sheets to wire racks; cool completely.

Yield: 5 dozen.

PRUNE PINWHEELS

2¼ cups sifted all-purpose flour
½ teaspoon baking soda
½ teaspoon salt
½ cup butter or margarine
1 cup firmly packed light brown sugar
1 egg
1 teaspoon vanilla
1 package (12 ozs.) pitted dried prunes, chopped
½ cup water
½ cup granulated sugar
½ teaspoon ground cinnamon

Sift flour, baking soda, and salt onto waxed paper.

Cream butter with brown sugar in a large bowl until fluffy-light; beat in egg and vanilla. Stir in flour mixture, part at a time, until well blended. Chill dough several hours, or overnight, until firm enough to handle.

While dough chills, combine prunes, water, granulated sugar, and cinnamon in a small saucepan. Heat to boiling; cook 3 to 5 minutes, or until thick; cool.

Divide dough in half. Roll out half to a rectangle ⅛ inch thick on a lightly floured cloth; spread half of the prune mixture over top. Starting at a long side of rectangle, roll up tightly, jelly-roll fashion. Wrap roll, seam side down, in waxed paper. Repeat with remaining half of dough and filling. Chill overnight.

Preheat oven to 400°.

Slice dough in ¼-inch-thick rounds with a sharp knife; place, 1 inch apart, on greased cookie sheets.

Bake 8 to 10 minutes, or until cookies are firm and lightly browned. Remove from cookie sheets to wire racks; cool completely.

Yield: 6 dozen.

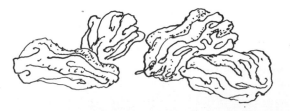

CHERRY BUTTERNUTS

1 cup butter or margarine
1 cup granulated sugar
2 eggs, separated
1 teaspoon grated lemon rind
⅛ teaspoon salt
2 cups sifted all-purpose flour
1 cup finely chopped California walnuts
15 candied red cherries, quartered

Cream butter and ¾ cup of the sugar in a medium bowl until fluffy-light. Beat in egg yolks, lemon rind, and salt. Stir in flour, then walnuts until well blended. Chill dough 2 hours, or until easy to handle.

Preheat oven to 325°.

Pinch off dough, a rounded teaspoon at a time; roll into balls; place, 1 inch apart, on lightly greased cookie sheets.

Bake 15 minutes.

While dough balls bake, beat egg whites in a small bowl until foamy; slowly beat in remaining ¼ cup sugar until meringue forms firm peaks.

Remove cookies from oven; quickly spread about ½ teaspoonful of the meringue over each; top with a piece of candied cherry.

Bake 10 minutes longer, or until meringue is golden. Remove from cookie sheets to wire racks; cool completely.

Yield: 5 dozen.

LEMON LOGS AND CRESCENTS

1 cup butter or margarine
  Confectioners' powdered sugar
3 teaspoons grated lemon rind
2 cups sifted all-purpose flour
2 cups finely chopped pecans

Cream butter with ⅓ cup confectioners' sugar in a large bowl until smooth. Stir in lemon rind and flour until well blended; stir in pecans. Chill dough several hours, or overnight, until firm enough to handle.

Preheat oven to 325°.

Pinch off dough, a scant teaspoon at a time, and roll into 2-inch-long logs between palms

of hands; place, 1 inch apart, on ungreased cookie sheets. Leave as straight logs, or curve each into a crescent shape.

Bake 15 minutes, or until cookies are firm and delicately golden; remove from cookie sheets. While hot, roll in confectioners' sugar; place on wire racks; cool completely. Roll again in confectioners' sugar to make a generous snowy coating.

Yield: About 8 dozen logs or crescents.

PISTACHIO TRUFFLES

¾ cup butter or margarine
1⅓ cups confectioners' powdered sugar
  Dash of salt
1½ teaspoons vanilla
1½ cups sifted all-purpose flour
1 cup finely chopped pistachio nuts
2 tablespoons dry cocoa
2 tablespoons milk
  Chocolate decorating sprinkles
  Candied red cherries, cut in half

Cream butter with ⅓ cup of the confectioners' sugar and salt in a large bowl until smooth; stir in 1 teaspoon of the vanilla, then stir in flour until well blended; stir in pistachios. Chill dough several hours, or overnight, until firm enough to handle.

Preheat oven to 325°.

Pinch off dough, 1 teaspoon at a time, and roll into small balls; place, 1 inch apart, on ungreased cookie sheets.

Bake 20 minutes, or until cookies are firm. Remove from cookie sheets to wire racks; cool completely.

Mix remaining 1 cup confectioners' sugar, cocoa, milk, and remaining ½ teaspoon vanilla in a small bowl until smooth.

Holding each cookie at top and bottom with fingers, frost lower half; roll in chocolate sprinkles to coat well. Top each with a half cherry held in place with a dot of frosting. Let cookies stand on wire racks until frosting is firm.

Yield: About 3½ dozen.

CHERRY-PECAN CRESCENTS

1 cup butter or margarine
1 cup sifted confectioners' sugar
1 teaspoon vanilla
2 cups sifted all-purpose flour
1 cup very finely chopped pecans
¾ cup canned ready-to-spread cherry frosting

Cream butter and confectioners' sugar in a large bowl until smooth; stir in vanilla, then flour until well blended; blend in pecans. Chill dough several hours, or overnight, until firm enough to handle.

Preheat oven to 300°.

Pinch off dough, a level tablespoon at a time, and roll on a lightly floured cloth with palms of hands to a 9-inch-long log; cut in thirds. Place each on an ungreased cookie sheet; curve both ends to form a crescent.

Bake 20 minutes, or until cookies are firm but not brown. Remove from cookie sheets to wire racks; cool completely.

Put each two cookies, bottoms together, with about ½ teaspoon of the frosting. Stir just enough water into remaining frosting in a cup to make a thin glaze; drizzle over cookies. Let stand until glaze is firm.

Yield: About 4½ dozen.

PISTACHIO FINGERS

¾ cup butter or margarine
⅓ cup sifted confectioners' powdered sugar
    Dash of salt
1 teaspoon vanilla
1½ cups sifted all-purpose flour
1½ cups very finely chopped pistachio nuts
½ cup semisweet chocolate pieces
1 tablespoon shortening

Cream butter with confectioners' sugar and salt in a large bowl until smooth; stir in vanilla, then slowly stir in flour until well blended; stir in 1 cup of the pistachio nuts. Chill dough several hours, or overnight, until firm enough to handle.

Preheat oven to 325°.

Pinch off dough, a level teaspoon at a time, and roll into a 3-inch-long log with palms of hands; place on ungreased cookie sheets.

Bake 15 minutes, or until cookies are firm but not brown. Remove from cookie sheets to wire racks; cool completely.

Melt chocolate pieces with shortening in a cup over hot water; cool slightly. Spread remaining ½ cup pistachios on waxed paper.

Dip ends of cookies into chocolate, letting excess drip back into cup; dip into pistachios. Let stand on wire racks until frosting is firm.

Yield: About 4 dozen.

BUTTER-PECAN CRISPIES

1¾ cups sifted all-purpose flour
¾ teaspoon baking soda
¼ teaspoon salt
⅓ cup butter or margarine
⅓ cup shortening
½ cup granulated sugar
½ cup firmly packed light brown sugar
1 egg
1 teaspoon vanilla
½ cup finely chopped pecans

Sift flour, baking soda, and salt onto waxed paper.

Cream butter and shortening with granulated and brown sugars in a large bowl until fluffy-light; beat in egg and vanilla.

Stir in flour mixture, part at a time, until well blended; stir in pecans. Shape into 2 rolls, each about 10 inches long and 1½ inches in diameter, on waxed paper; wrap tightly in paper. Chill several hours, or overnight.

Preheat oven to 375°.

Slice dough into ¼-inch-thick rounds with a sharp knife; place, 1 inch apart, on greased cookie sheets.

Bake 8 to 10 minutes, or until cookies are firm and golden. Remove from cookie sheets to wire racks; cool completely.

Yield: About 7½ dozen.

BERLIN GARLANDS

1 cup butter or margarine
1 cup sifted confectioners' powdered sugar
2 eggs, separated
½ teaspoon almond extract
2¼ cups sifted all-purpose flour
Dash of salt
Green candied cherries, quartered
Red candied cherries, halved

Cream butter with confectioners' sugar in a large bowl until fluffy-light; beat in egg yolks and almond extract. Stir in flour and salt until blended. Chill dough several hours, or overnight, until firm enough to handle.

Preheat oven to 375°.

Beat egg whites in a cup until foamy.

Pinch off dough, a level tablespoon at a time, and roll with palms of hands on a lightly floured cloth to a log about 8 inches long. Shape into a wreath, overlapping ends. Place, 1 inch apart, on greased cookie sheets. Brush with beaten egg whites; press green and red candied cherries onto dough to resemble holly.

Bake 10 minutes, or until cookies are lightly golden. Remove from cookie sheets to wire racks; cool completely.

Yield: About 2½ dozen.

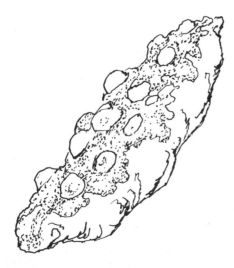

SERINA CAKES

2 eggs
1¼ cups granulated sugar
2½ cups sifted all-purpose flour
1 teaspoon baking powder
Dash of salt
¾ cup butter or margarine
1½ teaspoons vanilla
Red and green decorating sugars
Red and green gumdrops

Separate one of the eggs, placing white in a small bowl and yolk in a cup. Beat white until foamy; slowly beat in 2 tablespoons of the granulated sugar until meringue forms firm peaks.

Sift flour, baking powder, remaining granulated sugar, and salt into a large bowl. Cut in butter with a pastry blender until mixture forms fine crumbs.

Beat in egg yolk, remaining whole egg, and vanilla; stir in meringue until no streaks of white remain. Chill dough several hours, or until firm enough to handle.

Preheat oven to 350°.

Pinch off dough, a teaspoon at a time, and roll into 1-inch balls; roll in red or green decorating sugar. Place, 1 inch apart, on greased cookie sheets; flatten slightly. Or flatten balls first, then top with a small red gumdrop, slivers of gumdrops, or a tree shape cut from a green gumdrop.

Bake 10 minutes, or until cookies are lightly golden around edges. Remove from cookie sheets; cool on wire racks.

Yield: About 5½ dozen.

(Clockwise from top) ▶
ORANGE FIG WAFERS (p.531)
LEMON LOGS AND CRESCENTS (p.542)
BUTTER TREES (p.555)
CHOCO-PEPPERMINT TRIANGLES (p.533)
CHOCOLATE CUTOUTS (p.550)
JEWELED FRUITCAKE BARS (p.535)
PISTACHIO PINWHEELS (p.541)
CHERRY CHEWS (p.531)

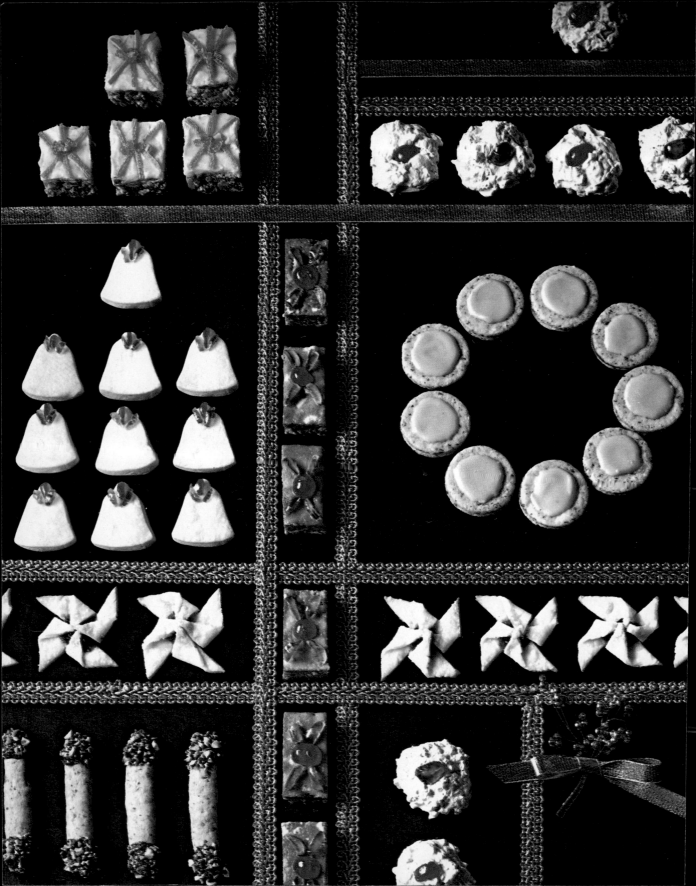

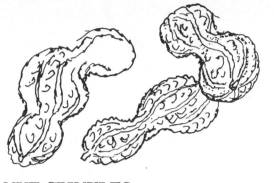

PEANUT CRINKLES

1¾ cups sifted all-purpose flour
½ teaspoon baking soda
¼ teaspoon salt
½ cup regular wheat germ
1 cup butter or margarine
⅔ cup peanut butter
½ cup firmly packed light brown sugar
1 egg
⅓ cup milk
2 cups cornflakes, finely crushed (½ cup crumbs)
  Peanuts

Sift flour, baking soda, and salt into a medium bowl; stir in wheat germ.

Cream butter with peanut butter and brown sugar in a large bowl until fluffy-light; beat in egg and milk. Stir in flour mixture to make a soft dough. Chill at least an hour.

Preheat oven to 350°.

Pinch off dough, a heaping tablespoon at a time, and roll into balls; roll each in cornflake crumbs to coat completely. Place, 2 inches apart, on greased cookie sheets. Flatten each ball slightly with fingertips. Decorate top of each with several peanuts.

Bake 15 minutes, or until cookies are puffed and lightly crackled. Remove from cookie sheets to wire racks; cool competely.

Yield: About 2½ dozen.

◄ *(Clockwise from top left)*
FIG BLOSSOMS (p.533)
COCONUT KISSES (p.530)
LINZER ROUNDS (p.547)
CHERRY SPINNERS (p.546)
HOLLY BARS (p.536)
PISTACHIO FINGERS (p.543)
SHORTBREAD BELLS (p.551)

SANDKAKER

⅔ cup butter or margarine
⅓ cup granulated sugar
1 egg yolk
1¼ teaspoons almond extract
  Dash of salt
½ cup ground or finely chopped almonds
1¾ cups sifted all-purpose flour
  Confectioners' powdered sugar
  Currant jelly

Cream butter with granulated sugar in a large bowl until fluffy-light; beat in egg yolk, almond extract, and salt. Stir in ground almonds and flour until blended. Chill dough several hours, or overnight, until firm enough to handle.

Preheat oven to 325°.

Pinch off dough, a little at a time, and press into well-greased 2-inch tart-shell pans to fill ⅛ inch from top. Place pans on a cookie sheet for easy handling.

Bake 25 minutes, or until tarts are firm and golden. Cool 5 to 10 minutes in pans on wire racks; turn pans upside down and tap lightly with a knife handle to loosen tarts; lift off pans. Cool tarts completely. (If you do not have enough pans to bake tarts all at once, be sure to wash and grease them again before shaping another batch. Between bakings, keep remaining dough chilled.)

Just before serving, sprinkle tarts with confectioners' sugar; top each with jelly.

Yield: About 2 dozen.

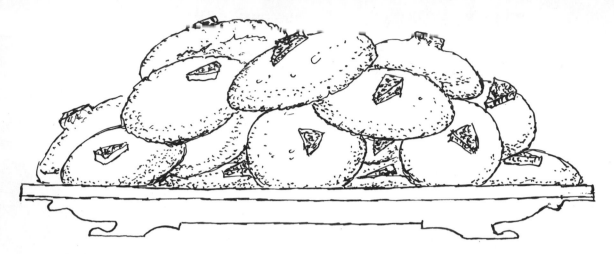

CANDY-BAR JINGLES

2¼ cups sifted all-purpose flour
¾ teaspoon baking soda
¼ teaspoon salt
½ cup butter or margarine
⅔ cup granulated sugar
1 egg
3 tablespoons dairy sour cream
1 teaspoon vanilla
4 bars (3 ozs. each) triangle-shaped Swiss milk chocolate candy with almonds

Sift flour, baking soda, and salt onto waxed paper.

Cream butter with sugar in a medium bowl until fluffy-light; beat in egg, sour cream, and vanilla. Stir in flour mixture until blended. Chill dough several hours, or overnight, until firm enough to handle.

Preheat oven to 375°.

Roll out dough, half at a time, ⅛ inch thick, on a lightly floured board; cut into 2-inch rounds with a floured cookie cutter; place, 1 inch apart, on greased cookie sheets.

Break each candy bar into 12 triangles; place one in the center of each cookie round.

Bake 10 minutes, or until cookies are firm and lightly golden around edges. Remove from cookie sheets to wire racks; cool completely.

Yield: 4 dozen.

CHERRY SPINNERS

1¼ cups sifted all-purpose flour
3 tablespoons granulated sugar
½ teaspoon salt
½ cup shortening
1 package (3 ozs.) cream cheese
1 tablespoon cold water
1 teaspoon grated lemon rind
¼ cup cherry preserves

Sift flour, sugar, and salt into a large bowl. Cut in shortening and cream cheese with a pastry blender until well mixed. Stir in water and lemon rind until dough holds together and cleans the side of bowl. Chill several hours, or overnight, until firm enough to handle.

Preheat oven to 400°.

Roll out dough, half at a time, on a lightly floured cloth to a 10-inch square; cut into 2-inch squares.

Place ¼ teaspoon of the preserves in center of each square; cut small slits in each corner to within ½ inch of preserves; fold every other corner over preserves to make a pinwheel shape; press lightly to hold in place. Place on greased cookie sheets.

Bake 6 minutes, or until cookies are firm and lightly golden. Remove from cookie sheets to wire racks; cool completely.

Yield: About 4 dozen.

ROLLED COOKIES

LINZER ROUNDS

    1 cup sifted all-purpose flour
 1/3 cup granulated sugar
      Dash of salt
 1/2 cup butter or margarine
    1 cup ground filberts
 1/2 cup raspberry preserves
 1/2 cup sifted confectioners' powdered sugar
2 1/2 teaspoons milk
 1/2 teaspoon vanilla
      Red food coloring

Sift flour, granulated sugar, and salt into a medium bowl; cut in butter with a pastry blender until mixture forms fine crumbs. Stir in filberts. (Dough will be crumbly.) Shape into two balls with your hands. Chill several hours, or overnight, until firm enough to handle.

Preheat oven to 350°.

Roll out dough, half at a time, 1/8 inch thick on a lightly floured cloth; cut into rounds with a 1 1/2-inch cutter; place on ungreased cookie sheets.

Bake 6 minutes, or until cookies are firm but not brown. Remove from cookie sheets to wire racks; cool completely.

Put each two cookies, bottoms together, with 1/2 teaspoon of the preserves.

Blend confectioners' sugar, milk, and vanilla in a small bowl until smooth; tint pink with food coloring. Spread over cookies; let stand until frosting is firm.

Yield: 4 dozen.

GINGER FANTASIES

2 1/2 cups sifted all-purpose flour
    1 teaspoon ground ginger
 1/2 teaspoon ground nutmeg
 1/2 teaspoon ground cinnamon
 1/2 teaspoon salt
 1/2 cup shortening
 1/2 cup granulated sugar
 1/2 cup light molasses
 1/2 teaspoon baking soda
    2 tablespoons hot water
      Decorating Frosting (recipe on page 490)
      Red, green, and yellow food colorings

Sift flour, ginger, nutmeg, cinnamon, and salt onto waxed paper.

Cream shortening with sugar in a medium bowl until fluffy-light; beat in molasses.

Dissolve baking soda in hot water in a cup. Stir into sugar mixture, alternately with flour mixture, until well blended. Chill dough several hours, or overnight, until firm enough to handle.

Preheat oven to 350°.

Roll out dough, half at a time, 1/8 inch thick, on a lightly floured cloth; cut into animal, bird, and flower shapes with floured cutters. Place on greased cookie sheets.

Bake 6 to 8 minutes, or until cookies are firm. Remove from cookie sheets to wire racks; cool completely.

Make Decorating Frosting; divide into custard cups; tint pink, red, green, and yellow with food colorings. Working with one color at a time, spoon into a cake-decorating set; attach writing tube. Press frosting out onto cookies in designs of your choice. Let cookies stand until frosting is firm.

Yield: 9 dozen 2-inch cutouts.

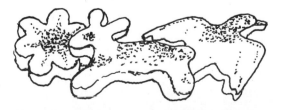

RASPBERRY MACAROON MINIATURES

1¾ cups sifted all-purpose flour
  2 tablespoons granulated sugar (for dough)
  ½ cup butter or margarine
  3 eggs, separated
  ½ teaspoon almond extract
  1 tablespoon ice water
  1 cup granulated sugar (for meringue)
  1 cup cookie coconut
1½ cups red raspberry preserves

Sift flour and the 2 tablespoons sugar into a medium bowl; cut in butter with a pastry blender until mixture forms fine crumbs.

Beat egg yolks with almond extract and water in a small bowl until blended; stir into flour mixture with a fork until blended; knead dough in bowl several times until smooth. Shape into a ball; chill at least an hour.

Roll out dough, half at a time, ⅛ inch thick, on a lightly floured pastry cloth; cut into 2-inch rounds with a floured cookie cutter. Place, 2 inches apart, on ungreased cookie sheets. Chill while preparing meringue.

Preheat oven to 350°.

Beat egg whites in a medium bowl until foamy; beat in the 1 cup sugar, 1 tablespoon at a time, until sugar dissolves completely and meringue forms stiff peaks; fold in coconut.

Spoon meringue into a pastry bag. Press out around edge of each cookie to form a border about ¼ inch high.

Bake 15 minutes, or until meringue is firm and lightly golden. Remove from cookie sheets to wire racks; cool completely.

Just before serving, spoon preserves into center of each cookie.

Yield: About 4½ dozen.

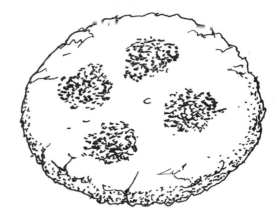

LEMON SAUCERS

3 cups sifted all-purpose flour
1 teaspoon baking powder
½ teaspoon baking soda
½ teaspoon salt
½ cup butter or margarine
1 cup granulated sugar (for cookies)
1 egg
1 teaspoon lemon extract
½ cup dairy sour cream
  Currants
2 tablespoons granulated sugar (for glaze)
1 tablespoon lemon juice

Preheat oven to 400°.

Sift flour, baking powder, baking soda, and salt onto waxed paper.

Cream butter with the 1 cup sugar in a large bowl until fluffy-light; beat in egg and lemon extract. Stir in flour mixture, alternately with sour cream, until blended.

Roll out dough, half at a time, ¼ inch thick, on a well-floured cloth; cut into rounds with a 4-inch cookie cutter; place on greased cookie sheets. Press 3 or 4 currants into center of each round.

Bake 10 minutes, or until cookies are firm and lightly golden. Remove from cookie sheets to wire racks; cool 5 minutes.

Combine the 2 tablespoons sugar and lemon juice in a cup; brush over warm cookies; cool completely.

Yield: 1⅓ dozen.

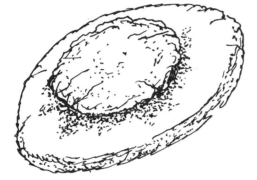

SCOTTISH JEWELS

2¼ cups sifted all-purpose flour
1 teaspoon baking powder
½ teaspoon baking soda
½ teaspoon salt
1 cup butter or margarine
1½ cups firmly packed light brown sugar
2 eggs
2 teaspoons vanilla
2½ cups quick-cooking rolled oats
½ cup currant jelly

Sift flour, baking powder, baking soda, and salt onto waxed paper.

Cream butter and brown sugar in a large bowl until fluffy-light; beat in eggs, 1 at a time; beat in vanilla. Stir in flour mixture until blended; stir in rolled oats. Chill dough several hours, or overnight, until firm enough to handle.

Roll out dough, a third at a time, ¼ inch thick, on a floured pastry cloth; cut into 3-inch-long ovals with a floured cookie cutter; cut a 1-inch round from center of half of the ovals.

Preheat oven to 350°.

Spoon ½ teaspoon of the jelly onto center of each whole oval; top with a cutout oval; press edges together with a fork to seal. Place on ungreased cookie sheets.

Bake 15 minutes, or until cookies are firm and lightly golden. Remove from cookie sheets to wire racks; cool completely.

Yield: About 4 dozen.

SUGAR BALLS AND CANDY CANES

1¾ cups sifted all-purpose flour
½ teaspoon baking powder
¼ teaspoon salt
6 tablespoons butter or margarine
½ cup granulated sugar
1 egg
1 teaspoon lemon extract
   Decorating Frosting (recipe on page 490)
   Red food coloring
   Red and green decorating sugars

Sift flour, baking powder, and salt onto waxed paper.

Cream butter with sugar in a medium bowl until fluffy-light; beat in egg and lemon extract. Stir in flour mixture until blended. Chill dough several hours, or overnight, until firm enough to handle.

Preheat oven to 350°.

Roll out dough, half at a time, ⅛ inch thick, on a lightly floured board; cut into ball or candy-cane shapes with floured cookie cutters. Place on lightly greased cookie sheets.

Bake 12 minutes, or until cookies are firm and lightly golden. Remove from cookie sheets to wire racks; cool completely.

Make Decorating Frosting; leave white or tint pink or red with a few drops of food coloring. To decorate balls, spread frosting in bands over middle of cookies; sprinkle red or green sugar over frosting. To trim canes, use a cake-decorating set and pipe red frosting over cookies to resemble stripes. Let cookies stand on wire racks until frosting is firm.

Yield: 2 dozen 3-inch balls or 2½ dozen 4-inch canes.

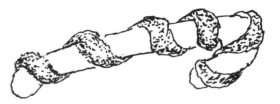

CARDAMOM SNOWFLAKES

1½ cups sifted all-purpose flour
1¼ teaspoons baking powder
¼ teaspoon salt
¼ teaspoon ground cardamom
⅓ cup shortening
¾ cup granulated sugar
1 egg
2 teaspoons milk
5 tablespoons boiling water
1 package vanilla glaze mix
2 cups cookie coconut

Sift flour, baking powder, salt, and cardamom onto waxed paper.

Cream shortening and sugar in a large bowl until fluffy-light; beat in egg. Stir in flour mixture, alternately with milk, until well blended. Chill dough several hours, or overnight, until firm enough to handle.

Preheat oven to 400°.

Roll out dough, half at a time, ⅛ inch thick, on a lightly floured cloth; cut into 2½-inch snowflake shapes with a cookie cutter, or cut around your own cardboard pattern. Place on lightly greased cookie sheets.

Bake 5 minutes, or until cookies are firm and lightly golden around edges. Remove from cookie sheets to wire racks; cool completely.

Place cookies in single layers on wire racks set over sheets of waxed paper or foil.

Stir boiling water into glaze mix until smooth in a small bowl. (Mixture should be thin enough to pour from a spoon.) Spoon over cookies to cover. (Scrape any glaze that drips onto paper back into bowl and beat until smooth, then use again. If mixture becomes too stiff to pour, add more boiling water, a few drops at a time.) Cover cookies with coconut. Let stand until glaze is firm.

Yield: About 3 dozen.

CHOCOLATE CUTOUTS

2½ cups sifted all-purpose flour
1 teaspoon baking powder
½ teaspoon baking soda
¼ teaspoon salt
⅔ cup butter or margarine
1 cup granulated sugar
1 egg
1 teaspoon vanilla
2 squares unsweetened chocolate, melted and cooled
2 tablespoons milk
Decorating Frosting (recipe on page 490)
Green and yellow food colorings

Sift flour, baking powder, baking soda, and salt onto waxed paper.

Cream butter with sugar in a large bowl until fluffy-light; beat in egg, vanilla, and chocolate.

Stir in flour mixture, alternately with milk, until well blended. Chill dough several hours, or overnight, until firm enough to handle.

Preheat oven to 325°.

Roll out dough, part at a time, about ⅛ inch thick, on a lightly floured pastry cloth; cut into small shapes with floured cookie cutters of your choice. Place, 1 inch apart, on lightly greased cookie sheets. Reroll trimmings and cut out.

Bake 10 minutes, or until cutouts are firm. Remove from cookie sheets to wire racks; cool completely.

Make Decorating Frosting; divide into custard cups. Leave one white and tint the others with food colorings. Working with one color frosting at a time, spoon into a cake-decorating set; attach writing tube. Press out onto cookies in designs of your choice. Let stand until frosting is firm.

Yield: About 13 dozen 2-inch cutouts.

SHORTBREAD BELLS

1 cup butter or margarine
½ cup granulated sugar
3 cups sifted all-purpose flour
 Red and green candied cherries, sliced

Cream butter and sugar in a large bowl until fluffy-light; stir in flour until blended, then knead dough in bowl until smooth. Chill several hours, or overnight, until firm enough to handle.

Preheat oven to 300°.

Roll out dough, half at a time, ¼ inch thick, on a lightly floured cloth; cut into 1½-inch bell shapes with a floured cutter. Place on ungreased cookie sheets; trim top of each with bits of red and green cherries.

Bake 20 minutes, or until cookies are firm but not brown. Remove from cookie sheets to wire racks; cool completely.

Yield: 6 dozen.

PEPPERKAKER

1¾ cups sifted all-purpose flour
½ teaspoon baking soda
½ teaspoon salt
1¼ teaspoons ground ginger
½ teaspoon ground cinnamon
¼ teaspoon ground cloves
⅓ cup butter or margarine
⅓ cup granulated sugar
⅓ cup light molasses
 Decorating Frosting (recipe on page 490)
 Red, green, and yellow food colorings
 Small colored candies

Sift flour, baking soda, salt, ginger, cinnamon, and cloves onto waxed paper.

Cream butter with sugar in a large bowl until fluffy-light; beat in molasses. Stir in flour mixture until blended. Chill dough several hours, or overnight, until firm enough to handle.

Preheat oven to 375°.

Roll out dough, a third at a time, ⅛-inch thick, on a lightly floured cloth; cut into shapes of your choice with floured cookie cut-

ters. Place cutouts, 1 inch apart, on greased cookie sheets. Reroll all trimmings and cut out.

Bake 5 minutes, or until cookies are firm. Remove from cookie sheets to wire racks; cool completely.

Make Decorating Frosting. Divide into custard cups and tint pink, green, and yellow with food colorings. Working with one color at a time, spoon into a cake-decorating set; attach writing tube. Press frosting out onto cookies in designs of your choice; trim some with colored candies. Let stand until frosting is firm.

Yield: About 9 dozen small cutouts or 4½ dozen large ones.

STRAWBERRY JIM-JAMS

1 package piecrust mix
6 tablespoons strawberry preserves
 Milk
 Granulated sugar

Preheat oven to 400°.

Prepare piecrust mix with water as label directs; divide in half.

Roll out, half at a time, ⅛ inch thick, on a lightly floured cloth; cut into rounds with a 2½-inch biscuit cutter. Reroll trimmings and cut out to make 36 rounds in all.

Place half of the rounds on a large cookie sheet. Spoon 1 teaspoon of the strawberry preserves onto center of each; top each with a plain round. Press edges together with a fork to seal. Prick top of each several times with a fork to let steam escape. Brush rounds with milk; sprinkle sugar generously over tops.

Bake 15 minutes, or until tarts are golden. Remove from cookie sheet to a wire rack; cool completely.

Yield: 1½ dozen.

MOLDED COOKIES

BIRD'S NESTS

2¼ cups sifted all-purpose flour
¼ teaspoon salt
1 cup butter or margarine
½ cup granulated sugar
2 eggs, separated
1 teaspoon almond extract
1 cup finely chopped almonds
¼ cup confectioners' powdered sugar
  Tiny jelly beans

Preheat oven to 350°.

Sift flour and salt onto waxed paper.

Cream butter and granulated sugar in a large bowl until fluffy-light; beat in egg yolks and almond extract. Stir in flour mixture until well blended.

Beat egg whites slightly in a small bowl; spread almonds on waxed paper.

Pinch off dough, a teaspoonful at a time, and roll into balls; dip in beaten egg whites, then roll in almonds. Place on greased cookie sheets; press a hollow in center of each ball with thumb.

Bake 15 minutes, or until cookies are firm and lightly golden. Remove from cookie sheets to wire racks; cool completely.

Mix confectioners' sugar with just enough water to form a paste in a cup; place a dot in hollow in each cookie; top with 1 or 2 jelly beans to resemble bird's eggs.

Yield: About 4 dozen.

PEANUT-BUTTER SNOWBALLS

1¼ cups graham-cracker crumbs
¼ cup granulated sugar
¾ teaspoon ground cinnamon
½ cup chunky peanut butter
⅓ cup light corn syrup
¼ cup unsifted confectioners' powdered sugar

Mix graham-cracker crumbs, granulated sugar, and cinnamon in a medium bowl; stir in peanut butter and corn syrup until well blended.

Roll mixture, a scant teaspoonful at a time, into ½-inch balls between palms of hands; place on a large plate or tray. Chill several hours until firm.

Measure confectioners' sugar into a pie plate; roll each ball in sugar to coat well.

Yield: About 3 dozen.

ORANGE OATMEAL ROUNDS

2 cups sifted all-purpose flour
1 teaspoon baking soda
¾ teaspoon salt
1 cup shortening
1 cup firmly packed light brown sugar
1 cup granulated sugar
3 eggs
1 tablespoon grated orange rind
2½ cups quick-cooking rolled oats

Preheat oven to 350°.

Sift flour, baking soda, and salt onto waxed paper.

Cream shortening with brown and granulated sugars in a large bowl until fluffy-light; beat in eggs, 1 at a time, and orange rind.

Stir in flour mixture until well blended; stir in rolled oats. Pinch off dough, a teaspoonful at a time, and roll into 1-inch balls; place, 2 inches apart, on lightly greased cookie sheets.

Bake 12 minutes, or until cookies are firm and golden. Remove from cookie sheets to wire racks; cool completely.

Yield: About 5 dozen.

COCOA TRIFLES

1 cup fine vanilla wafer crumbs
1 can (3 ozs.) pecans, finely chopped
1 cup confectioners' powdered sugar
1 cup regular wheat germ
3 tablespoons cocoa powder
⅛ teaspoon salt
¼ cup orange juice
¼ cup honey
1 teaspoon vanilla
   Multicolored decorating sprinkles

Mix wafer crumbs, pecans, powdered sugar, wheat germ, cocoa, and salt in a large bowl. Stir in orange juice, honey, and vanilla until mixture is evenly moist and well blended.

Shape into small balls, using a rounded teaspoonful for each; roll in decorating sprinkles on waxed paper. Store in a tightly covered container at least overnight to mellow flavors.

Yield: About 3½ dozen.

APRICOT MINIATURES

2¾ cups sifted all-purpose flour
½ teaspoon baking soda
½ teaspoon salt
⅔ cup butter or margarine
¾ cup granulated sugar
3 eggs
1¼ cups apricot preserves
2 teaspoons grated orange rind
1 teaspoon grated lemon rind
1 cup mixed candied fruits
1 cup dark raisins
1 cup snipped dried apricots
1½ cups chopped California walnuts
1½ cups finely chopped California walnuts

Preheat oven to 325°.

Sift flour, baking soda, and salt onto waxed paper.

Cream butter with sugar in a large bowl until fluffy-light; beat in eggs, 1 at a time, until fluffy again; beat in ½ cup of the apricot preserves and orange and lemon rinds.

Beat in flour mixture until well blended; stir in candied fruits, raisins, apricots, and chopped walnuts.

Spoon into greased 1¾-inch muffin-pan cups. (If you don't have enough pans to bake all of the cakes at one time, place remaining batter in the refrigerator until first batch is finished.)

Bake 30 minutes, or until cakes are golden and a wooden pick inserted into top comes out clean. Loosen cakes around edges with a knife and carefully remove from pans to wire racks; cool completely.

Spread remaining ¾ cup apricot preserves over tops of cakes; dip each in finely chopped walnuts. Store in a single layer in a tightly covered container until ready to serve.

Yield: 5½ dozen.

PEANUT CRUNCH BALLS

1½ cups sifted all-purpose flour
1 teaspoon baking powder
¼ cup shortening
½ cup peanut butter
½ cup granulated sugar
3 eggs
2 teaspoons grated orange rind
1 teaspoon vanilla
4 cups fortified high-protein cereal flakes
1 cup finely chopped salted peanuts

Sift flour and baking powder onto waxed paper.

Cream shortening with peanut butter and sugar in a large bowl until fluffy-light; beat in eggs, 1 at a time, until fluffy again; beat in orange rind and vanilla. Stir in flour mixture until well blended; fold in cereal flakes.

Preheat oven to 350°. Spread peanuts on waxed paper.

Roll dough, a scant teaspoonful at a time, into ¾-inch balls with palms of hands; roll in peanuts. Place, 1 inch apart, on lightly greased cookie sheets.

Bake 12 minutes, or until cookies are firm and lightly golden. Remove from cookie sheets to wire racks; cool completely.

Yield: About 5 dozen.

RASPBERRY RIBBONS

1 can (8 ozs.) shelled California walnuts
2/3 cup granulated sugar
2 egg whites
2/3 cup raspberry preserves

Grease a large cookie sheet; dust lightly with flour, tapping off any excess.

Preheat oven to 350°.

Grate walnuts, a few at a time, in an electric blender. (Walnuts should be dry and powdery—not ground and oily.) Place in a medium bowl; stir in sugar.

Beat egg whites in a small bowl just until foamy; stir into walnut mixture, a part at a time, until evenly blended and mixture forms a paste. Shape into 2 rolls about 10 inches long and ¾ inch in diameter. Place rolls on prepared cookie sheet. Using your finger or the handle of a wooden spoon, make a tunnel about ½ inch deep down center of each roll to within ¼ inch of ends. (You may find it easier to shape rolls on a sheet of waxed paper and, using paper as a lifter, flip rolls over onto cookie sheet.)

Bake 25 minutes, or until rolls are firm and golden brown. (Rolls will spread and flatten somewhat during baking.) Place cookie sheet on a wire rack.

While rolls bake, heat preserves slowly, stirring several times, until thin and syrupy in a small saucepan. Spoon into tunnels in hot cookie rolls; cool.

Cut each in half crosswise; cut each half into 6 slices.

Yield: 2 dozen slices.

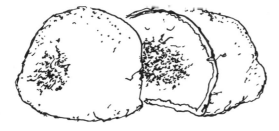

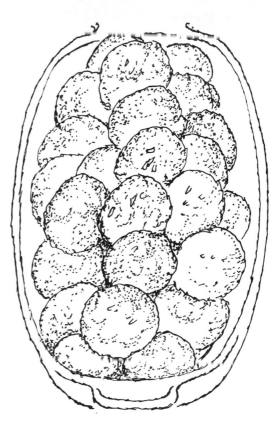

APRICOT-RUM BALLS

1 cup finely chopped dried apricots
1/3 cup boiling water
¼ cup light rum
1 package (7¼ ozs.) vanilla wafers, crushed fine (2 cups)
2/3 cup sifted confectioners' powdered sugar
1 cup chopped California walnuts
Orange decorating sugar

Combine apricots and boiling water in a small bowl; let stand until liquid is absorbed. Stir in rum.

Mix wafer crumbs and confectioners' sugar in a large bowl; blend in apricot mixture and walnuts. Shape into 1-inch balls; roll in orange sugar. Place on wire racks until sugar dries. Store in a tightly covered container for 2 to 3 days to mellow flavors.

Yield: 4 dozen.

PRESSED COOKIES

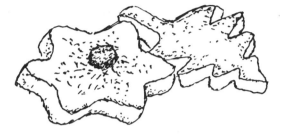

ORANGE SPRITZ

  4 cups sifted all-purpose flour
  1 teaspoon baking powder
1½ cups butter or margarine
  1 cup granulated sugar
  1 egg
  2 teaspoons grated orange rind
    Colored decorating sugars and sprinkles

Preheat oven to 400°.

Sift flour and baking powder onto waxed paper.

Cream butter and sugar in a large bowl until fluffy-light; beat in egg and orange rind. Stir in flour mixture until well blended.

Spoon dough, a fourth at a time, into an electric or manual cookie press; attach design plate of your choice. Press out onto cold un-

greased cookie sheets; sprinkle colored sugars or decorating sprinkles over each.

Bake 8 minutes, or until cookies are lightly golden. Remove from cookie sheets to wire racks; cool completely.

Yield: About 9 dozen.

BUTTER TREES

  3 hard-cooked egg yolks
 ¾ cup butter or margarine
 ½ cup granulated sugar
 ½ teaspoon salt
1¼ teaspoons rum extract
  2 cups sifted all-purpose flour
    Green decorating sugar

Press egg yolks through a sieve into a small bowl.

Cream butter with sugar and salt in a medium bowl until fluffy-light; stir in sieved egg yolks, rum extract, and flour until mixture is smooth and well blended. (Do not chill.)

Preheat oven to 350°.

Spoon dough, a part at a time, into an electric or manual cookie press; attach tree plate. Press out onto cold ungreased cookie sheets; sprinkle green sugar on top.

Bake 10 minutes, or until cookies are firm but not brown. Remove from cookie sheets to wire racks; cool completely.

Yield: About 5 dozen.

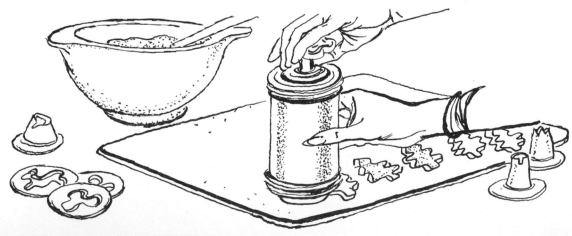

SANDWICHES AND SNACKS

ANY TIME IS THE RIGHT TIME FOR A SANDWICH. Everyone can get into the cooking act, and it's fun, once in a while, to plan a sandwich supper or picnic so that everybody in the family, of almost any age, can be his own chef. Supermarkets help, too, by offering us a bountiful array of makings—sliced meats and cheeses, canned fish and seafood, ready-prepared spreads, vegetables, relishes, fruits, pickles, breads, rolls, and muffins.

When you're making lots of sandwiches for lunch boxes or freezer, save yourself time. Line up the bread slices so that buttering, filling, and packing can move along assembly-line style. First spread all of the slices with soft butter or margarine right to the edge to keep the filling from soaking in. Then add the filling to every other slice; close, cut, and wrap.

For a change of pace with bread slices, pair one of white and another of whole-wheat instead of two of the same flavor; pack halves of two different kinds of sandwiches rather than a whole one of the same kind; make an open-faced sandwich occasionally; cut sandwiches in rectangles, triangles, squares, and thin strips as well as in halves, and cut them invitingly small for children. Vary spreads, too, adding herbs or spices, grated orange or lemon rind, finely chopped nuts, or grated cheese to butter or margarine for a livelier flavor.

If you're planning sandwiches as the whole meal, build them high and husky so they'll be satisfying. Read on for plenty of suggestions for fast-fix fillings—some to put together as you go; others to make ahead and keep on hand in your refrigerator.

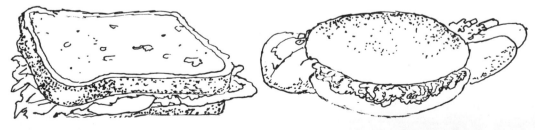

HOT AND HEARTY SUPPER CHOICES

RIVIERAS

1 thin loaf French bread
½ cup process Cheddar cheese spread
2 packages (6 ozs. each) sliced boiled ham
2 eggs
1 cup milk

Preheat oven to 350°.

Cut 16 half-inch-thick slices from bread; use remainder another day.

Spread cheese on bread, using about ½ tablespoon for each slice. Top 8 slices with ham, cutting meat as needed to fit; put together with remaining bread to make 8 sandwiches.

Beat eggs slightly with milk in a pie plate. Dip each sandwich into egg mixture, turning to coat both sides. Place on a greased cookie sheet.

Bake 15 minutes; turn; bake 15 minutes longer, or until sandwiches are crusty brown.

Yield: 4 servings.

CHEESEBURGER SQUARES

1 lb. ground beef
1 single-serving envelope onion soup mix
1 package refrigerated Parker House rolls
4 teaspoons prepared mustard
1 medium tomato, cut in 4 slices
4 tablespoons shredded sharp Cheddar cheese

Preheat oven to 375°.

Mix ground beef and dry onion soup mix in a medium bowl; lightly press into an even layer in a baking pan, 8x8x2 inches.

Bake 15 minutes; cut into 4 squares.

While meat bakes, unroll Parker House dough; separate into 5 sections about 4 inches square, pinching together at perforations. Leave squares flat and place on a greased large cookie sheet.

Bake in same oven with meat 10 to 12 minutes, or until puffed and golden. Remove 1 square from cookie sheet and set aside for nibbles.

Spread 1 teaspoon of the mustard over each of the remaining 4 squares; top each with a meat square and a tomato slice; sprinkle cheese over tomatoes. Return to oven for 2 to 3 minutes, or until cheese melts.

Yield: 4 servings.

TURKEY RAREBIT STACKS

2 tablespoons butter or margarine
2 tablespoons all-purpose flour
½ teaspoon salt
1 cup milk
1 cup shredded sharp Cheddar cheese (4 ozs.)
½ teaspoon Worcestershire sauce
4 slices white toast
2 packages (4 ozs. each) sliced turkey loaf
1 large tomato, cut in 4 slices
  Paprika

Preheat oven to 350°.

Melt butter in a small saucepan; stir in flour and salt. Cook, stirring constantly, until bubbly. Stir in milk; continue cooking and stirring until mixture thickens and boils 1 minute. Stir in cheese until melted and Worcestershire sauce; remove from heat.

Place toast in a single layer in a baking pan, 9x9x2 inches. Top each slice with turkey, then a tomato slice. Pour cheese sauce over all; sprinkle paprika on top.

Bake 15 minutes, or until sauce bubbles up and sandwiches are heated through.

Yield: 4 servings.

CORNED BEEF CRUNCHIES

1 can (12 ozs.) corned beef
6 tablespoons butter or margarine
1 teaspoon prepared horseradish-mustard
8 slices white bread
4 slices process American cheese
2 eggs
2 tablespoons milk
½ cup crushed cheese crackers

Cut corned beef into 8 slices. (If meat is chilled in can for several hours, it will slice neatly.)

Mix 4 tablespoons of the butter and mustard in a cup; spread on bread. Top each of 4 slices with corned beef, cheese, and remaining bread slices.

Beat eggs with milk in a pie plate; sprinkle crackers on waxed paper. Dip sandwiches in egg mixture, then in crackers to coat both sides.

Preheat grill or griddle as manufacturer directs; grease with remaining 2 tablespoons butter.

Place sandwiches on grill. Sauté, turning once, until sandwiches are golden and cheese starts to melt. Cut each in half diagonally; serve hot.

Yield: 4 servings.

RHINELANDERS

1 can (16 ozs.) sauerkraut
1 teaspoon caraway seeds
1½ lbs. ground beef
1 tablespoon bacon-flavored vegetable-protein bits
½ teaspoon salt
¼ teaspoon pepper
2 long slices Swiss cheese, cut in half crosswise
4 large hard rolls
2 tablespoons butter or margarine

Preheat broiler.

Combine sauerkraut and liquid with caraway seeds in a small saucepan; cover. Simmer 20 minutes; drain; keep warm.

Combine ground beef, protein bits, salt, and pepper in a large bowl; mix lightly. Shape into 4 patties ¾ inch thick. Place on rack in broiler pan.

Broil, 4 inches from heat, 4 minutes; turn; broil 3 minutes. Top each patty with a slice of cheese; broil 1 minute longer for rare, or until beef is as done as you like it.

While patties cook, split rolls; toast on a cookie sheet in oven. Spread butter over each; place on serving plates. Spoon sauerkraut onto one half of each roll and place a meat patty on the other half. Serve hot.

Yield: 4 servings.

NEST EGGS

4 large round soft rolls
5 tablespoons butter or margarine, softened
4 eggs
Dash of salt
Dash of pepper
3 tablespoons all-purpose flour
1½ cups milk
1 jar (5 ozs.) bacon-cheese spread
½ teaspoon prepared mustard

Preheat oven to 325°.

Cut a 2-inch round from the top of each roll, cutting only about ½ inch deep; lift out sections and save to make bread crumbs.

Spread 2 tablespoons of the butter in hollows in rolls; place rolls on a cookie sheet. Break an egg into each hollow; sprinkle salt and pepper lightly over eggs.

Bake 30 minutes, or until eggs are as firm as you like them.

While eggs bake, melt remaining 3 tablespoons butter in a small saucepan; blend in flour, then milk. Cook, stirring constantly, until sauce thickens and boils 1 minute; stir in cheese spread until melted, then add mustard. Heat slowly to boiling.

Place each roll on a serving plate; spoon cheese sauce over top.

Yield: 4 servings.

PEANUT-BACON CRISPIES

    8 slices bacon, cut in 1-inch pieces
⅓ cup creamy peanut butter
    2 tablespoons mayonnaise or salad dressing
    1 teaspoon prepared mustard
⅓ cup chopped celery
    8 slices whole-wheat bread
    3 tablespoons butter or margarine

Preheat oven to 400°.

Sauté bacon until crisp in a small skillet; remove and drain well on paper toweling.

Mix peanut butter, mayonnaise, and mustard in a small bowl; stir in bacon and celery. Spread mixture on 4 slices of the bread; top with remaining slices. Spread about 1 teaspoon of the butter on each side of sandwiches; place on a cookie sheet.

Bake 7 minutes; turn; bake 7 minutes longer, or until sandwiches are crusty-brown. Cut each sandwich diagonally in half.

Yield: 4 servings.

LAMB BURGERS

    1 lb. ground lamb patties
    1 cup bran flakes cereal
    1 tablespoon instant minced onion
½ teaspoon salt
    1 can (10½ ozs.) pizza sauce with pepperoni
    1 tablespoon salad oil
    4 hamburger buns, toasted

Mix lamb with cereal, onion, salt, and ¼ cup of the pizza sauce in a medium bowl; shape into 4 patties. Brown slowly, turning once, in salad oil in a medium skillet; pour all fat from skillet.

Stir in remaining pizza sauce; heat to boiling. Simmer, turning patties once, 15 minutes.

Place patties on bottom halves of buns on serving plates; spoon any remaining sauce over meat; cover with tops of buns. Serve with potato chips and celery sticks if you like.

Yield: 4 servings.

FRANKFURTER SALAD ROLLS

    1 lb. frankfurters
    1 small onion, peeled and quartered
    2 hard-cooked eggs, diced
¼ cup chopped dill pickle
¼ cup chopped celery
½ cup mayonnaise or salad dressing
    1 tablespoon mustard pickle relish
¼ teaspoon salt
    6 large hard rolls, split
    6 slices process American cheese

Put frankfurters and onion through a food grinder, using a coarse blade; place mixture in a medium bowl. Add eggs, dill pickle, and celery.

Preheat oven to 400°.

Mix mayonnaise, pickle relish, and salt in a cup; stir into frankfurter mixture. Spread a generous ½ cup on bottom half of each roll; top each with a slice of cheese; cover with tops of rolls. Wrap each sandwich in foil.

Bake 5 minutes, or until sandwiches are hot and cheese starts to melt. Serve hot.

Yield: 6 servings.

STROGANOFF SHORTCAKES

    4 beef cube steaks
    2 tablespoons butter or margarine
1½ cups water
    1 envelope Stroganoff sauce mix
    1 cup (8-oz. carton) dairy sour cream
    4 toaster cornmeal cakes
    1 tablespoon chopped parsley

Brown steaks quickly in butter in a large skillet; remove from pan.

Stir water, then sauce mix into drippings; simmer 10 minutes. Stir about ½ cup of the hot mixture into sour cream in a small bowl; stir back into skillet until smooth; place steaks in sauce. Heat slowly just until hot. (Do not boil.)

Heat cornmeal cakes as label directs; place on serving plates. Top each with a steak, then sauce. Sprinkle parsley over all.

Yield: 4 servings.

TURKEY BOATS

4 small hero rolls
¼ cup butter or margarine
2 teaspoons prepared horseradish-mustard
2 cups diced cooked turkey
1 cup shredded process American cheese
1 small onion, minced (¼ cup)
1 jar (2 ozs.) sliced pimientos, drained and
    chopped
½ cup thinly sliced celery
¼ teaspoon pepper
½ cup mayonnaise or salad dressing
1 medium tomato, cut in 12 thin wedges

Preheat oven to 400°.

Cut around the top of each roll about ¼ inch in from edge; scoop out insides to make boat-shaped shells.

Blend butter and horseradish-mustard in a cup; spread over hollows in rolls.

Mix turkey, cheese, onion, pimientos, celery, pepper, and mayonnaise in a medium bowl until blended; pile into rolls; place on a cookie sheet.

Bake 15 minutes, or just until cheese starts to melt. Garnish with tomatoes.

Yield: 4 servings.

GRILLED HAM SANDWICHES

1 package (4 or 5 ozs.) sliced boiled ham
2 packages (9 ozs. each) frozen French toast
1 jar (7¾ ozs.) junior applesauce
3 teaspoons cinnamon-sugar
    Pancake syrup

Preheat sandwich grill or griddle as manufacturer directs.

Cut ham slices in half crosswise; arrange evenly over 6 slices of French toast. Spread applesauce over ham; sprinkle cinnamon-sugar over applesauce; top with remaining French toast.

Lightly grease grill; place sandwiches on grill. Heat 8 to 10 minutes, or until sandwiches are hot and crusty. Serve hot with syrup.

Yield: 6 servings.

PIZZA CUTS

1 lb. ground beef
¼ cup grated Parmesan cheese
1 can (8 ozs.) tomato sauce
½ teaspoon dried oregano, crushed
½ teaspoon salt
⅛ teaspoon pepper
1 long loaf French bread
½ cup sliced pimiento-stuffed green olives
2 long slices mozzarella cheese, cut crosswise in
    ½-inch-wide strips

Preheat broiler.

Combine ground beef, Parmesan cheese, tomato sauce, oregano, salt, and pepper in a medium bowl; mix lightly.

Split French bread lengthwise; spread meat mixture on cut surfaces; place on a cookie sheet.

Broil, 8 to 10 inches from heat, 10 minutes; remove from broiler.

Arrange olive slices over meat; lay cheese strips diagonally on top.

Broil 2 minutes longer, or just until cheese starts to melt. Cut each half crosswise into thirds. Serve with green onions and celery sticks if you like.

Yield: 6 servings.

FRANKFURTER BOATS

8 frankfurters
4 small sweet pickles, cut in thin strips
8 frankfurter rolls
2 packages (3 ozs. each) pimiento cream cheese

Cut a slit in each frankfurter almost to bottom and ends; stuff pickle strips into slits, dividing evenly.

Preheat oven to 400°.

Open frankfurter rolls and hollow out both top and bottom halves of each just enough to hold frankfurters. Spread cream cheese generously in hollows; place frankfurters, pickle side up, in rolls. Wrap each in foil.

Bake 5 to 7 minutes, or until frankfurters are hot and cheese starts to melt. Serve hot.

Yield: 4 servings.

SAUCY FISH BUNS

1 package (9 ozs.) frozen fish sticks
2 tablespoons butter or margarine
2 tablespoons all-purpose flour
½ teaspoon salt
1 cup milk
1 teaspoon Worcestershire sauce
1 hard-cooked egg, chopped coarsely
2 tablespoons chopped parsley
4 frankfurter rolls

Preheat oven to 425°.

Place fish sticks in a shallow baking pan; heat in oven as label directs.

While fish heats, melt butter in a small saucepan; stir in flour and salt; cook, stirring constantly, until bubbly. Stir in milk; continue cooking and stirring until sauce thickens and boils 1 minute. Stir in Worcestershire sauce, egg, and parsley; keep hot.

Toast rolls in oven with fish; place each on a serving plate. Place fish sticks in rolls; spoon sauce over fish.

Yield: 4 servings.

DANISH SALMON LOGS

1 large cucumber, sliced thin
½ cup dairy sour cream
2 tablespoons snipped fresh dill
2 teaspoons lemon juice (for cucumbers)
1 teaspoon salt
⅛ teaspoon pepper
1 can (16 ozs.) salmon, drained, boned, and flaked
½ cup finely chopped celery
1 small onion, minced (¼ cup)
1 egg, beaten
½ cup fine saltine crumbs
¼ cup milk
1 tablespoon lemon juice (for salmon)
6 frankfurter rolls

Combine cucumber, sour cream, dill, the 2 teaspoons lemon juice, ½ teaspoon of the salt, and pepper in a small bowl; chill well.

Preheat oven to 350°.

Combine salmon, celery, onion, egg, saltine crumbs, milk, remaining ½ teaspoon salt, and the 1 tablespoon lemon juice in a medium bowl; mix lightly until well blended. Shape into six 5-inch-long rolls. Place in a greased shallow baking pan.

Bake 30 minutes, or until crusty brown.

While salmon bakes, toast rolls in same oven; place each on a serving plate. Top half of each roll with a salmon log and the other half with cucumber mixture. Garnish cucumbers with a sprig of fresh dill and serve with cherry tomatoes and a slice of lemon if you like.

Yield: 6 servings.

CHICKEN BUNS

3 boneless chicken breasts or cutlets, weighing about 10 ozs. each
1 egg
2 tablespoons water
¼ cup dry bread crumbs
1 package (8 ozs.) Neufchatel cheese
¼ cup finely chopped green onion
1 tablespoon chopped parsley
3 tablespoons milk
6 large round hard rolls

Preheat oven to 400°.

Cut each chicken breast in half; pound thin between sheets of waxed paper.

Beat egg well with water in a pie plate; dip chicken into egg mixture to coat well, then into bread crumbs. Place pieces in a single layer in a buttered shallow baking pan.

Bake 40 minutes, or until chicken is tender and golden.

While chicken cooks, mix cheese, green onion, parsley, and milk in a small bowl.

Split rolls; toast in oven with chicken; spread cheese mixture on all halves. Place each two halves together, sandwich style, with a half chicken breast. Serve with spiced crab apples if you like.

Yield: 6 servings.

WAFFLED STEAK SANDWICHES

4 individual beef steaks or 4 slices beef eye of
    round, cut ¼ inch thick and weighing about
    1 lb.
½ teaspoon unseasoned instant meat tenderizer
2 tablespoons butter or margarine
⅛ teaspoon dried basil, crushed
2 English muffins, split
  Salt

Preheat waffle iron to highest temperature
as manufacturer directs.

Moisten steaks well with water; sprinkle
tenderizer over meat and pierce with a fork as
label directs.

Grease waffle iron and arrange steaks on
grids; close iron. Cook 2 to 2½ minutes.

While steaks cook, blend butter and basil in
a cup and toast muffin halves. Place each half
on a serving plate; top with a steak. Salt steak
lightly, then spread seasoned butter over
each.

Yield: 4 servings.

RANCHER'S HEROES

1 lb. ground beef
½ lb. sausage meat
1 egg
½ cup fresh bread crumbs (1 slice)
¼ cup milk
1 tablespoon instant minced onion
1 teaspoon salt
1 large onion, peeled and sliced
1 large green pepper, quartered, seeded, and
    sliced
1 tablespoon salad oil
4 small hero rolls
2 tablespoons butter or margarine
  Red-pepper relish

Preheat oven to 375°.

Combine ground beef, sausage meat, egg,
bread crumbs, milk, instant onion, and salt in a
large bowl; mix lightly. Shape into 4 logs
about 5 inches long. Place on rack in broiler
pan.

Bake 30 minutes, or until crusty and meat is
no longer pink.

Sauté sliced onion and green pepper in
salad oil in a medium skillet until crisp-
tender; keep warm.

Cut a thin slice from the top of each hero
roll; scoop out insides to make boat-shaped
shells.

While meat bakes, toast rolls and top slices
on a cookie sheet in oven; spread butter into
hollows in rolls.

When ready to serve, spoon onion mixture
into each roll; top with a meat log, then a
spoonful of red-pepper relish; set tops of rolls
back in place. Serve hot.

Yield: 4 servings.

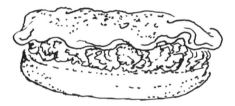

FINGER BEEF PIES

2 packages refrigerated buttermilk biscuits
¼ cup chopped celery
1 tablespoon butter or margarine
1 can (15 ozs.) barbecue sauce with ground beef
2 tablespoons chopped pimiento-stuffed green
    olives
⅓ cup shredded sharp Cheddar cheese

Preheat oven to 450°.

Roll each biscuit to a 4-inch round; place 10
rounds, about 1 inch apart, on greased cookie
sheets.

Sauté celery in butter until soft in a medium
skillet. Stir in barbecue sauce and olives; heat
to boiling. Spoon about 3 tablespoons in
center of each biscuit on cookie sheets.
Sprinkle cheese over meat mixture.

Cut one or two slits in each remaining biscuit to let steam escape; place over rounds on
cookie sheets. Press edges with a fork to seal.

Bake 8 minutes, or until pies are golden and
filling bubbles up.

Yield: 4 to 6 servings.

TURKEY SPOONBURGERS

2 cups diced cooked turkey
3 tablespoons salad oil
1 medium onion, chopped (½ cup)
½ green pepper, chopped (½ cup)
1 teaspoon chili powder
1 can (15 ozs.) herb-tomato sauce
1 teaspoon salt
¼ teaspoon Worcestershire sauce
⅓ cup water
4 hamburger buns, toasted
½ cup broken corn chips

Brown turkey lightly in salad oil in a large skillet; push to one side.

Stir onion and green pepper into drippings; sauté until soft. Stir in chili powder; cook 1 minute, then add tomato sauce, salt, Worcestershire sauce, and water. Heat to boiling; simmer 15 minutes.

Place each two bun halves on a serving plate; spoon turkey mixture over each; sprinkle corn chips on top. Serve as open-face sandwiches.

Yield: 4 servings.

TURKEY DUGOUTS

4 large hard rolls
1½ cups finely diced cooked turkey
½ cup chopped celery
½ cup shredded sharp Cheddar cheese
2 tablespoons chopped parsley
½ cup dairy sour cream
¼ teaspoon salt

Cut a thin slice from the top of each roll; set aside. Hollow out rolls to leave shells about ⅛ inch thick.

Preheat oven to 400°.

Combine turkey, celery, cheese, and parsley in a medium bowl. Blend sour cream and salt in a cup; stir into turkey mixture. Spoon into hollows in rolls; replace tops.

Wrap each sandwich in foil; place on a cookie sheet.

Bake 20 minutes, or until filling is hot. Serve hot.

Yield: 4 servings.

BARBECUED PORK TOASTIES

1 lb. lean boneless pork shoulder
2 tablespoons salad oil
1 medium onion, chopped (½ cup)
½ cup chopped celery
1 cup chili sauce
1 tablespoon brown sugar
1 teaspoon salt
2 tablespoons Worcestershire sauce
1 tablespoon cider vinegar
½ cup water
8 toaster cornmeal cakes

Cut pork into ½-inch cubes; brown slowly in salad oil in a medium skillet; push to one side.

Stir onion and celery into drippings; sauté until soft. Stir in chili sauce, brown sugar, salt, Worcestershire sauce, vinegar, and water. Heat to boiling; cover. Simmer 1 hour, or until pork is tender.

Heat cornmeal cakes as label directs; place 2 on each serving plate; spoon meat mixture on top. Serve hot with dill pickles if you like.

Yield: 4 servings.

WHITECAP SPAGHETTI ROLLS

1 can (15 ozs.) spaghetti rings and little meatballs in tomato sauce
1 teaspoon prepared hot spicy mustard
2 large round hard rolls
1 large tomato, cut in 4 thick slices
1 tablespoon melted butter or margarine
4 square slices mozzarella cheese

Preheat broiler.

Mix spaghetti and mustard in a medium bowl.

Split rolls; place halves in a large shallow baking pan. Spoon spaghetti mixture over rolls, spreading to edges. Top each with a tomato slice; brush melted butter over tomatoes.

Broil, 6 inches from heat, 2 to 3 minutes; place cheese over tomatoes.

Broil 1 minute, or until cheese melts. Serve hot.

Yield: 4 servings.

BAKED HAM STACKS

1 cup biscuit mix
½ teaspoon dried shredded parsley
¼ cup milk
4 large thin slices cooked ham
2 tablespoons mayonnaise or salad dressing
1 tablespoon hot-dog relish, drained
1 large tomato, cut in 4 slices
2 long slices Cheddar cheese, cut into 8 triangles

Preheat oven to 425°.

Combine biscuit mix and parsley in a medium bowl; stir in milk until mixture is evenly moist. Turn out onto a lightly floured board; knead a few times. Roll out to a 7-inch square; place on a cookie sheet. Arrange ham slices in a single layer over square.

Mix mayonnaise and relish in a cup; spread over ham slices.

Bake 10 minutes, or until biscuit is golden around edges; remove from oven.

Place tomato slices over ham; arrange two cheese triangles over each slice.

Bake 4 to 5 minutes, or until cheese melts. Cut into 4 squares. Serve hot.

Yield: 4 servings.

SAUCY SAUSAGE BUNS

1 medium onion, chopped (½ cup)
½ cup chopped green pepper
2 tablespoons salad oil
2 cans (5 ozs. each) Vienna sausages, drained
    and sliced ¼ inch thick
1 can (8 ozs.) tomato sauce with mushrooms
¼ cup chili sauce
4 large round hard rolls, split and toasted

Sauté onion and green pepper in salad oil until soft in a medium skillet; push to one side. Stir in sausages; brown lightly.

Stir in tomato and chili sauces; heat slowly to boiling; cover. Simmer, stirring once or twice, 15 minutes, or until slightly thickened.

Spoon sausage mixture into toasted rolls; place on serving plates. Serve with corn chips and crisp celery sticks if you like.

Yield: 4 servings.

MEATBALL HEROES

1 small onion, chopped (¼ cup)
1 tablespoon butter or margarine
1 can (8 ozs.) tomato sauce
½ teaspoon dried thyme, crushed
1 can (15 ozs.) meatballs in brown gravy
4 frankfurter rolls
4 tablespoons shredded sharp Cheddar cheese

Sauté onion in butter in a medium skillet until soft; stir in tomato sauce, thyme, meatballs and gravy. Heat slowly, stirring several times, to boiling; simmer, 15 minutes.

While meatballs heat, hollow out bottom halves of rolls slightly to make boats; toast rolls; place each on a serving plate.

Spoon meatballs and sauce into rolls; sprinkle 1 tablespoon of the cheese over filling in each. Serve hot to eat knife-and-fork style.

Yield: 4 servings.

GUACAMOLE STEAKBURGERS

1 small avocado
2 teaspoons minced onion
2 teaspoons lemon juice
  Salt
4 beef cube steaks, weighing 1 lb.
2 tablespoons butter or margarine
4 hamburger buns, toasted
1 large tomato, cut in 4 thick slices

Cut avocado in half; peel, pit, and mash in a small bowl. Stir in onion, lemon juice, and ¼ teaspoon salt.

Brown steaks, turning once, in butter in a large skillet about 6 minutes for rare, or until beef is as done as you like it. Sprinkle lightly with salt.

Spread avocado mixture on both sides of buns. Top bottom halves with a steak, then a slice of tomato and top of bun. Serve hot with potato chips and carrot curls if you like.

Yield: 4 servings.

BURGERS DIABLO

  2 lbs. ground beef
1½ teaspoons salt
  ⅛ teaspoon pepper
  3 tablespoons chili sauce
  1 tablespoon brown sugar
  1 tablespoon lemon juice
  1 tablespoon prepared hot spicy mustard
    Few drops red-pepper seasoning
  ⅔ cup fine dry bread crumbs
  6 hamburger buns, toasted and buttered
  1 large tomato, cut in 6 slices
  1 small sweet onion, peeled and cut in 6 slices

Combine ground beef, salt, and pepper in a large bowl; mix lightly. Shape into 6 patties about 1 inch thick.

Preheat broiler.

Mix chili sauce, brown sugar, lemon juice, mustard, and red-pepper seasoning in a cup; sprinkle bread crumbs on waxed paper. Spread chili mixture on each side of meat patties, then dip each in bread crumbs to coat well. Place on rack in broiler pan.

Broil, 4 to 6 inches from heat, 3 minutes; turn; broil 2 minutes longer for rare, or until beef is as done as you like it.

Place each meat patty in a bun; top with tomato and onion slices. Serve hot with extra mustard if you like.

Yield: 6 servings.

TURKEY BURGERS

  1 cup fresh bread crumbs (2 slices)
  1 envelope instant chicken broth
  ½ cup boiling water
  1 egg
1½ cups finely chopped cooked turkey
  2 tablespoons chopped onion
  ¼ cup chopped celery
  2 teaspoons lemon juice
  ½ teaspoon salt
  ¼ teaspoon liquid red-pepper seasoning
  4 hamburger buns
  1 medium tomato, cut in 4 slices

Combine bread crumbs, chicken broth, and boiling water in a medium bowl; stir well; let stand 20 minutes, or until liquid is absorbed.

Beat in egg; stir in turkey, onion, celery, lemon juice, salt, and red-pepper seasoning. Pile onto bottom halves of buns; place in a large shallow pan.

Preheat oven to 500°.

Bake sandwiches 5 minutes; place top halves of buns in same pan; continue baking 3 minutes, or until turkey mixture is heated through and tops are toasted.

Place tomato slices over turkey halves; cover with tops of buns. Serve hot.

Yield: 4 servings.

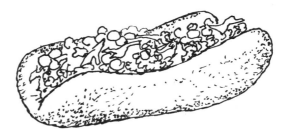

YANKEE TACOS

  ½ lb. ground beef
  1 can (16 ozs.) pork and beans in tomato sauce
  2 tablespoons chili sauce
  2 tablespoons instant minced onion
  ¼ teaspoon salt
  1 cup shredded sharp Cheddar cheese (4 ozs.)
  4 frankfurter rolls, toasted
  1 cup coarsely chopped iceberg lettuce

Shape ground beef into a patty in a medium skillet; brown in its own fat, turning once, then break up into chunks.

Stir in pork and beans and sauce, chili sauce, onion, and salt. Heat slowly, stirring several times, until bubbly. Stir in cheese; heat very slowly, stirring gently but constantly, until melted.

Place each roll on a serving plate; spoon bean mixture over top; sprinkle lettuce over filling. Serve hot to eat open-face style.

Yield: 4 servings.

BIG CHIEF SPOONBURGERS

1 large onion, chopped (1 cup)
1 large green pepper, quartered, seeded, and chopped (1 cup)
3 tablespoons salad oil
1½ lbs. meat-loaf mixture (ground beef, pork, and veal)
1 can (10¾ ozs.) condensed tomato soup
1 can (8 ozs.) tomato sauce
2 teaspoons sugar
1½ teaspoons salt
1 teaspoon dried basil, crushed
¼ teaspoon pepper
Few drops red-pepper seasoning
2 packages (10 ozs. each) frozen whole-kernel corn
12 hamburger buns, toasted

Sauté onion and green pepper in salad oil in a kettle until soft; push to one side.

Add meat-loaf mixture to kettle; brown well; break up into chunks. Spoon any excess fat from kettle.

Stir in soup, tomato sauce, sugar, salt, basil, pepper, red-pepper seasoning, and frozen corn. Heat slowly, breaking up corn with a fork, to boiling; cover.

Simmer 30 minutes; uncover; stir well. Simmer, uncovered, 30 minutes longer, or until thickened.

Spoon mixture into toasted buns, using about ½ cup for each. Serve with dill pickles if you like.

Yield: 12 servings.

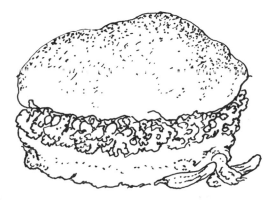

NEW ENGLAND BEAN BURGERS

2 lbs. meat-loaf mixture (ground beef, pork, and veal)
1¼ teaspoons salt
¼ teaspoon pepper
1 can (8 ozs.) pork and beans, drained
2 tablespoons catsup
2 tablespoons bacon-flavored vegetable-protein bits, crumbled
6 large sesame rolls, toasted
6 tablespoons red-pepper relish

Combine meat-loaf mixture, salt, and pepper in a large bowl; mix lightly. Shape into 12 very thin patties.

Preheat broiler.

Mix beans, catsup, and protein bits in a small bowl. Spoon about 1 tablespoon onto each of 6 of the patties; top with remaining patties; press edges together to seal. Place on rack in broiler pan.

Broil, 4 to 6 inches from heat, 3 minutes; turn; broil 5 minutes longer, or until meat is no longer pink on the inside. Place each meat patty in a toasted roll; spoon relish on top.

Yield: 6 servings.

PENNY PIZZAS

4 English muffins
1 can (8 ozs.) tomato sauce with mushrooms
¼ teaspoon dried oregano, crushed
¼ teaspoon dried basil, crushed
4 frankfurters, sliced into thin rounds
4 long slices mozzarella cheese

Preheat oven to 400°.

Split muffins; place halves, cut sides up, in a single layer in a large shallow baking pan.

Mix tomato sauce, oregano, and basil in a small bowl; spread about 1 tablespoon over each muffin half; arrange frankfurter slices over sauce.

Cut each slice of cheese into 8 squares; place 4 over each muffin half.

Bake 15 minutes, or until cheese melts and browns lightly. Serve hot.

Yield: 4 servings.

DEVILED DOG ROLLUPS

8 frankfurters
½ cup shredded process Old English cheese
1 tablespoon well-drained hot-dog relish
1 tablespoon mayonnaise or salad dressing
1 package refrigerated crescent rolls

Cut a slit lengthwise in each frankfurter not quite to bottom or ends.

Mix cheese, hot-dog relish, and mayonnaise in a bowl; spoon into slits in frankfurters.

Preheat oven to 375°.

Separate crescent rolls into triangles; flatten each slightly with hand or a rolling pin. Place a stuffed frankfurter on the wide end of each triangle; roll up as label directs. Place, stuffed side up, on an ungreased cookie sheet.

Bake 15 minutes, or until rolls are golden and frankfurters are hot.

Yield: 4 servings.

SAUSAGE PIZZA ROUNDS

4 pita or pocket breads
1⅓ cups meatless spaghetti sauce (from a 15-oz. jar)
4 precooked smoked sausage links, cut crosswise into thin rounds
1 package (8 ozs.) Muenster cheese, shredded
2 tablespoons grated Parmesan cheese

Preheat oven to 400°.

Press each pita bread as flat as possible with hand; place, crust sides down, on two large cookie sheets.

Spread ⅓ cup of the spaghetti sauce over each bread; top with sausage slices. Sprinkle the Muenster, then Parmesan cheeses over sausage.

Bake 15 minutes, or until cheese melts and sauce bubbles up. Cut each bread in half. Serve hot.

Yield: 4 servings.

BOLOGNA-BEAN DOGS

1 can (8 ozs.) pork and beans
1 tablespoon hot-dog relish
8 frankfurters
1 package (6 ozs.) sliced ham bologna
¼ cup bottled barbecue sauce
8 frankfurter rolls, toasted

Drain liquid from beans; mash beans with a fork in a medium bowl; stir in hot-dog relish.

Preheat broiler.

Slit frankfurters lengthwise not quite to bottom; stuff with bean mixture. Wrap a slice of ham bologna around each frankfurter; fasten with wooden picks. Place on rack in broiler pan. Brush all over with barbecue sauce.

Broil, 6 inches from heat, turning and brushing often with more barbecue sauce, 8 minutes, or until glazed. Serve in frankfurter rolls with extra relish.

Yield: 4 servings.

FRANKFURTER REUBENS

8 frankfurters
1 can (16 ozs.) sauerkraut, drained
¼ cup bottled Russian salad dressing
8 frankfurter rolls
4 long slices Swiss cheese, cut crosswise into strips

Preheat broiler.

Place frankfurters on rack in broiler pan.

Broil, 6 inches from heat, turning several times, 5 minutes, or until puffed and hot.

While frankfurters heat, combine sauerkraut and Russian dressing in a small saucepan; heat slowly until bubbly.

Open frankfurter rolls flat; place cheese strips on each. Broil 2 to 3 minutes, or just until cheese starts to melt.

Place each frankfurter in a roll; spoon sauerkraut mixture on top. Serve hot.

Yield: 4 servings.

TORPEDOES

1½ lbs. ground beef
⅓ cup bottled plain barbecue sauce
1 teaspoon salt
⅛ teaspoon pepper
1 small loaf French bread
1 package (4 ozs.) frozen French fried onion rings
½ cup prepared sandwich spread
4 slices process white American cheese, cut in half diagonally
2 medium tomatoes, sliced thin

Preheat broiler.

Combine ground beef, barbecue sauce, salt, and pepper in a large bowl; mix lightly. Shape into 6 patties about ½ inch thick. Place on rack in broiler pan.

Split bread lengthwise; place on a cookie sheet. Place onions in a shallow pan. Toast bread and heat onions in oven; keep onions warm. Spread sandwich spread over bread; keep warm.

Broil beef patties, 4 inches from heat, 2 minutes; turn; broil 1 minute longer for rare, or until beef is as done as you like it.

Overlap patties on bottom half of bread; arrange cheese over meat; return to oven until cheese melts. Place tomato slices on remaining half of bread; place both halves on a platter. Sprinkle onions over meat.

To serve, cut each half loaf crosswise into quarters.

Yield: 4 servings.

BARBECUED TURKEY BURGERS

1 medium onion, chopped (½ cup)
1 cup chopped celery
3 tablespoons salad oil
2 cups diced cooked turkey
1 tablespoon brown sugar
½ teaspoon dry mustard
¾ cup catsup
2 tablespoons cider vinegar
4 hamburger buns, toasted

Sauté onion and celery in salad oil until soft in a medium skillet: push to one side. Stir in turkey; brown lightly.

Stir in brown sugar, mustard, catsup, and vinegar; heat to boiling. Simmer 20 minutes, or until thick.

Spoon into toasted buns; place on serving plates. Serve with potato chips.

Yield: 4 servings.

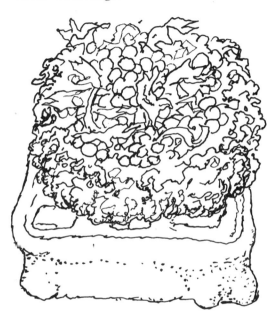

OPEN-FACE TACOS

½ lb. ground beef
2 tablespoons salad oil
1 small onion, chopped (¼ cup)
1 can (16 ozs.) barbecue beans
2 teaspoons prepared mustard
4 frozen round waffles
1 cup shredded sharp Cheddar cheese (4 ozs.)
1 cup shredded iceberg lettuce

Shape ground beef into a patty. Brown, turning once, in salad oil in a medium saucepan, break up into chunks; push to one side.

Stir onion into drippings; sauté until soft. Stir in beans and mustard; simmer 5 minutes.

While beef mixture cooks, toast waffles as label directs; place each on a serving plate. Spoon bean mixture onto waffles; sprinkle cheese and lettuce on top. Serve hot.

Yield: 4 servings.

AT-HOME LUNCH SPECIALS

TOASTED HAM-AND-CHEESE STICKS

1 can (4½ ozs.) deviled ham
1 tablespoon catsup
1 tablespoon sweet pickle relish, drained
8 slices frozen French toast
1 jar (5 ozs.) process Old English cheese spread

Preheat oven to 400°.

Mix deviled ham, catsup, and pickle relish in a small bowl; spread on 4 slices of the frozen French toast. Spread cheese on remaining 4 slices; put slices together to make sandwiches. Place on an ungreased cookie sheet.

Bake 15 minutes, or until hot and crusty. Cut each sandwich into three strips. Serve hot.

Yield: 4 servings.

CHILI ROLLS

1 can (15 ozs.) ring-shaped spaghetti in tomato and cheese sauce
1 can (8 ozs.) chili con carne
4 frankfurter rolls, toasted and buttered
½ cup shredded process American cheese

Preheat oven to 400°.

Mix spaghetti and chili con carne in a medium bowl; spoon into rolls. Stand rolls, filling side up, in a shallow baking pan; sprinkle cheese over filling.

Bake 15 minutes, or until hot.

Yield: 4 servings.

BOLOGNA BUNS

1 piece bologna, weighing 12 ozs.
2 packages (3 ozs. each) chive cream cheese
3 tablespoons chopped dill pickles
2 tablespoons chopped parsley
¼ teaspoon salt
4 large round hard rolls

Preheat oven to 400°.

Peel casing from bologna; dice meat and combine with cream cheese, pickles, parsley, and salt in a medium bowl.

Cut a thin slice from the top of each roll; hollow out insides to leave shells about ¼-inch thick. Spoon bologna mixture into hollows, using about ½ cupful for each; replace tops. Wrap each sandwich in foil; place on a cookie sheet.

Bake 15 minutes, or until hot.

Yield: 4 servings.

REUBEN LOAF

1 loaf unsliced light rye bread, about 9 inches long
2 cups shredded romaine or iceberg lettuce
¼ teaspoon caraway seeds
½ cup bottled Thousand Island salad dressing
2 packages (3½ ozs. each) sliced corned beef
1 package (8 ozs.) sliced Swiss cheese
6 cherry tomatoes, stemmed

Slice bread lengthwise into quarters, keeping slices in order.

Toss romaine, caraway seeds, and 2 tablespoons of the salad dressing in a medium bowl.

Spread 3 tablespoons of the dressing on bottom slice of bread; top with corned beef, second slice of bread, and romaine mixture.

Spread remaining dressing over third slice of bread; stack on top of romaine mixture; top with Swiss cheese and fourth slice of bread.

Thread cherry tomatoes on each of 6 long skewers. Stick into loaf to hold together. To serve, cut crosswise into thick slices with a serrated knife and a sawing motion.

Yield: 6 servings.

TURKEY SHORTCAKES

1 package (8 ozs.) process American cheese, cut up
¼ cup milk
2 cups cubed cooked turkey
1 can (about 8 ozs.) peas, drained
2 tablespoons drained chopped pimientos
   Few drops red-pepper seasoning
8 small frozen waffles, toasted

Combine cheese and milk in a medium saucepan; heat slowly, stirring constantly, until cheese melts and sauce is smooth.

Stir in turkey, peas, pimientos, and red-pepper seasoning; heat until bubbly.

Spoon over waffles on serving plates.
Yield: 4 servings.

BROILED PEANUT-HAM SANDWICHES

4 slices white bread
½ cup peanut butter
1 package (4 ozs.) sliced boiled ham
1 can (8 ozs.) crushed pineapple in juice, drained
2 tablespoons butter or margarine, melted

Preheat broiler.

Place bread slices in a single layer on a cookie sheet; toast on one side in broiler.

Spread peanut butter over untoasted sides; top with ham, folding slices to fit, if needed. Spread pineapple over ham; drizzle melted butter over top.

Broil, 4 to 6 inches from heat, 2 to 3 minutes, or until heated through. Serve hot.
Yield: 4 servings.

WIENER BURGERS

8 frankfurters
½ cup catsup
1 envelope green-onion dip mix
¼ cup finely chopped celery
8 hamburger buns, toasted

Cut frankfurters in half crosswise; score every ¼ inch not quite to bottom. Place in a medium skillet; add water to cover; cover skillet. Heat very slowly 10 minutes, or until frankfurters are hot.

Combine catsup, dip mix, and celery in a small saucepan; heat slowly to boiling; simmer 5 minutes to blend flavors.

Drain frankfurters; place 2 pieces on the bottom of each bun; spoon sauce on top. Cover with tops of buns.
Yield: 4 servings.

FRANKFURTER PONYTAILS

4 frankfurters
1 cup shredded sharp Cheddar cheese
2 tablespoons chili sauce
2 tablespoons drained sweet-pickle relish
4 frankfurter rolls

Preheat oven to 400°.

Slit each frankfurter lengthwise not quite to bottom.

Mix cheese, chili sauce, and relish in a small bowl; stuff into frankfurters; place in rolls. Wrap each in foil, twisting ends to seal.

Bake 15 minutes, or until hot.
Yield: 4 servings.

TURKEY SMORGASBORDS

¼ cup mayonnaise or salad dressing
2 tablespoons drained sweet-pickle relish
4 slices cracked wheat bread, toasted
4 large thin slices cooked turkey
4 hard-cooked eggs
2 slices process American cheese

Preheat broiler.

Mix mayonnaise and pickle relish in a cup; spread on toast; top with turkey.

Slice eggs lengthwise; cut cheese into 8 strips. Arrange eggs over turkey; crisscross 2 strips of cheese over eggs on each sandwich; place on a cookie sheet.

Broil, 4 to 6 inches from heat, 1 to 2 minutes, or until cheese melts. Serve hot.
Yield: 4 servings.

CALICO EGG WHOPPERS

2 tablespoons butter or margarine
2 tablespoons all-purpose flour
¼ teaspoon dried thyme, crushed
1 cup milk
1 can (8 ozs.) peas, drained
¼ cup chopped pimiento
4 frozen waffles
1 can (4½ ozs.) deviled ham
3 hard-cooked eggs, sliced

Melt butter in a small saucepan; stir in flour and thyme; cook, stirring constantly, until bubbly. Stir in milk; continue cooking and stirring until sauce thickens and boils 1 minute. Stir in peas and pimiento; heat to boiling.

Toast waffles; spread deviled ham over each; overlap egg slices on top of ham. Place on plates. Spoon sauce over all.

Yield: 4 servings.

HAMBURGER JUMBLES

¾ lb. ground beef
1 tablespoon salad oil
1 small onion, chopped (¼ cup)
1 tablespoon all-purpose flour
2 tablespoons catsup
1 teaspoon prepared hot spicy mustard
¼ teaspoon salt
⅛ teaspoon pepper
½ cup dairy sour cream
4 hamburger buns, toasted

Brown ground beef in salad oil in a medium skillet; push to one side. Stir in onion and sauté until soft.

Sprinkle flour over meat mixture, then stir in with catsup, mustard, salt, pepper, and sour cream. Heat slowly, stirring several times, until hot and blended.

Spoon into toasted buns; serve hot.

Yield: 4 servings.

BOLOGNA ROLLUPS

2 medium seedless oranges
3 cups finely shredded green cabbage (about ¾ lb.)
1 tablespoon finely minced onion
½ cup dairy sour cream
2 teaspoons sugar
¼ teaspoon salt
2 teaspoons lemon juice
2 tablespoons butter or margarine
4 slices Vienna bread
1 package (8 ozs.) sliced large bologna

Pare oranges and section, discarding white membrane. Cut fruit into bite-sized pieces and place in a medium bowl. Add cabbage and onion.

Mix sour cream, sugar, salt, and lemon juice in a cup; stir into cabbage mixture; chill.

Just before serving, spread butter on bread. Spoon cabbage mixture onto bologna slices; roll up, jelly-roll fashion; place two rolls on each slice of bread. Serve open-face with corn chips and halved cherry tomatoes if you like.

Yield: 4 servings.

SHRIMP REMOULADE BOATS

2 cans (4½ ozs. each) deveined shrimp
¾ cup mayonnaise or salad dressing
2 tablespoons chopped green onions
1 tablespoon drained capers
1 teaspoon Worcestershire sauce
1 teaspoon prepared horseradish
2 teaspoons chopped parsley
　Few drops red-pepper seasoning
4 club rolls
　Romaine

Drain shrimp and rinse; chop coarsely and place in a medium bowl.

Mix mayonnaise with onions, capers, Worcestershire sauce, horseradish, parsley, and red-pepper seasoning in a small bowl. Fold into shrimp; chill.

Cut a thin slice from the top of each roll; hollow out insides to make boat-shaped shells. Line hollows with romaine; spoon shrimp mixture into hollows; replace top slices. Serve with small celery sticks and a wedge of lemon.

Yield: 4 servings.

FISH BURGERS

1 package (8 ozs.) frozen fish cakes
1 can (10¾ ozs.) condensed cream of celery soup
1 can (8 ozs.) peas and carrots, drained
½ teaspoon dried basil, crushed
4 hamburger buns

Heat fish cakes as label directs; keep hot.

Combine soup, peas and carrots, and basil in a small saucepan; heat slowly, stirring several times, to boiling.

Toast hamburger buns; place bottom halves on 4 serving plates. Top with a fish cake, then spoon vegetable sauce over each; replace tops of buns.

Yield: 4 servings.

GERMAN SUBMARINES

6 fully-cooked bratwurst
4 tablespoons butter or margarine
6 frankfurter rolls
1 jar (16 ozs.) red cabbage, well drained

Preheat oven to 425'.

Brown bratwurst in a skillet as label directs.

Spread butter on rolls; place a bratwurst in each; spoon red cabbage on top. Wrap each sandwich in foil. For easy handling, place in a shallow baking pan.

Bake 15 minutes, or until sandwiches are hot. Serve hot.

Yield: 6 servings.

PEANUT-BACON BUILDUPS

¾ cup peanut butter
2 tablespoons chopped sweet pickles
2 tablespoons chopped pimiento-stuffed green
    olives
8 slices white bread, toasted and buttered lightly
8 slices bacon, cooked crisp
1 small tomato, cut in 4 slices

Mix peanut butter, pickles, and olives in a small bowl; spread on 4 slices of the toast. Top each with 2 slices of bacon, 1 slice of tomato, and a remaining slice of toast. Cut each into triangles.

Yield: 4 servings.

HAM-AND-EGG WHOPPERS

4 hard-cooked eggs, chopped
½ cup chopped celery
½ cup mayonnaise or salad dressing
1 tablespoon chopped parsley
½ teaspoon salt
⅛ teaspoon pepper
8 slices rye bread
2 long slices Swiss cheese, cut in half crosswise
1 package (4 or 5 ozs.) sliced boiled ham

Combine eggs and celery in a medium bowl. Blend ¼ cup of the mayonnaise, parsley, salt, and pepper in a cup; fold into egg mixture.

Spread remaining ¼ cup mayonnaise on bread. Place a half slice of cheese on each of 4 slices of bread; top with egg salad, then ham and remaining slices of bread. Cut each sandwich in thirds.

Yield: 4 servings.

BROILED BACON BUNS

4 frankfurter rolls
¾ lb. sliced bacon, crisply cooked
1 cup shredded sharp Cheddar cheese (4 ozs.)

Preheat broiler.

Place rolls in a shallow pan; toast in broiler. Top each half with bacon and cheese.

Broil 3 minutes, or until cheese melts.

Yield: 4 servings.

TURKEY TRIANGLES

⅓ cup mayonnaise or salad dressing
¼ cup prepared cranberry-orange relish
8 slices whole-wheat bread, toasted
2 packages (3 ozs. each) sliced pressed turkey
4 slices Muenster cheese
  Iceberg lettuce

Blend mayonnaise and cranberry relish in a cup; spread on toast.

Stack each of 4 slices with turkey, cheese, lettuce, and remaining slices of toast. Cut diagonally in half.

Yield: 4 servings.

BEEF STACKS

1 can (15 ozs.) roast-beef hash
2 tablespoons butter or margarine
2 medium tomatoes, cut crosswise in half
1 carton (8 ozs.) prepared onion dip
3 tablespoons milk
4 small frozen waffles

Open both ends of roast-beef hash can and push hash out in one piece; cut into 4 rounds.

Melt 1 tablespoon of the butter in a medium skillet; add hash rounds and sauté, turning once, until crusty brown.

Sauté tomatoes, without turning, in remaining 1 tablespoon butter in a second skillet just until hot.

Combine onion dip and milk in a small saucepan; heat slowly, stirring several times, until hot. (Do not boil.)

Toast waffles as label directs; place each on a serving plate. Top with a hash round, tomato slice, and onion sauce. Serve hot.

Yield: 4 servings.

PARISIAN CHEDDAR STACKS

2 medium-sized red apples
2 tablespoons lemon juice
⅓ cup thinly sliced celery
¼ cup finely chopped dates
¼ cup chopped California walnuts
6 tablespoons mayonnaise or salad dressing
8 slices raisin bread
4 long slices sharp Cheddar cheese

Core apples but do not pare; slice in thin rounds; place slices in lemon juice in a pie plate to prevent darkening.

Mix celery, dates, walnuts, and 3 tablespoons of the mayonnaise in a small bowl.

Spread rest of mayonnaise on bread; fold each cheese slice in half and place on a slice of bread. Top with apple slices, date mixture, and remaining slices of bread, spread side down. Cut each sandwich in half.

Yield: 4 servings.

PEANUT CLUBS

8 slices bacon
¾ cup chunky peanut butter
1 can (8 ozs.) crushed pineapple, drained
3 tablespoons butter or margarine
12 slices cracked-wheat bread, toasted
2 small tomatoes, sliced thin
  Iceberg lettuce

Cut bacon slices in half crosswise. Sauté until crisp in a medium skillet; remove and drain on paper toweling; keep warm.

Mix peanut butter and pineapple in a small bowl.

Spread butter on toast, then spread pineapple mixture on 4 slices. Top with tomato slices, another slice of toast, bacon, lettuce, and last slice of toast. Hold in place with wooden picks. Cut each sandwich diagonally in quarters.

Yield: 4 servings.

JUAREZ TURKEY BUNS

1 small onion, chopped (¼ cup)
¼ cup chopped green pepper
2 tablespoons salad oil
1 teaspoon chili powder
1 can (8 ozs.) red kidney beans
1 can (8 ozs.) tomato sauce
¼ teaspoon salt
8 small thin slices cooked turkey
4 hamburger buns
4 pitted ripe olives, sliced crosswise

Sauté onion and green pepper in salad oil in a medium skillet until soft. Stir in chili powder; cook 1 minute.

Stir in kidney beans and liquid, tomato sauce, and salt; heat to boiling; cover. Simmer 10 minutes. Place turkey in sauce; heat 5 minutes longer.

Toast buns; place each two halves on a serving plate; spoon turkey and sauce over top. Garnish with olive slices.

Yield: 4 servings.

TOASTED PEANUT SANDWICHES

2 cups oven-toasted crisp rice cereal
2 eggs
¼ cup milk
¼ teaspoon salt
12 frozen waffles
6 tablespoons chunky peanut butter
6 tablespoons apricot preserves

Crush cereal with a rolling pin to make about 1 cup crumbs; spread on a sheet of waxed paper.

Beat eggs with milk and salt in a pie plate. Preheat oven to 400°.

Cut waffles apart. (No need to thaw.) Spread 1 tablespoon of the peanut butter on 6; spread preserves on remaining 6; put one of each kind together to make sandwiches.

Dip sandwiches into egg mixture, turning to coat both sides, then dip into crumbs to coat well. Place on a greased cookie sheet.

Bake 20 minutes, or until crisp and golden. Serve hot.

Yield: 6 servings.

LIVERWURST WHOPPERS

8 slices bacon
½ cup mayonnaise or salad dressing
2 tablespoons chili sauce
2 large round hard rolls, split
½ lb. sliced liverwurst
½ medium-sized sweet onion, peeled and cut in 4 slices
   Boston lettuce
1 large tomato, cut in 4 slices
½ medium-sized firm ripe avocado, peeled and cut in 4 rings

Sauté bacon slices until crisp in a large skillet; remove and drain on paper toweling.

Mix mayonnaise and chili sauce in a cup; spread about ½ tablespoon on each half roll. Top each with liverwurst, an onion slice, 2 slices of bacon, lettuce, a tomato slice, and an avocado ring. Spoon remaining dressing into avocado rings. Serve on plates to eat, knife-and-fork style.

Yield: 4 servings.

CONFETTI TURKEY TRIANGLES

1½ cups finely diced cooked turkey
1 large carrot, pared and shredded (1 cup)
3 tablespoons chopped sweet pickles
1 package (3 ozs.) cream cheese
2 tablespoons mayonnaise or salad dressing
1 tablespoon milk
¼ teaspoon salt
8 slices Vienna bread
   Iceberg lettuce

Combine turkey, carrot, and pickles in a large bowl.

Blend cream cheese, mayonnaise, milk, and salt until smooth in a small bowl; stir into turkey mixture. Spread on 4 slices of the bread; top with lettuce, then remaining slices of bread.

Cut each sandwich in half diagonally.

Yield: 4 servings.

BARBECUED CHICKEN BOATS

2 cans (4¾ ozs. each) chicken spread
¼ cup bottled plain barbecue sauce
2 tablespoons drained sweet pickle relish
2 teaspoons prepared mustard
4 sesame-seed rolls
2 tablespoons butter or margarine
  Boston lettuce
1 medium tomato, cut in 4 slices

Combine chicken spread, barbecue sauce, pickle relish, and mustard in a medium bowl; mix well.

Cut a thin slice from the top of each roll; hollow out bottoms with a fork to make shells about ¼ inch thick. Spread butter in shells, then line with lettuce and fill with chicken mixture. Cover each with a tomato slice; replace tops of rolls. Place on serving plates. Serve with potato chips if you like.

Yield: 4 servings.

TURKEY TOASTIES

4 slices whole-wheat bread
2 tablespoons prepared sandwich spread
1 can (2¼ ozs.) deviled ham
4 large thin slices cooked turkey
1 large tomato, cut in 4 slices
4 slices process Old English cheese

Preheat broiler.

Place bread slices in a single layer on a cookie sheet; toast on one side in broiler.

Spread sandwich spread, then deviled ham on untoasted sides of bread; top with turkey, tomato slices, and cheese. Return to cookie sheet.

Broil, 4 to 6 inches from heat, 2 to 3 minutes, or until cheese bubbles up.

Yield: 4 servings.

BEEF-AND-CABBAGE TRIANGLES

2 packages (3½ ozs. each) sliced corned beef
½ cup finely shredded green cabbage
¼ cup chopped celery
¼ cup chopped green pepper
½ cup mayonnaise or salad dressing
2 tablespoons chili sauce
8 large slices rye bread

Shred corned beef with a sharp knife. Combine with cabbage, celery, and green pepper in a medium bowl.

Blend mayonnaise with chili sauce in a cup; stir into corned beef mixture. Spread on 4 slices of the bread; top with remaining slices of bread. Cut each sandwich diagonally into quarters.

Yield: 4 servings.

BACON-AND-EGG ROUNDS

6 slices bacon, cut in 1-inch pieces
6 hard-cooked eggs
½ cup diced celery
¼ cup chopped ripe olives
2 tablespoons chopped green onions
½ cup dairy sour cream
1 tablespoon horseradish-mustard
¼ teaspoon salt
  Dash of pepper
4 hamburger buns

Sauté bacon until crisp in a medium skillet; remove with a slotted spoon and drain on paper toweling.

Chop eggs; combine with celery, olives, and onions in a medium bowl.

Mix sour cream, horseradish-mustard, salt, and pepper in a cup; stir into egg mixture.

Open buns flat and place each on a serving plate; spoon about ¼ cup of the egg mixture onto each half; sprinkle bacon on top.

Yield: 4 servings.

PEANUT-ORANGE TOASTIES

⅔ cup peanut butter
2 teaspoons grated orange rind
8 slices unfrosted raisin bread
1 egg
½ cup milk
  Dash of salt
  Butter or margarine

Mix peanut butter and orange rind in a small bowl. Spread on 4 slices of the bread; top with remaining slices to make sandwiches.

Beat egg with milk and salt in a pie plate. Dip sandwiches into mixture to coat both sides.

Sauté in butter in a large skillet, turning once, until sandwiches are golden. Serve hot.

Yield: 4 servings.

HEARTY HAM HEROES

3 hard-cooked eggs
2 tablespoons mayonnaise or salad dressing
1 tablespoon hot dog relish
1 tablespoon chopped parsley
½ cup cold pack Cheddar cheese food
4 frankfurter rolls
  Iceberg lettuce
4 thin slices cooked ham

Chop eggs in a medium bowl; stir in mayonnaise, hot dog relish, and parsley until well blended.

Spread cheese on bottom halves of rolls; layer lettuce, ham, lettuce, and egg mixture over cheese; replace tops of rolls. Serve with potato chips and carrot sticks if you like.

Yield: 4 servings.

GOLDEN HAM ROLLS

4 frankfurter rolls
2 tablespoons butter or margarine
  Iceberg lettuce
2 packages (4 ozs. each) sliced boiled ham
4 square slices Muenster cheese, each cut in two triangles
1 can (11 ozs.) mandarin orange segments, well drained
½ cup mayonnaise or salad dressing
¼ teaspoon sugar
1 tablespoon milk
1 tablespoon lemon juice

Open each roll and place flat on a serving plate. Spread butter over each, then top with lettuce, ham, and cheese; arrange orange segments over cheese.

Mix mayonnaise, sugar, milk, and lemon juice in a cup; spoon part over each sandwich.

Yield: 4 servings.

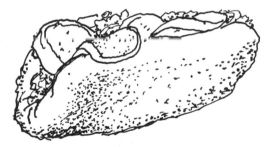

BOLOGNA LOAVES

½ cup French fried onions (from a 3-oz. can)
4 club rolls
1 package (3 ozs.) pimiento cream cheese, softened
1 package (8 ozs.) sliced bologna

Place onions in a medium skillet; heat slowly, shaking skillet constantly, 2 to 3 minutes, or until hot.

Make a diagonal cut in rolls from end to end, cutting not quite to bottom crust.

Spread cream cheese over cut surfaces; fold each two bologna slices and tuck into a roll with a big spoonful of onions.

Yield: 4 servings.

BROILED BACON BUNS (p.572) ▶

GOOD TRAVELERS FOR LUNCH BOXES

PETER RABBIT SQUARES

⅓ cup peanut butter
¼ cup chopped raisins
¼ cup grated raw carrot
¼ cup chopped celery
   Dash of salt
 2 tablespoons mayonnaise or salad dressing
 8 slices whole-wheat bread

Mix peanut butter, raisins, carrot, celery, salt, and mayonnaise in a small bowl; spread on 4 slices of the bread; top with remaining bread.

Cut each sandwich in half lengthwise and crosswise to make 4 small squares.

Yield: 4 servings.

POLKA-DOT CHEESE TREATS

 1 package (3 ozs.) cream cheese, softened
¼ cup drained chopped cooked prunes
¼ cup coarsely chopped peanuts
¼ cup orange marmalade
 8 slices white bread

Blend cream cheese with prunes until smooth in a small bowl; stir in peanuts.

Spread ½ tablespoonful of the marmalade on each slice of bread, then spread cheese mixture on 4 slices; top with remaining slices. Cut each sandwich lengthwise and crosswise into quarters.

Yield: 4 servings.

◄ *(Clockwise from top)*
CHICKEN BENEDICT (p.182)
CHILI CHICKEN (p.181)
PILGRIM'S DRUMSTICKS (p.182)

HAM-AND-CHEESE STACKS

6 tablespoons prepared sandwich spread
8 slices cracked-wheat bread
1 package (8 ozs.) sliced ham-and-cheese loaf
1 cup coleslaw (from delicatessen department)
2 small tomatoes, sliced thin

Spread sandwich spread on bread. Layer each of 4 slices with ham-and-cheese loaf, coleslaw, and tomato slices. Top with remaining slices of bread, spread side down.

Cut each sandwich in half diagonally. Serve with potato chips if you like.

Yield: 4 servings.

PEANUT DOUBLE DECKERS

½ cup creamy peanut butter
½ cup finely diced unpared apple
 2 tablespoons bacon-flavored vegetable protein bits, crumbled
 8 slices cracked-wheat bread
 4 slices process American cheese
   Iceberg lettuce

Blend peanut butter, apple, and protein bits in a small bowl; spread on 4 slices of the bread.

Top each with a slice of cheese, lettuce, and a remaining slice of bread. Cut each sandwich in half.

Yield: 4 servings.

NEW ENGLAND CHICKEN SQUARES

1 can (4¾ ozs.) chicken spread
3 tablespoons chopped celery
1 tablespoon mayonnaise or salad dressing
8 slices white bread, toasted
6 tablespoons bottled cranberry-orange relish

Mix chicken spread, celery, and mayonnaise in a small bowl. Spread on 4 of the toast slices; spread cranberry relish on remaining 4 slices. Put slices together to make sandwiches.

Cut each in half lengthwise and crosswise to make 4 small squares.

Yield: 4 servings.

PEANUT-CHEDDAR STRIPS

4 slices bacon, cut in ½-inch pieces
1 jar (5 ozs.) Old English cheese spread
⅓ cup peanut butter
2 tablespoons butter or margarine
8 slices whole-wheat bread
  Iceberg lettuce

Sauté bacon until crisp in a small skillet; remove from skillet and drain on paper toweling.

Mix cheese spread, peanut butter, and butter until smooth in a medium bowl; stir in bacon. Spread on 4 slices of the bread; top with lettuce, then remaining bread. Cut each sandwich lengthwise into thirds.

Yield: 4 servings.

DUBLIN DANDIES

2 cans (4½ ozs. each) corned-beef spread
2 tablespoons minced onion
2 teaspoons prepared mustard
8 large slices pumpernickel
1 jar (5 ozs.) Old English cheese spread
2 medium tomatoes, sliced thin
1 can (16 ozs.) sauerkraut, well drained

Mix corned-beef spread, onion, and mustard in a small bowl; spread on 4 slices of pumpernickel. Spread cheese on remaining 4 slices.

Place tomatoes, then sauerkraut on top of corned-beef layers; put together with remaining slices of bread, cheese side down.

Cut each sandwich in thirds diagonally.
Yield: 4 servings.

HAM-AND-CHEESE HEROES

4 small hero rolls
1 package (8 ozs.) cream cheese
1 teaspoon sugar
½ teaspoon grated orange rind
3 teaspoons orange juice
1 package (4 or 5 ozs.) sliced boiled ham

With a sharp knife, cut each roll in quarters diagonally, cutting not quite to bottom.

Blend cream cheese with sugar and orange rind and juice until creamy-smooth in a small bowl; spread 1 heaping tablespoon of the cheese mixture into each cut in rolls.

Leave ham slices stacked together as they come from the package, then cut in half lengthwise and in sixths crosswise to make 12 squares in all. Stuff one stack into each cut in rolls.

Yield: 4 servings.

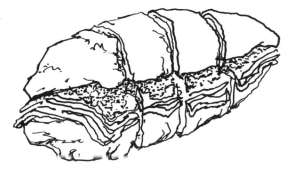

HAWAIIAN CHICKEN BUNS

1½ cups chopped cooked chicken
1 can (8 ozs.) crushed pineapple in juice, well drained
¼ cup chopped celery
⅓ cup mayonnaise or salad dressing
2 teaspoons prepared hot spicy mustard
1 tablespoon chopped parsley
¼ teaspoon salt
4 large round hard rolls
2 tablespoons butter or margarine
  Iceberg lettuce

Combine chicken, pineapple, and celery in a medium bowl.

Blend mayonnaise, mustard, parsley, and salt in a small bowl; stir into chicken mixture.

Cut a thin slice from the top of each roll; set aside. Hollow out bottoms of rolls to make shells about ¼ inch thick; spread butter over hollows. Line hollows with lettuce; spoon in chicken mixture; replace tops.

Yield: 4 servings.

TUNA CLUBS

2 packages (3 ozs. each) cream cheese
2 tablespoons drained chopped pimientos
1 tablespoon milk
 Salt
1 can (7 ozs.) tuna, drained and flaked
¼ cup drained finely chopped pared cucumber
¼ cup mayonnaise or salad dressing
12 slices white bread

Combine cream cheese, pimientos, milk, and a dash of salt in a small bowl; mix until well blended.

Combine tuna, cucumber, mayonnaise, and ¼ teaspoon salt in a second small bowl; mix until well blended.

Spread cheese mixture on 4 slices of the bread; spread tuna mixture on another 4 slices. For each sandwich, stack a cheese slice, tuna slice, and plain slice of bread. Cut into quarters.

Yield: 4 servings.

FRUITED CHEESE TRIANGLES

1 package (3 ozs.) cream cheese
1 tablespoon orange juice
1 teaspoon sugar
⅓ cup chopped peanuts
¼ cup snipped pitted prunes
¼ cup chopped light raisins
4 tablespoons butter or margarine
8 slices whole-wheat bread

Combine cream cheese, orange juice, and sugar in a medium bowl; stir in peanuts, prunes, and raisins until blended.

Spread butter on bread; spread cheese mixture on 4 of the slices; put together with remaining slices to make sandwiches. Cut each in half diagonally.

Yield: 4 servings.

SHRIMP HEROES

1 can (4½ ozs.) deveined shrimp
½ cup finely diced celery
1 tablespoon instant minced onion
½ cup mayonnaise or salad dressing
⅛ teaspoon salt
4 frankfurter rolls
 Iceberg lettuce
2 small tomatoes, each cut into 4 slices
2 hard-cooked eggs, sliced

Drain shrimp and rinse; dice. Combine with celery, onion, mayonnaise, and salt in a medium bowl; mix well. Spread evenly on bottom halves of rolls; top each with lettuce.

Cut each tomato slice in half; arrange 4 half slices in a row on top of lettuce in each sandwich. Place egg slices over tomatoes; replace tops of rolls.

Yield: 4 servings.

DEVILED EGG TRIANGLES

4 hard-cooked eggs
1 can (4½ ozs.) deviled ham
¼ cup chopped celery
2 tablespoons sweet-pickle relish, drained
1 teaspoon lemon juice
1 package (3 ozs.) chive cream cheese
8 to 12 slices whole-wheat bread
 Iceberg lettuce

Dice eggs; place in a medium bowl. Stir in deviled ham, celery, pickle relish, and lemon juice until well-blended.

Spread cream cheese on bread; spread egg mixture on 4 to 6 of the slices. Top each with lettuce and remaining slices of bread to make sandwiches.

Cut each sandwich into 4 triangles.

Yield: 4 to 6 servings.

MAKE-AHEAD FILLINGS

These savory meat, cheese, egg, seafood, and peanut butter spreads go together quickly and will keep for two or three days if stored, covered, in the refrigerator. Use about ¼ cup for each sandwich.

Mexican Corned Beef—In a medium bowl, combine 2 cans (4½ ozs. each) corned-beef spread, 2 tablespoons finely chopped onion, 2 tablespoons chopped seeded green chili peppers (canned variety), and 1 teaspoon Worcestershire sauce; mix well. *Yield:* 1½ cups.

Western Egg—Chop 6 hard-cooked eggs and place in a medium bowl. Stir in ¼ cup chopped onion, ¼ cup chopped green pepper, 1 tablespoon baconion seasoning, and ½ cup prepared sandwich spread. *Yield:* 2¼ cups.

Ham-and-Swiss—Grind enough cooked ham and enough Swiss cheese (4 ozs.) to measure 1 cup each; place in a medium bowl. Stir in ¼ cup chopped bread-and-butter pickles and ⅓ cup mayonnaise or salad dressing. *Yield:* About 2 cups.

Scandinavian Sardine—Drain oil from 2 cans (3¾ ozs. each) sardines; mash sardines in a medium bowl. Stir in ½ cup finely chopped celery, ¼ cup chopped onion, ¼ cup softened butter or margarine, and 1 tablespoon lemon juice. *Yield:* 2 cups.

Liverwurst—Peel casing from 1 chunk (8 ozs.) liverwurst; mash liverwurst in a medium bowl. Stir in ½ cup finely chopped celery, ¼ cup chopped onion, ¼ cup dairy sour cream, and 2 teaspoons prepared horseradish-mustard. *Yield:* 2 cups.

Chicken-and-cheese—Drain liquid from 1 can (5 ozs.) boned chicken; chop chicken and place in a medium bowl. Stir in 1 package (8 ozs.) Neufchâtel cheese, ¼ cup chopped pimiento-stuffed green olives, 1 tablespoon milk, and ⅛ teaspoon pepper. *Yield:* 1⅔ cups.

Smorgasbord Tuna—Drain 1 can (7 ozs.) tuna and flake in a medium bowl. Pare, chop, and drain enough cucumber to measure ½ cup; stir into tuna with 2 tablespoons chopped pimientos, 1 teaspoon dillweed, ¼ teaspoon salt, and ⅓ cup mayonnaise or salad dressing. *Yield:* 1⅔ cups.

Fruited Pork—In a medium bowl, shred 1 can (12 ozs.) pork luncheon meat with a fork. Stir in ½ cup finely chopped unpared apple, 1 can (8 ozs.) drained crushed pineapple in juice, and ¼ cup mayonnaise or salad dressing. *Yield:* About 3 cups.

Hearty Corned Beef—In a medium bowl, shred 1 can (12 ozs.) corned beef with a fork. Stir in ¼ cup chopped onion, ⅓ cup catsup, and 1 tablespoon prepared horseradish. *Yield:* 2 cups.

Relish Cheese—Press 1 container (16 ozs.) creamed cottage cheese through a sieve into a medium bowl. (Or twirl in an electric blender.) Pare and shred 1 medium carrot; stir into cottage cheese with 2 tablespoons minced parsley, 2 tablespoons mayonnaise or salad dressing, ½ teaspoon salt, and a few drops red-pepper seasoning. *Yield:* 2 cups.

Shrimp Louis—Drain and rinse 1 can (4½ ozs.) deveined shrimp; chop coarsely and place in a medium bowl. Chop 2 hard-cooked eggs and stir into shrimp with 2 tablespoons thinly sliced green onions, ⅓ cup bottled Thousand Island salad dressing, 2 teaspoons lemon juice, and ¼ teaspoon salt. *Yield:* 1⅔ cups.

Peanut-prune—In a medium bowl, blend 1 cup chunky peanut butter, 1 jar (8 ozs.) unsweetened applesauce, ½ cup finely chopped pitted prunes, and 2 tablespoons honey. *Yield:* 2 cups.

Old-fashioned Bean—In a medium bowl, coarsely mash 1 can (16 ozs.) barbecued beans. Drain liquid from 1 can (5 ozs.) Vienna sausages; slice sausages in thin rounds and stir into beans with 3 tablespoons drained sweet pickle relish. *Yield:* 2¼ cups.

Turkey-cranberry—Drain liquid from 2 cans (5 ozs. each) boned turkey; chop turkey and place in a medium bowl. Cut 1 can (8 ozs.) jellied cranberry sauce into small cubes; stir into turkey with 2 tablespoons chopped toasted slivered almonds, 2 tablespoons mayonnaise or salad dressing, 1 teaspoon lime juice, and ¼ teaspoon salt. *Yield:* 2 cups.

CANDIES AND CONFECTIONS

HOMEMADE CANDY IS A TRADITION AT CHRISTMAS, for special occasions such as Valentine's Day and Easter, and for birthdays and parties of all kinds. And for generations it's been a thoughtful gift for students away from home.

To be a blue-ribbon candy maker, you need to know a few simple rules. Most important is temperature, for sugar syrups change character the longer you cook them. To insure top results, invest in a good candy thermometer and use it along with the cold water test to determine the exact cooking stage specified in your recipe. (See page 583 for a review of cooking temperatures and tests.)

Unless the recipe you're following directs otherwise, it's best to keep the heat low to medium. Cooking may take a little longer, but there's less chance of burning or scorching.

Choose a clear, cool, dry day for your candy-making spree. Rain, wet snow, or high humidity may prevent candy from hardening or cause it to be grainy.

If you need more than one batch of candy, make two separate ones. Doubling a recipe is risky since the cooking time for a large amount may change and give you less than perfect results.

Now look through the recipes on the next few pages. Time-tested favorites such as chocolate and brown-sugar fudge, divinity, peanut brittle, and caramels are all here. With them are timesaving ideas that call for frosting mix, marshmallow cream, and sweetened condensed milk to streamline fixing. And for those who prefer little or no cooking at all, there are suggestions for fondant, dried fruit, and popcorn treats that satisfy a demanding sweet tooth. No matter which you try, follow the directions exactly for sweet success every time.

How to use a candy thermometer
Check the accuracy of your thermometer each time you use it. Here's how: Let it stand in a pan of rapidly boiling water for about 10 minutes. If the mercury registers 212° while it's in the water, the thermometer is accurate. If it's lower or higher than 212°, subtract or add the same number of degrees to the temperature specified in your recipe.

When cooking candy mixtures, be sure that the bulb of the thermometer is completely covered with boiling syrup—not foam. Make sure, too, that the bulb does not touch the bottom or side of the pan.

Always read the thermometer while it's in the cooking pan and read it at eye level. Watch the syrup carefully after it reaches the boiling point for the temperature rises quickly from then on.

When the candy has finished cooking, remove the thermometer from the pan at once and put it in a safe place to cool before it's washed.

GUIDE TO COOKING TEMPERATURES AND TESTS FOR CANDY-MAKING

Degrees	Stage	Description
230 to 234	Thread	Syrup will spin a 2-inch thread when dropped from a spoon.
234 to 240	Soft Ball	Syrup dropped into a cup of cold water forms a soft ball that flattens when removed from water.
244 to 248	Firm Ball	Syrup dropped into a cup of cold water forms a firm ball that holds its shape when removed from water.
250 to 266	Hard Ball	Syrup dropped into a cup of cold water forms a ball that's hard enough to keep its shape, yet pliable.
270 to 290	Soft Crack	Syrup dropped into a cup of cold water separates into threads that are hard but not brittle.
300 to 310	Hard Crack	Syrup dropped into a cup of cold water separates into threads that are hard and brittle.

How to cool and beat candy

Some recipes (fudge, for example) direct you to cool the candy mixture to lukewarm or 110° after it's cooked. A simple test is to feel the bottom of the pan with your hand. It should feel neither warm nor cool. If it's too warm when you start beating, the candy will be grainy. If it's too cool, beating will take longer, but the finished candy will be creamier.

Once you start beating, keep going until the candy is ready to pour into the pan. This doesn't mean that every stroke must be vigorous and hard, but it does mean steady. Another reminder for some types of candy: Never scrape the last little bit of syrup from the cooking pan. If there are undissolved sugar crystals clinging to the side, they'll cause the finished candy to lose its creaminess.

How to store candy

Most candies keep best in a cool, dry place unless your recipe specifically directs you to place them in the refrigerator. Leave fudge types in their pans and cover the pans tightly with foil or transparent wrap.

Layer other creamy kinds into containers between sheets of transparent wrap or waxed paper to prevent breakage, and cover tightly. Wrap caramels or hard candies individually and place in airtight containers.

Avoid boxing different kinds of candies together for storage. Hard candies may become sticky and creamy kinds may dry out.

OLD-FASHIONED CHOCOLATE FUDGE

2 cups granulated sugar
2 squares unsweetened chocolate
1 cup light cream
2 tablespoons light corn syrup
2 tablespoons butter or margarine
1 teaspoon vanilla
1 cup chopped California walnuts

Lightly butter a pan, 9x9x2 inches.

Combine sugar, chocolate, cream, and corn syrup in a heavy medium saucepan. Heat slowly, stirring constantly, until sugar dissolves and chocolate melts, then cook, without stirring, to 238° on a candy thermometer (soft-ball stage). Remove from heat.

Add butter and vanilla but do not stir in. Cool mixture at room temperature, without stirring, to lukewarm (110°).

Beat mixture just until it starts to hold its shape and lose its gloss; stir in walnuts. Quickly spoon into pan and spread in an even layer; mark top into 36 squares. Let stand until cool and firm; finish cutting into squares.

Yield: 3 dozen 1½-inch squares.

BITTERSWEET FUDGE

2 packages (12 ozs. each) semisweet chocolate
    pieces
1 can (14 ozs.) sweetened condensed milk
2 teaspoons orange extract
1 cup chopped pecans

Lightly butter a pan, 9x9x2 inches.

Combine chocolate and sweetened condensed milk in the top of a double boiler; set top over hot water. Heat, stirring several times, until chocolate melts completely and mixture is smooth; remove from hot water.

Stir in orange extract and pecans. Spoon into pan and spread into an even layer. Chill 3 hours, or until firm. Cut into squares. (If candy is too hard to cut, let stand at room temperature a half hour to soften.)

Yield: 6½ dozen 1-inch squares.

PENUCHE

¼ cup butter or margarine
1 cup firmly packed light brown sugar
1 cup granulated sugar
¾ cup whipping cream
1 teaspoon vanilla
1 cup chopped California walnuts

Lightly butter a pan, 8x8x2 inches.

Melt butter in a heavy medium saucepan; stir in brown and granulated sugars and cream. Heat slowly, stirring constantly, until sugars dissolve, then cook, without stirring, to 238° on a candy thermometer (soft-ball stage). Remove from heat.

Add vanilla but do not stir in. Cool mixture at room temperature, without stirring, to lukewarm (110°).

Beat mixture just until it starts to hold its shape and lose its gloss; stir in walnuts. Quickly spoon into pan and spread in an even layer. Mark top into 36 squares; press a walnut half into top of each if you like. Let stand until cool and firm; finish cutting into squares.

Yield: 3 dozen 1¼-inch squares.

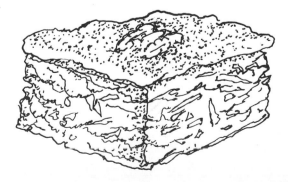

BUTTERSCOTCH PRALINES

1 package (3¼ ozs.) butterscotch pudding and pie
    filling mix
1 cup granulated sugar
½ cup firmly packed light brown sugar
½ cup evaporated milk
1 tablespoon butter or margarine
1 can (6 ozs.) pecans

Lightly butter a large cookie sheet.

Combine pudding mix, granulated and brown sugars, evaporated milk, and butter in a heavy medium saucepan. Heat slowly, stirring constantly, until sugars dissolve, then cook, without stirring, to 238° on a candy thermometer (soft-ball stage). Remove from heat. Cool at room temperature, without stirring, to lukewarm (110°).

Beat mixture just until it starts to thicken; stir in pecans. Quickly drop by teaspoonfuls onto cookie sheet. Let stand until cool and firm.

Yield: 2½ dozen 2-inch patties

PEANUT MELTAWAYS

2 cups granulated sugar
1 cup milk
1 jar (7 ozs.) marshmallow cream
1 cup peanut butter
1 teaspoon vanilla
1 cup chopped peanuts

Lightly butter a pan, 9x9x2 inches.

Combine sugar and milk in a medium saucepan. Heat slowly, stirring constantly, until sugar dissolves, then cook slowly, stirring several times, to 238° on a candy thermometer (soft-ball stage). Remove from heat.

Stir in marshmallow cream, peanut butter, vanilla, and peanuts; beat until blended with a wooden spoon. Pour into pan. Let stand until cool and firm. Cut into squares.

Yield: 6½ dozen 1-inch squares.

GLACEED ALMONDS

1 cup firmly packed light brown sugar
½ cup granulated sugar
½ cup evaporated milk
2 tablespoons light corn syrup
1 tablespoon butter or margarine
2 teaspoons vanilla
2 cups whole blanched almonds

Lightly butter a large shallow pan.

Combine brown and granulated sugars, milk, and corn syrup in a heavy medium saucepan. Heat slowly, stirring constantly, until sugars dissolve, then cook, without stirring, to 236° on a candy thermometer (soft-ball stage). Remove from heat.

Add butter and vanilla but do not stir in. Cool mixture at room temperature, without stirring, to lukewarm (110°).

Beat mixture just until it starts to lose its gloss; stir in almonds. Quickly spoon into pan; separate almonds with two forks. Let stand until cool and coating is firm.

Yield: 4 cups.

CHERRY PINK SNOWDROPS

2 cups granulated sugar
½ cup light corn syrup
⅓ cup water
2 egg whites
1 teaspoon vanilla
1 container (3½ ozs.) candied red cherries, chopped

Combine sugar, corn syrup, and water in a heavy medium saucepan. Heat slowly, stirring constantly, until sugar dissolves, then cook, without stirring, to 245° on a candy thermometer (firm-ball stage). Remove from heat.

While syrup cooks, beat egg whites in a medium bowl until they form firm peaks. Beating constantly, pour in hot syrup in a thin stream; beat in vanilla. Continue beating until mixture starts to form very stiff peaks that hold their shape; beat in cherries.

Drop by teaspoonfuls onto waxed paper, swirling top of each into a pretty peak with spoon. (If mixture hardens too quickly as you work, beat in one or two drops hot water.) Let candy stand until firm.

Yield: 3 dozen.

PEANUT BRITTLE

3 cups granulated sugar
2 tablespoons butter or margarine
1 can (12 ozs.) salted peanuts

Lightly butter a jelly-roll pan or large cookie sheet.

Measure sugar into a heavy large skillet; heat slowly, stirring constantly, until sugar melts into a smooth golden syrup. Stir in butter and peanuts.

Pour into pan and quickly spread into a thin layer with spatula. Let stand until cool and firm.

Break into serving-sized pieces with a kitchen mallet.

Yield: About 2 pounds.

VANILLA CARAMELS

1 cup whipping cream
1 cup granulated sugar
¼ cup light corn syrup
1 teaspoon butter or margarine
1 teaspoon vanilla

Lightly butter a pan, 9x5x3 inches.

Combine cream, sugar, corn syrup, and butter in a heavy medium saucepan. Heat slowly, stirring constantly, until sugar dissolves, then cook, stirring several times, to 248° on a candy thermometer (firm-ball stage). Remove from heat.

Stir in vanilla; pour into pan. Cool just until firm.

Loosen candy around edges of pan with a knife; turn out onto a cutting board. Cut lengthwise into quarters and crosswise into eighths with a heavy sharp knife. Cool caramels completely. Wrap each in a square of transparent wrap.

Yield: About 2½ dozen.

LEMON CREAM BONBONS

2 cups flaked coconut
   Yellow food coloring
1 package (8 ozs.) cream cheese, softened
7 cups confectioners' powdered sugar, sifted
1 teaspoon grated lemon rind

Measure coconut into a large jar with a tight cover; add 2 to 3 drops food coloring; cover. Shake until coconut is evenly tinted; spread out in a pie plate.

Beat cream cheese until fluffy in a medium bowl; beat in confectioners' sugar, about 1 cup at a time, until mixture is well blended and stiff enough to handle; beat in lemon rind.

Shape, 1 teaspoon at a time, into small balls; roll in coconut to coat generously. Place balls on a tray or large flat plate; cover with transparent wrap. Store in refrigerator.

Yield: 5½ dozen.

WALNUT BUTTER CRUNCH

½ cup butter or margarine
1 cup granulated sugar
⅓ cup water
¼ teaspoon salt
½ teaspoon vanilla
1 cup chopped California walnuts
4 bars (1¼ ozs. each) milk chocolate candy

Lightly butter a cookie sheet.

Melt butter in a medium saucepan; stir in sugar, water, and salt. Heat slowly, stirring constantly, until sugar dissolves, then cook to 285° on a candy thermometer (soft-crack stage). Remove from heat.

Stir in vanilla and ½ cup of the walnuts. Pour onto cookie sheet to make a thin layer. Let stand at room temperature until cool and firm.

Melt candy bars in a small saucepan over warm water; spread over cooled layer on cookie sheet; sprinkle remaining ½ cup walnuts over chocolate. Let stand until chocolate is firm. Break into serving-sized pieces with a kitchen mallet.

Yield: About 1 pound.

BUTTERSCOTCH DROPS

1 cup granulated sugar
⅓ cup firmly packed light brown sugar
½ cup butter or margarine
1 teaspoon vinegar
3 tablespoons water

Butter 2 large cookie sheets very lightly; set cookie sheets on wire racks.

Combine granulated and brown sugars, butter, vinegar, and water in a heavy medium saucepan. Heat slowly, stirring constantly until sugars dissolve, then cook, without stirring, to 290° on a candy thermometer (soft-crack stage). Remove from heat. (Watch syrup carefully as it cooks to prevent scorching.)

Working quickly, drop hot syrup from the tip of a teaspoon onto cookie sheets to form ¾-inch rounds. Let stand until cool and firm.

Yield: 7½ dozen.

SEAFOAM KISSES

1 lb. light brown sugar
1 cup granulated sugar
½ cup light corn syrup
½ cup water
2 egg whites
1 teaspoon vanilla
1 cup chopped California walnuts

Combine brown and granulated sugars, corn syrup, and water in a heavy medium saucepan. Heat slowly, stirring constantly, until sugars dissolve, then cook, without stirring, to 245° on a candy thermometer (firm-ball stage). Remove from heat.

While syrup cooks, beat egg whites in a large bowl until they form firm peaks. Beating constantly, pour in hot syrup in a thin stream; beat in vanilla. Continue beating until mixture starts to form very stiff peaks that hold their shape; stir in walnuts.

Drop by teaspoonfuls onto waxed paper, swirling top of each to a pretty peak with spoon. (If mixture hardens too quickly as you work, beat in one or two drops hot water.) Let candy stand until firm.

Yield: 5 dozen.

CHOCOLATE BUBBLES

2 tablespoons butter or margarine
¼ cup milk
1 package (14 ozs.) sour-cream chocolate fudge frosting mix
1 teaspoon rum extract
1 cup peanuts
1½ cups tiny marshmallows

Heat butter and milk in a medium saucepan to simmering; remove from heat. Stir in frosting mix.

Heat slowly, stirring constantly, until mixture is smooth and glossy; stir in rum extract, peanuts, and marshmallows.

Drop by teaspoonfuls onto waxed paper. Let stand until cool and firm.

Yield: 3½ dozen.

PISTACHIO ROLLS

1½ lbs. white chocolate
1 can (14 ozs.) sweetened condensed milk
1 teaspoon almond extract
  Green food coloring
1¼ cups finely chopped pistachio nuts

Combine chocolate and sweetened condensed milk in the top of a double boiler; set top over hot water. Heat slowly, stirring several times, until chocolate melts and mixture is smooth; pour into a medium bowl.

Stir in almond extract and a few drops food coloring to tint pale green. Chill mixture 1 hour, or until cool and firm enough to handle.

Pinch off mixture, 1 teaspoon at a time, and roll into 1-inch logs; roll in pistachio nuts on waxed paper. Place on waxed-paper lined cookie sheets and chill again until firm. (If mixture becomes too soft to handle as you work, return it to the refrigerator until firm again.)

Yield: 9 dozen.

Note: If you prefer to make fewer small candies, spoon half of mixture into a waxed-paper lined pan and cut into squares.

PEANUT CLUSTERS

1 package (3⅛ ozs.) vanilla pudding and pie filling mix
½ cup light corn syrup
¼ cup crunchy peanut butter
4 cups crisp presweetened corn cereal rounds

Blend pudding mix and corn syrup in a large saucepan. Heat slowly, stirring constantly, to boiling; continue cooking and stirring 1 minute; remove from heat.

Stir in peanut butter; stir in cereal until well coated.

Drop mixture by tablespoonfuls onto a waxed-paper lined cookie sheet. Let stand until cool and firm.

Yield: 2½ dozen.

POPCORN SCRAMBLE

6 cups freshly popped corn
2 cups bite-sized rice cereal squares
2 cups ring-shaped puffed oat cereal
1 can (6½ ozs.) salted peanuts (1 cup)
½ cup butter or margarine
1 cup firmly packed light brown sugar
¼ cup light corn syrup
¼ teaspoon baking soda
1 teaspoon vanilla

Mix popcorn, cereal squares, oat cereal, and peanuts in a large bowl.

Preheat oven to 250°.

Melt butter in a large saucepan; stir in brown sugar and corn syrup. Heat slowly, stirring constantly, to boiling; cook, without stirring, 5 minutes; remove from heat. Stir in baking soda and vanilla.

Drizzle over popcorn mixture; toss lightly until evenly coated. Spoon into a large shallow baking pan.

Bake, stirring several times, 1 hour; cool. Store in a tightly covered container.

Yield: 12 cups.

TAFFY CORN

1 cup granulated sugar
⅓ cup light molasses
½ teaspoon salt
½ cup water
2 tablespoons butter or margarine
10 cups freshly popped corn

Combine sugar, molasses, salt, and water in a medium saucepan. Heat slowly, stirring constantly, to boiling, then cook slowly, stirring once or twice, to 270° on a candy thermometer (soft-crack stage).

Remove from heat; stir in butter. Drizzle over popcorn in a large bowl; toss lightly until evenly coated.

Spread mixture onto a lightly buttered cookie sheet. Let stand until cool and firm. Break into pieces.

Yield: 10 cups.

CHOCOLATE-MARSHMALLOW CRISPIES

½ lb. marshmallows
1 package (6 ozs.) semisweet chocolate pieces
¼ cup butter or margarine
1 teaspoon vanilla
   Dash of salt
6 cups oven-toasted crisp rice cereal
1 cup coarsely broken California walnuts

Combine marshmallows, chocolate, and butter in the top of a double boiler; set over hot water. Heat, stirring several times, until mixture is completely melted and smooth; remove from heat; stir in vanilla and salt.

Drizzle over cereal and walnuts in a large bowl; mix until evenly coated. Press into a buttered pan, 9x9x2 inches. Let stand until firm.

Cut mixture lengthwise and crosswise into quarters.

Yield: 16 two-inch squares.

CARAMEL APPLE POPS

6 medium-sized firm apples
1 package (14 ozs.) light caramels
¼ cup evaporated milk
½ cup finely chopped California walnuts
¼ cup flaked coconut

Wash apples; push a wooden skewer into stem end of each. (Inexpensive bamboo chopsticks also make handy holders.)

Combine caramels and evaporated milk in the top of a double boiler. Heat over hot water, stirring once or twice, until caramels melt and mixture is smooth.

Spread walnuts and coconut onto separate sheets of waxed paper. Dip apples, one at a time, into caramel mixture, turning to coat all over; hold over pan a minute to let excess drip back, then roll half in walnuts and the rest in coconut. Stand sticks in a bowlful of sugar or a flower holder until apples are cool and coating is firm.

Yield: 6 candy apples.

CANDIED GRAPEFRUIT PEEL

2 large grapefruits
2½ cups sugar

Wash grapefruits and remove rind from each in 6 large sections. Scrape off as much of the white membrane from undersides as possible. (A sharp spoon makes the job go quickly.) Cut rind into strips about ¼ inch wide with kitchen shears. (There should be about 3 cups.)

Place rind in a large saucepan; pour in cold water to cover. Heat to boiling; drain off water. Cover with fresh water, heat to boiling, and drain two more times; return rind to saucepan.

Add 2 cups of the sugar and 1½ cups water. Heat slowly, stirring constantly, until sugar dissolves, then simmer, stirring several times, 40 minutes, or until syrup is almost absorbed and rind is translucent.

Lift rind from pan and place on wire racks over a jelly-roll pan to drain. When cool enough to handle, roll strips, a few at a time, in remaining ½ cup sugar to coat generously. Let stand on racks until sugar dries.

Yield: About ½ pound.

Note: To make candied orange peel, use thick-skin fruit. You'll need about 6 large oranges to measure the 3 cups peel specified in recipe above.

JAMAICAN DATES

1 package (3 ozs.) cream cheese
2 teaspoons finely chopped crystallized ginger
¼ cup granulated sugar
¼ teaspoon grated lemon rind
1 package (8 ozs.) pitted dates

Mix cheese and ginger in a bowl; mix sugar and lemon rind in a pie plate.

Cut a slit lengthwise in each date; stuff with about ½ teaspoonful cheese mixture; roll in lemon sugar to coat generously. Let stand on a wire rack until coating dries.

Yield: About 3 dozen.

APRICOT CHEWS

1 package (11 ozs.) dried apricots
2 cups water
1 can (3½ ozs.) flaked coconut
1 teaspoon grated orange rind
1 tablespoon curaçao
  Confectioners' powdered sugar

Combine apricots and water in a medium saucepan; heat to boiling; drain. Pat apricots dry with paper toweling.

Put apricots through a food grinder, using a coarse blade; combine with coconut and orange rind in a medium bowl. Stir in curaçao, 1 teaspoon at a time, until mixture is smooth and evenly moist.

Shape, 1 teaspoon at a time, in balls; roll each in confectioners' sugar. Place on wire racks and let stand until coating dries; roll in sugar again to make a generous white coating.
Yield: 3½ dozen.

HONEY CRUNCH

½ cup granulated sugar
½ cup firmly packed light brown sugar
⅓ cup honey
⅓ cup water
1 teaspoon vinegar
6 tablespoons butter or margarine
¼ teaspoon salt
2 cups plain granola-type cereal
6 cups freshly popped corn
½ cup broken California walnuts

Combine sugars, honey, water, vinegar, butter, and salt in a large saucepan. Heat slowly, stirring constantly, to boiling, then cook to 290° on a candy thermometer (soft-crack stage).

Quickly pour syrup over cereal, corn, and walnuts in a large bowl; toss with 2 large spoons until evenly mixed.

Spread mixture out onto a buttered large cookie sheet; let stand until cool and firm. Break up into chunks. Store in a tightly covered container.
Yield: About 1¼ pounds.

MARSHMALLOW PINWHEELS

1 can (3½ ozs.) flaked coconut
  Red food coloring
  Granulated sugar
24 large marshmallows
24 large red gumdrops
2 egg whites

Place coconut in a small jar with a tight lid. Mix several drops red food coloring with ½ teaspoon water in a cup; drizzle over coconut; cover. Shake vigorously until coconut is evenly tinted; spread out on waxed paper.

Sprinkle sugar generously over a cutting board. Roll marshmallows, one at a time, on board to an oval about 2½x2 inches; roll each gumdrop to a slightly smaller oval. Place each gumdrop on top of a marshmallow; roll up tightly, jelly-roll fashion, (Marshmallows will be sticky enough to hold rolls in place.)

Beat egg whites slightly in a pie plate. Dip rolls in egg whites to coat lightly, then roll in coconut. Let stand on a wire rack until coating dries.
Yield: 2 dozen.

GUMDROP SNOWBALLS

4 tablespoons butter or margarine
1 package (10 ozs.) large marshmallows
10 cups freshly popped corn
½ cup cut up gumdrops

Melt butter in a kettle; stir in marshmallows. Heat very slowly, stirring constantly, until marshmallows melt and mixture is smooth and syrupy; remove from heat.

Add popcorn and toss until evenly coated; sprinkle in gumdrops; toss again to mix.

Moisten hands lightly and shape mixture, about 1 cup at a time, into a ball. Let stand on a wire rack until cool and firm.
Yield: 8 large balls.
Note: If mixture cools and becomes too sticky-firm to work with easily, return to very low heat for several seconds until slightly warm.

SUGARPLUMS

18 large dried figs
1 package (12 ozs.) pitted large dried prunes
¼ cup granulated sugar
1 teaspoon grated orange rind

Trim stems from figs; cut each in half lengthwise.

Cut a slit lengthwise in each prune; stuff a half fig into each.

Mix sugar and orange rind in a pie plate; roll prunes in sugar mixture to coat generously. Place on a wire rack and let stand until sugar dries.

Yield: About 3 dozen.

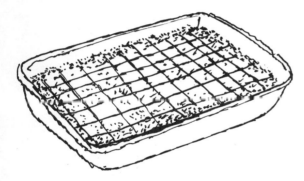

CHOCOLATE POPCORN BARS

4 cups tiny marshmallows
1 package (6 ozs.) semisweet chocolate pieces
4 tablespoons butter or margarine
2 tablespoons light corn syrup
1 teaspoon vanilla
12 cups freshly popped corn

Combine marshmallows, chocolate, butter, and corn syrup in a medium saucepan. Heat very slowly, stirring constantly, until marshmallows and chocolate melt and mixture is smooth; stir in vanilla.

Pour over popcorn in a large bowl; toss lightly until evenly coated. Press mixture into a buttered pan, 13x9x2 inches. Let stand until firm. Cut lengthwise and crosswise into sixths.

Yield: 3 dozen.

FRUIT SQUARES

1 package (8 ozs.) dried figs
1 cup pitted dried prunes
1 cup dried apricots
1 cup light raisins
1 cup California walnuts
⅓ cup orange juice
¼ teaspoon salt
  Confectioners' powdered sugar

Snip stems from figs. Put figs, prunes, apricots, raisins, and walnuts through a food grinder, using a medium coarse blade. Stir in orange juice and salt.

Spoon mixture into an oiled 1½-quart shallow baking dish; press down firmly into an even layer with back of spoon. Cover; chill overnight.

Cut fruit mixture into 40 small squares; lift each from dish with a small spatula and roll in confectioners' sugar to coat well. Let stand on a wire rack until coating sets.

Yield: 3⅓ dozen 1-inch squares.

COCONUT POPCORN BALLS

10 cups freshly popped corn
1 can (3½ ozs.) flaked coconut
1 package (14 ozs.) vanilla caramels
3 tablespoons water

Mix popcorn and coconut in a bowl.

Combine caramels and water in a medium saucepan; heat slowly, stirring several times, until caramels melt and mixture is smooth. Drizzle over popcorn mixture; toss lightly until evenly coated.

Moisten hands lightly; shape popcorn mixture into 2-inch balls. Let stand on wire racks until firm.

Yield: About 2 dozen.

GARNISHES

MAKING FOODS LOOK ENTICING is somewhat like painting a picture, yet you really don't need any special talent. What it takes, primarily, is imagination with a few simple ground rules.

For the most eye-catching platter or plate, mix colors—the pastels of greens or the bright hues of fruits and vegetables with the brown and golden tones of meat. Since garnishes should also be good to eat, blend flavors so that sweet contrasts with tangy and sharp with mild. One good example: Peach halves filled with tart cranberry sauce around a platter of roast chicken or pork. Keep textures in mind, too, for a dish made up of something crisp and something soft is much more interesting to eat than one that's the same all the way through. Croutons sprinkled over clear or cream soup illustrates this point.

Need more inspiration? Read through the ideas on the following pages. They tell you when to use a sprightly touch of parsley or go more elaborate with a homey tomato turned into a rose. They suggest ways to play up the season with tiny cheese apples for fall or dainty orange pumpkins for Thanksgiving. Both are whimsical, showy, edible—and excellent conversation pieces for parties or special dinners when you're in the mood to be fussy.

Remember, too—especially when time is short—that the foods themselves often double as the trim. A thick slice of white or red onion or a few big French fried onion rings atop a cheeseburger complement the meat and provide all the contrast that's needed in color, flavor, and texture.

VEGETABLE

Fluted Mushrooms—Remove stems from medium or large snowy white mushrooms. On rounded side of each cap, make 5 to 8 curved slits from center to outer edge. Make a second cut just behind each of the others, slanting knife in slightly; lift out the narrow strips between each two cuts. To keep mushrooms white, dip in lemon juice. Use for meat, sandwich, or salad plates, or vegetable dishes.

Turnip Daisies—Pare a small white turnip. Slice thin crosswise, then cut a small round from each slice with a cookie cutter. Cut V-shaped notches all around edge to form petals. Pare a large carrot and slice thin; to make a pretty edge, cut each slice with a tiny scalloped cutter. Attach a carrot slice to each turnip round with a dot of cream cheese or a short wooden pick. Use for meat, cold cut, sandwich, hors d'oeuvre, or salad plates.

Pickle Fans—Cut 4 slits lengthwise in small sweet or dill pickles, cutting from pointed end to within ⅛ to ¼ inch of top. Spread slices carefully to form a fan. Use for meat, sandwich, fish, hors d'oeuvre, salad, or relish plates.

Blackeye Carrot Curls—Pare carrots; shave lengthwise into long, paper-thin slices with a vegetable parer. Roll up slices and fasten with wooden picks. Chill in a bowl of ice and water until slices curl. Before serving, pull out picks; tuck a ripe olive inside each curl. Use for meat, sandwich, hors d'oeuvre, salad, or relish plates.

Celery Fans—Cut stalks of celery into 2-inch lengths. Cut narrow slits in each end, cutting not quite to center. Chill in a bowl of ice and water until ends curl. Use for meat, sandwich, hors d'oeuvre, salad, or relish plates.

Radish Puffballs—Trim stem and root ends of large radishes. Cut about 6 slits one way across root end, then the same number crosswise, cutting about three quarters of the way to bottom. Chill in a bowl of ice and water until cuts open into a fluffy, flowerlike ball. Use for meat, sandwich, hors d'oeuvre, salad, or relish plates.

Tiny Tomato Baskets—Remove stems from small cherry tomatoes. Cut a thin slice from rounded end of each. Hollow out inside, using the quarter teaspoon of a measuring-spoon set. Turn cups upside down on paper toweling to drain well. Fill hollows with tiny bouquets of parsley. Use for meat, sandwich, salad, hors d'oeuvre, or relish plates.

Frosted Carrot Sticks—Pare carrots; cut lengthwise into narrow strips about three inches long. Chill in a bowl of ice and water until crisp. Drain well and dry sticks on paper toweling. Dip one end of each stick into softened cream cheese, then into chopped parsley or watercress. Use for meat, sandwich, hors d'oeuvre, salad, or relish plates.

Cucumber Accordions—Split a medium cucumber in half lengthwise, pare, and cut into three-inch lengths. Place each piece, flat side down, and cut into thin slices not quite to bottom. Tuck a thin radish slice into each cut. Another time, use this same cutting trick for radish accordions. Start with long radishes; chill in ice and water until cuts open. Use for meat, sandwich, hors d'oeuvre, salad, or relish plates.

Olive Bundles and Dumbbells—Thread several small carrot or celery sticks through a large pitted ripe olive. Or place small pitted ripe olives on each end of 2-inch-long carrot sticks. Use for meat, sandwich, hors d'oeuvre, salad, or relish plates.

Tomato Sunbursts—Remove stems from large cherry tomatoes. Make 5 slits at equal intervals into each, cutting from stem end almost to bottom. Tuck a paper-thin slice of water chestnut into each cut. Insert a tiny sprig of parsley or watercress or a small celery leaf in top of each. Use for meat, sandwich, salad, hors d'oeuvre, salad, or relish plates.

Onion Ruffles—Trim tips of green onions; cut off tops, leaving about a half inch of the white attached. Shred top into narrow ribbons, cutting almost to white part. Chill in a bowl of ice and water until ribbons curl. Another idea: Cut green onions into 3-inch lengths; shred each end, cutting not quite to middle. Chill until curled. Use either for meat, sandwich, hors d'oeuvre, salad, or relish plates.

Snippets—Cut chives or green onion tops into tiny pieces with kitchen shears; sprinkle over soup, salad, cottage cheese, or a bowl of salad dressing for a colorful touch.

Olive Top Hats—Pare a small carrot; shave lengthwise into paper-thin slices with a vegetable parer. Roll each slice tightly around finger; tuck into a large pitted ripe olive. Insert a tiny sprig of chicory or a small celery leaf in top. Use for meat, sandwich, hors d'oeuvre, salad, or relish plates.

Cucumber Frills—Pull the tines of a fork lengthwise through the rind of a cucumber to make a ridged design; slice cucumber thin. Use for sandwich, salad, or relish platters.

Turnip Lilies—Pare a medium-sized white turnip; slice thin crosswise. Curve two slices together to form a lily-shaped cup; tuck a thin carrot stick in the center; hold in place with a wooden pick. Place in a bowl of ice and water until crisp. Use for meat, sandwich, salad, fish, hors d'oeuvre, or relish plates.

Tomato Roses—Place small tomatoes, stem ends down. Cut each into 5 or 6 wedges, cutting through skin but not to center or quite to bottom. Gently separate wedges to resemble petals; tuck parsley or watercress into centers. Another idea: Cut an X in the rounded ends of cherry tomatoes of any size; gently separate to resemble petals. Spoon a dot of sieved hard-cooked egg yolk or cottage cheese into center. Use either trim for meat, sandwich, salad, fish, hors d'oeuvre, or relish plates.

Carrot Chrysanthemums—Pare medium carrots; shave lengthwise into long, paper-thin slices with a vegetable parer. Trim slices to even lengths of 5 or 6 inches; round ends slightly. Thread about 8 slices through the middle onto a wooden pick, then spread the slices, flower-petal fashion. Chill in a bowl of ice and water until the ends curl. Use for meat, sandwich, hors d'oeuvre, salad, or relish plates.

Olive Links—Slice pitted ripe olives. Stand two whole slices in a row; make a cut in a third slice and place on top of the other two to join them together and form a chain. Use for sandwich, hors d'oeuvre, salad, or relish plates.

Cucumber Wedges—Cut a small cucumber into wedges about 2 inches long, but do not pare; dip pointed edge of each into paprika or finely chopped parsley. Try this same idea with lemon or lime wedges, too. Use for fish, sandwich, or salad plates.

Pimiento Cutups—Cut canned pimientos into diamonds, strips, stars, cubes, or other small fancy shapes with a knife or truffle cutters. Use for meat or salad plates, vegetable or dip bowls, or cheese balls or spread.

Carrot Accordions—Pare a large carrot; shave lengthwise into long paper-thin slices with a vegetable parer. Thread, accordion fashion, onto a wooden pick. Chill in a bowl of ice and water until crisp. Use for meat, sandwich, salad, hors d'oeuvre, salad, or relish plates.

Dressing Cups—Try green peppers or hollowed out tomatoes for serving salad dressings, dips, and seafood sauces. A large cucumber, hollowed out lengthwise to form a boat-shaped shell, looks equally attractive.

Easy Dressups—Tomato wedges, green and red pepper rings, sliced green onions, small or large white onion rings, sliced radishes and olives, and carrot pennies are simple decorations that go a long way to brighten all kinds of everyday foods.

Radish Trims—To make a star, trim root and top from radish. Make 6 evenly spaced cuts into root end, cutting about halfway down. For a rose: Trim root but leave about a half inch of green top on. Holding radish by the top, make 3 or 4 evenly spaced vertical cuts into side, leaving a bit of red between each. To make a domino: Trim root and top. Cut radish at root to form a deep X, then slice off a thin circle of red peel in center of each quarter. Chill all in a bowl of ice and water until cuts open. Use for meat, sandwich, hors d'oeuvre, or relish plates.

Borders—All varieties of lettuce, small spinach or celery leaves, watercress, parsley, and mint can be used around the edges of salads, meats, cheeses, and hors d'oeuvres to form frilly ribbons of color. Another idea: Shred or finely chop greens for a sprinkle of color on soups, salads, dips, deviled eggs, vegetables, or salad dressings.

FRUIT

Lemon or Lime Roses—Start at the stem end of a pretty lemon or lime, and, moving around and round fruit, cut off a thin continuous half-inch wide strip of peel. Carefully curl strip, rind side out, to resemble a rose. If needed, hold end in place with a short wooden pick. Use for meat, sandwich, hors d'oeuvre, or cake plates.

Lemon, Lime, or Orange Cartwheels—Slice fruit in rounds; cut even V-shaped notches into rind all the way around with a knife or scissors. Use for fish platters, vegetable dishes, or beverages in glasses or punch bowls.

Mandarin Pumpkins—Arrange 6 to 8 drained, even-sized mandarin-orange segments, standing up and touching each other, to form a miniature pumpkin; tuck a sliver of green pepper into top for a stem. Nestle in a bed of rice on a meat or salad platter so rice will hold pumpkin together.

Prune Frills—Pipe a ribbon of seasoned cream cheese on pitted prunes or dates. Use for a salad platter or a fruit-and-cheese tray.

Cranberry Cutups—Slice canned jellied cranberry sauce into thin rounds; cut each into a fancy shape with a cookie cutter. Use for fruit or salad platters, or place on a chicken or turkey pie after it comes from the oven.

Pineapple Twists—For each, use two pineapple slices and place one flat on plate. Make a cut into second slice and insert one end into hole in first slice; curl the rest of the slice towards the outside. Top with tiny pimiento cutouts for color. Use for a fruit or salad platter.

Gelatin Sparkles—Prepare a package of fruit-flavor gelatin with 1¾ cups water; pour into a shallow pan; chill until firm. Cut into tiny cubes or pull a fork through mixture to rice. Spoon around edge of cream puddings or cottage cheese plates.

Cherry Bouquets—Arrange maraschino or dark sweet cherries with the stems on in small clusters; trim with mint or watercress. Use for salad or fruit platters or bowls.

Pineapple Borders—Center whole slices of canned fruit with grapes or maraschino cherries; arrange with sprigs of watercress around a meat platter. Or cut pineapple slices in half; arrange, rounded side toward center, over a salad bowl. Place a grape or cherry in each hole.

Avocado Trims—Peel an avocado; cut in half and remove seed. Cut lengthwise into slices or crosswise into crescents, or dice or cube fruit. Or peel fruit, cut into rings, and gently push rings off seed with a knife. Dip fruit in lemon juice to prevent darkening. Use for salads, soups, open-face sandwiches, dips, or cheese platters.

Banana Trims—Peel bananas; draw the tines of a fork lengthwise down fruit to score. Slice or cut into small chunks; dip in lemon juice to prevent darkening. Pile chunks onto a salad platter or arrange slices, overlapping, in a ring on puddings, cakes, cream pies, or gelatin desserts. Place a stem-on cherry in center of ring.

Kabobs—Onto skewers, thread cubes of pineapple, maraschino cherries, firm strawberries, large grapes, apple or banana chunks dipped in lemon juice, or small orange wedges with the peel on. Use for cold beverages or salads.

Strawberry Sunbursts—Cut berries lengthwise in half; arrange in a circle, rounded sides up or down. Stand a whole small berry, pointed end up, in center. Use for desserts or salad platters.

Pineapple Sunflowers—Arrange pineapple tidbits, large end out, in a circle to form a flower; place a nut or small round of green pepper in center. Cut stems and leaves from green pepper. Use for fruit or turkey or chicken salads.

Peach Blossoms—Drain canned peach slices and arrange 6 or 7 in a circle, flat sides down. Place a half cherry, rounded side up, in center. Use on salads or desserts, or as a trim on baked ham.

CHEESE

Chevron Top—Cut cheese slices into inch-wide strips; arrange, chevron fashion, on top of a rectangular casserole or salad platter.

Lattice Trim—Cut cheese slices into strips and arrange in diagonal lines, crisscross fashion, on top of a rectangular or square casserole.

Whirling Star—Cut three square slices of cheese in half diagonally to form six triangles. Place a whole square on top of a round casserole or salad bowl; arrange the six triangles, points out, around slice in center.

Acorns—Cut balls from a chunk of cheese with a melon-ball cutter or quarter teaspoon of a measuring-spoon set. Cut tiny rounds from a slice of cheese with a truffle cutter; sprinkle with ground cinnamon and attach to balls with whole cloves for stems. Use for salad or fruit-and-cheese platters.

Blushing Apples—Moisten shredded cheese with a little mayonnaise or salad dressing and roll in balls. Poke a tiny hollow in top and bottom with tip of finger; stick whole cloves in tops for stems and slivers of green pepper in bottoms. Roll balls lightly in paprika to tint sides. Use for salad or fruit-and-cheese platters, or serve with apple or pumpkin pie.

Nougats—Roll seasoned cream cheese in small balls, then into chopped nuts. Use for salad, dessert, or fruit-and-cheese platters.

Creamy Cutouts—Spread cream cheese in a layer about ¼-inch thick on a cookie sheet dusted with confectioners' powdered sugar; chill until firm. Cut cheese into fancy shapes with truffle or small cookie cutters; sprinkle colored sugar lightly over tops. Lift cutouts with a pancake turner so they hold their shapes. Use for fruit salad or dessert plates.

HARD-COOKED EGGS

Whirligigs—Slice eggs into rounds; overlap slices in a ring; tuck a small green or ripe olive or a radish in center. Use for salad or vegetable bowls or casseroles.

Tulip Cups—Make even saw-tooth cuts around the middle of whole eggs, pushing knife in far enough to cut to center; gently pull halves apart. Remove yolks; press through a sieve. Moisten with a little mayonnaise and stuff back into whites. Use for salad, hors d'oeuvre, or sandwich plates.

Petaled Posies—Cut each egg into 6 thin wedges; arrange wedges, yolk side up, in a circle; tuck a sprig of parsley in center and smaller ones between wedges. Another idea: Arrange wedges; white side up; place a small spoonful of sieved egg yolk in center. Use for salad bowls or cold-cut platters.

Mimosa—Press eggs, either white and yolk or yolk alone, through a sieve onto the top of a salad, vegetable bowl, tureen or plate of soup, or an open-face ham or tuna salad sandwich.

Baskets—Make deviled eggs; press each two halves back together to form whole eggs. Pipe ribbons of cream cheese over cut edges. Use for luncheon meat or salad plates.

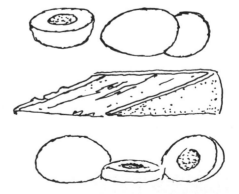

BREADS, BISCUITS, AND PASTRY

Ring-a-rounds—Cut rings or rounds from bread with a biscuit cutter; butter each lightly; arrange, overlapping, on casseroles about 15 minutes before they come from the oven. Rounds will bake just long enough to turn toasty golden.

Stars—Cut slices of buttered toast in quarters diagonally to form triangles. Place triangles, points toward center, around the top edge of meat pies or stews baked in round dishes. Another idea: Cut a 3-inch cross in 8- or 9-inch pastry rounds for the tops of meat pies or casseroles. Turn points back; the filling will show through in a small square.

Checkerboards—Cut bread into 1-inch cubes. Line up cubes in rows, checkerboard fashion, on top of square or rectangular casseroles. Bake about 10 minutes to toast cubes.

Pastry Ropes—Twist strips of pastry into ropes and place diagonally over tops of meat pies or casseroles.

Rings and Rounds—Separate refrigerated biscuits and cut small rounds from each with the inside of a doughnut cutter. Lift off the outside rings and use as toppers for meat pies; arrange small rounds in clusters of three to form another design.

Four-leaf Clovers—Separate refrigerated biscuits; make 4 evenly-spaced cuts into each biscuit around edge; separate cuts slightly to form petals. Use as toppers for meat pies or stews.

Cornbread Toppers—Prepare a package of corn-muffin mix; spoon over meat pies in diagonal ribbons so the filling shows through. Another idea: Spoon batter around edge of dish, leaving center open; sprinkle chopped parsley over batter.

Truffle Trims—Instead of cutting slits in the top crusts for main dish or fruit pies, go fancy and cut out tiny shapes such as leaves, animals, or fruits with a truffle cutter. Lift cutouts carefully and place them over the pastry between the holes. Brushed with beaten egg yolk mixed with a little water, they bake to an inviting golden brown and give pies a truly professional look.

OTHER GARNISHES

Bacon Curls—Sauté bacon slices until almost crisp; before removing from skillet, wind each slice around the tines of a fork to make a curl. Drain on paper toweling. Use for casseroles or salad or sandwich plates.

Tinted Coconut—Combine 2 or 3 drops food coloring with 1 teaspoon water in a jar with a tight lid; add coconut; cover tightly. Shake jar until coconut is evenly tinted. Use for cakes, pies, candies, or molded or frozen desserts.

Chocolate Curls—With a vegetable parer, shave thin strips from a square of unsweetened or semisweet chocolate, or a plain chocolate candy bar. Chocolate should be room temperature to make neat even curls, and to avoid breaking them, lift, one at a time, with a wooden pick. Use for desserts or ice cream.

Marshmallow Stirrers—Thread marshmallows onto cinnamon sticks or slim peppermint candy sticks. Use for cocoa or chocolate beverages. For cider or hot apple or fruit punches, use plain cinnamon sticks.

Chocolate Cutouts—Melt ¼ cup semisweet chocolate pieces with ½ teaspoon shortening in a cup; spread in a thin rectangle about 6x5 inches on a sheet of foil. Chill 15 minutes, or just until firm enough to cut. Using truffle cutters, cut into diamonds, triangles, rounds, flowers, or other fancy shapes. Use for pies, cakes, or ice-cream desserts.

Tureen Toppers—Float crumbled crisp bacon, croutons, popcorn, French fried onion rings, chopped green or red peppers, sliced olives, or diced cooked sausages on soup. Just remember that whatever you choose should complement the soup in color, texture, and flavor.

Frosted Glasses—To make beverages look extra-cool, serve them in frosted glasses. Dip the top half inch of each glass into fruit juice, then into white or tinted granulated sugar. Let stand at room temperature or in the refrigerator until the sugar dries.

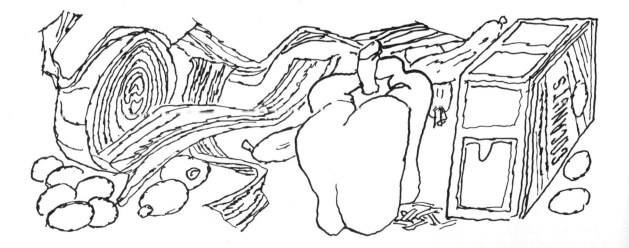

CANNING AND FREEZING

FOR SOME OF US, having our own year-round supply of food packed away in jars is a means of saving money; for others, it represents a great sense of accomplishment and a way to creativity.

Freezers, too, long viewed as a convenience, have taken their rightful place as a savings bank for foods. Managed with an eye on economy of all types, a home freezer pays dividends these ways: Enables you to stock up on family favorites when they're in season or on sale; affords you an opportunity to prepare special dishes when you have the time and the cost of the ingredients is lower; preserves leftovers that might otherwise be wasted; provides mealtime insurance for spur-of-the-moment guests; saves last-minute cooking when company's coming; makes it possible to serve family specialties that money can't buy; and finally, minimizes trips to the market.

Whether you devote your efforts to canning or freezing, the first step is the same: Plan ahead. Familiarize yourself with the how-to's on doing the job right, then get the tools you need and make sure they're in good working order and ready to go when the food is. Keep a watchful eye on what's plentiful and the best quality—for whatever comes out of a jar or a package is only as good as what went in.

If you have a freezer, remember that it's good economy to keep it full, but a waste to pack it with foods you use constantly. Label and date all packages and keep an inventory as a reminder to use them quickly. Pay attention to storage times and rotate packages so you can use the oldest first.

On the following pages, you'll find detailed directions for canning fruits and vegetables, and for freezing a variety of foods. For specific information on canning meats, poultry, fish, and prepared foods, or for canning at high altitudes, check with your local extension office or the home-service department of your local utility company.

THE HOW-TO'S OF CANNING

Even if you've never done any canning before, you needn't be timid about trying your hand at the job now. The basics are easy, but must be followed exactly if you're to achieve success.

The proper combination of processing time and temperature is the most important rule. While a boiling-water bath of 212° for a given length of time is sufficient for high-acid foods, all low-acid varieties require an above-boiling temperature for safety, and must be processed at 240°.

To handle both jobs, you need two basic pieces of equipment: a water-bath canner and a steam-pressure canner. High-acid foods include all fruits, tomatoes, pimientos, sauerkraut, pickles, and relishes. All other vegetables, meats, poultry, fish, and soup fall into the low-acid category.

Types of canners—The water-bath canner is simply a large deep kettle with a rack and a tight-fitting lid. Buy one specially made for canning, or use one you already have, providing it is deep enough to allow 2 to 4 inches of water to boil briskly over the tops of the jars during processing. It should also be big enough so that the jars do not touch one another or the sides of the kettle. The rack, which can be either metal or wood, keeps the jars off the bottom of the kettle, and if it has dividers, prevents them from bouncing about as the water boils. Use this type of canner for all high-acid foods.

A steam-pressure canner, similar to a pressure cooker, is a heavy seamless kettle with a rack, a locking lid with gasket, a pressure gauge, and a safety valve. The gauge may be either a spring dial or a weight. When the pressure holds at 10 pounds for a specific time, the food inside is being processed at 240°—an absolute must for low-acid foods.

A good precautionary measure is to have the pressure gauge on your canner checked at the start of each canning season. Your local extension office or the manufacturer of the canner can tell you where.

If your steam-pressure canner is deep enough, it can double as a water-bath canner. In this case, cover the canner with the lid but do not fasten it, and leave the petcock or vent wide open so the steam can escape rather than build up inside.

Jars and lids–Always use mason or glass jars. They come in a wide variety of sizes, and are tempered to take the heat and pressure of canning as well as to withstand the cold temperature of freezing. Never use mayonnaise, peanut butter, coffee, baby food, or any other jars originally filled with commercial foods. They may break or fail to seal tightly, and because there are so many different sizes and shapes, they may throw off the processing time.

Lids are available in two styles: A two-piece kind with a flat disc and a screw band, or a one-piece glass or porcelain-lined zinc cap to be used with a rubber ring. Be sure you have the correct kind and size for your jars. Screw bands and zinc or glass caps can be reused unless they're rusted, bent, or otherwise damaged; rubber rings and the flat lids that contain a sealing compound must be new each time. Always read package directions that tell you how to use and adjust the particular closures you buy.

Getting started–Check jars to make sure there are no nicks or cracks around the rims that might cause breakage or prevent a tight seal. Wash all jars, lids, screw bands, and rubber rings in hot soapy water; rinse well in hot water, then let them stand in hot water until you're ready to fill them.

Filling jars–Certain procedures are the same no matter which of the two processing methods you're following. In putting foods into the jars, there are also two ways to do the job: Raw (or cold) pack and hot pack. Either is suitable for most foods.

If you choose to use cold pack, place raw or unheated foods firmly into hot containers and cover with boiling syrup, water, or fruit juice, leaving the head space (or room at the top) that's specified for that particular product. Some need more than others, since they expand during processing. A handy tip: Setting the jars on a clean dish towel while you're filling them prevents slipping and catches any spills.

For the hot pack method, fill hot jars loosely with precooked foods and cover with boiling liquid, leaving specified head space.

After filling each jar (either type of pack), run a narrow rubber spatula down into the jar between the food and the side to work out any air bubbles. Be careful as you move the spatula around so you don't break or mash the food. If necessary, add more boiling liquid. Wipe off the rims of the jars with a damp cloth and add the caps, following manufacturer's directions. Pack only one jar at a time, and after it's capped, place it on the rack in the canner so it can start to heat up while you're filling the next one. Re-cover a water-bath canner each time you add a jar so the steam doesn't escape.

Processing–If you're using a water-bath canner, start the water heating before you begin to fill the jars. Pour 4 to 5 inches of water into the canner and place it over the heat. At the same time, heat more water in a kettle so it will be hot by the time the food is packed. As soon as the last jar has been put into the canner, check to make sure the jars aren't touching each other, then add enough more hot water to bring the level 2 to 3 inches over jar tops. (Pour the water down the side—not directly on jars.) Cover the canner, heat to a brisk rolling boil, and start timing at this point. Adjust the heat under the canner so the water will boil gently during the entire processing time. If necessary during processing, add more boiling water to keep jars covered. Stop counting the processing time until the water returns to a full boil, then start again.

When processing is finished, remove the jars from the water with a can lifter or tongs, place them on a rack away from drafts and each other so the air can circulate around them, and finish the sealing, if necessary, as manufacturer directs.

For steam-pressure canning, follow the manufacturer's directions for the model you're using. Fill only as many jars as the canner will hold at one time, and always can just one type of food and like jar sizes in the same load. While it's always more efficient to fill the canner completely each time, a smaller number of jars doesn't affect processing time or quality. With a steam-pressure canner, start counting processing time when the gauge reaches 10 pounds.

After canning is finished, turn off the heat or move the canner off an electric burner. Let the pressure fall normally to zero—usually from 15 to 25 minutes. Do not try to rush cooling by running water over the canner. When you open the canner, lift the cover away from you to avoid a blast of hot steam. If the food in the jars is still bubbling, wait a few more minutes, then take the jars out of the water and place them in a draft-free spot; adjust seals at once. For any type of canning, do not open a hot jar to add more liquid if part has boiled out during processing. Simply finish sealing the jar as if it were full.

Testing the seal–This is the final step that proves whether or not your efforts have been a success. Different types of closures require different tests, so it's best to follow the manufacturer's directions.

Generally speaking, seals on jars with rubber rings can be tested by tipping the jar slightly. If there's any leaking or bubbles that start at the lid and rise through the jar, the seal is not airtight.

Two-piece vacuum lids are another story. While they're cooling, you may hear some loud pinging noises. These sounds occur when the vacuum inside the jar suddenly pulls down on the metal lid to make an airtight seal. However, it doesn't always happen, so look for the dip in the center of the lid and feel it with your fingertip. If it doesn't push down, the jar is sealed. If it pushes down and then springs up, the closure is not tight. Any jar that has not sealed properly should be refrigerated so the food can be used immediately.

If the lid is not concave, but pushes down and stays there, the seal is questionable. In this case, carefully remove the screw band and lift the jar by the edges of the lid—only a fraction of an inch. A lid that comes off answers your sealing question.

After you're satisfied that the seals are tight, gently remove the screw bands. If left on, they may become corroded and make jars difficult to open later on. If a band sticks, covering it for just a few moments with a hot, damp cloth may help to loosen it sufficiently. Before storing, wipe off all jars with a damp cloth, then label them and place in a dry, dark place—preferably one that's below 70°.

Detecting spoilage–Before you serve any jar of home-canned foods, inspect it carefully by using your eyes, your nose, and a little common sense

Leaking from jars, bulging lids, mold, and a foamy or cloudy appearance tell you that the food should be thrown out. During and after opening, look for these signs: Spurting liquid, gas bubbles, an unpleasant aroma, food that is soft, mushy, or slimy—all of which mean that the product is not safe.

Some spoilage is not easy to detect, and for this reason, all home-canned vegetables, meats, poultry, fish, and soup should be boiled for 10 minutes before tasting or eating. (Spinach and corn require 20 minutes.) During heating, any food that looks spoiled, foams, or develops an off-odor should be discarded where it can't be touched by people or animals. Be safe; never taste any low-acid food cold from the jar.

CANNING FRUITS

Select firm ripe fruits at their peak of quality, and work quickly with small batches, handling them as little as possible. At the proper stage of maturity, fruits are also the most fragile. Remember, too, that for canning purposes, tomatoes are handled like fruits and, therefore, are covered in this section.

Your first steps–Start by washing the fruit well, several times if necessary, but do not let it stand in water or some of the food value will be lost.

Apples, apricots, peaches, and pears darken when cut and need to be treated with an ascorbic-acid color keeper and water as they're being prepared. Follow manufacturer's directions for proportions. Or you can drop the fruit into a mixture of 2 tablespoons salt and 2 tablespoons vinegar or lemon juice per gallon of water. However, vinegar may affect flavor, so let the pieces stand in the mixture for only a few minutes, then drain and rinse well.

Sweeten to taste–Sugar helps canned fruits keep their flavor, shape, and color. Most is called for in the form of syrup; to suit your preference and the sweetness of the fruit, you may use either light, medium, or heavy syrup. In each case, start with 4 cups of fruit juice or water, then add the following amounts of sugar for each type:

> Light: 2 cups; makes 5 cups syrup.
> Medium: 3 cups; makes 5½ cups syrup.
> Heavy: 4¾ cups; makes 6½ cups syrup.

To prepare, combine water and sugar in a saucepan and heat, stirring constantly, until sugar dissolves; skim if needed. Lower the heat to keep the syrup hot—but not boiling—as you work. You'll need from 1 to 1½ cups of syrup for each quart jar of fruit.

To make fruit juice, crush fully ripe, soft juicy fruit with a potato masher. Place it in a kettle or large saucepan and heat slowly to simmering. Strain through a jelly bag or a cloth; discard pulp.

Sugar-free fruits–All fruits may be canned successfully without sugar since it isn't needed to ensure keeping quality. If this is your choice, heat the fruit to boiling, then pack it hot into hot jars. Cover with boiling fruit juice or boiling water and process in a water-bath canner the same as sweetened fruits.

Directions for preparing and processing fruits are given in the chart on the following pages, but you'll need to choose between cold or hot pack when both are listed.

PREPARING AND PROCESSING FRUITS

Fruit	Preparation	Total Minutes For Water-Bath Processing
Apples (2½ to 3 pounds yield 1 quart)	*Hot Pack:* Prepare syrup. Wash apples; pare, core, and cut in pieces. Use ascorbic-acid mixture. Boil pieces in syrup 5 minutes. Pack hot pieces into hot jars, leaving ½ inch head space. Cover with boiling syrup, leaving ½ inch head space. Adjust lids; process.	Pints - 15 Quarts - 20
Applesauce (6 to 7 pounds yield 1 quart)	Wash apples; quarter and core. Use ascorbic-acid mixture. Make into applesauce; leave plain or sweeten to taste. Pack hot into hot jars, leaving ¼ inch head space. Adjust lids; process.	Pints - 10 Quarts - 10
Apricots (1½ pounds yield 1 quart)	*Raw Pack:* Prepare syrup. Wash fruit; halve; pit enough for one jar at a time. Use ascorbic-acid mixture. Peel or not as you wish. Pack into hot jars, leaving ½ inch head space. Cover with boiling syrup, leaving ½ inch head space. Adjust lids; process.	Pints - 25 Quarts - 30
	Hot Pack: Prepare fruit as above, except heat fruit through in syrup. Pack hot apricots into hot jars, leaving ½ inch head space. Cover with boiling syrup, leaving ½ inch head space. Adjust lids; process.	Pints - 20 Quarts - 25
Berries, except strawberries (1 to 2 quarts yield 1 quart)	*Raw Pack:* Use for soft berries. Prepare syrup. Wash fruit; drain; stem if needed. Pack into hot jars, leaving ½ inch head space. Cover with boiling syrup, leaving ½ inch head space. Adjust lids; process.	Pints - 10 Quarts - 15
	Hot Pack: Use for firm berries. Wash fruit; drain; stem if needed. Combine ½ cup sugar with each quart of berries in a saucepan; heat slowly, covered, to boiling. Shake pan to prevent sticking. Pack hot fruit into hot jars, leaving ½ inch head space. Adjust lids; process.	Pints - 10 Quarts - 15
Cherries (2 to 2½ pounds unpitted yield 1 quart)	*Raw Pack:* Prepare syrup. Wash cherries; stem; pit or not as you wish. Pack into hot jars, leaving ½ inch head space. Cover with boiling syrup, leaving ½ inch head space. Adjust lids; process.	Pints - 20 Quarts - 25

Fruit	Preparation	Total Minutes For Water-Bath Processing
	Hot Pack: Prepare fruit. Combine ½ cup sugar with each quart of cherries in a saucepan; add a little water only if cherries are unpitted; cover. Heat to boiling. Pack hot into hot jars, leaving ½ inch head space. Adjust lids; process.	Pints - 10 Quarts - 15
Peaches (2 to 3 pounds yield 1 quart)	*Raw Pack:* Prepare syrup. Wash fruit; peel. For easy peeling, dip fruit into boiling water, then into cold water. Halve and pit; use ascorbic-acid mixture. Pack into hot jars, leaving ½ inch head space. Cover with boiling syrup, leaving ½ inch head space. Adjust lids; process.	Pints - 25 Quarts - 30
	Hot Pack: Prepare fruit as above, except heat thoroughly in syrup. Pack hot fruit into hot jars, leaving ½ inch head space. Cover with boiling syrup, leaving ½ inch head space. Adjust lids; process.	Pints - 20 Quarts - 25
Pears (2 to 3 pounds yield 1 quart)	*Raw Pack:* Prepare syrup. Wash fruit; pare; halve; core. Use ascorbic-acid mixture. Pack into hot jars, leaving ½ inch head space. Cover with boiling syrup, leaving ½ inch head space. Adjust lids; process.	Pints - 25 Quarts - 30
	Hot Pack: Prepare fruit as above, except heat through in syrup. Pack hot fruit into hot jars, leaving ½ inch head space. Cover with boiling syrup, leaving ½ inch head space. Adjust lids; process.	Pints - 20 Quarts - 25
Plums (1½ to 2½ pounds yield 1 quart)	*Raw Pack:* Prepare syrup. Wash plums and drain; prick skins if canning fruit whole. Or halve and pit if you wish. Pack into hot jars, leaving ½ inch head space. Cover with boiling syrup, leaving ½ inch head space. Adjust lids; process.	Pints - 20 Quarts - 25
	Hot Pack: Prepare fruit as above, except heat to boiling in syrup. Pack hot fruit into hot jars, leaving ½ inch head space. Cover with boiling syrup, leaving ½ inch head space. Adjust lids; process.	Pints - 20 Quarts - 25
Rhubarb (1 to 2 pounds yield 1 quart)	*Raw Pack:* Prepare syrup. Wash rhubarb; trim; cut into ½ inch pieces. Pack into hot jars, leaving ½ inch head space. Cover with boiling syrup, leaving ½ inch head space. Adjust lids; process.	Pints - 10 Quarts - 10
	Hot Pack: Prepare fruit as above, except heat rhubarb through in syrup. Pack hot fruit into hot jars, leaving ½ inch head space. Cover with boiling syrup, leaving ½ inch head space. Adjust lids; process.	Pints - 10 Quarts - 10

PREPARING AND PROCESSING FRUITS

Fruits	Preparation	Total Minutes For Water-Bath Processing
Fruit Juices	Wash fruits; pit; crush with a potato masher. Heat to simmering; strain through cheesecloth. Add 1 cup sugar for each 4 quarts juice; reheat to simmering. Pour hot into hot jars, leaving ½ inch head space. Adjust lids; process.	Pints - 5 Quarts - 5
Fruit Purées	Wash firm ripe fruit; pit. Cut large fruits into pieces. Simmer until soft, adding only enough water to keep fruit from sticking. Strain or put through a food mill. Add sugar to taste. Reheat to simmering. Pack hot purée into hot jars, leaving ½ inch head space. Adjust lids; process.	Pints - 10 Quarts - 10
Tomatoes (2½ to 3½ pounds yield 1 quart)	*Raw Pack:* Use only firm, ripe, red tomatoes. (Overripe ones will not contain enough acid; those with soft or decayed spots aren't suitable.) Peel by dipping into boiling water for ½ minute, then into cold; remove skins. Leave whole or cut in half or quarters. Pack into hot jars, leaving ½ inch head space. Add ½ teaspoon salt to pints and 1 teaspoon to quarts. Do not add water. Adjust lids; process.	Pints - 35 Quarts - 45
	Hot Pack: Quarter peeled tomatoes; heat to boiling in a saucepan, stirring several times to prevent sticking. Pack boiling hot into hot jars, leaving ½ inch head space. Add ½ teaspoon salt to pints and 1 teaspoon to quarts. Adjust lids; process.	Pints - 10 Quarts - 10
Tomato Juice	Use only firm ripe, red, juicy tomatoes, with no soft or decayed spots. Wash; cut into pieces. Simmer, stirring often, until soft; strain. Add 1 teaspoon salt to each quart juice. Reheat to boiling; pour into hot jars, leaving ½ inch head space. Adjust lids; process.	Pints - 10 Quarts - 10

STRAWBERRY-PINEAPPLE CROWN (p.357) ▶

CANNING VEGETABLES

Even though they vary widely in color, shape, flavor, and texture, almost all vegetables—except tomatoes—are low in acid and must be processed in a pressure canner at 10 pounds pressure. Only if they are made into pickles, relishes, or sauerkraut with vinegar added can they be safely processed in a water-bath canner.

For the best results, start with fresh tender young vegetables, and get them into the jars as quickly as possible. This means having lids, jars, kettles, canner, and any other equipment you need ready. As with fruits, working with only a small batch at a time helps maintain quality.

Thorough washing is a must, but it's important not to let vegetables stand in water. To avoid bruising and overhandling, lift each type up and down in a sinkful of water, changing the water as often as needed. Lift the vegetables out of the water before it's changed; otherwise, the soil will resettle on them as water drains off.

Packing the jars—Potatoes, corn, peas, and lima beans expand while being processed, so it's necessary to allow 1-inch head space at the top of each jar. With all other kinds, ½ inch is enough.

Choose between raw or hot packs. For hot pack, use the liquid in which the vegetables were cooked unless it's murky, gritty, dark, strong-flavored, or there isn't enough. Then substitute boiling water. Add ½ teaspoon of salt to each pint and 1 teaspoon to each quart. Since salt is a seasoning in this case and not a preservative, you can omit it for those on salt-free diets.

Directions for preparing and processing vegetables (except tomatoes) are given in the chart on pages 610-613. For safety, follow it exactly for type and time of processing, adjusting pressure where needed for altitudes that are more than 2,000 feet above sea level.

◀ *(Clockwise from top)*
LUMBERJACK BURGOO (p.58)
GLAZED STUFFED PORK (p.108)
BOMBAY CHICKEN (p.172)

PREPARING AND PROCESSING VEGETABLES

Vegetable	Preparation	Total Minutes For Steam-Pressure Processing
Asparagus (2½ to 4½ pounds yield 1 quart)	*Raw Pack:* Wash asparagus thoroughly. Trim off scales and tough ends; cut into 1-inch pieces. Pack into hot jars, leaving ½ inch head space. Add salt. Cover with boiling water, leaving ½ inch head space. Adjust lids; process.	Pints - 25 Quarts - 30
	Hot Pack: Prepare asparagus as above. Cover pieces with boiling water in a kettle; heat to boiling; boil 3 minutes. Pack hot into hot jars, leaving ½ inch head space. Add salt. Cover with boiling cooking liquid, leaving ½ inch head space. Adjust lids; process.	Pints - 25 Quarts - 30
Beans, green and wax (1½ to 2½ pounds yield 1 quart)	*Raw Pack:* Wash beans thoroughly. Tip and cut into 1-inch lengths. Pack into hot jars, leaving ½ inch head space. Add salt. Cover with boiling water, leaving ½ inch head space. Adjust lids; process.	Pints - 20 Quarts - 25
	Hot Pack: Prepare beans as above. Cover with boiling water in a kettle; heat to boiling; boil 5 minutes. Pack hot into hot jars, leaving ½ inch head space. Add salt. Cover with boiling cooking liquid, leaving ½ inch head space. Adjust lids; process.	Pints - 20 Quarts - 25
Beans, lima (3 to 5 pounds in pods yield 1 quart)	*Raw Pack:* Shell beans; wash; sort into sizes. Pack into hot jars, leaving 1 inch head space. Do not shake jars or press beans down. Add salt. Cover with boiling water, leaving 1 inch head space. Adjust lids; process.	Pints - 40 Quarts - 50
	Hot Pack: Prepare beans as above. Cover with boiling water in a kettle; heat to boiling. Pack hot beans loosely into hot jars, leaving 1 inch head space. Add salt. Cover with boiling cooking liquid, leaving 1 inch head space. Adjust lids; process.	Pints - 40 Quarts - 50

PREPARING AND PROCESSING VEGETABLES

Vegetable	Preparation	Total Minutes For Steam-Pressure Processing
Beets (2 to 3½ pounds yield 1 quart)	Wash beets, leaving root and 1 inch of tops on. Cover with boiling water; cook 15 to 25 minutes, depending on size. Cool just until easy to handle; slip off skins and trim. Leave tiny ones whole; slice large ones. Pack hot into hot jars, leaving ½ inch head space. Add salt. Cover with boiling water, leaving ½ inch head space. Adjust lids; process.	Pints - 30 Quarts - 35
Carrots (2 to 3 pounds yield 1 quart)	*Raw Pack:* Wash carrots thoroughly; pare; slice or dice. Pack tightly into hot jars, leaving 1 inch head space. Add salt. Cover with boiling water, leaving ½ inch head space. Adjust lids; process.	Pints - 25 Quarts - 30
	Hot Pack: Prepare carrots as above. Cover with boiling water in a kettle; heat to boiling. Pack hot into hot jars, leaving ½ inch head space. Add salt. Cover with boiling cooking liquid, leaving ½ inch head space. Adjust lids; process.	Pints - 25 Quarts - 30
Corn, whole-kernel (3 to 6 pounds yield 1 quart)	*Raw Pack:* Husk corn and remove silks. Wash ears. Cut from cobs at two thirds the depth of kernels; do not scrape cobs. Pack corn loosely into hot jars, leaving 1 inch head space. Add salt. Cover with boiling water, leaving ½ inch head space. Adjust lids; process.	Pints - 55 Quarts - 85
	Hot Pack: Prepare corn as above. Add 2 cups boiling water to each 4 cups corn in a kettle; heat to boiling. Pack hot, loosely, into hot jars, leaving 1 inch head space. Add salt. Cover with boiling cooking liquid, leaving 1 inch head space. Adjust lids; process.	Pints - 55 Quarts - 85
Corn, cream-style (1½ to 3 pounds yield 1 pint)	*Raw Pack:* Use pint jars only. Husk corn and remove silks; wash ears. Cut from cobs at half the depth of kernels; scrape cobs. Pack into hot pint jars, leaving 1½ inches head space. Add salt. Cover with boiling water, leaving ½ inch head space. Adjust lids; process.	Pints - 95

PREPARING AND PROCESSING VEGETABLES

Vegetable	Preparation	Total Minutes For Steam-Pressure Processing
Okra (1½ pounds yield 1 quart)	*Hot Pack:* Wash pods; trim. (Can only tender pods.) Leave whole or cut into 1-inch pieces. Cover with boiling water in a kettle; heat to boiling; cook 1 minute. Pack hot into hot jars, leaving ½ inch head space. Add salt. Cover with boiling cooking liquid, leaving ½ inch head space. Adjust lids; process.	Pints - 25 Quarts - 40
Peas, green (3 to 6 pounds in pods yield 1 quart)	*Raw Pack:* Shell peas; wash. Pack loosely into hot jars, leaving 1 inch head space. Add salt. Cover with boiling water, leaving 1½ inches head space. Adjust lids; process.	Pints - 40 Quarts - 40
	Hot Pack: Prepare peas as above. Cover with boiling water in a kettle; heat to boiling. Pack hot into hot jars, leaving 1 inch head space. Add salt. Cover with boiling cooking liquid, leaving 1 inch head space. Adjust lids; process.	Pints - 40 Quarts - 40
Potatoes, sweet (2 to 3 pounds yield 1 quart)	*Dry Pack:* Wash potatoes. Cook in boiling water 20 to 30 minutes, depending on size; drain; remove skins; cut up. Pack hot potatoes into hot jars, leaving 1 inch head space. Do not add liquid or salt. Adjust lids; process.	Pints - 65 Quarts - 95
	Wet Pack: Wash potatoes. Cook in boiling water until skins slip off easily; drain; remove skins; cut up. Pack hot potatoes into hot jars, leaving 1 inch head space. Add salt. Cover with boiling water, leaving 1 inch head space. Adjust lids; process.	Pints - 55 Quarts - 90
Pumpkin; acorn, Hubbard, and butternut squash (1½ to 3 pounds yield 1 quart)	Wash; cut in half; scoop out seeds. Pare; cut into cubes. Barely cover cubes with water in a kettle; heat to boiling. Pack hot into hot jars, leaving ½ inch head space. Add salt. Cover with boiling cooking liquid, leaving ½ inch head space. Adjust lids; process.	Pints - 55 Quarts - 90
	Mashed pumpkin or squash: Prepare as above; cook in a small amount of boiling water in a kettle until tender. Put through a food mill. Heat again until hot, stirring often to prevent sticking. Pack hot into hot jars, leaving ½ inch head space. Do not add liquid or salt. Adjust lids; process.	Pints - 65 Quarts - 80

PREPARING AND PROCESSING VEGETABLES

Vegetable	Preparation	Total Minutes For Steam-Pressure Processing
Spinach and other greens (2 to 6 pounds yield 1 quart)	*Hot Pack:* Pick over leaves, using only fresh tender ones for canning. Wash thoroughly; cut off stems and remove coarse ribs. Place about 2½ pounds at a time in a cheesecloth bag and steam 10 minutes until wilted. Pack hot, loosely, in hot jars, leaving ½ inch head space. Add salt. Cover with boiling water, leaving ½ inch head space. Adjust lids; process.	Pints - 70 Quarts - 90
Squash, yellow and zucchini (2 to 4 pounds yield 1 quart)	*Raw Pack:* Wash squash but do not pare; trim ends. Cut squash into ½-inch slices, cutting large ones into halves or quarters to make even. Pack raw tightly into hot jars, leaving 1 inch head space. Add salt. Cover with boiling water, leaving ½ inch head space. Adjust lids; process.	Pints - 25 Quarts - 30
	Hot Pack: Prepare squash as above. Barely cover with boiling water in a kettle; heat to boiling. Pack hot into hot jars, leaving ½ inch head space. Add salt. Cover with boiling cooking liquid, leaving ½ inch head space. Adjust lids; process.	Pints - 30 Quarts - 40

MAKING SWEET FRUIT SPREADS

Six members belong to this popular family: Jelly, jam, preserves, marmalade, conserve, and fruit butters. Because their ingredients and cooking methods are similar, their names are often used interchangeably, but strictly speaking, each has its own identity. Briefly, here's how they differ: *Jelly* is clear, firm, and shimmery and made only from strained fruit juice. *Jam* starts with crushed or ground whole fruits, and while it may be firm enough to hold its shape, it is softer than jelly.

Preserves consist of a thick syrup containing whole or cut up fruit. *Marmalade* resembles jelly, but in addition, has pieces of fruit or fruit peel mixed throughout. *Conserve* looks a bit like jam, but combines several fruits—usually one citrus—and nuts. *Fruit butters* are made only from fruit pulp.

Ingredients–Regardless of type, sweet spreads call for four common items: Fruit, pectin, acid, and sugar. For a successful product, use in the proper proportions.

Fruit provides the flavor and color, and quality is the key, the same as in any other type of preserving. In this case, fruit that is barely ripe, or slightly underripe is best.

Pectin is the ingredient that makes the product gel (or set). All fruits contain some naturally, but in varying amounts. Tart apples, blackberries, cranberries, currants, gooseberries, Concord grapes, and sour plums have a considerable amount; apricots, blueberries, cherries, peaches, pineapple, rhubarb, and strawberries have much less. Slightly underripe fruit contains more pectin than does fully ripe. That's why many recipes call for a commercial fruit pectin, either in liquid or powdered form. The two types are not the same and cannot be substituted for one another, so be sure to follow recipes that have been developed specifically for each of these products.

For flavor and gelling, all spreads need acid, while sugar enhances flavor, acts as a preservative, and also aids gelling.

Equipment you'll need–An 8- to 10-quart kettle with a broad flat bottom is a must for jelly-making. While it seems and sounds large in proportion to the amount of ingredients you'll have, the space is needed so the jelly or jam mixture can boil briskly without spilling over.

A jelly bag for separating fruit pulp from juice is a handy item to have. Buy one, if you like, but you can also improvise by making one from cheesecloth or a square of muslin.

In jars and glasses, there are many sizes and shapes that are suitable for jellies and jams, but it's a good idea to stick to those that can take the temperature of the hot food as well as the boiling water that's needed for sterilization. Where possible, choose regular half-pint canning or jelly jars made by canning manufacturers.

Preparing glasses and jars–If food is to be processed, wash jars, lids, and bands in hot soapy water and rinse well with hot water, then turn jars upside down to drain. Or you can wash both jars and lids in your automatic dishwasher, providing the rinse cycle is very hot; leave them there until needed so they'll stay warm.

For jelly that will not be processed, place clean glasses, lids, and bands in a deep kettle, cover with water, and boil 10 minutes. Remove them from the water after jelly has cooked 5 to 10 minutes; drain glasses.

Working with paraffin–A clean 1-pound shortening or coffee can with a plastic lid is ideal for this purpose. Place the paraffin—one bar is enough at a time—in the can and set it, uncovered, in a saucepan containing about an inch of water. Heat until paraffin melts, then keep it hot until you're ready to use it. Never melt paraffin over direct heat; it may splatter and catch fire.

When putting paraffin onto jelly, rest the spoon on the edge of the glass or jar and tilt it to let the paraffin flow onto the surface. With the tip of the spoon, gently spread it around until it covers the surface and touches the edge of the glass completely. The layer should be only about ⅛ inch thick. If air bubbles appear, prick them, for they turn into holes as the paraffin hardens. After paraffin is cold and firm, put caps on jars. Cover any unused paraffin and store it in the can for another day.

To fix fruit juice–Soft fruits and juicy berries simply need to be crushed with a potato masher. Work with only one layer at a time. Strain the crushed fruit through a jelly bag, or place several layers of cheesecloth loosely into a colander as a liner, then set the colander in a large deep pan or bowl to catch the juice. Tie the corners of the cloth together to form a bag so you can lift it up easily to let the juice drip.

Firm fruits such as apples have to be cooked first. Cut up the fruit but do not pare or core it since these parts contain the most pectin. Place fruit in a kettle with just enough water to prevent sticking; cook until fruit is tender. Strain through a bag the same as crushed fruit. Avoid squeezing the bag or little bits of pulp will also run through and result in cloudy jelly.

Regardless of how much juice you have, never double a jelly recipe. It's much easier—and safer—to make the recipe over again than it is to cook larger amounts at one time. As a rule of thumb, cook in batches of 4 to 6 cups.

How to tell when jelly is done–Many jelly and marmalade recipes specify cooking the fruit mixture until it sheets from a spoon. The amount of time it takes to reach this point will vary from batch to batch and from recipe to recipe.

To make the sheeting test, dip a cool metal spoon into the bubbling jelly, lift out a spoonful, and tilt the spoon so the mixture flows back into the kettle. At first, drops will be light and syrupy. As cooking progresses, drops will become heavier and fall from spoon two at a time. Finally, drops will run together and break from the spoon in a sheet or flake. This is the jellying point.

Filling jelly jars–If you're using jars with vacuum lids and screw bands, it's necessary to work quickly—otherwise the jelly will start to set and the jars will not seal properly. To speed things along, place a funnel firmly in the jar and pour in the boiling hot jelly to within ⅛ inch of the top. Wipe around the rim with a damp cloth and adjust lids; screw bands on evenly and tightly. Turn the jar upside down for a few seconds so the hot jelly heats the lid and sterilizes it, then turn it right side up again and let it cool. When cold, check seals the same as for other canning; remove screw bands and store jars in a cool, dark, dry place.

If you're using regular jelly glasses, leave ½ inch space at the top and cover immediately with paraffin. Let glasses stand in a draft-free spot until paraffin hardens, then add jar caps.

When making other spreads–Prepare jars and lids the same as for jelly. Follow your recipe directions for fixing and cooking the fruit, since marmalades, butters, preserves, and conserve will vary slightly. As soon as the mixture is cooked, remove it from the heat and skim off the foam with a metal spoon. Ladle into jars, cap, and process as directed.

Freezer spreads–Because these foods are not cooked and are so easy to fix with fresh, frozen, or canned fruits, they rate high in popularity. Most can be stored in the freezer up to a year, but once opened, should be placed in the refrigerator to use within three weeks.

THE HOW-TO'S OF FREEZING

Luscious berries, blush-cheeked peaches and nectarines, rosy cherries, tender young vegetables, meat, poultry, and fish—plus homemade dishes of all kinds—take happily to this method of preserving. And done properly, freezing, particularly, helps fruits and vegetables keep their bright colors, fresh flavors, and nutritive values. Another advantage: Meal-fixing is often cut to a minimum since a great deal of the preparation is done before freezing.

About packaging and packing–All foods, raw and cooked, must be wrapped or boxed carefully if they're to retain their high quality while in the freezer. This means that wraps and containers have to be airtight and moisture- and vaporproof. Supermarkets, as well as department and housewares stores, stock a wide variety of wraps, jars, boxes, bags, cartons, plates, pans, casseroles, sealing tapes, and markers for you to choose from. Before you buy, read labels so you'll get what's best for your purpose. Keep in mind that whatever you use must be durable, easy to seal airtight, and stackable both in the freezer and in your cupboard when not in use.

In using wraps, it's important to press all of the air out of the package and seal it tightly. Otherwise, the food may develop freezer burn. This term simply means that the dry air in the freezer has touched an exposed part of the food, causing it to develop a dry, pithy, tough surface.

Since many foods expand when frozen, it's necessary to have what's known as head space at the top of the containers. In wide-mouth pint containers, leave ½ inch, and for quarts, 1 inch, if the food is packed in liquid or packed solidly. (Applesauce and mashed pumpkin are two examples of solid-pack.) Only ½ inch is needed for fruits and vegetables packed dry in any size container; loosely packed vegetables such as peas can go right to the top of the container.

Fast freezing a must–Any type of food must be frozen quickly after it's packed. As a general rule, add unfrozen foods in small quantities—only as much as will freeze firm within 24 hours. Stated another way, this means 2 to 3 pounds of food per cubic foot of freezer space. Overloading simply slows down freezing, may raise the temperature inside the freezer, and causes foods to lose quality.

When you're freezing a maximum amount, it's a good idea to turn the temperature control to its coldest position and leave it there for a day, then turn it back to the storage marking.

Place all unfrozen packages against the freezing coils (either at bottom or sides) and leave space between them so the air can circulate. After they're frozen solid, they can be stacked or moved.

What not to freeze–While the list of fresh or prepared foods that can be frozen successfully is almost endless, there are others that are totally unsuccessful. To be avoided are fluffy cake frostings or those made with egg whites, meringue, cream pies and custard, hard-cooked eggs, mayonnaise, boiled potatoes as used in stews, jelly in sandwiches, and vegetables to be served raw.

Season prepared freezer dishes well as you fix them, but remember that some ingredients, such as salt, lose flavor, whereas others, such as onions, pepper, and cloves, get stronger. If needed, you can always add more as the food is reheated.

When cooked food is frozen–Guideline number one is to cool it quickly. Place the hot food in the refrigerator or in a sink or roasting pan filled with ice and water if the container is unbreakable. Since large quantities of hot foods will raise the temperature inside your refrigerator, it's best to transfer the food to one or more shallow pans, then set these pans in larger ones of ice and water. Another reminder: For safety, speed cooled foods into the freezer. If allowed to stand at room temperature in a hot kitchen, they may not be safe to eat.

To save space and keep from tying up favorite dishes, try this: Cool prepared food as directed above. Then line a second casserole or kettle that's the same size and shape with heavy foil, allowing a 3-inch overhang. Spoon in the cooked food and freeze until almost firm. Lift foil and food from casserole, overwrap tightly, and return to freezer. At mealtime, remove the block of frozen food from foil, put it back in its original cooking container, and reheat as recipe directs.

Baked pies, cakes, cookies, breads, and rolls may be cooled at room temperature, then wrapped and frozen.

Thaw foods safely–While freezing slows the growth of bacteria, it doesn't kill them, and as food defrosts or warms up, they start growing again. This is why it's so important to thaw foods carefully. Call on your refrigerator to do the job. Simply place the container or package in the refrigerator, allowing about 24 hours for a pound of meat or a quart of food.

If you have a microwave oven, you can use the defrost cycle, following manufacturer's directions.

When you're in a hurry, foods such as soups, broth, or sauce can be thawed by placing the container in a pan of cold water. Leave it just long enough to thaw around the edges, then empty the food into the cooking pan. Heating will take care of the rest.

Prepared dishes that are to be baked needn't be thawed at all. If they're packed in ovenproof containers, remove any outer wrappings, then start heating them in a cold oven to save energy and breakage. (Recipes included in this chapter are handled this way.) Most will take from 30 to 45 minutes extra baking, depending on size, so watch the timing carefully.

Keep tabs on temperature–If your freezer holds a constant 0° temperature or less, foods will be safe to eat almost indefinitely, but flavor and quality do deteriorate with time. It's best to keep a constant check on the temperature with a thermometer specifically designed for this purpose. If the temperature runs higher, especially in freezer compartments of combination appliances, plan to use foods within two weeks. A very general guide: Unless your freezer keeps ice cream so hard you can't scoop it easily, avoid using it for long-term storage.

When your freezer breaks down–If there's a power failure or a mechanical problem that causes your freezer to stop, keep the door closed. Opening it only lets out cold air and shortens your safety time. A fully loaded freezer at 0° temperature will stay cold for as long as two days; one that's only partly full will hold foods frozen for a day.

If you know that your freezer will be off even longer, pack it with dry ice. (Local ice suppliers usually have some on hand.) Work quickly when you put in the ice, handling it with gloved hands and placing pieces on thick cardboards on top of the foods—not directly on the packages. While you're working, keep the room well ventilated. If this problem-solver doesn't help you, perhaps you can transfer the food to a neighbor's unit or, in some cases, to a community locker plant.

If the food has already thawed, follow these guidelines in deciding what to save and what to throw out:

(1) If the food still has ice crystals in the center, it may be refrozen safely.

(2) If meat, poultry, or fish has warmed to room temperature, discard it.

(3) If vegetables and fruits have thawed and warmed, but still have a fresh aroma, cook them for immediate use.

FREEZING FRUITS

Most fruits freeze satisfactorily, although quality will depend on the kind of fruit, how ripe it is, and how you pack it. Wash and drain the fruit first, working with only a small quantity at a time to save handling and bruising. Avoid letting fruits stand in water, since they lose flavor and food value. As a rule of thumb, most fruits keep their textures and flavors best if packed in sugar or syrup, although some also freeze successfully without sweetening.

In making syrups, dissolve the sugar in either hot or cold water. If hot, cool the syrup before you pour it over the fruit; otherwise, it softens the fruit. To save time, you can also make the syrup a day ahead and store it in the refrigerator.

In packing, be sure the syrup covers the fruit so the top pieces keep their bright color and flavor. To prevent floating, press the fruit down into the syrup, hold it in place with a small piece of crumpled waxed paper or transparent wrap, then seal as usual.

When using dry sugar, sprinkle it over prepared fruit in a shallow dish or bowl and mix well—but gently—until the juices start to flow and the sugar dissolves. Then spoon into packing containers and seal.

Some fruits (peaches, for example) that turn dark when cut need to be treated with ascorbic-acid mixture before they go into the containers. Buy it as powder, crystals, or tablets and use as labels direct.

The chart on pages 621-622 will give you the specifics on most fruits.

FREEZING FRUITS

FRUIT	PREPARATION	PACKAGING	STORAGE AND USE
Apples (1¼ pounds yield 1 pint)	Peel, core, and slice into mixture of 2 tablespoons salt for 1 gallon water; drain. Or make into applesauce and sweeten to taste.	Pack slices, unsweetened, or applesauce, in containers. Leave ½ inch head space in pint applesauce containers. Seal; label; date; freeze.	8 to 12 months. Use slices for pies or baked desserts. Thaw applesauce sauce and use as is or in cooking.
Apricots (1½ pounds yield 1 quart)	Halve, pit, and peel. Use ascorbic-acid mixture as label directs. Mix with ½ cup sugar per 4 cups fruit.	Pack into containers, leaving ¼ inch head space in pints and ½ inch in quarts. Seal; label; date; freeze.	8 to 12 months. Thaw until halves can be separated easily. Use as fresh.
Blueberries (1 to 1½ pints yield 1 pint)	Stem. For serving cold, use syrup of 4¾ cups sugar per 4 cups water.	Pack berries in syrup in containers, leaving ¼ inch head space in pints and ½ inch in quarts. Or freeze whole berries dry on a tray, then loose-pack in containers. Seal; label; date; freeze.	8 to 12 months. Use frozen in cooking. Or thaw and serve while icy.
Cantaloupe (1¼ pounds yield 1 pint)	Remove seeds and pare. Cut into ¾-inch cubes, balls, or slices.	Pack in bags. Seal; label; date; freeze.	8 to 12 months. Thaw and serve while icy.
Cherries, sour (1½ pounds yield 1 pint)	Stem and pit. Mix with 1 cup sugar per 4 cups fruit. Or use syrup of 4¾ cups sugar per 4 cups water.	Pack into containers, leaving ¼ inch head space in pints and ½ inch in quarts. Seal; label; date; freeze.	8 to 12 months. Use for pies or other cooked desserts.
Cherries, sweet (1½ pounds yield 1 pint)	Stem and pit. Use ascorbic-acid mixture as label directs, plus syrup of 4¾ cups sugar per 4 cups water.	Pack into containers, leaving ¼ inch head space in pints and ½ inch in quarts. Seal; label; date; freeze.	8 to 12 months. Thaw and serve cold or use in cooked or uncooked desserts.
Cranberries (1 pound yields 1 quart)	Stem. Leave as is or make into cranberry sauce and cool.	Pack dry berries in bags or containers. Pack sauce in containers, leaving ¼ inch head space in pints and ½ inch in quarts. Seal; label; date; freeze.	8 to 12 months. Use dry pack, frozen, in cooking. Thaw sauce and serve.

FREEZING FRUITS

FRUIT	PREPARATION	PACKAGING	STORAGE AND USE
Peaches or Nectarines (1 to 1½ pounds yield 1 pint)	Peel, halve, pit, and slice. Use ascorbic-acid mixture as label directs. Mix with ⅔ cup sugar per 4 cups fruit.	Pack in containers, leaving ¼ inch head space in pints and ½ inch in quarts. Seal; label; date; freeze.	8 to 12 months. Thaw just until slices can be separated. Use as fresh.
Plums (1 to 1½ pounds yield 1 pint)	Leave whole. Or halve and pit. Mix with 1 cup sugar per 5 cups fruit.	Pack whole in bags, filling space as much as possible. Pack sweetened fruit in containers, leaving ¼ inch head space in pints and ½ inch in quarts. Seal; label; date; freeze.	8 to 12 months. Thaw until fruit or slices can be separated. Use as fresh.
Raspberries (1 pint yields 1 pint)	Remove stems. Leave plain or gently mix with ¾ cup sugar per 4 cups fruit.	Pack plain in bags. Pack sweetened fruit in containers, leaving ¼ inch head space in pints and ½ inch in quarts. Seal; label; date; freeze.	8 to 12 months. Thaw and serve while icy. Or use in uncooked desserts.
Rhubarb (1 pound yields 1 pint)	Trim and cut into 1-inch pieces. Leave plain or mix with 1 cup sugar per 4 cups fruit.	Pack plain in bags. Pack sweetened fruit in containers, leaving ¼ inch head space in pints and ½ inch in quarts. Seal; label; date; freeze.	8 to 12 months. Use frozen in cooking.
Strawberries (1½ pints yield 1 pint)	Hull. Leave whole, halve, or slice. Mix with ¾ cup sugar per 4 cups fruit.	Pack whole in bags. Pack sweetened fruit in containers, leaving ¼ inch head space in pints and ½ inch in quarts. Seal; label; date; freeze.	8 to 12 months. Thaw and serve while icy. Or use in other desserts.

FREEZING VEGETABLES

Select tender top-of-the-season vegetables at their peak in quality—and this means neither under- nor overripe. If at all possible, process them on the day you buy them.

To start, wash all vegetables first in cold water, then peel or pare, trim, and cut into even-sized pieces the same as you would if serving them fresh. Almost all need to be blanched or heated briefly in rapidly boiling water before they go into the containers. A large blanching kettle or a steamer is handy for this job. Use about a gallon of water for each 1 to 2 pounds vegetables, and make sure the water is boiling when you add the vegetables. Cover the kettle; keep the heat high, and start counting the time immediately. After heating, plunge the vegetables into ice water to stop the cooking, then drain them well. Let them stand in water only until cooled; otherwise, they lose color, flavor, and nutrients.

The chart below and on the following pages will give you the exact directions for most vegetables.

FREEZING VEGETABLES

VEGETABLE	PREPARATION	PACKAGING	STORAGE AND USE
Asparagus (1½ pounds yield 1 pint)	Trim stalks; remove scales. Leave whole or cut into even 1-inch pieces. Blanch small spears or cut pieces 1½ minutes and large ones 3 minutes; chill; drain.	Freeze spears on trays, then pack into containers or bags. Pack cut pieces in bags or containers, leaving ½ inch head space. Seal; label; date; freeze.	8 to 12 months. Cook without thawing 5 to 10 minutes.
Beans, green or snap (1 pound yields 1 pint)	Tip and cut into pieces or slice lengthwise, French style. Blanch 3 minutes; chill; drain.	Freeze cut beans on trays and loose-pack in containers. Or pack into containers, leaving ½ inch head space. Seal; label; date; freeze.	8 to 12 months. Cook without thawing 5 to 10 minutes for French style and 12 to 18 minutes for cut beans.
Beans, lima (2½ pounds in pods yield 1 pint)	Shell and sort, according to size. Blanch 1 to 3 minutes; chill; drain.	Pack into containers, leaving ½ inch head space. Seal; label; date; freeze.	8 to 12 months. Cook without thawing 5 to 15 minutes, depending on size.
Beets (1½ pounds without tops yield 1 pint)	Remove tops; cook beets until tender. Cool; slip off skins. Leave whole or quarter, slice, or dice.	Pack into containers, leaving ½ inch head space. Seal; label; date; freeze.	8 to 12 months. Thaw until they can be separated; heat and season.
Broccoli (1 pound yields 1 pint)	Trim stalks; soak in mixture of 4 teaspoons salt and 1 gallon water for ½ hour to remove any insects. Cut stalks lengthwise in uniform pieces. Blanch 3 minutes; chill; drain.	Pack into containers with some heads at each end to save space. Or chop stalks coarsely and pack into containers, leaving ½ inch head space. Seal; label; date; freeze.	8 to 12 months. Cook without thawing 5 to 8 minutes.

FREEZING VEGETABLES

VEGETABLE	PREPARATION	PACKAGING	STORAGE AND USE
Carrots (1½ pounds yield 1 pint)	Scrape or pare; leave small ones whole or dice, slice, or cube. Blanch whole ones 5 minutes and pieces 3 minutes; chill; drain.	Freeze whole ones on trays, then pack into containers. Pack pieces in bags or containers, leaving ½ inch head space. Seal; label; date; freeze.	8 to 12 months. Cook without thawing 10 minutes for whole ones and 5 to 8 for pieces.
Cauliflower (1½ pounds yield 1 pint)	Trim; break into flowerets of even size. Blanch large flowerets 3 minutes in 1 gallon water to which 4 teaspoons salt have been added; chill; drain.	Pack into containers. Seal; label; date; freeze.	8 to 12 months. Cook without thawing 5 to 8 minutes.
Corn (2½ pounds yield 1 pint)	Husk; remove silks. Blanch ears 7 to 11 minutes, depending on size; chill; drain. Leave ears whole or cut kernels from cobs.	Wrap whole ears individually and pack into bags. Pack kernels into containers, leaving ½ inch head space. Seal; label; date; freeze.	8 to 12 months. Thaw ears; cook 3 to 4 minutes. Cook kernels without thawing 3 to 5 minutes.
Greens (beet, mustard, turnip, kale, chard, spinach, collards) (1½ pounds yield 1 pint)	Trim tough stems and coarse ribs; remove imperfect leaves. Blanch collards and spinach 3 minutes and the other varieties 2 minutes; chill; drain.	Pack into containers, leaving ½ inch head space. Seal; label; date; freeze.	8 to 12 months. Cook without thawing 5 to 15 minutes, depending on variety.
Herbs	Wash well and dry, but do not blanch.	Wrap a few sprigs in freezer film and place in bags. Seal; label; date; freeze.	8 to 12 months. Leave whole or chop and add to cooked dishes.
Peas, green (2½ pounds in pods yield 1 pint)	Shell and sort, according to size. Blanch 1½ minutes; chill; drain.	Pack into containers, leaving ½ inch head space. Seal; label; date; freeze.	8 to 12 months. Cook without thawing 5 to 10 minutes.
Peppers, sweet green or red (¾ pound yields 1 pint)	Remove stems and seeds. Halve peppers, dice, cube, or cut into strips. Do not blanch if using in uncooked foods. To use in cooked dishes, blanch strips 2 minutes and halves 3 minutes; chill; drain.	Pack any style into containers, leaving ½ inch head space for blanched peppers only. Seal; label; date; freeze.	8 to 12 months. Thaw and add to uncooked foods. Use frozen in cooked dishes.

FREEZING VEGETABLES

VEGETABLE	PREPARATION	PACKAGING	STORAGE AND USE
Pumpkin (3 pounds yield 2 pints)	Halve; scoop out seeds; cut pumpkin into pieces. Cook, covered, in boiling water 25 minutes, or until tender-soft; drain. Scoop pulp from rind; mash or press through a sieve or food mill; cool.	Pack into containers, leaving ½ inch head space. Seal; label; date; freeze.	8 to 12 months. Thaw and use in pies, breads, cookies, cakes, or other cooked dishes.
Squash, yellow and zucchini (1¼ pounds yield 1 pint)	Trim; slice ½ inch thick. Blanch 3 minutes; chill; drain.	Pack into containers, leaving ½ inch head space. Seal; label; date; freeze.	8 to 12 months. Cook without thawing 10 to 15 minutes.
Squash, acorn, Hubbard, and butternut (3 pounds yield 2 pints)	Halve; scoop out seeds; cut squash into pieces. Cook, covered, in boiling water until tender-soft; drain. Or bake squash halves at 375° until tender. Scoop pulp from rind and mash or press through a food mill; cool.	Pack into containers, leaving ½ inch head space. Seal; label; date; freeze.	8 to 12 months. Heat without thawing 15 minutes.
Tomatoes, cooked	Core, cut into pieces, and cook until soft. Press through a sieve or put through a food mill; cool.	Pack into containers, leaving ½ inch head space. Seal; label; date; freeze.	8 to 12 months. Use in recipes calling for purée or sauce.

FREEZING MEATS, POULTRY, AND FISH

For these three families of foods, freezing holds their fresh qualities better than any other method of preservation. Most important: Freeze only high quality products; an inferior one will not get any better after it's frozen. Make sure, too, that the food and anything that comes in contact with it is clean. Freezing is not a sterilizer—the low temperature only slows down the changes that lower quality or cause spoilage.

Equip yourself with proper packaging materials and wrap packages tightly. If you buy meats, poultry, or fish in plastic or film coverings, remember that these are not designed for long-term freezer use. Take the item out of its store package, remove as many bones as possible to save space, and rewrap the product in freezer paper, using the drugstore method of sealing off air and moisture. Here's how: Place food in the center of a rectangular piece of freezer paper or heavy foil that's large enough to go around the food and allow for folding at top and sides. Cushion any protruding bones with small crumpled up pieces of foil. Bring the two sides up and over the food to the center and fold over about a half inch. Make a crease the entire length, then make a second fold to bring the paper down to the surface of the food. Press out air through ends. Mold the wrapping to the shape of the food; fold ends up and over, continuing to press out air before sealing. Tape ends to hold wrapping in place.

For convenience and to avoid thawing more than you need, package foods in meal-sized portions or in quantities to be cooked at one time. Place two layers of paper between small items such as meat patties, individual steaks, chops, boneless chicken breasts, and fish fillets, then bag like items together. This way, individual pieces can be separated while frozen if you don't want to cook them all at once. Try not to overthaw meats. They'll be at their juicy best if you cook them while they're still icy.

Directions for freezing different types of meats, poultry, and fish are given in the chart below and on the following page.

FREEZING MEATS, POULTRY, AND FISH

FOOD	PREPARATION	PACKAGING	STORAGE AND USE
Roasts (beef, pork, lamb, veal)	Trim any excess fat. Pad sharp bones with foil to avoid puncturing paper.	Wrap tightly in freezer paper or heavy foil. Seal; label; date; freeze.	6 to 12 months for beef; 6 to 9 months for lamb and veal; 4 to 8 months for pork. Thaw all meats and cook the same as fresh.
Steaks, chops, cutlets	Trim any excess fat.	Separate pieces with double-thick waxed paper. Wrap in meal-sized quantities in freezer paper or heavy foil. Seal; label; date; freeze.	6 to 12 months. Thaw and cook the same as fresh.

FREEZING MEATS, POULTRY, AND FISH

FOOD	PREPARATION	PACKAGING	STORAGE AND USE
Stewing and ground meats	Separate into recipe quantities; shape ground meat into patties if you like.	Wrap or pack in containers, separating patties with double-thick waxed paper. Seal; label; date; freeze.	3 to 4 months. Thaw stewing cubes until they can be separated easily. Thaw patties almost completely to avoid over-cooking.
Variety meats	Trim any excess fat.	Wrap tightly in freezer paper or heavy foil. Seal; label; date; freeze.	3 to 4 months. Thaw and cook the same as fresh.
Sausage, fresh	Buy in bulk or as links.	Wrap meal-sized quantities tightly in freezer paper or heavy foil. Seal; label; date; freeze.	1 to 2 months. Thaw and cook the same as fresh.
Ham and bacon	Trim any excess fat from ham; cut ham into halves or slices.	Wrap ham tightly and over-wrap bacon in freezer paper or heavy foil. Seal; label; date; freeze.	1 to 2 months. Thaw and cook the same as fresh.
Poultry (chicken, turkey, duckling, goose)	Rinse whole birds; do not stuff. Rinse parts and sort according to recipes.	Wrap whole birds tightly in freezer paper or heavy foil. For faster thawing, wrap parts individually. Wrap giblets separately or pack into containers. Seal; label; date; freeze.	6 months for whole or cut-up birds. 2 months for giblets. Thaw and cook the same as fresh.
Fish (whole, fillets, steaks)	Clean and prepare as for cooking. Rinse and leave wet. Do not bread any fish product.	Wrap pieces individually or pack meal-sized amounts in bags or cartons. Whole fish may be frozen in a container filled with water, leaving ½ inch head space. Seal; label; date; freeze.	6 months for cod, flounder, sole, and haddock. 3 months for bluefish, mackerel, perch, and salmon. Cook frozen or partly thawed.
Shellfish (shrimp, clams, oysters, lobster, crab)	Rinse, peel, and devein raw shrimp. Shuck clams and oysters. Cook lobster and crab and remove meat.	Freeze shrimp on a tray; pack loose in containers. Pack clams and oysters in containers with juice, adding enough brine (1 teaspoon salt to 1 cup water) to cover. Pack lobster and crab meat in containers. Seal; label; date; freeze.	3 months. Thaw just enough to separate easily.

FREEZING MAIN DISHES, BREADS, AND DESSERTS

When you fix your own special casserole or meat recipes for the freezer, cook the foods slightly underdone or just to the tender stage; they'll cook further during reheating and keep their textures better. If one ingredient doesn't freeze well, leave it out of the recipe, then plan to add it when reheating the dish for serving.

To avoid leftovers, package all foods to fit your family's appetites. Since most prepared foods are stored only a month or two, you can use any airtight packaging that's convenient in size and shape. Seal casseroles that have loose-fitting lids with tape, or overwrap the dish with freezer paper, then seal it.

Follow the chart below and on the next page as your guide to freezing prepared foods.

FREEZING PREPARED FOODS

FOOD	PREPARATION	PACKAGING	STORAGE AND USE
Breads (loaves, rolls, sweet rolls, coffee cakes)	Make and bake as usual; cool. Slice loaves if you like.	Place loaves in bags. Freeze rolls on cookie sheet, then bag. Seal; label; date; freeze.	3 months. Thaw in package at room temperature. Or remove from package and warm in oven.
Cakes (layer, loaf, angel, chiffon, sponge, fruit; cupcakes)	Make and bake as usual; cool.	Wrap layers separately. Freeze large cakes or frosted ones on a cookie sheet first, then box. Seal; label; date; freeze.	3 months for plain cakes; up to 12 months for fruitcakes. Thaw layers and other plain cakes, then frost or glaze. Thaw frosted ones at room temperature or in refrigerator.
Canapes	Make open-face varieties as usual, spreading filling to edge.	Place in a single layer on cookie sheet; freeze. Pack in cartons with freezer paper between layers. Seal; label; date; freeze.	2 months. Remove from carton and place in single layer on a tray or cookie sheet; cover. Thaw in refrigerator.
Casseroles	Prepare and cook dishes with favorite recipes or follow those in this chapter. For maximum storage time, underseason with onions and spices; cool.	Freeze in baking dish. Or empty into freezer containers, depending on type of food. Seal; label; date; freeze.	3 months. Thaw in refrigerator, then heat as usual. Or take dish from freezer, unwrap, and bake immediately, allowing extra time.
Cookies	Make, bake, and cool. Shape refrigerator cookie dough into long rolls.	Pack in boxes or bags with freezer paper between layers. Wrap unbaked rolls in freezer film, then bag. Seal; label; date; freeze.	6 months. Thaw baked cookies. Thaw rolls until soft enough to slice; cut and bake as usual.

FREEZING PREPARED FOODS

FOOD	PREPARATION	PACKAGING	STORAGE AND USE
Cooked meat and poultry	Slice, cube, or chop meat and combine with gravy or broth to keep it moist and flavorful. Remove stuffing from poultry immediately after cooking and freeze separately.	Pack in meal-sized or recipe amounts in containers, leaving ½ inch head space. Seal; label; date; freeze.	3 months. Thaw and heat or use in recipes.
Meat loaf	Prepare and freeze unbaked. Or prepare, bake, and cool.	Wrap either in freezer paper. Or freeze unbaked loaf on a cookie sheet, then wrap. Seal; label; date; freeze.	1 to 2 months. Bake frozen loaf according to recipe, but allow extra time. Bake cooked frozen loaf until heated through.
Pastry	Prepare, roll out, and cut into rounds to fit pie plates.	Stack unbaked rounds with freezer paper between in freezer containers. Or stack on foil-covered cardboard with paper between, then wrap or bag. Seal; label; date; freeze.	2 months. Thaw, fit into pie plate, and continue according to recipe.
Pies	Prepare two-crust fruit pies, but do not cut steam vents. Make chiffon fillings, spoon into crust, and chill until firm.	Freeze fruit pies unbaked, then wrap or box. Freeze chiffon pies; bag or box. Seal; label; date; freeze.	6 to 8 months. Cut slits in top crusts of fruit pies; bake frozen. Thaw chiffon pies completely in refrigerator.
Sandwiches	Make with chicken, cheese, sliced roasts, peanut butter, egg-yolk and meat spreads, and fish. Omit mayonnaise, egg white, and crisp vegetables. Spread bread with butter or margarine to keep filling from soaking in.	Wrap individually in freezer paper; stack in box or bag. Seal; label; date; freeze.	1 to 2 weeks. Pack frozen in lunch boxes. Or thaw about 3 hours in refrigerator.
Stew	Prepare and cook, omitting potatoes until serving time; cool. Skim any fat from top.	Pack in meal-sized amounts in containers. Seal; label; date; freeze.	3 months. Thaw in refrigerator; add cooked potatoes; heat as usual.
Soup and broth	Make as usual, but omit cream or milk until serving time; cool. Strain broth; remove fat.	Pack in containers, leaving ¼ inch head space in pints and ½ inch in quarts. Seal; label; date; freeze.	3 months. Heat or use in recipes.

HOME CANNING SPECIALTIES

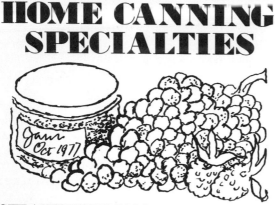

STRAWBERRY JAM

4 pints fully ripe strawberries, washed and hulled
1 package (1¾ ozs.) powdered fruit pectin
7 cups sugar

Place strawberries, one layer at a time, in a large bowl; crush with a potato masher.

Measure 4½ cups crushed fruit into a kettle; stir in pectin.

Heat quickly, stirring constantly, to boiling; add sugar all at once and stir in. Heat again to a full rolling boil; cook rapidly, stirring constantly, 1 minute; remove from heat. Skim off foam with a metal spoon. Continue stirring and skimming 5 minutes.

Ladle hot into hot jars, leaving ¼ inch head space. Adjust lids as manufacturer directs. Process 15 minutes in water-bath canner.

Cool jars, test seals, label, date, and store.
Yield: 8 half-pints.

CONCORD GRAPE CONSERVE

2½ pounds ripe Concord grapes
4 medium sized seedless oranges
2 small lemons
4 cups sugar

Wash grapes and pull from stems. Squeeze pulp from skins, placing pulp in a kettle and skins in a medium bowl. Heat pulp to boiling; cover. Cook 15 minutes, or until soft; press through a sieve into a medium bowl.

Squeeze juice from oranges; measure 1 cup.

Squeeze juice from lemons; measure ¼ cup; combine with orange juice.

Scrape white part from 1 orange and 1 lemon rind with a spoon. Place rinds and enough water to cover in a small saucepan; heat to boiling. Cook, uncovered, 20 minutes, or until tender; drain; chop rinds coarsely.

Combine grape skins, pulp, the 1¼ cups juice, chopped rinds, and sugar in a kettle. Heat slowly, stirring several times, to boiling; cook rapidly, uncovered, stirring once or twice, 40 minutes, or until mixture sheets from a spoon; remove from heat. Skim off any foam.

Ladle hot into hot jars, leaving ¼ inch head space. Adjust lids as manufacturer directs. Process 15 minutes in water-bath canner.

Cool jars, test seals, label, date, and store.
Yield: 5 half-pints.

SUMMER GARDEN CHUTNEY

15 large ripe tomatoes, peeled, cored, and chopped (10 cups)
4 large apples, pared, quartered, cored, and chopped (4 cups)
2 large sweet red peppers, quartered, seeded, and chopped (1½ cups)
2 large cucumbers, pared, seeded, and chopped (2 cups)
3 medium onions, chopped (1½ cups)
1 hot red pepper, quartered, seeded, and chopped
1 cup light raisins
3 cups firmly packed brown sugar
3 cups vinegar
1 clove garlic, crushed
3 teaspoons ground ginger
1 teaspoon ground cinnamon
1 teaspoon salt

Combine all ingredients in a large kettle; heat slowly, stirring several times, to boiling; cover. Simmer, stirring once or twice, 1½ to 2 hours, or until thick.

Ladle hot into hot jars, leaving ¼ inch head space. Adjust lids as manufacturer directs. Process 10 minutes in water-bath canner.

Cool jars, test seals, label, date, and store.
Yield: 6 half-pints.

FREEZER RASPBERRY JELLY

3 pints fully ripe red raspberries, washed and
   stemmed
5 cups sugar
2 tablespoons water
½ bottle liquid fruit pectin

Place berries, one layer at a time, in a large
bowl; crush with a potato masher. Place
crushed fruit in a jelly cloth or bag and extract
juice. Measure 2½ cups into a large bowl; stir
in sugar; let stand 10 minutes.

Stir water into pectin in a small bowl; stir
into juice mixture; continue stirring 3 minutes.

Ladle into sterilized jelly jars. Adjust lids as
manufacturer directs. Let stand at room temperature 24 hours until set. Label, date, and
store in freezer.
Yield: 5 half-pints.

SPICED APPLE SLICES

10 large firm tart apples (about 5 lbs.)
   Lemon juice
 4 cups sugar
 4 teaspoons whole cloves
 6 two-inch sticks cinnamon
 2 cups white vinegar
   Red food coloring

Pare apples, quarter, and core; cut each
quarter into 3 thick slices. Place in a large
bowl of water and lemon juice to keep slices
from darkening.

Combine sugar, cloves, cinnamon sticks,
and vinegar in a kettle; tint bright pink with
food coloring. Heat to boiling; simmer 10
minutes.

Drain apple slices; add only enough to
syrup at one time to make one layer deep in
kettle. (It will take about 2½ cups raw slices to
fill 1 pint jar.) Heat to boiling; cook 2 minutes,
or just until apples are tender but still firm.

Ladle hot into hot jars; add a stick of cinnamon and a few cloves from kettle to each;
cover with boiling syrup, leaving ¼ inch head

space. Adjust lids as manufacturer directs.
Process 15 minutes in water-bath canner.

Cool jars, test seals, label, date, and store.
Yield: 6 pints.

CUCUMBER CHOP-CHOP

 8 large cucumbers, pared, seeded, and chopped
   (8 cups)
 3 large sweet red peppers, quartered, seeded,
   and chopped (2 cups)
 3 large green peppers, quartered, seeded, and
   chopped (2 cups)
 1 large onion, chopped (1 cup)
 1 tablespoon turmeric
 ½ cup salt
   Cold water
 1 tablespoon mustard seeds
 2 teaspoons whole cloves
 2 teaspoons whole allspice
 2 four-inch sticks cinnamon
 1½ cups firmly packed brown sugar
 4 cups vinegar

Combine cucumbers, red and green peppers, and onion in a large bowl; sprinkle turmeric over top; stir in salt and 2 quarts cold
water. Let stand 3 to 4 hours; drain. Cover
vegetables a second time with cold water; let
stand 1 hour; drain well.

Tie mustard seeds, cloves, allspice, and
cinnamon in a small cheesecloth bag; combine with brown sugar and vinegar in a
medium saucepan. Heat, stirring until sugar
dissolves, to boiling; pour over vegetable mixture; cover. Let stand 12 to 18 hours in a cool
place.

Pour vegetable mixture into a kettle; heat to
boiling. Ladle hot into hot jars, leaving ⅛ inch
head space. Adjust lids as manufacturer directs. Process 10 minutes in water-bath canner.

Cool jars, test seals, label, date, and store.
Yield: 6 pints.

TOMATO PRESERVES

4 large fully ripe tomatoes (about 2½ lbs.)
1 package (1¾ ozs.) powdered fruit pectin
1 small seedless orange, quartered and sliced
thin
1 small lemon, quartered, seeded, and sliced thin
4½ cups sugar

Dip tomatoes into boiling water, then into cold; peel off skins. Cut tomatoes into quarters and core; place in a kettle. (Do not add any water.)

Heat slowly to boiling; cover. Simmer 15 minutes, breaking up tomatoes with a spoon. Measure, then return 3 cupfuls to kettle.

Stir in pectin and orange and lemon slices (including rind); heat rapidly, stirring once or twice, to boiling. Stir in sugar; heat to a full rolling boil; boil hard, stirring constantly, 1 minute; remove from heat. Skim off foam with a metal spoon. Continue stirring and skimming 5 minutes.

Ladle hot into hot jars, leaving ¼ inch head space. Adjust lids as manufacturer directs. Process 20 minutes in water-bath canner.

Cool jars, test seals, label, date, and store.
Yield: 6 half-pints.

OLD-FASHIONED APPLE BUTTER

10 large tart apples (about 5 lbs.)
4 cups apple cider
2 cups sugar
3 three-inch sticks cinnamon
10 whole cloves
½ teaspoon ground nutmeg
⅛ teaspoon ground allspice

Quarter apples and core. (No need to pare.) Combine with cider in a large kettle; heat to boiling; cover. Cook 20 minutes, or until apples are tender.

Preheat oven to 350°.

Drain liquid from apples into a small roasting pan; press apples through a food mill to remove skins; stir purée into liquid in pan. Stir in sugar and spices.

Bake, uncovered, stirring every 30 minutes,

for 4 hours, or until mixture is thick and golden.

Ladle hot into hot jars, leaving ¼ inch head space. Adjust lids as manufacturer directs. Process 10 minutes in water-bath canner.

Cool jars, test seals, label, date, and store.
Yield: 7 half-pints.

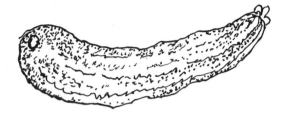

DILLED ZUCCHINI

10 medium zucchini, each about 7 inches long
(about 3 lbs.)
6 small white onions
2 tablespoons salt
Ice
2 cups sugar
1 tablespoon dill seeds
2 cups white vinegar
Fresh dill

Trim zucchini but do not pare; cut each in half lengthwise and crosswise; cut each quarter into 3 sticks. Peel onions, slice thin, and separate into rings.

Layer zucchini, onions, and salt into a large bowl; cover with a deep layer of ice; cover bowl. Let stand 4 hours; drain off all liquid.

Combine sugar, dill seeds, and vinegar in a kettle; heat to boiling. Add only enough zucchini and onion rings to syrup at one time to make one layer deep in kettle. (It will take about 15 zucchini sticks and 4 or 5 onion rings to fill 1 half-pint jar.) Heat to boiling again.

Pack hot into hot jars; add a sprig of dill to each; cover with boiling syrup, leaving ¼ inch head space. Adjust lids as manufacturer directs. Process 15 minutes in water-bath canner.

Cool jars, test seals, label, date, and store.
Yield: 8 half-pints.

PICKLED BEETS

9 lbs. small beets
2 cups sugar
1 tablespoon whole allspice
2 four-inch sticks cinnamon
1½ teaspoons salt
3½ cups vinegar
1½ cups water

Scrub beets; leave roots in place but trim tops, leaving stems 2 inches long.

Place beets in a kettle; add water to cover; heat to boiling; cover. Cook 15 minutes, or until tender. Cool until easy to handle. Then trim root ends and slip off skins. (Beets should measure about 12 cups.)

Combine sugar, allspice, cinnamon, salt, vinegar, and water in a large saucepan; heat to boiling; simmer 15 minutes. Remove cinnamon sticks.

Pack beets into hot jars, leaving ½ inch head space; cover with boiling syrup, leaving ½ inch head space. Adjust lids as manufacturer directs. Process 30 minutes in water-bath canner.

Cool jars, test seals, label, date, and store.
Yield: 6 pints.

GINGERED PEAR MARMALADE

4 large firm ripe pears, peeled, quartered, cored, and diced (4 cups)
2 cans (20 ozs. each) crushed pineapple in syrup
1 large seedless orange, halved lengthwise and sliced thin (including rind)
2½ cups sugar
½ cup chopped crystallized ginger
1 teaspoon ground cinnamon
⅛ teaspoon ground cloves

Combine pears, pineapple and syrup, orange slices, sugar, ginger, and spices in a kettle. Heat slowly, stirring constantly, to boiling, then simmer, stirring several times, 30 minutes, or until mixture sheets from a spoon.

Ladle hot into hot jars, leaving ¼ inch head space. Adjust lids as manufacturer directs.

Process 10 minutes in water-bath canner.
Cool jars, test seals, label, date, and store.
Yield: 6 half-pints.

SWEET CHERRY MARMALADE

1 large seedless orange, chopped (including rind)
4 cups pitted dark sweet cherries (about 4 lbs.)
3½ cups sugar
¼ cup lemon juice

Place orange in a small saucepan; add enough water to cover. Heat to boiling; cover. Cook 15 minutes, or until rind is soft; pour mixture into a kettle.

Stir in cherries, sugar, and lemon juice; heat slowly, stirring several times, to boiling; cook rapidly, stirring often, 30 minutes, or until mixture sheets from a spoon.

Ladle hot into hot jars, leaving ¼ inch head space. Adjust lids as manufacturer directs. Process 10 minutes in water-bath canner.

Cool jars, test seals, label, date, and store.
Yield: 4 half-pints.

PILGRIM'S PRESERVES

2 packages (16 ozs. each) cranberries, washed and stemmed
3 large tart apples, pared, quartered, cored, and chopped (3 cups)
1 large seedless orange, chopped (including rind)
3 cups sugar
½ cup honey
2 cups water

Combine cranberries, apples, orange, sugar, honey, and water in a large saucepan; heat slowly, stirring several times, to boiling. Simmer, stirring once or twice, 30 minutes, or until mixture sheets from a spoon.

Ladle hot into hot jars, leaving ¼ inch head space. Adjust lids as manufacturer directs. Process 10 minutes in water-bath canner.

Cool jars, test seals, label, date, and store.
Yield: 8 half-pints.

RED PEPPER RELISH

9 large sweet red peppers, quartered and seeded
6 large sweet green peppers, quartered and seeded
2 large onions, peeled and quartered
¼ cup salt
3 cups sugar
1 tablespoon mustard seeds
2 teaspoons celery seeds
1 teaspoon turmeric
2 cups cider vinegar
2 cups water

Put red and green peppers and onions through a food grinder, using a coarse blade. Combine in a large bowl; stir in salt; cover. Let stand 4 hours. Rinse mixture well with water; drain.

Combine sugar, mustard seeds, celery seeds, turmeric, vinegar, and water in a kettle; stir in vegetable mixture. Heat slowly, stirring several times, to boiling; simmer 3 minutes.

Ladle hot into hot jars, leaving ¼ inch head space. Adjust lids as manufacturer directs. Process 10 minutes in water-bath canner.

Cool jars, test seals, label, date, and store.
Yield: 6 pints.

FREEZER BLUEBERRY JAM

2 pints blueberries, stemmed and washed
4 cups sugar
1 teaspoon grated orange rind
½ teaspoon ground cinnamon
2 tablespoons lemon juice
½ bottle liquid fruit pectin

Place blueberries, one layer at a time, in a large bowl; crush with a potato masher.

Measure 2 cups crushed fruit into another large bowl; stir in sugar, orange rind, and cinnamon; let stand 10 minutes.

Stir lemon juice into pectin in a small bowl; stir into fruit mixture; continue stirring 3 minutes.

Ladle into sterilized jars, leaving ¼ inch head space. Adjust lids as manufacturer directs. Let stand at room temperature 24 hours until set. Label, date, and store in freezer.
Yield: 6 half-pints.

HOME FREEZING SPECIALTIES

COUNTRY VEAL PIE

¾ lb. ground veal
 1 tablespoon salad oil
 1 medium onion, chopped (½ cup)
 1 can (6¾ ozs.) chunked and ground ham. drained and flaked
¾ cup shredded Swiss cheese
 1 egg, beaten
 3 tablespoons chopped parsley
½ teaspoon salt
¼ teaspoon pepper
 1 package piecrust mix
 1 egg yolk
 1 tablespoon water
 2 tablespoons minced onion
½ teaspoon paprika
 2 tablespoons butter or margarine
 1 can (10¾ ozs.) condensed golden mushroom soup
¼ cup dairy sour cream

Shape veal into a large patty. Brown in salad oil in a medium skillet; break up into chunks; push to one side.

Stir chopped onion into drippings; sauté until soft. Pour any fat from skillet; cool mixture slightly. Combine with ham, cheese, egg, parsley, salt, and pepper in a medium bowl; mix well.

Prepare piecrust mix as label directs. Roll out half on a lightly floured board to a 12-inch round; fit into a 9-inch pie plate; trim overhang to ½ inch. Spoon veal mixture into shell.

Roll out remaining pastry to an 11-inch round; place over filling. Trim overhang to ½ inch; turn top and bottom edges under flush with rim of pie plate; flute. Freeze pie until firm, then wrap tightly; seal, label, date, and return to freezer.

About 55 minutes before serving, preheat oven to 400°.

Unwrap pie; cut several slits in top to let steam escape. Beat egg yolk with water in a cup; brush over pie.

Bake 45 minutes, or until golden.

While pie bakes, sauté minced onion with paprika in butter until onion is soft in a small saucepan; stir in soup and sour cream. Heat slowly just until hot.

Cut pie into wedges; top with mushroom sauce.

Yield: 4 to 6 servings.

MEXICAN CHILI CHOPS

 6 pork loin chops, cut ¾-inch thick (about 2½ lbs.)
 1 large onion, chopped (1 cup)
 1 clove garlic, minced
 3 teaspoons chili powder
 1 can (28 ozs.) tomatoes
 1 can (4 ozs.) green chili peppers, drained, seeded, and chopped
 1 teaspoon salt
½ cup sliced pitted ripe olives
 Hot cooked rice

Trim any excess fat from chops. Melt enough of the trimmings in a large skillet to make 3 tablespoons drippings; discard trimmings.

Place chops in skillet and brown slowly on both sides; remove from skillet to a plate and set aside.

Stir onion and garlic into drippings; sauté until soft. Stir in chili powder; cook 1 minute.

Stir in tomatoes, chili peppers, and salt; place chops in sauce. Heat to boiling; cover. Simmer 45 minutes, or until chops are almost tender.

Place chops and sauce in a 2-quart shallow freezer-to-oven dish; cool quickly; skim off any fat that rises to top. Wrap dish tightly; seal, label, date, and freeze.

About 2 hours before serving, unwrap dish but leave covered; place in cold oven. Set temperature control at 350°.

Bake 1¾ hours, or until bubbly. Sprinkle olives on top. Serve over plain steamed rice.

Yield: 6 servings.

HAM-AND-CHEDDAR PINWHEELS

1 lb. cooked ham, ground
1 small onion, minced (¼ cup)
1 egg, beaten
½ cup finely chopped celery
2 tablespoons chopped parsley
2 teaspoons prepared mustard
2½ cups sifted all-purpose flour (for dough)
3 teaspoons baking powder
1¼ teaspoons salt
½ cup shortening
2½ cups milk
3 tablespoons butter or margarine
3 tablespoons all-purpose flour (for sauce)
⅛ teaspoon pepper
1 cup shredded sharp Cheddar cheese (4 ozs.)

Combine ham, onion, egg, celery, parsley, and mustard in a medium bowl; stir to mix well.

Sift the 2½ cups flour, baking powder, and 1 teaspoon of the salt into a medium bowl; cut in shortening with a pastry blender until mixture forms coarse crumbs. Stir in 1 cup of the milk with a fork until mixture is evenly moist.

Turn dough out onto a lightly floured board; knead 20 times; roll out to a 12-inch square. Spread ham mixture over square; roll up, jelly-roll fashion; pinch edges and ends to seal. Cut crosswise into 12 one-inch slices.

Place slices on an ungreased cookie sheet; freeze firm. Remove from cookie sheet; wrap tightly; seal, label, date, and return to freezer.

About 50 minutes before serving, preheat oven to 400°.

Unwrap rolls; place on a lightly greased cookie sheet.

Bake 40 minutes, or until golden.

While rolls bake, melt butter in a medium saucepan; stir in the 3 tablespoons flour, remaining ¼ teaspoon salt, and pepper; cook, stirring constantly, until bubbly. Stir in remaining 1½ cups milk; continue cooking and stirring until sauce thickens and boils 1 minute; stir in cheese until melted and sauce is smooth.

Place rolls on a large serving plate; serve with cheese sauce.

Yield: 6 servings.

HAM-AND-ASPARAGUS ROLLUPS

24 stalks fresh asparagus
  Salt
2 packages (4 ozs. each) sliced boiled ham
4 tablespoons butter or margarine
4 tablespoons all-purpose flour
2 cups milk
3 tablespoons dry sherry
½ cup fresh bread crumbs (1 slice)
3 tablespoons grated Parmesan cheese

Break tough woody ends from asparagus; wash spears. Remove scales with a small sharp knife; wash spears again. Trim each to a 6-inch length. (Save trimmings to add to soup.)

Tie spears in several bundles; stand upright in a deep saucepan. Pour in boiling water to a 1-inch depth; salt lightly; cover. Cook 8 minutes, or just until asparagus is crisp-tender; drain carefully. Cool slightly.

Place 3 asparagus spears at one end of each ham slice; roll up, jelly-roll fashion; place in a row in a freezer-to-oven dish, 11¾x7½x1¾ inches.

Melt butter in a medium saucepan; stir in flour; cook, stirring constantly, until bubbly. Stir in milk; continue cooking and stirring until mixture thickens and boils 1 minute; remove from heat. Stir in sherry. Spoon over ham rolls to cover completely; cool quickly.

Mix bread crumbs and Parmesan cheese in a small bowl; sprinkle over sauce. Wrap dish tightly; seal, label, date, and freeze.

About 1¼ hours before serving, unwrap dish; place, uncovered, in cold oven. Set temperature control at 350°.

Bake 1 hour, or until bubbly and topping is toasted.

Yield: 4 servings.

BARBECUED RIBS

4 lbs. pork spareribs
⅓ cup bottled teriyaki sauce
2 tablespoons all-purpose flour
1 bottle (18 ozs.) barbecue sauce
⅓ cup water

Preheat oven to 350°.

Cut pork into serving-sized pieces of two ribs each. Place, meaty side up, in a single layer in a large shallow baking pan.

Bake 2 hours; pour fat from pan.

Mix teriyaki sauce into flour in a medium bowl until smooth; stir in barbecue sauce; brush part over ribs.

Continue baking, brushing once or twice with more sauce, 45 minutes, or until meat is tender.

Place ribs in a freezer-to-oven dish, 13x9x2 inches; cool quickly. Mix remaining barbecue sauce with water; pour into dish. Wrap tightly; seal, label, date, and freeze.

About 1¼ hours before serving, unwrap dish but leave covered; place in cold oven. Set temperature control at 350°.

Bake 1 hour, or until ribs are hot and bubbly.

Yield: 4 to 6 servings.

VEAL PARMIGIANA

2 lbs. veal leg cutlets or veal for scallopini
1 egg
1 tablespoon water
1 cup fine dry bread crumbs
4 tablespoons grated Romano cheese
½ teaspoon salt
¼ teaspoon pepper
⅓ cup salad oil
1 jar (21 ozs.) Italian cooking sauce
3 long slices mozzarella cheese

Cut veal into serving-sized pieces, if needed.

Beat egg with water in a pie plate. Mix bread crumbs, 2 tablespoons of the Romano cheese, salt, and pepper on waxed paper. Dip veal into beaten egg, then into crumb mixture to coat both sides well.

Preheat oven to 350°.

Brown veal slowly, part at a time, in salad oil in a large skillet.

Pour half of the cooking sauce into a shallow freezer-to-oven dish. Place veal in sauce; pour remaining sauce on top; cover.

Bake 45 minutes, or until veal is almost tender; cool quickly. Wrap dish tightly; seal, label, date, and freeze.

About 1½ hours before serving, unwrap dish but leave covered; place in cold oven. Set temperature control at 350°.

Bake 1 hour, or until bubbly.

While veal heats, cut mozzarella cheese into triangles or strips; place over veal; sprinkle remaining 2 tablespoons Romano cheese on top.

Bake 15 minutes longer, or until cheese melts and browns lightly.

Yield: 8 servings.

CHICKEN MADRAS

6 boneless chicken breasts, weighing about 5 ozs.
    each
4 tablespoons butter or margarine
1 medium onion, chopped (½ cup)
1 large tart apple, pared, quartered, cored, and
    chopped (1 cup)
1 clove garlic, minced
2 teaspoons curry powder
4 tablespoons all-purpose flour
1 teaspoon salt
¼ teaspoon pepper
½ teaspoon ground ginger
⅛ teaspoon ground cardamom
1 can (13¾ ozs.) chicken broth
    Water

Rinse chicken breasts and pat dry with paper toweling.

Brown chicken slowly in 2 tablespoons of the butter in a large skillet; place in a single layer in a freezer-to-oven dish, 11¾x7½x1¾ inches.

Add remaining 2 tablespoons butter to skillet; stir in onion, apple, and garlic; sauté until soft. Stir in curry powder; cook 1 minute.

Stir in flour, salt, pepper, ginger, and cardamom; cook, stirring constantly, until bubbly.

Combine chicken broth with enough water to measure 3 cups; stir into flour mixture; continue cooking and stirring until sauce thickens and boils 1 minute. Pour over chicken in dish; cool quickly. Wrap dish tightly; seal, label, date, and freeze.

About 1¾ hours before serving, unwrap dish but leave covered; place in cold oven. Set temperature control at 350°.

Bake 1½ hours, or until bubbly and chicken is tender. Serve with plain or saffron-seasoned rice and condiments such as pineapple chunks, raisins, sliced radishes, sliced cucumbers, chopped hard-cooked eggs, chopped peanuts, and diced green pepper.

Yield: 6 servings.

MAJORCAN LAMB BAKE

1½ lbs. ground lamb
1 clove garlic, minced
½ teaspoon dried rosemary, crushed
2 teaspoons salt
½ teaspoon pepper
1 large eggplant, weighing about 1¼ lbs.
    Salad oil
1 large onion, chopped (1 cup)
3 large tomatoes, cored and chopped (3 cups)
2 cups water
1 envelope instant onion broth
1½ teaspoons dried basil, crushed
¼ teaspoon sugar
1 cup uncooked regular rice

Combine lamb, garlic, rosemary, 1 teaspoon of the salt, and ¼ teaspoon pepper in a large bowl; mix lightly until well blended. Shape into 36 small balls.

Pare eggplant and cut into ½-inch thick slices. Brown, a few slices at a time, in salad oil in a large skillet; remove from skillet and drain on paper toweling.

Place lamb balls in skillet and brown, adding oil as needed; remove with a slotted spoon to a bowl.

Stir onion into drippings; sauté until soft. Stir in tomatoes, water, instant onion broth, basil, sugar, and remaining 1 teaspoon salt and ¼ teaspoon pepper. Heat slowly to boiling; simmer 5 minutes.

Preheat oven to 350°.

Layer half each of the eggplant, lamb balls, dry rice, and sauce into a 3-quart freezer-to-oven dish; repeat layers; cover.

Bake 45 minutes. (Not all of the liquid will be absorbed.) Cool quickly. Wrap dish tightly; seal, label, date, and freeze.

About 2¾ hours before serving, unwrap dish but leave covered; place in cold oven. Set temperature control at 350°.

Bake 2½ hours, or until bubbly.

Yield: 6 servings.

Chicken Madras
Oct. 1977

CHICKEN-CORN BAKE

1 broiler-fryer, weighing about 2½ lbs.
1 small onion, peeled and sliced
　Few celery tops
6 peppercorns
2 teaspoons salt
2 cups water
1 cup thinly sliced celery
1 small onion, chopped (¼ cup)
¼ cup butter or margarine
¼ cup all-purpose flour
⅛ teaspoon pepper
1 cup milk
2 eggs
1 can (12 ozs.) whole-kernel corn, drained
1 can (3 ozs.) chopped mushrooms
1 jar (4 ozs.) pimientos, drained and chopped
1 cup fresh bread crumbs (2 slices)
½ cup shredded process American cheese

Rinse chicken; combine with sliced onion, celery tops, peppercorns, 1 teaspoon of the salt, and water in a kettle; heat to boiling; cover. Cook 40 minutes, or until chicken is tender. Remove from broth and cool until easy to handle. Take meat from bones; cut into cubes. (There should be 3 cups.) Strain broth into a small bowl.

Sauté celery and chopped onion in butter in a large saucepan until soft; stir in flour, remaining 1 teaspoon salt, and pepper. Cook, stirring constantly, until bubbly. Stir in 1 cup of the chicken broth and milk; continue cooking and stirring until sauce thickens and boils 1 minute.

Beat eggs in a small bowl; slowly stir in one quarter of the hot sauce, then stir back into remaining sauce in pan. Cook slowly, stirring constantly, 2 minutes; remove from heat. Stir in cubed chicken, corn, mushrooms and liquid, and pimientos; spoon into a 1½-quart freezer-to-oven dish; cool quickly.

Mix bread crumbs and cheese in a small bowl; sprinkle over chicken mixture. Wrap dish tightly; seal, label, date, and freeze.

About 2¼ hours before serving, unwrap dish; place, uncovered, in cold oven. Set temperature control at 350°.

Bake 2 hours, or until bubbly and topping is toasted.
Yield: 6 servings.

SHORTRIBS CARBONNADE

4 lbs. beef shortribs
3 medium onions, peeled and sliced thin
1 clove garlic, minced
⅓ cup all-purpose flour
1 can (12 ozs.) beer
1 cup water
2 teaspoons salt
1 teaspoon sugar
1½ teaspoons vinegar
1 teaspoon dried oregano, crushed
1 bag (16 ozs.) frozen small whole carrots
1 package (10 ozs.) frozen peas

Ask your meatman to cut shortribs into 2-inch pieces. Brown slowly, part at a time, in their own fat in a heavy kettle or Dutch oven; remove from kettle.

Stir onions and garlic into drippings; sauté until soft. Stir in flour until blended; stir in beer, water, salt, sugar, vinegar, and oregano; heat slowly, stirring constantly, to boiling. Place shortribs in kettle; cover. Simmer 1¾ hours. Remove any loose bones from kettle.

Stir in frozen carrots; heat to boiling; cover. Simmer 15 minutes.

Stir in frozen peas; cover. Simmer 15 minutes, or until beef is tender. Let stand a few minutes until fat rises to top, then skim off. Spoon mixture into a 2½- or 3-quart freezer-to-oven dish; cool quickly. Wrap dish tightly; seal, label, date, and freeze.

About 2½ hours before serving, unwrap dish but leave covered; place in cold oven. Set temperature control at 350°.

Bake 2¼ hours, or until bubbly in center.
Yield: 4 to 6 servings.

CASEROLE BEEF JUMBLE

1 package (8 ozs.) elbow macaroni
1 package (8 ozs.) cream cheese
1 lb. ground beef
1 medium onion, chopped (½ cup)
½ cup chopped green pepper
1 can (15 ozs.) tomato sauce
1 teaspoon salt
¾ teaspoon dried thyme, crushed
¼ teaspoon pepper
1 cup shredded sharp Cheddar cheese (4 ozs.)

Cook macaroni in a kettle as label directs; drain; return to kettle. Cut cream cheese into small pieces and stir into macaroni until melted.

Shape ground beef into a large patty; brown in its own fat, turning once, in a large skillet. Break up into chunks; push to one side.

Stir onion and green pepper into drippings; sauté until soft. Stir in tomato sauce, salt, thyme, and pepper; cover. Simmer 15 minutes.

Pour over macaroni mixture; stir in half of the Cheddar cheese. Spoon into a 2-quart freezer-to-oven dish; cool quickly. Sprinkle remaining Cheddar cheese on top. Wrap dish tightly; seal, label, date, and freeze.

About 2¼ hours before serving, unwrap dish but leave covered; place in cold oven. Set temperature control at 350°.

Bake 1¾ hours; uncover. Bake 15 minutes longer to brown top lightly.

Yield: 6 servings.

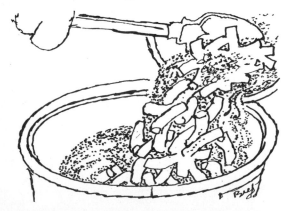

COMPANY CHICKEN RAMEKINS

1 broiler-fryer, weighing about 3 lbs., cut up
1 teaspoon salt
4 peppercorns
   Few celery tops
2 cups water
½ cup thinly sliced celery
½ cup chopped leeks
6 tablespoons butter or margarine
¼ cup all-purpose flour
1 egg yolk
2 tablespoons dry sherry
½ cup light cream
1 cup fresh bread crumbs (2 slices)
2 tablespoons chopped parsley
2 tablespoons grated Parmesan cheese

Rinse chicken; combine with salt, peppercorns, celery tops, and water in a large skillet; heat to boiling; cover. Cook 45 minutes, or until chicken is tender.

Remove from broth; cool until easy to handle, then take meat from bones and dice. Strain broth; return to skillet; cook down rapidly until it measures 1½ cups.

Sauté celery and leeks in 4 tablespoons of the butter in a medium saucepan until soft. Blend in flour; cook, stirring constantly, until bubbly. Stir in the 1½ cups broth; continue cooking and stirring until mixture thickens and boils 1 minute.

Beat egg yolk in a small bowl; slowly beat in half of the hot mixture; stir back into saucepan. Cook, stirring constantly, 1 minute; remove from heat. Stir in sherry, cream, and diced chicken. Spoon into 4 baking dishes.

Melt remaining 2 tablespoons butter in a small skillet; add bread crumbs and parsley; toss to mix. Sprinkle over chicken mixture, then sprinkle cheese on top. Wrap dishes tightly; seal, label, date, and freeze.

About 50 minutes before serving, uncover baking dishes; for easy handling, set dishes in a large shallow pan. Place in cold oven. Set temperature control at 350°.

Bake 50 minutes, or until bubbly in center.

Yield: 4 servings.

SLOPPY JOE BAKE (p.276) ▶
HEAVENLY HASH PARFAITS (p.429)

EVERYDAY HELPS

WITH ALL OF OUR MODERN KITCHEN APPLIANCES, minute minders, and space savers, cooking is a joy, yet push buttons just can't do everything. Recipes still call for a human touch, and here's where it pays to know the techniques and shortcuts that will make the job easier and the results surer.

This chapter was planned to give you quick answers to many of your daily cooking questions. How-to's on measuring ingredients and utensils help guarantee success and become second nature once you learn the right way. If you want to know how many whole onions it takes to make a cupful after they've been chopped, look here for a handy chart listing a number of foods.

For easy at-home reference—perhaps when you're planning meals or making up your shopping list—another table tells you what size cans certain foods come in so you can pick the pack that best fits your needs. Still another will guide you through emergency situations when you've started a recipe and find you've run out of a particular item you thought you had on hand. Sometimes there's an equally good counterpart you can use in its place, and this chart includes a few that have been worked out scientifically to eliminate mistakes and failures.

Finally, for these days when everyone's trying to save energy, there are tips to help you conserve it as well as get the most from what you do use.

BASIC COOKING TERMS AND WHAT THEY MEAN

BAKE: To cook food by dry heat in an oven or oven-type appliance.

BARBECUE: To roast or broil food on a rack or spit over or under a heating unit. Usually a special sauce is brushed over the food as it cooks.

BASTE: To moisten food as it cooks to prevent drying and add flavor. Pan drippings, fruit juices, salad oil, or special sauces are most often used.

BEAT: To make a mixture smooth with a quick even motion, using a spoon, wire whisk, or hand or electric beater.

BLANCH: To dip into boiling water to loosen skin from some foods or to scald as a step in preparing vegetables for freezing.

BLEND: To thoroughly mix two or more ingredients. Or to prepare food in an electric blender.

BOIL: To cook in liquid in which bubbles constantly rise to the surface and break.

BRAISE: To cook food slowly in a small amount of liquid in a tightly covered pan.

BROIL: To cook by direct heat on a rack or spit.

CARAMELIZE: To heat sugar slowly in a skillet until it melts and turns golden-brown.

CHILL: To refrigerate food or let it stand in a pan of ice and water until cold.

CHOP: To cut into small pieces with a knife or electric blender.

COAT: To cover all sides of food with another ingredient such as flour or bread crumbs.

CREAM: To make a mixture soft and smooth by beating with a spoon or electric mixer. Usually refers to blending fat and sugar together. Another meaning is to cook food in, or serve it with, a white or creamy sauce.

CRISP: To make a food firm and brittle by letting it stand in ice water or heating it in the oven.

CUBE: To cut food into cubes.

CUT: To combine shortening or solid fat with flour or other dry ingredients by using a pastry blender to distribute the shortening evenly.

DEEP-FRY: To cook in hot fat that's deep enough so the food floats on top.

DEVIL: To combine foods with one or more spicy-hot seasonings.

DICE: To cut foods into very small cubes, usually about ¼ inch.

DOT: To scatter bits of an ingredient such as butter or margarine over the surface of another food.

DREDGE: To coat or cover food with some dry ingredient such as flour, cornmeal, or sugar.

DUST: To sprinkle food with a dry ingredient such as flour or confectioners' powdered sugar.

FOLD: To combine delicate ingredients with other foods by cutting vertically down through the mixture with a spoon or spatula, sliding it across the bottom of the bowl, and bringing some of the mixture up and over the surface.

FRY: To cook in hot fat.

GRATE: To cut food into fine particles by rubbing it against a grater.

GREASE: To rub the surface of dish or pan with shortening or other fat to keep food from sticking.

GRILL: To cook by direct heat.

GRIND: To cut food into tiny particles by putting it through a grinder.

JULIENNE: To cut food into long, slender strips.

KNEAD: To work a food mixture with hands by folding it toward you, then pressing down and pushing it away.

LARD: To cover meat with strips of fat or to insert them into meat to add flavor and prevent drying.

MARINATE: To let food stand in liquid for a period of time to enhance flavor or produce tenderness.

MELT: To use heat to turn a solid food into liquid.

MINCE: To cut into very fine pieces.

MIX: To combine ingredients until evenly blended.

PANBROIL: To cook, uncovered, in a skillet without fat.

PANFRY: To cook in a skillet in a small amount of fat.

PARBOIL: To boil food until partly cooked.

PARE: To trim skin, peeling, or outer covering from food with a knife or vegetable parer.

PEEL: To pull outer covering from food with hands.

PIT: To remove seed.

POACH: To cook gently in simmering liquid.

PUREE: To press food through a fine sieve or food mill, or twirl in a blender, until it becomes smooth.

RECONSTITUTE: To add water to concentrated food to return it to its natural form.

ROAST: To cook, uncovered, by hot air.

SAUTE: To cook in a small amount of hot fat.

SCALD: To heat a liquid to a point just below boiling.

SCORE: To make shallow cuts or slits in the surface of food to prevent fat from curling, to decorate, or to increase tenderness.

SEAR: To brown the surface of meat quickly by intense heat.

SHRED: To cut food into thin strips or slivers with a knife or shredder.

SIFT: To put through a sieve or sifter.

SIMMER: To cook slowly in liquid with the surface of the liquid barely rippling.

SKEWER: To fasten with wooden or metal pins.

STEAM: To cook directly over boiling water in a tightly covered container.

STEEP: To extract color and flavor by letting food stand in hot liquid.

STEW: To simmer in liquid.

STIR: To mix food with a circular motion for uniform consistency.

TOAST: To brown by dry heat.

TOSS: To mix foods lightly by lifting them with two forks or spoons.

WHIP: To beat rapidly to incorporate air and expand volume.

THE RIGHT WAY TO MEASURE

Start with proper equipment. Every cook should have these basics: a set of four nested measuring cups for dry ingredients, a 1-cup measure for liquids, and a set of four measuring spoons.

Nested—or graduated—cups in metal or plastic include ¼-, ⅓-, ½-, and 1-cup sizes. Liquid measures, available in glass or plastic, are designed with a rim above the cup level to prevent spilling, as well as lines that mark less than 1-cup amounts. For measuring larger quantities or bulky foods such as bread cubes or apple slices, pint and quart sizes are also handy. Standard measuring-spoon sets include a quarter and half teaspoon, one teaspoon, and one tablespoon.

To measure dry ingredients. Lightly spoon flour, granulated sugar, or confectioners' powdered sugar into cup or spoon until it overflows, then level it off with the edge of a spatula. Two other reminders in measuring flour: Be careful not to pack it down and never shake or tap the cup.

On the other hand, pack brown sugar into the cup with the back of a spoon, then level off. If properly measured, the sugar should hold the shape of the cup when it's turned out.

Solid shortening also calls for nested cups. Spoon the shortening directly from can to cup, packing it down lightly; level off; scrape the cup out cleanly with a rubber spatula.

Most stick butter and margarine comes in wrappers that are designed with tablespoon measurements, so it's easy to cut off what you need with a knife. If your particular brand isn't marked, remember that one-quarter pound or one stick makes ½ cup. For smaller amounts, follow the rule for solid shortening.

For all other solid ingredients—fruits, nuts, cereals, grated cheese, coconut, bread crumbs, biscuit mixes, and rice—use your nested cups.

Many times a recipe calls for ⅛ teaspoon of some ingredient such as salt, an herb, or a spice. In this case, measure ¼ teaspoon and level off, then divide the amount in half by drawing a knife lengthwise through the center. Push half back into the bottle or jar and use the other half.

To measure liquids. Place cup on a level surface and fill it to the line marked on the side, then bend down so you can read the amount at eye level. For spoon measurements, pour the liquid right to the rim but don't let it spill over. Never measure, even small amounts, directly over the food to which the liquid is being added. Your hand may tremble or slip and pour out more than you need.

Measure liquid shortening, salad oils, and melted butter or margarine the same as milk, water, fruit juices, wine, or other liquids.

HOW TO MEASURE PANS AND MOLDS

For best results, it pays to use the exact size pan, casserole, or mold called for in your recipe. This ensures attractive foods and even cooking, and avoids spillovers.

Many manufacturers stamp the size or capacity on the bottom of baking pans and dishes, pie plates, custard cups, and molds. But if you should have some that aren't marked, here's how to determine their size:

Casseroles and molds: Pour measured amounts of water into the utensil up to the rim. The total amount tells you how many cups or quarts the utensil holds.

Round cake pans and pie plates: For diameter, use a ruler and measure across the top from inside edge to inside edge. If it's depth you need, stand the ruler straight up alongside.

Rectangular or square pans: Use your ruler again to measure length and width.

FOOD EQUIVALENTS

FOOD	WHEN YOUR RECIPE CALLS FOR:	YOU'LL NEED:
Almonds, sliced	1 cup	4-ounce can
Almonds, slivered	1 cup	4-ounce can
Apples, sliced	4 cups	4 medium
Bananas, mashed	1 cup	3 medium
Beans, dried, small	6 cups cooked	1 pound
Beans, green, cut	4 cups cooked	1 pound
Beans, lima, shelled	1 cup	1 pound in shell
Bread, slices	16 to 18	1-pound loaf
Bread crumbs, dry	1 cup	5 slices
Bread crumbs, fresh	1 cup	2 slices
Bread cubes, small	1 cup	2 slices
Bread stuffing mix	4 cups	8-ounce package
Butter or margarine	½ cup or 8 tablespoons	1 stick or ¼ pound
Cabbage, shredded	4 cups	1 pound
Carrots, grated	1 cup	1 large
Carrots, whole	10 medium	1 pound
Cheese, Cheddar, grated	1 cup	4 ounces
Cheese, cottage	1 cup	8 ounces
Cheese, cream	6 tablespoons	3 ounces
Cherries, red sour	1 cup pitted	4 cups unpitted
Chicken, cooked	4 cups diced	1 five-pound chicken
Chocolate, unsweetened	1 square	1 ounce
Chocolate, semisweet pieces	1 cup	6-ounce package
Citron, chopped	½ cup	4-ounce container
Coconut, flaked	1⅓ cups	3¼-ounce can
Corn, fresh, kernels	1 cup	4 ears
Cornflakes	1 cup crushed	3 cups
Corn meal	1 cup cooked	¼ cup uncooked
Crackers, graham	1 cup fine crumbs	12 square crackers
Crackers, saltines	1 cup coarse crumbs	20 square crackers
Cranberries, whole	4 cups	16-ounce package
Cream, sour	1 cup	8-ounce carton
Cream	1 cup whipped	½ cup whipping cream
Currants, dried	2 cups	11-ounce package
Dates, pitted, chopped	1¼ cups	8-ounce package
Flour, all-purpose	3½ cups	1 pound
Gelatin, unflavored	1 tablespoon	1 envelope
Lemon juice	3 tablespoons	1 large lemon
Lemon rind, grated	1½ teaspoons	1 large lemon

FOOD	WHEN YOUR RECIPE CALLS FOR:	YOU'LL NEED:
Lime juice	2 tablespoons	1 large lime
Macaroni, elbow	4 cups cooked	8-ounce package
Milk, evaporated	⅔ cup	1 small can
Milk, evaporated	1⅔ cups	1 tall can
Noodles, fine	5½ cups cooked	8-ounce package
Noodles, regular	4 cups cooked	8-ounce package
Onion, chopped	½ cup	1 medium
Orange juice	1 cup	3 medium
Orange rind, grated	1 teaspoon	½ orange
Peaches, fresh, sliced	4 cups	8 medium
Peanuts, chopped	1⅓ cups	6¾-ounce can
Peas, fresh shelled	1 cup cooked	1 pound in shell
Pecans, shelled	1½ cups	6-ounce can
Potatoes, diced, raw	1 cup	1 medium
Potatoes, sliced, raw	1 cup	1 medium
Prunes, pitted and cooked	2 cups	12-ounce package
Raisins	3 cups	15-ounce package
Rhubarb, 1-inch pieces	3 cups	1 pound
Rice, long-grain, cooked	4 cups	1 cup uncooked
Rice, packaged precooked	2 cups prepared	1 cup
Rice, wild, cooked	3 cups	1 cup uncooked
Strawberries, sliced	2 cups	1 pint
Sugar, brown, firmly packed	2¼ cups	1 pound
Sugar, granulated	2⅓ cups	1 pound
Sugar, confectioners' powdered	4 cups	1 pound
Sugar, loaf	120 pieces	1 pound
Tomatoes, fresh	3 medium	1 pound
Tomatoes, canned	2 cups	16-ounce can
Walnuts	1 cup	4-ounce can

FAMILIAR CAN SIZES

NET WEIGHT OR FLUID MEASURE	CUPS	SERVINGS	PRODUCT PACKED
8 ounces	1	1 to 2	Fruits and vegetables; *specialties.
10½ to 12 ounces	1¼	2 to 3	Condensed soups; some fruits, vegetables, meats, and fish; *specialties.
12 ounces	1½	3 to 4	Mostly vacuum-pack corn
14 to 16 ounces	1¾	3 to 4	Pork and beans; baked beans; meat products, cranberry sauce; blueberries; *specialties.
16 to 17 ounces	2	4	Fruits and vegetables; some meat items; ready-to-serve soups; *specialties.
20 ounces or 18 fluid ounces	2½	5	Juices; ready-to-serve soups; pineapple; apple slices; pie fillings; *specialties.
27 to 29 ounces	3½	5 to 7	Fruits, some vegetables such as pumpkin, sauerkraut, spinach, and tomatoes.
51 ounces or 46 fluid ounces	5¾	10 to 12	Fruit and vegetable juices; juice drinks; pork-and-beans.

*Specialties include such items as macaroni-and-cheese, Spanish rice, Mexican foods, and Chinese foods.

Juices now come canned or bottled in several sizes besides 18 or 46 fluid ounces.

Infant and junior foods are available in small cans and jars suitable for small servings. Check labels for content.

INGREDIENTS AND SUBSTITUTES

FOOD	MEASURE	SUBSTITUTION
Butter or margarine	1 cup	1 cup solid shortening plus ½ teaspoon salt.
Chocolate, unsweetened	1 square	3 tablespoons unsweetened dry cocoa powder plus 1 tablespoon butter or margarine.
Cream, light	1 cup	¾ cup whole milk plus ¼ cup melted butter or margarine.
Cream, whipping (not to be whipped)	1 cup	¾ cup whole milk plus ⅓ cup butter or margarine.
Egg yolks	2	1 whole egg.
Flour, all-purpose (for thickening)	2 tablespoons	1 tablespoon cornstarch or 4 teaspoons quick-cooking tapioca or 2 teaspoons arrowroot.
Flour, cake	1 cup sifted	1 cup minus 2 tablespoons sifted all-purpose flour.
Garlic, fresh, crushed	1 clove	⅛ teaspoon garlic powder.
Milk, sour or buttermilk	1 cup	1 tablespoon vinegar or lemon juice plus enough fresh whole milk to make 1 cup liquid.
Milk, whole	1 cup	½ cup evaporated milk plus ½ cup water or 1 cup reconstituted nonfat dry milk plus 2½ teaspoons butter or margarine.
Mustard, dry	1 teaspoon	1 tablespoon prepared mustard.
Onion, chopped	¼ cup	1 tablespoon instant minced onion.
Syrup, corn, light	1 cup	1¼ cups sugar plus ¼ cup liquid.
Tomato juice	1 cup	½ cup tomato sauce plus ½ cup water.
Yeast, compressed	1 cake	1 package active dry yeast.

WAYS TO SAVE ENERGY IN THE KITCHEN

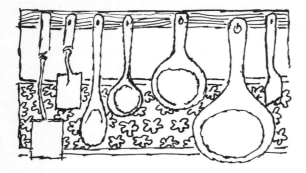

Consider appliances. Buy only as many as your family really needs and uses, and where possible, stick to the multi-purpose items rather than those that do a single job. Bypass any with a capacity larger than you ordinarily use, for they simply waste space and electricity. At all times, keep appliances in good repair so they operate at peak efficiency.

Defrost refrigerators and freezer compartments regularly so frost does not build up beyond ¼ inch. A thick layer only insulates the cooling coils and makes the appliance work harder to do its job.

Keep your freezer filled. It takes less energy to maintain a low temperature in one that's full than it does a half-filled or nearly empty one. Bread is a good space filler and can be used up quickly when you need room for other foods.

Plan ahead and thaw frozen roasts or large family-sized steaks in the refrigerator rather than cooking them from a frozen state. Defrosted, they take considerably less time, and therefore energy, to cook. Refrigerator thawing also helps cut down on the operating cost of this appliance.

Make the most of your oven. Many foods such as meat, vegetables, or baked fruits do not require a preheated oven. Preheat it only for leavened products—breads, cakes, cookies, or biscuits—or for ready-prepared convenience items such as pizza.

If you're going to fix a roast, take advantage of oven heat and cook the rest of the meal in the oven, too. Or consider cooking an extra dish or two for the freezer or a dessert for tomorrow's dinner at the same time.

For small jobs, think about a broiler or toaster oven. Either uses much less energy than a full-sized range oven. And do get in the habit of opening oven doors—refrigerator and freezer doors, too—only when necessary since reheating or recooling any appliance takes energy.

Avoid foil wraps for baking potatoes or roasting a turkey because foil insulates the foods and lengthens the cooking time.

Top-range cooking. If you have a choice of fixing a meal on top of the range or in the oven, chances are you'll save energy by picking the top-range way. For greater efficiency, make sure the cooking pans fit the burners and keep the lids on to shorten cooking time—preserve food value, too.

Saving water saves energy. It's always good homemaking practice to run hot water only when necessary. If you're rinsing dishes before stacking them or loading your dishwasher, place a little hot water in the sink or a dishpan and swish the dishes around in it rather than running a steady stream. When washing dishes by hand, wash a stack and rinse them all at once. Letting hot water run to rinse each piece separately is literally throwing money—and energy—down the drain.

Fill your dishwasher to capacity before you turn it on. Whether it's full or not, it uses the same amount of hot water so you might as well get as high a return as possible on your energy investment. And let dishes air-dry instead of using the hot-air drying cycle on your dishwasher. This means a saving of about half the energy it takes to wash a full load.

WEIGHTS, MEASURES, AND CONVERSION FACTORS

METRIC WEIGHTS AND MEASURES
Weights
1 kilogram = 1000 grams
1 gram = 1000 milligrams
1 milligram = 1000 micrograms

Conversion Table
1 kilogram = 2.2 pounds
454 grams = 1 pound
28 grams = 1 ounce
100 grams = 3½ ounces
227 grams = 8 ounces

Volumes
1 kiloliter = 1000 liters
1 liter = 1000 milliliters

Conversion Table
5 milliliters = 1 teaspoon
15 milliliters = 1 tablespoon
.24 liters = 1 cup
(240 milliliters)
.48 liters = 1 pint
(480 milliliters)
.95 liters = 1 quart
(950 milliliters)
3.79 liters = 1 gallon

Temperature Conversion
To change a Fahrenheit reading to the Celsius reading, subtract 32 from the Fahrenheit number, then multiply by 5/9.
To change a Celsius reading to the Fahrenheit reading, multiply the Celsius reading by 9/5 and add 32.

WEIGHTS AND MEASURES
Dash (liquid) = Few drops
Dash, pinch, or
few grains (dry) = Less than ⅛ teaspoon
3 teaspoons = 1 tablespoon
1½ teaspoons = ½ tablespoon
4 tablespoons = ¼ cup
5 tablespoons
+ 1 teaspoon = ⅓ cup
8 tablespoons = ½ cup
10 tablespoons
+ 2 teaspoons = ⅔ cup
12 tablespoons = ¾ cup
16 tablespoons = 1 cup
2 cups = 1 pint
4 cups = 1 quart
2 pints = 1 quart
4 quarts (liquid) = 1 gallon
8 quarts (dry) = 1 peck
4 pecks = 1 bushel
2 tablespoons = 1 ounce (liquid)
1 cup = 8 ounces (liquid)
1 quart = 32 ounces (liquid)
16 ounces = 1 pound

FRACTIONAL MEASURES
Half of ¼ cup = 2 tablespoons
Half of ⅓ cup = 2 tablespoons
+ 2 teaspoons
Half of ½ cup = ¼ cup
Half of ⅔ cup = ⅓ cup
Half of ¾ cup = ¼ cup + 2 tablespoons

OVEN TEMPERATURES

	Fahrenheit
Very Slow	250° - 275°
Slow	300° - 325°
Moderate	350° - 375°
Hot	400° - 425°
Very Hot	450° - 475°
Extremely Hot	500° - 525°

INDEX